DATE DUE

DEMCO 38-296

MAN OF THE PEOPLE

Also by Alonzo L. Hamby

The New Deal:
Analysis and Interpretation

Beyond the New Deal:
Harry S. Truman and American Liberalism

Harry S. Truman and the Fair Deal

The Imperial Years:
The United States since 1939

Liberalism and Its Challengers:
1st ed.: *F.D.R. to Reagan*
2nd ed.: *F.D.R. to Bush*

MAN

OF THE

PEOPLE

A Life of Harry S. Truman

ALONZO L. HAMBY

New York   Oxford
Oxford University Press
1995

Oxford   New York
Athens   Auckland   Bangkok   Bombay
Calcutta   Cape Town   Dar es Salaam   Delhi
Florence   Hong Kong   Istanbul   Karachi
Kuala Lampur   Madras   Madrid   Melbourne
Mexico City   Nairobi   Paris   Singapore
Taipei   Tokyo   Toronto

and associated companies in
Berlin   Ibadan

Copyright © 1995 by Alonzo L. Hamby

Published by Oxford University Press, Inc.
198 Madison Avenue, New York, New York 10016

Oxford is a registered trademark of Oxford University Press

Library of Congress Cataloging-in-Publication Data
Hamby, Alonzo L.
Man of the people:
a life of Harry S. Truman /
Alonzo L. Hamby.
p.   cm.
Includes bibliographical references and index.
ISBN 0–19–504546–7
1. Truman, Harry S., 1884–1972.
2. Presidents—United States—Biography.
3. United States—Politics and government—1945–1953.
I. Title.   E814.H28   1995   973.918′092—dc20   [B]   94–43806

9 8 7 6 5 4 3 2

Printed in the United States of America
on acid-free paper

FOR
THE OHIO GANG

Preface

This volume is the product of a scholarly engagement with Harry S. Truman that has occupied me, off and on, for more than thirty years. My quasi-obsession is more than an academic manifestation of the enduring fascination Harry Truman has possessed for the American public over the same period. Truman was part of my life from the time I developed a consciousness of the outside world. My first dim historical memory is of hearing the radio announcement that Franklin D. Roosevelt had died. A five-year-old boy in a tiny southwestern Missouri town, I understood that something important had happened, and ran to tell my mother.

I soon realized that while my parents had revered FDR, they also were firm backers of the new president, because he was a Democrat and a fellow Missourian. Their stance was not a popular one in a region that since the Civil War had regularly returned heavy majorities for Republican candidates. Politics and political allegiances were still deeply felt in those days, not least in my own family. I went through grade school with Harry Truman, prematurely politicized and, thanks to some of my schoolmates, acutely conscious that I was a member of a triple minority group— red-headed, fat, and Democratic. None of their reminders ever caused me to waver in the family affection for the president.

As I got older, I learned that Truman and I had some things in common. His ancestors had come to Missouri from Kentucky in the midnineteenth century; so had mine. They had fought for the Confederacy in the Civil War; so had mine. He had been raised in an unwaveringly partisan Democratic family; so had I. He was a product of small-town mid-America; so was I. He had been drawn to Kansas City as a young man; so was I. His second full-time job was with Commerce Bank; so was mine, at a salary even lower than his when adjusted for inflation. However superficial these commonalities, I have always believed that they gave me a special feel for Truman's life and for the environment in which he functioned.

By and large, only scholars recall that Truman left the presidency widely discredited. A partisan, controversial figure of low public standing during his last two years in the White House, he rose in public regard as a plain-speaking former president and became an American icon in the years after his death. It tells us much about the course of American historical scholarship and the radicalization of the intelligentsia in the 1960s and 1970s that as he steadily gained in public esteem he came to be increasingly debunked in the academy. The iconography reached unrealistic proportions; the academic critique was so steeped in ideology that it persuaded only those who needed no persuading.

My own view of Harry Truman and of the course of American intellectual life evolved in contrary directions. Striving to develop a critical (that is, evaluative) scholarly mentality, I could no longer give Truman the reflexive support I had learned in my youth. Moreover, the 1960s and 1970s left me convinced that Democratic party social welfarism had its limits. Thus I began this project with considerably more skepticism about the quality of Truman's liberalism than had been the case in my earlier book *Beyond the New Deal: Harry S. Truman and American Liberalism* (1973). But I am still persuaded of the basic validity of his view of international politics and his definition of America's role in the world.

I remain fundamentally positive in my view of the man. Limited in some respects, he nevertheless possessed virtues that considerably outweighed his flaws. Attempting a measured evaluation, I have sought to demythologize him, but not to debunk him. He is relevant to those who seek meaning in our past precisely because of the mixture of virtues and vices, strengths and limitations, one finds in his personality. Truman is significant not simply as one of the most important American presidents of our era, but also as a case study in American democracy, social and political, from the closing years of the last century to the middle years of this one. Born to no special class with no ready-made identity, his life exemplifies the stresses of self-definition, risk, failure, success, compromise, mobility, and idealism characteristic of the American experience.

For reasons legitimate and otherwise, political biography has become an unfashionable enterprise in contemporary academia. It amounts to a daring gamble for a historian who (unlike myself) is untenured. Increasingly in recent years, it is a genre that has been abandoned to popularizers who at their best tell good stories and reduce the historical process to the interplay of great men; at its worst, it delves into private lives and mongers gossip. At times, one has sensed a sort of literary Gresham's Law at work.

The academic unfashionability of political biography (and political history in general) is also the result of an ideological viewpoint that prefers to ignore the success of liberal democratic politics in America. The latest generation of scholarly ideologues focuses single-mindedly on varieties of social history that with varying degrees of persuasiveness emphasize oppression or injustice, rather than liberty, democracy, or opportunity, as the great constant of American history. Harry Truman's story largely refutes them.

Great men and women are not free agents who stride across a historical landscape and transform it at will, but their individuality can profoundly affect the course of events. Who would dare claim that the course of the twentieth century would have been about the same had Churchill been killed during the Boer War, Hitler fatally gassed in World War I, Stalin a victim of smallpox as a child, and Franklin Roosevelt shot dead by Zangara? I confess to a belief that this century might have been greatly different had Harry Truman been a fatality (as he almost was) of the World War I artillery skirmish in the Vosges that he and his men called the Battle of Who Run. I also believe that the distinction between social and political history is misconceived and that biography, by placing its subject within his or her context, can be a species of social history.

All very well, a skeptic may declare, but why on earth do we need another big biography of Harry Truman? I have learned from all my predecessors from Jonathan Daniels to David McCullough, but for reasons I discuss in the Bibliographic Essay, I am convinced that none of them has adequately measured the man and the worlds in which he lived. I have attempted to write the most thorough account yet of Truman's pre-presidential life while providing a self-conscious interpretation of the overlapping worlds in which he grew up, became a soldier, went into local politics, and served as a United States senator. I have sought to write a concise account of the Truman presidency—about half the length of Robert J. Donovan's—that gives us some sense of the ways in which Truman felt the institution's impact. I also have attempted to relate his White House experience to the larger themes of the Cold War, McCarthyism, the changing character of the Democratic party, and the redefinition of liberalism in the post-Roosevelt years.

Although I have drawn on *Beyond the New Deal*, I have not rewritten it. I prepared this interpretation with far better source material than was available in the early 1970s, a different sense of purpose, and a considerably different viewpoint. I have above all attempted to present Harry Truman as a historical figure in whose career one finds not just an interesting and vivid individual, but a picture of the evolution of American social and political democracy in the first half of the twentieth century. Only readers can judge whether I have come close to fulfilling so grand a design. I hope that they will feel that at the very least, I have told a crackling good story. Harry Truman deserves nothing less.

Athens, Ohio   A.L.H.
March 1995

Acknowledgments

In a very real sense, this book represents the culmination of thirty years of work. Thus, just as I refer the reader to my earlier work *Beyond the New Deal: Harry S. Truman and American Liberalism* for supplementary documentation, I also refer to the acknowledgments in that book.

Authors are seldom iron men capable of writing big books by the midnight oil after a normal workday. A large study of this sort requires time and funding beyond that normally accorded a university professor. Ohio University provided two sabbatical leaves, a summer research grant, and a John C. Baker Fund grant. The National Endowment for the Humanities awarded me a summer grant. The Harry S. Truman Library Institute, which has supported my work generously over the years, made me the recipient of its Senior Fellowship in 1986/1987 and thereby provided me an opportunity to spend several months in Independence researching and writing the early chapters. A fellowship from the Woodrow Wilson Center in Washington, D.C., allowed me to do much of the writing on the Truman presidency in the center's extremely supportive and stimulating surroundings.

Time and money provide an opportunity. People provide the tangible help that a serious project requires. I am indebted to Benedict K. Zobrist and the entire staff at the Harry S. Truman Library. Over the years, I have come to feel like a member of their family and hope they feel like members of mine. Without slighting the efforts of others, I especially want to thank Dennis Bilger, Erwin Muller, Niel Johnston, Sam Rushay, Philip Lagerquist, and, above all, Elizabeth Safly. Only those other Truman scholars who have needed long-distance assistance with a stray citation, a runaway document, or an obscure fact can fully appreciate the reassurance that one receives when calling the library research room and hearing at the other end of the line: "This is Liz. May I help you?"

Thanks also go to Charles Blitzer and his wonderful staff at the Wilson Center; Nancy Lankford and the archivists at Western Historical Manuscripts, Columbia, Missouri; and David Wigdor at the Library of Congress. Among my research assistants at the Wilson Center, Joseph Budney and Mytheli Sreenivas were especially helpful. At Ohio University, I benefited from the help of Campbell Craig, Don Illich, Mark Sonntag, and Brent Lundy.

Richard Kirkendall first steered me toward Truman over thirty years ago. This biography makes use of ideas I stole from him then and have been running with ever since. Fred Greenstein has been a long-standing source of concepts and encouragement. George Elsey's interest in this work has improved it enormously. These gentlemen have been mentors and friends. I am very grateful to them. Please don't blame them for my mistakes.

Gerry McCauley provided all the things one can expect of a good literary agent. Nancy Lane believed in this project from the start and displayed courage in signing it. I hope its readers will think her judgment was good. I am proud to have her faith in my capabilities. Kathy Banks played an indispensable role in the final development of the manuscript. In addition, I thank Irene Pavitt for her careful editorial work, Elizabeth Jones for her copy-editing, and Thomas LeBien for his careful handling of numerous important production details.

Joyce Litton Hamby helped a lot on the early phases before veering off to projects of her own. She always has understood the importance of this study to me and has been a source of support in so many ways that it is impossible to enumerate them.

I shall not name individually the people collectively recognized in the dedication. It has been a privilege to have them as colleagues. I thank them for their company and their stimulation.

Contents

Book II   American President, 1945–1972

Contents

Politics . . . takes both passion and perspective. . . . [M]an would not have attained the possible unless time and again he had reached out for the impossible. But to do that a man must be a leader, and not only a leader but a hero as well, in a very sober sense of the word. And even those who are neither leaders nor heroes must arm themselves with that steadfastness of heart which can brave even the crumbling of all hopes.

Max Weber, "Politics as a Vocation"

It takes men to make history, or there would be no history. History does not make the man.

Harry S. Truman, Memoirs: Year of Decisions

BOOK I

AMERICAN DEMOCRAT
1884–1945

1

"I Was Kind of a Sissy":
In Search of Self, 1884–1906

"Mr. President, was you popular when you was a boy?"

"Why, no, I was never popular," the old man told the crowd of school children in the Truman Library auditorium. "The popular boys were the ones who were good at games and had big, tight fists. I was never like that. Without my glasses I was blind as a bat, and to tell the truth, I was kind of a sissy. If there was any danger of getting into a fight, I always ran. I guess that's why I'm here today."[1]

It was one of Harry Truman's rare moments of candor about his childhood. A man who gloried in a public role as a gutsy, bourbon-drinking, poker-playing, frank-speaking fighter, he admitted, if just for an instant, that his difficulties in life had gone beyond hard election campaigns and bad luck in business. Behind his confession lay years of struggle to become the sort of man who would win the respect of his peers and, above all, that of his father. The tension of becoming something he wasn't strengthened him in many ways, but it also left scars: an inordinate touchiness, a quick temper, and an insatiable demand for recognition that stayed with him throughout his life.

Much of the story of Truman's life consists of alternating episodes of struggle and accommodation—to his physical limitations and to the rapidly changing social and economic conditions of twentieth-century America. Such was the fate of many of the children and grandchildren of the American frontier.

II

America was a land of democracy, individualism, and opportunity in 1846 when Anderson Shippe Truman and his bride settled near Westport

Landing, Missouri, not too far from another couple they had known back in Kentucky, Solomon and Harriet Louisa Young. Everyone was, in theory, equal; everyone had a chance in life. A vast, sparsely settled land offered resources apparently without end to those who had the initiative and hardihood to claim them. The Trumans and the Youngs displayed both qualities.

Anderson Truman and his wife, Mary Jane Holmes, were of the yeoman gentry of the upper South. Their parents had been part of the early wave of settlement from Virginia to the dark and bloody ground of Kentucky in the early days of the republic. The Trumans and Holmeses had fought Indians, staked out lands, raised crops, acquired a few slaves, and prospered. Thus, went the prevalent assumption, might any ambitious young couple willing to move west over trails blazed by the Indian traders, risk the scalping knife, and work hard at carving out for themselves a small slice of the nation's destiny.

The Trumans could be all the more assured of success with a bit of help from well-to-do parents and in-laws. Anderson Truman purchased 200 acres of prime farmland; his mother-in-law, Nancy Tyler Holmes, gave the newlyweds some slaves as a wedding gift. The couple lived in comfortable prosperity, leading figures in the Baptist Church and mainstays of their community. They raised five children; the third, John Anderson, was born in 1851. In 1853, the family moved just north of the Missouri River to a farm in Platte County, a quiet Kentucky-like area with a plantation culture. There they lived for the next thirteen years.[2]

In the same Kentucky that produced the Trumans, Sol Young, an orphan at the age of twelve, had made his way in the world. Twenty-three years old in 1838, he married nineteen-year-old Harriet Louisa Gregg, herself an orphan at ten. It is unclear whether Young benefited from an inheritance or made himself a man of means solely through muscle and ambition. It is indisputable that both he and his new wife possessed the limitless energy and self-reliance of archetypical American pioneers.

In 1841, the Youngs sold 800 acres that Sol had accumulated on the Little Bullskin River and, with their two children, took a steamboat down the Ohio, up the Mississippi, and westward on the broad Missouri. Just south and east of the great bend where the Missouri turns north, they settled near the jumping-off point for the great West at the confluence of the Missouri, Kansas, and Blue rivers in Jackson County.

Sol restlessly acquired and sold large tracts of land. He also hauled freight and led cattle drives west. Spending three years raising cattle in California, he acquired a Spanish land grant that purportedly included much of the present city of Sacramento; ultimately, he disposed of it for $75,000. He missed some main chances but cashed in on others. Louisa stayed at home, bore seven more children, ran the farm, and balked only at joining him in the West. By 1861, he was back in Missouri, a prosperous farmer and businessman who owned 1,300 acres.

During the Civil War, the Trumans and the Youngs sympathized with the South, more out of ties of kinship and culture than personal economic considerations. Both families suffered in the nasty guerrilla warfare along the Missouri–Kansas border. In 1861, Louisa was tending the farm by herself during one of her husband's absences when the Unionist Jayhawker Jim Lane and his Redlegs raided the property, made her cook biscuits for them until her hands were blistered, slaughtered the hogs for their own use, shot the chickens, burned the barns, and stole her silver. They repeatedly hanged her son Harrison, a boy of thirteen, by the neck, nearly strangling him to death in an effort to make him admit that his father was in the Confederate Army. (Actually, he was taking a load of freight across the Great Plains, but the eldest son, William, was a Confederate soldier.) On four other occasions, Union troops confiscated the Youngs' livestock and property.

In July 1862, Young signed an oath of loyalty to the United States, but in August 1863, his family still fell prey to Union Order No. 11, which mandated the internment of all Confederate sympathizers in Jackson and two and a half other counties. Sol was away again; Louisa and the six children still at home loaded as much as they could in an oxcart and followed it into Kansas City. Their house and whatever the Union irregulars did not loot went up in flames. Louisa and her children spent the next few months confined to a federal "post" and then made their way to Platte County, where they spent the duration of the war. For the rest of their lives, they harbored an unquenchable hatred for Abraham Lincoln, blue uniforms, and Kansans.

A quarter-century later, after Congress had passed a law permitting loyal citizens to request compensation for Civil War losses, Sol and Louisa filed for $21,442. The claim itemized the confiscation of 224 head of livestock, 1,500 bushels of corn, 43,000 fence rails, 1,200 pounds of bacon, 7 wagons, and a "house used for guardhouse." It remained unsettled at Sol's death, unpaid at Harriet's. Their heirs and attorneys would finally divide just $3,800.

The Trumans were luckier. At the beginning of the war, they took their few slaves to Kansas and set them free. Their farm was relatively unmolested. (Order No. 11 did not include Platte County.) Anderson signed a loyalty oath near the end of April 1863. Nonetheless, he was restricted to his home county. His family also lived in fear of the Redlegs and once spent a cold autumn night hiding from them in a cornfield.[3]

III

In all, the Youngs and the Trumans escaped the war relatively unscathed. The Trumans moved back to Jackson County and established themselves on 200 acres near Hickman's Mills. Mary Jane died in 1879. Anderson's oldest son, William, had gone off on his own, but John stayed to help run the farm. The Youngs acquired nearly 400 acres a few miles away, out-side the town of Grandview. Sol registered the property in Louisa's name, built a big house on it, and made his last trip west around 1870. He con-tinued to buy and sell land actively; by the end of 1869, he and Louisa held over 2,200 acres.

Both families were prominent. Both were Baptists, the Trumans vehemently so.[4] It must have seemed a natural match when on Decem-ber 28, 1881, John Truman married Sol's eighth child, Martha Ellen. The newlyweds moved to the town of Lamar, about 100 miles south. For $685 John bought a large lot with a small frame house and a big barn; he went into business as a livestock trader. Anderson sold his farm and moved in with them.

John Truman was thirty years old when he married, left his father's farm, and started out on his own. He was a bantam of a man, about five feet, four inches tall. As his children told it long after his death, he was a gentle father who seldom spoke a harsh word to them, had a soft voice, loved music, and sang as he worked. He also groped after the success his father and father-in-law had achieved but became bitter as he eventually found it out of reach in the more settled world of the late nineteenth cen-tury. One Lamar old-timer remembered him as a hot-tempered little man with a high-pitched voice who spoke in what some local residents took for an "English brogue."[5]

In a culture in which it was relatively common for men to come to blows over differences, John Truman never hesitated to resolve disputes with his fists. Once, after he had moved his family to Independence, he was testifying in a lawsuit when the lawyer for the opposition called him a liar. He jumped from the witness stand, fists flying, and chased the at-torney, a six-footer who weighed well over 200 pounds, into the street. After a while, he returned alone. "Did you get him, John?" asked the judge. "No, he got away." The response from the bench indicated how close western Missouri still was to the frontier: "Too bad. That fellow really had a good beating coming to him."

A shrewd, persuasive trader, John managed to walk the fine line between good salesmanship and outright crookedness. His honesty won wide recognition, but as his elder son later put it, after he closed a deal, "the other fellow was never sure he had all his hide." A trader and specu-lator, he strove to get ahead much as his elders had, through a combina-tion of hard work and risky enterprise.[6]

His bride was two inches taller than he and at twenty-nine years old had been an old maid in the eyes of her relatives and acquaintances. An alumna of Central Female College in Lexington, Missouri, where she had studied art, music, and literature, Martha Young Truman was a talented amateur artist, a devotee of the piano, and a lover of English literature who never lost her admiration for Alexander Pope. Like many rural and small-town wives, she had a considerably better education than her hus-band and saw the transmission of learning and culture to her offspring as one of the duties of motherhood. She also was a fun-loving woman who called herself a lightfoot Baptist because she ignored condemnations of social dancing and enjoyed a good party. But she was not a frail, over-cultured female unsuited to a tough environment. Very much the daughter of her strong pioneer mother, Martha ran things in the sphere she carved out for herself and usually got her own way. She handled a 16-gauge shotgun as well as most men. Independent, opinionated, and assertive, she was as tough as a barrel of roofing nails.[7]

John and Martha lived in Lamar for about three years. Her first pregnancy resulted in a stillbirth. The second was successful. On May 8, 1884, she bore a healthy baby boy. It was symptomatic of her ability to have her way that they named him Harry for her brother Harrison and gave him the middle initial "S.," which could be represented as abbreviating her father's first name or her father-in-law's seldom-used middle name.*

John Truman apparently found himself unable to make a good living on livestock trading alone. Two months before Harry's first birthday, he sold the Lamar property for $1,600. The family moved back north, briefly to Harrisonville, and then to a farm near Belton in Cass County, a few miles from the Young and Truman homesteads across the Jackson County line. There on April 25, 1886, Martha gave birth to a boy, John Vivian. The following year, they moved to Grandview to manage the Young farm. Anderson Truman died there a few months later. Harry, barely three, heard someone say "He's gone," came into the room, and tugged at the old man's beard in an effort to awaken him.[8]

The Grandview years were good for the Trumans. John not only managed the Young farm, but purchased 120 acres for himself, 40 of them from his father-in-law. On August 12, 1889, Martha gave birth to their third child, a daughter they named Mary Jane, after John's mother. For Harry, surrounded by loving relatives, the time at Grandview was memorable. When Harry was six, old Sol, by then a white-haired man with a long beard, took him to the Cass County fair at Belton to watch the horse races from the judges' box. Uncle Harrison, a muscular, six-foot bachelor, brought him and the other children candy and gifts from Kansas City. Harry and Vivian lived a Norman Rockwell childhood, romping through pastures and riding ponies, secure and innocent in a small, benign world.

Even in Arcadia, of course, all was not perfect. Harry occasionally learned the hard way. One day, while riding with his father, he fell off his Shetland pony. An angry John Truman snapped that any boy who could not stay on a pony at a walk ought to walk himself and made him return to the house leading the animal on foot. "Mamma thought I was badly

---

*This is as good a place as any to address the inevitable assertion that there should be no period after the "S" in Truman's name because it stood for nothing. It stood for both Solomon and Shippe. Truman often used the period when signing his name and invariably when typing it. Moreover, that form was the official standard during his presidency. Thus shall it be in this book.

mistreated, but I wasn't," he recalled seventy years later. "In spite of my crying all the way to the house, I learned a lesson."

Harder lessons began to come at the age of five. Under his mother's tutelage, Harry had begun to read, but he displayed difficulty with anything other than the large-type family Bible, which he eventually read twice in its entirety. A doctor diagnosed malformed eyeballs and prescribed thick, expensive, fragile glasses. It was not until he began elementary school three years later that Harry was fitted with them. But already he had been set apart. Suddenly, the little boy's weak vision made many of the normal childhood activities that he had enjoyed seem hazardous. He helped in the kitchen. He attended to his baby sister, regularly fixing her hair and rocking her to sleep. ("Mama, make Harry bye-o," she would cry when she wanted attention.) He spent more and more time reading. The adjustment would have been difficult enough in the secluded little environment in which he lived; it no doubt became even more trying when the family made yet another move.

However good the years on the Young farm had been, John was a man with wider ambitions. Martha had bigger dreams also—for her children, especially Harry. The rural schools, she told her husband, were not good enough. They had to move to town so that Harry could get a first-class education. In 1890, the family left the farm for Independence.[9]

IV

A growing county-seat city of 6,000, ten miles east of the emerging metropolis of Kansas City, Independence promised opportunities to an ambitious speculator. Poised in midstage between a frontier past and a twentieth-century future, southern in its atmosphere, it was still vividly mindful of three separate Civil War battles. The veterans of Quantrill's raiders, the most notorious of Missouri's Confederate guerrillas, held annual reunions. Young Harry probably did not yet know that in 1873 the first husband of his Aunt Sallie, a rogue named James (Jim Crow) Chiles, had been killed in a gunfight with Deputy Marshall Jim Peacock on the courthouse square. The old outlaw Frank James lived a few miles away near Kearney and drew crowds of admirers on his infrequent visits to town. (In 1902, James's former associate, Cole Younger, was released from the Minnesota state penitentiary; he settled in nearby Lee's Summit and supported himself by giving public lectures on the wages of sin.)

Business centered around the courthouse square, bounded by posts swagged with heavy chains to which horses and wagons were tied. In rainy weather, the dirt streets became avenues of mud, studded during the summer with discarded watermelon rinds. Most men wore boots with their trousers tucked into the tops; many still carried knives or guns. Covered boardwalks lined the storefronts on all sides of the square. The saloons were perpetually busy. Fistfights were common, especially on election days, when the voters of each of the city's four wards cast their ballots at different corners of the square. Nighttime holdups and burglaries were surprisingly frequent, many of them pulled off by blacks who disappeared into their districts of Kansas City.

When the Trumans moved to Independence, it had no water system, no paved streets or sidewalks, no electricity. Wood was the fuel commonly used for heating and cooking. A trip to Kansas City was an all-day experience in good weather, an impossibility in bad. The city showed a veneer of civilization—numerous churches, schools, a library, two newspapers, and a substantial educated class. Still, the transition from farm to town was easy. For John Truman, who planned to concentrate on livestock trading, it was more akin to a move of the farm to town.[10]

Truman purchased a big house with a white cupola on Crysler Street, not far from the Missouri Pacific Railroad tracks. The neighborhood consisted of prosperous upper-middle-class homes, displaying those little touches of the extravagant characteristic of Gilded Age architecture. John bought two adjacent lots, fenced his property, probably built a barn or an animal shed, and conducted what appears to have been a thriving livestock business. He hired a black couple, Caroline Hunter and her husband, Letch Simpson, to do household work. Their children usually came along to do small chores or play with the Truman youngsters in the big yard. In keeping with the attitude toward blacks that his family taught him, Harry would take time from his duties as president fifty years later to facilitate assistance for one of them who had fallen on hard times.

The family found a natural-gas deposit on the property and used it for winter heating. (It was characteristic of John Truman that he became embroiled in a lawsuit with the driller. It was probably in this case that he chased the attorney who insulted him into the street.) When the gas ran out in 1895, John traded the Crysler property for an equally big house with a huge lot on Waldo Street. In partnership with a man named Oscar Mindrup, he went into the real-estate and grocery businesses. An inventor who held at least two patents, he developed an idea for an automatic railroad switch, a device with substantial profit potential; but when he demanded too high a royalty from interested railroads, they came up with an alternative. He also began to speculate profitably in commodity futures.[11]

By the turn of the century, John's livestock enterprise took him as far south as Texas. On at least one or two occasions in the 1890s, the entire family took train trips there to visit John's older brother, William, who had moved to the Southwest in the early 1870s shortly after the death of his first wife. He had left behind his son, Ralph, who was passed around from one family of Missouri Trumans to another until he joined the army during the Spanish-American War. He had a near-brotherly, and sometimes tempestuous, relationship with Harry that endured throughout their lives.

If the Trumans were a relatively cohesive family, the Youngs long had been at one another's throats. When Sol Young died in 1892 without a will and leaving 1,520 acres of land, his children soon were bitterly disputing his estate. On one side were Harrison and Martha; on the other, William and two sisters: Laura and Sallie. The groups traded accusations that the other had already received substantial "advancements" from Sol's estate and thus should be disqualified from any further share. At this point, the Trumans were the only losers; John had to deed the 80 acres he had acquired in 1889 to "the heirs of Solomon Young," probably because Sol had held a mortgage on it or had otherwise financed it. In October 1894, all parties signed an agreement to acquiesce in whatever differential awards the court might choose to make. The Trumans realized 160 acres and $286. The following year, they purchased another 40 acres from Harrison.

Sol's widow must have watched with anger and despair. The owner of 398 acres in her own name, Louisa already had assented to accept a child's share of the estate, rather than the half interest to which she was entitled. In 1893, after her home at Grandview had burned to the ground, she had moved into Independence to stay with the Trumans while Harrison saw to the building of a new, considerably less pretentious farmhouse. It seems clear that she felt estranged from her other children. On March 30, 1895, she signed a last will and testament; it provided $5 for each of them except the two that she felt were taking care of her, Harrison and Martha. They were to receive all the rest of her property. John's attorney, J. M. Callahan, witnessed and probably drafted the document.[12] It provided a powerful incentive for the Trumans to help out Louisa in every way, for it meant an eventual half-ownership of the 518 acres of prime farmland that she possessed after the settlement of Solomon's estate. For the Trumans, this prize must have seemed the future capstone of a life that was already prosperous.

For many Americans—workers in industrial towns and cities made jobless by a severe depression, farmers in the plains states and the South facing falling crop prices and foreclosure—the 1890s were desperate years, scarred politically by the Populist revolt and the bitter Bryan–McKinley presidential campaign of 1896. But for much of the middle class living in well-kept houses on elm-lined streets, the decade *was* the Gay Nineties. The Truman family belonged to this group. As he moved through his forties, John Truman could count himself among the lucky.

When he was interested in something other than his businesses, it was usually politics. In the tradition of the Trumans and the Youngs, he was an intensely partisan Democrat whose attachment to his party went beyond ideological considerations. When Grover Cleveland won the election of 1892, he nailed a flag to the cupola of the Crysler house in celebration. He supported Bryan, Cleveland's ideological antithesis, with equal enthusiasm in 1896. In 1900, he attended the Democratic National Convention, held in Kansas City, to cheer Bryan's second nomination. He watched from the box of his host, prominent Kansas City banker William Kemper. Clearly, he had moved a few steps away from the ragged farmers and workers whom Bryan vainly attempted to unite, but it mattered little. The party allegiance that John Truman inherited from his father was not based on class conflict; it was a product of the guerrilla warfare along the Missouri–Kansas border. He passed his faith along to his children, and they accepted it without question.[13]

V

Harry's early years in Independence produced some fond memories. The Truman house, with its big yard and farm animals, was a gathering place for neighborhood children. John Truman had a little wagon made for Harry and Vivian; a leather worker named Henry Rummell crafted a set of harnesses for a team of goats; and the children paraded around the neighborhood in the rig. Harry did his share of the chores, most of them farm work—milking the cows, herding them to pasture and back, currying the horses, taking the animals to a big public spring two blocks south for water, weeding the garden. He and Vivian sold newspapers for a time, not with a lot of business sense, he recalled: "We usually spent the capital and profit for ice cream sodas and then our father would have to finance us again but we had a lot of fun."[14]

In the fall of 1892, fitted at last with thick eyeglasses, Harry began the first grade at the age of eight. The Independence school instructors taught basic reading, writing, and arithmetic in the no-nonsense pre-progressive tradition. A handbook of rules and regulations issued in 1909 expressed the tone of the school during Harry's years in it. Students were expected "to be punctual and regular in attendance; obedient in spirit; orderly in action; diligent in study; gentle and respectful in manner."

Harry no doubt received strong injunctions from his mother to study hard and obey the teachers—most of them unmarried women and all with names that personified the small-town, Victorian Midwest: Miss Myra Ewin, Miss Minnie Ward, Miss Jennie Clements, Miss Mamie Dunn, Aunt Nannie Wallace. He was a good, earnest student, if far from brilliant, and probably a favorite among them. Years later, he recalled, probably accurately, that none of his teachers had been bad: "They gave us our high ideals, and they hardly ever received more than forty dollars a month for it." He also remembered how at an early age he had learned the way to get ahead: "Whenever I entered a new school room I would watch the teacher and her attitude toward the pupils, study hard, and try to know my lesson better than anyone else."[15]

In January 1894, both he and Vivian contracted diptheria. There was no known antitoxin; the doctors prescribed ipecac and whiskey; fifty years later, Harry claimed (despite his fondness for bourbon) still to hate the smell of both. Vivian recovered quickly. Harry lingered for months, his throat and right side paralyzed. On his tenth birthday, he was unable to walk and had to be moved about in a baby buggy. Soon afterward, he was well and never critically ill again for the next sixty years. Sent to summer school to make up for the half-year of second grade he had missed, he did so well that in the fall he was placed in the fourth grade, joining his own age group for the first time.

He enlarged his horizons in other ways. The town had a good public library with about 3,000 volumes; he spent a lot of time there, browsing through encyclopedias and other works. He read avidly at home as well, mostly books checked out of the library but also some his mother bought for him. When he was ten, she gave him a four-volume set edited by Charles F. Horne, *Great Men and Famous Women*, a beautifully bound, lavishly illustrated collection of biographical articles from leading adult periodicals. The first volume, *Soldiers and Sailors*—with its sketches of such leaders as Alexander the Great, Hannibal, and Charles Martel—especially captured Harry's imagination.

He also became a devoted reader of Mark Twain. A Missourian raised in a southern-style environment, a writer capable of dealing with great themes in prose that a child could read, a commentator who addressed contemporary manners and morals with ironic, blunt, and pithy epigrams, Twain had a special appeal that endured through Harry Truman's life. Both to the boy and to the mature man, Twain was the sort of figure that Benjamin Franklin had been to an earlier generation of Americans—an inspirational, practical philosopher who won adherents with elemental, easily remembered maxims. One that Harry learned early and frequently repeated as an adult was "Always do right. This will gratify some people and astonish the rest."[16]

For a few months, shortly after he began high school, Harry got up early every morning to open Clinton's Drugstore on the town square, sweep the sidewalks, dust off the bottles on the shelves, crank the ice-cream freezer, and take care of a few early customers. His most lasting impressions came from church members and Anti-Saloon Leaguers who slipped in after breakfast every day for a 10-cent shot of whiskey. They initiated a lasting skepticism about "the public front of leading citizens and 'amen-corner-praying' churchmen."

As he remembered it twenty years or so later, Harry did not do much at Clinton's: "I ate ice cream and candy and usually failed to show up when windows were to be washed." But others recalled it differently. Long afterward, Mary Paxton Keeley remembered—or thought she remembered—her friend Bessie Wallace remarking that she wished Harry did not have to work so hard. Piled on top of piano lessons, chores at home, and school assignments, the job was too much for him. He was proud of the $3 a week he was making, but his grades began to slip. His father told him to quit the job and spend more time studying.[17]

Independence High School offered only a three-year curriculum. Old-fashioned, solid, and not terribly different from the education that Franklin D. Roosevelt was receiving at Groton at about the same time, it emphasized the classics, rhetoric, logic, mathematics, natural science, history, and English literature. As a teenager, Harry read Cicero, Plutarch,

Caesar, and Marcus Aurelius, learning and never forgetting the vices and virtues of the ancients. He emerged from the experience a truly educated man, short on vocational skills perhaps, but well grounded in the liberal arts.

One thing that his education did not provide—here also one senses a parallel to Groton—was a sense of complexity and relativity. Standards were clear, fixed, and simple. Harry's schooling conspired with his moral and religious upbringing to leave him with the conviction that personal behavior, and by extension that of societies and nations, should be guided by universally understandable Victorian maxims, that distinctions between good and evil were unambiguous, that there were few gray areas in life. As with Roosevelt's education at Groton, moreover, Truman's schooling embodied the Victorian assumption that the history of mankind was a story of progress; thus it reinforced the pioneer optimism of his forebears.

It was equally consistent with his upbringing and his environment that he learned to interpret virtue in ways other than the heroic. At the age of fifteen, he wrote a short essay on courage. It began by quoting Emerson: "Behavior is the Mirror in which each man shows his image." Then it defined the topic: "The virtue I call courage is not in always facing the foe but in taking care of those at home. Courage does not always come in battle but in home communities." A man who cared for plague victims at the risk of his own life displayed courage. Robert Morris had demonstrated courage by pledging his fortune to the American Revolution. "A true heart, a strong mind, and a great deal of courage and I think a man will get through the world."

Truman also enjoyed poetry. Tennyson was among his favorites. Several stanzas from "Lockesley Hall" affected him so deeply that he copied them and carried them with him for the next fifty years:

> For I dipt into the future, far as human eye could see,
> Saw the Vision of the world, and all the wonders that would be;
> Saw the heavens fill with commerce, argosies of magic sails,
> Pilots of the purple twilight, dropping down with costly bails;
> Heard the heavens fill with shouting, and there rained a ghastly dew
> From the nations' airy navies grappling in the central blue;
> Far along the world-wide whisper of the south-wind rushing warm,
> With the standards of the people plunging thro the thunderstorm;
> Till the war-drum throbbed no longer, and the battle-flags were furl'd
> In the Parliament of Man, the Federation of the World.
> There the common sense of most shall hold a fretful realm in awe,
> And the kindly earth shall slumber, lapt in universal law.[18]

The most indelible interest that he carried away from his school days was the study of history. Like many a bookish boy and very much in tune with his times, he developed a fascination with the exploits of great men, especially soldiers and political leaders. Cincinnatus, the Roman farmer-soldier, was a special hero; so was Robert E. Lee. Unlike his mother, he eventually came to regard Lincoln as a great leader and the preservation of the Union as a good thing. But, no doubt with her encouragement, he developed a lifelong distaste for New England in all its political and cultural manifestations.

At some point, he developed a rough philosophy of history that emphasized personalities and assumed patterns. By current academic standards, his view of the historical process seems simple-minded; in an age that read Plutarch and venerated Carlyle, it appeared very much the common sense of things. "I saw that it takes men to make history, or there would be no history," he wrote after a lifetime of experience. "History does not make the man." He came to believe that while history moved generally in the direction of progress, in the course of its ups and downs, it repeated itself. "What came about in Philadelphia in 1776 really had its beginning in Hebrew times," he would assert in his memoirs. It followed that the leaders who made history move in the right direction were men who, drawing on the lessons of the past, avoided the mistakes of those who had preceded them—whether in investigating the conduct of a war, dealing with foreign aggressors, facing a modern-day witch-hunt, or handling an obstreperous general.[19]

VI

His mother decided that Harry should learn to play the piano. When he was eleven, he began to take lessons from Miss Emma Burrus, whose family lived next door. He displayed remarkable aptitude; after two or three years, he had learned all she could teach him. Martha then arranged for twice-a-week lessons in Kansas City with Mrs. E. C. White, who had studied with, among others, Theodor Leschetizky (a teacher of Ignacy Paderewski), Anton Rubinstein, and Josef Lhevinne. Sitting at an imposing Steinway in her big brick house at Twenty-seventh Street and Brooklyn Avenue, Harry played the works of Beethoven, Mozart, Chopin, and other greats. In 1900, when Paderewski performed in Kansas City, Mrs. White took Harry backstage to meet the maestro and learn firsthand how to execute a difficult "turn" in one of his own compositions.

In his early teens, Harry seriously aspired to a career as a concert pianist, rising every day at 5:00 A.M. for two hours of practice on the family's Kimball upright before going off to school. Mrs. White considered him one of her most promising pupils. "She gave a recital once in a while and she always gave me a showy, brilliant piece to play," he told a friend fifty years later. "The mothers of her other pupils always said she played favorites with the boys—maybe she did."

It was not easy in turn-of-the-century Independence for a boy to stay with the piano, but Harry did, probably all the way through high school and afterward until he had neither the time nor the money to continue. Yet after he quit, he never looked back. "I thought once I'd be an ivory tickler," he wrote to Bess Wallace in 1911, "but I am glad my money ran out before I got too far." Decades later, he simply said, "I wasn't good enough." (In company he liked, he joked, "My choice early in life was either to be a piano player in a whorehouse or a politician—and to tell the truth there's hardly a difference.")[20]

He retained a lifelong love for classical music and enjoyed it openly when he was president. One senses nonetheless that his attraction to the piano as a career was always tentative. He wanted to please his mother and teacher and was happy to be recognized as the best at something. But he also wished to win the recognition of the boys who sometimes jeered at him as he walked past with his music rolls. And he wanted most of all to emulate his father. By the time he was forced to abandon his lessons, he had a clear understanding that he could not achieve all these objectives as a pianist. He may already have possessed a dim awareness that he might attain them as a politician.

Harry Truman's childhood was not that of a miserable outcast, but his thick eyeglasses amounted to a handicap of sorts in a youthful world where learning counted for less than athletic prowess. His malshaped eyeballs were not an obvious, crippling disability. Still, their impact is suggested by Truman's private remark at the age of sixty-five that they were a "deformity" and by his belief that his parents might have found a specialist who could have corrected his vision through eye exercises.[21]

Young Harry learned to get along. Following the orders of his eye doctor and mother, he never fought, ran away when he had to, and rarely, if ever, participated in rough sports. But he was not an insufferable sissy, and he no doubt had learned very early from his egalitarian parents that it was wrong to flaunt his learning or to act superior. He naturally enough wanted to be liked and accepted, and he worked at it. Just as he tried to please his parents and teachers, he strove with some success to win over his playmates. "He just smiled his way along," his first-grade teacher, Myra Ewin recalled fifty years later.[22]

The lesson stayed with him: "Because of my efforts to get along with my associates, I usually was able to get what I wanted. It was successful on the farm, in school, in the Army, and particularly in the Senate."[23] What he perhaps did not fully understand, even as an old man, was the psychic cost of that mode of success. Having been taught the virtue of male aggressiveness and inner direction, as exemplified by his father, Truman found himself forced into a conciliatory, other-directed style of behavior that clashed with his ideas of what a man should be.

He had a few friends who must have been about as bookish as he—most notably Charlie Ross, the son of the local jailer, and Elmer Twyman, whose father was the family doctor. They studied Latin and literature together. Once they constructed a model of Caesar's bridge across the Rhine. Charlie edited the first school yearbook, *The Gleam*, named for Tennyson's "Follow the Gleam." Harry worked on the staff. Soft-faced, bespectacled, physically underdeveloped, a bit pudgy, he was never a leader in any group. He developed something of a reputation as an arbiter of disputes that might have erupted into fistfights, and he occasionally umpired baseball games for the other boys. Yet for all his goodwill, he seems to have been forced to endure more than his share of teasing and name-calling.

"I was always afraid of the girls my age and older," he remembered.[24] The only exceptions seem to have been his sister, Mary Jane, and his first cousins, Ethel and Nellie Noland. It was a fear that must have been rooted in his sense of inadequacy and his need to expend so much energy on getting along with boys. He dealt with it through a common defense mechanism, the impossible romance. In Sunday school at the age of five, he met a little girl with golden curls and beautiful blue eyes. He fell in love at once, he recalled. Astonishingly, his devotion, although not directly expressed to her and certainly not reciprocated, lasted through his school years and beyond.

That little girl, Bess Wallace, was from one of Independence's best families. Her grandfather George P. Gates had moved to Missouri from Vermont after the Civil War, had co-founded a successful milling company, and had built a big gingerbread house at 219 North Delaware Street (just across from a more modest structure that would be occupied by Harry's cousins, the Nolands). Her father, David W. Wallace, was reputedly the handsomest man in town. Her mother, Madge Gates Wallace, had been a beauty whose likeness adorned the milling company's Queen of the Pantry flour sacks. However egalitarian their ideals, the people of Independence understood social distinctions—and felt them all the more keenly because they were at variance with the prevailing democratic myth. Young Harry had to be aware that the Wallaces belonged to a class apart. The Wallaces were established and moneyed; the Trumans were a new family of uncertain and insecure fortune. The Wallaces were Presbyterian and Episcopalian; the Trumans were Baptists.

Bess herself was attractive, intelligent, high-spirited, and athletic. She could play tennis, baseball, and the new sport of basketball better than Harry. His admiration for her must have been clear enough, but there is no indication that during their school days their relationship went beyond occasional walks home with Harry carrying her books. In high school, they frequently studied Latin together with the Noland sisters. But at social gatherings in which boys and girls paired up, Harry usually escorted his cousin Ethel, whom he credited with teaching him "how to be polite."[25] Because boys and girls did not date in the contemporary sense and because so much socializing was organized around church membership, Harry and Bess were probably only seldom at the same occasions. It is doubtful, moreover, that she took him any more seriously than did his male friends. A smart boy and nice enough, she probably felt, but not the one she would marry. Chances are that Harry understood her feelings perfectly, even as he cultivated his infatuation.

Harry's relationship with his father and brother must have gnawed at his self-esteem. Perhaps because he sensed from the beginning that Harry was his mother's favorite, Vivian became his father's boy. He was not interested in schooling, refused to take piano lessons, and liked the outdoors. Avidly adopting his father's interest in livestock trading, he practically became a junior partner. By the time he was twelve, Vivian had his own checkbook and was trading on his own account. Harry must have sensed that while his father treated him decently, he did not have a full measure of paternal respect. Perhaps in an attempt to win it, at the end of his first week at Clinton's Drugstore, he actually tried to give his earnings to his father; no doubt he was disappointed when told to save the money for himself.

Sometime during his high-school years, Harry tried to change his image. He brought fencing foils along to his Latin study sessions with the Noland sisters and Bess. During study breaks, the adolescents played at the sport on the porch. (One need not be a hard-core Freudian to discern a certain significance here.) Ethel and Nellie gave him the nickname Horatio, after Hamlet's decisive friend, and he gloried in it. After the beginning of the Spanish-American War in the summer of 1898, the neighborhood youngsters, like children all over the country, formed a drill company. They marched through the streets, camped out in the woods just north of town, elected new officers every day, and occasionally shot stray chickens with their .22 rifles. Harry began to dream about becoming a professional soldier.

During his second year of high school, he and a friend, Fielding Houchens, tried to prepare for the military academies. They took special tutorials in history and geography with one of their teachers, Miss Maggie Phelps. Harry had his heart set on West Point. He gave up shortly after his graduation, when he went to the Army Recruiting Station in Kansas City and discovered that his eyesight disqualified him for a regular army commission. The experience was yet another—probably not unexpected—disappointment. (Houchens made it to the Naval Academy, only to flunk out.)

Harry Truman, Fielding Houchens, Charlie Ross, and Elmer Twyman were four of only eleven boys who graduated along with thirty girls in the Independence High School class of 1901. They all posed as a group, dressed in their Sunday best, on the front steps of the school for the class picture. Charlie, the valedictorian, sat at one end of the front row. Harry stood inconspicuously near the middle of the back row. A very pretty Bess Wallace displayed her most fetching smile two rows farther down. The stained glass over the school door bore the legend "Juventus Spes Mundi": "Youth, the Hope of the World."

VII

John Truman was worth $30,000 or $40,000 and looked to a future without limit. Harry felt no sense of urgency about getting a job. He took a short trip to Murphysboro, Illinois, where he visited with his Aunt Ada and her family. On the way back, he stopped in St. Louis to see relatives there. They took him to the races, where he bet $5 on a long shot named Claude, a fine mud horse who ran poorly on dry tracks. A rainstorm blew in just before post time, Claude won going away, and Harry collected $125. Like his father, he was attracted to long shots; his initial experience with one was encouraging.

In September, he and Cousin Ralph, recently discharged from the army, went down to Texas for a visit with Ralph's father. They traveled like hobos, grabbing rides on freight cars. Ralph had become a strapping young man—loud, rough, toughened by military life. In Dallas, Harry trailed along while Ralph and an acquaintance did the town. Whatever the activity, seventeen-year-old Harry did not participate. Years later, he wrote to Ralph, "I was a damn fool about that time. If it had been a year or two later I'd had as good a time as you did. It don't take a fellow long to learn in the National Guard."[26]

In the fall of 1901, Charlie Ross and Elmer Twyman went off to the University of Missouri. It appears that the Trumans could have afforded to send Harry to Columbia with them, although his father may have already begun to have cash problems. In those days, a university education did not seem essential for a bright young man, and Harry seems to have wanted to continue his Kansas City–based piano lessons. He enrolled in Spalding's Commercial College in downtown Kansas City, learning typing in the summer and "debit and credit and Pittman shorthand" during the fall semester. His business education, such as it was, would leave him with an understanding of the rudiments of bookkeeping; but he rarely used a typewriter and may never have employed whatever shorthand he acquired. He typically left home early in the morning with trolley fare and a quarter for lunch, attended his classes, had a piano lesson with Mrs. White (probably twice a week), and returned in the afternoon. Occasionally, he had an ice-cream soda at a downtown shop run by Jesse James, Jr.

Harry quit Spalding after only one semester and began to work with his father and Vivian in the family business, most likely keeping the books while the other two did the trading. He may have left business school as quickly as he did because the family was already experiencing financial difficulties. (In March 1902, they raised money by selling the 160 acres that Sol Young had left Martha.) His father was making large—and disastrous—commitments to grain-futures contracts. By midsummer 1902, the family's losses were massive and irreversible.[27]

There was nothing to do but sell every asset. Harry and his father took the train down to Thayer, just a mile or so from the Arkansas line, to inspect forty acres of land that John had acquired sight unseen. Renting a buggy and team of horses, they took a twisting road some eight miles along the Eleven Point River, which was raging along at flood stage. At what must have been considerable risk, they forded the river thirteen times. As Harry remembered it fifty years later, the property ran up the side of a mountain and "was more perpendicular than horizontal."

After John Truman returned to Independence, he sold the livestock, the remaining forty acres near Grandview, and, in September 1902, the big house on Waldo Street. The family rented a residence at 902 North Liberty Street, but stayed there for only a few months. In April 1903, they moved to Kansas City, purchasing a two-story house at 2108 Park Avenue. The neighborhood immediately to the south was a respectable one with some fine homes, but the Truman residence was modest. John still liked to think of himself as a livestock dealer, but he had to settle for a job as night watchman. Still a tough, feisty man, he seems never to have recovered his self-confidence. The reversal came at a critical stage of Harry's life. He would spend much of his young adulthood seeking the sort of business success that had eluded his father and would become increasingly touchy about any disparagement of his family.[28]

VIII

"It took all I received to help pay family expenses and keep my brother and sister in school," Truman recalled of those hard times. In August 1902, he took a mailroom job for $7 a week at the *Kansas City Star*. Two weeks later, he found better-paying work. His bookkeeping class and good reputation landed him the position of timekeeper for the L. J. Smith Company, a railroad construction firm doing a project for the Santa Fe line. The pay was $35 a month and board. Because John had not yet gotten his night watchman's job, Harry's was probably the Truman family's only regular income at that time.

Driving a hand-propelled "tricycle car," Harry, just eighteen, moved between three construction camps about five miles apart and recorded job attendance for each member of the crew. A few of the workmen were farmers using their teams and wagons to make some extra money; others were semiskilled specialists such as blacksmiths and cooks. The manual laborers were hobos who worked a ten-hour day for 15 cents an hour. Every two weeks, Harry paid them off in some saloon; most of them promptly spent every penny on a weekend drunk. Eating and living in the camps, he discovered what alcohol could do to men and learned, he recalled, "all the cuss words in the English language, not by ear, but by note." He remembered with pride a foreman's assessment of him: "He's all right from his asshole out in every direction."[29]

The construction project concluded toward the end of February 1903. Harry spent the next several weeks at home, helping with business matters and assisting in his parents's move to Kansas City. Shortly before his nineteenth birthday, the National Bank of Commerce hired him as a clerk at $35 a month. That June, after leaving high school (he seems never to have graduated), Vivian also got a job at Commerce, at $15 a month.[30]

In his later years, Harry had nothing but bad memories of the bank and its management, remembering especially the way in which the vice president in charge of personnel, C. H. Moore, delighted in dressing down clerks who made mistakes. But Moore never had much cause for complaint with Harry, who after six months was put in charge of the bank's filing vault. The job was an important one. The reports from A. D. Flintom, an intermediate supervisor, were uniformly glowing:

> October 13, 1903
>   Is an excellent boy—does his work well—is kind and obliging. . . . Habits and appearance good.

> April 14, 1904
>   He is an exceptionally bright young man and is keeping the work up in the vault better than it has ever been kept. . . . almost always here and tries hard to please everybody. We never had a boy in the vault like him before.

Vivian did not fare so well. Paid a miserable salary and given routine work in an environment alien to his temperament, he periodically rebelled. A few months after starting, he demanded a salary increase and stalked out of the bank when refused. Two days later—no doubt after being told by his mother, his father, and possibly Harry that the family had to settle for what it could get—he returned and was reinstated. Flintom judiciously evaluated the younger boy:

> He writes a miserable hand, but is a good worker and a good collector. His appearance is good and he is seldom absent from duty and his habits are also good. He appears to be without ambition. . . . At times he is anxious to work . . . and at other times he will sulk. . . . I don't think the boy will ever make a success as a bank clerk.[31]

After two years, Harry had managed a raise to $40 a month. "If a man got an additional five dollars on his monthly pay, he was a go-getter," Truman recalled forty years later, "because he had out-talked the bawler-out and had taken something from the tightest-wad bank president on record." In March 1905, his parents, with whom he and Vivian continued to live, traded their house in Kansas City for eighty acres near Clinton, Missouri. Both Harry and Vivian quit their jobs, helped with the move, and may have expected to stay and help run the new farm. By the beginning of April, however, they were back at Commerce Bank, applying for and receiving their old jobs.

Neither stayed long. After six weeks, Harry quit to take a similar job at Union National Bank. As he recalled it, the starting pay was $60 a month, and he soon had won a raise to $100 a month, very good money for a bank clerk in those days. In July, Vivian left for a job at the First National Bank. Harry recalled the supervisors on his new job as kind and sympathetic. He made friends easily; on occasion, he would take some of them out to his grandmother's farm for a country dinner followed by a horseback tour of the property.[32]

IX

Harry found it a good life. Kansas City was a rough, rollicking, wide-open river town, but it seems unlikely that he sampled its opportunities for sin. Save for an occasional burlesque show, his fun was of the innocent variety. After his parents moved to Clinton, he stayed briefly with his father's sister, Emma (Mrs. Rochester Colgan), on Twenty-ninth Street, and then moved into a boardinghouse run by Mrs. Trow at 1314 Troost Avenue. The guests lived two to a room, paying $5 a week for bed, breakfast, and dinner. Harry customarily purchased a 10-cent box lunch at a shop on East Eighth Street. One of his fellow boarders, a young man named Arthur Eisenhower from Abilene, Kansas, worked at Commerce Bank while Harry was still there; he recalled that he and Harry had about $1 a week for riotous living. (Arthur stayed at Commerce Bank, becoming a senior executive before his retirement at about the time his brother Dwight succeeded Harry as president of the United States.)

Life was comfortable and civilized. Harry from time to time played Mrs. Trow's piano for two young ladies who lived in the house. As his income increased, he and his friends enjoyed occasional evenings at one of the city's steak houses. On many weekends, he went to Clinton to see his parents or out to Grandview to see his grandmother and Uncle Harrison.

He was capable of cruel practical jokes. He and his cousin Mary Colgan tricked her brother Fred and a fellow bank clerk into believing that a note they had put in a bottle and tossed into the Blue River had been retrieved by a southern belle in Mississippi. Weeks of correspondence followed, culminating with the young lady's declaration that she had fallen in love with them. At a party, Mary produced the young men's letters, sent back to her by a friend who had provided a mailing address in Greenville, Mississippi. She read them aloud. A grinning Harry announced that he had dictated the imaginary belle's epistles and Cousin Mary had written them.

Harry likely attended services at the Benton Boulevard Baptist Church fairly regularly. It was there that he felt a sense of salvation, was baptized, and was accepted as a member. The Trumans probably had not attended church regularly in Independence, and Harry's own attendance eventually became infrequent. Nevertheless, the Baptist faith meant a great deal to him, however much in his subsequent years he would ignore its prohibitions against liquor, cards, and swearing. He found intellectual solace in being a member of a faith that allowed the common man direct access to God. The lines of church authority ran from the bottom up; the worship services were simple and unpretentious. The Bible also had great importance for him; throughout his life, he prayed when he needed guidance. Fundamentally a tolerant man, he nevertheless always retained just a bit of distrust for Catholics and Jews.[33]

In 1905, soon after his twenty-first birthday, he and some friends from the bank joined a new National Guard artillery battery, commanded by Captain George R. Collins. For Truman, the move was a matter of patriotism and a modest fulfillment of his military aspirations. It was also a way of making connections with other ambitious young men like himself and getting to know senior notables like Collins. The officers took their duties seriously, and many had military backgrounds. However, no one entered the command ranks without some political attachments.

Harry soon discovered that not everyone in his family was thrilled about his decision. Shortly after signing up, he made the mistake of wearing his dress blues with red striping down the legs—ominously similar to the garb of Jim Lane's men—out to Grandview to display to Grandmother Young: "She looked me over and I knew I was going to catch it. She said, 'Harry, this is the first time since 1863 that a blue uniform has been in this house. Don't bring it here again.' I didn't."

He found the Guard experience, especially summer training camp, exhilarating. It provided a sense of comradeship, shared effort, and achievement. He liked to recall how the men would sing on the way to and from camp, how they had learned to drill and to fire light artillery pieces, how they occasionally harassed unpopular officers. He met some important associates, among them Lieutenant Fred Boxley, a prominent attorney with political and military connections, and one of the sergeants, an overweight bank clerk named Arthur Elliott. He was soon promoted to corporal and made battery clerk. The thrill of that first promotion, he later felt, was never surpassed, not even when he received a captaincy signed by Woodrow Wilson himself. Once he was awestruck when Captain Collins asked him for help in removing his boots.

Still, he kept his sense of humor. One evening in 1906 or 1907, he signed up a new recruit, a young English immigrant and veteran of the Grenadier Guards, Ted Marks. Marks always remembered Truman asking him how long he had been in the country. "Six months," Marks had replied. "You speak pretty good English for someone who's only been in the United States for six months," Truman remarked with a straight face.[34]

His favorite civilian diversion was the theater. On Saturdays, he worked as an usher at one of the vaudeville houses, where he saw all the famous acts of the era, including the Four Cohans, Eddie Foy, and Sarah Bernhardt. He attended grand opera, performances by famous pianists, Shakespeare plays, contemporary dramas, and light musicals. He recalled such experiences with a special fondness decades later.[35]

Only one thing seems to have been missing from a generally satisfactory existence. If Truman had anything approaching a serious relationship with a young woman, it is lost to history. He still frequently escorted Cousin Ethel, but they apparently never allowed their relationship to go beyond a mutual fondness. In a reminiscence written around 1920, he described one of the female boarders at Mrs. Trow's house "that we all thought a great deal of," a pleasant, nice-looking schoolteacher named Cosby Bailey. Perhaps he was attracted to her; clearly, he enjoyed her companionship, but his passing mention of her leaves the impression that he did so in the company of the other boarders. Some people vaguely remembered that he was interested for a time in someone else, but no evidence survives. He rarely, if ever, encountered Bess Wallace in Independence.

Bess's own life had been blighted by an unmentionable personal tragedy. Shortly after Harry had started to work at Commerce Bank in mid-1903, her father, suffering (according to some memories) from throat cancer and deeply in debt, sat down in the bathtub shortly before dawn one morning, put a pistol to his head, and killed himself. Madge Wallace took the children to Colorado for a year, and then returned to Independence and moved into her father's big house on North Delaware Street. Bess attended day classes at a finishing school in Kansas City for the next two years, graduating in 1906 and staying with her mother, who suffered from chronic health problems. A succession of beaux courted Bess, but Harry was not prominent among them, quite probably not among them at all.

That he thought and dreamed about her seems certain. It is less clear why he did not after a time give up and begin to take a practical survey of more available women. Of course, he lived in an age in which men tended to marry later in life than they do today, and was of a culture in which male–female relationships tended to be stilted and uneasy. Moreover, he undoubtedly continued to harbor within himself the exaggerated fear of the opposite sex that had possessed him as a child; he still coped with it by fixating on an unobtainable love.[36]

X

Whatever his difficulties in relating to women, Truman had done well for himself in other ways. He had many friends, had begun to establish a banking career, and enjoyed the cultural variety of city life. Remarkably, he decided to give it up.

His parents had stayed in Clinton for only a year. Bad luck had followed them; John Truman had grown a fine crop of corn, only to see the Grand River spill over its banks and wipe it out. In October 1905, at Grandmother Young's request, John, Martha, and daughter Mary Jane moved back to Grandview to take over the management of the farm from Uncle Harrison, who preferred the high life of the city to agricultural drudgery. They asked Harry and Vivian to come and help. Vivian left the First National Bank sometime in late 1905 or early 1906. Harry agreed to quit his job in mid-1906.

Why did he do it? Years later, he said that he had grown tired of looking at rows of figures. Perhaps he appreciated that his family was in line to inherit the prime spread and that someday part of it would be his. Perhaps he simply felt a sense of responsibility. Surely, he was reluctant to let his father down. The passage of time between his parents' move to Grandview and his resignation at the bank suggests that the decision was difficult.

One thing is certain. Like many a twenty-two-year-old, he had not yet established a firm sense of purpose in his life. Lacking competing ties to a wife or fiancée, not absolutely determined to be a banker, and possibly sensing an occasion to prove his masculinity, he found it easy enough to accede to his father's call and shift from one tentatively established life pattern to another. What he could not have foreseen was a future of eleven years of hard, unrewarding labor.

2

"I Tried to Dig a Living Out of the Ground": J. A. Truman & Son, Farmers, 1906–1914

"All sorts of wagers were made that I wouldn't stay over ten days, two weeks, a month, a year at the outside," Truman recalled twenty years later. The hard life of the farm was in fact alien to his temperament, if not his physique; but whatever his motivation, he came determined to stick it out. He retained his outside interests and developed several new ones, but for the next nine years his primary occupation was simply "farmer." It was a calling that became less attractive with each passing year.[1]

II

The Young farm, only a mile from the town of Grandview, consisted of 598 acres, 80 of them owned by Uncle Harrison and 518 by Grandmother Young. It was about four times the size of the average midwestern farm. The rolling, fertile, eighteen-inch-deep prairie topsoil of Jackson County, probably the most valuable in the state, was worth around $150 an acre in 1910. In what historians have called the Golden Age of American agriculture, it must have seemed a sure and secure source of wealth.

Digging those riches from the ground was nevertheless hard work. Agricultural mechanization had progressed no farther than steam-powered threshers; the Trumans rented one from a neighbor for a few days every year at harvest time. Their own equipment—a gangplow, a corn planter, a grain drill, a manure spreader, a binder—moved along behind the plodding gait of a horse or a mule. From the biting, windy days of March through the scorching summer into the fall harvest season, Harry spent hours in the fields sitting on some piece of machinery and contemplating the tail of the animal pulling it. The rest of the work had only one source of energy, the muscle and endurance that they and hired hands could muster. No matter how valuable the land, even the prosperous farmer shucked corn, bucked bales of hay, and wrestled livestock.

John, Harry, Vivian, and the hired help regularly put in crops of corn, wheat, oats, hay, clover, and potatoes. They raised hogs and cattle, rented livestock pasture to other farmers, hired out registered Hampshire hogs and shorthorn bulls for breeding, sold seed for wheat and oats, even marketed their own homemade sausage. A vegetable garden and a small orchard were directly behind the house, primarily for their personal use.[2]

They farmed during years of rising prices and, in Jackson County, generally favorable weather. The elder Truman managed the farm with his customary intensity, regularly rising before dawn and rousting his sons and hired men out of bed for a workday that usually lasted until dusk; he gave meticulous attention to every detail of maintenance, cultivation, and animal husbandry. Harry kept the books and managed the money. Indications are that the family bank account was kept in his name in order to keep his father's creditors from attaching it. He also read up on the latest developments in agricultural science and did his share of hard outdoor labor. They preserved the land by rotating crops methodically. Vivian, who seemed born to the soil, was a valuable co-worker. Aside from an unsatisfactory few weeks in 1907, when he once again tried employment as a bank clerk, he stayed with the family until his marriage in October 1911.

The family was never poor and no doubt did quite well at times; however, when a much older and overly nostalgic Harry Truman told Jonathan Daniels that the farm made as much as $15,000 a year, he must have been remembering (and possibly exaggerating) the very best year of World War I. (He seems to have been a haphazard bookkeeper, and there is no indication that he ever did a profit-or-loss accounting for any enterprise with which he was connected.) Surviving records indicate that the Trumans took in many small sums but few big profits. Diversification provided insurance against disaster, but also created multiple opportunities for smaller losses from crop failure and livestock disease. In the summer of 1911, the farm suffered weeks of drought while neighbors twenty miles away received enough rain to get by. In 1912, hog cholera wiped out most of the swine. In another year, some mysterious disease killed a hundred steers.

Personal mishaps got in the way, too. At the end of 1910, John Truman broke his leg in a barn accident. He was hardly able to get around three and a half months later when an obstreperous calf knocked Harry down and fractured his leg. The two casualties made efficient farming all but impossible that year. Truman was closer to the truth about the farm's profitability in 1951 when he wrote, "We always owed the bank something—sometimes more, sometimes less—but we always owed the bank."[3]

The house in which they all lived was considerably more modest than the imposing dwelling that Sol Young had acquired and enlarged after the Civil War. After it burned down in 1895, Louisa and Uncle Harrison had built a two-story farmhouse typical of the style prevalent in the rural Midwest—white, T-shaped, a comfortable porch extending across most of the front, a back porch accessible from the sitting and dining rooms. The indoor plan was simple—a sitting room on one side of a center hallway, a parlor on the other, dining room and kitchen to the rear, three bedrooms upstairs. Rows of fine maple trees, set out a generation earlier, lined a long front yard. A small cemetery lay across the road; the men sometimes found themselves pressed into grave digging.

In common with virtually all farmhouses of the time, the dwelling had neither indoor plumbing nor electricity. A well and a cistern provided the water supply. The women or their household help cooked with coal or wood in the winter, used a coal-oil stove in the summer, did the laundry largely by hand, and cleaned house with a broom. Kerosene lamps provided lighting. Only the downstairs rooms were heated, each with its own stove. About the only resemblance to the living conditions Harry had known in Kansas City was a rural telephone service, an unimagined luxury in most agricultural areas. For $3 a month plus tolls for calls to Kansas City, the Trumans were on a ten-party line operated by Home Telephone. To ring up families and businesses served by the Bell system in Kansas City, it had to go through a central switching office, a process that was often time consuming and frustrating.[4]

Nevertheless, thanks to the telephone, communication with the outside world was still not so difficult as in most midwestern agricultural regions. The train station at Grandview, moreover, was only a mile or so away; both the Frisco and Kansas City Southern tracks ran right through the farm. The Trumans went to Kansas City frequently for business, shopping, and entertainment. The closeness of the city must have sharpened the family's sense of living primitively, especially when some emergency presented itself. In March 1914, the family summoned a local doctor when Martha complained of severe abdominal pain. The physician, in turn, sent out a call for a specialist, who after a quick examination found a serious hernia and decided that immediate surgery was required. "There was a long incision made in her right side and some parts removed," Harry recounted. "I had to stand and hold a lamp while it was going on. I hope never to witness another one."[5]

III

The extended family with which Harry lived for some ten years molded his character and personality as much as any other force. Presiding over them for three years was Grandmother Young. Once formidable, she was in her eighty-eighth year when Harry moved to the farm in 1906. We know little about her physical health or clarity of mind as she moved toward the tenth decade of her life. Some fifty years later, a neighbor recalled her as silent and apparently uncomprehending. Surely, she required and received some special care and attention from the one daughter able and willing to come back to the farm and look after her.[6]

Martha (still "Mamma" to Harry, "Mat" or "Mattie" to her friends) remained a source of stability and support in Harry's life. She probably disliked farm life about as much as he; hired help often did the cooking and the washing, but she worked hard and seemingly without complaint. She doubtless encouraged Harry to continue with literary and musical endeavors that most of their neighbors—and probably his father—considered a bit odd for a farm boy. However much Harry wanted his father's respect, he knew that he had received his values from his mother. Applying for a Modern Woodmen insurance policy in 1911, he was required to respond to the question, "Which do you resemble in general characteristics, father or mother?" He wrote, "mother."[7]

John (whom Harry would always call "Papa") was important in one crucial way. Harry seems to have felt inadequate in comparison with his father; he probably hoped that he could earn the older man's respect by dint of his hard work. After Vivian went off on his own, John and Harry became more dependent on each other than ever before. Harry would remember those difficult years with a degree of fondness: "We were real partners. He thought I was about right and I knew he was."

Actually, their relationship was not so simple. Part of the partnership that Harry valued so greatly was an agreement that he would "go in with daddy, even on his debts." Until the last several weeks of his life, John Truman gave the orders, and Harry followed them. John was surely grateful for his son's loyalty and seems to have been liked by his neighbors, but he was not an easy man to live with. In 1949, Harry recalled the way in which his father, a demanding perfectionist, needled him unmercifully over every mistake: "If a crooked row or a blank space showed in the cornfield or the wheat, I'd hear of it for a year."

Single-minded in his devotion to the farm, John openly and vociferously resented Harry's numerous outside activities—even as he himself retained a consuming interest in Democratic politics and expected his son to help him in that enterprise. As Harry's interest in Bess Wallace occupied increasingly large amounts of time, John appears to have become almost jealous and to have worried that he would lose an indispensable source of help. Whatever satisfaction it provided, Harry's relationship with his father made him an aging adolescent from age twenty-two until he was well past his thirtieth birthday, living in his father's house, following his father's orders, enjoying minimal privacy, never quite able to establish an independent identity.[8]

At this stage, Harry seems to have gotten along rather well with his younger brother, despite (or perhaps because of) their dissimilar interests. They divided the work amicably, and there is no record of serious conflict between them. Vivian's earlier move into full independent adulthood must have largely ended whatever normal brotherly rivalry they once felt. Gregarious, lively, and more independent than Harry, Vivian was also more prone to seek the company of farm people his own age. By 1911, he was courting seriously; when he married at the end of October, Harry was best man. Vivian worked rented land on adjacent property and occasionally helped out. But his own family, enlarged by the birth of twins in 1912, necessarily claimed top priority.[9]

Harry's relationship with Mary Jane oscillated, along classic sibling lines, between mutual support and frequent bickering. She remained at home, helping with everything her mother did and establishing what were to be the two consuming interests of her life: her memberships in the Eastern Star (the women's auxillary of the Masonic Lodge) and the Grandview Baptist Church. She shared Harry's love for the piano and gave lessons to a few girls from nearby farms. An occasional beau squired her around, but none of her friendships with men appear to have approached the point of marriage. To some friends and acquaintances, she already seemed an old maid, destined to spend her life looking after Mamma.

Although she and Harry advanced well into chronological adulthood during their years together on the farm, their relationship remained much like that of typical teenagers, filled with considerable teasing and fussing, much of it involving friendships with the opposite sex. Less than two months before Harry's thirtieth birthday, he wrote to Bess Wallace about how he had tormented his sister by ostentatiously trying to get Vivian's year-and-a-half-old twins to call her gentleman friend, Val Brightwell, "Uncle Val." Mary Jane retaliated by attempting to persuade the infants to call for "Aunt Lizzie," referring of course to Bess. "I nearly had to pour a glass of milk down her neck before she came to her senses," he told Bess.[10]

Uncle Harrison lived at various rooming houses in Kansas City but visited frequently, sometimes staying for days. He was in his late fifties when the Trumans took over the farm. Falstaffian in girth and in appetites, with a personal fortune estimated at $40,000, he remained a bachelor and appears to have made a conscious decision to spend his final years having fun in the city. In dramatic counterpoint to the Trumans' work ethic, he played cards for money, enjoyed good whiskey, and liked the company of younger women. Harry regarded him with alternate fondness and irritation—and with envy and a trace of avarice. Harrison demonstrated that decent men could conduct themselves in ways he had been taught to disapprove. Harrison also had a wad of money that Harry hoped to tap for investment opportunities that might bring profit to both of them. Harrison liked and encouraged his nephew, but harbored a healthy skepticism about his business judgment.

IV

Ten years of farm life left their imprint on Truman in other ways. It intensified his Missouri provincialism and chauvinism. Never a bigot in the ugly, emotional sense of the word, he nevertheless absorbed the rhetorical prejudices pervasive in a homogeneous rural environment and spewed them out at the slightest provocation. "I think one man is as good as another so long as he's honest and decent and not a nigger or a Chinaman," he wrote to Bess Wallace in 1911. His letters contain numerous nasty references to other races and ethnic groups. Yet he was equally capable of depicting America as a country whose greatness stemmed from mixing the best of many ethnic strains. Here, as in so many other ways, he exemplified the American democrat, insistent on social equality but suspicious of those who were unlike him.

Although he continued to enjoy the amenities and cultural opportunities of Kansas City, he frequently talked like a Jeffersonian democrat who believed that a growing urban immigrant population corrupted the American way of life. "If they had only stopped immigration about twenty or thirty years ago, the good Americans could all have had plenty of land and we'd have been an agricultural country forever," he commented in October 1911. "You know as long as a country is one of that kind, people are more independent and make better citizens. When it is made up of factories and large cities it soon becomes depressed and makes classes among people."[11]

The farm experience, moreover, strengthened his speculative bent. Farm life was, and remains, a gamble against nature and unseen market forces. He interpreted the business of making a living and getting ahead in the world as one of defying the odds. Never discounting hard work and talent, he nonetheless envisioned luck as the most important component of success. In large measure, this was an accurate reading of the farmer's condition: drought and disease frequently confound the best-laid plans. And it was consistent with the democratic viewpoint that he accepted; if luck, more than talent, determined material success, then all men were indeed equal. Such assumptions squared better with agrarian culture than with the world of business that he would enter one day.

The prospect of breaking out of a hard life into something new, promising, and profitable took on increasing allure with every disappointing year on the farm. Fresh air and hard work may have appealed to Truman at first, and there can be no doubt that it left him stronger and better developed physically than most city bank clerks. But years of work with little material gain sapped him psychologically. He was, as his bank supervisor had observed, a very ambitious young man; yet for all his effort, the possibility of a big payoff seemed steadily to recede over the horizon. As he passed his midtwenties, he must have felt keenly his lack of independence, of material possessions, of a full adult identity.

He did his farm work philosophically and brought to it what humor he could. (He named two of the sows Sarah Bernhardt and Carrie Nation; one of the cows, Nellie Bly.) Nonetheless, he came more and more to detest it. Its rigors dominated one letter after another to Bess Wallace. After pitching hay, "a forkful every two seconds or so," into a raucous binding machine, "my head roars, my eyes are full of mother earth and father fire and my arms ache like rheumatiz." On assisting at a swine vaccination, he remarked, "A two-hundred pound hog can almost jerk the ribs loose from your backbone when you grab him by the hind leg." A day of shucking corn "got my eyes so full of dust that I could almost scoop it out. . . . It is a job invented by Satan himself." Sausage making was an endurance test: "It's always my job to stuff the sausage into the sacks. . . . Always I put in some good hide off my own hands along towards the last because they blister and the blisters wear off. It doesn't injure the flavor of the sausage."[12]

V

The toil of farmwork must have been all the greater when divorced from clear ownership. The Truman family seemed on the verge of renewed independence and prosperity in 1909 when Grandma Young died and left her 518 acres to them and Uncle Harrison. However, four of her children launched a legal challenge to the will, questioning the old lady's competence and alleging that she had been manipulated. The Trumans and Harrison hired Harry's National Guard lieutenant, Fred Boxley, to defend them.*

As usual in complex and ambiguous civil suits, the case dragged on interminably, imposing a steady financial drain on all but the lawyers; it would not come to trial until 1913. Handling most of the pretrial preparation, Harry endured the strain most directly and felt the bitterness sharply. As he prepared for a deposition to be given by a once-cherished aunt, he anticipated the worst: "One hates to see a white-haired old lady, one he likes and respects, tearing up the truth just for a few dollars. . . . I like money as well as anyone but I think I'd do without it if I had to cast aspersions on my mother's character to get it."

The high-stakes suit hung over the family for four years. Harry estimated the property's value at $200 an acre and steadily increasing. A half-interest would be worth $50,000. If the other side prevailed, the Trumans would get a one-seventh interest worth $15,000. The costs stretched the

---

*From 1908 to 1917, Harry was also involved in a complex legal fight over a claim of unknown origin to 120 acres of wooded land in Shannon County, 200 miles away in southwestern Missouri. In July 1917, the Missouri Supreme Court heard the case on appeal, ruled against him, and assessed him a total of $117 in costs. The property's fair-market value was less than $7 an acre. He may have considered the case more a matter of principle than an opportunity for personal profit. This episode is treated definitively in Paul W. Barrett and John K. Hulston, "The First and Only Verified Autobiography of the 32nd President of the United States," *Missouri Law Review* 56 (Winter 1991): 85–101.

family's resources to the limit. In March 1913, a jury deadlocked after listening to a humiliating ventilation of family charges and countercharges. A second trial was scheduled for early 1914. Harry's frustration was intense. "Every trial costs about $3,000, whether it goes or not," he wrote in despair. "If you win, you lose. It's like the Board of Trade. The only sure winner is the middleman, the lawyer."

The death of Aunt Ada in February 1914 interrupted the second trial, which was adjourned without a decision. The other Young heirs, also overextended, made a last-ditch effort to persuade her husband, a man of considerable wealth, to bankroll the suit. Fortunately, he decided against it. In May, the two sides reached an out-of-court agreement. In return for a payment of $9,500, the plaintiffs signed quit-claim deeds to Harry S. Truman.

Harry felt he had achieved a considerable victory; he also felt, as he would so frequently in the future, that his work was unappreciated. He had carried the ball for his family throughout the ordeal and acted as principal for them in the final settlement. Uncle Harrison had offered him compensation a year earlier, and he had refused it. Now he was annoyed that no one wanted to give him anything. He fantasized about keeping the money or pressing the suit on his own after receiving the quit-claims. Of course, he had no serious intention of doing so. It would be enough, he told Bess Wallace, if Mamma got her farm and Harrison let him act as the agent when he sold some of his land.

He then prodded his mother and Harrison into making a formal division of the property. Harrison, he conceded, probably got somewhat the better of the bargain, but that was preferable to another family fuss. The old uncle leased the property back to Harry to work as part of the farm, just as always. In order to pay settlement costs and legal fees, Martha Truman mortgaged her half of the farm for $7,500. It seemed at the time more prudent than selling forty valuable acres to raise the money. At last, the family prospects seemed all but assured.[13]

VI

Drudgery and anxiety-ridden legal battles were not the only experiences of Truman's farm years. He went to Kansas City and Independence frequently to visit relatives, maintain established friendships, and pursue new ones. His social life was increasingly active, time consuming, and fulfilling. And as the years passed, he tended more and more to dream of a new life.

Relationships with other men were central to his existence. He continued in Battery B of the National Guard, going to the city often for drill and attending summer camp from 1906 through 1908. Finding it more and more difficult to meet his Guard obligations, he did not reenlist at the expiration of his second tour of duty in 1911. Yet he remained on close terms with his buddies and continued to attend battery social functions. He also joined the Kansas City Athletic Club, the Grandview Commercial Club (which made him its president), the town band (for which he tried to learn to play the clarinet), and the Woodmen of the World, a fraternal-insurance organization. When the Farm Bureau established itself in Jackson County in 1914, he was literally drafted to be president of the Washington Township chapter.

In 1909, sponsored by Frank Blair, cashier of the Bank of Belton and a reliable family friend, he won admission to the Belton Masonic Lodge. An intelligent and enthusiastic initiate, he rapidly mastered the order's ritual and gained the respect of its members. In 1911, he obtained permission to establish a lodge at Grandview, was elected its first master, then served for a time as its secretary, and was elected master once again. In 1912, he secured acceptance into the Scottish Rite and quickly moved ahead within it also. The Masonic Order became the focus of his social life, taking him away from the farm evening after evening for meetings and banquets all around Jackson County. Blair and other prosperous members of the order, impressed by his intelligence and earnestness, stood his transportation to statewide meetings and offered to finance his expenses for advancement.[14]

For all his social activity, he remained inordinately shy. In 1912 and again in 1913, he expressed his fear of giving talks to groups of schoolchildren. Acutely conscious of his somewhat effete appearance, he described himself as "a guy with spectacles and a girl mouth." He had achieved neither the confident, assertive masculinity so esteemed by the rural culture in which he lived nor the business success and independence so highly valued by the urban culture to which he was attracted. Within his unprepossessing exterior, he harbored strong feelings—romantic aspirations, ideals of public service, desperate hopes for financial success, anger at the greed of his relatives—that he repressed for fear of being seen as ridiculous or unattractive.[15]

He was most appealing to older men of the town and city business and professional classes; they regarded him as reliable, willing to accept responsibility, and capable of initiative. A winning personality, he neither smoked nor drank, dressed well when the occasion called for it, used polite language in polite company, and was deferential to his elders. As much as he valued his relationship with his farmer father, as much as he continued to profess rural egalitarianism, he also admired the respectable bourgeoisie, wanted its esteem, and sought its ideal of success.

On the farm, he seemed just a bit out of place. Although he did his share of work and helped out his neighbors when called on, he did not conceal his dislike of hard and dirty jobs. He resented farm labor all the more intensely because his other activities kept him out late night after night. Often he went for days at a time on four hours of sleep. He respected the value of farmland, but had little use for those who made a living from farmwork, especially if they were landless. "No man that's any good would be a farmhand," he remarked in May 1914. At social occasions, he was as likely to be found in the parlor playing the piano for the ladies as talking crops and weather with the men. His father fretted constantly about his refusal to give all his time and attention to the family enterprise.[16]

VII

The most dramatic development in his life—one that not only fulfilled deep longings but also gave focus and a sense of urgency to his hopes of being something more than a farm boy—was the renewal of his relationship with Bess Wallace. Toward the end of 1910, he made one of his numerous visits to the Nolands in Independence. Aunt Ella mentioned, perhaps casually, perhaps with design aforethought, that a cake plate needed to be returned to the Wallaces. The young man seized the occasion—and the plate—rushed across the street, knocked on the door, and found himself face to face with the young woman whose memory he had cherished for so long. At the age of twenty-six, he still found courtship difficult, but he had mustered the determination to attempt it.

The years since her high-school graduation could not have been easy for Bess. After completing her postsecondary education, she had become in many ways the mistress of her grandfather's mansion at 219 North Delaware, running the house and seeing to the care of her extended family: Grandmother and Grandfather Gates; her partially invalided mother; and her three younger brothers, Frank, George, and Fred. By the time Harry knocked on the door, the belle of Independence High School was twenty-five and on the brink of spinsterhood. The smiling face of the nice boy with whom she once had studied Latin must have been a pleasant surprise.

Other men came to call over the next few years, but Harry returned again and again, eventually monopolizing her weekends. Sleeping over at the Nolands, he customarily spent each Saturday and Sunday with Bess. The trips required walking a mile into Grandview, catching a train to Sheffield (a little industrial town just north of Kansas City), and then taking a streetcar into Independence, where he could get off a couple of blocks from the Wallace house. On Sunday evening, he would leave in time to catch the last train to Grandview, arrive at the station around midnight, and trek back home along a dark, lonely road, often glancing nervously over his shoulder, on the lookout for hobos who preyed on lone travelers after dark. Invariably, his father would call him out of bed at five the next morning.[17]

Each Monday, sometimes Tuesday if he was especially busy, Harry would write Bess a long letter that often ended with a phrase such as "I hope you'll consider this worth a reply." Almost always, the replies arrived on Thursday or Friday and left him encouraged. Unfortunately, none are available today; Bess, ever jealous of her privacy, reputedly destroyed them in her old age. One suspects that she was impressed by

Harry's effort to spend time with her. Doubtless she discovered that they had much in common. Both lived lives dominated by their duty to their families. Both read extensively for pleasure, most often popular magazine fiction and light novels, but also some weightier matter. Bess was fond of Dickens; in the political year of 1912, Harry read Plato.

Both enjoyed the theater in all its varieties—vaudeville, light musicals, grand opera, Shakespeare. Both loved music. Harry frequently entertained Bess, and tried to win over her mother, by playing the piano for them. They went to concerts in Kansas City. Sometimes they also had dinner downtown, at the plush dining room of the Baltimore Hotel or at a more modest eatery like the Tea Cup Inn, depending on how much money Harry happened to have.

There were some differences in their tastes. Bess was a sports and outdoors person to a far greater extent than Harry. She loved tennis, a game for which he had no use. When they went fishing, he brought along a book, baited the hook for her, and read. Her different preferences made her, if anything, more interesting to him. He even attempted to build a tennis court on the farm in the hope of luring her there for regular visits. She must have appreciated a man so determined to indulge her.

The relationship with Bess changed Truman's life, but the attempt to take a big step toward becoming a full-fledged adult was anything but easy. The rural, Protestant, Victorian culture in which he lived treated a young single man's normal interest in an unattached woman his own age as if it were a dirty secret. Wanting to be taken seriously, he resented kidding of any sort and doubly resented gibes about Bess. He obviously took pride in his friendship with her and displayed her picture, after he had cajoled one from her, on his bedroom dresser; but he seems to have discussed her as little as possible with his family and friends.

Even without cultural inhibitions weighing on him, he keenly felt the insecurities that one might expect to afflict a young man courting a girl he had envisioned for so many years as standing on a remote pedestal. After several months of seeing her regularly, he worked up the nerve to propose marriage, but not face to face. He asked her indirectly in the second paragraph of a long, rambling letter, dated June 22, 1911:

> I guess we'll all have to go to drinking whiskey if it doesn't rain very soon. Water and potatoes will soon be as much of a luxury as pineapples and diamonds.
>
> Speaking of diamonds, would you wear a solitaire on your left hand should I get it? Now that is a very personal or pointed question provided you take it for all it means. You know, were I an Italian or a poet I would commence and use all the luscious language of two continents. I am not either but only a kind of good-for-nothing American farmer. I've always had a sneakin' notion that some day maybe I'd amount to something. I doubt it now though like everything. It is a family failing of ours to be poor financiers. . . . Still that doesn't keep me from having always thought that you were all that a girl could be possibly and impossibly. You may not have

guessed it but I've been crazy about you ever since we went to Sunday
school together. But I never had the nerve to think you'd even look at me.
I don't think so now but I can't keep from telling you what I think of you.

. . . You said you were tired of these kind of stories in books so I am
trying one from real life on you. I guess it sounds funny to you, but you
must bear in mind that this is my first experience in this line and also it is
very real to me. Therefore I can't make it look or sound so well as Rex
Beach or Harold Mac[Grath] might. . . .

. . . Say, Bessie, you'll at least let me keep on being good friends won't
you? I know I am not good enough to be anything more but you don't know
how I'd like to be. Maybe you think I won't wait your answer to this in
suspense.

Still if you turn me down, I'll not be thoroughly disappointed for it's
no more than I expect.[18]

Apparently, Bess did not know how to react. Perhaps she seriously
considered the proposal; perhaps she was embarrassed. It could not have
been her first opportunity at marriage. Harry waited for nine days and
then wrote, "Did you get a letter from me not long ago? Please answer if
only to give me fits for being so fresh." Still no reply. On July 10, he wrote
again:

I have just about come to the conclusion that I must have offended you in
some way. If being in love with you is any offense, I am sorry but it can't
be helped you know. Anyway that shouldn't keep you from being real civil
anyway.

Won't you at least let me know you are not "mad," as Shakespeare
would say? . . .

Would you object to my coming down Saturday evening?

Her reply, a day or two later, was negative but kind and not altogether discouraging; most important, she did not tell him to stop seeing
her. "You turned me down so easy that I am almost happy anyway," he
responded. "I am more than happy to be your good friend for that is more
than I expected. So when I come down there Saturday (which I'll do if I
don't hear from you) I'll not put on any hangdog airs but will try to be
the same old Harry."[19]

VIII

So they settled for the next couple of years into an increasingly feigned
routine of "good friendship," with Harry visiting almost every week and
letters being exchanged with regularity. Exactly why Bess decided against
marriage in 1911 is a mystery; but she was not willing to send Harry out
of her life, and he was determined to keep trying. The main strike against
him, he quickly concluded, was his lack of success; he resolved that he
would not marry Bess until he had the means to support her independently. Until then, he would take as much of her time as she would give
him and would not let her forget his ultimate intentions.

Weekend after weekend, month after month, year after year, he showed up at 219 North Delaware. Bit by bit, he won her affection. He also established congenial relations with her brothers. Her mother was more difficult. She may have thought Harry a nice young man, but near-unanimous testimony has it that she never really considered him worthy of her daughter. He doubtless was right in understanding that his lack of financial independence was a big part of the problem—and a legitimate consideration for any mother or prospective bride. But there was more.

Madge Wallace was probably more emotionally than physically dependent on her daughter. Bess was the one consolation in her life. She had thought all Bess's suitors unworthy and had done what she could to discourage them. In the end, ironically, her possessiveness was to Harry's benefit. Where other possible husbands probably had slipped away because they found it impossible to accept Mother Wallace as a formidable presence in their lives, Harry did not shrink from the idea. His willingness to share Bess with her mother would make their marriage feasible.

In the fall of 1913, he scored a major triumph. One Sunday evening, she told him that she cared for him and may have said she would consider marriage. She underscored her feelings the next day with a letter. "I have been all up in the air clear above earth ever since it came," he wrote on November 4. "I guess you thought I didn't have much sense Sunday, but I just couldn't say anything—only just sit and look." He could not ask her to marry him until he had a decent home for her, but they could make a tentative commitment: "Let's get engaged anyway to see how it feels. No one need know it but you and me until we get ready to tell it anyway." If she found a man she liked better, it could be broken off easily enough. As for him, he meant to have her or no one at all. Whether Bess considered herself engaged after this episode is uncertain. Harry did not buy her a ring—he was never able to do so—but she had declared her affection in a decisive way.[20]

Harry fit in well with the gay young crowd that Bess was part of. Her best friend was probably Agnes Salisbury, a daughter of another elite Independence family that owned a sprawling horse farm just to the east of town. Agnes had married Harry (Pete) Allen, a boyhood friend of Truman, one of the most handsome men in town and a superb athlete; she had given birth to a daughter by him (Bess was the little girl's godmother), divorced him, and remarried. Near scandalous, this personal history demonstrated that the Salisburys followed their own rules in the game of life. Agnes's father was wealthy; her mother, the grande dame of the local Daughters of the American Revolution. An uncle, a crusty retired commodore in the navy, spent several months of each year with them. Agnes's brother, Spencer, was a tall, imposing, devil-may-care fellow who rode a motorcycle recklessly, had served a term as township constable, and was an officer in Independence National Guard Battery C. Possessing no clear career plan, he cultivated an image as a bit of a rogue and displayed a fine sense of humor. He and Harry became good friends.

Bess and Harry visited the Salisbury spread fairly often, occasionally spending well-chaperoned weekends with a crowd of young people. Years later, Mary Paxton Keeley recalled, "We had more fun at that farm than any place we went—saddle horse riding, ice skating on the ponds with bonfires to warm us and hayrides and dancing in the summer." This life was a step up from Harry's (at times, in order to save him the expense of renting a horse and buggy, he and Bess walked the two miles to the Salisbury farm), but it was one to which he reasonably could aspire.[21]

Truman reacquainted himself with many people he had known as an adolescent. Bess's middle brother, George, courted and married May Southern, the daughter of Colonel William Southern, publisher and editor of the *Independence Examiner*. Colonel Southern (the title was honorary) had made the *Examiner* the rural county's leading paper and himself a key figure in the local establishment. He wrote a regular column, "In the Missouri Language" (a phrase coined by Mark Twain), and signed it "Solomon Wise." A staunch Jeffersonian with loose ties to the "goat" faction of the local Democratic party, Southern was a devout Presbyterian with influence in church circles around the state, a committed prohibitionist, and a widely respected man of integrity. His brother, Allen, was a local judge cut from the same cloth but with vague connections to the "rabbit" Democrats. The colonel had known and liked John Truman; May surely favorably mentioned John's son to him. The developing relationship would be to Harry's great advantage.[22]

By the spring of 1914, Harry was able to see Bess more easily and frequently than ever. The settlement of the long civil suit gave the family some financial margin. Martha Truman let her son have $650 to buy a used Stafford automobile. He had long yearned for a car. He had the aggravations with it that all auto owners of that era endured—tire punctures, crankshaft stubbornness, engine stalls, drained batteries—and the bumps and bruises that often accompanied them. None of these irritations were as consequential as the sense of substance and mobility the auto gave him. He drove it everywhere, especially to Independence.[23]

IX

"Who knows, I may be his excellency the Governor of Montana someday," Truman wrote to Bess shortly before he proposed the secret engagement. "How would you like to be Mrs. Governor?"[24] The query, only half-jest, was emblematic of two important themes that had developed in his life. The first was a yearning to move off on his own, preferably to some place far away, begin life anew, and earn the fortune that eluded him on the farm. The second was the awakening of his own political aspirations.

From his relatives in Texas, he knew of the rapid development of the Southwest—and of quick increases in land values there. Intermittently, he tried to persuade Uncle Harrison and perhaps other relatives or friends to go in with him on speculative land purchases in the Pecos Valley of Texas or the Rio Grande Valley of New Mexico. Typically, he thought of only potential rewards rather than risks. He made trips to Texas and New Mexico in 1910 and 1912, returning filled with enthusiasm about the beauty and fertility of the land, the length of the growing season, and the potential for a prosperous living or quick land profits.

The other possibility, far more romantic, was to become a modern-day pioneer homesteading on the Great Plains. The supply of federal lands suitable for agricultural development had dwindled far below the potential demand, but as late as the early twentieth century some promising tracts, detached from Indian reservations, were released through a land-lottery system. An aspiring settler traveled to a city near the area to be made available, registered, and received a number. If it came up in a subsequent drawing, he was assigned a parcel of land. If after a specified period he did not take up residence, the property would be reassigned. The prospect of free, fertile, wheat-growing land in an age of rising grain prices was alluring to many midwestern farmers.

In October 1911, with his family's land title under legal challenge and memories of a disastrous growing season still vivid, Truman, his cousin Murray Colgan, and a neighbor took the train to Gregory, South Dakota, to register for a land drawing. They discovered that hordes of land seekers were filling up one special train after another to get there, frequently shouting "Sucker!" and sterner epithets at trains that passed on adjacent tracks. Gregory was jammed with would-be homesteaders. After registering, Truman wrote to Bess, "There are about four hundred claims that are worth from $8,000 to $12,000 each. Of course I'll draw one of those." He got nothing other than an exciting trip and a chance to see Omaha on the way back: "Omaha is a fine town, I think. Every street is as wide as Grand Avenue." From an exaggerated optimism, he fell into an equally exaggerated depression. "I am born under Neptune or some other far distant and unlucky star," he reported to Bess. "Just keep imagining that my luck will change someday."[25]

In September 1913, he was on the train to Glasgow, Montana, to participate in a Fort Peck–area land lottery with a group that included his father, possibly Vivian, and one or two neighbors. Soon after he returned, he received notification that he had drawn claim no. 6199 and would be able to take it in the first half of the following year. Elated, he joined the local Fort Peck Settlers Association, wrote optimistically about land values, and hyperbolically proclaimed to Bess his ambition to be governor of Montana and, on one occasion, "Chief Executive of the U.S." But Bess could not have been enthusiastic about moving to the frigid North. By the beginning of May, a month before he had to make a decision and with the family lawsuit settled, he began to back off. He still knew neither the location nor the value of his claim. He noted reports of a spring snowstorm and below-zero winters with trepidation: "Coal is only two dollars a ton . . . but I've an idea a person can burn some seventy tons a week." Toward the end of the month, he went up to have a look for himself and evidently did not like what he saw. The governorship of Montana disappeared from his list of ambitions.[26]

X

Politics in general did not, however. Truman's political interests usually were secondary concerns; he frequently was flip about them when he mentioned them to Bess. But a real seriousness underlay his clowning. In 1912, his father supported the renowned Missourian Champ Clark for the Democratic presidential nomination; Harry, probably displaying his bookish inclinations, liked Woodrow Wilson from the beginning. During the 1912 Democratic National Convention, he repeatedly took time from his plowing to get the latest reports at a telegraph station on one edge of the farm. When he heard that William Jennings Bryan had denounced Clark, he was "ecstatic." From 1912 on, Wilson was a special hero to him.[27]

Locally, Bess's brother Frank was active in the growing county organization of the Kansas City Pendergast machine, the goat faction of the party, opposed primarily by Joe Shannon's rabbits. John Truman's Democratic associations also had been with the goats. Soon Harry and Frank were attending goat meetings in Kansas City. Until 1912, Harry's political activity did not extend beyond being an election judge in Grandview; but in that year, he and his father worked hard in Washington Township for R. D. Mize, the goat candidate for eastern district judge of the county court. Harry came to feel so strongly about the campaign that in the general election he scratched two local nonmachine Democratic candidates in favor of a Republican and a Theodore Roosevelt Progressive.[28]

Mize won a hard fight and was scarcely installed in office before John Truman was campaigning vigorously to be appointed township road overseer. The job carried some public recognition and a small extra income; the road overseer could bill the county for work done by his teams and wagons when they were not needed on the farm. But it also would tie Harry down even more. He circulated petitions for his father, but told Bess, "I honestly hope he gets beaten." Small chance. John's opposition had been on the wrong side in the primary election, and his neighbors respected him as a man who would do the job honestly.

John won the appointment and threw himself into the task with an energy that delighted some, infuriated others, and cut into Harry's weekend time in Independence. He dragged the county court out on a tour of his rural roads in an effort to get more funds; he badgered farmers who failed to cut roadside weeds and trim their hedges. He was soon complaining about lack of cooperation and appreciation. When the editor of the *Belton Herald* called him one of the "henchmen of the Jackson County Court," he went to Belton to thrash the offending journalist, but luckily did not find him. An amused Harry told his father, "It was a very mild remark and should be accepted as a compliment to a man who has a political job."

If anything, John Truman delighted in the animosity he had attracted. He may actually have considered running for political office in the next election. Harry vowed to speak against him if he did. "Politics sure is the ruination of many a good man," he grumbled. "Still, if I were real rich I'd just as soon spend my money buying votes and offices as yachts and autos."[29]

Whatever the vicissitudes of local politics, things at home looked better than they had in years. John was livelier than ever. Even before the legal settlement, he was getting off the farm and attending weekend social affairs. Harry also became a political activist. When the postmastership of Grandview became vacant, he campaigned intensively for the position, although he expected to make little or no money from it. He no doubt saw it as a modest stepping stone. He enjoyed public service. Above all, he valued the confidence and backing of his neighbors. As he told Bess, when he wrote to his congressman, W. P. Borland, "I didn't ask him to appoint me straight out but asked him to make the appointment that the majority of the patrons of the office wanted."[30]

XI

By mid-1914, the Trumans had clear title to 300 acres of prime farmland and were counting on a bumper wheat crop to take them out of debt. Then luck of the worst kind struck again. Working on the roads, John Truman attempted to lift a large rock and injured himself. X-rays revealed not a simple hernia, but an intestinal tumor that had been developing for years. Apparently, the road injury aggravated its effects, creating a near-total intestinal blockage. The doctors told him that surgery was his only chance—and that his chances of surviving it were less than 50–50.

For weeks, the old man refused the operation. Harry took him to a Chinese physician in Kansas City who claimed to be able to effect a cure without it. John kept as much a hand in the management of the farm as he could muster and continued to display mastery as a livestock trader. Still, he could barely get out of bed, and Harry hardly dared leave him. At the end of September or beginning of October, John finally agreed to an operation at the Swedish Hospital in Kansas City. Soon he was convalescing at home, but displaying little improvement. Harry stayed as close to him as possible while trying to keep up the road responsibilities and run the farm. On the evening of November 3, he was at his father's bedside. "I had been sitting with him and watching a long time," he remembered. "I nodded off. When I woke up, he was dead."

It was hard for Truman to come to grips with his father's death, harder than for most sons because he had never escaped paternal domination. It was hard, he told Bess, to imagine going on about the business of running the farm alone, supervising hired men who could be unruly and unreliable, bargaining over livestock, keeping the general management of the place up to his father's high standards.[31] Yet John Truman's death, although deeply and sincerely mourned by his son, was in a very real sense a liberation. Harry could now move out on his own in a fashion that would have been difficult as long as his father was alive. He would continue active management of the farm for another year, but his interests increasingly were elsewhere. He was finally free to follow his real ambition: to become an entrepreneur.

3

"My Ship's Going to Come in Yet": Misadventures in Venture Capitalism, 1915–1917

With the death of his father, Truman found himself able at last to decide his own aspirations without inhibition. He must have felt mixed emotions—gradually receding sorrow over the loss of a parent, a fair amount of anxiety over the existential prospect of self-definition that lay before him, and above all optimism that he could make himself into the substantial citizen that his sweetheart deserved and his prospective mother-in-law demanded.[1]

His quest for success inevitably took him from the farm. Memories of his father, his own sense of inadequacy as a farm manager, and the disappointing financial results of his years at Grandview were all too strong for him to stay on. He continued to dabble in politics, but his major ambition was the achievement of wealth. His experience was primarily with the land or with products extracted therefrom; it was here that he would try his luck. The next two and a half years were a roller-coaster period in which hopes rode high but disappointments prevailed.

Harry Truman at the age of thirty was a product of the century of American experience that had preceded him; it had been represented well by Solomon Young, less so by his father. From his family and from his larger environment, he inherited the attitudes that had dominated the westward movement and that were more appropriate to a nineteenth-century frontier society than to the rapidly maturing twentieth-century

Midwest—a willingness to take chances in hope of riches, a tendency to envision wealth in the form of natural resources, a faith that fortunes could be built from small stakes. He and his culture clung to a vision of success as the result of both luck and pluck. One was not quite ready to assume all the blame if a venture went sour; nevertheless, failure suggested a deficiency of character. By his thirty-third birthday in May 1917, Truman still had hope for the future, but his confidence in himself must have been considerably deflated.

II

Less than a month after his father's death, he won the political office for which he had been campaigning. With Congressman W. P. Borland's endorsement, he was appointed postmaster of Grandview on December 2, 1914. He quickly discovered that political success could be about as onerous as political failure. He did not have time to run the operation himself, and eager job seekers begged for it. In the end, he retained a widow, Ella Hall, who already had been doing the job, and gave her his salary of $41.92 a month. On April 27, 1915, apparently tired of tending his white elephant, he submitted his resignation. In late August, he turned the position over to a successor. Auditors subsequently billed him for a 38-cent discrepancy in his accounts.[2]

Another public office engaged Truman's active attention. The family's political patron on the county court, Judge R. D. Mize, had him appointed to succeed his father as road overseer. He went at the job with the same zeal and combativeness. His work notes for the spring of 1915 indicate that he devoted at least ten days to his responsibility during the months of March, April, and May. When the new county highway engineer, Judge Allen Southern, backed by the local state senator, refused to pay him and numerous other overseers, he prepared a scalding letter:

> With all due respect to you and the Senator, it seems to me that you have a little too much law and not much common sense mixed in these questions and answers. . . . In order to get good men and good teams and a good day's work, it is necessary to pay the prevailing scale of wages. . . . [Y]ou have not figured correctly nor had much experience in either farm work or day labor. . . . [W]hen it comes to working at the figures you give and in the manner you suggest I can't see my way clear to do it.[3]

After writing in probably the most assertive language he had ever used, he decided against sending the letter and invited Southern to dinner. "I had Allen Southern out home Tuesday and gave him a sample of mamma's old roosters," he wrote to Bess. "He was very well pleased with my road district. I don't know if the rooster had any effect or not but he said I had the best kept in the county. So said Mize. Everyone seems to think I must place the ends against the middle to get by those two fellows."

Torn between the example of his father and the need to be liked that had dominated his own life, Truman frequently in the future would act out his anger on paper, and then resort to charm and reason with the object of his rage. The system may have said something about his psychology; it was also an intelligent way to handle many difficulties. It usually worked pretty well.

Judge Mize died in 1915. By then, Truman, attempting to make a going concern of a lead and zinc mine in Commerce, Oklahoma, was unable to devote much time to road work anyway. The county court promptly relieved him of his duties. Naturally enough, he resented being fired; thirty years later, he would write, "The presiding judge became dissatisfied because I gave the county too much for the money."

He sought to stay politically active by running as goat candidate for Democratic township committeeman. Part of his motivation was no doubt to seek vindication against the new powers on the county court. But his business obligations so curtailed his campaigning that he was away on election day. "Some of my best friends threw me over," he told Bess. "They thought I ran away on purpose."[4]

III

As always, his life revolved more than ever around Bess. On many weekends, they went to Kansas City to see the latest show. At other times, they enjoyed the company of friends (mostly Bess's). In April 1915, they spent a weekend at the Salisburys. Harry was a bit embarrassed a few days later to find his name in the social notes of the local paper. Cousin Ethel told him she was expecting a formal engagement announcement party at any time.

One major problem still stood in the way. His opportunities for advancement appeared forever blocked by his family's debts. Annual mortgate interest seemed to swallow most of the farm profits, leaving the family hard pressed to pay for necessary paint and repairs. At times, Harry thought of persuading his mother to sell out, but he knew she loved the old homestead too much to do so. "Financially I'm $12,500 worse off than nothing," he told Bess just after their weekend at the Salisbury farm. "But I'm not going to be for long, and if you'll only believe it I know I can make things come right yet." He admitted a fear of losing her good opinion, an event that "would be the last bitter drop in a cup that has been pretty full of disappointments in the last year or two." Through the spring and summer, he devoted his energy to the farm, hoping for the good crops and big profits he needed to start anew.[5]

In October, he and Bess went downtown to the Grand Theater to see the touring Broadway hit musical *The Girl from Utah*; it featured the romantic Jerome Kern song "They'll Never Believe Me." Afterward, perhaps alone in Bess's parlor, they talked of their future. He probably told her that he had decided once and for all to look beyond the farm for his future. She, as he put it thirty-two years later, told him that she would take a chance on him. He never forgot the song; he never forgot the evening.[6]

For capital, he looked once more to Uncle Harrison; for investment possibilities, to the newly opened lands of the Southwest. The old man was in precarious health, chronically ill, often drunk, and, Harry feared, "on the point of cashing in." Yet at times, he was his old bon vivant self, apparently healthy and in the best of spirits. On three occasions—September and November 1915 and February 1916—Harry traveled to Texas, always with groups of prospective land buyers, evaluating opportunities for himself and acting as a commission salesman for a land company. Harrison came along on the last journey, all the way out to Fort Stockton and San Angelo, enjoying the trip immensely. "He is able to lead every big lie that is told in his presence by a bigger one," Harry wrote to Bess. "When he can do that he's happy." Unfortunately, Harrison enjoyed the travel more than he did Texas; Harry's optimism sagged, although his uncle did promise to consider an investment closer to home.

Perhaps confirming Harrison's belief that Pecos Valley land was overpriced, an agent offered to let Harry have up to 640 acres with nothing down and five years to pay it off. On its face, the proposition was tempting; agricultural commodity prices and land values still seemed on a steady upswing. But it would involve either a move to Texas or absentee ownership with hired management. The first option was unthinkable without Bess; the second probably seemed too risky. After February 1916, the dream of riches in Texas went the way of homesteading in Montana.[7]

IV

About that time, another tempting venture materialized. A well-to-do older neighbor, Tom Hughes, the former sheriff of Cass County, introduced Truman to Jerry Culbertson, his one-time prosecuting attorney. Culbertson was a "promoter"—an individual who sought out get-rich possibilities and found partners to provide the financing. A type still common in the early twentieth century, he was neither an entrepreneur nor a manager—and was more adept at raising money than making it.

Lured by the boom in metals prices that had accompanied the first year and a half of World War I, Culbertson had acquired an option on a sub-par lead and zinc property, the Eureka Mine and Mill, at Commerce, Oklahoma, near Joplin, Missouri. His likely intention was to raise a quick stake from it while prices were high, and then to reinvest the proceeds into a higher-quality lease. He approached Hughes, who had previously bought into a couple of Culbertson's unprofitable mining ventures, persuaded him to take another gamble, and through him met Truman.

As he talked to his new acquaintance, sketching prospects of big payoffs, Culbertson scouted extremes of rhetorical excess. "The hinges of destiny," he declared, were greased on the door of opportunity. Truman was amused ("Jerry has oratorical ambitions I think") but receptive. He knew that Vivian's father-in-law and two partners had just sold a mine near Joplin at a profit of $75,000 and that "the old geezer" was making $1,000 a week from another one. Raw ore was selling at $115 a ton or more; the prewar price had been about $45.

On March 4, the three men drew up an agreement to establish the T.C.H. Mining Company. Truman and Hughes would contribute $5,000 for development of the property and $500 as a down payment to the sellers of the lease. (Truman's source of funds remains unclear. It seems definite that he pledged his livestock as loan collateral and probable that the creditor was Uncle Harrison.) Culbertson's option provided for a lump-sum purchase price of $10,000 or an installment price of $13,500, with payments to begin ninety days after taking possession of the property. Presumably, the partners expected to meet that obligation from mine earnings. Culbertson apparently would function as a fund-raiser, leaving Truman and Hughes responsible for management of the mine.

The next day, Truman wrote excitedly to Bess from Joplin as he waited for an engineer to give him a final report on needed repairs to the mill. Visions of riches filled his mind. He had been told that there was $4,000 worth of waste ore lying around the mill, accessible with an expenditure of only $1,500. When the mill was repaired, it would process enough ore to make $1,000 a day (half of which would be profit). He could find no one who thought the mine was a fake; it just needed $3,000 worth of work: "In six months we expect to be on velvet and an income of about $400 a week apiece. . . . I'm going to have the best farm in Jackson County and one in the Pecos Valley for winter with a Pierce-Arrow to ride in."[8]

Culbertson's door of opportunity was more like a trap door. He and his partners had purchased one of many marginal, run-down Joplin-area properties that were changing hands and being reopened in the unrealistic belief that the metals-price boom would last forever. In fact, the partners had come to the bonanza too late. They were wholly inexperienced in mining, unrealistic about the amount of capital required to put their acquisition into operating shape, and unable to distinguish between unreliable and good help. They failed to discern that prices had already peaked and were on the verge of collapse under an avalanche of new supply from dozens of tertiary operations such as the Eureka. Vivian's father-in-law had shown better judgment in selling.

Full of hope, Truman and Hughes moved down to Commerce. The tiny town had grown up a stone's throw from a string of a dozen or so mines. It had gone through one boom-and-bust cycle; renewed prosperity had not brightened its bleak appearance. Large slag heaps studded the landscape. The housing was shabby. For 50 cents each a night, Truman and his partner stayed for a few days at the "best hotel in town," an ill-constructed building with paper-thin walls, just four blocks from the mine shaft.

Carpenters worked on an addition to the mill; mechanics repaired the creaky old machinery; and men did some preliminary blasting down below. The new mine proprietors were hoping for a quick start-up. Instead, they ran into one delay and unexpected expense after another—high initial payrolls, costly supplies, and unanticipated equipment purchases. In the meantime, they established T.C.H. Mining as an Oklahoma corporation. The articles of incorporation, filed on March 27, 1916, authorized 8,000 shares of common stock with a par value (offering price) of $10 each. The financial structure of the corporation was indicative of its founders' optimism and of Culbertson's promotional tactics. It declared a value of $10 a share for 1,997 unsold shares, although the partners had each invested just a little more than $1 a share for their stakes. A total book value of $80,000 was thus proclaimed for a corporation that had been started up with less than a tenth of that amount.

Not surprisingly, no one was willing to buy a minority interest at so inflated a price. But then, as now, insiders who had already placed their funds at risk were free to value treasury stock at whatever price they deemed suitable. With metals prices soaring and engineering reports indicating potentially strong veins of marketable ore at the site, it was easy to be optimistic. Before they started up, Culbertson offered to buy Truman's stock for $5 a share. Affecting an amiable cynicism, he wrote to Bess, "I would take that much cash but not wind." In fact, it appears certain that he never seriously explored whether his partner could raise the cash to make good on the offer. He fully hoped to get rich.[9]

As soon as the carpenters had finished their work, Truman (apparently Hughes also) moved out to the mine, partly in order to save the $2.50-a-night cost of a watchman. Thereafter, Truman wrote his frequent dispatches to Bess on a table near a large air compressor. Two nearby mills worked through the night, one of them making "a racket like the German army," the other "a noise like a rattletrap Met streetcar." Night watchman or not, he told Bess, he had decided against sleeping with a double-barreled shotgun because "I'm more afraid of a gun than a possible intruder."

Night security was the least of his problems. All the mills in the vicinity operated with water pumped from underground and sent down a channel by a large mine situated on higher ground. Just as the mill was finally ready to run at the end of March, mine owners upstream diverted the water, forcing T.C.H. to rely on a pond. After a few days of negotiation, Truman got the original supplier to pressure the upstream competitors to send the water on through. It appears that they did so only sporadically. The ground boss showed up for work drunk, was fired, and got the rest of the crew to quit. The partners also decided that their mine superintendent either had cheated them or was incompetent and tried to get rid of him. "The superintendent won't fire worth a cent," Truman wrote to Bess on April 27. "Says he is going to stay until Saturday and

draw his fifty dollars. I suppose I shall have trouble with him on that day."
Apparently, the man talked them into keeping him on.

The first attempts to separate ore demonstrated that the mill needed
yet more investment. By the end of the first week in April, the partners
had sunk more than $3,000 into their enterprise and had produced no
more than two tons of marketable ore. On April 14, Truman and Hughes
renegotiated their partnership with Culbertson. The new agreement provided that any further investment by any of them would be treated as a
loan to the company rather than as a capital investment and would be
repaid before any dividends could be distributed from earnings.[10]

The Oklahoma environment provided no relief. Spring windstorms
and intermittent monsoon-like rains raked the area. The summer produced almost insupportable heat. Smallpox broke out in town; its victims were carted to a pest house just half a mile from the mine. Truman
and Hughes took their meals with a widow across the way. She and her
five children lived in a shabby, poorly furnished house that made Truman
long for the relative comfort and luxury of Grandview.

During the first month or so, he was able to make only two or three
trips home. He checked at the post office regularly twice a day for letters
from Bess. In addition to his desperate loneliness for her, he worried incessantly about his mother, who was seriously ill, and Uncle Harrison,
who was once again sick. Through correspondence and an occasional
long-distance telephone call, he kept in touch with the family and advised
Mary Jane on running the farm. Despite all the difficulties at the mine,
he remained optimistic. Initial work had turned up indications of unexpectedly rich veins of zinc. If sufficient ore could be brought to the surface before the company's funds were totally depleted, he could make it
yet. When he took a week off to go home and plant corn at the end of
April, he was still hopeful.[11]

V

A week or two later, the venture seemed a total loss. Bereft of funds,
its production tied up by creditors, unable to meet its first installment
payment to the former owners, the operation closed down early in May.
Back at Grandview, discouraged by his failure and worn down from sleepless nights with his failing uncle, Truman was at a low point. He wrote to
Bess:

> If I don't lose all the livestock I have, it will only be because I shall turn it
> over to Mamma. I shall join the class who can't sign checks of their own I
> suppose. . . . There was never one of our name who had sense enough to
> make money. . . . You would do better perhaps if you pitch me into the ash
> heap and pick someone with more sense and ability and not such a soft
> head. My position seems to be that of following a mule up a corn row rather
> than directing the centers of finance.

Remarkably, he bounced back. In a few days, he managed to talk his suppliers into renewing the company's credit, the former owners into deferring the installment payments, and his banker friend, Frank Blair, into making him a loan. At Blair's insistence, Culbertson assigned his rights to Truman until such time as the mine repaid Truman's investment. With by far the largest stake in the mine's success, Truman was more determined than ever to make a go of it.[12]

His sincere, engaging personality persuaded a good many people. One of the former Eureka lease owners paid his gas bill and put up bond on the one lawsuit that he could not settle. He found a reliable mine boss, a red-haired, "half cross-eyed" hoisting engineer named Bill Throop, who provided competent management, much-needed encouragement, and greatly appreciated friendship. Truman boarded with Throop's large family, drove them around on weekend outings, and vowed to give them a little stock if the mine became profitable. In order to keep the payroll as lean as possible, he did as much manual labor as he could and tried to function as maintenance engineer. His best efforts were not enough to prevent engines from stalling or boilers from blowing off. Just after he reopened, the gas engine broke down; a mechanic took seven days to fix it. Rich, unworked zinc veins took on the character of a mirage—always, it seemed, just another dynamite blast away.[13]

Near the end of June, Truman received a wire from Mary Jane informing him that she had been forced to fire one of the hired men and that the other had quit. Leaving Hughes, in whom he had lost confidence, he rushed back to Grandview, found some new help, and spent the next two weeks tending to wheat, oats, clover, and livestock. He also began his race for township committeeman and made occasional dashes back to Oklahoma to rectify Hughes's latest blunders. By late July, Truman was back at the mine. Hughes shortly afterward received notification that his barn had burned and rushed home. He returned briefly, left again, and never came back. Truman stayed in Commerce throughout August, cursing Hughes for his absence, Oklahoma days for their blistering temperatures, and Oklahoma nights for their swarming mosquitoes. Boiler problems shut down the mill for two days and cost $100 to fix. When all systems were running, the mine produced enough marketable ore to keep hopes of a big strike alive, but meeting the weekly payroll became an increasingly difficult challenge. Facing reality, Truman began to look for a buyer.[14]

If market conditions had been better, he could have found one. Instead, they steadily worsened. The price of ore at the mine was down to $80 a ton by late June and continued to fall. In Commerce, mines built up huge stockpiles in hopes of higher prices, thereby enlarging a surplus that could only drive prices down. By August, Truman was dependent on the continued help and patience of various suppliers and the town banker, who tolerated an overdraft of about $400. Culbertson and Hughes had become invisible.[15]

The venture came to an end in the first week in September. Unable to meet his payroll, Truman closed the mine down. He told one of the former owners that he would try to find more financing, but he soon abandoned the idea. He managed to raise enough money to pay off his work force and satisfy most of his suppliers. Not quite able to admit to himself that the enterprise had been misconceived from the beginning, he nevertheless conceded the impracticality of further operation. Bill Throop urged him to find another $2,500 or so and do some test drilling at a site north of nearby Pitcher, Oklahoma. The old engineer's instincts were sound, but Truman was broke; others would strike rich veins of lead and zinc at that location. All that was left to do was to tally up the costs of the Eureka operation. They amounted to $15,852.55, or approximately $5,284.18 a partner. Proceeds from the ore they had mined and from the sale of their machinery covered part of the expense. Years later, Truman estimated his loss at $2,000.[16]

Truman left Commerce with a few new friends and as good a reputation as could be expected from a losing effort. One might assume that his first experience as an entrepreneur would have left him profoundly discouraged. But like many American venture capitalists before him, he licked his wounds and attributed his failure to bad luck rather than bad sense. "You know a man's judgment is good or bad accordingly as he wins or loses on a proposition," he had told Bess in August. "It seems to me that it's one big guess and the fellow who guesses right is the man of good judgment. I am going to keep guessing."[17]

VI

In August 1916, desperately trying to save the Eureka mine and furious at partners whom he believed had deserted him, Truman had written to Bess that Jerry Culbertson "had the nerve to want me to buy some oil stock in a corporation he's working for so he could get a better job." Culbertson not only had nerve, but was ultimately persuasive. It was testimony to Truman's eagerness for wealth that he soon was again Culbertson's partner.

He was able to be an investor because Uncle Harrison had died during the final weeks of the Oklahoma enterprise. At the end of June, the old man had prepared his last will and testament. After making small bequests to several family members—with the explicit provision that these would be canceled if they contested the will—he left everything else to Martha, Harry, Vivian, and Mary Jane. His personal property estate inventory listed no cash on hand and less than $600 in tangible personal effects, although he had entertained the idea of purchasing Texas farmland just six months earlier. Probate court appraisers conservatively valued his 305 acres of land next to the Truman farm at $148 an acre. Harry's share of the inheritance was, at a minimum, $11,285. Harrison's losing investment in the Oklahoma mine appears to have been in the form of a

$1,500 note owed to the Bank of Belton. In order to retain the land inheritance intact, the Trumans would have to borrow money to pay off claims against the estate.[18]

Truman drew on the value of his newly acquired land to join with Culbertson and David Morgan, a Kansas-bred and -educated attorney, in yet another attempt to strike it rich with a limited investment, ebullient salesmanship, and lots of luck. Culbertson had run advertisements in Oklahoma newspapers stating an interest in acquiring cheap lands that could be classified as "possible oil-producing." His purpose was to use them as the basis for an oil syndicate that would sell stock to the public, drawing on the proceeds to acquire and develop other properties. Thus structured, the enterprise minimized its creator's risk while maximizing the exposure of his partners.

Culbertson's advertisement drew a response from Morgan, who had eight years of experience in the booming Oklahoma oil fields. They agreed to establish the Atlas-Okla Oil Lands Syndicate—Morgan contributing 1,540 acres of land in southeastern Oklahoma, Culbertson his office in downtown Kansas City and his abilities as a salesman. In addition, they formed a separate, related enterprise, Morgan & Company Oil Investments, a brokerage firm to deal in oil stocks, leases, and properties; it also might manage oil enterprises on a commission basis. Truman was induced to provide the only real cash.

On September 25, 1916, the three men signed an agreement establishing the brokerage firm. Each held 1,000 shares. Truman purchased his interest with five $1,000 notes, each co-signed by his mother; they may also have been the basis for his stake in Atlas-Okla. The company used them as collateral for a bank loan. Years later, Morgan recalled that "all 5 notes were paid off and retired from profits which accrued to the $\frac{1}{3}$ interest which Truman [had] acquired." Morgan was president, Culbertson secretary (actually sales chief), and Truman treasurer. Each man was entitled to a salary of $250 a month; but since Truman spent much of his time managing the farm, he never drew a cent.[19]

The price he paid for continuing his business aspirations was not cheap. He signed a quit-claim deed relinquishing to his mother his interest in the property inherited from Uncle Harrison. In February 1917, she mortgaged the entire combined farm to Frank Blair for $25,000. (It is unclear whether this sum was in addition to the $7,500 mortgage of 1914.) At least part of this loan probably covered the cost of Truman's oil ventures. The gamble must have seemed relatively small. At a possible actual market value of $175 an acre, the property would have been worth approximately $100,000.

Truman took an active role in his new investment. More than thirty years later, the firm's bookkeeper, J. K. Brelsford, recalled him coming into the office frequently: "Truman was surrounded with people, people, people. Salesmen, lease men, lease owners, scouts and what-have-you. Morgan had his duties but he shoved quite a burden of seeing people over to Mr. Truman." At times, Truman functioned as office head in Morgan's absence. The business was exhilarating. It carried none of the frustration of managing an exhausted mine and gave him an opportunity to meet people—he was, Brelsford recalled, "courteous and affable," altogether the most enjoyable person with whom to work. He frequently took prospects or associates to dinner at fine downtown steak houses.

Above all, the business carried the prospect of instant wealth. "I am simply on needle points," Truman wrote to Bess on company stationery in November. He was waiting for confirmation on a $300,000 deal they were brokering. Morgan was in Tulsa: "I suppose he is out showing old man Walker the $3,500,000 Cushing property. Should he succeed in selling that, I shall simply float away on air." The Atlas-Okla company seemed to be doing well also. Culbertson's sales campaign produced a steady stream of stock purchases, with Morgan & Company taking a small commission on each share. The sales also gave Atlas-Okla a small amount of capital for the acquisition and development of genuinely promising leases. Bess purchased some shares herself. In early 1917, as war with Germany loomed on the horizon, oil was an attractive speculation to many small investors. "It is now 8:30 P.M. and I haven't been to supper yet," Truman wrote to Bess on January 23. "We sold 636 shares and collected $1,592.50 today. I have just finished getting out yesterday's receipts. We got about $800 yesterday. . . . The money is coming in by the basketful."[20]

In March 1917, Atlas-Okla changed its name to Morgan Oil and Refining Company, possibly to avoid confusion with Atlas Petroleum, another locally traded company. Contrary to Morgan's memory a generation later, the structure of the business did not change from a "syndicate" to a common-law trust, but soon there was an important departure at the top. Culbertson sold out his holdings—"at a most satisfactory figure," according to his public announcement—and started another oil investment firm. Truman and Morgan later claimed that they had become uneasy with Culbertson's sales methods. In common with many other promoters, he engaged in inflated and misleading claims. His salesmen doubtless used high-pressure tactics on vulnerable customers. Morgan stock was not traded on any exchange, making its value whatever a huckster could talk a customer into paying. Some shares apparently changed hands at as little as $1 apiece.

But Culbertson's partners were probably more concerned about his expensive advertising and, so they believed, the excessive commissions he allotted to himself and his employees. Simply put, his high-cost effort was failing to produce enough revenue to justify it. Morgan lined up J. S. Mullen, an Oklahoma banker and millionaire, to buy Culbertson out at a comfortable profit and succeed him as secretary. W. H. Lynn, one of Culbertson's most productive stock sellers, took over sales. He was no more hesitant than his old boss to make the most of what he had to peddle.[21]

VII

Whatever the source of its financing—Morgan & Company profits, cash infusions by Mullen, stock sales—Morgan Oil had become more than a shoestring wildcatting operation by the spring of 1917. As speculative fever in petroleum heightened with the approach of war, it seemed that the company could only grow. On February 5, less than a week after Germany announced a policy of unrestricted submarine warfare, Truman acknowledged a purchase of five shares at $5 each; by the end of March, with hostilities near, the selling price was $25. On Sunday, April 1, the day before Woodrow Wilson was scheduled to ask Congress for a declaration of war, the company ran a large advertisement in the *Kansas City Star*. This asserted that wartime oil prices would "soar beyond all expectation and an investment in the shares of any oil company that has production and large holdings of proven properties . . . is beyond question an investment of rare opportunity."[22]

With the help of the other petroleum-wise investors, Morgan aggressively put the company's cash flow into a wide variety of promising leases. His chief field man was Truman's old friend Harry (Pete) Allen, Agnes Salisbury's former husband. On April 15, Morgan Oil and Refining issued a glossy brochure and prospectus, offering 10,000 shares for sale to the public at $25 each: "Upon the sale of the above allotment it is the intention of the company not to offer any more shares for sale, as we believe it will be unnecessary." The offering was, of course, managed by Morgan & Company, "The Oldest Exclusive Oil Investment Firm in Kansas City." The prospectus boasted ownership of the 1,540 Oklahoma acres that Morgan had contributed to the enterprise; leases on more than 40,000 acres in Kansas, Oklahoma, Texas, and Mexico; its own refinery; and two drilling rigs. It "conservatively" estimated the total value of these properties at $423,297.20. A valuation of $25 on each of its unsold 26,000 shares added another $650,000 in equity and put its net worth at over $1 million.

Additionally, the brochure listed net intangible assets of $15,000. It cited cash income of approximately $4,500 a month from producing properties and predicted that this stream of greenbacks would be increased by $2,500 a month (a rate of $30,000 a year) into the foreseeable future. It described the refinery as "thoroughly equipped" and "completely overhauled," serving 1,200 customers and capable of turning a $9,000 profit a month. Skeptics were assured that the organizers and managers had put in their own money and had received no free stock; in order for them to realize a profit, the company would have to start paying regular dividends as soon as possible. Operated "in a safe, conservative manner," Morgan Oil would forgo wildcatting until the shares had become "a dividend-paying proposition from the development of its present proven holdings." It would fulfill the investor's dream of "Big Profits in the Oil Business."[23]

Not pure hot air, these claims were nonetheless misleading. The company did own twenty producing wells in Kansas with a total output of seventy-five barrels a day. The $4,500-a-month cash flow from production was based on a reasonable value of $2 a barrel. (In mid-April, Pennsylvania-grade crude hit an all-time high of $3.10, with lesser grades at $2.20 to $2.40.) The refinery, however, was a small, outdated skimming plant, apparently purchased in the hope of new finds. Because Morgan Oil's production was not enough to justify operation, it never went into service; in 1951, Morgan remembered it as "window dressing." Far from being proven, most of Morgan Oil's leases were typical wildcat situations, chosen for their proximity to producing acreage rather than for any hard evidence of oil and gas deposits. The asset value that the company claimed for them was arbitrary and speculative. In support of a $20,160 valuation for the Mexican property, for example, the brochure declared: "Mr. H. L. Doherty stated to a member of this firm that it was impossible to put a true value upon this lease."

Despite success in raising some additional capital, the company's finances remained weak. Most of the income from producing wells must have been needed to meet payroll and other regular expenses. Only about 1,000 of the 10,000 shares offered in mid-April were sold, and one doubts that installment payments came in as pledged. An equity infusion of about $25,000, instead of the hoped-for $250,000, left insufficient margin for error. Wartime regulations on petroleum processing foreclosed opening the refinery. A manpower shortage forced higher wages. Truman and Pete Allen opted for military service, leaving the burden of day-to-day operations on Morgan.

During the war, Morgan continued to acquire leases, came close to big strikes a couple of times, but somehow always missed the main chance. The company raised money by selling the refinery (for scrap metal, according to Morgan), its drilling rigs, and some of its leases. In widely separated parts of Texas, Morgan drilled three unproductive holes in a row. He gave up on one of them, near Wichita Falls, after coming up dry at a depth of 2,500 feet. A few years later, another company went down to 3,000 feet and opened up a major field. Near Eureka, Kansas, he became discouraged at 1,500 feet and sold the lease to Empire Oil & Gas (later the Cities Service Company). Empire went farther down and opened up the Teter Pool, one of the major oil fields in Kansas. Morgan Oil could not afford to renew its leases on 144,000 carefully selected acres near Phillipsburg, Kansas; in later years, hundreds of profitable wells dotted that landscape.[24]

VIII

After the war, Morgan sold out his interest in both the exploration and brokerage firms. Truman, after some hesitation, did the same. Clearly, the enterprises were not the total loss that the mining venture had been, but neither had they made him rich. From time to time in later years, his attempt to become an oil baron would come back to haunt him. Political enemies would call him a scoundrel who had swindled widows and orphans.

In fact, Morgan Oil's marketing tactics were legal and common. The lure of quick riches for ordinary people from the bounty of an abundant land had long been part of the American democratic myth. Morgan Oil was only one of many firms—Quadrangle, Okmulgee, Arrow Rock, Plantation, Neosho, Combination, Iroquois, Kansas Star—that sold stock by direct sales and newspaper-coupon advertising, made hyperoptimistic claims, and wound up in the graveyard of failed venture-capitalist enterprises. Some may have been cynical scams. Most were operated by wildcatters who really believed in the game they were playing and frequently risked their own assets. Truman fell in the latter category, and Morgan Oil was more substantial than many other midcontinent oil firms.[25]

In later years, Truman sometimes thought about how different their lives might have been if he had stayed at home and influenced Morgan to keep drilling outside of Eureka. In sober moments, he realized it probably would have made no difference, but the dream was hard to shake. "Well, Dave," he wrote to Morgan after entering the White House, "if we had carried that well on down and opened up the Teter Field with all that oil, it's a cinch I would not be President today."[26]

4

"Our Young Man Was a True Patriot": The Forge of War, 1917–1919

"I was stirred in heart and soul by the war messages of Woodrow Wilson. . . . I thought I ought to go. . . . I felt that I was a Galahad after the Grail. . . . I rather felt we owed France something for Lafayette." Thus Truman about two decades later recalled his feelings about possibly the most momentous decision of his life. One looks in vain for hidden impulses. Like a substantial majority of Americans, he had supported Britain and France from the start of World War I. He no doubt shared in the tidal wave of national outrage against unrestricted submarine warfare that compelled Woodrow Wilson to ask Congress for a declaration of war. He envisioned the forces of the Kaiser as barbarians who had to be beaten at any cost. "I do want to be in on the death of this 'Scourge of God,'" he would tell Bess just before leaving for France. "Just think of what he'd do to our great country and our beautiful women if he only could." Convinced that he had a duty to his loved ones and to America, he behaved, he later thought, as "a true patriot."[1]

His course was pure choice. He was past draft age and had left his National Guard battery six years earlier. As a farmer, he could rightly claim to be performing an important service for his country by staying at home. His business ventures were at such a critical point that it was quixotic to leave them. Bess was not simply ready to marry him, but was eager to do so in order to keep him from endangering his life. These considerations argued powerfully against the course he took. Yet in the end, his democratic idealism prevailed—and possibly the hope that war service would reveal new dimensions in his personality and bring him a more satisfying sense of identity.

II

In 1916, Truman's old National Guard Battery B and the state's two other batteries, A (St. Louis) and C (Independence), had been called to federal service to spend nearly six months on the Mexican border as regular army forces went into Mexico in pursuit of Pancho Villa. Truman had regretted being unable to go with his many friends among the officers of the Kansas City and Independence units. In June 1917, two months after the American declaration of war against Germany, he reenlisted in the Guard, cheating on the eye test (the first of several that he somehow would talk his way through in the next year) and joining energetically in a successful recruiting drive to expand Batteries B and C into a regiment. The new Kansas City–area unit, the Second Missouri Field Artillery Regiment, consisted of six combat batteries, A through F, organized into two battalions, supported by headquarters and supply companies, sanitary and veterinary detachments; it numbered 1,300 men.

While still Guardsmen, the troops elected their officers at the battery level. Truman, a bit to his surprise and certainly to his delight, was chosen a first lieutenant in Battery F; his old friend Pete Allen was made its captain. The battery officers then selected a senior command team. Truman disappointed his Independence friends by vocally supporting a successful ticket backed by his old Kansas City Guard buddies. Its head, Karl D. Klemm, was a wealthy West Point graduate and former cavalry lieutenant; he became colonel and commanding officer. Klemm's opponent, Major E. M. Stayton, heretofore the senior Missouri National Guard field artillery officer, did not speak to Truman for a time after that. Refusing a subordinate command, he raised a battalion of combat engineers.[2]

The Guardsmen quickly began to ready themselves for active duty. They purchased their own uniforms, drilled, and attended a training school every afternoon. The reaction of Truman's loved ones left him torn between a desire not to hurt them and a renewed appreciation of their affection. Tears came to his mother's eyes when he donned his uniform to go to a lodge meeting. He wore it to Bess's house on the Fourth of July, and she cried on his shoulder. Her tears, he later wrote, were "worth a life time on this earth." She wanted to marry him. On the night that he accepted his officer's commission, he wrote her a refusal:

> I don't think it would be right for me to ask you to tie yourself to a prospective cripple—or a sentiment. . . .
> . . . [Y]ou may be sure that I'll be just as loyal to you as if you were my wife. I'll try not to extract any promises from you either if you want to go with any other guy, why all right, but I'll be as jealous as the mischief although not begrudging you the good time.
> Bess, this is a crazy letter but I'm crazy about you and I can't say all

these nutty things to you without making you weep. When you weep, I want to. If you'd looked right closely the other night, you might have discovered it, and a weeping man is an abomination unto the Lord.

On August 5, Truman's outfit was federalized as the 129th Field Artillery Regiment, one of three in the Sixtieth Field Artillery Brigade, attached to the Thirty-fifth Division, a National Guard infantry unit composed of volunteers from Kansas and Missouri. After being billeted for nearly two months at the Kansas City convention hall and at armories in Kansas City and Independence, the Guardsmen departed on September 26 for serious army training.[3]

III

Their destination, Camp Doniphan, was part of the vast Fort Sill military reservation on the plains of southern Oklahoma. There they lived in Spartan conditions, five to a tent, each of which had a wood floor, four-foot-high wooden walls, a stove, and individual bunks. The drinking water, piped from five miles away, was brackish and foul smelling. Hot-water heaters (which usually worked) were put in the bathhouses. The encampment was set up along macadam roads lined with bright electric street lamps, which gave a deceptive aura of comfort to what were actually primitive living conditions.

Soldiering for the Guardsmen became a never-ending battle against Oklahoma dust blowing at as much as sixty miles an hour into their quarters, food, equipment, and eyes. In the midst of one of the worst storms, Truman wrote to Bess, "A tent fifty yards away is invisible. Dust is in my teeth, eyes, hair, nose, and down my neck. The cook next door bought me a piece of apple dumpling . . . when I ate it there was a grinding sound. . . . I ate it anyway, sand and all." Day-to-day life for both men and junior officers settled down to a dreary regimen of fighting dust, drilling, caring for horses, digging trenches, marching long distances, standing inspections, and attending evening instructional sessions after a bone-wearying day.[4]

In this difficult environment and later in France, Truman made lasting friendships among fellow officers, whom he liked and admired. They became comrades, financial backers, and political supporters in later years. Much like him, they were drawn to military service not by any danger of conscription, but by a sense of patriotism and duty mixed with a spirit of adventure and ambition. As a group, these men were competent and courageous. Some were successful professionals or businessmen: Colonel Klemm; Lieutenant Colonel Arthur Elliott, a banker who had clerked with Truman a dozen years earlier; Major John Thacher, a prominent Kansas City attorney; Major Marvin Gates, a well-to-do real-estate developer and the commander of Truman's battalion. Others were aspiring politicians, including Major John Miles, soon to become sheriff of Jackson County, and Captain Roger Sermon, who would return home to become mayor of Independence.[5]

The most important friendship of all was one Truman crafted with James (Young Jim) Pendergast, the son of Jackson County goat leader Mike Pendergast and nephew of Big Jim, the deceased founder of Kansas City's dominant political faction. There is a story, without a shred of evidence to corroborate it, that the friendship began when Truman, serving on a court-martial board, voted to absolve Pendergast of responsibility for a training-camp accident. More likely, they just found a lot to like and respect about each other. Like Truman, Young Jim went on to become a battery commander (Battery A, 130th Field Artillery Regiment) who served with distinction and won the affection of his men.[6]

Truman became an even closer friend of Spencer Salisbury, captain of Battery E and the brother of Bess's close friend Agnes. Standing six feet, two inches in his army boots, Salisbury was an experienced, first-rate officer who cut a dashing figure. Seventy years later, one of his privates, Bill Hamby, remembered him as a "wonderful" commander. Salisbury enjoyed the nickname "Captain Carranza," stemming from his service on the Mexican border; his men were called the "gorillas," an Americanization of guerrillas.

Salisbury was a practical joker, capable of slaughtering a goat (the mascot of a Kansas unit), stewing it, and feeding it to the battalion officers as beef pot roast. A nonconformist who detested piety, he sometimes held mock YMCA meetings, leading his fellow officers in hymns. He made a virtue of cutting corners. In combat, he fired his initial rounds deliberately long while still calculating his necessary trajectory. The practice was good for morale, he argued; others wondered if he hoped unwary superiors might confuse quick firing, however slapdash, with efficiency. In France, he and his men, expert scavengers capable of liberating equipment and creature comforts wherever they found themselves, picked up a modified nickname, "Carranza and His Forty Thieves." Truman liked him and probably envied his dash and confidence.[7]

IV

The regiment had hardly established itself at Camp Doniphan before most of its members realized the need to establish some mechanism for the purchase of the little luxuries and near-necessities of life that the army did not issue—tobacco, candy, soft drinks, snacks, stationery, pens, pencils. The closest retail merchants were in Lawton, five miles away, and, as Truman put it, sold "to the soldiers at a fair profit, plus all the traffic will bear." Colonel Klemm authorized him to organize a regimental canteen and ordered each man in the slightly understrength regiment to contribute $2, giving the young lieutenant initial capital of about $2,200.

On September 28, Truman set up a beginning in a tent, selling tobacco, apples, and a drink called Puritan (probably a near-beer). Soon he was selling his goods to the entire division, operating out of a frame building, and running barber and tailor shops. As his assistant, he secured an old acquaintance from the Commerce Bank days. "I have a Jew in charge of the canteen by the name of Jacobson and he is a crackerjack," he wrote to Bess. Each battery and company contributed a clerk, who had his pockets sewed up to prevent pilfering. Truman deposited receipts daily and kept the books in meticulous shape.

In later years, he would say that Eddie Jacobson had done most of the work, but it is clear that he devoted a lot of his own time to the enterprise, especially in the crucial first couple of months of its existence. In December, the canteen paid a dividend of $3,000, approximately $1.36 for every $1 invested. By the time it was liquidated, it had distributed another $12,000. In any setting, this performance would have been considered a remarkable display of entrepreneurial and managerial skill. At Camp Doniphan, where other regimental canteens collapsed with dreary regularity, it made Truman's career. By February 1918, his was the only canteen still functioning in the entire camp. Some of his colleagues dubbed him "Trumanheimer." Laughing off the imputed Jewishness, he basked in the attention of his superiors.[8]

He ran the canteen as an addition to all his regular duties; yet he did very well at those also. Despite his meager formal education, rudimentary summer camp training, and lack of active-duty experience, he was a good soldier. He took well to the theoretical aspects of artillery training, stood up under the physical demands of his job, and displayed initiative. He even brought down his car and let the battery use it as a utility vehicle. When Pete Allen gave him a glowing efficiency report, Klemm sent it back with the comment, "No man can be that good." In late December or early January, he was one of ten officers from the regiment selected for the division's Special Overseas Detail, a group that would receive early training in France and, in turn, act as teachers when rejoining their outfits.[9]

Truman poured out his experiences, hopes, and anxieties in letter after letter to Bess and longed to see her. She joined the 129th's women's auxiliary, participated faithfully in its work, and to Truman's delight became good friends with Mrs. Klemm. He hoped that somehow this friendship would give her an excuse to come down to the camp. She never did, but in November she sent him a picture. The card that came with it said, "You didn't expect me at Fort Sill so soon did you? I'm depending on this to take you to France and back all safe and sound." For the next year and a half, he carried the photo constantly in his left breast pocket.

When he could not get a pass home for Christmas, his mother and Mary Jane took the train down to see him. Mamma was sixty-five, disappointed that Harry could not be in Grandview, and worried sick about him. She smiled and told him to do his best for his country; he learned later that she had cried all the way home. Shortly after the first of the year, he managed to wrangle five short days at home, returning to camp just ten minutes before his time expired.[10]

V

The Doniphan experience included encounters with regular army officers who rarely bothered to conceal their contempt for National Guard personnel. The brigade commander, Brigadier General Lucien T. Berry, an old Indian fighter who sported an oversize mustache, regularly told young Guard officers of their unfitness, delighted in the slightest excuse to chew them out, and routinely denied weekend-leave requests, no matter how merited. Truman, who called him "Old Handlebars," hated him.

Sometime in early 1918, Berry had a brigade officers' meeting. He arrived a few minutes early, called those present to attention, and picked out Truman and began to give him "unshirted hell" about some minor inspection demerits in the canteen. At that point, a group of young second lieutenants from the 130th, unaware of the early start, came through the door laughing and talking. Berry turned around, glared at the new arrivals, selected the biggest man among them, and spent the next few minutes telling him why he was a disgrace to his uniform. Truman slipped back into the ranks. Berry, apparently having forgotten about him, moved on to another item of business. After the meeting ended, Truman thanked Lieutenant Harry H. Vaughan for getting him off the hook. He could not have begun to imagine how often he would return the favor in the future.[11]

Not all professional soldiers inspired the same mixture of fear and loathing. At the end of December, Klemm and Elliott were sent off to a special training school for senior officers. Klemm's interim replacement was Lieutenant Colonel Robert M. Danford. Scholarly, yet charismatic, Danford was the co-author of the standard army work on field artillery, an excellent organizer, and a demanding leader who saw his charges as men to be made into rounded soldiers rather than as objects of abuse. The entire regiment, especially the junior officers, revered him.

Danford influenced Truman enormously: "He taught me more about handling men and the fundamentals of artillery fire in six weeks than I'd learned in the six months I'd been going over to the school of fire and attending the regimental schools." Truman, in turn, became one of Danford's favorite young officers. In early March, after Klemm returned, Danford was reassigned, soon to become a brigadier general and later commandant of cadets at West Point.

To the annoyance of some senior officers, he let Lieutenant Truman have his saddle horse for $100, a third or a quarter of its value. Truman shipped it to Grandview; it was too fine a mount to take into combat. "You lucky Jew you get all the plums that fall, don't you?" Klemm told Truman in a less than congenial tone. Truman responded, no doubt with his characteristic smile, that he took them when they were thrown at him. Whether because of this incident or because of events that would occur in France, Truman's relationship with the colonel he once had so eagerly supported became increasingly tenuous.[12]

It was on Danford's recommendation that three lieutenants—

Truman, Ted Marks, and Newell Paterson—were examined for promotion to captain on February 22. Old General Berry himself presided, after keeping them waiting in frigid weather that left them with terrible colds. Truman recalled the ordeal sixteen years later:

> When we could answer, it displeased him but when we couldn't he'd rattle his false teeth, pull his handlebar mustache and stalk up and down the room yelling at us: "Ah, you don't know, do you? I thought you were just ignorant rookies. . . . [I]t will be a disaster to the country to let you command men."

Truman stammered his way through the procedure and went away convinced that he probably had failed. A few days later, he discovered that the general had passed Marks; then he got indirect word that he also was on the promotion list. He was waiting for his commission when he finally left for France.[13]

He doubtless was not entirely surprised at this latest achievement. Occasionally, he experienced spasms of self-doubt; even after being chosen for the Special Overseas Detail, he worried that he might be sent home. Yet he was aware that he had made a superior record for himself. The success of the canteen was his pride and joy; his strong showing in artillery theory and practice was also a great confidence-building experience. He conducted himself with the surface modesty he had been taught to affect as a child and realized that new challenges lay ahead; but at bottom, he had more faith in himself than at anytime in his life.

VI

Early on the morning of March 20, the Special Overseas Detail boarded a train for the first leg of its journey to France. By 5:00 A.M., it was in the switchyards in Kansas City. Truman scrambled off, found the yardmaster, and asked for a phone. The office had only a Bell connection; thus it was possible to call Bess but not Mamma and Mary Jane. The official told Truman, "If she doesn't break the engagement she really loves you." Madge Wallace answered and summoned Bess, and the couple talked for a few minutes before the train pulled out. The detail arrived at Camp Merritt, New Jersey, late on the night of March 23; its members found that they had missed their boat and had the next few days to see New York.

Establishing a pattern that would characterize the next year, Truman was an indefatigable, but resolutely skeptical, tourist. "I am in the most touted town on earth and it is a vast disappointment," he told his cousins. Nothing—not Broadway, not Fifth Avenue, not the vaudeville stage— could match Kansas City. When Grant's Tomb was pointed out to him, the young officer stole a line from Mark Twain: "Is he dead?" (The view from the Woolworth Building, he reluctantly admitted, was spectacular.) He disliked New York mostly because he was lonely. "I'm almost homesick for you and Mamma and Mary," he wrote to Bess. "If only I could have stayed these two days in Kansas City instead of this —— Kike town, I'd have felt much better."

On March 29, Truman's detail boarded the USS *George Washington*. The next evening, the big transport ship steamed out of New York Harbor. Thoughts of his mother and Bess must have crossed his mind. He vowed that he would have nothing to do with French women, that he would be as clean in France as would his intended in America. He and Newell Paterson stood on the deck until the city lights vanished, thinking of submarines in the Atlantic and of all the hazards that awaited them in France, wondering if they would ever see the Statue of Liberty again. Then they went below and played poker for the rest of the night.[14]

VII

On April 13, after a safe, uneventful voyage, the *George Washington* and its sister vessels arrived at Brest, France. Truman and his fellow officers were billeted in luxury hotels until April 21. For six sybaritic days, they spent their time learning how to eat French food and drink French wine, and going to movies, stage shows, and the opera.[15] Those six days in a busy cosmopolitan port city left Truman with a feeling of ambivalence toward France, and by extension Europe, that would never leave him. He continued to believe unquestioningly in the mission that had brought him across the Atlantic. He delighted in the courtesy and sense of deliverance that the French extended toward American soliders. He understood the incredible sacrifices they had made—he wrote to Bess of a mother who had lost nine sons. Yet he could take neither the people nor their culture altogether seriously; and like an archetypical American provincial, he was constantly wary of being flimflammed by wily Europeans.

He joked about the way $10 purchased wads of bills and piles of coppers, about the elaborately decorated French military costume, about the tall tales that French tour guides inflicted on him. He complained about hustlers and price gougers and shared the widespread suspicion that Americans were charged ten times as much as the French in restaurants. The French railway system, with its "little bitsy engines" and "peanut roaster whistles," did not escape his satiric gaze.

By April 21, he and his fellow officers were on one of those trains; it took them to Montigny-sur-Aube, a tiny, hospitable, well-kept village clustered around a large sixteenth-century chateau that served as barracks and classroom building for the American advanced artillery school. The commander, Colonel Dick (By God) Burleson, a profane, no-nonsense Texan, put his charges through their most rigorous intellectual and physical exercises yet. Their day began at 7:00 A.M. and ended at 9:30 P.M. "When I come home I'll be a surveyor, a mathematician, a mechanical draftsman, a horse doctor, a crack shot, and a tough citizen if they keep me here long," Truman wrote to Bess. The curriculum, with its emphasis on geometry and trigonometry, was exceedingly difficult; and despite his good physical condition, the exercise routine was almost too much for him. "I am dizzy most of the time," he told Bess, "but I hope to come out on top."

The light artillery piece they learned to use, the French 75mm field gun, was the best of its kind. Its advanced recoil mechanism allowed for quick, accurate firing without a need for manual repositioning after each shot. It accepted twelve- to twenty-pound shells (high explosives, gas, shrapnel) slightly less than three inches in diameter and could hurl them nearly five miles. Crack demonstration teams could get off twenty to thirty rounds a minute; a more realistic, but still fearsome, rate in sustained combat conditions was three or four a minute. Pulled by a team of six or eight horses, the gun was theoretically highly mobile. Military planners assumed, usually with insufficient attention to real-world logistical difficulties, that it could keep up with advancing infantry and maintain an offense with one barrage of withering fire after another. To command 75s meant to be on the move, operate close to the front lines, and provide the main artillery support for ground troops who faced barbed wire, machine-gun fire, and enemy shells.[16]

On June 8, Truman and most of the other officers found they had graduated. Major Gates, who had become a friend and mentor, achieved special distinction. Qualified to function as effective artillery instructors or commanders, Truman and his comrades rejoined their regiment, now headquartered in the small village of Brain-sur-l'Authion, just four miles east of the old provincial city of Angers. By now, Truman received confirmation of his elevation to captain through reading a promotion list. Although the official orders had not yet reached him, the regiment gave him his second bar; for the next four months, he would function at that rank while drawing the pay of a first lieutenant. Gates resumed his position as Second Battalion commander; Truman did double duty as his adjutant and as an artillery instructor.

A number of the officers, Truman apparently among them, were billeted in the neighboring village of Andard at a crossroads inn, the Silver Pot Hook. Neither here nor anywhere else did he socialize with his French hosts, to whom he related along the classic lines of the American tourist. Too busy to learn more than a few phrases of French, he made a virtue of his ignorance: "I can tell 'em I don't understand and ask for des oeufs sur la plat and that's about all. I pronounce fromage frummage and say Angers like she's spelled but the French insist on saying fromaag and Onjay. I'll never comprehend it." Nonetheless, he enjoyed his comfortable quarters and picturesque surroundings. Occasionally, he got into Angers for dinner and a movie or for sightseeing. Perhaps the most memorable tourist experience was the old Bishop's Palace, a museum of religious art. Its greatest treasure was the Tapestry of the Apocalypse, a medieval masterwork consisting of seventy large panels that powerfully depicted St. John's vision of the end of the world and the second coming of Christ. Many panels, no doubt, were in a poor state of restoration.

Truman typically shrugged them off. He did like some of them, he told Bess, such as the one that showed "St. John sticking a dragon and the blood running out and every thing just as natural." But one that his guide thought especially outstanding looked like "a dirty tablecloth."[17]

On July 4, the regiment observed Independence Day with athletic events and a picnic on the grounds of a nearby chateau. All of France celebrated the American national day also. Across the doorway of the old church at Brain, the local townspeople hung a large English-language banner: "God Bless America." Three days later, the 129th Field Artillery left the village for its final precombat training with the advice of seasoned French officers at Camp Coetquedon.[18]

VIII

They had been there only a day when Colonel Klemm called Truman in. He waited nervously in the commander's outer office, wondering what he was to be dressed down for. Finally, he was admitted:

> "Harry, how would you like to command a battery?"
> "Well sir, I hope to be able to do that some day."
> "All right, you'll take command of D Battery in the morning."

Truman said nothing, saluted, about-faced, and left the office, wondering if Klemm was trying to get rid of him.

Battery D was the most insubordinate in the regiment. Made up predominantly of Kansas City Irish Catholics along with a few men of German descent, it had compiled a record of rowdyness and inefficiency that had led the colonel to give serious thought to dispersing its personnel. Its first captain had been cashiered at Camp Doniphan; its second had been hated by the men and all but run out of the battery. The third, John Thacher, had won their love and respect, but was too old for combat and slated to become First Battalion adjutant. Fearful that he would fail and be sent home, Truman told Gates that his days in France were numbered.[19]

When he assumed command at reveille the next morning, he faced a group of soldiers proud of their standing as a problem unit, bitterly resentful that Thacher had been taken away from them, disdainful of Protestants from the country, and prone to regard anyone who wore eyeglasses as a sissy. Truman understood that his first task was to restore discipline and effectiveness, but that his second and more important would be to make them want to follow him under fire. Very scared at his first review of his new troops, he put up a tough front, looking them over in silence with as cold and steely-eyed a gaze as he could muster, saying nothing, and dismissing them. The same day, they staged a fake stampede of the horses, which failed to impress him. That night, they got into an after-hours brawl in the barracks, resulting in broken furniture and four infirmary cases.

The next morning, Truman laid down the law to his sergeants and corporals: "I didn't come over here to get along with you. You've got to get along with me. And if there are any of you who can't, speak up right now and I'll bust you right back now." In the next few weeks, he demonstrated that he could put into practice the ideals he had learned from Robert Danford.

"The very first man that was up before me for a lack of discipline got everything I was capable of giving," he told Bess. "I took the battery out to fire the next day and they were so anxious to please me." He demoted and promoted without hesitation and kept a little black book that contained entries for each of his men. "Absolutely worthless," he wrote of one man. "Court martialed . . . [penalized] $2/_3$ of 4 mo. pay." After the name of an unreliable private, he wrote, "1st AWOL in France, gave him hell and extra duty." Other examples of misbehavior were less egregious and more easily dealt with. "Made him write his mother," he wrote of one minor miscreant. He did not hesitate to recognize those who lived up to his expectations. He helped one of his men win admission to West Point and got another into officers' training school over the personal opposition of Colonel Elliott. He persuaded his charges that he was fair, if tough; that he would recognize accomplishment; and that he was proud of them as a group.[20]

Over the next month, he worked the battery hard during long days replete with drills, inspections, and incessant firing practice. By and large, the men responded. Just three days after taking over, Truman was writing (perhaps with a bit of his determined optimism) that they seemed to like him. In less than two weeks, his outfit was winning battalion competitions. He was elated when Major Gates praised the battery and ecstatic when Gates brought Captains Allen and Salisbury "over to see how it should be done." Above all, he was happy and maybe a bit surprised that he had established himself as a leader of men. "Can you imagine me as the hard-boiled captain of a tough Irish battery?" he asked Bess.

His success reinforced his other ambition—to reach the front and prove himself as a combat officer. His one aim, he wrote time and again, was to fire at least one volley at the Hun. He faced the prospect serenely, telling his correspondents that he trusted in the Lord and that his men would take care of him.[21]

IX

On August 17, the 129th entrained for Alsace. Politically a part of the German Empire since 1871, the region was also heavily Germanic ethnically and culturally. Its beautiful, rugged, green Vosges Mountains and narrow, twisting roads reinforced the supremacy of the defensive that had characterized the conflict from its earliest months. The focus of combat was to the north and west, from Saint-Mihiel, Verdun, and Reims to the Somme and Flanders. For three years, the Vosges had been almost a rest-

and-recreation area for tired French and German troops. To American commanders, it seemed a perfect sector in which to give marginal National Guard units their initial combat experience.

Suddenly, the war was on the verge of becoming an actuality. Truman admitted to "a real creepy feeling" and wondered whether he would stand firm under fire. He, Lieutenant Gordon Jordan, and a couple of his sergeants formed an advance party to meet Major Gates at Kruth, a small Germanic mountain village where the 129th established headquarters. With Gates, they rode on horseback to meet with the French group commander, based in the mountains above the town. When they arrived at midday, the Germans were shelling a nearby crossroads. To the untried captain, Camp Doniphan all at once seemed very pleasant and very far away.

The French officer insisted on inviting the Americans to one of those extended, multicourse French lunches that infuriated Truman: "It takes them so long to serve a meal that I'm always hungrier when I get done than I ever was before." Then he assigned a lieutenant to guide Truman and his party to Battery D's position in a forested area near the Herrenberg Pass. The altitude was about 4,000 feet. Truman picked out a site for his field kitchen, a place for the horses, and an emplacement for his guns at the edge of the woods about 215 yards away. On the night of August 25, the rest of the battery came up from Kruth. The horses pulled the artillery pieces and around 7,500 pounds of shells up a wet dirt road that rose at a fifteen-degree angle; the men carried other supplies and equipment by hand.

For the next two days, the battery lived in rain and mud, and Truman meticulously plotted his firing plan. On August 28, he scrapped it after receiving orders to move his pieces a mile and a quarter closer to the enemy in preparation for a gas barrage to be fired the following evening. That night, they hauled the guns and ordnance up and down steep, muddy roads again, this time to the edge of a forested area at the top of a hill not far from the village of Mittlach.

At precisely 8:00 P.M. on August 29, in tandem with the rest of the regiment, Battery D began a gas barrage against German positions. The four 75s discharged 500 rounds in thirty-six minutes, exactly on schedule, and then prepared to evacuate before the Germans could return fire. For some reason, the First Sergeant, who had been put in charge of the horses a considerable distance away, failed to show up on time. The men waited anxiously until he appeared at about 9:00. Hastily, they hitched up the guns; then the First Sergeant ordered two of them pulled out in the wrong direction, dangerously close to the steeply sloping hillside. Truman mounted his own horse. At 9:30, just as they were evacuating, enemy shells began to fall.

The horses bolted in every direction, two teams breaking away from the pieces at the edge of the hill. A German shell landed, spewing out shrapnel a few yards from the captain; Truman's mount went down, perhaps hit, perhaps simply spooked and slipping in the mud. Lieutenant Vic Housholder ran to pull him out from under the animal. Simultaneously, the First Sergeant, badly frightened, yelled, "Run for the dugouts, fellows. They've got a bracket on us." Housholder, Chief Mechanic McKinley Wooden, Sergeant Eddie Meisburger, Private Al Ridge, Private William O'Hare, and numerous others waited for their commander's orders. The rest of the men disappeared into the forest. The two horseless pieces slipped downhill into a bog of mud. Truman, unhurt by his fall and in the heat of action unafraid, was furious.

The enemy's return barrage ceased quickly. Those who held their ground were unscathed; four horses were dead or mortally wounded. Truman and one of his lieutenants rounded up the surviving animals. Unable to extricate the other two guns, they camouflaged them with tree branches until a party could return for them the next day. The enraged captain's next job was to regroup his men; he did so, using every bit of profanity that he had picked up from Missouri farmhands and professional soldiers. The "no-good Irish sons-of-bitches" sheepishly came straggling back. Finally, in the early-morning hours of August 30, they returned to their base position and eagerly devoured a hot meal. At about 4:00 A.M., their weary captain went to his tent and fell asleep; he awoke twelve hours later.

As Truman would put it after the war, "It was the first time for the whole bunch to be at the wrong end of a trajectory and they didn't know exactly what to do." Consequently, a lot of them "had distinguished themselves as foot racers." The men, both embarrassed by their behavior and elated that they all were unharmed, dealt with the incident by joking about it. Since no one wanted to admit that he had been among the panicky, somebody dubbed it "the Battle of Who Run." They developed an exaggerated sense of their ability to survive German fire and a conviction that their commander was a human good-luck token who would lead them through the war without injury. "We have a captain who cannot be beaten," O'Hare wrote to his father.

The episode demonstrated gaps in the training that both the enlisted men and the officers had received. Neither Truman nor anyone else seems to have realized that it was one thing to leave guns in the heat of an artillery duel or with the enemy advancing, but quite another to seek temporary cover in the midst of an evacuation. Still, the disorderly flight that had occurred was both unmilitary and dangerous. The behavior of his top noncommissioned officer revealed that Truman, for all his promotions and demotions, had been a poor judge of character in at least one instance, although the First Sergeant was an experienced Guard veteran. It remains uncertain whether the responsibility for the late arrival of the horses was that of the First Sergeant, whether his commander had ordered them billeted farther away than necessary, or whether they were all victims of darkness and difficult terrain.

No one was more deeply self-conscious about what had happened

than Truman. On August 31, he and the other battery commanders received orders to leave their positions and return to Kruth. Although he
had fired his rounds with apparent effectiveness, had come back with all
his men and guns, and had proved his own courage to himself, Truman
felt disgraced when he reported to his major. Gates simply told him it
was common for men to break their first time under fire and suggested
that he get a new First Sergeant.

Truman decided against a court-martial for the offender, busted him
to private, and got him transferred to another battery. Three weeks later,
the man would conduct himself bravely in the Meuse-Argonne offensive.
Truman also took a decision that implied that he had not yet gauged the
perils of combat; he unsuccessfully recommended three of the men who
had held their ground for Distinguished Service Crosses. With that, he
and Battery D put Alsace and the Battle of Who Run behind them. Having received their baptism of fire, they were to be shifted to the north to
participate in the decisive campaigns of the war.[22]

X

As they marched down from the Vosges, an incident occurred that presaged friction in the regiment. Colonel Klemm, noticing that most of the
men had disregarded a standing order to wear their metal helmets, rode
up and down the ranks pulling off their soft overseas caps and throwing
them away. Few of the Guardsmen admired so relentless an insistence
on the dress code; most, Truman recalled, thought he was drunk or
crazy.[23]

They went to Remiremont, several miles to the west, to entrain for
the front. The Battery D train left at 1:20 A.M., September 6; not told his
destination, Truman assumed at least a twenty-four-hour ride and went
to sleep. Three hours later, a lieutenant colonel, the regulating officer of
the Thirty-fifth Division, boarded the train when it stopped at the village
of Charmes. He awakened the sleep-dazed captain to tell him that they
were about to reach their destination, Bayon, about nine miles south of
Nancy; warned that the town was under constant daytime airplane attack; and advised him to get his men unloaded and under cover before
dawn. He then returned to the station to wait for the next train.

As the train pulled into Bayon, one of the first sights Truman saw
was two dead horses on the platform; he took them for victims of an air
attack. Badly frightened and with "absolutely no one to pass the buck
to," he rushed his men into a double-time disembarkment. They hurried
to a nearly wooded area suggested by the regulating officer and spent the
next day sleeping and then bathing in the Moselle. Grateful for the good
advice he had received, Truman met the battery supply train at noon;
passed the warning along to its commander, Colonel Elliott; and ostentatiously displayed the dead horses to him. Frightened that a squadron

of Hun planes would dive out of the sky at any moment, machine guns blazing away, Elliott unloaded in a frenzy, desperately searched for vacant wooded space, and finally jammed his charges in next to Battery D. To the relief and surprise of both men, no air raid marred a peaceful day. Then they discovered, to Truman's embarrassment, that the horses had been shot by an army veterinarian.

The regulating officer was Bennett Champ Clark, son of the renowned Champ Clark. Truman was not at the time terribly bothered by the incident. Yet in later years, as the two men's political careers bumped up against each other, it developed into a grievance that he never allowed to evaporate. He would persuade himself that Clark had played a practical joke on him. Clark's protests that his warning had been made in good faith from a village almost nine miles away and that he had not even known about the unfortunate equines would count for little.[24]

From Bayon, the regiment began a series of forced marches, undertaken after dark to avoid enemy detection. One night after another, each enlisted man carrying sixty to eighty pounds of equipment on his back, the regiment competed with other units for the right of way on overburdened roads, the men enduring a cold rain that seemed to follow them as they went. During the day, they bivouacked in a woods or village, eating and trying to catch a little sleep. Riding on the caissons or supply wagons was strictly prohibited. Even Captain Truman hitched his horse to a wagon and walked along in front of his troops. Tempers flared easily. The first night out, a high-ranking infantry officer ordered the artillery off the road to make way for his troops. Truman vowed to "bust" the man after the war.

On the night of September 12, they marched through Nancy; the black skies lighted up as a massive artillery barrage signaled the beginning of a major American offensive to push the Germans out of the Saint-Mihiel salient. The 129th camped in the woods for three days, waiting in reserve, horses hitched to guns and wagons; the call never came. Then the march resumed, this time to the west and north toward the Argonne Forest and Verdun. Sometimes proceeding at a snail's pace because of road blockages, sometimes moving at a fatiguing double time, the regiment and the entire Thirty-fifth Division struggled forward in the darkness. Horses driven beyond their limits dropped in their traces, were shot, and were left by the roadside. Trucks carrying infantrymen and equipment contested for the right of way. Dust from the French crushed-rock roads choked the men and covered the entire procession—except on those nights when chill autumn rains made the march even more miserable.

Probably on September 20 (remembered by the regimental historian as the worst single day of the ordeal), Colonel Klemm, attempting to keep the line moving, rode up alongside the worn-out, stumbling men of Battery D; condemned their appearance; and demanded to know their unit. Truman, who had been marching on foot with them, stepped forward. Klemm ordered him to call them to attention and double-time them up a hill a third of a mile away. Instead, as soon as the colonel rode off, Truman marched them into a woods to bed down for the night. He went down the road, explained his actions to the colonel, and persuaded him to let the battery get the rest it needed. The process could not have been easy. Truman wrote in his diary, "The Colonel insults me shamefully. No gentleman would say what he said. Damn him."[25]

At last, on September 22, having marched almost fourteen miles on one hour's sleep, the battery reached a muddy encampment near Rarecourt, about twelve miles from the front. "We were so tired," Eddie Meisburger recalled twenty years later, "all we thought about was slum, bread, and sleep." Their rest was short-lived; Truman got orders to move his guns and firing personnel to the front as soon as it was dark.[26]

XI

After an exhausting struggle, they got the wagons, guns, and gun crews—who rode for the first time in weeks—out onto a good, wide national route filled with trucks heading north. They moved rapidly up a pitch-dark, rain-slickened highway, always at a trot, sometimes at a gallop, occasionally moving carefully into fields to bypass stalled or overturned vehicles. Flares from the front line and flashes from enemy artillery illuminated the northern skies. By 2:00 A.M., September 23, they were at the ruins of the town of Neuvilly, just east of the Argonne Forest.

The battery moved off the road over a field of mud toward their positions on Hill 290, three miles east of Neuvilly at the edge of the Hesse Forest. Their speedy pace came quickly to an end. All at once, movement became, as Truman put it, "a heartbreaking job." Somehow the worn-out horses and men managed to get the pieces in place after three hours of falling into shell holes and pushing through a mire that was sometimes axle-deep. At 5:00 A.M., they were theoretically ready to face the enemy; actually, they were at the point of collapse. They luckily faced no immediate action. As soon as he had set up his tent, Truman fell across his bed and slept until noon.

The next day, he decided to move his quarters closer to the battery; a few hours later, German artillery scored a direct hit on his first site. The incident was typical of the random harassing fire from enemy gunners who had to shoot without benefit of precise direction from observers. Most of their shells landed long or short or wide, but they managed to destroy a field kitchen and an ammunition dump, annihilate Pete Allen's quarters, and inflict on the regiment its first two deaths by enemy action. For two days, men and officers waited, the battery commanders plotting possible firing trajectories, the men digging in, all of them wondering whether the next shell would find them.

On the evening of September 25, the line officers received notice that the long-awaited final drive of the war was to begin the following morning. The 129th was in the middle of perhaps the most strategic sector, running from the Argonne Forest to the Meuse River. To push the enemy decisively across to the east bank of the Meuse would create enormous pressure on German lines all the way west to the English Channel and open the way for an attack into Germany itself. The regiment's mission was to provide support for Thirty-fifth Division infantrymen who would assault German positions four and five trench lines deep beginning at Boureuilles, only about three miles up the national route and extending to Buzancy, another twelve and a half miles to the north.

No one slept that night. Far to the rear, big guns began firing at 11:00 P.M. The regiment had breakfast at 2:30 A.M. At 4:20, it began its participation in a mighty one-hour barrage, designed to chew up the barbed-wire emplacements in front of Boureuilles and destroy the powerful German strong point at Vauquois Hill. Then, after ten minutes of silence, the regiment made its contribution to a rolling barrage that moved progressively north toward Varennes and Cheppy for the next two and a half hours. Months later, Truman recalled the experience:

> There was more noise than human ears could stand. Men serving the guns became deaf for weeks afterward. The sky was red from one end to the other. . . . Daylight came about 6:30. It was a smoky, foggy morning. We could see our observation balloons beginning to go up behind us . . . evenly spaced and all ascending together. The guns got very hot. It was necessary to keep them covered with wet gunny sacks and to swab after every second or third shot.

As quickly as possible, the regiment pulled out to follow the infantry, which charged through enemy positions with a dash that demonstrated both valor and lack of professional training. Many of its units bypassed silent pillboxes, assuming that they had been vacated or destroyed, only to take withering machine-gun fire from the rear. The men nevertheless advanced rapidly. Overwhelming the first and intermediate German defense lines, they moved to the north of Varennes and Cheppy, gaining almost four miles.

The artillery once again faced its most difficult obstacle, the rain and mud of northern France. Denied the use of the national route, the artillerymen switched double teams of horses from one gun to another and supplemented horsepower with their own backs, bringing their pieces forward with painful slowness, experiencing the way in which chance and weather usually make a hash of exquisitely devised war plans.

By 1:00 P.M., the 129th was near Boureuilles, but stymied by a wrecked bridge. Klemm ordered Battery D into temporary position to support a tank company in front of Varennes. Gates, Truman, and Lieutenant Jordan waded the Aire and walked toward the front, looking for targets and attempting to find the tank commander. They were pinned down for a time by machine guns, unable to find either artillery objectives or anyone in charge of the tank attack. In a surreal incident, the trio encountered an American brigadier general and his orderly—riding through the battle zone in dress uniform as if on parade—and asked them to give their horses to the artillery. Finally, with machine-gun fire coming closer, an infantry lieutenant advised Truman and his companions to return to their position, where they learned that the entire 129th had narrowly escaped destruction from a German near-miss.

Klemm decided to push ahead to a position near Vauquois Hill. Once again, the regiment struggled through the mud, moving a gun at a time with infinite effort. German artillery harassed them. A direct hit demolished Battery E's instrument wagon. A dud landed directly between the legs of a Battery D private as he rested in a shell hole. Another dud hit a couple of feet from Truman's old friend, Captain Ted Marks. At 4:00 A.M. on September 27, the regiment reached its new position, fortunate to have lost only a couple of men wounded and several horses (most to exhaustion rather than enemy fire). The men were literally asleep on their feet. Truman had been awake for forty-eight hours. As he crawled between his blankets and began to doze off, he noticed that it was starting to rain.

His rest lasted about an hour. He was awakened and ordered to begin a rolling barrage in support of nearby infantry at 5:30. As he recalled it, his response was "Go to hell! But I'll try." After figuring a rough trajectory, he realized that he could not place his guns at a steep enough angle. Batteries A and B, on the slope of a hill, were able to use the terrain. Salisbury angled one of his Battery E pieces in a shell hole. The regiment's other guns had to remain silent. The episode was emblematic of a general deterioration in artillery backing that made further progress slow and costly for Thirty-fifth Division infantry. At 11:00 A.M., the Second Battalion dragged its guns and wagons across a shorter area of mud and moved onto the road to Cheppy.

XII

Into what had been enemy territory the day before, they encountered the debris of combat. The usual chatter and joking stopped quickly. The terrain they had pounded the day before, Eddie Meisburger wrote, "looked like humans, dirt, rock, trees, and steel had been turned up by one plow." Wounded Americans and German prisoners moved toward the rear. Meisburger would never forget a smiling, freckle-faced doughboy, one leg blown off at the hip, who sat calmly on a horse rolling a cigarette—and died just as he reached the dressing station.

Alongside the road, they saw the bodies of fourteen infantrymen killed by a single German shell (one of them a major whose body had been split open) and then more bodies, some of them severed by murderous machine-gun fire. One of the sergeants said, "Now you sons of bitches, I guess you'll believe you're in a war." A hysterical French officer jumped on top of an automobile and shouted, "Go back! The Boche are coming!" A Battery D private named Casey knocked him down. As they turned through what was left of Cheppy, machine-gun fire was very close.

Early in the afternoon, the battalion established itself in an orchard between Cheppy and Varennes to give close-in support to infantry engaged in a desperate battle against a German counterattack at Charpentry, less than two miles north. Gates warned the men that if the Germans broke through, they should be prepared to fire their guns at point-blank range, defend themselves with revolvers, and above all ensure that the firing pins were pulled off the 75s if they had to be left behind. He ordered harassing barrages against the Germans in Charpentry and sent Truman and a small party forward with a field telephone to establish an observation post.

Truman and Lieutenant Les Zemer reached a hill just about 750 yards south of Charpentry. A few enlisted men trailed them, struggling to keep the phone line intact. Infantry commanders were nowhere to be found in the confusion; from the hill, the two officers observed a see-saw struggle. American tanks assaulted the village, only to be driven back by hostile artillery fire. The telephone line failed to work. A German plane flew overhead and dropped a "potato masher" grenade that exploded near Zemer, blowing the telephone set off his head but leaving him unhurt. An infantryman who encountered them told them that his unit was falling back and that they were in no-man's-land. Hastily, they withdrew, found tank headquarters, used it as a new observation post, and redoubled efforts to establish a functioning phone connection. At 5:30 P.M., they finally were successful.

With the aid of a flare dropped by an American reconnaissance plane, Truman had located a German battery outside the regiment's sector. Disregarding standing orders, he relayed coordinates to Battery D for a barrage. It was too dark to observe the effect. Klemm later threatened him with court-martial for firing outside his area. He himself always would be convinced that he had destroyed the enemy position. He and Gates returned the next day and with a functioning telephone managed to direct effective fire against a German observation post and an enemy artillery column before receiving orders to stop because the advancing infantry claimed that it was taking friendly fire from the rear.

Truman's battalion spent the next four days firing from a new position just off the Varennes–Cheppy road. (It had left its original placement after being spotted by German planes. Shortly afterward, enemy artillery plastered the site.) On September 28, Miles's First Battalion "leap-frogged" them to provide close support to American troops. Just a short distance in front of Miles, remnants of the shattered 140th Infantry Regiment, rallied by Harry's cousin Captain Ralph Truman, desperately struggled to hold back a German counterattack. Major Stayton's 110th Engineers abandoned their road-repair work and moved up to the front with rifles. Wounded men were sent up from the triage if they were capable of handling a weapon. The line held.

Increasingly, the Second Battalion was in the rear echelon, still taking occasional return fire but farther removed from the fighting as the infantry held on, then slogged ahead. Battery D nevertheless remained very busy, firing two or more barrages every day, occasionally facing incoming rounds, but incurring no losses. On September 29, the Thirty-fifth Division, having suffered 50 percent casualties among its rifle units, was pulled out and replaced by the more battlewise First Division, which pushed ahead over the next week and a half to take another four miles, sustaining terrible losses in the process. The artillery continued in support for a couple of days. On the afternoon of October 2, a squadron of German airplanes attacked Truman's battalion with machine-gun fire and bombs, but managed only to wound a private in Battery F. That evening, Truman received orders to move all the way back to Seigneulles, a little village near Bar-le-Duc, for rest, resupply, and reassignment.[27]

XIII

Truman's battery was probably the luckiest in the regiment. Its only casualties had been two men wounded while on duty with the ammunition train. (One of them, a young draftee from Texas who was a recent addition, would die in the hospital. He would be Battery D's only combat fatality.) Yet all the men could feel that they had done their duty bravely. They knew that they were far more fortunate than the infantry, but that realization did nothing to relieve the strain they had felt. The days and nights of imminent danger without sleep and regular meals had, as Truman put it, left them all nervous wrecks and as thin as scarecrows. They went back to the rear as living demonstrations that there was no easy combat duty.

The trauma of combat contributed to Truman's growing disenchantment with France and the French. Seigneulles had gone through the entire war close to the front. Just off the main supply road between Bar-le-Duc and Verdun, it (like many similar villages) had been all but overrun by the military since the earliest days of the war. With most of its able-bodied young men away in the French army, it was a town of women, old men, and children, playing host to a procession of French and American units that claimed shelter in their houses and placed intolerable stress on their short supplies of staple foodstuffs.

To Truman and many other American soldiers, Seigneulles was populated by greedy profiteers who charged outrageous prices for the smallest luxuries. "These people love francs better than their country," he told Bess. Seigneulles was also a "dirty little village." (It was not uncommon for the inhabitants of French farming settlements to stack piles of manure against their houses, nor was the distinction between the living quarters of people and livestock always clear.) Truman wrote to Bess:

> You can always tell a French village by day or night, even if you can't see anything. They are very beautiful to stand off and look at, nestling down

in pretty little valleys, as they always do, with red roofs and a church spire. But when you arrive there are narrow dirty streets and a malodorous atmosphere that makes you want to go back to the hill and take out your visit in scenery.

Still, the days at Seigneulles were not all bad. Truman's commission as a captain finally caught up with him, enabling him "to accept" it and begin drawing pay commensurate with his rank. Klemm soon forgot the threat to court-martial him and perhaps tried to make up for it by taking him and Marks into Bar-le-Duc for dinner. Truman rested, gained back some weight, and wrote to Bess. He sent her three letters in six days. "The great drive has taken place and I had a part in it," he told her with pride in himself and his battery. He knew that the part he had played in the war was small, and he accompanied every declaration of his achievements with a feigned modesty. Nevertheless, he was a man with a newfound confidence that lifted his spirits above the muck and gore that surrounded him.[28]

The regiment moved out of Seigneulles for the front on October 12. On October 16, it moved into new positions just to the east of Verdun. The city had long since ceased to be the focal point of the war, but the landscape displayed vivid scars of the long siege of 1916, when men on both sides had been chewed up by the hundreds of thousands. Battery D took up a position for a week near Somedieue to the southeast, and then moved to the north near a strategic railway tunnel close to Fort de Tavannes; Truman set up his command posts in dugouts on barren hillsides. All around him were fields of mud and shell craters and blackened, limbless tree trunks. In the moonlight, he imagined them as a sorrowful parade of the ghosts of the 500,000 soliders who had been slaughtered there.

"There are Frenchmen buried in my front yard and Huns in the back yard and both litter up the landscape as far as you can see," he wrote to Bess from his second command bunker. "Every time a Boche shell hits in a field over west of here it digs up a piece of someone." He walked into Verdun one day to find it a ruin—not a civilian in town, not a building untouched by enemy artillery, the cathedral a shambles, with only its twin towers intact. Walking four miles to his observation post near the famous Fort Douaumont, he found a few poppies and other wildflowers growing in the rubble; he picked them to send to Bess, Ethel, Nellie, and other loved ones.[29]

The 129th's new positions were essentially defensive, but only a few miles from the front lines. Enemy artillery harassed them intermittently, at times with gas shells. German reconnaissance and attack planes were in the air daily. Truman saw one German plane go down in flames. Another made a crash landing; its two aviators surrendered and seemed happy for the security of a prison camp. (The Americans to whom they gave up picked them clean of anything that might be considered a war trophy. As Truman told Bess, there was a saying that Germany was fighting for territory, France for patriotism, Britain for control of the seas, America for souvenirs.) Some days he did nothing; on others, he fired barrages or figured artillery problems or adjusted his firing ranges with a few test rounds.

In early November, the Germans having been pushed across the Meuse, the infantry in front of Verdun began to take the offensive. Battery D remained in its strategically important spot and fired new long-range shells to the east toward the villages of Grimacourt and Hermeville. On November 11, Truman finally received a long-awaited word: "Hostilities will cease on whole front at 11:00 hours this morning."

At 11:00 A.M., Truman recalled, the front became "so quiet it made your head ache." Infantrymen on both sides emerged from the trenches and cheered. Farther back, the artillerymen stayed at their positions until night. By evening, the French had managed to bring up cases of wine. Soon they were all marching past Truman's tent, saluting, and shouting, "Vive Président Wilson! Vive le capitaine d'artillerie américaine!"[30]

XIV

Truman was justifiably proud. He had performed effectively and bravely, had lost only one man at the front, and had been twice commended for the excellent maintenance of his guns, once in writing by the commanding general of the Thirty-fifth Division. (He inserted a memorandum into the military record giving all credit to Chief Mechanic McKinley Wooden, but he told Bess, "I am going to keep the original letter for my own personal and private use. It will be nice to have someday if some low-browed north-end politician tries to remark that I wasn't in the war when I'm running for eastern judge or something.") In January 1919, Gates gave him a sterling evaluation: "an excellent battery commander . . . excellent instructor . . . resourceful and dependable." In May, despite the fact that he wanted only to go home, his new regimental commander, Colonel Emery T. Smith, would deliver almost as strong an appraisal and recommend him for the rank of major in the regular army.[31]

He also had an opportunity to get away from the dreary battlefront villages and see more of the France that he had enjoyed during his first months in the country. On November 26, he, Gates, Elliott, and one or two other officers were given leave. They spent thirteen days in Paris, Marseilles, and Nice; Truman would remember the experience vividly for the rest of his life.

In Paris, he viewed the Arc de Triomphe and the Alexander III Bridge, admired the imposing Gothic mass of Notre-Dame and the Hellenic grace of the Madeleine, made a reverent visit to Napoleon's Tomb, dined at Maxim's ("the restaurant in *The Merry Widow*," he reminded his cousins), and saw a performance of *Thaïs* at the Paris Opéra (the building alone, he remarked, was worth the price of admission). He even took in the Folies Bergère. (Forty years later, he would remember the performance as "a disgusting experience," but at the time he was more down-to-earth. "What you'd expect at the Gaiety only more so," he reported to Ethel and Nellie.) He missed only the Louvre; there was no use starting it, he told his cousins, unless one had three weeks.

In Marseilles ("some town") he heard the famous chanteuse Gaby Dileys and managed to catch a bouquet she threw into the audience. At Nice (also "some town"), he stayed in a huge room overlooking the sea at the Hotel de la Méditerranée ("some hotel"). "There is no blue like the Mediterranean blue," he wrote to Bess, "and when it is backed by hills and a promontory with a lighthouse on it and a few little sailing ships it makes you think of Von Weber's *Polacca Brilliante*." In Monte Carlo, not allowed in the gaming rooms, Truman and his friends spent an evening in the casino restaurant, where they witnessed a grand entrance by the princess. Elliott, who had the best view, reported to the others, "Oh hell, she's taking beer! Can you imagine a princess drinking beer?"[32]

After his furlough, Truman faced the frustration of every combat soldier who survives a war intact: the long wait to go back home. First the battery lived in primitive quarters at Camp La Beholle, in the woods about four miles from Verdun, and then in the village of Rosières, near Bar-le-Duc. Both places were ideal breeding grounds for lice and other parasites; personal hygiene was difficult and easily neglected. (In February, a medical inspection revealed 149 cases of lice in the Second Battalion, about evenly divided among the three batteries.) Officers and men alike fought off boredom with nonstop poker sessions; it was probably at this time that Truman developed his lifelong fondness for the game. Morale sagged.

Truman increasingly resented the discipline that was enforced on him and that he was expected to apply to others. Suddenly, it seemed, the senior officers who had commanded them in war were transferred one by one and usually replaced by inexperienced and none-too-bright martinets obsessed with book regulations, dress codes, drills, and inspections. What had seemed meaningful while training in anticipation of combat now appeared mindless. The constantly overcast skies, the cold, and the rain all reinforced a general state of melancholy.

Some of his friends, including Salisbury and Allen, asked for regular army commissions (Allen would receive one); others signed up for the reserves. Truman applied for "full and immediate separation."[33] Like most of the troops, he saw the situation in the simplest terms—they had beaten the Hun, and it was time to go home. As the peace conference in Paris dragged along, international politics seemed to be keeping them in the mud longer than necessary. For the first time, he was critical of his political hero, Woodrow Wilson. "I am very anxious that Woodie cease his gallavantin' around and send us home at once and quickly," he told his cousins.[34]

When the time came, he hated to give up his artillery pieces: "If the government would let me have one of them, I'd pay for it and pay the transportation home just to let it sit in my front yard and rust. . . . It's like parting with old friends who've stood by me through thick and thin." Once again, he felt let down by Klemm, who refused to recommend either him or any other line officer in the regiment for a medal. Nor did it sit well that both Klemm and Elliott took opportunities to go home early. Truman was determined that Klemm should be barred from marching in the regiment's victory parade. Many of the other officers agreed; ultimately, their elected commander would be absent from his regiment's final celebration.[35]

XV

Amid the gloom, there were bright spots. Perhaps the most memorable was a happy Christmas celebration in the mud of La Beholle. On December 24, Christmas packages from home had not arrived, the regiment seemed forgotten by the army ration system, and Truman had only a 330-franc allotment from the regimental mess fund. His predecessor as commander of Battery D, John Thacher, found another 500 francs, and Truman apparently supplemented it. The two officers sent chow scouts out to comb every nearby village for fresh meat, poultry, eggs, and wine. They were successful, if at exorbitant prices. "We bought a hog," Truman told Bess. "Now what do you reckon that cursed hog cost in honest-to-goodness money? Just $235.00. Dollars, real dollars, not francs."

The entire battery dinner must have cost them $500, but it was worth every penny, he concluded. The troops decorated the mess hall, a tar-paper shack surrounded by frozen mud and snow, with a Christmas tree, ornaments fashioned from old tin cans and tinfoil, mistletoe, red berries, and evergreen sprigs. They feasted on chicken, duck, roast pork, potatoes, gravy, corn, jam, peach and cherry cobbler, and abundant *vin rouge*.

Each of the officers made a brief speech. The battery quartet, accompanied by a piano that somehow had been found for the occasion, sang a full repertoire that ranged from sentimental ballads to rousing tunes such as "Keep Your Head Down Allemand." Someone played several melodies on a violin. Sergeant Tommy Murphy, a charming young Irishman with lethal fists and a beautiful tenor voice, sang some solos.[36] Even on Christmas, the entire regiment had boxing and wrestling matches. Although Murphy, an amateur lightweight champion, was barred from competition, Battery D carried off most of the honors. After the scheduled fights were over, the proceedings nearly declined into a general free-for-all.

Through the rest of the winter, athletics provided an outlet for the energies of aggressive young men. On January 2, 1919, a showdown match between Batteries D and E was the highlight of the boxing card; both units put down bets lavishly. Two generations later, Chief Mechanic Wooden remembered the event (and a referee's biased decision) vividly.

Truman wrote of the result to Bess, "My Sergeant Meisburger lost the decision over a gorilla named Hamby,* and I lost 1,000 francs. . . . [T]he other fellow had to be carried from the ring and my man walked out." He added, "I'd rather have been beaten by anyone on earth than one of Salisbury's outfit."[37]

On February 17, General John Pershing, accompanied by the Prince of Wales, inspected the regiment, along with the entire Thirty-fifth Division and Sixtieth Field Artillery Brigade. As usual, the day was overcast and rainy, but just as the artillery brigade paraded past Pershing and unfurled its colors, the sun broke through, highlighting the unit against gray, misty hillsides on the horizon. The general and the prince inspected each battery. Pershing congratulated Truman (and all the other officers) on the fine moral and physical condition of his men. Neither he nor the prince heard (or perhaps chose not to hear) the private in the rear ranks, who said, "Captain, ask that little son-of-a-bitch when he's going to free Ireland."[38]

On April 9, the regiment boarded the captured German transport ship *Zeppelin* for the voyage home. The eleven-day trip was miserable. Improperly loaded, making its first Atlantic crossing, and run by American officers unfamiliar with its navigational characteristics, the *Zeppelin* pitched and rolled violently. Truman was constantly seasick; at his low point, he told Bess, he wanted only to go back to the Argonne and die honorably. He lost nearly twenty pounds.

On the morning of April 20, the men awoke to find themselves in New York Harbor, greeted by the mayor's welcoming boat, complete with a band playing "Home, Sweet Home." "Even the hardest of hard-boiled cookies had to blow his nose a time or two," Truman recalled. All the social service agencies had something for them when they disembarked: handkerchiefs from the Jews, chocolate from the YMCA, cigarettes from the Knights of Columbus, homemade cake from the Red Cross, free telegrams home and chocolate Easter eggs from the Salvation Army.

They spent a week and a half at Camp Mills, which after France seemed a luxury resort. Gorging himself on ice cream and enjoying (in company with most of the battery non-coms) an enormous Italian dinner prepared by the sister of his "Dago barber," Frank Spina, Truman regained his weight. He did a little sightseeing and took in several shows in New York, but remained determined not to be impressed by the city: "Went to Bronx Zoo. It's about like Swope."[39]

On April 30, the men boarded trains for home. At 7:00 A.M., May 3, they pulled into Union Station at Kansas City and found it crowded with family and friends. At 9:00, the regiment formed and marched downtown—through streets lined with cheering well-wishers—and underneath a triumphal arch to the convention hall, where they resumed their reunion

---

*Private Finis H. Hamby, a Texan, who does not appear to have been even a distant cousin to the simian who wrote this book.

with loved ones, had a large meal, and received a silver cup from the women's auxillary.

That afternoon, they marched back to the station to entrain for Camp Funston, Kansas, where they turned in their equipment. On May 6, Truman, like the rest of the men, was given his uniform, including overcoat and raincoat, steel helmet, gas mask, final pay, a $60 bonus, mileage money to his home, and a "full and immediate separation" from the U.S. Army.

5

"June 28, 1920 One Happy Year . . . June 28, 1922 Broke and in a Bad Way": Family, Fraternity, and Commerce in the 1920s

The wedding, the *Independence Examiner* reported, had been one "of unusual beauty and interest." Miss Wallace, attended by two cousins and given in marriage by her brother Frank, wore a gown of white georgette and a hat of white faille; she carried a bouquet of Aaron Ward roses. Captain Truman wore a new suit tailored by his best man and close army comrade, Ted Marks. Daisies, hollyhocks, and larkspur decorated a candlelit altar. Bride, groom, and guests heard music by Mendelssohn and Gounod. After a brief pause for photographs, the couple departed in Truman's new Dodge roadster for their honeymoon. The date was June 28, 1919.

The marriage marked Truman's entry at the age of thirty-five into a world of full adulthood, requiring a decisive attempt at self-definition and bringing unexpected disappointments. Writing to Bess thirty-eight years later, he recalled their first twelve months as "one happy year." He also remembered their situation by their third anniversary: "broke and in a bad way."[1]

II

The newlyweds lingered in Chicago. ("Remember the Blackstone?" Harry asked Bess thirty years later.) They visited Detroit, and then spent days on the beach at Port Huron. But they could not escape a persistent reality that would be a part of their life together for the next thirty-three years. From the time her daughter left the altar, Madge Wallace displayed psychological withdrawal symptoms. Writing to Bess at the Blackstone on July 5, her youngest brother, Fred, reported, "Mom says if she doesn't hear from you, she's going to telegraph the hotel." After three weeks, they returned home and established their residence at 219 North Delaware with Bess's mother.[2]

The young couple had talked of living in Grandview, but family responsibilities aside, such could hardly have been an attractive prospect to Bess; nor did it comport well with Harry's business requirement of easy access to downtown Kansas City. Mrs. Wallace periodically suffered from sciatica, which had a way of becoming especially difficult at times when one of her children was on the verge of establishing independence. Bess's elderly Grandmother Gates still lived at the big house and also required caring attention. (Grandfather Gates had died a year earlier.)

Bess herself apparently was torn between the resumption of her long-standing family duties and a desire to live separately with her new husband. Harry never attempted to force the issue. As Bess's sister-in-law May Wallace put it some sixty years later, "Bess thought they should stay until her mother got used to the idea. . . . [M]other never got quite settled enough for Bess to leave. And Harry liked it that way." Thus they settled into a life of middle-class respectability, Bess periodically entertaining her bridge club and holding teas for church groups, Harry devoting himself to business and civic activities.[3]

Truman worked hard at nurturing what seems to have been a sincere and mostly unreciprocated devotion to his mother-in-law. Whatever discomfort he may have felt over his residence was more than mitigated by his understanding that Bess was probably happier with it than any other possibility. The convenience and lack of expense doubtless helped also. He seems generally to have given people a Kansas City business address for correspondence; on those rare occasions when Bess was away, he retreated to Grandview or to a Kansas City hotel.

He had, in effect, taken up life in a Wallace family compound. At Madge's instigation, Grandfather Gates had subdivided lots from the back of his spacious property, had built bungalows fronting on Van Horn Street (now Truman Road), and had presented them to Bess's married brothers. The oldest, Frank, worked for the family business, Waggoner-Gates Milling. George, the second son, was an order clerk in a lumber mill. Every evening, Frank spent at least a half-hour with his mother; George, by contrast, saw little of her. The youngest brother, Fred, a college student at the time of Bess's marriage, lived in the big house after his graduation, pursued a quasi-active career as an architect, and allowed his mother to smother most of his normal drives toward maturity and independence.

Inside 219 North Delaware, Grandmother Gates lived in a downstairs bedroom until her death in 1924. Bess's mother occupied the master bedroom; the Trumans and Fred had rooms down the hall. Shortly after Grandma Gates died, Madge moved to the ground floor in order to avoid painful daily walks up and down the stairs. The Trumans relocated to the master suite.

Business, politics, and fraternal obligations kept Truman away from home on many evenings over the next fifteen years. When the entire family was present for dinner, they ate formally and a bit stiffly, Harry at one end of the table, Madge at the other. The women wore good dresses; the men, jackets and ties. Mother Wallace customarily finished the day doing needlework in her rocking chair, chatting softly with Fred, and listening to music on the radio. Harry might play the upright piano in the music room or retreat to a small nook he used as a study and reading area. He favored history and biography; Bess enjoyed mysteries.[4]

Truman's own relatives rarely, if ever, set foot inside 219 North Delaware. Yet living a remarkably compartmentalized family life, he maintained close relations with all of them. Mamma and Mary Jane remained on the old home place just outside Grandview, renting out their farmland to a nearby operator. By now, it was pretty apparent that they always would be together. As years passed, Mary Jane could be defensive about her status as an old maid and a bit resentful that she had been stuck with the job of caring for Mamma. She found consolation in the Baptist Church and the Eastern Star. She had title to eighty acres of the property as her share of Uncle Harrison's legacy. Vivian had taken sixty-five acres, which he farmed himself.

Mamma was seventy in 1921, but still mentally alert and physically fit. From time to time in the middle of the decade, Vivian's son J. C. would come over with his .410 shotgun, and the two of them would tramp through nearby woods searching for rabbits. Martha carried a big 16-gauge shotgun and rarely missed a target. "It seemed natural enough to a 12-year old boy at the time to go hunting with Grandma," J. C. marveled years later.

She was as tough as ever. It was around this time that a hobo showed up at the door and asked for a meal. Martha seated him on the porch with a plate of food and a cup of coffee. Realizing that the old lady was alone in the house, the tramp became insolent and menacing. Calling her out, he told her to warm up his coffee. She nodded, took the cup, and went back inside. Returning with her shotgun, she sent the man scurrying for his life through the screen door. The story would be treasured within the Truman family.

Years later, Ted Marks recalled escorting Martha Truman as the wedding party watched Harry and Bess depart for their honeymoon. "I said to her, 'Well, now, Mrs. Truman, you've lost Harry.' And she looked up at me with those little blue eyes and said, 'Indeed, I haven't.'" Harry spent every Sunday afternoon with her at Grandview; Bess usually accompanied him. Dinner was almost always country-fried chicken—it was the one dish that Martha had learned to cook well. Mary Jane usually would have been there; Vivian probably frequently dropped by. They shared local gossip and always talked politics. Mamma Truman was plainspoken; her sons followed her example. The atmosphere was commoner and easier than at the Wallace house. Bess liked her mother-in-law's uninhibited bluntness and seems to have enjoyed the visits as much as did her husband.[5]

Harry devoted much of his spare time to public service and fraternal activities. He was a leading member of the Triangle Club, a young businessmen's civic association in Kansas City. Rising steadily in the Masonic Order, he became deputy district director for Jackson County and a figure of note in statewide Masonic activities. He was active in the American Legion and belonged to a downtown Kansas City post of the Veterans of Foreign Wars. He became a prominent member of the National Old Trails Association. Few men in Independence could claim recognition and achievement in so wide a range of service and fraternal groups.

As he was getting started in business in 1919, he joined the elite Kansas City Club and the Lakewood Country Club. He surely valued from an economic standpoint the contacts with important business and professional men that these memberships entailed. They must have been equally important to him as signaling acceptance as a junior member of the local establishment and as continuing his easy association with wartime comrades of money and status such as Marvin Gates and John Thacher. With his marriage into the Wallace family and his admission to exclusive clubs, he seemed to have crossed an important social threshold.

Yet his new life had its share of troubles. Most deeply felt was Bess's difficulty in having a child. Soon after they were married, she became pregnant; in early 1920, she suffered a miscarriage. In mid-1922, as Harry was campaigning for nomination to the county court, she endured another one. He began to fear that he never would become a father. His dream of finally becoming a successful businessman also unraveled. As early as the fall of 1920, his finances were so straitened that he could not afford the $250 annual dues of the Kansas City Club, nor could he meet his bills at the Lakewood Club. With what must have been enormous disappointment and embarrassment, he resigned from both. No doubt, Bess felt herself a source of distress to her husband, while Harry, beset with demands from creditors, must have felt that he had failed his wife. It says much about their commitment to each other that they overcame these strains.[6]

III

As deep as was Truman's attachment to Bess, it could not override the pull of another affiliation that he once had wanted to put behind him. He soon discovered that he missed the army. He craved not the exhilaration of physical danger, not the narrow rigidity of the military outlook, and certainly not the mindless discipline. Rather, he missed the association with men like himself, who—in the tradition of Cincinnatus—had responded to a call to arms and served their country without abandoning their civilian vocations. Ted Marks and Spencer Salisbury already had accepted reserve commissions. In December 1919, hardly half a year since he had rejoiced in his discharge, Truman applied for appointment as a major in the reserves.

It was a natural enough step. Many of the men of Battery D saw him regularly and considered him their leader; some sixty or seventy of them presented him and their other beloved captain, John Thacher, with large silver loving cups. The inscription on Truman's read:

> CAPTAIN HARRY S. TRUMAN
> PRESENTED
> By The
> Members of Battery D
> In Appreciation of His
> Justice, Ability and
> Leadership

He cherished the trophy. After he and Eddie Jacobson opened their haberdashery in downtown Kansas City, the cup stood on prominent display, and the store became a hangout for his former soldiers. Under the genial patronage of Captain Harry, it functioned as a meeting place, a small-loan agency, and an employment bureau. Former private Al Ridge, who had stood firm at the Battle of Who Run, spent hours in the back room studying law; eventually, he became a judge and a firm Truman political ally.

It is difficult to estimate how many of the battery boys maintained a close relationship with Truman. No army officer is universally popular; the men whom he had demoted were surely happy to forget about him. Others who liked him found themselves separated by geography; only a few remained in touch by letter. Around a hundred seem to have remained in the Kansas City area; from that number, the five dozen or so who paid for his loving cup constituted a devoted following.

During the war, Truman had always been willing to lend a few dollars to almost any of his men who were broke. Even as his own finances tightened painfully, he appears to have continued the custom as best he could. Eddie Jacobson recalled years later that if a man came in and addressed his business partner as "Captain Truman," he likely was a cash customer; if he used the phrase "Captain Harry," a request for credit or a personal loan was likely to follow. Truman also scouted out jobs for the men, no small task in the tough times of 1921 and 1922. He found former private James "Abie" Burkhardt employment as a security guard (for cousin Ralph, working in Springfield, Missouri, as head of security for the Frisco railroad). Truman then sent Burkhardt the .45 that he had carried through the war, telling him, "Please don't lose it but if you do come and see me all the same because I value your friendship higher than a U. S. Army gun."[7]

The annual ritual that reinforced such ties was the St. Patrick's Day banquet, a custom begun in March 1918 at Camp Doniphan and maintained with gusto in the postwar years. The occasions invariably began with an invocation and always contained a tribute to the memory of the battery's six dead. (Five had died in France of noncombat causes.) Then the boisterous partying instinct took over. The 1920 gathering may have been comparatively quiet because several female singers and musicians were among the entertainers. The infamous 1921 dinner, held at the Elks Club, labored under no such inhibitions. An abundant supply of bootleg booze fueled a sense of energy and a lack of restraint. Before the evening was over, dishes and glassware were flying through the air. When the Elks management attempted to quell the disturbance by bringing in the police, they had the misfortune to get a cop who was himself a Battery D veteran. His old mates promptly disarmed him and stripped him to his underwear.

A few days later, Truman received a bill for an extra $17.80 to cover broken dishes, shattered tumblers, shredded napkins, crushed artificial flowers, and extra cleaning. "We regret very much the occurrence of that evening and realize that the officers were not responsible for the acts of the individuals," wrote the lodge's secretary. He did not, however, invite the battery back. The banquet moved around a lot in those years.[8]

Rollicking male comradeship that sometimes got out of hand exemplified one aspect of Truman's postwar military life. There were serious sides, too: patriotism and pride of service, a continued faith in the ideal of the citizen-soldier, an ambition to move ahead in the world. The Thirty-fifth Division Association held annual conventions. In 1926, Truman won election as a member of its executive committee; in 1939, he became its president.

Like so many war veterans, Truman gravitated naturally to the American Legion. It gave him a chance to renew and cement old associations with friends in the officer corps, among them Young Jim Pendergast. The state Legion meetings were many things—exercises in nostalgia, loud and frequently disorderly celebrations, perpetual fights for office between Kansas City, St. Louis, and the rest of the state—but above all they involved the organization and expression of political power. Referring to the men around him at the St. Joseph state convention in 1921, Truman wrote to Bess, "The next twenty years will see them running the country." By then, with the men's-furnishings business going poorly, Truman may have been thinking of himself as one of those who would do a bit of the running. Through the Legion, he became acquainted with others who possessed the same aspirations, among them Bennett Clark, Tuck Milligan, and Lloyd Stark.

Throughout 1921, he was one of many Legionnaires involved in planning for the organization's national convention, held that November in Kansas City. Picked to serve on the beautification committee, chaired by his old major, Marvin Gates, Truman became its most active member and eventual acting chairman. He drafted the Triangle Club into the effort and worked with leaders of nearly two dozen other business organizations to clean up unsightly areas of the city. "We expect . . . to decorate about 65 or 70 blocks of the down-town district with bunting and the Allied flags, suspended from the trolley poles," he told a supplier from whom he requested bids. Utilizing Boy Scouts, he also undertook a "Tag Your Home with a Flag" drive designed to get the Stars and Stripes flying from the front of 100,000 residences.

The effort seems to have enjoyed considerable success, but few remembered the Legion convention because of it. Writing of the Legionnaires at St. Joseph, Truman had told Bess, "They're just young and full of pep and they have to explode someway." When they came to Kansas City from all over the country, the national convention delegates hit the city with the force of an artillery barrage. They created a bonanza for pimps and bootleggers, tossed ladies' undergarments from hotel windows, rolled dice in the streets, took over taxis for a unique version of polo involving car bumpers and trash cans, invaded the stages of burlesque performances, and brought a befuddled steer into a sixth-floor party at the Baltimore Hotel.

Truman himself likely took no part in the more spectacular shenanigans, but one responsibility was especially memorable. As acting chairman of the decorations committee, he presented flags of the United States, Great Britain, France, and Italy to military leaders of the Allied powers at the dedication of Kansas City's World War I monument, the Liberty Memorial. The committee's work solidified his standing in the local American Legion post, involved him with numerous influentials in a significant community effort, and enhanced his reputation as a can-do person.

At a time when failure was closing in on him from all directions, the Legion and the other organizations kept alive the memory of shared effort, success, affection, and respect that had marked the greatest endeavor of Truman's life. The veterans' groups also helped him develop valuable political contacts locally and around the state. He never progressed beyond vice-commander of the local Legion post—holders of public office were ineligible for elective Legion offices. But the memories of France and his sense of himself as a citizen-soldier continued to be paramount aspects of his own conception of his identity.[9]

IV

Truman's reserve service also became an integral part of his life. The Organized Reserve Corps was simply a cadre of officers who could be called to active duty in an emergency. Those who wished to move ahead improved their skills through a series of correspondence courses, which occupied many hours of Truman's time throughout the 1920s and early 1930s. Beginning in 1923, the reserve officers undertook two weeks of field training with National Guardsmen each year at a nearby military base.

Although serious in the actual drilling and artillery practice, the camps were less than rigidly formal in their organization. In 1927, Truman took his friend and associate Rufus Burrus along as a guest trainee. Harry Vaughan, the young officer who years earlier had saved Truman from the wrath of General Lucien Berry, gave Burrus a "promotion" each day by adding stripes to his shirtsleeve with a piece of chalk, and then "broke" him to buck private after a week. (Burrus enjoyed the experience enough that he enlisted after returning home.) After hours, the older men generally managed to sucker some green lieutenant into being the goat in a fraudulent little exercise called a badger hunt. A stag dinner, the tone of which was somewhere between that of a Rotary luncheon and a Battery D banquet, concluded the fortnight.

Truman participated in all these activities, training at Fort Leavenworth, Kansas, in 1923; at Fort Riley, Kansas, from 1925 through 1931; at Camp Ripley, Minnesota, in 1932; and at Camp Pike, Arkansas, in 1933. (He skipped camp in 1924 because of a difficult primary-election campaign.) Always he faithfully wrote to Bess, telling her how much he missed her. No doubt he did, but the emotional fulfillment he derived from summer training made the sacrifice worthwhile. Among his associates were Karl Klemm, Arthur Elliott,* Spencer Salisbury, and Ted Marks. He developed a special relationship with E. M. Stayton, who along with John Miles constituted the examination board that promoted him to lieutenant colonel in 1925. Three of his closest and most loyal friends were Vaughan, still loud and irrepressible; John W. Snyder, an Arkansas banker; and Eddie McKim, a Battery D enlisted man who had qualifed as a reserve lieutenant.

The summer camps were important for what the upwardly mobile of a later generation would describe as networking. A few regular army men, some of them individuals of distinction, supervised the training activities or were otherwise present. (Truman recalled going to a party held in celebration of George M. Patton's promotion to higher rank and leaving early because, as he enigmatically put it, "it was too rough for me.") But far more helpful were the contacts with other ambitious

---

*Truman effected at least a partial reconcilation with Klemm and Elliott, who as Klemm's second in command had also earned his wrath. Both men came to unfortunate ends. In 1925, Klemm, apparently deeply depressed about the collapse of an important business deal and possibly about family difficulties, killed himself with his old army revolver. With what one assumes to be unintentional irony, his comrades established a marksmanship award in his honor. (A few days later, Klemm's successor as commander of the 129th Field Artillery, Lieutenant Colonel Emery T. Smith, hanged himself at Fort Leavenworth. A student at the General Command and Staff School, he was making failing grades.) Arthur Elliott, a man whose physique long had been characterized by obesity and general unfitness, suffered a fatal heart attack just after eating a big Thanksgiving Day dinner in 1930 (*KCT* and *KCS*, November 6, 16, 1925; November 28, 29, 1930).

midwestern men who like Truman saw the reserves as a way of both ful-filling a patriotic duty and getting to know others like themselves. One of the most significant such acquaintances was with the Nebraskan Dwight Griswold, later the governor of his state and, after that, President Harry Truman's representative in Greece during the insurgency of 1947.[10]

Truman wanted the Reserve Corps to be more than two weeks of semiserious summer camp for adults. In November 1921, he, Stayton, Klemm, Elliott, and Major E. E. McKeighan met for lunch at the Hotel Baltimore. After some discussion, they decided to organize a Kansas City–area Reserve Officers Club. Typically, Truman shouldered most of the organizational work. He then served a one-year term as the club's first president.

He started the Reserve Officers Club off along the lines that he envi-sioned for all his military activities: practical instruction and social fellow-ship. A series of luncheons featured lectures on military subjects by regular army officers from Fort Leavenworth. The highlight of the first year was a dinner at which the guest speaker was Assistant Secretary of War Jonathan Wainwright, who twenty years later would be known to every American as the heroic defender of Battan. Truman apparently liked him from the first and later admired him greatly.

In subsequent years, the club flourished. The luncheon meetings became Wednesday dinners; the lecture series, a twenty-eight-week evening course with an average attendance of 150 officers. Operating at first out of the 110th Engineers National Guard Armory, the organiza-tion managed to finance a club building, which went up next door. It had living quarters for army officers assigned to reserve duty in the area, head-quarters offices, a social lounge, a pistol range, and a large lecture room. Truman was near the center of all these developments as a director of the club and a member of key committees. In his years as presiding judge of the county court, he saw to it that the county provided a subsidy for reserve officers' training activities. As late as 1937, his third year in the Senate, he was a member of five organization committees.

Extraordinarily proud of his reserve activities, he liked to consider the Kansas City club the founding chapter of what became the national Reserve Officers Association. That claim was probably an exaggeration; there were other local associations that appear to have been more inter-ested in establishing some sort of national structure. It does seem clear, however, that the Kansas City organization was one of the first and a strong example for similar groups.[11]

In mid-1932, Truman won promotion to the rank of colonel. He was by this time commanding officer of the 381st Field Artillery Regiment. (Lieutenant Colonel John Snyder was second in command; Major Ted Marks was a battalion commander.) But politics were closing in on this part of his life. His primary campaign for the Senate in 1934 again forced him to miss summer camp. In 1935, after he took his Senate seat, the army (following established policy and irritating him mightily) relieved him of his reserve command and put him on "general assignment." His solid military career might be at an end, but the expertise he had developed would become a valuable political asset.[12]

V

From the moment of his return to the United States in 1919, Truman was determined to abandon agriculture as a way of life and go into business. The farm had prospered under Mary Jane's management and with the assistance of good hired men. Harry had left 16 swine; he returned to a herd of 230. As he remembered it, they brought in $4,000. Despite the fact that the enterprise was experiencing its most profitable years, he announced to his mother and sister that he was leaving it and wanted to liquidate it to raise capital for his new ventures.

On September 23, 1919, he held a big auction at the farm, selling the swine and every other head of stock, every bushel of grain, every implement, and one Kimball organ. Thirty years later, he told Jonathan Daniels, possibly engaging in an unconscious adjustment for inflation, that the sale had netted $15,000. How the cash was divided among himself, Mamma, and Mary Jane is uncertain. (Since his marriage, Vivian had run his own operation and was not a partner to this one.)[13]

Truman may have taken only a third of the proceeds, although he had been primarily responsible for the farm since his father's death and with some justification considered the stock and equipment his. Perhaps he took a greater share and used much of it to pay off remaining prewar debts. (Aside from a $1,000 note that he mentioned to Bess in early 1918, it is impossible to fix the amount of debt he owed before going into the army.) He renounced any interest in his mother's property by signing a quit-claim deed; he had already quit-claimed his share of Uncle Harrison's property in 1916.

In 1919, the other family members had negotiated mortgages with the Bank of Belton. Mary Jane took $5,200 on her 80 acres, Vivian $2,100 on his 65 acres, and Martha $6,200 on the 160 acres of her brother's property remaining to her. (The last obligation was apparently a rollover of the $6,000 loan that the three of them had taken out on Harrison's legacy in 1917.) Its implications were ominous. The family had failed to work down its debt during the prosperous war years. Mary Jane and Vivian had taken on fairly manageable burdens. But Martha was now mortgaged for a total of $31,200 (including the $25,000 owed to Frank Blair), with an annual interest of $1,872—a burden in good times, a peril in lean ones.[14]

In November 1919, Truman unsuccessfully attempted to sell the 160 acres his mother had obtained from Harrison for $50,000 ($312.50 an acre).[15] In 1922, as hard times had begun to appear for every member of the family, he undertook a more modest plan, dividing 55 acres of the Harrison Young legacy just east of the Kansas City Southern tracks into eleven lots and platting them as a tract called Truman's Subdivision. Working through a Kansas City realty firm, his mother sold seven and a half lots that year for a total of $14,450. The results looked impressive, but at least some of the payments were in the form of mortgages negotiated directly with the owner. Survey, plat registration, and brokerage costs took first claim on the up-front cash. Harry himself, by this time in desperate financial straits, used the money from at least one sale to pay off a $1,700 note and possibly from another to satisfy a $1,000 obligation.

In mid-1922, Martha was able to reduce her $6,200 mortgage of 1919 by $3,400 and secure clear title to the subdivision, including some lots she already had sold. The family nonetheless continued to be chronically delinquent on its remaining mortgage obligations. Inexplicably, the remainder of Truman's Subdivision lingered unsold until 1932, probably because Martha found it difficult to part with any more of her property than was absolutely necessary. As each year passed, the mortgages hung more menacingly over it.[16]

Another matter that engaged Truman on his return from France was his disaffiliation with the Morgan enterprises. Although he talked up the prospects of the Morgan companies to acquaintances he had induced to invest, he was ready to bail out. Morgan himself had already sold his interest in Morgan Oil and Refining to J. S. Mullen, the Oklahoma millionaire who had joined them in 1917, evidently receiving in return Mullen's interest in Morgan & Company Oil Investments. Truman followed suit rather quickly. The nature of his compensation is unknown; if paid at the par value of $1 per share, he would have received $1,000.

Other than whatever he received from farm operations, Truman had no visible source of income in mid-1919. Yet he purchased a new car, took his bride on an extended honeymoon, and made cash contributions of $2,000 to his new business, Truman & Jacobson, all before his farm sale. In later years, he remembered that he had broken even or made a small profit on his oil-exploration enterprise. It is a good bet that his memory was correct.

That left the oil investment firm, in which Truman, now Morgan's sole partner, held 1,000 shares, to Morgan's 2,000. With the price of oil slipping sharply, Morgan & Company had little to commend it as an investment. No one appeared to snap up Truman's interest. In December 1919, Morgan signed over to the enterprise numerous oil leases he had personally owned. In return, and with Truman's apparent consent, he gave himself 97,000 shares of new stock, thus reducing Truman's ownership stake to 1 percent. Shortly thereafter, Morgan sold all his holdings to one Charles S. Lips. Truman, as far as one can discern, received nothing for his shares, which were (as a practical matter) worthless. In December 1920, nonetheless, Morgan transferred to Truman a large house he owned on Karnes Street, in a substantial Kansas City residential district just south of Penn Valley Park. It came encumbered with an $8,500 mortgage, but probably had a reasonable net value close to Truman's original investment. Truman apparently accepted it as final payment for his interest in the Morgan brokerage firm.[17]

The Morgan house gave Truman entrée into another business line that long had appealed to him, that of real-estate speculator and trader. The house had not been Morgan's residence and probably came with a tenant. Located in a desirable area, it was a good long-term holding; Truman envisioned it as a means of leverage. In late March 1921, in partnership with real-estate broker George Cheney, he traded the house for a three-story apartment building at 3932–34 Bell St. It came with three mortgages totaling $17,600. Truman gave title to Cheney, who accepted responsibility for the first two mortgages ($12,600), and Truman took on the third. While riskier than the Karnes Street house, the Bell Street property was also an attractive holding; a solid brick house with two large apartments on each floor, it was located in an area of middle-class homes. It probably produced enough income to service the substantial debt that Cheney and Truman had taken on.

Truman looked for an even better opportunity. He soon found a 160-acre farm just across the state line in Johnson County, Kansas. The grounds and buildings were run-down, but with a bit of improvement he thought he could turn the farm over at a considerable profit. That July, he worked out a deal with the farm's owner, Felix Gay, in which he swapped his interest and obligations in the Bell Street apartment house for Gay's farm. His new property came with two mortgages: one to the Merriam Mortgage Company for $3,500, and the other to F. E. Goodway for $5,300.

Truman valued his equity stake at $5,000, an estimate that put his total purchase at $13,800, or $86.25 an acre. It was a measure of the escalation of farmland values during the second decade of the century that just twelve years earlier the same property had changed hands for $2,250. Nonetheless, its new owner considered it a bargain. He contracted with a tenant named Ed Beach to live on the place, farm it on a share-crop basis, and fix it up. Clearly, he hoped for a reasonably quick sale and may have seen this as the last hope for a bailout of his main enterprise, Truman & Jacobson.[18]

VI

From his army discharge through 1921, Truman & Jacobson was at the center of Truman's life. It took up most of his time and ultimately claimed nearly all his capital, emotional as well as monetary. He and Eddie Jacobson had decided as they waited to be shipped home from France that they could duplicate the success of the Camp Doniphan regimental canteen in downtown Kansas City. On May 27, 1919, scarcely three weeks after being mustered out, they signed a five-year lease at $350 a month on a choice downtown site at 104 West Twelfth Street.

The location was on the ground floor of a five-story apartment build-ing that was being converted into a modern hotel, the Glennon. The building's owner, prominent real-estate developer Louis Oppenstein, reserved five store fronts on the ground floor. Considering the premium rent, the space was small, an 18-foot frontage and a 48-foot depth, along with 400 square feet of basement storage. The provisions of the lease were straightforward and standard. The new tenants paid the first three months in advance.[19] As workers labored on the hotel and the street-level shops through the summer and fall, the partners secured bank financing, estab-lished credit with suppliers, built an inventory, and purchased equipment.

Only fragmentary records remain. A few ledger sheets detail the start-up phase thoroughly; a separate invoice ledger fully covers the finances of their relations with suppliers. It is impossible to recount accurately the ebb and flow of the store's sales from late 1919 to early 1922, but the available materials indicate that the operation was very shaky from the beginning. Its financing was excessively leveraged. It began opera-tions with a negative cash flow that it may never have reversed. It also faced stiff competition that could have done in the best management.

On November 28, 1919, the day after Thanksgiving and the start of the Christmas shopping season, the shop opened for business. Start-up expenses had been heavy: $1,050 advance rent and $6,835.82 for fixtures, advertising, and inventory. The proprietors were already $5,000 in debt to the Security State Bank. Truman provided the only cash, $4,000 in all. Jacobson apparently contributed only his expertise in the men's cloth-ing business, but Truman clearly considered him an equal partner.[20]

Christmas shoppers jammed the streets and kept the partners busy. "We are very much encouraged," Truman wrote to his old lieutenant, Vic Housholder. The store handled men's underwear, socks, handker-chiefs, shirts, collars, ties, belts, gloves, and hats—all perfect items for the gift trade or for hotel guests who found themselves short on items of apparel. It specialized in high-quality (presumably also high-margin) brands and featured such items as silk shirts and ties and kid-leather gloves.

Truman & Jacobson was at the busy center of the business and en-tertainment district. Kansas City's finest hotel, the Baltimore, was just around the corner to the north; the newer and equally posh Muehlebach was across the way on the south side of Twelfth Street. Across from the Muehlebach was the Dixon Hotel, with two wide-open gambling parlors in play around the clock. A half-dozen large movie houses were within a few blocks. So were another six or so theaters running live entertainment for every taste. Nearby supper clubs featured name singers and musicians; jazz, hitherto centered a mile to the east on Vine Street, was making in-roads into such establishments. In theory, Prohibition had eliminated the alcoholic beverages that long had fueled downtown night life; in fact, the saloons and bars continued to do business. A bustling commercial cen-

ter during the day, downtown after dark had something for everyone—
late shopping, movies, burlesque, vaudeville, legitimate drama, hot music,
liquor, crap games, and the girls who worked the streets.[21]

The partners tailored their hours accordingly. They were open from
eight in the morning until nine at night. Jacobson managed the inventory; Truman kept the books. Both attended to customers; for a time they
employed a clerk—until they discovered that he was stealing from them.[22]
Every few weeks, they hired a professional display man to change the front
window arrangement. They paid themselves only $40 a week each.

Still, their thrift and hard work was no guarantee of success. The
canteen at Camp Doniphan had prospered in the beginning largely because the partners had more business savvy than other amateurs; in the
end, with the failure of one canteen after another, it had enjoyed a monopoly position. Kansas City was another story. The competition was
intense and highly professional: large department stores such as the Jones
Store and Emery, Bird, Thayer; and posh clothing firms such as Woolf
Brothers (which operated a small men's-furnishings shop directly across
the street in the Muehlebach). These and other competitors had solid
finances, established reputations, and the size to cut better deals with
suppliers.

Truman later asserted that the store had a flourishing first year in
which it did $70,000 worth of business. Almost certainly, he was once
again engaging in the nostalgic exaggeration to which he was prone with
the passage of time. He may in fact have been thinking about sales for
the store's entire existence. Surviving ledger sheets indicate that expenses
exceeded gross receipts for the first two months of the enterprise's existence—without taking into account the prepaid rent. In early 1920, the
partners faced the prospect of building an inventory for the spring and
summer trade and also beginning to pay monthly rent. That January, they
borrowed an additional $2,500, bringing their total bank debt to $7,500.

The business struggled along, making enough money to pay the rent
and utilities, adroitly juggling bank debt and supplier invoices, but in a
slippery situation. From January to July, Truman & Jacobson purchased
nearly $19,000 in inventory. It does not appear to have paid a single in-
voice until July 26. Using proceeds from a healthy spring and early-
summer trade, it paid off most of its suppliers, a few of which had been
waiting since December. It repeated the act on a smaller scale for the fall—
winter season, buying slightly less than $7,000 in new inventory. Evidently
doing a brisk Christmas trade, it cleaned up most of its bills in December
1920 and January 1921. It does not seem to have reduced its bank debt.[23]

Like typical small-business operators, Truman and Jacobson went
into debt, worked hard for little money, stalled their creditors on past-
due invoices, and barely survived. By early 1921, they faced a sharp economic recession; the bubble prosperity of the wartime era had burst in
the middle of the previous year. Agricultural prices, land values, wholesale and consumer prices for virtually everything—all were in free fall. A

general deflationary spiral threatened to pull under economic players who were small, weak, and saddled with debt.

In February 1921, the partners attempted to raise money by establishing the business as a corporation with 100 shares of common stock and 200 shares of 8 percent preferred, both types valued at $100 a share. Their listing with the state of Missouri provided a rosy picture of their situation, right down to claiming the unexpired value of their lease as an asset rather than a liability. Read carefully, it revealed a company with a nearly empty treasury and a lot of debt. Using their claimed net worth of $15,900, Truman and Jacobson assigned themselves all the common stock (50 shares each) and 59 shares of preferred (30 to Truman, 29 to Jacobson), thus ensuring that they would have voting control of the company. That left 141 shares of preferred to be sold at $100 each to gullible investors or generous friends. The purchasers, who included several old army comrades and Frank Wallace, were probably all in the latter category. Years later, Truman thought they had raised $12,000.[24]

VII

Incorporation provided nothing more than a breathing spell. During 1921, Truman and Jacobson somehow managed to talk their suppliers into providing them with approximately $10,765 in merchandise. They apparently worked down their stock in the early part of the year, and then rebuilt it in the spring and summer with another $8,000 in purchases. Meanwhile, business conditions continued to deteriorate throughout the country. When Warren G. Harding was inaugurated in March, most businesses were suffering. Sears, Roebuck, in those days primarily a catalog retailer catering to a rural clientele, reported sales for the first six months of 1921 down 36.8 percent from the same period a year earlier. The haberdashery was probably hit about as hard; it had to withstand the blows with infinitely fewer resources.

In 1921, Truman & Jacobson fell steadily behind in payments to suppliers, many of which in turn appear to have cut off its credit. The Christmas season evidently did not provide the sales needed for a bailout. The ledger shows no purchases for 1922. At the beginning of that year, the partners owed their suppliers approximately $8,219. Their debt to Security State was at least $5,000; the bank, itself in precarious financial condition, had been merged into Continental National Bank in December 1921. In January 1922, the business negotiated a $2,500 loan from the Twelfth Street Bank. Truman and Jacobson probably hoped, in vain as it developed, for a good Easter season. They hung on through the summer; but in September, after Truman had been nominated for county judge, the partners held a going-out-of-business sale and closed their doors for good.[25]

In later years, Truman asserted that he had been the victim of a monetary squeeze engineered by Harding's secretary of the treasury, Andrew

Mellon. An examination of the surviving business records, however, supports the conclusion that Mellon had virtually nothing to do with Truman's difficulties. The credit squeeze, fundamentally a natural deflationary one, had begun under Woodrow Wilson's Federal Reserve Board. Mellon, no friend of easy money, may have encouraged credit policies that were tighter than conditions warranted; but during his first year as secretary of the treasury, interest rates declined, although they remained high in real terms.

Truman & Jacobson, in fact, appears to have been unable to make money *before* the squeeze started. As in his earlier mining and oil-exploration ventures, Truman built his quest for success around the ethic and assumptions of the nineteenth-century entrepreneur, but he lived in a world of business increasingly dominated by large corporations. He suffered the usual fate of the small competitor who tries to play in the same league as the big boys while lacking new ideas, special advantages, or strong financing. Weakly capitalized, the haberdashery was vulnerable to hard times. Truman, understandably enough, refused to look at things in this fashion. He had worked hard, stocked quality merchandise, and dealt honestly with customers and suppliers. Rather than conclude that he had made an expensive mistake, he found it much more comfortable to embrace the populistic folklore of the small entrepreneur and combine it with the partisan political outlook absorbed from his childhood.

His immediate problem, and his alone, was how to get out from under the business's heavy debt. With the best intentions in the world, Jacobson had lost nothing much beyond two and a half years of effort. He possessed no assets. Truman had already invested $4,000 and stood to lose much more. Their attorney, Phineas Rosenberg, wrote to each of their suppliers, offering a settlement based on the proceeds of a close-out sale and assuring that his clients would attempt to make payment in full over the long haul. (Some at least did receive eventual payment in full.) Almost all agreed; the Cluett-Peabody Company, the manufacturer of Arrow shirts, seems to have been the only holdout. In January 1924, it got a judgment against Truman and Jacobson in a justice-of-the-peace court for $238.54. A year and a half later, the manufacturer managed to attach an account Truman held with the City Bank of Kansas City.

There was also the lease. It ran until December 1, 1924. Assuming that the last monthly rental payment was for September 1922, Truman and Jacobson still owed Louis Oppenstein at least $9,100. Oppenstein found new tenants, undoubtedly at lower rates, and went to court to recover his losses. In January 1924, he received a judgment for $3,222.87. Truman ignored it for nearly ten years, allowing accrued interest to bring the total to more than $3,900; in 1933, he and Oppenstein agreed to what he described as a settlement of "about 50 cents on the dollar."

The bank debt presented the most difficult problem. Truman hoped to meet it by selling his Johnson County farm. By the summer of 1922, having become a candidate for county judge, he had no income whatever and could not even meet the interest payments on his mortgage to F. E. Goodway, who was himself in sinking financial condition. Desperately but unavailingly, Truman advertised the farm. That October, when he and Jacobson negotiated the latest rearrangement of their debt with Security Bank (now Continental National), bringing it to $6,800, Truman gave it his encumbered title to the acreage as collateral and agreed that income from Beach's farming operations would go directly to the bank.

In 1924, one of Goodway's creditors, the Hartford Steam Boiler Inspection and Insurance Company, forced a sheriff's sale of the property as a means of collecting a judgment against Goodway. Less than two years earlier, Truman had tried to sell the Johnson County farm for $20,000. Hartford Steam submitted a high bid of $4,490.22. Truman could only watch helplessly. Whether Continental National made a bid is unknown. It credited Truman $1,043.58 in income realized from Beach and informed him that he still owed $6,261.44 in principal and accrued interest. Truman thought that the bank had squandered a valuable property that should have been accepted as payment in full. He ignored the bill.

Continental National Bank itself had been merged with Commerce Trust Company in December 1923. Commerce Trust was controlled by William T. Kemper, a leading figure in state and local Democratic politics; one of its vice presidents was Jo Zach Miller III, a close associate of Truman's in the army reserve. Perhaps because of these connections, the bank appears to have made no attempts at collection for the next five years. By 1929, however, long-standing legal action against Continental National left Commerce Trust unable to be complacent about any of its uncollected debts. In April, it got a court judgment against Truman for $8,944.78. The following year, Continental's assets passed into the hands of a court-appointed receiver. From then on, attorneys attempted with scant success to attach Truman's bank accounts, especially during election years, when he would be subject to maximum embarrassment. There would be no final settlement until he reached the Senate. In 1935, Continental's assets were liquidated at a sheriff's sale. After considerable maneuvering, Vivian Truman acquired the note for $1,000 and returned it to his brother.

The relationship with Twelfth Street Bank was more amicable. Truman gave the bank two mortgages that his mother had received for the sale of lots in Truman's Subdivision as collateral. He (perhaps with some help from Jacobson) worked the $2,500 debt down slowly over the next two years, making payments of as little as $25. In August 1924, having brought the principal down to $1,925, he suddenly reduced it to $200, using the proceeds from a mortgage paid off on one of the Truman's Subdivision lots. In December, he paid the balance in full.

It had been, he later wrote in his memoirs, a hard experience. Perhaps hardest of all was the continuing pressure from dissatisfied creditors. Jacobson found it intolerable. In February 1925, he declared bankruptcy, listing personal assets of $507 and debts of $10,658.50. It was the only way in which he could get a new start.

Jacobson's bankruptcy threw all the burden of payment on his partner. Yet Truman refused Jacobson's legal solution, however much he took it in the practical sense of insolvency and nonpayment. The ethic by which he had been taught to conduct his life told Truman that the formal, legal renunciation of debts was disgraceful, that it was better to live with the burden of his obligations and the possibility of their redemption than to commit the sin of renunciation. There was a pragmatic consideration also. Bankruptcy would hinder his move into another occupation that always had fascinated him: politics.[26]

6

"I Became a Member of a Fighting County Court": The Darwinian World of Jackson County Politics, 1922

As Truman later depicted it, his decision to go into politics was a matter of simple solicitation. Young Jim Pendergast's father, Mike, came into Truman & Jacobson one day early in 1922 and asked him to run for eastern judge. Mike, Truman believed, was not even aware that the business was on the brink of failure.

But why had Mike, a shrewd if inarticulate political commander, picked Truman? He may have known Truman vaguely ever since Frank Wallace had begun to take his young friend to goat political club meetings. He certainly had heard glowing reports from Young Jim, probably did know the haberdashery was in trouble, and may have wanted to help his son's friend. All this would have meant little, however, if Truman had not possessed a strong independent appeal that the organization needed.[1]

He probably did not hesitate long about accepting the opportunity. He had talked semijokingly about holding public office so frequently that it was obvious a serious desire lay behind his flippancy. Thus he made his entry as a candidate into a political world that was in many ways a microcosm of the larger country. It was also a world of complexity and intrigue that fully merited the adjective "Byzantine."

II

Jackson County, Missouri, unlike most similarily compact areas in the United States, contained virtually all the forces that made American politics especially turbulent in the 1920s.

Much of it was still traditionally rural–small town culturally and economically. Outside Kansas City, the electorate consisted predominately of old-stock Americans who lived in villages with three-digit populations or on semi-isolated farms. They favored laws that encoded traditional Protestant moral strictures. Bad roads and poor communications reinforced localism. Independence was in many respects the bastion of their culture.

Kansas City, with its population of 325,000, the nineteenth largest city in the United States, was not so heavily immigrant as many larger urban centers. Its population was nevertheless heterogenous; most visible were Irish, Italians, Germans, Jews, and blacks. In many respects, the city was a smaller replica of its great neighbor, Chicago, 500 miles to the northeast. Not quite the hog butcher to the world and not so ethnically diverse, Kansas City had its own sprawling stockyards, slaughterhouses, factories, and mills, manned primarily by a work force of muscular immigrants and poor old-stock whites. Like Chicago, it was a swinging, wide-open town in which law and order ran distinctly second to the easy availability of the illicit and the pleasurable. Like Chicago, it was ruled by politicians who had little use for the moralistic values of traditional America.

The most important of them, Tom Pendergast, was heir to a political organization founded in the 1890s by his older brother, Alderman Jim. Jim, the second son of an Irish immigrant family, had moved to Kansas City in 1876 as a young man of twenty. He worked in a packing house and an iron foundry, scored a big win betting on the horses, and purchased his own saloon. It became a social center where workers cashed their paychecks, drank, chatted with friends, and gambled upstairs. By the 1890s, Jim Pendergast was Big Jim, the political boss of the First Ward, the sprawling, industrial West Bottoms area. He voiced the interests of workingmen and advocated increased municipal services for the ordinary people. Like all great bosses, he was a philanthropist who invariably managed a handout for the needy; during the great flood of 1903, he distributed massive aid to hard-hit constituents.

By then, he was a major power in other working-class wards, able to swing huge blocs of votes with his word and with little or no fraud. His support made a young lawyer with formidable oratorical powers, Jim Reed, mayor of Kansas City in 1900 and helped him on to the United States Senate in 1910. Big Jim controlled hundreds of patronage jobs, including appointments to the police force. Personally wealthy from saloons, gambling rake-offs, and the liquor business, he coexisted uneasily with more traditional civic leaders and took a genuine interest in the city's future.

Disregarding his own interests, he supported the construction of a new union railroad terminal outside his ward. A move that lessened the value of his property and entailed the departure of many rail workers from the Bottoms, it also consolidated Kansas City's position as a midwestern rail center, contributed greatly to the city's development, and produced one of the Midwest's architectural masterpieces. When he died in 1911, even his opponents mourned. A public drive quickly raised funds for a statue of him; placed in Mulkey Square near the bluffs, it overlooked the West Bottoms. A plaque paid tribute "to the rugged character and splendid achievements of a man whose private and public life was the embodiment of truth and moral courage."[2]

Alderman Jim's successor, his brother Tom Pendergast, had made another brother Mike his lieutenant. A third, John, ran the family saloons. Thirty-nine years old at his brother's death, Tom Pendergast was a formidable, experienced politician who had dispensed patronage as Kansas City's superintendent of streets and had held elective office as county marshal (chief law-enforcement officer) and city alderman. Like all the Pendergasts, he was a strong, stocky man with a beer-barrel build. A man of explosive temper, he might strike at targets that most would handle gently. He lacked his brother Jim's scruples, lived lavishly, ate immoderately, smoked big cigars, and (in his later years) gambled compulsively. A legion of sycophantic followers seized every opportunity to assure him that he was the tribune of Kansas City's ordinary people and a civic leader of incomparable stature.

He was also a devoted husband and father, faithful to his wife, solicitous of the character and education of his children. A tireless worker, he regularly arose early and often attended Mass before proceeding to his political headquarters. Sitting in an unpretentious office, the door of which was invariably open, he spent hours every day listening to one supplicant after another. When he gave his word, he kept it. He understood power, had a talent for organization, and adapted flexibly to the political requirements of a growing city.

Almost the cartoon image of a political boss, often underestimated in his early years as a machine leader, Pendergast coolly understood both the limits of his power and the possibilities for its enlargement. A no-quarter fighter against opponents he could beat, he usually knew when to compromise. Like many machine leaders, he carefully cultivated an image of strength by giving his backing in close situations to men of independent appeal; he endorsed nonentities only in races that could not be lost. At the height of his power in the 1930s, he would be a man of national notoriety, hated and feared by many Kansas Citians, loved by many others. In 1922, he was one of two local barons engaged in a struggle for supremacy, made all the more complex by lesser semi-independent lords and insurgent commoners.

III

Joe Shannon was the major opponent of Tom Pendergast in an off-and-on struggle for power that had become a way of life for both by the time

Harry Truman entered politics. Shannon also was a tough Irishman who had made his way up in a hard political world by winning the loyalties of the poor and the working classes. He controlled three wards in eastern Kansas City, an area of lower-middle-class homes, rooming houses, and a crowded black ghetto.

Both organizations had popular names. The Pendergast followers were the "goats," allegedly because they had climbed up the steep bluffs from the Bottoms or because many families in their wards actually kept goats in their small yards. The Shannon crowd had become the "rabbits," because their political tactics were swift and agile, because they had voracious appetites for spoils, or perhaps because wild rabbits roamed the East Side.

Shannon's experience surpassed that of Tom Pendergast. In 1895, two years before his thirtieth birthday, Shannon had become political master of his faction and a natural opponent to Jim Pendergast. Thereafter, he alternately battled the Pendergasts and cooperated with them. Together they overthrew the old "combine" that had dominated Kansas City politics. At other times, they fought bitterly over important local and county offices, often allowing Republicans to win elections. In the aftermath of such a debacle, they would generally negotiate a new alliance and agree to split patronage 50–50. At best fragile, the 50–50 agreements invariably crumbled under pressure from job seekers, whose numbers multiplied in Malthusian fashion, always outstripping any administration's ability to satisfy them.

Shannon had moved quickly and adeptly to extend his influence beyond the city. Aside from a general devotion to the ideals of Thomas Jefferson, nothing in his political identity appealed to rural voters, but the votes he controlled in Kansas City were attractive to politicians who had to win countywide elections. His support made G. L. Chrisman of Independence the presiding judge of the county court in 1898, established him as a kingmaker willing to work with rural politicians, and facilitated the development of a strong county organization. For the next twenty years, the Pendergasts found themselves playing catch-up.[3]

As formidable as they were, Pendergast and Shannon were not the whole show. As Shannon expanded his reach, he relinquished day-to-day control of the Sixth and Eighth wards to a lieutenant, Casimir Welch. In his youth, a two-fisted, pistol-toting Irish brawler, Welch was by 1922 an elected justice of the peace who for a dozen years had held daily court at his headquarters at Fifteenth and Charlotte streets. There he settled numerous petty civil and domestic disputes, dealt out sentences for misdemeanors, and provided cheap, efficient marriage ceremonies.

Forty-nine years old in 1922, Welch was a big, physically powerful man, who wore expensive tailored suits, secured his neckties with diamond stickpins, and sought the company of women more genteel than he. His income came from multiple sources—"honest graft" from business dealings with the city, shares in enterprises that needed influential friends, illicit ventures run by gangsters with whom he openly associated. In the manner of all ward bosses, he recycled much of his cash to his poor constituency. He also distributed food, coal, and clothing to those in need. He sought and received heavy support from black constituents. At once tough and likeable, capable of mayhem and benevolence, he was more admired and loved than hated and feared. By 1922, he was absolute boss of his wards. He was at once Tom Pendergast's political enemy, personal friend, and business partner. Still a faithful follower of Shannon, he was above all a realist.[4]

Welch endured in large measure because he understood his position in the natural order of things. The same could not be said for the other notable subchieftain, Miles Bulger. In his temper and physical characteristics, Bulger resembled John Truman. A tough, wiry little man with a low boiling point, he was quick to use his fists against opponents twice his weight. He had started out in life, like Welch, as a plumber's apprentice and had become the wealthy owner of a cement company. The opportunities for public contracts quickly brought him into politics.

By the second decade of the century, Bulger was the Little Czar of the North Side's Second Ward and a Pendergast ally. Like Welch, he attracted the poor and blacks with charitable beneficence while using not-so-subtle means of intimidation to take care of any opposition. Cocky, feisty, boastful, he had a Napoleonic ambition. In 1914, Tom Pendergast backed Bulger for presiding judge of the county court and R. D. Mize for eastern district judge. The result appeared to be a great victory; nominated and elected, Bulger and Mize seemed to establish goat dominance over the entire county. Actually, by putting up a Kansas Citian for presiding judge, Tom had done little to strengthen his rickety county organization. And he had bet on the wrong man. Bulger saw his new office and its substantial patronage as a power base from which he would make himself the new boss of all of Jackson County.

IV

Mize's death in 1915 and his replacement by Allen Southern shifted control of the court away from Bulger. (Road overseer Harry S. Truman was one of the casualties.) Bulger bided his time and received Pendergast's support for a triumphant reelection in 1918, despite the misgivings of goat lieutenants who paid attention to county affairs. In 1920, as Tom Pendergast lay dangerously ill with a mastoid infection, Bulger openly proclaimed his intention of taking over the machine. He increased the number of road overseers from forty-two to fifty-nine in an effort to build a stronger personal base in the eastern district. (One of the new appointees was Vivian Truman.) He also authorized construction projects and road work as if the county treasury had no bottom.

His challenge seemed at first credible, but he did not have enough jobs and money to dismantle the complex webs of patronage and personal loyalty that the Pendergasts had constructed. Joe Shannon rebuffed overtures for an alliance and put together another 50–50 slate with Tom. They swept the primary. In the general election, Republicans, riding the Harding tide, won several county offices, including the western district judgeship. Shannon man James Gilday won the eastern district, establishing a claim on county patronage that reduced Bulger's leverage. Two years later, a healthy Pendergast and Shannon negotiated a new 50–50 agreement, one with no room for Miles Bulger. County newspapers ran story after story, criticizing Bulger's alliances with crooked contractors who built shoddy "pie-crust roads" and reminding voters that the court was piling up an unprecedented debt. The Little Czar suddenly was on the verge of going into exile.[5]

Goats, rabbits, and followers of the Little Czar constituted the most visible part of the Jackson County political spectrum, but the Republicans could not be ignored. Although a woeful minority in both city and rural areas, they won offices frequently when the Democrats split at election time; they also benefited enormously from the GOP presidential landslides of the 1920s. Moreover, the Ku Klux Klan was beginning to organize in Jackson County. It was a potential political force that might hold the balance of power in a close election.[6]

The Pendergasts had developed little more than a makeshift eastern district organization headed by Mike Pendergast, who possessed the aggressive temperament of his older brothers but lacked the slightest glimmer of their coolheadedness. Of all the goat leaders, he was the most belligerent, openly contemptuous of 50–50 agreements, dedicated to the extermination of all rabbits, and perfectly willing to lead the charge in person. No goat captain was more skilled at organizing the takeover of polling places by gangs who formed lines at the entrance and discouraged opposition or unknown voters.

As befitted a Pendergast, Mike had held several offices—circuit court clerk, county license inspector, and city clerk—learning in each instance multiple opportunities for patronage and honest graft. By 1922, he was president of the Eureka Petroleum Company, a concern whose major customers tended to be governmental bodies. He lacked only one requisite of the old-time boss: he could not make a speech. In 1923, he found himself unable to go through with a major oration at his newly organized Ninth Ward Democratic Club; his son Young Jim stepped in and spoke for him. Mike became Truman's political mentor, almost a surrogate father who was always supportive. Truman would give Mike what he wanted above all else—dominance over the rabbits in the rural district.[7]

For all their mutual hatred, there were no differences of principle or ideology between the rabbits and the goats. If Shannon preached Jeffersonianism more loudly, Pendergast men also subscribed to the sacred creed in political speeches. In office, neither faction let the ideals of small and frugal government stand in the way of self-indulgence. The leaders of both factions wanted power and the wealth that came with it. Their followers wanted public jobs; their contributors wanted public contracts. This was what Jackson County politics was all about.

The system infuriated reformers who actually believed in disinterested, efficient public service. Kansas City's most powerful newspaper, the *Star*, preached the virtues of good government by nonpartisan, businesslike professionals. Colonel Southern's *Independence Examiner* asserted the same values. Their circulations increased; their preachments won few converts. Few middle-class professionals were willing to commit to politics as a profession; fewer still would have had a prayer of winning wide public support. Efficient government was a nice abstraction, but the boss system (as it operated in Kansas City and elsewhere) was a fairly standard outgrowth of an American democracy historically more concerned with tangible individual gain than with a platonic public interest. The boss system's patronage, philanthropy, and many special favors provided real benefits to many citizens.

It also provided grand public entertainment. The *Star* and its morning edition, the *Times*, might demand a moral reformation, but their news stories—in the style of H. L. Mencken—usually played the antics of Tom, Joe, and their assorted henchmen for laughs. Farmers who found it difficult to get into the city relished political diversions. Political rallies, politicians speaking at nearby picnics, contests between the rabbits and the goats—all were rural equivalents of a good vaudeville show or a double-header between the Kansas City Blues and the Toledo Mud Hens.

V

All the same, the act appears to have been wearing just a bit thin. For many ordinary citizens, the old system was becoming less tolerable because it was interfering with the nation's top priority: the construction of a sound, reliable road system. In 1922, paved thoroughfares remained relatively rare outside urban areas; even main trunk highways, most of them following major trails laid out during the nineteenth century, might degenerate into crushed rock between cities. Secondary rural roads were usually dirt or gravel, negotiated at one's own risk during rainy seasons. Frequently not adequate for horse-drawn buggies or wagons, they were in a state of perpetual collapse under the stress of trucks and automobiles. The Jackson County system was no different. Perceptive observers realized that old construction techniques were inadequate without quite knowing what might take their place. The immediate issue, however, was the county court's expensive, third-rate implementation of those techniques.

In Jackson County, all political factions had a pet road-oil company, pet cement suppliers, and pet road contractors. Cement and road oil, if overpriced, tended to be of acceptable quality. Pet road contractors, by contrast, did shoddy work. They won assignments on the basis of unrealistically low bids, negotiated loophole-riddled agreements, billed the county for expenses beyond their original estimates, and generally collected. The most notorious operator was W. A. "Willie" Ross, the son of Pendergast lieutenant Mike Ross.

Willie Ross's most infamous project was a three-mile stretch of macadam known as the Ross–Pryor Road, to the west of Lee's Summit. Begun in 1920, it had been built one mile at each end with rock taken from a quarry Ross dug in the middle section. There he stopped, using the exhaustion of the road fund that year as an excuse to avoid completion. To travel the road's entire distance, drivers had to detour into a cornfield in order to avoid a ten-foot drop into the quarry. For this, the county paid Ross nearly $20,000 more than his original bid for the entire three miles. Republicans noted that he had managed to build as far as farms belonging to himself and John Pryor, another contractor with close Pendergast ties. A friendly justice of the peace dismissed charges of fraud; a county grand jury controlled by an equally friendly prosecutor produced no indictments.

Miles Bulger saw the Ross–Pryor Road as no problem. He announced in January 1922 that the county would take bids from contractors (Willie Ross included) to build the central section, estimated that it would cost another $20,000, and declared, "I have the power." His critics denounced "Bulgerism": a debt-ridden road fund, poor county roads, and political road overseers.[8]

VI

Truman, unlike most potential goat candidates, could appeal to genuinely independent Democrats. Organizational support was crucial, but in itself not enough to deliver a county nomination. Many primary voters were either nonaligned or casual in their factional loyalties. No group was more independent than the returned soldiers, a powerful force at a time when the comradeship of shared danger was still deeply felt by veterans. In 1920, Truman's old major, Marvin Gates, had won election as a Republican to the Kansas City Board of Aldermen. The commander of the 129th's First Battalion, John Miles, also a Republican, had been elected county marshal; Truman had campaigned openly for him and had accepted an honorary appointment as a deputy marshal. Colonel E. M. Stayton, a man of wide influence and considerable respect, urged Truman to run for political office. A respected veteran with a wide network of acquaintances, he would be attractive to the electorate in general and the doughboy vote in particular.

Tom Pendergast and Joe Shannon had reached amicable agreement on all county offices except eastern district judge. Given their strength in the rural districts, the rabbits would have a clear edge unless the goats could find an unusually strong personality with wide appeal. Their last strong entry in the eastern district, Judge Mize, had been such a person— a highly respected, well-known Independence druggist who had won the all-out support of the *Examiner*. Truman possessed similar assets and could count on sympathetic mention from Colonel Southern, who as George Wallace's father-in-law was practically a member of the family.

By March (after Judges Bulger and Gilday had renewed Vivian Truman's appointment as a road overseer), the Truman campaign was ready to get under way, its kickoff and early weeks calculated to depict Truman as an independent veteran. With Stayton doubtless orchestrating the arrangements, the commander of the Lee's Summit American Legion post called a general meeting of "ex-service men and their friends." Perhaps 300 individuals squeezed into the small auditorium of the town's memorial building. Groups of Truman and Stayton friends came from all over the county. Others simply sought an evening of relaxation with old comrades.

The program, conducted amid clouds of smoke emanating from cigars handed out by the organizers, exemplified the way in which politics and entertainment meshed in rural Jackson County:

> Clarence Anderson and Robert Shawhan, both of Lee's Summit, 160-pound class wrestling match, 15 minutes.
>
> Battling Dixon, Independence, v. Sol Salzberg, Kansas City, 90-pound class boxing match, four two-minute rounds.
>
> Durard Meyers v. Martin Meyers, eight- and nine-year-old brothers, Buckner, 60-pound class wrestling match.
>
> Speeches: Colonel E. M. Stayton; Major Harry S. Truman.
>
> Tommy Murphy and Harry Mills, both of Kansas City, exhibition boxing match, three two-minute rounds.
>
> Mrs. Ethel Lee Buxton, accompanied on the piano by Miss Roe Roberts, singing "Can't You Hear Me Calling You, Caroline," "When Irish Eyes Are Smiling," and a parody on "Smiles" written for her by soldiers she entertained in France during the war.
>
> Comedy sketch by Apec and Garrison.
>
> Buck and wing dancing by Thompson, accompanied by Garrison with the ukelele.
>
> Mrs. Buxton singing "Mother Machree."

Stayton's talk centered on themes of public service, honesty, and patriotism; asserted that veterans should do their part to see that the right men held public office; and urged Truman to run for eastern judge. Truman, nearly overcome by stage fright, declared his candidacy stammeringly. Only a few disgruntled factionalists abstained from applauding. The next day, although Colonel Southern surely knew better, the *Independence Examiner* declared that Truman ran "without any organization or factional endorsement whatever."[9]

VII

Truman had four opponents in the Democratic primary. James V. Compton, sixty-three, had served briefly on the county court by gubernatorial appointment in 1916. An advocate of honest, efficient government and "the higher ideals of morality," he was an exemplary public servant with no machine support and no chance of winning.[10] George Shaw was also sixty-three, an independent and honest contractor with extensive road-building experience; widely respected, a political outsider, he was a sure loser. Tom Parrent, forty-eight, president of the county road overseers association and Bulger's man, promised road improvements for every town he visited, while also pledging to retire the county's debt. E. E. Montgomery, a Blue Springs bank president, was the rabbit candidate. A self-made man of fifty, he claimed strong credentials as a financial manager qualified to handle the county's debt problems—for which the rabbits escaped accountability because of Bulger's high visibility as a spender.[11]

Against Montgomery, Truman needed, and possessed, large assets of his own. Only thirty-eight, he was the candidate of youth and managed to capture much of the idealism associated with that image.[12] His campaign literature capitalized on his military record, often identifying him by his reserve rank of major. A frequent speaker at his rallies was Colonel Ruby D. Garrett, a powerful orator and politically ambitious veteran of the Argonne campaign. Men from Battery D were usually around wherever Truman spoke. If anyone asserted that the former captain had been unpopular with the troops, written refutations with long lists of signatures quickly appeared. Fellow officers, including Ted Marks, Spencer Salisbury, and Roger Sermon, worked for him. Marshal Miles observed the proceedings with a benevolent neutrality.

At times, the campaign may have overdone what Truman later called "the soldier stuff." His backers left an exaggerated impression of the time Truman's battery had spent in serious combat. They also occasionally asserted that he had been involved in road building while in the army. Still, the military image of patriotic duty and deeply felt personal loyalties was a great asset, blending well with youth and idealism. All these themes may have inspired Eddie McKim's idea of flying the candidate into a large Democratic picnic at Oak Grove in July. The plane circled the grounds, dropped leaflets, and swooped down to a bumpy landing that ended in a panic stop a few feet in front of a fence. Truman climbed out and heaved his lunch onto the turf. Then, with more determination than enthusiasm, he worked the crowd and made the most publicized speech of his campaign.[13]

Another motif was the repeated assertion that Truman was an able young businessman. It was a good issue in an era that perceived no conflict between business success and idealism. Write-ups repeatedly emphasized his achievement with the canteen at Camp Doniphan and mentioned his Kansas City enterprise, however fleetingly, in the hope of convincing undecided voters that Truman could manage county funds as well as Montgomery. He secured an endorsement from his downtown Kansas

City service organization, the Triangle Club, that probably helped even if none of its members voted in the eastern part of the county.[14]

The Truman drive worked hard at maintaining the increasingly tenuous appearance of an independent candidacy. On May 11, Truman backers formed the Men's Rural Jackson County Democratic Club; they praised their candidate as "a farmer and a business executive of marked ability and sterling integrity," unsullied by previous political experience. The *Independence Examiner* went along, describing the organizers as mostly "young men who have not heretofore been identified in county politics." In fact, the temporary secretary of the organization was longtime goat Frank Wallace. *Examiner* editor Southern, most likely motivated by both family ties and genuine admiration for Truman, had knowingly gone along with the deception. A month later, the paper declared, "Harry Truman of Independence is credited with the Goat support, although he came out without consulting either the Goats or the Rabbits. The Jackson County Democratic Club, which is said to be a Goat organization, has endorsed Mr. Truman." The Pendergasts were apparently jumping on the Truman bandwagon.

Such news items in the rural county's most influential paper were more valuable than dozens of columns of advertising. The *Examiner*'s refusal to make an official endorsement made favorable mention in it seem objective. Other village weeklies, typically two- or three-person operations that also avoided endorsements, often reprinted *Examiner* articles.[15] Truman did no display advertising, although he purchased the tiny classified announcements of his candidacy that the small papers expected of every candidate. He may have indirectly bought the support of a couple of small sheets that printed his leaflets, but it is unknown whether he patronized them to get their backing or because he already had it.

By and large, he campaigned the old-fashioned way, as did almost every rural Missouri candidate in an era when radio had penetrated to few farms and daily newspaper delivery was rare outside of cities. As he recalled it, he put two sacks of cement in the rear of his 1919 Dodge roadster, bounced the vehicle over one deep-rutted, pot-holed secondary road after another, and set out to meet every voter he could. His slogan, embossed on his campaign literature, was simple and effective: "My Platform: Good Roads, A Budgeted Road Fund, Economy, A Day's Work for a Day's Pay, Fewer Automobiles and More Work for County Employees."

He would give his card to a farmer or small-town resident, chat for a few minutes, ask for consideration, and move on. He was at his best in these encounters: still youngish, flashing a big smile, radiating a simple charm. A poor speaker, he rarely talked at length to large gatherings. Of the three major candidates, he was the only one from Independence. He had the added advantages of a second "hometown" in Grandview. His county Masonic associations were an asset. He circulated easily at local picnics and political rallies, at small lawn parties held by supporters, and at weekend picnics with crowds of a thousand or more.[16]

VIII

The speech he had made after his panic landing at Oak Grove was widely disseminated. Probably reading better than it had been spoken, the speech restated his local roots, his farm years, his business experience, and especially his military achievements. It also turned charges that he had deserted his party to vote for John Miles in 1920 into an asset:

> I have seen him in places that would make hell look like a play-ground. I have seen him stick to his guns when Frenchmen were falling back. I have seen him hold the American line when only John Miles and his three batteries were between the Germans and a successful counter-attack. He was of the right stuff and a man who wouldn't vote for his comrade under circumstances such as these would be untrue to himself and his country. . . . John Miles and my comrades in arms are closer than brothers to me.

Then he moved to his platform. The county's money needed to be budgeted intelligently. He was against the construction of macadam roads that would fall apart under modern traffic. Oiled dirt roads would stand up far better and could be maintained for a fraction of the cost. He would hire road overseers who knew their job and wanted to work. There would be enough money left in the road fund to begin construction of permanent highways on main traffic routes. Rational budgeting required fixed legal limits; the legislature should forbid county courts from going into debt; existing debt should be paid off.[17]

A forceful declaration, it (like most campaign speeches) ignored the practicalities that intervene between aspiration and accomplishment. A couple of weeks later, the *Examiner* prominently featured it: "Truman Speaks Out. Would Budget County Funds, Pay County Debts, and Bring System Out of Financial Chaos." The story declared that only Truman had submitted his platform to the paper. Actually, Truman's declarations differed little from those of Montgomery, and both goats and rabbits knew that the race was really over who would control jobs and contracts. Seasoned observers described the contest as the hottest in county history.[18]

Election day, August 1, provided two challenges for each candidate: getting a maximum vote out to the polls, and keeping a sharp eye out for cheating. The numbers were smaller in the eastern district than in Kansas City and the practices generally cleaner, but ballot-box skullduggery was not unknown. The close race sent the distrust index soaring to new highs. A week earlier, the *Examiner* had indignantly reported a rumor that "negroes who can be handled are to be voted at the Democratic primary." (While careful to denounce vote sellers and vote purchasers of all colors, it had gone on to declare, "Missouri is far enough south to adopt the plan of white votes only in a Democratic primary.") For their part, the rabbits were outraged by an anonymous flyer, circulated on election eve by either the Parrent or the Truman forces, accusing Montgomery of corruption and corrupt intent.

Sometime during the day, Joe Shannon picked up a rumor that the goats were planning to grab the election by stuffing the ballot boxes at Fairmount Junction, to the west of Independence. Deciding to steal a march on the opposition, he telephoned for three carloads of thugs to come from Kansas City, invade the polling place, and appropriate the boxes. Then he proceeded to Fairmount himself, determined to stop any early malfeasance by the nefarious goats. Once again, Truman was helped by his Wallace family ties. His forces got word of Shannon's plans through Albert Ott, a loyal rabbit who had a quaint belief in honest elections and also happened to be the father of Frank Wallace's wife, Natalie.

An appeal went out to Marshal Miles, who sent two deputies: his brother, George, and John Gibson, a veteran of the 129th Field Artillery. When Shannon arrived at the polling place, a crossroads house, he found all in order under the watchful eye of rabbit county clerk Pete Kelly. In short order, the deputies drove up. Kelly ran out frantically in a vain attempt to head off the Kansas City goons, who were due at any moment. The automobiles from the city arrived just after George Miles and John Gibson had stationed themselves on the porch and assured Shannon of their good intentions. Three or four of the rabbit toughs were carrying guns. As one took aim at Miles, Gibson, probably terrified, pushed his .45 into Shannon's stomach: "Mr. Shannon, your gang may get Miles, but I will get you." Shannon threw his hands in the air and shouted, "Go away, boys, go away; everything is all right here!"[19]

The rescue of the Fairmount boxes from the predatory rabbits may have made the difference for Truman. He won the election by fewer than 300 votes with 4,230 (35.6 percent), against 3,951 (33.3 percent) for Montgomery, 2,172 (18.3 percent) for Parrent, 1,437 (12.1 percent) for Shaw, and 81 (0.7 percent) for Compton. Montgomery charged fraud and filed for a recount. Truman responded with his own allegations. With the two candidates looking on tensely, a commission examined the returns and found not a single irregularity.[20]

Plenty of bitterness remained. Writing to cousin Ralph, Truman declared, "I won the dirtiest and hardest fought campaign Eastern Jackson Co. has ever seen without money or promises. . . . [Montgomery] spent somewhere near $15,000 it is said and his gang made me every kind of an S. O. B. the army or civil life either ever produced but I beat him anyway with a clean campaign."[21]

IX

Truman now found himself contending with the emerging Ku Klux Klan. To many in Jackson County, it was a strong, mysterious protector of 100 percent Americanism, a benefactor of the Protestant churches, a guardian of traditional morality, and a zealous advocate of good government. Near the end of August, a long Klan motorcade paraded through Independence. Meeting in an open field to the south, Klansmen burned a fiery cross and initiated, they claimed, 900 new members.

A week and a half later, a similar scene occurred near Lee's Summit, this time with a reputed 500 initiates. An estimated 4,000 attended, with hundreds of the curious looking on from a distance. "In the crowd were scores, yes, hundreds of men of high standing in official, in professional and in business life," admitted the *Examiner*, a critic of the Klan. "It was a clean-looking up-standing sort of a crowd, with none of the ordinary mob spirit." In October, 20,000 Klansmen filled the Kansas City Convention Hall for a meeting that had not been publicly advertised. The speakers, including two local Disciples of Christ ministers, attacked Catholics and political bosses and urged support of Protestant candidates in the upcoming election.

It is hardly surprising that Truman, like many young politicians, flirted with membership in the Klan. Truman's version of what happened is generally accepted and is more plausible than other accounts. He met with a Klan organizer named Jones (probably at the Baltimore Hotel just a few days after the primary), handed over the $10 initiation fee, may have taken a membership oath, and possibly signed a membership card. Told that if elected eastern district judge he would be expected to give county jobs only to Protestants, he refused and took back his $10.

On the Sunday before the election, Klansmen in street clothes passed out copies of a sample ballot on the steps of several Protestant churches in Independence. It endorsed only one Democrat and one independent candidate, both of them running for judicial positions. Opposite Truman's name was the notation "Church affiliation protestant, endorsed by Tom and Joe." For the benefit of the densest among the faithful, the leaflet identified Tom and Joe as "two Roman Catholic Political Bosses."

Even so, the general election was a walkaway. According to Truman's official report of expenses, he spent nearly $520 in his race for the nomination and $275 on the general election. His Republican opponent, Arthur Wilson, the owner of an Independence lumberyard, was a maverick who got no help from GOP regulars. Truman nevertheless campaigned intensively. He won by a final count of 9,063 to 6,314 and was the leading vote getter among the Democratic candidates for legislative and executive offices.

Truman, declared the *Independence Examiner,* had made a clean campaign and would go into office with no promises to compromise him. The *Lee's Summit Journal* said, "We are safe in predicting that Truman will make good and help give Jackson County a real business administration—one that will be open and above board." Such was Truman's aspiration also. Reality was about to set in.[22]

7

"McElroy and I Ran the County Court and Took All the Jobs": Ideals and Realities, 1923–1924

Truman had demonstrated a flair for electoral politics. Now he had to show his constituency that he could deliver on his promises. The job would tax to the limit his ability to mobilize others, win the cooperation of co-workers, and put into effect ideals of efficient, constructive government. He also had to deal with the realities of the patronage-driven system that had brought him to power. In the end, he and his goat colleague, as he later put it, "took all the jobs," precipitating a fight that would make him a casualty in a political struggle beyond his control.[1]

II

The county court was a product of earlier, simpler times in which local governments had been run by "courts" with judicial and administrative powers. It no longer heard civil or criminal cases, although it claimed a theoretical power of imprisonment for contempt. The court was a commission of two district judges and one presiding judge with general authority over the budgets of elected county officials, penal and eleemosynary institutions, and, most crucially, local road systems. Its meetings rotated monthly between courthouses in Independence and Kansas City.

The court had little jurisdiction in the city, but Kansas Citians held the preponderance of power in choosing the presiding judge (elected every four years by the county at large) and had the exclusive voice in chosing the western district judge. (District judges stood for election every two years.) As eastern district judge, Truman represented the rural, small-town county and had special responsibility for the road system.

County finances were rickety. Property taxes, the only significant source of revenue, were not due until October 31. Every year, the court sold "anticipation notes" each month for up to 10 percent of anticipated annual tax revenues until cash began to flow into the treasury around the end of October. Short-term debt—and the accompanying interest costs—thus had become the unavoidable method of current financing.

The county paid its bills by issuing warrants—drafts against its various operating funds. If the appropriate fund was solvent, recipients could cash or deposit a warrant as if it were a check. If not, they could sell the warrant at a discount to an individual or institution willing to hold it until the cash materialized. Or they could treat it as a certificate of deposit; it bore 6 percent interest. Those who took the latter alternative had to wait until sufficient overdue taxes were collected for the year in which the warrant had been issued; the obligations were paid in strict numerical order. It was not until January 1923 that money became available to pay the last $50,000 of 1920 warrants.[2]

Truman and his colleagues inherited an enormous budget deficit, conservatively estimated at $750,000 after collection of back taxes. County employees, unable to cash their December salary warrants, had financed their Christmases by selling them at 80 percent of face value. State institutions to which the county sent mental cases, the feeble-minded, tuberculosis patients, and juvenile criminals were refusing to accept new admittees because the county had not paid them for 1922. The Bulger court had set new standards of irresponsibility; the new court had to make restoration of the county credit its highest priority.

Bulger's excesses obscured a fundamental underlying problem: the Jackson County property tax system did not provide enough revenue to meet the growing demand for public services—foremost among them adequate roads—no matter how frugal and efficient the court might be. Few taxpayers were prepared to face that conclusion, especially in the hard economic climate of the early 1920s. Machine politics—an army of patronage appointees, Willie Ross's sham roads, rigged contracts—made it easy to believe that the county needed only honest government.

Jackson County reformers, led by *Independence Examiner* publisher Southern, espoused a narrow but popular variety of progressivism. Rooted in the moral outlook and economic needs of the taxpaying middle classes, it envisioned reform not as developing new social services for the underprivileged, but as bringing an honest business outlook to government, establishing hard-and-fast budgets, and implementing economies. Truman had campaigned on this ethic and these assumptions even as he accepted the backing of a goat machine hungry for jobs and contracts.[3]

It is hard to say just how Truman had developed a view of government akin to Southern's. Most fundamental surely was the ethic of honesty and hard work that his parents had instilled in him. If his father had sought political appointment and additional income as a road overseer, he also had worked tirelessly at the job. The emphasis on efficiency in Truman's military service contributed to his outlook. And from his first bookkeeping class at Spalding's Commercial College, he had cultivated the attitude of the earnest young businessman. He assured an official of the Kansas City Chamber of Commerce that he intended "to be the county's servant just the same as if I were president of a private corporation."

Such was the ideal; Truman sincerely believed in it. At the same time, he knew from experience that reality usually stood in the way of a full realization, that successful politicians needed organizational support, that organizations expected tangible payoffs, that wholly disinterested advocates of good government rarely won elections. Through a process that was probably not fully conscious, he juggled idealism and realism awkwardly for the rest of his public life. He made concessions to practicality in order to maintain political power, hoping that he could more than compensate by advancing the public interest. He salved his conscience by rejecting the deals and kickbacks that many officeholders took for granted, even if it meant remaining in debt, even if it meant being unable to help his beloved mother.

His conduct was sensible enough, if not fully thought out. It is uncertain whether he ever explicitly contemplated the futility of trying to separate himself from all the evil in the world, but he knew that those who pretended to earthly sainthood were guilty of hypocrisy. Never forgetting Solomon Young's admonition to keep a close eye on those who prayed the loudest in the amen corner, he was always quick to cite contradictions between private behavior and public morality in others. It was an easy move to the conviction that men like Tom Pendergast were fundamentally more decent than the do-gooders who attacked them.

Such reasoning provided a deeply needed self-justification, but Truman seems never to have achieved a fully satisfactory rationale for the political compromises he had to make. He managed without too much difficulty in his first elective office; but as his career progressed, the problem plagued him in a deeply personal way. It created emotional tensions that he could not resolve, provoked behavior that appeared awkward or erratic, did much to generate a reservoir of anger that seethed beneath the surface of his normally genial personality, and brought him on occasion to the verge of physical exhaustion.[4]

Neither of the men with whom Truman served on the court seems to have been troubled by such conflicts. The new presiding judge, Elihu Hayes—Truman remembered him as "a good old man"—was a Kansas Citian and a rabbit slated for the post as part of the 50–50 agreement. A decent individual, he was also a strong factional advocate. Sociable with his fellow judges, especially Truman, he was reduced increasingly to sputtering protest or obstructionism on substantive matters. H. L. McElroy, the western district judge, was a shrewd accountant, Tom Pendergast's point man on the court, and single-mindedly devoted to the interests of the goats. Tall, ascetic, and thoroughly unpleasant, he was a bully. Truman followed McElroy's lead, but usually avoided his abrasiveness.

III

The new court began its duties at the beginning of January 1923 in an atmosphere of businesslike harmony. It authorized an independent audit of the county accounts, ordered the termination of all nonessential county activities, and prohibited the personal use of county cars. Each member expressed determination to pay off the county debt and avoid unnecessary spending. Truman declared, "If we could close up all the offices until we get down to bed rock, it would be a good thing." Personal priorities and factional rivalries soon overwhelmed the good intentions.

Truman's first imperative was to gain control of the road program, his area of special accountability and his main source of patronage. The official with direct responsibility for road construction and maintenance, however, was county surveyor and ex officio highway engineer Leo Koehler. A Republican, Koehler had won a four-year term in the Harding landslide of 1920. A canny politician with a shrewd aptitude for self-aggrandizement—Truman privately believed he took rake-offs on road contracts—he would continue to ride Republican presidential tides and would be an irritant to Truman for the next decade.

Koehler had enjoyed a cozy day-to-day relationship with Bulger, who supported an increase in his salary and appears to have worked out comfortable arrangements for the sharing of patronage and other benefits with him. Controlling dozens of jobs, a fleet of county automobiles, and an armada of road equipment, Koehler drew an annual salary of $8,000 ($3,000 as surveyor and $5,000 as highway engineer), a higher total than that of any county or state official, including the governor and chief justice.[5]

Truman and McElroy began their offensive at once and with no pretense at gentility. With typical bluntness, McElroy told Koehler, "You are a damn poor adviser. You are not competent to advise anybody and we don't want any of your advice at all." In the first week of its existence, the court knocked Koehler's engineer salary down to $3,000 (Truman, reporters noted, listened to the order with an especially big smile on his face), appointed two new road superintendents and a new blacksmith, and ordered the sale of numerous department automobiles.[6]

Koehler struck back. Asserting that he, not the court, controlled the road fund, he refused to approve payment of the $291 a month that each judge was to receive as a road commissioner. He also persuaded rabbit county clerk Pete Kelly to hold up their January salary warrants. The judges thereupon declined to issue warrants for Koehler's salary. Koehler then secured a temporary circuit court injunction against the sale of thirteen cars, six of which he chained together in the departmental garage, although the county court already had auctioned them off.

On March 17, 1923, Truman, who had avoided being served with the injunction, invaded the garage with a squad of carefully selected goats (at least one of them armed), unchained the captive Studebakers, and presented them to their new owners. The following Monday, a judge grilled him on the witness stand for forty-five minutes, but decided that he could not be held in contempt.

Bulger did what he could to help Koehler. Elected to the state legislature in 1922, he pushed through a bill to reorganize Jackson county government in ways that would maximize the authority of the highway engineer, only to run into a veto from Republican governor Arthur Hyde. He also engaged in more direct hostilities. In early March on a trip back to Kansas City, he caught Judge McElroy by surprise, lashed into him with fists flying, and left him on the ground bloody and bruised.

In mid-May, a circuit judge ruled that the county court had the right to buy and sell highway department equipment, but that the highway engineer could hire and fire department employees. This ruling and the sheer necessity of getting on with the work forced an accommodation. The judges and Koehler stopped blocking each other's salaries; Koehler got six deputies, each with his own car, and dismissed fourteen goats who had been inflicted on him.[7]

Hacking away at the rabbits was the next Truman–McElroy priority. Had the 50–50 agreement simply provided for an even division of candidates on the Democratic ballot, or did it require a down-the-line split of all patronage jobs? Truman wanted and needed patronage to build a personal machine. (The organization had told him he could have the poor farm, the garage, and the road overseers—all the traditional prerogatives of the eastern judge.) McElroy believed as a matter of principle that the spoils belonged to the victors. And Tom and Mike Pendergast were determined to strengthen the rural organization.

At the beginning, the goat judges threw a few jobs to the rabbits. Truman boosted Fred Boxley—his attorney, good friend, and "favorite rabbit"—for county counselor; but the appointment went to outgoing criminal judge Ralph Latshaw, beloved by the goats for his management of grand juries that met and adjourned without returning indictments. After cutting the number of road overseers to forty-five, Truman let Judge Hayes name nine of them. He and McElroy also permitted the appointment of rabbit Eugene Jarboe as county purchasing agent, a post with vast opportunities for honest graft. Still, the patronage split was more like 80–20 than 50–50. Unhappy rabbits began to talk privately with Koehler and Bulger about an alliance. Relations were not improved when Truman and McElroy, who had declined county cars, made Hayes give up the chauffeured Packard that Miles Bulger had passed on to him.

On June 1, Truman and McElroy unleashed phase two of their offensive for total power. A large crowd, drawn by rumors of fireworks, packed the county courtroom. The two goats voted to fire Jarboe, who hardly had moved into his office, and replace him with William Kirby, county license inspector, alderman from Kansas City's Tenth Ward, and close friend of Mike Pendergast. They then gave Kirby's old county job to goat stalwart Jack Tolliver.

Hayes was furious. Jarboe, who was present, demanded to know why he had been fired. McElroy refused to answer. Thereupon, the dismissed rabbit, described as "red with rage and trembling," told McElroy, "I don't give a damn for you politically or any other way. My opinion of you personally is that you can stand flat-footed and kiss a gnat's ass." He wheeled around and stalked out of the room. Brought back, he apologized half-heartedly, and then was sentenced by vote of Truman and McElroy to two days in jail for contempt. A real judge subsequently voided the action.

Hayes, furious at the dismissal of his only significant appointee, bitterly charged his colleagues with grand-scale patronage jobbing and waste of county funds. Unruffled, McElroy and Truman announced that they intended to contract out all work that could not be handled by the road overseers and close the county garage. This move left Koehler with a half-dozen deputies who supervised the overseers, a few office employees, and little else. The goat judges had effectively taken all the jobs. They also had guaranteed that every non-goat job seeker in the county would join an embittered opposition in the 1924 primary.[8]

IV

The destruction of the latest goat–rabbit truce made it all the more imperative for Truman and McElroy to establish a record that would attract independent-minded voters. Not unblemished, their performance would be a considerable improvement over that of the previous court. The happiest hunting involved further attacks on the Bulger court that also contributed to the new team's budget-minded image. Their independent audit of county finances by the Arthur Young accounting firm fixed the county debt at an astounding $1.2 million.[9] They demanded, and in at least one case obtained, refunds on expensive county insurance policies, none of which appear to have been written by goat agents. They also refused to open and operate the former presiding judge's monument to himself, the lavish Miles Bulger Industrial Home for Negro Boys. (Bulger understood the importance of the black vote. "Aren't negroes human?" he had asked in his 1918 campaign.) The decision alienated Kansas City blacks. The Pendergasts, and eventually Truman, would avoid future provocations.[10]

Other economy moves were of dubious effectiveness. An investigation of the charity rolls turned up numerous doubtful cases. At the end of May 1923, the McElroy–Truman court (as it had become known) ended individual payments and initiated subsidies to private charities. In the abstract, there was much to be said for the new policy; for actual persons, many of whom appeared at the courthouse seeking help, the transition was difficult. The savings, if any, were negligible.[11] McElroy and Truman charged that the county juvenile homes, controlled by the circuit judges sitting as the county parole board, were mismanaged and demanded direct control. The move was widely viewed as a patronage grab. McElroy made things worse by engaging in his customary hectoring of anyone who disagreed with him. The normally sympathetic *Independence Examiner* curtly defended the judges, one of whom was the publisher's brother, Allen Southern. In January 1924, the Missouri Supreme Court upheld the judges in every respect. (A year later, after Republicans took control of the court, it reversed itself.)[12]

In most respects, however, McElroy and Truman looked good. Independent critics still complained of too many patronage payrollers, but admitted that the number had decreased. The court not only held the line on county employment, but actually did away with the position of assistant county counselor, thereby forcing the chief lawyer of the county to pay significant attention to its legal business for the first time in years. The court also adopted a strict policy of accepting only the lowest bid (subject to the meeting of specifications) for any county business in which a bidding process was feasible. It was able to demonstrate apparently impressive savings on items ranging from county printing to road oil to interest costs on bank loans. By midyear, it had covered all delinquent balances owed to state institutions, which, in turn, lifted their prohibition on patients from Jackson County. By late fall, it was clear that the county would achieve a surplus for 1923, and—most importantly in the minds of many residents—without a property tax increase.[13]

The court could not entirely escape the cultural and moral conflicts that dominated American politics through much of the 1920s. Rural citizens demanded enforcement of Prohibition and suppression of a variety of urban immoralities facilitated by the automobile. Republican marshal John Miles, Truman's close friend, was a religious fundamentalist who, in earlier times, might have been a major in Cromwell's army. The court was generous in allocating him deputies, cars, and motorcycles, with which he attempted to subdue the speakeasies, speeding, drunken driving, and roadside sex that seemed to be coming out of Kansas City and engulfing the rural county. Urban sophisticates viewed Miles's largely futile efforts as comic, but his crusade was popular in the eastern district. It also reflected Truman's personal morality.

If he did not mind a drink or two of watered whiskey in the company of his friends, Truman was aware of the damage alcohol could do to men. His wife's life had been heavily conditioned by the effects of drink on her father and brothers. He had no sympathy for those who ran the roadhouses and little for those who patronized them. His own sexual behavior was undiluted high Victorian. He wrote to himself of the need for men to control their carnal impulses and viewed with outrage the vogue of Freudian psychology (as vulgarized for popular consumption). In 1934, he concluded an angry diary entry:

> Some day we'll awake, have a reformation of the heart, teach our kids honor and kill a few sex psychologists, put boys in high schools to themselves with *men* teachers (not sissies), close all the girls finishing schools, shoot all the efficiency experts and become a nation of God's people once more.

Such declarations fully refected the values of his eastern district constituency.[14]

V

Truman's main concern was the 1,600-mile rural road system. Maintenance involved tough judgments in matching surfaces to traffic loads, stretching resources to meet as many needs as possible, monitoring the work of forty-five road overseers, and intermittently dueling with Koehler. The court was also expected to undertake new construction wherever it was most needed; not surprisingly, most areas of the county felt it was desperately needed. Yet funds were embarrassingly small.

Truman traveled extensively around the county, investigating problems as mundane as blocked culverts and weed patches, constantly reminded of the primitive conditions that county motorists faced. In June 1923, he rode in a taxi to Kansas City; the driver took Independence Road, the heavily traveled northern route to downtown. The vehicle careened over rough rock and negotiated one or two steep grades that were nearly impossible in bad weather. The route had to be virtually rebuilt every year. "I watched the judge as we went along and one time his head came pretty near hitting the top of the car and his glasses came very near bouncing off," the driver told the *Examiner*. "He knows that this road needs some attention." In 1924, the court let out a contract to pave it.

Everyone favored a rational plan of road development, but each advocate assumed that rationality started with his own town. Every part of the county wanted better access to Kansas City. Suburban property developers worked for road construction along their subdivisions. Truman and McElroy made a decision that was commendable on its merits and finessed the political problem about as well as possible. With Hayes abstaining, they appointed two eminent engineers, Republican Louis R. Ash and Democrat E. M. Stayton, Truman's old military associate, to examine "the entire highway system of Jackson County" and develop "a complete, comprehensive and systematic plan for the economical and effective improvement and maintenance of the roads."

Stayton and Ash produced a program for maintenance and improvement of existing roads. Their one recommendation for new construction was for the Washington Park Boulevard (soon to be known as Winner Road) in Independence. Justifiable on the basis of numbers affected, the project was hailed in Independence and widely resented in the rest of the county, especially in the southeast around Lee's Summit, which perceived itself as neglected. Truman handled complaints with as much tact and good humor as he could muster. McElroy was invariably abrasive. He did Truman no good when he insulted the editor of the *Lee's Summit Journal*.[15]

Aside from filling potholes, the major form of maintenance was oiling the secondary dirt roads that constituted the greater part of county mileage. In previous years, county workers had applied the oil. In line with its policy of taking as much as possible out of Koehler's hands, the new court let out the operation to Pendergast-owned Eureka Oil and goat contractor Paul Patton. Critics screamed patronage and favoritism. Truman and McElroy claimed that the new arrangements would cut costs in half; in fact, the county probably did spend less per mile on oiling.[16]

Much of the rest of the road maintenance (patching, grading, clearing culverts, undertaking small-scale construction) was the work of the road overseers. Under the general supervision of Koehler and his deputies, subjected to considerable informal monitoring by Truman, they appear to have performed effectively. In 1923, the McElroy–Truman court spent $288,153 less than had the Bulger court in 1922 with no apparent sacrifice in quality. In September, it began to plan a system of rural roadside parks. Truman was increasingly aware, however, of an important underlying question: Could Jackson County ever have a first-class road system, given the financial limitations within which the court had to work?[17]

One other issue connected with the roads returned to the court like the bad penny it was. The controversy over the infamous Ross–Pryor Road seemingly had been resolved in 1922 when Ross Construction's attorney agreed to return a $19,000 county warrant. In September 1923, Mike Ross, the power behind his son's company, gave the warrant to county counselor Latshaw with the proviso that it would be a charitable donation toward the recently announced park system. The act was designed to give the company a nice tax deduction, an unmerited reputation as a public benefactor, and favorable consideration for some new bids.

Feelings about the Rosses and the $19,000 warrant, stemming from factional considerations and simple public indignation, were intense and not entirely rational. When the court met to consider Ross's offer, it faced opposition spearheaded by Judge William H. Wallace (no relation to Bess)—one of the leaders of the Missouri bar, a near-candidate for governor, and a powerful orator. In the twilight of his life, Wallace had appointed himself an advocate of strict honesty and economy in government; he tended to be a critic of whatever court was in power and a transitory ally of whatever Democratic faction was on the outside. Most politicians did not like to tangle with him; McElroy, who wanted to accept Ross's deal, was an exception. When he fired off a salvo of condescending sarcasm, the old man stepped up to his desk and pounded it:

"You can bulldoze some of the people that come into this court, but you are not going to bulldoze me."

Truman watched with what must have been considerable amusement. Aside from his sense of the public interest, he had personal reasons for wanting to take a shot at the Ross family. One of Mike Ross's sons had served in the army under the command of cousin Ralph and had spent a fair amount of his hitch in the guardhouse. After the war, the Rosses had made a clumsy and unsuccessful attempt to frame Ralph for extortion. When Ralph exhorted him to take Ross "to a genuine cleaning," Harry replied, "If I can put a crimp in him, it won't take me long to do it."

Judge Hayes asked Counselor Latshaw for the warrant. Latshaw responded that he had given it to McElroy, who refused to produce it unless it was accepted as Ross had specified. Truman offered a motion for the return and cancellation of the warrant; Hayes sided with him to carry it. McElroy still declined to give it up. "Let Ross go into the circuit court to collect it and see how far he gets," Truman declared. Ross did not go to court. The contracts that he had wanted remained in abeyance for the rest of the year.[18]

The break with McElroy on the Ross warrant was Truman's most visible display of independence during his two-year term as eastern district judge. There were other instances, demonstrating a decency that McElroy rarely displayed. Unlike McElroy, Truman took no joy in harassing minor supplicants if they had some connection with the rabbits; many of them were people he knew personally. But on the big issues, he followed McElroy's lead, right down to awarding a $97,417 contract to Ross Construction in May 1924. It was the low bid, but past Ross fiascoes had started out the same way. Truman's independence was more symbolic than significant.[19]

VI

Despite their strong 1923 record, Truman and McElroy faced serious challenges for reelection. Their races were part of the continuing struggle for power between Tom Pendergast and the disaffected Democratic factions. At stake was control of Jackson County, statewide influence, and control of the governorship whenever the Democrats returned to power. Through the first half of 1924, however, Tom Pendergast and Joe Shannon adhered scrupulously to a 50–50 division of offices—with the understanding that, as in 1922, there would be an all-out contest for eastern district judge.

Pendergast could nevertheless move against Bulger, whom he despised as a renegade. On March 7, 1924, the date for choosing delegates to the state convention, goat forces took control of the Democratic caucus in Bulger's Second Ward stronghold. The grab was a spectacular exhibition of the "mob primary"; toughs and party workers took over the caucus room and denied admission to factional opponents. This action set off a pitched street battle in which goat street thugs and party workers overwhelmed the Little Czar's forces. The following week, a Pendergast gang took control of two Second Ward polling places in the Democratic primary election for delegates to the city party convention.

The city election, held on April 8, was a blow to Joe Shannon, who saw rabbit Mayor Frank Cromwell easily beaten by a Republican. The loss of the mayor's office, allocated to the rabbits by the 50–50 agreement, made the contested eastern district judgeship all the more important to Shannon. As Pendergast's strength loomed menacingly, rabbits, Bulgerites, and Klan-affiliated Independent Democrats banded together in an effort to control the county administration.[20]

Given the normal rabbit strength in the eastern district, Truman's strategy was to emphasize his image of quasi-independence and managerial competence. He once again gave Judge Hayes nine of the road overseer appointments, an act for which he won ostentatious praise in the *Examiner*. A second Arthur Young audit, presented to the court in March, made Truman and McElroy appear to be financial managers without peer. The rabbits quibbled with the figures and accurately predicted an imminent deficit. They could not deny, however, that an operating surplus had been achieved in 1923 and that, for the moment, one existed for 1924. In June, the county accountant affirmed that these surpluses had cut the cumulative county debt by more than half. The *Kansas City Star*, rarely attracted to Democrats, lavished editorial praise on Truman and McElroy while condemning the waste of Mayor Cromwell's administration. The Kansas City Chamber of Commerce issued an unusual commendation of the two judges. Truman's opponents lacked any serious issue that could be used against him. They produced instead inaccuracies and irrelevancies.[21]

Truman realized nonetheless that the organizational clout of the rabbits could not be underestimated. He once again waged an intensive campaign, speaking at one gathering after another, hoping to rouse the goat faithful and persuade the independent-minded voters. He skipped army reserve camp. "I am in the midst of the hottest and dirtiest campaign," he wrote to his commander. "I have had speaking dates at the rate of two a night and usually one an afternoon all during July." His opponent, Robert Hood of Independence, was a decent man, but Hood's supporters held back no tactic. Truman bitterly resented what the *Star* characterized as a "whispering campaign" against him; he also received threats. It had been customary for goat and rabbit candidates to speak at the same Democratic rallies. Now the rabbits held their own meetings and denied the platform to goats. The Independent Democratic–Klan faction designated only four county offices as targets; one was the eastern district judgeship. A Klan sample ballot endorsed Hood.

A somewhat better and more confident speaker than in 1922, Truman was still no orator. Ruby Garrett or Colonel Stayton might either warm up the crowd or serve as the main attraction. Truman would deliver a speech filled with facts and figures: 538 miles of dirt road oiled, another 110 miles graded, 75 miles of rock road filled and graded, 80 bridges and culverts built or repaired. He also threw high hard ones: Joe Shannon, he alleged, wanted to put "the scoop shovel gang back in the county treasury."

Emblematic of the tone of the campaign was a Saturday afternoon picnic at Judge Wallace's farm near Blue Springs. An outgrowth of the old man's blasts at the court, it was in effect a late campaign rabbit rally. Truman, who had attempted without success to invade other opposition meetings, requested an invitation. Wallace obliged, declaring that he was holding "just a Democratic picnic for the farmers of eastern Jackson County."

Around noon, farm families with baskets of food began to arrive in Model Ts and Chevrolets. They ate their dinners and drank from barrels of ice water in a large grove not far from their host's pre–Civil War mansion. At three o'clock, the speaking began, first with Hood charging that the county was at the mercy of rampaging spendthrift goats, and then with Truman responding. He rapidly delivered his standard speech, reminding the audience that a surplus was a surplus, however one wanted to figure it. Angered by anonymous circulars, he added, "I will not object to anything that is said of my official record, but the writers of these unsigned communications had better leave me and my family alone." He stepped down to little applause and a few loud, hostile remarks. "Better stay a while," someone shouted. "I will," he replied. "I'm not ready to leave yet." Questioning Hood in face-to-face debate, Truman then got him to admit in effect that the goats were telling the truth about county finances. The episode was not mentioned in major newspaper accounts the next day, but the Truman camp got it into the *Star* a couple of days later.

Truman and McElroy got one final lift before the August 5 primary. At the end of July, the nonpartisan Kansas City Public Service Institute praised them for having cut the cost of county government by 21 percent in 1923. Riding high, Truman declared in one of his last speeches that he and McElroy were one term away from eliminating the county deficit. Then it would be possible either to build roads on a larger scale or to cut the tax levy. Praised by the *Kansas City Star*, the *Independence Examiner*, and the *Sentinel*, Independence's other paper, he was the clear favorite.[22]

The results were a goat sweep. Truman won 6,833 to 5,234 (56.6 percent to 43.4 percent), apparently establishing himself as the most important figure among the eastern district Democrats. Independent Democratic leader Todd George of Lee's Summit was trounced in his race for county treasurer. Shannon's gubernatorial candidate, Floyd Jacobs, lost the state primary badly to Pendergast-endorsed Arthur Nelson, destroying Shannon's hopes of statewide influence. But an unpleasant implication lay beneath these triumphs. Both George and

Shannon, facing political eclipse, would have little to lose by knifing the ticket in the fall.[23]

VII

The general election would not be the cinch it had been in 1922. The entire Democratic ticket, state and local, faced an uphill fight. Democrats everywhere were bitterly divided over Prohibition, the Klan, and the legitimacy of the newer immigrant groups. In April, the state Democratic convention degenerated into a "riot" in a dispute over an anti-Klan resolution. In June, the national Democratic party burned itself out during the worst convention struggle in its history. The splits between urban and rural Democrats in Jackson County were as deep. Truman had to walk a difficult line between these two distinct groups.

County finances also turned against him. A week and a half after the primary, Truman and McElroy admitted that the road fund was depleted and ordered an end to all work other than emergency jobs done by county gangs. Taken reluctantly, and too late to avoid a 1924 deficit, the move was not popular with those voters still waiting for their annual road maintenance.[24]

Truman's opponent was an unlikely choice who would have been a pushover in most years. Put into the race by John Miles, Henry Rummel was the harness maker who thirty years earlier had fabricated the reins for the team of goats that Harry and Vivian had driven around their Crysler Street neighborhood. When Truman defeated Hood, Miles tried to persuade Rummel to withdraw. But the old man knew he had a good shot at victory and liked the prospect of having the title "judge" in front of his name. A good campaigner, Rummel capitalized on his lifelong residence in Independence and developed a set speech on restoring business methods to the court.

Miles had won the Republican primary contest for the new patronage-heavy office of county sheriff, which merged the old offices of marshal (criminal-law enforcement) and sheriff (civil-law enforcement). Truman again backed him and actually raised some $500 for him from their old military associates, whether for the primary or for the general election is unclear. (Miles's opponent in the general election was a former rabbit mayor of Independence. The Pendergasts would not have been terribly disturbed.)[25]

The most notable anti-Truman offensive was in the pages of the Kansas City newspapers owned by Walter S. Dickey, a millionaire businessman and local Republican organization leader. The Dickey papers (the *Journal* in the morning, the *Post* in the afternoon, the *Journal-Post* on Sundays) were widely circulated and blatantly partisan. Dickey had a strong personal motive to dispose of Truman and McElroy; they had refused to have the county build roads for a residential subdivision he was developing.

On September 28, the *Journal* began a daily series of articles and editorials designed to pull together every resentment against the court majority. A blend of fact, fiction, misrepresentation, and innuendo, it was Truman's first contact with the mode of political combat that a later generation would call McCarthyism. Aimed primarily at Truman, the series devoted its greatest attention to road work. Its central theme was that "the goat majority" consisted of two wasteful, extravagant patronage politicians masquerading as efficiency experts. Some of the complaints were legitimate, if exaggerated. Many others were capricious and devious. A few were viciously personal. The paper laid out Vivian Truman's road overseer payroll without demonstrating any irregularities. It carped at a reduction of $1.75 in Martha Truman's property tax and exhorted its readers to investigate Judge Truman's personal property taxes.

More often than not, the *Journal*'s facts were accurate, but the presentation was slanted. At most, it demonstrated that the court was run by politicians who rewarded their friends and tended to put county funds and projects where the votes were. The graft it revealed, petty compared with that of many other administrations, still aroused the opposition. Truman's own partisanship could only have been intensified by the experience.[26]

Demoralization among the Democrats added to Truman's problems. The lackluster national ticket of John W. Davis and Charles Bryan inspired little enthusiasm. Gubernatorial candidate Arthur Nelson, initially considered a strong runner with heavy rural support and an untarnished image, was shown to have flirted with the Ku Klux Klan. Truman's biggest worry was the local Democratic schism. Rabbits, Bulgerites, and Independents reached a secret patronage agreement with the Republicans and deserted the Democratic ticket. Bulger campaigned hard against Truman and other goats in the eastern district. The Independent Democrats openly supported the GOP.[27]

Truman, like any incumbent, had to face a bundle of accumulated grievances. In 1923, the court had oiled only a little more than a third of the total road mileage; in 1924, it would manage only a quarter. Around Lee's Summit and Lone Jack, road work lagged badly, partly because of bad weather. Paving of the Independence Road went on into the fall, creating serious hardship for Mount Washington and Fairmount merchants. Leo Koehler asserted that he could have done the job quicker and cheaper.

The Truman–McElroy claim of budgetary efficiency also eroded further. At the beginning of September, the court had to cancel W. A. Ross's contract to finish the five-and-a-half-mile Hickman Mills–Lee's Summit Road. Several days later, Republican county treasurer J. H. Fayman and rabbit county clerk Pete Kelly refused to pay a $19,200 county warrant drawn against the road fund, claiming that no more money was available. McElroy protested that the warrant fell within estimated revenues, but the account's depletion, if only for the moment, was undeniable.[28]

VIII

In a speech near the end of the campaign, Truman laid out his values and aspirations. Keenly aware of the inadequacies of the system he was part of, he promoted change: efficient government with such nonpolicy offices as county clerk and assessor made appointive and professional; a scientifically planned road system capable of standing up under modern traffic loads; a county hospital for the indigent elderly. These improvements all could happen, he said, if the people wanted it. Campaigning strenuously during the latter half of October, he was cautiously optimistic. He even seems to have thought Davis would carry Missouri and win nationally over Coolidge. With the *Star* and the *Examiner* behind him, he could hope for the votes of independent-minded Democrats and Republicans.

Twenty-five years later, he told Jonathan Daniels a dramatic story. The Klan had threatened to kill him:

> I went out to one of their meetings and dared them to try. This was a meeting of Todd George's "Independents" at Lee's Summit. I poured it into them. Then I came down from the platform and walked through them to my car. There I met my gang with a load of shotguns in a car. It was a good thing they did not come earlier.

He later told Merle Miller that the meeting had been in the daytime and "in the eastern part of the county" and that the Klansmen had not been in their regalia.

There is no record of such an incident; yet it is doubtful that the story was a conscious invention. Truman was likely recalling his talk at Judge Wallace's Democratic "meeting." The atmosphere had been hostile and a bit menacing; many in the audience probably had been Klan members; he had warned unnamed individuals to stop harassing him and his family. It is also entirely possible that as he left, Truman had met some armed friends who thought he needed protection. But the meeting was covered by the press, and the possibility of violence was minimal. This recollection exemplified more than a normal impulse to embroider good stories; it also showed the Walter Mitty–like tendency of a man, keenly aware of his inadequacies, to rewrite his personal history in a way that demonstrated uncommon daring and command.[29]

In one of his advertisements, Truman asked for endorsement of his management of "your county business" on the basis of the voter's identity "as a Stockholder and Taxpayer." In line with the ethos of the 1920s, invoking the values of commerce, the appeal optimistically assumed that people would rationally evaluate his managerial talent. But he was caught up in a web of emotions and ambitions he had done little to create: the Democratic factional fights; the gathering Coolidge tide; the Klan drive to purge American politics of Catholics, Jews, and "alien elements." On election day, Klansmen stationed themselves in several churches and tugged at the bell ropes from the time the polls opened until they closed. A Truman precinct captain in Englewood, west of Independence, told a friend, "They're tolling the bell on me, it's driving me crazy."

The Republicans swept nation, state, and county. Rummel won with 11,587 votes (52.5 percent) to Truman's 10,721 (47.5 percent). The opposition of the Klan and its fellow travelers had been telling. Truman ran 1,822 votes behind gubernatorial candidate Nelson, who had the strong support of the Klan. If Truman had run even with Nelson, he would have defeated Rummel. McElroy lost in Kansas City. The single Democratic victor was the rabbit candidate for public administrator, an office without a single patronage deputy. Still, the rabbits exulted in the goat defeat and looked hopefully to their patronage deal with the Republicans; the Lee's Summit Independents celebrated openly.

Yet Tom Pendergast's defeat carried the seeds of an all but total strategic victory. Shannon's deal with the Republicans had alienated two key associates. Cas Welch made a separate peace with the goats and returned customary Democratic majorities in the Sixth and Eighth wards, leaving Shannon with control of only his home Ninth Ward. Another Shannon friend, James Aylward, the widely respected county Democratic chairman, repudiated the rabbits. Pendergast made him a close lieutenant and adviser. Shannon in fact had all but disemboweled himself politically. The rabbits would not get enough patronage from the Republicans to sustain them, forcing Shannon to make an accommodation with Pendergast on the latter's terms by 1926. The two of them got along well once there was no doubt about who was the big boss. Elected to the House of Representatives in 1930, Shannon would remain there, a vocal advocate of old-time Jeffersonianism, until his death in 1943.

As for Miles Bulger, the realization that he never would regain his old clout was brought home to him the day after the election as he stood waiting for a streetcar. A big limousine pulled up. Tom Pendergast emerged, his glowering face betraying homicidal intentions. Bulger hesitated only long enough to thumb his nose, and then ran for his life. Rushing past a startled friend, he was heard to say, "Pendergast had a gun."[30]

A few days later, Truman met a friend for dinner at the Kansas City Club. He found sixty-five men waiting for him, about half of them Battery D boys, about half political associates. After the group finished eating, the men gave him a white-gold wristwatch. An engraving on the back of the case read:

> Judge Harry S. Truman
> from his
> Buddies and Friends
> November 18, 1924

The judge, reported the *Examiner*, "was entirely unable to respond and could only repeat how surprised and gratified he was."

The event might have been a fitting conclusion for Truman's first term. Unfortunately, the denouement was much less happy. Beginning on November 10, warrants on the road fund began to be registered as nonpayable; in short order, 205 were listed, for a total of about $200,000. Quickly thereafter, other funds were exhausted. By December 31, the current account for 1924 would show a deficit of nearly $511,000. It was small consolation that the record was still better than Bulger's.

In addition, the two judges incurred a lot of criticism when they appointed three new justices of the peace. Known locally as "jackrabbit judges," they earned fees from judgments they routinely rendered against debtors. The posts themselves were disreputable; the men appointed to them were all easily identifiable as goat patronage hounds. The *Star* commented of the justice-of-the-peace courts: "The hardships they have worked on persons of small means . . . far outbalance any good they may do."

Worse yet, on December 31, Republican county treasurer J. H. Fayman, claiming that he acted on the advice of Counselor Latshaw, accepted and paid off the notorious $19,000 Ross warrant, which with accrued interest came to $23,875. Both Truman and McElroy repudiated Fayman's action, but many observers believed they had known what was going to happen.

The *Kansas City Star* summed up a widespread impression: the court had been tarnished by the jackrabbit-judge appointments and the Ross warrant scandal: "It might have gone out with the merited respect of the community. Instead, in yielding to the demands of politics, it goes out under the cloud of public disfavor. Too bad."[31]

8

"Enough Left for a Living": Family, Business, Service, 1925–1934

The defeat of Truman in 1924 came at another difficult time in his life. When he left office, he had a new daughter less than a year old to add to his already heavy family responsibilities. He was loaded down with debts. He also had to look after the needs of his mother, sister, and brother. Increasingly, he would also be under pressure to help out his in-laws. For a time, he returned to salesmanship in one form or another and managed, as he put it, to make "enough for a living" for himself and his loved ones. Problems of debt aside, however, his personal life was probably never more satisfactory than in the decade or so after his first political loss.[1]

II

On February 17, 1924, four days after her thirty-ninth birthday, Bess gave birth to a healthy baby girl. Expecting another miscarriage, she was so pessimistic that she had resolutely forbidden the purchase of a bassinet or baby clothing; her depression was so deep that she broke into tears when informed that her child was a girl rather than the boy Harry had wanted. For a day or two, until Truman could purchase more suitable accommodations, the infant slept in a bureau drawer.

Whatever his gender preference had been, Truman was elated by his daughter. Momentarily, the stormy county court of early 1924 basked in goodwill as the new father passed out cigars and received the congratulations of political friends and enemies alike. The parents squabbled over a name. Bess preferred Margaret (after her mother); Harry insisted on Mary. Sometime before the child's fourth birthday, they reached an agreement; at an Episcopal ceremony, she was christened Mary Margaret. Harry's apparent victory was superficial, however; surrounded by Wallaces, the little girl was called Margaret from the beginning.

Like most middle-aged men who have fathered a child, Truman doted on his baby. He was a kindly, permissive parent. For Bess, motherhood was harder. She had to assume the physical effort of child care at an age when most mothers were watching their children finish high school. She also had to balance Margaret's demands with those of her mother. Harry, constantly on the go with business, social, and political obligations, left Bess with an unusually large share of the burden of child care. Like nearly all parents of that era, she expected obedience as a matter of course and did not hesitate to use the paddle. Many years later, Margaret, recalling that her mother had usually addressed her as Marg, wrote that the nickname "still rebounds in my ears with orders, impatience, and discipline in it."

Both Bess and Margaret were fortunate that the other Wallaces lived so close by. Frank, Natalie, George, and May provided the girl with ample attention, creating a warm, protective environment that went beyond what she could have experienced from her parents alone. Aunt May was especially important. She and Margaret frequently played together in the little house on Van Horn Street. A favorite game was "shoe store"; May would empty her closet of all her shoes, and the two would take turns playing clerk and customer. She and George often took Margaret to Saturday movie matinees, and then to the drug store for ice-cream sodas.

By the time she was eight, Margaret was at the center of a small group of neighborhood girls who had formed a little club, the Henhouse Hicks. They put out a newspaper and staged plays. At times frail in appearance because of a susceptibility to tonsilitis and bronchial ailments, she was still a bit of a tomboy. George and May once took her golfing. "I toddled around the practice tee," she recalls, "picking up everyone's golf balls and refused to stop until they gave me a club and ball of my own." Her relationship with her mother was at times tense. At the age of eight or nine, probably having just read some story about an orphan taken in by another family, she asked, "Mother, am I adopted?" Bess replied, "No. If you were, we would have done better."

Even her father, for all his indulgence, did not fully understand her. On Christmas morning, 1934, she rushed downstairs expecting to find an electric train. Instead, she saw a baby-grand piano that Harry had purchased for her. She burst into tears.[2]

Harry got on well with Bess's brothers, but found himself obligated to help them out once he was back in public office. As presiding judge, he gave Fred architectural contracts for the new county hospital, a new Negro Girls' Home, and renovation of the Independence courthouse. George had a drinking problem serious enough to hospitalize him once or twice. Fred drank heavily also. After George lost his job during the Depression, Truman had to find work for him with the county at a time when he was laying off some 200 public employees. Madge Wallace seems by the 1930s to have run through her inheritance and become semi-dependent on her son-in-law.[3]

Truman's own family also had difficulties. Vivian, who would have enjoyed nothing more than his independence on the land, was discovering (like many others in the 1920s and early 1930s) that hard farmwork was no guarantee of a decent living. Harry's return to office in 1927 assured him county employment that kept his farm afloat. A filling station on Mary Jane's property increasingly failed to provide a satisfactory income.

Mamma's finances grew more precarious by the year. Her farm income probably barely covered day-to-day expenses. Harry gave her and Mary Jane money on a fairly regular basis. The big problems she faced were the $25,000 mortgage that she had negotiated in 1917 and the $6,200 mortgage of 1919. Both hung over the property until 1932. His worst fear, Harry told Bess in early 1931, was that if there should be a foreclosure, "that good old woman who made me an honest man would pass on." Somehow, the family met the interest payments. After difficult efforts at refinancing, Harry and Vivian negotiated a new $25,000 mortgage, signed on July 30, 1932, with Anna Lee Rosier, a wealthy director of the Bank of Belton.

At the end of that year, they finally sold the remaining three and a half lots of Truman's Subdivision to Willock Realty for a purported $5,000. (Given the economic conditions of the time, it was a good price; Truman's political enemies spread rumors that Willock, who was distantly related to Bess, was paying him off for favors rendered in connection with county land deals.) The Trumans apparently used whatever they received to pay $3,200 on the smaller note. In January 1933, the Bank of Belton refinanced the $3,000 balance. These transactions did little more than buy time, but that in itself seemed a precious commodity to Harry.*[4]

III

Despite his financial burdens and personal cares, Truman continued to live a remarkably fulfilling social life built around the Masonic Order, the Reserve Officers Corps, and (during his two years out of public office) his lead-

---

*Richard Lawrence Miller believes that a $5,500 mortgage to Kansas City Life Insurance Company signed by Vivian Truman and his wife on May 29, 1935, was actually negotiated for Martha's benefit (*Truman: The Rise to Power* [New York: McGraw-Hill, 1986], 340–41). The issue, however, is ambiguous. The mortgage included both Vivian's property and a hitherto unencumbered segment of property that Martha had deeded over to Vivian on March 29 of that year. The motive may have been to keep this land in the family if the bank foreclosed on the rest of Martha's farm and had to go after additional holdings to recover the mortgage total.

ing role in Independence's Tiery Ford American Legion post. (The last affiliation may indicate that he finally was beginning to think of himself as an Independence man rather than as a Kansas Citian.) These activities produced valuable contacts and friendships in Jackson County and around the state. Once or twice a month, he spent an evening drinking and playing poker with the Harpie Club, a group of friends and political cronies who met in a shabby upstairs room overlooking the Independence square.[5]

In September 1923, Truman had enrolled as a student at the Kansas City School of Law. The institution, located in a downtown office building above a piano store, was Kansas City's only law school. It held all its classes at night and charged $80 a year for tuition. The faculty consisted of leading local attorneys, most of them active in politics; Truman knew several either as friends or as political foes. Instruction was serious; grades were based solely on a final examination. The students were predominantly young men employed in junior managerial or professional positions during the day; a few were women. One of the men was Charles E. Whittaker, who would be a justice of the United States Supreme Court, from 1957 to 1962. Another was William Boyle, whom Truman would one day make chairman of the Democratic National Committee.

The school's earnestness extended to its social occasions. The annual Washington's Birthday banquet in 1925 featured short talks entitled "The Organic Law v. Child Labor," "Law and Manners," "Loyalty," "Progress and the Future Lawyer," and "Congress and the Supreme Court." Truman's old corporal, Albert A. Ridge, class of 1925, spoke on overlegislation; Truman himself addressed the group on the topic "Honor and Government."

The night classes must have been grinding. Truman took a reduced load during his sophomore year, when he was running for reelection as eastern district judge and then attempting to reestablish himself in business. It was testimony to his vigor that despite his stressful and demanding political duties, his performance was superior. In all, he took fourteen courses, made one C (in sales law), ten Bs, two As, and one A+ (Blackstone's *Commentaries*).

He did not return for his junior year. Two decades later, he said that he had given up law school because "I had so many people interested in the welfare of the county who wanted to see me that I couldn't study law." No doubt he was regularly pestered by job seekers and constituents, but he quit only after he had been voted out of office. The demands of providing for his family likely had become so heavy that by mid-1925 he had neither the time nor the money to continue. In 1945, the school (by then part of the University of Kansas City) would award him an honorary degree.[6]

Truman crowded one new interest into his busy life. Since his elementary-school years, he had been a history buff especially fascinated by the exploits of pioneers and western leaders. Since his days on the farm, he had worked for improved roads and highways. He became a member of the National Old Trails Association, an organization that fused these two themes, and extended his network of personal contacts. In 1926, he was elected its president. What made the association especially attractive to Truman was its effort to obtain funding for transcontinental highways along the routes of the old National Road, the Santa Fe Trail, and the Santa Fe extension to Los Angeles. The organization never had anything approaching a mass membership, but its chapters stretched from Ohio to California. It had especially close links to the Daughters of the American Revolution (DAR) and less formal ties to the American Automobile Association and other good-roads groups.[7]

Truman headed a multistate membership drive. He also worked closely with the national DAR to select towns in twelve states as sites for monuments commemorating pioneer mothers. (His acquaintance with Spencer Salisbury's mother, an important DAR official, was helpful.) These tasks required considerable diplomatic skill and fairly extensive travel. As always, he could muster the former when necessary, while enjoying new sights and new people. It is unclear when he formally relinquished his post or how long the organization continued; but for three years, he was an active and effective leader.

In November 1926, he traveled through Kansas to hear the cases of competing towns. (His mother told him to keep an eye out for the family silver that Jim Lane had stolen in 1861.) Then he went to Dayton to effect a merger with the National Highway Boosters' Clubs. In 1927, he made trips that took him as far east as Wheeling and as far west as Albuquerque. He met local officials and community leaders at every stop, relished the attention they gave him, made friends, and further enlarged his horizons.

The highlight of his Old Trails experience came in April 1928, when he delivered a report to the national congress of the DAR in Washington. It was his first time in the capital. The only other guest speakers were three cabinet members and President Coolidge. He admitted to nervousness; one suspects that the talk reads better than it was delivered. But it was a nice blend of history, humor, and human interest; it seems to have gone over well with the audience. The DAR women, he told Bess, were formidable but sociable, rather like Mrs. Salisbury.

Over the next year or so, he was at most of the ceremonies dedicating the monuments. The twelve identical statues, called *Madonna of the Trail*, depicted a hatchet-faced pioneer mother attired in bonnet, long dress, and boots. She held an infant, carried a rifle, and stood protectively over a small boy who clung to her skirts. The artistic merit was questionable; the appeal to Truman's sentiments, deep. His speeches reflected his profound sense of identification with the history of his own family, especially that of the women in it, and a feeling for the American national experience. And they universalized his devotion to his mother: "We owe all we are or ever expect to be to our mothers. They gave us birth, taught us our first words and our first prayer, gave us our morals and our understanding of life. There she stands—the Mother of the Mississippi Valley!"[8]

IV

Truman's search for a new livelihood led him back to the path he had tried with little success in the past: sales. In February 1925, he became membership secretary of the Automobile Club of Kansas City. An independent body that rejected affiliation with the Automobile Club of Missouri, the Kansas City group provided services that ranged from emergency towing to insurance and advocated a variety of safety measures. It enjoyed the support of the business elite and maintained a country club–style facility just a few miles from Grandview. Through it, Truman maintained his tenuous ties to the city's civic leaders and made solid contacts throughout the metropolitan area's growing middle class.

His compensation, either entirely or primarily on a commission basis, depended on the number of memberships he could bring in. It was his toughest test yet as a salesman, an organizer, and a judge of men; he seems to have passed it well. He "tried out" sixty men and wound up with a sales force of five go-getters, who did most of the actual selling. Spencer Salisbury, who had a federal civil service position with the Bureau of Internal Revenue, apparently helped out by giving Truman access to area tax and income records. Undertaken in booming automobile years, the hunting was very good.

The operation lasted for twelve to eighteen months; Truman severed his connection to the Automobile Club when he returned to active political involvement and became more deeply involved in banking. As he remembered it eight years later, the drive grossed $15,000 (approximately 1,000 new members at $15 a head), $10,000 of which went to expenses, primarily the salesmen's commissions. If his memory of the figures was correct and his stint with the club lasted for about a year, he had earned close to his $5,000 county judge salary. If the net was for a year and a half (an annualized $3,333), it was still good; in 1926, the average wage earner made $1,375 a year.[9]

This comfortable middle-class income did not satisfy him. Painfully aware of the debts that hung over him, he dispersed his funds among several banks to hide them from creditors like Cluett-Peabody, which in mid-1925 had attached an account to satisfy an old haberdashery debt.[10] He may also have held unusually large amounts of cash. In such circumstances, Truman needed more than simply good earnings. Seeking other ways in which to deploy his energy, he turned to banking.

V

The career of his old associate Arthur Elliott, the "fat colonel," provided inspiration. Elliott had prospered during the early 1920s as manager of the Kansas City and St. Louis branches of an aggressive mutual savings and loan association, Farm and Home, based in Nevada, Missouri. Mutual savings and loan associations are owned by their depositors, who possess shares in direct proportion to the size of their deposits. They generally are created and run by management groups that are paid by the association and often perform such related services as the writing of insurance on property put up by borrowers. In those days, before government deposit insurance, an energetic, responsible management could be an invaluable asset, deserving generous remuneration. The greater its success in adding to deposits, the stronger the association would be in times of economic downturns and loan defaults. But with management usually free from supervision by shareholders, abuse was not uncommon. Farm and Home itself, while apparently flourishing, nearly went under because of lavish fees paid to Elliott and other officials.

For the first half of 1925, Truman worked for Elliott (as did their fellow 129th officer Newell Paterson), most likely using his Automobile Club sales force to solicit deposits (in other words, sell stock) for Farm and Home. He must have felt a trace of envy at his old friend's *haute bourgeois* life-style, which included a farm outside the city and a home in the posh Country Club district.[11]

Elliott provided an example. Lou Holland was instrumental in giving Truman an opportunity. A few years older than Truman, Holland made his home in Englewood, an unincorporated community just west of Independence. He was one of Jackson County's civic leaders. A self-made man who had taught himself photo engraving, he had founded Holland Engraving with backing from local advertising agencies. He was president of the Associated Advertising Clubs of the World, a founder of the Kansas City Better Business Bureau, active in the Automobile Club, and a power in the Kansas City Chamber of Commerce. His two pet causes were good roads and a municipal airport. Like Truman, he was a Mason and a Democrat; like Truman, he envisioned progress as modernization. They admired each other enormously.[12]

Holland was vice president and dominant member of the board of directors of a small bank, Citizens Security, in Englewood. Its manager and cashier was Paul E. Cole, a rough-and-ready figure who had won local acclaim when he mortally wounded a fleeing robber. His brother-in-law was Missouri secretary of state Charles U. Becker. The tiny institution, like many small midwestern banks, was highly vulnerable to economic recession or mismanagement. At the beginning of 1924, its assets (mostly loans) amounted to only $100,000, against liabilities (mostly deposits) of $85,000. As with all banks, its solvency depended on the quality of its loan portfolio. It seemed prosperous; in February 1925, it paid a 10 percent cash dividend to its stockholders and with Holland's enthusiastic participation embarked on a successful program of attracting new local depositors.[13]

In September 1924, Citizens Security officials, possibly in partnership with Spencer Salisbury, obtained a controlling interest in a tiny Kansas City mutual S&L, took over its management, moved it to the Citizens Security building in Englewood, and renamed it Community

Savings and Loan. Although a separate business, Community functioned as an affiliate of Citizens Security Bank. It had only a few thousand dollars in assets, but seemed a good bet to grow with a suburban economy that was making a strong recovery from the 1921 and 1922 recession. However, despite a torrid building boom, Community faced strong competition for savings from many other S & Ls and experienced little or no growth. As of August 31, 1925, its assets totaled just $6,613.

Salisbury and Holland probably played primary roles in persuading Truman to transfer his S&L solicitation efforts from Farm and Home to Community Savings and Loan. On or about October 1, 1925, Truman established a management company in partnership with Salisbury and Arthur Metzger (an important local goat attorney and politician) under the name Harry S. Truman and Company. Although the original agreement is no longer extant, it appears that both Salisbury and Metzger contributed $400 to the partnership. It is uncertain whether Truman was expected to raise $400 also or whether his existing sales organization was to be his only contribution. The company's contract with Community gave it effective control of the S&L. In return for assuming all operating expenses, it would receive a 2 percent commission on stock sold (deposits received).

Undertaking a vigorous campaign to attract money to Community Savings and Loan, the partnership established an office just off the square in Independence and utilized Ted Marks's tailor shop in downtown Kansas City. It promoted installment savings plans with payments of as low as $5 a month, engaged in a modest advertising campaign, and did telephone solicitation. By the end of February 1926, the effort had raised Community's total assets to $27,714. Truman's control of Community became all but total when he, Holland, and others took over Citizens Security Bank in February 1926. Truman became president of Community. Salisbury resigned his position with Internal Revenue to replace Paul Cole as treasurer of Community. During the next several months, Truman cleaned out the old board of directors and appointed such friendly figures as old Jim Clinton, the druggist for whom he had worked as a child.[14]

In April 1926, moreover, he brought in an important new partner, H. H. Halvorson. A good friend of Tom Pendergast and a well-to-do real-estate developer, Halvorson contributed $750 in cash to the partnership, allowed his downtown office to be used as a branch, and contributed space for another branch office in a building he owned in the West Bottoms. Halvorson was to receive rent for the latter branch as soon as it was profitable; he also was to share equally in the profits (or losses) of the partnership. To Halvorson's frustration, however, Truman refused to make the West Bottoms office the company headquarters. Much of the business of the American Savings and Loan Association, a Pendergast-controlled S&L, came from the Bottoms, and Truman was unwilling to compete vigorously against it on its own turf. Instead, he moved the main office from Englewood to 204 North Liberty Street in Independence, where he also maintained an insurance agency in partnership with a friend and political associate, Robert Barr.[15]

Truman's successful campaign for presiding judge in 1926 and the exercise of his official duties was probably good for Community's growth. By August 31, 1927, its assets were $110,176; almost all the total consisted of soundly based loans, government bonds, and cash. Yet Truman's management partnership was shaky. Commissions had failed to keep pace with expenses. As of August 31, 1927, an audit of Harry S. Truman and Company, likely undertaken at the instigation of Metzger and Salisbury, revealed a net loss of $1,200 and showed that Truman had been a decidedly sloppy bookkeeper. It is probable that his inability to render a satisfactory accounting to his partners had led to the audit. No doubt responding to the sentiments of Salisbury and Metzger, the audit declared that he was obligated to contribute $400 to the operation.

Further complicating matters, Truman, as presiding judge, was unable to provide rewarding patronage jobs for Salisbury or, apparently, Metzger. He initially made Salisbury purchasing agent for eastern Jackson County. "Mike [Pendergast] didn't like it," Salisbury told Jonathan Daniels twenty-five years later, "so Harry canned me and gave me a job to collect interest due on county school funds held by the county court and I got a little rough making 'em pay so he canned me, but I had made a contract so he paid me $3,000 to quit." After that, the Truman–Salisbury friendship was history.[16]

Several weeks after the audit, the partners signed a revised agreement that changed the name of their management agency to the Community Investment Company. It established a rent of $75 a month for Halvorson's West Bottoms building "to be paid out of profits accruing in the future." To Truman's embarrassment, it listed the contributions of each partner: Halvorson, $750 and use of his downtown office; Metzger, $400 and certain personal services; Salisbury, $400 plus $184 in unpaid commissions; Truman, only the original contract between himself and Community Savings and Loan. Truman could argue that this arrangement was fair enough. His reputation, contacts, and sales force were, after all, substantial, if intangible, assets. Salisbury and Metzger saw it differently.[17]

VI

Community Investment Company's losses continued to increase apace with Community Savings and Loan's steady growth. On January 14, 1928, the partnership had less than $76 on hand with which to meet nearly $418 in salaries and bills payable. "We *must* raise the difference today," declared a statement, probably typed by Salisbury. A month later, the partners nearly closed the West Bottoms office because of another cash crunch. The economic slump after the 1929 stock-market crash required further sacrifices.

Salisbury seems to have worked harder than anyone else at making a go of the enterprise. He continued to defer collection of commissions due him, made a $450 loan to the company sometime in 1927, and in 1929 and 1930 drew less than half his $1,800 annual salary. Halvorson watched his rent account pile up without receiving a cent. Metzger apparently chipped in about $250 toward the speculative purchase of a house in Independence. Truman, busy with the county court and probably sensing that the business was going nowhere, became increasingly disengaged—just as Jerry Culbertson had when things began to go poorly at the Oklahoma mine.

A final accounting of the partnership's lack of progress was made as of September 30, 1930. It showed a net loss of $6,023.32, apportioned as follows: Metzger, $138.54; Salisbury, $2,171.26; and Halvorson, $3,713.52. Truman received credit for all but 71 cents of the long-disputed $400 cash subscription: $149.27 in the form of commissions he never had collected; $150.02 for cash he claimed to have put into the company; and $100.02 for his 25 percent share of the $500.11 capital balance the partnership showed on August 31, 1927. None of the loss was apportioned to him. Although he still was listed as president of Community Savings and Loan, he had been effectively dealt out of the management company.[18]

The three remaining partners—acting without Truman's involvement—reestablished Community Investment as the Rural Investment Company, a general financial services corporation. It was to manage Community Savings and Loan, deal in depressed rural real estate, and sell insurance through an agency that moved into the offices of the recently dissolved Truman–Barr partnership. From the beginning, the venture was riddled with dissension. Perhaps because he liked Truman or understood the business value of the presiding judge's goodwill, Halvorson urged Salisbury, as treasurer, to issue Truman 25 percent of the stock. Metzger was vocally opposed. Salisbury refused to act.

Truman was bitter. "My private business has gone to pot," he wrote to himself probably in late 1930. "I'll be worse than a pauper when I'm done." He blamed Salisbury, "who used me for his own ends, robbed me, got me into a position where I couldn't shoot him without hurting a lot of innocent bystanders and laughed at me." A few months later, unwilling to fight for worthless stock but equally unwilling to leave quietly, he sent Halvorson an assignment of his "undivided one-fourth (¼) interest in and to the partnership." Halvorson returned it and made one last effort to bring Truman on board. He assured him that Salisbury was willing to issue shares to him "as soon as you made some settlement of the affairs that have led to a disagreement between you, Metzger, and himself."

Truman's response was curt:

> The only reason I made this assignment to you was because I felt that I should make some reparation for getting you into the organization. So far as Metzger and Salisbury are concerned I am thru with them in a business

way, and they can take the Community and run it into the ground or any place else they care to.

By this time, he appears to have been encouraging friends and associates to withdraw their deposits. Toward the end of 1931, he asserted that he was responsible for the pulling of at least $25,000.

Salisbury did his part toward making the break irreparable by telling Halvorson (and presumably others) that the West Bottoms rent would have been paid despite the Depression "if Truman had kept only part of his numerous promises made to all of us." Halvorson thereupon left the partnership, demanding payment of back rent and alleging pettiness, unfriendliness, and dishonesty.[19]

The situation was hardly a simple one. Truman understandably resented the constant pounding he had endured for not having made a cash investment. But Salisbury had made considerable sacrifices and had kept Community going through the Depression. By 1934, it qualified for a federal charter and deposit insurance with solid assets of nearly $484,000. Unfortunately, both Truman and Salisbury were too much men of their culture to forgive and forget.

In 1934, Salisbury ostentatiously campaigned against Truman in the senatorial primary, and then worked against him in every subsequent political race. Five years later, Truman would strike back. As a United States senator, he encouraged federal banking officials to investigate irregularities in Salisbury's management. After they discovered that he had signed an audit misrepresenting the S&L's shaky assets, Community Savings was liquidated with no loss to depositors. Salisbury pled guilty to bank fraud and served a year in the federal penitentiary at Leavenworth. He spent the rest of his life as a convicted felon, making a living as a tavern owner and bail bondsman. As president, Truman, rejecting many requests from old friends, refused to pardon him.[20]

VII

Truman and his partners had earlier heroically rescued Citizens Security Bank from near-collapse and then, knowingly or not, returned it to its enemies. Despite its surface profitability, Citizens Security remained shaky, primarily because of Paul Cole's loan practices. In February 1926, Truman, Metzger, Salisbury, and Colonel E. M. Stayton purchased the controlling interest held by Cole and John Hoover. Salisbury replaced Cole as cashier at Citizens Security at the same time he became treasurer of Community Savings and Loan. Lou Holland, who probably arranged the transaction, agreed to serve as temporary president.

For Truman, Salisbury, and Metzger, control of Citizens Security promised obvious advantages in tandem with Community Savings. The terms, moreover, were unusually attractive. Asking not a cent in cash, Cole and Hoover accepted notes for a total of $9,900. The new owners quickly discovered that they had bought enormous problems. They later told the *Kansas City Star* that the sale was based on an audit of January 25, 1926. When they took control a week later, they found new, highly questionable items totaling $15,250. An audit on February 16 estimated that $12,362 in real-estate loans were uncollectable. It also found dubious personal loans, including $950 to a brother-in-law of Cole. These fishy deals had been facilitated by Secretary of State Becker's deposit, under his own name, of $10,000 in state auto-license receipts.

A generous analysis of the situation might indicate that Becker was a bit careless in his handling of money. Truman was less charitable. Becker, he commented privately, was "the crookedest secretary of state the world has ever seen."[21]

The new managers moved rapidly to save the bank, salvage their own reputations, and avoid damage to their main interest, Community Savings. They attached the deposits of one debtor and seized the car of another. They pressured Cole into returning their $9,900 in notes and made these part of the bank's asset base. The move was a big risk for all of them. If the bank failed, Truman, assuming he had a one-quarter interest, faced the prospect of having another $2,475 added to his debt burden. Cole raised additional money to cover other questionable transactions he had authorized. He probably did so by getting Holland and three other holdover directors to give the bank notes for $730 each, which he secured with some real estate he owned. (He apparently never paid these; when Citizens Security eventually failed, Holland and the others found themselves stuck for the full amount.)[22]

The bank had been pulled back from the brink of failure, but Truman and his partners faced considerable risk that they were in no position to handle. Elementary prudence dictated quick extrication. In April, the partners received an offer from a group headed by two local real-estate brokers: B. Manley Houtchens (the brother of the boyhood friend with whom Truman had studied for military academy examinations) and Novus Reed, Houtchens's brother-in-law. Truman agreed to retain two shares of stock and stay on the board of directors for thirty days; then he transferred his interest to his friend Rufus Burrus, who handled much of the legal business for both Citizens Security and Community Savings.

It is unclear whether at the beginning they realized that the moving force behind the Houtchens–Reed group was Paul Cole, whom the new owners promptly reinstalled as cashier. Holland privately alerted the state finance commissioner to the change in management. Publicly, however, there was little to do but put as good a face as possible on developments and hope for the best. Holland, Truman, and Salisbury all cited the pressure of other commitments. These excuses were not falsehoods; neither were they the entire story.

Truman's candidacy for presiding judge in 1926 had something to do with his silence, but an open attack on Cole as incompetent or dishonest would surely have doomed the bank to a fatal run by depositors. Neither Truman nor his associates wanted to touch off a bank failure or be open to a slander suit. The earlier problems had been handled quietly. Houtchens's integrity was unquestioned, the bank was reasonably sound, and Cole was still popular. It was possible to believe that he had learned his lesson.

One nagging problem remained. The day after the bank changed hands, Holland wrote to Secretary of State Becker requesting the routine release of a bond that the outgoing owners had given for the protection of state funds. Becker responded, "I will do this at the earliest date possible." The release never came, leaving Truman and his friends under potential liability for the safety of funds they long since had ceased to manage. On August 7, Citizens Security was padlocked by the state finance commissioner.[23]

Cole and Becker, in league with Novus Reed, had recycled large deposits of state money to themselves in the form of unsound loans. Houtchens, who had been shamefully suckered, made a valiant effort to save the institution. Unable to help financially, Truman lent his public backing. After Houtchens put $26,000 of his own and other people's money into Citizens Security, state examiners informed him that the bank remained insolvent, that its assets would be liquidated, and that its depositors would be lucky to get 50 cents on the dollar. Soon afterward, he killed himself.

Truman and his associates found themselves threatened with a suit by Becker, who claimed that their bond was still enforceable. They produced in response Becker's four-month-old promise to release them. Becker got little cooperation from his Republican rivals in Jefferson City. After some complex legal and political maneuvers, the state reclaimed Becker's deposits; other depositors got nothing. Truman and his partners, fairly enough, emerged unscathed. So did Cole. Becker was reelected secretary of state in the Republican sweep of 1928.[24]

VIII

Truman's latest ventures had kept him afloat—and perhaps persuaded him that no good deed went unpunished. He had conducted himself honestly, given due consideration to the interests of others, and—most important from his point of view—preserved his honor. By mid-1926, he had a solid marriage, many friends, and wide public respect. He also had further confirmation that he possessed little business aptitude. Politics, public service, and a reunited Democratic organization beckoned again.

9

"Am I an Ethical Giant . . . or Just a Crook?": Achievement and Doubt, 1926–1934

Truman's return to politics was the stuff of dreams. It brought him genuine power, gave him an opportunity for meaningful public service, and culminated in near-visionary achievement. By the end of his first term as presiding judge of the county court, he enjoyed bipartisan acclaim as the best occupant of the office in its history. Yet he also faced episodic public criticism as a partisan politician unable and probably unwilling to cut himself loose from a corrupt machine. The conflict between the ethic of disinterested public service and the requirements of politics periodically gnawed at him and left him anguished.[1]

II

In 1925, Tom Pendergast had made himself the undisputed master of Kansas City politics by co-opting a middle-class business-oriented reform movement. The reformers, spearheaded by the Kansas City Public Service Institute, had proposed a new city charter. The document redrew ward lines and reconstituted the city council in a fashion calculated to make machine dominance considerably more difficult. It prescribed a nonpartisan election system and an appointive city manager, who presumably would run civic affairs in a nonpolitical businesslike manner. Boss Tom confounded the reformers by endorsing the new charter and getting out the goat vote for it. It swept to approval with Joe Shannon and the rabbits the only organized force in opposition. The Pendergast machine then won control of the new city council by a vote of 5 to 4.

Stunned municipal reformers then watched as the council selected H. L. McElroy to be city manager. Given broad powers by the reform charter, he would remain in the post for fourteen years, boasting that he was giving Kansas City the best and most economical administration it ever had, presiding over an era of civic improvement akin to that experienced by many American cities in the latter half of the 1920s. Running the city with his usual domineering arrogance, he advanced the interests of the local Democratic party and, especially, of Tom Pendergast. He rigged contracts, juggled books, and handed out patronage in a fashion that mocked his claims. Only the police, controlled until 1932 by a board of commissioners appointed by Republican governors, remained outside his authority, if not beyond his challenge.

Shannon and his rabbits had no choice but to come back into the organization on a basis that left Pendergast the boss of bosses in Kansas City politics. The Shannon organization remained sizable and with Pendergast's blessing claimed substantial patronage, but the days of 50–50 were over. Thanks to the defection of Cas Welch, now a quasi-independent leader of the new Second Ward, the rabbits could be only spoilers; they concluded that a third or so of a loaf was better than nothing. The goats hailed the return of the prodigals and all Democrats looked forward to the next election.

As Truman sought a place on the sure-to-win county ticket, he was no doubt motivated by both the prospect of political vindication and a genuine attraction to public service; but he was also drawn by the lure of money. The county collectorship, compensated on a fee basis that could bring in up to $25,000 a year, promised an honest income that would support his family in comfort and allow him to pay off his many debts. Politicians fight for such prizes. Truman's strongest card was his close friendship with Mike Pendergast. The two men liked and respected each other enormously. In some ways, they had similar personalities—warm and personable with individuals or in small groups, uneasy in front of crowds, at times impulsive, usually tempted to fight for their objectives rather than to compromise, always passionately loyal to friends. Mike surely regarded Truman as his prime political asset in the county's eastern district. Just possibly he also saw a political pupil who had become a surrogate son. Truman himself later said of Mike, "I loved him as I did my daddy."[2]

With Mike running interference, Truman seemed at first to have the job locked up. In March 1926, the organization leaked a unity ticket slating him for collector. The designation drew sharp opposition from William T. Kemper, the most powerful banker in Kansas City and Missouri's man on the Democratic National Committee. Like many pragmatic Kansas City businessmen, Kemper was willing to work with Pendergast, but only as an equal. He adamantly pushed John Ranson, a competent organization man to whom he was close. Ranson, who had been passed over for the job once, declared he would fight for it. When the final machine endorsements came out, Ranson was in the collector's slot and Truman was the candidate for presiding judge.

Truman, already furious at the refusal of Kemper's Commerce Trust to settle his long-standing debt, privately seethed. Several years later, he wrote to himself that the office was a gold mine taken away from him by the "money boys" in the party. "It is my opinion that Kemper got most of the gold," he added. "He usually does." Mike offered his backing for a primary fight, but Truman wisely accepted the inevitable—which was not without its attractions. If it offered no financial relief, it promised far more influence and potential for political advancement. The machine all but guaranteed him control of the county court by slating for eastern district judge his good friend Robert Barr.[3]

The primary was a walkover; the general election, almost as easy. The incumbent Republican court had been neither venal nor incompetent, but it had failed to rise above the routine. It had maintained a bloated patronage payroll, played politics with sensitive positions that should have been nonpartisan, and fought a losing battle to keep the roads drivable.[4] Truman ran with the usual rhetoric about businesslike management and assiduously promoted Democratic unity. Sure of an overwhelming machine turnout in Kansas City, he profited outside the city (as did Barr) from a glowing endorsement in the *Independence Examiner*. On election day, he polled approximately 56 percent of the vote; Barr won comfortably in the eastern district. Now in control of county government, Truman hoped to establish himself as more than another in a line of crooks and mediocrities.

III

The first challenge facing the court was to appease hordes of Democratic job seekers who literally descended on the courthouse. Nothing was more central to the survival of the organization. Tom and Mike Pendergast and numerous machine captains decided most of the appointees. Even Truman had relatively limited clout, as demonstrated by his inability to provide Spencer Salisbury with a comfortable county job.

The new court took office on January 3, 1927. Expensive floral tributes from well-wishers gave the ceremony a springlike fragrance. Mamma and Bess were among the women who gathered to watch their men being sworn in. Most of the individuals who filled the room and jammed the corridors, however, were there to get work. After the pleasantries and formalities, Judge Barr moved the acceptance of a list of appointments, Judge Howard Vrooman seconded the motion, and clerk Eddie Becker read them off name by name. As the room began to empty, Truman rose to make a short declaration of policy: "We will appoint all Democrats to jobs appointable, but we are going to see that every man does a full day's work for his pay. In other words, we are going to conduct the county's affairs as efficiently and economically as possible." It is uncertain whether he ever believed such a policy could be satisfactorily implemented. He could expect little positive support for it from his colleagues.[5]

Western judge Howard Vrooman, a well-to-do Kansas City real-estate developer, was supposedly the protector of the rabbits. Amiable and weak-willed, more interested in philandering and gambling than in public service, he rarely quarreled with Truman and lasted for only one term. His easygoing accommodation to goat control enraged the rabbits; the messy breakup of his marriage ended whatever appeal he may have had to the independent-minded middle-class. Truman felt amused contempt for him.

Eastern judge Robert Barr—West Point graduate, World War I army officer, and president of the county Farm Bureau—initially had Truman's respect and friendship. Early in 1927, the two men became partners in an insurance agency that shared office space with Community Savings and Loan just a couple of blocks from the Independence courthouse. Their relations gradually frayed. Truman privately criticized Barr as overly self-interested and lazy, lacking the idealism that one expected in a West Pointer. He also resented Barr's occasional independence. Barr probably expected Truman to do more for his political ambitions. In 1929 or early 1930, the insurance partnership ended; the political partnership lasted only a bit longer.

On slow days, presumably when the courtroom was empty or nearly so, Barr and Vrooman amused themselves on their hands and knees behind the judges' bench shooting craps while Truman read orders and motions. They paid little attention and provided affirmative votes when asked. Thus functioned good government, Jackson County style.[6]

In 1929, the rabbits replaced Vrooman with Thomas B. Bash, who had resigned as chief of construction for Kansas City Power & Light to begin his own electrical-equipment business. Blunt and strong-minded, an afficionado of shotguns, hunting dogs, and long-eared Missouri mules, Bash was no pushover. He fought for more jobs for the rabbits, regularly voted against what he regarded as unbalanced appointment lists, and freely criticized his colleagues. Truman had to mollify him with increased patronage.

Bash also took care of his former employer. In 1929 and early 1930, he and Truman engaged in a sharp public struggle over whether Kansas City Power & Light would provide the electricity for the new county farm. Truman had disliked Power & Light since it had demanded an exorbitant fee for hooking up his mother's farmhouse; he stubbornly fought for a county generating plant or for a contract with a smaller utility. Bash argued, apparently correctly, that Power & Light was the cheapest, surest alternative; Barr went along. Angry at losing to a "representative of the Power Trust," Truman had by this time developed a cordial dislike for Bash. He probably heaved an enormous—and, as it developed, premature—sigh of relief when Bash, afflicted by business difficulties and affected by the death of his brother, declined to run for reelection in 1930.[7]

For county counselor, Truman insisted on Fred Boxley, his long-time friend, legal adviser, and supporter. As Boxley's assistant, he appointed Rufus Burrus. They were in many respects an ideal team. Boxley, despite his long relationship with Truman, was identified with the rabbits and could be counted as an important patronage concession to them; Burrus long had run with the goats. Both were totally loyal to Truman. Burrus handled the county's routine legal business. Boxley functioned as Truman's confidential adviser. In his capacity as county attorney, he could be counted on to sustain the presiding judge's authority to do virtually anything he wished.[8]

IV

From the day he took office, Truman pursued one overriding objective, the building of a modern highway system for rural–small town Jackson County. To the needs of farmers had been added those of suburbs growing rapidly in the unincorporated areas just outside the eastern and southern boundaries of Kansas City. The collapsing nineteenth-century road system was a formidable barrier to their development. The Republican court had expended the entire road fund on maintenance and done so honestly, but it could not keep up with the punishment that twentieth-century vehicles inflicted on oiled-dirt and macadam crushed-rock roads. Cries for new construction, especially from the booming "intercity district" between Kansas City and Independence, had gone unmet. By 1927, no court could ignore the need for change.

Truman faced two possibilities. One was to double the road-fund tax levy to its legal maximum of 25 cents. At best, this action would produce enough revenue to provide adequate maintenance of the old system and allow for the building of several miles of modern paved highway each year. The other possibility, much more alluring to an administrator determined to propel Jackson County into the twentieth century, was to plan an entirely new primary road system, finance it through a major bond issue, and construct it all at once. In the end, it would be cheaper than patching up and rebuilding the decrepit old roads every year. The idea had been floated two years earlier by Leo Koehler, still the county highway engineer. The influential William Southern, usually a foe of bond issues, leaned toward it.

Yet neither alternative seemed to have a lot of popular support. By state law, bond issues had to achieve a two-thirds majority vote in a special election. The bulk of those votes had to come from Kansas City residents who felt no compelling interest in rural roads. Most tellingly, there was massive skepticism about any large-scale public-works program that would be managed by the Pendergast organization. In 1926, the public had voted down bonds for a new Kansas City courthouse, a jail, and a county hospital. Truman faced the biggest selling job of his career.[9]

He moved quickly to revive the 1923 idea of a nonpartisan road commission. Less than three weeks after taking office, the new court hired E. M. Stayton again and teamed him with a young Kansas City Republican, N. T. Veatch. (L. R. Ash had died during Truman's years out of office.) They were delegated the task of developing a comprehensive county road plan, one that would start from scratch and create the county's basic traffic pattern for the next generation. A political master stroke, the move brought the judges wide acclaim. Stayton's reputation as a straight-shooter, reserve officer, and veterans' leader was immense. He had just completed a term as state commander of the American Legion. Veatch, who had worked with Stayton on Kansas City sewer projects, was a top-notch civil engineer at the beginning of a remarkable career. Well connected, he had great credibility among Jackson County Republicans.

Leo Koehler praised the appointments of Stayton and Veatch and never questioned the road plan—in part because Truman privately warned him that the court would attempt to reduce his salary if he did, but also because he had advocated the basic idea himself. Retaining substantial responsibility for ordinary road maintenance, Koehler instead argued for replacing the fifty court-appointed road overseers, mostly farmers unable to do more than grade dirt roads, with a half-dozen well-qualified deputy highway engineers. The net savings, he argued, would allow the county to purchase and operate modern road-maintenance equipment. A creative suggestion for efficiency and modernization, the idea got nowhere. Representing the reservations of his colleagues, Barr shot back that it was better to have Democratic road overseers than Republican road supervisors. Efficiency, after all, had its limits.[10]

The campaign for a new road system got under way at once. Outside Kansas City, Truman, Stayton, and Barr carried the major part of the burden, speaking to one group after another. Given assurances that the road program would be the real thing rather than just another boondoggle for crooked contractors, the county residents would turn out for it in droves. The bigger problem was to convince Kansas City.[11]

Truman had no problem with the machine leaders. But in order to get the two-thirds majority he needed, he had to persuade the organization's opposition. He drew on the most appealing aspect of his political identity, that of the idealistic businessman in government. He lined up the Taxpayers League, headed by his old battalion commander Marvin Gates, by taking Gates and other league officials on bumpy rides over broken-down county roads. He developed a close relationship with leaders of the Kansas City Chamber of Commerce, the director of which was his good friend Lou Holland. A new road system, he argued, would greatly stimulate the development of both city and county. He also began a warm association with the Kansas City Public Service Institute, depicting the road program as part of a larger design to modernize Jackson County. He even won over the machine's most visible enemy, the *Kansas City Star*. By election day, he had much of the city establishment behind him.

The plan itself fully justified Truman's choice of his engineers; it envisioned a highway system that would make Kansas City and the most remote parts of the county accessible to each other, while putting virtually every farmer within two miles of a hard-surfaced road. The cost was heavy—$6.5 million—but the specifications were rigorous and up-to-date: 34 miles of asphalt, 190 of high-stress concrete. At a time when major highways between Missouri cities still were not entirely paved, Stayton and Veatch's plan was an ambitious leap into a new era.[12]

Truman hoped for a quick bond election, perhaps in the fall of 1927, but a strange alliance of the Pendergast organization and the civic establishment developed multitudinous other projects. By the time they were finished, the highway bonds were a relatively small part of a huge $31 million package of city and countywide projects. In all cases, the issues carried the endorsements of notables, were supported by the *Star*, and were accompanied by assurances that elite committees would oversee expenditures.[13] Campaigning hardest for the highway plan, Truman argued that it would cost the taxpayers less to approve the bonds than to stay with the old roads. He promised honest management by pledging that Stayton and Veatch themselves would handle the entire enterprise. He made a county geriatric hospital his second priority.[14] On May 8, 1928 (Truman's forty-fourth birthday), a wary citizenry went to the polls. The county hospital and the highway system were big winners. In Kansas City, the voters rejected all but two municipal projects.

One large blemish marred the election. In the Italian-American northeastern ward, John Lazia, a young underworld leader, seized power from Tom Pendergast's absentee boss, Mike Ross. Lazia's thugs abducted Ross's lieutenants and held them until the polls closed. (Only one Ross man, a 300-pounder, staved off Lazia's kidnappers; they were unable to muscle him into their car.) Pendergast quickly recognized Lazia as the new ward leader. Lazia's seizure of power seemed just another chapter in the seamy history of Kansas City politics. Yet it would alter the character of the Pendergast machine and Kansas City politics in ways that no one could have imagined on that bright spring day.[15]

V

Stayton and Veatch solicited what the *Independence Examiner* described as "sensational" low bids from honest contracting firms throughout the Midwest. In September 1928, the county awarded the first three contracts: two of them to an Iowa construction company and the third to a Kansas City, Kansas, firm with no machine affiliation. The *Kansas City Star* praised the court's "elimination of politics" from the bidding.[16]

Shortly thereafter, Truman received a phone call from Tom Pendergast: "Harry, I'm in trouble. I wish you'd come over." The command-invitation was to a meeting at, as Truman recalled it, Pendergast's political headquarters, the Jackson Democratic Club at 1908 Main. A little two-story building adjacent to the Pendergast-owned Monroe Hotel, 1908 Main housed a wholesale linen business and a café on the street level.

Tom Pendergast's offices were upstairs. The neighborhood might be a bit tawdry, the office space cramped, and the decor strictly functional, but the office nonetheless was a center of unbridled authority. Kansas Citians called it "the powerhouse."

When Truman arrived, he found waiting for him the boss and his three "pet contractors": William D. Boyle,* John J. Pryor, and Willie Ross. He surely knew that Tom Pendergast was a silent partner of all three. As Truman told it in later years, Pendergast declared, "These boys tell me you won't give them contracts." The contractors then argued that tax-paying local businessmen like themselves deserved an inside track. Truman sometimes described his response as a little rough, but he probably delivered it with his big trademark smile and firm but gentle words. He told them that he had promised fair bidding to the voters of Jackson County, that he had done so with Pendergast's approval, and that contracts would go only to low bidders who met specifications. He also declared that his honor was at stake. Pendergast then said, "Didn't I tell you boys, he's the contrariest cuss in Missouri." The boss dismissed his unhappy friends and told Truman, "You carry out your agreement with the people of Jackson County."[17]

Truman told this story so often and so consistently that at some point he probably came to believe it. Perhaps it was a result of what became a fierce determination not to speak or think ill of Tom Pendergast. A description of the meeting written in Truman's hand just a couple of years later tells a different story. Pendergast was furious. Eulogized by his followers as "the Man Whose Word Is Good," he nevertheless (possibly in the presence of the pet contractors) called Truman a sucker who was forgoing a chance to get rich while giving his consulting engineers a free national reputation. Harry, he said, your honor isn't worth a pinch of snuff.[18]

It was to Truman's great credit that he stood firm under such pressure and perhaps to Pendergast's that he knew when to stop. The boss could have controlled Truman's two associates and subverted the road plan, but doing so would have been exceedingly messy and would have doomed future bond issues. It was far better to let Truman provide an example that might seduce the voters into approving public works that others would manage. Moreover, Pendergast knew that his Ready-Mixed Concrete Company would make enormous profits. For years, prudent contractors had given it an effective monopoly. On city paving projects, it charged approximately twice the usual market price and probably expected to get about the same on the county system.

As Truman later remarked, "All the county court had to do was to let contracts to the lowest and best bidders. Where they got their concrete and other material did not concern us." In addition, the new high-

*Not related to William M. Boyle, Jr., aide to Senator Truman and Democratic national chairman under President Truman.

way projects would provide plenty of jobs for the machine's soldiers; the court required the majority of workers to be locals, and most of the placements were on a patronage basis. The public interest that Truman so courageously defended was frequently consistent with that of the machine.[19]

The construction of the new highway system provided Jackson County with an example of governmental efficiency unlike any it had seen before. Stayton and Veatch enforced strict quality standards; work proceeded at a pace that later generations would find hard to imagine. In the fall of 1930, Presiding Judge Truman, on his way to an overwhelming reelection victory, was able to announce the near-completion of the entire system with savings that made it possible to add seven miles of pavement. He could declare with pride that he had taken farmers out of their isolation and had made the rural beauty of the county accessible to the city, while increasing the value of farmland by an average $50 an acre. In one Sunday edition after another, the *Star* ran maps outlining scenic drives on the new roads. Plans for another bond issue and more construction loomed.[20]

At about the same time, the new county hospital opened. It also provided jobs for the party faithful, foremost among them Fred Wallace, who served as chief architect, thanks to a lot of pressure from Bess, Madge Wallace, and possibly Fred himself. Inwardly, Truman resented having to name his "drunken brother-in-law," but whether despite Fred or because of him, the hospital came in at about 81 percent of budget. Desperately needed, it was a godsend to the elderly infirm.[21]

VI

The highway system and the hospital were only the visible tip of Truman's aspirations. Despite his alliance with the Pendergast organization, he sought to be a reformer who would modernize Jackson County government, bringing to it an ethic of economy and efficiency it never had known. He also envisioned himself as a master regional planner.

By now, he had added a new element to what was becoming a complex political identity. He had begun his public life primarily as another traditional politician, connected to the machine by his father's goat affiliations and a network of friendships; his initial entry into politics had drawn heavily on other personal ties, especially military and Masonic. Throughout his county years, he distributed public jobs to machine loyalists, close friends, and needy relatives. Becoming de facto organization leader for eastern Jackson County after Mike Pendergast died in 1929, he functioned, in Richard Miller's apt phrase, as a "master machinist."

Yet there had always been another side to him, manifested in his support of Woodrow Wilson instead of Champ Clark in 1912 and his repeated invocations of the ethic of business efficiency in government. At heart, he was, as he remarked privately from time to time, an "ideal-

ist" about the purpose and potential of public service. A typical midwestern insurgent progressive, he hated big business and finance much
in the manner of the great leaders of midwestern insurgency, Robert
La Follette and George Norris, both of whom he admired greatly. Yet
like La Follette and Norris, he did not engage in a backward-looking rejection of modernity. He detested only centralized private economic
power, not the modern ethics of organization, efficiency, and expertise.

Although the Pendergast machine was his indispensable political
base, Truman broadened his support by appealing to the modernizers of
the community. Primarily development-oriented businessmen and educated professionals, the modernizers favored policies that encouraged
economic growth and expanded public services. Demanding honesty and
efficiency in government, they envisioned public administration as a science that required both special skills and a degree of independence. Many
of Truman's friends and supporters came from this camp: Tom Evans, a
young pharmacist with whom he had once attended goat political meetings, owned a group of drugstores; Marvin Gates was a real-estate developer; Lou Holland had a printing and engraving business that surged or
ebbed with the economy; *Examiner* publisher William Southern was a
prominent civic booster. They provided Truman with points of entry into
a larger community that had little use for the Pendergast view of politics;
increasingly, they viewed him as the one figure in county government who
wanted to put their values into practice.

The ethic of modernization most clearly converged with day-to-day
politics in the Kansas City Public Service Institute (later the Civic Research Institute). Funded by the Chamber of Commerce and other civic
groups, the institute was dedicated to the belief that "democratic government can be efficient." Its director, Walter Matscheck, was a graduate of the academic citadel of progressivism, the University of Wisconsin. The institute stood for what had become the progressive definition
of local reform. Rather naïvely, it envisioned municipal and county government as a nonpolitical service enterprise to be run on a businesslike
basis by educated technicians. Its biggest achievement—the successful
fight for city-manager government—tellingly defined both its viewpoint
and its naïveté. Both advocate and watchdog, the institute promoted new
trends in public administration and exposed waste in local government.
Isolated by the Pendergast grip on the "reformed" city administration, it
needed Truman at least as much as he needed it.[22]

As an exercise in planning, expertise, and cost efficiency, Truman's
county highway program exemplified the Public Service Institute's ideals. Displaying his ability to unite modernizers and traditionalists behind
specific common causes, it was the most successful of several projects that
Truman undertook, usually with the counsel of the institute, in an attempt to modernize county government. Other efforts were less happy.

In 1927, Truman and the institute got the county court to form a
special sewer district for the rapidly developing intercity area. The pro-

cess was highly elitist and well removed from the threat of a popular vote—reflecting the modernizers' reliance on the authority and knowledge of the educated few. Affected homeowners, however, already possessed private septic systems put in at their own expense. They felt no need for sewers, resented steep tax assessments levied without their assent, and tended to be Jeffersonian minimalists in their political worldview. A mass protest movement developed almost overnight. By late 1929, it claimed about 2,500 members and was a powerful force in county politics. In June 1930, a local judge who earlier had facilitated the sewer district's creation halted planning and construction, killing the idea for the remainder of Truman's years as a county official. Contrasting strongly with the sensitive development of support for the highway system, the controversy was a compelling demonstration of what could happen when elite modernizers failed to get public consent.[23]

Truman also struggled unsuccessfully to acquire state authorization for county-court zoning authority over unincorporated areas. Perhaps motivated in part by the need to generate more county revenues during the Great Depression, he also backed major tax-assessment reforms. His proposals, similar to methods used in Cincinnati, Ohio (a model to many good-government strivers), were simple, systematic, and free from political favoritism. They were blocked by machine politicians with whom he got along on less rarified matters.[24]

Truman envisioned a thoroughly reorganized county governmental structure—one in which lines of authority were clear and direct, overlapping responsibilities consolidated, and many elective offices abolished. In 1932, a Kansas City Chamber of Commerce subcommittee, chaired by Matscheck and including Truman, produced a draft bill for the state legislature. It would have abolished five elective offices, replacing them with three new departments to be headed by qualified appointees. In theory, the bill would streamline county administration, cut costs, eliminate waste, and make maximum use of trained professional administrators. The *Kansas City Times* praised the plan as "sound, modern, and necessary to improved and less expensive administration." Truman proclaimed that it would save $500,000.

The bill made the presiding judge the "chief administrative officer" of the county, vesting in him the power to name appointive officials (with the concurrence of at least one of the other two judges) and giving him unlimited authority to remove them. Subcommittee member Manvel Davis, a Republican state senator, grumbled that such provisions made the presiding judge a monarch. Possibly thinking of the way city-manager government worked in Kansas City, he warned that the draft bill contained no real checks on abuse of power. His objections were well considered. The proposal was possible only because Truman had brought the post of presiding judge into such high repute. It would have seemed unthinkable if Miles Bulger still had been at the head of the county administration, and Bulger exemplified the local norm far more faithfully than Truman.

The bill reflected Truman's own passion for control. Ever since he had worshiped great men as a boy, he had in effect accepted the principle of a strong executive. His experience on the court had increased his dedication to the concept and had left him convinced that he alone among elected county officials was dedicated to the public welfare. A chart illustrating the proposal dramatically demonstrated his concept of administrative reform. It placed the presiding judge, subject to only the voters, squarely at the top of a complex, specialized hierarchy, all lines of responsibility running directly to him.

The reformers loved the concept; the political professionals were less impressed. State senator M. E. Casey of Kansas City, chairman of the Judiciary Committee and a rabbit, saw only a disguised goat power grab and refused to report the bill.[25]

Truman by then had identified himself with changes calculated to outrage approximately three-quarters of local Missouri officeholders. On November 28, 1931, testifying before a state legislative committee, he argued for the consolidation of Missouri's 114 counties into 30, advocated countywide mergers of local boards of education, and counseled the elimination of some state boards. Among the public officials whose number would be reduced were many of the legislators whom he was trying to influence. Unsurprisingly, his vision of a restructured state failed to win much enthusiasm among them. It reflected what had become an infatuation with rational, "scientific" administration. It also demonstrated a developing tendency to believe that good causes could be advanced through the simple act of testimony, whatever the practicalities of the real world.

A few piecemeal acts were about all that came of these ideas. Most notable was a law that established a uniform county budget system, designated the presiding judge as the chief budget official, and forbade deficit spending. Truman also helped arrange statewide seminars, sponsored by the American Political Science Association and the University of Missouri, on budgeting and management for county judges and other officials.[26]

If one word could have summarized Truman's ambitions and objectives, it would have been "planning." In 1930, he advocated a "ten year plan for Independence" and chaired the meeting that established a state planning association, later a state agency.[27] Two years earlier, he had taken the lead in creating the Regional Plan Association, composed of officials from six counties in the Kansas City metropolitan area and patterned after the fifteen-county Chicago Regional Planning Association. Its immediate objectives were to rationalize road-building plans and provide a survey map. Truman hoped that the association would manage regional development by coordinating zoning regulations and sewage requirements; he also envisioned a planned multicounty system of parks and recreational facilities.

The Regional Plan Association may have served a useful consulta-
tive function, but it seems to have produced little more than the survey
map. The Great Depression made growth and development issues academic, while choking off funding from governmental and private
sources. When Truman entered the United States Senate, the association appears to have dissolved. It nevertheless provided eloquent testimony to his faith in science, reason, and technocracy. He despaired that
a shortage of funds seemed to prevent the realization of a grand goal.
"Oh! If I were only John D. or Mellon," he wrote to himself in May
1931, "I'd make this section the world's real paradise." With his customary determined, if misplaced, optimism, he added, "What is the use
wishing. I'm still going to do it."[28]

In the end, the Jackson County highway system was his great planning triumph. It both anticipated and channeled future growth while
improving the quality of life for city, suburban, and rural residents.
Truman celebrated the achievement in a small book that recounted the
history of the program and contained artful photographs of the rustic
countryside. It was fittingly entitled *Results of County Planning*.[29]

VII

Truman's forays into reform caused no discernable break with the machine. Tom Pendergast and his henchmen did not think in terms of planning; they welcomed the jobs and public contracts it delivered. Perhaps
they were annoyed with some of the blunter rhetoric produced by
Truman. "There are too many people on the county payroll and a lot of
money is foolishly spent," he admitted in 1930. But he quickly added that
both parties were at fault and that the state legislature was ultimately
responsible because of its devotion to antiquated county government
organization. To blame everyone was to blame no one.[30]

Truman was not the only Pendergast man with a reputation for good
administration. City Manager McElroy, although thoroughly dishonest,
built a reputation as an efficient, tight-fisted, irascible guardian of the
public treasury. County prosecutor Jim Page was an independent advocate of law and order, but he lacked the resources needed to break Kansas City's elaborate system of graft and organized crime. Like Truman,
he did what he could for better government and spread the blame to one
and all when he denounced civic corruption. If the machine could tolerate an independent prosecutor, it could take Truman's good-government
strivings in stride. In fact, as Kansas City became progressively wide-open,
corrupt, and gangster-dominated, Truman provided a veneer of respectability. Esteemed by many Republicans and endorsed by the *Star*, he
coasted to reelection in 1930. Efforts to use his continued indebtedness
as a campaign issue only confirmed that he did not take payoffs. On
November 4, 1930, he beat his hapless Republican opponent by a mar-

gin of 58,000 votes, running barely behind Judge Allen Southern as the biggest vote getter on the ticket.[31]

Yet he was a troubled man. He had made no mention of an impending deficit during his reelection campaign, but he must have known that big economic and political problems lay ahead. With the onset of the Great Depression, county finances were turning sour. In December, county salary warrants bounced, as they had in the early 1920s. Employees sold them at a steep discount, cut back on their Christmas spending, and began to worry about layoffs.[32]

Truman was at least equally bothered by the ambiguous political situation in which he found himself. On November 24, 1930, all too obviously under a machine dictate, he appointed two goat loyalists as justices of the peace; as Bash was out of town and Barr out of the courtroom, Truman acted without a legal majority. Moreover, the appointments were in contravention of a recently enacted state law abolishing "jackrabbit judges." Overnight, Truman moved from being one of the most respected men in Jackson County politics to being one of the most criticized. His explanation was lame: the legal system needed more judges, and he wanted to test the law. His demeanor betrayed intense discomfort. The *Star* and the county bar association rejected his story; Page moved to oust the new justices. Eventually, the Missouri Supreme Court decided in favor of the jackrabbits, but its decision provided scant vindication.[33]

Truman found the contradiction between his identity as an advocate of good government and his role as a master machinist to be a source of considerable psychic tension. From time to time in 1930 and 1931, he laid his feelings out on paper. His surviving "diary memoranda" were written on stationery bearing the letterhead of the Pickwick Hotel, an undistinguished establishment in downtown Kansas City, which was owned by a machine ally. Truman stayed there from time to time when events necessitated that he spent the night in the city.

The Pickwick provided him with a supply of stationery that probably would be deemed sufficient for an entire floor of rooms in such hotels today. One imagines him sitting at the desk and writing by the light of a small lamp, perhaps late at night with a bourbon and water (still illegal but readily available) to the side. Here he poured out on paper the most bitter thoughts he would leave behind.

None were aimed at Tom Pendergast, whom Truman could not bring himself to denounce even in private. Tom was a "real man" who kept his word, although "he gives it very seldom and usually on a sure thing." The real venom was aimed in other directions, at

> *Robert Barr*
> a dud, a weakling, no ideals, no nothing

> *Thomas B. Bash*
> I wonder what the "B" stands for—"Bull" or "Baloney"*

*It stood for Benton.

Leo Koehler
>   His ethics were acquired in a north end precinct. . . . He can't be
stopped

Spencer Salisbury
>   used me for his own ends, robbed me

Fred Wallace
>   my drunken brother-in-law

He could muster only contempt for most machine notables, including

Cas Welch
>   a thug and a crook of the worst water

Joe Shannon
>   hasn't got an honest appointee on the payroll

Mike Ross
>   just a plain thief

Willie Ross, who had recently died
>   I suspect his sales of rotten paving have bankrupted the government
of hell by now

Perhaps, he admitted, he had erred in thinking that most people were
fundamentally honest. The boss had told him that the vast majority would
steal if they thought they could get away with it. Pendergast's cynicism,
both a rationalization for his own corruption and a reasonably sound
evaluation of human nature, provided Truman some justification for his
own allegiances. The reformers, he wrote, were more contemptible than
the crooked politicians: "Who is to blame for present conditions but sniv-
eling church members who weep on Sunday, play with whores on Monday, drink on Tuesday, sell out to the Boss on Wednesday, repent about
Friday, and start over on Sunday. I think maybe the Boss is nearer heaven
than the snivelers."

How near to heaven, then, was Harry Truman? He agonized over
the problem of his own virtue: "I wonder if I did right to put a lot of no
account sons of bitches on the payroll and pay other sons of bitches more
money for supplies than they were worth in order to satisfy the political
powers and save $3,500,000?" (The figure referred to half the value of
the road bonds.) At other times, he worried about having looked the other
way as various associates enriched themselves at the taxpayers' expense.
He took refuge in two arguments. The first was that his small sins had
been committed in order to head off larger ones by others. To have striven
for perfect virtue would have meant loss of office and control of the county
by crooks; they would have stolen far more. The second was that "I'll go
out of here poorer in every way than when I went into office."

Truman's sneering dismissal of the reformers was shabby. Still, his
rationale had much to commend it. In a fashion that a later generation
might have called Niebuhrian, he rejected the perfectibility of man and
society, made the necessary compromises to function within a system he

had not created, and left Jackson County far better off than he had found it. He took too much pride in his own honesty; it was, after all, no more than he rightfully owed the people who had elected him. He was too prone to tell himself that his lack of business success and relative "poverty" testified to his personal virtue. (Actually, his public pay of $5,000 to $6,000 placed him squarely in the upper-middle-income bracket, even if it did leave him considerably less affluent than most other organization leaders.) Nonetheless, given his position, his Niebuhrian compromise was about the best he could have done.

It was to his credit, moreover, that he was anything but complacent about the contradictions in his public life. "Am I a fool or an ethical giant?" he asked himself in one of his most agonized memos. "I don't know. . . . [A]m I just a crook to compromise in order to get the job done? You judge it, I can't."[34]

10

"A Tremendous Amount of Strain": Crisis and Anxiety, 1931–1934

"I don't know whether you appreciate the tremendous amount of strain that's been on me since November," Truman wrote to Bess in February 1931. "My two former associates as you know were just full of anxiety to obtain any funds that they could because of their positions, the finances of the county were never in such shape since Miles Bulger handled them, and every person I've ever had any association with since birth has wanted me to take pity on him and furnish him some county money."[1]

Years later, Truman liked to remember his second term at the helm of the county court as a triumphal encore to the first. In fact, despite his continued accomplishment and growing personal stature, it was a harrowing experience dominated by the crisis of the Depression and the increasingly notorious excesses of the Pendergast machine.

II

On January 1, 1931, the new county court was sworn into office amid an atmosphere that mingled celebration and apprehension. Truman still controlled it. His new eastern district judge was E. I. "Buck" Purcell, a reliable, much-liked goat wheelhorse and Independence businessman with a gift for gab. "I expect to get in hot places occasionally," he said, "but if a man can't stand the heat he ought to stay out of the kitchen." Truman appropriated the homey epigram and subsequently made it famous. The new western district judge and rabbit man on the court, William O. Beeman, was a Kansas City meat wholesaler. Truman privately and a bit contemptuously called him a "meat-cutter." He served for one term and was succeeded by Battle McCardle, another Kansas City rabbit. Beeman and McCardle were occasional nuisances, but Truman's main preoccupation was an endless budget crisis.[2]

From the time he took the oath of office for his second term as presiding judge, Truman experienced the grim verity that comes sooner or later to all career managers: when there is a lot of money to allocate, the going is good; in times of stringency, there are no easy choices and few accolades. The imperatives of patronage politics had left Jackson County little financial leeway even in the best of times. The economic contraction just beginning to be felt at the beginning of 1931 sent county finances reeling.

The visible signs of joblessness and hunger were clearest in the city. Organization leaders worked overtime to distribute food baskets. In 1931, Cas Welch fed an estimated 10,000 blacks and whites at segregated sites on Thanksgiving Day. In 1932, Jim Pendergast's Eleventh Ward Democratic Club distributed 2,000 bushel baskets of food at Christmastime. Other machine captains sent food and coal to the needy in their domains. Tom Pendergast's Christmas dinners drew several thousand. Cynics might complain that Cas and Tom financed their charitable activities with only a bit of the boodle they kept for themselves, that the poor had to scrounge for adequate nourishment the other 363 days of the year, that an organized welfare system probably would distribute assistance more equitably and efficiently. Still, the organization gave handouts year-round and does not appear to have been very selective. (The distribution of jobs, few and far between, was obviously a different matter.) The Depression underscored the image of Pendergast as a philanthropist.[3]

It offered no such opportunities to Harry Truman. Machine charity does not appear to have been very extensive outside the Kansas City limits. Instead of building a reputation as a friend of the poor, Truman found himself administering constant cuts and disappointments on his constituency, while vainly fighting to reduce the county budget as fast as county revenues dwindled.

Even in flush times, the Truman court had failed to stay in the black. During every year of its first term, current expenditures outran current revenues, although tax payments increased each year. The court finessed the shortfall by issuing "judgment bonds" to pay off outstanding county warrants. The expedient was palatable because the bonds carried a lower interest rate than the mandatory 6 percent on warrants. With these paid off, back taxes could be applied to current expenditures, producing a balanced budget. Nevertheless, the increased bonded indebtedness had to be paid off; there was a limit to the possibilities of financial juggling. When the books on 1930 were tallied, Truman and his colleagues discovered that although tax revenues were at an all-time high of $3,245,000, they had run up a deficit of $1,189,000, making Miles Bulger look like a piker. In 1931, tax collections would be $90,000 lower, in 1932, down by another $697,000.

The road and county hospital bonds, like all bond issues, had been passed in the expectation that better and better times would provide the funds to pay them off. Instead, they became a serious burden on taxpayers, who in increasing numbers simply could not pay up; at the nadir in 1933, the county collected only 67 percent of taxes due. In 1933, the court had to almost double the tax levy for payment of bonds. In response to popular pressure, it compensated a bit by shaving 2 cents off the levy for ordinary operations. Yet it was easier to talk about making cuts in county activities than to enforce them; the court's authority over the staffing and spending of independently elected officeholders was tenuous and rarely tested. Little wonder that Truman spent much of his second term arguing for reforms in tax assessment and county administration!

In January 1931, Truman, relying on fragile authority, announced that county expenditures would have to be sliced by 15 percent, through either firings or pay reductions. He also got the court to take the long-overdue move of cutting the number of road overseers from fifty-one to sixteen. As he slashed jobs and salaries, he found himself beseiged by jobholders, each with a tale of woe. Headaches and sleepless nights followed; they would be all too common during his second term.[4]

An initial challenge came from county prosecutor James Page. Although often paired with Truman as one of the machine's ornaments, Page heartily disliked the presiding judge, who fervently returned the sentiment. Refusing to reduce his budget, Page asserted that the court had no authority to cut his staff, which was established by the circuit court. Other elective officials grudgingly complied in one fashion or another, but Page stood his ground. News reports speculated that he would take the issue directly to Tom Pendergast; if he did, Pendergast had enough public-relations sense to support him. On April 4, Truman backed off "for the time being."[5] He struggled with other items, ranging from the trivial to the vital. By the end of 1931, it appeared that he had been successful. Total county expenditures were down by about 22 percent from 1930 and nearly $250,000 less than total revenues (although the current operating deficit was $466,000). In January 1932, the court retained existing cuts but planned no new ones.[6]

The collapsing economy overwhelmed the court's intentions. The state Board of Equalization made them impossible by ordering a 10 percent lowering of property assessments throughout Missouri. In April, the court eliminated another 300 jobs, ended dental services for inmates at the county homes, and returned 200 nonviolent mental patients to their families. Truman called on all elective officials to take a voluntary 10 percent pay cut. He and his two associate judges were the only volunteers. In the months that followed, some county offices ran weeks behind on their payrolls. The court eventually saved fifty-eight jobs by getting a general agreement on a 10 percent pay reduction and a one-month unpaid "vacation" for all employees. Truman spent much of his time seeking state and federal grants for the needy. As year-end neared, despite all the slashing, a deficit of more than $900,000 loomed in the current operating account.[7]

The trauma of 1932 probably did much to concentrate Truman's attention on the "scientific" property-assessment and administrative reforms he championed in the early 1930s. The crisis may have made them seem achievable. The effort brought him little more than a well-deserved reputation as a thoughtful and responsible public official, but it did result in a 1933 state law mandating a county budget system along lines he advocated (although he was more than a little annoyed that Governor Guy B. Park commended the bill to the legislature as the only way of making Jackson County conduct its finances responsibly). The law required counties to balance their budgets, designated presiding judges as chief budgetary officers, and gave them strong authority over spending. It said much for Truman's sense of duty that he was prepared to work for enhanced budget power and practice it at a time when the task was akin to administering an orderly sinking of the *Titanic*.[8]

The county court invoked the new budget bill immediately, although it was not mandatory until January 1, 1934. Truman announced that another 202 employees would get the ax and managed to make the cuts stick after conferences with factional leaders. Even so, the county remained unable to pay election workers, maintain social services, and meet its reduced payroll. In August 1933, the court put every county employee on half-time duty for the remainder of the year. The new budget process, good for the county in the long run, had the immediate effect of more pain for Truman's constituents. The acquiescence of political spoilsmen like Tom Pendergast and Joe Shannon was a telling indication of the county's hopeless finances.[9]

The greatest resistance came from the new sheriff of Jackson County, Truman's old enemy Tom Bash, elected to the post in 1932. Bash was strong-minded, energetic, and adept at self-promotion. His rabbit faction had been frozen out of the Kansas City police force. By nature as well as by political conviction, he was, as Truman told Bess, "a contrary boy." Nonetheless, he went along at first, slashing his employee force from eighty-one to sixty-one and instituting strict financial controls. In August, however, after he gunned down two underworld hit men and became a public hero, he pressed for higher appropriations. Once again, the Truman court was in the impossible position of having to say no to an esteemed law-enforcement official. Bash turned down a special medal, declaring that he needed more deputies instead. "If he can tell me where the money will come from, we'll be glad to employ more men," Truman protested. The *Kansas City Times*, normally a strong supporter of Truman's management, responded, "He needs an adequate staff. The county can afford it."

A wave of public adulation could not print greenbacks. Bash got no more deputies and was told that the ones he had would have to go to half-time status. He responded with a suit alleging that the new budget law was invalid, holding up full implementation for nearly a year. In mid-1934, the Missouri Supreme Court upheld the act, but Truman had been denied an opportunity to make full use of it. It would be a legacy to his successor, Buck Purcell.[10] Right up to his final day as presiding judge, Truman preached budgetary responsibility and tried to find some way to maintain county services. The struggle was a losing one, characterized by successive plans for layoffs and salary payments in "red" warrants that speculators bought at discounts of up to 50 percent. By the end of 1934, the county was in effect bankrupt.[11]

III

Truman had taken wartime combat more easily than the task of inflicting unemployment and salary cuts on constituents and county workers, many of whom he knew personally. As early as February 1931, he seized on an inspection trip of urban courthouses as an excuse to get away. From Little Rock, he wrote to Bess:

> I was becoming so keyed up that I either had to run away or go on a big drunk. . . . My head hasn't ached and I've slept like a baby because I know the phone's not going to ring, and that no one's going to stop me with a tale of woe when I walk down the street.[12]

The 1931 trip illustrated a recurrent tendency in his career. When the going got tough, he would feel overwhelmed and exhausted. He would try to get away, preferably for a week or two, sometimes just for a night at a hotel. Invariably, he would return refreshed and ready to resume his duties. Although understandable, the pattern hardly fit his effort to appear combative and decisive.

Another long-running tendency emerged: an inordinate touchiness about his newspaper coverage. He often fumed about the *Kansas City Star*. Yet aside from a rare incident like the jackrabbit-judge appointments, the *Star* all but eulogized him. A 1933 editorial managed to mention in one sentence his "enthusiastic devotion to county affairs," the "wonderful road system developed under his direction," and "his desire to preserve the natural beauty of the countryside." He received similar notices in the *Kansas City Journal-Post* after Pendergast ally H. L. Doherty purchased a half-interest in it. Although the *Independence Examiner* continued to say nice things about him, he groused about the self-righteousness of Colonel Southern.[13]

Truman did face intense resentment from dismissed employees and endured charges of favoritism in hiring. In June 1932, for example, pro-testers from Marlborough, just south of the Kansas City limits, com-plained that the county had taken on only five local men for a nearby road project and had handed out twenty-one scarce jobs to Grandview resi-dents. By the spring of 1933, he was warning Bess, apparently in all seri-ousness, not to eat any foodstuffs sent to her through the mail.[14]

The ultimate insult came that fall when Jim Page, now a circuit judge, ordered a grand jury to investigate rumors that the county court was paying exorbitant sums to acquire rights-of-way for highway projects. Grand jury foreman Russell Grenier recalled years later that Page had issued specific instructions to obtain evidence for an indictment of the presiding judge. Truman, aware that he was a target, sent a letter to Grenier, which he released to the press: "I should be more than glad to appear before the grand jury, waiving immunity, if you desire it, and fur-nish you with any information you desire. . . . I am inviting the closest investigation because I am proud of the record of the County Court."

There was no indictment. Page died a year later, but Truman's hatred for him endured. Reminded of the incident in 1949, he described Page as "unscrupulous and heartless," adding with his customary exaggera-tion: "After I finished talking to the Grand Jury they came very nearly indicting Page himself and would have done it if I had urged it." The incident surely strengthened Truman's conviction that Tom Pendergast was more trustworthy than "uplifters" like Page and Grenier.[15]

Jobs for family members also became an increasing problem. It was always necessary to provide additional income for Vivian, who could not make farming support his wife and five children. He held a number of county jobs under Harry's presiding judgeship, working as a deputy high-way engineer after Alex Sachs (an old Truman friend and conduit to the Jewish community) ousted Leo Koehler in 1932.[16] The brothers-in-law also had to be taken care of. After the completion of the county hospital, Truman gave Fred the job of rebuilding the Independence courthouse and tried to drum up state business for him.[17] George lost his job as a lumber-mill clerk and began to drink heavily. In 1933, just as he was announcing 202 layoffs, Truman placed George in the highway engineer's office, where he spent the rest of his working career (although he never fully surmounted his alcoholism).[18]

Margaret, always prone to respiratory infections in the drafty old house on Delaware Street, came down with pneumonia and rheumatic fever in the spring of 1933. In April, acting on the advice of a family physician, Truman took Bess, Margaret, and a practical nurse down to the Gulf Coast so that his daughter could recuperate in a warm climate. They rented a cottage with a big yard near the water. Harry spent a couple of weeks helping them get settled, and then returned to Kansas City and the budget crisis.

He found the absence of his wife and daughter a wrenching experi-ence that could not have come at a worse time. He was announcing layoffs, fussing with Tom Bash, getting George Wallace settled in his new job, advising the Wallaces in a business dispute, and dodging anguished county jobholders. He divided his time among 219 North Delaware, his mother's farmhouse at Grandview, and downtown hotel hideouts. He wrote daily to Bess of his troubles. Margaret recuperated nicely, but Bess—cut off from the rest of her family at a trying time—was about equally lonely and unhappy. In mid-May, Truman finally was able to break away for Mississippi, spend another fortnight with his family, and take them back home.

By then, he had just authorized advertisements for bids on the largest single piece of construction and most durable monument he would leave behind him.

IV

The Depression did not brake the political establishment's drive for public improvements. In the spring of 1931, it was still easy to believe that the economic downturn was only temporary and to view more bonded indebtedness as a painless investment in the future. Truman's new highway system had demonstrated to the voters that their money could be employed constructively. Civic leaders pressed for a huge program of bond-funded improvements for Kansas City and Jackson County. The county bonds totaled just under $8 million: $3.5 million for further highway improvements, $200,000 for a thorough renovation of the Independence courthouse, $250,000 for a new county detention home, and $4 million for a new courthouse in downtown Kansas City. The city bonds came to an astounding $32 million for sixteen different projects, including a new city hall, hospitals, a municipal auditorium, and an airport.

Worked out by a committee of business leaders, the improvements were promoted as a ten-year plan that would bring greatness to Kansas City. Sponsors responded to fears of corruption by pledging that a blue-ribbon group would oversee implementation. In fact, however, the machine could find ways around any watchdog committee. Well-meaning promises of honesty notwithstanding, the city establishment had made an alliance with its own local devil. On the surface, Tom Pendergast conceded everything and assumed the role of a statesman advocating vital public needs. By allowing Truman to play it straight with $7 million in 1928, he had gained a $32 million opportunity. The momentum was irresistible, the opposition all but invisible. The improvements would stimulate local business and provide jobs for the unemployed. The major city and county newspapers fell in behind the entire basket. On May 26, 1931, the voters overwhelmingly approved every single project.[19]

Truman once again vindicated their trust. The second phase of the county highway system moved ahead quickly and professionally under the direction of E. M. Stayton and N. T. Veatch. They and their contractors gave the machine some patronage and its leaders some supply business without compromising quality or efficiency, while building eighty-five miles of highway and constructing numerous bridges and viaducts in about a year. As before, they came in under budget. Truman used the excess funds to pay for a huge barbeque held on Columbus Day, 1932.[20]

Fred Wallace remade the old Independence courthouse, a somewhat somber brick building with a large clock tower at one end, into a stately, pillared neocolonial structure with the clock moved to a cupola in the center of the roof. The building would be the centerpiece of Independence's civic life for the next generation. Truman arranged an imposing dedication for it. The city held a parade, band concerts, athletic events, contests in events ranging from horseshoe pitching to "Negro dancing," a bathing-beauty competition, and a historic pageant. Governor Park was the featured speaker, but it was the presiding judge's day. With pride and a sense of accomplishment Truman declared, "Here is your courthouse, Jackson County, finished and finished within the budget set aside to build it." Such occasions lifted public morale in the bleak days of the Depression. This one was probably especially theraputic for Harry Truman.[21]

The biggest single construction project for which Truman was responsible was the $4 million Kansas City courthouse. Its cost was rivaled only by the projected new city hall, also budgeted at $4 million, and the new municipal auditorium at $4.5 million. These three projects alone surely stretched the capacity of Pendergast's Ready-Mixed Concrete to the limit; they also held out the promise of gain to real-estate speculators and sharp operators of all sorts. Truman had to fight off City Manager McElroy, who wanted to put the new city hall and county courthouse on one block in order to hold down the cost of land acquisition (no doubt with the intention of funneling the savings into friendly pockets).

The personal relations between the two men had changed enormously from the days when Truman had followed McElroy's lead on the county court. Truman felt contempt for the way McElroy posed as a tight-fisted guardian of the public treasury while facilitating the routine bid rigging that characterized the city's public business; perhaps most of all, he resented the private wealth that McElroy had acquired in the process. McElroy was offended by the increasing prominence and ostentatious independence of his former junior partner. The two men engaged in a semipublic squabble over site location. Determined to uphold the autonomy of the county government, Truman wanted his new courthouse to have dignity and aesthetic appeal; he also wanted to demonstrate that he long since had quit following instructions from H. L. McElroy.[22]

Truman decided to locate the courthouse on an entire block bounded by the south side of Twelfth between Oak and Locust streets. Friendly real-estate agents quietly acquired options on much of the property before the location was announced in December 1931. McElroy, constrained by a public pledge to build the city hall somewhere north of Twelfth Street, placed it directly to the north. He would at least be able to take consolation in his decision for a building that was considerably taller; he would place his office near the top in order that, some have alleged, he could look down on Truman.

William Scarritt, a real-estate developer who had invested heavily in options on an alternative site, filed a nuisance suit; this delayed land purchases until the end of May 1932, when a local judge dismissed it, and property owners on the Truman site paid Scarritt $35,000 not to file an appeal. As Truman saw it, the episode was yet another example of the hypocritical venality of Kansas City's respectables. Noting that Scarritt was "rated as a high class, ethical, Christian gentleman," he declared, "If there is any difference between this procedure and heaving a bomb through a dry cleaner's window to make him pay to a racket, I fail to see it."[23]

But how clean were Truman's hands? Seven years later, the *Star* briefly investigated allegations by realtor George Tracy. Tracy claimed that he, acting for the county, had accumulated options on the Truman site and that Truman, working through Fred Boxley and realtor Thomas Y. Willock, had forced him to kick back $16,000 of $24,000 in commissions. Tracy asserted that the funds had been used to meet payments on Martha Truman's Grandview mortgage. As Richard Miller has pointed out, the story has some plausibility. In December, Willock purchased the long-unsold three and a half lots in Truman's Subdivision. The Grandview mortgages already had been renegotiated shortly after Scarritt dropped his suit, although the principal was not reduced. The *Star* poked around, found nothing, and never used the story, although by then the paper was no longer friendly to Truman.[24]

Even before the bond vote, Truman had begun to explore contemporary public architecture. His trip south in February 1931 had been for the purpose of inspecting some of the region's newer courthouses. Although he doubtless cared about the practicalities of interior arrangements, he seems to have put a big investment of his ego into the aesthetics of exterior design. He wanted to leave behind a monument to his administration.

He estimated at the time that he traveled 2,400 miles looking at courthouses across the country.* From the start, he was most impressed by the new Caddo Parish Courthouse at Shreveport, which he considered an ideal blend of the traditional and the contemporary. He engaged its architect, Edward Neild.

The final design, based on Neild's concept but modified by a group of Kansas City architects, was impressive. A twenty-eight-story, two-tier building, it had bulk and dignity appropriate to its purpose. Bas-relief

---

*Years later, he recalled the trip as one that meandered from Shreveport and Houston to Denver, Milwaukee, and Brooklyn. The mileage expanded in his mind to 24,000. A quick glance at a map and an estimate of the time needed for the travel that Truman described leaves no doubt that he had merged in his mind a number of trips.

friezes at its main entrance illustrated the origins of civilization and justice. A marbled, Art Deco interior combined style and authority. New York sculptor Charles Keck, an artist renowned for his heroic equestrian works, did a life-size statue of Andrew Jackson on horseback to be placed in front of the main entrance.[25]

Construction moved rapidly. The initial low bid came from a Chicago firm. Yet perhaps because of pressures to employ local contractors or perhaps because of quality considerations, the work went to Swenson Construction of Kansas City. Swenson's bid was $98,000 higher; but the company, untainted by accusations of corruption, was probably the city's best. If, like most other local contractors, Swenson used Pendergast cement, Tom at least provided a quality product.[26] One episode, early on, demonstrated both Truman's determination to get the job done and the style of his progressivism. Tough Teamster organizers, trying to get recognition from a local trucking company, brought the project to a halt. To the acclaim of the local business community, Truman broke the strike, threatening to hire non-union labor if the regular unionized force did not return.[27]

The courthouse dedication in December 1934 was his last official act as a county judge. United States Supreme Court Justice Pierce Butler delivered the major address. Employing a Masonic rite reputed to be the same followed by King Solomon for his great temple, Truman sprinkled corn, wine, and oil over a plaster miniature of the new structure. He devoted it to virtue and ethical conduct, to honor and good government, to law and justice.[28] The ceremony ended a difficult second term on a note of triumph. Truman declared that the new structure would serve the county for fifty years. It remains scarcely less impressive or less functional after sixty years. The county was insolvent and facing yet more reductions in services and personnel, but Judge Truman could take solace in the understanding that this problem was no fault of his and that he had left behind an enduring monument.

V

The courthouse dedication honored a spirit of civic achievement and municipal progress that coexisted uneasily with Kansas City's graft, crime, and ballot tampering. During Truman's second term as presiding judge, the city won a reputation less for its growth and accomplishment than for the way in which its political structure fostered lawlessness and corruption so gross as to constitute a national concern.

As always, the evolution of the Democratic organization dominated local happenings. The machine's character had been altered powerfully by the emergence of John Lazia as boss of the northeastern Italian-American ward in 1928. Lazia was an archetypical example of a peculiarly dark variant of the American dream: the poor immigrant boy made good as gangster, the gangster as businessman and community godfather.[29] After a botched holdup and a shootout with police in 1918, Lazia, then a young school dropout, was convicted of highway robbery and sentenced to twelve years in the state penitentiary. He served for eight months and seven days before being issued a special pardon. James Aylward, responding to requests from political leaders in Lazia's ward, was among those recommending the action. Returning to Kansas City, Lazia declared that the "wild boy" had learned his lesson. He settled down to quieter and more lucrative pursuits.

By 1928, he had acquired the muscle to depose Mike Ross and make himself new Democratic boss of the northeastern ward. His method epitomized his new style. "Why not kidnap 'em?" he asked. "You don't hurt 'em and they don't hurt you. And they're easier to keep out of sight in good health than they are when their heads are bloody." He easily reached an understanding with Tom Pendergast, who was both a realist and (thanks to enormous gambling losses) in need of an ever-greater cash flow.

After a meeting with Al Capone, in which the Chicago gang lord recognized him as the chief of the Kansas City underworld, Lazia preached the virtues of nonviolence and declared his concern for the safety of the city's citizens. All the same, he owed his position to a small army of enforcers, including Charles "Pretty Boy" Floyd and other free-lance desperados. In turn, they used Kansas City as a sanctuary when the going got tough out in the law-abiding world. Lazia tried to build an image as a businessman and philanthropist. He had interests in a soft-drink company (whose product enjoyed a phenomenal market share in Kansas City), a finance company, a beer distributorship (after repeal of Prohibition), a nightclub, and a dog-racing track. When the Depression hit, he set up a breadline in his ward, distributed clothing to the poor, and handed out money freely.

Slight of build, handsome in the manner of a jockey or a matador, soft-spoken, a natty dresser, he mixed as much as he could with the local elite, spending his weekends at Lake Lotawanna, where he built an expensive second home and raced a powerful speedboat. Like Mike Ross, he moved his residence out of his ward to a posh midtown apartment on Armour Boulevard, but he kept in close touch and delighted in depicting himself as the benefactor of his people: "I've done a lot for the Italians in Kansas City. I've been fair with everybody. . . . I don't need a bodyguard. No one's mad at me."

In what had to be an object lesson for Truman, Lazia's rise paralleled the fall of his old friend and hero, John Miles. In 1929, Republican governor Henry Caulfield had made one last effort to clean up Kansas City by appointing Miles as chief of police. Miles, the iron-willed artillery major who had held the line in the Argonne, never had a chance. He was unable ever to establish firm administrative control of the police department. A fair number of his men were corrupt, and many of the rest were indifferent to crime. Both attitudes were understandable in a city where machine-dominated courts usually found reasons to release gamblers and bootleggers. City Manager McElroy, fearful that Miles might actually establish effective law enforcement, held up police paychecks for months before finally being overruled by the Missouri Supreme Court.

Personally inflexible, Miles made himself ridiculous by being excessively tenacious in the pursuit of insignificant targets. He ordered more than a hundred raids on the East Side Musicians Club, a "Negro boogie-woogie joint" that he believed to be a gambling den. He never obtained a conviction. Doc Fojo Wilson, the club's president, announced that on the hundredth raid he intended to serenade the chief with a special arrangement of "I Can't Give You Anything But Love, Baby." Miles was further embarrassed by having to fire his trusted deputy John Gibson—the same John Gibson who had guarded the ballot box at Fairmont crossing in 1922—when Gibson was involved in an auto accident under the influence of alcohol. Miles's attempts to get rid of crooked Republican cops drew the wrath of GOP politicians. In April 1930, he resigned under pressure, sadly ending an honorable career. He never had regular employment again.[30]

Miles had put a little heat on the gamblers, pimps, and liquor dealers, but he had never seriously threatened them. The demand for their services was too great to be blocked by law-enforcement officials. Kansas City was the metropolis between Chicago and Denver where it was easiest for any man with a wad of bills to find a game of chance, a willing girl, a shot of whiskey, and night-long jazz. Many local citizens reveled in the city's reputation. Others thought it good for business. The rest simply kept their distance.

Gambling was the king of the city's vices, operating openly and attracting five-figure wagers from the high and the mighty and five-buck bets from the lowly—all attracted by what local journalist William Reddig called the faith that "America offered endless opportunity to every man willing to put some dough on the name of a nag or the turn of a card." In July 1931, the *Kansas City Post* ran a series of reports documenting the proliferation of crap-shooting parlors throughout the downtown area and concluding: "Games doing business in Kansas City at this time do not even pretend to give the sucker an even break. . . . [T]he operators doctor their dice in such a manner as to make a loss to them a gravitational impossibility."[31]

Such was the atmosphere that existed with a Republican police force. Then, in March 1932, the Missouri Supreme Court removed the police department from state control. John Lazia now acquired a new role. Already head of organized crime in Kansas City, he became de facto chief of police.

VI

Tom Pendergast had reached the height of his power and notoriety. In May 1929, he moved into a mansion he had built on fashionable Ward

Parkway. A news story observed that among its adornments were three fireplaces "in the style of Louis XIV, Louis XV, and Louis XVI." At his daughter's lavish wedding, looking altogether out of place, he posed for the photographer in formal morning dress. He took up horse breeding, traveled on grand tours of Europe, and had an audience with the pope. By 1933, he was getting mostly favorable national attention. An *American Magazine* profile of him began, "In Tom Pendergast you may recognize the man who runs your town."[32]

Sixty years old in 1932, Pendergast resembled an aging football lineman who had gone to fat but might yet be able to take out anyone who crossed him. Often seen with a cigar in his mouth, he was the very caricature of the Irish political boss; but none questioned his mastery of his political territory. His admirers asserted that he exemplified the kind of steadiness and strength that the Depression-gripped city needed. The respectables who had allied with him on the city's ten-year plan saw him as a roughneck and a ballot-box stuffer, but also as an agent of progress; most of them respected the quality of his overpriced cement and believed him guilty of little more than the "honest graft" in which all machine politicians indulged.[33]

Beneath the appearance of unchallenged supremacy, however, was an unfolding tale of personal disintegration. Unlike many men of power, Pendergast was not a womanizer. Unlike the cliché Irishman, he had no fatal attraction to whiskey. But he had one weakness: horses and an uncontrollable impulse to bet on them. Initially small and affordable, it grew into a self-destructive obsession. Eventually, it would cost him his political soul.

At first, it all seemed a rather charming hobby. He began to raise thoroughbreds, one of which he ran in the Kentucky Derby. Employing a number of legal dodges, he opened up a racetrack in Platte County and frequented it daily. In the late winter, he might travel to New Orleans for the opening of the racing season. In May, accompanied by a trainload of friends as diverse as Cas Welch and clothing-store magnate Herbert Woolf, he went to Louisville for the Derby; in June, he journeyed to Saratoga.[34] Reports of his betting on these occasions were innocuous. Like most high rollers, he talked about his winnings and kept quiet about his losses. He could stand the expense of his stables and his trips. What wounded him was a pattern of almost daily losses to bookmakers; as the sums grew to five, even six, figures, he was increasingly desperate for income. His secret political life departed from his old pattern of honest graft as he financed his addiction more and more by outright theft, big-time bribery, and underworld payoffs.

A rapid physical deterioration accompanied his moral disintegration. In March 1933, he was hospitalized for "exhaustion," and then spent weeks at home suffering from "artificial sunlight burns" and "nervous indigestion." When he finally reemerged at 1908 Main, he had lost fifty pounds. Less than two months later, he left Kansas City for three months of relaxation in the East. The following year, he spent much of the summer in the Colorado mountains. More and more, Young Jim assumed the day-to-day duties of organization leadership.[35]

In the meantime, Kansas City had developed a reputation as a national crime center. With Jim Page kicked upstairs into a judgeship, the new prosecuting attorney was Waller W. Graves, Jr. Not only was Graves complacent about organized crime, but his connections with it became increasingly intimate. Arson, bombings, kidnappings, and warning shots fired through windows became a routine part of the daily news, giving the lie to the argument that officially tolerated vice victimized no one. In the summer of 1933, as Tom Pendergast rested and played the horses in New York, two sensational incidents graphically underscored the lawlessness that had overtaken the city.

The first occurred on June 17, 1933, at Union Station, where federal agents, local police, and an Oklahoma lawman were transferring bank robber Frank Nash from a train to an automobile that would return him to the federal prison at Leavenworth. Verne Miller, Nash's old partner, enlisted the notorious gunmen Pretty Boy Floyd and Adam Richetti in an attempt to free Nash. At 7:20 A.M., the trio, armed with submachine guns and an automatic pistol, hit the lawmen as they were hustling Nash into their car across from the station's main entrance. In the murderous gunfire that followed, Nash and four of his escorts were killed. Two other federal agents were wounded; Floyd, it was later discovered, took a bullet in the shoulder. Government agents later learned from an underworld turncoat that John Lazia had arranged medical treatment for Floyd and helped the three killers slip out of town. The incident propelled Lazia and the Pendergast machine toward the top of the feds' priority list.[36]

The other episode was in its way even more dramatic. On Saturday morning, August 12, Kansas Citians who got the *Times* read the following center front-page headline:

3 SLAIN ON ARMOUR
Sheriff's Car into Path of Men Driving Away After
Bootlegger Is "Put on Spot"
BASH KILLS TWO

Sheriff Tom Bash had happened onto the killing of Ferris Anthon, "Kansas City Tony" to his Chicago connections—an associate of the Joe Lusco gang and Cas Welch. The sheriff, cool and deadly with an automatic shotgun, killed two of John Lazia's lieutenants; a third, Charles "Gus" Gargotta, surrendered after taking several shots at him. Bash became an instant hero. The *Star*, never before one of his boosters, pictured him holding a submachine gun. The caption read "A Fighting and Straight-Shooting Sheriff Who Fears No Criminal."

Bash followed up by declaring war on crime and getting into his budget dispute with Truman. He also said he had one regret: he had not killed Gargotta when he had the chance. His apprehensions were well founded. Relying on perjured testimony from L. L. Claiborne, an investigating police detective who placed Gargotta's gun far from where he actually had dropped it, prosecutor Graves refused to press charges. Gargotta evaded a trial for years before copping a plea for a token sentence in the state penitentiary. Bash clearly had visions of higher office; instead, the Pendergast organization, unnerved by his interest in law enforcement, would drop him from the ticket in 1936.[37]

The machine's excesses grew with those of Kansas City's underworld; indeed, by 1934, the distinction between the two was hard to discern. Unhindered by external checks, exhibiting an unprecedented arrogance of power, the organization took vote fraud to spectacular lengths. Some precincts reported totals that exceeded the number of registered voters, who in some cases exceeded the recorded population of voting age. Election judges openly boasted of their malpractices. So immense an exercise in ballot theft was unnecessary: as later events would prove, Pendergast men could win honest elections in Kansas City. But ward captains received patronage in direct ratio to the votes they turned out, and the machine needed to counter the growing power of a suddenly large St. Louis Democratic vote in statewide elections. Perhaps most fundamentally, the ballot was debauched as never before simply because it was now possible.[38]

Even worse was the open rough stuff that reached a peak in the municipal elections of March 27, 1934. Facing a challenge from a well-organized Citizens-Fusion movement, the machine struck back brutally. Dozens of unlicensed cars filled with armed thugs cruised the streets, searching for targets. One pack of hoodlums pounced on a Citizens candidate for city council, his bodyguard, and a *Star* reporter, beating them all savagely. The reporter fled; the gunsels pursued him in a car chase to the front door of the *Star* building. Infighting within the machine was bloodier. A gang, identified as "Italian," invaded a polling place in a black precinct with the apparent aim of mauling one of the election judges; when another judge whipped out a revolver, they shot and killed him instead. Other thugs, involved in a bitter power struggle within the rabbit faction, set out to kill a deputy sheriff who was on the other side. After an exchange of gunfire, Deputy Lee Flacy and mobster Larry Cappo were mortally wounded; an innocent bystander was killed instantly. The police coped with the violence by arresting fourteen Citizens workers. A civic embarrassment, the election drew the attention of outsiders who rethought the assumption that Tom made the city work.[39]

He did keep the organization together, acting himself to solve the rift among the rabbits by giving a comfortable job to Shannon's disaffected lieutenant Pete Kelly (a veteran of the 1922 Fairmont Junction episode). Neither Shannon, happy enough as the reigning Jefferson authority in the United States House of Representatives, nor Cas Welch, aging rapidly and in poor health, was disposed to challenge him.

External pressures were more ominous. The *Star* began an antimachine crusade that far surpassed its previous perfunctory efforts. On the other side of the state, the St. Louis newspapers, led by the Pulitzer flagship *Post-Dispatch* and always quick to look askance at Kansas City, began to devote tons of newsprint to the sins of the Pendergast organization. If not visibly mightier than that of the sword, the power of the press could nevertheless reach into many places.

One of those places was Washington. President Franklin Roosevelt, mindful that Pendergast had been no help at the 1932 Democratic National Convention, would do him no favors. Missouri's one Democratic senator, Bennett Champ Clark, owed Tom nothing. In early 1933, when John Lazia was indicted for income tax evasion, Pendergast attempted to use his influence in Lazia's behalf, only to be brushed off. A year later, Lazia was convicted; Judge Merrill Otis, never a jurist to take lightly the misdeeds of gangsters and Democrats, sentenced him to a year in prison. As his attorneys appealed, Lazia faced his first hard time since 1918. The Kansas City underworld and the Pendergast organization had dozens of figures vulnerable to the same charges.[40]

In the spring of 1934, his victory in the local elections notwithstanding, Pendergast surely understood that he needed to reassert his mastery of state politics. To the surprise of many, his instrument would be Harry S. Truman.

John and Martha Truman on their wedding day, December 28, 1881. (Courtesy of the Harry S. Truman Library)

Harry, age six, with Vivian, age four, in 1890. (Courtesy of the Harry S. Truman Library)

Harry, probably at age eleven or twelve. (Courtesy of the Harry S. Truman Library)

Graduation day, the Independence High School class of 1901. Harry is fourth from left, back row. Bess smiles fetchingly at far right, second row. Charles Ross is at far left, front row. (Courtesy of the Harry S. Truman Library)

The young National Guardsman poses proudly in his dress uniform, 1905. (Courtesy of the Harry S. Truman Library)

No. 50873

AMERICAN
EXPEDITIONARY FORCES
Corps Expéditionnaires Américains
IDENTITY CARD
Carte d'Identité

Name Harry S Truman
Nom
Rank Captain 129 FA
Grade

Duty
Fonction

Signature
of Holder

Major, AGD USA
Adjutant General

Signature
du Titulaire Harry S Truman

Captain Truman in 1918. Photo taken from Truman's military identification. (Courtesy of the Harry S. Truman Library)

Wedding day, June 28, 1919. Captain and Mrs. Truman pose with Bess's bridesmaids, Captain Ted Marks (rear left), and Bess's oldest brother, Frank Wallace. (Courtesy of the Harry S. Truman Library)

Power and accomplishment. At the dedication of the county road system, October 12, 1932, Presiding Judge Truman poses with the associate judges who had served with him since 1927. From left: Thomas Bash, Robert Barr, Howard Vrooman, E. I. "Buck" Purcell, William Beeman. (Courtesy of the Harry S. Truman Library)

Happy days. Senator Truman at the 1936 Democratic National Convention with Tom Pendergast, James Aylward (whose refusal to run cleared the way for Truman's Senate race), Democratic National Chairman James A. Farley, and two delegates. (Courtesy of Bettmann Archive/Bettmann Newsphotos)

In 1934, the senatorial candidate poses with Margaret, age ten, and Bess, whose expression displays little enthusiasm for the endeavor on which her husband is about to embark. (Courtesy of the Kansas City Star)

Good friends, mutual benefactors. Robert Hannegan and Truman confer at the 1944 Democratic National Convention just days before Truman's nomination for vice president. (Courtesy of the St. Louis Post-Dispatch)

Senator Truman meets with Hugh Fulton (center) and an unidentified man. (Office of War Information, courtesy of the Harry S. Truman Library)

11

"I Have Come to the Place Where All Men Strive to Be": Questing for the Heights, 1931–1934

It was four o'clock in the morning on May 14, 1934, when Harry Truman began the last of his soul-searching diary memoranda on Pickwick Hotel stationery: "I have come to the place where all men strive to be at my age and I thought two weeks ago that retirement on a virtual pension in some minor county office was all that was in store for me." He reviewed his life and education, his attraction to the stories of great men, the lessons he had learned from history, his love for his wife, his war experience, his business failures, his triumphs on the county court. "And now I am a candidate for the United States Senate. If the Almighty God decides that I go there I am going to pray as King Solomon did, for wisdom to do the job."[1]

As he wrote by the light of his desk lamp in that small hotel room, Truman must have felt deeply mixed emotions. There was no reason for him to be away from home other than Bess's frosty coolness toward any position that would take her so far from her mother. Surely he was hurt that she had so little regard for his aspirations. Yet he was equally filled with excitement. He had longed for a higher office—the governorship, the United States Congress—that might actually allow him to make a difference on state or national issues. Unable to sleep, he once again resorted to pouring his emotions out on paper. His nervous energy was an early indicator of the intensity with which he would wage the hardest campaign of his life.

II

Located at the center of the nation, Missouri was a crossroads state, never more complex in its political geography and demographics than at the time Truman began his rise out of Jackson County.[2] Its politics stemmed largely from historical settlement patterns and deeply felt partisan allegiances traceable to the Civil War. The state had first been settled along the Missouri and Mississippi rivers by slave-owning border-state Southerners like Truman's own ancestors. The impact of that migration endured most pervasively in an area popularly known as Little Dixie, stretching from north of Hannibal on the Mississippi south to somewhere above St. Louis and then west with the Missouri River perhaps as far as Independence. The names of prominent towns—Macon, Marshall, Boonville, Richmond, Lexington—revealed the origins of the area's pioneers.[3]

An equally Democratic area was the northernmost extension of the cotton-growing Mississippi Delta, beginning below the river town of Cape Girardeau and extending down the Missouri bootheel. Much of it recently drained swampland, the bootheel lacked the long history of Little Dixie; but its agriculture and, even more fundamentally, its race relations dictated a traditional, southern, conservative Democratic loyalty. It could be of immense strategic significance in a tight election.

To the north and west of the bootheel, the Democrats were strong in the lead-belt mining counties and the eastern Ozarks plateau. Also leaning toward the Democrats were the rich farm counties of the Osage Plains to the south of Kansas City; the area still bore the imprint left by Kansas marauders in the Civil War. Farther south, the lead and zinc mines around the city of Joplin had generated some pro-Democratic labor-union strength. North of Kansas City, the Democrats controlled the Missouri River city of St. Joseph, the state's third largest city with a population of 80,000, and nearby counties. West of St. Joe and north of Little Dixie, northern Missouri was in many ways an economic and cultural extension of Iowa; more heavily settled by Yankees than the rest of the state, its counties were split between Democrats and Republicans.

Missouri possessed two reliable areas of Republican power. A German influx into and around St. Louis had been instrumental in holding Missouri for the Union in 1861. The "Rhineland" area, including St. Louis County and extending west from it, tended to be safe for the Republicans. German settlement along the Mississippi to the south as far as Cape Girardeau gave the Republicans a fair chance in several counties. Unionists from Appalachian Kentucky and Tennessee had peopled much of the southwestern Missouri hill country before secession and had been loyal Republicans ever since. Economically underdeveloped and culturally isolated, the western Ozarks counties were the state's most impoverished. Nonetheless, they would resist the blandishments of the New Deal and remain heavily Republican throughout the 1930s. Only in Springfield, Missouri's fourth largest city with a population of 57,000, did the Democrats have a significant organization and a shot at political power.[4]

As for the state's two big cities, Kansas City (population, 400,000) had been the center of Democratic strength in Missouri throughout the 1920s, and St. Louis (population, 821,000) had tended to be Republican since the early twentieth century, when Joseph W. Folk had broken the Democratic machine run by Ed Butler in a reform movement immortalized by Lincoln Steffens's *Shame of the Cities*. World War I had turned St. Louis's German vote against the Democrats; the prosperity of the 1920s seemed to entrench GOP rule. In 1926, however, local Democratic leader Harry Hawes had nearly carried the city in his victorious campaign for the United States Senate; the Depression would bring the Democrats back to power.[5]

According to the 1930 census, the urban and rural populations were almost equal in number, thereby creating a situation in which candidates had to vie not simply for the support of city machine leaders who delivered votes by the thousands, but also for the endorsements of small-town newspaper publishers and courthouse bosses. A statewide candidate had to speak at dozens of rural picnics and county fairs to farmers who might grow corn in the north or cotton in the southeast, at meetings of chambers of commerce in a like number of county-seat towns, and at labor gatherings and party rallies in the two big cities; he worked knots of idlers and daytime shoppers who might be collected on main streets from Braggadocio and Hayti in the distant southeast to Tarkio and Rockport in the far northwest.

III

As early as September 1929, the Henry County Association of Kansas City adopted a resolution sponsoring Judge Harry S. Truman for governor of Missouri. Shortly afterward, the newspapers of the Henry County seat, Clinton, published articles commending Truman. William Southern wrote an effusive editorial in the *Independence Examiner*.[6] To be a governor seemed more imposing in 1929 than it would a half-century later. The prestige, responsibility, and opportunity for public service doubtless outweighed in Truman's mind the colder truth that the governorship of Missouri, limited to one term, had been a political dead end for most of its holders.

His significant early promoters were Southern and Judge Robert Barr. Southern had numerous important contacts among Democratic party activists and Presbyterian church leaders around the state. Barr, at this point still a political friend, was a native of Clinton, well known and much admired in his hometown. He doubtless arranged the endorsement of the Henry County Association. He also planted an article in the *Clinton Democrat*; it declared that Truman was "a former Clintonian" and had attended high school there. (Two years later, Truman, indulging in Mark

Twain–style creative exaggeration, claimed the nearby hamlet of Urich as his birthplace when he was the featured speaker at its homecoming.)[7]

The movement, such as it was, remained quiescent for more than a year; it resurfaced after Truman won reelection as presiding judge in 1930. A new supporter was Peter T. O'Brien, a Sedalia attorney with strong Pendergast connections and ambitions for office in the American Legion. Other backers—Colonel Southern was probably the ringleader—drove over to neighboring Lafayette County and talked the editor of the *Odessa Democrat* into running an editorial endorsing Truman for governor. Probably written by Southern, it extolled the vitality of the Jackson County Democracy, praised Truman's road-building record, and cited his relative youth.[8]

The mention of Truman's age was doubtless meant to contrast him to his strongest potential opponent, Francis Wilson. A prominent attorney from nearby Platte City, Wilson did most of his business in Kansas City, where he maintained a residence. He long had been loosely allied with the Pendergast machine. With imposing outstate support, he had been the top vote getter on the Democratic ticket in the losing effort of 1928. A dignified, mustached little man who looked like the classical cartoon conception of John Q. Public, he nevertheless called himself "the red-headed peckerwood of the Platte." If the election returns are a reliable indicator, the sobriquet helped him out with the good old boys in rural Missouri.[9]

Truman had a politically attractive mix of rural and urban experience and backing. He was building up substantial credit with independent good government groups. He already had many contacts around the state among good-roads advocates, the Masons, the veterans' groups, the Reserve Officers Corps, and the National Guard. What he did not have was statewide political visibility and meaningful support outside his home county. He knew that he could not beat Wilson, but also that Wilson had a weak heart and might not run. A preliminary campaign would be a no-lose chance to make new friends and develop a state organization.[10]

Cousin Ralph, back in Kansas City as an insurance investigator and steadily rising in the National Guard, worked hard and successfully to drum up support among the Guard leadership. Harry also relied on him to develop alliances in Springfield and the surrounding area. Working with factional leader Dan Nee and an ambitious young attorney named James Ruffin, Ralph started a Truman-for-governor club with members from Springfield and several nearby counties. The people affiliated with it were more ambitious than powerful, but they amounted to an entering wedge.[11]

In the spring of 1931, Truman also explored what seemed a natural alliance with Bennett Clark, who had announced for the Senate. Clearly, the judge hoped—and it was not a bad idea—to work out a Kansas City–St. Louis alliance, while attaching himself to Clark's coattails outstate. Clark seems to have been receptive, perhaps encouraging. On the evening of April 21, 1931, a meeting of veterans, orchestrated by Ralph Truman, met in downtown Kansas City to form a Truman-for-governor, Clark-for-senator club. A *Kansas City Post* editorial, doubtless facilitated by city editor and Battery D veteran Eddie Meisberger, hailed the development.[12]

Truman and his backers planned to take his drive public, first with a talk to the American Legion at Clinton over Memorial Day weekend, and then, a week later, with an appearance at a Democratic rally in Houston, a county-seat town east of Springfield. On May 30, Tom Pendergast blindsided them with a declaration that he would support Charles Howell for the Senate and Wilson for governor, "provided Wilson makes the race." As long as Wilson did not make an announcement, Truman felt free to move ahead—but his alliance with Clark was shattered. The events of the next few weeks demonstrated the limits of his appeal as a candidate.[13]

The meeting in Clinton no doubt went over nicely; Truman would have been at his best speaking to a group of Legionnaires with whom he was very comfortable. The following weekend, he went to southwestern Missouri. Accompanied by Ralph and Pendergast operative R. Emmett O'Malley, he stopped at Monett to attend a gathering of American Legion officials and then talked with National Guard officers in Pierce City. At Springfield, he met Ralph's friend James Ruffin for the first time. On Saturday, June 8, they all drove to Houston, where he was the featured guest for a six-county Democratic rally. A gathering thunderstorm kept the crowd down to only 200 or 300.

Truman's speech, probably planned as an outright declaration of candidacy, was carefully hedged. His supporters would proclaim the event a great success; Wilson's friends would call it a bust. Given Truman's weak speaking skills and history of freezing on such occasions, the Wilson partisans were doubtless closer to the truth. As summarized in the *Examiner*, the talk was a graceful blend of pride and modesty in which Truman described his life as a farmer, soldier, and public servant and then talked of his successes in managing Jackson County. But as to whether he was a candidate for governor, he was almost incoherent:

> I have been in no sense a candidate, yet I would hardly be human nor fair to my friends if I did not say at this time that their loyalty and interest in my behalf creates a situation which, if developed, might find me ready at their command to enter the lists.[14]

His appearance—neat, dapper, citified—and his lackluster oratory surely failed to satisfy the longing for entertainment and partisan extravagance that constituted the main appeal of such occasions to hard-working Ozarkians. As he sat down to polite applause, the meeting's local sponsor, Bill Hiatt, introduced the next speaker with the remark "Now let's have some old-fashioned Democratic gospel." Will Zorn, a West Plains newspaper publisher and local Democratic party power, privately called the meeting "a frost" and commented that Truman was "not one around whom the gallus Democracy of this section would rally."[15]

Truman made several other talks outside Jackson County that summer. In June, on his way to the meeting of the National Conference on City Planning, he stopped in St. Louis to confer with Clark and some other local politicians. They encouraged him to stay in the race. Perhaps in a fighting mood, perhaps simply hoping that Wilson might not run, he wrote to Bess, "You may yet be the first lady of Missouri."[16] But he would have been guilty of gross political stupidity if he had allowed himself to be used by Clark and the St. Louis gang. As the summer ended, the Truman boom petered out.[17] Wilson meanwhile traveled around the state convincing the locals, and himself, that he was in fine health and holding Truman's private pledge of "wholehearted" support.[18]

However disappointing this tentative bid, Truman had not in any way hurt himself. Maybe he was unable to excite an audience, but he made a good impression as an earnest young businessman-politician. Careful not to alienate Wilson's supporters, he became a second choice for many of them. "Judge Truman is a mighty fine man and is qualified for most any office in the gift of the people of Missouri," Wilson himself wrote to a supporter. "I trust someday to see him elevated to other offices."[19]

As it was, Truman spent 1932 working hard for Wilson and Howell—when he could take time away from the financial woes of the county, road construction, and plans for the new courthouse. He struck his most effective blow in the Democratic primary, asserting that Russell Dearmont (who was running as an alternative to the Pendergast-tainted Wilson) had earlier explored with him the possibility of a Pendergast endorsement. Dearmont denied the charge, but it likely had some basis. Wilson won easily. Truman had both underscored his loyalty to the organization and established his potential as a statewide candidate.[20]

IV

Wilson's victory in the gubernatorial primary was only part of a triumph that made Tom Pendergast the preeminent political figure in Missouri. The Great Depression had submerged the urban–rural conflict that had split Missouri Democrats in the 1920s. The party took control of the legislature in 1930 and by 1932 was poised to sweep the statewide races. Because Republican governor Henry Caulfield and the Democratic legislature had deadlocked on congressional redistricting, all candidates for the Democratic nomination to the United States House of Representatives had to run at large. The result was a field of fifty-six aspirants for thirteen seats. One after another, the candidates came to Kansas City seeking Tom Pendergast's support. Tom, with his usual prudence, assented graciously to entrenched veterans like Clarence Cannon and Ralph Lozier, both from Little Dixie districts, and John Cochran of St. Louis. He gave formal endorsement to twenty-two candidates, Joe Shannon the only Kansas Citian among them, but told his lieutenants to concentrate on a more select list.

Four incumbents, running without the Pendergast seal of approval, lost. Most of the winners enjoyed Tom's favor; five were nonincumbents, who in each case got about half their votes from Jackson County. Jim Claiborne (St. Louis County), Dick Duncan (St. Joseph), Frank Lee (Joplin), Jim Ruffin (Springfield), and Rube Wood (Springfield) went off to Washington with a "made in Kansas City" label. Pendergast now had a political network that covered much of the western half of the state and extended into the environs of St. Louis. The St. Louis Democrats, by contrast, had not been nearly so effective in concentrating their votes or picking winners. Most working politicians read the results as evidence that Tom Pendergast delivered in a way that St. Louis could not and that he could swing statewide contests.*[21]

Pendergast was equally fortunate with the gubernatorial campaign, if not in the way he had expected. Francis Wilson, still denying rumors of ill-health and coasting to an easy victory, collapsed and died in mid-October. Wilson doubtless would have met Pendergast's needs, but probably would have maintained a degree of independence. The party's state committee, a body in which Pendergast had considerable leverage, filled the vacancy. It rejected Russell Dearmont and some strong Wilson supporters, including Major Lloyd Stark of Louisiana. Truman's name seems never to have been in play. The selection was Judge Guy B. Park, whose only qualification was that he had been Wilson's close friend and alleged personal choice as a successor. In 1932, qualifications were not much of a problem; any Democrat was sure to win. A decent man and in most respects a good governor, Park acceded to Pendergast's every wish over the next four years. Humorists would call the capitol building "Uncle Tom's cabin."[22]

Pendergast suffered one setback. His candidate for the Senate, Kansas City attorney Charles Howell, ran up against Bennett Champ Clark. A gifted orator with extensive statewide contacts, possessor of the greatest name in Missouri politics, Clark was formidable. A resident of St. Louis County, he easily united the St. Louis city Democratic factions behind him, exerted a powerful regional appeal throughout the eastern part of the state, and won the endorsement of the still-influential Jim Reed. In the primary, Clark devastated Howell and a third major opponent, Charles Hay. The result demonstrated once again that Pendergast, although he had delivered 101,000 votes to Howell, could not put over a candidate devoid of outstate appeal. But Howell's loss appeared considerably less important than Park's victory and the congressional outcomes.

---

*Pendergast's one loser, John Taylor, failed woefully at drawing outstate votes. He may also have been the victim of some creative counting. Four days after the election, 25 percent of the rural precincts were still out, the majority of them in Representative Milton Romjue's Little Dixie–northern Missouri district. On November 6, Romjue, still 13,000 votes away from the thirteenth position, claimed victory on his expectations of results that had not yet been reported. These boosted his final total from 117,000 to 185,000 and returned him to Congress. Taylor finished fourteenth (*PD*, November 6, 1932).

One statistic was ominous. In St. Louis, the Democratic gubernatorial primary vote, only 37,000 in 1928, had gone up to 90,000. A strong, unified St. Louis organization turning out a huge vote might enable the Democrats to win one statewide contest after another; it equally would pose a challenge to Tom Pendergast's continued supremacy. In April 1933, Democrats captured the St. Louis municipal government and its 7,000 patronage jobs. With the resources to build a formidable machine, new mayor Barney Dickmann and city party chairman Bob Hannegan were forces to be reckoned with. Moreover, St. Louis soon had a specific grievance to add to its traditional rivalry with Kansas City. The Pendergast-influenced legislature drew up new congressional districts that shamelessly overrepresented Jackson County while blatantly underrepresenting St. Louis. Those who looked ahead already could foresee a showdown in the 1934 senatorial primary.[23]

V

In October 1933, Truman got a second job, thanks in large measure to Senator Clark. Clark—with Missouri's thirteen-man Democratic delegation in the House behind him—demanded the ouster of Republican Martin Lewis as director of the Federal Reemployment Service in Missouri. Reluctantly, for Lewis was doing a solid, nonpartisan job, Secretary of Labor Frances Perkins complied.[24]

Asked to recommend a successor who could win Senator Clark's approval, Lewis submitted three names. Two were Republicans; the third was Harry Truman, one of Lewis's best Democratic friends. Labor Department official Walter Burr, a former University of Missouri professor close to Truman, shepherded the nomination to approval. It was apparently he who described Truman as "said not to be identified with any factional organization." Clark, probably less than ecstatic with the lack of choice given him, acquiesced. While not his man, Truman had either the active backing or the passive acceptance of most of the House delegation, as well as enthusiastic support from the Pendergast machine and Governor Guy Park in Missouri. Summoned to Washington, Truman sought assurances that Lewis was not being put out on the street. Satisfied on that score, he agreed to become the director of the Federal Reemployment Service in Missouri. The compensation was $1 a year plus expenses; the appointment allowed him to continue as presiding judge of Jackson County.[25]

Truman's new job was important, but less imposing than the title made it sound. He was responsible for establishing a system of local employment bureaus that would register the jobless, certify their eligibility for government relief, and attempt placements in either government work programs or private openings. The task was urgent because Washington was implementing the first of the New Deal's massive work-relief programs: the Civil Works Administration (CWA). Truman, operating with a small Jefferson City staff, soon established 109 bureaus. Over the next several months, he dealt with at least a dozen job-generating federal and state agencies, each with its own imperatives and procedures. He negotiated with labor unions, which at times wanted to control hiring processes. On Mississippi River projects, he worked with the Reemployment Service directors of other states.[26]

Truman insisted that he would administer the reemployment program nonpolitically. His patronage possibilities were relatively small. Certification for eligibility was largely a matter of following federal guidelines, which were occasionally abused by both applicants and certifiers. There were a half-dozen state-level positions to fill and a few jobs to distribute in every county; no doubt, they generally went to good Democrats, some of whom may have pestered their staff and relief recipients for petty kickbacks. Department of Labor careerists in Missouri grumbled about the political types Truman brought on board, but it seems unlikely that they seriously compromised the functioning of the service. The important spoils were in the hands of those officials who had the actual power to put people on relief jobs.[27]

The effort was chaotic from the start. Truman was appalled by the overlapping bureaucracies, the duplication of effort, the proliferation of forms, the requests for detailed reports, the complexity of regulations, the denials of what he considered valid expense claims, and, above all, the uncertainty of funding. "All I am trying to do is to keep the situation from becoming ridiculous," he declared in a letter of complaint to Washington. "People down near to the soil pretty soon will come to the conclusion that people on travel pay are using up more money than the man on the ground is getting for relief and employment."[28]

Whether out of disgust or simple exhaustion, he tried to resign in February 1934. Unable to devote more than a couple of days a week to the job, much of it on the road, he found himself relying heavily on Martin Lewis, when Lewis was available. Truman must have felt he was neglecting the desperate financial situation in Jackson County. Because his proposed successor, Neal Williams, was unacceptable to Washington, he stayed on until his senatorial candidacy mandated his resignation.[29]

The effort enhanced Truman's name recognition and enlarged his network of acquaintances around the state. It also brought him into working contact with a national administration for the first time in his life. Going to Washington twice for conferences, he met and instantly admired Franklin Roosevelt's impressario of relief, Harry Hopkins. Although only a peripheral part of massive relief assistance that provided over 100,000 jobs for Missourians during the winter of 1933/1934, the Reemployment Service had played a useful role. Truman could take pride in his work.[30]

VI

Yet he must have wondered just what the experience was preparing him for. It was valuable for a man who had designs on higher office, but indications are that Truman could not make up his mind whether that was what he wanted. The only upscale option for 1934 was Washington; presumably that meant a place in the House of Representatives. In early 1933, with the Democrats in full control of the state government, new House districts were being drawn up; Jackson County would get two of them. Joe Shannon, the only resident of the county on Capitol Hill, would retain one. Truman used such independent influence as he had in Jefferson City to make certain that the other would be as rural as possible; he was a natural for the product that emerged in the spring of 1933. His major opposition seems to have come from home; Bess continued to be against any move that would take her away from her mother.[31]

That left only some local alternative. None had the power and responsibility of the presiding judgeship, which Truman (in accordance with the informal two-term limitation for the office) would have to give up in 1934. The county collectorship entered his thoughts again. The Depression had reduced the income available from it, but he figured it would clear $10,000, more than half again his judge's salary and a substantial income. In April 1933, shortly after taking Bess and Margaret to Mississippi for their long stay there, he conferred with Tom Pendergast on county affairs. He also brought up his political future, making specific reference to both the House and the county collectorship. Pendergast amiably promised to support him for either office and told him to decide early in 1934.

Truman wrote to Bess of the encounter in a way that could have left little doubt about his personal preference:

> Congressman pays $7,500 and has to live in Washington six months a year, collector will pay $10,000 and stay at home; a political sky-high career ends with eight years collector. I have an opportunity to be a power in the nation as a Congressman. I don't have to make a decision until next year. Think about it. [32]

If Bess ever produced an answer, it was not the one that Truman wanted. Instead of coming to a quick decision and entrenching himself against all opponents, he engaged in not-so-private equivocation all through the year and into 1934. William Southern boomed him for Congress through the *Examiner*, but could not get a declaration. As late as March 2, 1934, the *Missouri Democrat* reported that Truman had not made up his mind, but seemed to be leaning toward the collectorship.[33]

At the beginning of May, Pendergast made up Truman's mind for him. He gave the congressional nod to Judge C. Jasper Bell, an aggressive young politician who had been a faithful supporter on the city council. Stunned and unhappy when he got the news in a personal meeting with the boss, Truman faced the prospect of political vegetation and $10,000 a year. He may even have told Pendergast in a moment of pique that he would quit and go back to the farm. To his astonishment and utter disbelief, Pendergast told him that if things worked out as expected, he would endorse Truman for the Senate instead. As Truman recalled it a year or two later, he told Pendergast not to kid him, only to have Tom reply in a somewhat offended tone, "Harry, I'm not kidding, and if the opportunity comes I'll be for you whether you like it or not."[34]

Only one serious contender had announced for the senatorial primary: Jacob L. (Tuck) Milligan, World War I hero, six-term congressman, and close friend of Bennett Clark. Milligan looked like a formidable candidate. Especially popular among veterans and the natural candidate of the rural–small town areas, he could count on Clark to work hard for him in St. Louis and around the state. His younger brother, Maurice, United States attorney for the western district of Missouri, was beginning a series of potentially embarrassing investigations of the Pendergast machine. If Tuck won, Bennett Clark could persuasively claim the leadership of the state Democratic party. The assertion would be all the more convincing in view of the elimination, thanks to redistricting, of two of the congressmen (Lee and Ruffin) for whom Pendergast had provided the margin of victory in the at-large election of 1932.

Against this threat, Tom Pendergast for months had done no more than talk with Jim Reed and Joe Shannon about making the race, while floating an occasional trial balloon for the hopeless Charles Howell. Reed, who hated Roosevelt's New Deal, dithered, said nothing, and finally declined. Shannon talked about the greatness of Thomas Jefferson and eventually decided he was happy enough in the House. He was also on the verge of a nervous collapse that would incapacitate him for more than a year. Howell concluded that his private law practice was preferable to another losing race. Pendergast then turned to Jim Aylward. Known and well connected in Democratic circles throughout the state, a capable speaker, a longtime preacher of party harmony, Aylward would have been a tough candidate, although he had never run for elective office. He too said no. Congressman Ralph Lozier of Carrolton was willing, but Pendergast apparently decided that he could not beat Milligan.

That left only Harry Truman.

Both the tight chronology and Truman's own memory suggest that Tom had decided that Harry Truman was his man for the Senate before he allowed Jasper Bell to file for the House. No other possibility, not even Aylward, had the same blend of rural and urban appeal along with so wide a network of contacts around the state. In order to unite the locals, Pendergast went through a quasi-public ritual of offering the Senate endorsement to Reed, Shannon, Howell, and Aylward. One by one, each declined, thereby assuaging the feelings of followers who might have been angry and uncooperative if they thought their man had not received proper deference from the boss. Less than two weeks after Bell had announced for the House, Pendergast was ready to call on Truman.

The presiding judge had embarked on a statewide speaking tour, campaigning for a $10 million state bond issue to finance the state's contribution to federal work projects. In town after town, he vindicated Pendergast's judgment by impressing local influentials as an earnest public servant. Typically, he set a hard pace. Accompanied by Martin Lewis and Neal Williams, he spoke in three or four places a day. Lewis, who frequently shared a hotel room with him, remembered that each evening after dinner, Truman would telephone Bess and Margaret, and then would take two books to bed with him—a serious piece of history or biography and a Western. He would read the heavier work until he began to feel drowsy, and then switch to the Western and fall asleep with it on his chest. The next morning, he would be up before six and ready to go.[35] At the little northern Ozarks town of Warsaw, he received a call to come to Sedalia at once to meet with Aylward and Jim Pendergast. It was May 8, his fiftieth birthday.

Young Jim and Aylward met every objection Truman raised. He would rather wait until 1936 and run for governor. No, the organization needed him for the Senate. He did not have the money. They would see that he got the funding he needed. He needed Aylward to run the campaign. Aylward agreed to do it, assured him that the state would vote for him over Milligan, and promised to line up friendly bosses in St. Louis. Truman assented to the race.[36]

At last, he had acted on a sense of his own destiny.

VII

Truman's announcement of his candidacy on Monday morning, May 14, 1934, quickly drew warm support from Jackson County. The *Kansas City Post* called him "an admirable candidate . . . a gentleman in the deeper sense of that term . . . a man of honor." The *Examiner* described him as a "country boy" and an honest administrator who would fit well into a legislative body "where thinkers are needed and where men of conscience stand for what they believe." Tom Pendergast stated his invaluable backing in a few sentences. Joe Shannon would barnstorm the state for him. It was equally important that with a few exceptions—Miles Bulger and Spencer Salisbury among them—Truman could count on the votes of most Jackson County Democrats who had no use for Pendergast.[37]

Reaction from St. Louis was very different. Editorial writers, motivated by the reputation of the Pendergast machine and by long-held feelings of cross-state rivalry, acted as if they had been confronted with the outrage of the year. A *Star-Times* editorial listed several great Missouri senators from the past who had "undoubtedly turned over in their graves." On May 21, Congressman John Cochran of St. Louis entered the race.[38] Among the city's opinion shapers, feeling ran so strong that even Truman's boyhood friend Charles Ross, now editorial-page editor of the *Post-Dispatch*, favored Cochran. Ross remembered Harry with some fondness and respect, but like the other eminences of the *Post-Dispatch*—Clark McAdams, O. K. Bovard, and publisher Joseph Pulitzer II—he was transfixed by the specter of Pendergastism. The paper made no outright primary endorsement, but was clear about the identity of its least favorite candidate.[39]

Cochran's entry transformed the race from a two-man contest (in which the St. Louis vote would have split) to a three-man* race. Truman had on his side not simply Kansas City, the Pendergast organization, and his own outstate network of supporters but also the backing of nearly the entire state administration and its several thousand patronage employees. Cochran had near-unanimous support in St. Louis; outstate, he at first had little more than the name recognition that brought him second place in the statewide 1932 congressional primary. Subsequently, an endorsement from William Hirth, the leader of the Missouri Farmers Association, would substantially increase his appeal in rural areas. As for Milligan, he now found himself a decided underdog who attempted—forlornly after Hirth's endorsement of Cochran—to depict himself as the only genuine candidate of rural Missouri.[40]

Truman had one other major asset: his energy. He wasted no time in beginning the first of three trips around the state, occasionally speaking to audiences but primarily lining up what support he could from the political influentials in smaller cities and many tiny villages. Hitting a half-dozen or more towns a day, he talked with county officials, newspaper editors, and anyone who resembled a Democratic activist.[41]

With Congress in session until mid-June, Truman had about a month with the field to himself. He was unusually appealing in one-on-one contacts. Richard L. Harkness, who covered Missouri politics for the United Press, wrote, "He is a personable, pleasant gentleman and has made friends rapidly, friends who will support him because they like him."[42] In some towns where he had friends and supporters, the results were gratifying. But often the quest was grinding and unsatisfactory, made up of hot, bumpy car rides, forgettable hamlets, meetings with strangers, and private doubts about pledges of support. His aide Fred Canfil was usually along, doing the driving when Truman did not feel like it; Rufus Burrus may have taken his place on some trips. Truman kept a pocket diary that detailed his mileage and contacts; he recorded a typical crowded day on a cramped page:

---

*There was a fourth candidate, James Longstreet Cleveland, an amiable and idealistic eccentric who preached the brotherhood of man and world democracy. He had grown up in a St. Louis orphanage; a few Austrian monarchists believed him to be the son of Crown Prince Rudolf, who had committed suicide with his lover, Baroness Marie Vetsera, at Mayerling. Cleveland himself claimed neither royal ancestry nor the Austro-Hungarian crown. His only political asset, the *Missouri Democrat* remarked, was a good Democratic name. As the *St. Louis Post-Dispatch* put it, reporting his death a few years later, "his political addresses always were free from personalities or local issues, his expenses negligible, his votes few" (*MD*, July 6, 1934; *PD*, July 3, 1938).

Tuesday, June 5, 1934
156th day—209 days to come

mi

2705   Indp. 7:15 A.M.

2780   Clinton 9:00 A.M. to 11:00 A.M.
Saw Poague, Floyd Sperry, Adair, and whole town. Grand reception.

2806   Osceola 11:45 A.M. to 12:30
Saw Pence, Cooper & Crooks, all OK

2819   Collins 12:45–1:30 Hotel man and his 84 year old friend OK

2827   Humansville 1:50 to 2:05
Mr. Jones & Mr. Reynolds OK

2840   Fair Play 2:45 Dr. Jones (Milligan)
No Democrats in town.

2849   Bolivar 3:00 to 4:00 P.M.
Stufflebaum—newspaperman for Milligan. Not a lot of Dems. Coon OK cleaner
& presser Legionnaire. Dr. Thomasson OK Vet for Co. Clerk. Mr. Moffitt OK
Stewart P.M. OK
Dr. Thomasson former county clerk & candidate again with Mr. Moffitt orga-
nizing a club for me. Say we can carry county. Vets not for Milligan.

2938   Carthage 6:00 P.M. Good meeting.

2947   at Carterville with all candidates[43]

Truman pushed Governor Park, not known for his strong will, to
pull every lever at his command. Writing to the governor from Joplin on
June 6, Truman revealed a bit of his own drive:

> I'm talking to some of my young Democratic friends down here; they tell
> me that some of the State employees are saying that I am a *nice* fellow and
> that they are for me but they think Cochran will win.
>   I'd rather be called any sort of a —— —— than to be damned with
> faint praise.
>   Thought perhaps you might be able to get them to say they think I
> can win and that I'll do the job when I do.[44]

Gubernatorial support, reinforced by Truman's local network, could
be formidable. On July 12, the *St. Clair County Democrat* of Osceola,
which had endorsed Milligan, printed a front-page editorial, "We Switch
to Truman." Appearing in the county's leading weekly, the new endorsement was a real triumph. Truman backer Harry Pence sent a copy of the
editorial to Governor Park, remarking of its author, "The old boy came
across in good shape when we put the pressure on him."[45] (Milligan would
nonetheless carry St. Clair County in the election.)

A Truman supporter prodded the governor to lean on the superintendent of the Federal Soldiers Home at St. James: "If he is for Truman,
and can control the Soldiers home vote, it will mean at least 400 votes."
After the primary, Truman's opponents charged that applicants for federal relief in Independence had been forced to sign Truman pledge cards.[46]

State workers drove from town to town passing out Truman literature; those who bucked the orders from above clearly jeopardized their jobs. Park nonetheless declared that Truman's opponents were lying when they asserted that the state government was threatening to discharge employees who supported Milligan or Cochran. "Every loyal friend of the Administration should resent this attack," he wrote to Orestes Mitchell, head of the state-appointed St. Joseph Police Commission. Mitchell replied with good-humored cynicism, "Rest assured that we will do our part here to resent this attack. The Grain Department and Police Department are thoroughly organized and there are few who have not fallen in line."[47]

Truman was not the only person to gain from heavy-handed political influence. St. Louis leaders had every city employee working for Cochran, including the entire police force; they controlled a couple of state agencies that used their personnel in the same fashion. Only Milligan was left out in the cold, although his opponents charged (probably spuriously) that Bennett Clark was shaking down federal appointees for campaign contributions and leaning heavily on them to aim benefits at Milligan's backers.[48]

After the July 4 holiday, with Congress adjourned and the election a month away, the campaign shifted into a demanding, intensive final phase. The ordeal was exhausting as the candidates and their supporters crisscrossed a drought-plagued state under a blazing sun in automobiles that must have seemed like ovens. Years later, Jim Aylward remembered, "The corn was burning up in the fields. . . . [Y]ou could even smell it." At times, the candidates drew large crowds in unlikely places. In the little town of Cameron, for example, Father M. F. Wogan, a shrewd entrepreneur, had transformed an annual church picnic into a gathering that attracted thousands who came to eat fried chicken, drink pop, and listen to speeches by the political leaders of the state (all of whom paid Father Wogan a fee for the privilege). More often, audiences numbered in the dozens or hundreds, assembled outdoors in shady areas on afternoons when the temperature was measured in triple digits, or in local parks after sundown.[49]

Not about to cede outstate to Milligan, Truman argued that he was the best friend of the farmer in the field. John Hulston recalls his father introducing Truman to a picnic crowd at Everton: "You folks won't get a chance very often to vote for a farmer for United States Senator. . . . He's our kind of people. Why, his hands fit cultivator handles just like owls' claws fit a limb." Someone, Hulston remembers, probably planted in the audience, threw his hat into the air with a whoop. Truman owned the crowd when he came forward.[50]

Nonetheless, he remained at best a mediocre speaker. Unable to hold the interest of a crowd for long, he kept his talks brief. At Father Wogan's picnic, for example, he observed a rule of avoiding politics on Sundays, uttered a few pleasantries, and commended the Catholic church for its efforts to clean up motion pictures. Occasionally, his speeches were shorter than those of long-winded introducers. He was fortunate to be campaigning in a state and a time when "retail" face-to-face politics could compensate for a poor platform presence.[51]

Through the last weeks of the campaign, he labored under a special handicap. Between Rolla and Jefferson City on July 6, his Plymouth collided with a car that cut in front of it. His head hit the windshield; two ribs were broken when they impacted the gearshift. A nearby garage straightened out the fender; presumably a local physician bound the damaged ribs. Truman proceeded to Jefferson City; making no public announcement of the accident, he delivered his talk with throbbing head and aching side. Then he went on to Columbia for his official campaign kickoff address. For the next four weeks, he continued his planned itinerary with his ribs taped—yet another example of the determination that had characterized every major effort of his life.[52]

VIII

Truman was running for the Senate at a time of great change. Franklin D. Roosevelt and his New Deal had become an overwhelming national presence—fighting the Great Depression by organizing agriculture, business, and labor through the Agricultural Adjustment Administration and the National Recovery Administration and by bringing the federal government to the relief of ordinary citizens by way of vast jobs programs, mortgage bailouts, and direct welfare payments. All the Democratic candidates lunged for his coattails, thus displaying the way in which the Depression and the New Deal had almost overnight pulled the Missouri Democracy away from its traditional literal-minded Jeffersonianism. Truman praised Roosevelt's "efforts to have the advances of social and industrial processes spell something for the great masses." One of his campaign slogans was "A New Deal for Missouri."[53]

Hard policy disputes among the candidates were minor. In perhaps the most significant one, Truman and Milligan advocated quick payment of the World War I veterans' bonus; Cochran did not. In general, Truman tried to establish himself as the most "populistic" candidate. Free of a Washington record, he capitalized on the merest hint that Cochran or Milligan was against any federal benefits and routinely asserted that they had not gotten the state its fair share of federal aid. The Senate, he argued, needed a man who, uncorrupted by residence in the District of Columbia, had been in daily contact with the political pulse of Missourians.[54] With little debate on the issues, the contest became a test of personalities and nonideological alliances—and eventually a test of namecalling abilities.

Truman's strongest card—the support of Tom Pendergast—was also his biggest problem. Both his opponents depicted him as the ineffectual tool of a corrupt urban boss bent on total domination of Missouri politics. In a fashion that foreshadowed his later career, he found himself transformed from an individual with a record of achievement and independence to a symbol of Pendergastism. The image was probably decisive in William Hirth's influential endorsement of Cochran. Truman responded by declaring his pride in being backed by the Kansas City organization and asserted (accurately in Cochran's case, questionably in Milligan's) that both had solicited Pendergast's support two years earlier.[55]

Events in Kansas City ran against him. In July, John Lazia's reign over the local underworld came to a sudden end. Riding high despite his conviction for tax evasion, Lazia still frequented Twelfth Street, hanging out in restaurants and drinking places, invariably accompanied by his driver and bodyguard, Charley (The Wop) Carollo. In the Italian neighborhoods on the North Side, he was a beloved godfather who had opened up a breadline during the worst days of the Depression and given assistance freely to the poor. In the evenings, he often made the rounds of local nightclubs with his young wife, Marie.

On the night of July 9, Lazia, Marie, and Carollo looked in on several downtown establishments. Shortly past midnight, Carollo drove the couple up to the front door of their Armour Boulevard apartment building. As Lazia stepped out of the car, a hail of machine-gun bullets and shotgun pellets mowed him down; his last order to Carollo was to get Marie to safety. He clung to life in the hospital for eleven hours, attended by a team of physicians headed by D. M. Nigro, a longtime machine lieutenant. As Lazia slid toward death, reporters overheard Nigro telephoning Tom Pendergast: "He is very low, Boss. He has spoken of you, Mr. Pendergast, and says he loves you as always."

Lazia's funeral, held on Friday, July 13, was one of the largest in Kansas City history. Thousands lined the city's grandest boulevard, The Paseo, for a glimpse of his cortege, and more thousands congregated in front of the small Catholic church where his funeral mass was celebrated. Among the mourners inside were Tom Pendergast, City Manager H. L. McElroy, Police Chief Otto Higgins, and Prosecutor Waller W. Graves, Jr. Truman, although scheduled to speak in the Kansas City vicinity that day, did not attend. The senatorial candidate surely was less impressed by the widespread mourning on the North Side than by the way Lazia's sensational death reminded the entire state of Kansas City gangsterism. Nor could he have been gratified by improbable rumors that Tom Pendergast had ordered the rubout to prevent Lazia, in a bid to avoid prison, from squealing to the feds.[56]

It did not help that a couple of weeks later a federal jury convicted Kansas City detective L. L. Claiborne of perjury, committed in an effort to clear Charles Gargotta of charges of attempted murder. The trial was the latest repercussion from Tom Bash's violent confrontation with the hit squad that had rubbed out Ferris Anthon.

A number of the newspapers that carried the story of the Claiborne conviction also featured another item. The receivers of the Security State Bank of Kansas City had highlighted the candidate's financial problems by obtaining a garnishment order against Independence banks in which

he might have deposited money. Such publicity had never hurt Truman
in past campaigns. During the Depression, it probably gained him the
sympathy of many ordinary people with similar problems, and it seemed
to demonstrate that he had not profited from Kansas City's rampant
corruption.[57]

In this regard, Truman could also capitalize on the valuable support
of editor Bill Southern, whom many Missourians knew as a great Bible
teacher. Introducing Truman to a convention of preachers and Sunday-
school instructors in Maryville, he told them, "Here is my boy. I vouch
for him, and don't pay any attention to what others may say about him."
The endorsement probably helped a lot in the state's smaller cities and
towns.[58]

Remarkably, given his subsequent career, Truman was widely perceived as the mildest-mannered and most gentlemanly of the candidates,
perhaps a bit of a wimp. All the same, he demonstrated that he could
give as good as he got. To nominate Milligan, he charged, would be to
give Bennett Clark an automatic second vote in the Senate; to nominate
Cochran would be to give St. Louis two votes and thereby ensure that
the interests of the rest of the state, including "good old country Missouri," would be ignored.[59]

Truman may have consciously goaded Bennett Clark into wild
swings, a strategy often used by small, nimble prize fighters against bigger, clumsier men. Truman made credible the charge that Milligan was
Clark's puppet while neutralizing the claim that Tom Pendergast was
using Truman in an attempt to dominate the state. Clark's massive ego
got in the way of his judgment. Instead of quietly lining up support for
Milligan in a way that would not overshadow his candidate, he made angry
speeches. His oratory, bombastic and rich with sarcasm, was the most
quotable in the campaign; by mid-July, it appeared that he, rather than
Milligan, was running against Truman.

The level of the Truman–Clark exchanges may have been entertaining, but it was seldom instructive:

CLARK: Harry Truman fears a boss in Missouri—God save the mark. . . .
    Why bless Harry's good, kind heart—no one has ever accused him of being
a boss or wanting to be a boss and nobody will ever suspect him of trying to dictate to anybody in his own right as long as a certain eminent citizen of Jackson
County remains alive and possesses his health and faculties.[60]

TRUMAN: His language . . . is in keeping with the hydrophobic stage he has reached
in realizing that he is a load on his sponsored candidate, Jacob L. Milligan.[61]

CLARK: My friend Harry must be affected by the heat because he is neither
vicious enough nor inventive enough to tell as many lies as he is telling in his
campaigning across the state.[62]

Other events that summer probably drew more interest. Dizzy Dean
was leading the St. Louis Cardinals toward a National League pennant;
he won his twentieth game on election day. In Chicago, FBI men gunned

down John Dillinger; in Texas, lawmen killed Bonnie Parker and Clyde Barrow. Most Missourians probably took a greater interest in the doings of the Gashouse Gang and the demise of the desperadoes than in the senatorial primary. A little angry rhetoric may have been necessary to attract their attention.

Goings-on abroad were far more ominous. In Germany, Chancellor Adolf Hitler slaughtered his rivals within the Nazi party in the "night of the long knives." Soon afterward, President Paul von Hindenberg died, and Hitler made himself an absolute dictator. In Austria, Nazi insurgents killed Chancellor Engelbert Dolfuss in a failed putsch. Remarkably, none of the candidates commented on the events in Europe; in fact, if any of them uttered a word about foreign policy, it is lost to history. They probably reflected the attitude of most of their constituents.

Shrewd observers discerned that behind all the noise, Truman was holding on to his lead and probably adding to his support. His campaign, expertly run by Aylward, never missed a bet. Using mailing lists probably obtained from state agencies, it sent form letters to veterans publicizing Truman's stand on the bonus and to licensed beauticians, asking them to use their influence with female customers. The Jackson County road overseers association sent out an endorsement of Truman to overseers all over the state. The Kansas City Building Trades Council, unflustered by the way Judge Truman had broken the Teamsters organizing drive, affirmed that he was a friend of labor. Aylward sent out a mailing to elderly persons reminding them that Truman had spoken out in behalf of a national old-age pension system. Truman got the support of numerous influential small-town newspaper editors, several of whom relied on state patronage and printing assignments.[63]

In the end, the result hung on two separate contests: one between the Kansas City and St. Louis politicians to see who could create the most votes, and the other among the three candidates outstate. Kansas City would win the first; Truman, the second.

As recently as 1932, outside observers had written of Tom Pendergast's ability to run up pluralities of as much as 50,000 for his favorites; by 1934, the number that generally appeared in print was 100,000. St. Louis, given its recent return to Democratic ranks and relative lack of political cohesion, was a much less certain proposition. Yet its Democratic captains were united behind Cochran, and it seemed probable that many St. Louis Republicans, faced with an unexciting primary, would request Democratic ballots and vote for him. A week before the election, the local Democratic chairman was predicting that Cochran would come out of the city of St. Louis with 125,000 votes, a total more than sufficient to offset Truman's expected Kansas City turnout and far above the 66,000 that St. Louis had given Clark two years earlier.[64]

Tom Pendergast planned accordingly. On election day, the machine was primed as never before in its history. One Kansas Citian recalled a family story to the effect that Truman visited a polling place to discover that the voting line was actually a circle in which people signed in under one name, cast their ballots for the organization slate, got back in line, signed in under another name, and voted again in a political version of perpetual motion that physics textbooks had not yet discovered.[65]

The final combined Kansas City–rural Jackson County vote was Truman, 137,529; Milligan, 8,406; Cochran, 1,525. In St. Louis, meanwhile, Cochran fell slightly short of his backers' predictions. The combined city and county of St. Louis vote was Cochran, 121,048; Milligan, 10,807; Truman 4,614. To cynics ever since, these contrasting figures have presented remarkable evidence of the high degree of refinement to which the rival machines had perfected the art of creative balloting. Still, it is equally realistic to observe that the percentages had some connection to the respect and esteem that Truman and Cochran had achieved in their home bailiwicks. In the most scrupulously honest election, each would have taken a huge percentage of the vote in his home territory; in each case, however, the totals would have been considerably smaller, thereby increasing the importance of the outstate results.

Outstate, Truman's own contacts and gubernatorial backing paid off. The totals were Truman, 134,707; Milligan, 128,401; Cochran, 113,532. Of the 112 outstate counties, Truman won 39; Cochran, 37; and Milligan, 36.[66] Truman gained perhaps as many as 25,000 votes from the support of Governor Park. Cochran had enjoyed the backing of the state's only significant farm leader. Milligan had been both the only indisputable representative of the countryside and the choice of the enormously popular Senator Clark. It would be facile to argue that all these considerations canceled one another out, but it seems fair to observe that William Hirth and Bennett Clark were formidable players on the state political scene. Beginning the campaign as a relative unknown outside of Jackson and adjoining counties, Truman had emerged as a candidate with a fair amount of personal appeal. Observers who saw only his massive machine support, his continued uneasiness when he spoke before large crowds, and his diffident bearing underrated his achievement.

IX

Win or lose, Truman had been prepared to make up with his Democratic opponents after the election, whatever the accusations of corruption and impropriety. But he had a special problem with Cousin Ralph. Ralph would have led the charge for Harry anywhere, anytime, had he not already been committed to Milligan. Harry obligingly enough had agreed that Ralph could not go back on his word, and Ralph had promised to refrain from personal attacks. The understanding was friendly, familial, and businesslike.

Unfortunately, neither self-restraint nor understatement had ever been among Ralph's virtues. If he kept the letter of his promise, he did not keep the spirit of it. He launched charges of corruption at the Truman campaign and all but made Harry an unindicted co-conspirator. He virtually accused Aylward of vote buying with an enormous slush fund. He fingered Truman's aide, Canfil, as the bag man who delivered payoffs. Infuriated, Harry reacted characteristically. A day or two after the election, Ralph telephoned to offer congratulations and support in the general election. The conversation was easygoing and good hearted. Then, most likely as soon as he hung up, Harry sat down and wrote Ralph a venomous letter. Ralph's second wife, Olive, dissuaded him from replying in kind. The cousins did not speak to each other for the next two years.[67]

Otherwise, postprimary recriminations were relatively few and mostly predictable. Many people in St. Louis, the *Post-Dispatch* editorial writers among them, continued to depict Truman as an obscure nobody put over by an alliance of Missouri's forces of political darkness. Most Kansas Citians, including the *Star*'s editorialists, thought him a worthy victor.[68] Among the politicians, the reaction was usually what one would expect from seasoned professionals. That fall, Bennett Clark spoke for Truman, ostentatiously visited Tom Pendergast, and consistently refused to assume the leadership of an anti-Pendergast faction within the Democratic party.[69] Cochran quickly came aboard also. The nominee for his House seat promptly withdrew, thereby allowing him to reclaim his old place on the ticket. He and Truman subsequently developed a cordial relationship. Truman traveled to St. Louis, spoke to a local party banquet, praised the city's leading Democrats, and asked for their backing. The *Post-Dispatch* called the occasion "a political love feast."[70]

Tuck and Maurice Milligan were less forgiving. Tuck gave Truman no more than perfunctory support during the campaign. Unlike Cochran, he had no prearranged mechanism for returning to the House. With Truman victorious, Maurice surely knew that his own position as United States attorney for the western district of Missouri was in danger. The Milligans persisted in their hostility to Tom Pendergast, Harry Truman, and everyone associated with the Kansas City machine, despite "get-along, go-along" advice from their political patron Bennett Clark.[71]

Truman established the tone of his fall campaign with a speech to the state Democratic convention on September 11. Calling himself a Roosevelt man first, last, and always, he advocated "unemployment insurance, old age pensions and further security in home ownership," aid to the farmer, reciprocal trade, payment of the World War I bonus, and generous veterans' benefits. He depicted the Republican establishment as a group of dishonest business tycoons heedless of human suffering and bent on resuming their exploitation of the masses. Senator Roscoe Patterson, Truman asserted about his Republican opponent, had been their faithful representative: "He is a rugged individualist, imbued with the cruelties of jungle strife. I am for the individual, the common run of mankind."[72]

Beginning on October 1 and running through election day, Truman barnstormed the state with an intensity hard to fathom when one considers the certainty of his victory. However hyperbolic his rhetoric might seem in a calmer, more prosperous atmosphere, he correctly perceived that there was a large audience for it. Moreover, it was a faithful expression of his personal point of view about the Republican elite, perfectly consistent with the deep-seated partisanship he had inherited from his parents and with the few comments he had made on matters of national concern during the 1920s. One senses that he was most comfortable speaking to rural audiences, to whom he mouthed Bryanite agrarian fundamentalism. His appeals to labor seem more general and less deeply felt. His conspiratorial explanations of the Depression implied that the economic crisis was little more than the creation of evil men. On occasion, he muted his partisanship enough to appeal for the votes of progressive Republicans who took their cues from a Robert La Follette or a George Norris.[73]

Patterson had little to offer in response other than charges that Truman was Tom Pendergast's tool in a master plan to dominate the state, bring big-time crime and vice to St. Louis, and destroy independent Democratic factions.[74] Truman doubtless resented such attacks on his integrity and may have begun to realize that he would never escape the accusation that he was soft on corruption.

He easily defeated Patterson, 787,110 to 524,954, carrying all parts of the state except the Republican southwest and the Rhineland area. He won Kansas City and Jackson County by almost 143,000 votes, St. Louis and St. Louis County by 48,600, outstate by 120,000. Patterson asserted bitterly that he had been the victim of ghost votes in Kansas City, but Truman had won every ward, machine controlled or not. The organization boys had simply added padding to what would have an impressive victory anyway. (What padding it was! If Kansas City figures were to be taken at face value, over 99 percent of the adult population had registered to vote. The comparable figure in St. Louis was 72 percent.)[75]

Truman's energetic campaigning may have helped, but he was little more than the beneficiary of a situation he did not make. Most Missourians surely had been more excited by the Cardinals' victory over the Tigers in the World Series. For thoughtful, independent-minded individuals, the campaign was a dreary affair, made all the drabber by the predictability of its outcome. The state's two leading papers, the *Kansas City Star* and the *St. Louis Post-Dispatch*, refused to endorse either candidate, although the *Star* extended cordial congratulations to Truman. As later in his career, he understood the limits of his appeal. Telling a reporter of his plans to look for living accommodations in Washington, he said with a smile, "It'll be safer to rent than to buy, of course."[76]

The eight weeks between Truman's victory and his swearing in as junior senator from Missouri were busy. He managed to take off a few days in Nebraska with his old friend Ed McKim, but most of his time was devoted to dealing with the county budget crisis and planning the move to Washington. On November 30, he and Jim Aylward left for twelve days there. They met briefly with President Roosevelt, had a longer visit with Democratic National Chairman and Postmaster-General Jim Farley, and saw assorted agency officials (including Reconstruction Finance Corporation executives from whom they vainly sought a loan for Jackson County). Truman attended the Gridiron Club dinner as the guest of Duke Shoop, the *Star*'s Washington correspondent, and looked up William Helm, the *Journal-Post*'s man in Washington.

He seemed to find the capital daunting. Perhaps without fully meaning it, he indulged in excessive self-deprecation. Stressing his feelings of unpreparedness, he said he would try to finish law school at Georgetown. Despairing of finding an affordable and decent place to live, he remarked, "I am undoubtedly the poorest Senator financially in Washington." Back in Kansas City, he spoke to the Elks Club: "I am just a farmer boy. . . . I won't be a James A. Reed or a Thomas Hart Benton. But I'll do the best I can. . . . All this precedence and other hooey accorded a Senator isn't very good for the Republic. . . . [A]ssociation with dressed-up diplomats has turned the heads of more than one Senator." The *New York Times* picked up the speech, misnamed him "Henry," and lampooned him as a rube from Pendergast land.[77]

Over the Christmas season, Truman passed along the presiding judgeship to Buck Purcell. The family packed for Washington, much to the dismay of Madge Wallace, who remained emotionally dependent on Bess. On December 15, 400 Independence residents jammed the basement of the First Christian Church for a farewell banquet. William Southern presided; Mrs. W. L. C. Palmer, who had worked in every one of Truman's campaigns, recalled his school days; E. M. Stayton talked of their experiences in war and highway building; Mary Chiles, representing the DAR, praised Truman's work with the Old Trails monuments; many other local dignitaries said their pieces. On December 28, the day after the dedication of the new Kansas City courthouse, Harry, Bess, and Margaret left for St. Louis, where they would catch a train to Washington. On December 31, 1934, they arrived at the capital, on the eve of a new year and a new life.[78]

12

"Wisdom to Serve the People Acceptably": Life in the Senate, 1935–1940

"I was timid as a country boy arriving on the campus of a great university for his first year," Truman recalled of his early days in Washington. He took his new seat in the Seventy-fourth Congress with a silent prayer "for wisdom to serve the people acceptably." The years ahead were to be stressfully busy and personally difficult, but Truman found that the Senate offered everything he craved—a sense of public service, an easygoing male camaraderie, recognition based on merit, and a feeling of belonging. These far outweighed the burdens of his still precarious finances, a mounting political insecurity, and strains in his family life.[1]

The Trumans rented a four-room apartment at 3106 Connecticut Avenue for an astronomical $150 a month. It was the first of a series of six-month leases at several addresses in the Northwest section of the city. The senator had to borrow money to buy some furniture and rent a piano; years later, speaking to a group of bankers, he thanked Washington's Hamilton Bank for its willingness "to float a little slow paper for me."[2]

He and Bess had come to Washington with the assumption that they actually would live there only from the beginning of a congressional session in January until adjournment in June. Normally, the expectation would have been reasonable. During a period of near-constant national and international emergency, it was usually unobtainable. His first year established the general pattern of their lives. As soon as Margaret's school was out in June, the family packed up, vacated the apartment, and drove back to Independence, where mother and daughter passed the latter half of the year. In no other way could Bess balance her obligations to her mother against those to her husband and daughter. Yet Congress was mired in debate over several controversial pieces of New Deal legislation. Harry returned to Washington, took up residence in a hotel room, and stayed until the session concluded near the end of August. From 1937 on, he had to return to the capital in the fall for special sessions and committee work. It was testimony to his ambition and growing devotion to the Senate that he persevered through these lonely, barely tolerable periods.

II

The Senate in which Harry Truman took his seat was caught up in a tug of war between continuity and change. It remained the world's most exclusive club, a ninety-six-person assembly in which elaborate courtesy to one's colleagues and deference to one's seniors were basic rules of conduct. It had only one woman member, the inconsequential Hattie Caraway of Arkansas. The dominant individuals commanded attention or wielded power by dint of ability and hard work, oratorical powers, or personal integrity. Some of the older figures—William Borah (the chamber's senior member), George Norris, and Burton Wheeler among them—were men Truman appears long to have admired.

In a nation not yet homogenized by mass electronic communications and personal mobility, regional differences remained pronounced. Older southern senators spoke and dressed almost like Fred Allen's comedy character, Senator Claghorn. Westerners and Midwesterners frequently professed neopopulist resentments dating back to the nineteenth century and recoiled from involvement in the evil affairs of Europe. Thirty senators could trace their Capitol Hill service back to Woodrow Wilson or beyond. Yet the chamber was in the throes of two revolutions that had neatly dovetailed to change the shape of American politics: the rise of the city and the transformation of the Democratic party by the Great Depression and Franklin D. Roosevelt. These developments brought political power to a newly articulate urban, immigrant-stock population and fostered a new style of urban liberalism stemming from the social democratic impulses of the industrial working classes.

By the time Truman took his seat, the GOP was down to twenty-five members, many of them progressive mavericks. The Democratic coalition that nominated Roosevelt had been heavily based on the predominantly rural southern and western wings of the party; but by 1935, the urban Democracy was the most visible and rapidly growing element of the party. The new urban Democrats—ethnic and religious minorities, devoted exponents of labor unionism, advocates of social-welfare programs geared toward the city poor—seemed alien to rural traditionalists in both parties. Some of the older progressives, most notably Norris, adjusted easily to the transformation; others, including Borah, held back. Truman entered the Senate as one of thirteen freshman Democrats at the early stages of the Rooseveltian transformation. He and most of his colleagues had only a vague sense of where it might lead, but he had in many respects followed his party's path from rural roots to an urban electoral base. Yet he would not discard his old identity even as he sought to represent a new constituency.

In many respects, Truman's most important—and touchiest—relationship was with Bennett Clark. The two seemed to resume their pre-1934 friendship with scarcely a ripple. They reached agreement on recommending Matt Murray, a vital cog in the Pendergast machine, to be Missouri director of the Works Progress Administration (WPA). For Truman, the accord was a triumph of sorts; for Clark, it was a peace offering to Tom Pendergast that would cement future support from Kansas City. The *Star* described them as a team that "functioned as smoothly as a Rockne Notre Dame football squad."[3]

Actually, their relationship was often tense. Clark had contacts on the Hill dating back to the years he had spent there with his father and could wield considerable influence. But he had only two years of Senate service more than Truman, delighted in oratory rather than in committee work, was contemptuous of detail, and drank too much good bourbon. Possessing an outsize ego, he considered himself the moral and ideological leader of the Missouri Democracy. He was much more consistently dedicated to Jeffersonian principles of government at the working level than was Truman, who talked Jeffersonianism but voted consistently in support of the New Deal. Truman found his colleague's pomposity and lack of sobriety irritating. The differences in their voting records and attitudes toward Roosevelt widened during Truman's first term and assumed the proportions of a chasm as foreign policy became a salient issue.

Truman and Clark would also have numerous patronage disputes, some of them bitter; Truman was invariably the loser. Clark once went directly to Pendergast to resolve a disagreement over a federal judgeship. (The appointment of Murray, for whom Truman had no respect, likewise was a recognition of the Pendergast machine, not of Truman.) In 1938, the Roosevelt administration, by then determined to prosecute Pendergast, rejected Truman's bid to the control of two of the most desirable federal jobs in western Missouri: the United States attorney and United States marshal. It also froze him out on federal judicial appointments.

In what Truman may have taken as the greatest affront of all, Roosevelt officials dismissed his nomination of his administrative assistant, Victor Messall, to be secretary of the Civil Aeronautics Authority (CAA), although the senator had been a key player in creating the agency and had fought for presidential control of it. He understandably felt that his support of the president was going unrecognized while Clark reaped rewards for disloyalty. "It looks as if the people with whom you are associated have a habit of taking all and giving nothing," he told CAA administrator Clinton Hester in August 1938. "The attitude of the Administration generally, so far as I am concerned, has not been at all courteous, and I don't hesitate to tell you that I don't like it."[4]

Whatever their differences, Clark and Truman needed each other. For Clark, Truman was a useful conduit to Tom Pendergast. To Truman, Clark was a source of numerous outstate contacts. They thus developed a working relationship despite numerous jealousies and conflicts. Each often considered the other an annoyance, but never an enemy. They also were disposed to provide each other with support against third-party challenges. The understanding would prove in the end more valuable to Truman than to Clark.

Far more than Clark, the dominating presence in Truman's political life during his first five years in the Senate was Tom Pendergast. Far from apologetic about the relationship, Truman made a point of displaying Pendergast's portrait in his office. Nonetheless, he surely knew that Tom allegedly told visitors he had sent his office boy to Washington. Truman rightly sensed that quite a few Republicans and independent progressives took the office-boy story literally and were cool to him. "This attitude did not bother me," he wrote two decades later. "I knew it would change in time." One doubts that he really was so cool and detached.[5]

Truman and Pendergast seem to have had an understanding that Tom would never make a serious effort to dictate a Washington vote. He may well have asked Truman to vote against the public utility holding-company bill of 1935, a piece of legislation vehemently opposed by utility interests to which he was close. But such requests were few and never pressed; Truman could, and did, reject them with no hard feelings.[6]

What Pendergast wanted from Truman was favors, not policy decisions. Having a senator who would intercede with Washington agencies on behalf of friends was what gave Pendergast happiness and, frequently, personal profit. The game was an old, established part of the political process, and Truman had no problem playing it. One of the few surviving examples was a letter dated January 13, 1939:

> Dear Senator:
>
> Charley Howell will be in Washington in a few days. He will talk with you about some matters in which Braniff Airways, Inc., are interested. I hope you are in a position to help him out as it means considerable to him.
>
> Sincerely yours,
>
> T. J. Pendergast
>
> [handwritten:]
> P.S. It means a great deal to more than Howell.   T.J.P.

Six months later, with Pendergast out of power, Truman testified before the Civil Aeronautics Authority in favor of awarding the Kansas

City–Minneapolis route to Braniff. The action upset a good many Kansas Citians, who favored their hometown airline, Mid-Continent (later TWA). Why Truman acted as he did—the merits of the case, Pendergast's request, an expectation of campaign donations from Braniff—is uncertain.[7]

Pendergast liked to hand out service academy appointments and may have leaned harder on Truman about these than anything else. In late January 1939, he wrote to ask for the appointment of William R. Cecil to the Naval Academy. The correspondence that followed displays how tough it was to take care of Tom's wishes: Truman wrote to Pendergast on January 31, 1939:

> I appointed the Hansen boy as the principal to Annapolis and the Cecil boy as first alternate.

Pendergast replied by telegram on February 1, 1939:

> NOT SATISFIED WITH ALTERNATE APPOINTMENT. MY WORD IS OUT FOR PRINCI-
> PAL APPOINTMENT. YOU HAVE TWO APPOINTMENTS. I AM ENTITLED TO ONE.

Truman countered by telegram on the same day:

> I APPOINTED HARRY HANSEN AS PRINCIPAL TO ANNAPOLIS AT YOUR SUGGESTION.

The exchange must have left Truman seething; but by the end of February, he was dutifully working with Congressman Jasper Bell to get young Cecil into Annapolis. Truman was no one's office boy—at least not on most matters. But as long as Tom ran Kansas City, the senator's independence was provisional.[8]

III

By the standards of a later day, a senator's resources were exceedingly modest. Truman's key employee, his administrative assistant, held the title of secretary; a couple of clerk-typists and an assistant in charge of his Kansas City office rounded out the official staff. He also could fill a few patronage jobs in such places as the Senate mailroom and levy occasional claims on the services of the appointees. His most complex piece of office equipment was probably a typewriter.[9]

Truman was fortunate in his choice of a secretary. Jim Aylward had introduced him to Victor R. Messall, a southwest Missourian who had been secretary to outgoing congressman Frank Lee of Joplin. As Messall recalled it years later, he was not enthusiastic about working for a Pendergast minion but agreed to show Truman around, help him buy some furniture, and assist in getting an office organized. Truman was uncertain about Messall, but he knew that he needed some Capitol Hill experience. Messall went on the payroll as acting private secretary the day Truman was sworn into the Senate, was soon given the job on a continuing basis, and stayed with Truman for six years. His wife, Irene, also worked in the senator's office from June 1937 to June 1941.[10]

A stylish dresser with smooth manners, Messall possessed political sense and seems to have been a tireless worker. He looked after Truman when Bess and Margaret were away, helped him find one apartment after another, and acted as a rental agent when the senator sublet to out-of-town visitors. He was additionally a stock-market adviser, a conduit to Missouri politics, and a manager of other delicate political tasks. As Truman's first term neared its end, Messall had acquired a sense of loyalty deep enough to manage an uphill reelection campaign.[11]

Back home, Truman relied heavily on Vivian, who acted as his brother's political operative. He had contacts all over the county, played the game by the patronage ethic both he and Harry had learned early on, and judged events with an elemental shrewdness. One senses that his advice, when offered, was rarely ignored.[12]

Another trusted assistant in Kansas City was Fred Canfil. A close aide for some years and chief custodian of the Kansas City courthouse, Canfil looked so much a machine man that his portrait might have been the work of a political cartoonist. Blunt in manner and (to Truman's distress) a chain-smoker who left a trail of cigarette ash in his wake, he had the appearance and charm of an aging saloon bouncer. Truman, valuing his loyalty and astuteness, indulged him with an air of amused resignation. The man exasperated him, he told Bess, but "he'd cut a throat for me." Indeed he would, although not necessarily a throat Truman would want cut; jealous of Truman's other friends, he often squabbled with them. His unsavory image, a rumored unfavorable FBI report on him, and his need of a job after 1939 made him a liability. Truman spent years trying to get a United States marshalship for him.[13]

Lacking today's array of legislative advisers and issue specialists, members of Congress voted largely according to personal preferences, partisan affiliation, and constituency interests or prejudices. Yet with the New Deal in full swing and the functions of the federal government expanding rapidly, legislators faced mounting pressures from individuals and interest groups anxious to land a government job or benefit. From the beginning, Truman found himself deluged by a flood of correspondence, set on by visitors from Missouri, and harassed. He told a *Kansas City Star* reporter in June 1935 that he was working from 7:00 A.M. until 7:00 P.M. and was still unable to keep ahead of his correspondence.[14]

In fact, Truman very likely spent more energy keeping up with Missouri contacts and developments than he did on legislating. Throughout his years in the Senate, he paid close attention to the details of Jackson County government and politics. Patronage became for him, as for many other politicians, almost an obsession. As late as 1941, he was involved in such local problems as the choice of a dentist for the county farm, the selection of a shop foreman for the county garage, and the designation of road overseers. He worked to either maintain or create jobs for numerous friends and war buddies.[15]

Probably the most frustrating situation that Truman faced involved postmasterships, for which there was intense rivalry. In many little Missouri towns, the job was one of the most lucrative to be had. In the cities, it was a plum that carried a nice salary and minimal demands. An applicant had to score well on a civil service examination; but in the absence of a strict numerical merit order, postal openings had a way of creating donnybrooks among local Democratic factions. Invariably, each candidate and his supporters labeled their opponents back stabbers who supported Truman's enemies; invariably, they described themselves as his only true-blue friends within the boundaries of the postal district. Truman often asked local political associates to make the choice for him. "Pass the buck on these post offices," Truman advised Independence mayor Roger Sermon. "Every single one of them is a hot potato and when you satisfy one fellow in the community you make fourteen mad."

Postmasterships as a rule were problems for congressmen, not senators. However, as Republicans began to recapture congressional seats in Missouri after 1938, Truman faced involvement in one fight after another. At times, he asked for trouble; for example, he twice intervened to secure the postmastership at Clinton for old Battery D men with minimal local support. From time to time, disputes erupted between Truman and Bennett Clark about who controlled what political turf. Supposedly, the two of them had divided the state on an east–west basis. But in 1943, Clark refused to concede control of the postmastership in El Dorado Springs, a town 100 miles south of Kansas City; Truman retaliated by claiming a veto over the postmastership of Hannibal, about an equal distance north of St. Louis. These disputes consumed valuable time while Truman was investigating the defense program, attracting attention as a spokesman on postwar foreign policy, and establishing himself as one of the leading Democrats in Washington.[16]

By contrast, the WPA was a patronage politician's dream. The huge federal relief agency conducted projects throughout the state. Favoritism did not blatantly dictate the distribution of ordinary jobs, but Matt Murray saw to it that district and local directors were friendly to the Kansas City organization. Several Truman associates—Harry Easley of Webb City, Frank Monroe of Sedalia, and J. V. Conran of New Madrid among them—used WPA posts both to assist Truman and to consolidate their own political positions. In the two-year period 1935 to 1937, the WPA paid out over $74 million to Missouri workers; in much of the state, it functioned as an extension of the Pendergast machine. Truman demonstrated his own attitude to a constituent who asked for help in getting a WPA job: "If you will send me indorsements from the Kansas City Democratic organization, I will be glad to see what I can do for you."[17]

IV

Truman got along well with his freshmen colleagues, assiduously cultivated the Washington representatives of the large Missouri newspapers, and sought the approval of the Senate establishment. Not only did the chamber's clubby male atmosphere appeal to him, but its ethic of quiet achievement harmonized with the career pattern he already had established. His quick acceptance by an older, senior leadership circle was not unlike his satisfying experience in the Masons. By now a shrewd natural psychologist who understood how to flatter men with large egos, he acted the role of a neophyte anxious to be instructed by his betters. With a reasonably straight face, he told *Kansas City Journal-Post* correspondent William Helm, "I came to see you first of all because you are a famous newsman and know all the ropes." Even men who recognized this sort of treatment for what it was nonetheless enjoyed it.[18]

Truman was determined to avoid being typed a show-off. Gerald Nye, the North Dakota isolationist who conducted a long investigation of the munitions industry, struck him as "one of the good-looking, egotistical boys who play to the gallery all the time." Many of the other "so-called progressives" left him about as unimpressed. His special bête noire was the flamboyant Huey Long. Twenty years later, Truman took great pleasure in recalling (probably with some embellishment) that in August 1935 he had been trapped in the presiding officer's chair as Long staged a filibuster. The Senate chamber emptied until only the two of them were left, Long reading one irrelevancy after another into the *Congressional Record*. After Long moved for adjournment, he asked Truman how he had liked the experience. Truman replied, "I had to listen to you because I was in the chair and couldn't walk out." It was his last exchange with the Kingfish, who was shot and killed in Baton Rouge shortly afterward.[19]

Those whom Truman respected were the "workers," men more in his own image who did the toil of research and legislative drafting, usually without benefit of lights, cameras, headlines, or rooms packed with interested spectators. With the conspicuous exceptions of Burton K. Wheeler of Montana and Robert F. Wagner of New York, they tended to be men of the center and the right: John Bankhead of Alabama, Carter Glass of Virginia, Alva Adams of Colorado, Pat Harrison of Mississippi, and, above all, Joe Robinson of Arkansas. Robinson, the majority leader in the Senate, was tough, energetic, and domineering; he was one of the most effective party chieftains in the chamber's history. He and James F. Byrnes of South Carolina (generally considered Roosevelt's man in the Senate) worked hard at winning over members of the freshman class. Truman admired them, doubtless appreciated their attention, and seldom let them down. He was even more impressed by the establishment's most colorful eminence, Vice President John Nance Garner of Texas. Often asked to join Garner and others in the then-frequent ritual of striking a late-afternoon blow for liberty in a private hideaway, he got to know such Garner protégés as Sam Rayburn, already one of the top Democrats in the House.[20]

A fair amount of the chamber's decision making occurred as a result of socializing in Capitol retreats stocked with good food and the best whiskey. Some of the participants were the workers; many others were men distinguished primarily for their bonhomie and skills as raconteurs. One of the latter was J. Hamilton Lewis of Illinois, the majority whip. "Don't start out with an inferiority complex," he told Truman. "For the first six months you'll wonder how you got here, and after that you'll wonder how the rest of us got here." Lewis's bluff self-deprecation captured the tone of many long lunches and after-hours drinking sessions. Some of these recreations were outside the Senate—chiefly with the Houn' Dawg Club, a poker group of Missouri politicians and newsmen. But most of Truman's convivial moments were with other senators, primarily from the more distant provinces, especially the South. (The Northeasterners customarily spent long weekends in their home districts.) They drank highballs and swapped jokes that none today would dare tell in the closest company. A lot of their stories were off-color; quite a few, based on common racial assumptions of the day, featured "nigga preachers," Stepin Fetchit–like buffoons, or hypersexual blacks. Truman thoroughly enjoyed them.[21]

Party affiliation may have been important in admitting one into the circle, but ideology had little to do with it. Truman's good friends were down-the-line New Dealers and devoted Roosevelt worshipers (Sherman Minton, Joe Guffey, Robert Wagner, Lew Schwellenbach), dissenting conservatives (Ed Burke and Pat Harrison), independent mavericks (Burton Wheeler), men of moderate temperament and generally liberal voting records (Alben Barkley, James Byrnes, Carl Hayden), and even Republicans (Charles McNary and Warren Austin). This assortment reflected both Truman's capacity for wide friendships and the pervasive affability of the Senate.

In August 1939, Truman related to Bess how he, Garner, and more than a dozen other senators of various ideological bents had lunched on a ham he had brought back from Missouri: "If you read the *Record* today, you'll wonder how that outfit could sit down together, but they did and had a grand time. Maybe Johnny Walker, Ballantine, and Mr. Gin had something to do with it." They all had expressed a hope he would be reelected in 1940. "I'm crazy enough to believe they meant it. Anyway they meant it while the alcoholic gentlemen mentioned above had control." They would have meant it if they had been reduced to bologna sandwiches and Coca-Cola. Truman had become one of the most popular men in the Senate.[22]

V

Truman's $10,000 salary carried roughly the purchasing power that a senator would receive fifty years in the future. Still, then as later, Washington was costly, and members of Congress had many extraordinary expenses. Like many a moderately prosperous member of the bourgeoisie,

Truman also faced demands on his income from other family members. He contributed to the support of his mother and probably continued to help out with the expenses of his mother-in-law. He was so concerned with money that on at least one occasion he rented the family's Washington apartment for a week or so to some tourists. He watched expenditures closely and groused about his relative poverty. In June 1935, he wrote to a friend who had returned a $24 check to him: "It just took about that much to make me solvent at the bank."[23]

By the measurements of the world in which he now functioned and the business elite to which he once had aspired, Truman's income and standard of living remained painfully modest. Unlike most of his fellow senators, he had no outside income and minimal savings. Like most senators, he readily accepted small gifts—a case of whiskey, say, or a turkey—from friends and constituents, but he steered clear of outright graft and declined payments for speeches and appearances. He even turned down a cash fee, apparently offered to every senator, for an advertising endorsement of Lucky Strike cigarettes; a nonsmoker, he reasoned, had no business playing that game. He told Bess that he did not want their friends to speculate about the amount of money it had taken to buy him. Without extra cash, the family maintained a marginal middle-class existence, living in comfortable but cramped apartments, managing to keep up senatorial appearances, but not getting ahead. It was symptomatic that Vic Messall could afford to buy a suburban Maryland home; Truman could not.[24]

Martha Truman, still alert and active in her early eighties, followed her elder son's career closely and probably wrote to him frequently. The only surviving letter tells a lot about their relationship. She thanked her son for a check (adding "have always hoped you could lay up something for a rainey [sic] day instead of helping everybody"), described visits with friends and family, and commended him for a strong denunciation of the Townsend old-age pension plan. "Hope you get along with your committees and make good in all but don't read too long and strain your eyes," she wrote. "Lovingly, Mamma Truman."[25]

The farm's financial status was more precarious than ever. The $25,000 mortgage negotiated with the Rosier sisters of Belton ran overdue at a time when the property was worth less than ever. In April 1938, after many efforts at refinancing, Truman arranged a politically embarrassing, nine-month, $35,000 loan from the Jackson County school fund. Vivian Truman and Fred Canfil co-signed the note. The *Star* observed that the farm's assessed value was $22,680 and that the much higher loan violated Missouri law. Clearly, the county court, still controlled by Pendergast goats, had put together a short-term bailout. In June 1939, with Pendergast control of the county government crumbling, the loan was six months overdue and under increasing attack. Back in Kansas City trying to set up yet another mortgage, Truman told a reporter, "You know how it is when you seem to owe more than you can pay."[26]

Mary Jane and Vivian were also hard pressed. The service station that Mary Jane had leased to a Standard Oil franchisee continued to produce an insufficient income; she staved off creditors and seems to have relied heavily on agricultural acreage allotment payments that were slow in coming. Harry had to keep up his assistance. Vivian still had his county job in 1935, but all county employees were on half-salary. In 1935, Victor Messall, undoubtedly acting on his boss's direct or indirect request, engineered employment for him with the Federal Housing Authority office in Kansas City.[27]

Truman apparently managed to accumulate some savings after a couple of years. A big financial worry was alleviated in 1935 when, after long and delicate negotiations, Vivian was able to purchase for $1,000 the last big outstanding haberdashery note at a court-ordered sale. It is unclear whether the senator or his friends provided the funds. By 1938, he had enough spare cash that he was engaged in small-scale stock speculation with some success. He half-seriously planned a family vacation in France that would include a tour of his old World War I battle areas.[28]

Aside from concern about her mother, Bess seems to have enjoyed life in Washington. The formal rounds of teas and exchanges of visits were not much different from social occasions in Independence and Kansas City. The wives of John Cochran and Bennett Clark went out of their way to be cordial to her, just as their husbands did with Harry. She frequented the comfortable Congressional Club, an organization for the wives of congressmen, many of them also new to the city. She had more time to spend with Margaret. The experience was good for both mother and daughter. They went sightseeing, shopped, made formal social calls, and visited ice-cream parlors. Margaret recalled this as the most relaxed time she had yet spent with her mother; Bess no doubt enjoyed her respite from the demands of Independence.[29]

One might have expected Margaret, pulled weeks before her eleventh birthday from the only home environment she ever had known, to find the transition immensely difficult, but she adjusted remarkably well. Her parents enrolled her in Gunston Hall, a private school. She has recalled that entering it midway through the fifth grade was not easy, but her natural gregariousness soon won friends. An unusual routine characterized the rest of her elementary and secondary education—the fall semester in the Independence public schools, the spring semester at Gunston Hall.

The moves back and forth may have been more painful for the young adolescent than she later remembered, but she never became a problem child. The enhanced relationship with her mother in Washington no doubt helped a lot. At home in Independence, the attention she received from aunts and uncles (Frank, for example, taught her how to drive a car) went far toward compensating for her father's frequent absences. Perhaps most important, Harry's single-minded devotion to her, so palpable in his letters, transcended his physical absence. It made little difference that he frequently talked about political preoccupations she neither understood nor cared about, or that at times he was so harried he could not remember what grade she was in at school. What was important to Margaret was that he wrote often and that his letters always included expressions of love and encouragement. Years later, she would remember him as her "knight in shining armor."[30]

Truman may have been a bit disappointed that his daughter never took to the piano, but he was pleased that she developed musical interests. She took up the study of voice and displayed some promise as a singer. On May 18, 1941, at the age of seventeen, she made her radio debut, singing on an NBC Sunday-afternoon show, *Women's Congress*. Her proud parents invested $3 in a recording of the event.[31]

One temporary apartment after another, worry about money, an overworked man facing enormous career uncertainty, and long periods of separation generated no more than a normal quota of minor disagreements and misunderstandings for the family. Harry at times thought Bess too extravagant. Bess occasionally reacted sharply to stories that her husband might be having a good time in her absence.[32] Both, however, were determined to make their marriage work and raise a daughter of whom they could be proud. In the world of the late twentieth century, one might gauge all the odds against a couple in their situation. In the Victorian world that had produced them, their course seemed the only natural and respectable one. They went about it with a minimum of friction and an absence of angst.

VI

Truman's new life was nonetheless stressful. In addition to the hard work and the family separations, there was the insoluble problem of Mamma's mortgage, the pressures of a long-running railroad investigation, attempts to push through major transportation legislation, and a deteriorating political situation in Missouri. These converged as his first term progressed and probably were central in producing ominous physical symptoms. Alone in Washington in late 1935 and early 1936, he wrote repeatedly to Bess about headaches. About the middle of 1937, well into the railroad investigation and after Majority Leader Robinson's sudden death had delivered a dramatic example of the dangers of stress and overwork, he began to suffer from headaches, occasional nausea, and constant fatigue. The symptoms were similar to those he seems to have experienced during the tough budget-cutting crises in Jackson County.

In August, he saw a physician at the Naval Hospital in Bethesda. A routine physical revealed no obvious problems; the doctor told him to lose some weight and put him on a strict diet. In five weeks, he shed ten pounds; he emerged from the experience feeling all the worse for it. In September, at Bess's urging, he went to the Army-Navy Hospital at Hot Springs, Arkansas, for a more thorough checkup. Close to exhaustion, he still insisted that nothing was really wrong with him. A week and a half at Hot Springs revealed little other than routine effects of stress, overwork, and lack of exercise—a mild inflammation of the heart muscles and a minor edema (excess fluid) around the ankles. None of this required medication; his doctor's chief recommendation was to forget about his diet, engage in greater physical activity, and enjoy more recreation. An eye examination suggested that his headaches might be cured by a new eyeglass prescription.

Truman left feeling relaxed, refreshed, and well fed. He wrote on his checkout sheet: "Excellent treatment by everyone. Remarkable rest and very pleasant environment." In this and subsequent consultations with military doctors, he clearly understood that his ills were largely a matter of nervous strain and workaholism. In the future, he would use the Hot Springs hospital, located in the midst of a popular resort area, almost as a vacation hotel when the pressures of work and everyday life left him worn down. He found that doing something about his work-aholism was harder than periodically succumbing to it. "There's a driving force inside me that makes me get into things," he had told Bess at the end of his first year in the Senate. "I can't sit still and do nothing."[33]

VII

Senator Truman in many ways had changed little from his years in local government. He still had a model family, lived a clean personal life, had a reputation for honesty, enjoyed the affection of his colleagues, and possessed their respect. He also remained the master machinist, operating now from the Senate Office Building rather than Jackson County courthouses. But his new position forced an act of self-definition that had been unnecessary in the days when he could present himself simply as an efficient businessman-progressive. Was he just an amiable, nonideological technician in government? Or did a stronger vision guide his political course? The Great Depression, the New Deal, and Franklin D. Roosevelt would require answers to these questions.

13

"Vultures at the Death of an Elephant": Insurgency, New Dealism, Interest Group Politics, and the Regulatory State, 1935–1940

Although he had professed unquestioning loyalty to Franklin Roosevelt while campaigning for the Senate, Truman exhibited conflicting tendencies that stemmed naturally from his earlier career. A product of the Missouri Jeffersonian tradition and a critic of bureaucratic government, he was often a rhetorical conservative; yet he became a champion of big government, embodied in the regulatory state. An heir to the tradition of Bryanite progressivism, he was often a militant opponent of big business and Wall Street, who saw himself as a friend of the small entrepreneur. A politician who worked with an urban machine, sought ties to the labor movement, and rode to Washington on Roosevelt's coattails, he was an operational New Deal liberal. Most fundamentally, he was a shrewd, pragmatic player of interest group politics.[1]

II

Truman had come to Washington openly prepared to vote against the president on renewal of the National Recovery Administration. Ham-fisted and bureaucratic, the NRA was a special nuisance to many small-business constituents with whom Truman identified. The Supreme Court, much to his delight, spared him a negative vote by ruling the agency unconstitutional.[2] As it was, his voting record went nearly down the line with the administration. On the few occasions during his first term that he broke with it, he was as likely as not to vote for a bigger spending alternative. Like most members of Congress, he was also prone to give the objectives of important constituency groups top priority. In 1935, he went against the administration on only two significant votes: he backed full, immediate payment of the veterans' bonus and supported an amendment to the public-works bill mandating "prevailing" local wages for WPA workers. The Roosevelt administration considered both items too expensive and secured their defeat. (The bonus, however, did pass Congress in 1936 over FDR's veto.)

Other breaks with the administration were few and far between. In April 1937, Truman voted for a measure, sponsored by James Byrnes, to outlaw sit-down strikes in the coal industry. In January 1939, he joined a narrow majority of the Senate in voting for an emergency relief appropriation $150 million lower than the administration had requested. Cast on relatively peripheral issues, both votes were symbolic declarations of independence and demonstrations of dissatisfaction with his treatment by the White House as much as they were expressions of principle.[3]

Truman's most important deviation came in July 1937, after the sudden death of Joe Robinson. He resisted administration pressure, applied through Tom Pendergast, to vote for Alben Barkley as the new Senate majority leader. His explanation was simple: Pat Harrison had asked for his vote first, and he had promised it. To make certain there was no doubt that he had kept his word (unlike Illinois senator William Dieterich, who reversed himself at the behest of Chicago boss Ed Kelly), he showed his marked secret ballot to Clyde Herring of Iowa. Aside from a determination to show that neither the president nor Tom Pendergast could dictate to him, Truman wanted to back the best man. He considered Barkley a fine storyteller and drinking companion; Harrison, a great legislator. Moreover, Harrison had been only marginally less supportive of the New Deal. Truman's action, principled and forthright, did nothing to damage his friendship with Barkley.[4]

Truman not only quietly voted for Roosevelt's programs, but was unyielding in his support for some of the most controversial. During his first year in the Senate, he was a vehement backer of the public utility holding-company bill, which was opposed by Bennett Clark, the *Kansas City Journal-Post*, and utility interests close to Tom Pendergast. He did not cast a vote on its passage in June 1935 because he was back in Missouri attending to previously scheduled obligations; he probably would have flown back to Washington had his vote been needed. His public comments on it were outspokenly unambiguous. "Some measure of protection must be given the investing public against the blue sky operators and the unscrupulous promoters who have used the holding companies as a means to rob the small investor," he told the *Kansas City Star*.[5]

After a bit of waffling, he was equally strong in support of Roosevelt's bill to add six new justices to the Supreme Court. He broke with numerous Senate friends (including Clark and Burton Wheeler), engaged in sharp exchanges with constituents who deluged him with letters of opposition, and defended the proposal before a crowd of 3,000 in Kansas City. His rhetoric, to be sure, lacked elegance and perhaps logical consistency. In his big Kansas City speech, he declared both that the Court could not really be packed (because appointees tended to be unpredictable) and that the bill was needed because the Court had been packed with conservatives for fifty years. Nor was he persuasive in asserting that "the people" supported the bill because most of his mail in favor was handwritten on cheap paper, and most opposed was typewritten on higher-quality stationery. "Down with the economic royalists who use typewriters, is Senator Truman's slogan!" lampooned a *Kansas City Times* editorial.

All the same, Truman's private references to the debates of the Constitutional Convention and to the dissents and warnings of the first John Marshall Harlan, John Clarke, Oliver Wendell Holmes, and Harlan Fiske Stone reveal a serious study of the Court and its place in the American constitutional system. His public pronouncements varied a bit in nuance and may have been designed to rebut accusations of rubber-stamping Roosevelt's proposal, but they left little room for doubt about his final position. The form letter he sent out to Missourians was intelligent, well argued, and clear enough in its conclusion: "The Constitution doesn't need an amendment at all. It merely needs a liberal interpretation."[6]

In March 1939, two months after joining the "anti-Roosevelt" forces in cutting relief appropriations, Truman provided crucial help to the president. At the request of the White House, he flew back from Kansas City through a heavy snowstorm to cast a decisive vote for the executive reorganization bill, a measure designed to give the president far-reaching powers over executive departments and agencies. He may have been motivated in part by a desire for recognition and patronage. He surely wanted to get some consideration for Tom Pendergast, whose political empire was beginning to crumble. Still, as he claimed at the time, his action was consistent with his long-held belief in executive authority.[7]

After voting, he called Roosevelt's assistant, Steve Early, to whom he angrily declared that he was sick and tired of being the White House office boy. Roosevelt invited the senator to the executive mansion the next day to express his thanks. It was the first of several meetings with Truman or his friends in which FDR shed a previous aloofness and provided some rhetorical encouragement. Truman got little more than that as he faced a difficult campaign for renomination in 1940. He had been neither as enthusiastic about the New Deal nor as innovative as, say, Bob Wagner, but the president had few more consistent supporters in the Senate and perhaps none for whom he had done so little. At times bitter about his lack of recognition, Truman was nevertheless philosophical. Writing to Bess, he analyzed his patronage frustrations as the result of "the rotten situation in Kansas City" and the jealousy of Bennett Clark. The president was unreliable, but "the things he's stood for are, in my opinion, best for the country, and jobs should not interfere with general principles."[8]

III

Despite the specifics of his voting record, Truman frequently sounded like an anti–New Dealer when he talked in generalities:

> January 24, 1936
>   I am against giving another nickel to those who can work, have the opportunity and won't do so.

> January 31, 1936
>   The money has been spent, and the bill must be paid. . . . I am ready to vote to cut down expenses and for any tax bill that will raise sufficient revenue to pay what we owe.

> February 7, 1936
>   No one wants to see the government in business. My pet aversion is a bureaucrat—a Washington bureaucrat is the worst form of political parasite.

> January 5, 1938 (on the best way for Congress to handle the growing economic recession)
>   Ease taxes on the little corporation, make labor and business cooperate, pass as little new legislation as possible, adjourn Congress and let the lawmakers go home. . . . [C]ome back here in 1939 and abolish the unnecessary boards, bureaus and commissions, and fashion an economical form of government.[9]

No doubt, such remarks—rarely very specific—were in part conscious rhetorical ploys, designed to give comfort to anti–New Deal Democrats. But they also reflected Truman's background as a budget-conscious administrator, a product of late-nineteenth-century liberal individualism, and a moral absolutist who believed deeply in the traditional values of the American middle class. He and other "insurgent progressives" in the Senate, Democrat and Republican, were cut from similar cloth. Identifying themselves with the common man (defined as individual worker, farmer, small enterpriser, or self-employed professional), usually small-town and Protestant in background, they faced a world of big cities, giant corporations, large labor unions, organized pressure groups, and faintly alien collectivist social ideologies. They adjusted uneasily to the world of the twentieth century and the New Deal.

Frequently their worldview seemed to be that of agricultural fundamentalists who accepted the Jeffersonian–Bryanite assumption that farms represented the essence of America. Their first impulse was to re-create an idealized past, usually through antitrust actions that would lead to the breakup of big business. Most of them came to realize that to some degree they would have to accept the world as it was, recognize the pervasiveness of the large organization in American life, acquiesce in a vision of reform built around centralized bureaucratic regulation and planning, accept some degree of collectivist welfarism, and embrace values that were more relativistic and pluralistic than those on which they had been reared. Even those who went farthest in that direction, however, did not repudiate their initial outlooks.

Like many liberal Democrats of the 1930s, Truman came to think of himself as a new kind of Jeffersonian. His view of American history largely revolved around an interpretation of the conflict between Jefferson and Hamilton: in this, Jefferson represented not so much small government as the welfare of the common person; Hamilton stood not so much for big government as for moneyed special interests. One rationale for New Deal bureaucracy was expediency: government had to do extraordinary things to meet an extraordinary emergency. Another was the need for the state to act "as a sort of umpire between producer and consumer, between bankers and their customers, and between railroads and their shippers." The selfishness of human nature dictated a need for social legislation and for action to prevent excessive concentration of economic power. Moreover, government had to take unprecedented remedial activities to solve problems it had created; agricultural distress, Truman insisted, was a consequence of encouraging farms to expand during World War I, then taking foreign markets away from them during the 1920s.

Although he believed in it deeply, Truman's liberalism was not simply an intellectual exercise, but also a matter of the practical politics of obtaining benefits for constituent interest groups. To represent the interests of labor might mean in the narrow sense to look out for the needs of the unions, an enterprise he did not shirk as a working politician. Yet, as he told an audience at Liberty, Missouri, "labor" was not just the relatively well-off rail brotherhoods or building trades unions, but "every man or woman who works with hand or brain for a living." All deserved a living wage based on reasonable hours. The Harry Truman of 1939 looked to the values of the past with nostalgia, was a Jeffersonian in some very deep senses of the word, and was also a New Dealer.[10]

IV

Truman's most important ongoing legislative work during the 1930s stemmed from his activity on the Interstate Commerce Committee and his long interest in transportation. Transportation policy attracted little public interest; nevertheless, it affected all freight shippers and passenger carriers, influencing the routes they traversed, the rates they charged, the jobs they had available, the wages they paid. Transportation policy might determine the very survival of small or medium-size enterprises; it was highly significant to many agricultural, business, and labor interest groups. A legislator who was influential on transportation matters could command the attention—and the campaign money—of those groups.

One of these was the emerging civil aviation industry. In the 1930s, numerous young airlines engaged in a fierce rivalry for federal routes and subsidies. But they also perceived a common interest in the development of a coherent, comprehensive regulatory structure that, whatever limits it imposed, would protect them from the ravages of unbridled competition. By 1937, work was well along in the Senate Commerce Committee on legislation to establish the Civil Aviation Authority, which would pull together the regulatory powers of four separate federal entities. Its primary sponsor was Commerce Committee chair Pat McCarran of Nevada.

Thanks to the disorderly structure of the Senate, the Interstate Commerce Committee, originally created to oversee the Interstate Commerce Commission (ICC) and develop railroad legislation, had an aviation subcommittee, headed by Truman. He paid little attention to McCarran's bill until it came to the floor of the Senate in 1938. Roosevelt loyalists demanded strong presidential power to appoint and remove members of the new body. Truman sponsored their alternative, which passed by a vote of 34 to 28, but subsequently was largely reversed in conference committee. The issue was narrow, but the argument was bitter. Because it involved executive authority, Truman considered it a matter of principle, not just an effort to ingratiate himself with the president. McCarran resented his interference. Both detested each other for the rest of their political lives.[11]

With considerable exaggeration, Truman claimed joint authorship of the Civil Aeronautics Act. His role had been small, but he had established a lot of prestige and visibility in the world of civil aviation—and no doubt staked a claim to election-time money. He continued to take a keen interest in the industry and its regulatory politics. *National Aeronautics* magazine hailed him in March 1939 as a "modest and capable Western statesman" who was a friend and promoter of air transportation.[12]

Truman's pet project was less noteworthy. In 1937, he introduced a bill that would have required all motor vehicle drivers who crossed state lines to hold state driver's licenses issued according to minimum federal standards. It was the work of a legislator who, whatever his Jeffersonian rhetoric, believed in the utility of a strong administrative state. Truman worked hard for the bill, but it had no strong constituency. It passed the Senate in 1938, but was never reported to the floor of the House.[13]

V

Burton K. Wheeler, chairman of the Interstate Commerce Committee, was from the beginning Truman's fastest political friend and most valued Senate mentor. An embodiment of progressive insurgency, a senator from Montana since 1923, the running mate of Robert La Follette, Sr., on the 1924 Progressive presidential ticket, a battler and a maverick, a crusader against corporate and financial power, Burt Wheeler deferred to no one, not even Roosevelt. Under Wheeler's guidance, Truman exercised his first major legislative responsibility, confirmed his outlook as a midwestern insurgent New Dealer, gained significant new contacts, and poised himself for reelection to the Senate. Eventually, Wheeler's opposition to World War II and his postwar career as a business lobbyist positioned him far from Truman ideologically. Still, in 1951, a harried president would write of his old friend: "I shall continue to like him as long as I live."[14]

In December 1936, Wheeler established a subcommittee that began a major inquiry into the condition of American railroads—one that would concentrate on a bête noir of western and midwestern insurgency: the malign influence of Wall Street. Insurgency in its most elemental form had always professed a generalized neopopulistic resentment on the part of self-styled "productive" classes—farmers, workers, small businessmen—against moneyed and presumably "nonproductive" groups. In the early twentieth century, when Truman's political consciousness was maturing, Louis Brandeis had given the faith a veneer of sophistication with his attacks on corporate bigness and denunciations of bankers who played with "other people's money." By 1937, Roosevelt's New Deal had veered sharply in that direction. Brandeis himself, now a justice of the Supreme Court, was a force in Washington, his influence felt in the persons of dozens of Harvard Law School graduates placed in strategic administration positions by his disciple, Felix Frankfurter. Truman eagerly put himself into an effort that combined emotional and provincial neopopulism with Brandesian economic analysis. Whether the combination was good economics is debatable. That it was good politics is certain.

In the insurgent mind of the early twentieth century, the railroads had been the most visible of corporate malefactors. The nation's largest economic enterprise, employing more workers than any other business, affecting the fortunes of millions of small enterprisers, controlling large holdings of land and natural resources, the rail corporations wielded enormous political power. Bryan, Brandeis, and other progressives had seen them as a many-tentacled octopus squeezing ordinary Americans everywhere while enriching the robber barons.

By the 1930s, however, the railroads were the sickest of American businesses; several leading lines were in bankruptcy, and most of the rest were on the verge. Only generous, and increasingly tenuous, Reconstruction Finance Corporation (RFC) loans kept the system afloat. The plight of the rails was largely the result of impersonal forces magnified by the Depression: competition, huge capital demands, heavy debt, overbuilding, inefficient regulatory constraints, high labor costs and antiquated work rules required by powerful unions, the lack of a coherent federal consolidation policy, increased freight-hauling competition from truck and barge lines, and the growing use of the automobile as a passenger vehicle. To Wheeler, Truman, and the Brandeisians, the blame could be easily assigned; it lay with inept corporate managers and rapacious Wall Street financiers.[15]

The rails, which owned substantial undervalued assets and generated a steady cash flow, seemed attractive to speculators, takeover artists, and would-be empire builders despite fundamental problems and uninspiring profits during the 1920s. When the federal government failed to achieve a reorganization mandated by the Transportation Act of 1920, private entrepreneurs attempted the task. Acting haphazardly, frequently paying excessive prices for acquisitions, and worsening the already rickety financial structure of their companies, they counted on a strong economy to generate the profits to pay off big debt loads.

The most famous of the private consolidators, Oris and Mantis Van Sweringen of Cleveland, acquired controlling interests in a half-dozen major railroads, including the Missouri Pacific. Although imposing, their rail empire was a jumble of holding companies and junk-bond financings. Yet as long as prosperity brought more and more business, heavy debt seemed manageable. Allegedly hard-headed investors cultivated a giddy optimism. On Wall Street, stock in the Van Sweringens' primary holding company, the Alleghany Corporation, soared from $24 to $56 in the summer of 1929. Pennroad Corporation, a holding-company subsidiary of the giant, supposedly rock-solid Pennsylvania Railroad, pursued its own large-scale acquisition program.

The Depression brought disaster. Alleghany stock traded as low as 12½ cents a share in 1933 and never got higher than $8.25 for the rest of the decade. The Van Sweringen brothers died broke in 1935 and 1936. Pennroad struggled to stay afloat. Small holders of stocks and bonds faced possible total losses. As rail business shrank, one line after another sought refuge in the bankruptcy courts, making a much-needed national reorganization and consolidation impossible. Management, labor, shippers, and various committees of stockholders and bondholders all fought for their own interests. The tangled financial structures of the lines and their holding companies would have taxed the wisdom of Solomon and the detective skills of Ellery Queen. By the end of 1936, the Missouri Pacific alone had issued twenty-four different series of corporate bonds and equipment trust certificates. Its balance sheet showed a deficit (negative stockholders' equity) of over $43 million.[16]

When Wheeler's subcommittee convened to investigate railroad financing in the 1920s, its key figure was its counsel, Max Lowenthal, a protégé of Frankfurter and a devoted acolyte of Louis Brandeis. A dedicated Zionist, a benefactor of socialist trade unions, and a shrewd Wall Street player, he was a near-prototype of an increasingly prominent liberal species: the wealthy Jewish reformer. In 1933, he had published *The Investor Pays*, a case study of the most inequitable rail bankruptcy reorganization of the 1920s—that of the Chicago, Milwaukee, and St. Paul.

It told a horror story of fleeced bondholders, overcompensated managers, unscrupulous attorneys, and predatory investment bankers. Liberals hailed the book as comparable in importance to Brandeis's classic *Other People's Money*.

Lowenthal managed the railroad investigation to demonstrate a preconceived thesis that the investing public and the American rail system had been victimized by a Wall Street cabal. Armed with subpoena power, his investigators searched through the archives of leading corporations, financial establishments, and law firms. Their ultimate objective was to lay the groundwork for legislation that would strengthen the railway regulatory system and perhaps lead to government ownership.[17]

Truman had not been involved in planning the inquiry; but after he displayed an interest, Wheeler appointed him to the subcommittee. After becoming leader of the fight against the Court-packing bill, Wheeler turned the investigation over to Truman and Lowenthal. By May 1937, Truman was acting chairman, determined to push the inquiry hard. It focused on such alleged predators as the old populist demons of the House of Morgan and the Kuhn, Loeb investment firm. It also went after famous old-line Wall Street law firms: Cadwalader, Wickersham & Taft; Cravath, de Gainsdorf, Swaine & Wood; Winston, Strawn & Shaw. As the hearings continued through the fall, Truman was consistently adversarial and hard hitting. Jousting with the cream of the Wall Street legal elite, he attacked excessive fees and perquisites.[18]

His bitterness was deepened by a personal affront. He went to New York to secure some information at the Chase National Bank. After obtaining it, he called on the bank's president, Winthrop Aldrich. Inexplicably, he was kept waiting in the outer office. After a bit, he got to his feet, said to his escort, "You tell the old S.O.B. I didn't want to see him anyway," and left. He never forgot the slight. Eight or nine years later, Aldrich went to the White House. As Truman recounted it to Cousin Ethel, "I let him cool his heels for about an hour, which, I'm sure, was no lesson to him, while I saw a half dozen *common* people ahead of him. Us Missourians are not vindictive, no, not at all. When he finally got in, I said nothing doing to his proposition."[19]

It was unlikely that Aldrich would have intentionally snubbed a United States senator; his father had been Senate Republican leader early in the century. He himself had been a vocal critic of the sort of speculation and insider preferences that Truman so vehemently condemned. All the same, the incident confirmed Truman's long-held sentiments toward the northeastern Republican elite and gave him yet another grievance against Wall Street.[20]

VI

Truman's most emotional hearings focused on the Missouri Pacific. He got into a name-calling contest with the line's treasurer, William Wyer, whom he accused of fraudulent reporting to the RFC, the federal bank-ruptcy courts, and several state utility commissions. Appearing before the committee, Wyer called Truman's statement a blend of "misrepresenta-tion, distortion, and libel"; he went on to assert that the investigation was "a project for the defamation of character." Truman retorted, "Mr. Wyer, I want to say to you I think your statement is exactly in line with your bookkeeping, and I do not think it conveys the truth."[21]

The committee staff may have uncovered some questionable ac-counting practices, although no criminal conviction resulted from its investigations. Mostly, they elaborately demonstrated that investment bankers tended to make big money, that railroad executives had made many bad acquisition decisions during the 1920s, that the railroads were broke, and that stockholders and bondholders had lost heavily. The guid-ing assumption was that the debacle was the result of immoral and illegal behavior for which someone had to take the blame. The investigation, and especially Truman, recklessly besmirched the reputations of numer-ous financiers, corporate executives, and public officials in ways uncom-fortably close to those employed against alleged Communists in the Truman administration a dozen years later.

There can be no doubt, however, that Truman was sincere in his bitterness and determination. "It has been a most trying and patience-straining week," he wrote to Bess. "I wanted to punch the witnesses rather than question them because they had robbed and abused a great prop-erty and a lot of the 'widows and orphans' you hear so much about."[22] Undeterred by a Morgan Guaranty demonstration that the first volume of the subcommittee hearings contained eighty-one different errors, vir-tually all of which had the effect of understating the firm's risk and exag-gerating its profit, he brushed off the complaint as a "publicity stunt."[23]

He probably received some pressure from his home state to lay off the Missouri Pacific. But Tom Pendergast does not appear to have inter-vened, and Truman's role as defender of the state's greatest railroad against outside predators was hardly a political liability. The investiga-tion gave him considerable national visibility and a modest reputation as a champion of the small investor; it even won him quite a bit of respect in the previously hostile editorial columns of the St. Louis Post-Dispatch.[24]

The inquiry also made him a figure of note among the old progressives in Washington. "Old Man Norris came up to me yesterday and said that he thought my rail hearing was the highlight of the special session," Truman told Bess in December. "I almost went out because he's hardly spoken to me since I've been here."[25] Max Lowenthal took him to tea at the home of Justice Brandeis. Proud and a bit awed, he wrote to Bess, "It was a rather exclusive and brainy party. I didn't exactly belong, but they made me think I did. The Justice spent more time with me than any of his other guests and seemed very much interested in what we are doing to the railroad and insurance companies."[26]

In June 1937, Truman delivered a major speech. "Some of the

country's greatest railroads have been deliberately looted by their financial agents," he asserted. He compared the lawyers, bankers, and stock-
brokers involved in bankruptcy reorganizations to "vultures at the death
of an elephant. . . . [T]hey get all the flesh and the stockholders and the
public get the bones." His formula for change? Abolish holding companies, get rid of the financiers, and turn the lines over to operators who
cared about the stockholders and the public interest.[27]

As Congress approached adjournment just before Christmas, he took
to the floor of the Senate to issue a second blast. In a passage possibly
composed by Brandeis or Lowenthal, he appealed to Judeo-Christian
fundamentalism:

> We worship mammon; and until we go back to ancient fundamentals and
> return to the Giver of the Tables of the Law and His teachings, these con-
> ditions are going to remain with us. . . .
>   I believe the country would be better off if we did not have 60 percent
> of the assets of all the insurance companies concentrated in four compa-
> nies. I believe that a thousand insurance companies, with $4,000,000 each
> in assets, would be just a thousand times better for the country than the
> Metropolitan Life, with $4,000,000,000 in assets. . . . I also say that a thou-
> sand county-seat towns of 7,000 people each are a thousand times more
> important to this Republic than one city of 7,000,000 people. Our unem-
> ployment and our unrest are the result of the concentration of wealth, the
> concentration of population in industrial centers, mass production, and a
> lot of other so-called modern improvements.[28]

Whatever the merit of such rhetoric, it was irrelevant to a looming
railroad crisis. Desperate for cash by the end of 1937, the companies
requested a 15 percent rate increase from the ICC. "I do not think it will
remedy their situation one mite," Truman asserted. He explicitly rejected
the Wall Street argument that the breakdown of the railroads was "the
result of the depression, of paying rail labor too much, of Government
regulation." Rather, "Wall Street brought about Government regulation
and the depression. If Wall Street had produced the necessary statesmen
to run the railroads, they would never have needed regulation."

Was there nothing beyond bashing Wall Street that needed to be
done? Truman was vague. Nationalization was not the answer, nor was
pouring more money into broken-down financial structures, nor was a
rate increase. "The whole structure must be overhauled," he declared.
"One thing is certain—no formula, however scientific, will work without
men of proper character."[29]

VII

By the beginning of 1938, with the economy sinking deeply into recession, the railroads were shakier than ever. Conferring with legislators,
managers, and union leaders in a series of White House meetings,
Roosevelt offered to back any remedy (short of outright nationalization

or endless government subsidies) that Wheeler and his House counterpart, Clarence Lea, could get through Congress. Wheeler took on the task
reluctantly and made Truman his lieutenant. Politically thankless, the job
involved difficult regulatory issues that the public neither understood nor
cared about. It would require dealing with various narrowly based interest groups, all of them fixated more on the prospect of immediate losses
than on the possibility of any long-term national gain. It amounted to a
walk through a political minefield.[30]

Truman believed strongly in the mission. The detailed task appealed
to the managerial side of his personality. He involved himself heavily in
the work and made a considerable investment of ego in the bargain. Aware
of the political risks, he doubtless understood that the assignment might
give him an accomplishment to flaunt in what looked to be a difficult
reelection bid. Handled properly, moreover, the effort could reinforce the
good relationship he had begun to develop with the powerful railway
unions.[31]

In the spring of 1938, Wheeler and Truman began to develop legislation designed to force meaningful rail reorganization over the next several years. They also supported a bill that provided more loans to the
companies. The process came to a dead halt when the rail lines, motivated by a cash-flow crisis, asked the ICC to sanction a 15 percent wage
cut. The request was not outrageous in the economic context of the
Depression. Politically, though, it was unwise in the extreme. Senate liberals and insurgent progressives, led by Robert F. Wagner and Robert
La Follette, Jr., blocked passage of the loan bill. A presidential fact-
finding committee considered the wage-cut request through the summer
and fall.

Wheeler and Truman were the most prominent among legislators
who testified against the wage cut. Invoking the findings of their investigating committee, they asserted that the railroads had been looted by
financiers. "Railroad labor is the most efficient in the country," Truman
asserted. The problem was "banker management." That such testimony
had little to do with current reality was irrelevant. The banker-piracy thesis
gave the unions an excuse for rejecting any of the pain associated with a
rationalization of the rail system; it was also the received wisdom of a
liberal–labor alliance whose consent was necessary for any legislation.[32]
After six months of delay, the fact-finding board and the ICC rejected a
wage cut. The effort for legislation resumed, made more difficult by hardened union attitudes and a tepid economic upturn that muted the sense
of crisis.

Brought together in the form of a presidential committee, labor and
management agreed on a compromise program in December 1938. Invoking the national interest and a planning ideal that had been attractive to
many turn-of-the-century progressives as well as to New Dealers, the
committee produced a report advocating benefits for the railroads and
their employees while prescribing regulation for their largely unregulated

competitors. Reformist language broadened the report's appeal to the relatively few voters who paid any attention to the debate. For most members of Congress, the salient questions were whether the labor–management alliance could hold together and whether those interests that felt threatened by the report would prove more powerful than those that had developed it.[33]

The truckers, already subjected to regulation in 1935 by another Wheeler-sponsored piece of legislation, reacted strongly; they depicted the purpose of the bill as the awarding of discriminatory advantages to railway-operated trucking lines. Other major opposition came from inland-waterway carriers, which operated freighters on the Great Lakes or barges on the nation's canals and major rivers. The water carriers and their constituencies were vociferous, but relatively limited in number and organizational clout. Largely free from regulation, they received invaluable indirect subsidies from the federal government in the form of Corps of Engineers dredging and channel-development projects along every major American waterway. In those areas where their routes paralleled rail lines, the water carriers enjoyed a significant cost advantage. Regulation and their effective integration into a national transportation grid dominated by the railroads would severely reduce their competitive edge.

For Truman, the issue was tricky as a matter of both principle and politics. He sought far more than the simple infliction of regulation on another kind of carrier. Furthermore, a senator from a state bounded by the Mississippi and bisected by the Missouri had to tread carefully. Missouri River barge traffic was not unimportant to Kansas City; St. Louis was a major terminus for commercial traffic on the Mississippi. It complicated matters even more that both Bennett Clark and the *Kansas City Star* championed the water carriers. In his communications with Missouri businessmen, mostly based in St. Louis, Truman consistently stressed the benefits of the legislation. He appears to have convinced some of them that regulation, presumably by promoting rate stability, could advance their interests.[34]

Over two and a half months in early 1939, Wheeler and Truman introduced four separate bills, providing for (1) stringent regulation of investments by railroads, (2) a special federal railroad bankruptcy reorganization court, (3) abolition of transportation holding companies, and (4) ICC jurisdiction over all common carriers in order to reduce "wasteful and destructive competition." This last objective was to be facilitated by a definitive codification of transportation policy as it had developed in legislation and judicial decisions since the passage of the original Interstate Commerce Act in 1887. The most ambitious effort to establish a national transportation code ever undertaken, the proposals drew comment ranging from warm support (mainly from the rail interests), to relatively disinterested and constructive criticism (from academic experts and technocrats), to reflexive hostility (primarily from those that felt endangered).[35]

Thus the Truman–Wheeler proposals were fed into the sausage-grinder of politics. The holding-company bill was soon dead for lack of support. The senators also quickly agreed to leave the airlines to the CAA. Unregulated freight forwarders (truckers who assembled small lots of goods into freight-car loads for long-distance shipping) also gained exemption. But much of the legislation remained intact despite vehement opposition from water carriers and increasing restiveness from various motor interests.[36] With Roosevelt still supportive, the ICC bill came before the Senate on May 25 and passed by a vote of 70 to 6. Two days later, the bankruptcy reorganization court bill also won easily on a voice vote.

The bills then went to Representative Lea's House Interstate and Foreign Commerce Committee, which shelved the reorganization court. The ICC bill emerged in a considerably altered state on July 14. Its most important provisions included ICC regulation of water carriers, more RFC loans for the railroads, voluntary rail consolidations and traffic pools subject to ICC approval, and investigation of regional rate differentials. One important addition was the Harrington amendment, which prohibited the layoff of railway workers as a result of consolidations.

The opposition fought hard to block the legislation on the House floor. Not conducted along partisan lines, the debate was a near-classic example of specialized interest group conflict in which labor and business were about as divided as Republicans and Democrats. In general, those groups with a stake in cheap, unregulated water transportation opposed the legislation; Secretary of Agriculture Henry A. Wallace, for example, attacked it as detrimental to farmers. Those attracted to protection of the railroads and to the idea of stable, profitable shipping rates supported it. Only a few individuals made their decisions on the basis of ideological proclivities for or against federal planning. On July 26, the bill passed by a vote of 273 to 100.[37]

Throughout the fall of 1939 and into the spring of 1940, a joint conference committee (of which Truman was a leading Senate member) worked to hammer out a compromise between the Senate and House bills. With every week, however, the issue seemed less urgent. War in Europe strengthened an economic recovery and posed a real chance that the endeavor might disintegrate from simple lack of interest. In April 1940, the conference group finally issued a report. Patterned in most respects on the Lea bill and abandoning the larger effort to codify interstate-commerce law, it must have disappointed Truman and Wheeler. Still, it contained most of the substantive provisions of their product, including regulation of water carriers and loans to the railroads. Its preamble stated the ambitious objective of an integrated, efficient national transportation system that would end wasteful competition. Roosevelt not only endorsed the legislation, but silenced Wallace and other administration officials who opposed it.[38]

Just as victory seemed within reach, the opposition found a powerful new ally in the balky railway labor brotherhoods. The conference committee had dropped the Harrington amendment on the assumption that with an improving economy, layoffs were a theoretical proposition. The unions were not willing to give up the protection. With a large number of labor-oriented congressmen defecting, the compromise bill was defeated in the House by a vote of 209 to 182.[39]

"I feel like four years and a half's work has been thrown into the river," Truman wrote to the president of the St. Louis Chamber of Commerce. With the bill apparently dead, he went into a tough primary race without a single major legislative achievement. He, Wheeler, and others worked to put the coalition back together in the only way possible—by giving the railway brotherhoods what they wanted. A few days after winning renomination, Truman returned to Washington as the House voted in favor of a new conference report that provided job protection for the rail workers. The Senate followed three weeks later; in September, President Roosevelt signed the legislation. Formally designated the Transportation Act of 1940, it is frequently also called the Wheeler-Lea Act. To Truman, it would always be the Wheeler-Truman Act.[40]

VIII

The final legislation seems unworthy of all the fuss. It neither destroyed the water carriers nor saved the railroads. By the time it became law, a gigantic expansion in American military spending was starting to propel the rails back to a heady, and deceptive, profitability. Over the longer run, however, no system of regulation could protect them against airplanes and modern highways. Viewed from the last decade of the twentieth century, the Transportation Act—with its denunciation of wasteful competition and its faith in the benign character of governmental regulation—seems quaint, nostalgic, even reactionary.

Truman repeatedly defined the issue as one of fairness to all, to be achieved through a regulatory process that would serve a larger public interest. Denying that regulation would increase the cost of transportation, he nonetheless observed (without ever being too specific on the implications) that business interests and other economic groups not only adjusted to regulation, but often requested more of it.[41] His faith, rooted in his insurgent viewpoint, represented a virtually unexamined consensus among New Deal liberals at the end of the 1930s.

Politically, Truman had served himself well. He had learned how to chair an investigation and publicize himself in the process. He surely lost no votes in Missouri by taking a stance as a defender of the Missouri Pacific and won friends nationally among rail bondholders.[42] Most important, by aligning himself with the railway brotherhoods, he had gained a powerful ally that would serve him well in a time of need. However faulty his economics, he had displayed the instincts of a smart politician.

14

"I'm Going to Lick that Double-Crossing, Lying Governor": Struggle for Vindication, 1937–1940

As Truman began the final year of his first term in the Senate, he could take satisfaction in the esteem of his colleagues, his work as a hard-hitting investigator, and his involvement in an unusually ambitious legislative effort. Yet his future was in serious doubt. Politically vulnerable, discredited in the eyes of many observers, he found himself engaged in a desperate struggle for vindication against a one-time friend he now described as "that double-crossing, lying governor."[1] Characteristically, he plunged into what many observers considered a hopeless fight.

II

Lloyd Crow Stark's inauguration as governor of Missouri in 1937 was a glittering affair that appeared to usher in a new era of style in state politics. Stark was by any standard an impressive figure. His ancestry, which he traced back to 1719, was packed with military leaders and pioneers. His great-grandfather had started the first commercial fruit nursery west of the Mississippi. His father, Clarence M. Stark, working with Luther Burbank, had developed a new variety of apple, marketed it as Stark's Delicious, and amassed a fortune selling fruit trees.

Two and a half years younger than Truman, Stark was born for leadership. A graduate of Annapolis, he had aborted a promising career as a naval officer to take over his father's business in 1912. Commander of an artillery battalion in World War I, he had served with distinction at Saint-Mihiel and the Meuse-Argonne. A founder of the American Legion, he participated in civic activities, bred show horses, and oversaw an expansion of the family business that even the Great Depression could not stop. By the mid-1930s, his nurseries, the oldest and largest in the world, employed 1,000 salaried workers and 21,000 commission salesman. Perhaps no name was better known in Missouri, whether to hard-scrabble farmers trying to raise apples on marginal land, businessmen who made him director of the state Chamber of Commerce, or his fellow members of the elite clubs of St. Louis. Wealthy, aristocratic in bearing, well connected across the country, he was a natural member of the governing class.[2]

Stark and Truman got to know each other through American Legion and civic activities; both were interested in highway improvement and state planning. They became close friends in the early 1930s as Stark, the governorship looming large in his ambition, sought lines to the Kansas City organization. Truman was not put off even when Stark remained neutral in the 1934 senatorial primary. By the spring of 1935, he was an enthusiastic promoter of Stark's gubernatorial aspirations.[3]

In October 1935, Pendergast announced that Stark was his candidate for governor; the choice was based primarily on Stark's outstate strength and popularity, but Truman's backing surely helped. The St. Louis organization, still divided and indecisive, fell in line. Anti-Pendergast farm leader William Hirth ran against Stark, only to be flattened by a 3 to 1 margin in the August primary. After Stark beat Republican Jesse Barrett by 250,000 votes in November, Truman predicted that he would initiate one of "Missouri's greatest administrations."[4]

Stark's governorship was progressive and altogether memorable. His wealth and success gave a touch of glamor to what had been a drab institution. He pursued a businessman-reformer's agenda of expanded welfare programs, highway construction, road safety laws, a state cancer hospital, and professional-level pay for legislators. Financed by gasoline and sales taxes, his program was little different from what Truman would have adopted had he realized his own gubernatorial ambitions.[5]

These considerable achievements were overshadowed by a growing rift with the Pendergast machine. Stark had made few explicit commitments, but Pendergast had expected a benign reciprocity. Instead, after several months of hesitancy, the governor fired state insurance commissioner Emmett O'Malley, who had taken huge bribes and funneled them to Pendergast; then he repudiated O'Malley's settlement of a long and bitter rate dispute with leading fire-insurance companies. Advocating a strong new voter-registration law, he ignored boss Tom's recommendations for the Jackson County election board and appointed a body that threw out fraudulent, machine-generated registrations by the tens of thousands.[6]

The final break came over a 1938 primary contest for the Missouri Supreme Court. Stark boldly and shrewdly supported James M. Douglas, a scholarly and independent St. Louis jurist, against Pendergast's choice, Democratic regular circuit judge James V. Billings of Kennett. Douglas was the better qualified candidate, could count on St. Louis support, had the fervent support from most of the metropolitan press, and got backing from such independent influentials as William Hirth. He easily defeated Billings; reformers hailed the result as a victory for the people—and for Lloyd Stark, Missouri's new top Democrat.

By now, Truman pictured Stark much in the way regular Democrats recalled Joseph W. Folk, the turn-of-the-century antimachine crusader who had cleaned up St. Louis. Lionized by Lincoln Steffens, Folk had become governor but had also wrecked the state Democratic party; to old-time loyalists, he was an ingrate and a back stabber. Truman still found it convenient, perhaps psychologically imperative, to remain loyal to Tom Pendergast. Toward the beginning of May 1938, he removed an autographed picture of Stark from his Senate office. Queried about its whereabouts, he announced, "I've put it face to the wall in the clothes closet."[7]

Stark was only one cloud on Truman's horizon. His old political enemy, United States Attorney Maurice Milligan, prosecuted Pendergast henchmen for vote fraud and racketeering. The local federal judges, Albert Reeves and Merrill Otis, intensely partisan Republicans, acted almost as cheerleaders. A federal grand jury, composed of individuals from outside Jackson County, returned indictments. One Pendergast operative after another, most of them pathetic small fry, many of them otherwise decent people numbed by pervasive corruption, faced conviction and heavy sentences for vote fraud. By the end of 1938, the toll was 278 indictments, 63 convictions, 196 pleas of guilty or no-contest, 72 prison sentences, and over $60,000 in fines.[8]

Truman saw Milligan not as a righteous prosecutor, but as an insulting patronage rebuff. It had been assumed that having been recommended by Bennett Clark in 1934, Milligan would be succeeded by a Truman-designated appointee when his term was up in 1938, and that the same fate would befall local United States marshal Henry Dillingham, also a Clark choice. By prosecuting Truman supporters, Milligan had staked a claim to keep himself and Dillingham in office. In late 1937, Truman received notice that the president and the Justice Department were prepared to force another Milligan term through the Senate without his consent. Governor Stark also revealed that he privately had urged the president to retain Milligan.[9]

The situation engaged Truman's worst instincts. Obviously, the politically smart, and moral, course would have been to express personal disappointment at the situation in Kansas City and acquiesce in Milligan's reappointment for the sake of ensuring that justice was done. Tom Pendergast had made it clear that he did not expect Truman to engage in an act of political self-immolation. Both the *Kansas City Star* and the *St. Louis Post-Dispatch* urged the senator, to whom they had been rather friendly, to step aside. Yet something within Truman made it impossible for him to take the expedient course. He believed that Milligan, Otis, and Reeves were moral hypocrites like all "do-gooders." Narrowing the focus of his relationship with the machine to one of reciprocal loyalty, he would not desert friends who had done him no harm—whatever their other failings.[10]

Speaking to the Senate, he declared that in deference to the president he would not try to invoke senatorial courtesy but would cast a personal vote against Milligan, whom he described as being unqualified "morally" and "professionally" and having been paid off for his role in an anti-Pendergast conspiracy with large bankruptcy fees awarded by Otis and Reeves:

> I say to the Senate, Mr. President, that a Jackson county Missouri, Democrat has as much chance of a fair trial in the Federal District Court of Western Missouri as a Jew would have in a Hitler court or a Trotsky follower before Stalin. Indictments have been wholesale. Convictions have been a foregone conclusion. Verdicts have been directed. This is Federal court justice in Western Missouri, on the face of it a conspiracy between the partisan Federal judges and their bought and paid for district attorney.[11]

The tirade brought Truman little but scorn and ridicule. The *Star* condemned him as morally obtuse and tactically stupid; the *Post-Dispatch* caricatured him as a ventriloquist's puppet, "Charlie McTruman." "Say not the struggle naught availeth," commented the *New York Times*. "Tom Pendergast may have lost the cemetery vote, but he can't lose Harry Truman."[12]

Truman was certain that he had done the manly thing, and his attack was not without substance. Otis, Reeves, and Milligan were indeed engaged in a vendetta, and none was immune to the lure of political back stabbing. (During Truman's presidency, Reeves and Milligan quietly passed along information about his business failures to hostile columnist Westbrook Pegler.)[13] Nonetheless, their flaws were minor compared with the gangsterism and corruption of Kansas City politics.

That left the United States marshal's job, which Truman was unable to get for Fred Canfil. By the fall of 1937, he had received assurances of Canfil's appointment from Justice Department patronage chief Joseph Keenan, but Milligan protested that he needed Dillingham. Truman dug in his heels: "They will either take Fred Canfil or there won't be a marshal in Kansas City." Justice never sent Dillingham's name up for reappointment, but argued that he could remain in office until a successor

was designated. After Pendergast was behind bars, Truman finally agreed
to Dillingham and received assurances, not honored until 1943, that a
federal job would be found for Canfil.[14]

At the beginning of 1939, Truman faced another scandal. The family was unable to pay the county-school-fund mortgage on Martha
Truman's farm when it came due on December 31, 1938. In mid-May
1939, with the Pendergast empire collapsing and the loan five and a half
months overdue, the *Kansas City Times* devoted much of an anti-Truman
editorial to the issue. It would come up intermittently on *Times* and *Star*
editorial pages for the next fifteen months. Truman never forgave the
publishers for what he chose to interpret as an attack on his aged mother.
Of course, it was more; everybody knew that a county court run by standards that Harry Truman had set would never have made the loan.[15]

III

Boss Tom's organization seemed about as strong as ever despite the vote-fraud cases. It went into the municipal election of March 29, 1938, with
50,000 names purged from the voter-registration rolls. It faced a reform
movement with moral support from the governor's mansion in Jefferson
City, the Justice Department in Washington, and, it appeared, the White
House itself. Yet in unusually quiet and orderly balloting, the machine
ran up majorities of 43,000 votes in the contests for mayor and at-large
council seats, carried fourteen of the city's sixteen wards, and established
absolute dominance of the city council. "The people" had spoken; Kansas
City was still Tom's town.[16]

The defeat of Pendergast in the 1938 Missouri Supreme Court primary a few months later was a serious, but hardly fatal, reversal. With
the rise of the St. Louis Democracy, he might be somewhat less dominant, but he still controlled a big bloc of votes. And Missouri governors
could not serve two consecutive terms. In 1939, gubernatorial aspirants
would be around soliciting Tom's support, knowing he would require
proof that he was not dealing with another Lloyd Stark.

But could the machine survive until then? By 1938, Kansas City was
a top Justice Department priority. A large force of Treasury agents and
FBI men searched through a maze of bribery, vice, fraud, and extortion
for evidence of income tax evasion.[17] In January 1939, a local grand jury
empaneled by Judge Allen Southern began its own inquiry. The flinty old
jurist, who had tangled with Truman over road-work reimbursements a
quarter-century earlier and had always gotten just a few more votes than
he in countywide elections, bypassed county prosecutor Waller W. Graves.
Using attorneys and investigators supplied by Governor Stark, the grand
jury issued 167 indictments by mid-March.[18]

Less than a month later, a federal grand jury directed by Judge Reeves
returned its own brace of indictments. The most important was against
Tom Pendergast for failure to declare as income $315,000 in bribes

received from the fire-insurance companies. Arraigned on April 7, 1939, Good Friday, Pendergast told bystanders, "They persecuted Christ on Good Friday and nailed him to the cross." He smiled, spoke with a steady voice, was fingerprinted, posted bond, and left the courthouse a picture of serene confidence.[19]

In Washington, Harry Truman told a journalist:

> My opinion is that the District Attorney at Kansas City is behind this, because of political animus.
>
> I am sorry it happened.
>
> My connection with Pendergast was, of course, purely political. He has been a friend to me when I needed it. I am not one to desert a ship when it starts to go down.[20]

Truman later claimed that he had used the phrase "ship in distress," but the original rendering was apt. In a matter of weeks, City Manager H. L. McElroy, Chief of Police Otto Higgins, and other key officials were forced to resign. On May 22, Pendergast entered a plea of guilty to a substantially enlarged indictment. The government agreed to accept $350,000, almost all of his net assets, to settle an estimated tax liability of $830,000. Judge Otis, displaying surprising leniency, fined him another $10,000 and sentenced him to fifteen months in prison—to be followed by five years of probation in which he would be barred from all political activity and specifically prohibited from setting foot inside the old power-house at 1908 Main. Seven days later, he walked through the gates of the federal penitentiary at Leavenworth, sixty-seven years old and in precarious health.[21]

Truman had done what he could for Tom in Washington that spring, but no one was interested in making a deal. He found some consolation in remaining unindicted and not even suspected of serious wrongdoing. He told Bess that fall:

> Looks like everybody got rich in Jackson County but me. I'm glad I can still sleep well even if it is a hardship on you and Margie for me to be so damn poor. Mr. Murray, Mr. McElroy, Mr. Higgins, and even Mr. P. himself probably would pay all the ill-gotten loot they took for my position and clear conscience. What think you?[22]

Reformers determined to eradicate the last vestiges of Pendergastism had different ideas about Truman's virtue. They saw him as the machine's last big survivor and waited for Lloyd Stark to declare for the Senate. Truman put up a brave front; two weeks after Pendergast's indictment, he declared that if Stark ran, "I'll beat the hell out of him." Subsequently, he cleaned up the line to "I am confident of victory." In fact, his confidence must have been thin to nonexistent. He had less than eighteen months to build a new political base and almost no resources.

By December 1939, Jackson County was administered by a new court, headed by reformer George Montgomery. It foreclosed on Martha

Truman's farm and fired Fred Canfil as chief custodian of the Kansas City courthouse. Truman put Canfil in charge of his Kansas City office. By May 1940, the Kansas City director of the Federal Housing Authority was trying to get rid of Vivian.[23] Depressed and privately aware that he was not without some small guilt for the Pendergast excesses, Truman asked Burton Wheeler whether he should resign. After Congress adjourned in late 1939, he took off with several Senate colleagues on a tour of army bases from Fort Knox, Kentucky, through Central America to Panama, and then up the West Coast. Political observers took his decision not to return home and start mending fences as a sign that he would not run for reelection. Actually, it was an indication of profound weariness and demoralization; he reacted as he had at such times in the past. "Things seemed to be getting worse and worse in Kansas City," he told John Snyder, "and I decided to run away from it for a while."[24]

IV

When he got back to Missouri, Truman faced the hard prospects of the 1940 primary. In Jackson County, he still had a lot of personal loyalists. The most important were Vivian, Fred Canfil, Independence mayor Roger Sermon (now an independent factional leader), Independence postmaster Edgar Hinde, and the ever-loyal Rufus Burrus. (Fred Boxley had died in 1936.) Jim Pendergast and much of the remnants of the organization would back him.[25]

But he was desperately weak in St. Louis, now the fulcrum of Missouri Democratic politics. There, the local kingpins, Barney Dickmann and Bob Hannegan, were steely-eyed professionals, primarily interested in being on the winning side. Truman's most important local contact was his close friend in the Reserve Officers Corps, John W. Snyder, a transplanted Arkansan and Reconstruction Finance Corporation official. Through Pat Harrison and John Snyder, Truman had met and forged a close relationship with James K. (Jake) Vardaman, Jr. Snyder's predecessor at the RFC, Vardaman was a St. Louis banker and son of a famous progressive-era governor of Mississippi. Truman's old friend Harry Vaughan was based in St. Louis as a salesman. By a generous estimate, these three were capable of swinging six votes—their own and those of their wives.[26]

The rest of the state provided at best a mixed outlook. Truman's "organization" was little more than a network of a few prominent Masons, army reserve officers, and National Guardsmen. To this group, he added some political allies acquired through his Pendergast associations and his uneasy concord with Bennett Clark. In northwestern Missouri, he could count on St. Joseph mayor Phil Welch and Congressman Richard Duncan; but it was doubtful they could prevail against hordes of state patronage workers. In northeastern Missouri, he had almost no prominent loyalists.[27]

In the southwestern region, Truman had the firm support of Vic Messall's old employer, former congressman and newspaper publisher Frank Lee of Joplin. In nearby Webb City, he had the devoted allegiance of Harry Easley, a banker whom he had met in the Masonic Order. In Springfield, local organization leader Sam Wear was his point man. Easley and Wear sometimes bumped up against each other, but in tandem with Lee they were capable of delivering to Truman most of the Democratic votes to be had in an obstinately Republican area.[28]

In central Missouri, rich in Democratic ballots, Truman's greatest friend was Tom Van Sant, a Fulton banker and Masonic associate. Frank Monroe, a former presiding judge of the Pettis County court, was Truman's man in Sedalia. In Jefferson City, several elective state officials, including Secretary of State Dwight Brown, had connections to the Pendergast machine. A sometime ally was Richard (Dick) Nacy, a banker and former state treasurer who had married into the Pendergast family.[29]

Truman developed some significant support in southeastern Missouri, thanks largely, it appears, to the good offices of Bennett Clark. In Caruthersville, he had the backing of Neal Helm, a prominent businessman, and Roy Harper, an ambitious young lawyer. His most important booster, however, was J. V. Conran, the tough prosecuting attorney of New Madrid County. Conran tolerated illegal gambling and other forms of "victimless crime," played rough-and-tough with the opposition, always kept his word, and delivered cotton-bale-size quantities of votes. By the late 1930s, he was close to the Pendergast machine, Matt Murray having given him control of the regional WPA. His view of the world reflected the sentiment of the propertied establishment throughout the cotton South. He enjoyed the respect, if not the affection, of many political professionals.[30]

In early 1940, there were numerous reports that Truman might accept a federal appointment. He denied it, but in fact he had received an indication that the president would appoint him to the Interstate Commerce Commission. He called a meeting of friends in St. Louis at the end of January to evaluate his prospects. Only a few persons showed up; most told him that he could not win. No major St. Louis figure was present. There was also little representation from Kansas City heavyweights, quite a few of whom were prepared to swallow hard and back Milligan (who at least was not a double-crosser like Stark).

The senator had wanted Dick Nacy to be his chief fund-raiser; Nacy was conspicuously absent. Roger Sermon agreed to take on the job, but with so little hope that immediately after the meeting he wrote to Bennett Clark asking him to help Truman secure a respectable federal appointment. Harry Easley, who subsequently begged off the assignment of campaign chairman, privately agreed that Sermon had taken the only practical course. The *Post-Dispatch* summarized the local political wisdom: "He is a dead cock in the pit."[31]

A week later, Truman filed for renomination.[32]

V

The senator's apparently suicidal decision may have stemmed from his determined optimism that hard work could overcome any obstacle, but it may equally have rested on a shrewd judgment that his potential support was far greater than it appeared and that Stark's liabilities were large. Truman still had a high personal reputation. His opponents asserted that he had walked too many miles too blindly with Tom Pendergast, but not that he was a crook. The foreclosure of his mother's farm less than a month before the primary underscored his honesty and attracted some sympathy. President of the Thirty-fifth Division Association in 1939, he had name recognition and popularity among veterans. He also was grand master of the Missouri Masons. That fall, asked whether the state leader of the Masonic Order was a person of low character, Republican gubernatorial candidate Forrest Donnell, himself a leading Mason, responded, "Of course not." Truman backers gleefully publicized the admission.[33]

His awkward alliance with Bennett Clark also helped. Envisioning himself as leader of the state Democratic party and a credible candidate for the presidency, Clark bitterly resented Stark's similar ambitions. He was not always wild about Harry, especially after the two of them differed vehemently on neutrality revision after the outbreak of war in Europe. Still, if Truman ran, Clark would be in his corner; the only question was with what intensity. In the summer of 1939, he told Truman that he might try to get one of the Milligan brothers into the race to split the antimachine vote.[34]

Truman was popular among rank-and-file Democratic party regulars all over the state. In January, he attended a Jackson Day dinner organized by anti-Stark Democrats in Springfield; the overflow audience of at least 700 people cheered lustily when Senator Tom Connally of Texas eulogized their senator; it jeered when a state official tried to read a message from the governor. Truman assured John Snyder that the demonstration was unplanned. There were also a lot of pro-Stark Democrats in Springfield, but so large a crowd could hardly be written off as a collection of Pendergast thugs—although that did not prevent the *St. Louis Post-Dispatch* from trying. Plainly there was a large residue of pro-Truman sentiment among party activists, who were most likely to vote, and bring others to the polls, in a primary election.[35]

Connally's praise underscored another Truman asset: his remarkable popularity in the Senate. In a fashion that was nearly unprecedented, about two dozen Democratic senators, ranging ideologically from Robert F. Wagner on the left to Pat Harrison and Kenneth McKellar on the right, endorsed him for renomination. Several, including Alben Barkley, came into the state to speak for him. Barkley used his frank to mail a pro-Truman speech by Senator Lew Schwellenbach to Missouri voters. James F. Byrnes secretly raised a critical $4,000 from financier Bernard Baruch.

Guy Gillette orchestrated a Senate investigation of Stark's campaign. Voters who paid attention got a loud and clear message.[36]

The railway labor unions paid Truman back for his support. The brotherhoods had about 50,000 members in Missouri; a few local leaders favored Stark, but the national officers were solidly for Truman. They sponsored large rallies for the senator in Kansas City and St. Louis. The railway workers put out a special issue of their weekly paper, *Labor*, filled it with testimonials for Truman, and distributed 500,000 copies around the state. The sheet-metal workers, electrical workers, and boilermakers had some presence in rail yards and frequently followed the cue of the rail unions. William Green, president of the American Federation of Labor (AFL), endorsed Truman. Stark had substantial union support, but Truman got the most visible and active labor backing.[37]

As spring moved into summer, the European war that had broken out in September 1939 became an international crisis. The Nazi blitzkrieg, the surrender of France, the British evacuation at Dunkirk—all stunned Missourians. Among Democrats especially, these events generated a lot of preparedness and interventionist sentiment. The week before the election, newspapers carried stories and photos of German bombing raids against England. Truman and Stark had no appreciable differences on the salient issues; both advocated preparedness while stopping short of endorsing a military draft or outright intervention. However, the possibility of war favored Truman. His own military experience, his membership on the Military Appropriations Subcommittee, and his long tour of military bases toward the end of 1939 qualified him as a defense expert whose credentials outshone Stark's. Even the *Post-Dispatch* could not avoid quoting him at some length on national defense needs.[38]

Even so, it was questionable that these assets, such as they were, would be sufficient against Stark's money, the power of the governorship, and the opposition of most of the state's large newspapers. Money was necessary for more than advertising. The Pendergast machine had never enjoyed a monopoly on ballot fraud. Dozens of ward bosses and courthouse rings around the state produced votes only in response to cash. "You know yourself what the fourth ward is in Maryville," a supporter told Truman. "Nobody ever got many votes down there without spending a lot of money." Here the governor's resources, both personal and official, were overwhelming.[39]

Truman had benefited enormously in 1934 from the backing of the state administration; now Stark had at his disposal several thousand state employees twisting arms, managing patronage, and handing out Stark literature. The gubernatorial machine could swing 25,000 votes or so outstate. Even some of the senator's old friends and supporters had been turned around. For example, Stark made Bob Walton, the influential publisher and editor of the *Armstrong Herald*, an honorary colonel and appointed him superintendent of the Confederate soldiers' home at an annual salary of $3,000. Walton had supported Truman in 1934; by 1940, he was more distant. He harbored private doubts about Stark, but it was unlikely that he would express them at the cost of giving up an income supplement that could buy him a new Buick annually.[40]

The big newspapers especially infuriated Truman. Only the *Kansas City Journal* backed him. The far more powerful *Kansas City Star* was of course hostile. The St. Louis papers—the *Post-Dispatch*, the *Star-Times*, the *Globe-Democrat*—were unanimously against him, all criticizing him for sticking with a machine that they deemed the antithesis of civic morality. On the eve of the primary, the *Post-Dispatch* thundered, "Should Truman be nominated, there would be shrill rejoicing among all the forces of evil in Missouri."[41] Stark epitomized the values and class consciousness of those who owned the metropolitan dailies and determined their editorial policies. The *Post-Dispatch* provided the sharpest example. Whether by inherited wealth and family tradition (as with publisher Joseph Pulitzer, Jr.) or by education and upward mobility (as with Truman's old friend Charles Ross), it was run by patricians sure of their virtue and their mission to provide leadership for others. However unintentionally, the paper had tellingly displayed this combination of class and values in April 1939 by illustrating a long, favorable feature article on Stark with a picture of the governor in full riding habit on his favorite show horse.[42] Truman's revulsion against such attitudes was instinctive.

Stark himself displayed personality traits not unknown to men of wealth and power: an exaggerated sense of his own importance and a pervasive insensitivity to others. Time and again, he displayed arrogance toward backers, leaving them demoralized and unenthusiastic. He often ignored requests for small favors, insensitively angered local influentials, and bypassed key legislative supporters.[43] His most serious political mistake was his cavalier attitude toward the St. Louis machine. Bob Hannegan, its chief patronage dispenser, appears to have received more than his share of turndowns from Stark and must have gotten tired of such admonitions as "Please try not to recommend anyone but top-quality men." By early 1939, the disgruntlement in St. Louis was common knowledge. Stark did little to mollify it, perhaps assuming that the organization would have to support him because of his regional affinity, newspaper backing, and general popularity. The St. Louis boys, however, cared nothing for the first two considerations, personally preferred Truman with his machine background, and inclined toward the governor only because he looked like the winner.[44]

Truman would capitalize on yet another of Stark's blunders, his thoughtless alienation of much of the state's black vote. Growing in visibility within the Democratic party when Stark became governor, blacks, to be sure, were still heavily controlled by city ward leaders. But increasing numbers looked to a growing educated class of professionals and political activists for leadership. This group, in turn, appears to have initially welcomed Stark, envisioning him as a sympathetic leader willing to go beyond the old politics. Instead, he was crudely manipulative, appointing a number of state commissions to study Negro problems, but never bothering to send formal notification to the members or to find meaningful funding for their work.[45]

When the United States Supreme Court ordered the state of Missouri either to admit blacks to the University of Missouri law school or to establish a genuinely equal alternative, the governor went along with state legislation that set up patently unequal facilities. The board of curators at Lincoln University, the state's only black institution of higher education, protested; Stark fired them all. In late 1938, black sharecroppers, evicted from their farms in New Madrid County, camped along the highway. Stark sent the highway patrol to maintain order; eventually, it forced the demonstrators from their camps. Old machine-oriented black leaders such as C. A. Franklin, the editor of the *Kansas City Call*, took such events as confirmation that the regulars, however limited their social outlook, were more reliable than reformers such as Stark. He and numerous other black leaders supported Truman.[46]

Truman took no position on either the law school or the sharecropper demonstration, but he recognized Negro leaders and dealt with them as an interest group. Unlike Stark, he would make a direct appeal for black votes, asserting frankly that although he did not believe in "social equality," he stood for equal opportunity: "I believe in . . . not merely the brotherhood of white men, but the brotherhood of all men before the law." In the Missouri of 1940, this was fairly strong stuff; his opponents did not rush to match it. Blacks attentive to issues found what they wanted to hear only in Truman's speeches.[47]

VI

At the beginning of 1940, however, it seemed that only the governor possessed what any candidate needed to win a primary election—an organization. Truman could find no major Democrat willing or able to manage his campaign. By default, the assignment went to Vic Messall, who resigned as the senator's secretary and took it on an unpaid basis. (Messall's wife went back on Truman's payroll to keep the family afloat.) David Berenstein, a St. Louis attorney and Zionist leader, volunteered to run the campaign there. He had no particular political weight; but he had a good reputation, was affiliated with a highly regarded law firm, and was well connected in the Jewish community. Truman gave him the imposing title of director-general of the campaign and unleashed him on the city. Brash, aggressive, and self-promoting, Berenstein got along poorly with Truman's older loyalists and awakened some latent anti-Semitism in Truman himself. But he established a facade of independent, non-machine St. Louis support and probably raised some campaign funds. Truman and his friends later disparaged Berenstein unmercifully; in fact, they were lucky to have him.[48]

Truman managed to keep a lot of supporters in the state WPA. After Matt Murray's forced resignation as state director in 1939, the administration appointed as his successor Marvin Casteel, superintendent of the Missouri Highway Patrol. Casteel, who had voted for Truman in 1934, was a nonpartisan figure with a mandate to depoliticize the WPA. If he succeeded, the net effect would be to help Stark. In a single devastating stroke at the beginning of 1940, he fired thirty-one officials in the Kansas City area, and then made scattered dismissals and issued numerous warnings elsewhere. Truman reacted sharply, complaining to administration officials and writing to Casteel at the end of February: "I am not at all happy with the situation and I am going to do something about it unless conditions change very radically." His allies throughout the state inundated Missouri Democratic congressmen with letters of protest.[49] Casteel was impressed enough to lay off, both because of Truman's wrath and because too many WPA officials enjoyed relationships with powerful local politicians. On election day in most of the state, the agency employees would get out votes for Truman.[50]

Casteel also backed off after Bennett Clark's imposing state network dominated the Democratic state convention in mid-April. Stark and his supporters had expected that the governor would be named head of the delegation to the Democratic National Convention pledged to support Roosevelt for a third term. This action would all but knock Truman out of the Senate race and make Stark a leading contender for the vice presidency (the presidency, if Roosevelt did not run). Instead, Stark walked into a buzzsaw. Clark forces throughout the state controlled one county caucus after another; remnants of the old machine dominated the Kansas City delegation; the St. Louis professionals made no fight. Stark, realizing that he had been beaten, conceded the delegation chairmanship to Clark without a struggle.

Stark sat grimly on the platform, not called on to speak, listening to talks by such machine types as former governor Guy Park and Representative Joe Shannon. Delegates booed mention of his name and cheered Jim Pendergast. It took the personal intervention of Clark, Bob Hannegan, and Truman to get the governor in the Democratic National Convention delegation. Truman helped write a convention platform that in effect rebuffed Stark's claim that he was the only true Roosevelt follower in Missouri.[51]

Stark put the best face he could on these events, but he had suffered a humiliating defeat that confirmed the deep dissatisfaction among the grass-roots partisans he would need in the primary. Yet the spectacle hardly presaged a groundswell for Truman. The atmosphere in Truman's hotel suite was still so subdued that J. V. Conran asked about a rumor that Jim Pendergast would throw his support to Maurice Milligan to make certain that Stark would be defeated. Truman responded sharply, "Conran, I am getting damn tired of everybody talking about beating Stark. I want . . . my friends to start talking Truman."[52]

Milligan had resigned as United States attorney and declared his candidacy for the Senate just a couple of weeks earlier, thereby converting the contest into a three-way race akin to that of 1934. It appears that Bennett Clark did indeed encourage him and may have brokered a deal that he would get his old job back if he lost. Milligan surely resented the way in which Stark had tried to monopolize the credit for overthrowing the machine. He could have run for governor and been elected easily, but the job was a political dead end with miserable pay. (A senator's salary was twice as much, and Milligan apparently expected to be able to maintain a Washington law practice on the side.) He drew support from the rabbit faction in Kansas City, but statewide—as Bennett Clark had predicted—he damaged Stark more than Truman.[53]

It soon became obvious that Milligan was going nowhere. He had started too late, had no flair for self-dramatization, and exhibited no aptitude for developing an organization. His ineptness ensured that Bennett Clark and his following would see Truman as the only realistic alternative to Stark. Milligan impartially assailed both his opponents, but he could say nothing about Truman that had not already been said. When he hammered Stark for soliciting Pendergast support for governor and joining the fight against the machine only when victory was in sight, he invoked issues that Truman could never credibly employ.[54]

One final consideration was critical. Whom did Franklin D. Roosevelt want? The president had protected Milligan's job in 1938 and had accepted his resignation with a letter of fulsome praise. He had met with Stark at the White House on numerous occasions, apparently had the most cordial of relations with him, and was rumored to have considered him for Secretary of the Navy in 1939. Stark, in turn, relentlessly curried favor with Roosevelt and, in his correspondence with the White House, depicted himself as the president's paladin in Missouri.[55] Truman had supported the administration on almost every important issue, but his relationship with Roosevelt had been rocky. In early 1940, he openly opposed a third term as a matter of principle, although he said he would make an exception for FDR. In the spring, he unsuccessfully fought an administration drive to bring the Civil Aeronautics Authority under Commerce Department jurisdiction. That summer, annoyed when Roosevelt vetoed a minor bill he had sponsored to provide government funds for rail bridges, Truman led the charge for a successful veto override.[56]

Roosevelt refused to state a preference. But in 1939, he made several private statements to friends of Truman and to Truman himself that seemed to indicate support for the senator's return. "I do not believe your governor is a real liberal. . . . He has no sense of humor. . . . He has a large ego," he told Truman in August 1939. Other senators came out of the White House saying that Roosevelt was for Truman. Yet whatever FDR said, his administration was distinctly unhelpful when Truman needed help. Roosevelt may have discerned (correctly) in Stark a resemblance to Harry Byrd, another apple grower, who had let him down after being elected to the Senate. Or he may have privately given the governor the same kind of encouragement he gave Truman. The senator, like the other two contenders, uncritically praised Roosevelt, but he was by now wise enough to expect nothing in return.[57]

VII

When Truman formally opened his campaign at Sedalia on June 15, 1940, his opponents had been speaking around the state for a month without arousing much response. Disinterested observers were beginning to think that he had a real chance. The rally attracted a crowd of 4,000 to 6,000 and included representation from each of Missouri's 114 counties. Truman's good friend Senator Schwellenbach was the major guest speaker. Also delivering addresses were General Stayton; Father M. F. Wogan, the Cameron priest; Colonel Edward Gorrell, chairman of the Air Transport Association; and leaders from the Railroad Conductors and the Sheet Metal Workers unions. Martha Truman, now eighty-seven years old, sat on the platform and greeted prominent attendees. Tom Van Sant recalled that she displayed acute judgment in discerning which of the politicians introduced to her were really for Harry.

Truman's own speech emphasized the need for a strong national defense, the expulsion of subversive elements from America, justice for the Negro, and fairness for the farmer. It established themes to which he adhered throughout the campaign. Truman would stress his own experience and strengths and leave Milligan and Clark to blast away at Lloyd Stark. He would capitalize on the world crisis without sounding overly warlike. Appealing to large and important voting groups that had benefited from the New Deal, he would identify himself with Roosevelt. (At Sedalia, Sam Wear introduced Schwellenbach as "a 100 per cent New Dealer" and declared, "I think his appearance here is an indication of where the President stands.")[58]

On June 20, Guy Gillette's Senate Campaign Investigating Committee, after quietly arranging the timing with Truman, charged that the governor was financing his campaign through state employee salary kickbacks. The committee asserted that he had extracted at least $28,000 in pledges and collected at least $11,000. Stark responded unconvincingly that the report was a smear. (Gillette privately told Truman that Stark, if elected, probably could not be seated in the Senate.) Milligan demonstrated his special value to the Truman drive by calling for the release of all the investigative data.[59] Of course, the governor had done no more than play politics as traditionally practiced in Missouri, but he had made the mistake of presenting himself as a moral exemplar. He was hurt by the allegations, and then further damaged when a former lobbyist for the Union Electric Company confessed to having funneled an illegal $4,000 in cash to Stark's 1936 campaign.[60]

The governor's greatest liability was his overweening ambition. As early as 1938, the St. Louis Advertising Club gridiron dinner featured a skit that lampooned his thinly veiled desire for the secretaryship of the navy. At the beginning of 1940, Bennett Clark declared that Stark was simultaneously running for president, vice president, secretary of war, secretary of the navy, high commissioner to the Philippines, ambassador to Great Britain, and United States senator. He added, "It is also rumored that he is a receptive candidate for the papacy and the archbishopric of Canterbury."[61] Clark's extravagant denunciation was effective because it had a factual basis. Stark had spent much of 1939 in a campaign of self-promotion that clearly envisioned the Senate as a secondary objective and included the presidency as a possibility. On June 29, 1940, amid rumors that he would be chosen for vice president, he met at his request with Roosevelt in Washington. On July 4, speaking to a large crowd in Sedalia, he offered himself to the people in "any capacity I may be called to serve." With Roosevelt still not having announced his own intentions, Stark's backers began floating his name for either end of the national ticket.[62]

Perhaps told by Roosevelt that he had a "green light," Stark let his name be put in nomination for the vice presidency at the Democratic National Convention. His boom lasted for two days. The convention nominated Roosevelt by acclamation; it then followed FDR's bidding by naming Henry Wallace as his running mate.[63] Remarkably, Stark did not realize that he had looked silly. He told a supporter that "thousands of people" were "furious" at Clark and Truman for keeping a Missourian off the ticket. Others knew better. Maurice Milligan skewered Stark as a politician who had "vowed to high heaven" that he was not running for vice president, only to reveal that he had been doing so for many months and that "his organization was complete even down to the distribution of free apples." Bennett Clark characterized the bid as an "ill-fated, short-lived, and ludicrous fiasco." Calling Stark a tireless "plum hunter," he revealed that six months earlier the governor privately had again expressed interest in the Navy Department.[64]

VIII

The candidates spent most of July campaigning around the state. For Truman, the experience was a replay of the grueling 1934 effort: driving for hours over dusty roads in oven-like automobiles, talking for fifteen minutes or so at county fairs or local picnics or political rallies, working the crowd for another fifteen or twenty minutes, and then moving on. He spoke in seventy-five counties. In the cities, he appealed to labor; in the rural areas, to farmers; almost everywhere, he mentioned his work for a strong national defense and cited his experience on Capitol Hill.[65]

He had barely enough cash to keep going, although the unions did a lot for him in the way of donated services and literature. (One such effort depicted Stark as a tax cheat and an employer who subjected his apple-nursery workers to poverty-level wages. It was entitled *By Their Fruits Ye Shall Know Them*.) There was also the $4,000 contribution from financier Bernard Baruch. Truman would report a deficit of $3,674, which he apparently covered himself over a period of years, just as he had handled his haberdashery debts. Just days before the voting, Stark charged that Truman was the beneficiary of a huge, boss-generated slush fund. Independent observers did not take the charge seriously. Actually, at the very time Stark made it, the senator requested an urgent loan against the value of his life insurance. It is uncertain whether he took it. A week before the primary, the Stark campaign reported that it had received the maximum $19,286 in cash allowed by the law.[66]

Truman could expect to carry Kansas City and Jackson County, but by much-reduced margins from 1934. With Stark controlling the gubernatorial apparatus and strongly supported by William Hirth, there was little prospect of repeating the 1934 outstate triumph. That situation made St. Louis crucial, especially since the Democratic vote (ghost and genuine) had expanded greatly there. By 1940, total voter registrations in Kansas City were 185,000. St. Louis tallied 390,000, perhaps 50,000 of which were fraudulent.[67]

The St. Louis politicians were mostly concerned with winning the gubernatorial race; the Hatch Act and WPA cutbacks left the statehouse, not Washington, as a primary source of spoils. Their candidate, local excise commissioner Lawrence McDaniel, was not an easy sell. Portly and jolly, he fit the cliché image of a machine politician. His opposition delighted in referring to him as St. Louis's "saloon commissioner." McDaniel's major opponent, Allen McReynolds of Carthage, had been an able good-government leader in the legislature, had an imposing outstate following, and was endorsed by the major newspapers.[68]

Through a tacit alliance with Stark, the St. Louis bosses hoped to make McDaniel palatable to the rest of the state. Mayor Barney Dickmann's sister, Mayme, was a prominent member of the Stark-for-senator club. McDaniel's wife, who was a Democratic national committeewoman, was also close to the governor. Mike Kinney, the most prominent St. Louis machine pol in the legislature, also backed Stark. The governor, in turn, did not endorse a candidate to succeed him, although about all of his vocal supporters favored McReynolds. One did not have to be a Machiavelli to discern an unspoken alliance of convenience.[69]

As Truman's support appeared to grow throughout the spring and summer, the St. Louis leaders leaned increasingly toward a straddle. On August 1, Bob Hannegan told reporters that "a poll of committeemen" of the city's twenty-eight wards showed ten each for Truman and Stark, two for Milligan, and six open. Truman leaders privately promised to back McDaniel. The deal nearly broke down after Truman's last big appearance in St. Louis flopped. A labor rally maladroitly scheduled for a Wednesday night, it drew only 326 people. On Sunday, August 4, two days before the election, the papers reported a massive machine swing to Stark.[70]

The Truman forces struck back hard. On Monday, Harry Easley, who privately favored his fellow Jasper Countian McReynolds anyway, fired off telegrams to Dickmann and McDaniel: "UNDERSTAND YOU HAVE TRADED OFF TRUMAN. COMMENCING IMMEDIATELY TO ORGANIZE THIS SECTION OF THE STATE FOR ALLEN MCREYNOLDS." J. V. Conran, Roger Sermon, and others sent similar wires. Dickmann responded with a denial, but also got on the phone. He promised Easley that Truman would carry twelve wards and claimed that only one was firm for Stark, one was questionable, and the rest were open. McDaniel, as Roger Sermon recalled it, told him fourteen wards for Truman, eight for Stark, and six open. Hoping that St. Louis really meant it, the Truman organization stayed with McDaniel.[71]

On the morning of election day, August 6, the senatorial primary was a toss-up. The *Post-Dispatch*, which had urged independents to vote in the Democratic primary, printed a front-page story that its editors probably knew was spurious; it charged that the Truman campaign was trying to shake down WPA workers. (Buried on page 2 was David Berenstein's explanation that some WPA workers had simply received a general form letter asking for contributions; it specifically cited the Hatch Act, which barred solicitations of federal employees.) Three days earlier, the *Kansas City Star* had printed a sixteen-month-old photo of Truman standing in front of a portrait of Tom Pendergast.[72]

The early returns from around the state left Truman in despair McDaniel was winning handily, but in the senatorial race Stark had a commanding lead of 11,000 votes at 10:30 P.M. Truman went to bed convinced that it was all over. In the middle of the night, Dave Berenstein called from St. Louis to congratulate him on being renominated. Bess took the call, believed it a prank, and slammed the receiver down in anger. It was no joke. St. Louis had come through with seventeen wards. Stark won outstate Missouri (including St. Louis County) by more than 24,000 votes. Truman ran ahead of Stark in Jackson County by a substantially diminished majority of 23,900; his vote there was little more than a third of his 1934 total. He carried the city of St. Louis by 8,391 votes; his statewide margin was 7,966.

J. V. Conran did yeoman work also. He managed to find 2,500 more votes in New Madrid County than had been cast in the 1934 senatorial primary and gave Truman a whopping margin. He also probably helped deliver some other southeastern counties. Sam Wear and Harry Easley produced a big bloc of southwestern counties. Truman carried several counties along the Missouri River, including Cole (Jefferson City), where the governor's influence was offset by other state officials allied to Kansas City. Although he lost the total outstate vote, Truman actually carried forty-four counties, five more than he had six years earlier.[73]

Stark and his supporters, noting that the primary turnout was much lower than in 1938, blamed the independent, good-government vote for failing to show and the weather for being sunny. "Due primarily to the severe drought, etc., about 100,000 of our rural vote, which is strong for me, did not turn out," he wrote to Roosevelt. He privately believed that the election had been stolen from him in the Pendergast wards of Kansas City, in St. Louis, and in southeastern Missouri. Perhaps he was right— assuming, of course, that no dishonest ballots were cast by his own people. (The ninth precinct of St. Louis's Fourth Ward had reported early on the evening of August 6: 118 for Stark, 0 for Truman.)[74]

Truman returned to the Senate on August 9. When he stepped into the chamber in the midst of a speech by Hiram Johnson, he was surrounded by exultant friends—Wheeler and Byrnes, Barkley and Harrison, Schwellenbach and Minton, Hill, Hatch, Stewart, and Chavez, even Republican leader and vice-presidential candidate Charles McNary. As the miffed Johnson asked for order, they went off to the cloakroom for a celebration. "I told them I was glad to be back with them for a little spell," Truman told a journalist.[75]

IX

In Washington, he found himself faced with a tough war issue that he had dodged during the campaign: conscription. "The Gallup poll shows Mo. overwhelmingly for it. . . . I don't like it but I guess I'll have to be for it," he wrote to Bess. As usual by now, Clark voted the other way. For Truman, the issue was overshadowed by final passage of the Transportation Act.[76]

Truman reluctantly agreed to recommend Milligan for reappointment to his old job as United States attorney. "Some of my Kansas City friends will be hopping mad about it. And I don't feel so good about it myself," he told Bess. His feelings toward Lloyd Stark were less generous. A friend of Stark inquired if he had heard from the governor since the election: "Told him I hadn't and didn't want to hear from the S.O.B. and that so far as I am concerned I didn't give a damn what he did or intended to do, and that I hoped he'd tell him just that." Truman and Clark got the Democratic National Committee to exclude Stark from any participation in the fall campaign. Stark, for his part, refused to endorse not simply Truman, but the entire Democratic ticket.[77]

Truman's Republican opponent was Manvel Davis of Kansas City, the civic leader who had criticized his county reform ideas nearly a decade earlier. Davis hammered away at Truman's Pendergast ties and got the active or passive support of numerous followers of Stark and McReynolds. Foreign policy, the third-term controversy, and continued passions over the New Deal bumped up against one another, making the election seem unpredictable. Truman's campaign organization was chaotic as Berenstein, Messall, and Canfil intermittently squabbled. Nonetheless, he was always at least a slight favorite; he campaigned vigorously in the fall, but without the sense of desperation that had been in evidence during the summer.[78]

On election day, Roosevelt led the ticket in Missouri, defeating Willkie by 958,476 (52.3 percent) to 871,009 (47.5 percent); Truman beat Davis by 930,775 (51.2 percent) to 886,376 (48.7 percent). Republican gubernatorial candidate Forrest Donnell upset McDaniel by 3,500 votes. Narrow as it was, Truman could rightly take his victory as a vindication. He lost outstate Missouri by nearly 27,000 votes, but carried Kansas City by almost 25,000 and St. Louis by over 46,000. Thus he emerged definitively as a candidate of the cities, an urban liberal. Moreover, his most important center of political strength was now in St. Louis. In a twelve-month period, he had remade his political base.[79]

He also hoped that he had remade his image. The Missouri Democrats unwisely attempted to contest the gubernatorial election; Truman remained aloof from the effort, which was widely called a "steal." Friends in Jackson County urged him to assume leadership of what was left of the Kansas City organization. Others wanted him to take over the state Democratic party and lead it back to victory. He displayed no appetite for either endeavor.[80] Instead, focusing on his role in Washington, he already had an idea for another investigation that he hoped would be good for the country, for Missouri, and for himself.

15

"We Saved the Taxpayers About Fifteen Billion Dollars": The Truman Committee, 1941–1944

"My investigating committee is getting really hot," Truman wrote to Bess in March 1941.[1] By then, investigations had become a way of life and a mode of political advancement for him. Bouts of exhaustion notwithstanding, he thrived on the work, the confrontation, and the ultimate sense of accomplishment. His new endeavor, he hoped, would bring greater efficiency to a burgeoning defense program, serve key Missouri constituencies, and increase his stature as a senator. On that day in 1941, however, he surely never imagined how far it would take him.

II

Washington in early 1941, like the country at large, had undergone an astonishing transformation. During the last six months of 1940, Congress had authorized $10.5 billion for defense alone, a sum greater than the entire budget of the United States for any of the Depression years of the 1930s. New agencies with mandates far more imposing than their actual statutory powers attempted to manage this massive mobilization. Businessmen from all over the nation bid for defense contracts that were let with more speed than caution. Unavoidably chaotic and inefficient, the situation offended virtually all of Truman's administrative instincts. Moreover, it generated intense unhappiness within the one group in American society with which he most closely identified—smaller regional businessmen who often found it impossible to deal with procurement officials drawn naturally to big, tested suppliers. The tribulations of Missouri friends and supporters goaded him to action. Military waste and excess in his own state provided him the examples to make his point.

Truman's old friend and supporter Lou Holland was the president of the newly established Mid-Central War Resources Board, founded to publicize and coordinate small-business resources as a means of attracting defense contracts to the region. Acting at Holland's behest and following his own impulses, Truman met personally with President Roosevelt on February 3, 1941, to plead the case of small business. He left doubting that he had gotten anything but FDR's usual "cordial treatment."

He also worried about waste, fraud, and extravagance. By early 1941, he had visited numerous defense camps in the course of initial construction or drastic enlargement (although not, as he later remembered it, in one grand 30,000-mile journey). At Fort Leonard Wood in southern Missouri, he was appalled by squandered material, idle workers, and exorbitant costs that seemed typical of camp construction around the nation.[2]

On February 10, 1941, Truman spoke to the Senate requesting an investigation of the national defense program. Complaining that small manufacturers were ignored and forced to sell out, he declared, "The policy seems to be to make the big man bigger and to put the little man completely out of business." Asserting that favoritism was rampant in the contracting process, he said, "I have had considerable experience in letting public contracts; and I have never yet found a contractor who, if not watched, would not leave the Government holding the bag." He also attacked unions for extracting high initiation fees from new members as the price of a job, warned that defense industry was dangerously concentrated in a few small areas, and argued against channeling workers into already crowded urban defense centers.[3]

The address showed that at heart Truman remained the insurgent type—populist, entrepreneurial, culturally traditional, yet enough of a modernist to couch his argument in terms of efficient use of resources. It also demonstrated a newfound confidence. No longer content to function as second banana to Burt Wheeler or any other senator, he wanted to head his own special investigating committee. Astutely realizing that probes of the defense program were sure to happen, he wanted to make one headed by himself attractive to Democratic leaders.

He followed up the speech with a resolution to establish a special committee that would be empowered to investigate virtually any aspect of the defense program. He countered the initial doubts of the Roosevelt administration by giving assurances of responsible cooperation, made it clear that he would work closely with the congressional leadership, and systematically built support among his many friends in the Senate. Just appointed to the Senate Military Affairs Committee, he secured a vote endorsing his resolution over the lone dissent of its ailing chairman, Morris Sheppard of Texas.

He then negotiated funding with James Byrnes, who still ran the Audit and Control Committee out of his hip pocket and functioned as Roosevelt's right-hand man in the Senate. Facing the prospect of investigations that might be controlled by such unfriendly characters as Eugene Cox of Georgia, Roosevelt and Byrnes agreed to support the Truman probe—with as little money as possible. Truman had asked for only $25,000 to get started; after a few days of haggling, he and Byrnes agreed on what he later called "the magnificent sum of $15,000."[4]

Truman, of course, would chair the new committee, but he had to bargain over the membership. He wanted Robert La Follette, Jr., but ran into a firm negative from a Democratic establishment offended by La Follette's isolationism and distrustful of his independence. The veto was to the new chairman's advantage. La Follette might well have overshadowed him; the committee as it turned out consisted mostly of competent younger senators whom Truman could manage and with whom he would form personal friendships that crossed party lines.[5]

Truman's seriousness of purpose made itself evident in the way he chose a staff. Ignoring applications from political friends, he asked Attorney General Robert Jackson to recommend for chief counsel "the best investigator you've got." Jackson sent him Hugh Fulton, a tough prosecutor who at the age of thirty-five had already rung up prison terms for a retired federal judge, a utility executive, and an investment banker. "He came in wearing a derby hat, a big fat fellow with a squeaky voice," Truman later recalled. "I said to myself, 'Oh shucks!'" But Fulton was no slob. Among Washington insiders, he had a formidable reputation; his presence would give the Truman committee instant credibility. He wanted assurances that the investigation was going to be more than a headline grabber (although events would demonstrate that he was not averse to some publicity for himself and his chief). Truman gave them and put him on the payroll at $9,000.[6]

Truman already had appointed as chief investigator Matthew J. Connelly, a thirty-three-year-old Massachusetts native whom he had met a few years earlier and who was friendly with Vic Messall. A Capitol Hill veteran, Connelly had six years of investigative experience with federal relief agencies and several congressional committees. He was loyal, smart in the ways of Washington, and politically shrewd. The rest of the staff consisted primarily of investigators and stenographers. One of the investigators, appointed on Truman's orders, was William M. Boyle, Jr., of Kansas City, whom Truman had known since they were fellow students at the Kansas City School of Law in the mid-1920s. Although personally honest, Boyle had been director of the Kansas City police department during Tom Pendergast's final year of power. Truman liked him, thought him loyal and competent, and used him primarily as a personal aide. After Harry Vaughan's departure for military service in 1942, he would serve as the senator's de facto private secretary. Another key individual was Walter Hehmeyer, officially an investigator but actually a public-relations man who effectively publicized the committee's accomplishments, especially those of its chairman.[7]

III

The committee held its first hearings in mid-April, looking into camp construction. Daringly, Truman broke off the initial inquiry to investigate a major strike of coal miners. On April 22, he announced that if the miners were not back to work in three days, he would call United Mine Workers president John L. Lewis and coal-company executives before the committee to explain why it was impossible to produce coal during a national emergency. If it should be necessary to "take them for a bus ride to get them together," he declared, the committee would do it.

Lewis seized the opportunity. The dominant labor leader of the day, a hulking man of formidable appearance and deep voice, a master of grandiose rhetoric, he asserted that the southern mine operators were the major obstacle to a settlement. Apparently persuaded, the senator threatened to call them before the committee. A few hours later, the strike was settled. Inevitably, it appeared that Truman had made the difference; he happily enough accepted the interpretation.[8]

Subsequently, motivated largely by genuine indignation but doubtless intending also to demonstrate his evenhandedness, Truman adopted an adversarial attitude toward work stoppages in the defense industry and lambasted what he saw as abuses of union power. Holding hearings on a major shipyard strike, he lectured American Federation of Labor president William Green on the need to bring it to an end. Throughout the year, he asserted in one form or another that "a profiteer is in the same class with a labor racketeer." He was not just striking a pose for the public.[9]

The committee then injected itself into another critical situation: a serious shortage of aluminum, which threatened airplane production. At the end of June, noting that the aluminum-production capacity of Germany was double that of the United States, the committee advocated a drastic, federally subsidized expansion; it strongly criticized inaction on the part of the Office of Production Management (OPM) and placed much of the blame on aluminum executives working as dollar-a-year men in the defense production bureaucracy while retaining their regular salaries. Its toughest finding was an assertion that Alcoa had discouraged enlargement of the industry in order to protect its privileged position. One consequence would be heavy federal support for Alcoa's only significant competitor, Reynolds Aluminum. Another, to which the committee pointed with pride, would be the renegotiation of generous subsidies that the government had given to Alcoa to build new facilities.[10]

Throughout the spring and summer, the committee engaged in hearings on military-camp construction and turned up one horror story after another of waste, fraud, abuse, and nepotism. Truman minced no words. In July, he declared, "You and I are going to have to pay for the cost, the waste and the inefficiency in the form of increased taxation for years to come." In mid-August, the committee issued a report documenting these and other fiascos. Speaking to the Senate, Truman asserted, "If our plans for military campaigns are no more extensive and no better than those for construction we are indeed in a deplorable situation."[11]

In a manner consistent with its original purpose, the committee pleaded the case for the small businessman. "Smaller firms are being cut out by priorities on essential materials and are having to close down," Truman asserted in early June. "There is no reason why these defense contracts should not be spread over all sections of the country." A month and a half later, he warned that he would "cause trouble" if the OPM attempted to requisition machine tools from small operators and move them out of the Midwest. Far from being complex, the problem was elemental: "The little fellow is being rooked."[12]

Fight waste, fraud, and abuse. Expose the selfish excesses of big business and big labor. Speak up for the little guy. Thus Truman had established the main lines of the inquiry. Each was popular. Still, continuance of the committee was by no means automatic. The Audit and Control Committee, now run by Scott Lucas of Illinois, balked at a request for $40,000; whether the hand of the president was behind its inaction is unclear. After four weeks of negotiation, the Senate gave the committee another $25,000 in August 1941.[13]

For the rest of the year, the committee conducted a variety of inquiries into camp construction, housing, shipping, and airplanes. Truman was in the news frequently—evaluating defense progress; making constructive-sounding suggestions for managing economic mobilization; giving the back of his hand with ostentatious impartiality to greedy big businesses, rapacious labor "racketeers," and obtuse bureaucrats; pushing the case of the little guy.[14]

His reputation soared, and he delighted in the development. Writing to Bess from Columbia, Missouri, he remarked:

> It's funny how things change around in thirteen months. I'm on the front pages of the *Kansas City Star*, *St. Louis Star-Times*, and *Kansas City Journal* for yesterday and am on the front page of the *Post-Dispatch* editorial section for today and mentioned in about three or four other places in the other parts of the paper and the *Globe*.[15]

The date of the letter was December 7, 1941. Shortly after writing it, Truman was awakened from an afternoon nap by an acquaintance who had just heard of the attack on Pearl Harbor. A call from Bess came quickly thereafter. He commandeered a private plane to St. Louis, and then made it onto a long, sleepless commercial night flight. He got back to Washington in time to vote for war against Japan.[16]

The conflict presented the committee with another crisis. Its enemies began to argue that it would get in the way of victory and that it might start meddling in strategy and tactics. On December 10, Truman attempted a preemptive strike. He read a statement into the *Congressional Record*, denying any intention of second-guessing the generals and admirals and insisting that the committee was needed more than ever to ensure an efficient war effort.[17] Predictably unpersuaded, Undersecretary of War Robert Patterson publicly called for the committee to disband. Truman arranged to plead his case with Roosevelt (Byrnes was by then on the Supreme Court). To Bess, he privately vented his love–hate feelings for FDR: "It must be done or I'd tell him to go to hell. He's so damn afraid that he won't have all the power and glory that he won't let his friends help." They met early in the new year. Truman emerged to announce that the president backed continuance of the committee.[18]

On January 15, 1942, he presented its first annual report to the Senate, a presentation that drew major attention. Blasting business and labor alike, he lashed into "gross inefficiency" and private greed, tore into the OPM and other federal agencies, and renewed his pleas for small business. The committee, he said, could serve a congressional oversight function of "incalculable value"; it could speed up necessary weapons production while staving off excessive militarization of the economy and preserving a sound civilian sector. He described the problems of defense production compellingly and, not inconsequentially, appealed to the prerogatives of the Congress. Roosevelt, intentionally or otherwise, had given him valuable help a couple of days earlier by abolishing the OPM and replacing it with the War Production Board (WPB). The Senate voted another $60,000 with which to set up a more permanent operation.[19]

The committee remained reasonably lean, with only about a dozen investigators and another twenty or so support personnel. Truman later calculated that during his three-and-a-quarter-year watch, it spent less than $400,000. Probably never before, certainly never after, was so much congressional influence leveraged on so small an expenditure.[20]

Truman more than anyone else had made the committee a success and would keep it in the spotlight. He left the detail work to Fulton and the staff and steered a general course that avoided the hazards of squabbling, partisanship, and blatant irresponsibility that had wrecked many congressional inquiries. He and Fulton met at 7:30 every morning when they were both in Washington, resolving whatever operational issues required Truman's decision. They worked well together. They carefully selected their targets and avoided spurious complaints from malcontents or win-the-war nostrums from crackpots.[21]

Truman saw to it that no one on the committee had a legitimate cause for dissatisfaction. Once a week or so, he presided over informal early-morning sessions that provided ample opportunities for members to discuss current issues or suggest future business. Making extensive use of a subcommittee system, he gave all of them responsible assignments and ensured that they would be involved in any investigation of a situation in their home states. If he attended a subcommittee hearing, he customarily sat to one side and let the regular members run the show.[22]

As at earlier times in his career, he displayed a remarkable talent for conciliation and bipartisanship. Often he met behind the scenes with administration representatives to resolve problems privately. During his tenure as chairman, every report was unanimous. In part, this outcome was possible because such issues as waste, production difficulties, labor abuses, and small-business opportunities lacked hard ideological edges and presented few occasions for emotional partisan outbursts. Still, given a venomous political atmosphere on Capitol Hill, the achievement was exceptional. Avoiding grandstanding, Truman saw to it that committee findings were backed by evidence that made them plausible, and appeared more like a disinterested public servant than a self-serving politician. "The chairman is a fine fellow," journalist Allen Drury confided to his journal in March 1944, "presiding like some trim, efficient, keen-minded businessman, which is just what he looks like, with his neat appearance, heavy-lensed glasses and quick, good-humored smile."[23]

IV

Within the Senate, Truman was successful in staving off occasional efforts to establish new panels that might be competitive. He encountered considerable criticism and hostility from the House Military Affairs Committee, but its chairman, Andrew Jackson May of Kentucky, was widely considered a small-bore politician and a mouthpiece for the military.[24] It seemed at first that Truman might have some serious competition from the House Select Committee on Defense Migration, headed by John Tolan of California. Well managed and responsible, the Tolan committee parlayed its mandate to look into labor migration as a justification for examining many issues that overlapped Truman's concerns. Much less successful at public relations, it probably never got a tenth of the attention accorded the Truman committee. In January 1943, it went out of business.[25]

From early 1942 on, the Truman committee delved into virtually every aspect of the war other than purely military strategy and tactics. Investigations of construction, abroad as well as at home, continued, but were increasingly overshadowed by other issues, ranging from the broad management of the wartime economy to specific examples of maladministration. Some of the committee activities represented public service and political leadership at its finest. Others seemed driven by headline potential and, at times, possessed only a slim factual basis.

One of the most important and constructive inquiries, undertaken in early 1942, was into the serious national rubber shortage. The committee levied its heaviest criticism at the defunct OPM for having freely allotted rubber to the auto companies before Pearl Harbor, thereby encouraging an "orgy of consumption" that left the United States with insufficient reserves. It also administered a light slap on the wrist to the federal Rubber Reserve Corporation and its head, Jesse Jones, for having failed to build up the rubber stockpile, questioned the military need for huge rubber allocations, and (with less justification) charged Standard Oil of New Jersey with not having moved to develop synthetic-rubber capacity in the prewar era.

Less important than apportionment of blame was the committee's prescription: a tough conservation program that included a low national speed limit, gasoline rationing, and a prohibition on individuals' owning more than five tires per automobile. The recommendations were largely adopted by the administration, although (to Truman's annoyance) not until they had been embraced by a presidential committee headed by Bernard Baruch, who promptly appropriated credit for them.[26]

In 1943, with synthetic-rubber development still hung up by squabbling personalities, conflicting interest groups, and arguments over synthetic production methods, the committee returned to the problem and issued a demand for a speedy resolution. Truman declared, "The War Production Board must exercise its authority in a *tough* manner. . . . Where necessary, heads must be knocked together." By then, he had enough prestige to speak as an arbiter of the public interest with the certainty that people would listen. He probably helped get synthetic rubber back on track. A year later, the new industry provided 87 percent of the American rubber supply.[27]

Other broad-gauged inquiries involved manpower policy, transportation, shipbuilding, steel, farm machinery, and aircraft production. Some reports were insightful and constructive. On manpower policy, for example, the committee consistently argued against overexpansion of the military to the detriment of the labor pool for civilian and defense industries; it promoted the full utilization of women, the elderly, and racial minorities. Exposing cases of labor hoarding, the committee prodded the War Manpower Commission (WMC) to develop a comprehensive manpower policy while supporting WMC's opposition to a labor draft and its insistence on civilian control of labor policy.[28]

A few investigations and recommendations were more attuned to politics than to the disinterested management of the war. One was a political whitewash; a brief report absolved Senator A. B. "Happy" Chandler of any corrupt intent in accepting a complimentary swimming pool from a defense contractor. Truman probably would have skewered himself on the nearest bayonet rather than accept such a gift, but he was perfectly willing to massage the sensibilities of a colleague—and pick up an IOU in the process.[29] Another, written at the urging of a friend and political backer, cotton broker Neal Helm, touted the alleged superiority of cotton cord over rayon cord in tires for military vehicles. In addition to helping out a pal, the senator was always happy to bash Du Pont, the leading producer of rayon. The document warned of the destruction of the South's economy in order to stoke the profits of the huge chemical concerns.[30]

A report on farm machinery ignored suggestions that farmers might pool equipment; it called for strong increases in machinery production along lines recommended by the Department of Agriculture and the Farm Bureau Federation. Truman himself issued a statement proclaiming the critical importance of food production, recalling his own experience on the farm and praising the patriotism of American farmers. Cynics were quick to discern a political purpose. Nevertheless, the position was in line with his general policy of supporting civilian needs.[31]

One of the committee's major purposes was to provide information; at times, this put it into the dangerous business of telling harsh truths that the American people did not want to hear. The first annual report of the committee asserted that airplane production had lagged badly; that those models currently available were at best mediocre, at worst obsolete; that first-rate designs had not yet made it off the drawing boards. Too bearish about future production, the report was otherwise right on target. In April 1943, the committee revealed that the Germans were still sinking Allied merchant shipping faster than it could be replaced. Accuracy did not prevent contractors, the military, and civilian defense officials from issuing denials. Usually, albeit after a delay, the committee received the recognition it deserved.[32]

By the fall of 1943, the committee correctly perceived that the battle for production had been won and that defense orders soon would be tapering off. Although it earlier had rightly criticized excessive tolerance of civilian production, it now held public hearings on reconversion and published a brief report urging a progressive phasing in of a postwar economy to ease the shock of the transition from war to peace. The most farsighted of all the Truman committee reports, the document met strong resistance from the military and its allies in the civilian bureaucracy. Truman intermittently returned to the issue until he was nominated for vice president. By the summer of 1945, little would be accomplished, and he would find himself facing a situation he had accurately forecast two years before.[33]

The committee might obtain positive results in specific cases. It probably contributed, for example, to the needed redesign of the B-26 bomber in late 1941 or early 1942, but Truman grossly exaggerated when he claimed single-handedly to have forced aircraft entrepreneur Glenn Martin to do the right thing. The committee did much to expose stunning incompetence in the Navy Bureau of Ships, which persisted in designing inadequate and unstable "tank lighters" (landing ships capable of carrying tanks) while refusing to commit to an effective model manufactured by Higgins Industries, a New Orleans shipyard. Committee pressure led Secretary of the Navy Frank Knox to order acceptance of the Higgins craft, which played a critical role in winning the war.[34]

The committee uncovered numerous examples of corruption. Empire Ordnance, a firm started with $42,500 in capital, had employed the Washington attorney Thomas Corcoran to gain entrée to defense officials, secured over $47 million in contracts for allied shipping, and then proceeded to build a shipyard in Savannah so defective that it had to be taken over by the Maritime Commission. Proving that no bad deed goes unrewarded, Empire eventually extracted a settlement of $1,285,000 for the government seizure of its shoddy facilities.[35]

The worst horror story was the discovery that company and army inspectors at the Wright Aeronautical engine plant in Lockland, Ohio, routinely approved faulty engines for military aircraft. Some observers argued that too much was made of one lapse in the corporation's general record as a producer of high-quality power plants for warplanes. Truman, who knew that Wright's overall performance would make little difference to a pilot in a tailspin, thought it was unconscionable.[36]

In later years, he liked to believe that he had been successful in sending some of the Wright Aeronautical inspectors to prison. Alas, he did not even come close. The War Department relieved two and then court-martialed three, who were punished by dismissal from the service. The Justice Department filed a civil suit against Wright, but effectively abandoned it and never brought criminal charges. Labor unions at the Lockland plant complained bitterly that their members were being smeared. To Truman's anger, production slowed to a crawl for a time. Wright instituted a large advertising campaign denying the charges and stressing its contributions to the war effort.[37]

In 1943, the committee investigated the Canol project, an enormously expensive army project to develop Yukon oil fields that would supply fuel to Alaska-based military aircraft. It found that Alaska could have been supplied by one medium tanker from the West Coast three times a month. The army stonewalled. Claiming "military necessity," Undersecretary of War Robert Patterson declared, "The War Department is proud of Canol," a statement to which Hugh Fulton responded with justifiable laughter. But the committee could not persuade Congress, paralyzed by the "military necessity" plea, to terminate Canol.[38]

The Truman committee could successfully police many production abuses, but it never forced determined military leaders to make a 180-degree turn. Nor could it impose its will on so massive an economic mobilization. War production meandered along like Old Man River, largely oblivious to the attempts of mortals to control it.

V

Through it all, Truman retained his fierce insurgent liberalism, hoping to cut down the power of big business and develop opportunities for small enterprisers. His efforts enjoyed scant success and at times did him little credit.

He wanted to get rid of the dollar-a-year men who staffed so much of the production bureaucracy. After Donald Nelson asserted that he needed them and promised to do as much as possible to control favoritism, Truman could only say, "I am not going to argue this question with you. . . . We are behind you to win this war."[39]

Pursuing his long-cherished goal of opportunities for small business, he got his friend Lou Holland named to head the federal Smaller War Plants Corporation. Holland was unable to steer much business to small manufacturers. His successors, including the redoubtable Maury Maverick, fared little better. In truth, the concept of bringing maximum efficiency to the war effort by involving tens of thousands of small enterprises was never feasible. Inexorably, the war made big manufacturing bigger.[40]

Truman remained reflexively hostile toward large corporations. He admired businessmen who built empires from small beginnings, such as Henry J. Kaiser and Andrew J. Higgins in shipbuilding and Richard Reynolds in aluminum. True to his insurgent outlook, however, he detested the large, usually eastern-based enterprises that had dominated the American economy since he was a child. Committee reports constantly charged these old-line giants with impeding the war effort for their selfish interests. Sometimes there was ample justification for such charges, sometimes not. For example, the auto companies, which had resisted conversion to defense production in 1940 and 1941, took hits. In the case of the worst offenders, however, the committee overreached by taking denunciation to the point of implicit accusations of pro-fascist behavior.

One conspicuous target remained Alcoa; hoping to dominate wartime aluminum production, it had initially negotiated very lucrative contracts with the government and attempted to prevent the subsidization of competitors. In addition, Alcoa, Dow Chemical, and Standard Oil of New Jersey were charged with delaying production of two vital resources— magnesium and synthetic rubber—because of cartel-style marketing and patent agreements these companies had made with the German industrial giant, I. G. Farben. In each instance, the facts yielded no such conclusion. Both industries had been retarded by low demand during the Depression, not by a conspiracy. Dow Chemical had produced sufficient magnesium to meet domestic needs in the 1930s. The mass-production of synthetic rubber had made no economic sense with cheap natural rubber readily available from Southeast Asia.

Blame for the shortages of 1942, as far as any could be assessed, lay primarily with officials who before Pearl Harbor had failed to plan for the stockpiles required to fight a global war. Nevertheless, the committee criticized Dow for having failed to expand magnesium capacity beyond any conceivable market demand, attacked Alcoa's dealings with Farben, and asserted in its published report on rubber that Standard had "engaged in activities helpful to the Axis Nations and harmful to the United Nations." Truman was even more vehement in a letter to a constituent: "The Standard Oil group, of course, are still trying to choke the country to death and I am trying to keep them from doing it, but I am only one voice in the wilderness."[41]

In 1943, the committee asserted that Carnegie-Illinois, a division of U.S. Steel, had knowingly sold substandard steel plate to the navy. The steel in question seems to have been perfectly sound, if not entirely within technical specifications, but Truman pushed the Justice Department to get indictments against the company on forty-seven counts of fraud. After a three-week trial in May 1944, an unimpressed jury returned a verdict of innocent on all charges. Hugh Fulton denied that the company had been completely exonerated. Few neutral observers agreed.[42]

Big-business bashing cost the committee some credibility among knowledgeable observers, but there was little political risk in asserting that a corporation founded by John D. Rockefeller or J. P. Morgan could do no right. There was even less in championing small enterprise. Most ordinary Americans were probably inclined to believe that the committee was on to something. As Eliot Janeway would later observe in his own opinionated study of World War II mobilization, "Statistically, the small business group is elusive, but sociologically and politically it is ubiquitous. . . . [S]mall business is a state of mind—it is *the* state of mind of the average American, rich or poor."[43]

Even those who deplored the committee's forays into neopopulism were inclined to believe that its investigations did more good than harm. What one could not do was cite large, quantifiable achievements or claim that the committee had engineered a major change in administration policy. Using that yardstick, one can only agree with Senator Joseph Ball's recollection, some forty years later, that the committee did "a good and worthwhile job, not earth-shaking but helpful."[44] It uncovered genuine fraud, compelled needed contract renegotiations, and (simply by its presence as a watchdog) prevented a lot of waste and inefficiency. For the rest of his life, Truman would boast that it had saved the country $15 billion. It is difficult to determine where he got the figure, much less verify it.[45]

To a great extent, the secret of the committee's success lay in Truman's insurgent-populist worldview. He specifically and the committee generally voiced the outlook of "little people" reflexively distrustful of big business and big labor, apprehensive about the way in which the growing defense program and its elephantine bureaucracy touched their lives, anxious about a frighteningly uncertain future. Presenting itself as single-mindedly dedicated to winning the war, the committee inevitably got a share of the credit for the enormous production turnaround that put America on the road to victory. Guilty of occasional excesses, it was more responsible than most Senate investigating bodies and earned a measure of trust that at times (the rubber-conservation problem, for example) allowed it to perform as an arbiter of the national interest. Not required to produce legislation, it was free to function as a roving critic. It concentrated its attacks on easy targets, never took on sleazy congressmen, and never went after Franklin Roosevelt. The last omission left Truman well positioned for higher office.[46]

VI

The achievement of the committee was fairly enough reflected in Truman's growing stature. He had conceived it, staffed it, and made the major decisions about its operations. Its public-relations staff issued a steady stream of press releases (headed "Truman Committee," not "Special Committee to Investigate the National Defense Program") that featured the senator's latest declarations and activities. By the time of the first annual report, Truman had reconstructed his image from that of a machine politician to a statesman of democracy.

Influential journalists praised him. In 1943, he was the subject of a *Time* cover story that characterized him as "a personally honest, courageous man" untouched by scandal, still a Pendergast loyalist because he would not kick a friend who was down, and a crusader for an effective war effort. In May 1944, a survey of fifty-two Washington newsmen conducted by *Look* named him one of the ten most valuable officials in Washington. He was the only member of Congress on the list. By then, he was widely considered a vice-presidential possibility.[47]

With a presidential election looming in 1944, committee bipartisanship became increasingly difficult to maintain. Some Republican members displayed quick-triggered tempers with witnesses who tried to score Democratic points. Among the Democrats, Truman may have had the lowest boiling point. He found himself more and more caught in an untenable contradiction between two identities: impartial chairman of a valuable investigating committee and leading national Democrat in demand as a partisan speaker all over the country. His position was made all the more difficult by Republican efforts to use committee findings as evidence of administration bungling in running the war. Increasingly, in the spring of 1944, he engaged in angry exchanges with his GOP friends on the committee.[48]

Nonetheless, he was as popular as ever within the Senate, considerably more powerful in Washington, and widely esteemed outside the capital. Happy and fulfilled, he probably contemplated his future: one or two more terms in the Senate after the war, probably a Democratic leadership position, and eventually a dignified retirement to Independence with Bess.

16

"Looks Like I've Arrived in the Senate": Statesman and Democratic Leader, 1941–1944

The Truman committee changed the life of its chairman in many ways. It made his personal existence more hectic and difficult than ever but also provided him the most prominence and power of his political career. He became a leading Democratic liberal and an advocate for a Wilsonian postwar world. The public persona he had half-consciously crafted for himself—that of an ordinary man functioning as a leader of democracy—was enormously attractive. By 1944, he found it leading him toward an awesome responsibility beyond leadership in the Senate and far more frightening.[1]

II

The war years were transitional for Truman's family. Margaret graduated from Gunston Hall in 1942, her father delivering a commencement address that urged the young ladies to devote themselves to supporting the war and the men in the armed forces.[2] That fall, still living with her parents, she entered George Washington University as a freshman majoring in history. On the side, she continued to take voice lessons in pursuit of her real ambition, the concert stage. As Margaret made her way into young adulthood, Grandmother Wallace found it more and more difficult to manage by herself. The family moved her to a small apartment in Independence, and then to Denver to live with her son Fred and his wife. In September 1944, she came to Washington to stay with Bess and Harry, sharing the second bedroom of the apartment with Margaret.[3]

Bess found the war years busy and difficult. She probably took satisfaction in her volunteer work at the Washington USO, but much of her life was frustrating. She and Harry were separated more than ever. She worried about her mother's declining health. She and Margaret took Madge Wallace to Denver in mid-1943. Truman encountered one delay after another in joining them for a planned family vacation. When he finally arrived, he had time only to put his ladies on a train back to Missouri before beginning a speaking tour. "Bess let him have it with both barrels," Margaret remembers. From Des Moines a day or two later, Harry wrote, "I had the dumps for most of the evening remembering what you said about my being a Senator (wish I'd stayed a clodhopper)."[4]

In 1941, when Victor and Irene Messall left the senator's employment, Bess quietly went on the payroll as Irene's replacement at $2,400 a year. When Vic's successor, Harry Vaughan, was called to active military duty, Bess became his replacement at $4,200, although Bill Boyle (officially associate counsel for the Truman committee) actually did the work. By 1944, Bess was making more than $4,500 and additional compensation that ranged from $24.16 to $36.25 a month, the maximum salary for a congressional employee.

She long had functioned as an all-around political helper and adviser to Harry; when her position became an issue, he claimed that he never wrote a speech or made a decision without consulting her. Moreover, she was not the only senator's wife to pull down a salary in her spouse's office. Both knew, however, that they were skirting impropriety. Bess never put in a standard forty-hour week at the office and, indeed, seems to have been seldom seen there. Financial pressures, including Margaret's college tuition, undoubtedly dictated the decision. Truman usually refused honoraria for speeches to interest groups; he probably thought that putting Bess on the payroll was a less objectionable way of meeting the family's needs.[5]

Mary Jane and Mamma also had to be taken care of. In January 1944, Truman appointed Mary Jane an "additional clerk," based in the Kansas City area at $1,800. Mamma was ninety on November 25, 1942, her eyesight was failing, and her health oscillated ominously. The Jackson County court still held her old farm, uncertain how to dispose of it. When Judge Fred Klaber, Truman's only friend on the county court, asked him for comments on a purchase offer in 1941, the senator retorted, "That old squint-eyed son-of-a-gun, who is the Presiding Judge [George Montgomery], . . . caused a lot of suffering to a grand old woman and I hope he's happy over it. You own the place, do as you please with it." His rage vented, Truman then sent a note to Jim Pendergast urging him to try to get the county's land business turned over to a pliable agent.[6]

The question of the farm would remain a running sore on Truman's psyche, but to his credit, he refused to accept questionable sources of help. When a constituent offered him the money to repurchase the farm in exchange for his influence in helping her sell a $250,000 property to the government, he responded, "In the first place I am not a good real estate salesman, and in the second place, the office of a United States Senator is not for private use at any price."[7]

III

Shortly after Pearl Harbor, Truman had offered himself to Army Chief of Staff General George C. Marshall for active duty. Whether he actually intended to resign from the Senate or simply take a leave is uncertain. He believed that he could run a training regiment capable of turning out good young artillerymen. As he recalled it, Marshall was curt: "He asked how old I was and I told him I was fifty-six years old. He pulled his reading glasses down on his nose, grinned at me, and said, 'We don't need old stiffs like you—this will be a young man's war.'"[8]

Cousin Ralph fared no better. He was summarily relieved of command of the Thirty-fifth Division in a systematic "purge" of National Guard officers from combat command positions. Senators Truman and Clark protested vehemently, but to no effect.[9] Other friends saw service. Fred Canfil spent more than a year as a training officer before being discharged because of age and rejoining Truman's staff. Called to active duty in 1941 and sent to the South Pacific, Harry Vaughan served as provost marshal of Brisbane until he was injured in a plane crash. Back in Washington, he became a military liaison to the Truman committee and functioned almost as a member of Truman's personal staff. Jake Vardaman, although past military age, managed to wrangle a naval commission, got an assignment as a liaison officer with army combat units, served with distinction in North Africa, was wounded in Sicily, and received the Legion of Merit. Truman's loyal Independence associate Rufus Burrus rose from lieutenant to colonel, serving in Italy.[10]

His young southeastern Missouri supporter Roy Harper went off to the Pacific as an enlisted man and returned as an officer. Truman, who had become enormously fond of him, was proud of his patriotism and received his letters almost as if they were from a son. With at least equal concern he watched as, one by one, his nephews went into uniform. All four would return unscathed. He followed the children of old comrades. "Had a letter from Abie Burkhart," he informed Bess in August 1944. "His boy was killed in action June 22 in the assault on one of those South Pacific islands. It was a pitiful letter because he was all wrapped up in that boy. I've been scared for Ed McKim's boy, but Ed doesn't seem to be as uneasy as I am. He's on Guam." Two or three days later, McKim got the dreaded telegram telling him that Marine First Lieutenant Eddie, Jr., was dead.[11]

Nothing preoccupied Truman more intensely than his investigating committee. The process of getting it started on the right foot and establishing its credibility was anxiety-producing and complicated by his uneven health. On April 13, 1941, just two days before its first public session, he awoke at 4:00 A.M. with severe pain in his abdomen and chest. X-rays confirmed a gallstone attack, and doctors put him on a strict diet.[12] By late June, with the aluminum investigation and camp construction hearings concluded, he was exhausted. Once again, he retreated to the Army-Navy Hospital at Hot Springs.

His initial interview there showed that he felt weighed down not simply by the hard pace of the past few months, but by emotional baggage he had been carrying for years—from his first race for the Senate in 1934, through the vilification he had endured in the 1940 campaign, to the hard work and hectic activity of the past few months. He had, the physician noted, reached a point at which "he felt he would be unable to continue his present pace."[13] He spent the better part of a week going through a number of diagnostic procedures, some of them primitive and revolting, and then another week resting. Finding nothing fundamentally wrong with him, the doctors gave him some minor stomach medication and recommended new eyeglasses; they also prescribed mineral baths, mild exercise, and a lot of sleep. The treatment, along with news from Washington that the committee was assured of extended funding, left him rejuvenated.[14]

He remained too intense a personality to achieve the rest, relaxation, and equanimity that would have been most therapeutic for him. In a moment of insight, he told Bess, "It's the strain that does the damage" (and anger at foes such as Judge Montgomery and Lloyd Stark, whom he vetoed for appointments so inconsequential that no one ever heard of them). He continued to suffer from frequent nausea. "My meals are staying down the last two days," he reassured Bess in late July 1942.[15]

The committee's success in becoming one of Washington's most esteemed institutions did nothing to make life easier. By mid-1943, he was frequently on the road as a much-coveted speaker before interest groups and Democratic gatherings. "I just don't see how you get around and do what you do," wrote his Springfield lieutenant Sam Wear in June 1943. "I would try to slow up a little." A few days later, Truman told Vivian, "I had the 'phone shut off because I had not had any sleep for a week and decided to spend about twelve hours in bed." A little more than a month later, he was off on a grueling two-week speaking tour through Kansas, Nebraska, and Iowa in the hottest days of midsummer. By September, he was back in the hospital at Hot Springs for another checkup; it disclosed nothing that a few days rest could not cure. Throughout the war years, his letters reveal a near obsession with the need for more peace and quiet and especially for adequate sleep.[16]

For a time, he closely identified himself with Moral Rearmament, a nondenominational religious movement that preached universal brotherhood and traditional morality. Its disregard of formal sectarianism and emphasis on Christian ethics were consistent with the directions in which

Truman's own religious quest had taken him. Moreover, the impending crisis of 1939 through 1941, and then the war itself, seemed to lend the movement special meaning and urgency.[17] From 1939 into 1944, he was an enthusiastic supporter who appeared at the organization's rallies, made radio broadcasts for it, and allowed it to use his name in its promotional material. He requested draft exemptions and military reassignments for movement activists, a favor he usually refused to constituents who requested it.[18]

Moral Rearmament had numerous prominent adherents in both political parties. President Roosevelt sent a message to one of its first large meetings. It had a lot of critics also. Many New Deal liberals, secular in outlook and conditioned by the experience of the 1930s to interpret politics as class conflict, recoiled from efforts to submerge class differences in a quasi-mystical exaltation of nationhood. They looked at Moral Rearmament and saw an incipient fascism. From his own perspective as a middle-class Protestant, Truman saw a force attempting to give birth to the world predicted in Tennyson's "Lockesley Hall." Nonetheless, he was practical enough to back away in 1944, when he began to receive warnings that the movement had a history that some interpreted as profascist and anti-Semitic. In August 1944, after being nominated for vice president, he told the *St. Louis Post-Dispatch* that he had backed the movement because it had done good morale work in defense plants.[19]

IV

Before 1941, few observers could have imagined that Truman would emerge as a major spokesman for an aggressive, idealistic internationalism during his second term in the Senate. In common with most Americans, his attention had been turned mainly inward during the 1930s, and he shared the widespread resentment at the failure of the World War I Allies to pay their war debts. "I spent a year in France, the hardest work that any man ever did, trying to save their country from the Germans, and after it was all done, I sincerely wished I had been on the side of the Germans, and I still feel that way," he told Carter Harrison in 1936. "The 'frogs' should pay us what they owe us." In common with most other members of the Senate, he voted for the Neutrality Acts of 1935, 1936, and 1937, which had the cumulative effect of removing the United States from serious participation in world politics at a time when a dwindling number of unsteady democracies desperately needed American leadership.[20]

Yet his outburst about the French notwithstanding, his votes for the Neutrality Acts were clearly a product of political calculation rather than principled conviction; he did not conceal his skepticism that they would keep the nation out of war.[21] Actually, his foreign policy views were strongly held and much at variance with the isolationist consensus of the country. They derived from his education and from his experience—as a partisan Democrat, a combat artilleryman, and a reserve officer.

Truman's education, like that of most young men of the late nineteenth century, uncritically accepted the concept that history was a story
of progress toward, among other things, a coming reign of peace as the
rule among civilized nations. It likewise assumed the primacy of English-
speaking culture as the basis for some degree of world union. His identity as a partisan Democrat had long committed him to a policy of free
trade, which assumed broad American involvement in the world and a
wide degree of international cooperation. The great Democratic president of his young manhood, Woodrow Wilson, had indelibly wrapped
all these cultural and economic assumptions into a stirring vision of a world
united by liberal values, free trade, and an international assembly—all to
be achieved by American leadership.

His personal experience as a soldier provided powerful reinforcement.
Immensely proud of his World War I duty, he found vindication for it in
the Wilsonian vision. That experience had also driven home to him the
importance of power in world affairs and the necessity of military strength.
It gave vivid reality to lessons he had absorbed from his boyhood study
of great generals, his observation of the strong current of physical aggressiveness in the Independence of his school days, and his personal contacts with men who had fought in the Civil War. Rather like Franklin
Roosevelt and a good many other people who had come to adulthood in
the first decade of the twentieth century, he arrived at a concept of foreign policy that amalgamated the realism of Theodore Roosevelt with the
idealism of Woodrow Wilson.

Ideals, he understood, had to be qualified by the realization that the
world was imperfect, human nature flawed, and the path of progress difficult. Civilized democratic nations might not require military power for
protection against one another, but they were obliged to safeguard themselves and the progress they had achieved from gangster regimes that
appeared steadily more menacing during Truman's first term in the Senate. Military training, if conducted to develop a broadly based citizen
army, also could build individual character and mold a sense of obligation to serve the common good. Truman was not a systematic thinker,
although his inclinations were more scholarly than those of most of his
Capitol Hill colleagues. Still, he had pondered the lessons of history; these
propelled him toward an activist internationalism.

As early as the spring of 1937, even before he cast his vote for the
last of the Neutrality Acts, he made it clear that his vision of the world
was neither isolationist nor pacifist. Speaking on April 20 in Larchmont,
New York, he assailed the Republican foreign policy of the 1920s: rejection of the Treaty of Versailles and "our responsibility as a world power,"
tariff barriers that attempted "to reap the benefits of world trade without
giving anything in return," naval arms agreements that had primarily
benefited Japan while leading to the dismantling of the United States
Navy. Warning that Europe could explode at any time and citing Japan's
ambitions, he declared, "In the coming struggle between Democracy and

Dictatorship, Democracy must be prepared to defend its principles and its wealth."

The logic of such a statement pointed toward an international alliance with Britain, France, and perhaps China. Truman understood that his Missouri Democratic constituency was not ready for such a move; possibly neither was he. Instead, he promoted military preparedness in a fashion that avoided head-on confrontation with most isolationists, calling for a big navy, "an air force second to none," and legislation to establish plans for industrial mobilization. Asserting that "we can and will fight for our rights, in spite of a small and vociferous pacifist group," he proclaimed, "I think that the old Puritan, who prayed regularly for protection against the Indians, was much safer when, at the same time, he prudently kept his powder dry."[22]

Truman recycled the Larchmont speech several times over the next two years; he became increasingly explicit about the threat to the United States and his conception of the American mission abroad. At St. Joseph in October 1938, less than a month after the collapse of democratic resolve at Munich, he envisioned the turmoil of Europe as perpetual unless the continent could be united. In a short (and superficial) historical survey, he cited four leaders—Julius Caesar, Henri IV of France, Napoleon, and Woodrow Wilson—who had tried and failed to establish a universal European order. The United States, he believed, would have to assume the Wilsonian mission or face another Dark Age in human history.[23]

The outbreak of war in Europe on September 1, 1939, called for hard decisions. Over the next two and a quarter years, Truman would make them with a minimum of political equivocation. In the fall of 1939, he voted for the cash-and-carry amendment to the Neutrality Act, a move that would permit Britain and France to buy military hardware in the United States. "I am of the opinion that we should not help the thugs among nations by refusing to sell arms to our friends," he told a crowd at Caruthersville, Missouri. "I think it is to our interest, our very selfish interest, to lift the embargo."[24]

In 1940, he made his support for a strong defense one of the main themes of his campaign. After winning renomination, he voted for the conscription bill. In 1941, he backed Lend-Lease, the extension of service terms for draftees, and the arming of American merchant ships for convoy duty to England. (His remarks about the French five years earlier were now long forgotten. "I never felt very badly about the fact the money we lent in Europe during the last World War was not repaid," he told Eddie Meisburger, "for I am sincerely of the opinion that we sent money instead of blood to the Front.")[25] To his good fortune, these votes required minimal political courage. A strong majority of Missouri Democrats approved of Roosevelt's foreign policies. Truman stopped short of advocating war against the Axis powers. Like Roosevelt and most other interventionists, he understood that the country would not yet accept so stark a prospect, that the message of preparedness and limited aid to Britain was far more acceptable, whatever its illogic.[26]

His private correspondence could be considerably blunter:

> We are facing a bunch of thugs, and the only theory a thug understands is a gun and a bayonet.

> As much as I dislike the thought of war, I still think the present plight of Poland, Holland, Norway, Belgium and the Balkan nations is much worse than war.

> Your quotation from the Holy Writ, "Righteousness Exalteth a Nation," is just as true now as it was in the day when the Prophet wrote it; but righteousness and liberty are things that have to be fought for, and we cannot obtain them by lying down to such people as Hitler, Mussolini, and the Japanese.[27]

After Pearl Harbor, he became an increasingly prominent advocate of American strength and continuing international involvement in the postwar world. In 1943, possibly acting with the encouragement of the White House, he did much to engineer a bipartisan Senate resolution, popularly known as B_2H_2 (for its sponsors: Senators Ball, Burton, Hatch, and Hill), committing the United States to a strong postwar international organization. Displaying the impatience of younger senators with the administration's caution, the resolution attracted much favorable attention. Three of the sponsors were members of the Truman committee; Truman made no effort to conceal his own fingerprints. He won wide approval both for the effort itself and for his willingness to share the limelight with other senators.[28]

The 1943 summer speaking tour that disrupted his family holiday was likewise in the service of the internationalist gospel. Sponsored by the United Nations Association, he traveled with Republican congressman Walter Judd of Minnesota. He returned to Washington encouraged. That fall, he was one of a bipartisan group of fourteen senators who fought successfully for adoption of the essence of B_2H_2 by the Senate.[29]

By 1944, Truman was defining the war aims of the United States as built around Roosevelt's Four Freedoms and requiring an "'improved' League of Nations . . . controlled by Britain, China, Russia and the United States in the name of all and for the welfare of all." The new order, he declared, could be attained only by "a new machine of peace . . . a powerful international police force."[30] At a point in history when all things seemed possible, he championed revolutionary arrangements for managing relations among nations. He assumed (as did most wartime internationalists) that a virtuous America would be the benign arbiter of the postwar world, that it would achieve peace by exporting its liberal-democratic values to less enlightened nations, and that it would exert moral hegemony over an international organization by the strength of its ideals.

He was prone to present himself, especially to constituents, as a plain-thinking, straight-talking country boy with no tolerance for devious diplomacy. Responding to a letter requesting his opinion on the position of China in the postwar world, he was also capable of succinctly discussing potential conflicts of interests among the United States, the Soviet Union, and Great Britain in East Asia. Then, having bared his understanding of power politics, he rushed to cover himself: "All these deep, dark ramifications are entirely too much for me to work out. . . . Diplomacy has always been too much for me."[31] He largely subscribed to such maxims as the primacy of national self-interest and the overriding importance of power in world politics. Like most Americans, he nonetheless found these distasteful and was far more comfortable in embracing an idealistic concept of American foreign relations as built around a secular missionary role of spreading liberal democracy. Like most American leaders of the twentieth century, he would struggle to reconcile the two views.

V

Generalities aside, how did he stand on the many specific issues that total Allied victory would raise? Two in particular would occupy much of his attention in the eight years after 1944: Zionism in Palestine and relations with the Soviet Union. In both cases, his attitude was cautious, restrained by considerations of personal political self-interest, by a sense that the national interest of winning the war was more important than ideals or personal attitudes, and by an apparent understanding that the shape of the postwar world was too fluid to permit absolute commitments.

As far as Zionism was concerned, Truman, like most liberal Democrats, was supportive. By World War II, he had many associations with Jews: Max Lowenthal remained a good friend and adviser, for example; David Berenstein, despite Truman's irritation with him in 1940, was one of several valued St. Louis Zionist contacts. In the 1930s, Truman had handled numerous requests to facilitate the emigration of Jews from Germany. While he refused for sound reasons to endorse the raising of a special Jewish Palestine liberation army or to make a public commitment to a Jewish state in Palestine, he had no hesitation about aligning himself with the general Zionist goals. Speaking in Chicago in April 1943, he publicly affirmed the thesis, still disputed, that the Nazis intended to slaughter European Jewry. He declared, "Today—not tomorrow—we must do all that is humanly possible to provide a haven and place of safety for all those who can be grasped from the hands of the Nazi butchers. Free lands must be opened to them."

This rhetoric earned Truman the plaudits and handshakes of his audience, a host of rabbis whom he described to Harry Vaughan as having whiskers ranging in style from Moses to Jeff Davis. But what did it mean? A St. Louis constituent wanted him to come out for a resolution endorsing a Jewish homeland in Palestine. Truman responded in a fashion that belied his occasional pretense that he was a naive country boy. The resolution, he warned, had strong implications for American relations with Great Britain and the Arab peoples. It had to be "very circum-spectly handled until we know just exactly where we are going and why." It would be unwise to add another element of discord to the problems of the alliance, but "when the right time comes I am willing to help make the fight for a Jewish homeland in Palestine."[32]

The Soviet Union presented in many ways a more difficult problem. Truman had next to nothing to say about the USSR in public during the 1920s and 1930s, but there can be little doubt that he regarded the So-viet experiment with loathing. A few cosmopolitan intellectuals might admire Soviet national planning and ideals of equality. Truman's insur-gent worldview also had room for a certain style of class conflict (the "little guy" against the "big guys") but not for class warfare, the eradication of the capitalists, the abolition of private property, or the dictatorship of the proletariat. Truman regarded Stalin's Soviet Union, whatever its professed social objectives, as no less a gangster regime than Hitler's.

Considerably more clear-eyed and pragmatic than that of a majority of the American intelligentsia, this view saw nothing inherently unnatu-ral about the Nazi-Soviet Pact. From the beginning of the war until mid-1941, Truman envisioned the USSR as an unfriendly power. Given that perspective, his remark to a reporter asking for his reaction to the Ger-man invasion of the Soviet Union in June 1941 was predictable, if im-practical: "If we see that Germany is winning, we should help Russia and if Russia is winning we ought to help Germany and that way let them kill as many as possible, although I don't want to see Hitler victorious under any circumstances."

Scholars have tended to invest this offhand comment with much more significance than Truman gave it at the time. Arthur Krock, who had observed Truman closely since 1935, wrote that the senator was speak-ing "not too seriously." Nor was the sentiment unique. George Norris, the most esteemed of all the Senate progressives, offered the same policy; like Truman, he would soon back away from it.[33]

Writing to Bess at the end of 1941, Truman commented that he still thought the Soviets were "as untrustworthy as Hitler and Al Capone," but his attitude (at least for public consumption) soon mellowed. He replied to a list of questions submitted to him by the *American Magazine* as follows:

> As far as I am concerned as long as the Russians keep the 192 Divisions of the Germans busy in Europe that certainly is a war effort that cannot be sneered at. . . .
>   I am perfectly willing to help Russia as long as they are willing to fight Germany to a stand-still.[34]

But what did such statements mean for the postwar era? Truman envisioned the Soviets as deserving allies; his speeches indicated that he was willing to accept them as partners in a new world order. But he never was swept up in the wartime euphoria that depicted the USSR as a new kind of democracy. His lack of illusions, far from disqualifying him from dealing with the Soviet Union, left him better prepared than many other leaders for a realistic postwar diplomacy.

VI

As Truman would tell his friend Mon Wallgren in late 1945, he thought of himself as a "little left of center." By 1944, however, he had become not merely a faithful follower of Roosevelt and the New Deal, but a leading figure in the liberal wing of the Democratic party. As historians Gary Fink and James Hilty have observed, his new position reflected in part the erosion of New Deal strength in the Senate under the stresses of World War II. But it also amounted to a continuation of the progression Truman had begun in the 1930s.[35] Consciously or unconsciously, he constructed a political image that reflected a new balance of power within a Missouri Democratic party increasingly finding its center of gravity in metropolitan St. Louis. In that city and in other urban centers around the state, the old machines were declining and being supplanted by two well-organized power blocs: the labor movement and an independent black vote.

The experience of what might be called the presidential wing of the Democratic party—the northern, metropolitan-centered forces that dominated the national convention and thereby controlled presidential nominations—was similar to that of Missouri. Thus as Truman's image altered in ways that responded to developments in his home state, he became a more plausible possibility for a national ticket. In the case of both labor and blacks, what changed was less a matter of substance than of tone. Truman had refrained from complete identification with both groups but had always enjoyed generally good relationships with them; they had been important in his 1940 renomination.

With considerable justice, Truman could consider himself an even-handed legislator on labor issues. As chairman of the Truman committee, he frequently criticized union excesses and made no secret of his loathing for John L. Lewis, who pulled the United Mine Workers off the job repeatedly during the war. Such actions, he told a correspondent, were "straight out-and-out treason."[36] Still, when it came to votes on issues, he usually supported labor objectives. In 1942, he opposed the Ball amendment to limit wage increases to 15 percent.[37] In 1943, he voted to recommit the Smith-Connally antistrike bill (although, following the Senate leadership, he did vote for the bill after recommittal was defeated); subsequently, he was in the minority that voted to sustain President Roosevelt's veto. He also introduced a Senate resolution that defended the railway brotherhoods in a wage-stabilization dispute.[38] Whenever the issue came up, he strongly opposed a labor draft.[39]

Truman criticized only a few individuals, primarily Lewis, at the national level. His biting attacks on wartime strikes created little enmity because, unlike Lewis, most labor leaders were pledged against them. Truman made a clear distinction between established big business, which he reflexively disliked, and big labor, which he usually supported. Political considerations go far to explain his position, but in his heart he found it impossible to envision men who worked with their hands as a threat to American values. By 1944, most labor chieftains considered him a friend.

Truman's relationship with black leaders was along the same lines. He never put civil rights at the top of his priority list, never advocated "social equality," and never considered most blacks the equal of most whites. But he continued to consider Negroes an important electoral constituency and a legitimate interest group. He was more attuned to the patronage needs of black political leaders than to civil rights grievances, although he always delivered sympathetic responses to such issues and may have been of some assistance in opening up skilled jobs for black workers in Kansas City defense projects.[40]

What changed during the war was his level of sensitivity. In his private life, it consisted of little things, such as a tendency to use the word "Negro" more frequently in his personal correspondence. In public, it meant a willingness to associate himself more clearly than ever with civil rights causes, despite private ambivalence. Late in his first term in the Senate and throughout his second term, he signed on as a sponsor of numerous bills designed to promote more equality for blacks.

His attitude seems to have passed down to his aides. In October 1941, Harry Vaughan was capable of privately referring to a black critic as "one of the particular class of humans to which I am allergic—an Ethiopian graduate of Harvard." In February 1945, as military aide to Vice President Truman, Vaughan wrote to a black soldier who had complained about discrimination: "That it is wrong—all right thinking people agree. You may count upon Harry Truman to do his utmost toward righting this wrong." By the standards of later generations, such gestures were inconsequential. In a political world characterized by assumptions of white superiority and widespread segregation, they were meaningful moves in a new direction.[41]

Truman decisively aligned himself with the forces of change on one other large issue: the transition to the postwar economy. The Truman committee's advocacy of planning for reconversion to a civilian economy had been vague and general. By mid-1944, however, Truman was prepared to be specific. At the urging of his good friend and Truman committee colleague Harley Kilgore, he signed on as co-sponsor of a bill to establish new bureaucratic machinery for managing a planned reconversion. Developed by liberal intellectuals, the legislation included generous unemployment benefits for workers making the transition from defense industry or military service to civilian employment. Assuming a revival of the New Deal and a continuation of the strong control over the economy that the government had assumed in World War II, it had the backing of organized labor and the New Dealish National Farmers Union.[42]

The Kilgore bill, eventually known as the Kilgore-Truman-Murray bill, was defeated in August 1944 by a Senate majority that thought it too liberal. But Truman's sponsorship was an important declaration. He had chosen sides in an ideological debate over the postwar political economy and had come down unequivocally with the Senate's liberals.

At the same time, he felt a fundamental ambivalence about many of his allies. His ties to the labor movement were loose. He had doubts about the intellectuals; like many insurgent progressives, he valued their advice as technicians but doubted their capabilities as public administrators. He received many complaints from constituents about the ineptness and downright stupidity of wartime regulations. From political associates, he heard repeated wails about the way in which special federal agencies were undermining local Democratic organizations. He usually replied with hearty agreement and might refer to the "pinheads" who had infiltrated the government. He and his correspondents were especially prone to knock the Office of Price Administration, the most conspicuous wartime refuge of the New Deal intellectuals. Writing to his old friend and supporter Marvin Gates in January 1942, he remarked, "The longer I am here, the more I hate the Bureaucrats. They have neither common sense [n]or judgement."[43]

On some issues, his thoughts were nearly identical to those of the thinkers and publicists who provided a definition of "liberalism" in the 1940s. They loved the way in which he went after Standard Oil and other old-line examples of robber-baron capitalism. They would have been delighted by his private detestation of General Brehon Somervell and other military bureaucrats who would "create a fascist government if Somervell can manage it." In fact, a *New Republic* survey of key votes in the Seventy-eighth Congress credited him with taking the liberal side on twenty-one of twenty-three roll calls. A scaling method gave him a score of 98 percent; Bennett Clark's was 35 percent.[44]

VII

Despite mixed impulses about New Deal liberalism and the groups that backed it, Truman had by 1944 positioned himself on the left wing of the Democratic congressional party and had gotten considerable praise from the liberals. He equally had made himself a leader of stature on Capitol Hill, and it is probable that—as he always protested—this was his only goal. Yet by conspicuously placing himself left of center, he diminished his chances of achieving a leadership position in the upper house. Whatever his intentions, he was both attractive and available to that other Democratic party, the one that might not command the Congress but had established its dominance over presidential, and vice-presidential, nominations.

17

"Bob, It's Truman.   F.D.R.": The Vice Presidency, 1944–1945

Truman increasingly found himself telling close friends, fellow Democrats, journalists, and perfect strangers, "I don't want to be Vice President." By mid-1944, nevertheless, there was a growing movement to put him into the office. Among Democratic leaders, he alone seemed capable of restoring a healthy relationship between president and Congress and assuming the presidency should a much-feared day ever come. At one level of his consciousness, he was surely sincere in his repeated declarations that he loved the Senate and wanted only to stay there. Yet he had launched his career on a flight path that seemed designed to put him on a national ticket.[1]

II

By the end of 1941, Truman had become the leading Democrat in Missouri. His new status, in part a consequence of Bennett Clark's isolationism and alcohol-related inattentiveness to constituents, became apparent only a few months after his investigating committee had gone into business. In September 1941, he issued a statement deploring the battered condition of the Democratic party in Missouri, criticizing the Roosevelt administration for its inattentiveness to "liberal" party regulars, and announcing that he would hold a series of meetings to try to rebuild the statewide Democracy.

In Kansas City near the end of the month, he took a suite in the Muehlebach Hotel, where he spent two days seeing a steady stream of visitors in a fashion consciously reminiscent of Tom Pendergast:

> I sat in the dining room at the head of the table so everybody in the living room could see me and then I put the customer with his back to the double doors, both open, and occasionally while he was telling me his tale of woe I'd smile and nod to someone waiting and you'd be surprised how fast they went through.

He must have seen a thousand people, he told Bess, all of them cussing Clark and imploring him to do something for "the poor old '*Party*.'"[2]

After a time, he shed his initial enthusiasm. He continued to keep a close eye on local politics and patronage, but soon discovered that he could not manage a wide range of local ambitions and rivalries from Washington. Realizing that he was in danger of being used in ways that might harm him, he wisely avoided every Missouri political battle he could dodge. As much as he hated the "reform" forces in Jackson County, he also decided against active participation in local campaigns despite pleas from his friends. He was smart enough to know that there were more political dividends in fights with large corporations, big labor, or the federal bureaucracy.[3]

The limits of Truman's influence in Missouri became clear in 1944, when (probably against his better judgment) he intervened in the state Democratic primary, endorsing Bennett Clark for renomination to the Senate and Independence mayor Roger Sermon for governor. In doing so, he violated a maxim he should have learned from Tom Pendergast: even the strongest boss needed to look for candidates with broad outstate support. By 1944, Clark, once the colossus of Missouri politics, had transformed himself into a midget. Sermon had no idea of how to wage a statewide campaign. Worse yet, the Clark and Sermon forces seemed more interested in working out deals with the other's opposition than in establishing an alliance. On the first Tuesday in August, Missouri attorney general Roy McKittrick edged Clark, and state senator Phil Donnelly easily beat Sermon.[4]

The results were an embarrassment for Truman, and it was as well for him that they came after the Democratic National Convention. He had little personal enthusiasm for either candidate, but felt compelled by past favors and relationships to give them his backing. As was so often the case with him, the primary endorsements were a matter of loyalty and locality prevailing over calculations about issues or personal prestige. He delivered his blessing and asked his friends to help as much as possible, but avoided intensive personal campaigning. Unfortunately, the 1944 experience established a precedent for other contests in which Truman would back his friends and keep his agreements at the cost of identifying himself with inept losers and organization hacks.[5]

However limited his influence in local contests, Truman became steadily more important in Washington. His new stature began to translate into the most visible kind of political power—patronage clout. Early in 1942, he nominated his 1940 benefactor, Bob Hannegan, to be federal collector of internal revenue for St. Louis. A two-month minitempest ensued as antimachine Missourians vented their outrage. Truman set his feet in concrete, and on May 4, 1942, Roosevelt named Hannegan to the post. Hannegan's subsequent rise was meteoric. With Truman's backing, Roosevelt brought him to Washington as commissioner of internal revenue in the fall of 1943. A couple of months later, Truman turned down the chairmanship of the Democratic National Committee (DNC) and recommended Hannegan. On January 22, 1944, Hannegan, by now one of Truman's closest associates and biggest political debtors, took over the party machinery.[6]

Other triumphs were equally sweet. Congressman Richard Duncan, Truman's close friend from St. Joseph, had lost his seat in the Democratic rout of 1942. Despite the open, vehement opposition of Bennett Clark and the quieter but equally determined resistance of Attorney General Francis Biddle, the senator insisted on making Duncan a federal district judge. After a protracted deadlock, Clark grudgingly gave in; Truman agreed to support Clark's associate, Rubey Hulen, for another judicial appointment. On orders from the White House, Biddle acquiesced. The appointment of Duncan demonstrated that, as the *Kansas City Star* put it, "Harry S. Truman has emerged top man among Missouri Democrats at the White House."[7]

Soon afterward, Biddle found himself fighting another hopeless delaying action against Truman's nomination of Fred Canfil as United States marshal for the western district of Missouri. Finally appointed and confirmed by the Senate on January 12, 1944, Canfil was sworn into office by Judge Duncan. He would be less concerned with marshaling than with continuing to act as one of Truman's political lieutenants in the state.[8]

The new recognition had not come easy. The administration had regarded the Truman committee as a nuisance during the first year or two of its operation. As late as mid-1943, James Byrnes, working out of the White House as a de facto "assistant president" in charge of the domestic war effort, had criticized it; he asserted that it hampered the prosecution of the war.[9]

Mindful of Roosevelt's sensitivity, Truman walked a fine line, attempting to critique the way in which the war was being managed without criticizing FDR. In general, he was successful. Early on, however, he made one notable slip that surely caught the attention of the White House. On August 14, 1941, speaking on the committee's initial findings and justifying a new appropriation for it, he engaged in a colloquy with Republican senator Arthur Vandenberg:

MR. VANDENBERG: In other words, the Senator is now saying that the chief bottle-neck which the defense program confronts is the lack of adequate organization and coordination in the administration of defense?

MR. TRUMAN: That is exactly what the hearings before our committee will prove.

MR. VANDENBERG: Who is responsible for that situation?

MR. TRUMAN: There is only one place where the responsibility can be put.

MR. VANDENBERG: Where is that—the White House?

MR. TRUMAN: Yes sir.

MR. VANDENBERG: I thank the Senator. (Laughter)[10]

Over a year later, Truman did a ghosted piece with the *American Magazine*. The reporter, who interviewed him in August 1942, caught him in a mood of anger at the fumbling of the rubber situation and the widespread disarray in defense production. Truman spoke frankly and bluntly, primarily with the hope of getting stronger leadership out of War Production Board chief Donald Nelson. Several days later, a young woman from the magazine came to his office with a manuscript for his approval. Pleading a tight editorial deadline, she asked him to act on it at once. Doubtless already feeling harassed and overworked, he displayed a trait that would hurt him in the future. Wanting to get it out of the way, he read through the copy quickly and initialed each page.

Sometime later, reality set in. Despite his later claim that the magazine had taken advantage of him, the article faithfully reflected Truman's attitude and accurately reproduced his words. He began to realize that they were too strong, that some of them were too clearly aimed at Roosevelt, and that the magazine would hit the newsstands just about a month before the midterm elections. Frantically, he tried to kill the article, even ordering Hugh Fulton to ask for a federal court injunction against its distribution. "The more I think of it, the worse it gets from a political angle," he told Bess. "I was feeling hostile over the rubber thing and went off half prepared—and it doesn't pay. That's why I need help and advice so badly."

Impolitic judgment was, of course, no grounds for prior censorship, and Truman's initials throughout the manuscript made it impossible to argue that he had been misrepresented. Citing space considerations, however, the magazine cut out the senator's more inflammatory remarks. What remained was a good, hard-hitting piece that proclaimed the need for strong leadership to cut through red tape, enforce cooperation, and weed out incompetence. Its message was that defense production desperately needed a tough, effective civilian czar with a wide grant of authority. When Truman read the article as published in the November 1942 issue, he was relieved. All the same, Harley Kilgore remembered it as leaving Roosevelt unwilling to speak to Truman for months.[11]

By mid-1943, nevertheless, the relationship between Truman and Roosevelt was a good one. Truman had become one of the president's most consistent supporters on the Hill. In one speech after another to Democratic meetings throughout the first half of 1944, he praised Roosevelt and advocated a fourth term. By now, he was enough of a force in Washington that a *New York Times* reporter could call his endorsement a strong boost for FDR.[12]

III

As early as the beginning of 1943, Missouri backers were beginning to talk about Truman as a vice-presidential candidate.[13] By midyear, the real prospect of a 1944 vacancy in the office loomed.

Vice President Henry A. Wallace was on the surface one of the strongest and most active individuals ever to function in a traditionally inconsequential position. An effective secretary of agriculture in the 1930s, vice president since 1941, he had occupied important positions in the defense production program and was the nation's strongest spokesman for New Deal liberalism. He was a favorite of both the president and Eleanor Roosevelt. Yet Wallace had been a flop on Capitol Hill. A shy, awkward teetotaler, he had no independent electoral constituency, no knack for the glad-handing camaraderie of the Senate, and no talent for the politics of conciliation and compromise. He lacked every quality that had endeared John Nance Garner to most senators. Conservative Democrats detested him. His reputed religious mysticism, ineptness at practical politics, and increasing ideological rigidity led moderates, nonideological professionals, and even a few liberals to worry that an unguided missile was just an uncertain heartbeat away from the presidency. Allen Drury summed it up in his diary: "He looks like a hayseed, talks like a prophet, and acts like an embarrassed schoolboy."[14]

Wallace characteristically inflicted the most telling wound on himself in mid-1943 when he went public in a long-simmering dispute with Secretary of Commerce Jesse Jones, the administration figure most revered among congressional conservatives. Roosevelt, angered at the appearance of a confused war effort, gave both combatants slaps on the wrist and reshuffled some lines of authority. But Wallace emerged as the clear loser. He was left with no substantive job and, most of Washington suspected, a less than 50–50 chance of renomination.

It was two weeks after Wallace's first shot at Jones that Truman's friend and colleague Joe Guffey asked him "*very confidentially*" what he thought of Wallace. Truman responded, "Henry is the best Secretary of Agriculture we ever did have." The remark, no doubt accompanied by a big grin, drew a laugh, an assent, and then a serious question: If necessary, would Truman help out the ticket in 1944 by accepting the vice-presidential nomination? "I told him in words of one syllable that I would not," Truman wrote to Bess. Guffey may well have been collecting intelligence for Roosevelt, Wallace, or some other hopeful. The first breezes of a draft had nonetheless made themselves felt.[15]

Truman was sincere in his response. He loved the Senate, basked in the mostly favorable public attention he was getting, and understood full well just how insignificant a vice president could be. But how firm was his resolve? It was one thing to say no to a second-line colleague who could deliver nothing beyond a good jolt of bourbon. Would he give the same answer to a group of party leaders who had real authority? To the president?

As it was, the campaign for the vice presidency proceeded along various indirect lines. Wallace attempted to reinforce his urban-labor-liberal constituency with one strong speech after another, hoping to establish himself as an asset too valuable to discard. His major unannounced rival was James Byrnes, who harvested much of the credit for awesome increases in defense production and was a favorite of those who wanted an archetypical Washington man in the vice presidency.

A few congressional notables waited with varying degrees of anticipation for lightning to strike. Senate Majority Leader Alben Barkley was probably the most receptive; Speaker of the House Sam Rayburn perhaps was also amenable to a draft. Truman continued to reply with a vigorous no every time the issue came up; by early 1944, he was boosting Rayburn at every opportunity. Yet Rayburn, a good friend whom Truman sincerely liked and admired, was an unlikely candidate on several counts, not least among them a strong challenge to his renomination in his home district. At no time did Truman make a public endorsement of Byrnes, a far more realistic possibility.[16]

In the end, as everyone knew, only Roosevelt would make the final decision; an open campaign by any aspirant would be counterproductive. The contest for the vice presidency thus was a matter of trying to influence the judgment of a tired, unwell chief executive who had to devote most of his attention to the diplomatic and military aspects of the greatest war in American history. In the spring of 1944, as the country began to focus on the political conventions, Wallace and backers of numerous other candidates did what they could to make an impression at 1600 Pennsylvania Avenue. Wallace's appearances around the country revealed a devoted following, including the unions in the Congress of Industrial Organizations (CIO), but his political advisers could charitably be described as amateurs. Barkley and Rayburn, receptive if asked, had no organization whatever. One small group, centered around cabinet members Harold Ickes, Francis Biddle, and Henry Morgenthau, Jr., talked up Supreme Court Justice William O. Douglas.[17]

In such a political environment, the party leaders were an influential force. They included Bob Hannegan; Postmaster General Frank Walker and New York leader Ed Flynn (both of them predecessor DNC chairmen); DNC treasurer Edwin Pauley, a wealthy California independent oilman; and DNC secretary George Allen, a Mississippian whom Pat Harrison had brought to Washington. Most influential among the bosses were Frank Hague of Jersey City and Ed Kelly of Chicago. As a group, these men were personally a bit conservative but professionally nonideological. Above all, they wanted Democratic ascendancy and all the power that accompanied it. Their primary aim was a winning ticket; given Roosevelt's questionable health, their secondary goal was a potential successor with whom they could work. Any of the alternatives (other than Douglas, who never had a real chance) was acceptable, but their favorites were Byrnes and Truman.

Roosevelt heard suggestions from a variety of sources but kept his counsel. Perhaps he wanted to put off an unpleasant decision; perhaps he enjoyed playing the contenders against one another; perhaps he was simply too distracted by the war. One move, however, was portentous. In May, he sent Henry Wallace on a vague, extended mission to China and Soviet East Asia, thereby removing him from the country at a critical time.

After sending Wallace abroad, Roosevelt gave Byrnes strong encouragement, at first indirectly through Hannegan and others and then personally. In June and early July, the president saw many other people who had an interest in the nomination and invariably told them things they wanted to hear. On June 27, talking with three of his aides, Roosevelt threw out several names—Wallace, Truman, John Winant, Henry Kaiser, Byrnes. He seemed to believe that both Wallace and Byrnes had serious liabilities.

On July 6, he told Harold Ickes and Sam Rosenman, perhaps his closest White House aide, that he thought Byrnes would be a poor candidate. On July 10, he left Ickes and Rosenman with the impression that he favored Douglas; he then sent them to meet Henry Wallace, just back from China, with the suggestion that he should withdraw. Wallace refused to discuss the matter with them. Obtaining a personal meeting with Roosevelt, he got the president to promise a letter to the convention declaring that the nomination was open but that he was FDR's personal choice. Decidedly lukewarm in tone, it would be read to the Democratic delegates on July 20.

On the night of July 11, Roosevelt dined with Hannegan, Walker, Flynn, Kelly, Pauley, and Allen. They discussed one possibility after another. Ed Flynn led the charge against Byrnes, arguing that he would alienate labor, blacks, and Catholics. (Perhaps he felt as he did because Byrnes two years earlier had been delegated to tell Flynn that the Senate would not confirm him as ambassador to Australia; Truman had supported Flynn's nomination to the end.) Kelly was alone among the pols in displaying any enthusiasm for Douglas. Truman drew the most support, and Roosevelt *apparently* agreed to him.

It was probably at that point, or perhaps the next day, that he gave Bob Hannegan a postdated handwritten letter, which was also typed for his signature:

July 19, 1944

Dear Bob:—

You have written me about Harry Truman and Bill Douglas. I should, of course, be very glad to run with either of them and believe that either one of them would bring real strength to the ticket.

Always sincerely,

Franklin D. Roosevelt*

The next day, after Frank Walker told Byrnes of a shift toward Truman, Byrnes called the president, who told him, "You must not get out of the race. If you stay in, you are sure to win." In a personal meeting on July 13 and another phone conversation on July 14, Roosevelt remained encouraging. In two separate discussions with Byrnes, Hannegan could only affirm Roosevelt's indication of Truman or Douglas and say, "I don't understand it." (According to Byrnes, he said nothing about a letter.) The convention was scheduled to begin in Chicago on Monday, July 17. The principals in the vice-presidential drama must have been utterly confused and possibly wondering if they had somehow been transported back in time to Caligula's court.

What did Truman know of all this, and when did he know it? Doubtless he realized that Hannegan and other professionals were boosting him for the vice presidency, but he resisted pressure through the spring and summer to indicate, however quietly and confidentially, that he was available. His attitude probably was that if Roosevelt laid hands on him, all right; he would take the nomination. If not, fine. On the eve of the convention, he was still telling all comers that he was not a candidate.

That was also what he said to Byrnes when the South Carolinian

---

*As Grace Tully, Roosevelt's secretary, recalled it, she was ordered several days later (after Hannegan met with Roosevelt at the Chicago rail yards) to change the order of names in the letter from "Douglas and Truman" to "Truman and Douglas." Hannegan's own account of that meeting is that he came to ask the president for a change in the statement that Roosevelt had promised Wallace. After "a rather heated discussion," he got an alteration that considerably softened FDR's declaration of preference for the vice president. The handwritten and typed letters that name Truman first were given to him by Hannegan's widow in 1960, but do not seem to be included in Truman's papers; copies are in the Robert Hannegan Papers, Truman Library. Apparently, no "Douglas and Truman" letter, if there ever was one, still exists. It is possible that Grace Tully had made such a change some days earlier at the White House, but she and her assistant, Dorothy Brady, were convinced that it was done on the train. For Hannegan's account, see Robert Hannegan to Samuel Rosenman, May 25, 1949, and telephone message from Hannegan, June 8, 1949, as summarized by Rosenman's secretary in Rosenman Papers, Franklin D. Roosevelt Library. Two drafts of the Wallace letter, addressed to Senator Samuel Jackson, temporary chairman of the convention, coexist with the final product in PSF (Democratic Convention File), Franklin D. Roosevelt Papers, Roosevelt Library. I am grateful to Robert Hannegan's son, William Hannegan, for providing me with copies of these and numerous other relevant documents. For Tully's memories, see Grace Tully, *F.D.R.: My Boss* (New York: Scribner, 1949), 275–77.

called on July 14 to ask if he was running. Byrnes thereupon asked Truman to make the nominating speech for him. Truman readily agreed and pledged his full support. In later years, he would bitterly assert that Byrnes must have known he was Roosevelt's choice and was engaged in an effort to preempt him. No political naïf, Byrnes was capable of such a ploy, but he clearly did not believe that Truman was a firm choice. In fact, Roosevelt had not yet indicated a final decision to anyone; rather, he had written two letters naming three people and had given extraordinary oral encouragement to Byrnes, who logically felt that he still had a strong chance.

Was Truman playing games of his own? It is hard to believe that Hannegan or another participant did not get word back to him about the July 11 meeting, but he later claimed no knowledge of it before the convention. It is more credible that he knew but, like most of the participants, did not regard it as a definitive decision in his favor. He still had no direct indication from the president. Soon after taking Byrnes's call, he received a similar request from Barkley, which he declined on the basis of his prior commitment to Jimmy. He left for Chicago the next day ready to work for Byrnes unless and until destiny intervened.

Byrnes's account of the next few days confirms the uncertainty of the situation. On Saturday morning, July 15, Kelly called him from Chicago with the news that he and Hannegan would meet the president's train, confer with him once again about the vice presidency, and transmit their opinion that Byrnes would not drive away black votes. Sometime later, he called again to say that Roosevelt "has given us the green light to support you and he wants you in Chicago." The next day, meeting personally with Byrnes in Chicago, Hannegan and Kelly reported that Roosevelt definitely wanted Byrnes; at an evening gathering, other party leaders rallied around and talked of a first-ballot nomination. Then, according to Byrnes, just as the conclave was breaking up, Hannegan said, "Ed, there is one thing we forgot. The President said, 'Clear it with Sidney.'"[18]

Was Hannegan playing out a charade he had prearranged with Roosevelt? If so, he never admitted it. Had Roosevelt consciously plotted to embarrass Byrnes? There is no reason why he would have wanted to injure a loyal and trusted aide. The most likely explanation is that a tired, distracted president had been caught in an attempt to please everyone. Whatever the truth, Byrnes's aspirations quickly unraveled.

Sidney Hillman, now chairman of the powerful CIO Political Action Committee, would not support Byrnes. On the evening of July 17, at Ed Flynn's insistence, Flynn, Hillman, and CIO president Philip Murray telephoned Roosevelt from Hannegan's hotel suite in the presence of Byrnes's close friend Leo Crowley. As Crowley reported it later, Hillman and Flynn insisted repeatedly to the president that Byrnes would alienate labor and blacks, dragging the ticket down to defeat; Roosevelt thereupon said he "would go along with their desire to nominate Truman."[19]

Truman by then was in Chicago, to all appearances engaged in a good-faith effort to line up votes for Byrnes. He breakfasted with Hillman (who by lucky coincidence was a longtime friend of Max Lowenthal) and learned that the labor leader was dead set against Byrnes, but willing to take either Truman or Douglas. Truman recalled getting the same message from Philip Murray, rail-brotherhood chief A. F. Whitney (although Byrnes believed that Whitney was a strong supporter), and AFL president William Green. At some point (Truman probably was wrong in remembering it as Tuesday evening, July 18), Hannegan showed Truman a note written on a White House scratch pad: "Bob, it's Truman.   F.D.R." Truman's Senate colleagues Millard Tydings and George Radcliffe of Maryland, neither of them close friends, offered to back him. "I reported all these conversations to Byrnes in detail," Truman writes. "Every time I gave him the information Byrnes told me just to wait, that the President would straighten everybody out in plenty of time."[20]

On Tuesday, Byrnes's hopes collapsed. That morning, he got Roosevelt on the phone. The president denied dropping him, but had to admit that he had written a letter giving his approval to Truman or Douglas. By then, according to Byrnes, Truman had already been told by Hannegan that Roosevelt wanted him for vice president and wanted Byrnes to release him. That afternoon, Byrnes dictated a letter asking the South Carolina delegation to refrain from nominating him. According to the diary of Walter Brown, one of Byrnes's closest aides, Truman met with Byrnes on Wednesday in a state of embarrassment. He expressed regret and declared that he had not been a part of any conspiracy against him. Byrnes responded that Truman was not to blame for the "duplicity and hypocrisy which had been practiced by the President."[21] He then released his letter and asked his friends to vote for Truman. The next day, he left town.

Yet Truman did not make himself unequivocally available for the vice presidency until Thursday afternoon. A great part of his continued reluctance was no doubt traceable to Bess's vehement opposition. A smaller part may just have been a determination to get definitive word from Roosevelt himself. Called to Hannegan's suite at the Blackstone, he listened to Roosevelt's voice booming from a telephone:

> "Bob, have you got that fellow lined up yet?"
> "No, he is the contrariest Missouri mule I've ever dealt with."
> "Well, you tell him if he wants to break up the Democratic party in the middle of a war, that's his responsibility."

Roosevelt hung up, slamming his receiver with an impact that may have sounded like an artillery shell to Truman. FDR still had made no direct request. Truman sat for a minute or two, then got up, walked around the room, and finally said, "Well, if that is the situation, I'll have to say yes, but why the hell didn't he tell me in the first place?"[22]

That night, nonetheless, the Wallace forces almost stampeded the convention for their man; Ed Pauley would never forget having to threaten mayhem on the sound system to get the organist to stop playing "Iowa, Where the Tall Corn Grows." But the pros never lost control. They let the Wallace forces have their demonstration and got the session adjourned without taking a ballot. The next day, they played the convention like a violin.

On Friday morning, with utter assurance, a smiling Truman told newsmen that it was "all over"; he was going to be the vice-presidential nominee. Convention chairman Samuel Jackson read Roosevelt's perfunctory statement of preference for Wallace; it was dated July 14. Hannegan then released Roosevelt's declaration of willingness to run with Truman or Douglas; tellingly, it was dated July 19. (Hannegan surely preferred Truman above all other possibilities, but he took greater satisfaction in beating Wallace. "When I die," he later said, "I would like to have one thing on my headstone—that I was the man who kept Henry Wallace from becoming President of the United States.")

Although he trailed Wallace on the first ballot, Truman got the votes he needed at the end of the second as the favorite-son states switched to him. He had to be aware that Byrnes's supporters, almost to a man, backed him. He went to the platform; in fewer than a hundred uninspired words that read like a parody of convention rhetoric, he expressed a sense of humility, indicated his appreciation for the great honor that had come to Missouri, said he would assume the great responsibility, and expected to continue the efforts he had made to shorten the war and win the peace under that great leader Franklin D. Roosevelt.

Whatever happiness he felt, it had to be highly qualified. The nomination would force him to leave his committee at once and eventually to resign his Senate seat. It presented the prospect of political insignificance if Roosevelt survived a fourth term in good health, unthinkable challenge if he did not. Truman knew that Bess dreaded the spotlight and that there would be controversy about her paid office position. On the hot, crowded convention floor, she and Margaret already were besieged by reporters and well-wishers when Harry joined them. Margaret was elated; Bess, unhappy and apprehensive. With a wedge of Chicago policemen slowly pushing them through a wild crowd, they finally got into a waiting car. Bess, Margaret recalls, glared at her husband and asked, "Are we going to have to go through this for the rest of our lives?"[23]

IV

Truman would be an active participant in the 1944 campaign but never a major issue, despite the best efforts of his opponents. After an emotional resignation from his investigating committee, he met on August 18 with Roosevelt for the first time since the nomination. The encounter consisted of little more than genial pleasantries, the new nominee tendering his thanks and Roosevelt, as Truman recalled it, giving him "a lot of hooey about what I could do to help the campaign." They lunched in the open behind the White House under an enormous oak planted by Andrew Jackson more than a hundred years earlier. Not having seen FDR face-to-face for more than a year, he was shocked by Roosevelt's haggard appearance and the way his hands trembled as he attempted with little success to pour cream into his coffee. But he told reporters afterward, "The President looked fine and ate a bigger meal than I did. . . . He's still the leader he's always been and don't let anybody kid you about it. He's keen as a briar."[24]

Party leaders soon developed a grueling campaign schedule in which Truman would be the workhorse, criss-crossing the country to rouse the troops. Roosevelt would play the role of incumbent commander-in-chief, making trips and appearances designed to remind the people that he was at the head of a winning war effort and holding the partisan speech making to a few appearances during the last weeks of the campaign. Truman's small staff included his two most trusted committee aides, Hugh Fulton as campaign manager and chief speechwriter and Matt Connelly as an all-around arrangements man. The national committee's publicity director, Paul A. Porter, a bright, liberal young Kentuckian, helped intermittently with press relations. George Allen came along. (A year or so later, introducing Allen to his mother, Truman informed her that, growing up in Mississippi, Allen had not seen a Republican until he had reached the age of twelve. The old lady replied, "You didn't miss much.")

Although he had financial carte blanche from the national committee, Truman endeavored to raise enough money to cover the vice-presidential campaign himself. His old friend Tom Evans was campaign treasurer; Eddie Jacobson worked Jewish contributors. They deposited the funds in John Snyder's St. Louis bank. Ed McKim, increasingly at Truman's side, came along less for any practical purpose than for the long friendship that seemed somehow more important to both men since the death of Eddie, Jr. Harry Vaughan, still on active military duty, provided encouragement from the sidelines.[25]

Like many vice-presidential candidates, Truman became a lightning rod for the attacks of the opposition. The campaign against him was nasty. Republican writers all but called him a gangster who, in the words of Missouri Democrat-turned-Republican Ewing Mitchell, had been one of the "four horsemen of the Pendergast machine," had been elected to the Senate with stolen ballots, and had devoted his career to misgovernment.[26] Truman was especially wounded by criticism of Bess's position on the public payroll. Clare Booth Luce weighed in with some comments that appear to have been little noticed, but Truman never forgot them. Westbrook Pegler snidely riposted that "some petty white graft" was probably a necessity of life for a poorly paid senator. The opposition also dredged up the farm mortgage foreclosure and Vivian's FHA job.[27]

Rumors about Roosevelt's deteriorating health made Truman-bashing an especially pertinent line of attack. The *Chicago Tribune*, picturing him as a Throttlebottom fronting for the city machines, warned that "a vote

for Roosevelt is very likely to be a vote for Truman for President."[28] Other
attacks were more sinister, if ultimately inconsequential. Truman's old
enemy Todd George and a few other Klansmen reemerged to assert that
he had once been a member of the Klan. The story was easily put down,
although with no mention of the $10 initiation fee that Truman had briefly
tendered in 1922. Rabbi Samuel Mayerberg, one of the leaders of Kansas City Jewry, spoke up for him. So did Eddie Jacobson, although he
engaged in creative exaggeration when he claimed, "He and his family
have been on intimate terms with me and my family, and we often have
been his guests and he has been ours."[29] (A few right-wing crazies added
credibility to the denials of the Klan charge by asserting that Truman was
actually Jewish. [His middle initial stood for Solomon, didn't it?] Truman
simply responded, "I am not Jewish, but if I were I would not be ashamed
of it.")[30]

If he attracted none of the negative emotions that Henry Wallace had
evoked, Truman drew little positive passion. Assessing himself candidly,
he told Senate journalists, "The trouble with me is that I'm not photo-
genic and I'm a hell of a public speaker." Louis Johnson reported to Steve
Early that Truman had "flopped" in a joint appearance with Republican
vice-presidential candidate John Bricker.

He committed a fair-sized blooper also. In Massachusetts, he told
newsmen who asked him how he could support Democratic isolationist
Senator David Walsh: "Oh, his term has two more years to go. Maybe
we can reform him." Walsh, still a major figure in the state's politics, was
not amused; he subsequently required a lot of stroking from the White
House. There were reports that Roosevelt had personally ordered George
Allen to stop Truman "from making all those damn fool statements."[31]

All the same, Truman's campaign, like that of most vice-presidential
aspirants, was little more than a sideshow. *Time* probably expressed the
consensus of those who attempted an objective look at him; in a relatively
friendly article, it described him as "unsophisticated" and "homespun,"
not superficially impressive but solid and capable: "There is no reason to
suspect he would make a great President—and there is no reason to believe that he would be the worst."[32]

Roosevelt was the focus of the campaign. When he seemed to regain
his old vitality as a speaker and rode through the boroughs of New York
for hours in the rain, the outcome was sealed. On election day, the Old
Master won for the fourth time. Truman sent him a congratulatory telegram: "I AM VERY HAPPY OVER THE OVERWHELMING ENDORSEMENT WHICH YOU
RECEIVED. ISOLATIONISM IS DEAD. HOPE TO SEE YOU SOON."[33]

V

"Your note about the gal on the piano is one hundred per cent right,"
Truman wrote to Eddie McKim in February 1945. "You should see the
letters I have from the old ladies."[34] No image is more remembered from

his vice presidency than that of the beautiful, young Lauren Bacall on top of an upright piano at the National Press Club, displaying a lot of leg (by 1945 standards) and smiling down at a grinning Truman. No matter that the vice president had been the victim of a publicity stunt or that his grin was a cover for his discomfort; the scene was a little too akin to that of a piano player in a whorehouse. It became a classic example of the triviality to which the office lent itself.

One of the least attractive aspects of the vice presidency—and one that Harry and Bess especially resented—was its empty celebrity status. With the president wrapped in a public cloak of wartime security and military-diplomatic leadership, the number-two man and his family became targets of hostesses, Democratic fund-raisers, and gossip columnists. Bess, already infuriated by the Bacall photo, felt that the press, especially the *Kansas City Star*, depicted her and Harry as provincial rubes unaccustomed to associating with the rich and famous.[35] Harry attempted to be more philosophical. He wrote to Lou Holland:

> High society never interested me much, and I am not going into it any more than I have. Nearly all the parties I have attended were occasions where my attendance was a necessity, and things which were mostly given by people with whom I had been associated for many years past. . . . [S]ince I am living in a glass bowl, they created comment, which was to be expected.[36]

On January 26, Tom Pendergast died. Vice president for a week, Truman issued a public statement: "He was always my friend and I have always been his." Commandeering an air force bomber, he flew to Kansas City for the funeral. The overflow crowd at Kansas City's Visitation Church included Bennett Clark and former governor Guy Park, but none of the new city and county political establishment. Truman believed that he had taken the only decent course. The opposition, which acted as if Truman's plane had been pulled directly from a combat run over Tokyo, saw his pilgrimage as an outrage that reaffirmed his loyalty to a crooked machine and underscored his status as a political hack. The event became a talking point used against him for years.[37]

Appearances aside, he was far more effective as vice president than Wallace and potentially more useful to Roosevelt than John Nance Garner, who had spent much of his tenure disagreeing with FDR. Truman was determined to make his mark. Ten years later, he would write, "The Vice-President's influence on legislation depends on his personality and his ability, and especially the respect which he commands from the senators. Here is one instance in which it is the man who makes the office, not the office the man."[38]

Roosevelt started him out with a make-or-break assignment. On Inauguration Day, FDR "accepted the resignation" of Jesse Jones as secretary of commerce and federal loan administrator, informing Jones that Henry Wallace, having expressed an interest in both positions, would be his successor. Told of the decision just before Roosevelt released it to the press, Truman, as Jonathan Daniels later expressed it, "dropped two words from the New Testament" and went to work to pacify the Senate.

Wallace remained personally unpopular with a majority of senators. Jones, who openly led the opposition, not only retained his prestige in the upper chamber, but added to it considerable sympathy for the shabby way in which he had been fired. Roosevelt had handled the entire affair so maladroitly that some observers took it as a plot to get rid of Wallace. With a stiff battle looming in the Senate, FDR secretly left the country on January 22 to meet Stalin and Churchill at Yalta.

Operating with no resources other than the respect and friendship he enjoyed, Truman acted as midwife for a compromise that severed the post of federal loan administrator from the secretaryship of commerce, thus assuring a few fence-straddling senators that Wallace would not have billions of dollars with which to destroy the republic and/or further his own ambitions. He had to cast two tie-breaking votes and, on one occasion, make extraordinary use of his power to choose which senators to recognize. When Wallace was finally confirmed as secretary of commerce on March 1, 1945, it was in no small measure Truman's achievement. Despite a lack of personal enthusiasm for the appointment, he had shown that he would loyally and effectively carry water for the administration.

Truman then got the ultimately impossible assignment of managing Senate approval for the southern liberal Aubrey Williams to head the Rural Electrification Administration. He also annoyed liberals by referring to the hostile Commerce Committee a bill to establish the Missouri Valley Authority. Although he insisted that he had no choice, he could have sent the legislation to a more sympathetic committee. His decision reflected a long-held commitment to a comprehensive flood-control scheme for the Missouri River basin, open doubt that the bill in question was technically practical, and a wholly accurate understanding that the full Senate was not about to approve another Tennessee Valley Authority.[39]

Chatting with a group of Capitol Hill journalists on March 3, Truman disingenuously remarked (probably with his usual smile) that he had no influence on the Williams controversy: "After all, I'm just a—what do they call it?—political eunuch." Allen Drury thought not, remarking to himself that Truman was "beginning to emerge as a V.P. who may presently become a very powerful man. . . . He is no man's stooge, and he goes about the business of politics with a youthful enthusiasm and a mature skill." FDR, he anticipated, might find "Harry, with the Senate behind him, doing the dictating on a number of things."[40]

Truman certainly expected to wield some clout. He secured the appointment (this one not controversial) of his old corporal Al Ridge to be a federal judge. To the dismay of Attorney General Biddle, he told the Justice Department that he did not want Maurice Milligan reappointed as a United States district attorney.[41] Still, his main ambition appears to have been to serve the president. Unfortunately, between January 20 and

April 12, the president was in Washington for only about thirty days; according to the White House records, Truman met personally with him only twice.

A letter written by Truman on April 5 demonstrates the distant superficiality of their working relationship:

> Dear Mr. President:
>
> Hope you are having a good rest. Hate to bother you, but I have a suggestion to make.
>
> Why don't you make Frank Walker Federal Loan Administrator and make Bob Hannegan Postmaster-General?
>
> Seems to me this would make everybody happy and solve the situation.
>
> Hannegan did the P.M.G.'s job in the campaign as well as it was ever done and he is entitled to the recognition.
>
> Walker is as able a businessman and administrator as the country has. Both are 100% for you.
>
> Hope you'll like my suggestion.
>
> Sincerely   Harry[42]

The letter was that of an emissary from the party organization, making an almost apologetic suggestion to an imperial president. FDR responded encouragingly.

Underneath Truman's efforts to create a role for himself, there existed a pervasive fear that his days in the vice presidency would be few. Roosevelt, he told Harry Easley after the election, had the pallor of death on his face. He had similar conversations with other close Missouri friends. On February 20, while presiding over the Senate, he was informed of a rumor that Roosevelt was dead. Probably thinking that a personal call would be unseemly, he went to the office of the new Senate secretary, Les Biffle, and asked him to contact the White House. Biffle relayed the news, still secret, that the president's appointments secretary, General Edwin "Pa" Watson, had died at sea on the way back from Yalta.

When the president arrived in Washington, his wasted appearance left Truman shaken. Roosevelt's report to Congress, delivered on March 1, confirmed his fears. The president gave the address sitting down and mentioned in public for the first time the steel braces that he wore to support his legs. His voice was hollow; the cadence and construction of his message were marred by maladroit ad-libs. Truman preferred in later years to recall the episode as a remarkable display of will and courage. At the time, he told reporters who asked him for a reaction quote that the speech was "one of the greatest ever given," and then laughed heartily. Privately, he and everyone else understood that the president had fumbled an important occasion. Roosevelt told Truman that he was worn out but that two or three weeks' rest would put him back in trim. On March 30, he left for his retreat at Warm Springs, Georgia. The will to believe his prediction was likely nowhere stronger than in Harry Truman's mind.[43]

Writing to Mamma and Mary Jane on April 11, he recounted his new routine—dropping Margaret off at George Washington University first thing in the morning, getting to the office at the unaccustomedly late hour of 8:30, managing a foot-high stack of mail, receiving visitors in his old Senate office, seeing more supplicants in the vice president's Capitol suite, opening the daily session of the Senate ("it's my job to get 'em prayed for—and goodness knows they need it"), seeing senators about various bits of business, meeting curiosity seekers "who want to see what a V.P. looks like and if he walks and has teeth," and often attending a late meeting before going home.[44]

The next day, Thursday, April 12, while presiding over the Senate, he wrote another letter to his mother and sister. When the session was over, he walked to Sam Rayburn's hideaway—"the Board of Education"—for a late-afternoon bourbon and some good conversation to be followed by an evening of poker at Eddie McKim's suite in the Statler Hilton. When he arrived, Rayburn told him that Steve Early at the White House had just called and had to get in touch with him right away. Truman telephoned at once; the strain in Early's voice was evident and his message terse: "Please come right over and come in through the main Pennsylvania Avenue entrance."[45]

Truman's rational impulse was not to make too much of the call; Roosevelt probably had sneaked back into town for the funeral of an old friend, Episcopal bishop Julius Atwood, and wanted to see him before heading back to Georgia. But his intuition told him something else. One of the men in the room later described him to Alfred Steinberg as ashen-faced, blurting an expletive, and saying, "Boys, this is in this room. Something must have happened." He quickly went back to his office and got his hat. Without bothering to inform his Secret Service guard, he ran through the basement of the Capitol to meet his chauffeur. He arrived at the White House at 5:25 P.M.

Immediately taken up to the living quarters on the second floor, he found Eleanor Roosevelt waiting for him. Years later, he vividly recalled her tenderness and dignity as she put her arm on his shoulder.

"Harry, the President is dead."

BOOK II

AMERICAN PRESIDENT
1945–1972

18

"I Feel Like I Have Been Struck by a Bolt of Lightning": Confronting the Presidency, 1945–1947

"In the long cabinet room he looked to me like a very little man as he sat waiting in a huge leather chair," Jonathan Daniels wrote of the new president. "I feel like I have been struck by a bolt of lightning," Truman later told John Snyder. Visiting the Capitol the next day, he told a group of reporters that he did not know if any of them had ever had a load of hay fall on them but that he felt like the moon, the stars, and the planets had all fallen on him. "Boys, if you ever pray, pray for me now," he said. He clearly felt small, overwhelmed, and in something of a state of shock. The days and weeks ahead would be filled with numerous policy decisions for which he had been left totally unprepared. A stream of people would leave and enter a new administration. Above all, he would have to get a grip on the levers of power and the institution of the presidency.[1]

II

Truman managed the immediate transition well. Members of the cabinet, also summoned by Steve Early, began to arrive. Secretary of State Edward Stettinius suggested a cabinet meeting. At about 6:00 P.M., Truman called the meeting to order. He formally reported the death of FDR., quoted Eleanor Roosevelt as saying that her husband had "died like a soldier," promised to try to carry on as he would have wished, and asked them to stay in their posts. Stettinius observed Secretary of Labor

Frances Perkins quietly praying. The cabinet officers delivered brief pledges of support. They all decided that the oath of office should be administered immediately, and someone called for Chief Justice Harlan Fiske Stone.[2]

At a few minutes after seven, with Bess and Margaret at his side, Truman took the oath of office, his left hand holding a Bible that had been found in the office of Correspondence Secretary Bill Hassett. The chief justice reminded him to raise his right hand and began, "I, Harry Shippe Truman . . ." The new president, without missing a beat, responded, "I, Harry S. Truman . . ."; he kissed the Bible when he was finished. The room was crowded with administration officials, leading members of Congress, newsmen, photographers, and film cameramen. The ceremony was repeated for the benefit of the picture takers. It had been done, James Forrestal thought, "with dignity and firmness."[3]

Truman then conferred briefly with Early regarding funeral arrangements and authorized Stettinius to announce that the San Francisco Conference, to establish the United Nations organization, would begin as scheduled on April 25. He emphasized his determination to meet the international responsibilities of the presidency and promised the secretary of state his full support. Stettinius thought that he seemed "a simple sincere person, bewildered, but who is going to do everything in his power to meet this emergency." He had imparted "no feeling of weakness whatever."[4]

By 9:30 P.M., Truman was back at 4701 Connecticut Avenue. The next-door neighbors provided him and his family with something to eat. Then, as he put it in an account written a few days later: "Went to bed, went to sleep, and did not worry any more."[5]

Friday, April 13, 1945

Truman got up at his usual hour, had a quick breakfast, and met with Hugh Fulton, who had come to offer his services. The Secret Service escorted them down the back stairs to avoid the newsmen and curiosity seekers gathered at the front of the building. As they got into the presidential limousine, Truman spied Tony Vaccaro, Washington correspondent for the Associated Press, and invited him to ride to the White House with them. Shortly after 9:00 A.M., he walked into the Oval Office as president for the first time. Roosevelt's belongings were still everywhere; reluctantly, Truman called for a White House employee to clear the desk. As he did so, a train bearing his predecessor's remains was moving toward Washington, to be met by grieving crowds all along the way.

Truman tried to sort out his new position in a series of meetings, some unfocused, others very purposeful. First, there was a quick interview with Secretary of State Stettinius on problems with the Soviet Union and a briefing from Stettinius's aide Charles Bohlen. Then followed a rambling discussion of "nothing of any importance" with Fulton, Eddie

McKim, and Leonard Reinsch, a radio executive who had advised Truman on his speaking technique in the 1944 campaign. Next military leaders briefed him on the state of the war. With remarkable conservatism, they told him that it would take six months to finish Germany and another year and a half to defeat Japan.[6]

The big event of the day was a luncheon with seventeen leading legislators on Capitol Hill, a symbolic gesture meant to underscore the warmth of his feeling for his Washington roots and to assure the Congress that the new president would accept it as an equal. It was an unprecedented move that left a lot of good feeling in its wake. "It shattered all tradition. But it was both wise and smart," Senator Arthur Vandenberg wrote in his diary. "It means that the days of executive contempt for Congress are ended." Before sitting down with the smaller party, Truman stationed himself in the office of the secretary of the Senate to meet other colleagues and to say hello to the reporters who had covered him as a senator. It was then that he asked for their prayers—a sincere, heartfelt, and unwise request that did nothing to establish him as a leader.[7]

Back at the White House, Truman spent a half-hour or so discussing Soviet–American relations with James Byrnes. Byrnes pledged to provide his own notes on the Yalta Conference, and Truman all but promised to appoint him secretary of state. After a brief visit with Duke Shoop and Roy Roberts from the *Kansas City Star*, Stettinius and Bohlen came again to discuss at length Soviet intransigence in Poland and to outline a message to Stalin. By then, Truman recalled, his desk seemed loaded down with papers, and he found himself doing more reading than he had thought possible. It was evening by the time he left the office, carrying a group of documents that required his immediate attention. A Secret Service motorcade took him uptown to his apartment.

Saturday, April 14, 1945

Up at dawn, Truman worked at home on his first speech to Congress and read more briefing papers before leaving for the White House. He was in the Oval Office at 8:30 A.M. His first visitor, a half-hour later, was John Snyder, just back in Washington. Overriding Snyder's objections, Truman told his old friend that he would be named federal loan administrator. Then Secretary of the Treasury Henry Morgenthau, Jr., came in to talk about war financing and pledge his support. After that, flanked by James Byrnes and Henry Wallace, whom he had chosen to join him in a display of unity, Truman went to Union Station to meet Roosevelt's funeral train.[8]

The procession that followed was the occasion for a national catharsis. Roosevelt's casket, resting on a horse-drawn caisson and escorted by an honor guard, moved slowly from the station to the White House to the accompaniment of dirge and muffled drums. Behind it crept automobiles with the new president, other officials, and family members.

Crowds of spectators all along the route watched, some curious, some silent, many weeping openly. Truman remembered most vividly the sight of an old Negro woman sitting on the curb and pressing her apron to tear-filled eyes. Untold millions listened on their radios to Arthur Godfrey, struggling to hold back his emotions as he told his audience in a broken voice how the fallen president had taken so much for all of the ordinary people, and then declaring, "God bless Harry Truman!"[9]

Back at the White House, Truman took a few minutes to accept the respects of Andrew J. Higgins, the Louisiana shipbuilder he had championed as a congressional investigator. Then he closeted himself for an hour and a half with Harry Hopkins, who, gaunt and spectral, had left a hospital bed at the Mayo Clinic. Picking at a lunch sent up from the kitchen, they talked extensively about Hopkins's role in wartime diplomacy, and Truman tried to persuade him to stay on in his administration.

After a short talk with Ed Flynn, Truman spent two hours with Byrnes and Admiral William Leahy, going over war-related issues brought up in messages from Churchill. By then, it was time to go to the White House funeral services for Roosevelt. The mourners, overwhelmed by grief and fixated on the memory of FDR, neglected to rise when the new president entered the room. If Truman noticed, he gave no indication.[10] According to observers, he sat unmoving through the twenty-five-minute service, his eyes fixed on the casket. Late that evening, accompanied by Bess and Margaret, he followed Roosevelt's body back to the train, which they boarded for the overnight trip to Hyde Park.

Sunday, April 15, 1945

The next morning, they attended the burial services, Truman comporting himself as circumspectly as possible in the knowledge that many observers were examining him. United Press correspondent Merriman Smith thought (no doubt correctly) that he seemed tired and uneasy. Back on the train, he visited with many members of Congress and with the Roosevelts. Then, as they got under way, he closeted himself with George Allen, Byrnes, Early, and Snyder to work on the speech he would deliver to Congress the following day. Back in Washington, the family spent their last night at 4701 Connecticut Avenue. The next day, they would move to Blair House, the fine old presidential guest residence where they would stay until Eleanor Roosevelt could move out of the White House.[11]

Monday, April 16, 1945

At 1:00 P.M., Truman delivered a nationally broadcast address to a joint session of Congress. One miscue indicated that he had yet to internalize his new position: after entering the chamber of the House of Representatives and ascending the rostrum to a wild ovation, he attempted to begin his speech as if he were still a senator. Sam Rayburn broke in, "Just a minute. Let me present you, will you, Harry."

The speech itself, not especially memorable now but meaningful at the time, emphasized Truman's intention to carry on with Roosevelt's policies. He drew his greatest applause with a strong line affirming his continuing dedication to the war policy of unconditional surrender. No one then or ever would accuse him of speaking as well as Roosevelt or displaying quite the same flair for leadership, but his determination came through strongly. He had scored a triumph.[12]

Tuesday, April 17, 1945

Another big test: the first press conference. Reporters, 348 of them by Assistant Press Secretary Eben Ayers's count, packed the Oval Office and spilled out onto the terrace. Whether intentionally or not, a *New York Times* description implicitly contrasted Truman with the wheelchair-bound, unwell Roosevelt: "He stood behind his desk, a compact, active, vigorous figure with a complexion which glowed a healthy pink." He was affable. His answers to a variety of questions were crisp and decisive. He displayed good judgment in firmly declining comment on matters for which he either was not prepared or did not wish to discuss. The new president, Ayers thought, had made an excellent impression. And so he had, but then he had not been compelled to field anything very difficult. The press, like the rest of the country, wanted reassurance, hoped the president would succeed, and was not yet in a mood to push him. They applauded him when the conference ended.[13]

Tuesday was Truman's sixth day in office; he could hardly have been blamed if on the seventh day he had rested. He had mostly done all the right things and had gone far toward establishing himself in the popular consciousness as a president America could accept. Even his mother had added to the widespread goodwill with a statement that she released to the press:

> I can't really be glad he's President because I am sorry President Roosevelt is dead. If he had been voted in, I would be out waving a flag, but it doesn't seem right to be very happy or wave any flags now. Harry will get along all right. . . . Everyone who heard him talk this morning will know he's sincere and will do what's best.[14]

Truman was at the beginning of a honeymoon period that would last through the remainder of the year. In June, the Gallup organization found an 87 percent approval rating for him; in October, 82 percent. People liked what they saw of their president—modest, unassuming, determined to be an ordinary fellow, yet apparently on top of his job. Citizens who never would have thought of addressing Roosevelt as Frank called him

Harry. The attitude stemmed in part from what seemed to many Americans a refreshing change in style after Roosevelt's grandeur. As Harry Vaughan put it, "After a diet of caviar, you like to get back to ham and eggs." On the surface, moreover, things seemed to go so well in those first several months during which Truman presided over America's greatest military victory.[15]

Yet the exultation of triumph would pass, to be succeeded by a host of underlying anxieties about the future. Furthermore, Truman's style of presenting himself as the ordinary American democrat carried with it real perils. The common people might love to see someone who looked like one of them do well, but would they believe that over the long run he had what it took to handle the presidency? How many had that much faith in themselves? Eighty percent approval ratings could not last, and Truman had enough common sense to know it. It is doubtful, however, that he ever considered the pitfalls of the way in which he had packaged himself. By then, in any event, he knew no other way.

III

"Well, I'm getting organized now," Truman told Bess in June. "It won't be long until I can sit back and study the whole picture and tell 'em what is to be done in each department. When things come to that stage there'll be no more to this job than there was to running Jackson County and not any more worry."[16] The remark is incredible. Did he really believe it? Most likely, it was yet another indication of the determined—at times, desperate—optimism that had characterized so much of his life. It also displayed his understanding of the importance of organizing a White House staff that would be loyal to him and fit his administrative needs.

The presidency into which he had stepped was an institution of enormous power, but without the formal resources to wield that power effectively. The staff he inherited (omitting clerical, security, and logistical personnel) was scarcely skeletal: a half-dozen administrative assistants; secretaries in charge of appointments, press relations, and correspondence; a special counsel; a personal military chief of staff; a military aide (who in the case of Roosevelt's General Edwin Watson had doubled as appointments secretary); and a naval aide. The Executive Office of the Presidency included the Office of War Mobilization and Reconversion (OWMR), renamed to take into account the winding down of the war, and the Bureau of the Budget; the heads of both agencies served in effect as members of the president's immediate staff. Beyond this formally designated group, one could find various individuals on the payroll of some executive departments and a few strictly informal advisers. Fifty years later, presidents would preside over a staff of several hundred.

Of course, Truman was less concerned about the size of his staff than he was with finding people who had his trust and who could do the job.[17] Many of the Roosevelt people were not interested in staying on. Some could not imagine themselves working for any other president; others, having spent years as poorly paid federal employees, could not afford to remain; a few were not well. For one combination or another of these reasons, Truman was unable to retain Harry Hopkins, whom he desperately wanted; Steve Early, whom he long had respected; and Jonathan Daniels, who would have remained only in the unavailable position of press secretary. William Hassett would stay on as correspondence secretary for Truman's entire administration, and Eben Ayers would continue as assistant press secretary. Both men did competent and useful work, but in truth neither added much to the new administration. Another Roosevelt holdover, David K. Niles, was a valuable liaison to black civil rights and Jewish groups.

The most significant retention was Admiral William Leahy, the presidential military chief of staff. Just a few weeks short of his sixty-eighth birthday, Leahy had filled one post after another—a battleship command, chief of naval operations, ambassador to Vichy France—with distinction. A crusty old man who had, in the words of Charles Bohlen, a "snapping-turtle manner," he warned Truman that he always spoke his mind. The president assured Leahy that he wanted just that and added, "You may not always agree with my decisions, but I know you will carry them out faithfully."[18] It was the beginning of a relationship characterized by mutual trust and affection until Leahy retired in 1949.

Two other key individuals agreed to remain for a year or so: Special Counsel Samuel I. Rosenman and Bureau of the Budget director Harold D. Smith. Rosenman, a man of considerable ability, had become Roosevelt's chief speech writer and one of his strongest aides. Although devoted to his old chief and determined to return to his legal practice in New York, he felt constrained by a sense of duty to stay for a transitional period. Rosenman would serve Truman well, render occasional services for his presidency, and earn his lifelong friendship. Smith, who had developed the Budget Bureau into a major legislative review and program-coordination agency, was among the most able bureaucrats in Washington. He was an effective adviser before leaving to become vice president of the World Bank in June 1946. His relationship with Truman seemed cordial; yet for reasons not altogether apparent (perhaps Smith's didactic attitude toward the president or the budget director's uneasy relations with John Snyder), Truman would remember him in later years as an "A 1 conniver." Thoroughly undeserved, the remark illustrated one of Truman's more unpleasant qualities: a peevish tendency to dislike people who made him or his friends uncomfortable.[19] The president would relate more easily to Smith's successors—James E. Webb, Frank Pace, and Frederick Lawton.

For the key position of appointments secretary, Truman quickly chose Matt Connelly, whom he considered loyal, reliable, and politically shrewd. Connelly would stay in that position for almost the next eight years. Never an all-powerful gatekeeper, he was at his best discreet and tactful in sorting out who really needed to see the president and handling the requests of others. He also functioned as a contact with the Democratic pols, acting as an intermediary on patronage requests and campaign fund-raising. (Truman had learned early on to avoid involvement in raising money—or for that matter to ask many questions about where it came from.) Connelly would become a lightning rod for partisan critics and a target of muckrakers. In the end, whether fairly or not, he would pay a heavy price for his years in the White House. Pursued by the Eisenhower Justice Department, he was prosecuted and convicted for income tax evasion.

Remarkably, Truman decided against giving Hugh Fulton any position in his administration, although Fulton had been his right-hand man for four years. The few terse explanations that have been given for this decision verge on the absurd; if taken literally (as they must be in the absence of other evidence) they reveal in Truman a deep-rooted insecurity that could sometimes manifest itself in petty ways. Truman supposedly was upset because Fulton, on going into private practice after the election, had sent out business cards noting that he had been chief counsel to the Truman committee. Margaret Truman is a little more direct: "Dad soon heard from friends that Mr. Fulton was telling everyone in Washington that he was going to be the acting President—the implication being that Harry S. Truman did not have the talent to do the job." According to Merle Miller, Truman would not discuss Fulton's postcommittee career other than to say that "he got too big for his breeches."[20]

If Margaret Truman, relying on family lore or possibly her direct memory, states the heart of the matter, could Truman really have believed that Fulton was fool enough to go around telling "everyone in Washington" that he was going to run things? Did Truman never consider that his "friends" (Harold Gosnell implies they were Connelly, Snyder, and Vaughan) might be jealous of Fulton and out to get him?[21] One wishes Truman had made a rational decision, however dubious, that Fulton, while a good investigative attorney, was not an executive type. Unfortunately, there is not the slightest indication that he did.

He was surely acutely aware that a lot of people believed that Fulton deserved most of the credit for the success of the Truman committee, thereby giving short shrift to his own exhausting work. It followed that Fulton already had gotten more recognition than he deserved; he was not going to be a reputed de facto president. No one knows whether Fulton would have been a strong chief of staff or attorney general. It is hard to argue that the administration was enhanced by his absence.

For press secretary, Truman from the beginning wanted his old friend Charlie Ross. When Ross at first declined, feeling that he could not give up his $35,000 salary with the *St. Louis Post-Dispatch* for a $10,000 White House job, Truman settled for Leonard Reinsch, who had intermittently acted as press liaison for him when he was vice president. Never officially designated press secretary, Reinsch functioned as such for a couple of weeks and created a stir among print reporters angered by the use of a radio man to handle press relations. Ross solved the problem by deciding that he had a duty to sign on. Reinsch went back to private employment and served as an occasional consultant on speaking technique to Truman.[22]

One of the most esteemed journalists in Washington, Ross seemed an inspired choice. But like most individuals who accept assignments out of a sense of obligation, he was unhappy (and looked it) from his first day on the job. A year and a half younger than Truman, he nonetheless lacked the president's stamina, chain-smoked, and appeared constantly tired. A better newsman than news handler, he never established a policy of coordinating news releases throughout the executive branch, frequently fumbled details, never developed (probably never thought of developing) a strategy for marketing the president's image, and failed to establish a strong press office. Ross's strength was his integrity, which earned him the affection and respect of most White House journalists. He would have been better appointed an all-around policy adviser, a function he also exercised freely and usually with good judgment. His loyalty to Truman was absolute but never sycophantic. The president became devoted to him. When Ross's heart gave out late one afternoon in December 1950, Truman suffered probably the greatest personal blow of his administration.[23]

Truman's press conferences hewed to existing rules about attribution and quotation that many contemporary journalists would find intolerable. Even so, his meetings with reporters, like Roosevelt's, were more useful to those who attended them than are today's televised extravaganzas. He held them about once a week, usually with several dozen White House correspondents in his office. By April 1950, however, the growth of the Washington press corps would require him to move these affairs to the more formal Indian Treaty Room in the adjacent Old Department of State Building. His day-to-day relationship with the White House press corps was superficially good, although privately he distrusted reporters as a group. Occasional unpleasantries involving presidential snappishness or exclusive interviews were no more numerous than had occurred under Roosevelt.[24] Lacking Roosevelt's presence, however, Truman suffered more from them. Seldom able to retrieve an angry moment or a misstatement gracefully, he was fortunate to miss the era of live televised conferences.

Ross was the happiest example of the president's early tendency to surround himself with old friends, Missourians or quasi-Missourians, and seemingly to do so with more regard for their loyalty than for demonstrated ability. Truman had been in office only a matter of days before some observers, perceiving a similarity to the atmosphere of the Harding administration, were writing of a "Missouri gang" taking control of the government.[25] Actually, the simile was never very accurate and the imputation of pervasive crass mediocrity much overdone. The White House was never stuffed to the rafters with Missourians, and the relative few who made it there varied greatly in talent, manner, and quality of service. Still, the phenomenon got wide notice in the early months of the administration; inevitably, the least attractive examples of it attracted the most attention. Truman's need to have his friends around was understandable; he would have served himself much better, however, if he had been more selective about it.

The most prominent member of the gang—never mind that he was a transplanted Arkansan—was Truman's longtime comrade John Snyder. In little more than a year, Snyder moved from federal loan administrator (April–July 1945), to director of OWMR (July 1945–June 1946), to secretary of the treasury (June 1946–January 1953). The *New Republic* exaggerated when it asserted, "It is cruel to plunge a man of this caliber into the duties of Secretary of the Treasury."[26] Nevertheless, Snyder had few obvious qualifications for so important a post. A capable regional banker and second-tier Reconstruction Finance Corporation official, he had no standing in the financial world and no credentials as an economist. At that, however, he was about as well qualified as his predecessor, Henry Morgenthau, Jr., a point that no one seemed to notice. Snyder filled the position adequately but with little flair. An ideological conservative, he became a bête noir of the liberal-left wing of the Democratic party. He may have influenced the president on matters of tactics from time to time, but clearly not on grand strategy, which by and large never concerned him. As with Ross, Truman valued his friendship and absolute loyalty.

Other Missourians were less consequential but equally visible and no credit to Truman's judgment. Probably his single worst appointment was of Eddie McKim as chief administrative assistant. McKim had no Washington experience, no sympathy for New Deal liberalism, and little administrative ability. He lasted about six weeks in his White House job, was shuttled over to the Federal Loan Administration to work under John Snyder, and soon thereafter was back at his insurance company in Omaha.[27]

Truman appointed Harry Vaughan as his military aide with the rank of brigadier general. Largely ceremonial in nature, the post should have attracted little attention, and the rank was probably one to which Vaughan's military service entitled him. Although Vaughan handled a few responsibilities involving veterans' issues and for a time was the president's connection to FBI director J. Edgar Hoover, Truman no doubt saw Vaughan primarily as a close friend with whom he could play poker and swap jokes over a bourbon and branch water at the end of the day. Unfortunately, Vaughan emerged as a bull in constant search of a new china shop. Equipped with absolutely no sense of public relations, he seemed to specialize in the maladroit quote and the unseemly act, whether pulling strings for a friend or accepting a military decoration from the notorious Argentine dictator, Juan Peron. Few people could have imagined that in his private life he was a Presbyterian Sunday-school teacher and an abstemious social drinker. And none of his adventures dimmed Truman's feelings for his old pal. The more Vaughan came under attack in the press, the more Truman was prone to defend him. He would be with Truman all the way to 1953.

As his naval aide, Truman selected Jake Vardaman, promoting him from captain to commodore. He related to Vaughan almost as if he were a matching bookend. More circumspect about his public dealings, Vardaman nevertheless shot himself in the foot by becoming a know-it-all nuisance around the White House; when he started to interfere with Bess Truman's staff, his days were numbered. In January 1946, Truman displayed another unfortunate trait. He appointed the commodore as a governor of the Federal Reserve Board, a post for which his qualifications were insubstantial (although he had nearly been appointed by Roosevelt in 1937). Raking over charges of fraud in a bitter lawsuit involving the failure of his old St. Louis shoe company, the Senate took two months to confirm him. He spent twelve years on the board, behaving from time to time like an unguided missile.[28]

Vardaman's successor as naval aide—his assistant, Captain Clark M. Clifford—attracted little notice at the time, but was already well on the way to making himself an indispensable man at the White House. A native of St. Louis, Clifford came from a family that the social arbiters would have described as good but not distinguished. His father was an executive with the Missouri Pacific Railroad; he was named for his mother's brother, Clark McAdams, a one-time editor of the *Post-Dispatch*. After graduating from Washington University of St. Louis in 1928, Clifford began a legal practice that by World War II would make him a leading local trial lawyer; one of his clients was Jake Vardaman.

In 1944, although he was thirty-seven years old, Clifford requested a commission in the Naval Reserves and volunteered for active duty. After a stint in the Pacific Naval Supply Offices, he was brought to the White House as Vardaman's assistant. In view of his lifelong silence about how he had sided in the senatorial primaries of 1934 and 1940, it seems a pretty good bet that Clifford had voted for Cochran and Stark. He had met Truman briefly in 1938 and 1944, but it is doubtful that the president remembered him and perhaps amazing (considering his family connection to the *Post-Dispatch*) that Truman let him into the White House. (When queried on this point nearly forty years later, Clifford merely smiled and said, "Mr. Truman was a very tolerant man.")[29]

Tall, handsome, articulate, and married to a charming and elegant woman, Clifford would have attracted attention at the most glittering occasions. His years as an attorney had made him an eloquent advocate who chose his words carefully and spoke precisely, with just a bit of an Upper South drawl. With little to do as Vardaman's aide, he made himself ad hoc assistant to Special Counsel Sam Rosenman. Before long, he had acquired as his own aide a young naval officer named George Elsey; an activated reservist who had done graduate work in history at Harvard, Elsey had run the White House Map Room (the international communications center). Only twenty-seven years old in 1945, single and at loose ends, but handsome, polished, and intelligent, Elsey worked well with Clifford.

Clifford was surely as motivated by an honest desire to render public service as he had been when he volunteered for active military duty. He also doubtless sensed that Washington offered opportunities for recognition, power, and wealth far greater than those in St. Louis. And he knew a vacuum when he was in the middle of one. Contemplating the imminent departure of Rosenman and surveying the rest of the White House staff as it was then constituted, he could rightly conclude that no one stood between him and a position of much greater influence than he could have thought possible a year earlier. When Rosenman resigned as special counsel in January 1946, Truman did not plan to replace him. In June, however, implicitly endorsing Clifford's judgment, he reinstated the position and appointed the St. Louisian to hold it. George Elsey came along as Clifford's aide.

Despite impressions that Clifford would cultivate later, he was never the master strategist of the Truman administration, never Truman's chief of staff, never quite the dominating figure in the White House. Moreover, his gift for getting his name into newspapers and magazines surely annoyed Truman. Yet, in so many ways, he *was* an indispensable man—an astute manager of the speech-writing process, a policy catalyst, a political adviser, even an amateur foreign policy analyst. It was not that Truman moved in directions he would have avoided in Clifford's absence; it was that Clifford was a gifted facilitator whose presence and advice strengthened Truman's instincts. He was also a natural leader toward whom some of the more able staffers gravitated. Even his self-promotion was good for the administration; many journalists rightly found him impressive and by extension granted Truman more credibility than they might have otherwise.

In December 1946, Truman appointed as "the assistant to the president" John R. Steelman, a labor mediator who had succeeded Snyder as director of OWMR. The ideologically minded would soon envision the White House as torn in a power struggle between the "liberals" headed by Clifford and the "conservatives" headed by Steelman. In fact, the rivalry between the two men was more over public recognition and White House turf than differences of social vision. Clifford's liberalism, such as it was, derived largely from political pragmatism; Steelman, very much a product of New Deal labor policies, had no ideological agenda. He handled a wide variety of what might be called administrative matters, resolving minor problems between departments and agencies, pushing routine paper, and leaving the president's desk clear for bigger things. His policy influence was limited to his own areas of expertise: labor issues and, during the Korean War, economic mobilization. There is no indication that he was ever interested in challenging Clifford on a range of policy issues—or that Truman perceived him as doing so.[30]

By and large, Truman avoided informal advisers. But for a time in 1945 and 1946, George Allen was highly visible around the White House and widely believed to have influence that extended far beyond his formal assignments of, first, assisting in the liquidation of war agencies and, then, serving as a director of the Reconstruction Finance Corporation, where Truman put him in the hope of avoiding financial raids on the agency.[31] New Deal Democrats (who tended to pass quickly over the unfortunate fact that he had been a fixture in the Roosevelt administration) saw Allen, with some justification, as crass and overly business-oriented. Truman, who had revered Allen's mentor, Pat Harrison, liked him and considered him useful. In 1946, his refusal to support extravagant RFC financing for the Lustron Corporation and other manufacturers of prefabricated homes would lead to the resignation of Housing Expediter Wilson Wyatt. The episode infuriated the liberals; yet Allen was justified in his belief that Lustron was not creditworthy. After he left the RFC at the end of 1946, Lustron lavishly purchased influence on Capitol Hill, got a $32.5 million loan from the RFC, and promptly began to lose money at the rate of $1 million a month. It would end up in bankruptcy, the federal loan a total loss; Allen, one need hardly add, got no retrospective praise from his critics.[32]

Allen was in fact a crude self-promoter. How else could one describe a man who later wrote a book entitled *Presidents Who Have Known Me?*[33] Clearly, he was no New Dealer. All the same, he handled his assignments with reasonable competence. During Truman's first year in office, he helped write speeches, involved himself in a wide range of matters, and enjoyed Truman's friendship. A member of the administration faction skeptical about economic controls, he had a part in some significant tactical decisions on economic reconversion. Allen's relationship with Truman became increasingly distant after he left the White House. When he attached himself to Dwight Eisenhower in the 1950s, Truman curtly dismissed him as a "fixer."[34]

By the end of 1946, the structure of the Truman White House was set. Some important men would eventually leave, most notably Clifford in early 1950 (to be succeeded by Charles Murphy). The staff of Truman's second term was on the whole more professional, scholarly, and impressive than that of his first. From time to time, new appendages would appear. The Council of Economic Advisers was created in 1946. In 1951, the Mutual Security Agency would be established with Averell Harriman as its director. The Korean War would bring a new economic stabilization bureaucracy.

In general, Truman preferred administrative simplicity and sharply defined lines of authority—all of which led up to him. Acting as his own chief of staff, he met daily with aides, most of whom were assigned some distinct function. The special counsel was inevitably a generalist involved in almost every policy issue. The very compactness of the staff made hierarchical levels of administration unnecessary and encouraged a collegial atmosphere. Rivalries existed, to be sure, but not vicious infighting. Truman expected his helpers to get along or get out.

IV

Truman also had to manage the cabinet. He wrote about the task five years later in a letter he decided not to send to Jonathan Daniels. His mordant evaluations were not always fair, but he was correct in believing that he had been left a less than sterling support group:

> *Edward Stettinius*
> *(State)*
> a fine man, good looking, amiable, cooperative, but never an idea new or old
>
> *Henry Morgenthau, Jr.*
> *(Treasury)*
> block head, nut
>
> *Henry L. Stimson*
> *(War)*
> a real man—honest, straightforward and a statesman
>
> *Francis Biddle*
> *(Justice)*
> make your own analysis
>
> *Frank Walker*
> *(Post Office)*
> my kind of man, honest, decent, loyal—but no new ideas
>
> *Frances Perkins*
> *(Labor)*
> a grand lady—but no politician. F.D.R. had removed every bureau and power she had
>
> *Henry Wallace*
> *(Commerce)*
> no reason to love me or to be loyal to me
>
> *Harold Ickes*
> *(Interior)*
> never for anyone but Harold, would have cut F.D.R.'s throat or mine for his "high-minded" ideas of a headline—and did
>
> *Claude Wickard*
> *(Agriculture)*
> a nice man, who never learned how his department was set up
>
> *James Forrestal*
> *(Navy)*
> Poor Forrestal. . . . He never could make a decision[35]

A lot of these dominoes fell quickly; but as often as not, Truman failed to replace them with sturdier stuff. Postmaster General Walker, happy enough to go back to New York was succeeded by Hannegan in a classic case of Tweedledum and Tweedledee. Secretary of Labor Perkins, who had little support among union leaders, was replaced by Truman's old friend Lew Schwellenbach. (Truman confided to his staff that he really didn't want a woman in the cabinet anyway.)[36] Organized labor approved, but Schwellenbach was in poor health and never up to the job; John Steelman would partially fill the vacuum. Secretary of Agriculture Wickard eagerly accepted a demotion, the still-vacant directorship of the Rural Electrification Administration. His successor, Clinton Anderson of New Mexico, had been a first-rate congressman with a strong reputation on Capitol Hill.

Attorney General Biddle had clashed with Truman too often to have any realistic expectation of staying on; nevertheless, when he got a phone call from Steve Early asking for his resignation, he petulantly insisted on a face-to-face meeting with the busy new president. It was pleasant enough, but Biddle was horrified to discover that his successor would be Assistant Attorney General Tom Clark, whom he had been planning to dismiss for being overly political in prosecutorial decisions. Truman likely considered Clark's political consciousness meritorious; in addition, Clark possessed strong backing from Sam Rayburn and had been probably the only Justice Department official willing to give Truman minor patronage appointments when he was a senator. Few thought then or would think later that he was an improvement over Biddle.[37]

Other changes seemed far more solid. As soon as the San Francisco Conference was over, Stettinius was made United States ambassador to the United Nations and was replaced by Byrnes. The appointment won general approval, not least because the existing presidential succession law placed the secretary of state next in line for the White House when there was no vice president. Byrnes was also widely respected and thought to be more informed in diplomacy than he actually was.[38] Morgenthau was soon gone because of foreign policy disagreements with Truman; his replacement was OWMR director Fred Vinson, who had been an influential Kentucky congressman and later a federal judge. Vinson had no particular credentials for the Treasury Department, but was a shrewd politician with considerable support in Congress; he enjoyed Truman's absolute confidence. In 1946, the president made him chief justice of the United States and sought his advice on a variety of issues for the next six years. In September 1945, Stimson, seventy-eight years old and unable to continue in office, resigned. Overlooking past clashes, Truman named Stimson's trusted deputy Robert Patterson to run the War Department. It was a splendid appointment.

By the autumnal equinox, Truman had in effect a new cabinet, but whether it was stronger than the one he had inherited could be questioned. The three survivors were all special cases. Henry Wallace was a powerful symbol to the liberal Democrats; Truman felt it vital to hang onto him. Ickes, a doughty old independent progressive, also had a wide following among liberal Democrats and reform-minded independents. Forrestal—well, Truman was not so certain, but he was at the least a capable man worth keeping until an appropriate successor could be groomed.

Truman expected that successor to be Edwin Pauley, whom Roosevelt had intended to make assistant secretary of the navy. Truman probably envisioned Pauley, not Forrestal, as the first secretary of defense after the unification of the armed forces. The California oilman, he later told Jonathan Daniels, was a "tough, mean son of a bitch" who might have been able to whip the military establishment into line. Pauley had been Truman's choice for United States representative to the Allied reparations commission (taking along with him as an assistant Colonel Dick "By God" Burleson, Truman's old artillery instructor); he had done a solid job, establishing a reputation as a tenacious negotiator.[39]

In February 1946, following through on Roosevelt's original intentions, Truman nominated Pauley to be undersecretary of the navy, only to see the appointment derailed by the determined and vocal opposition of Secretary Ickes, who undoubtedly would have remained quiet if FDR had still been president. Ickes, remembering Teapot Dome as if it had happened the day before yesterday and incensed at the thought of an oilman having jurisdiction over the naval oil reserves, charged that Pauley had attempted to get him to deliver favors to oil interests as a way of facilitating fund-raising during the 1944 campaign. Plausible enough, although Pauley denied it, the charge had little to do with the undersecretaryship of the navy, but it was enough to block the nomination. Ickes also resigned. Truman—his image tarnished by the episode—replaced him with Julius Krug, another refugee from the wartime bureaucracy.

By the end of 1946, Henry Wallace would be gone, fired as the result of a spectacular foreign policy controversy. Snyder would by then be secretary of the treasury. Byrnes would be preparing to go back to South Carolina, leaving the way for George Marshall to become secretary of state. Forrestal would be the last survivor of FDR's cabinet.

Truman, Harold Smith believed, had come into the presidency failing fully to understand the distinction between cabinet officers and staffers. Cabinet members were frequently prominent individuals with independent reputations and followings; they all had distinct constituencies, whether farmers, businessmen, Foreign Service officers, the military, or civilian bureaucracies. Staffers existed only to meet the needs of the president; they alone could pursue his objectives unimpeded by other considerations. Apparently motivated by Truman's practice of establishing committees of cabinet members to lobby members of Congress, Smith delivered a brief lecture to Truman on this point in February 1946.[40] It probably annoyed the president, but perhaps contributed to his decision to revive the post of special counsel a few months later. Yet Truman never faced the real problem: a staff too small for the responsibilities of the presidency. Eisenhower would undertake a drastic enlargement.

Whether cabinet members were staff or quasi-independent operators was less important to Truman than his dominance over them. Hoping to revive the cabinet as an institution of government, he encouraged general discussion of issues in it and on occasion took straw votes. He considered it, he said, "a Board of Directors appointed by the President, to help him carry out policies of the Government." As such, it was very much the president's institution. At a cabinet meeting on May 18, 1945, Truman established the rule by relating the famous story of Abraham Lincoln putting a proposed policy to a vote, getting a unanimous nay from his cabinet members, and then announcing he was voting aye and that the ayes had it. When Forrestal, intrigued by the British system of cabinet government, proposed such ideas as a cabinet secretariat and informal cabinet lunches without the president's attendance, Truman squelched them.[41]

Truman may never have accepted the distinction between staff and cabinet as an abstract proposition. As a working one, however, he would find it easy to deal with cabinet members as quasi-independent operators to be managed, even negotiated with—Wallace for much of 1946, Marshall in the spring of 1948. At no point, however, would he let permanent control of an issue in which he was interested be taken away from him. As a matter of both constitutional theory and self-respect, he was determined to leave the presidency at least as powerful as he had found it.

V

Truman would have to make major reorganizations in the executive branch not only to accommodate his style, but also to facilitate the new domestic responsibilities undertaken by the New Deal and to meet the needs of the "imperial" situation in which the United States found itself after World War II. The logic of events, his passion for administrative clarity, and his determination to establish mechanisms for presidential control led Truman to support a major alteration of the executive branch: the establishment of what historians have (usually with disapproval) called the "national security state." This was largely the result of the National Security Act of 1947, which created a triad of agencies charged with managing various aspects of American foreign policy.

Its most visible achievement was the "unification" of the armed forces. By the end of World War II, there was wide acceptance of the need for some sort of consolidation of the chaotic, antagonistic bureaucracies responsible for the military. Truman, here as elsewhere wanting order, supported the goal. Still, adjusting differences among the army, navy, and a newly independent air force was a herculean task probably accomplished only because of the emergence of the Cold War. With Clark Clifford doing much of the coordinating from the White House end, the job involved complex negotiations between the War and Navy departments and leading members of Congress.

The act created the National Military Establishment, headed by the cabinet-rank secretary of defense, who in theory would supervise and coordinate the operations of subcabinet departments of army, navy, and air force. In fact, the act gave the new position minimal authority, stopping well short of the power that Truman and Secretary of War Patterson would have preferred. Truman offered the position to Patterson, who declined it and left the administration to return to private legal practice. Then the president gave it to James Forrestal, who as secretary of the navy had voiced the strongest opposition to the concept. For a year and a half, Forrestal nonetheless worked tirelessly to make the new office effective. In early 1949, having reached a point of nervous collapse, he would be eased out for Louis Johnson. Amendments to the act strengthened the office's power and established a full-fledged Department of Defense but hardly ended interservice rivalry.[42]

The National Security Act also established the Central Intelligence Agency. The CIA succeeded the Central Intelligence Group, which Truman had established in 1946 to absorb the activities of the wartime Office of Strategic Services and to coordinate army and navy intelligence activities. It never actually centralized all foreign intelligence, but even so constituted a powerful new tool for diplomatic-military planning and action in the Cold War world. Its directors under Truman were all military figures: General Hoyt S. Vandenberg (nephew of Senator Arthur Vandenberg) of the air force, Rear Admiral Roscoe Hillenkoetter, and General Walter Bedell Smith of the army. Truman himself had mixed feelings about the entire enterprise. On the one side lay his liking for centralization and clear lines of responsibility; on the other, his fear that he might be creating a "Gestapo."

Years later, he would condemn the CIA's excesses in the use of covert operations under Eisenhower; yet such activities began on a more modest scale during his presidency and almost certainly with his knowledge. Given the near impossibility of access to CIA files, a historian cannot know for certain just how limited they were. In the immediate postwar years, it would be the CIA that would funnel subsidies to anti-Communist politicians and labor unions in France and Italy, thereby countering money coming from Moscow. The objects of that covert support, however, would be democrats rather than dictators, and the agency itself was staffed by officials sympathetic to the non-Communist left.[43]

The third creation of the act was the National Security Council, established to coordinate diplomatic and military policy. Its original membership consisted of the president; the secretaries of state, defense, army, navy, and air force; and the chairman of the National Security Resources Board (another creation of the act, envisioned as more important at the time than it would turn out to be). The NSC exercised a general supervisory authority over the CIA and authorized early covert activities. In 1949, Truman, probably feeling that the council was too packed with military influence, would obtain from Congress the deletion of the three service secretaries and the addition of the vice president.

The NSC had been pushed with special vigor by Forrestal, who may have seen it as another step toward the cabinet government ideal. It also had origins in the already functioning joint planning committee of the State, War, and Navy departments. Truman had not been interested in it while the National Security Act was being formulated, but once it came into being he was determined to control it. In his remarks at the NSC's first meeting, he stressed that he considered it *his* council. Periodically over the next few years, he felt that Forrestal, and then Louis Johnson, was trying to make the NSC into a super cabinet, a development with which he had no patience.

Particularly in the early years of the NSC, control meant limitation. Before the Korean War, Truman rarely attended the meetings, in part to allow greater freedom of discussion, in part to emphasize his determination that the NSC was an advisory committee established to assist the president, not a policy-making body. The meetings themselves were small, with most aides and briefcase carriers excluded. The group discussed current problems and crises, but also devoted itself to reviewing basic policy over an array of diplomatic-military matters. Its recommendations, many of them on quite broad issues, would go to the president for approval. In a series of papers accepted by Truman over the next several years, the NSC defined the main lines of American foreign and military policy in a way that not only expressed a cabinet consensus, but also embodied the will of the president.

Council operations were managed by a compact staff, headed by an executive secretary (an early draft of the National Security Act had said director; Truman had insisted on the title change). Under Truman, the NSC secretaries were nonpolitical, anonymous bureaucrats—first, Rear Admiral Sidney Souers, who had briefly headed the Central Intelligence Group, followed by James S. Lay, Jr., a civil servant who continued in the position into the Eisenhower administration. Respecting established lines of authority and easily annoyed by large egos, Truman did not want "*his* Council" to be run by an alternative secretary of state. Flawed in some respects but reasonably flexible, the new national security apparatus gave Truman far more resources for the making of foreign and military policy than he possessed for most areas of domestic policy, where he had to resort to ad hoc committees and working groups. As Truman saw it, and by and large as things actually functioned under him, the National Security Act greatly expanded the power of the presidency.[44]

The evolution of the presidency was, of course, an ongoing process throughout Truman's seven and three-quarters years in office. It had scarcely begun as he faced pressing concerns that could make or break him in his first few months in office.

19

"I AM HERE TO MAKE DECISIONS": POTSDAM AND HIROSHIMA, 1945

Truman became president at a time when events were taking charge of international history to so great an extent that the most experienced statesmen were scrambling to keep pace. Knowing little more about diplomatic arrangements and military progress than what one would read in a good newspaper, he suddenly found himself responsible for overseeing the end of the war and the establishment of a new global order.

Like most Americans, he envisioned victory as a first priority to which all else had to be subordinated, but he also saw the new order as an essential vindication of the costs and human sacrifices of World War II. Like most Americans, he expected the United States to be first among equals in the postwar world, realized that Britain and France had become secondary powers, and understood that the Soviet Union would be the only other imposing nation to emerge from the war.[1] Securing the peace would be in large measure a matter of maintaining the wartime alliance; yet even as victory came closer, the alliance seemed shakier.

Truman also understood that no natural basis existed for Soviet–American friendship—not in shared social and political values, or in geography, or in most conventional definitions of national interest. Still, he knew that Americans expected him to make an effort, and he thought that a good relationship with the USSR was possible. Here, as in so many other ways, he shared the reflexive outlook of a majority of his countrymen. Not a hard-edged ideologue, he was unable to believe that ideological differences made conflict between nations inevitable. Convinced that men, not abstract forces, made history, he thought that relations between nations had a large personal component. Finally, he approached diplomacy as he had every other problem in his life—with a determined, quintessentially American optimism.

Above all, he had a firm conviction that the presidency was a job that required choices, often difficult, and that he would not shirk the responsibility. Meeting with Anthony Eden about a month after becoming president, he said, "I am here to make decisions, and whether they prove right or wrong I am going to make them."[2]

II

When Truman became president, World War II was rapidly concluding in Europe. American troops had been across the Rhine for more than a month and were advancing rapidly through southern Germany toward Czechoslovakia. Soviet forces were in a titantic battle for Berlin. On April 28, the new president's sixteenth day in office, Italian partisans captured and killed Mussolini. Two days later, Hitler committed suicide. In Reims, France, on the night of May 7, Nazi general Alfred Jodl signed the instrument of surrender and was taken off to prison. The United States observed V-E Day on May 8, Harry Truman's sixty-first birthday. The nation celebrated in subdued fashion, certain that a long road lay ahead in the Pacific war.

During those early hectic weeks, Truman had to devote most of his attention to diplomatic controversies with the Soviet Union. Fundamental issues that had been evaded for the sake of preserving the wartime alliance had to be faced: a Soviet drive for dominance in Eastern Europe that focused on Poland and threatened to shred the Yalta agreements; a tendency to counter any American complaint by presenting obstacles to the establishment of a workable United Nations; recent accusations (which had angered Roosevelt) that the United States had sought a separate peace with Germany. Even more troubling than the specifics was the deteriorating tone of the American–Soviet relationship. Yet Truman and all the planners around him believed that Soviet participation was absolutely essential for the quickest possible defeat of Japan.

As president, Truman continued to regard the USSR with the same combination of skepticism and pragmatism that he had formulated as a senator. A memorandum he wrote to himself on May 23, 1945, demonstrated both a clear-eyed understanding of the Soviet system and a fuzzy conception of human nature:

> I've no faith in any totalitarian state, be it Russian, German, Spanish, Argentinian, Dago, or Japanese. They all start with a wrong premise—that lies are justified and that the old, disproven Jesuit formula, the end justifies the means, is right and necessary to maintain the power of government.

I don't agree, nor do I believe that either formula can help humanity to the long hoped for millennium. Honest Communism, as set out in the "Acts of the Apostles," would work. But Russian Godless Pervert Systems won't work.

Anyway, the human animal can't be trusted for anything *good* except en masse. The combined thought and action of the whole people of any race, creed, or nationality will always point in the Right Direction—"As ye would others should do unto you do ye also unto them." Confucius, Buddha, Christ, and all moralists come to the same conclusion.[3]

The memorandum expressed much of the political philosophy that Truman had acquired over a lifetime—partly from reading but mostly from his own experience and intuition. It was also very much in line with the neo-Wilsonian and New Deal idealism that had been carried into foreign affairs to justify the American effort in World War II. "The people," it held, were fundamentally good; evil rested in individuals and the systems of power they created for their own aggrandizement. But it was equally the case that the existence of evil in the world was an inescapable fact and that the realities of life often required an accommodation with it. Truman had learned the lesson early in his association with Tom Pendergast; he would seek to apply it to his relationship with Joseph Stalin. The idea that Stalin could be thought of as a tough political boss analogous to Tom Pendergast, Ed Kelly, or other such American types was widespread in the America of 1945; it was among the most distinctive expressions of the innocence with which the United States began its assumption of world leadership.

Truman's view of diplomacy as an extension of domestic politics did not stop with unwise, if widely held, analogies; it also left him with an intense distrust of Foreign Service professionals, whom he considered a pretentious, self-contained elite. He habitually referred to them as the "striped pants boys" or the "cookie pushers." He liked to repeat a story that Alben Barkley had told him about visiting Cairo and being escorted by the American chargé d'affaires: "He wore a checked suit, carried a cane, wore a cap, and talked with an Oxford accent. Barkley kept looking at him and wondering if the gentleman could have been reared in Egypt. Finally he asked him what his antecedents were. The man said he was a native of Topeka, Kansas."[4]

Such mannerisms were worth a good laugh, and maybe they bespoke a certain smug shallowness that extended to the policy side of Foreign Service analysis—but perhaps the style of dress and the Oxford accent also proved helpful in a place that had a long history of British cultural dominance. Although Truman was on firm ground in believing that it was up to politicians like himself to define the national interest, his visceral reaction against the professionals was unwise. His episodic conviction that they were trying to undermine him only got in the way of a smoothly functioning foreign policy. And despite his dislike, the professionals would be largely responsible for the making of his foreign policy.

There was no other feasible way to manage the myriad problems of diplomacy. The Foreign Service officials would be most effective, however, when their views were transmitted through shrewd mediators whom Truman liked and respected: Averell Harriman, George Marshall, and Dean Acheson.

As it was, two and a half months into his administration, Truman was writing to himself that America's "three ablest foreign policy men" were Cordell Hull, Joseph Davies, and Harry Hopkins![5] Hull, the aged and ailing former secretary of state, had been consistently bypassed by Roosevelt; Davies, as United States ambassador to the Soviet Union and afterward, was a witless celebrant of Stalin; although intermittently an important emissary to Churchill and Stalin during the war, Hopkins had never held a full-time diplomatic post in his life.

To the triad of Hull, Davies, and Hopkins, Truman added James Byrnes—"my able and conniving Secretary of State." Truman meant the phrase as a compliment. He saw Byrnes as a man very much like himself in outlook, extraordinarily able, and (because he had been at the Yalta Conference) well versed in the mainstream concerns of American diplomacy. Byrnes also had a jaundiced view of the professionals and believed that with a few close aides he could handle the issues that really mattered. Truman was convinced that he had acquired a top-notch lieutenant: "My but he has a keen mind! And he is an honest man."[6]

III

Truman faced two urgent issues: Soviet behavior in Eastern Europe, especially Poland, and the need to establish the United Nations, an endeavor for which Soviet cooperation was essential. Soviet flouting of the Yalta accords in Poland was detailed in frequently acrimonious cable traffic that had come into the White House during the last month of Roosevelt's life.

Yalta had promised freely elected governments throughout liberated Europe. Instead, the Russians already had established a Communist-dominated government in Poland, had refused to deal with the London-based government-in-exile, and had arrested Polish leaders who went to Moscow under pledges of safe conduct. American protests during the last weeks of the Roosevelt administration had led to infuriating Russian countercharges of anti-Soviet collaboration with the Nazis. Reading Roosevelt's last communication with Stalin, Truman found this angry passage: "I cannot avoid a feeling of bitter resentment toward your informers, whoever they are, for such vile misrepresentations of my actions or those of my trusted subordinates." Reading his predecessor's last message to Churchill, he saw: "I would minimize the general Soviet problem as much as possible. . . . We must be firm, however, and our course thus far is correct."[7]

Such documents gave Truman a sense of direction; analyzing the problem and setting a specific course were more difficult. Conferring with advisers on April 13, he asked Secretary of State Stettinius why relations with the USSR were poor. Stettinius replied, as he summarized it in his diary, "There was no explanation other than the fact that Stalin had his own political problem within the Soviet Union and perhaps certain influences were being brought to bear on him from within that country." Truman took this misreading of Stalin's power seriously and from time to time returned to it in the future. He nevertheless did not view it as a justification for appeasement. The United States had to stand up to the Russians, he responded, and not be easy with them.[8]

Truman got reinforcement in this determination from a new figure in his political life: Averell Harriman, United States ambassador to the Soviet Union. Disillusioned after a year and a half of frigid hostility in Moscow and convinced that the Soviet Union was bent on domination of as much of Europe as possible, Harriman had returned to the United States in the hope of influencing the new president. He met Truman for the first time on April 20. The Soviet leadership, he said, was unwilling to settle for a simple sphere of influence in areas it occupied. As Poland already was demonstrating, the USSR wanted total control. The Soviets, moreover, were under the Marxian illusion that the United States would be in desperate need of a trading relationship with the USSR after the war and therefore would not resist Communist expansionism. What was occurring, he asserted, was no less than a "barbarian invasion of Europe." The American reaction, Harriman believed, had to be one of firmness and tough dealing—not unmitigated hostility, but a hard-headed determination to use all American cards, including financial aid, in the pursuit of an acceptable modus vivendi between the two great powers.

It was the sort of talk that appealed to all of Truman's instincts. The Russians needed us more than we needed them, he responded. Maybe we could not get 100 percent of what we wanted, but we should be able to get 85 percent. Settlement of the Polish question, he thought, would be absolutely necessary to get the UN treaty through the Senate. What if the Russians balked? Harriman asked. What if they pulled out of the conference? Facing, if not resolving, the dilemma in front of him, Truman replied that "the truth of the matter was that without Russia there would not be much of a world organization."[9]

That evening, Truman undertook what was probably his first full reading of the Yalta minutes and agreements, discovering their haziness firsthand. Queried on the point, Stettinius told him that Roosevelt "had tried to get it clear cut and definite but it had been impossible to do."[10] Truman also met with British foreign secretary Anthony Eden, who was in Washington attempting to do what he could for the London-based Polish government-in-exile, to which the British, having been unable to defend Poland in 1939, felt a special responsibility.[11] Feeling that the spirit of Yalta had been betrayed and knowing that Roosevelt seemed to have been moving toward a tougher stance, Truman was inclined to stand firm.

He had his first chance when Soviet foreign minister Vyacheslav

Molotov visited Washington on April 22 and 23. Officially, Molotov was stopping simply to make a courtesy call en route to the San Francisco Conference, which he was attending in response to an American demand for his presence as a symbol of Soviet support for the United Nations. Truman and administration foreign policy leaders saw an opportunity to achieve a compromise settlement on Poland. The president received his Soviet guest cordially on April 22. He promised faithfully to carry out all agreements and to continue Roosevelt's policy of friendship with the Soviet Union. The meeting was pleasant and insubstantial. Then Molotov, Stettinius, Eden, and their aides conferred on the Polish question. It was quickly apparent that there was no hope of compromise from the Soviet side. At 2:00 P.M. on April 23, Truman convened his major foreign and military advisers.

Stettinius began with a summary of the negotiations, declaring, according to Forrestal, that Soviet behavior was "directly contrary to the Yalta understanding." (The statement reflected the views of Undersecretary of State Joseph Grew and the department's top resident Soviet expert, Charles "Chip" Bohlen.) Truman spoke his own mind. As Bohlen summarized it, he declared that "agreements with the Soviet Union so far had been a one way street and that could not continue; it was now or never." The United States would go on with the plans for the United Nations and if the Russians did not wish to join in, "they could go to hell."

Most, but not all, of those gathered around the table seemed supportive. Among the civilians, Stimson demurred most strongly, arguing for deference to Soviet concerns. Forrestal asserted that Poland was simply part of a larger pattern of unilateral Soviet expansionism and thought "we might as well meet the issue now as later on." Harriman agreed strongly. General John Deane, chief of the United States Military Mission in Moscow and a veteran of equally frustrating experience, backed him up fully. Admiral William Leahy wanted the United States to promote Polish independence, but doubted that it could be achieved and was unwilling to break with the USSR over the subject. Backing Stimson, Army Chief of Staff George Marshall cited worries about the need for Soviet cooperation in the war against Japan. Truman found nothing in the discussion to change his mind.[12]

Later that afternoon, the president met with Molotov again. Also present were Stettinius, Harriman, Leahy, Bohlen (who translated from English to Russian), Ambassador Andrei Gromyko, and Vladimir Pavlov, Molotov's interpreter. Deliberately blunt, Truman promised again to carry out all American obligations but asserted that the USSR had not done so in Poland. Warning explicitly that only public confidence and support could get measures to aid the Soviet Union through Congress, he made it clear that Poland was a test case with the American people. Bohlen's diplomatic notes on the meeting refer to the president as speaking "with great firmness" and replying "sharply." Everyone there, however, remembered one telling exchange:

MOLOTOV: I have never been talked to like that in my life.

TRUMAN: Carry out your agreements, and you won't get talked to like that.

When Molotov tried to persist in arguing, Truman handed him a communication to Stalin and curtly dismissed him. By then, he had developed a hearty dislike of the Soviet foreign minister and would retain it throughout his life.[13]

"How I enjoyed translating Truman's sentences," Bohlen wrote a quarter-century later, still convinced that Truman, perhaps with a few rough edges, was following the policy that Roosevelt had left him. Stettinius went off to San Francisco to tell the story proudly to the American delegation to the United Nations conference. Senator Arthur Vandenberg, the delegation's leading Republican, was ecstatic: "F.D.R.'s appeasement of Russia is over. . . . [I]t is no longer going to be all 'give' and no 'take.'" The incident was exhilarating to numerous Americans who had been involved firsthand in dealing with the Soviet Union.[14]

IV

Reality soon set in. In Poland and throughout Eastern Europe, the Soviets were on the ground, in effective control, and unwilling to budge. Churchill opposed the withdrawal of American troops from the Soviet zone of occupied Germany and urged a Big Three meeting as soon as possible. On May 12, he warned, "An iron curtain is drawn down." Truman may have hoped that a delay would provide some leverage, for American troops stayed in the Soviet zone for another few weeks; it was all but unthinkable, however, that the United States would renege on the zonal frontiers set at Yalta. The USSR, furthermore, refused to discuss occupation arrangements for Berlin or Vienna until it had full military control of its zones. In mid-June, American troops began to leave.[15]

In San Francisco, the USSR had the power to obstruct, delay, and ultimately block the establishment of an effective UN organization—by walking out if need be. Truman might tell his advisers that the Russians could either go along or go to hell, and Vandenberg might be ready to try to launch the international body without them. But the prospect of a failed conference was in fact intolerable. According to the Gallup organization, more than 80 percent of the American people thought it was "very important" to join a world organization to maintain the peace.[16] Editorial writers and cartoonists depicted a functioning United Nations as the only protection against World War III. Truman had advocated a strong international organization in speech after speech. The San Francisco Conference could not be allowed to break up without Soviet adherence to the United Nations. Nor could Truman face the possibility that the USSR might retract a secret pledge made at the Teheran and Yalta conferences to enter the war against Japan three months after the end of the European conflict.

No one who gave the matter any deliberate consideration believed that a "meaningful international association" could exclude the USSR, and almost no one was willing to declare the concept itself an oxymoron. However a few exasperated diplomats and policy makers might feel, many Americans, including most of the New Dealers, still considered the Soviet Union a valiant ally. Truman's own emotional investment, that of the liberal Democrats, and that of the larger electorate virtually dictated a new attempt at settlement of the Polish issue and gave Stalin great leverage.

Another incident damaged relations with the Soviet Union. On V-E Day, the president signed an order terminating Lend-Lease except for supplies needed to support allies in the Pacific war. He later claimed that the order had been put in front of him by Undersecretary of State Grew and Foreign Economic Administrator Leo Crowley, who told him Roosevelt already had approved it, and that he thereupon went ahead and signed it without reading it. Crowley enforced the order with a meat-ax, ordering ships en route to both the Soviet Union and Great Britain to return to the United States.

Truman had been willing to use Lend-Lease shipments as a bargaining card with the Soviet Union, but it seems fairly certain that he had not intended anything so drastic. With the advice of Harriman, he quickly altered the order to allow for shipments of aid on a reduced basis to both countries. He also began to look around for a new foreign economic administrator; by October, Crowley was out of the administration. However, the Soviets (and the British) had been given another grievance to pound when convenient. With the end of the Pacific war, Lend-Lease, which Congress had authorized only as a war measure, would be phased out for once and for all.[17]

By mid-May, the prospective postwar world appeared grim and threatening. Deadlock at San Francisco demonstrated to Truman that his tough approach was getting nowhere. Yet his situation demanded an understanding with the USSR, and he was determined to have one. Influential voices in his own party and administration—including Joseph Davies, Eleanor Roosevelt and her family, Henry Stimson, Henry Wallace —wanted conciliation. Harriman, who had been in San Francisco with Stettinius, now began to argue for a new approach. With Chip Bohlen, he conceived of the idea of sending Harry Hopkins to Moscow to make a direct appeal to Stalin on the Polish problem and to discuss all outstanding differences. Personal diplomacy seemed attractive to Truman and to most Americans. No matter how obstinate Molotov had been, perhaps one could deal with Stalin on the same man-to-man basis that one dealt with a tough American politician. Harriman, and especially Bohlen, should have known better; instead, they reinforced Truman's misconceptions.[18]

The president hesitated, but not because, as Harriman mistakely recalled, he was uncomfortable with Hopkins. He was probably reluctant to send a person of such fragile health halfway around the globe. On

May 13, he asked Davies, who declined, arguing his own poor health; subsequently, Davies would go to London to discuss matters with Churchill. On May 19, Hopkins agreed to the mission. Truman told him to assure the Russian dictator that the United States would carry out its obligations to the letter and expected him to do the same—and that in conveying the message "he could use diplomatic language, or he could use a baseball bat."

But to what purpose? Four days after his meeting with Hopkins, Truman wrote to himself that he had given Hopkins instructions to tell Stalin that for the sake of peace "Poland, Rumania, Bulgaria, Czecho-slovakia, Austria, Yugo-Slavia, Latvia, Lithuania, Estonia, et al[.] make no difference to U.S. interests"—that a free election for Poland could be as free as Boss Hague or Tom Pendergast might stage it. The same day that he saw Hopkins, he made a note on his appointment calendar refer-ring to "the agreements, purported to have been made at Yalta." The phrase showed how far he had come in addressing another problem; like most Americans, he was torn between an impractical but morally desir-able universalistic idealism and a practical but morally distasteful real-politik. For the sake of a deal with the Soviet Union, Truman was ready to give up on Eastern Europe for the time being at least.[19]

The policy displayed a healthy understanding that the United States had no real power to affect the situation in countries occupied by Soviet troops. Yet it had built-in pitfalls also. Could a totalitarian dictator such as Stalin be content with the limited power of a Hague or a Pendergast (especially if he was aware of what had happened to the latter)? Were Stalin's ambitions limited to Eastern Europe, or did they extend to areas that could not be written off? Perhaps most fundamental of all, it was one thing to lay down such a policy in private on a piece of paper. How could any president gain support for it from the American people? For the sake of getting Soviet acquiescence to the United Nations organiza-tion and ultimate participation in the war against Japan, Truman was playing power politics. Such a Faustian bargain was possibly unavoid-able, but would not be easy to explain.

Truman may have found it hard to explain even to himself. Reports came across his desk daily of brutal Soviet action in repressing democratic-minded opponents. Toward the end of May, for example, Bulgarian Agrarian party leader G. M. Dimitrov found himself forced to seek asy-lum at the house of Maynard Barnes, the American political representa-tive in Sofia. Several hundred Communist militiamen armed with tommy guns surrounded the structure. A tense standoff lasted until August, when Dimitrov was finally allowed to go into exile in the United States. Hague-or Pendergast-style control was one thing; the naked police tactics going on in Eastern Europe were another. Truman wanted no more than a fig leaf, perhaps just as a concession to his sense of moral decency; but he would doggedly insist on that.[20]

By mid-May, he had adopted another postulate of the pro-Soviet conciliators, a stance of neutrality between the Soviet Union and Great Britain. "The difficulties with Churchill are very nearly as exasperating as they are with the Russians," he wrote to Eleanor Roosevelt. He ludicrously overstated differences of opinion about the future of the British Empire, postwar aid to Great Britain, and multitudinous, if small, operational frictions between the two nations. Following an idea propagated by Davies, he refused to meet separately with Churchill before seeing Stalin. The fear was that the Russians would think the English and Americans were ganging up on them. Superficially attractive, the concept made little sense. The collapsing British Empire and the emerging Soviet one were hardly equivalent, either morally or geopolitically; they in no way represented equal challenges to American interests. Truman adopted the stance because, very much like Roosevelt before him, he knew he could take British friendship for granted and was desperate for an understanding with the Soviet Union.[21]

Davies accomplished little but to annoy Churchill. Hopkins, who long had been committed to close American–Soviet relations and was in no physical condition for arduous negotiations, returned from Moscow after several amiable talks with Stalin; he carried with him a series of agreements to break the deadlock at San Francisco and to recognize a slightly reorganized Polish government. Publicly and privately, Truman was pleased with the efforts of both his emissaries and positively elated with the Hopkins–Stalin agreement. In substance, the pact was a defeat for American policy, but it wore the fig leaves that were vital to him. Stalin had conceded on UN-related matters of no importance to him; Truman had caved in on Poland, but few Americans cared.[22]

It was now possible to declare victory and move on with the effort to maintain the Grand Alliance. It also seemed possible to deal with the Soviets—at least if one bypassed Molotov, broke through the palace guard, and went right to Uncle Joe. On June 26, the San Francisco Conference concluded on a high note with agreement on the United Nations Charter. Many Americans believed that the event inaugurated a new era of human history. Truman addressed the closing session, his final words epitomizing the grand hopes of the occasion: "Let us not fail to grasp this supreme chance to establish a world-wide rule of reason—to create an enduring peace under the guidance of God."[23]

V

Diplomatic issues stemming from the termination of the European war and the establishment of the United Nations necessarily occupied much of Truman's attention during his first three months in office, but the war against Japan was never far from his attention. On April 1, twelve days before he took office, American troops had landed on Okinawa, just 400 miles from the southernmost Japanese home island of Kyushu. Allied forces, mostly American but including a British naval contingent, had overwhelming superiority. Okinawa was smaller than Rhode Island. Nevertheless, the battle that followed lasted for nearly three months and was the most terrible of the Pacific war. More than 100,000 Japanese troops defended the island, fighting with suicidal tenacity. Offshore, waves of kamikaze planes attacked the American fleet, inflicting greater losses than the Japanese navy had managed over the past year. On April 11, a kamikaze hit the USS *Missouri*. When Truman heard the news, he must have thought at once of his nephew J. C., a crewman on the great battle-ship. (J. C. was uninjured and the heavily armored *Missouri* scarcely nicked.)

Two days later, Truman, now president, began to receive daily reports on the battle. A few would have read as follows:

April 30
   In a massive air–naval engagement, the United States loses 20 ships; another 157 are damaged. The Japanese lose 1,100 planes.

May 5
   Kamikazes sink another 17 American ships.

May 8–18
   U.S. Marines cross the Asa estuary and advance on Naha, the island's capital. In ten days of intense combat, marines take Sugar Loaf Hill, suffering nearly 2,700 casualties.

May 11
   U.S. aircraft carrier *Bunker Hill* is hit and damaged by air attacks.

May 19
   Japanese defenders repel an American offensive against Ishimmi Ridge.

May 27–28
   Japanese air attacks sink 2 American destroyers. Japanese losses are estimated at 200 planes.

June 5
   American fleet is pounded by a typhoon that damages 19 big warships, 11 destroyers, and many auxiliary vessels.

June 6
   American troops finally capture the last enemy airfield.

June 12
   Japanese troops, defending the last 1,000 square yards of unconquered territory, commit suicide in large numbers.

June 17–21
   Japanese Admiral Minoru Ota and Lieutenant General Mitsuru Ushijima commit hara-kiri. United States Army Lieutenant General Simon Bolivar Buckner is killed by a Japanese artillery shell.

June 22
Okinawa campaign is declared over. American losses number 12,500 soldiers, sailors, and marines killed and 36,600 wounded; 36 ships; 800 planes. Japanese losses are 110,000 defenders killed; 180 ships; 7,800 planes.

June 27
Another kamikaze wave hits the *Bunker Hill*, killing 373 crewmen.[24]

As Truman read these reports, he must have thought of his own combat experiences—Cousin Ralph holding a shattered infantry force together against a German counterattack, John Miles and his battalion standing firm, the corpses along the road to Cheppy, perhaps the dying freckle-faced kid, the scattered remains of unknown soldiers heaved from shallow graves by German artillery shells east of Verdun. And he must have thought of Eddie McKim, Jr., and Abie Burkhart's son, and the still-living children of other friends.

On June 18, the day he would have received news of General Buckner's death, the president met with his top civilian and military officials to discuss the endgame in the war against Japan. The imposing group around the conference table had directed a military effort without parallel in American history. They were Admiral William D. Leahy (the president's personal military chief of staff), General George C. Marshall, Admiral Ernest J. King, Air Force Lieutenant General I. C. Eaker (representing General Hap Arnold), Secretary of War Henry Stimson, Assistant Secretary of War John J. McCloy, and Secretary of the Navy James Forrestal.

They recommended an invasion of Kyushu no later than November 1. The operation would be enormous: 766,000 American assault troops engaging an estimated 350,000 Japanese defenders. This would be simply the essential first step in a plan to take the other home islands. Everyone present assumed that the decisive campaign would occur in 1946 with a massive invasion of the main island of Honshu.

Would the Kyushu operation, Truman asked, be "another Okinawa closer to Japan"? The military chiefs of staff thought that the casualties might be somewhat lighter. They believed that *during the first thirty days*, the Kyushu campaign would exact about the same price as had the battle for the Philippine island of Luzon: 31,000 casualties. Admiral Leahy thought their estimate was low. In the end, Truman gave his reluctant approval. Returning again to the Okinawa experience, he said that he had hoped "there was a possibility of preventing an Okinawa from one end of Japan to another."

In fact, Pentagon planners were at work on estimates that projected 132,000 casualties (killed, wounded, missing) for Kyushu, and another 90,000 or so for Honshu. Of these, probably a quarter would be fatalities. These figures were not wholly worked out by the June 18 meeting, but Truman would become aware of them. In later years, he exaggerated them; but at their most conservative, they made any alternative a compelling option.[25]

The president and everyone else at the meeting knew that a possibile alternative existed. It was discussed but not taken into account in a serious way because it was still a prospect, not an existing reality. Two years earlier, Truman had tried to investigate a vast, expensive secret operation known as the Manhattan Project. He had backed off at the personal request of Secretary Stimson, who had told him only that the super-secret effort was attempting to develop a new and powerful explosive device. He had gotten basic information from Byrnes and Stimson a day or two after Roosevelt's death. He had had an extended conference with Stimson on April 25 at which he had learned that the scientists involved in the Manhattan Project were building an atomic bomb and that, as Stimson put it, "within four months, we shall in all probability have completed the most terrible weapon ever known in human history."[26]

Despite his willingness in later years to assume full and sole responsibility for use of the atomic bomb, Truman dealt with the impending event in the fashion of a circumspect chairman of the board: in early May, he appointed a committee to recommend a course of action. However incongruent with his self-manufactured image, this was a prudent course. The Interim Committee, headed by Stimson and containing Byrnes as Truman's personal representative, was certain to recommend use of the device when it was ready.

A number of Manhattan Project scientists who had been impelled to work on the bomb out of a hatred of Nazism now realized that the weapon would likely be used against Japan. Led by Leo Szilard, they tried to gain an audience with Truman, but he diverted them to Byrnes. The subsequent Byrnes–Szilard meeting served mainly to leave both men with a negative impression of each other. (In England, Churchill had a similar experience with Niels Bohr.)[27]

The Interim Committee saw the bomb, however terrible and unprecedented, as a proxy for the thousand-plane raids that already had devastated numerous German and Japanese cities and thus as neither so terrible nor beyond human comprehension. Neither Szilard and his group nor the stellar group of scientists on the committee and its advisory panel understood the horrifying radioactive side effects of atomic warfare. On June 1, citing all the uncertainties of employing an unprecedented weapon, the Interim Committee recommended its use against Japan without warning.

No one doubted that Truman would accept the advice.

There the situation stood when the Truman met with his military advisers on June 18. The bomb, still untested and unmanufactured, could not be assumed to be a winning weapon that would make a land invasion unnecessary, but they discussed it—and did so in the atmosphere of total war that had hardened decision makers around the world to mass slaughter. The Okinawa experience made the device, should it prove workable, seem a moral alternative. McCloy alone argued for informing the Japanese of American possession of atomic weapons and perhaps staging a demonstration. Military leaders wanted the shock value of surprise. James Byrnes, not yet secretary of state and not at the meeting but very influential with Truman, was in full agreement.

Was it possible that the war might be ended without either invading Japan or dropping the bomb? The United States already had exacted unconditional surrender from Germany. Should it, could it, accept less from Japan? Leahy was most emphatic in asserting that it should. Japan could not menace the United States in the foreseeable future. The demand for unconditional surrender could only encourage fanatical resistance. Stimson and McCloy favored giving the Japanese guarantees that they could keep the emperor. Truman appeared somewhat sympathetic, said he had left the door open for Congress to alter the unconditional surrender policy, but felt that he could not take action to change public opinion.

One wonders if he had thought his position through. It amounted to an implicit belief that it would not be possible to allow an utterly defeated Japan to retain the emperor under terms that still could be called "unconditional surrender" and that the American people would prefer another devastating year of war. Byrnes, who worried intensely about the domestic political repercussions of the emperor issue, may have been a decisive—and wholly negative—influence on Truman at this stage.[28]

VI

After considerable hesitation, Truman had agreed to meet Churchill and Stalin in mid-July for a conference near Berlin in an effort to settle a multitude of issues arising from the end of the war. At this point, any connection between the bomb and relations with the Soviet Union was peripheral in his mind, but he could not ignore the probability that a functioning atomic bomb would represent a substantial enhancement of American power. This, in turn, *should* be of some value in dealing with the Soviet Union. If nothing else, it would greatly reduce the urgency of Soviet intervention in the Pacific war. Thus he may well have delayed the meeting in the hope he could go to Germany with a successful atomic test behind him. It was not to be. Preparations moved slowly. On July 7, Truman left for Europe on the cruiser USS *Augusta*, still uncertain whether he had a superweapon and therefore required to lay out a game plan that assumed he did not. By the time confirmation came, he would find it difficult to reconceptualize the problem.

The prospect of dealing on high-stakes issues with his formidable counterparts had to be intimidating to any new chief executive, especially one of Truman's meager diplomatic background. The continual difficulties with the Soviets and the need to win the Pacific war could only increase his anxiety. En route to Potsdam in mid-July, he wrote to Bess, "I sure dread this trip worse than anything I've had to face."[29]

The postponement probably owed something to Truman's sense of dread, but other problems had gotten in the way of an earlier gathering. The San Francisco Conference had to be concluded in order to allow the president and his diplomatic advisers to concentrate on one set of issues at a time, keep the United Nations off the discussion list, and allow the transfer of the secretaryship of state from Stettinius to Byrnes. In Germany, functioning zones of occupation and a working Allied council had to be established. Hoping (futilely) to remove Poland from the agenda of running diplomatic sores, the United States and Britain waited for a respectable-looking coalition government; they recognized one on July 5. Nationalist China and the USSR needed to work out the details of concessions to which Roosevelt had agreed at Yalta; final agreement was still pending in early July.

Domestic matters, superficially more mundane but dictated by the change-over in administration and by legally mandated timetables, also held up an early conference. With the fiscal year ending on June 30, Truman had to send a budget to Congress. His administrative background impelled him to take the responsibility seriously, and events required important recalculations. The revised War Department authorization bill, the biggest component of the budget, did not go to Congress until June 11.[30] In addition, the process of setting up and settling into a new administration was time consuming and far from finished by the beginning of July.

The leisurely trip across the Atlantic gave Truman plenty of time for rest and relaxation as well as for numerous meetings with advisers. While he spent hours with huge briefing books, he also enjoyed the company of a few close friends who had been brought along largely for their entertainment value—Vaughan, Vardaman, and Canfil. (Still the practical joker, Truman would delight in introducing Canfil to Josef Stalin: "Marshal Stalin, meet Marshal Canfil." He liked to believe later on that Stalin and the Soviet delegation took Canfil for an unknown field marshal.)

Aside from securing Soviet participation in the Pacific war, Truman had to negotiate a range of questions involving the future of liberated Europe, the political and economic destiny of Germany, and the postwar Far East. He expected to make his way through this daunting agenda by engaging in point-by-point bargaining with his allies. What chips did he have?

Conventional military power? It could not be used so long as the United States was soliciting Soviet intervention in the Far East. And even in the absence of that contingency, it was hardly a credible threat in the absence of a frontal challenge from the Soviet ally.

The atomic bomb? If it worked, it would add enormously to American power. Truman, Byrnes, and Stimson all hoped that a successful test would increase American leverage; none had yet gotten beyond that vague expectation.

Economic aid? This probably seemed to Truman the most likely instrument of persuasion. Both Leahy and Harriman advocated using it. The USSR, they and others believed, would need substantial American assistance for postwar reconstruction. Pauley, whose hard-minded approach Truman admired, opposed unilateral concessions to the USSR in reparations negotiations. Hypersensitive to possible domestic political implications, Byrnes probably saw Soviet concessions as an essential precondition for American assistance.

Still vaguely envisioning himself as a broker between Churchill and Stalin, Truman continued to be influenced, albeit to a declining extent, by Joseph Davies, who discussed the meeting with him, prepared extensive memoranda for his consideration, participated in the conference itself, and met privately with both the president and Byrnes.[31]

Clearly, both Truman and his secretary of state believed that they could make deals with Stalin. Neither was yet receptive to the naysayers. Harriman, whose skepticism about the USSR was stronger than ever, attended the entire conference but felt that his advice was unwanted. He also developed an antipathy toward Byrnes. Forrestal, the most anti-Soviet member of the cabinet, had been left behind. He flew to Potsdam anyway, wrangled some time with Truman near the end of the meeting, and found him optimistic about a relationship with Stalin.[32]

Neither Truman nor Byrnes paid any attention to the Foreign Service and thereby denied themselves a resource that—however imperfect in its own attempts to comprehend the USSR—could have supplemented and possibly altered their own limited frames of reference. A frustrated Chip Bohlen found himself relegated to the periphery as a translator and excluded from personal conferences between Byrnes and the president. The two chief aides on whom Byrnes relied—Benjamin V. Cohen, an idealistic New Dealer, and Donald Russell, a South Carolina political associate—had no discernible qualifications for their positions. Yet Truman was not concerned and wrote in his diary the day he left America: "The smart boys in the State Department, as usual, are against the best interests of the U.S."[33]

Truman and Byrnes shared one central experience: that of being successful politicians and United States senators. However acrimonious the proceedings might get, their legislative colleagues had shared the same fundamental preconceptions of an interest group democracy in which the deal was the path to success. With no other perspective, the president and secretary of state assumed that world politics would be an extension of their previous careers. Prepared to engage in high-level logrolling, they expected Stalin to be a shrewd, hard bargainer, but ultimately reasonable and willing to trade.

The president and his party arrived in the Berlin suburb of Potsdam on the evening of July 15. They were put up in a mansion that Truman described as a dirty yellow and red French château that some German architect had ruined in an alteration that made "the place look like hell but purely German." The beginning of the conference had been delayed to July 17 because Stalin had suffered what the Russians called a mild heart attack.

In the morning, Churchill came to call. Meeting for the first time, the two men were more interested in getting acquainted than in discussing conference business. Truman enjoyed the conversation, but wrote about it several hours later in a determinedly skeptical manner:

> He is a most charming and a very clever person—meaning clever in the English and not the Kentucky [horse] sense. He gave me a lot of hooey about how great my country is and how he loved Roosevelt and how he intended to love me etc. etc. Well I gave him as cordial a reception as I could—being naturally (I hope) a polite and agreeable person.

For Churchill, the visit was an exercise in political and diplomatic courtship not all that much different from his efforts to woo Roosevelt five years earlier. In the manner of overly ardent suitors, he laid the praise on so thickly that he aroused suspicion. "I am sure we can get along if he doesn't try to give me too much soft soap," Truman wrote. "You know soft soap is made of ashhopple lye and it burns to beat hell when it gets into the eyes."

That afternoon, he toured the rubble of Berlin, seeing all around him nothing but "absolute ruin . . . old men, old women, young women, children from tots to teens carrying packs, pushing carts, pulling carts, evidently ejected by the conquerors and carrying what they could of their belongings to no where in particular." No young, able-bodied men in view, he assumed that they had been impressed into slave labor. The unhappy panorama, he wrote, was the ultimate result of Hitler's folly. Looting and pillaging, the Soviets had exacted "retribution to the nth degree."

The scene affected him deeply and was made tolerable only by the knowledge that the Germans had done the same thing to the Soviets, who now were practicing the Golden Rule in reverse. "What a pity that the human animal is not able to put his moral thinking into practice!" he mused. "I fear that machines are ahead of morals by some centuries." Perhaps thinking of the bomb, he added, "We are only termites on a planet and maybe when we bore too deeply into the planet there'll be a reckoning—who knows?"[34]

Truman may well have written those lines after meeting between 7:30 and 8:00 P.M. with Secretary Stimson, who presented him with a top-secret message he had just received from his closest aide, George Harrison. It obliquely summarized the results of the first atomic explosion, near Alamogordo in the New Mexico desert:

> Operated on this morning. Diagnosis not yet complete but results seem satisfactory and already exceed expectations. Local press release necessary as interest extends great distance.[35]

At noon on July 17, Truman had his first meeting with Stalin. For two hours, the two had a broad discussion of conference issues. Only two other Soviets, Molotov and Pavlov, and two Americans, Byrnes and Bohlen, were present for the entire session. While anxious to feel out Stalin on the issues, Truman was obviously most interested in arriving at a personal impression of his Soviet counterpart and establishing a good relationship. In that sense, as in most of what transpired at Potsdam, his approach was little different from Roosevelt's.

With a smile on his face, he called Stalin Uncle Joe, described himself as no diplomat, and declared that he usually answered yes or no after hearing all the arguments. Stalin, he thought, liked the approach. He listened as the Soviet leader brought up demands, many of which he had not previously addressed, for a share of the German fleet, reparations, more concessions on Poland, division of the Axis colonies among the Big Three, and the overthrow of the Franco government in Spain. Some of them, Truman thought, were "dynamite"; others, especially the ejection of Franco, he could live with. On such matters as Soviet intervention in the Pacific war and open access (the "Open Door," Stimson called it) to postwar Manchuria, Stalin appeared forthcoming and cooperative. Above all, Truman liked the Soviet leader and thought he had established a good working relationship with him. "I can deal with Stalin," he wrote a few hours later. "He is honest—but smart as hell."[36]

That afternoon, the conference held its first session; largely organizational, it lasted for only 105 minutes. Truman and the senior American delegates—Brynes, Leahy, and Davies—sat together occupying approximately a third of the circumference of a large round table; also with them was Charles Bohlen, who acted only as an interpreter. Directly behind sat other American delegates: Harriman, Pauley, and several Department of State officials. As the only head of state present, Truman chaired the meeting.

Calling for agenda items, the president put four American concerns on the table. Two, a council of foreign ministers to draw up peace treaties with the Axis powers and an Allied control council for Germany, were unncontroversial. Two others, an assertion that the Yalta agreements still needed to be implemented in the Eastern European nations and a call to recognize Italy as a rehabilitated nation by admitting it to the United Nations, were unlikely to win quick assent from the Soviet Union. Churchill added the Polish problem to the list. Stalin weighed in with eight items, ranging from the spoils of war (division of the German fleet and reparations) to trusteeships in areas well outside the traditional Soviet orbit.

The differing lists foreshadowed profound differences in approaches and objectives that made a truly successful conference unlikely. Even so, Truman felt good about the opening session. He had proceeded crisply. He informed the Russians and British that he wanted issues decided expeditiously ("something in the bag each day," as Churchill put it) and that he was prepared to go home rather than engage in endless discussion. (He may or may not have realized that he was copying a tactic

Woodrow Wilson had used at Versailles.) Churchill and Stalin were amiable, Churchill displaying his command of the English language and power at debate and Stalin exhibiting a wry wit.[37]

Truman subsequently added to the American proposals a request (also reminiscent of Wilson at Versailles) for the internationalization of the major waterways of Central and Eastern Europe—the Kiel Canal, the Rhine, the Danube, the Turkish straits. Stalin (like later radical American historians) probably considered it a none-too-subtle proposal for Western capitalist penetration of the Soviet sphere. It would have had that effect; it also would have economically and politically enriched the lives of the Eastern European peoples. Of course, it got nowhere; nor did other Western attempts to moderate the increasingly heavy-handed pro-Soviet governments being established in Eastern Europe.

The conference was held up for a couple of days by the unexpected defeat of the Conservatives in the British elections. Truman took to the new Labour prime minister, Clement Attlee, a mild-mannered Oxford don, far more than to his foreign secretary, Ernest Bevin, a dockworkers' union leader whose appearance and plebian manner reminded the president of John L. Lewis. He also observed that Stalin seemed rather disappointed by Churchill's exit. Perhaps the Soviet dictator preferred the devil he knew to the one he did not; possibly he realized that Bevin was a tough-minded anti-Communist likely to entertain even fewer illusions than Anthony Eden about the continuance of the alliance.[38]

The conference did not come close to achieving Truman's hopes for quick, favorable results. Dragging on for thirteen sessions, it finally ended with more of a whimper than a bang at 12:30 A.M. on August 2. Aside from reaffirmation of the Soviet pledge to declare war on Japan, it reached no significant substantive decisions.

If grueling and frequently frustrating, the Potsdam trip had its pleasant aspects. Truman visited with his nephew Harry, an artillery sergeant, and with his beloved old World War I friend Father Curtis Tiernan, still a military chaplain. He interviewed and acquired a White House physician, Wallace Graham, a bright young army surgeon who was the son of an old Kansas City friend. The banquets the leaders hosted for one another were glittering affairs; Truman and Stalin, both devotees of classical music, produced some of their finest concert talent as entertainers. On the way home, Truman had a brief visit in England with George VI and took an instant liking to the "Limey King."[39]

On the whole, he left Potsdam in good spirits. He could hope that once the procedural machinery began to function, the issues of Germany and Eastern Europe could be worked out. The president was still pleased that he had gotten his top priority, the Pacific war pledge. No solid reparations agreement had been reached, but he had avoided any arrangements that might commit the United States to long-term support of the German people and thereby underwrite their reparations to the USSR and other allies.

Above all, he thought (as had Roosevelt) that he had established a good relationship with Stalin. The Soviets, he told Mamma and Mary Jane, were "pig-headed," and he wished he would never have another conference with them. But he thought that Stalin was different. "I like Stalin," he wrote to Bess on July 29. "He is straightforward. Knows what he wants and will compromise when he can't get it. His foreign minister isn't so forthright." He left Potsdam hoping that Stalin's health would allow him to hold on as Soviet dictator and fearing that he might be overthrown by a less accommodating military clique. The impression would stick. Four years later, Truman would tell Jonathan Daniels, "Stalin is as near like Tom Pendergast as any man I know."[40]

VII

Finally, Truman left Potsdam elated that he had a weapon that would probably end the war no matter what the Russians did. On the morning of July 18, Stimson had given him another enigmatic message from Harrison in Washington. The key sentence read, "The light in his eyes discernible from here to Highhold and I could have heard his screams from here to my farm." Highhold was Stimson's estate on Long Island, 250 miles away; Harrison's farm was in Upperville, Virginia, 50 miles distant. Truman, Stimson wrote in his diary, was "highly delighted . . . evidently very greatly reinforced."

On July 21, a much fuller report by General Leslie Groves arrived. It contained specific data on the explosion: a force of 15,000 to 20,000 tons of TNT, a fireball lasting for several seconds and shining as brightly as several midday suns, a mushroom cloud rising to 41,000 feet above sea level, secondary explosions within it, a 1,200-foot crater, the evaporation of the 100-foot tower from which the bomb had been suspended, the destruction of a 70-foot steel tower a half-mile away. Groves also reported his feelings of "profound awe" and included the emotional reactions of others.

The most eloquent was General Thomas Farrell:

> No man-made phenomenon of such tremendous power had ever occurred before. The lighting effects beggared description. . . . It was that beauty the great poets dream about but describe most poorly and inadequately. Thirty seconds after the explosion came first, the air blast pressing hard against the people and things, to be followed almost immediately by the strong, sustained, awesome roar which warned of doomsday and made us feel that we puny things were blasphemous to dare tamper with the forces heretofore reserved to The Almighty.[41]

Stimson read the report to Truman and Byrnes. "They were immensely pleased," he wrote shortly afterward. "The President was tremendously pepped up by it and spoke to me of it again and again when I saw him. He said it gave him an entirely new feeling of confidence and he thanked me for having come to the Conference and being present to help him in this way." Because the British had been partners in the Manhattan Project, Churchill was fully informed. Stimson shared Groves's report with him. Gunpowder, he declared, had become trivial and electricity meaningless; the bomb was "the Second Coming in Wrath." Truman told himself, "It may be the fire destruction prophesied in the Euphrates Valley Era after Noah and his fabulous Ark."[42]

For all his solemn forebodings, Truman was elated. The bomb had given him a sense of enormous power and at a stroke had changed his position from that of a supplicant in quest of an ally against Japan to a more-than-equal partner now able to be indifferent. Churchill had observed on July 21 that Truman was markedly more assertive and considerably firmer in rejecting Soviet demands. After reading Groves's report, he understood why.[43]

What should the Soviets be told? At this point, even Stimson, who later would favor more openness, was pessimistic about future relations with the USSR and not inclined to tell Stalin too much. His attitude approximated a consensus that quickly developed between the British and the Americans. At the conclusion of the day's negotiations on July 24, Truman, leaving Bohlen behind, walked over to Stalin; as the president recalled it, he "casually mentioned . . . that we had a new weapon of unusual destructive force."

Stalin, poker-faced, merely said that he hoped the United States would make good use of it against the Japanese, asked no questions, and made no further comments. Of course, thanks to his espionage ring at Los Alamos, he actually was well informed about the Manhattan Project, although he may not have known of the successful test. The Americans and British, many of them puzzled at his lack of interest, did not realize that they had witnessed the first display of an interim Soviet strategy for dealing with the bomb—to behave as if it were irrelevant, even to treat it as a joke, until the USSR could produce its own.[44]

As Truman remembered it seven years later, he called a meeting of Secretaries Stimson and Byrnes, Admirals Leahy and King, and Generals Marshall and Arnold to discuss use of the atomic bomb. Asked about likely casualties in the planned invasions of Kyushu and Honshu, Marshall estimated around 250,000 Americans and at least an equal number of Japanese. However, there is no reference to this meeting in the voluminous official Potsdam record or in Truman's own diary. It is more likely that he conflated numerous individual discussions in his mind.[45]

Whatever the extent and quality of Truman's advice, numerous historians and journalists have argued that he knew about and ignored Japanese attempts to achieve peace. These involved primarily approaches to the Soviet Union. United States intelligence was intercepting diplomatic transmissions from Foreign Minister Shigenori Togo to Ambassador Naotake Sato in Moscow revealing that Japan wanted to discuss ending the war and hoped that the Soviet Union would be a sympathetic go-between. The intercepts also revealed, however, that the Tokyo government was at an impasse, despite the hopelessness of its situation.

Truman was briefed on these exchanges and probably saw copies of Sato's telegram to Togo, dated July 12. With a bold directness and despairing eloquence, Sato asserted that the time was past for negotiation, that the Japanese homeland was in peril, that the Soviets had nothing to gain by assisting Japan. "We ourselves must firmly resolve to terminate the war," he declared. "Is there any meaning in showing that our country has reserve strength for a war of resistance, or in sacrificing the lives of hundreds of thousands of conscripts and millions of other innocent residents of cities and metropolitan areas?" Asking Togo's pardon and begging for his understanding, he concluded, "In international relations there is no mercy, and facing reality is unavoidable."[46]

What could Truman and those around him have thought of the Togo–Sato exchanges? It was reasonable to assume that the men in Tokyo were going to try to fight to the end and that they had to be dealt a cataclysmic blow in order to obtain a surrender.

Truman also knew that just before the conference, the Japanese Foreign Ministry, employing a communication signed by the emperor, had asked the Soviet government to receive Prince Fumimaro Konoye as a special envoy. Konoye's mission, never clearly stated, would relate to "the termination of the war." Making a remarkable stretch, some writers have depicted this as an indication that Japan was prepared to surrender unconditionally; yet Togo explicitly told Sato that Japan was *not* ready to do that.

To Truman and his advisers, the proposal probably seemed reminiscent of a suggested meeting between Konoye and Roosevelt that the Japanese government had floated in the fall of 1941 before the attack on Pearl Harbor. In the absence of specific negotiating points from Japan, the Roosevelt administration had rejected it. Moreover, Konoye's visit to Moscow could reasonably be interpreted as a tactic to delay Soviet entry into the war. Most likely, it was an indication of the state of gridlock and denial in Tokyo. And to civilian officials who (unlike Sato in Moscow) faced the real possibility of assassination, it was a way of delaying the inevitable necessity of advising surrender. Clearly, it was not an offer to surrender, either unconditionally or conditionally.[47]

Stalin, bent on war with Japan and territorial gains in Northeast Asia, rejected the Japanese initiative. Acting the role of the faithful ally, he told Churchill and Truman about it on July 18, the same day that Truman got George Harrison's second report. Truman wrote in his diary:

> Discussed Manhattan (it is a success). Decided to tell Stalin about it. Stalin had told P.M. [Churchill] of telegram from Jap Emperor asking for peace. Stalin also read his answer to me. It was satisfactory. Believe Japs will fold up before Russia comes in.
>
> I am sure they will when Manhattan appears over their homeland. I shall inform Stalin about it at an opportune time.[48]

The refusal to face reality in Tokyo imparted nearly unstoppable momentum to the planning for military use of the bomb. Of those with whom Truman talked in the final stages, no one was more important than Stimson, who had his total respect and was directly responsible for the Manhattan Project. When Stimson insisted on dropping Kyoto from the target list for the atomic bomb, Truman concurred, in Stimson's words, "with the utmost emphasis." The military saw Kyoto as a prime industrial target; Stimson saw it as a city of shrines and cultural centers that could not be destroyed without alienating the Japanese population.[49]

Stimson was probably also the key figure, if only through his refusal to wield a veto, in persuading Truman to adopt a strategy of dropping the first two bombs in rapid succession; the idea was to convince the Japanese that the United States had a large stockpile. As to the decision to use the bomb, there was no dissent among the primary advisers. On July 25, Truman gave Stimson a final go-ahead, and the secretary returned to Washington. Militarily, the project was now on automatic pilot. Sometime during the first ten days of August, the bomb would be used against Hiroshima, Kokura, or Nigata in that order of choice. This could be stopped only by a Japanese agreement to surrender unconditionally. That, in turn, might depend on what sort of an ultimatum Japan received.

Issued from Potsdam on July 26 in the names of Truman, Attlee, and Chiang Kai-shek of China, the proclamation demanding the unconditional surrender of Japan was a stern document that presented as the alternative "the inevitable and complete destruction of the Japanese armed forces and . . . the utter devastation of the Japanese homeland." In accord, however, with the decision already made in Washington, it did not mention an atomic bomb. Nor—and here Byrnes prevailed over Stimson —did it state that Japan would be allowed to retain its emperor. Truman apparently still felt that such a concession was too emotionally and politically charged.[50]

Two days later, Japanese prime minister Kantaro Suzuki issued a statement at a press conference rejecting the Potsdam ultimatum with a verb that could be translated as "treat with silent contempt" and declaring that Japan would "resolutely fight for the successful conclusion of the war."[51]

Unconditional surrender had by now become a wartime objective carved in stone; having exacted it from Germany, no American president could appear to negotiate something less with Japan. Nevertheless, it is puzzling that the United States did not make it clear, either publicly or through diplomatic back channels, that unconditional surrender would not mean removal of the emperor. Whether Japan would have responded to such an initiative cannot be surmised. But since that was the policy the United States followed anyway, one can only regret that it was not made explicit before the obliteration of two cities. As it was, Truman allowed things to go forward, increasingly buoyed by a belief that the war would soon be ended without a massive invasion of Japan.

He was not entirely comfortable with what he had done. Writing in his diary, he portrayed his orders to Stimson in terms that in his heart he had to know were unrealistic:

> I have told the Sec. of War, Mr. Stimson, to use it so that military objectives and soldiers and sailors are the target and not women and children. Even if the Japs are savages, ruthless, merciless and fanatic, we as the leader of the world for the common welfare cannot drop this terrible bomb on the old Capitol [Kyoto] or the new [Tokyo].
> He & I are in accord. The target will be a purely military one.[52]

At approximately 8:11 A.M. on August 6, a B-29, the *Enola Gay*, piloted by Colonel Paul Tibbets, dropped an atomic bomb over the city of Hiroshima from an altitude of 31,600 feet. Executing a maneuver he had practiced incessantly, Tibbets veered sharply and increased the speed of his engines as soon as the device cleared the bomb-bay doors. The explosion, which occured at 2,000 feet, nonetheless shook his craft. Observers in a trailing B-29 witnessed the phenomenon that had overwhelmed the men at Alamogordo—the blinding fireball, the shock wave, the mushroom cloud rising miles into the sky. The central city of Hiroshima, built on a level plain, was instantly in flames; almost nothing remained standing within a one-mile radius of ground zero. Perhaps 75,000 people, mostly civilians, were killed instantly; more tens of thousands would eventually die from the effects of radiation. No single device in the history of warfare had ever displayed an ability to kill so many people so indiscriminately.

The news reached Truman aboard the *Augusta* at least twelve hours later. Eating lunch with the crew, he received a terse message from Stimson: "Big bomb dropped on Hiroshima at 7:15 P.M. Washington time. First reports indicate complete success which was even more conspicuous than earlier test." A confirming message came a few minutes later. Elated, convinced that the war soon would be over, and cognizant of the unprecedented military and scientific implications, Truman declared, "This is the greatest thing in history." Some would criticize the statement as callous, but Truman was celebrating the end of a war. And if by "greatest" he meant most important, who will say he was wrong?[53]

The *Augusta* docked at Newport News just before 5:00 P.M. on August 7; Truman was the White House by about 11:00. The next day, he conferred with Stimson, who gave him photographs and a written report detailing the damage at Hiroshima. He examined them thoroughly and remarked that the destruction placed a terrible responsibility on himself and the War Department. Stimson expressed his hope that the United States would make it as easy as possible for Japan to surrender and would treat the defeated enemy with tact and leniency. That afternoon, Truman personally announced to White House reporters that the USSR had declared war on Japan. With no surrender offer, no word at all, coming from Tokyo, he did not interfere with the plan for dropping the second bomb.

On August 9 at 11:00 A.M., it hit Nagasaki, a tertiary target selected because of bad weather and poor observation conditions at Kokura and
Nigata. The death and devastation were perhaps half those at Hiroshima,
but still beyond imagination.

Should there have been a longer interval between the use of the two
bombs? Would the Japanese have surrendered had they been given more
time to contemplate the totality of the destruction at Hiroshima? No one
can say. They realized that an event of unique horror had occurred there
and that the United States claimed it had been inflicted by an atomic
bomb. Civilian officials wanted to surrender, but the military leaders,
driven by a deeply internalized warrior code, found the prospect unbearable. Just before midnight on August 9, the civilian-military Supreme War
Council met in the presence of the emperor. After each side made its
presentation, Hirohito declared emotionally and firmly, "I swallow my
own tears and give my sanction to the proposal to accept the Allied proclamation on the basis outlined by the Foreign Minister."[54]

The Japanese surrender offer was put before Truman on August 10.
Strictly speaking, it still was not unconditional, but was posited on retention of the emperor. (Truman, of course, was not aware of Hirohito's
role in breaking the Japanese gridlock.) Leahy, Stimson, and Forrestal
favored acceptance; Byrnes leaned toward rejection. Truman opted for a
response asserting that the Japanese message met American terms with
the understanding that the emperor would be subject to the Allied supreme commander. There would be no more atomic bombings, he told
the cabinet. He had withheld permission to ship components for a third
bomb to the Pacific. Henry Wallace recorded his attitude: "He said the
thought of wiping out another 100,000 people was too horrible. He didn't
like the idea of killing, as he said, 'all those kids.'"[55]

He also declared ("most fiercely," according to a dismayed Wallace)
that he expected the Russians to stall on the surrender in order to grab as
much of Manchuria as possible. If China and Britain agreed to the American formulation, he told them, he would not wait for the Russians.[56]

It remains an article of faith among scholars of the left that the bombs
were dropped not to compel a Japanese surrender, which they believe was
already imminent, but to intimidate the Russians and bring the war to a
close before the USSR could occupy Manchuria. These assertions rest
primarily on circumstantial evidence and implication. There is no credible evidence in Truman's personal contemporary writings or his later
accounts that he saw the *use* of the bomb as a way of making a point to
the Soviet Union. (Obviously, he thought its *existence* would strengthen
the United States.) Nor is there any reason to believe that he was bam-
boozled by others.

Later on, he would throw out varying exaggerated estimates of the
number of lives saved by the bomb: 500,000; 250,000; 100,000. His critics
have observed that some military planners had argued that Japan, bombed
out by conventional ordnance and blockaded, would be forced to sur-

render in a matter of months for lack of food and matériel. It is doubtful that their estimates ever reached Truman, and they were not accepted by the American military high command, which continued to assume suicidal resistance. Okinawa had made an indelible impression.

One consideration weighed most heavily on Truman: the longer the war lasted, the more Americans killed. Some critics have suggested that he should have engaged in a grim calculus, that it would have been the moral thing to accept a "worst case estimate" of an additional 46,000 American deaths without use of the bomb.[57] No one who might conceivably have been president of the United States in the summer of 1945 would have withheld the bomb while facing that prospect. Perhaps Japan, hammered by cumulative defeats, facing an unbreakable naval blockade, and shocked by Soviet intervention, would have shortly surrendered anyway.[58] But in the end, a brutal certainty remains. Japan was unable to muster the will to quit until two atomic bombs had been dropped.

Almost all veterans of the Pacific war heartily supported Truman's course. One of them was Second Lieutenant Francis Heller, a young man who had fled Austria with his parents a decade earlier. Assigned to the first wave of the planned invasion of Honshu, Heller instead that fall found himself wading ashore on a quiet beach where he had expected to face withering fire. Years later, he told a historian how he felt as he stepped out of the surf: "I thought this is where I would have been killed if not for the atomic bomb." The thought must have entered his mind many times nine years later when he helped Harry Truman write his memoirs.[59]

Truman, the old artilleryman who had seen war close-up, understood from his own experience the hopes and fears of the Francis Hellers of the world—young combat officers dreaming of families and futures, just as he had a generation earlier. Their survival would be the ultimate vindication of his decision.

VIII

The Allies (including the Russians) gave their approval to American terms. Yet final acceptance did not come from Japan. On August 13, Truman authorized one last terrible 1,000-plane raid on Tokyo. In Japan, die-hard army officers invaded the Imperial Palace, killed the commander of the emperor's guard, and searched in vain for Hirohito's recorded surrender speech. The next day, Japanese radio ran the emperor's address, and the nation surrendered. On the evening of August 14, the president announced that World War II was over and declared a two-day holiday. Americans celebrated, at times wildly, in the streets of every town and city. For a moment, it was possible to hope that the destruction of the enemy meant the birth of a new and better world.

20

"I'M TIRED BABYING THE SOVIETS": THE COLD WAR EMERGES, 1945–1946

The postwar world fell woefully short of any utopian expectations. Leaving behind a world in disarray, the war largely destroyed an old Eurocentric order based on capitalism and empire, but erected nothing to replace it. American foreign policy found itself dealing, one step removed, with the collapse of old imperial orders and attendant communal violence on the Indian subcontinent, in Southeast Asia, and in Palestine; with revolution and chaos in China; with famine in much of the world. Truman handled all these issues in a manner that tried to blend American idealism and national self-interest. It was possible to leave some crises—India, Indochina, Indonesia—to wartime allies. Others—Palestine, China, and world hunger—could not be avoided.

One big issue, however, eclipsed even these matters (which themselves would once have been considered herculean in the challenges they presented). This was the central problem Truman had faced at Potsdam: establishing a working relationship with the Soviets. He had returned from Potsdam thinking it difficult but possible. During the next year, the bumps he had expected began to take on the dimensions of mountains that more and more looked impassible. As late as the fall of 1946, he presided over a foreign policy that was more a response to disparate crises than a strategically unified whole, more a matter of atmospherics than of careful conceptualization. Nonetheless, after a lot of uncertainty, its direction was clear and vividly expressed in an admonition to Jimmy Byrnes: "I'm tired babying the Soviets."[1]

II

Eastern Europe remained the focus of contention. In one country after another—Poland, Hungary, Romania, Bulgaria, Yugoslavia, Albania— Communists backed by Russian military forces steadily increased their power and drove the opposition to the margins of politics. The United States could do little other than withhold recognition and attempt to use the peace process established at Potsdam as a means of obtaining more open regimes. In September 1945, the first Council of Foreign Ministers meeting in London demonstrated just how weak the American hand was.

Byrnes, still conceiving of diplomacy as a series of ad hoc, Senate-like negotiations, thought that he had two powerful aces in the hole: postwar American aid conditioned on Soviet cooperation and all the power that resided in the atomic bomb. He soon had it brought home to him that diplomacy was not seven-card stud. Although the USSR had requested a large postwar loan, it was unwilling to make concessions for one. Determined to dominate Eastern Europe whatever the hardships, the Russians had created a situation in which a loan would be gravy if granted, grievance if denied. As for the bomb, there was no real possibility of it being used short of the improbable contingency of a Soviet attack against Western Europe.

In London, Molotov moved from Stalin's Potsdam stance of studied indifference toward the bomb to one of open ridicule. At his first meeting with Byrnes, he asked the secretary of state if he had brought an atomic bomb along in his pocket. A few days later at a banquet, he proposed a toast to the secretary, declaring, "Of course, we all have to pay great attention to what Mr. Byrnes says, because the United States are the only people who are making the atomic bomb." Thereafter, the Soviet foreign minister missed few opportunities for similar snide references, thus demonstrating to the Americans what John Lewis Gaddis has tellingly characterized as "the impotence of omnipotence." The meeting adjourned with no agreements and not an inch more of breathing space for democratic elements in the emerging Soviet empire. Shortly afterward, Truman and Harold Smith found themselves talking about difficulties with the Soviet Union. The budget director remarked that Truman, after all, had an atomic bomb up his sleeve. Truman simply responded, "I am not sure that it can ever be used."[2]

Byrnes had misgauged the Russians, whom he expected to wilt in the reflection of American nuclear energy. But both the American and British governments still felt a strong need to express a principled opposition to total Soviet dominance (as opposed to a less heavy-handed sphere of influence) in Eastern Europe. Some of the harsher moments of the London conference, in fact, transpired between British foreign minister

Bevin and Molotov. Yet principle, however admirable, did not necessarily constitute a compelling national interest. Neither the United States nor Britain was ever seriously willing to contemplate forcing the USSR out of its new possessions.

Truman, increasingly preoccupied with domestic reconversion, appears to have paid only limited attention to diplomacy after Potsdam. When he made comments about foreign policy in press conferences and in a couple of speeches, he assumed that the United States would continue to play a dominant role in world affairs while acting in the service of American idealism and the goals of the United Nations. He advocated a precedent-breaking program of universal military training (UMT) for young men, although he soon realized he probably could not get it through Congress. And while he rhetorically committed himself to a strong military, he likely had not begun to realize the yawning gap between his budgetary plans and his military aspirations. As for relations with the USSR, his mind remained divided, one side wanting to stand on principle and assert American power and ideals, the other wanting to work out a compromise with the Soviet Union. For the time being, he was willing to leave specifics to Byrnes, who quickly and rashly assumed the same latitude he had exercised as unofficial "assistant president" under Roosevelt.[3]

One undeniable lesson of London was that the atomic bomb had unavoidably become central to American foreign policy. Truman squarely confronted the problem on September 21, 1945, at what was possibly the most memorable cabinet meeting in American history. Henry Stimson, seventy-eight years old, perhaps the most respected elder statesman in American politics, had spent the past several months of his tenure as secretary of war focusing his attention almost exclusively on the atomic bomb and its implications for the future of the world. His concern very quickly became a question of how to relate the new weapon to the more general problem of dealing with the Soviet Union. His own attitude had swung back and forth between hope and apprehension; the authoritarian atmosphere surrounding the Soviet presence at Potsdam had left him briefly uncertain that it was possible to work with the Soviet Union. In the end, however, he had fallen back on the lessons and values of his patrician youth and education. Now he argued for extending them to atomic diplomacy.

Far from being the master card of American diplomacy, Stimson argued, the bomb had become a liability in Soviet–American relations; it inspired suspicion and rivalry that might not otherwise exist. Not just another powerful weapon, it constituted "a first step in a new control by man over the forces of nature too revolutionary and dangerous to fit into the old concepts." Thus an unprecedented situation required the United States in cooperation with Great Britain to make "a direct and forthright approach" to the USSR with a program of atomic disarmament and joint development of atomic energy "for commercial and humanitarian purposes." The proposal was deliberately sketchy; almost certainly, however, it would involve some sharing of scientific development with the Soviet

Union. And given past American experience with the secretive and often hostile Soviet regime, it manifestly assumed that the United States and Britain must be willing to accept Russian assurances on many key points. Stimson underscored the point by declaring, "The chief lesson I have learned in a long life is that the only way you can make a man trustworthy is to trust him; and the surest way to make him untrustworthy is to distrust him and show your distrust."[4]

Reaction around the table ranged from strong support (Undersecretary of State Dean Acheson [Byrnes was at the London conference], Undersecretary of War Patterson, Undersecretary of the Interior Abe Fortas, Secretary of Commerce Wallace) to equally vehement disagreement (Secretary of the Treasury Vinson, Secretary of the Navy Forrestal, Secretary of Agriculture Anderson, Attorney General Clark) to relatively noncommittal declarations (OWMR director Snyder, War Production Board chairman Krug). Truman's remarks indicated considerable sympathy for Stimson's position. Then and in both private conversations and press conferences later on, the president appeared to accept the key concept of the proposal: it was practical to withhold the techniques for manufacturing a bomb while sharing scientific information and engaging in joint peaceful development.[5]

Through the fall, moreover, Truman's occasional private and semiprivate remarks about the USSR indicated a belief that it was both possible to deal with Stalin and necessary to work out agreements with his country; indeed, his greatest fear was of Stalin's demise and the difficulties that some obstreperous successor (possibly Molotov or General Georgi Zhukov) likely would present.[6] It therefore seemed natural enough for him to move ahead on atomic energy. In a hurried (and poorly planned) conference held in Washington that November, he got British prime minister Attlee and Canadian prime minister Mackenzie King to assent to the principle of an international control plan. In early 1946, two of the most impressive subcabinet members of Truman's administration, Acheson and Tennessee Valley Authority (TVA) head David Lilienthal, began work on a plan for international control that might be placed before the Soviets and submitted to the United Nations.[7]

III

Byrnes in the meantime had decided to undertake a new and conciliatory initiative addressing a wide range of major problems stemming from Soviet behavior since V-J Day: atomic energy, the consolidation of Communist power in Eastern Europe, early pressures on Turkey for "joint control" of the straits between the Black Sea and the Mediterranean, establishment by Soviet troops of a pro-USSR secessionist government in the northwestern Iranian province of Azerbaijan, the unilateral establishment of a sphere of dominance in Manchuria and northern Korea, demands for a role in the occupation of Japan. With no progress appar-

ently possible through normal diplomatic channels, Byrnes followed the
course that by now was becoming second nature to American diplomats:
the direct appeal to Stalin. With the grudging acquiescence of Bevin, he
managed to get another Council of Foreign Ministers meeting scheduled
for Moscow in December 1945. In all of this, he appears to have had
Truman's support. There is no indication that the president objected at
this juncture to what had become an established policy of leaving the
details to Jimmy.

Yet both in public and behind the scenes, pressure was building.
Senator Vandenberg and congressional Republicans saw the Moscow
initiative as a return to softness toward the Soviet Union. From Undersecretary of State Acheson down, the foreign policy professionals were
unhappy with Byrnes's cavalier attitude toward them; Acheson himself
would offer his resignation in the spring of 1946. Within the White House,
Admiral Leahy, who had all but given up on the hope of accommodation
with the USSR, was a frequent sniper at the secretary.

Even Truman, seemingly willing to give Byrnes a lot of latitude,
complained caustically to Harold Smith of weak administration at State.
On November 28, he listened sympathetically as Henry Wallace went after
Byrnes. At a staff meeting on December 12, Truman displayed open
annoyance about, as he put it, having to read the newspapers to find out
about United States foreign policy. He vented his feelings to Frank Walker,
who repeated them to Averell Harriman. The president was clearly displeased, although he was focusing more on style than on substance; characteristically, he could not bring himself to have a direct discussion with
Byrnes about it. Whether the secretary of state realized it or not, he needed
a triumph at Moscow.[8]

After the first meeting in Moscow, Ambassador Harriman asked
Byrnes whether he should draft a report for the president or whether
Byrnes preferred to do it. Byrnes retorted, "The President has given me
complete authority. I can't trust the White House to prevent leaks." Several days later, Chip Bohlen, brought along primarily as an interpreter,
attempted to suggest to his boss that it might be well to send back regular reports to the president. As Bohlen recalled it, "I was put in my place
and I stayed there."[9] Byrnes's motivation remains murky. Too savvy to
be innocent of growing criticism at home, he may have feared that daily
reports to the president would fall into the hands of individuals who would
selectively leak bad news. Truman, always amiable and eager to oblige in
face-to-face meetings, had indeed approved a State Department document that amounted to a full delegation of power. Yet it is remarkable
that such an astute politician had become so insensitive to his relationship with his chief that he took it for granted.[10]

Nor was there much to be said for the manner in which Byrnes conducted himself in Moscow. Showing little interest in the opinions of
Harriman or embassy counselor George F. Kennan and hardly conde-

scending to consult with the British delegation, he attempted to conduct diplomacy in the improvisational manner of FDR. But Byrnes lacked Roosevelt's presence and depth; and his task, the establishment of a post-war order, was different from Roosevelt's imperative of holding a fragile wartime alliance together. Good atmospherics could be purchased only by concessions that could not be frankly acknowledged as such. Kennan described Byrnes and his objectives caustically in a diary entry dated December 19, 1945:

> He plays his negotiations by ear, going into them with no clear or fixed plan, with no definite set objectives or limitations. He relies entirely on his own agility and presence of mind and hopes to take advantage of tactical openings. . . . [H]is main purpose is to achieve some sort of an agreement, he doesn't much care what. The realities behind this agreement, since they concern only such people as Koreans, Rumanians, and Iranians, about whom he knows nothing, do not concern him.[11]

In Washington, Truman had been set on in the meantime by the entire membership of the Senate Atomic Energy Committee, including Senators Tom Connally and Arthur Vandenberg. Alienated by Byrnes's offhand treatment, they entertained exaggerated fears that he might give away America's nuclear monopoly. When Truman assured them that was not possible, they asked for a copy of his directive to Byrnes. To Truman's embarrassment, the document clearly gave the secretary latitude to do anything he wished on atomic policy. Truman stood by Byrnes, asserting that nothing was to be given away in Moscow and leaving a fuming Vandenberg to record in his diary: "For some inscrutable reason, the President seemed to fail to grasp our point." Truman then had Acheson, acting secretary of state in the secretary's absence, inform Byrnes of the meeting with the committee and of his pledges to it that there would be no untoward concessions on atomic energy without full review and discussion by president and Congress. Byrnes responded with assurances of his own, and the issue seemed closed.[12]

The senators had been needlessly overwrought. Truman had handled the episode well. Nevertheless, it must have bothered him to discover that Byrnes had handled the influentials of the Senate so badly; it also must have rankled him no end to be told that he did not understand a directive he had signed. Byrnes's subsequent failure to send any report until December 24 could hardly have improved Truman's temper—all the more so as, in Truman's later words, the communication was "like one partner in a business telling the other that his business trip was progressing well and not to worry."[13]

The president's bleak personal life also must have contributed to his annoyance. Bess, her mother, and Margaret all left for Independence on December 20. Truman stayed in Washington until the morning of Christmas Day, and then flew to Kansas City in weather so bad that the *New*

York Times and the *Washington Post* editorially criticized him for reckless self-endangerment. Bess, tense and unhappy over his absence and his dangerous flight, berated him for having stayed in Washington so long. On December 27, as his brief respite with family and friends was coming to an end, he received from the State Department the text of Byrnes's communiqué on the conclusion of the Moscow conference—an hour after it had been released to the news media. He was also the recipient of another alarm on the atomic-energy issue from Vandenberg.[14]

Truman flew back to Washington the next morning after yet another quarrel with Bess over his quick departure. Probably while still on the plane, he scribbled an angry letter to her and had it sent special delivery. Shortly afterward, he had cooled down enough to call Margaret, tell her to contact Independence postmaster Edgar Hinde, have him intercept the letter, and burn it. At the end of the day, he sat down and wrote, but did not send, a contrite missive expressing his unhappiness and feelings of inadequacy:

> You can never appreciate what it means to come home as I did the other evening after doing at least 100 things I didn't want to do and have the only person in the world whose approval and good opinion I value look at me like I'm something the cat dragged in and tell me I've come in at last because I couldn't find any reason to stay away. . . . You, Margie and every one else who may have any influence on my actions must give me help and assistance, because no one ever needed help and assistance as I do now. . . . Kiss my baby and I love you in season & out.[15]

The final agreements at Moscow amounted to little, but what there was seemed mostly concessions to the USSR, unbalanced by reciprocal concessions to American concerns. The ministers agreed to the establishment of a UN atomic-energy commission that presumably would be a vehicle for international control of the atom, to token Soviet participation in the occupation of Japan, and, in effect, to Western recognition of the Romanian and Bulgarian governments. At best, the results could be seen as an exercise of Rooseveltian pragmatism, recognizing the realities of power and seeking only an atmosphere of goodwill. At worst, they could be seen as a prelude to an atomic giveaway and a surrender of principle.

Continuing to be deeply unhappy with his family life and finding little merit in Byrnes's agreements, Truman received Vandenberg. With Acheson's assistance, they produced a press release promising that no production secrets for the atomic bomb would be given away without an effective international inspection system. Then the president left the White House for a few days on the White House yacht, the *Williamsburg*, where he planned to work on a major speech designed to address the frustrating blockage of his domestic program in Congress and an increasingly vexing economic situation. He expected also to spend at least a part of his time escaping from his personal melancholy.[16]

On December 29, stopping to refuel in Newfoundland, Byrnes telegraphed the State Department. He asked Acheson to have the White House arrange air time for a radio report he intended to make the following evening. With Acheson's encouragement, Truman instructed the secretary of state to report to him first. Tired and annoyed by the further hop to Quantico, Virginia, Byrnes met with Truman that afternoon on the *Williamsburg*; both men felt put upon, but neither (despite Truman's later version of the event) was willing to express his emotions. Truman would write later that he had brusquely demanded that Byrnes do a better job of keeping him informed and had extracted an apology from him. Byrnes's account, probably more accurate although self-serving, stresses the cordiality of the meeting while making it clear that Truman at least raised questions about the lack of contact and the timing of the final communiqué. Truman had the secretary stay for dinner and invited him back for New Year's Eve. And, of course, he raised no objection to a radio broadcast, which Byrnes delivered on the evening of December 30.[17]

However pleasant the event, Truman was more accurate than Byrnes in his understanding of the Moscow agreements. Byrnes depicted his mission as one that had accomplished American objectives and restored good feeling among the allies; years later, he would persist in quoting Truman, Vandenberg, and Walter Lippmann as among those delighted with his achievements. In fact, Truman soon came to the conclusion that Byrnes had done nothing to resolve the manifold problems of United States–Soviet relations. He set down his thoughts in a longhand letter to Byrnes, dated January 5, 1946. It displayed his continued unhappiness at the lack of consultation from Moscow, and then went on to address some of the major issues. Citing a report (nearly a month old by the time Truman received a copy of it) by special envoy Mark Ethridge on the brutal establishment of Communist-dominated regimes in Romania and Bulgaria and deploring the presence of Soviet troops and political agitation in Iran, Truman declared his patience at an end:

> There isn't a doubt in my mind that Russia intends an invasion of Turkey and the seizure of the Black Sea Straits to the Mediterranean. Unless Russia is faced with an iron fist and strong language another war is in the making. Only one language do they understand—"how many divisions have you?"
>
> I do not think we should play compromise any longer. . . . I'm tired babying the Soviets.[18]

Truman would claim in his memoirs that he actually read this letter to Byrnes when they met that day. Almost certainly, he did not. He probably had it on his desk and may have referred to it from time to time as he made his points in his typical friendly and nonconfrontational fashion. And even the letter did not declare that Byrnes had been too soft; rather, it criticized the USSR for presenting him with an "accomplished fact" in Iran and behaving in a unilateral, totalitarian fashion. The document was more subtle than Truman later presented it, and one may be certain that his oral delivery had an even softer focus.

IV

Byrnes nonetheless would get the point, if not from Truman then from Vandenberg and Connally, both of whom accompanied him to the United Nations session in London that January. Vandenberg constantly leaked criticism of Byrnes's conciliatory attitude toward the Russians to journalists, who printed it with no real effort to conceal their source. Worse yet, Byrnes's approach bore no fruit. Through January and February, every problem with the USSR continued to fester, and American opinion, both in Washington and throughout the country, rapidly turned against the Soviet Union.

In August 1945, the Gallup Poll had reported that 54 percent of the American people felt that the USSR would cooperate with the United States in building the postwar world; by mid-October, the figure was 44 percent; at the end of February 1946, it had fallen to 35 percent. By mid-March, only 7 percent were willing to say that they "approved" of Soviet foreign policy. Rather than a valiant ally, Stalin's USSR appeared to more and more Americans truculent, totalitarian, and imperialistic. Truman's changing feelings mirrored those of most Americans. He had long harbored a deeply felt anti-Communist and anti-Soviet attitude, had repressed it in the interest of winning the war and the hope of securing the peace, and now found it once again foremost in his mind.[19]

The events of early 1946 did much to push the change along. During January and February, at the organizational meeting of the United Nations in London, bickering and discord characterized the exchanges between the Soviet and American delegations. In Moscow on February 9, Stalin delivered a tough speech that predicted the final crisis of capitalism and exhorted the Russian people to prepare for conflict and sacrifice. It read, William O. Douglas told Secretary Forrestal, like "the Declaration of World War III."[20]

On February 22, George Kennan, temporarily in charge of the American embassy in Moscow, sent the Department of State a lengthy communication analyzing United States–Soviet relations. Stripped to its essentials, it argued that the Stalinist regime was implacably hostile to the democratic West, not amenable to conciliation, and expansionist. It could, however, be contained by a policy of firmness, by the advocacy of American values, and by a positive program for the rest of the world. Truman read it and almost certainly was influenced. Forrestal saw to it that the so-called long telegram was widely disseminated in the upper levels of the administration. Kennan, acting at a strategic moment, had delivered an explanation of Soviet conduct that probably would have been ignored a year earlier but now won an enthusiastic response in Washington. Soon he would be on his way back home to speak to community leaders around the country and to lecture at the National War College.[21]

As much of high-level Washington absorbed Kennan's confidential analysis, Vandenberg went public with a speech to the Senate on February 27. Presented as a report on the London UN meeting, it dwelt heavily on Soviet behavior, depicted the USSR as expansionist, and called on the United States to speak "as plainly upon all occasions as Russia does," vigorously to sustain "its own purposes and its ideals upon all occasions as Russia does," to "abandon this miserable fiction, often encouraged by our own fellow-travelers, that we somehow jeopardize the peace if our candor is as firm as Russia's always is," and to "assume a moral leadership which we have too frequently allowed to lapse." Ostentatiously omitting any praise for Byrnes, the speech attracted praise and wide attention. It also amounted to a demand for a hard line if the Michigan senator and his followers were to continue support for a bipartisan foreign policy.[22]

Byrnes had gauged the direction of the wind, but it is likely that more than politics was involved in his conversion. By the end of February, conciliation had reached a dead end. The concessions in Moscow had in fact produced nothing, not even a better atmosphere, much less the liberalization of the Romanian and Bulgarian governments. By now, the secretary may well have felt worn down and tired of traveling a one-way street. It was one thing, moreover, to give in on two Balkan countries where the United States could do little to contest Soviet control. It would be quite another to acquiesce to a long-term Soviet presence in Iran. Furthermore, in January the USSR had formally demanded joint control (certain in practice to be unilateral Soviet control) of the Turkish straits. Byrnes may have been pushed along by Truman and Vandenberg, but he was no appeaser.

On February 28, one day after Vandenberg's address, Byrnes delivered a "get tough" speech of his own to the Overseas Press Club in New York. The United States, he declared, wanted the Soviets as friends and partners, but "in the interest of world peace and in the interest of our common and traditional friendship we must make it plain that the United States intends to defend the [United Nations] Charter." The United States would oppose such behavior as the stationing of foreign troops in sovereign nations that had not consented to their presence, the seizure of property without reparations agreements, and aggressive designs on the territory of others. America would "act as a great power" in order to preserve both its own security and world peace. Byrnes's new tone struck a responsive chord in Truman, who read an advance copy, underscored several of the tougher passages, and returned it with the notation "Jim, I've read it and like it—A good speech!"[23]

Byrnes had retrieved his position with both the Senate and the president, but it was clear that he no longer could operate with his old freedom of action. In April, after a routine physical examination appeared to show evidence of "myocardial damage" to his heart, a physician warned him that the time had come to slow down. Byrnes did so by confidentially submitting his resignation to Truman to take effect on July 1 or after the completion of the postwar peace treaties. It is revealing that he made no attempt to rescind his resignation when subsequent examinations indicated that the April diagnosis had been faulty.[24]

The next shoe would drop on March 5; former British prime minister Winston Churchill visited the United States at Truman's invitation to speak at Westminster College in Fulton, Missouri. The train trip that Churchill and Truman made to Fulton has generated some wonderful stories: of Truman donning an engineer's cap and driving the locomotive for a short distance; of the way in which the president and his guest quickly moved to a "Harry" and "Winnie" basis; of Churchill's seeming befuddlement at the American game of poker ("Harry, I think I'll risk a shilling on a couple of knaves" and "Harry, what does a sequence count?"); of Churchill's taste for alcohol ("When I was a young subaltern in the South African war, the water was not fit to drink. To make it palatable we had to add whiskey. By diligent effort I learned to like it"); of Churchill's petulance when it proved difficult to find liquid refreshment for him in the dry town of Fulton ("I didn't know whether I was in Fulton, Missouri, or Fulton, Sahara").

But it was the speech that drew the attention of the world. Churchill declared that Russia was drawing an iron curtain down across Europe and called for an Anglo-American "fraternal association" in opposition to Soviet expansion. Tougher and more uncompromising in its implications of near-inevitable East–West hostility than the prior pronouncements of Vandenberg and Byrnes and coming from a figure of world renown, the address forced the attentive portion of the public to undertake a reappraisal of United States–Soviet relations. Scarcely less memorable than Churchill's oratory was the image of President Harry S. Truman sitting on the stage in apparent approval.[25]

Truman nevertheless took care to remain at arm's length from Churchill's message. Officially, he declared that he had not read the speech in advance, although he had been given a detailed overview of it by Byrnes and then by Churchill himself and had sneaked a look at it on the way to Fulton. Writing to his mother and Mary Jane six days later, he said, "I think it did some good, although I am not yet ready to endorse [it]." Byrnes took the same tack. Quite a number of leaders of opinion, however, *were* ready, among them *Time*, the *New York Times*, and the *Wall Street Journal*. Polls demonstrated that Americans deeply distrusted the USSR, but found only 22 percent of Americans willing to endorse an alliance between Britain and the United States. Instinctively or otherwise, Truman had accurately measured popular opinion.[26]

V

By March, the increased tension with the USSR over Iran was reaching a peak, with Soviet troops still sustaining the puppet Azerbaijani regime. In Truman's mind, the issue was one of stark aggression demanding a response. In his January 5 letter to Byrnes, he had laid out his feelings:

Iran was our ally in the war. Iran was Russia's ally in the war. Iran agreed to the free passage of arms. . . . Without these supplies furnished by the United States, Russia would have been ignominiously defeated. Yet now Russia stirs up rebellion and keeps troops on the soil of her friend and ally— Iran.

The analysis was perhaps a bit too pat, but not fundamentally wrong-headed. A March 2 deadline for the withdrawal of Soviet troops passed with no action and soon gave way to a brief war scare fueled by reports of unusual Soviet troop movements. Some alarmists feared a Russian move to occupy Teheran and perhaps also an invasion of Turkey.

Publicly, Truman said nothing to inflame the situation. Privately, he told the new United States ambassador to Moscow, Walter Bedell Smith, "to tell Stalin I had always held him to be a man to keep his word. Troops in Iran after Mar. 2 upset that theory." Stiff diplomatic protests, strong public support for Iran in the UN Security Council, a nationwide radio address by Byrnes calling for Soviet withdrawal, and Smith's own strong representations to Stalin apparently were instrumental in persuading the USSR to back off. Soviet diplomats saved a bit of face by negotiating an agreement (repudiated by the Iranians as soon as it was safe to do so) for an oil concession. The administration would continue to worry about Soviet designs on Iran for months, but the salience of the issue progressively diminished. Truman exaggerated six years later when he declared that he had sent an "ultimatum" to Stalin, but he and Byrnes had engaged in what might be taken as the first successful application of Kennan's formula of containment.[27]

The administration also took steps to reassure Turkey. That March, in a pointed display of courtesy, it sent the USS *Missouri* to Istanbul with the remains of the recently deceased Turkish ambassador to the United States. Six months earlier, Truman had been annoyed at Turkish refusal to include the straits in his scheme for the internationalization of European waterways; he had doubted at that time that the United States could prevent a Soviet seizure. By early 1946, he was focusing single-mindedly on Soviet imperialism. The use of a seagoing hearse equipped with nine sixteen-inch guns may have lacked the virtue of subtlety, but by then the president had decided, as he would later put it, "that Russia would understand firm, decisive language and action much better than diplomatic pleasantries." Originally, the administration had planned to send a full naval task force in the wake of the *Missouri*. Various operational needs, however, prevented one from being assembled until August; then, built around the new aircraft carrier *Franklin D. Roosevelt*, the task force was sent to the eastern Mediterranean to establish an American presence that has endured in the area ever since.[28]

The decision to send the navy was part of a larger assessment of American interests and capabilities. On August 15, Truman approved a State, War, Navy Coordinating Committee policy memorandum that stated a vital interest in protecting Turkey, especially the Turkish straits, against Soviet attack or encroachment. Transmitting the document to Byrnes, who was in Paris for a Council of Foreign Ministers meeting, Dean Acheson informed him that the president had "stated he was prepared to pursue it 'to the end.'" Forrestal wrote in his diary that Truman had remarked, "We might as well find out whether the Russians were bent on world conquest now as in five or ten years." Acheson recalled that it was at this meeting in the Oval Office that one of the military leaders—he inaccurately remembered him as General Eisenhower—whispered a request that Acheson make certain the president understood that he was embarking on a course that could result in war. Truman thereupon took a map of the Middle East from his desk and delivered a brief lecture on the immense strategic importance of the area. "When he finished," Acheson later wrote, "none of us doubted he understood fully all the implications of our recommendations."[29]

By mid-August, the most critical issue of all, the atomic bomb, had to all intents and purposes been hashed out with the Soviet Union. On March 17, in the midst of the Iranian crisis, the Acheson–Lilienthal group finished its recommendations for a plan for the international control of atomic energy. Acheson, probably its dominant spirit, still considered himself a reverent disciple of Henry Stimson; he was determined to find a way of ending the military application of atomic energy. Consequently, the Acheson–Lilienthal proposal omitted detailed enforcement procedures in the belief that the USSR would subscribe to only a nonintrusive plan. The plan assumed that cheating by one power could be rather easily detected and that other powers then either would take steps to enforce atomic disarmament or would initiate their own programs—in brief, an international control treaty would be either self-enforcing or self-destructive. Its authors believed that no other possibility existed for achieving such an agreement and that once it was under way it might be carried along by its momentum. Such assumptions were debatable but worthy of discussion and respect. Unfortunately for Acheson, Lilienthal, and their associates, the plan was politically dead on arrival.

Given the intense concern of Vandenberg and other political leaders on the issue since late 1945 and given the skepticism of such cabinet members as Vinson and Forrestal, it is unlikely that an international control plan of the Acheson–Lilienthal variety ever could have been sold politically. In the wake of the iron curtain speech, the Iranian controversy, and continuing pressure on Turkey, it was certain to be a lost cause. Acheson's first intimations of this came quickly when Byrnes, enmeshed in negotiating the postwar treaties and probably not eager to get involved in the atomic control issue, told him that Bernard Baruch would serve as a special envoy to the United Nations to present an international control plan that would use Acheson and Lilienthal's proposal as a point of departure.[30]

At one level, the choice of Baruch was astute; the old man had great prestige among the general public as a renowned adviser to presidents.

He enjoyed widespread influence on Capitol Hill, where his sage counsel may have been less important than his timely campaign contributions, including the cash infusion that had helped Truman in 1940. Yet Baruch knew nothing about atomic energy, and after one session with him, the Acheson–Lilienthal group despaired of teaching him anything. He also had a massive ego that annoyed everyone with whom he came in contact. "He wants to run the world, the moon, and maybe Jupiter," Truman commented to himself. Most distressing to the drafters of the Acheson–Lilienthal recommendations, he was intent on putting his own brand on the proposal.[31]

In the weeks that followed, the Acheson–Lilienthal proposal became the Baruch Plan. The major alterations in it involved an elaborate series of safeguards, including the suspension of great-power veto rights in the United Nations Security Council on atomic control issues. Baruch presented it to the United Nations General Assembly with great flair ("We face a choice between the quick and the dead"), and then the plan died a slow diplomatic death of endless debate, argument, charge, and counter-charge. Acheson, Lilienthal, and their colleagues were heartsick. The Soviet alternative, a nonenforceable resolution to outlaw all atomic weapons, had no credibility. In the end, the Baruch Plan would serve as little more than a talking point for Truman and his diplomats, providing a vital part of the mythology of Cold War diplomacy—proof of the selflessness of the United States in offering to give up the bomb and share the secrets of peaceful development of atomic energy with the rest of the international community.

Critics asserted that the plan was one-sided and blatantly stacked in favor of the United States. It would have forced the Soviet Union and every other nation interested in atomic development to cease independent development, whereas the United States would retain its own atomic weapons until the final phase of implementation (when they would be handed over to UN control). To use a poker analogy, it would have required all other players to fold their hands while the United States decided whether it wanted to continue playing the game. But only the United States had much of a hand to begin with, and, of the other players, only the USSR had major objections to the Baruch Plan. "For Stalin the danger was not the atomic bomb as such, but the American monopoly of the bomb," writes David Holloway. "The obvious solution . . . was a Soviet atomic bomb."[32]

How did Truman feel? On a personal basis, he undoubtedly preferred Acheson, with whom he had forged a good working relationship, and Lilienthal, whom he positively admired, to Baruch. In his memoirs, he would call the Acheson–Lilienthal report "a great state paper" on one page, but on another "a working paper" that still needed to be shaped into a formal proposal. On a policy basis, he appears to have felt that Baruch was more realistic. Unequivocally aligning himself with the Baruch Plan, he told the old statesman in July, "We should not under any circumstances throw away our gun until we are sure the rest of the world can't arm against us."[33]

However one-sided such an attitude may have been, it presented the only possible hope of negotiating an agreement that would get the support of the Senate and the American people. Public-opinion surveys displayed not only mounting distrust of the USSR, but enormous majorities in favor of producing and maintaining exclusive control of atomic weapons.[34] Perhaps, as the critics have argued, Truman could have successfully overcome these majorities as he would surmount similar formidable opposition to a loan to Great Britain. But it is foolish to compare the two issues on any basis of intensity of feeling or salience in the public consciousness.

Truman and Byrnes, having dealt with the frantic fear of an atomic giveaway expressed by Vandenberg, Connally, and other senators, were tuned in to the real world and established their policy accordingly. Those who thought it possible to have a relationship of trust with Stalinist Russia believed their course disastrous. Those who doubted such a possibility saw it as a prudent expression of the national interest.

VI

Other events and nonevents confirmed the growing chasm between the two major powers of the postwar era. In early 1946, the administration negotiated a $3.75 billion loan to Britain and got it through Congress that summer. The anti-Communist implications—the need to prop up Britain as a barrier to Soviet expansion into the Middle East—were a major consideration in swaying Congress. Truman involved himself in a major way as a leading lobbyist and chief strategist.[35] In the meantime, a Soviet request for a substantial loan became "lost" somewhere in the subterranean reaches of the State Department. Throughout the year, relations with Marshal Tito's pro-Soviet government in Yugoslavia worsened, reaching bottom when the Yugoslav air force shot down two United States Army transport planes in August.

In May 1946, the last vestiges of Soviet–American cooperation in Germany broke down. General Lucius D. Clay and the other Western commanders suspended deliveries of interim reparations to the Soviet zone in retaliation for the USSR's lack of cooperation in establishing a stable German currency and its refusal to send any East German agricultural production to the Western zones. That summer, the United States and Britain merged their areas of occupation into a single economic unit, popularly known as Bizonia. The French, conspicuously independent as always and harshly punitive in their attitude toward Germany, would resist being drawn in until 1948. Already, however, the framework for a separate West German state was being established.

The next step would come on September 6, when Secretary Byrnes would deliver a remarkable speech to a carefully selected group of anti-Nazi German leaders in Stuttgart. There Byrnes declared that it was the

policy of the United States to rehabilitate Germany politically and economically, to establish a liberal democratic government, to assist in rebuilding the German economy, and to readmit Germany to the company
of free nations. In case anyone was unclear about the motivation behind
the speech, key passages clarified it:

> If complete unification cannot be secured, we shall do everything in our
> power to secure maximum possible unification. . . . We do not want Ger-
> many to become the satellite of any power.
> [A]s long as there is an occupation army in Germany, American armed
> forces will be part of that occupation army.[36]

America, Byrnes had declared, wanted to rebuild Germany, protect
it from the Soviet Union, and (implicitly) make it a democratic bulwark
against Soviet expansion. The phrase "Cold War" had not yet made its
way into popular discourse, but chill winds already were blowing with
increasing intensity over Europe.

Sometime that summer, Truman, frustrated and concerned with the
growing agenda of American–Soviet disagreement, asked Clark Clifford
to prepare a summary specifically enumerating all the agreements that
the USSR had broken. Clifford turned the assignment over to George
Elsey, who devoted much of his time to it for several weeks and then gave
it to Clifford, who added his signature and a covering letter of transmittal. It would reach Truman's desk on September 24, 1946, four days after
the ejection of Henry Wallace from the cabinet. The report, more than
fifty pages long when it finally was printed as an appendix to the memoirs of Arthur Krock in 1968,[37] was meant primarily to be a compendium
rather than a policy paper. It nonetheless reflected Elsey's perspective as
a talented amateur who had witnessed diplomacy with the USSR firsthand during the presidencies of both Roosevelt and Truman and was
attempting to provide a coherent, overall reference point both for himself and for the president.

Drawing heavily on the pessimistic analyses of George Kennan and
perhaps hoping to influence Truman toward a more generous defense
budget, he produced a document that defined the problem of Russia as
ideological in origin and military in practical application. He may have
misunderstood Kennan in emphasizing military containment, but if so it
was a common misunderstanding—so common that it indicates an im-
precision in Kennan's own thinking. The relevant points could be found
in an outline that Elsey placed at the beginning of the report:

> Soviet leaders believe that a conflict is inevitable between the U.S.S.R. and
> capitalist states, and their duty is to prepare the Soviet Union for this con-
> flict. . . .
> Soviet-American agreements have been adhered to, "interpreted," or
> violated as Soviet officials from time to time have considered it to be in the
> best interests of the Soviet Union in accordance with the Soviet policy of
> increasing their own power at the expense of other nations. . . .

The U.S.S.R. is improving its military position with respect to the United States. . . .

The U.S.S.R. is seeking wherever possible to weaken the military position and the influence of the United States abroad, as, for example, in China.

The U.S.S.R. is actively directing subversive movements and espionage within the United States. . . .

. . . [T]he United States must assume that the U.S.S.R. may at any time embark on a course of expansion effected by open warfare and therefore must maintain sufficient military strength to restrain the Soviet Union.

The United States should seek, by cultural, intellectual, and economic interchange, to demonstrate to the Soviet Union that we have no aggressive intentions and that peaceable coexistence of Capitalism and Communism is possible.

Much of the report was matter of fact, but its conclusion, "United States Policy toward the Soviet Union," contained a series of recommendations that dwelt heavily on military preparedness. Its most memorable declaration, oft quoted by historians, was fearful: "The United States must be prepared to wage atomic and biological warfare if necessary."[38]

Truman had to cope with this problem in the context of a rapidly changing political situation that left him far from being a free agent in foreign policy. Congress, as personified by Senators Connally and Vandenberg, pushed him in the general direction of a hard line toward the Soviet Union. Neither man could be ignored, in part because of the political and institutional forces they represented, in part because both had well-developed senses of their own importance.

The congressional climate was also influenced by constituency pressures that were especially telling within the Democratic party. The increasing Soviet grip on Eastern Europe stirred outrage among working-class ethnoreligious blocs that appeared to have been cemented into the party by the New Deal. Restiveness among Polish-Americans, for example, was especially discernible in Vandenberg's Michigan; there were similar stirrings among other Eastern European groups throughout the industrial heartland. An overlapping commitment to Catholicism intensified a vehement anti-Soviet attitude. Neither Truman nor any other Democrat with a memory could have failed to recall that the same sort of cracks had occurred within the party during the Spanish Civil War. Republicans could see emerging problems with the USSR as an opportunity; Democrats, as a threat to the retention of a core constituency. Northern Democrats in Congress, many of whom had been caught up in the pro-Soviet tide during the war, quickly backtracked in 1946, either standing mute or looking for plausible straddles. The most vocal of those who kept the faith, such as Claude Pepper of Florida and Glen Taylor of Idaho, came from states not known for large ethnic-Catholic working classes.

Within the administration, moreover, what might loosely be called the pro-Soviet group declined in size and influence. Truman had become president at a time when the USSR was still an ally; he had inherited a large group of subordinates and advisers who were dedicated to the belief that the alliance could be held together and the new United Nations made to work. Some were fundamentally patrician conservatives (Stimson, Acheson); others were New Deal liberals (Hopkins, Wallace, Eleanor Roosevelt). With the exception of Joseph Davies, none were uncritical of the Soviet state; but cognizant of its overwhelming sacrifices during the war, they were prepared to be forgiving.

Davies, very influential with Truman through Potsdam, had become a peripheral figure by the beginning of 1946, his advice no longer sought by either Byrnes or Truman. Hopkins was dead. Eleanor Roosevelt, appointed to the American delegation to the United Nations, remained optimistic but was already in the early stages of a disillusionment that would convert her, in Joseph Lash's phrase, into a "reluctant Cold Warrior." Only Henry Wallace clung doggedly to his hopes.

The anti-Soviet group had become more influential than anyone might have supposed possible in April 1945. Leahy had the president's ear daily. Forrestal, although not high in Truman's personal esteem, got his message across through sheer persistence. By mid-1946, Stimson was a supporter of the Baruch Plan and an advocate of building a nuclear stockpile if the Soviets did not accept it. Acheson, acting secretary of state during Byrnes's frequent absences and increasingly influential with Truman, time and again counseled firmness toward the Soviet Union.

What was most important, however, was a movement into the anti-Soviet camp of aides and advisers who had staked out no previous turf on foreign policy, people who like Truman were fundamentally centrists. They included Fred Vinson, Clinton Anderson, and newcomer Clark Clifford. All—like Truman—were liberal-minded pragmatists, sensitive to political considerations to be sure, but also sharing a frame of reference dominated by the experience of making compromises built on shared assumptions. Gradually, they came to the conclusion that the Soviet leaders possessed a very different view of the world, that therefore no tolerable compromises were likely with them, and that Stalin was more than just a tough political boss. Truman's own conceptual journey appears to have been very similar to theirs.

VII

It was against this backdrop that Truman had to deal with Henry Wallace's efforts to change the direction of American foreign policy. Wallace presented a difficult problem for Truman on personal, political, and policy levels. He was the person from whom Truman had taken away the vice presidency and, by extension, the presidency—a fact that neither could forget. To almost all New Deal Democrats, he was the legitimate heir of FDR, still a figure with such clout that Truman told Byrnes he was one of only two people who *had* to be kept in the administration. (The other was Eleanor Roosevelt.)[39] Both these considerations made Truman uncomfortable with a man who, reserved and other-worldly in manner, was not easy to deal with in the best of circumstances.

Wallace himself, as his diary indicates, was a decent individual who wanted to do the right thing. He also had little respect for Truman and harbored a bit of resentment toward him. All things considered, he would have been less (or possibly more) than human had he felt otherwise. The emerging Cold War poisoned what would have been a touchy but probably manageable relationship in more normal times. By September 1946, Wallace was the last major American politician to remain a true believer in the wartime alliance and World War II Popular Front against fascism.

After the September 21, 1945, cabinet meeting on atomic energy, Wallace became almost obsessively concerned with Soviet–American relations and the atomic bomb. The major threats to world peace and stability, he believed, came from Great Britain, the Catholic Church, and the remnants of fascism that they backed. The USSR, by contrast, appeared passive, peace loving, interested only in protecting itself, and incessantly provoked by the atomic monopoly enjoyed by the United States. American militarists, he was convinced, wanted to "encircle" the Soviet Union through the construction of a ring of air bases from the Aleutians to Iceland. It is no exaggeration to say that by the end of 1945—through a process of discarding inconvenient facts, accepting improbable accusations, and imputing the worst motives to those with whom he disagreed— Wallace had codified these musings into a unified conspiracy theory. Increasingly, he saw his primary mission less as managing the Department of Commerce than as reversing Truman's foreign policy.[40]

He missed no opportunity to give Truman unsolicited foreign policy advice, all of it slanted in the direction of conciliation and economic ties with the Soviet Union. It was not that he was unreservedly pro-Soviet— he criticized Communism as an economic and political system—but he was willing to extend the benefit of the doubt to Russia at every step. He urged Truman to support a loan to the USSR, seeing such a move as the basis of a mutually supportive economic relationship that would provide a foundation for closer political ties. Above all, he privately criticized the Baruch Plan and argued that it should be considerably loosened to respond to Russian complaints.

His behavior must have annoyed Truman from several different directions: a secretary of commerce ranging far outside his responsibilities, opinions with which he disagreed but could not shut off because of Wallace's political importance, and a probable sense that he was being patronized by a subordinate who thought the wrong man was president. All the same, persuaded that he had to string Wallace along, Truman was friendly and went out of his way to agree with him on such generalities as the need for peace, balance between Britain and the USSR, and atomic control.

On July 23, 1946, Wallace gave Truman a letter containing what amounted to his full blueprint for improved Soviet–American relations.

Truman expressed interest, avoided dispute, and promised to pass the letter along to Byrnes. Of course, nothing happened. Truman was trying to manage Wallace in much the same way as Roosevelt had dealt with Stalin during World War II—by a policy of amiable postponement of differences to achieve the objective of preserving a winning coalition. In politics as in diplomacy, such an act could not go on forever. Truman apparently hoped to avoid discord at least until after the midterm elections. Wallace, who probably planned to resign toward the end of the year, gave no indication that he wanted a confrontation.[41]

Instead, things came to a head unpredictably. Wallace, scheduled to speak at a rally of left-liberal groups at Madison Square Garden in New York on September 12, let himself be persuaded to make a foreign policy address. As drafted, the speech was his fullest public statement yet of views that clearly diverged from administration diplomacy. Instead of submitting the speech to the State Department for clearance, he took it directly to Truman on September 10.

After a brief discussion of Wallace's recent trip to Mexico, the secretary thrust the speech in front of Truman and insisted on going over it with him "page by page," as Wallace wrote in his diary. Truman, preoccupied by domestic problems that included a major shipping strike and an emerging meat shortage, foolishly accepted what should have been a staff function. Lacking the time and circumstances for reflection, eager to mollify Wallace, distracted that he was falling behind in his appointment schedule, and led along by his subordinate, he failed to grasp the significance of what he was reading. For example, Wallace emphasized the innocuous sentence "I am neither anti-British nor pro-British, neither anti-Russian nor pro-Russian." Truman declared, "By God, Henry, that is our foreign policy!" At other, doubtless similar, points, he indicated enthusiastic approval.

Wallace got Truman's permission to communicate their agreement, although it appears that Truman thought it applied to only the sentence about maintaining detachment from the ambitions of both Great Britain and the Soviet Union. Returning to his office at the Commerce Department, Wallace remarked to his chief assistant that he was uncertain whether Truman had understood the implications of the speech. He did not call the president to check on the point; nor did he refrain from putting out advance word of White House approval along with the text of the speech itself. Truman would pay a stiff price for this lack of punctiliousness.[42]

On the afternoon of September 12, Truman held a press conference at which a reporter asked if he agreed with Wallace's address. Yes, Truman replied. Just the passage about standing between Britain and Russia or the whole speech? The whole speech, declared the president, charging into territory that demanded a long, elliptical detour. Did he regard it as a departure from Byrnes's policy. He did not. The thoughts of the two men were "exactly in line." Truman had just shown how his "crisp and decisive" style could turn a contretemps into a disaster.[43]

The effect of the speech suddenly became all the greater. Wallace delivered it that evening to an audience that was heavily pro-Soviet; when it booed some passages critical of the USSR, he deleted others. His talk was the most moderate of the evening; in fact, it came in for some strong criticism the next morning in the Communist party paper, the *Daily Worker*. Yet in the real world that existed outside the left-wing hothouse that Madison Square Garden had become that night, the speech had approximately the impact of a medium-size asteroid colliding with the earth. Truman could agree with much of the address, but there was one serious sticking point: Wallace explicitly endorsed a Soviet sphere of political influence in Eastern Europe. Even here, he did not go beyond what seems to have been Truman's personal impulse a year earlier, and he explicitly argued for an economic open door in the region. But neither did he face up to events of the past year that had demonstrated that the USSR had no interest in so limited an arrangement; nor did he mention Iran, Turkey, or other points of difficulty.[44]

What he had done was go just far enough to indicate serious disagreement with the public foreign policy that Byrnes was advocating at that moment, at yet another Council of Foreign Ministers conference in Paris. Furthermore, his address could be seen as a reply to Byrnes's speech at Stuttgart just six days earlier. It was not altogether surprising that Truman could give the address a quick read under somewhat difficult circumstances and decide he could go along with it. Yet given the setting in which it was delivered—at a rally of the far left, with Byrnes in Europe trying to squeeze a modicum of representation for democratic forces in Eastern Europe—it was less surprising that the result was a diplomatic and political firestorm. Byrnes, backed by Connally and Vandenberg, was furious; they all informed Truman that the cabinet was not big enough for two secretaries of state.

Quickly realizing the dimensions of his mistake, the president spent the next week trying to recover; he looked for some formula that would allow him to keep both Byrnes and Wallace in the cabinet. He had not meant to approve the speech, Truman lamely announced, just Wallace's right to deliver it. Then, to try to satisfy Byrnes, he negotiated, or thought he had, an agreement that Wallace would make no more foreign policy speeches for the duration of the Paris conference.

All to no effect. Wallace's July 23 policy letter to Truman was leaked to the press in another misunderstanding with the White House. From Paris, Byrnes, with Connally and Vandenberg at his side, still demanded Wallace's head. Wallace himself, displaying all the instincts of a kamikaze pilot, made it clear that any silence would be brief and that he would continue to speak out on foreign policy. Backed into a corner, Truman found himself with no choice but to request Wallace's resignation.

Throughout the entire episode, Truman had been outwardly cordial with Wallace, even through a meeting on September 18 in which he and Charles Ross spent nearly two and a half hours negotiating with the wayward cabinet member almost as if he were a visiting head of state. Characteristically, however, Truman seethed inwardly. The day after the September 18 meeting, he had written in his diary:

> He is a pacifist 100 percent. He wants us to disband our armed forces, give Russia our atomic secrets and trust a bunch of adventurers in the Kremlin Politbureau. I do not understand a "dreamer" like that. The German-American Bund under Fritz Kuhn was not half so dangerous. The Reds, phonies and the "parlor pinks" seem to be banded together and are becoming a national danger.
>
> I am afraid they are a sabotage front for Uncle Joe Stalin.[45]

The next day, he sent Wallace a furious handwritten letter, probably somewhat along the lines of the diary entry, asking for his resignation. Wallace complied at once. In a demonstration of his innate decency, he also called Truman and offered to return the letter with the promise that it would not be copied. Truman, agreeable as always in direct conversation, thanked him, sent someone from the White House to get it, and apparently had it destroyed. With that lame ending and final personal embarrassment, Byrnes had been vindicated, the administration had regained some semblance of unity, and the single most charismatic leader of the Democratic party had become a loose cannon in the world of American politics just six weeks before the congressional elections.[46]

VIII

Truman, feeling depressed and beaten down, told Charlie Ross that he was going to make a hermit of himself for a while. He then left to spend the weekend on the *Williamsburg*. It was from there that he would appoint Averell Harriman, who had left Moscow to become United States ambassador to Britain, as secretary of commerce. A widely praised selection, it did a bit to ameliorate a bad situation. As he invariably did after a weekend on the yacht, the president returned to the White House refreshed, ready for another week, and disposed to look at the bright side of things.

Yet he must have been puzzled by the way in which events had broken. Truman in fact still believed that his disagreements with Wallace on foreign policy were less than fundamental. Far from being led along by warmongers, as Wallace believed, he seems to have felt that military conflict with the Russians was never a real possibility. It is doubtful that he would have committed American forces had Soviet troops marched into Turkey or Iran. The day after firing Wallace, he wrote to John Nance Garner:

> There is too much loose talk about the Russian situation. We are not going to have any shooting trouble with them but they are tough bargainers and always ask for the whole earth, expecting maybe to get an acre. The situation, I think, is cleared up since yesterday and from now on we will have smoother sailing.[47]

After reading the Clifford–Elsey report, which came to him on September 24, he was so alarmed by its belligerent tone that he rousted Clifford out of bed at 7:00 on a Sunday morning and told him to get every extant copy into a safe at the White House. No doubt a large part of his motivation was fear of leaks to the press, which might print selected passages as confirmation of Wallace's warmongering charge. But it seems equally true, as he told Wallace on two separate occasions in September, that he had not yet fully given up on a general accord with the Soviet Union, especially if he could deal on a man-to-man basis with Stalin. He even told Wallace that he was willing to work to get a loan to the USSR through Congress once all the peace treaties were signed.[48]

At the same time, Truman could wax indignant about Soviet behavior that offended liberal and democratic principles or threatened the sovereignty of smaller nations. Here he lacked Wallace's illusions—or willingness to look in the other direction. As late as September 1946, his personal attitudes toward the USSR remained mixed and allowed room for hope about the future. He did not believe that his move in the direction of a hard line was irrevocable. What he did not fully understand was that events would soon make it so.

21

"BEING PRESIDENT IS LIKE RIDING A TIGER": THE TRIALS OF LIBERALISM IN A CONSERVATIVE AGE, 1945–1946

Before V-J Day, war and diplomacy had occupied most of Truman's time. Suddenly, it became necessary for him to address domestic problems in a reasonably comprehensive fashion. On September 6, just days after the Japanese had signed the instrument of surrender aboard the battleship *Missouri*, he submitted a 16,000-word, 21-point message to Congress. Designed to maintain prosperity beyond the war years and to demonstrate that "the foundation of my administration" would be "liberalism and progressivism," it laid out in overwhelming detail the president's program for America. A constant undercurrent ran through it: a sense of confidence that after fifteen years of depression and New Deal and wartime big government, the American people wanted an expanding welfare state and a quasi-controlled economy.[1]

The issue found a focus in the problem of "reconversion." The term suggests a set of crashingly dull and technical problems in economics. Yet in 1946, it encompassed the hopes of real people who wanted, after years of sacrifice, to live the good life but feared more deprivation. Truman and many other Americans remembered the way in which the post–World War I reconversion had degenerated into a ruinous boom-and-bust. Others recalled the Great Depression, listened to economists and policy makers debate whether it was going to return, and wondered whether they would find jobs as they left the armed forces or were laid off from defense plants.

Reconversion also involved a struggle between the political parties that had been reshaped by the Great Depression. It pitted most Democrats (heavily influenced by liberals, labor, and the interests of the urban working classes) against most Republicans (prone to represent the business-oriented middle classes and commercial farmers). Individuals on either side typically counted themselves among the virtuous, struggling against either entrenched greed or class envy. Although not without applicability to the real world, this dualistic viewpoint obfuscated as much as it revealed. At another, more basic, level, reconversion was less a struggle between two large contending forces than a pluralistic scramble in which many different groups pursued their own material interests with little regard to the needs of others. It marked a demoralizing end to the sense of national purpose that had been central to the war years and now was replaced by perceptions of social dislocation and individual inconvenience. Without depression and mass unemployment, moreover, there was no natural, responsive coalition for a Democratic president to rally.

Truman's task was somehow to manage the largest economic transition from war to peace in American history in a way that would secure prosperity, maintain the loyalty of Democratic core constituencies, make the case for his larger liberal agenda, and attract sufficient votes from the larger middle class to continue the Democrats as a majority party. Instead, by the end of 1946, his popularity was at a low point and his party defeated. The greater part of his problem stemmed from the frustrations of economic reconversion, but that and other aspects of his domestic program had a common feature—an attempt to govern by the principles of New Deal liberalism in a conservative age.

II

As the summer of 1945 ended, a majority of Americans regarded Truman as a "middle-of-the-road" president, liked him in that role, and wanted him to maintain it.[2] He nevertheless issued a contrary political self-definition in his September 6 message to Congress. The document was put together in the crowded days at the end of the war largely by Sam Rosenman, following a general mandate from the president. Far too long and dull to be an oral address, it probably was read in its entirety only by those whose profession required it. Essentially, it consisted of two lists.

The first explained the basic policies and objectives of reconversion: the rapid demobilization of the armed forces, expeditious transition to a consumer economy, and temporary continuance of wartime economic controls, which would be phased out as soon as the economy had converted back to its normal civilian character.

The second list itemized Truman's twenty-one-point legislative program. It ranged from the mundane to the near-revolutionary: from expansion of such New Deal programs as unemployment compensation and the minimum wage to executive reorganization and disposal of surplus property; from "full-employment legislation" and retention of the wartime Fair Employment Practices Committee (FEPC) to continuance of the military draft and universal military training; from extensive housing legislation and establishment of a National Science Foundation to small-business assistance and enhanced veterans' benefits; from large-scale public-works programs, including "regional development of the natural resources of our great river valleys," to fair settlement of Lend-Lease obligations and international economic development. The message also promised bills for a national health insurance plan, an expanded Social Security system, and an education program. The health plan followed in November; the Social Security and education programs would come later.[3]

Perceiving the document as "a combination of a first inaugural and a first State of the Union message," Truman regarded its transmittal as the defining act of his presidency, a chance to tell the nation (and perhaps more importantly the Democratic party) just who he was ideologically and politically. He had chosen, without any real qualms, to cast himself in the tradition of Franklin Roosevelt, partly in the belief that such was good politics but also because he was more comfortable with New Dealism than with any other political worldview. It was not that he cared to appeal to the "professional liberals." Upon hearing that *PM*, the left-wing New York tabloid, was ecstatic about his manifesto, he remarked to his staff that possibly he was on the wrong track after all. But he took pride in the draftsmanship of Roosevelt's old speech writer Rosenman, a liberal whom he admired as a man of practicality.[4]

Nonetheless, the message was the literary equivalent of a copious kitchen sink overflowing with pots, pans, and dinnerware of wildly diverse patterns and origins, probably because Rosenman had no mandate to edit out proposals from various executive agencies. The document mixed domestic and foreign policy, mingled important policy initiatives with housekeeping measures, and demonstrated no sense of priorities. In all, it presented a case study of how not to lead Congress.

Truman, in fact, was less concerned with leading Congress than with catering to its sensibilities while staking out his own positions. Having been a senator under Roosevelt, he was acutely aware of the seething resentment that he and many of his colleagues had felt at being pushed around by a strong president. Overconfident in his ability to deal with leading members of Congress on a personal basis, he believed that conciliation and quiet negotiations might yield more results than demands.[5]

The president met about once a week with the "Big Four" Democratic leaders in Congress (Speaker of the House Sam Rayburn, House Majority Leader John McCormack, Senate Majority Leader Alben Barkley, and Senate President Pro-tem Kenneth McKellar). On these occasions, he stated his priorities and pressed for action, however tactfully. At the beginning of 1946, he reluctantly—and ineffectively—decided to try the Roosevelt method of appealing directly to the people in a radio address. Its failure to accomplish much left him less leverage on Capitol Hill than ever. (Remarkably, few commentators at the time recalled that such tactics had worked well for Roosevelt only during the early New Deal, when he had a Congress that fairly demanded presidential direction and was ideologically compatible. Truman never would be so lucky.)

How much of the September 6 message he expected to see translated into legislation is uncertain. No politician with a grip on reality could have expected the FEPC to survive a Senate filibuster. Despite (or perhaps because of) the war, universal military training had scant public support. National health insurance was little more than a hobbyhorse of liberal reformers inspired by the example of the British Labour government. A National Science Foundation had no influential constituency. The proposals relating to economic reconversion faced substantial opposition from Republican and southern Democratic conservatives, antagonistic toward generous social programs and vociferously hostile toward centralized economic management. Truman had to know that a few of his proposals were dead on arrival and that substantial compromise would be necessary on others. Not insincere in recommending them, he was too pragmatic to expect their passage.[6]

In a very real sense, he damaged himself with voters who wanted "moderation" by advocating a left-of-center program. Knowing that Congress would not give him some of the most important items, he also had risked being typed as a failure. Yet it would have been out of character, and quite probably politically dangerous, for him to spend the next three years as a chief executive who stood for nothing much of anything. The state of the Democratic party forced him to make choices; liberals, conservatives, labor, blacks, farmers, and businessmen all demanded to know his stance on policies vitally important to their interests and view of the world. And there was no reason to believe that a mushy middle-of-the-roadism would appeal to the larger electorate over the long haul. After September 6, 1945, everyone who listened *knew* where Harry Truman stood.

III

Many of the issues before Truman involved practical urgencies related to economic reconversion. At least four, however, had other implications. Civil rights, full-employment legislation, universal military training, and management of atomic energy possessed an especially strong ideological tone that overshadowed practical policy implications. The positions that Truman took on each told a lot about both the range and the inner contradictions of his worldview.

His civil rights record displayed a surface consistency that belied deeply ambivalent feelings, exemplified by the paternalistic racism of his youth, his deep faith in equal opportunity, his distaste for social mixing, and his politician's instinctive respect for all interest groups, blacks included. He remained a racist only in the narrowest sense of the word and was considerably less so than the vast majority of white Americans in the years after World War II. In private discourse, he was still capable of resorting to "nigger" to describe a black man he disliked, but in public he was more careful about his language on race than on most matters. Withal, he could be especially touchy about being challenged or questioned by a black man. At his first press conference, a black journalist asked him to outline his position on civil rights. He retorted, a bit sharply and defensively, "I will give you some advice. All you need to do is read the Senate record of one Harry S. Truman."[7]

It was in that spirit that Truman supported the retention of the beleagured Fair Employment Practices Committee, albeit with little hope that Congress would buy the proposal. His relative lack of passion would be mistaken for hypocrisy by some civil rights advocates at the time and by numerous scholars later. As it was, Congress grudgingly gave the FEPC enough money to wind up its affairs by early 1946; Senate filibusterers easily blocked anything more. In December, as the agency was being talked to death on Capitol Hill, its most prominent member, Charles H. Houston, resigned after the White House refused to let it release a directive of questionable legality. The other members stayed on only after Truman signed an executive order affirming the committee's continuance and issued a directive for fair employment in the executive branch.[8]

One other embarrassment occurred in October 1945, after the Daughters of the American Revolution refused to allow black pianist Hazel Scott, the current wife of Representative Adam Clayton Powell, Jr., to perform in Constitution Hall. Powell asked Bess Truman to boycott a tea that the DAR had scheduled in honor of the First Lady. Bess issued a reply deploring the DAR policy, but stating that she would attend the function as scheduled; Powell characterized her as "the last lady of the land." Enraged at Powell, whom he accurately saw as engaging in self-promotion, Truman released a statement backing Bess's decision. An easily dramatized event, it made him look like a segregationist. Privately referring to Powell as "a smart aleck and a rabble rouser," the president barred him from the White House.[9]

Truman looked around for other ways to appease black voters and advance the cause of civil rights. About a month after Houston's resignation, he fired the governor of the Virgin Islands, a white politician who had treated the job as a sinecure, and appointed in his place William Hastie, a black federal judge who had been a Roosevelt appointee.[10] As welcome as it might be, the appointment did nothing for the average black person.

Periodically informed of violent attacks, some of them deadly, against blacks, the president decided in September 1946 to appoint a committee to study problems of racial violence. "I am very much in earnest on this thing," he wrote in a memorandum to his minority affairs aide David Niles, "and I'd like very much to have you push it with everything you have." Niles and Attorney General Tom Clark suggested an investigation of the broader state of civil rights. At the beginning of 1947, Truman named a committee of prominent civil rights activists. It was likely to advocate major adjustments to the status quo.[11]

While civil rights was important to the black community, the issue was far overshadowed, even among the most devout liberals, by the fight for full employment. A full-employment bill, directly descended from the Kilgore-Truman-Murray bill of 1944, embodied the new liberal consensus on economic policy and the maintenance of prosperity. Using Keynesian economics as an intellectual point of departure, it required the government to commit itself to a "full employment budget," engaging in whatever compensatory spending was necessary to ensure a job for virtually everyone in the workforce. Henry Wallace forcefully stated the formula in his little book *Sixty Million Jobs* (1945), written with the assistance of about every major liberal economist in the country. Thus in supporting the full-employment bill, Truman reaffirmed a position that he had taken as a senator and, one might think, established himself as a liberal leader.[12]

Conceptually and politically, however, the stance was probably ill-advised. A full-employment budget could be a useful tool of economic policy, but to make it a rigid requirement was to substitute a near-algebraic formula for creative leadership. Nor, to use a later phrase, could one be certain that even wise policy makers were capable of "fine-tuning" the large and complex American economy. Politically, the bill had to go through a Congress run by moderate to conservative Democrats reflexively skeptical of neo–New Dealish nostrums. Ideologically concerned with much more than civil rights, they openly expressed their feelings that a higher minimum wage was bad for business, that generous unemployment compensation encouraged idleness, and that labor unions were conspiracies against the public interest. Truman's revered old friend Sam Rayburn, possibly spooked by the right-wing effort to defeat him in 1944, gave administration liberal initiatives lip service, but made no secret of his discomfort with them.[13]

Truman had no problem with the conceptual aspects of these proposals, which probably appealed to the rationalist, administrative side of his personality. Politically, he surely saw his support as an asset in his relationship with the liberal–labor forces. He took the bill seriously, spoke out vigorously for it, and personally lobbied key legislators. To get it through Congress, he appointed a cabinet committee chaired by Fred Vinson.[14] Nevertheless, by the time it got out of the Senate, the bill had been shorn of provisions affirming the right to a job and stating a federal policy of underwriting full employment. Alben Barkley grumbled that it now "promised anyone needing a job the right to go out and look for one."[15] In the House, the legislation was thoroughly redrafted. What finally emerged for a vote was, in the eyes of the original sponsors, a pathetic shadow of their creation. Yet the administration decided that it was better than nothing. With Vinson and Wallace pushing hard, despairing liberal Democrats cast their votes for the House substitute and hoped for the best in a conference committee.

The result, the Employment Act of 1946, contained an affirmation of the goal of maximum employment, required the president to submit an annual economic report to Congress, established the Council of Economic Advisers (CEA) to assist him, and set up the Joint Committee on the Economic Report in Congress. The act contained no guarantees, no firm policies or policy mechanisms, no embodiment whatever of the liberal Keynesian ideal—and no political credit for Harry Truman.

On this and numerous other issues, liberal Democrats increasingly saw the president as ineffective; they developed a nostalgia for Franklin D. Roosevelt, who became in their memories an overpowering leader capable of blasting needed legislation out of Congress with a single radio address. Given Truman's clear weaknesses as a public speaker, the comparison, however historically inaccurate, was devastating.[16]

The new Council of Economic Advisers provided no services that could not have been supplied by the Bureau of the Budget, but at least it established an institutionalized mechanism for presidential economic initiatives. The liberal Democrats hoped to staff it with progressive politicians (such as lame-duck senator Robert La Follette, Jr.) and dynamic, policy-oriented New Dealish economists.[17] Truman decided on a more diverse group, neither excitingly liberal nor neanderthal conservative, capable of providing him with advice but unable to seize control of economic policy: Edwin Nourse of the Brookings Institution, chairman; John D. Clark, businessman and former dean of the University of Nebraska School of Business; and Leon Keyserling, New Deal bureaucrat and former aide to Senator Robert F. Wagner.

On matters of policy, Nourse and Clark were middle-of-the-roaders open to Keynesian formulas; Keyserling was a dedicated social reformer. But in their conceptions of their jobs, they differed considerably. Nourse, a former president of the American Economic Association who was a year older than Truman, saw his function as that of a nonpartisan technician.[18] Keyserling envisioned his mission as that of aide to the president and policy advocate. Clark was willing to follow whichever cues he received from the Oval Office. In the beginning, Truman himself was probably drawn to both conceptions. But after a time, the needs of the practical politician would overwhelm the ideals of the disinterested administrator.[19]

IV

During the first few months of the atomic era, Truman had been forced to concentrate on the international ramifications of the weapon that had ended the war. By the late fall of 1945, however, he had to confront the problem of nuclear control at home. In a special message to Congress on

October 3, he requested the establishment of the United States Atomic Energy Commission, with full control over atomic research and broad authority to engage in scientific research and development. Because of the thinness of the White House staff and a multiplicity of pressing concerns, he let the War Department draft the legislation. At stake were issues of military versus civilian control and presidential power.[20]

The initial bill, sponsored by Representative Andrew Jackson May of Kentucky and Senator Edwin Johnson of Colorado, provided for substantial military membership on a part-time commission that would appoint a full-time administrator, likely an army general. In effect, it would continue the administrative structure of the wartime Manhattan Project. At a press conference on October 18, Truman responded, perhaps evasively, to the question of whether he was satisfied with the May-Johnson bill by saying that he thought so but had not studied the details.[21]

If he did not know by then, he doubtless soon learned that the atomic energy administrator would not be a presidential appointee. May and Johnson's bypass of the presidency must have redoubled already considerable qualms about handing over control of atomic energy to a clique of bureaucrats in uniform. In early 1946, he endorsed an alternative bill sponsored by Brian McMahon of Connecticut, chairman of the newly established Select Senate Committee on Atomic Energy. It provided for strong presidential control over a wholly civilian commission. When Secretary of the Navy Forrestal and Secretary of War Patterson continued to back the May-Johnson bill, Truman ordered them to cease their support.

After a long legislative fight, the Atomic Energy Act passed Congress in substantially the form proposed by McMahon; Truman signed it on August 1, 1946. To appease the armed forces and their advocates, the final version provided for a military liaison committee; a general advisory committee, designed to give representation to the needs of nuclear scientists, balanced even this modest (and prudent) input. To demonstrate his seriousness about strong, liberal, civilian leadership for the new Atomic Energy Commission, Truman appointed as its first chairman David E. Lilienthal.

One of Truman's first acts as president had been to reappoint Lilienthal to the directorship of the Tennessee Valley Authority over the opposition of the powerful, curmudgeonly Tennessee senator Kenneth McKellar. ("McKellar will have a shit hemorrhage," he had told Jonathan Daniels with twinkling eyes and a laugh.) In early 1947, Lilienthal came up for confirmation before a Senate controlled by Republicans, many of whom saw him as a fuzzy-minded enemy of private enterprise and soft on Communism. After weeks of controversy in which Truman never wavered, Lilienthal won confirmation. By then, he had developed a deep affection and admiration for the president who had twice stood by him.[22]

Despite his firm antimilitary stance on atomic energy, Truman's repeated espousal of universal military training for able-bodied young men marked him as a militarist in the eyes of many of his critics. In fact, UMT was yet another example of his wariness of the professional military and an affirmation of the American ideal of the citizen soldier. He wanted all young men between the ages of eighteen and twenty to receive a year of basic military training without actually being inducted into any of the armed services. They then would spend several years in a general reserve that could be activated quickly and divided among the specific forces in times of national emergency. In tandem with a substantially enlarged regular reserve and national guard, the structure theoretically would allow the rapid mobilization of millions of civilians, trained and ready, while avoiding the expense and undemocratic influence of a large, permanent military caste.

Truman's enthusiasm for UMT doubtless stemmed from his own experience in the National Guard—the discipline, the learning, the comradeship, the training in leadership, the sense of pulling together in a mighty endeavor. In his more lyrical descriptions, he made the program sound like an extended post-secondary-school class in citizenship and physical fitness. It was not just as a matter of political tactics that he preferred to drop the word "military" and call it a universal training program.[23]

Universal military training never came close to passage. In reality, it would have been both expensive and unlikely to produce graduates able to spring into military service without extensive retraining. Many critics thought that it possessed totalitarian implications. In the end, Truman's biggest problem may have been with the mothers of America, who had been taught by the war to regard military service as life threatening and were not inclined to send their children off to any kind of training camps. Although Gallup Polls taken in late 1945 seemed to show overwhelming public support, there was little passion behind it. The opposition, by contrast militant and well organized, included numerous labor unions, the churches, and many educators.

The rapid reduction of the armed forces also removed any sense of need. By early 1947, the military draft seemed so unnecessary that Truman did not request its renewal. A year later, it would be brought back in response to the Czech crisis, but calls would be light. However much it might do to improve general levels of health and citizenship, UMT could claim immediate relevance only if the United States were going to maintain a mass army, which Truman did not want. Indeed, he never faced the apparent contradiction between cutting military strength to the bone and advocating an expensive plan of universal training.[24]

V

An emerging food crisis overlay the first two years of the Truman presidency. Vividly demonstrating the difficulties of satisfying domestic consumers while meeting larger national obligations and moral imperatives, it also called into question liberal efforts at economic management that generally had served the country well in depression and war.

Just as American industry had done so much to supply the Allies during the war, so had American agriculture fed and clothed them with a rapid expansion of production, achieved through policies that combined patriotic exhortation, high prices, and federal subsidies. Controls and allocations then had directed key commodities, primarily cotton and grain, toward war use rather than civilian consumption. The achievement, if great, had not been without political pain. Farmers resented wartime controls, especially those administered by the Office of Price Administration (OPA), widely considered a refuge for New Dealers who believed in centralized state economic management and thought only of the interests of urban consumers.[25]

Truman did not have much time to think about agricultural issues in the early months of his presidency, but as they emerged, they centered on three points: (1) political reconciliation in the form of programs to bring farmers, primarily midwestern grain and livestock producers, back into the Democratic party; (2) supply and demand management in the form of a government policy that would avoid the enormous surpluses and catastrophic price collapses of the early 1920s while promoting the abundant harvests that would meet the needs of both American consumers and a temporarily dependent wider world; and (3) humanitarian relief in the form of energetic action to stave off a possible global famine.

Hoping to build a bipartisan consensus, Truman conferred on these problems with leading Republicans, including Herbert Hoover, whom he called to the White House as an expert on World War I food policy and famine relief. Hoover's visit was the beginning of a useful, if intermittent, collaboration and (in the years after Truman left the White House) a warm friendship. The old man, grateful for the attention, came through with a clarion call for action to prevent a disaster in Europe, announcing, "It is now 11:59 on the clock of starvation."[26]

Truman's choice for secretary of agriculture was Democratic congressman Clinton P. Anderson of New Mexico, a hard-headed, self-made millionaire close to the president's good friend Senator Carl Hatch. Anderson's background as a businessman and his instincts as a politician led him to believe that there was a single answer to the Democratic political problem and the supply difficulties—to decontrol agriculture as quickly as possible. Farmers able to produce and sell under the rules of an unregulated market, he believed, could provide for America and the world, even if at prices higher than wartime ceilings.

From a viewpoint of basic economics, Anderson's argument was hard to challenge. Politically, its consequences were less certain; higher farm prices would mean higher food prices that likely would draw the wrath of workers already prone to strike for large wage increases. Within the administration, Anderson's preferences represented a special challenge to the OPA, with its commitment to low, controlled prices for the urban consumer. As no one seriously believed that all controls could be lifted overnight, the administration succumbed to the temptation to throw out the most unpopular ones (rationing) while keeping those that possessed mass appeal (price controls).

At the beginning of 1946, it became obvious that European requirements had been woefully underestimated and that the Continent was suffering one of the most dreadful famines in its history. Low grain production in many parts of the world meant that only the United States could meet the crisis. But largely because of the diversion of unprecedented amounts of wheat to livestock feeding (the most profitable use as long as prices were held to a low level), supplies for Europe were drying up.

Truman acted quickly. Although he had preferred to avoid the political pain of demanding sacrifice from the American people, he also believed that the United States had a mission to prevent mass starvation. On February 6, 1946, acting on the recommendations of a special cabinet committee, he issued a number of conservation orders that had the effect of diverting grain and dairy products to famine relief. In terms of practical everyday life, the program meant no real hardship: darker bread; some continued scarcity of such items as beer, whiskey, cheese, ice cream, butter, and oleomargarine; but no hunger or malnutrition. It did not even reestablish meat rationing. Throughout 1946, the American people would remain the world's best fed, consuming twice the calories of the average European; still, their small sacrifices would add one more irritation to the annoyances of daily life in a reconverting society.[27]

With the clock now at one minute before midnight, Truman brought back Herbert Hoover to serve as honorary chairman of the Famine Emergency Committee and as his personal representative on an around-the-world trip to assess the situation. A good many New Deal Democrats gnashed their teeth as Hoover proceeded around the globe with maximum fanfare. His final report, which appears to have underestimated the extent of need, was of questionable value. Nevertheless, the mission was a shrewd ploy that made the crisis bipartisan and focused public attention on it for weeks. Truman did his part with both policy initiatives and appeals to conserve, but he was realistic in his understanding that no one could approach Hoover's authority on this issue.[28]

The government had to acquire and deliver 6 million tons of wheat to Europe in the first half of 1946. Speeches could not produce a bushel. Requisitioning was unthinkable; efforts to limit livestock feeding were impractical. The reimposition of rationing on meat would take weeks and likely lead to a consumer revolt. The only course was to make it more profitable for farmers to sell wheat than to use it as a feed grain. The administration could not bring itself to scrap price controls altogether. But with bonus payments and sharply higher price ceilings, it refilled nearly empty federal granaries. By July 1, 5.5 million tons had been shipped to Europe with another 500,000 at the docks. In the end, all Americans would pay higher prices to save Europe, but considering the alternative, only the meanest-spirited could begrudge the cost. Truman and Anderson may have been slow to grasp the dimensions of the crisis. Yet it was to their credit that when they did, they acted, displayed flexibility, and chose rightly among difficult alternatives.

VI

No representative tale could encompass millions of individual experiences in coping with the economic transition that Truman had to manage. One that was revealing in the broadness of its applicability, however, was that of recently discharged Sergeant Robert J. Donovan, who returned to his job at the *New York Herald-Tribune* in the fall of 1945 from service in the European theater. Donovan walked the streets of Manhattan searching vainly for a clothing store with an acceptable suit that would fit his tallish but standard frame. At times, he found himself forced off the sidewalk by picketing strikers. A couple of days later in his hometown of Buffalo, he was finally able to outfit himself at a secondhand shop. At last free of military khaki, he stood in front of a mirror, viewed himself in preworn civvies, and felt "just like Doug Fairbanks."[29]

Most Americans in 1945 and 1946 went through some such experience whether shopping for clothing or food or a car or housing. Everything was in short supply; rationing, price controls, and raw-material allocations continued almost as if the war were not over; but patriotic sacrifice was no longer at the top of many agendas. Ordinary Americans, rich as never before thanks to wartime savings, wanted the comforts and small luxuries of the good life: new clothing, beefsteak, bonded whisky, a new auto, decent housing. All such things, when they could be found, were likely to be available only via "the black market"—backroom transactions, lavish tips to salespersons, extra payments passed under the counter—all off the books, illegal, and designed to beat price controls. Naturally, most consumers preferred to pay the official, lower prices for the goods they coveted. A substantial majority were more than willing to give their endorsement to the OPA's efforts to control prices. That same majority, however, was equally willing to patronize the black market in order to satisfy its desires. That such contradictory impulses were normal made them no less difficult for the politicians who had to manage the economy.

Truman had come to the presidency with no ready-made formula for reconversion and with a jumble of contradictory attitudes. Of course, he considered himself a "progressive" or a "liberal" or a "New Dealer" or, as he remarked to Mon Wallgren in December 1945, "a little left of center."[30] From the beginning of his political career, he had solicited the support of organized labor, but he also had been through turbulent relations with individual unions and their leaders—the Kansas City Teamsters, John L. Lewis, Sidney Hillman. By experience and temperament, he was also a small businessman with deeply internalized individualistic and entrepreneurial values reflected in his frequently stated distaste for government bureaucracy. Some of his best friends and most reliable supporters—Lou Holland, Tom Evans, Neal Helm—were successful regional business figures; he admired them and took their opinions seriously. John Snyder, midwestern banker and self-described conservative, was perhaps his closest and most trusted associate.

He had attempted to reconcile the contradictions in his mind by defining the working man as almost anyone—blue-collar laborer, farmer, businessman—who toiled hard at making a living. In the end, he would have to balance his middle-class, business-oriented values against the political realities of Democratic party leadership. The process, affecting as it did virtually all the domestic controversies of the first year and a half of his presidency, was intellectually messy and in many ways contributed to the disorderliness of reconversion itself.

Unavoidably, there would be considerable transitional friction involved in any industrial conversion from wartime to civilian goods, but one agent seemed most active in jamming the gears of American capitalism: the labor movement. As soon as the war was over, strikes burst out everywhere and seemed to bring production of much-coveted consumer goods to a grinding halt, all for the sake of what many Americans considered incredible wage demands. Labor leaders argued that the big increases amounted to fair compensation for years of wartime restraint and that high pay for the workingman would generate the mass purchasing power the economy needed and thereby underwrite general prosperity. They also asserted that the level of corporate profits had been so high during the war that big raises could be instituted without corresponding price increases, a contention angrily rejected by business.

The argument had some economic validity—a well-paid working class was an essential component of prosperity—but it was also obviously self-serving and disingenuous. It resonated poorly among most non-unionized Americans, who distrusted the labor movement, saw it as a greedy special interest, and often linked it to alien collectivist ideologies. (Communist influence was in fact readily discernible in some large industrial unions and not effectively purged from all of them until the end of the decade.) Even during the depths of the Depression, organized labor had enjoyed only minimal public support. Much of that had eroded during the war, because of a relatively few but highly visible strikes or threatened strikes; moreover, the awesome industrial production that won the conflict for America had restored the standing of the leaders of American business. From mid-1945 on, one public-opinion poll after another showed large majorities agreeing that labor had too much power or was making excessive demands or needed to be restricted.[31]

Labor aggressiveness in one controversy after another made reconversion especially difficult for Truman. Not only his inner attitudes, but also his duties as a party leader were contradictory. The Democratic "presidential party" (the Democratic organizations in the large urban states that swung presidential elections) had by 1945 come very close to being an American variant of the British Labour party. Union labor was its most important and active constituency, surpassing the old machines as mobilizers of the vote. Liberal policy activists hoped to put over a social-welfare agenda on a tide of union money and ballots. Truman sympathized with many of these objectives and had no trouble accepting labor as a critical segment of the Democratic party. Yet aside from his own longstanding personal qualms about labor excesses, he had to attempt to build majority support for his party—and for himself. He could not align himself unequivocally with the demands of the unions even if he had wanted to do so.

His administration's task was to find a policy that would secure industrial peace, maintain price stability, and achieve a reasonably fast, relatively painless reconversion. The assumption was that labor could be placated without long strikes and that controls, somewhat loosened, could continue for a year or two after the end of the war. Such a vision embodied the faith of the Democratic party intelligentsia that administrators motivated by a vision of the public interest could manage the economy in a disinterested fashion. Reality provided scant vindication.

A president capable of eloquently stating a clear policy track might have been able to give reconversion more direction, although one doubts that anyone could have mastered the scramble for group advantage. Truman's efforts were unproductive in part because he remained a poor speaker, but also because his administration's policy, reflecting to a large extent his own mixed attitudes, never achieved coherence. Somewhat misleadingly, these conflicting impulses came to be symbolized by the rivalry between OPA head Chester Bowles and Office of War Mobilization and Reconversion director John Snyder.

Snyder had become head of OWMR when Truman made Fred Vinson secretary of the treasury in July 1945; he held the post until June 1946, when Truman designated him to succeed Vinson at the Treasury Department. (John Steelman took over OWMR until its termination at the end of the year.) Snyder was openly skeptical of New Dealism, broad-gauged social programs, and intellectuals who believed the economy could be run from Washington. Because he looked and talked like a small-town banker, the liberals immediately targeted him as the éminence grise of the administration.

Yet whatever his private preferences, he never advocated immediate cold-turkey decontrol. He accepted the liberal vision of a managed process to a surprising degree and for a time received much of his economic advice from fire-breathing liberal economists he had inherited from Vinson.[32] Still, he differed with the liberals on important matters of emphasis that came to be seen as differences in kind. He thought that the control system was at best a necessary evil to be phased out as quickly as possible, not a socially desirable restraint on the greed of business. While it existed, he wanted to administer it in what he considered an equitable fashion—one that would take into account the demands of both business and labor.

Bowles, a member of one of the most distinguished families of Connecticut, a successful advertising man, and an idealistic New Dealer, combined a generous, deeply felt liberalism with a gift for self-promotion. He had run the OPA during the most successful period of its existence, effectively administering a tough "hold-the-line" policy on prices—at least as measured by the "on-the-books" economy. Where Snyder was inclined to tilt toward business and was dubious about economic controls, Bowles leaned in the direction of labor and believed strongly in the efficacy of economic management. By and large, the policy bureaucracy in both OPA and OWMR aligned itself with Bowles. Richard Gilbert and Robert Nathan of the OWMR, for example, largely accepted the labor case for lifting or at least relaxing controls on wages but not prices. In the end, such a direction was irresistible because it meshed wonderfully with the political self-interest of both Bowles and Truman.

VII

Despite the Truman committee's wartime exhortations, virtually nothing had been done to plan for reconversion when Truman became president. With the rush of events and the midsummer change of command at OWMR, little more had been accomplished by V-J Day. On August 16, 1945, after forty-eight frantic hours of discussion, Truman issued a statement laying down guidelines for reconversion. Its key provision declared that "there is no longer any threat of an inflationary bidding up of wage rates by competition in a short labor market"; therefore, unions might seek voluntary wage adjustments "upon condition that they will not be used in whole or in part as the basis for seeking an increase in price ceilings."

With that declaration, giving presidential imprimatur to the idea that the lid could be taken off wages but not prices, Truman flashed a green light to an era of industrial turmoil. He pretty clearly had acted on the basis of a perceived political imperative, but also on the recommendation of his economic policy team, including Snyder (however reluctant) and Bowles. What they all had created was an unmanageable monster. As Snyder confided to journalist Frank McNaughton two months later, "If we increase wages now, we have got to increase prices, and there you get on the old, old merry-go-round of inflation."[33]

The original intention probably had been to allow token wage increases. Instead, major labor unions demanded raises in the neighborhood of 30 percent (a figure that would preserve the take-home pay from the standard defense plant forty-eight-hour week) and called one strike after another. Truman, who believed that labor leaders had given him a no-strike pledge, felt betrayed. He called a labor–management conference to establish a workable wage–price formula. But the meeting could not be convened until early November, when the cycle of charge and countercharge had gone too far to permit any agreement; it adjourned at the beginning of December, having accomplished nothing.

Truman himself zigged and zagged, attempting to promote economic stability while preserving the Democratic party's special relationship with labor. In mid-September, he impulsively fired William H. Davis director of the Office of Economic Stabilization, after being told (misleadingly) by Lew Schwellenbach that Davis had advocated 50 percent wage increases. Yet Truman continued to support some unspecified wage adjustment. In November, with the national labor–management conference at midpoint, the United Auto Workers began the biggest industrial action yet by shutting down General Motors, the nation's largest producer of automobiles, at a time when consumer demand for new cars was unprecedented. The president refused to endorse the UAW's 30 percent wage demand, but he did call on GM to open its books and reveal the size of its profits to outsiders.

Did this act put the president back on the side of labor? Not exactly. Shortly after the breakup of the labor–management conference, he asked Congress for legislation, patterned after the Railway Labor Act, to prevent major strikes. Featuring cooling-off periods and federal fact-finding boards, the proposal was mild compared with others on Capitol Hill. Nevertheless, the labor establishment erupted with the fury of Vesuvius. Philip Murray, president of the CIO, declared that the request was designed "to weaken and ultimately destroy labor organizations."[34] The UAW indignantly rejected a separate presidential entreaty for the auto workers to return to the assembly lines pending a federal fact-finding report. By mid-December, both Murray, by then persona non grata at the White House, and his counterparts in business were alienated from the administration.

In the meantime, strikes continued. Throughout late 1945 and early 1946, the White House involved itself in labor disputes on a scale without precedent in peacetime. Steelman, Snyder, and, to a lesser degree, Schwellenbach usually acted as principals for the president. But only Truman could use the weapon of last resort. Employing wartime seizure powers, the president brought under temporary government management the anthracite coal mines, much of the meat-packing industry, twenty-six oil companies, and the Great Lakes Towing Company.[35] At best, however, seizure was a short-term fix, keeping workers on the job and giving both sides added incentives to settle. Furthermore, it could achieve that limited usefulness only as long as workers were unwilling to strike against the government.

On January 20, 1946, with the UAW still out at General Motors, the steelworkers shut down U.S. Steel. Faced with immense pent-up consumer demand for durable goods and with a labor–management crisis that threatened to pull down the economy, the administration pushed hard for settlements and found they required concessions to both sides at the expense of the general public. It was at this point that the rivalry between Bowles and Snyder became most manifest. Bowles, while not contesting labor demands, fought to hold the line on prices. As the official with overall responsibility for reconversion, Snyder had to make the real-world deals required to get the economy moving—and Truman as president had to sanction them.

The price–wage settlements in auto, steel, and other major industries in early 1946 resulted in pay increases of around 18 percent and in a significant "bulge in the price line." Such outcomes may have been realistic, but they pleased almost no one and damaged the administration. The results probably would have been about the same had the administration merely phased out controls and allowed labor and management to bargain freely. Instead, the attempt to maintain selective controls made it a party to one unsatisfactory settlement after another.

By the spring, Truman was furious about the difficulties the labor movement was making for him. Two incidents precipitated a showdown. On April 1, John L. Lewis called the United Mine Workers out once again. As fruitless negotiations with management went on for more than a month, the economy, heavily dependent on coal, began to be dragged down into a morass of reduced railway schedules, factory layoffs, and electrical brownouts. Truman long had hated Lewis, had been especially bitter about his World War II strikes, and now saw his behavior as a personal challenge. Writing to Charles Sawyer, he paired the UMW chief with Soviet foreign minister Molotov as the "principal contenders for top rating as walking images of Satan."[36] Lewis, even more prone to personalize disputes than Truman, displayed open contempt for the president. On May 21, after a futile effort to get the contesting sides to agree to arbitration, Truman seized the coal mines, only to discover that the miners would not obey his back-to-work order. A settlement would not be reached until the end of the month, the president all the while seething in outrage.

By then, Truman had seized the railroads. Rivalry among the railway brotherhoods had resulted in protracted negotiations over a postwar contract. A. F. Whitney and Alvaney Johnston, the two most militant brotherhood leaders, turned down a settlement personally offered by Truman, although the other eighteen brotherhoods accepted it. On May 17, Truman issued a seizure order. At his personal appeal on May 18, the union leaders postponed the strike for five days. On May 23, defying the government, the two brotherhoods walked out, creating a disastrous transportation crisis that threatened to bring the economy to a halt and, by interfering with grain shipments, cause starvation in Europe. As Truman later remembered it, his last words to Whitney and Johnston were, "You are not going to tie up the country. If this is the way you want it, we'll stop you."[37]

Nearly a million persons had been idled by strikes. Truman was sick to death of the situation. Over the first thirteen months of his presidency, he had been pulled back and forth between foreign and domestic crises. He had been through the bruising and unnecessary Ickes–Pauley controversy. Now Americans from the editorial offices of the *New York Times* ("weak and spineless") to every rail station in the country were describing him as inept.[38]

However much he had tried to align himself with labor in the past, Truman was not immune from the wide public perception that the unions were demanding huge increases far beyond what other Americans could expect, that they were willing to hold the economy hostage in order to achieve their objectives, and that by extension they were responsible for the shortages and high black-market prices that were the lot of the American consumer. Sometime that spring, probably not too long before the coal and rail crises, he scribbled out a few angry thoughts on White House stationery. These were built around a fantasy of calling in several major labor leaders:

> Tell them that patience is exhausted. Declare an emergency—call out troops. Start industry and put anyone to work who wants to go to work.
> If any leader intervenes, court martial him.
> Lewis ought to have been shot in 1942, but Franklin didn't have the guts to do the job.[39]

Building on his already intense feelings, he prepared a "draft" of a speech to Congress, tearing into the recalcitrant unions and asking for authority to force strikers back on the job. It was an emotional catharsis and a rough indication to his speech-writing team (Clark Clifford, Sam Rosenman, and Charlie Ross) of the tone he expected from them. It also revealed an angry, harassed chief executive, who if taken literally had gone well beyond the point of rationality. Beginning by contrasting the wartime sacrifices of American soldiers with the egoistic greed of union leaders, the draft charged that the labor bosses had lied to him and cared for nothing other than their own comfort. It concluded by calling for a lynch mob:

> I think no more of the Wall Street crowd than I do of Lewis and Whitney. Let's give the country back to the people. Let's put transportation and production back to work, hang a few traitors and make our own country safe for democracy.
> Come on boys, let's do the job![40]

The writing team toned down the speech, of course, but it still was tough. Truman delivered one version as a radio address on the evening of May 24. Speaking to Congress the following day, he attacked "the obstinate arrogance" of rail-union leaders Johnston and Whitney and, in bombshell fashion, asked for emergency legislation "to authorize the President to draft into the Armed Forces of the United States all workers who are on strike against their government." Fortunately for all concerned, he was handed a message just after reading those lines and could say, "Word has been received that the railroad strike has been settled, on terms proposed by the President!" He asked Congress to give him his legislative request anyway. Henry Wallace, however, observing the president's demeanor at a cabinet meeting, thought that a now-cooler Truman would not be unhappy if Congress rejected the bill. In any event, it was blocked in the Senate by labor-oriented liberals headed by Claude Pepper and legalistic conservatives headed by Robert A. Taft.[41]

VIII

The episode revealed a lot about Truman. He had responded to a drastic crisis with an equally drastic solution that made no virtue of moderation. Following every cue that his social background and political education had given him, he had attempted to present himself as a tough, decisive leader. Persuaded that he represented the public interest, he believed that the labor leaders were indifferent to the needs even of their own members, let alone the general public. He was carried away by an anger so intense that it could interfere with his perceptions of reality. He stunned Bob Hannegan by declaring to the cabinet that Whitney's Brotherhood of Trainmen had never supported him for the Senate. When corrected, he said, "Well, they didn't come in until the last minute."[42]

Considering the seriousness of the situation, one could make a case for his legislative request. What must have seemed scary to those who witnessed him close up was the way in which his rage shaded into irrationality. He had a great deal to be angry about, but one senses that the behavior of Lewis, Johnston, and Whitney had also provided a focus for a deeper, more generalized anger that long had been part of his emotional baggage and already had surfaced from time to time against targets of varying merit—Spencer Salisbury, Tom Bash, the Kansas City reformers, the *Kansas City Star*, railroad financiers, Lloyd Stark, Standard Oil. Dealing with it would be a constant problem throughout his presidency. He understood the dangers of both being out of control and seeming to appear that way. Hence his frequent resort to writing out his fury; pieces of paper could be filed away—at least as long as they never made it into the mail.

What he had achieved for the time being was the settlement of two major strikes. Few doubted that his big stick had brought the unions around. On the whole, the public probably approved of his behavior,[43] but all the irritations of reconversion remained to annoy Mr. and Mrs. John Q. Public. And Truman faced the cold reality that he *had* to have labor support. On June 11, he vetoed a severely restrictive labor bill sponsored by Representative Francis Case of South Dakota; Truman argued, persuasively in the opinion of many observers, that his request for temporary powers to meet an emergency was one thing, legislation designed to weaken organized labor as an institution was another.[44]

When Sidney Hillman wrote to thank him, Truman responded irritably, "It has been the policy of some labor leaders to throw bricks and bark at their best friend at every opportunity. I have never seen any of them come forward to defend the President when he is right."[45] The tone of the letter demonstrated that there was still a lot of damage to repair.

Hillman's death in July would not help matters. The veto of the Case bill left the door open for a reconciliation, but the relationship between labor and the White House remained distant.

Price stabilization was as critical—and as difficult—as labor–management relations. Here all of Truman's options were unpromising. The decision to allow wage increases had fundamentally undercut any hope of freezing prices. Price controls delivered benefits to consumers who could actually buy goods at the official prices, but they also clogged the economy in many ways and thereby got in the way of resuming full production. With every month after the end of the war, resistance to them increased and placed impossible strains on enforcement mechanisms. In an age of family-owned and -operated retail businesses, it was impossible to control individual transactions effected by tens of thousands of automobile dealers, furniture stores, local groceries, and the like. Consumers who paid $1,000 or more above the list price for a new car might feel gouged, but they paid. Without a consumer strike, price controls were doomed.

Chester Bowles, director of the OPA, had become a hero to liberal Democrats. Focusing on the price demands of a handful of large corporations, they saw a need to control the rapaciousness of big business and looked to right-minded intellectuals and technicians to run the economy in the public interest, which they largely defined as that of workers and middle-class consumers. John Snyder, head of the OWMR, had become a natural foil for Bowles. Bowles believed in controls as the ultimate protection of the ordinary American; Snyder increasingly doubted their effectiveness. Truman's own attitudes on both a personal and a policy level were distinctly mixed, possibly hopelessly confused. Personally, Snyder was among his best friends. Bowles was, Truman told Harold Smith, "a grand guy" who concentrated too much on headlines and periodically made him as mad as the devil.[46]

Through the spring of 1946, Congress debated whether the OPA, set to expire on June 30, should be renewed with full authority. The debate, ideological rather than pragmatic, polarized conservatives and liberals. Each side had its demons: for the liberals, greedy businessmen; for the conservatives, arrogant bureaucrats. Liberals lamented the way in which the consumer was exploited; conservatives told tales of local grocers being fined for selling cans of asparagus at 2 cents above the control price. Truman endorsed renewal as a means of both protecting consumers and appeasing the liberal–labor forces, but Snyder and other business friends kept him aware of OPA red tape and pricing policies that in some cases (men's shirts, for example) made it impossible to sell a product profitably. Writing to Bess, Truman remarked, "Office of Price Administration is a mess, brought on principally by the pinheads who have administered it."[47]

The bill hammered out in Congress extended OPA in name, but gutted the price control system in fact. The liberals, convinced that

Truman's leadership had been limp, blamed the president for the bill's weakness. Truman could cite vigorous statements in favor of a strong OPA, but presidential activity was probably irrelevant. On Capitol Hill, business in the form of small enterprisers had the attention of a clear majority. Dominated by rural, small-town America, Congress as a body was unlikely to be moved by either presidential rhetoric or large pro-OPA demonstrations organized by labor unions. The debate never really focused on the central questions of whether controls worked and whether they were facilitating or hindering reconversion. Instead, it involved conflicting ideologies and interest group aspirations.

The OPA renewal bill came to Truman's desk near the end of June. To sign it would be to accept a system that everyone agreed could not work; it would also be taken as a declaration that Truman was aligning himself with business and "special interests" against the "ordinary people." To veto it would mean doing away with any vestige of a control system on the hope that popular anger would compel Congress to enact something stronger. A veto also would enrage a majority of legislators, including such influentials as Barkley and Rayburn.[48]

Reasoning that there was nothing to gain from signing a bill that was unworkable, Truman opted for a veto. He accompanied it with a stinging message to Congress and a radio address in which he accused the opposition of "shortsightedness and impatience . . . partisanship and greed." His words briefly elated OPA supporters and elicited congratulations from Bowles, who resigned to return to Connecticut. They accomplished little else. Congress was no more willing than before to give Truman what he wanted. In the meantime, prices shot up. After three weeks, the legislative branch sent Truman another extension bill, somewhat different in form but equally ineffective. Having decided it was the best he could get, the president signed it.[49]

Truman's performance was terrible. He appeared to have danced around every side of the issue. He was weak, then strong, then weak again. He seemed to lack any direction, had forfeited any claim to leadership in the fight against inflation, and had earned no credit from the critics of controls. "Harry Truman," *Time* congressional correspondent Frank McNaughton told his New York office on July 26, "could not carry Missouri now."[50]

IX

Far from feeling beaten down in mid-1946, Truman was determined to go on the offensive. Disgusted with the tepid support he had received from congressional Democrats, he focused his outrage on Roger Slaughter, a Kansas City Democrat and longtime friend who had succeeded Joe Shannon in the House of Representatives after the old rabbit chief had died in 1943. Slaughter had landed a prized seat on the Rules Committee because Truman put in a good word for him with the House leadership. Then, despite what Truman considered firm promises to the contrary, he had proceeded to vote a straight anti-administration line and establish himself as a leader of the young conservative Democrats on the Hill.

Truman took Slaughter's behavior as a personal affront and was determined to get rid of him. Jim Pendergast, following family tradition, considered Slaughter's district a rabbit preserve. Truman bludgeoned him into line:

> Now if the home county organization with which I have been affiliated slaps the President of the United States in the face by supporting a renegade Congressman it will not be happy for the President nor for the political organization. . . .
> Slaughter is obnoxious to me and you must make your choice.[51]

Young Jim (now known to the remnants of the machine as Big Jim) selected a reliable goat named Enos Axtell to go up against Slaughter. Truman pulled two other old lions—Jim Aylward and Roger Sermon—into tandem with Pendergast. All the same, in the disorganized world of Kansas City politics, Axtell stood a fair chance of losing. Two and a half weeks before the election, Truman used a press conference less to endorse Axtell, whose first name he could not remember, than to blast Slaughter. On August 6, Axtell barely won a tight, three-man race.[52]

The purge had a high price. Slaughter charged massive fraud. The following year, after the Justice Department refused to act, the Jackson County prosecuting attorney got indictments of seventy-one people for ballot-box stuffing in favor of Axtell. They escaped trial after a lurid middle-of-the-night caper in which thieves, somehow undetected, managed to enter the county courthouse, blow a safe, and steal the evidence. By then, Axtell had lost to his Republican opponent, Albert Reeves, Jr., son of the federal judge whom Truman hated so intensely. The president had gotten an even less friendly congressman and gained a scandal in the bargain.[53]

The Slaughter purge was an unhappy beginning to a midterm campaign that would be a referendum on the president's first year and a half in office. Organized labor, unsure whether he was friend or foe, was apathetic. The Henry Wallace fiasco caused many people to doubt Truman's competence and highlighted a sizable pro-Soviet, Popular Front faction on the left wing of the Democratic party. The general public felt battered by the chaos of reconversion.

One final issue, growing out of reconversion, drove the last nail in the Democrats' coffin. The OPA renewal provided a moratorium of about a month before reimposing price controls on meat. Predictably, farmers and feedlot operators rushed their product to market in advance of the reversion to controlled prices on August 20; after that date, many of them held back their already depleted stocks in what amounted to an informal strike.

In one city after another, beef and pork disappeared from butcher shops and grocery stores. A frustrated, weary public tended to blame the administration. Four Connecticut Democratic congressmen, in mortal (and, as it developed, entirely justified) terror of losing their seats in November, sent a letter to the president that stated the issue starkly: "Party workers canvassing the voters are being told by Democrats 'No meat, no votes.'" Truman watched as eighteen months of exhausting effort addressing titanic problems at home and abroad came down to what Sam Rayburn called "a damn *beefsteak* election."[54]

He had reason to be bitter. Believing that the public (at least his Democratic urban core constituencies) wanted the OPA, he had suppressed his instinctive doubts about price controls. Now he faced mass resentment from a nation that wanted both low prices and meat on the table. By mid-October, he and everyone around him realized that there was nothing to be gained by fighting the market. Decontrol was the only way out—and, in truth, always had been the only policy that made economic sense.

To work off his own frustration, Truman wrote an angry message to the American public somewhat in the vein of his railroad-strike speech draft. It contrasted the reign of selfishness with the heroic patriotism of Medal of Honor winners and informed the people that the fault lay with them—not with a president who was trying to provide leadership in the tradition of a Wainwright, a Stilwell, or the more anonymous brave men of the war. The concluding passage read:

> You've deserted your president for a mess of pottage[,] a piece of beef—a side of bacon. . . . If you the people insist on following Mammon instead of Almighty God—your President can't stop you all by himself. . . .
>
> I can no longer enforce a law you won't support. . . . You've gone over to the powers of selfishness and greed.
>
> Therefore I am releasing the controls on meat and will proceed to release all other controls. . . .
>
> Tell 'em what will happen and quit[.][55]

Truman's actual speech on the evening of October 14 was considerably softened and more "presidential." It drew an enormous radio audience. But although he gave his listeners the decontrol most of them wanted, he hurt himself by sounding, as Robert Donovan recalled it, "strained and tired."[56] The tone represented the president's emotional state. On September 26, he had written a memorandum to himself recalling the beginning of the Argonne offensive twenty-eight years earlier and the way "a service man of my acquaintance" had commanded a battery of French 75s, had come home, watched the political and economic follies of the 1920s, lived through the Depression, supported a great leader in war and peace, and finally had taken over for him:

> Then the reaction set in. Selfishness, greed, jealousy raised their ugly heads. No wartime incentive to keep them down. Labor began to grab all it could

get by fair means or foul, farmers began blackmarketing food, industry hoarded inventories and the same old pacifists began to talk disarmament.

But my acquaintance tried to meet every situation and has met them up to now. Can he continue to outface the demagogues, the chiselers, the jealousies?[57]

Truman clearly doubted it. So did Democratic party leaders, who advised him against campaign appearances in the final weeks before the midterm election. With few illusions about the likely outcome, he went off to Independence to cast his ballot.

The results were devastating for the northern liberal Democrats with whom he had tried to identify himself. The Republicans swept to power in the House of Representatives by a margin of 246 to 188; they captured the Senate more narrowly (only one-third of the incumbents were up for reelection), 51 to 45. The presidential train came into Washington's Union Station late the following evening. The chief executive of the United States found waiting to greet him a reception committee of one: Acting Secretary of State Dean Acheson.

X

What had gone wrong? In the large sense, Truman's presidency to November 1946 had been a successful one. Yet what loomed large were the failures, slipups, and fiascoes. In a curious reversal of the old maxim that the whole may be less than the sum of its parts, the parts at the time seemed much less than the whole. Even the president's achievements looked like failures.

He had attained a firm grip on foreign policy by November 1946 and was well along in an effort to formulate a coherent policy in the national interest. The immediate fruit of that endeavor, however, had been the Wallace debacle. Toughness toward the USSR had alienated and demoralized the left wing of the Democratic party and had intensified an already existing split in New York, California, Minnesota, and other northern states where the influence of fellow travelers was strong.

The split over Wallace in turn highlighted the Communist issue and rendered vulnerable any Democrat who tried to straddle the emerging fissure within the party or who might be credibly painted pink. The most notable example was Representative Jerry Voorhis of California, unseated by a former naval officer named Richard Nixon.

Reconversion was, of course, far more decisive in the Democratic defeat. In large measure, the election results amounted to an expression of mass irritation over multiple shortages and inconveniences. Yet beneath the surface, reconversion was working, however bumpy the ride. Industry had retooled, made settlements with labor, and begun to produce all the items that an economy of mass consumption demanded. There had been a lot of transitional unemployment, comfortably buffered by generous federal benefits, but no mass long-term jobless problem. Most important, there had been no real depression.

Americans *had* experienced a sharp, unavoidable inflation, first in the off-the-books black market, and then after the demise of price controls in the on-the-books market. Still, there was no bust on the horizon to follow the boom. Inflation, which ran around 10 percent in 1946 (much higher according to some recent estimates, a bit lower by the reckoning of others),[58] was probably the inevitable result of wartime policies that financed the conflict heavily by debt instead of taxes and rejected forced savings in the form of compulsory war-bond purchases. Truman could do little to prevent it.

Federal macroeconomic policy was not perfect, but it largely was what the country needed. This was a remarkable achievement because it seems to have been the outcome of scattered decisions made before and during the early months of the Truman presidency by functionaries in OWMR, the Treasury, the Bureau of the Budget, and congressional tax committees. Perhaps someone had a conception of it as a whole, but there is no indication that Truman, Snyder, or Vinson was among them. Its most dissonant element, the attempt to preserve a full-blown control system, delayed settlement of many labor disputes and introduced numerous distortions into the economy. Other aspects of economic policy, however, were well suited to the situation.

Tax Policy

Truman wanted to keep the fiscal 1946 deficit as small as possible and run a surplus for fiscal 1947. Hence he resisted big general tax cuts. A course he would follow for the rest of his time in office, this meant no big addition to already massive consumer purchasing power; it dampened inflationary pressures. Here Truman was motivated by the experience of having been a county chief executive who had to balance his budget, or at least come close, but he was aware of the large-scale economic impact of his tax policies. Whether he or anyone else planned it that way, they were consistent with the use of fiscal tools that the original full-employment bill would have required. Corporate tax legislation, however, gave business generous benefits for new investment in plants and equipment; to use the jargon of a later generation, it gave a boost to the supply side that was especially useful at the time.

Monetary Policy

From the beginning, the Treasury pressed for and the Federal Reserve acquiesced in a policy of low interest rates and easy money. In order to keep government interest costs as low as possible, the Federal Reserve had made massive purchases of war bonds from 1942 on and thus had injected huge amounts of cash into the economy. Supporting government bonds at par was a matter of public honor with Truman and of convenience with his secretaries of the treasury. The Treasury–Federal Reserve agreement would therefore endure throughout his first term. A growing supply of cheap money in the private sector fueled reconversion and did much to ensure that there would be no postwar bust. The inflationary impact was at least partially offset by high personal income taxes and federal spending restraint.

However good the fundamental policies, Truman surely never saw them as a coherent whole and thus was never able to explain them to the American people, a task that in any case would have been extraordinarily difficult. With the Council of Economic Advisers just getting organized, he had no well-defined clearinghouse for economic policy.

In the end, he was his own biggest liability. His imperfect grasp of what was happening was the smallest part of the problem. On the big, visible issues that grabbed public attention, he had seemed indecisive and had given the appearance of a president not in control—whether the subject was the OPA, Henry Wallace, or red meat. His weaknesses as a public speaker magnified the impression. Although he was not on the ballot, the election was primarily a defeat for Truman and widely perceived as such. Senator J. William Fulbright underscored the point by suggesting that the president should unify the government by appointing a Republican leader, possibly Senator Vandenberg, as secretary of state (then next in the line of presidential succession), and resign in his favor.

The suggestion, widely discussed in the press, infuriated Truman. Speaking to the Gridiron Club in mid-December, he made light of it, quoting Gladstone to the effect that the Constitution was the most wonderful document ever produced by man. Then, in a not very indirect reference to Fulbright's Oxford education, he observed that Gladstone was evidently no longer taught at Oxford and "maybe we'd better educate our statesmen in our own land grant colleges." Privately, so the story goes, he referred to Fulbright as Senator Halfbright.[59]

If the president was going to rebound, he would have to convince people that he could master events rather than be mastered by them. At the end of 1946, almost no one thought he could do it. Yet, the emerging political and diplomatic situations held numerous possibilities for a resourceful chief executive, and at this point he had nothing to lose. "I'm doing as I damn please for the next two years and to hell with all them," he wrote to Bess from his new vacation retreat at Key West.[60]

Possibly even then, he recalled that Harry Truman had been underestimated before.

22

"WE MUST ASSIST FREE PEOPLES": THE TRUMAN DOCTRINE AND THE MARSHALL PLAN, 1947–1948

When Truman appeared before a joint session of Congress on March 12, 1947, to request emergency aid to Greece and Turkey, the atmosphere was expectant. Focusing on major pressure points in an emerging struggle with Soviet Communism, he at last took the decisive step into what soon would be called the Cold War and articulated a strong, easily comprehended rationale. Unlike his twentieth-century Democratic predecessors, Woodrow Wilson and Franklin Roosevelt, he was not meeting so obvious a threat as German unrestricted submarine warfare in 1917 or the Nazi conquest of Western Europe in 1940. Both events had led to war, a development that neither Truman nor sober observers anticipated.

What Truman promised was a long engagement with the wider world in the interest of defending democracy against totalitarianism. How long the struggle would be no one could say, but his statement promised no quick and easy termination. Proclaiming what journalists quickly dubbed the Truman Doctrine, he declared, "I believe that it must be the policy of the United States to support free peoples who are resisting attempted subjugation by armed minorities or by outside pressures."[1]

II

At the beginning of 1947, Truman accepted the long-arranged and amicable resignation of James Byrnes and appointed General George Marshall
his new secretary of state. "He's the great one of the age," Truman noted
on his appointment calendar. "I am surely lucky to have his friendship
and support."[2] Truman never wavered in that admiration. He felt that
many of the people who served him were in one respect or another more
talented than he, but Marshall may have been the only one whom he
considered a better man.

The general could be courtly and charming in casual social contacts
with women; he was unreservedly devoted to his wife and their model
Victorian marriage. But to the people with whom he worked, he was distant and aloof. Allowing no one, not even the president, to address him
by his given name, he understood that a professional relationship required
candor with one's superior and unsentimental evaluation of one's subordinates. He reserved his personal feelings, he remarked, for Mrs. Marshall.
Secure in his sense of identity, exuding a rectitude that sometimes annoyed others but more often impressed them, selfless, patriotic, always
gentlemanly, he possessed the aura of a distinguished commander. The
moment he entered a room, Dean Acheson recalled, everyone in it felt
his presence.

Marshall's only genuine foray into diplomacy, an attempt to settle
the Chinese civil war, had ended in failure. Still, he was at least as suited
to be secretary of state as Byrnes or Stettinius or Cordell Hull. In truth,
the choice was an inspired one. Above all, Marshall generated more reverence than any other figure in American life. He was for Truman the
perfect symbol for a foreign policy that had to transcend party lines.
Marshall commanded the confidence of a large majority in Congress. To
the general public, he was a figure of unimpeachable integrity beyond the
self-seeking hurly-burly of politics. In foreign countries, he was instantly
recognizable as a leader of great standing.

Moreover, he was a master organizer brought in to preside over a
department that demanded those skills after all the years of being casually bypassed by Roosevelt, and then virtually ignored by Byrnes. Unlike
his predecessor, Marshall knew his limitations, by way of both professional background and innate human capacity. One thing he had learned
as chief of staff of the army was the necessity of a large, well-structured
effort in the management of vast problems; he had no illusions that he
could negotiate by the seat of his pants. He welcomed strong, capable
assistants and backed them to the limit.

One of his first acts was to establish the Policy Planning Staff to be
headed by the Foreign Service's new star, George Kennan. His instructions, as Kennan remembered them, consisted of one two-word sentence:
"Avoid trivia." He expected policy recommendations to be brief summaries on one sheet of paper with boxes that allowed him to indicate ap-

proval, disapproval, or a need for modification. In practice, his mode of operation empowered the Foreign Service—Truman's "striped pants boys"—to take control of American foreign policy.[3]

Involving as it did a willingness to have a foreign minister of greater stature than himself, Truman's appointment of Marshall was courageous—all the more so because Marshall, unlike Byrnes, was either oblivious to or contemptuous of domestic political considerations. The president must have realized that if push came to shove, Marshall would be much harder to rein in than Byrnes. But Truman also probably felt that Marshall's sense of rank and duty would ultimately prevail in any conflict between them.

The temporary retention of Dean Acheson as undersecretary of state eased the transition. Marshall needed Acheson's experience and advice. As acting secretary of state during much of 1946, Acheson had worked closely with Truman and had established himself as a loyal, sensible liaison to the foreign policy bureaucracy. Truman remembered vividly Acheson's lone display of fidelity as the presidential train arrived at Union Station after the congressional elections. Whether it was motivated simply by devotion to the presidency or also by a hope for eventual appointment as secretary of state mattered little to him.

The relationship that already had developed between Truman and Acheson was, on the face of it, curious and unpredictable. The patrician, Ivy League–educated Acheson seemed the social antithesis of Truman. Yet something had clicked between them. Truman doubtless was receptive to Acheson's deference to the presidency, liked his no-nonsense manner, and respected his competence. (Acheson, with his bristling mustache and tailored suits, might seem the epitome of one of the striped-pants boys; actually, however, he had almost as little regard for them as did Truman.) Acheson found Truman's directness refreshing after the condescension of Roosevelt. He developed a liking for his new chief's character that matured into strong respect and affection.

Acheson would leave the department in June 1947 to resume the practice of law and strengthen his finances. His successor, Robert Lovett, was in many respects his equal in ability and by far his superior in political tact. An investment banker and business partner of Averell Harriman, a superb administrator, he was sober and cautious in his approach to foreign policy commitments, but convivial and effective in selling them to a doubting Congress. Truman never developed as close a relationship with him as with Acheson, but obviously understood his value.

III

The Truman Doctrine was a decisive move in the implementation of a policy of containment that had begun with Truman's support of Iran and Turkey in 1946. What was important was that a heretofore unclear national goal had been stated bluntly and invested with the prestige of the presidency. In the simplest geopolitical terms, Truman and the makers of American foreign policy had accepted the need to assume the role of the British Empire in the eastern Mediterranean. Less the product of a consciously formulated strategy than of a rush of events that demanded a decision, the new course had been the outcome of Britain's inability to continue as the guarantor of an independent, pro-Western Greek government.

The situation of Greece presented more formidable problems than that of Turkey, which was united in a determination to resist encroachment from its traditional Russian enemy to the north. Possessing a substantial military capability, it was fully mobilized and ready to fight, requiring primarily economic assistance to maintain its solvency. Greece, ravaged by World War II, lay in a state of economic near-ruin, was bitterly divided, and was poorly led. Whereas Turkey faced naked outside pressure, Greece confronted a left-wing guerrilla insurgency, the character of which was less obvious.

A faint odor of fascism emanated from the reactionary Greek government, which was controlled by a discredited oligarchy and had unrealistic dreams of border concessions from its northern Communist neighbors. Dean Acheson described its premier, Constantine Tsaldaris, as "a weak, pleasant, but silly man" who expected the United States not only to support his hopeless territorial demands, but also to fork over $6 billion in economic aid. Some members of the Tsaldaris government had competence, vision, and perhaps even sympathy for the common people; but no honest observer could describe the regime as in the vanguard of liberal democracy. As would be the case many times in the future of the Cold War, the most compelling argument for assistance was the alternative.[4]

Early warning that American help was needed in Greece had come throughout 1946 from Ambassador Lincoln MacVeagh, who minced no words in asserting that the USSR was bent on total domination of the country. (Critics at the time and historians later would argue that the insurgency was indigenous, but the post-1945 experience with Communist-front insurgencies around the world casts doubt on such assertions. Furthermore, the Greek guerrillas undeniably relied on assistance from the pro-Soviet regimes of Bulgaria, Yugoslavia, and Albania—so much so that, after the Yugoslav break with Moscow, the uprising would collapse.)[5]

In the summer of 1946, a Greek mission, which met briefly with Truman, had engaged in discussions on American assistance. As early as November, the State Department was contemplating an indirect transfer (with Britain as intermediary) of arms. In December, the administration dispatched Paul Porter to do a firsthand evaluation of Greek economic needs. On Friday, February 21, 1947, Secretary Marshall gave the final go-ahead for a plan of comprehensive economic and military assistance to Greece. On Monday, the February 24, the department received formal confirmation of the long-expected British withdrawal—in just six weeks. Given the preparation that had gone before, it took only a couple of days to hammer out the essentials of a stopgap aid program: $250 million to keep Greece afloat economically, another $150 million for Turkey. The map of the Middle East that Truman kept in his desk and used as a basis for short lectures provided ample evidence of his intense interest in the region. He quickly approved the proposal.

On February 27, he presided over a meeting at the White House that included Marshall, Acheson, and congressional leaders from both parties. Truman informed the guests from Capitol Hill of his forthcoming request and asked Marshall to summarize the new policy recommendations. The impact of what he said remains a matter of dispute; the content does not. Marshall bluntly stated the American interest in the eastern Mediterranean; warned that if either Greece or Turkey fell to the Soviet Union, the other would soon follow it; and raised the specter of a long row of falling dominoes: "It is not alarmist to say that we are faced with the first crisis of a series which might extend Soviet domination to Europe, the Middle East and Asia." Truman would recall several years later that the legislators appeared "deeply impressed."

Acheson, probably influenced by Marshall's decision to end his statement with a list of needed legislation, was not so certain. He was convinced, as he later put it, that "my distinguished chief, most unusually and unhappily, flubbed his opening statement." With Marshall's permission, he launched one of his own. It did not differ in substance, but was more passionate in tone. As Acheson recalled it, a long silence followed, and then Senator Vandenberg said, "Mr. President, if you will say that to the Congress and the country, I will support you and I believe that most of its members will do the same."[6]

On March 7, Truman met with his cabinet. He told the members, as Forrestal summarized it, that he "faced a decision more serious than ever confronted any President." Conceding the corrupt, inefficient character of the Greek government, he outlined the situation, stated his intentions, and asked for reactions. Clearly not called to discuss the merits of aid to Greece and Turkey, the session appears to have been designed to elicit a display of support. If Truman took anything out of the gathering, it was the need to make a strong, unhedged declaration before a joint session of Congress. With Marshall going off to Moscow for another meeting of the Council of Foreign Ministers, Truman made one concession; he would not mention the Soviet Union by name.[7]

IV

When he went to the Capitol four days later, however, no one had doubts about the import of the address. Its attacks on armed insurgents "led by Communists" and its identification of Poland, Romania, and Bulgaria as countries that had suffered the imposition of totalitarian governments "in violation of the Yalta agreement" left no ambiguity. The president conceded that the Greek government was not perfect, but argued that—whatever its "mistakes"—it was, unlike the regimes he had named, fundamentally democratic and capable of being set on a better course.

The heart of the talk lay in its depiction of a world in which nations faced two stark alternatives: liberal democracy or totalitarianism. The United States had to support "free peoples" who wanted to choose the first. However, the speech did not say "free peoples *everywhere*." It also declared, "Our help should be primarily through economic and financial aid which is essential to economic stability and orderly political processes." All the same, the sense of urgency and universal commitment was overpowering. Never specifically alluding to national economic or geopolitical interests, the president warned of the possibility of "confusion and disorder" spreading throughout the Middle East, claimed that the effects of failure to help Greece and Turkey would be "far reaching to the West as well as to the East," demanded "immediate and resolute action," and talked of the "great responsibilities" that events had imposed on America.[8]

By the time he had finished, no one could doubt that the nation faced a historic decision and that its second postwar era of the century would bear few resemblances to the first.

In one sense, the policy had been prepackaged for him by America's chief diplomats and the emerging national security apparatus, but his acceptance of it was equally a matter of the worldview he had brought to the presidency. Most fundamentally, it reflected both his long-held view of totalitarianism (whether of the left or the right) as an implacable enemy of human freedom and his faith (embodied in his reverence for Tennyson's "Locksley Hall") in the eventual triumph of a universal world order based on liberal values. In this, he almost instinctively had grasped what was perhaps the central issue of the twentieth century.

Sophisticates might argue that a dualistic view of international politics was too simple and that universal aspirations were doomed to disappointment. Yet Truman believed, on the whole rightly, that he had stated larger truths; he was not much concerned with the subtle shadings that are a part of any large picture. The intellectuals might refine ideas to death, elaborate on them, and even argue about whether a totalitarianism of the left was possible. Truman had arrived at his own ideas less through such processes than through his own experience. In a very real sense, he embodied Daniel J. Boorstin's argument that American political ideology is inherent in the environment. Most ordinary Americans found Truman's explanation of the world intellectually congenial and rhetorically effective.

Exhausted from hard work and the ordeal of decision, Truman left Washington for a week at Key West. Shortly after his arrival, he wrote a letter to his daughter that displayed both the toll of the past several weeks and the distance he had traveled in thinking about foreign policy:

> No one, not even me (your mother would say I) knew how very tired and worn to a frazzle the Chief Executive had become. . . .

> The attempt of Lenin, Trotsky, Stalin, et al., to fool the world and the American Crackpots Association, represented by Jos. Davies, Henry Wallace, Claude Pepper and the actors and artists in immoral Greenwich Village, is just like Hitler's and Mussolini's so-called socialist states.
>
> Your pop had to tell the world just that in polite language.[9]

The subsequent debate, argued on a somewhat more elevated plane, demonstrated the way in which the administration had seized the tactical high ground. The most vociferous opposition came from the independent, but Democratic-inclined, liberals, now led by Henry Wallace. Speaking at enthusiastic rallies across the country, using his recently acquired post as editor of the *New Republic* to attack the Truman Doctrine in print, Wallace had a strong appeal to those on the left who continued to think of the Soviet Union as a wartime ally rather than a hostile power. Many other liberals, moreover, were distressed by the failure to use the United Nations as a forum for settling the Greek–Turkish issues and managing whatever aid needed to be distributed. All the same, a visible and prestigious minority, mostly affiliated with the new Americans for Democratic Action (ADA), was willing to embrace an anti-Soviet policy. Wallace and his following presented a potential political problem for Truman, but they could not stop his program.[10]

The conservatives were even less of a problem. A good many of them on the Republican side were old isolationists and instinctive critics of any new spending program, but they also were visceral anti-Communists who would find it difficult to vote against containment measures. Many of them also realized that a public that had supported a war to liberate Europe would not be inclined to withdraw in the face of a perceived Soviet challenge. Senator Robert A. Taft was the foremost example of the conservative predicament. One of the two GOP leaders in the Senate, already known as "Mr. Republican," Taft was a formidable opponent, an intense partisan, and an aspirant to the presidency. Despite their scrupulous observance of the civilities of public life, he and Truman disliked each other cordially. Taft attacked the Greek–Turkish aid bill from virtually every angle and then wound up voting for it. Others would follow his example, leaving the bitter-end resistance of the right numerically insignificant.[11]

Having planted itself firmly in the most strategic position of American politics, the center, the administration had to deal primarily with practical issues of detail raised by Democrats and Republicans in the same ideological vicinity. Many moderate liberals would be satisfied with the argument that the United Nations, still young, semiorganized, and hobbled with the Security Council veto, could not handle the Greek–Turkish issue. Economizers who worried about cost would be reminded that Truman was asking for about one-tenth of 1 percent of the cost of fighting World War II; they would be admonished that to do nothing might well be more expensive in the long run. Prudent men on either side of the aisle who raised the question of open-ended commitments got assurances that the United States was not going to extend aid continually to any country, any time, anywhere.

In a Congress controlled by the opposition, Republican support was all important. Vandenberg, functioning almost as an emissary of the administration, brought along a majority of Senate Republicans and neutralized the UN argument by sponsoring an amendment that gave the United Nations a symbolic role. In the House, Christian Herter of Massachusetts and other East Coast Republicans pushed the bill along. Richard Nixon and other young conservative veterans of World War II, who probably would have been staunch isolationists a decade earlier, tended to support it also. After two months, the Greek–Turkish aid bill, and implicitly the Truman Doctrine, passed Congress by votes of approximately 3 to 1 in both houses. The margins and patterns of regional support were roughly similar to those for Lend-Lease six years earlier.[12]

V

In a sense, the Truman Doctrine had been a relatively easy beginning. As aid to Greece and Turkey moved through Congress, foreign policy planners had to come to grips with a much vaster reality: two years after the war, all of Western Europe still suffered from an economic malaise that threatened to destroy free institutions throughout the Continent. Postwar relief had done little more than keep the Europeans alive, albeit malnourished. The big loan to Great Britain had accomplished nothing more than the postponement of national bankruptcy. To many American observers in fact, Western Europe appeared on the brink of collapse, renewed misery, and chaos or Communism.

For the United States, the stakes were clear and compelling. The biggest specter and spur to action was the possibility of Soviet dominance, first through the election of Communist governments in France and Italy, and then surely over the rest of Europe. Even without the Soviet threat, any American administration might have been forced to develop some sort of aid program out of both humanitarian impulses and the general realization that an impoverished, unstable Europe was a long-term danger for the rest of the globe. Of course, it is questionable that such a program would have been politically sustainable.

Finally, the revival of Europe and its integration into a liberal global economy were central to the neo-Wilsonian vision for which many Democrats believed World War II had been fought. To put it a bit simply, to Woodrow Wilson, Franklin Roosevelt, and most of their foreign policy thinkers, the formula could be stated as follows: (relatively) free trade among nations begat prosperity for all concerned; prosperity begat freedom and world peace. The alternatives were autarkic self-aggrandizement, beggar-thy-neighbor trade policies, and war. From Truman on down, the idea that liberal trade was the basis for liberal political institutions constituted a near-monolithic consensus within the administration. The president stated this view concisely in a major speech at Baylor University just six days before making the Truman Doctrine address to Congress.

In the real world, as Truman had long since learned, the constraints of professional politics prevented rigid adherence to the theoretical free-trade tradition of the Democratic party. If the claims of an industry could not be ignored, he preferred to meet them through such nontariff methods as subsidies, which at least had the merit of not directly challenging liberal precepts. At Baylor, he engaged in a lot of hedging, right down to the point of asserting, "All that is contemplated is the reduction of tariffs, the removal of discriminations, and the achievement, not of free trade, but of freer trade."[13] For purposes of public discussion, the political debate centered on bilateral reciprocal-trade agreements, which were far more easily explained and defended. Nonetheless, despite all the rhetorical backing and filling, American diplomats were already in the early stages of developing machinery for multilateral trading arrangements that would take the non-Communist world a step farther toward their ultimate ideal. The result would be the General Agreement on Tariffs and Trade, established in 1948.

Truman later dated his own realization of the gravity of the European economic crisis to General Marshall's return from the Moscow conference near the end of April 1947. In fact, however, the issue had already received discussion in cabinet meetings and was being addressed by the State, War, Navy Coordinating Committee (in a loose sense, the precursor of the National Security Council). Marshall's homecoming and his vivid, firsthand account of the distress he had witnessed in Europe underscored the urgency of the problem. The secretary ordered George Kennan and the new Policy Planning Staff to bring together a general plan for European recovery as rapidly as possible.[14]

As the realization dawned that European recovery would be unimaginably expensive, the administration began to prepare the public. Dean Acheson, speaking in Mississippi on May 8, delivered the first major statement of the need for a comprehensive European recovery program, but the remote location of the address and poor press work by the State Department caused the speech to get little attention. Three weeks later, Communists seized power in Hungary, adding to the administration's sense of urgency. Queried about the event at a press conference, Truman called it "an outrage."[15]

The declaration that at last made an impact on the attentive public came when Marshall delivered the commencement address at Harvard in June. After Marshall's talk, the new proposal could be called the Marshall Plan. The president, who dismissed Clark Clifford's suggestion that it should bear his name, sincerely wanted Marshall to have whatever honor might attach itself to the proposal. He also knew that the general could do a much better job of selling it.[16] The Marshall Plan, as it existed by early June, consisted of little more than the open-ended proposition that a European recovery plan had to be comprehensive rather than piecemeal and should be based on cooperative transnational planning. Implicitly, such a program looked to the vision of an economically unified Europe that would shake off old national rivalries and attach less importance to political boundaries. In theory, if not in intent, it differed sharply from the Truman Doctrine, the purpose of which was the containment of totalitarian expansionism. The Marshall Plan, by contrast, envisioned the spread of economic development and prosperity to all comers.

It followed that the Soviet Union and its Eastern European satellites had to be given a chance to participate. For both diplomatic and domestic political reasons, the United States could not accept the moral responsibility for the division of Europe that inevitably would follow a refusal to invite the Soviet bloc. Privately, administration planners anticipated that the USSR likely would reject an invitation. Joining the Marshall Plan would have been of benefit to the Soviet peoples, but likely fatal to the Soviet system. Participation would require the USSR to divulge extensive and detailed information about its economy, make contributions of raw materials to the common effort, and risk being drawn into the Western capitalist orbit.

Everyone from Truman down realized that acceptance by the USSR would make the struggle for congressional funding infinitely more difficult. That June, at a foreign ministers conference in Paris, Molotov rejected Soviet participation, and the administration heaved a collective sigh of relief. The consequences, however, were portentous. Subsequently, the USSR forced all the Eastern European nations under its control, as well as still-independent Czechoslovakia, to reject the plan also. The next step was an agreement, the Molotov Plan, that established an Eastern economic bloc linked to the Soviet Union. In large measure a formalization of an already well-developed situation, these events nevertheless marked the more or less formal division of Europe.

A transnational recovery plan for all of Europe also implied a commitment to the economic rehabilitation of Germany. Although the administration had never accepted Henry Morgenthau's plan for German deindustrialization, the effect of the four-power occupation had been much the same. The French, as much as the Russians, feared a revival of German power and pressed hard for a punitive peace. Allied agreements placed limits on German industrial redevelopment. By the spring of 1947, however, the British and the Americans were prepared to support full economic reconstruction.

The catalyst was a special report prepared for the president by Herbert Hoover. It argued cogently that German recovery was the indispensable prerequisite to European recovery, that Germany drove the economies of the rest of Europe. Even so, the prospect of a resurgent German nation was hard to swallow just two years after the end of the war. Some high-ranking State Department staff members objected. So did Truman's close friend and former reparations commissioner Ed Pauley. So did John Steelman.

Truman did not formally approve the Hoover report, but neither did he reject it. (It is likely that both he and Hoover remembered vividly the

perceived economic consequences of Versailles.) Pauley's protests appear
only to have taken him definitively out of the foreign policy loop. Steelman's fears went unheeded. Acheson, with Marshall's backing, overruled
objections from within State. Averell Harriman, Clinton Anderson, Robert
Patterson, and Budget Director James Webb all seem to have been supportive of Hoover. In May, Acheson made the reconstruction of Germany
one of the major points in his Mississippi speech. In the summer, the
United States and Britain consummated an economic union of their zones
of occupation; by the fall, the French were induced to join.[17]

VI

From the beginning, even before the numbers were firm, everyone realized that the Marshall Plan would involve an enormous commitment of
American resources, which, in turn, were tightly limited by the material
demands of Americans unwilling to accept more years of deprivation.
Higher taxes, stringent economic controls, and curtailment of civilian
consumption were all beyond consideration. Truman, determined to be
a strong budget manager, would not accept large-scale, inflationary deficit
spending to finance an activist foreign policy. The only course was to
establish two priorities that were explicitly understood within the administration but never set forth in a clear fashion to the public. One was to
concentrate on bailing out Western Europe while deemphasizing the East
Asian mainland, specifically China. The other was to spend on economic
reconstruction at the expense of the defense budget. Understandable,
perhaps nearly inevitable, both decisions would boomerang on the
administration.

In China, the end of World War II had allowed for the resumption
of a long-dormant civil war between Communist forces of Mao Zedong,
based in the north, and the American-recognized Nationalist regime of
Chiang Kai-shek. Given aid (although not direct military support) by
Soviet occupiers in Manchuria and seemingly enjoying a large popular
following, the Communists quickly emerged as a formidable force. Chiang's
government, by contrast, seemed to display all the vices of traditional
Asian powers—corruption, nepotism, lethargy, incompetence. Yet Chiang
had been publicized in the United States as a great leader who embodied
the aspirations of his people.

Chiang's support was strong among conservatives, especially heartland Republicans influenced by a widespread Christian missionary impulse. They included Truman's colleague on his 1943 internationalist
speaking tour, Representative Walter Judd of Minnesota, and the far more
powerful Henry Luce, publisher of *Time*. In late 1945, the United States
ambassador to China, Patrick J. Hurley, resigned, blasting his Foreign
Service aides there as pro-Communist. A New Mexico Republican who
was arguably Roosevelt's least successful venture into bipartisanship,
Hurley repeated his charges before a congressional committee, thereby

foreshadowing a specter that would haunt the State Department a few years later.

Truman, desiring peace in China and certainly aware of the political dynamite in the conflict there, sent General Marshall in 1946 to mediate between the two forces. The effort, which displayed a profound misunderstanding of both Asian culture and the unbridgeable ideological gap between the two sides, was sure to fail. Marshall's goal, a coalition government that would include both Chiang and Mao, was about as likely as a collaboration between a scorpion and a tarantula. After protracted negotiations—during which the main objective of both sides was to cast blame for lack of results on the other party—Marshall returned to the United States with nothing to show for months of hard work, unhappy with both sides, but rather more disgusted with the Nationalists.

State Department thinking, heavily influenced by Marshall's jaundiced view of the Nationalist government and by the tendency of its own China experts to emphasize the progressive and reformist aspects of Maoist Communism, moved rapidly toward withdrawal. Neither Marshall nor the State Department professionals welcomed the probable coming to power of the Communists, but they believed that China probably could not be saved by any amount of aid. Given limited resources and the necessity for choice, there could be only one hard, unsentimental conclusion: Europe was salvageable and vastly more important to the United States.[18]

Most of the American diplomatic leadership, moreover, was Europe-centered, with a relatively short attention span for the Asian mainland. As Walter Isaacson and Evan Thomas have commented, the "wise men" who formulated the Marshall Plan understood well the calculus of national self-interest, but they also felt a deep attachment to Europe and to the liberal ideals of Western civilization. So did Truman, whose own cultural upbringing had not been very different. Against these realities, what could be the pull of a primitive Asian nation presided over by an unfit leader who called himself a generalissimo? Some might talk in geopolitical terms. Truman preferred to focus directly on Chiang, whom he later dismissed to an old Missouri friend as head of "the most corrupt government in the history of the world." China was effectively written off by mid-1947—without preparing the American people for the probable consequences.[19]

The defense budget also experienced a severe reduction. Truman's fiscal conservatism was one driving force behind the push. He hoped to whittle down the federal budget in general and was convinced that military spending as a matter of principle should be in a range of one-quarter to one-third of the total. He also appears to have worked from the assumption that—given the devastation inflicted on it by the war and given the American atomic monopoly—the Soviet Union would not openly attack areas it already did not occupy. Until the Korean War, he would make the policy stick despite cries of anguish, bureaucratic guerrilla warfare, and intermittent open rebellion from various corners of the Pentagon. Many members of Congress were more than willing to go along, many liberals feeling that the military had to be taken down several pegs, many conservatives favoring strict economy. As Secretary of Defense Forrestal, the man in the middle of some of the most contentious disputes, put it, "In the person of Harry Truman, I have seen the most rock-like example of civilian control the world has ever witnessed."[20]

Truman could and did argue that the American military establishment remained at record peacetime strength. The navy and air force were each the largest in the world; the army, far above its levels of the 1930s. Still, the reduction was draconian. The president's motivation had several sources, among them his firm belief in a small standing military and the citizen-soldier ideal, his fiscal conservatism, and his estimate of congressional attitudes. To the extent he assumed that Congress would place a strict limit on national security spending and opted to divert as many resources as possible into foreign economic aid, such a decision had much to commend it. But he also locked himself into a rigid and dangerous budgetary formula that tolerated a growing disparity between escalating commitments and military capabilities.[21]

In fact, considerable wishful thinking and downright willful avoidance of reality pervaded the defense budget. Even after the Czech coup and resultant war scare of March 1948, Truman would support only limited increases in defense spending. "We must be very careful that the military does not overstep the bounds from an economic standpoint domestically," he told Council of Economic Advisers chairman Edwin Nourse. "Most of them would like to go back to a war footing—that is not what we want."[22] When Congress, following the recommendations of an administration committee headed by Thomas Finletter, appropriated funds for a big enlargement of the air force, the president impounded the money. In fiscal year (FY) 1948 (July 1, 1947–June 30, 1948), total military spending was only $13 billion. Truman originally hoped to bring it under $10 billion for FY 1949; as it was, he would acquiesce in $13.1 billion of actual spending. This was about $10 billion below what military leaders insisted they needed.

Even granting the probability of a fair amount of fat in these requests, it is impossible to avoid discerning a reality gap in Truman's planning. As Robert Pollard has observed, administration strategy was to "set defense spending levels according to what the President and the Budget Bureau determined the economy could withstand, rather than what the administration's own foreign policy commitments seemed to require." Far from being impressed with a potential problem, however, Truman was increasingly put out with what he considered the insubordination of military brass and his service secretaries, especially Stuart Symington (air force) and Kenneth Royall (army). Fed up with what he considered Secretary of Defense Forrestal's "weakness," he planned to dispose of him for a new man who would be a tough budget enforcer.[23]

The American nuclear monopoly provided no persuasive justification for Truman's approach. Clear-eyed analysts understood that it was a transitory phenomenon. Moreover, throughout Truman's first term, the United States lacked a sufficient bomb stockpile, adequate delivery systems, or a viable strategy for a nuclear war. (When his old lieutenant Victor Housholder visited the White House in February 1947, Truman casually, and astonishingly, told him that the United States had only fourteen atomic bombs.) In addition, Truman's private remarks about the bomb from the fall of 1945 on leave the impression that he envisioned it as an instrument of indiscriminate slaughter and would have authorized its use only in the most extreme situation. It is clear that he never undertook a close analysis of the relationship between power and commitments. He surely doubted, moreover, that Congress would back both a bigger defense budget and the Marshall Plan. In the very short run, Truman's defense spending policy was viable. But hinging as it did on transitory Soviet postwar difficulties and on exclusive possession of the atomic bomb, it was untenable over a longer haul that—as it developed—would not be very long at all.[24]

VII

Truman took a relatively low-profile role in the selling of the Marshall Plan. He commented on it at numerous press conferences but carefully, and surely intentionally, avoided putting himself at the head of a media campaign. He knew that an overly personal identification with it would do it no good in a Republican Congress. He may even have known that so friendly a figure as Vandenberg rather huffily rejected the idea that there was such a thing as "the Truman Doctrine."[25] He used the power of the presidency in other ways, naming two "blue-ribbon commissions" headed by Secretary of the Interior Krug and Secretary of Commerce Harriman to study the implications of the Marshall Plan for American resources and economic progress; he gave the Council of Economic Advisers a similar assignment. To no one's surprise, all three endeavors produced reports that extolled the manifest necessity of the plan and minimized any adverse effects on the country. Beyond that, the president wisely relied on Marshall's enormous prestige and Undersecretary Robert Lovett's consummate skill as a lobbyist.

The plan attracted support from numerous interest groups that were either politically powerful or articulate and influential in the political dialogue. At the top of the prestige scale was the Committee for the Marshall Plan, with Henry L. Stimson as honorary chairman at the head of a list of board members who were bipartisan and impeccably establishmentarian. The two major labor federations, the AFL and the CIO, added their support; so did the most important farm group, the Farm Bureau. The Committee for Economic Development, a group of progressive business leaders, not only supported the plan, but made major contributions to its content.[26]

For Truman, perhaps the most fortuitous political spinoff from the Marshall Plan was the way in which it isolated the pro-Soviet left within the Democratic party. Insignificant on Capitol Hill, the Popular Fronters had remained strong at the grass roots. Mobilized around the still-formidable Henry Wallace, they presented the prospect of a sizable group of demoralized, disaffected Democrats in 1948 at best, a third-party challenge at worst. Attacking the Truman Doctrine as negative and militaristic, Wallace had seized what many liberals considered the high ground in the foreign policy debate. The Marshall Plan forced a reconsideration. Wallace waffled for months, and then came out against it. The anti-Communist Americans for Democratic Action embraced it as a fulfillment of the ideals of Franklin Roosevelt and endorsed it in a widely distributed pamphlet, *Toward Total Peace*. They also pictured Wallace as a deluded idealist who had been taken in by the Communists. Many liberal Democrats who had been tolerant of the Popular Front would back the Marshall Plan, become increasingly anti-Soviet, reject Wallace, and find themselves behind Truman.[27]

In Congress, the plan had near-unanimous support from the Democrats in both houses. Two additional developments put it over the top: firsthand contact with the appalling conditions in Europe and strong backing from the internationalist Republicans. In late 1947, perhaps half the members of Congress traveled to Europe; almost all came back converts. Eugene Cox of Georgia, widely considered one of the shabbiest demagogues on the Democratic side of the House, was reported to have shed tears and given away most of his wardrobe to ragged unfortunates. Influential Republican representative Everett Dirksen, from isolationist downstate Illinois, returned to the United States to pledge his support. Representative Richard Nixon, convinced that he had seen a continent on the brink of starvation, chaos, and Communism, traveled up and down his California district explaining the need for the Marshall Plan to a constituency that, according to public-opinion surveys, opposed it by a 3 to 1 margin.[28]

The internationalist Republicans, some convinced by their travel abroad, many for the plan from the beginning, did most of the truly effective and critical work in Congress. Overcoming their own instincts for rigid economy and willing to precipitate a party split, they fought effectively and, despite a temporary setback on appropriations in the House, prevailed. Vandenberg assumed the most visible and active role, acting as a mediator between the administration and the Capitol Hill Republicans, suggesting alterations that made the legislation more palatable to the GOP without harming it, and putting his prestige on the line to achieve a restoration of appropriations that his fellow partisans had reduced in the House.[29]

Ultimately, the reason for the program's passage with full appropriations was anti-Communism. The Truman Doctrine had been the call to arms of the Cold War. The Marshall Plan, first presented as an attempt to transcend the Cold War, became an extension of containment once the Soviet Union rejected it. In doing so, the USSR saddled itself with the responsibility for the division of Europe and virtually ensured that Congress would approve the administration request. In December 1947, Congress passed an interim aid bill to carry Western Europe through the winter. Everyone realized that it was a first step in a long-term, comprehensive program.

During the first half of 1948, the USSR appeared increasingly menacing, aggressive, and unpredictable. In February, Communists seized power in Czechoslovakia, thereby eliminating the last independent democracy in Eastern Europe and consolidating Soviet control of the region. Czech foreign minister Jan Masaryk, the Eastern European leader most esteemed in the West, died shortly thereafter in a fall from his apartment window. With hindsight, one might observe that the USSR was simply rationalizing its "sphere of influence," however painful the process might be for millions of Czechs. Yet at the time, the takeover of a small nation incapable of threatening Soviet interests and the probable assassination of Masaryk sent shock waves through Western Europe and across the Atlantic.

In March, General Lucius D. Clay, United States commander in Germany, warned Washington that an armed attack from the east might be possible. Truman went before Congress to request resumption of the draft and subsequently received it. Meanwhile, under strong pressure from the USSR, Finland agreed to a mutual-security treaty. Britain, France, Belgium, the Netherlands, and Luxembourg responded to Soviet actions by agreeing to a collective-defense treaty. At the time and later, critics of the Truman administration would argue that it had contrived a "war scare" in order to push through the Marshall Plan and engage in a military buildup. It is just possible, however, that reasonable people—Democrats and Republicans, Americans and Europeans—faced with the events of early 1948 might perceive an imminent threat. In April, they could take heart from two events that seemed to show that the tide was running against Moscow. Congress approved the Marshall Plan, although final budgetary authorization would not come until June. And anti-Communist forces won the Italian elections; American aid to Italy may have been decisive.

In the meantime, the Western powers had moved ahead with the merger of their occupation zones into a more unified West Germany. After they introduced a new currency and thereby deprived the USSR of the power to sabotage the economy, the Soviet Union began to blockade land routes to Berlin. It remained unclear until well into the summer whether the Soviets contemplated temporary and sporadic harassment or whether a serious new crisis was beginning. With this latest ominous development in the background, Congress passed a $6 billion foreign aid appropriation. It included approximately $5 billion for the Marshall Plan, a sum that was about 12 percent of the entire federal budget and 2 percent of the gross national product.

In the end, Truman had only one disappointment. He had wanted Dean Acheson to head the program; but Vandenberg, speaking for himself and other Republicans who had gotten the Marshall Plan through Congress, wanted a nonpartisan businessman. He insisted on Paul Hoffman, president of the Studebaker Corporation and chairman of the Committee for Economic Development. Disgruntled, Truman wrote in his diary on April 3, 1948: "[Vandenberg] said the Senate wanted no one connected with State Dept. Silly idea. Want some industrialist without experience."

Truman may have toyed with the idea of trying to appoint Acheson anyway. He called the next day to try to get him to accept the position. Acheson wisely refused to touch it without Vandenberg's approval. In the process, he saved Truman from a bad mistake, held himself in continued availability for the post of secretary of state, and made it likely that Vandenberg would feel compelled to support him should that designation come. On April 5, the White House announced the appointment of Hoffman. For the next two years, given a free hand by the White House, he ran the Marshall Plan with distinction, resigning in 1950 to become an avid promoter of foreign-economic-development programs and to be remembered as one of Truman's best choices for high office.[30]

Upon signing the original authorization bill, Truman issued a statement that commended the Congress for its bipartisanship, called the act a triumph for democracy, and praised it as "perhaps the greatest venture in constructive statesmanship that any nation has undertaken."[31] He was right on all counts. And while he had avoided personal identification with the legislation, he doubtless took satisfaction in the probability that historians would place it among *his* greatest achievements.

23

"A DISCOURAGING PROSPECT INDEED": THE PALESTINE CONTROVERSY AND THE BIRTH OF ISRAEL, 1945–1948

While the Marshall Plan made its way through Congress, Truman had to grapple with another issue that seemed in one sense a sideshow, yet had epochal significance.[1] The drive to establish a Jewish homeland in Palestine confronted him with a bewildering series of conflicts involving morality, politics, and the national interest—even as it also presented a challenge to his authority as president. Moreover, the outcome would have a major impact on American diplomacy and self-interest in the Middle East for the next half-century.

During the first three years after the end of World War II, the Palestine controversy was a classic example of a worst-case scenario in the politics of foreign policy. On the one hand, a crucial constituency irrevocably committed to an absolutist solution sought to determine the administration's position. On the other, a Foreign Service establishment, backed to the limit by a secretary of state with unparalleled prestige, defined the national interest with no reference to domestic political realities (or increasingly to those in Palestine) and attempted to impose its will on the president.

For Truman, caught in the middle, the result was an embarrassing no-win situation that threatened his control of foreign policy and left him a victim of something akin to political combat fatigue. In one of his more reflective moments, he told David Niles: "I surely wish God Almighty would give the Children of Israel an Isaiah, the Christians a St. Paul and the Sons of Ishmael a peep at the Golden rule."[2]

II

Truman, of course, had quietly committed himself to Zionist objectives while in the Senate. For him, as for many other members of Congress, the issue had been an easy one: American Jews, preponderantly advocates of Zionism in the wake of Nazi persecutions and the Holocaust, had money and votes; their opponents were all but invisible. Some had been among his political supporters in Missouri. A core constituency within the Democratic party, Jewish voters were an absolutely critical bloc in New York state, whose forty-five electoral votes made it the biggest prize in any presidential election. Furthermore, if the Jewish vote was the Democratic party's to lose, the Republicans were doing their best to attract it. New York governor Thomas E. Dewey was an ardent suitor as well as the likely Republican presidential nominee. So was his major Republican rival, Senator Taft. Many other Republicans who had no presidential ambitions, including the aged farm-state senator Arthur Capper of Kansas, had likewise aligned themselves with Jewish aspirations in Palestine.

Whether a matter of political opportunism or moral conviction, support of Zionism seemed cost-free. Truman understood the political calculus and could sound cynical about it. In 1946, he met with American Middle East diplomats who warned him that American prestige in the region was sinking because of statements indicating sympathy with the Zionists. His response: "I am sorry, gentlemen, but I have to answer to hundreds of thousands who are anxious for the success of Zionism; I do not have hundreds of thousands of Arabs among my constituents."[3]

Clearly, however, there was more to it than simple cynicism. At one level, he must have felt a sense of reciprocal loyalty to Jewish groups that had supported him on the same basis that he had felt an obligation to Tom Pendergast, and he understood their concern for their persecuted European cousins. Moreover, his religious heritage and his reading of ancient history predisposed him to the idea of a Jewish state in Palestine.[4] But if all these considerations pushed him toward Zionism, his responsibilities as president made it impossible for him to ignore the problem of the national interest in the Middle East, as pressed on him by the Department of State and by numerous national security officials, most notably James Forrestal. The result was a mix of rhetorical sympathy and practical inaction that made all sides unhappy.

When Truman became president, Palestine was in effect a British colonial possession, acquired from the Ottoman Empire at the end of World War I and managed under a mandate from the League of Nations. In 1917, British foreign secretary Arthur Balfour had endorsed the concept that it could be the location of a Jewish "national home." Under terms specifically provided in the league mandate, Britain allowed self-supporting Jews to settle there in the 1920s and 1930s without significant restriction.

By the outbreak of World War II in 1939, nearly 500,000 Jewish settlers, many of them fleeing Nazi persecution, had formed the core of a militant nationalist movement and had attracted Arab hostility so intense that their settlements were armed camps. Britain envisioned a communal war in which its overstretched armed forces would be caught in the middle. Faced with growing pro-Nazi sentiment throughout the Arab world, apprehensive about their long-run position there, and hoping to stabilize an explosive situation, the British placed strict limits on further Jewish immigration.

Such was the inheritance of Truman, Attlee, at least 100,000 survivors of the Holocaust desperate for a new life, and their Jewish supporters in America. In Palestine, Jewish armed forces began an insurgency against both British and Arabs. In the United States, Jews, who had been predominantly assimilationist before the war, now overwhelmingly endorsed the Zionist dream. So did many Gentiles, who felt an obligation to what was left of European Jewry and had little sympathy for Arab attitudes that seemed indistinguishable from Nazi anti-Semitism.

From the beginning of his presidency, Truman was the object of intense lobbying by Zionist supporters. Eddie Jacobson and other Kansas City Jewish friends pressed their case with him. So did Max Lowenthal. Bob Hannegan and other Democratic pros might not be Jewish themselves, but they understood the importance of this constituency and reminded the president of it incessantly.[5] The major advocate of Israel was Administrative Assistant David K. Niles, a Roosevelt holdover and long-designated contact with northeastern Jewish liberals, most of whom were ardent Zionists. Niles had Truman's confidence and affection almost from the beginning. He spent part of every week in Boston and New York, meeting with ethnoreligious groups whose importance Truman appreciated but with whom he communicated poorly. Not simply a liaison to the Zionists, Niles was their spokesman within the White House. His hand, generally well hidden even from his White House colleagues, played a central part in Truman's key decisions.[6]

Acting from conviction, compassion, and political expediency, Truman identified himself with the general cause of Jewish immigration to Palestine. Its specific embodiment was a Zionist demand for the immediate admission of 100,000 refugees. The British government, caught between its fear of chaos and its need of American support, fixed on a strategy of delay. In November 1945, the administration reluctantly agreed to the appointment of the Anglo-American Committee of Inquiry, which would study the issue and make recommendations. Zionists and their sympathizers argued that the committee was no more than a ploy to avoid action. In response, Truman wrote but did not send a letter to his old Senate colleague Joseph Ball of Minnesota:

I told the Jews that if they were willing to furnish me with five hundred thousand men to carry on a war with the Arabs, we could do what they are suggesting . . . otherwise we will have to negotiate awhile.

. . . I don't think that you or any of the other Senators would be inclined to send half a dozen Divisions to Palestine to maintain a Jewish state.

What I am trying to do is to make the whole world safe for the Jews. Therefore, I don't feel like going to war for Palestine.[7]

By then, Truman had committed himself to a policy that Dean Acheson would describe as follows: "first, immediate immigration into Palestine of one hundred thousand displaced Jews from Eastern Europe; second, the determination to assume no political or military responsibility for this decision."[8] The president surely was correct in feeling that the larger American public would never have countenanced the use of military force in Palestine, but his policy pleased no one, especially after the Committee of Inquiry came out with a report the following spring recommending Jewish immigration and the British responded with further stonewalling.

Negotiations led to the short-lived Morrison-Grady Plan, which would have allowed the immigration of 100,000 and partitioned Palestine into four provinces: Arab, Jewish, Jerusalem, and the Negev. But Zionists rejected both British control of further immigration and the territorial division itself. Moreover, the entire plan required an initial Arab agreement that was highly unlikely without extensive talks and Jewish concessions. Truman, seeing it as a way to solve the refugee problem, was inclined to support it, but backed off after a blast of criticism from the Zionists and their allies. At a cabinet meeting on July 30, 1946, he vented his frustration with the Jews, declaring, as Henry Wallace recorded it, "Jesus Christ couldn't please them when he was here on earth, so how could anyone expect that I would have any luck?"[9]

III

By this point, the political pressures were intense. Taft had denounced the president's failure to achieve a satisfactory solution. New York Democratic leaders wrote that their state ticket was doomed unless something could be accomplished. Dewey, up for reelection as governor, was poised to make a declaration of his own. On Yom Kippur, October 4, 1946, Truman issued a release that in his memoirs he would disingenuously describe as a routine holiday statement. In fact, it had been originally drafted by Zionist leader Eliahu Epstein, working with David Niles, and then mildly toned down in the State Department (apparently by Dean Acheson). Recapitulating his efforts to obtain Jewish immigration to Palestine, Truman declared his belief that "public opinion in the United States" would support "the creation of a viable Jewish state in control of its own immigration and economic policies in an adequate area of Palestine." In language that was very direct by diplomatic standards, he thus had endorsed Zionist objectives without meaningful qualification.[10]

The Yom Kippur statement did little for the New York Democrats (Dewey quickly topped it by calling for the immigration of "several hundred thousand" Jews to Palestine), but it set off sparks around the world. King Ibn Saud of Saudi Arabia protested vehemently and sent two princes of the royal family to Washington to register their dissents in a personal meeting with Truman. Clement Attlee, representing the feelings of an outraged British government, sent an angry communication to the president. By the fall of 1946, Truman felt positively persecuted and profoundly ambivalent toward Jewish leadership at home and abroad. Writing to Ed Pauley in October, he remarked of the Jews: "They seem to have the same attitude toward the 'under dog' when they are on top as [that with which] they have been treated as 'under dogs' themselves." The only person who suffered in such situations, he concluded, was "the innocent bystander who tries to help." He would "spend the rest of my time here at this place working for the best interest of the whole country and let the chips fall where they may."[11]

Truman's rather self-pitying conception of himself may be appropriately dismissed as that of a political warrior trying to advance in the midst of a murderous crossfire—hazardous and unpleasant, the situation nonetheless came with the job. Still, he was not engaged in a simple act of self-deception when he declared his dedication to larger objectives. Fundamentally tolerant, whatever angry words might occasionally cross his lips, he really cared about the plight of all displaced persons, not just Jews. He advocated liberal immigration policies that would let many of them settle in the United States. To Senator Walter George, he wrote, "I am interested in relieving a half million people of the most distressful situation that has happened in the world since Attila made his invasion of Europe."[12]

By early 1946, the British occupation of Palestine had become the focus of Zionist wrath and extremist violence. On July 22, 1946, Jewish terrorists bombed Jerusalem's King David Hotel, a British army center; ninety-one persons were killed. In February 1947, the British, seeing no light at the end of the tunnel, announced that they were turning the issue over to the United Nations with the intention of relinquishing their mandate. Speaking to a cheering House of Commons, Ernest Bevin, intensely frustrated at Jewish violence against the British military and at the failure of continued efforts to broker an agreement between Jews and Arabs, personally denounced Truman for playing politics on Palestine. Perhaps because the undiplomatic attack had more than a grain of accuracy, Truman never quite forgave him.[13]

The British decision meant that Palestine would consume even more diplomatic effort, marked by increasing friction between Truman and State Department officials. State, along with the rest of the national security establishment, placed little value on the moral claims of the Jews; it agonized instead about the hostility of the Arab world and the availability of vital energy resources. Not motivated by anti-Semitism, the position was a perfectly respectable interpretation of the long-term national interest, but it spoke neither to Truman's political needs nor to his larger view of foreign policy as a moral mission. It also reawakened his long-held hostility toward professional diplomats.

In January 1947, after appointing Marshall as secretary of state, he had written to Mamma and Mary Jane, "I am hoping that Gen. Marshall will take the striped pants boys for a ride. There are more tea hounds and S.O.B.s in that place . . ." Fourteen months later, he was lamenting that even Marshall hadn't been able to get the job done: "I had thought . . . he'd set them right but he has had too much to do and the 3rd & 4th levels over there are the same striped pants conspirators. . . . [T]hey have completely balled up the Palestine situation."[14]

Truman's language in both communications was revealing. Groping for a way to explain a foreign policy that threatened to destroy him politically, he emphasized the alleged effete and duplicitous characteristics of Foreign Service professionals, while engaging in a near-total misreading of Marshall's conception of his relationship with them. Because he did not want to admit to himself that the political dimension was part of his own motivation, he could not deal with Marshall's assumptions that politics should have nothing to do with foreign policy and that it was the job of the secretary of state to advocate the national interest, largely as defined by Foreign Service professionals.

Truman avoided indicting the two State Department officials with whom he dealt directly—Marshall, whom he so admired, and, after mid-1947, Robert Lovett, who had been as successful in cultivating the president as he had with members of Congress. He found the prospect of conflict with either man politically and emotionally intolerable. To attack the diplomats, by contrast, was a natural manifestation of the populist outlook that long had led him to disparage most professional administrative types, in both government bureaucracies and large corporations.

At David Niles's suggestion, Truman had John Hilldring, a State Department official close to Acheson and to American Jewish leaders, placed on the United States delegation to the United Nations before the Palestine debate. The appointment of someone who would, in effect, serve as Truman's own man demonstrated how the president had come to think of State almost as enemy country; it is also noteworthy that the maneuver was managed through Lovett rather than Marshall. Hilldring reported directly to Niles. According to Evan Wilson, "The Department often did not know what was being reported to the White House or what instructions Niles was passing on to Hilldring."[15]

IV

Truman also faced continued pressure from the Jewish community and its allies. During the latter half of 1947, approximately 135,000 letters, telegrams, petitions, and the like came to him, almost all of them backing the Jewish cause. Understandably, his reaction was one of varying degrees of irritation, depending on the source of the pressure. Rabbi Abba Hillel Silver of Cleveland, the American leader of the more militant Zionists and a Republican who was close to Senator Taft, especially infuriated him. Responding to a memo from Niles, the president, implicitly admitting the political considerations, lumped the rabbi with Irgun and Stern Gang terrorists: "We could have settled this Palestine thing if U.S. politics had been kept out of it. Terror and Silver are the contributing causes of *some*, if not all, of our troubles."[16]

Conversely, he does not seem to have lost his balance with Rabbi Stephen Wise, also a dedicated Zionist but more moderate than Silver (who was his primary rival in the movement) and a longtime liberal reformer with ties to the Democratic party. And, of course, his relationship with Jacobson and Lowenthal suffered not at all. Eleanor Roosevelt, by now a Zionist fellow traveler, was, as always, handled with the softest of kid gloves.[17] For all his resentment of Zionist demands, moreover, Truman continued to tilt in the direction of the movement.

It was a leaning that appears to have been confirmed at a crucial point by a meeting that Hilldring and Niles arranged between the president and the great Zionist Chaim Weizmann in November 1947. Weizmann may have been welcome in part because a year earlier he had narrowly lost his bid for reelection as president of the World Zionist Congress—the opposition having been orchestrated by, among others, Rabbi Silver. By then, the United Nations was close to a vote to partition Palestine into Jewish and Arab states; the focus of the debate was the distribution of territory. A gentle scholar and idealistic visionary, Weizmann spoke to Truman of the way in which the Jews could rebuild Palestine, make the desert bloom, and build a nation that could serve as a model for the region. He pressed the Jewish case for the Negev and an outlet to the Gulf of Aqaba. Truman liked what he heard and instructed the United States delegation at the United Nations to support the Jewish claim. After some confusion it would do so.[18]

The president prevailed without much difficulty on this matter, which involved a relatively moderate adjustment in the American negotiating position. On November 29, 1947, the United Nations voted for a partition plan that divided the country between Arabs and Jews while maintaining Jerusalem as a separate entity. The Zionists saw the resolution as a victory; the Arabs angrily rejected it. By early 1948, Jews and Arabs were engaged in open warfare, and the whole question of how to enforce partition was unanswered. The British, wanting only to extricate themselves, set May 15 as the date at which they unilaterally would end their mandate.

As a practical matter, the options were to establish a large-scale UN peacekeeping force in which the United States would necessarily be a major participant, or to let the two sides fight it out to a result that surely would differ from the UN settlement. Diplomatically, either option was certain to intensify the enmity that the Arabs already felt toward the United States. In addition, as Western Europe experienced the Czech coup and the March war scare, conflict in Palestine appeared to be a distraction that the United States could do without. Secretary of Defense Forrestal used every forum at his disposal to argue against going forward with partition. Clark Clifford recalled him as asserting, "You just don't understand. Forty million Arabs are going to push four hundred thousand Jews into the sea. And that's all there is to it. Oil—that is the side we ought to be on." State Department officials began to turn toward postponement of partition and the maintenance of Palestine as one nation under a UN trusteeship. Inside the White House, however, Clifford made common cause with Niles and urged Truman to stand firm behind partition. Attuned to the politics of the issue, he well understood that the consequences of reversal would be catastrophic.[19]

Just how catastrophic was demonstrated on February 17 by a special congressional election in New York City. Running in a heavily Jewish district in the Bronx, American Labor party (ALP) candidate Leo Isaacson easily defeated the Democratic nominee, polling 56 percent of the vote in a four-man contest. Henry Wallace, who was capitalizing on the Palestine issue, had campaigned hard for him. The ALP was able to throw its workers from all over the city into the district, and Communists got out the vote for the winner also. These extenuating factors did not prevent most political analysts from seeing the result as an early warning for the White House: New York Jews would stand for no equivocation on partition. Liberal Democrats, who had the most to lose from a Jewish defection, reacted with hysterical visions of disaster in November.

Yet Truman wavered. On February 21, aboard the presidential yacht, *Williamsburg*, at the beginning of an official visit to Puerto Rico and the Virgin Islands, he received a communication from the State Department. It outlined a speech that Ambassador Warren Austin was to deliver to the UN Security Council, arguing that the council did not have authorization to enforce partition with military force and suggesting that if partition was no longer possible, the United States might have to back trusteeship. Truman, almost certainly acting with the advice of Clifford, responded, "I approve in principle this basic position. I want to make it clear, however, that nothing should be presented to Security Council that could be interpreted as a recession on our part from the position we took in the General Assembly. Send final draft of Austin's remarks for my consideration." Soon thereafter, he received the final text accompanied by the assurance that he had requested, and approved it. After Austin delivered the speech, however, most observers interpreted it as the first step in a probable retreat, and Zionists strongly protested to the White House.[20]

Meeting with Marshall and Lovett on March 8, Truman was informed that the Security Council was not prepared to accept the General Assembly partition resolution. The two men proposed trusteeships as a fallback position and presented the president with a draft of remarks along those lines for Ambassador Austin to deliver. Truman, apparently not yet fully comprehending what he was getting into, acquiesced. Most likely, he was thinking of trusteeship as a temporary postponement rather than a final denial of Jewish statehood.[21]

V

By now, the president was so fatigued from the pounding he had taken that he declined to see any Zionist leaders, including Chaim Weizmann. On March 13, Eddie Jacobson visited him at the White House, broke into tears, and pleaded with him to grant another audience to Weizmann. As Jacobson recalled it, Truman's rage at Jewish leaders who had criticized and been disrespectful to him had left him "at that moment as close to being an anti-Semite as a man could possibly be." Reminding his old friend that Weizmann would be the last person in the world to insult him, Jacobson said, "It doesn't sound like you, Harry, because I thought you could take this stuff they have been handing out to you." Truman turned in his swivel chair, looked out at the White House rose garden for a minute, and then turned around again and replied, "You win, you bald-headed son-of-a-bitch. I will see him."[22]

On Thursday, March 18, Weizmann secretly visited the White House and talked for forty-five minutes with Truman; once again, he set forth his dreams of Israel as the garden of the Middle East and a refuge for persecuted Jews. There can be no doubt that he left thinking that the president remained committed to partition, although Truman conceivably raised the possibility of delay. On Friday, March 19, Ambassador Warren Austin spoke to the Security Council, proposing suspension of partition and a temporary trusteeship. Jewish leaders across the country and around the world denounced the American about-face.

Weizmann said nothing, but his silence lends little credence to Truman's later assertion that the two of them had reached a meeting of minds on the course of American policy. It was largely the result of a back-channel communication by Sam Rosenman, who delivered Truman's personal assurance that Austin's speech did not represent his policy.[23]

In fact, Truman had been stunned by the speech. Shortly after hearing of it, he wrote in his diary:

> The State Dept. pulled the rug from under me today. . . . This morning I
> find that the State Dept. has reversed my Palestine policy. The first I know
> about it is what I see in the papers! Isn't that hell! I am now in the position
> of a liar and a doublecrosser. . . .
>
> There are people on the third and fourth levels of the State Dept. who
> have always wanted to cut my throat. They've succeeded in doing so.
> Marshall's in California and Lovett's in Florida.[24]

Of course, Truman should not have been astonished. What had happened? Robert Donovan, the most careful and sensitive interpreter of the zigs and zags over Palestine, suggests that Truman had been diverted by events in Europe (which had led to his "war scare" address to Congress on March 17); that he had assumed the State Department would take steps to prepare public opinion for a retreat from partition; that he had been given no advance warning of the date of Austin's talk; and that he did not understand (because State did not explain it to him) that a UN vote for trusteeship would likely cancel the partition resolution.[25] All these explanations are plausible.

One might add another. The sequence of events also demonstrated the thinness of the presidential staff. Able as he was, Clifford had too many balls to juggle; he could neither provide continual input on any one issue nor monitor the way in which it was being handled by a cabinet department. Truman needed a larger immediate support group for foreign affairs, one that could do more to help him define his foreign policy, ensure that his interests were being protected, and ascertain that his wishes were carried out.

Instead, Truman appears to have been overwhelmed by the Palestine issue. He was subjected to intolerable pressures and given impossible alternatives of either alienating his Jewish constituency or sending American troops as part of a UN force to impose partition. He did not want to get into a fight with Marshall and Lovett. And he had to come to grips with a morally ambiguous situation that made the European crisis easy by comparison. One senses that some sort of a mental withdrawal process occurred. Truman was too experienced a politician to have no sense of the emotions that American Jewry had invested in partition, too much a politician to the core to have overlooked them because of the European crisis. It seems more likely that—confronting a situation he had described as "insoluble" fifteen months earlier[26] and wanting to avoid conflict—he agreed with Marshall and Lovett, reassured Weizmann, and convinced himself that he was following a consistent policy until reality hit him like a sledgehammer on March 19.

Over the next few days, Truman and his aides attempted to pick up the pieces. "Clarifications" by Marshall and the president underscored the concept that trusteeship was meant as only a temporary expedient, not a substitute for partition. These were enough to prevent at least one disaster; Eleanor Roosevelt was persuaded to withdraw her resignation from the American delegation to the United Nations. Behind the scenes, Clifford undertook an investigation of whether State had "doublecrossed" the president and found himself forced to conclude that Austin's statement, however clumsily made, had been properly cleared. Thereafter, he acted as White House liaison on Palestine, apparently clearing all communications between the State Department and Austin.[27]

In theory, there was much to be said for the idea of a temporary trusteeship, accompanied by a truce between Arab and Jewish armed forces who would then engage in negotiations to work out a permanent political settlement. "The first thing to do is to restore peace in the Holy Land, try to see if we can't arrange a settlement that will stop the bloodshed," Truman told a press conference. "I don't want to see people killed any more." A noble sentiment. As a practical proposition, however, it had little support on either side. Writing to Truman on April 9, Chaim Weizmann declared that partition was unavoidable; it already existed on a de facto basis in much of Palestine, and the choice for the Jews was "between Statehood and extermination."[28]

Moreover, it seemed that trusteeship unavoidably would imply a substantial commitment of American military power at a time when Europe was in crisis. The Joint Chiefs of Staff estimated that approximately 100,000 troops would be required for a UN peacekeeping force to police an armed truce and that the United States probably would have to provide nearly 47,000 of them. This number would be, as Forrestal subsequently made clear, "substantially our entire present ground reserve." What would happen if war broke out in Europe? And however much the Jewish vote might welcome it, what would be the larger political consequences of committing military personnel, at least a few of whom would certainly be killed and wounded? Truman shrank from the possibility, but finally authorized Austin to say, as Forrestal summarized it, that "we would participate in the implementation of the trusteeship mandate by the associated allied nations (UK, US, and France) up to the limit of our ability."[29]

VI

For the next several weeks, American diplomats worked without success for an Arab–Jewish truce, accompanied by acceptance of temporary trusteeship. Neither side got much beyond public-relations gestures. The Zionists were relatively open in proclaiming their confidence that they could prevail in a military struggle. Increasingly, they were more interested in obtaining an end to the American policy of prohibiting arms sales to either side than in stopping the fighting. Furthermore, neither the British nor the French were willing to commit themselves to material support of a continued trusteeship. As the clock ticked down toward May 15, State relentlessly pursued a policy that was going nowhere, and Truman found himself under intense pressure to recognize the new Jewish state that was certain to be proclaimed as the British mandate ended.

Given the lack of progress under the official policy, it is remarkable that there was much doubt about the outcome. Still, it was no easy matter to turn the State Department around. The entire foreign policy apparatus, after all, had been lobbying for trusteeship at the United Nations and in Foreign Offices around the world. To reverse course would be at the least embarrassing; in some individual instances, it could lay American diplomats open to charges of bad faith.

On April 30, Truman met with Dean Rusk, who as director of State's Office of United Nations Affairs had become deeply immersed in the controversy. Rusk still believed that a truce was possible. When he warned Truman that the Arabs might accept one and the Jews refuse, the president replied, "If the Jews refuse to accept a truce on reasonable grounds they need not expect anything else from us." He seemed willing to take whatever heat might come his way if the diplomats could stop the fighting and he could represent himself as a successful peacemaker. He concluded by telling Rusk, "There is no other answer to this situation. Good luck to you and let me know if there is any way in which I can help."[30]

But what if the fighting did not stop? Inside the White House, Clifford counseled flexibility. On May 8, reporting a discussion with Rusk, he told Truman:

> I urged that the United States take no position between now and the 15th which would tie the hands of the United States after May 15th. I pointed out the likelihood that the Jew and the Arab States would be proclaimed and the United States should then be in a position to deal with the result.[31]

One did not have to be a cryptographer to discern the word "recognition" between the lines. By May 11, Rusk seems to have known that it was likely. In a telephone conversation with UN delegation members Philip Jessup and John Ross, he declared that the distinction between partition and trusteeship had been overblown. The objective always had been peace. Barring last-minute developments, what was likely to come out of the White House was that "something has happened in fact over there . . . a community in existence over there running its own affairs." Speaking of Truman, he continued, "I don't think the boss will ever put himself in a position of opposing that effort when it might be that the US opposition would be the only thing that would prevent it from succeeding."[32]

Marshall was not prepared to accept such a culmination. On the afternoon of May 12, he, Lovett, and a couple of other State Department officials were summoned to the White House to meet with the president, Clifford, Niles, and Matt Connelly. Truman began by indicating his concern about what would happen after May 15. Lovett responded that there was no longer any possibility of a truce. Jewish forces had achieved a temporary military ascendancy, planned to proclaim an independent state, and expected to work out an arrangement in which King Abdullah of Transjordan would take possession of the Arab area of Palestine. Still not prepared to confront Marshall directly, Truman had asked Clifford to make the case for recognition. Using as his point of departure a proposed presidential statement produced by Max Lowenthal and redrafted by George Elsey, Clifford argued that American policy had lost touch with reality, that a truce was unlikely, and that partition had been accomplished in fact. The statement itself, which he proposed for Truman to read at a press conference the next day, in effect urged the establishment of a Jewish state and promised immediate recognition.

Lovett and Marshall argued against recognition at a time when the issue was before the Security Council and the entire thrust of American policy was still in the direction of trusteeship. Both believed that it would be perceived as a transparent bid for the Jewish vote. Marshall declared that to follow Clifford's advice would be to subordinate an international problem to domestic politics, to diminish the dignity of the presidency, and to lose Truman his own vote if Marshall were to vote in the general election.

Tempers flared on both sides. Clifford recalled Marshall asserting "in a righteous God-damned Baptist tone" that the special counsel was a political functionary who should not even be present. Clifford responded that the State Department had no policy except to wait on events. Truman, surely taken aback, adjourned the meeting, stating, according to Marshall's summary, "that he was fully aware of the difficulties and dangers in the situation, to say nothing of the political risks involved which he, himself, would run." His precise position remains uncertain, but he did initial a position paper that would continue American efforts at the UN along the same lines as before.[33]

If Marshall appeared to have won a victory, Lovett sensed that it was illusory. The argument appears to have been more about the timing of recognizing a Jewish state than whether the deed would be done. If such was the case, it would be unreasonable to expect Truman to delay for the sake of established diplomatic protocol or to save the face of various diplomats. In profound disagreement with recognition, but also fearful of a break between Truman and Marshall that might have disastrous ramifications for European policy, Lovett met separately with Clifford and Marshall to pave the way for the inevitable. The Marshall Plan appropriation bill was at a crucial juncture in Congress; in terms of immediate need, Palestine must have seemed a comparatively small matter.

Lovett and Clifford agreed that it would be at least somewhat more acceptable for the president to recognize the new state in response to a request, however speedy, than to promise recognition in advance. Lovett was successful in convincing Marshall that the president properly had the final constitutional authority in such issues; for the secretary to resign in protest would be tantamount to a military officer's quitting in the midst of a campaign because he disagreed with a superior's tactical decision.

Truman's own thoughts and emotions as time went by remain unrecorded. On May 13, he received another appeal from Weizmann. On May 14, Clifford told Lovett that the president "was under unbearable pressure." By then, Clifford already had arranged with Eliahu Epstein, the new state's Washington agent, to request instant recognition in identical letters to the president and the secretary of state.

At about 5:45 P.M. on May 14 (11:45 P.M. in Palestine), Clifford phoned Dean Rusk to inform him that the state of Israel would be proclaimed at 6:00 P.M. Truman would issue a statement granting immediate recognition, and the UN delegation should be informed. Receiving the news in New York, Ambassador Austin, stunned and angered, went home without even informing his colleagues. A few minutes later, the news swept across the floor of the General Assembly, throwing it into pandemonium. Americans had to physically restrain the Cuban delegate, who had been hauled along on trusteeship, from taking the rostrum to denounce the United States and declare his country's withdrawal from the United Nations. At 6:15, Rusk got a call from Marshall instructing him to rush to New York and stop the entire delegation from resigning en masse.[34]

VII

In Tel Aviv, the new Israelis celebrated, and then prepared to repel the attacks they knew would come from the Arab world. Lovett wryly commented that Truman's advisers, having failed to make him the father of the new state, had at least made him the midwife.[35] On May 25, Chaim Weizmann would visit the White House, this time openly and, as president of Israel, accorded all the honor of a chief of state. Standing in front of a battery of photographers, he presented a Torah to a smiling Truman.[36] In Israeli folklore, the American president would become a father of sorts, to be honored along with the founders of the nation.

In fact, although recognition was a symbolic crossing of the Rubicon, it did not lay the Arab–Jewish issue to rest even temporarily. Syria and Lebanon invaded Israel on the very day it declared statehood; Iraq followed one day later. Truman still faced demands for termination of the arms embargo, for financial aid, and for de jure recognition. And, however he felt about it, the de facto recognition appeared so blatantly political that it did him no good among the wider voting public.

The Palestine issue in retrospect may be considered from numerous perspectives: as a study in contrasts between the culture of diplomacy and that of politics; as an example of the frequent conflict between morality and self-interest in diplomacy and of the ambiguity of morality itself in conflicts between peoples and nations; as a lesson in the power of strategically placed interest groups in democratic politics. What Truman made of it is less certain. No doubt he wanted to do the right thing and was persuaded that he had. One suspects, however, that he felt less like a triumphant national leader than a pummeled survivor who had hung on through one tough round after another—and faced yet more in a hard struggle.

24

"CONGRESS MEETS—TOO BAD TOO": POLITICS, POLICY, AND THE EIGHTIETH CONGRESS, 1947–1948

"Nobody here in the White House is downhearted," Charlie Ross told his sister a week after the 1946 election. "The consensus is that President Truman is now a free man and can write a fine record in the coming two years."[1] When one considers the depth of the repudiation that both Truman and the Democrats had suffered, the remark conveys an unreal optimism seldom seen in the visage of the sad-faced press secretary. Nevertheless, whether accurately conveying the White House mood or desperately searching for a silver lining, Ross was on to something.

Five months later, in March 1947, Frank McNaughton wrote that Truman had finally grown into his office: "He is confident, assured, and considerably something of a president, compared with the scared little man who stepped shaking into Roosevelt's larger shoes." As McNaughton saw it, Truman had suddenly metamorphosed from a sure loser, incapable of providing leadership, into a strong chief executive, dealing shrewdly with Congress, capturing major issues, projecting an attractive public image, and placing himself in a strong position for reelection. There were tentative plans, he reported, to have Truman tour the country by train after Congress adjourned—making a few major speeches, but mostly just shaking hands from the rear platform and letting people see him. The trip never came off, probably because of the pressure of events in 1947, although Truman made numerous appearances, frequently quite effective, out of Washington. The idea, however, was a good one: the president's strength was in "retail" face-to-face campaigning, and the country once again felt comfortable with him.[2]

What had happened, of course, was less a rapid personality transformation than a confluence of events that made it possible for Truman to look like a leader who had a grip on events rather than one who was gripped by them. Once again, he was on an ascending trajectory in his remarkably uneven relationship with the American people.

II

The president's revival rather clearly began with his decision to take on John L. Lewis in a fight to the finish shortly after the November 1946 election. Almost as if determined to maintain his position as the most unpopular public figure in America, Lewis had called yet another coal strike in violation of the contract he had signed with the government the previous May. As Robert Donovan has so aptly put it, "Déjà vu did not just afflict the country—it possessed it." Among politicians, editorial writers, respected commentators, and the general public, the predominant reaction was sheer outrage. Only labor unionists and their liberal allies could muster sympathy for the miners' union—and even the liberals gave it grudgingly, as a matter of principled solidarity rather than an expression of identification with Lewis.[3]

Truman's own intense hatred of the UMW leader had, if anything, simply grown over the months. In May 1946, he had lamented to Dick Duncan that Lewis was "giving us no ground on which to crack down but I'll try to meet it when it comes up."[4] After the election, he had little to lose and was spoiling for a fight. John Steelman, the administration's chief contact with Lewis, thought he had worked out an oral deal with the union boss, but quickly discovered that the president wanted no part of it. Urged on by Secretary of the Interior Julius Krug (who was responsible for government operation of the mines), Attorney General Tom Clark, and Clark Clifford, Truman was ready to fight it out. Refusing to accept telephone calls from Lewis, he told the Justice Department to move against him. The government got federal district judge Alan Goldsborough to issue an injunction forbidding a strike. The judicial action, authorized by the Smith-Connally Act of 1943, was possible because the country was legally still in a state of war.

Lewis thereupon overreached himself. Gambling that the courts might rule that the anti-injunction provisions of the Norris-LaGuardia Act of 1932 were controlling in this case, perhaps hoping through the sheer power of his presence and personality to win a duel with the administration, he allowed the miners to walk out on November 20. On November 26, writing to his old friend Sherman Minton, then a federal circuit judge, Truman remarked, "I am certainly sorry that we can't try

Lewis in your Court. I am sure he would get a fair trial and then be hanged."[5]

By those lights, Goldsborough did almost as well. On December 3, he ruled that Norris-LaGuardia did not apply to strikes against the government, and then fined the union $3.5 million and Lewis $10,000. Four days later, announcing that he would accept the judgment of the Supreme Court when it heard the union's appeal, Lewis ordered the miners back to work. Basking in wide public acclaim, Truman wrote in his diary that in the end Lewis had been, like all bullies, "as yellow as a dog pound pup" and that he and his loyal team had "whipped a damned traitor." The following March, the Supreme Court would sustain the substance of Goldsborough's decision, although it reduced the penalties he had imposed.[6]

Strictly on the merits, there was much to be said for Truman's tough stance. But the exhilaration of victory carried far beyond a sense of triumph in a labor dispute. When Congress convened in January 1947, Truman was ready for a scrap.

Controlled by Republicans, the legislative branch now presented Truman with a new range of opportunities. In the Senate, the GOP leadership—Vandenberg on foreign policy, Taft on domestic issues, both of them backstopped by Majority Whip Eugene Millikin of Colorado—was relatively moderate and frequently constructive. It provided a reasonably attractive counterpoint to a number of undistinguished right-wing partisans, among them Kenneth Wherry of Nebraska, Homer Capehart of Indiana, and John Bricker of Ohio. Given the narrowness of their control of the Senate, moreover, the Republicans had to be somewhat accommodating.

The House, however, was a different story. Here Truman might be able to count on an occasional helping hand from Speaker Joe Martin, but a far greater percentage of the Republican leadership consisted of anti–New Deal conservatives who had learned nothing, forgotten nothing, and hoped to move at least part of the way back toward the golden days of the 1920s. Among them were Charles Halleck of Indiana, Brazilia Carroll Reece of Tennessee (the Republican National Committee chairman), Leo Allen of Illinois, Jesse Wolcott of Michigan, and John Taber of New York. Firmly entrenched in the party leadership by virtue of long seniority, enjoying a comfortable margin of party superiority, and ideologically compatible with the southern Democrats on many issues, the House Republicans were more openly partisan, very conservative, and combative. They would be a perfect foil for Truman, who in the end would use them to define the image of the Eightieth Congress.[7]

Republican control of Congress also removed the impulse to identify with it and try to lead it through a process of negotiation and compromise, as Truman had been tempted to do time and again in 1946. He still made an occasional nostalgia-laden trip to Capitol Hill, but he may have begun to realize that familiarity with the president bred more contempt than cooperation. Republican ascendancy removed any possibility of acting as a prime minister. He could now at last be, for lack of a better word, "presidential." He seemed, Frank McNaughton thought, finally to be "growing into his White House job instead of trying to grow back to Congress."[8] There was much to be said for a strategy of partisan confrontation. Standing apart from an inherently unruly legislative branch and cloaking himself in the aura of his office, he could with some care build an image as a strong leader and representative of the general public interest.

One of the first occasions he seized was his nomination of David Lilienthal to head the Atomic Energy Commission (AEC). From the start, he indicated that this would be a fight to the finish that would culminate in a recorded Senate vote. Widely esteemed, a leading representative of New Deal liberalism, Lilienthal could count on support from most of the surviving Democrats in the upper chamber. Thus his nomination became a problem for the Republicans. If they threw up a solid front to defeat him, they would bear the responsibility of having driven an attractive figure from public life. If they split, they would squabble among themselves and Truman would score a big victory. One need not question Truman's genuine desire to have Lilienthal at the AEC in order to appreciate the political strategy.

At one point during the confirmation fight, he drafted a statement, probably meant for delivery to a press conference, calling the Senate hearings a "fiasco," condemning the Congress for taking "a low party viewpoint," dismissing accusations that Lilienthal was pro-Communist, and concluding that as a matter of principle "we cannot let the peanut politicians ruin a good man for their personal satisfaction and the detriment of the country and the world." After consulting with Charlie Ross and possibly Clark Clifford, he put the draft away—no doubt feeling all the better for having written it—said little in public, and did his lobbying behind the scenes.[9]

The debate divided Vandenberg and Taft. In the end, nearly half the Republican delegation in the Senate followed Vandenberg and supplied the votes to put Lilienthal over the top. Truman could feel principled pride in the success of his nominee, political satisfaction at having driven a wedge into Republican unity, and surely a fair amount of glee at having drubbed Taft.

The Lilienthal debate also in many respects established a paradigm for future conflict between Truman and Congress. Although control of American atomic energy resources had foreign policy implications, domestic ideological issues—Lilienthal's New Dealism and alleged softness on Communism—were at the root of the controversy. Vandenberg and a relatively moderate group of Republican senators supported Truman, just as they would on one key foreign policy issue after another. Taft led the opposition, backed by hard-line conservatives usually less flexible than he.

For the next two years, Truman, utilizing presidential powers as commander-in-chief and dominant maker of foreign policy, would (with the notable exception of the Palestine muddle) state the national interest so compellingly and work for it so shrewdly that Vandenberg and his followers would come along as effective and critical co-workers, much to the dismay of the Taft group. Taft himself, after criticizing the administration's foreign policy initiatives, would in the end throw in the towel and vote for them.

The difference between Democrats and Republicans would be argued primarily in terms of domestic issues, usually relating to the legacy of the New Deal and management of the economy. The Republican assault against some of FDR's accomplishments would enable Truman to cast himself as a protector of treasured programs rather than as an advocate of more change. The end of economic controls and easing of most consumer shortages would allow him to take credit for prosperity rather than be blamed for inflation and scarcity. More effectively than perhaps even he realized, the president had given himself a formidable position on the political high ground. The Republicans, mostly cooperating with him on foreign policy, would spend the next year and a half hurling themselves at his domestic program with abandon and an apparent lack of understanding of the way in which they were weakening themselves for the 1948 election.

III

Among the trickiest and most important domestic issues that Truman faced was the postwar position of the labor movement. The Democrats were badly divided between anti-union Southerners and liberal Northerners with close ties to labor. The Republicans, dominated by the perspective of traditional, business-oriented, middle-class America, faced no such split. Whatever differences of detail or degree they might have among themselves, almost all agreed that the unions had become far too powerful and needed to be restrained. One poll after another seemed to demonstrate that a healthy majority of the public was on their side.[10]

Truman continued ambivalent in his own mind. He already had been badly burned in his relations with the unions. At the beginning of 1947, many labor leaders probably saw him more as the chief executive who had threatened to draft the rail strikers and used the injunction against the miners, less as the president who had vetoed the restrictive Case bill of 1946. Yet he was capable of making a distinction between slamming individual irresponsible labor chiefs—Whitney, Johnston, Lewis—and bashing the entire labor movement. Valid enough as a matter of principle, it also was a distinction mandated by his political situation. He could not afford to sign a bill designed to punish a constituency whose support was absolutely crucial in a presidential campaign. He dealt with the problem by depicting himself as an impartial arbiter of the public interest, perhaps willing to accept a labor bill if it was fair and moderate all around.

Truman's public statements were cautious and restrained. In his State of the Union Address, delivered on January 6, 1947, he called for laws to curtail a few abuses—jurisdictional strikes, secondary boycotts, work stoppages resulting from contract interpretation disputes—but these were peripheral issues. To deal with the larger problem of economically traumatic strikes in basic industries, he simply recommended the appointment of a temporary study commission to suggest legislation, all the while protesting that he would not accept anything designed to damage organized labor.[11]

In a "Personal and Confidential" letter written to his old friend and colleague Senator Joseph Ball on January 8, 1947, he warned that he would veto anything that looked like a rewrite of the Case bill, but also said that "the labor situation can be worked out if those of us who are really interested in it go to work on it and work at it as it should be done." Inviting Ball to join in a constructive effort, he declared as his objective "a program which will keep our industrial plants operating and . . . cause a better understanding between industrial management and these all too powerful labor organizations."[12]

Just what he had in mind is hard to say. Perhaps just a nod in the direction of the powerful antilabor sentiment around the country. Perhaps a genuine desire for some undefined labor bill that somehow could satisfy both the unions and a big segment of the non-union public. Whatever he wanted to accomplish, Truman was smart enough to stand clear of any involvement in the actual legislative process. Having invited Congress to pass a labor bill he could sign, he sat back, made no effort at active involvement, and let the Republicans on Capitol Hill get on with the job.

In the House, they went at it with gusto. Under the chairmanship of Fred Hartley of New Jersey, the Labor Committee turned out a bill filled with ammunition for union haters. The Senate Labor Committee under the leadership of Taft produced considerably more moderate legislation, reflecting in part Taft's own instincts and presidential ambitions, in part the much closer ideological balance in the upper house. The result, after a series of compromises in a conference committee, came to the White House on June 9 as the Taft-Hartley bill.

Although considerably softened from the House version, the legislation imposed numerous restrictions, some of them resurrected from the wartime Smith-Connally Act (no longer in effect as a result of Truman's termination of the World War II national state of emergency). The most important of its provisions allowed the president to block major strikes by obtaining an injunction in the federal courts for an eighty-day "cooling-off" period; specified unfair practices in which unions could not engage; prohibited union contributions to candidates in federal elections; outlawed "closed shop" hiring practices, in which employment could be offered only to union members; and specifically sanctioned state "right-to-work" laws, which prohibited "union shop" procedures that required new employees to become union members.[13]

As late as May, Truman had given indications that he might sign a "moderate" bill, but Taft-Hartley far exceeded the few specifics to which he had committed himself in January. Given the president's past record of ambivalence toward union labor, he probably thought that the legislation had some merit. He knew also, however, that labor opposition was bitterly emotional and that his decision would be the acid test of his relationship. If he signed the bill, he would alienate, probably irretrievably, a core constituency. A majority of Americans might support the bill, but the greater part of that majority was Republican and would not vote for him anyway. The smaller part was less intensely engaged with the issue and capable of being won over as part of an electoral majority.

Politically, then, a decision to veto was almost automatic. Whatever the merits of Taft-Hartley, moreover, it hardly presented an issue of stark, overriding principle. Rather, it was largely a matter of interest group politics and partisan calculation. Truman made a show of deliberation, and then on June 20 issued a long, stinging veto message. That evening, he delivered a national radio address depicting Taft-Hartley as "a shocking piece of legislation" that attacked all labor unions, would "take fundamental rights away from our working people," and intensify class conflict in America.

Swiftly, the House overrode the veto by a vote of 331 to 83, a majority of the Democrats joining a nearly united Republican delegation. The Senate, however, presented an uncertain prospect. Truman invited eleven Democratic supporters of Taft-Hartley to a White House luncheon and made a strong plea for their votes. To no avail. On June 23, the upper house disregarded a last-minute, written plea from the president and overrode him, 68 to 25.[14]

"The veto was good politics—provided only that it is overridden," Frank McNaughton had commented in advance of the outcome. If it should be sustained, the country would blame Truman for every union abuse, real or imagined. But if it should be overridden, Truman would have the credit with labor without any real ill-will from ordinary voters who thought labor needed some restraint. It is tempting to assume that Truman planned it that way or at least analyzed the situation similarly.

Once Taft-Hartley became law over his veto, the president announced he would respect Congress's decision and enforce the new legislation. He would use the antistrike injunction several times during the remainder of his presidency. (The first invocation was against the UMW in 1948.) Even so, the controversy deepened his hostility toward the act's sponsors. "I've come to the conclusion that Taft is no good and Hartley is worse," he wrote in a draft letter to his sister. It is too simple to say that Truman saw himself as acting out a charade; yet it is probable that he was not altogether displeased to have the powers that Taft-Hartley gave him and convinced that, as a friend of labor, he could wield them fairly.[15]

A few critics argued that Truman could have done more to obtain a satisfactory bill or to have his veto sustained. But it is hard to see how an elaborate process of negotiation with the Republicans could have done anything other than to saddle him with the most visible responsibility for a law that would have made no one happy. Nor can one make a persuasive case that presidential rhetoric, patronage, or some other inducement could have created shifts on a large enough scale to make a difference. A later generation, aware that Taft-Hartley did not bring ruin to the labor movement, may be puzzled by all the emotion invested in the debate. At the time, nevertheless, the feelings were strong and earned Truman accolades from union leaders and the liberals who identified with their cause. The *Nation* declared that he had "given American liberalism the fighting chance that it seemed to have lost with the death of Roosevelt."[16]

IV

Truman also moved to make the economy an issue that helped rather than damaged him. Inflationary pressures continued unabated throughout 1947, pushed upward by a steady demand from both American consumers and European recipients of American aid. Housing and numerous manufactured goods remained scarce. Soaring food prices affected virtually every family in America. According to federally gathered data, the average price of a five-pound bag of flour in 1946 had been 35.4 cents; in 1947, it was 48.2 cents. Pork chops went from 48.5 cents a pound to 72.1 cents, eggs from 58.6 cents a dozen to 69.6 cents, and so on. The increases continued, albeit at a considerably more modest rate, into 1948. In terms of real dollars, many basic foodstuffs cost the average family more then than they did forty years later and consumed a larger proportion of its income.[17]

For the most part, there was no practical way to deal with high prices but to let them move on into the stratosphere until the economic law of gravity set in. Having rid himself of the price-control issue, Truman let the Republicans deal with the short-run consequences of free-market economics. Senator Taft obliged with one of the most maladroit soundbites in the history of American politics. Asked how he would advise families to deal with high food prices, Taft matter-of-factly declared, "Eat less meat, and eat less extravagantly." Under the circumstances, it was the most honest advice that could be given. The Democrats, who usually shortened it to "eat less," loved it.[18]

Truman had no better advice to offer. Dominant supply–demand imbalances would have made any fight against inflation little more than a Fabian one. Tax increases were obviously impossible in a Congress determined to cut taxes. Monetary policy remained handcuffed to low interest rates by the need to support government bonds at par, an absolute imperative for the president, Secretary of the Treasury Snyder, and (rather bafflingly since the policy was economically unsound) the Council of Economic Advisers. That left only the option of a return to economic controls. When Congress began a special session in November

1947, primarily to consider interim aid to Europe, Truman presented it with a comprehensive program for consumer credit controls, selective price controls, allocations, and rationing. Reacting with predictable over-statement, Senator Taft described it as "the end of economic freedom."[19]

Actually, a more appropriate reaction would have been to wonder why Truman would want to return to a program that had gotten him into so much trouble in 1946. Many observers then and historians since have assumed that the request was made for political effect with no expecta-tion of action. There can be no doubt that the president wanted to capi-talize on the widespread understanding that the Republicans had been the most ardent foes of price controls and leave the impression that there-fore they were responsible for persistent inflation. It would have been fairer to criticize their insistence on tax cuts, but no votes were to be gained along that path.

It was also true that the Council of Economic Advisers had recom-mended the control package and that many policy intellectuals retained a faith in the idea of a managed economy. The CEA, however, had stated a clear preference for high taxes, postponement of unnecessary government expenditures, and tighter credit policies. It may have genuinely thought a control program possible, but certainly not as a favored alternative.

As it was, and as widely expected, the Republicans did Truman a great favor. Three rather small items aside, they rejected his proposals, thereby not saddling him with an unworkable and unpopular program that probably would have done more harm than good to the economy. They also gave him an opportunity to pin the blame for inflation squarely on them. Signing the bill that he received, Truman cited "the pressure of exorbitant prices" and lambasted Congress for enacting legislation "that is pitifully inadequate as a weapon against the high cost of living." It was a theme to which he would return time and again in the coming year.[20]

The inflation problem forced Truman to deal with an increasingly restless Federal Reserve Board; led by Chairman Marriner Eccles, it was on the verge of revolt in late 1947. Eccles, yet another of those trouble-some human monuments from the New Deal, criticized the adminis-tration's credit and interest rate policies openly in testimony before Con-gress at the end of 1947. An aggressive tight-money policy could, he argued, lick inflation without controls. Eccles was probably correct, but his suggested course would mean higher mortgage and auto-loan rates for every American. It also would require abandonment of support for government bonds. Both Truman and Snyder considered such policies morally and politically intolerable. Near the end of January 1948, Truman had John Steelman tell Eccles that he would not be reappointed as chair-man when his term expired on February 1, although he was asked to stay on as a member of the board; Eccles rather astonishingly complied.

The episode earned the president a fair amount of criticism from lib-erals, who had an inflated idea of Eccles's economic radicalism, and from much of the financial community, which recognized the Fed chairman for the sound Mormon banker that he was—at least on monetary policy. Eccles's demotion was an indication of Truman's neopopulistic attachment to low interest rates as well as of his determination to enforce his policies throughout his administration. Privately, he told Sherman Minton that Eccles (along with Civil Aeronautics Board head James Landis) had given him "a first-class doublecrossing." Eccles's successor, Thomas McCabe, would hold his peace until after the election, but the administration's troubles with the Fed were far from over.[21]

V

"Truman's order to root out subversives from government employment hit a solid note with Congress and further pulled the rug from under his political detractors," Frank McNaughton observed in his exposition of the president's enhanced standing at the end of March 1947. "The charge of 'Communists in government' and nothing being done about it, a favorite theme of reactionaries, simply will not stick any longer."[22] McNaughton had accurately evaluated one aspect of a complex problem that Truman had to face by early 1947, but politics was only a part of it.

For years, it had been a staple of Republican right-wing rhetoric that the Democrats were leading the country down the road to socialism, Communism, and totalitarianism, but such charges had been little more than ideological red meat for the true believers. The emergence of the Cold War had changed all that.

Henry Wallace, if no longer in the administration, remained a compelling demonstration that "softness" toward the USSR was a significant force on the left wing of the Democratic party and, by implication, probably still present in some recesses of the bureaucracy. Softness of this sort, of course, could have many motivations other than an affinity for Stalinism; however, neither the Republicans nor many Democrats were prone to make fine distinctions between pro-Communists and other anti–Cold War types. Moreover, it was impossible to argue that under the new conditions of Cold War no security problem existed, however grossly exaggerated it might be in the mind of the right. Few sober observers believed that the federal bureaucracy was riddled with subversives. Yet, especially after USSR embassy clerk Igor Guzenko revealed a major spy ring in Canada, no one could deny that there was a Soviet espionage network operating in North America.

Thus some procedures in at least some areas of the government were merited. Inevitably, they would involve a degree of inquiry into personal convictions and political affiliations. All this might be distasteful, but it could be tolerable if done with detachment, restraint, and safeguards for accused individuals. By and large, the administration program would fail each test.

That it did so was less the result of Truman's will than of carelessness, bureaucratic incompetence, and Cold War hysteria. Truman himself detested the idea of snooping into people's lives—in no small part, one imagines, because it had been done to him during the 1930s. His association with Max Lowenthal, still a frequent informal adviser, doubtless confirmed his instincts. During the 1944 campaign, quite possibly acting at Lowenthal's behest, he had written to Harry Mitchell, the president of the Civil Service Commission, to protest the lack of procedural safeguards in its wartime loyalty investigations.[23]

Nevertheless, Truman put his signature on an executive order that not only continued the flaws of the World War II loyalty program, but institutionalized them in a fashion almost guaranteed to inconvenience and harass many more federal employees, while wasting the time and energy of countless administrators. Produced by the Temporary Commission on Employee Loyalty, which Truman had appointed in November 1946, the new program was hurriedly thrown together in order to preempt legislative action by the Republicans—partly, no doubt, for political advantage, but also out of a fear that Congress likely would devise something even more draconian.

None of the commission's members was noted for a concern with civil liberties. Attorney General Clark's memorandum to the members, furthermore, largely defined the situation: although the number of disloyal employees was not large, the committee should weigh the problem "from the viewpoint of the serious threat which even one disloyal person constitutes to the security of the government of the United States." With any sense of proportion thus airily dismissed, the commission's product was predictably large, grotesque, and indiscriminate. It required full-scale loyalty investigations of every new federal employee, whether an atomic scientist at Los Alamos or a janitor in a Department of Agriculture office in Peoria. It also required each department and agency to establish procedures to verify the loyalty of existing employees.

The result was the establishment of a series of loyalty boards throughout the government and the advisory Loyalty Review Board in the Civil Service Commission—all given the duty to investigate the character and loyalty of individuals against whom some accusation had been made or rumor had circulated. Standards of evidence, procedural safeguards, even a working definition of "loyalty" were nowhere to be found.[24]

Truman issued an executive order establishing the new program on March 21, 1947, nine days after the Truman Doctrine speech. Here, as on numerous other matters, the smallness of the White House staff made him a prisoner to whatever was recommended by a cabinet department. In the circumstances, to reject the proposal entirely would have been unthinkable. To send it back for a thorough overhaul would be to surrender the initiative to a Congress obsessed with subversion. To do a fast reworking inside the White House was not a live option.

A good many observers praised the loyalty program as a much-needed domestic counterpart to the president's anti-Communist foreign policy. Nonetheless, there are some indications that he had misgivings from the beginning. The way in which the FBI moved to establish itself as the investigator of loyalty cases, thereby substantially increasing its appropriations and personnel, infuriated him. FBI agents appear to have done investigations more professionally than Civil Service Commission personnel, but Truman trusted them less. He had been around Washington long enough to know that half the members of Congress believed that J. Edgar Hoover had damaging information on them. And he disliked the FBI director with a passion. The president, George Elsey noted, "wants to be sure & hold FBI down, afraid of 'Gestapo.'"[25]

If the FBI did not abuse its power, the program still functioned in unhealthy ways. Numerous scholars, writing as if it launched a reign of terror through the entire federal bureaucracy, have probably overstated its impact. The statistics are slippery, but it appears that during Truman's presidency 400 to 1,200 employees were dismissed under its procedures and 1,000 to 6,000 resigned—out of a total of some 2.5 million government workers.[26] Most people who appeared before loyalty boards were cleared. Inevitably, however, the program led to some injustices, some of them to individuals who had been guilty of nothing more than questionable judgment on tricky foreign policy questions.

The responsibility for these cases lay not with J. Edgar Hoover but with others. "I wanted security with the Bill of Rights, I wanted security with the rights of individuals protected," Truman privately commented in 1954, "but Clark and his assistants would always come back with a secret police proposition."[27] Tom Clark and his commission did indeed bear substantial responsibility for the excesses of their creation. Ultimately, however, the buck stopped with Harry S. Truman, who discovered that it was far easier to create a loyalty program than to control it.

VI

Truman's standing, as measured by occasional opinion polls, nevertheless grew through 1947. By that spring, Roosevelt had been gone for two years; increasingly a less vivid presence for most Americans, he was no longer an awesome reference point against which to measure the new president. Instead, Truman looked more like a reasonably strong and decisive leader dealing with a Congress that, as always, appeared divided and relatively rudderless. The public approved of his foreign policy, had no qualms about his domestic anti-Communism, and seemed to see him as a likable, if not charismatic, president.

His Gallup Poll approval rating climbed steadily from 35 percent in January to 60 percent by the end of March, just after the Truman Doctrine and the loyalty order. It leveled off just a bit in the summer and fall, but was still at 55 percent in October. In Gallup's hypothetical presidential contests, Truman ran ahead of Taft, Stassen, and Vandenberg and about even with Dewey.[28]

By early 1947, the entire White House seemed to be a much more professional, smoothly functioning operation. Much of the credit went to Clark Clifford. It was impossible for journalists and other political observers not to notice Clifford's tall good looks, smooth persuasiveness, intelligence, and political shrewdness. As Truman's chief speech writer and high-profile aide on such controversial issues as the Lilienthal appointment to the AEC, he attracted a lot of attention. In the words of Patrick Anderson, he emerged as the White House golden boy, his name appearing increasingly in articles about the administration—often with the assumption that he was the brains behind the president.

Others contributed to the new sense of White House effectiveness. George Elsey performed skillfully as Clifford's one-man support staff. Charles Murphy, a smart, quiet attorney with years of experience on Capitol Hill, became an administrative assistant. Another new face was Donald Dawson, a native of El Dorado, Missouri, but not an old friend of Truman. Working with Matt Connelly and the chairman of the Democratic National Committee, Dawson handled personnel matters for the White House and brokered patronage for much of the federal establishment. John Steelman began his tenure as the assistant to the president.

Clifford moved to establish himself as a political strategist and idea man. Along with Oscar Ewing, acting chairman of the Democratic National Committee, he established an informal brain trust that met each Monday evening in Ewing's apartment at the Wardman Park Hotel. Clifford and Ewing were joined regularly by a group of the younger and more dynamic New Deal liberals in the administration: Assistant Secretary of Agriculture Charles F. Brannan, Assistant Secretary of the Interior C. Girard Davidson, Assistant Secretary of Labor David Morse, and Leon Keyserling from the Council of Economic Advisers. Clifford was probably the most ideologically moderate member of the group, but his inclinations were in the same direction.

Clifford later—and with considerable exaggeration—depicted the Wardman Park group as pulling and heaving at one end of a tug of war for Truman's ideological soul. Leon Keyserling gave it credit for persuading Truman to veto the Taft-Hartley Act. It was true, of course, that the president had a few conservative to moderate friends and advisers, including John Snyder, Sam Rayburn, and (possibly on some issues) Alben Barkley. There were, additionally, a few signs at the beginning of 1947 that Truman hoped for a cooperative relationship with Congress. Still, he had pretty much typed himself as a New Deal liberal by 1947; a 180-degree turn was never in the cards. Both his aggressive impulses and his finely tuned political antennae indicated a fight with Congress and an effort to rally the Roosevelt coalition. The Wardman Park group, with Clifford as its intermediary, from time to time provided Truman with tactical ideas, rhetorical flourishes, and arguments. It changed neither his basic ideological direction nor his political style.[29]

In November 1947, Clifford gave Truman a long memorandum on political strategy for the 1948 campaign. The document certainly reflected the thinking of the Wardman Park group, but it had originated with James

Rowe, Jr., an insider from the Roosevelt White House and a law partner of Thomas Corcoran. Knowing full well that Truman loathed Corcoran and anyone connected with him, Clifford reworked the memo a bit and gave it to the president under his signature. It contained a series of recommendations that were mostly astute—and mostly redundant.

Clifford correctly predicted that the Republicans would nominate Thomas E. Dewey and that Henry Wallace would declare a third-party candidacy. He urged Truman to rally the Democratic coalition through an approach that emphasized the neo–New Deal character of his administration, reminded constituent groups of what the Democratic party had done for them since 1933, and held out the promise of more in the future.

These suggestions meant talking about such development programs as reclamation and flood control in the western states, Democratic backing for the workers in the cities, and agricultural price supports in rural areas. It meant civil rights legislation for blacks, support for Zionism for Jews, displaced-persons legislation for other ethnoreligious minorities, and anti-Communism for Catholics.

The strategy entailed discounting the old-line Democratic machines, already visibly on the decline in many cities, and appealing to labor unions. It involved cultivating the liberals, "idea men" whose significance far outstripped their numbers. It required a no-compromise battle with Congress on domestic issues with a greater interest in defining differences than in obtaining legislation.

Written before Truman sent a civil rights program to Congress, the memo contained one enormous blooper: "The South, as always, can be considered safely Democratic." So it must have seemed to anyone who looked back at Roosevelt's four consecutive sweeps of the region.

The memo also had some advice for polishing the presidential image that may have given Truman a few laughs. He should display his more reflective side by recommending a good book to reporters once in a while, thereby dispelling the impression that poker was his only form of recreation. He should invite the great personages of America to lunch and ask their guidance on such nebulous matters as the state of the nation and the struggle for peace; Clifford mentioned labor leaders, industrialists such as Henry Ford II, thinkers such as Albert Einstein. Truman wrote this counsel off as silly and artificial, thus sparing himself and Einstein an improbable confrontation.

The president discussed the memorandum at length with Clifford and implemented one of its tactical suggestions: the establishment of a small campaign research staff in the Democratic National Committee. He would follow its strategic course for the most part, but this amounted to little more than staying on a path he already had taken.[30]

Perhaps as early as the Lilienthal appointment and certainly after Taft-Hartley, he was in a fight with Congress in which he pitted an aggressive New Deal liberalism against a dominant Republican conservatism. The veto of Taft-Hartley, if the most memorable of Truman's presidency, was only one of several he unleashed at the Eightieth Congress. And he made most of them stick. On June 16, 1947, he vetoed a Republican tax-cut bill, arguing that it emphasized relief for the rich and was inflationary. A month later, he vetoed a nearly identical bill. At the end of June, attacking the legislation as a step backward toward economic isolationism, he killed a trade bill that would have raised the tariff on imported wool. On August 6, vetoing the removal of newspaper vendors from the Social Security system, Truman assailed the bill as part of an effort to undermine the program. All of these actions were successful, and all pointed toward a strategy of open confrontation with Congress on domestic issues.[31]

The administration also pushed forward on other fronts, advocating strong housing legislation, federal aid to education, and national health insurance. A number of conservative Republicans, led by Taft, were not prepared to reject such programs in toto. On housing, Taft actually moved so far beyond the Republican consensus that he had no significant differences with Truman; a bill that he co-sponsored with Democrats Robert F. Wagner and Allen J. Ellender got through the Senate, only to be killed by House Republicans. However, Taft wanted education and medical care programs that would be far less sweeping, expensive, and Washington-centered than the president's. An accommodationist president might have tried to split the difference. Truman preferred to emphasize the gap between them on these social-welfare issues and on their approaches to economic management. He went out of his way to denounce the Ohioan as an advocate of boom-and-bust economics in a long statement to the press on June 5, 1947, fifteen days before vetoing the Taft-Hartley Act.[32]

Such a strategy carried dangers. Above all, Truman had to insulate the struggle against a spillover into foreign policy. It was difficult, moreover, to maintain the distinction between the real object of attack, the Republicans who controlled Congress, and the institution itself. Off and on, many Democratic leaders felt that they were being used as expendable shock troops in a negative campaign; instead of working for real results, they were waging political war on fellow members of Congress with whom they were supposed to have a collegial relationship. Truman, so long an admirer of executive authority, may not always have kept the difference between the Congress and the Republican party clear in his own mind. "Congress meets—Too bad too," he wrote in his diary on January 6, 1948. "They'll do nothing but wrangle, pull phony investigations and generally upset the affairs of the nation."[33]

Sam Rayburn in the House and Alben Barkley in the Senate functioned as effective leaders of the opposition, but they had only sporadic contact with the president and at times found themselves surprised by White House initiatives. "This is like playing a night ball game," Barkley complained in early 1948 after not being told in advance about tax proposals in the president's State of the Union Address. "I'm supposed to be the catcher and I should get signals. I not only am not getting the signals but someone actually turns out the lights when the ball is tossed."[34]

Yet, as with Taft-Hartley, the objective was not to achieve compromise legislation that all sides probably would consider flawed. It was to underscore ideological differences for a presidential campaign. In achieving this goal, Truman was extraordinarily effective. The dozen or so significant vetoes he issued in 1947 and 1948 underscored differences between Democrats and Republicans on such issues as income equity, labor–management relations, regulation of business, and the New Deal welfare state.

VII

"I've got to make a speech to the Society for the Advancement of Colored People tomorrow and I wish I didn't have to make it," Truman wrote to his sister on June 28, 1947. Referring to another featured speaker, he continued, "Mrs. Roosevelt has spent her public life stirring up trouble between whites and black[s]—and I'm in the middle. Mamma won't like what I say because I wind up by quoting old Abe. But I believe what I say and I'm hopeful we may implement it."[35] The lines expressed the way in which Truman remained torn between tolerance and tradition in race relations. (Mary Jane preferred to see her brother as a more one-dimensional figure: "Harry isn't anymore in favor of nigger equality than I am," she told Jonathan Daniels in 1949. It is entirely possible that he on occasion encouraged that belief.)[36]

The speech itself was a major event. No president had ever before addressed the National Association for the Advancement of Colored People, and none had ever spoken so unequivocally for the rights of Negroes (the preferred term in those days). It was his decision to talk strongly about civil rights. Speaking to a crowd of 10,000 spectators at the Lincoln Memorial, his words internationally broadcast, the president left no doubt about his position. America, he declared, had "reached a turning point in the long history of our country's efforts to guarantee freedom and equality to all our citizens." Twice emphasizing that he meant *all* Americans, he asserted that the national government had to lead the way in guaranteeing a list of rights that ran from the classical civil liberties, to such economic entitlements as decent housing, education, and medical care, to protection from prejudice and discrimination: "Each man must be guaranteed equality of opportunity. The only limit to an American's achievement should be his ability, his industry, and his character."[37]

Truman also mentioned the forthcoming report of his Civil Rights Committee, predicting that it would produce "a vigorous and sensible program for action by all of us." That October, the committee presented Truman with a bold and far-reaching document, *To Secure These Rights.* It advocated antilynching legislation, abolition of the poll tax, voting-rights statutes, a permanent Fair Employment Practices Committee, desegregation of the armed forces, a permanent and adequately staffed civil rights division for the Justice Department, administration support for civil rights

suits in the federal courts, and establishment of the United States Commission on Civil Rights.[38]

A half-century later, with these objectives all achieved, it is hard to
conceive just how path-breaking and controversial the report was. In 1947,
segregation was rigidly enforced by law throughout the states of the old
Confederacy and (to a somewhat lesser extent) in Maryland, West Virginia, Kentucky, and Missouri. In the North and West, it was a widely
prevalent, if somewhat less formal, part of the structure of society. The
Brooklyn Dodgers had just fielded the first black baseball player in major-
league history; and although Jackie Robinson was undeniably a great
talent, his presence had incited anger and debate among players and fans
from Boston to St. Louis. Even outside the South, it was not uncommon
to address an adult black male as "boy." In the world of popular entertainment, blacks might win some white admiration as musicians or singers, but otherwise they still tended to be comedic buffoons: Rochester,
the Kingfish, Charlie Chan's chauffeur.

The white South was outraged at what it considered an attack on its
historic institutions and customs; in several states, Democratic leaders
began to talk of insurgency. In the North, blacks, labor leaders, and white
liberals praised the report. *Washington Post* cartoonist Herblock drew
Truman as a determined little man ringing the Liberty Bell.[39] But beyond the vocal and visible reactions, feelings were mixed and lukewarm.
Republicans, once the friends of blacks, might have some concern for civil
rights, but no longer enough to bring many of them behind a massive
attack on "states' rights." Few among the white working classes shared
the racial liberalism of their leaders; many in fact felt at least as threatened by blacks as did the meanest southern redneck and had even less of
a basis for communication.

Truman understood these realities. He might well have preferred to
dodge the issue as, by and large, had Roosevelt. Clearly, he wanted to
hold the Democratic coalition together, an objective that required him
somehow to continue the balancing act of uniting a party that now had
large contingents of both black civil rights activists and vociferous southern segregationists. Yet he also apparently realized that evasion was no
longer an option. Unlike Roosevelt, he had no personal claim on a black
vote that could hold the balance of power in a presidential election. His
probable Republican opponent, Governor Thomas E. Dewey, had a well-
established record as a friend of civil rights. Henry Wallace, still nomi-
nally on the left wing of the Democratic party, was talking civil rights as
well as foreign policy and acting more like a third-party candidate with
each passing week. Even so, the political consequences of presidential
support for civil rights were as likely to be negative as positive. In moving
as he did, Truman followed his best instincts.

In December, adhering to one of the Civil Rights Committee recommendations, he authorized the Justice Department to file an amicus
curiae brief seconding the arguments of civil rights forces in *Shelly* v.

Kraemer, an important case involving the enforceability of restrictive housing covenants. A few months later, the Supreme Court, perhaps encouraged by the cue from the administration, declared restrictive covenants unconstitutional. On the basis of this one act, no one could yet predict just how far the new amicus policy might go, but friends of civil rights could take heart from the administration's direction.

At the beginning of February 1948, Truman, perhaps prodded by Wallace's now-declared candidacy, sent an extensive package of civil rights legislation to Capitol Hill and announced that executive action would shortly follow to end discrimination in the civil service and to desegregate the armed forces. The reaction was little short of politically disastrous. A Gallup Poll taken a month later and released on April 5 could find only 6 percent support nationally for the legislative program. Among non-southern whites, 21 percent supported it, 15 percent were negative, and the rest had no knowledge or opinion. White Southerners declared by 51 to 34 percent that the administration had treated their region unfairly. Polls released a few days later showed that Truman had a 57 percent disapproval rating in the South and that countrywide he was running behind Dewey, Vandenberg, Harold Stassen, and Douglas MacArthur in presidential trial heats.[40]

No perceptive observer of Congress, moreover, expected the civil rights bills to get anywhere. In fact, Minority Leader Barkley, not wanting to touch off a filibuster that would disrupt other legislation, put off introducing them. Nor were the executive orders forthcoming; alarmed at the fury of southern members of Congress, whose votes were imperative for passage of the Marshall Plan, the White House put the drafts on the shelf. By early spring, although it had gone farther down the civil rights road than any before it, the administration was caught between unhappy Southerners and equally unhappy civil rights advocates. For the time being, it was unwilling to move in either direction.

VIII

By early 1948, Truman's public approval was once again on a downward trajectory. Despite his mostly shrewd judgments on domestic issues and his remarkable foreign policy achievements, he was in serious political trouble. According to a Gallup Poll taken in early April, his approval rating had plunged all the way from 55 percent in September 1947 to 36 percent. In January, a trial-heat poll had shown him beating Dewey 46 to 41 percent; in mid-April, another trial heat showed him losing, 39 to 47 percent. (Both polls showed 7 percent for Henry Wallace.) The nadir came in May, when another trial-heat survey estimated that Harold Stassen—in those days a serious, well-regarded candidate—would beat him 56 to 33 percent, with 5 percent for Wallace.[41]

What had happened? The civil rights program was a big part of the problem. It may have been the right thing to do, and it had strong political appeal to a black vote that he could not take for granted. White feelings, however, ranged from bitter hostility in the South to at best tepid support in the North. The prospect of interference in hiring decisions remained especially unpopular.[42]

All the waffling on Palestine, embarrassingly manifest by the spring of 1948, also surely contributed to the plunge. There is no satisfactory opinion-survey data on the subject, but Truman's behavior had to leave an impression of a president pulled one way, then the other, unable to make up his mind, presiding over a policy in disarray. Palestine not only damaged Truman with an important Democratic interest group, but also made him seem to a wider public weak and not in control of his administration. It is probably no coincidence that both the 36 percent approval rating and the devastating trial-heat loss to Stassen occurred during the interval between the reversal of policy on partition (March 19) and the recognition of Israel (May 14). Thereafter, Truman would do a bit better in such exercises, although he still would be a loser.

The simple fact of Henry Wallace's candidacy also seemed to ensure Truman's certain defeat. Few observers expected Wallace to get as much as 10 percent of the vote. But he drew large, passionate crowds and expertly played to the Democratic left on the emotional issue of peace, asserting that Truman had needlessly scrapped the wartime alliance with the Soviet Union. He and his followers also established themselves as strong proponents of Jewish objectives in Palestine, thereby reaping the political advantage of another "hot-button" issue.

If Wallace could not win, so the reasoning went, he could inflict severe damage. Leo Isaacson's victory in the Bronx special congressional election had stunningly underscored the point. The first (and, as it turned out, last) Wallace Progressive member of Congress, Isaacson imparted a grossly inflated illusion of the party's strength. Still, the coolest observers might doubt that a Truman candidacy could survive even much smaller defections by a left wing concentrated in the crucial big cities of the large industrial states.

Other things hurt Truman also. The dismissal of Marriner Eccles did him little good with those individuals who followed financial matters or who resented the toppling of yet another totem from the New Deal. Perhaps even more damaging was another decision, taken at about the same time. At the end of 1947, the president informed another old New Dealer, James M. Landis, the respected chairman of the Civil Aeronautics Board, that he would not be reappointed. As Landis recounted it, Truman said, "When I became President, Ed Flynn told me that I'd have to be a son of a bitch half the time. This is one of the times." The reasons for the firing of Landis remain murky. The widespread assumption in Washington was that the president, an old hand at air-transportation politics, had caved in to pressure from the airlines in the hope of substantial campaign donations.[43]

All these incidents began to remind people that Harry Truman might be a nice enough, ordinary guy, rather like themselves, but because he was so much like themselves, he was not big enough for the presidency. With his unprepossessing appearance, mediocre speaking ability, and lack of a firm sense of direction, he now once again began to seem a poor second choice to such competent Republicans as Dewey, Stassen, and Vandenberg. A Roper survey taken in March 1948 discovered that even his supporters were not enthusiastic; they described him as "an average American trying to do his best in the world's toughest job." Some of his opponents criticized him for not carrying out Roosevelt's policies, but more used phrases like "weak sister," "has done a bad job," "tied up with the Pendergast machine," "just a politician, not a statesman." Liberal journalist James A. Wechsler quoted the old St. Louis Cardinal pitcher Mike Gonzales's evaluation of a so-so rookie: "Good field, no hit."[44]

With Truman's stock in an apparent free-fall, many of the liberals and some of the party bosses began to look elsewhere. Inevitably, they soon fixed, indeed fixated, on General Dwight D. Eisenhower—perhaps the most attractive figure in American public life, widely believed to be liberal in his inclinations, not known to be a Republican and therefore possibly a Democrat.

Some of the same thoughts had occurred to Truman. In 1945 at Potsdam, he had chatted with Eisenhower about what might become of the war's great leaders. No doubt, he was preoccupied and probably feeling a bit overwhelmed. As Eisenhower recalled it, Truman impulsively and unexpectedly said, "General, there is nothing you may want that I won't try to help you get. That definitely and specifically includes the Presidency in 1948." Dismissing the offer with a courteous smile, Eisenhower told Truman that whoever his opponent might be, it would be someone else. Returning to the United States to become army chief of staff, he continued to be one of America's most admired heroes. In the fall of 1947, using Secretary of the Army Kenneth Royall as an intermediary, Truman seems to have offered the general his backing for the presidential nomination with himself as the vice-presidential candidate. Eisenhower declined with thanks and would continue to resist a draft throughout the spring of 1948.[45]

Was Truman serious? Did he expect Eisenhower to be a figurehead president who would let the second in command run things? Did he simply want to escape back to the familiar security of the Senate? Or did he expect Eisenhower to decline and thereby remove himself from the race at an early date?

There is no direct written documentation, but perhaps a clue may be found in a letter Truman sent to a friend toward the end of November 1947, when he still was high in the polls: "The family are going to spend Christmas at the White House this year because it probably will be the last chance for such a performance."[46]

Whatever Truman's earlier feelings, by mid-1948, there would be no question about his determination to run. He was not about to go out when people were calling him a loser. He may have been obliged to run away from fist fights as a child, but he had never run away from a political one in which he was an underdog—not in 1924 or in 1940. He was fully prepared to put everything he had into what he saw as yet another campaign for vindication.

25

"HE DONE HIS DAMNDEST": THE PRECAMPAIGN CAMPAIGN OF 1948

"Mr. Truman's time is short; his situation is hopeless. Frankly, he is a gone goose." Thus declared Clare Boothe Luce, Truman's least favorite female politico, to a cheering audience at the GOP convention in Philadelphia on June 21, 1948. If Truman watched this declamation on the television set that had just been installed in the White House, he must have realized that Luce was not just engaging in partisan hyperbole but repeating the conventional wisdom. The apparently strong Wallace candidacy (exemplified by Leo Isaacson's Bronx victory), the Palestine muddle, the reaction against the civil rights program—all had imbedded in the public mind the idea that Truman was a bumbler and a sure loser. None of this daunted a president who was beginning to glory in a newly developed reputation as a fighter. Speaking in Arizona the week before, he had adopted as his own the epitaph at the grave of Jack Williams in Tombstone: "He Done His Damndest."[1]

II

By the spring of 1948, Truman's domestic policy strategy of presenting himself as a fighting New Deal liberal was well established. It needed to be supplemented with a more pleasing personal image, the biggest obstacle to which was the president's stiff, stumbling way of reading a speech. With the encouragement of Clifford, Murphy, and Ross, Truman began to experiment with an off-the-cuff style of speaking, at times simply departing from a prepared text to make a few extemporaneous remarks, on other occasions referring only to note cards. The great virtue of the new speaking style was that it allowed Truman to be himself, a usually genial Mr. Everyman speaking plain, unaffected English, the words flowing from the heart.[2]

Its first major tryout came on the evening of April 17, when he spoke to the annual meeting of the American Society of Newspaper Editors. His formal speech, a radio address that promoted the administration's anti-inflation program, was competent in construction and delivery, but it was a dreary topic for a group of informed journalists who knew that economic controls were not about to be reinstated by Congress.

Once he was finished and off the air, however, the president informed his audience that he wanted to speak off the record about the escalating tensions with the Soviet Union. Here—less than two months after the Czech coup, just weeks after Truman had called for a resumption of the draft—was a topic guaranteed to get attention. The way in which he handled it was compelling. He spoke directly and personally of his hopes for good relations with the USSR, his initial liking of "Old Joe," his disappointing discovery that Stalin and his associates "have a different code of morals from ours—if they have any."

As Jonathan Daniels put it, "He was suddenly a very interesting man of great candor who discussed the problems of American leadership with men as neighbors." His first address had received only polite applause at the end; this one received numerous interruptions of approval. Most of the members of the audience, Eben Ayers later wrote, had never seen the president before; knowing him only from his radio speeches, they found his informal talk "a revelation" characterized by "intense sincerity and obvious honesty." One of them, a Maine Republican, told Ayers that if Truman went out and talked to the people like that he might well be re-elected. In fact, the reception guaranteed, as Robert Donovan later put it, "that he would adopt a style of campaigning that two-thirds of them would denounce on their editorial pages."[3]

Truman himself appears to have been surprised and a bit insecure about the entire business. He repeated his April 17 remarks to an informal press conference of business editors on April 23, spoke from an outline to another group on May 1, and used the technique for a speech carried on national radio on May 6. The following day, he wrote in his diary with mixed satisfaction and trepidation, "Returns from the radio on the family life speech are very satisfactory. Looks as if I'm stuck for 'off-the-cuff' radio speeches. It means a lot of hard work, and the head at 64 doesn't work as well as it did at 24."

A week later, he did another nationally broadcast speech without a prepared text, this time at the Young Democrats meeting. In a minor way, it displayed the risks of his words outrunning his calculation. Near the end, he declared, "I wish we had an Isaiah or a Martin Luther to lead us out of this moral despond into which we have fallen." William Batt, Jr., the head of the new research staff that Clifford had set up at the Democratic National Committee, told Clifford, "Reference to Martin Luther was resented by some Catholics listening. The hope that somehow great leaders may arise was negative." Whatever the ill effects, they were overshadowed by another presidential declaration: "I want to say to you that for the next four years there will be a Democrat in the White House, and you are looking at him!"[4]

III

Looking at the president was just what Truman and his advisers wanted as many people as possible to do. They all understood that he was most appealing in person. In April, the White House announced that he would accept a standing invitation to speak at the commencement ceremony of the University of California at Berkeley. Moreover, rather than fly to California and return immediately to Washington, he would travel by train, speak frequently from the rear platform, and make several major speeches at other locations. To the outrage of the Republicans, the administration would consider the journey an official presidential trip to be funded by public money—although everyone realized that it was a dry run for the fall campaign. Whether infuriated or bemused, few political observers thought either at the beginning or at the end that it represented a formula for victory in November.[5]

Truman traveled in the special presidential car, the "Ferdinand Magellan," a 142-ton armored behemoth with virtually all the comforts of the White House, including an oak-paneled living room, a luxurious dining area, and five bedrooms with private baths. The rear platform, roomy enough for a half-dozen or so persons, carried the presidential seal below its railing and had a built-in lectern wired to loudspeakers mounted overhead. It was the last piece of rolling stock on a seventeen-car train that carried approximately 125 persons, 59 of whom were reporters, the rest train crew and presidential support staff. The Army Signal Corps kept the train in constant touch with Washington. Other cars provided working space for presidential staff and newsmen; one served as a reception area in which the president met groups of local dignitaries.

The train left Washington late on the night of June 3. The next day at noon, it made its first stop at Crestline, a small town in northern Ohio. About a thousand persons crowded around the back of the train to hear a few pleasantries from Truman. Later in the day, at Fort Wayne and then at Gary, Indiana, he spoke more substantively about foreign relations and his personal quest for world peace, about the high cost of living and Republican indifference to the needs of the common man. That evening in Chicago Stadium, he delivered a nationally broadcast speech to the Swedish Pioneer Centennial Association in which he urged liberalized immigration laws and advocated his domestic legislative agenda as the best means of fighting Communism. Then he was back on the train for a night ride across Iowa and a day in Omaha, where he participated in the annual reunion of the Thirty-fifth Division, made two informal talks, and delivered a major agricultural address.

Thus went the pattern as the train chugged through the Northwest, over the continental divide, down the Pacific coast, and back to Washington. In a two-week period, Truman would give six major speeches and eleven times as many informal talks. All but one of the big speeches were from prepared texts and devoted to important issues. The informal talks were usually from outlines, occasionally purely extemporaneous. Sometimes, especially on Sundays, they consisted of nothing but amiable generalities: "I have made it a rule never to make political speeches or speeches of any other kind on a Sunday." But once in a while even on Sundays and continually on other days, he hurled stinging attacks at the misdeeds of the Eightieth Congress.[6]

The whistle-stop was not much different in tone and character from the kind of personal campaigning Truman had done in Missouri. He always began a talk by alluding to some bit of local history, perhaps fed to him by the campaign research staff, perhaps dredged up from his own historical knowledge or his prior travels across America. He always introduced Bess ("the Boss") and Margaret ("the Boss's Boss"), giving the crowd a look at the womenfolk and a sense of his model middle-class family. He always displayed his customary smile and increasingly seemed to take a genuine delight in his fleeting contacts with the average Americans who came down to the station; many of them, in turn, saw someone who might be running a local bank or small business: decent, respected, well traveled, but not much different from themselves. The train would depart with the presidential family on the rear platform waving good-bye; sometimes Margaret would throw a rose to the crowd.

There were mishaps aplenty. Thanks to Eddie McKim's inept management of local arrangements in Omaha, Truman spoke to a mostly empty auditorium; newspapers across the country printed photos of seemingly endless rows of empty seats. In Carey, Idaho, an appalling misunderstanding led the president to try to dedicate a new airport in the presumption that it was named for a fallen war hero rather than a young civilian woman who had been killed in a plane crash. After apologizing to her parents, he called a staff meeting; but he was temperamentally incapable of giving his aides the dressing-down they deserved.[7]

A couple of times, Truman's mouth got ahead of his political sense. At the end of his talk in Pocatello, he declared that he wanted the people to see and listen to him in person, and then make up their own minds about him: "I have been in politics a long time, and it makes no difference what they say about you, if it isn't so. If they can prove it on you, you are in a bad fix indeed. They have never been able to prove it on me." Spoken in an even voice with a big grin, quickly followed with the standard introduction of Bess and Margaret, the comment made little impact on the crowd. In print, it looked like a defensive retort to charges of Pendergast-era corruption.

A few days later, in Eugene, Oregon, he returned to what was becoming a habitual misinterpretation of Soviet politics. Speaking off the top of his head about relations with the USSR, Truman said, "I like old Joe! He is a decent fellow. But Joe is a prisoner of the Politboro. He can't do what he wants to." Displaying journalistic enterprise that the president could have done without, Robert J. Donovan dashed off a quick story, picked a trustworthy-looking woman out of the crowd, gave her a $20 bill, and got her to phone the copy to the *New York Herald-Tribune* in time for its morning edition. Undersecretary of State Lovett was soon on the phone, asking Clark Clifford to get the president's commitment never to state that bizarre view again. Clifford and Ross met with Truman and informed him as tactfully as they could that he had made a damaging blunder. After a moment of silence, the president replied, "Well I guess I goofed." He never repeated the statement in public.[8]

To those who expected dignity in presidential appearances, Truman could be downright offensive. Presented with boots and spurs in Nebraska, he talked about taking Congress for a ride. Partisans loved such rhetoric. "Pour it on, Harry!" someone shouted in Bremmerton, Washington. "I'm going to—I'm going to!" Truman responded. More than once, he appeared late at night in pajamas and bathrobe to greet crowds that had waited to see him. "I thought I would let you see what I look like, even if I didn't have on any clothes," he said in Missoula, Montana.

Speaking to—of all groups!—the ultra-conservative Union League Club of Philadelphia, his sense of propriety offended and his partisan reflexes all but uncontrollable, Senator Taft declared that Truman was "blackguarding Congress at whistlestops all across the country." The Democratic National Committee loved the charge; its publicity director, Jack Redding, wired the mayors of thirty-five towns and cities through which Truman had passed. Did they consider their municipalities whistlestops? The answers were predictable. After a tumultuous welcome in Los Angeles, Truman informed the Angelenos that their town was "the biggest whistlestop." A few hours later in San Bernardino, he accepted a basket of eggs and responded to the suggestion that he might throw them at Taft by saying: "I wouldn't throw *fresh* eggs at Taft!"[9]

As poor as always in his political judgment, Taft had given the campaign a name and had called attention to the sharp ideological edge that Truman was trying to give it. In one talk after another, the president accused the Republicans of responsibility for every ill that afflicted the country, with special emphasis on the high cost of living and the continuing housing crisis. He also had discovered that there were many people outside Washington who liked his blasts at Congress, accompanied by such descriptions as "worst," "do-nothing," "good-for-nothing," or controlled by "the special privilege boys." Excited spectators shouted for him to lay it on.

How people responded to all this depended on their political affiliation and expectations of presidential behavior. It was true enough that at times, Truman behaved rather like a warm-up act for Edgar Bergen and

Charlie McCarthy. The *Washington Evening Star*, Republican and a bit stuffy, declared, "The President in this critical hour is making a spectacle of himself that would reflect discreditably on a ward heeler." Before the trip was finished, reporters had developed a "many-versed song" celebrating its farcical aspects. A few of the more memorable lines, sung to the tune of "Oh Susannah," were

> They can't prove nothing
> They ain't got a thing on me
> I'm going down to Berkeley
> To get me a degree.

But whatever the impression of fumble and stumble, shrewd observers realized that the president was peddling ideas with his personality and that, although he still had an uphill fight, the combination had electoral potential.[10]

IV

Truman returned to Washington on June 18, his elation dampened by the emergence of a dangerous crisis in the heart of Europe. On that same day in Germany, the Western allies had taken the decisive step in the movement toward economic unification of their zones of occupation by introducing a new currency. Denouncing the move as illegal, the USSR retaliated by interfering with ground traffic into Berlin; by June 24, the Western powers faced a full-scale blockade.

In a series of conferences over the next three or four days, the president authorized a middle-of-the-road response. Meeting with Secretaries Forrestal, Lovett (acting for Marshall), and Royall on June 28, Truman reportedly declared, "We would stay, period." Still, he was cautious. There would be no attempt to break the ground blockade; West Berlin would be supplied by air. The strategy was precarious; in the beginning, it seemed unlikely that transport planes could bring in enough food and fuel to keep the city going over the long haul. Worried military officials kept coming back for renewed authorization. Truman reaffirmed the decision twice in the next three weeks. "We'll stay in Berlin—come what may," he wrote in his diary on July 19. Complaining that Forrestal wanted "to hedge" and was giving him "alibi memos," he continued, "I don't pass the buck, nor do I alibi out of any decision I make."[11]

As another sign of determination, the United States sent three squadrons of B-29 bombers to England and Germany. These were not modified to carry atomic bombs, but the president and his advisers clearly hoped that the Soviets would think they might be. It was as close as Truman ever came to playing the nuclear card during his presidency. At a high-level meeting on July 21, he curtly rejected a request to hand over custody of the atomic stockpile to the military, a move that he believed would jeopardize his control over it. His remarks, summarized by David

Lilienthal, showed just how far his thinking had progressed almost three years to the day since he had received word of the first atomic-bomb test in the New Mexico desert:

> I don't think we ought to use this thing unless we absolutely have to. It is a terrible thing to order the use of something that [pause], that is so terribly destructive, destructive beyond anything we have ever had. You have got to understand that this isn't a military weapon. It is used to wipe out women and children and unarmed people, and not for military uses. So we have got to treat this differently from rifles and cannon and ordinary things like that. . . . You have got to understand that I have got to think about the effect of such a thing on international relations. This is no time to be juggling an atom bomb around.[12]

Two days later, probably to mollify Forrestal, perhaps because he was genuinely undecided, Truman told the secretary that political considerations were influencing his decisions. After the election, he said, he would take another look at the picture. The next day, he issued a statement on "two years of experience with the Atomic Energy Act" that unostentatiously but pointedly emphasized civilian control and presidential responsibility.[13]

Yet the problem of the bomb would not go away. Civilian and uniformed military leaders pressed Truman as to whether it could be used if war broke out. With round-the-clock flights into Berlin intermittently harassed by the Soviets, with allied ground forces unable to resist a Soviet takeover of the city, the question had more than academic relevance. Meeting with Forrestal and others again on September 13, Truman said, as Forrestal recorded it, "that he prayed that he would never have to make such a decision, but that if it became necessary, no one need have a misgiving but what he would do so." In his own diary, the president wrote, "I have a terrible feeling afterward that we are very close to war."[14]

V

Truman had arrived back from California just a few days before the beginning of the Republican National Convention and about three weeks before the Democrats would meet. However well he felt he had done on his trip, he had neither dispelled the atmosphere of impending doom that hung over his party nor disturbed the Republican sense of inevitable victory. He needed to placate the South without losing northern blacks to Henry Wallace, stave off a growing dump-Truman movement, and find a vice-presidential candidate who would add luster to the Democratic ticket.

The South and the entire issue of civil rights presented a serious threat not only to Truman's reelection, but to the structure of the Democratic party. The administration's civil rights legislation was dead in the water on Capitol Hill. Wallace was refusing to appear before segregated audiences and making strong appeals to the black vote. Independent civil rights leader A. Philip Randolph was leading a crusade against military segregation and threatening to mount a black draft-resistance movement. Almost the entire white South was livid, and some leaders talked about yet another third-party revolt that almost surely would take some states of the Solid South away from the Democrats.

Truman's instincts were to be conciliatory toward Southerners, with whom he felt a common identity. He had made his point with the civil rights program and had no intention of abandoning it. But the time had come to unite the party. His strategy was logical enough: appease the South at the convention and stave off another new party; then, no doubt, make gestures to northern blacks sometime before the general election. Behind this course was the belief that somehow southern segregationists and northern civil rights activists could coexist within the Democratic party.

The president's word to the party platform committee was to write a brief, innocuous civil rights plank that avoided mention of specifics, including the administration's program. A classic "old politics" ploy, it was to run up against a drive by the Americans for Democratic Action (ADA) for a strong civil rights plank that would place the party unequivocally on the liberal side of the issue, whatever the risks of a southern revolt. This stand was good ideology. Truman wrongly believed that it was not good politics.

The ADA bedeviled Truman in an even more fundamental way. It headed an effort to drop him from the ticket. The organization's leadership conceded that the president had largely followed in the footsteps of Franklin Roosevelt and had pretty much pursued the lines that it recommended as the only means of reconstituting a viable non-Communist liberal movement—social legislation and economic management at home, European reconstruction abroad. The problem was not Truman's program; it was Truman. He was not FDR. His voice did not resonate with the northern intelligentsia. He was taking the party to a crushing defeat.

Chester Bowles, running for governor of Connecticut, was convinced that he was sunk with Truman at the head of the ticket. Minneapolis mayor Hubert Humphrey, running for the Senate, looked to the fall in despair: "We not only face defeat in November, we face a disintegration of the whole social-democratic block in this country." James Loeb, executive secretary of the ADA wrote, "We cannot compete with the Wallace crowd unless and until we have a national Presidential figure to crusade for. Harry Truman is ADA's great frustration."

How to deal with that frustration? In April, the ADA called on the Democratic party to nominate the most charismatic and electable individual in American public life: General Eisenhower. Numerous labor leaders, a few Democratic bosses, and FDR's two eldest sons, James and Franklin, Jr., registered their support. As Loeb and others from the ADA would explain in later years, Ike seemed the champion and personification of the common man. He therefore had to be a liberal. In truth, however, the prospect of certain victory made it easy for them to postpone a close examination of his ideas.[15]

Truman was furious—and with considerable justification. He had little use for the liberal intellectuals, many of the labor leaders, and such old rogues as Mayor Frank Hague of Jersey City, all of whom wanted to get rid of him. To him, the draft-Eisenhower movement confirmed their shallowness and lack of character. But he took the defection of the Roosevelt sons as a personal affront. In Los Angeles, he had met privately with Jimmy Roosevelt, giving the younger man a sharp lecture that a Secret Service man remembered as follows:

> Your father asked me to take this job. I didn't want it. I was happy in the Senate. But your father asked me to take it, and I took it. And if your father knew what you are doing to me, he would turn over in his grave. But get this straight: whether you like it or not, I am going to be the next President of the United States. That will be all. Good day.[16]

Nor was he any longer willing to pass along the job to Eisenhower. Although Ike had consistently refused to declare a candidacy, his boosters kept insisting that he had not shut the door, double-bolted it, and barricaded himself against the possibility. Truman, who knew that the general probably could prevail at the Democratic National Convention, remained jittery.

His mood could not have been improved by a scheduled train trip to Bolivar, Missouri, where he and the president of Venezuela dedicated a statue of Simón Bolívar on July 5. The greatest event in the little town's history took place in oppressive heat. The temperature was over 100 degrees in the shade, what there was of it. Returning from this needless distraction, tired and tense, the president got a copy of Eisenhower's latest declaration: "I will not at this time identify myself with any political party and could not accept nomination for any public office." Jumping on the phrase "at this time," he told Eben Ayers that the statement was weasel-worded and Eisenhower a "shit ass." Three days later, Eisenhower issued another statement, so Sherman-like as to discourage the most determined political press gang. Truman would have only kind words for him for the next three years.[17]

The last remaining obstacle to the nomination was insignificant. Senator Claude Pepper offered himself, only to be rejected by an ungrateful party that saw him as dangerously close to Wallace on foreign policy, not of presidential caliber, and altogether unelectable. Winifred Galbraith Todd, "Miss Equestrienne of 1948," nevertheless attempted to stampede the convention by riding into the hall on a horse festooned with a "Pepper for President" banner. An assistant sergeant-at-arms stopped her at the door, declaring, "Hey lady, he can't come in here. He hasn't got a badge."[18]

VI

The convention opened in Philadelphia on July 12 in an atmosphere of depression and lethargy accentuated by summer heat fully as strength sapping as that encountered by Truman in Bolivar. The Republicans had met in the same hall three weeks earlier in slightly more moderate temperatures and in a mood of gaiety and impending triumph. Their nominees—Dewey of New York for president and Earl Warren of California for vice president—gave all the appearance of an unbeatable dream ticket. Few doubted that Clare Boothe Luce had correctly called the political future of the country. The polls seemed to back her up.

Two events brought the convention back to life. The first was Alben Barkley's keynote address. A performance in the grand tradition of American political speech making, it excoriated the failures of the Republicans, quoted every patron saint of the Democratic party from Jefferson to FDR, expropriated Lincoln along the way, cited a text from the Book of Revelation, and invoked "the Divine obligation" that God had entrusted to America and, presumably, the Democrats. The old Kentuckian's stemwinding oratory roused the convention and set in motion a well-planned vice-presidential draft movement.[19]

The second event was the ADA-led civil rights fight. Over the opposition of Truman, the ADA put together a coalition of labor leaders, liberals, and big-city bosses. Galvanized by the impassioned oratory of Hubert Humphrey ("the time has arrived for the Democratic party to get out of the shadow of states rights and walk into the bright sunshine of human rights"), the delegates rejected the vague lines of the draft platform and substituted a plank commending the administration's program in all its specifics.

The impact of the civil rights revolt was profound. It had been carried through by the same forces that had wanted to draft Eisenhower. Thus it displayed the tenuousness of Truman's grasp on the party's levers of power and the precariousness of his nomination. It also was a symbolic demonstration that the Democratic party *stood* for civil rights, that the northern liberals and their allies were in the clear ascendancy, and that the liberal agenda of the postwar era (quite unlike that of the Depression years) gave the issue its highest priority.

A good many Southerners were unwilling to reconcile themselves to that message. "We bid you good-bye," declared an Alabama delegate just before he marched out of the hall with half of his state's representatives and the entire Mississippi contingent. Most of those who remained did so only to vote against Truman's nomination. The final result, 947.5 for Truman and 263 for Senator Richard Russell of Georgia, would demonstrate graphically how the South had moved from being a dominating force to a marginal minority at Democratic presidential conventions. By the time Truman arrived in Philadelphia to make his acceptance speech, everyone knew that the southern rebellion had laid the basis for yet another protest party that might be able to deny the presidency to Truman and the Northerners in a close election.

By the end of the month, southern insurgents had formed the States Rights' Democratic party, or Dixicrats, which nominated Governors J. Strom Thurmond of South Carolina and Fielding Wright of Mississippi for president and vice president. Given Truman's weakness in the polls and Wallace's challenge in the liberal northern states, the South had taken on a new electoral importance, however irrelevant it might have been to Roosevelt. How many states could Thurmond carry? How many could Truman afford to lose?

For vice president, Truman had wanted William O. Douglas, whose relative youth, dynamism, and aggressive liberalism would attract the northern constituencies that were crucial to victory in November and that might otherwise be drawn toward Wallace. Douglas, moreover, had roots in the western neo-Brandeisian insurgency that Truman had adopted as his creed. On July 12, the first day of the convention, the justice called to decline. Truman's annoyance would have been considerable under the best of conditions. A report from Burton Wheeler escalated it: Douglas had told Tommy Corcoran he did not want to be a number-two man to a number-two man.

There was nothing left to do but take "old man Barkley," as Truman privately called him, although Barkley would add little to the ticket's electoral appeal, was six and a half years older than Truman, and, in the president's estimate, had been a mediocre Senate Democratic leader. Inwardly, too, Truman seethed at the way Les Biffle, acting as convention sergeant-at-arms, was "running Barkley for President." As usual, however, he was the epitome of geniality when he talked with Barkley on the telephone: "Why didn't you tell me you wanted to run, Alben? That's all you had to do."

"I stuck my neck all the way out for Douglas, and he cut the limb out from under me." Such was the wonderful mixed metaphor the president delivered to his staff on the morning of July 13. He was blunt. Barkley was not the best candidate, but one had to be cold-blooded about it. If the convention wanted Barkley, it could have him. Truman was more excited about his acceptance speech, in which he would announce a special session of Congress; this would say in effect to the Republican party: "Now, you son of a bitch, come on and do your god-damndest." During the next six months, he told his aides, we will all have more fun than ever in our lives.[20]

In Philadelphia, the platform fight ran over to July 14, throwing Truman's nomination far behind schedule and leaving him furious at the "crackpots" who were trying to force the South to bolt. It was not until 7:00 P.M. that he boarded his train for the convention. It was 9:42 when he arrived at the convention hall with no quick end in sight to the balloting. For a while, he waited in Democratic National Chairman McGrath's hot, airless office, and then went out onto a ramp—"a balcony," he later called it—at the back of the hall. He received "a horde of politicians, masculine and feminine," and then chatted with Barkley. From time to time, they glanced out at the view—railroad tracks and an occasional passing train. Tom Evans marveled at the way in which the president seemed cool and immaculate in his white linen suit.

Three hours to the minute after he had arrived at the convention hall, Truman finally was nominated. Then it took another hour to present Barkley and designate him the vice-presidential nominee by acclamation (an honor denied to the president). At approximately 1:45 A.M. on the morning of July 15, the ticket finally appeared on the platform to receive what little acclaim the exhausted delegates could muster.[21]

One final fiasco occurred. National committeewoman Emma Guffey Miller of Pennsylvania, the sister of Truman's old Senate colleague Joe Guffey, presented the president with a floral Liberty Bell, releasing from within it a flock of white pigeons—symbolic doves of peace. The plan had been for the birds to swoop dramatically over the convention floor. Instead, frantic from the awful heat and their close confinement, they scattered and looked for the nearest place to perch. One of them landed in front of Permanent Chairman Sam Rayburn, who grabbed it, tossed it out toward the audience, and shouted, "Get those damned pigeons out of here." (Truman thoroughly enjoyed the spectacle. Later, as he did so frequently, he would improve on the story: "One perched on Sam Rayburn's head. Was Sam disgusted. Funniest thing in the convention." Rayburn, not amused, always denied Truman's account.)

After a few minutes, the pigeons dispersed, most of them making for the rafters and the breezes of the cooling fans. The comic relief had been scant. The delegates were in no mood to give their nominees a long ovation. Barkley spoke for only a few minutes. At about 2:00 A.M., Truman stepped in front of the microphones, aware that the nationwide audience he had hoped to reach had dwindled to a mere blip on the rating chart. As would be the case with George McGovern twenty-four years later, it was prime time in Guam.[22]

Speaking from an outline in a tight, clipped, angry voice that doubtless drew much of its emotion from the frustrations of the past few weeks, he came out swinging: "Senator Barkley and I will win this election and make these Republicans like it—don't you forget that!" The delegates, so tired and limp a moment earlier, came out of their seats yelling encouragement. In the same tone, he went on to list all the achievements of the Democratic party over the past decade and a half, all the things he as president had tried to do for "the common everyday man," all the sins of the "worst 80th Congress."

Then, surveying the platform adopted by the recent Republican Convention, he depicted it as a list of cynically hypocritical promises committing the party to a liberal legislative program. After that came the stunner: "I am therefore calling this Congress back into session July 26th." On that day, "Turnip Day" in rural Missouri, he would send up a multipoint program to Capitol Hill: economic controls, housing, aid to education, national health insurance, civil rights, a higher minimum wage, extended social security, publicly owned electric-power development, liberalized immigration for displaced persons.

If Congress believed in the Republican platform, it would pass the whole list: "They can do this job in 15 days if they want to do it. They will still have time to go out and run for office." Invoking the traditions and emotions of the Depression decade, he declared, "And in the record is the stark truth, that the battle lines of 1948 are the same as they were in 1932, when the nation lay prostrate and helpless as a result of Republican misrule and inaction."[23]

Like most political oratory, the speech contained gross exaggerations and was inflammatory. Drawing on continued widespread uncertainty about the staying power of postwar prosperity, it played to fears more than to hopes. The delegates loved it. First Barkley's keynote, then the civil rights fight, now Truman's acceptance speech—all had injected excitement into a dispirited gathering. In one way or another, each had done so by expressing the spirit of New Deal liberalism, no matter if the emerging postwar world was fundamentally conservative.

Many voters, and especially many Democratic activists, still possessed a worldview that had been forged in the different days of the 1930s. The extent of this ideological lag would be decisive in Truman's campaign. The self-conscious New Deal liberals, who had so recently scorned him, were especially stirred. "It was fun to see the scrappy little cuss come out of his corner fighting . . . not trying to use big words any longer, but being himself and saying a lot of honest things," wrote "T.R.B." (Richard L. Strout) in the *New Republic*. "Unaccountably, we found ourself on top of a pine bench cheering."[24]

Truman got quite a lift from the experience also. Writing to his old friend General Louis Pick, he gave the impression of a man spoiling for a fight and fully expecting to win: "When I get through with these counterfeits there won't be anything left but a small cloud of dust."[25]

26

"I'LL GIVE 'EM HELL":
THE CAMPAIGN OF 1948

The acceptance speech set the tone for one of the most memorable campaigns in American political history. Departing fromWashington two months later for his most ambitious cross-country tour, Truman left his vice-presidential candidate and other party leaders with words that would become his slogan: "I'll mow 'em down, Alben, and I'll give 'em hell."[1]

II

On July 26, the first day of the special session of Congress, Truman moved to make the most of the civil rights developments at the convention. With the States' Rights party now an unavoidable reality, there was no longer any potential gain from hedging. The White House issued executive orders promoting equal opportunity in the federal civil service and, most consequentially, in the armed forces. Asked at a press conference whether this meant an eventual end to military segregation, Truman replied with one word: "Yes."

With that stroke, the president all but forced A. Philip Randolph to put his draft-resistance movement on the shelf and deprived Henry Wallace of a potent issue. The integration of the armed forces would not occur overnight. The process over the next two years would be resisted at almost every turn by army leaders skilled in bureaucratic Fabian tactics. But in the summer of 1948, what loomed large was Truman's commitment—one that in fact he would keep despite the misgivings of the military.[2]

The special session itself was predictably unfruitful. Truman went before it on July 27 to deliver a special message demanding a long list of legislation. The Republicans, every bit as furious as one might expect, gave him practically nothing. When Congress adjourned after a couple of weeks, the White House released a long "Summary of Action by the Congress on the President's Recommendations." The phrase that appeared most frequently was "Failed to Act."[3] Thus the president had a lengthy compilation of issues for the campaign.

Perhaps the most notable thing about the list was that foreign policy matters were almost entirely absent from it, aside from such peripheral matters as a displaced-persons immigration law, the International Wheat Agreement, and a loan to the United Nations. The president had defined the difference between Democrats and Republicans as almost exclusively about domestic policies; he was shrewd in perceiving that here he had a distinct edge. As for the Republicans, they could claim their share of credit for important foreign policy innovations only by admitting that they had supported administration initiatives, not exactly the sort of thing likely to rouse the faithful or sway the independent voter.

One event during the special session might in ordinary times have left the administration badly damaged. In testimony before the House Committee on Un-American Activities, Elizabeth Bentley, Louis Budenz, and Whittaker Chambers identified a number of government employees, including former State Department official Alger Hiss, as having once belonged to the Communist party and in some cases (although not initially that of Hiss) having been involved in Soviet espionage operations.[4]

At a press conference on August 5, Truman responded to a reporter's question, "Mr. President, do you think that the Capitol Hill spy scare is a 'red herring' to divert public attention from inflation?" He read a statement denying congressional committees access to classified personnel files, observed that they had uncovered nothing not already known by the FBI, and denounced the hearings for "seriously impairing the morale of Federal employees, and undermining public confidence in the Government." Then, off the cuff, he added a sentence that repeated a phrase from the journalist's original question: "And they are simply a 'red herring' to keep from doing what they ought to do." Inevitably someone asked, "Mr. President, can we use a part of the quote there, that last: they are simply a 'red herring,' etc.?" Genuinely indignant over the committee proceedings, Truman unwisely agreed, thereby reducing a dull and not very quotable statement to a sound-bite that would redound hard against him in the future.[5]

As a campaign point, however, the "red herring" statement was worthless. It was hard to use the Communist issue against Truman as long as Henry Wallace was running to his left. The Progressive party convention had just given the country a vivid example of Popular Front politics and pro-Soviet advocacy. Spending much of their time attacking Truman's foreign policies, determinedly refusing to criticize the USSR, and openly accepting Communist support, the Progressives had begun a process of political self-destruction that would accelerate during the fall.

Wallace, personally embittered at Truman and opposed as a matter of principle to his foreign policy, had embarked on his campaign determined to bring down the president. Instead, by accepting a role as the focus of pro-Soviet sentiment in American politics, he did Truman a favor. Clare Boothe Luce, who took no prisoners with her oratory, called the Progressive leader "Stalin's Mortimer Snerd."[6] Unhappily, he would spend the campaign justifying the description.

The administration itself capitalized on anti-Communist feeling in a number of ways. Truman used the issue rarely, but at strategic points. On March 17, for example, making a nationally broadcast speech to a major St. Patrick's Day dinner in New York, he appealed to an audience of vehemently anti-Communist Irish Catholics and, by extension, to all American Catholics. Denouncing Communist tyranny and atheism, he declared "I do not want and I will not accept the political support of Henry Wallace and his Communists." (Not, of course, that there was any danger of it being offered!)[7]

On July 20, less than a week after the Democratic National Convention, a federal grand jury indicted twelve leaders of the Communist party for having violated the Smith Act. The crime was conspiracy "to organize as the Communist Party of the United States a society, group or assembly of persons who teach and advocate the overthrow and destruction of the Government of the United States by force and violence." The Smith Act had been passed in 1940, and the administration could claim simply to be enforcing it. Still, the criminalization of teaching and advocacy raised grave constitutional questions that far transcended the contemptible character of the indictees. Truman told a press conference, presumably truthfully, that he had not known about the indictment in advance. He probably was not proud of it, for it was at variance with attitudes he expressed privately and publicly. His memoirs would make no mention of it. Like the loyalty program, the Smith Act prosecutions were an embarrassment foisted on him by the temper of the time and, to some extent, by an administrative style that gave the cabinet departments wide discretion in the formulation and execution of their policies.[8]

Truman spoke extensively about Communism on only one occasion during the campaign. At Oklahoma City on September 28, his main target was the Republicans, whom he accused with considerable justice of demagoguing the issue. His one swipe at Wallace and the Progressives was a roundhouse aimed more at Dewey: "Just why are the Communists backing the third party? They are backing the third party because they want a Republican victory in November."[9] A tough statement, on the surface a bit demagogic, it was at least essentially accurate. Both Wallace and the Communists surely believed that a Democratic loss would increase their leverage in American politics, although both would have been much happier with the isolationist Taft than the internationalist Dewey. It is unclear whether there was a strategic decision that the president would not spend much time bashing domestic Communists or whether Truman avoided such exercises as distasteful. Democratic surrogates spent considerably more time on the issue, especially in urban areas with large Catholic populations.

III

Truman opened the 1948 campaign on Labor Day with a major speech to a huge labor rally in Detroit's Cadillac Square. He made six rear-platform appearances the same day, the first at 9:10 A.M. in Grand Rapids, the last at 11:55 P.M. in Toledo. The one-day tour was an exhausting foretaste of what was to come.

It was no longer possible to pretend that Truman's journeys were nonpolitical. Financing the rail trips, radio addresses, and other campaign events was a constant problem. Truman had asked Bernard Baruch to be the party's chief fund-raiser, only to receive a rejection. Baruch stated that he had never served in such positions and that Roosevelt had approved of the policy. His communication also made a request that read rather like a command: that the president send no representative other than the duly appointed ambassador (Baruch's brother) to the jubilee of Queen Wilhelmina of the Netherlands. Infuriated, Truman responded, "A great many honors have passed your way, both to you and your family, and it seems when the going is rough it is a one-way street. I am sorry that this is so." Baruch would not enter the White House again during Truman's presidency. Any small chance of reconciliation was quashed in December 1950, when columnist Westbrook Pegler quoted Baruch as calling Truman "a rude, uncouth, ignorant man."[10]

The finance chairmanship instead went to Louis Johnson, a Washington attorney and former national commander of the American Legion, who had served with distinction as assistant secretary of war for a time under FDR. Johnson threw all his energy into the campaign, but Truman had to involve himself more actively than he ever had done in the past. Speaking to groups of contributors at White House receptions, he stood on a chair begging for money that would allow him to carry the Democratic message to the people. Near the end of the first big whistle-stop trip, it appeared briefly that there was no cash to get the train out of Oklahoma City. Governor (and senatorial candidate) Robert Kerr brought the president together with a group of oilmen who produced the funds needed. Payment for presidential radio speeches was frequently a very near thing; on at least one occasion, Truman was cut off the air when he ran overtime.

As was common in those days, some of the fund-raising was irregular. A prominent St. Louisian liked to tell associates in later years that he had carried a suitcase full of cash across the state to Kansas City and personally delivered it to a federal judge who also was a close friend of the president. Perhaps accurate, perhaps a malicious exaggeration by a person who had an ax to grind, the story nonetheless carried a certain poetic truth in its revelation of how a lot of political money was still handled. Yet despite the impression of a near-constant crisis, the Democrats actually appear to have spent $2.7 million, compared with the overconfident Republicans' $2.1 million. However the cash was generated, one consequence was unavoidable: if reelected, Truman would face a long line of individuals and interest groups expecting favorable consideration on appointments to office or policy decisions.[11]

The biggest of the whistle-stop trips began on September 17 and lasted for fifteen days. A swing through the country comparable to the trip to Berkeley, it went through seventeen states from Pennsylvania to California. Truman delivered thirteen major speeches and made as many as a dozen rear-platform appearances a day. It was on this trip that two things were forever established: the character of the campaign and the ambiance of "the train." In many ways, both reproduced the California trip of June. Truman spoke much as he had then, presenting his attractive "ordinary fellow" personality, introducing his family, saying a bit about the history of the latest stop. Using an outline, he then moved to issues of special interest to the audience. The president threw everything he had at the Congress and told the crowds that the Republicans were responsible for the high cost of living, the housing shortage, declining farm prices, or the oppression of labor; that they would neglect development of the West; and that they cared for only the rich.

Years later, Robert J. Donovan, looking back on an event he had covered as a journalist, described Truman's oratory with a peculiar mixture of fondness and censure: "sharp speeches fairly criticizing Republican policy and defending New Deal liberalism, mixed with sophistries, bunkum piled higher than haystacks, and demagoguery tooting merrily down the track." Clark Clifford recalled the situation as akin to that of a football team down by several touchdowns well into the second half: "We were on our own 20-yard line. . . . [W]e had to throw long passes—anything to stir up labor and the other mass votes."[12]

Speaking to 80,000 farmers at Dexter, Iowa, Truman described the opposition as "gluttons of privilege," using the phrase a half-dozen times. He also declared, "This Republican Congress has already stuck a pitchfork in the farmer's back." (The line was so good, he could not suppress a good-natured laugh.) Rarely did he forget to recall the Depression and remind an audience in one way or another that it could happen again if the Republicans should be returned to office. Nor was he shy about charging that the GOP was ready to take away from the American people everything they had gained under sixteen years of Democratic rule. Delivering a model specimen of redundant rhetoric, he told a crowd in Akron, Ohio: "The Republican politicians don't like the New Deal. They never have liked the New Deal, and they would like to get rid of it—repeal it—put it out of existence."[13]

Thus Truman peddled issues in practically every appearance, but many of those with him would equally recall the experience of the train

itself. One stop after another, the marathon race to produce speech outlines, reporters running time and again to the rear of the train to hear a
talk, then racing to get back on. Clark Clifford, Wallace Graham, or some
other staffer would mingle with the crowd—and occasionally incite it with
a shout of "Give 'em hell, Harry!" if a local spectator had not done so
after a couple of minutes.

Eighty-three-hundred miles the first time around. Forty-four years
later, Donovan remembered it as a great time, a grand tour of America.
Others complained about days without a shower and not enough sleep.
An altogether unreal environment, it wore down some press people, all
of Truman's staff, and members of the president's family. Clifford recalled
that for years he had "a recurring nightmare of being trapped on that
train." When Eben Ayers went to meet the returning presidential party
on October 2, he greeted Margaret with a "How are you?" As young,
energetic, and vivacious as she was, she replied, "Just glued together."[14]

No other campaign swing was so extended, but all were grueling:
October 6 to 16, ten northeastern and midwestern states for eight major
speeches; October 18 to 19, to Miami and Raleigh by air for two major
speeches; October 23 to 30, ten states from Rhode Island and Massachusetts to Missouri for twelve major speeches. On almost every day of
the rail trips, Truman made six, eight, or even ten rear-platform appearances. How did he do it? Rubdowns between stops, quick naps, occasional shots of bourbon, and enormous reserves of energy. Most of all
perhaps, he had patterned his life in a way that allowed him to direct all
the unfocused anger within himself against a single target. Somehow, no
one on the train seemed fresher, more optimistic, more ready for the next
crowd.

He played his homespun charm for all it was worth. He estimated
the size of the crowd at Dexter, for example, by telling a local reporter
that it was simple: 16 acres, 5,000 persons to an acre, 80,000 people. It
was there that he got the votes of one Republican family by providing
autographs for their children; a few weeks later, Governor Dewey would
be too busy to do so. At one stop, the president stepped down from the
platform for a look at a horse, examined its teeth, and correctly guessed
its age. At another, he got off to shake hands with a group of first-graders
who were unable to see him from the back of the crowd.[15]

His talks combined fire-and-brimstone oratory, wisecrackery, and a
tendency to scold anyone who might be thinking about voting Republican. One of his favorite smart-aleck appeals was to ask voters to return
him to the presidential mansion so that he would not have to worry about
coping with the housing shortage. At other times, however, his rhetoric
spun out of control. In Chicago on October 25, his prepared speech implicitly compared Dewey with Hitler, Mussolini, and Tojo. A good many
journalists assumed that such excesses would backfire. Yet Truman's
crowds grew perceptibly through October until they were at least equal
in size to Roosevelt's in 1944.

Most observers dismissed the phenomenon. James Reston, who covered both candidates, wrote that neither was capable of lighting fires in audiences, which were merely friendly, curious, and enjoying the pageantry of a presidential campaign. Roosevelt had made a "great experience" out of his campaigning. Dewey was not particularly convincing. And Truman was "a mild man": "He has the words but he doesn't get the melody. He says he is mad at everybody, but he doesn't really look as if he's mad at anybody."[16]

But what was Dewey's melody? His competence was undeniable. He had been an effective governor of New York, had come closer than any other opponent to beating Roosevelt, and was a forward-looking moderate. Always neat and unruffled, with wavy dark hair, a nicely trimmed mustache, and a well-modulated baritone speaking voice, he might seem an ideal chief executive. Yet to many observers, close-up and distant alike, there was something artificial about Dewey—too flawless, too self-contained, too calculating. "The little man on the wedding cake," said a number of his detractors. He seemed an organization man, acting more like a chief executive officer of a corporate venture than a leader of the people. Walt Kelly, later to win fame as the creator of "Pogo," depicted him in *New York Star* political cartoons as a pint-sized robot-computer with a human head.

Dewey's emotions broke through the facade only once during the campaign. After he had finished a rear-platform speech at Beaucoup, Illinois, the engineer threw the locomotive into reverse, the usual procedure for loosening a taut string of railcars. The movement went a moment too long, raising the fear of a crash into the crowd. Then the train stopped and lurched forward. Dewey, startled and angry, said something to the crowd over the still-functioning microphone about a fool who ought to be shot at sunrise. The reaction was understandable—and counterproductive. Labor unions used the incident to portray the governor as an enemy of the workingman. James Reston recalled in later years (a bit inaccurately) that he concluded his own *New York Times* report of the incident with a double entendre: "The train moved forward with a jerk."[17]

None of these gaffes were necessarily fatal. But where was Dewey going to lead America? In his own bland way, he was as negative as Truman and much less specific. He seldom got beyond talking about "unraveling and unsnarling" the mess the Democrats had made of the country. Forty years later, Dewey's campaign manager, Herbert Brownell, listened to a recording of a major Dewey speech that he had helped write. At the end, the old man shook his head. "There's nothing there," he concluded. By refusing to answer Truman's charges, Dewey made them believable.[18]

How, then, did everyone assume the race would culminate in an easy Dewey victory? The Democrats were divided; the polls indicated a big margin for Dewey; local pundits, analyzing one state after another, agreed. The New York–based journalists probably were more influenced by Henry

Wallace's considerable strength in their state than by whatever understanding they had of the collapse of the Wallace insurgency almost everywhere else in the country. Washington-based experts, isolated either in the capital or aboard the campaign trains, accepted the consensus with few questions. The *New York Times* summed up the conventional wisdom with a seemingly authoritative survey the weekend before the election: Dewey, 345 electoral votes; Truman, 105; Thurmond, 38; Wallace, 0; doubtful, 43. The Republicans would retain control of Congress.[19]

Truman had different ideas. Campaigning through New York City on October 29, he declared that the people would "throw the Galluping polls right into the ashcan—you watch 'em."

Did he really believe that he could win? No one can say for sure. But on October 13, he had given George Elsey a list of the states he expected to carry, with a total of 340 electoral votes. He wrote to Eddie Meisburger on October 17: "I am of the opinion that the trend our way has set in, in dead earnest." When Clark Clifford tried to sneak past him a week or so later with a *Newsweek* survey of fifty journalists unanimously convinced that he was a loser, Truman took a quick look at the article, and then told Clifford, "I know every one of those fifty fellows, and not one of them has enough sense to pound sand into a rathole." If the confidence was not real, it was ersatz of the highest quality.[20]

Of course, there was more than tone and mood to the campaign. It had a grand strategy: to bring together the old Roosevelt coalition. The tactical course was quickly established and consistently pursued: to emphasize, according to location and specific audience, the various benefits that Roosevelt and the New Deal had delivered to the American people. In the West, Truman talked about dams, irrigation, and cheap, government-generated electricity; in the farm belt, agricultural price supports and rural electrification; in urban areas, the housing shortage and support of labor unions; in a historic appearance in Harlem, civil rights. If at times, as in the Harlem speech, he spoke of new directions, his basic appeal was a simple "Don't let them take it away from you."

Farmers got the message with unexpected directness as the harvest season progressed. Throughout the farm belt, wheat, corn, and oats came in more abundantly than anyone had foreseen—just as European reliance on American grain was at last declining sharply. The collapse of corn prices was especially dramatic: from $2.25 a bushel in July to $1.26 by the end of October. The Commodity Credit Corporation support price of $1.53 provided some relief for farmers who could find CCC storage facilities, but by October these were filled to overflowing.

Truman, who during the summer had criticized Congress for not appropriating sufficient funds for storage bins, suddenly had real validation of his charge that the Republicans had imbedded a pitchfork in the farmer's back. Grain farmers might be excused for seeing depression hurtling down the track at them like a runaway locomotive. The Democrats looked like the safe party and Harry Truman, former man behind a cultivator, considerably more understanding than a big city boy like Tom Dewey. Truman pounded away at the issue in one appearance after another through October. "That's how they love the farmers!" he told a St. Louis crowd in his last big speech. "They want to bust them just like they did in 1932."[21]

IV

Foreign policy was an insignificant component of Truman's rhetoric. Occasionally, he might talk about America's mission in the world or remind his audiences of his leadership in the struggle against Soviet Communism, but he rarely criticized the Republicans. Nevertheless, the foreign issues of 1948 could not altogether be excluded from the political process. Two inevitably intruded: the Berlin blockade and the continuing demands of Israel.

As the tense Berlin situation continued into the fall, Truman faced above all his genuine fear that war might erupt in central Europe and that he might have to confront the possibility of using the bomb. There can be little doubt that this weighed on his mind more heavily than the politics of the crisis, which on balance helped him. Soviet behavior in Berlin had driven the final nail into the coffin of Henry Wallace's campaign, alienating all but the most pro-USSR elements of the Democratic left.

Even so, to resolve the crisis in a fashion that would preserve the Western position in Berlin without significant concessions to the USSR would be a stunning political accomplishment that might overcome Dewey's lead in the polls. Even more important, it would mean that the atomic stockpile would remain safely locked away. Given those considerations, it is not surprising that Truman fell back on an enduring illusion—that a direct approach to Good Old Joe Stalin, cutting through the obstructions thrown up by the professional diplomats, might yield results.

In July, National Farmers Union president James G. Patton had urged Truman to arrange a personal meeting with Stalin to resolve the crisis and to do so in mid-October for maximum political benefit.[22] There is no indication that Truman ever seriously considered such a move, but it may have made him receptive to an alternative course. It might be worth sending another special envoy, trying another Hopkins mission. Two temporary speech writers, David Noyes and Albert Carr, made the suggestion to Matt Connelly; he took it directly to Truman.

Who in American public life had Hopkins's tact, common sense, and negotiating skills? The answer (or so the president believed) was Truman's old and trusted friend Chief Justice Fred Vinson. Without bothering to consult with Department of State officials, Truman resolved to go ahead. Vinson, flattered by the request, protested feebly, and then acquiesced. When told about the plan, Clark Clifford tried unsuccessfully to change the president's mind. On October 5, Charlie Ross moved to arrange air time for a speech, written by Noyes and Carr, announcing the Vinson mission; in the process, he had to tell network executives, off the record, what the proposed "nonpolitical" address would be about.

Truman clearly expected to present State with a fait accompli. One version of the story has him waiting until Ross was arranging radio time and then calling Robert Lovett, acting secretary while Marshall attended yet another interminable and unproductive foreign ministers conference— where Berlin was obviously a major object of negotiation. Lovett's recollection was that he first learned about the proposal when a copy of the president's notification to Ambassador Walter Bedell Smith in Moscow was routed to his desk from the State Department code room. He read it, ordered his official car, and sped to the White House with sirens blaring.

Lovett knew when to bend to the president's needs, even if it meant working around Marshall; he also knew that this was not one of those occasions. He remembered telling Truman that the scheme was utterly unacceptable and surely would result in Marshall's resignation. Truman thereupon decided to cancel the mission. Other versions of the incident include a transatlantic teleconference between Marshall and the president. Marshall's biographer, Forrest Pogue, thinks it unlikely that the secretary ever directly threatened to resign, but also believes that the Vinson incident sealed his determination to leave after the election.[23]

Of course, the idea had been a terrible one, but not because Truman was trying to "play politics" with foreign policy, as many Republican critics charged. It was terrible because it was poor diplomacy. Its inspiration, the 1945 Hopkins mission, had accomplished nothing except to provide a fig leaf for capitulation to Stalin's demands on Poland. Sending a diplomatic amateur like Vinson to meet with the Soviet dictator on his own turf likely would have resulted in a similar agreement or nothing. Both scenarios would have been bad for Truman and for the nation.

As it was, the president got a free ride. The secret plan inevitably became public knowledge. But Marshall did not resign, Dewey said little about it, and the continuing success of the airlift provided an ongoing example of Truman's determination to hang tough against Soviet aggression. At the same time, many of the anti-Wallace liberals were heartened by even an abortive display of Truman's quest to avoid war. Truman needed their votes badly. George Elsey commented retrospectively, "I think that people said to themselves, 'Harry Truman is trying to do something for peace, but the State Department has blocked him again.'"[24]

V

Politically, Palestine was an even more explosive problem for Truman. The recognition of Israel had not made the Palestine controversy go away; rather, it had raised new issues: de jure recognition, definitive boundaries, an end to the arms embargo, a loan to the new nation. Pressure from the Israelis and the American Jewish community was intense. Writing to Clark Clifford on August 3, Eliahu Epstein all but demanded White House assistance in obtaining an Export-Import Bank loan: "I do not believe that the President can know how repeatedly we have been put off on this matter. . . . The quota of empty words which we have received in this delaying action must set some kind of a record."[25]

The Department of State remained as standoffish as ever, leaving Clifford and other political operatives desperately concerned. As early as the end of July and through the fall, rumors circulated that the Dewey campaign was dealing secretly with the Zionists and about to outbid the administration for their support. Truman himself nervously sought some middle ground that would satisfy Secretary Marshall, advance his own interests, and be defensible as the right thing to have done. In mid-August, apparently unwilling to risk a clash with Marshall, he pressed the more politically attuned Lovett to expedite a loan.

The incessant pressure on this issue continued to anger him and wear him down. It seemed impossible to satisfy the Jews, he told his staff on September 9. They wanted to be a persecuted people. Although he never mentioned it, he also had to be aware that they were among the party's biggest potential campaign contributors. A few days later, he initially accepted a memo that Clifford had drafted for him to send to Marshall; it ordered de jure recognition and economic assistance. Apparently, he had second thoughts because the document never reached the State Department.[26]

The diplomats persisted in efforts to impose a partition settlement put forth by UN mediator Count Folke Bernadotte and unsatisfactory to the new Israeli state. Israel's requests for a loan languished through the fall in the Washington bureaucracy. Throughout the Northeast, as the fighting escalated in Palestine, Democratic candidates bombarded the White House with pleas to do something for the Jewish state. At Clark Clifford's behest, the president forbade the State Department and the UN delegation to comment on the issue without presidential clearance.

When Dewey issued a statement on October 22 condemning administration vacillation and disorganization regarding Palestine, Truman retaliated with a declaration of strong support for Israel; it included backing for the boundaries the Israeli government demanded, for de jure recognition as soon as elections were held, for economic assistance, and for an eventual end to the arms embargo. The opposition could charge, with a fair amount of justice, that words were no substitute for action. Some leading Zionists endorsed Dewey; some stayed with Truman; others sat on the fence. Still, given the delicate nature of his relationship with Marshall, it was the best the president could do.[27]

VI

On November 1, the day before the election, Truman was back home in Independence. The Gallup organization published its final poll, based on interviewing done from October 15 to 25; it gave Dewey a solid lead of 49.5 percent to 44.5 for Truman, 4 for Wallace, 2 for Thurmond. Its tally of states in which one or the other had a "substantial lead" showed twenty in which Dewey had an apparent lock and nine for Truman. It listed Missouri as one of fifteen states that might go either way. That evening, Truman made a brief radio address from 219 North Delaware, soberly proclaiming that only the Democratic party could preserve peace and prosperity, urging Americans to think about the issues and to vote their consciences.[28]

To all appearances, he remained serenely confident. He and Bess and Margaret voted at 10:00 A.M. on Tuesday morning. Then he attended a stag luncheon party hosted by Roger Sermon and joked with old friends about bygone days of county politics. That afternoon, he slipped away, accompanied by only a few trusted Secret Service agents, to spend the evening at a resort hotel in nearby Excelsior Springs. Why he went off to leave his family besieged by the press remains a mystery. No doubt, he was dead tired; any sixty-four-year-old man who had maintained his pace and lived with the burdens of his responsibilities had a right to be. But very possibly he also felt more than a flicker of doubt and preferred to take the blow of defeat, if it came, alone.

A Turkish bath, a ham sandwich and a glass of milk at 6:30 P.M., early election returns over the radio, a shot of bourbon, and he was in bed, sound asleep. Awakened at midnight, Truman listened to NBC radio pundit H. V. Kaltenborn proclaim him ahead by 1.2 million votes, but still likely to lose. He went back to sleep until 4:00 A.M., when agent Jim Rowley roused him and turned up the radio; to the consternation of the broadcasters, he was ahead by 2 million. The time had come, he told his bodyguards, to go into Kansas City "because it looked very much as if we were in trouble for another four years." They poured celebratory drinks and then had breakfast.[29]

By 6:00 A.M., he was in the presidential suite at the Muehlbach Hotel. Soon he was surrounded by jubilant aides and supporters. Dewey's concession came at 10:14 A.M. In Independence, the din of horns and whistles filled the air. That afternoon, he and Bess and Margaret received the cheers of an estimated 40,000 people in the town square. The celebration, he told them in a moment of ebullience, was not just for him: "It is for the whole country. It is for the whole world."

The next day, they took the train back to Washington. At St. Louis, someone gave the president a copy of the election-night issue of the *Chicago Tribune* with its headline "Dewey Defeats Truman." He held it aloft in triumph, providing the most memorable photograph of his political career. He made two more whistle-stop talks along the way; like the one in St. Louis, they were short, graceful, and humble.

In Washington, on November 5, the drive from Union Station to the White House was a triumphal parade past 750,000 cheering people. Congratulatory banners hung from the sides of many edifices. The one on the *Washington Post* building read: "Welcome Home from the Crow

Eaters." (Truman declined an invitation to preside over a banquet of pollsters and commentators eating "breast of tough old crow en glace.") As Margaret Truman remembered it, "bands, official and impromptu, seemed to be playing 'I'm Just Wild About Harry' on every corner."[30]

The letters of congratulations poured in from all over the country. Truman probably especially cherished one of them. At no point, wrote Dwight D. Eisenhower, did the political history of the United States "record a greater accomplishment than yours, that can be traced so clearly to the stark courage and fighting heart of a single man."[31]

VII

The unexpected victory of the little guy over the organization man captured the imagination of much of the country. Seeming in some way to affirm the country's promise, it made Americans feel good about themselves. Whatever the transcendental implications, the pragmatic consequence was that Truman had managed to pull together enough of the old Roosevelt coalition to eke out a narrow victory. He took 49.5 percent of the vote to Dewey's 44.5, 303 electoral votes to 189 for Dewey. Thurmond and Wallace each got about 2.5 percent, and Thurmond won 39 electoral votes, 1 of them from a "faithless elector" in Tennessee.[32]

It was hard to say that any single element was decisive. "Labor did it!" Truman is supposed to have declared at first blush. Organized labor was undeniably important, but its impact was uneven. In some cities, the unions outdid the machines in getting Democratic voters to the polls. However, a lot of railway workers, remembering 1946, appear to have left the presidential line of their ballots blank. Labor support certainly facilitated Truman's wins in all thirteen American cities with populations of more than 500,000. This feat, which duplicated Roosevelt's in 1944, also stemmed from a wide appeal to ethnoreligious minorities. Most ethnic groups supported his calls for generous displaced-persons legislation. Catholics liked his anti-Communism. And he had done enough for Israel to win a solid majority of the Jewish vote.

He also ran unexpectedly well in rural agricultural areas, thanks to the grain-storage fiasco. Dewey himself, and many of his advisers, attributed the Republican defeat to a late shift in the farm vote. Truman carried six of the eight big corn-growing states and lost the other two by narrower margins than had Roosevelt in 1944. The mid-American farm vote was Republican by culture and tradition. It was also volatile, receptive to anti–Wall Street rhetoric, and quick to turn to the Democrats when prices were falling.

There were other aspects of the election returns to which one could look for explanations. Truman ran strong in the West, seemingly having convinced the region that the Democratic party was its friend. His victory in California, the home of Dewey's running mate, was especially notable. He lost only four southern states and thereby apparently dem-

The new president is sworn in by Chief Justice Harlan Fiske Stone as political notables look on at 7:30 P.M., April 12, 1945. From left: Secretary of Labor Frances Perkins, Secretary of War Henry L. Stimson, Secretary of Commerce Henry A. Wallace, War Production Board Administrator Julius Krug, Secretary of the Navy James V. Forrestal, Secretary of Agriculture Claude Wickard, Deputy War Manpower Commission chairman Frank McNamee, Attorney General Francis Biddle, Secretary of State Edward R. Stettinius, Bess, Secretary of the Interior Harold Ickes, Speaker of the House Sam Rayburn, War Mobilization and Reconversion Director Fred Vinson, House Minority Leader Joseph Martin, Representative Robert Ramspeck, House Majority Leader John McCormack. Margaret is obscured by Chief Justice Stone. (National Park Service–Abbie Rowe, courtesy of the Harry S. Truman Library)

President Truman with James Byrnes, whom he soon would appoint secretary of state, and Secretary of Commerce Henry Wallace at Washington's Union Station waiting for the train bearing President Roosevelt's remains, April 14, 1945. (Office of War Information, courtesy of the Harry S. Truman Library)

Meeting at Potsdam: I. Churchill, Truman, and Stalin at the beginning of the conference. (Courtesy of the British Information Service)

Meeting at Potsdam: II. Attlee, Truman, Stalin, and their chief aides at the conclusion of the conference. Second row: Admiral William Leahy, British Foreign Secretary Ernest Bevin, Secretary of State James Byrnes, Soviet Foreign Minister Vyacheslav Molotov. (U.S. Army, courtesy of the Harry S. Truman Library)

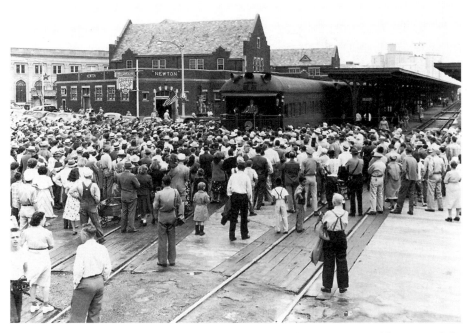

Whistle stop. The president speaks at Newton, Kansas, June 16, 1948. (Courtesy of the Harry S. Truman Library)

Home again. The first family returns to Washington at the conclusion of Truman's September whistle-stop tour, October 2, 1948. (National Park Service–Abbie Rowe, courtesy of the Harry S. Truman Library)

Chief Justice Fred Vinson administers the oath of office to new Secretary of Defense Louis Johnson. Outgoing Secretary James Forrestal looks on, March 28, 1949. (National Park Service–Abbie Rowe, courtesy of the Harry S. Truman Library)

Fond encounter. The president and General Douglas MacArthur at Wake Island, October 15, 1950. (U.S. Department of State, courtesy of the Harry S. Truman Library)

Happy days. The president, staff, and guests at Key West, December 19, 1949. Front row: Phillip Maguire, Bruce Forsyth (chief dental officer, U.S. Public Health Service), George Elsey, Joseph Feeney, David Lloyd, Stephen Spingarn. Second row: Clark Clifford, William Hassett, Secretary of the Treasury John Snyder, Truman, John Steelman, Charles Ross, Frank Pace. Back row: Charles Murphy, General Robert Landry, Admiral Robert Dennison, General Harry Vaughan, General Wallace Graham, David Niles, Donald Dawson. (U.S. Navy, courtesy of the Harry S. Truman Library)

The national security team. Truman with Secretary of State Dean Acheson, Mutual Security Administrator Averell Harriman, and Secretary of Defense George Marshall, July 13, 1951. (National Park Service–Abbie Rowe, courtesy of the Harry S. Truman Library)

Strained amiability. The president and Adlai Stevenson in the Oval Office, August 12, 1952. (National Park Service–Abbie Rowe, courtesy of the Harry S. Truman Library)

Good friends, happy occasion. The president presents yet another decoration to General Dwight Eisenhower, February 7, 1948. (National Park Service–Abbie Rowe, courtesy of the Harry S. Truman Library)

The president and Mrs. Truman with friends at the dedication of the Truman Library, July 6, 1957. From left: Eleanor Roosevelt, Chief Justice Earl Warren, President Herbert Hoover, Basil O'Connor. (Courtesy of the Harry S. Truman Library)

Final days. Artist Thomas Hart Benton sketches the aging statesman in 1971. (Randall Jessee, courtesy of the Harry S. Truman Library)

onstrated that it was not suicidal for a Democrat to back civil rights forthrightly. Up north, his biggest loss—New York—would have been a landslide victory if Wallace had not polled 500,000 votes; as it was, Dewey won the state by only 61,000 of more than 6 million ballots.

As numerous analysts pointed out, the nation was overwhelmingly prosperous, despite such irritants as inflation, some continuing consumer shortages, and credit controls. The American people had never made a habit of throwing out governments that seemed to be giving them the good life. Some—most notably the astute journalist Samuel Lubell—rejected the plausible Republican alibi that the GOP had been a victim of an extraordinarily low voter turnout. The stay-at-homes, Lubell asserted, had not been primarily overconfident Republicans; instead, they had been apathetic Democrats. If there had been a high turnout, he declared, Dewey would have received a drubbing akin to the one experienced by Landon in 1936.

Thus, it seemed, Truman had maintained the Democratic party as the ascendant majority party of the nation, the sun in the political heavens, eclipsing a Republican moon. As if to prove the point, the Democrats won solid majorities in both houses of Congress. But what had this "maintaining election" maintained?

One could find a clue in the narrowness of Truman's win. Nationwide, more people had voted against him than for him. He had won key states by razor-thin margins: California by 18,000 of 4 million total votes; Illinois by 33,000 of nearly 4 million ballots; Ohio by 7,000 of 3 million. He almost surely would have lost Illinois if not for the candidacies of Paul Douglas for the United States Senate and Adlai Stevenson for governor; both men won by large margins, providing their president with a reverse coattail effect. Truman could blame Wallace for narrow losses in Michigan and New York, but not for Pennsylvania and New Jersey, two northeastern industrial states that Democratic candidates in the wake of the Roosevelt revolution were supposed to carry.

And although the president had managed to hold onto most of the South, Thurmond had carried four states. For the time being, it was unclear whether the States' Rights campaign was a dud or the first skirmish in an ongoing revolution. One thing was certain, however; if Thurmond had carried all eleven states of the old Confederacy, he would have thrown the election into the House of Representatives. Roosevelt had swept the Solid South in each of his elections, but had never required a single electoral vote from the region for his four consecutive majorities in the electoral college. The 1948 results delivered a message that the South could not be so easily taken for granted and that a growing States' Rights party would endanger Democratic control of the presidency.

What Truman had done was to maintain a Democratic coalition that was badly frayed around the edges. It is tempting to observe that the addition of Thurmond's and Wallace's votes to his give the Democrats 54 percent of the total. In fact, however, many of those votes no longer could be counted on by a party adjusting to the early stages of the civil rights revolution and the Cold War. Truman was proud that he won the election despite defections from the industrial Northeast and the Solid South; however, the results demonstrated the precariousness of the Democratic electoral base.

The president could take pride in the belief that his win amounted to a personal endorsement and a vindication of sorts from the electorate. There was a great deal of merit to this interpretation, but it also revealed weakness. His qualities, if hard to quantify, were real to millions who voted for him; throughout America, whether workers, farmers, or small businessmen, the individuals who crowded around rear platforms to see the candidates were far more likely to identify with him than with Dewey. Yet personal appeal, especially that of being ordinary, provided a flimsy mandate for governing and especially for implementing major new programs.

It was questionable whether the election produced a mandate for anything beyond a continuation of the status quo—the logical response to Truman's "don't let them take it away from you" appeal. Yet labor-liberal groups critical to the Democratic party expected big change. In the end, what the election had maintained was the Democratic coalition with all its internal contradictions and potential for deadlock.

Harry Truman had won vindication. He had also—to use the phrase he uttered to his Secret Service man the morning after the election—won himself more trouble than he could have imagined.

27

"The Great White Sepulcher of Ambition": Living with the Presidency, 1945–1953

The presidency, Thomas Jefferson declared, is a "splendid misery." The phrase is dramatic, the description often apt. Still, even the unhappiest chief executives have enjoyed moments of triumph and delight in the office. Conversely, the lightest-hearted have fought off doubt, melancholy, and, on occasion, sheer despair. Truman, as much as any president in American history, experienced a full range of ups and downs.

A splendid misery to Jefferson, the presidency was more like enforced confinement to Truman or, whatever one makes of it, death. Thus the White House became the "great white jail," or the "great white sepulcher of ambition."[1]

II

President Harry Truman customarily arose at 5:00 A.M., shaved, dressed, and in the company of Secret Service guards took a vigorous one- or two-mile walk at the army marching pace of 120 steps per minute. Returning to the White House, he frequently had a shot of bourbon, followed by a rubdown, and breakfast. He ate lightly, maintained a weight in the neighborhood of 175 pounds, and boasted of being able to wear suits he had purchased during his first year as a senator.

As early as 7:00, he might be poring over documents and reports in the Oval Office. He would meet with staff between 9:00 and 10:00, and then plunge into a round of appointments. When possible, he lunched with his family, took a short afternoon nap, and then went back to his office to see more "customers." Frequently, he managed to work in several laps in the White House swimming pool; utilizing an awkward stroke that kept his head out of the water, he wore his eyeglasses. At 5:00 or 6:00 P.M. in the evening, he would leave the office for the day. Often he carried a stack of documents to review after dinner.

He and Bess would have cocktails, usually "dry Old Fashioneds," two ounces of bourbon on the rocks garnished with orange slices. When Margaret was at home (most of the time during his first term), she would join them for dinner. So would Bess's mother, who continued to live with them. If the president had no paperwork, the family might spend the evening talking or listening to music; at times, they watched a movie, usually a musical selected by Margaret. Once or twice a week, Truman would slip away to a stag poker party, usually held at a private home; often he did not return until after midnight. He and Bess slept in adjoining bedrooms.[2]

From November 21, 1948, to March 27, 1952, the Trumans lived across Pennsylvania Avenue in Blair House. During the president's first term, the White House had displayed signs of structural weakness, the most dramatic occurring when a leg of Margaret's grand piano fell through the floor of her sitting room. Architects decided that the old central executive mansion would have to be gutted and rebuilt, although the presidential office was maintained in the West Wing. Truman, who had an antiquarian's interest in the history of the building, had already mandated the erection of a balcony on the South Portico, just outside the upstairs oval study. He had done so despite widespread opposition, insisting (wrongly) that it had been in the original design and that it would beautify the building. His judgment was good. Once the total reconstuction was decided on, he took a strong interest in it and great pride in its successful completion.

All the same, both Harry and Bess enjoyed their return to Blair House. They liked the residence and took positive delight in its smaller, less formal character. It also provided an excuse for a more relaxed social pace. Receptions and state dinners were fewer and smaller; Truman banned the formerly obligatory white-tie-and-tails costume for men at evening functions. With mixed feelings, they moved back across the street in the spring of 1952.[3]

III

Truman's daytime appointment list consumed much of his working time. Matt Connelly attempted to handle most requests from Capitol Hill, but many members of Congress could not be denied personal access. Neither could assorted senior military officers, executive-branch officials, businessmen, and writers. In these meetings, usually fifteen minutes in length,

the visitors inflicted on the president their wisdom on major issues, their
patronage demands and job ambitions, or their justifications for pet pork-
barrel projects. Truman was invariably attentive. Harley Kilgore, one of
his close friends from the Senate, recalled that he would always rise to
meet a guest, shake hands, ask him to be seated, then go back to his desk,
listen carefully, and take notes on a legal pad.[4]

Privately, Truman regarded many such encounters with a mixture
of annoyance and wry amusement; from the first, he documented them
with tart summary remarks:

Irving Brant
　　To tell me how to run the State Dept. & the Supreme Court.

Herman Baruch
　　Flatterer. Wants to be ambassador to France. Conniver like his Brother.

William Randolph Hearst, Jr.
　　Told me what papa thought. Explained, diplomatically, I didn't give
a damn.

Congressman Vito Marcantonio
　　An ax to grind for Italy. N.Y. politics.

Congressman Samuel Dickstein
　　An ax to grind for some Jews.

Senator Joseph O'Mahoney
　　Wanted a western man for Interior, himself preferably.[5]

No matter how busy the day, he always had a few minutes for old
friends. One of them was Fred Whittaker, a Kansas Citian whom Truman
had put on the Senate payroll in the 1930s and had used as an informal
aide. A big, exuberant teller of tall tales, he provided the president with
a lot of enjoyment. Toward the end of 1948, Whittaker, who had become
the manager of a Ford dealership, took his boss, Jack Gross, to meet the
president. Gross recalled forty years later that they had spent at least an
hour in the president's office, chatting aimlessly and telling off-color stories—with two senators waiting outside.

Meeting the president for the first time, Gross was slightly shocked
when Whittaker prompted him to tell a dirty story and a bit more shocked
when Truman enjoyed it. He was even more taken aback by the presidential response when he delivered a fulsome compliment to Truman's
great courage and monumental achievement in winning the 1948 election:

　　He didn't answer for a full minute, then leaned back in his swivel chair,
　　staring at the ceiling, eyeglasses glinting, and as if we weren't there spoke
　　slowly with each word sharply emphasized, "Yes, I taught those sons of
　　bitches a thing or two, didn't I." It sent a chill down my back.[6]

Old army friends could always get time with the president. Many
received favors of one sort or another. Vic Housholder, the strapping lieutenant who had pulled him out from under his horse at the Battle of Who

Run, got special assistance in an effort to find the remains of a son killed during the war. He was an overnight guest at the White House. The president told White House personnel specialist Donald Dawson to "pull the necessary strings" to get Gordon Jordan, another fondly remembered lieutenant, the postmastership of Amarillo. Former corporal Joseph Coyle, wounded in action three decades earlier, gained appointment as postmaster of Kansas City, Kansas, over the outrage of the leaders of all Democratic factions. Presidential intervention helped Pete Allen and John Miles, among others, gain admission to crowded veterans' hospitals for medical treatment.[7]

Truman's generosity spilled over to his White House employees, aides, and associates. With astonishing unanimity, they remembered him as unusually egalitarian, kind, and considerate. He customarily introduced guests to the servants, probably embarrassing a few of them in the beginning but in the end leaving them delighted. His relations with his immediate professional staff were proper, formal, and friendly. George Elsey, Leon Keyserling, and Richard Neustadt all recalled him as tolerant and easygoing. They also expressed some puzzlement at his later indulgence in profanity, having heard little of it during the years they worked for him. He knew about their personal problems and did what he could to help. David Niles, seriously ill and incapacitated for much of Truman's second term, remained on the payroll until his death. Niles's assistant, Philleo Nash, earlier received a long leave of absence to deal with a serious family emergency.[8]

Roger Jones, a Bureau of the Budget official, recalled a cherished incident. At the end of 1949, the president came into a meeting of White House and Budget staff with four dozen or so Christmas neckties hanging from an extended arm: "They're pretty awful, but take your pick; the haberdasher's back in business."[9]

Few presidents have been so willing to massage the egos of their staff members. When, for example, Eben Ayers complained about an inscription on an autographed presidential photo, Truman produced a substitute with more pleasing lines and apologized for any unintentional offense. After being excluded from morning staff meetings, Ayers balked at attending them in Charlie Ross's absence until Truman personally invited him. Ayers refused to work for Ross's successor, Joseph Short; Truman found him other duties and brought in a new assistant press secretary. Remarkably, Ayers, who had the good fortune never to work for Lyndon Johnson or Richard Nixon, saw nothing extraordinary in such incidents.[10]

Truman's private secretary, Rose Conway, was a shy, discreet, and (in later years) formidable woman who had begun to work for him while he was vice president; she would remain in his employ until he died. He treated her as he did all women—with the utmost propriety and unfailing courtesy. Speaking to Merle Miller in 1961 or 1962, she commented, "In all this time, he has once to say a harsh word."[11]

IV

The employee for whom Truman in later years had the deepest feelings may have been Leslie Coffelt, a White House police private. On November 1, 1950, as Truman lay upstairs for a brief after-lunch nap, two would-be assassins, Puerto Rican nationalists Oscar Collazo and Griselio Torresola, attacked Blair House. Because of its close proximity to the street, the residence was far more vulnerable than the White House. After no more than two minutes of gunfire, three White House policemen had been hit; the two terrorists were down, never having penetrated the entrance.[12]

Coffelt, mortally wounded by three point-blank shots from Torresola's Luger, had managed nonetheless to draw his own weapon. He took aim at his assailant, who was exchanging shots with Private Donald Birdzell, hit in both legs but still firing from a prone position on Pennsylvania Avenue. With a last effort of supreme concentration, Coffelt put a bullet into Torresola's head, killing him instantly. Collazo was seriously wounded in an exchange of shots with Private Joseph Davidson and Secret Service agent Floyd Boring. Another White House police private, Joseph Downs, had taken three rounds from Torresola's gun and lay badly hurt just inside the basement door.

Truman, hearing the noise, rushed to an open window. Down on the street, one of the presidential guards saw him and shouted, "Get back! Get back!" He withdrew, dressed, and, after the Secret Service had decided all was safe, surveyed the scene firsthand. Displaying characteristic bravado, if poor judgment, he insisted on keeping a scheduled appointment to speak at an outdoor ceremony. Only after he returned did he learn that Coffelt, a much-liked man with a wife and stepdaughter, had died.

The assassination attempt possessed all the elements of a Keystone Kops plot transferred to a film noir. Collazo and Torresola thought that the murder of Truman would plunge the United States into revolutionary turmoil and allow Puerto Rico to declare independence. They carried only pistols, no explosives. The two either did not know or did not care that Truman was shortly scheduled to appear at an event where they would have stood a good chance at getting off some shots at him. They had no idea where to find the president inside the house. Had they made it to the entrance, they would have been mowed down by a Secret Service man who had armed himself with a Thompson submachine gun. Still, by the standards of a generation that has seen terrorism become a skilled trade, security was astonishingly light. A well-equipped and -trained suicide squad might well have killed the president.

As it developed, he was left resignedly resentful at much tighter restrictions on his movements. No longer could he walk across the street to the White House; he was driven in an armored limousine. For a time, the Secret Service dissuaded him from taking his morning walks; at his insistence, however, his agents drove him to different parts of the city each day, where he enjoyed his traditional exercise escorted by a heavy guard.

The attempt on Truman's life occurred two days after a failed effort against Governor Luis Muñoz Marín in Puerto Rico. The island was wracked for days with disturbances and acts of terrorism designed to disrupt an election in which Puerto Ricans were to vote on a new constitution, giving them full commonwealth status. Federal investigators were convinced but unable to prove that the Blair House episode was part of a much larger conspiracy orchestrated by leaders of the island's nationalist party.

Collazo insisted that he and Torresola had acted alone and had intended only a "demonstration." A jury found him guilty of murdering Coffelt, attempting to murder the president, and assaulting the two wounded guards with intent to kill. Judge Alan Goldsborough, the jurist who a few years earlier had come down so hard on John L. Lewis, sentenced him to death. On July 24, 1952, one week before the execution was scheduled to take place, Truman commuted the sentence to life imprisonment. Although he never publicly explained the decision, it was widely interpreted as a goodwill gesture to Puerto Rico in particular and to Latin America in general. The president may also have been moved by the fact that Collazo himself had done no more than inflict one wound on Private Birdzell. Surely, however, he could never have imagined that twenty-seven years later Jimmy Carter would pardon Collazo and that he would return to Puerto Rico acclaimed as a hero by the still-small, still-fanatical nationalist party.

"I've been shot at by experts and unless your name's on the bullet you needn't be afraid," he told his cousin Ethel Noland, "and that of course you can't find out, so why worry." Yet as he told Ethel and numerous others, he did worry about the men who guarded him. He could not conceal his emotions about Coffelt's death. A week after the event, speaking to a huge luncheon in Independence, he accepted a check for $1,000 to begin a fund for Coffelt's family. Choking with emotion, he told the crowd, "You can't understand just how a man feels when somebody else dies for him."[13]

V

Like all presidents, but with less success than many, Truman attempted to maintain a public identity characterized by reserve and dignity. Outside his immediate family circle, he could express himself freely only with close friends, in and out of Washington. He maintained an extensive private correspondence with dozens of trusted associates in which he spoke his mind without inhibition. (Such letters never got into the official White House files; they remained jealously guarded for the rest of his life by Rose Conway.) In Washington, he delighted in the companionship of his close friends, including Chief Justice Fred Vinson, Charlie Ross, Harry Vaughan, Sam Rayburn, Clinton Anderson, and John Snyder.

Poker was his premier recreation. Implicitly rejecting the assumption that it was, or should be, a game of skill, he played it recklessly and enjoyed bizarre wild-card variations that revolted purists. The presidential rules established a loss limit for individuals around the table and required winners to donate a portion of their chips to a bank from which the unlucky could draw. As he saw it, the purposes of the poker sessions were to drink a few well-watered bourbons, tell good stories, and enjoy the company of men like himself. Winning or losing money was a minor consideration; memories of fun and an addition to one's stock of good tales were far more important.

Chief Justice Vinson, a man who took the game seriously, provided one of the best yarns. On the evening of his birthday in 1947, he, Truman, and a few other friends met for dinner and poker at Clark Clifford's residence. During one hand, a game of high-low, the pot grew to about $3,000. With most of the cards face up, everyone could tell that Vinson needed only a jack or lower to rake in at least half of the stakes. He confidently told Truman, who was the dealer, to hit him.

The president, presumably dealing off the top of the deck, presented his old friend with the queen of spades. Momentarily, the chief justice forgot the protocol that he had faithfully followed since April 12, 1945. "You son of a bitch!" he blurted. Then, thoroughly flustered, he said, "Oh, Mr. President, Mr. President . . ." The room erupted with laughter, awakening Clifford's mother from a sound sleep in her second-floor bedroom. Truman thereafter delighted in recalling the incident and charging the chief justice with *lèse-majesté*.[14]

The poker sessions were what a later generation would call power events. An invitation was a mark of prestige; the chance to host one, a singular honor. To be known as a regular was to be invested with the cachet of easy access to the president. Even cabinet members prized the opportunity, although sometimes the reality was less attractive than the expectation.

One of the most curious such evenings occurred in the fall of 1946 at the home of Secretary of the Navy Forrestal, among the least likely members of the administration to fit in on such occasions. The guests included Vinson, Averell Harriman, Les Biffle, and Senator Warren Magnuson. Forrestal, who planned for the occasion with a mixture of anticipation and anxiety, spent much of the day trying to get his alcoholic and borderline-schizophrenic wife out of the house. To his horror, when the president arrived, she came down the stairs to greet him. Truman chatted with her for a few minutes; then Forrestal, saying, "Now Josie, you know this is a stag party," adroitly eased her out of the way.

Once the game got started, the secretary was hopelessly out of sync with its easygoing rhythm. The personification of competitive intensity, he had no jokes to tell. Repeatedly, he left the table to make or receive phone calls, turning over his place to his aide, Captain William Smedberg. The president, although a consistent loser that night, nonetheless seemed to enjoy himself. "He drank bourbon continuously but never got tight," Smedberg recalled. "He just got exhilarated and told terrible stories." When the party broke up, Truman left with his customary geniality—but surely also with a sense of puzzlement about his enigmatic cabinet official.[15]

For Truman, the poker games were therapeutic. To many in the general public, gambling and bourbon swilling, however low key, were not quite presidential. Neither was the intemperate "give 'em hell" campaign style nor the occasional profane phrase uttered in public. Poker exemplified a larger problem: the tension between his attempts at an image of leadership necessarily a cut above the ordinary and an informality that at times appeared to verge on crudeness.

VI

Truman remained always a person who exemplified traditional values and sentiments. "I am not a religious man," he told Thomas Murray. "Mrs. Truman takes care of that." But although his church attendance was sporadic, he continued to be deeply religious in a larger sense. He often resorted to a prayer he had learned as a child, asking God to make him "truthful, honest, and honorable in all things" and to give him "the ability to be charitable, forgiving, and patient with my fellow men." The prayer became public knowledge in 1952, when (with Truman's consent) William Hillman included it in *Mr. President*, a collection of Truman's writings. "Most men are timid when things of this sort come to light," Truman admitted to the Reverend Edward Pruden. "So am I. But I have been saying this prayer since my youth. It has been a great help."[16]

Of all the ceremonial occasions, none moved him more than Congressional Medal of Honor awards. Recognizing the highest qualities of courage and self-sacrifice, the honor seemed to him a greater one than the presidency itself. A young man in a wheelchair, both legs gone, told him, "Mr. President, my life is my country's and my country may still have it." Another recipient was a "skinny pharmacist's mate" who had been a conscientious objector; serving in the naval hospital corps, he had carried one wounded man after another back from the front lines on Okinawa. Hit by an enemy bullet himself, he had refused evacuation and had gone on tending the other casualties. Truman, who normally detested pacifists, was moved when the young man said he had wanted to serve the Lord and was willing to do so under fire if he did not have to try to kill anybody. "I always fill up when I read those citations," he told Bess.[17]

On his 1947 visit to Mexico City, he made a point of laying a wreath at the monument to the *Niños Héroes*, young military cadets who had defended the city's last redoubt against Winfield Scott's American troops a century earlier. No doubt, the gesture was calculated, but it also was from the heart. Truman admired courage, felt that it was limited to no nationality, and wanted to honor it. Besides, he recalled later, "I thought more of them than I did of General Scott anyway."[18]

He remained a relentless foe of all the manifestations of modernity in American culture. "School system needs overhauling," he wrote to himself in May 1945. "Kids should learn more fundamental 'reading, writing, and arithmetic.' Freud psychology and 'nut doctors' should be eliminated." Complaining to Assistant Secretary of State William Benton in April 1947, he took aim at avant-garde American art being exhibited in several European cities: "I am of the opinion that so-called modern art is merely the vaporings of half-baked lazy people. . . . [T]he ability to make things look as they are is the first requisite of a great artist. . . . There is no art at all in connection with the modernists in my opinion." For a sophisticate like Benton, such cultural conservatism might be a source of amusement. It equally was an example of the way in which Truman remained close to the pulse of ordinary Americans, who might not agree with his public-policy liberalism but identified with his deeper values.[19]

VII

As befitted a traditionalist, he cared about nothing more than his family. Here he suffered a grievous loss in 1947. That February, Mamma fell in her Grandview home and broke a hip. She was ninety-four. In those days, replacement surgery had not yet been developed. The most likely prognosis for such cases was confinement to bed, complications, and eventual death. Between mid-February and early May, Truman made four trips to Missouri to see her, all of them scheduled around the urgent foreign policy decisions and domestic conflicts of early 1947.

Shortly after he had returned to Washington from a Mother's Day visit, the president received word that she had suffered a stroke and was not expected to live. He flew back once again and stayed for nearly two weeks. Dividing his time between the Muehlebach Hotel and her home in Grandview, he handled the business of the nation as best he could while waiting for the worst. Remarkably, she rallied once more; emerging from a near-coma, she asked for a slice of watermelon.

Truman went back to Washington at the end of May. On July 26, he received word that she had developed pneumonia and was failing rapidly. He was on the way to Kansas City in his plane, asleep in his cabin, when his physician, Wallace Graham, awoke him to report a radio message that she had just died. He was convinced that in his dreams he had just seen her, telling him good-bye and admonishing him to be a good boy. At last, she had lost her son in the only way possible.[20]

Mamma's death made Bess and Margaret even more important to him. Both were at difficult times of their lives. He understood their situations and sympathized warmly with them. Bess found the position of first lady no more attractive with time. Like a good soldier, she performed her duties gracefully but made little attempt to conceal her preference for private life. In 1946, an interviewer asked, "If it had been left to your own free choice, would you have gone into the White House in the first place?" Her response was nothing if not candid: "Most definitely would *not* have." Every summer, she returned to Independence for weeks on end—determined to escape not from the heat (Independence's summer climate was near-tropical), but from the fishbowl environment of Washington. In July and August 1948, probably anticipating a return to mid-America after the election, she and Margaret painted the kitchen of the old Wallace house. One can safely conclude that her feelings about Harry's victory were mixed.[21]

Truman periodically erupted at any affront directed at Bess. Dean Acheson has remembered, with perhaps a bit of embellishment, how he was directed to declare Soviet ambassador Nicolai V. Novikov persona non grata for insulting Mrs. Truman in the fall of 1946. Novikov, a dour individual whom Truman liked to call Old Novocaine, had declined to attend a state dinner at which the first lady would have been the hostess. Acheson and Chief of Protocol Stanley Woodward attempted vainly to explain that the "snub" was actually the fault of a State Department functionary who had mistakenly placed the representatives of the Lithuanian government-in-exile on the invitation list. Under such circumstances, no Soviet ambassador could have attended. As visions of a diplomatic crisis raced through Acheson's head, the phone rang; Bess, at the other end, joined him in persuading the president to drop the issue.

"I guess you think I'm an old fool, and I probably am," Truman told him, reaching across the desk and showing him a photograph framed in gold filigree. It was the one Bess had given him to take to France nearly thirty years earlier. As Acheson and Woodward left, Truman fired one parting shot at them: "Tell Old Novocaine we didn't miss him!"[22]

He became even more emotionally engaged with Margaret's decision, after her graduation from George Washington University, to pursue a career as a coloratura soprano.[23] Bess had her doubts about the enterprise. Madge Wallace, who had grown increasingly outspoken with age, made it clear that she thought all show-business people, including those in classical music, were trash with whom her granddaughter should not associate.[24] By contrast, Harry gave Margaret nothing but encouragement. Her aspirations were of the sort he could understand: choose a goal, no matter how difficult; work hard, and go after it single-mindedly. And if it was a long shot, well, zinc mining and oil wildcatting had been long shots, too. It was better to pursue dreams and take chances than to settle for second best and spend a lifetime regretting it.

Accompanied by the family's aging black servant Vietta Garr, Margaret moved to New York and began a demanding series of voice lessons. In March 1947, she made her debut on national radio with the Detroit Symphony. In August, she delivered her first stage performance with the Hollywood Bowl Symphony, and then embarked on a thirty-city tour. Charging a midrange fee of $1,500 a concert, she did well financially. Her assets went well beyond her name. She had a superior voice, a wholesome personal charm, a girl-next-door attractiveness, and a great stage presence. Audiences sensed her guileless vulnerability, wanted her to do well, and instinctively loved her. In Oklahoma City, she had to make twenty-one curtain calls to please them.

Yet her career trajectory was that of a prodigy rather than that of a singer of promise. If she had wanted only to be the next Rosemary Clooney, she would have been a noncontroversial success. As it was, she aspired to a calling about as exclusive as that of a major-league baseball player and had cast herself in a role akin to that of a college phenom suddenly thrown into the starting lineup of the (then) perennial-world-champion New York Yankees. In fact, she was somewhat more like a promising rookie with considerable natural talent, but requiring a few years of development in the minors. The music critics suggested, sometimes politely, sometimes bluntly, that she needed more training.

No one rooted for her more than her father. He welcomed letters from friends and (often sycophantic) politicians praising his daughter's accomplishments. He tended to write off the professional critics as influenced by Republican newspaper publishers or mean-spirited. "A critic is a person who can do nothing himself and who tries to tear down those who do things," he told his sister. He correctly perceived that some anti-administration columnists, including the acid Westbrook Pegler, saw Margaret as a convenient target of opportunity. But only sporadically could he even hint to himself that the genuine music critics might be onto something.[25]

The pressures of the presidency and Truman's absorption with Margaret's career converged dramatically on the evening of December 5, 1950, the day of Margaret's first Washington concert. Truman's presidency was at one of its lowest points: American troops were in full retreat in Korea: British prime minister Attlee had flown to Washington for urgent, difficult discussions; and, shockingly, Charlie Ross had fallen over dead just before a late press briefing. An anxious president concealed the news of Ross's death from his daughter, went to hear her sing, and took some consolation in the warm ovations she received from a friendly crowd.

Early the next morning, before going to his office, he read Paul Hume's review in the *Washington Post*. An attractive and appealing personality, the critic admitted, but unable to handle even a lightweight program: "She is flat a good deal of the time. . . . She communicates almost nothing of the music she presents. . . . [T]he performance . . . was no more than a caricature of what it would be if sung by any one of a dozen artists today." It was "an extremely unpleasant duty to record such unhappy facts," Hume concluded. "But so long as Miss Truman sings as she has for three years and does today, we seem to have no recourse unless it is to omit comment on her programs altogether."[26]

A furious president reached for some stationery and wrote out an angry reply:

Dec. 6, 1950

Mr. Hume:—I've just read your lousy review of Margaret's concert. I've come to the conclusion that you are an "eight-ulcer man on four-ulcer pay."

It seems to me that you are a frustrated old man who wishes he could have been successful. When you write such poppycock as was in the *back* section of the paper you work for it shows conclusively that you're off the beam and at least four of your ulcers are at work.

Some day I hope to meet you. When that happens you'll need a new nose, a lot of beef steak for black eyes, and perhaps a supporter below!

Pegler, a guttersnipe, is a gentleman alongside you. I hope you'll accept that statement as a worse insult than a reflection on your ancestry.

H.S.T.[27]

The letter soon became public and caused a sensation. Margaret, at first embarrassed, was later gratified by her father's support. Hume, who apparently accidentally leaked the document, at first shrugged it off as the impulse of a chief executive carrying a "terrible burden." A couple of months later, he sold it to a collector. Truman never repented writing it and liked to believe that the parents of America understood his behavior and identified with it. (He and Hume finally would meet face to face in Independence seven years later. The encounter would be utterly friendly.) Westbrook Pegler issued a blast at the president's "nasty malice" and said, "Let us pray." It is pointless to speculate about who "came out best" in this exchange, but certain that Truman had needlessly lowered his stature at an already bad time.[28]

VIII

Truman remained in close touch with the remainder of his family in Missouri—Mary Jane, Vivian, Ralph, and cousins Ethel and Nellie Noland. He regarded each of them with a mixture of affection, comradeship, and concern that in one way or another they were harmed by their relationship to him.

He inquired after Mary Jane's financial needs and gave her constant encouragement in her difficult quest to become grand worthy matron of the Missouri Eastern Star, a post analogous to the grand mastership he had held in 1940. He believed, probably with some accuracy, that at least part of the opposition to her was a way of striking at him. "Don't let that bunch of trash entice you into the Grand O.E.S. again," he wrote to her in a dark humor on the day he fired Henry Wallace. "They'll simply mistreat you again for malicious political purposes against your brother." She persisted and won the position in 1950. He participated in her installation with pride and pleasure, while she doubtless took natural satisfaction in having matched one of her brother's accomplishments.[29]

Vivian pursued the largely separate track he had established since childhood, dividing his time between the farm, which remained his primary devotion, and his federal job in Kansas City. He watched with a satisfaction that Harry surely shared as his five children settled into marriage and responsible adulthood with, as far as one can discern, none of the scandals or ostentatious neuroses that have more recently been considered mandatory for those related to the famous and powerful.

The two brothers had plenty of family business to handle, but the topic that consumed much of their correspondence was local Missouri politics. "Sam Wear is asking me for reappointment as United States Attorney for the Western District of Missouri," Truman wrote to Vivian in March 1949. "What about it? I won't reply to his letter until I hear from you."[30] Vivian had become Harry's principal source of intelligence on Missouri politics. And why not? Vivian had no agenda of his own. His personal interests and loyalties were nearly identical to those of his brother. He was shrewd. And if he had no vision beyond that of courthouse jockeying and patronage jobbing, well that was what politics was all about.

Why did Harry care? Hadn't he gotten past that level long ago? The truth seems to be that, whatever one side of his personality told him, he could not entirely let it go. Local politics, along with its ethic of personal loyalty and patronage, continued to appeal to him—probably because it had a simple, elemental character that stood in vivid contrast to the complexity of the presidency. Moreover, isolated in the White House, Truman seems to have become a bit distrustful of the motives of almost everyone, even longtime supporters, back in Missouri. He knew he could trust Vivian. The situation made the two of them closer than probably they ever had been.

The earlier ups and downs of his relationship with cousin Ralph had given way to a reassertion of the friendship of their boyhood years. They both watched Ralph's son, Louis, rise through the regular army; the young man eventually would become a lieutenant general. Living in retirement in Springfield, Missouri, Ralph was one of Harry's most vocal supporters; he also was as hot tempered as ever. On April 23, 1951, less than three weeks short of his seventy-first birthday, he wrote Harry a letter masterfully blending contrition and self-satisfaction and detailing the way in which he had taken a swing at a "smart aleck" of about thirty-five for insulting the president: "I levelled off at him and putting all the power I had behind it very nearly upset him, at that time some of my Legion friends stepped in and stopped the contest." He was sorry, he said, but obviously not much. Neither was Harry: "I am glad you took a poke at that guy and my only regret is that you didn't get a chance to leave some marks on him."[31]

Ethel and Nellie had never married. They had supported themselves as schoolteachers and still lived across the street from the Gates–Wallace house, in the home their parents had moved into shortly after the turn of the century. Intelligent, well educated, and more serious in their intellectual interests than Bess, they were absolutely discreet and among Harry's closest confidants. He wrote to both of them often, but seems to have felt closer to Ethel. It was indicative of the special relationship they had enjoyed since childhood that he continued to correspond with her even after disputes estranged her from the rest of the family.

Ethel had appointed herself the unofficial Truman family genealogist, had engaged at considerable expense an English researcher, and had received a long study arguing (with some persuasiveness) that the name Truman was a variant of the Norman-French Tremaine. Harry intermittently kidded her about the discovery—especially after he learned that a popular brand of English beer was named for Ben Truman, a seventeenth-century brewer with a son who had emigrated to America. "Now I don't think there is anything to all that fancy name spelling," he told her in 1946. "It is my opinion that our people came from the English 'Beer Baron.'" A few years later, informed that the researcher had uncovered a Tremaine-Truman coat of arms, he promised to pass along the news to Ralph: "I'll tell him it is three hands each holding a bottle of the famous Truman ale."[32]

Other communications were more reflective, with thoughts on human nature, education, the vagaries of Washington life. Some vented anger and frustration with Republican politicians (including "a pathological liar, now in the U.S. Senate from Wisconsin, and a block headed undertaker in the same 'great body' from Nebraska"), renegade Democrats (especially Byrnes and Wallace), Douglas MacArthur ("the 'Right Hand of God'"), and others. Some were tinged with irony. "It is very remarkable, these days, how anxious people are to be, even distantly, related to me," he wrote in May 1948. Several letters commiserated with the cousins about all the difficulties of being a close relative of the president, and not a few underscored the burdens of the office itself: "Nobody but a damn fool would have the job."[33]

IX

As his relationship with Vivian demonstrated, Truman could not abandon his interest in Missouri politics. Yet his 1946 success in purging Roger Slaughter notwithstanding, he rarely could control what went on there. His efforts to do so, which generally boomeranged against him, provide case studies in the limitations of presidential power.

During Truman's presidency, political power in Missouri was even more diffuse than in the 1930s.[34] Kansas City remained largely under the control of the predominantly Republican (although they avoided that label) reformers who had overthrown Tom Pendergast. Under Tom's successor, Jim, the old organization shattered into factions that frequently seemed more devoted to fighting one another than to regaining control of the city. Republicans governed St. Louis from 1941 to 1949, thanks to the disintegration of the fragile confederation of ward leaders that Bob Hannegan had constructed in the 1930s.

Truman had no use for the two Democratic governors who served during his presidency: Phil Donnelley, whom he considered "just a little bit further right than Harry Byrd and Louis XIV," and Forrest Smith, to whom he wrote in early 1950, "You have been associated with the Democratic faction in Missouri that does not give much weight to promises when they are made."[35] For most of his time in office, the state's two United States senators were conservative Republicans: Forrest Donnell (1945–1951) and James P. Kem (1947–1953).

The Second Hatch Act (1940) had sharply limited the political activities of state employees funded by federal appropriations; postwar prosperity and the New Deal welfare state eliminated much of the social and economic function previously served by the machines. In both St. Louis and Kansas City, labor unions, pursuing their own independent political agendas, possessed far more political clout than machine politicians. The outstate political structure remained fractionated among literally hundreds of local influentials. Two of the most powerful were Truman's old friends J. V. Conran, who controlled several southeastern counties, and Dick Nacy, who used his position as a Jefferson City banker to raise money for obliging Democrats and attract state deposits to his and cooperating institutions. But Conran, Nacy, scattered urban ward bosses, and rural leaders controlled relatively small fiefdoms; given their notoriety, their support could be counterproductive; and many (unlike the reliable Conran) were far better at promising votes than at delivering them.

With no core of leaders able to join in mobilizing an overwhelming political voting bloc and with the governor no longer able to deploy small armies of state workers for political campaigns, statewide politics tended toward a classical pluralistic system in which candidates exploited personal or regional appeal and negotiated evanescent coalitions. In such an environment, the president of the United States could be at best one of several important actors. Truman wisely stayed out of the Byzantine factionalism of Kansas City politics and never attempted to influence a gubernatorial race. Understandably, however, he felt he had a right to have a say in senatorial races, and he was determined to oust Donnell and Kem. He would achieve his objective, but manage to look bad in the process.

At the end of 1949, after meeting with Governor Smith and other party leaders, he agreed to support state senator Emery Allison for the Democratic nomination for United States senator and subsequently discouraged state attorney general J. E. (Buck) Taylor from running. On January 5, 1950, Truman publicly announced his support for Allison. The ploy had one desired effect; it headed off a possible candidacy from Phil Donnelly. But it did not stop an announcement by Thomas Hennings, Jr., of St. Louis; Truman blamed Smith, probably wrongly, for failing to stop Hennings, harshly criticized the governor in private, and stopped barely short of calling him a double-crosser in public. With the governor brought into line (whether or not it was necessary) and the president working for him, Allison triumphantly carried 101 counties—and lost the primary to Hennings, who carried St. Louis with a 61,000-vote plurality. Hennings went on to defeat Donnell in November. He became an effective senator and a loyal Truman supporter.[36]

History repeated itself two years later in the Democratic primary to select an opponent to Kem. This time, Truman endorsed Buck Taylor but failed to head off a candidacy by Stuart Symington, another St. Louisian. Truman indicated to Roy Harper (whom he had made a federal judge) that he felt he owed Taylor something for staying out of the race in 1950. He also seriously underrated Symington, thinking that he would be weak outstate and that (as in the old days) Missouri would not accept two senators from St. Louis. In fact, as Hennings had demonstrated, a candidate able to pull together the different St. Louis Democratic groups (ward bosses, labor, and the relatively independent middle class) had at least as much strength as a Pendergast designee in the 1930s.

Symington did that and more. He campaigned hard, brought Lloyd Stark out of political limbo to speak for him, and defeated Taylor easily, carrying sixty-four counties. Eighty percent of his 188,000-vote plurality came from St. Louis city and county. Truman took the defeat philosophically and predicted that Symington would be a good senator. Two wrong picks in as many years, however, demonstrated that in Washington he had lost touch with a state whose political topography had changed dramatically. His misadventures in Missouri, furthermore, displayed a larger blind spot. Democratic politics across the nation were moving in the same direction. A substantial part of the explanation for his own declining popularity was his continued affinity with old-style organization types who were falling into increasing disrepute with the new post–New Deal Democrats.[37]

X

The presidency colored Truman's every act, affected members of his family in ways that distressed him, restricted his physical movements, made him a target for critics of all stripes, and subjected him to the threat of assassination. Not surprisingly, he tried to escape from it as much as possible. His two main vehicles were the presidential yacht, *Williamsburg*, and the naval base at Key West, Florida.

Originally a private luxury vessel called the *Aras*, the *Williamsburg* had been rechristened after it was requisitioned by the navy in 1941. Refitted and used as an auxiliary gunboat during the war, it was reconverted to its original purpose in 1945 and made available to the president. Slightly more than three-quarters the length of a football field, it displaced 1,900 tons. Its draft was shallow, leaving it prone to pitch and roll spectacularly in rough waters, despite the placement of several hundred tons of scrap iron as ballast in its bilge. Its furnishings were comfortable but not ostentatious. It contained spacious quarters for the first family, four guest staterooms, and two lounges.

Truman loved it. It became a favorite weekend hideaway, cruising languidly down the Potomac and around Chesapeake Bay, the president and friends taking in the sun or playing cards on deck in good weather. The presidential party was almost always all male. Reporters usually were not allowed on board; a few regular White House journalists might follow at a safe distance on a rented boat. Sometimes Truman used the yacht for official state visits, but more often it gave him a couple of days to set his own pace, forget about a suit and tie, sleep late, not worry about shaving, have a morning drink or two if he wished, and, inevitably, play poker.[38]

Key West was also a joy. He first went down there after the 1946 elections, suffering from a nagging cold and a normal sense of depression at the Democratic loss. The town, as Robert J. Donovan remembers it, was far from the upscale retirement haven it later would become. It was more like a sleazy Caribbean port of liberty patronized largely by sailors on shore leave, the downtown dominated by bars and strip joints. Street vendors sold turtleburgers for a dime apiece.

The naval base was quite different. Truman was delighted with the big commandant's house, the sun, the beach, the boating and fishing. Here he was largely free to indulge himself as he did on the *Williamsburg*, and here also the parties were usually stag. Rarely seen in suit and tie, he enjoyed showing off loud vacation shirts. His stays normally lasted for a week or two, with part of each day allotted to business. Reporters covered the president on a more official basis than on the *Williamsburg*, but often participated in off-the-record evenings of poker playing (euphemistically designated in the official log as "visits" between the president and other members of the party). In all, Truman spent 175 days of his White House years there—and remembered the trips so fondly that he returned five times after he left office.[39]

That still left the presidency as a day-to-day confrontation. His struggles with the office had good moments and bad: the awkward combination of personal insecurity and bracing public support in the months after Roosevelt's death, the difficult decisions of the Cold War, the breaks with Wallace and Byrnes, the disasters of postwar reconversion, the 1946 election repudiation, the Palestine fiasco, the uphill political fight of 1948, the elation of victory, the Fair Deal disappointments, the Korean slough of despond during the last two and a half years of his tenure. Truman was naturally affected by the ebb and flow of events. What damaged him and ultimately took away much of his effectiveness as a national leader was his inability to maintain the appearance of assurance and optimism that Americans expect from the inhabitant of the White House. For far too much of his time in office, much of the public perceived him as erratic, petty, and a cut or two below his responsibilities.

Some presidents, to use James David Barber's terminology, have been "active-positive" types, brimming with confidence in themselves, delighting in the powers of the presidency, enjoying public attention; Franklin Roosevelt was the preeminent twentieth-century example. At the other end of the psychological continuum, "active-negatives" have exhibited lower levels of self-esteem, immersed themselves in detail work, and frequently seemed uncomfortable with their position; the most recent example in Truman's experience had been Herbert Hoover.[40]

In his presidential behavior, Truman moved back and forth between both models, but often he seemed active-negative. When the going was good, he enjoyed the perquisites and duties of his office: the yacht, the vacations, the press conferences, the ceremonial meetings with foreign leaders. When it was tough, the yacht and the vacations became refuges, the press conferences and other duties, ordeals. More revealingly, when things were neither great nor disastrous—the usual state of affairs—he was as often as not short-tempered and prone to feel that he was either persecuted or at least insufficiently appreciated.

A product of a relatively egalitarian society that gave him no predetermined status as a member of a ruling elite, Truman, quite unlike Franklin Roosevelt, had struggled over the first sixty years of his life to construct a satisfactory identity. His personal and professional experience, like that of many men, had been an ambiguous blend of success and failure. Only after being unable to make it in business had he turned to the rough-and-tumble, insecure, and low-status career of politics. The security and confidence he had achieved were fragile.

From an early age, he had displayed the syndrome popularly known as workaholism, a tendency to seek a sense of achievement through exhausting effort. If, on the whole, it had paid off, it also had sometimes landed him exhausted at the Army-Navy Hospital in Hot Springs during his senatorial career. Writing in 1968, Dean Acheson praised the president's endless capacity for hard work and found a serenity in one of his attributes: "He slept, so he told us, as soon as his head touched the pillow, never worrying, because he could not stay awake long enough to do so."[41] But had Acheson described a confident serenity or a harrowed exhaustion?

At his relaxed best, Truman was an attractive individual—an exemplar of traditional values, considerate, reflective, charming, capable of making hard choices and assuming responsibility for them. Yet he often felt suspicious of those around him, was capable of considerable vindictiveness, seethed with unfocused hostility, and, above all, dealt poorly with stress. He long had nurtured an often justified, if not altogether healthy, resentment at not being taken seriously by his peers. In truth, he possessed at least a bit of the self-destructive attitude that Harold Lasswell ascribes to the "respect-centered character": easily wounded pride, antagonism toward those who receive credit to which the person feels entitled and anger at those who misdirect it, a tendency to overpersonalize criticism of public acts, a perpetual need for reassurance.[42]

He had written to Cousin Ralph after his first try for county judge in 1922 that he had won "the dirtiest and hardest-fought campaign" that the eastern half of the county had ever seen. More than a quarter-century later, as a triumphantly reelected president of the United States, he wrote out a preamble (not delivered) to his 1949 State of the Union Address asserting that during his first term he had been subjected to "a campaign of villification, misrepresentation and falsehood . . . unequaled in the history of the country—I might say in the history of the world." He could complain to William Southern about not being mentioned in the *Independence Examiner* and protest to Roy Roberts about being omitted in the Kansas City centennial edition of the *Star*.[43]

His irritation with the press bordered on the obsessive. He liked to think that he had a quarrel with only the plutocrats of the fourth estate— publishers with names such as Hearst, McCormick, Patterson, Pulitzer, and Roy Roberts; columnists such as Drew Pearson, Walter Winchell, and Westbrook Pegler. "Our press is controlled by Bertie M[c]Cormick, a moron, and anemic Roy Howard, whose snotty little sheet in Washington is among the worst, and the Hearst papers," he wrote in his diary in August 1952. "The Hearst papers reflect the morals and ethics of William Randolph Hearst. He had no morals and no ethics."[44]

As for the offending columnists, they were chronic liars and smear artists, or worse. And although Truman may have reserved a special place at the top of his hate list for a few select pundits, he was capable of striking out at almost anyone. "I am sorry to see you, in your old age join these prostitutes of the mind of our great Republic," he wrote after reading an especially critical piece by the respected conservative Frank Kent in September 1951. "Your article today is rank prostitution in its worst form." Fortunately, he refrained from sending the letter. There were ivory-tower columnists and guttersnipe ones, he told Claude Bowers, "and not one of them tells the truth except by accident."[45]

In fact, while Truman had a hierarchy of pet dislikes, he believed that most journalists and their publications were irresponsible with regard to the national interest and especially dedicated to attacking him. The *Denver Post*, he told Mape Harl (after Harl had sent him an editorial of support from it!), was a "dirty sheet." The *St. Louis Post-Dispatch*, he informed Edwin Pauley, was "the dirtiest outfit in the country." "Anything with the word Star in it is against us everytime," he wrote to Mary Jane, adding that the conservative *New York Sun* and the liberal *Chicago Sun* had something in common: "Neither of 'em with the honor and morals of a cornfield negro in pre–civil war days."[46]

At times, his complaints could verge on the irrational, as when he assailed newspapers and magazines for endangering national security by printing maps showing locations of defense plants and reproducing aerial photographs of Washington and other big cities. "Stalin needs no spy system to tell him our 'top secrets,'" he declared to Roy Roberts—as if such information could be kept secret. (Roberts, displaying remarkable patience, responded at length.) "The main difficulty with most newspaper editors is that they have no comprehension of the magnitude and responsibility of the Presidential Office," he told James Cox. "Some of their antics in the last campaign were next door to treason."[47]

At bottom, his grievances were deeply personal. Convinced of the perfideousness of almost every major newspaper and byline columnist, he privately lashed out at them all without regard to partisan or ideological slant. At times, he fantasized about libel suits. While he seems genuinely to have liked most of the reporters who actually covered him, he was privately wary of them also. Understanding that they had other interests, he misconceived the difference. Harry Vaughan's problem, he wrote to Cliff Johnson, was that he could not keep from talking to newspapermen: "He sometimes can't remember that they are out to embarrass the President whenever they get a chance."[48]

XI

"I have been with the president on occasions when he had what appeared to me to be a perfectly normal and amiable conversation with a caller," Admiral Robert Dennison recalled years later. "After the caller left, he would say to me, in effect, 'I certainly set him straight,' or 'I let him have it.' The president's remarks seemed to me to have no conceivable relation to the conversation I had just heard."[49]

Dennison did not realize that he was describing a common behavioral pattern: the friendly conversation that smoothed over or failed to touch on some difficulty with another person, then the surging feelings of aggression when that individual was out of range—at times discharged orally to a third party, at other times committed to paper in the form of an angry memorandum or letter that often was filed and forgotten but occasionally made its way to the addressee. Enough such missives would be discovered in his presidential papers to provide the material for a small book.[50]

In 1949, Truman had put into the mail an angry, although not intemperate, letter to Frank Kent, who had rather unfairly criticized the presidential expense account. When Kent replied indignantly, Truman, following a characteristic pattern, apologized; he accepted Kent's offer to return the document uncopied and unpublicized. Roy Roberts responded to a waspish letter by saying that he would consider it a communication from Harry Truman, Jackson Countian, and that, given the world crisis, he thought the president of the United States should receive only his best wishes. But Kent, Roberts, and other recipients of Truman's wrath, however silent they were about specific incidents, could not avoid feeling that they were dealing with a national leader who was inordinately touchy and perhaps dangerously erratic. Among the communications that became public, his blast at the Marine Corps "propaganda machine" and the letter to music critic Paul Hume were among the highlights of the last half of 1950. Even those who laughed off such outbursts were likely a bit uncomfortable with them.[51]

In April 1950, Raymond Brandt of the *St. Louis Post-Dispatch*, in an insightful and generally friendly article, observed that Truman's humility appeared to have evaporated after the 1948 election. "He is almost arrogant at times, telling visitors that he knows more about the budget, China and national security than anybody else." The president's attempts to appear decisive often backfired. At press conferences, he exhibited a tendency to speak before he thought. Sometimes the results were serious, as with the "red herring" comment on the Hiss case or his inadvertent remark that commanders in Korea might be allowed to use the atomic bomb. Faced with the adversity of the Korean War, he became more snappish than ever. In 1952, the Pulitzer Prize editorial cartoon depicted him angrily confronting a group of reporters and declaring, "Your editors ought to have more sense than to print what I say!"[52]

In March 1951, Truman's new assistant press secretary, Roger Tubby, privately described his chief—hammered by McCarthyism, domestic scandals, an inflationary economy, and the impending decision to dismiss Douglas MacArthur—as "burdened and psychologically worn." Truman was near a low point at that time, but the same could have been said of him at numerous other moments during his White House years. His physician, Wallace Graham, understood the problem; like the doctors at Hot Springs several years earlier, he recommended ample rest, recreation, and exercise. The morning walks, the swims in the White House pool, the poker games, the weekends on the *Williamsburg*, the extended trips to Key West—all were ways of dealing with stress. So were the angry letters—as long as they did not get out of the White House. So were diary memoranda that purged overflowing rage by talking about hanging John L. Lewis or nuking the Soviets.[53]

Truman's anger and hostility had a way of erupting spectacularly in the fashion of a geyser, then quickly receding. Perhaps the central image problem of his presidency was to contain its excesses and present his better side to the public. In the end, he lacked the self-control and the preparation to manage the task. Franklin Roosevelt, supremely self-confident and born to lead, could absorb the blows of his critics and strike back devastatingly by labeling them abusers of his little dog, Fala. Truman was more prone to threaten to beat them up.

Functioning in the dawn of the contemporary media age, he was subjected to more journalistic attention than any of his predecessors. His own miscues and his uneasiness with the presidency highlighted his mistakes and detracted from his accomplishments. During the later years of his presidency, the public increasingly would see not his fundamental generosity or his great decisions, but his gaffes, pettiness, and unpredictability.

28

"A Fair Deal": Liberalism and the Web of Government, 1949–1950

Harry Truman was at the height of his prestige and national goodwill when he appeared before the Eighty-first Congress on January 5, 1949, to deliver his State of the Union Address. Shorter than the first major message he had sent to the Hill three and a half years earlier and forcefully spoken, it contained a policy agenda fully as ambitious: widespread economic controls; new taxes to balance the budget and lower the national debt; repeal of Taft-Hartley; a higher minimum wage; an agricultural program providing "abundant farm production and parity income"; major resource-development projects and the creation of new valley authorities based on the TVA; large-scale extensions of the Social Security program; "a system of prepaid medical insurance" and other health initiatives; federal aid to education; creation of a cabinet-level department to manage health, education, and Social Security; an extensive housing bill emphasizing slum clearance and public housing for the poor; a fairer and more generous immigration bill aimed at the admission of greater numbers of displaced persons; comprehensive civil rights legislation.

"Every segment of our population and every individual," he concluded, "has a right to expect from our Government a fair deal."[1] With that line, employing a phrase he had used occasionally in the past, he gave his domestic program a name that distinguished it from Roosevelt's New Deal and threw it into a legislative process that had yet to yield productive results for him.

II

Before the political struggle began, however, there was time for celebration. The Republicans, expecting a triumphant return to power, had appropriated a record sum of money for the inauguration; the Democrats proceeded to make the most of it.

Truman displayed his own newfound aggressive confidence on the evening of January 19 at a white-tie dinner for presidential electors and some 1,500 other eminences. Recounting his election-night experiences, he surprised and delighted his audience by launching what *New York Times* reporter Anthony Leviero called "a surprise attack" on NBC news commentators H. V. Kaltenborn and Richard Harkness.

Actually, it was more a good-natured lampoon, but no one could doubt that the president was in fine fettle. As the other guests at the head table—Dean Acheson, Alben Barkley, Sam Rayburn, Fred Vinson—looked on, he stood on tiptoes, fists clenched, in front of the microphone. His passing-good impression of Kaltenborn's clipped delivery—"Although Pre-see-dent True-man is leading"—left the crowd convulsed with laughter. Bess, Margaret Truman remembered later, was less amused, although after nearly thirty years with Harry she was probably not very surprised.[2]

The next day was bright, cold, and crisp. Truman began it by meeting ninety-seven of the men from Battery D for a 7:00 A.M. breakfast. None of that "Mr. President" business, he ordered. Here it would be "Captain Harry." Resurrecting his best military style, he told them that after the inaugural address, "I don't give a damn what you do, but I want you to stay sober until then." They gave him an ebony cane with a solid-gold handle engraved with "D-129." He promised to use it daily and pass it along to his daughter in the hope that someday it would be used by a grandson. Later in the day, they flanked his car in the parade, all swinging identical canes of their own.[3]

The inauguration itself was solemn and dignified. It took place at the east front of the Capitol before nearly 18,000 invited guests and at least 100,000 other spectators stretching back toward the Supreme Court and the Library of Congress. A Baptist minister, a Jewish rabbi, and a Catholic archbishop all led the crowd in prayer. Chief Justice Vinson administered the oath of office as Truman's left hand rested on the same Bible with which he had taken the oath on April 12, 1945, and on an expensive Gutenberg replica given him by friends and supporters from Independence. The president's speech, devoted to America's mission to lead the world, was perhaps the best of his career.

Then the fun began.

Truman and Barkley rode at the head of what may have been the longest parade in Washington's history, accepting the cheers of perhaps a million people. Reaching their destination at the White House, they transferred to a glass-enclosed, inadequately heated reviewing stand. Bess and Margaret would leave early, but the president and vice president spent the next three hours watching a varied spectacle: the marine band, cadets from West Point and the Virginia Military Institute, midshipmen from Annapolis, Generals Bradley and Eisenhower, Admirals Nimitz and Halsey; hometown bands from across the country, state floats filled with pretty girls and touting leading products or attractions; a steam calliope playing "I'm Just Wild About Harry"; Missouri mules; a vast array of personages, many of them unknown beyond their own bailiwicks.

The one untoward moment came when the car bearing Dixiecrat Strom Thurmond passed by. Truman, who until then had displayed intense interest in everything passing in front of him, turned his back until it was well past. The actress Tallulah Bankhead, one of the guests and a product of Alabama's greatest political family, "let out a foghorn of boos." A moment of unexpected levity came later in the increasingly frigid afternoon as the Texas delegation came by, led by an open car whose occupant was identified (with chilling accuracy) by a banner that read "Lieutenant Governor Shivers."

After the last float, beauty queen, marching band, and semiunknown politician had gone by, the president moved on to a reception at the National Gallery of Art, where he shook an estimated 7,500 hands. Then it was off to the Inaugural Ball, where he did not dance himself but watched the festivities with Bess until the wee hours of the morning. When he finally went off to bed, no one doubted that he had enjoyed every minute of the day of his greatest victory.[4]

It was also to be the best day of his second term.

III

For all the acclaim of Inauguration Day, Truman faced serious problems for which there were no easy answers. His foreign policy, successful in Europe, was on the verge of coming unwound in Asia with devastating political consequences. His domestic agenda faced a doubtful future in Congress. Reduced to an embittered minority, the Republicans were spoiling for a fight on policy issues, ready to see Cold War reverses as evidence of administration softness on Communism, and determined to exploit any individual character flaw, real or contrived, as revelatory of pervasive corruption within the White House orbit. A very few right-wing Democrats would cheer them on; many others would be indifferent.

Amazingly, the president found it difficult to get Senate confirmation for any appointment that seemed vulnerable. His designation for the Supreme Court of Sherman Minton, a competent federal judge and popular former senator, attracted twenty-one negative votes for no particular reason. When he tried to reappoint zealous regulator Leland Olds to the Federal Power Commission, oil and gas interests dredged up anticapitalist articles that Olds had written twenty years earlier as an idealistic young socialist; numerous senators, including freshman Lyndon Johnson of

Texas, called him a menace to the American way of life. Truman worked hard for Olds and characteristically lost his temper. He wrote a sharp letter to one of Olds's opponents, Senator Edwin Johnson of Colorado: "I am extremely sorry that the special interest groups seem to have completely and thoroughly smeared a good public servant. I am also sorry that Senators seem to have been taken in by that approach."[5] The scolding was merited—and wholly unhelpful. Olds was rejected by a crushing 53 to 15.

Truman appointed instead his old senatorial buddy Mon Wallgren, whom he earlier had nominated to be chairman of the National Security Resources Board, and then had withdrawn after the Senate Armed Services Committee had refused to act. The Senate was willing to accept Wallgren as a member of a commission, but not as the head of an important administrative agency. His confirmation may also have been motivated by the intuition that Wallgren would be kinder than Olds to the oil and gas producers.

Most incredibly, due to the continuing enmity of Truman's old nemesis Pat McCarran, the president was unable to secure Senate Judiciary Committee approval for the reappointment as a United States marshal of his old aide Fred Canfil. Ever the bull who careened through his own China shop, Canfil had roughed up a photographer in Springfield, Missouri, and reportedly had replied to the cameraman's invocation of the First Amendment: "To Hell with the Constitution!" Truman kept him on just as Roosevelt had retained Marshal Henry Dillingham in the 1930s: by refusing to nominate a successor. Such rejections were the exception; yet they were remarkable for a well-liked, just elected chief executive.[6]

Truman's fundamental difficulty was not simply guerrilla attack by an opportunistic and frequently irresponsible opposition. It was the larger question of the mandate he had received from the voters in 1948. His rousing, heartening victory amounted to less than the sum of its parts; in fact, gridlock was inherent in its character. He had won the election by mobilizing a number of different constituencies—blacks, organized labor, farmers, ideological liberals, traditional Democrats—that had little in common with one another. He also had played to the anxieties of a broadly diverse middle class uncertain whether the postwar prosperity it was just beginning to enjoy would continue under the Republicans.

From these sources, Truman had received just under 50 percent of the popular vote. On the surface, his plurality was a continuation in diminished form of the old Roosevelt coalition, a vindication of the New Deal, and an implicit endorsement of more change. Yet aside from the ideological liberals, the voters had thought of specific, immediate objectives, not of a broad reform agenda.

In the harsh environment of the Great Depression, Roosevelt had succeeded briefly in giving his movement a unifying vision, but that had been lost even before World War II. Truman had a broad sense of liberalism that appeared in his better campaign speeches, but he was never very good at articulating it. Moreover, even if he had possessed a voice that surpassed FDR's, it probably would have made little difference. The emerging postwar prosperity encouraged individual and group ambitions while removing any broadly based sentiment for wholesale social change.

With the Depression and the war behind him, Harry Truman was fated to be the first president to preside over an era of pluralist liberalism—one in which Democratic presidents would attempt to fashion majorities composed of discrete interest groups with specific goals, joined together by a facade of unity supplied by the liberals but not deeply felt by others in the coalition. This was not his creation; indeed, he did not welcome it. It was the relatively natural consequence of a prosperous society in which the dispossessed were relatively few and personal advancement would be the primary concern of the many.

Nor could Truman expect much help from the new Democratic Eighty-first Congress, which was only marginally more obliging than the Seventy-ninth Congress of 1945 and 1946. In 1945, the Democrats controlled the Senate by 56 to 38, with two independents (La Follette and Shipstead) often inclined to vote with them on domestic issues; in 1949, their margin was only 54 to 42. In the House, their representation had increased from 242 in 1945 to 263 in 1949; however, that was only two more than in the Seventy-sixth Congress of 1939, which had given birth to the conservative coalition and ended the New Deal. Raw numbers aside, few Democratic members of Congress could have felt they owed their election to Truman. Many had actually run well ahead of him in their own states or districts.

If the numbers were not encouraging, neither was the congressional leadership. In the House, it consisted of the same old team of Sam Rayburn and John McCormack, friendly toward the president and wanting to help him but deeply attached to the mores of Capitol Hill and convinced that the esteem in which they were held was directly related to the lightness with which they exercised their leadership. In the Senate, always a collection of individualists, the situation was worse. Alben Barkley, as vice president, might preside over the upper house, but he had little more than moral authority. His successor as majority leader, Scott Lucas of Illinois, was usually loyal to the administration, worked so hard that he developed serious ulcer problems, and discovered that he was a general leading charges with precious few troops behind him.

In many respects, the de facto leader was Richard Russell of Georgia, one of the most able men in the Senate and the acknowledged chief of a disciplined bloc of southern Democrats, organized primarily to filibuster against civil rights legislation but fairly cohesive on many other issues. If Russell had come from a border state, Truman later wrote, he might well have become president.[7] Instead, he was a formidable adversary and the Senate linchpin of the conservative coalition.

As for the liberal Democratic senators, they appeared an impressive lot, highlighted by Claude Pepper of Florida, Frank Graham of North Carolina, Estes Kefauver of Tennessee, James Murray of Montana, Joseph

O'Mahoney of Wyoming, Paul Douglas of Illinois, Hubert Humphrey of Minnesota, Herbert Lehman of New York (after November 1949), and William Benton and Brien McMahon of Connecticut. In reality, they amounted to little more than a collection of individuals who rarely acted in concert and had little weight among their fellows. As Truman might have put it, they were better at talking than doing. Their vision of themselves as independent statesmen meant that they felt free to criticize the administration—and make life difficult for the president—whenever the spirit moved them. Truman long had considered Pepper a nuisance; he would add Douglas and Kefauver to the list; he appears to have possessed little respect for Lehman.

Could Truman have provided more leadership? A myth would develop that he lost an opportunity to develop a congressional strategy by vacationing at Key West after the election. Aside from discounting the factor of exhaustion and a need to recharge batteries, such an interpretation would seem to place a heavy burden on two weeks in the sun concluded a month and a half before the new Congress convened. And far from taking "a breather," as David McCullough has put it, during the first six months of 1949, the president worked hard at trying to get his program across.[8]

A good many liberal observers at the time thought that Truman could have done more to recruit congressional support, either personally or through the efforts of a Tommy Corcoran–style arm-twister. In fact, he might well have established a stronger congressional liaison operation. But he never would have employed Corcoran-type tactics, which had affronted his own sensibilities when he was in the Senate. He does seem to have spent considerable time meeting personally with members of Congress or lobbying them on the telephone. Perhaps Truman might have done more to mobilize the sizable classes of freshmen Democrats in the House and Senate, but there is no indication that they were prepared to challenge the seniority rules (as would an extraordinary freshman class in 1974). Some critics still lamented that he could not deliver a speech calling the nation to action in the style of FDR. But neither strong-arm tactics nor oratory had served Roosevelt well on domestic issues after 1937, and there is no indication they would have worked in 1949.

What we know of public attitudes, as measured by opinion surveys in 1949 and the first half of 1950, demonstrates a mixed sentiment in the country for major new federal initiatives.[9] From the beginning, the housing bill drew heavy majorities in the polls. By midyear, substantial public support existed for federal aid to education, but sharp lines also were drawn between Protestants and Catholics over whether parochial schools should be eligible for aid. As for civil rights, a big majority favored abolition of the poll tax, but barely more than a third of those asked favored a strong fair-employment bill. A solid plurality, including presumably a number of individuals who had voted for Truman, wanted to retain the Taft-Hartley Act. The administration's new agricultural program, the

Brannan plan, could muster little enthusiasm even from the farmers it was supposed to benefit. The national health insurance plan never came within sighting distance of a majority.

These snapshots are, to be sure, only a rough approximation of what a mythical unified public opinion may have felt, but most issues did not attract whopping popular support. It is hard to escape the conclusion that Truman's problem was less one of technique than a continuation of the difficulties faced by liberalism in a conservative age.

IV

Many of the liberals for whom Truman's Fair Deal was tailored expected a legislative blitzkrieg and a sweep to total victory. In fact, the more realistic outlook was for long, grinding trench warfare, characterized more by small, difficult gains than by big advances. Truman's legislative frustrations seemed more apparent at the time; but although he failed to obtain his big, dramatic goals, he eventually compiled a list of achievements commensurate with the modest nature of his mandate and the unpromising structure of public opinion.

The congressional session started out well enough when, with the backing of Sam Rayburn, the House of Representatives adopted new processes that curtailed the power of the House Rules Committee to keep legislation from coming to the floor. As it turned out, however, the victory was hollow. The new procedures were difficult to apply in real legislative situations, and the committee was controlled by a bipartisan conservative group headed by Eugene Cox of Georgia. The decision to press for procedural change, rather than to try to force proto-Dixiecrats off the committee, amounted to a confession of weakness.[10]

The less-than-halfway reform of the Rules Committee exemplified the continuing power of the Southerners. Although the administration would countenance the expulsion of outright Dixiecrats from the Democratic National Committee, it prudently decided against any effort to eject Thurmond supporters from the House Democratic Caucus. Such a move, however richly merited, would only have increased the alienation of a South that the Democrats needed for both electoral and legislative majorities. The States' Rights insurgency had accomplished more than the election results signified.

The growing gulf between Truman and the South, with which he once had been so comfortable, took on a personal dimension in the disintegration of his friendship with James Byrnes. In 1947, Byrnes had published a memoir of his tenure as secretary of state, *Speaking Frankly*. It maximized his role as a maker of American foreign policy and depicted Truman, in Robert Messer's words, as a "consistent supporter of everything Byrnes did and said." In 1948, with Truman desperate for support in the South, Byrnes refrained from making a presidential endorsement. By the spring of 1949, already planning to run for governor of South Carolina, he was speaking out against Truman's entire domestic program, most notably in a commencement address at Washington and Lee University.

Up to that point, Truman and Byrnes had maintained a friendly correspondence. But at the end of a genial letter to his old friend, Truman impulsively wrote a postscript: "Since your Washington and Lee speech I know how Caesar felt when he said 'Et tu Brute.'" Byrnes responded sharply, "I hope you are not going to think of me as a Brutus, because I am no Brutus. I hope you are not going to think of yourself as a Caesar, because you are no Caesar." They never exchanged words again. Three years later, Truman sent Byrnes a beautifully bound copy of *Mr. President*, a collection of his writings that included the written reprimand ("I'm tired babying the Soviets") of January 1946. Byrnes, who probably had never seen the document, felt "traduced." Truman's inscription read: "To my former good friend, with kindest regards, whose friendship I would still value most highly." "To this I could not respond," Byrnes later wrote in his memoirs.[11]

Byrnes's Washington and Lee speech was delivered after Truman's civil rights program had collided with a Senate filibuster—not on the legislation itself, but on a proposal to change the cloture rules in a way that would make it easier to cut off debate. Truman himself pledged not to compromise an inch on civil rights; he endorsed cloture by a simple majority of those present and voting instead of by two-thirds of the whole Senate. In March, as he vacationed at Key West, the Senate defeated cloture reform by a vote of 46 to 41, creating a major embarrassment for the president. He would provide comfort to the civil rights forces in other ways—a few symbolic appointments, very important support for their legal causes in the federal courts, unremitting pressure for military desegregation—but as a practical matter, civil rights legislation was a lost cause.[12]

By May 31, with little accomplished, Senate Majority Leader Lucas met with the president and then told reporters that possibly this session of Congress could concentrate on only the repeal of the Taft-Hartley Act. The rest of the administration's agenda would wait for 1950. The trial balloon attracted a deluge of criticism; its sole objective, put forth in deference to the labor movement, was as dead a horse as the civil rights bill. Congress dragged on into October, and Taft-Hartley repeal got nowhere.

Aid to education likewise was ground to death in a legislative process that took on the appearance of a religious war in which Protestant and Jewish Democrats fought the demands of Catholic Democrats for assistance to parochial schools. On Capitol Hill, House Education and Labor Committee chairman John Lesinski (Polish and Catholic) of Michigan and Graham Barden (Anglo-Saxon and Protestant) of North Carolina vividly displayed all the fault lines of the Democratic party in their dispute on the issue. In New York, Eleanor Roosevelt and Francis Cardinal Spellman engaged in a nasty episode of mutual criticism.

Truman, Baptist that he was, clearly sympathized with the Protestant side. (Writing privately to Eleanor Roosevelt, he expressed his condolences over her difficulties with the "meddlesome prelate.") But he equally recognized that Catholics were a core Democratic constituency, and as a practical politician he was more interested in getting a bill through than in defending an abstract principle to the death. Teaming the New Dealish Lesinski with the reactionary Spellman and the first lady of American liberalism with the conservative, segregationist Barden, the issue laid bare all the hostilities that coexisted within the Democratic party and the difficulties of leading it in any direction.[13]

The agricultural issue presented an equally confusing spectacle. Truman's new secretary of agriculture, Charles F. Brannan, proposed a radical departure from commodity price supports; he favored direct income-maintenance payments to family farmers only, an objective to be achieved by an upper limit on payments to any single enterprise. In theory, the Brannan plan was an attractive policy that would preserve a rural America of relatively small farms while letting the prices of agricultural products fall to a natural market level, with all the implicit benefits for urban consumers. It reflected Brannan's long record as a liberal Democrat and his former association with the neopopulistic National Farmers Union (NFU), the dominant farm organization in the Great Plains wheat belt.[14]

Politically and emotionally, the Brannan plan had great appeal to Truman and the Democrats. Yet in practice, it posed the possibility of intrusive and expensive bureaucratic monitoring of the precise level of production on every small and medium-size farm in the country. Its opponents charged, moreover, that because the plan pegged its payments to a formula weighted toward the sky-high prices of the war and postwar years, it would be extremely costly. Most agricultural economists agreed. The extent to which Truman understood these difficulties is uncertain. His personal papers leave no doubt, however, that he involved himself in the details of the plan before signing off on it. He obviously liked the idea of supporting only working family farmers and hoped that the plan would cement them into the Democratic coalition.[15]

The greatest practical obstacle that Brannan would encounter was mobilizing enough support to get his program through Congress. He could (more or less) bring the Farmers Union behind him, but it is doubtful that the backing of its leadership trickled down very far into its rank-and-file membership, most of whom had joined the organization for its insurance and cooperative marketing programs, not for its ideology. The National Farm Bureau Federation, the largest and most influential of the farm groups, was adamantly opposed. In part, the difficulty was that its leadership was predominantly Republican. But, more fundamentally, the Farm Bureau represented the aspirations of relatively substantial farmers who had found the old price-support system fairly unintrusive and personally profitable; furthermore, they were unlikely to take kindly to any program that, by limiting payments, placed a cap on their ability to expand their operations. The Farm Bureau and most commercial farmers wanted a continuation of price supports at as high and as rigid a level as possible—preferably 100 percent of parity, but at least 90 percent.

In Congress, a third force—led in the Senate by Democrat Clinton Anderson of New Mexico and by Republican George Aiken of Vermont—proposed a modified continuation of the program enacted by the Eightieth Congress. The Anderson-Aiken bill pegged price supports to production levels on a "sliding scale" of 75 to 90 percent of parity: the greater the surplus of any commodity, the lower the support level (subject to numerous loopholes and exceptions that had been necessary to get it out of committee). Unpopular in the big agricultural states and supported by neither the administration nor the farm organizations, Anderson-Aiken in many respects made the most economic sense, although it required some interesting contortions from its Democratic sponsor. ("I am sure some people have tried to tell you that I have masterminded the campaign against the Brannan Plan," Anderson wrote to Truman. "Nothing could be more dishonest than to say that.")

After a confusing, disorderly legislative struggle, neither Anderson nor Brannan achieved his objective. With the Brannan plan dead in the water and the Anderson-Aiken bill unpopular in the farm belt, the administration decided to go with the Farm Bureau position; Vice President Barkley cast the tie-breaking vote for it in the Senate. The Agricultural Act of 1949 provided for a continuation of the price-support system at 90 percent of parity. In the end, what had prevailed was neither ideology nor political strategy, but a triumph of classic interest group politics in which conservatives, liberals, and moderates from the farm states came together to bring home the benefits for their constituents. Envisioning the Brannan plan not just as a farm program, but as a political and ideological strategy, Truman, Brannan, and some other Democrats hoped in vain that it could be revived in 1950.[16]

In the meantime, the national health insurance program had been all but lost in the legislative melee. Few sober observers had expected it to be enacted, but its backers hoped to give it a good launch. Instead, it ran into a devastating counteroffensive from the American Medical Association, which called it socialized medicine and depicted it as an early-warning sign of incipient totalitarianism. The negative ramifications extended beyond the proposal itself: it inflicted damage on those individuals who had promoted it and, more generally, on the entire administration. The heaviest fallout hit Oscar Ewing, a strong campaigner for Truman in 1948, an ardent proponent of the insurance program, and one of the most conspicuous liberals in the government.

As administrator of the Federal Security Agency, Ewing headed what was probably the largest subcabinet entity in Washington. Established in 1939 as part of Franklin Roosevelt's reorganization of the executive branch, it had jurisdiction over a wide range of federal health and welfare programs. In the abstract, its size and scope entitled it to cabinet status; in the practical world, its controversial functions and visibly political chief guaranteed that such recognition was unlikely to be accomplished quietly on the basis of simple administrative logic. On June 20, 1949, Truman sent to Congress a reorganization plan providing for a department of welfare based on the Federal Security Agency. By doing so, he was making a statement about the importance of social welfare in his vision of American life. No one doubted, moreover, that the first secretary of welfare would be Oscar Ewing. Two months later, the Senate rejected the reorganization by a vote of 60 to 32, twenty-three Democrats joining thirty-seven Republicans in a textbook demonstration of the strength of the conservative coalition. It would be left to President Dwight Eisenhower to get congressional assent to the Department of Health, Education, and Welfare.[17]

By the end of 1949, the administration had achieved only one major objective: its long-sought-for public-housing and slum-clearance legislation. Even here, despite substantial public sentiment favoring the bill, the margin was narrow and the final product circumscribed from the original proposal. It probably would have joined other major administration initiatives in the legislative graveyard if not for the support of Robert A. Taft, who accepted a somewhat watered-down version of the administration's initial plan. Even so, it survived a key test in the House by only five votes.

The Housing Act of 1949 authorized the renewal of blighted urban areas by the construction of 810,000 units of public housing over the next six years. Representing the beginnings of large-scale ongoing federal involvement in housing the poor, the act stated the national goal of decent housing for every family. Liberals saw it as a major breakthrough in the evolution of the welfare state; Taft and some other conservatives, as a humane necessity. At the signing ceremony, Truman declared, "This far reaching measure is of great significance to the welfare of the American people. It opens up the prospect of decent homes in wholesome surroundings for low-income families now living in the squalor of the slums."[18]

How hollow such words would ring to a later generation! The public-housing revolution quickly became a creeping movement as a result of widespread local opposition and inadequate appropriations. When Truman left office, only 61,000 units had been built and twenty-six slum-clearance projects begun. Given what one knows of the big projects that did eventually emerge from the 1949 act and its successors, however, one hardly dares argue that construction at the original schedule would have amounted to progress. Opponents of the bill had fixated on the sins of socialism. Advocates had assumed that higher-quality housing transformed human nature and produced virtuous citizens. Instead, especially in its early high-rise form, public housing tended to degenerate into instant slums. Ill maintained, dirty, crime ridden, and dangerous, the projects added a new dimension to the social malaise they were supposed to ameliorate. The generous hopes of the more moderate conservatives and the Fair Dealers did not always materialize in the real world.[19]

V

Truman faced another test in 1949. For a time, it appeared that the economy was running out of steam, that the long-feared postwar depression might actually materialize. Confronted by an unexpected economic downturn, the president reacted with prudence and flexibility. Truman, his advisers, and most economists had begun the year assuming a continued inflation-prone economy stretched to the limit by domestic consumer demand, capital investment, and the needs of European recovery. Committed to an easy-credit policy in order to support government bonds and hold down federal interest costs, Truman, John Snyder, and the Council of Economic Advisers had hammered out a policy of containing economic excesses through high taxes and tight-fisted budget management. The administration asked Congress for an additional $4 billion in revenues and for standby economic control authority. Throughout 1949, it hacked away relentlessly at defense expenditures. Truman himself continued to approach his economic managerial functions very much as if he were chief executive of Jackson County, concerned primarily with balancing income and outgo, striving for a budget surplus that would allow him to hack another several billion dollars off the cumulative national debt.

Then it became increasingly apparent that the economy was slipping. Through the first half of 1949, unemployment moved up, peaking at about 6 percent in July. Consumer prices actually began to slip back a couple of percentage points. Farm income slipped perceptibly. Nonetheless, the administration stuck to its program, even as more hysterical observers proclaimed the opening stages of a new depression.

By July, however, Truman and his economic advisers were concerned enough to make a midcourse correction. In his midyear economic report, the president abandoned his request for tax increases and actually advocated a few tax breaks for businesses. He had decided to ride out what still appeared to be a modest recession without engaging in major stimulative activity. But he also abandoned his objective of a balanced budget.[20] Given his fiscal conservatism, this was a significant concession, the product of his political instincts rather than his economic thinking. More important, it was the right decision. During the latter half of the year, the economy began a slow, steady comeback.

Although short-lived, the recession served as a wake-up call to an administration that had conceived of economic policy as mainly the containment of the postwar economic boom. By reminding Truman and those around him that the business cycle still existed, it set the stage for an important shift in liberal thinking about economic policy and brought to center stage the most controversial of his economic advisers, Leon Keyserling.

By the fall of 1949, Truman had wearied of Council of Economic Advisers chairman Edwin Nourse, who declined to involve himself in promoting the president's legislative program and had privately offered to advise Robert A. Taft during the 1948 campaign. Nourse assuredly saw his behavior as a principled assertion of professional economic expertise; Truman considered it disloyal. Increasingly at odds with his council colleagues over how to deal with the recession, Nourse made intermittent offers to resign during 1949. In October, making a speech in Washington, he indicated serious concern with the growing budget deficit. Asked to comment in an off-the-record press conference with radio news analysts, Truman said, "Dr. Nourse didn't know what he was talking about. Although he is an economist, he knows absolutely nothing about Government financing." Later in the day, he accepted Nourse's resignation.[21]

Nourse's successor, Leon Keyserling, already had won Truman's appreciation by serving as an active partisan who had participated in campaign strategy sessions, provided material for the president's political speeches, and (Nourse's disapproval notwithstanding), testified before Congress in support of the White House legislative program. A former aide to Senator Robert Wagner, he was more a political operative than an academic economist. He understood that public men had a limited tolerance for "objective" economic discourse. His aggressive liberalism, relative lack of concern with budget deficits, and close ties to labor made him an object of suspicion among such relative conservatives as John Snyder and John Steelman; it was probably their opposition that caused Truman to delay into the spring of 1950 before naming Keyserling as permanent chairman of the CEA. As acting chairman from the date of Nourse's resignation, however, he quickly set a new economic tone for the administration.

From the beginning, Keyserling advocated above all government promotion and management of a rapid rate of economic growth—an important shift in emphasis from the redistributionism of New Deal economics. Precisely how this might be accomplished remained a bit fuzzy. A few of the congressional liberals, who had at least intellectual ties to Keyserling, talked of direct government investment in those areas of the economy—steel manufacturing, for example—in which capacity remained inadequate. Keyserling himself was too good a politician to get out on so isolated an ideological point. He always talked of growth as a private-sector function and made periodic efforts to butter up the business community. After mid-1950, he never needed to get beyond the rhetorical; the demands of the Korean War and a comprehensive defense buildup would provide growth stimulus aplenty. John F. Kennedy, working with Walter Heller, would pick up the growth imperative as the basis of his own presidential social-policy engineering.

Keyserling's phrasings in his economic reports, consciously and enthusiastically accepted by Truman, provided a general indication of where the president would take the economy: toward government-stimulated and -managed economic expansion, providing maximum employment and generating benefits for all groups in American society. The role of government would be large and would employ a fiscal policy in which the primary objective would be economic growth above all else (including, apparently, budget balancing). There would be strong measures to deal with depressed areas and "economic stagnation anywhere," build up natural resources, preserve competition, maintain collective bargaining, and encourage expanded opportunities for private enterprise.[22]

Whether Truman himself was prepared to buy every single aspect of Keyserling's growth program, and especially to relegate a balanced budget to a secondary priority, may be doubted. He continued to worry about the budget deficit and to blame it on the tax cut passed by the Eightieth Congress. Clearly, however, the president liked the general direction of his CEA chairman's policy and found the expansiveness of his vision exciting. Speaking on September 29, 1949, using figures supplied by Keyserling, he sketched out a glittering future for the American economy —a 50 percent increase in the national income and a movement of most Americans into the middle class, all accomplished with the benign guidance of a government actively reclaiming and irrigating arid lands, providing public power, aiding education, raising levels of public health, and ignoring "the backward-pulling boys" who claimed it couldn't be done.[23]

VI

Even as Truman tried to define his presidency on so lofty (and favorable) a level, other politicians were acting in one fashion or another to bring it down. One of the most effective methods, involving as it did Democratic investigators as well as Republican partisans, was to charge administration officials with corruption and (by implication) to remind the nation of the president's old Kansas City–machine associations. Truman, displaying an ill-formed sense of public relations, was not just inept in dealing with such charges; he behaved so willfully as to seem almost a conscious co-conspirator with his enemies.

His major problem in 1949 and 1950 was his military aide, Harry Vaughan, who was under nearly constant attack for sins as diverse as accepting a decoration from the Argentine government of Juan Perón, helping various small-time business operators who needed something from the bureaucracy, and consorting with Washington fixers. Whether individually or in the aggregate, the charges did not amount to much. Frank McNaughton expressed a common sentiment when he described Vaughan as "a big mud-brained jerk throwing his weight around for small favors in return."[24] No one thought that Vaughan was evil or deeply corrupt; he seemed merely morally obtuse, insensitive, and a bit stupid. The effect nevertheless was almost equally damning and far more difficult to handle. Truman would get rid of a patently crooked associate, but he might not turn out a friend guilty of no more than bad judgment.

For a time in 1945, Vaughan installed John Maragon, a Kansas City hustler whose last recorded legitimate occupation was as a Senate bootblack, in the White House as coordinator of transportation. Allegedly, Maragon had a police record in Washington; eventually, he would be convicted of perjuring himself before a Senate committee. ("He is of foreign appearance and might easily be taken for a gangster," Eben Ayers confided to his diary.) Having established his entrée to the White House, Maragon soon began operations as a lobbyist, working on behalf of various small-time enterprisers who needed some government favor.

One of them, whether at Maragon's behest or Vaughan's, provided a half-dozen scarce freezers ("deep-freezes"), which Vaughan distributed to various friends, including Bess Truman, who installed it in the house in Independence. The appliances were in short supply in those days, and the largesse would surface in 1949 as a minor scandal. Ironically, they were substandard rejects; the one given to the Trumans failed a few months after it was fully loaded with meat. Vaughan's also wound up in a garbage dump after a few years.[25]

Through 1949, Vaughan was under attack from columnist and radio commentator Drew Pearson. One of Truman's least favorite newsmen, Pearson shared the president's populist liberalism, but combined it with a journalistic style that drew on malicious gossip and muckraking personal attack. Still, he seems to have been basically accurate in accusing Vaughan of having pulled strings to secure building-materials priorities for a racetrack developer in 1946. Speaking at a Reserve Officers Association testimonial dinner for Vaughan on February 22, Truman issued a strong defense of his military aide and told the audience in a clear reference to Pearson that "any s.o.b." who thought he could force the dismissal of a presidential assistant had another think coming. Although the official transcript of the talk deleted the phrase, Truman's use of it became widely known. Pearson declared his new title stood for "servant of brotherhood." Truman's statement took a few more inches off his public stature.[26]

Vaughan also became the focus of a Senate investigation into influence peddling in Washington; J. William Fulbright, the chairman of the investigating committee, made himself even less loved around the White House than he had at the end of 1946, when he had suggested that Truman might resign. In an indirect way, the episode was a demonstration of the continuing southern backlash against the civil rights program. Although Fulbright, like every other southern Senator, was a Democrat, the investigation probably helped him in Arkansas, where he was up for reelection in 1950 and Truman was unpopular.

The Fulbright investigations, which continued into the spring of 1951, looked into the deep-freezes, the racetrack construction, and Vaughan's connections with various influence purveyors who became known as 5 percenters because they charged clients 5 percent of the proceeds from any government contracts or loans they facilitated. In itself, the 5 percent levy was no more illegal than any other commission fee. The larger question, however, was whether federal largesse was being purchased indirectly. The practice seemed illicit to many ordinary Americans, especially if types such as Maragon were engaging in it. If one could link the 5 percenters to a presidential intimate, Truman could not avoid damage. Whether Vaughan was guilty of a crime, an impropriety, or simple stupidity mattered little. The president's determined loyalty to his friend no doubt impressed some people, but it surely seemed a flaw in either his judgment or his character to many others.

Fulbright's committee also investigated allegedly improper Reconstruction Finance Corporation loans, leaving a largely justifiable impression that considerable RFC money moved in directions dictated more by political clout and personal influence than by the merits of the applicants. Perhaps zeroing in on him because he happened to be a native of Missouri, the committee took an especially hard look at the activities of Donald Dawson, Truman's administrative assistant in charge of personnel and patronage.

Its findings amounted to very little. Dawson had helped RFC applicants make appointments with loan officials. He also had accepted several nights' free lodging at a Florida hotel that had received an RFC loan. Such revelations were not exactly devastating, especially when Dawson protested that numerous senators often received similar consideration. Years later, he recalled that he had traveled to Florida to speak at a charitable event and had assumed that the gratis hotel bill had been arranged by the organizers. Even so, Dawson came out of the inquiry with a reputation that made him something of a liability. Truman, on the whole fairly and rightly, kept him on.[27]

The individual who caused Truman the most trouble in the entire RFC investigation was a person whom he probably hardly knew, E. Merle Young. A native Missourian who bore a resemblance to Truman, Young had let the impression get around that he was related to the president. The supposed connection may have landed Young a job with the RFC. (He had given Truman as one of his references and routinely spoke of the president as if they were very close.) As an RFC examiner, he had approved a loan for the notorious Lustron Corporation and then left the RFC to accept a lucrative job with Lustron while holding a well-paid position with another corporation, F. L. Jacobs, that also had been an RFC beneficiary. His wife, Lauretta, reinforced his claims to presidential access; she had landed a clerical job with Truman when he was a senator, had moved to the White House with him, and worked as Rose Conway's assistant.

By late 1949, Drew Pearson was getting stories that Young was soliciting RFC loan applicants for "commissions," apparently on behalf of new Democratic National Committee chairman William Boyle. Young also maintained a close relationship with Donald Dawson, and—to the annoyance of many of Truman's aides—was frequently seen around the White House, meeting with Dawson, using the West Wing driveway as his customary all-day parking space, and meeting his wife at the end of the day. By the time the Fulbright committee questioned Young, Lauretta was wearing an expensive mink coat, courtesy of a Washington attorney who specialized in helping businesses get RFC loans.

When this information began to come out in 1950, there was not much Truman could do about it. But he might at least have ordered Young's White House pass canceled, told Dawson to break off his relationship with Young, and had Rose Conway pass the word to Lauretta that mink coats were not suitable apparel for White House stenographers. He did none of these things. Predictably, news photographers soon were taking pictures of Merle and Lauretta leaving the White House. Eventually, Young would serve a prison term for perjury. Before then, however, he did grievous damage to Truman. Lauretta Young's mink coat became a symbol of Democratic corruption, most memorably invoked in Richard Nixon's declaration that Pat had no mink coat, just a "good Republican cloth coat."[28]

Whatever Dawson, Young, and some weak, politically motivated RFC directors might have been legally guilty of, there can be little doubt that the agency had become a hotbed of political favoritism and an embarrassment. Why did Truman fail to act? The answer seems to reside in his own political experience, going all the way back to Mike Pendergast's Democratic club and his father's patronage appointment as a road overseer. He still seems to have regarded his mission as the achievement of personal virtue within a messy, ethically ambiguous political system that could not be changed. Patronage and money made the system function. And why shouldn't the recipients of government favors, whether jobs or loans, kick back a little?

Even a president could not fight the system, Truman apparently had decided in 1948, when he fired the respected James Landis as chairman of the Civil Aeronautics Board. The best one could do was take no money for oneself, avoid handling it, let others do the dirty work, and—when the pressure got a little heavy—attack the uplifters, who no doubt were concealing sins of their own. A blend of realism and evasion, Truman's outlook was probably shared by a majority of American political leaders during his lifetime.

Truman gave himself another millstone to carry by naming Bill Boyle as chairman of the Democratic National Committee. Boyle, who had replaced J. Howard McGrath when McGrath succeeded Tom Clark as attorney general, had only one qualification for the job: his long association with Truman. He also had a history of affiliation with the Pendergast organization that shone more glaringly than his apparently honest public record. Having worked for a few years as an attorney with clients who did business with the government, he was almost a sure bet to be charged with influence peddling.

By appointing Boyle, Truman had thrown up a clay pigeon for Republicans, southern Democrats, and anti-administration journalists to blast away at. A few early rounds already had been fired by September

1949, when Truman addressed a testimonial dinner for Boyle in Kansas City. "Bill's all right!" he declared. "Don't let anybody tell you differently!" The event damaged the public image of both Truman and Boyle. As Robert Donovan recalled it, "The number of crooks and racketeers at the dinner with a president was a scandal in itself." Some prominent newspapers (the *Washington Post*, for example), along with many hostile editorialists and columnists, took notice.[29]

One of those gangsters in civic life was Charles Binaggio, the more or less lineal successor to John Lazia and Charley Carrollo as top capo of the Kansas City underworld, the boss of the northeast ward, and a member of the Boyle testimonial organizing committee. To an outsider such as Americans for Democratic Action field worker William Leuchtenburg, he seemed "the most frightening character I've ever laid eyes on." To Kansas Citians, he was merely the latest holder of what had become an institutionalized political role. On April 6, 1950, Binaggio and his lieutenant, Gus Gargotta (the same man whom Sheriff Tom Bash regretted not having killed in 1933), were gunned down in their ward clubhouse. Newspapers and magazines across the country carried pictures of their bodies sprawled out underneath a huge poster photo of Truman. The visual association was devastating.

One rumor was that Binaggio and Gargotta were murdered because they were about to rat to a grand jury; another, that they had taken huge payoffs to open up the city to outside gamblers, and then had failed to deliver. Repeatedly asked at a press conference whether he would order an FBI investigation, Truman responded, reasonably enough, that the president of the United States did not involve himself in local law enforcement. The answer did nothing for his standing. Missouri Republican Dewey Short, a vocal political primitive, observed that Binaggio had fallen out with the Pendergast faction and intimated on the floor of the House of Representatives that Truman himself might have ordered the hit.[30]

The peccadillos of Vaughan, Dawson, and Young; the investigations by Fulbright; the appointment of Boyle; the assassination of Binaggio and its evocation of the seamy Kansas City politics that Truman had once been a part of—all underscored weak spots in the president's image, but left him far from destroyed by the middle of 1950. The stage was now set, however, for more of the same and for an increasingly credible claim that the president of the United States tolerated corruption, consorted with crooks, and might be at least a bit of a crook himself. Truman should have seen it coming.

VII

In addition to charges of corruption, Truman had to deal with foreign policy reverses, spy scandals, and charges of Communist influence in the State Department throughout the latter half of 1949 and the first of 1950.

As measured by public-opinion surveys, the hammering took its toll. Truman's approval rating, 57 percent at the beginning of 1949, was 45 percent by January 1950. A month later, more Gallup respondents disapproved (44 percent) of his performance as president than approved (37 percent). These surveys probably accurately measured an erosion of confidence. Yet one senses that he remained popular, even respected, as an individual. Just after Thanksgiving in 1949, Gallup asked people to name the man, anywhere in the world, they admired most. Truman was most frequently mentioned—ahead of Winston Churchill, Dwight Eisenhower, Douglas MacArthur, Herbert Hoover, and Pope Pius XII.[31]

The Democrats, moreover, scored some signal victories in the scattered 1949 off-year elections, perhaps most notably that of Herbert Lehman over John Foster Dulles in the New York senatorial contest. Truman could take such results as an endorsement of his leadership (he campaigned for Lehman), his party, and his program. When he got out of Washington, he still drew large, enthusiastic crowds reminiscent of those he had attracted during the 1948 campaign.[32]

The administration slowly but surely began to squeeze some results out of Congress—not the big, flashy Fair Deal measures, but significant bread-and-butter additions to already established programs. In 1949, Truman obtained a raise in the minimum wage from 40 to 75 cents an hour. The Social Security Act of 1950 increased coverage and extended benefits to a degree that made it nearly as significant as the original act of 1935. Congress also came through with additions to public power, reclamation, and other programs. However modest its record, the Eighty-first Congress was the most liberal since the great days of the New Deal.[33]

And although stymied by what political scientists called "veto groups" on his more controversial programs, Truman could use the veto himself to block measures to which he was opposed. The most important of these was the Kerr natural-gas bill, which Congress sent to the White House in April 1950. It would have effectively decontrolled the price of natural gas, thereby raising energy costs at least a bit for millions of Americans. Its sponsor, Senator Robert Kerr of Oklahoma, was founder of and chief stockholder in a major domestic energy corporation.

The bill split the Democratic party down the middle between what many observers saw as its liberal and conservative factions, which coincided fairly neatly with the representatives of energy-consuming states and those of energy-producing states. The entire Texas delegation, led aggressively by Sam Rayburn, voted for the bill, as by and large did the congressmen from one producing state after another. The liberals, motivated by a visceral hatred of the oil and gas interests, called the legislation a "ripper bill" that would pick the pocket of the American consumer; they retained an unquestioning faith in the benign and constructive effects of regulation. Conservatives, southern Democratic and Republican, defended the law as a way of relieving American business of unfair restraints and letting the efficiencies of the market work.

From the perspective of a generation rocked by an energy crisis and characterized by an eclipse of the old-time faith in the beneficence of regulation, the conservative viewpoint made considerable sense. An analysis prepared by the new White House special counsel, Charles Murphy, concluded that substantial price increases were unlikely in the near future. But on both sides the emotions were intense; from Truman's perspective, the bill required a difficult political decision about which part of the Democratic party he was willing to alienate. He tried to conciliate Rayburn, but was deluged with calls for a veto.

In the end, Truman followed his instincts and ranged himself on the side of the little guy against the big, predatory interests. He issued a veto that was hailed by the liberals. Politically, he had satisfied the northern, urban center of gravity of the Democratic party—but, once again, at the cost of alienating many Southerners and Westerners. The veto also placed Texas votes more at risk than ever before in upcoming presidential elections. Possibly he expected a more moderate Federal Power Commission, with his friend Wallgren in Leland Olds's former seat, to take care of the legitimate demands of the producers. In fact, it would do so, but that alone would not repair the political damage.[34]

Truman understood these realities and was determined to be more than a passive observer to the disintegration of his party. By the time he vetoed the Kerr bill, he was involved in a long-term effort to try to remake the Democratic party along the lines of the 1948 victory into a farmer–labor coalition in which the South would be less influential and perhaps unable to block key legislation.

The Brannan plan was the most tangible embodiment of this aspiration, claiming as it did to meet the needs of both family farmers and urban workers. The fundamental impulse, however, had long been a major theme of American liberalism—from Jacksonian Democracy to the insurgent progressivism that still in so many ways defined Truman's worldview. Encouraged by the administration, CIO union leaders and their counterparts in the National Farmers Union held joint conferences meant to be the first step in the forging of a working political coalition. Speaking to a labor gathering, Brannan himself said, "Farm income equals jobs for millions of workers. Together, let workers and farmers unite in achieving a full employment, full production economy." In the spring of 1950, Undersecretary of Agriculture Albert Loveland won a hard-fought Iowa Democratic senatorial primary on a pro-Brannan plan, farmer–labor alliance platform.[35]

Truman took to the rails that May on a ten-day tour through the West and Midwest. Reminiscent of the 1948 campaign with its eleven addresses and many whistle-stop talks, the trip nonetheless lacked much of the fire and brimstone of the earlier effort. It was impossible to attack a Democratic Congress as easily as a Republican one. But Truman's pronouncements were filled with issues and ideas. He once again reminded crowds of what the Democratic party had done for them, identified himself with the cause of progressive government, and pressed the unfinished aspects of his program. "The Democratic Party, today, is the party of the mainstream of American life," he declared in one speech. "It is the party of progressive liberalism." The crowds were large and enthusiastic.[36]

When the president returned to Washington in mid-May, it seemed conceivable that the party, especially its liberal wing, could make gains in the fall elections and shift the ideological balance on Capitol Hill. No one could have imagined that the Fair Deal had reached its peak and that the nation stood on the edge of developments that would submerge the cause of liberal politics for the next decade.

29

"A Period that Will Be Eventful, Perhaps Decisive": Triumph and Travail in Foreign Relations, January 1949–June 1950

Truman began his second term with an inaugural address devoted entirely to foreign policy. Brief and eloquent, it laid out once again his commitment to a struggle on behalf of liberal democracy against Communist totalitarianism, proclaimed American unselfishness, and hailed the achievements of the Marshall Plan. He told the large crowd that had gathered at the east front of the Capitol: "Today marks the beginning not only of a new administration, but of a period that will be eventful, perhaps decisive, for us and for the world." American foreign policy, he declared, rested on four points: (1) "unfaltering support to the United Nations"; (2) "our programs for world economic recovery"; (3) pacts to "strengthen freedom-loving nations against the dangers of aggression"; and (4) "a bold new program . . . for the improvement and growth of underdeveloped areas."[1]

The months that followed seemed an appropriate sequel to Truman's well-received manifesto. Dominated by American influence, the United Nations reliably supported American policy. The Western Europeans began to make encouraging moves toward economic integration. They also negotiated a mutual-defense treaty, to which the United States would adhere in a historic departure from its old taboo against entangling alliances with European powers. The Soviet Union gave up the Berlin blockade. The bold new program for the underdeveloped world began, albeit slowly, to take shape in Congress.

Yet other events, less foreseen, would clash with the administration's optimistic scenario: a stunning reversal in China, a Soviet atomic capability, a collision between the president's budget priorities and the nation's defense needs, a politics of foreign policy infected by charges of Communist subversion in the State Department. By mid-1950, these elements dominated public discourse on American diplomacy and had put the administration on the defensive—just when it would have to face a wholly unexpected military challenge.

II

Truman began 1949 with a new national security team. At the beginning of the year, George Marshall, unwell and not altogether happy with his relationship to Truman, announced his resignation. Truman continued to revere him, and Marshall, in turn, extended his respect and friendship, if on a perhaps more qualified basis. His service as secretary of state had given Marshall a claim to historical greatness that would have been denied him on the basis of military achievements alone. It had given Truman and the nation a foreign minister of nonpartisan integrity, far more capable of compellingly stating and embodying the national interest than the president.[2]

Although brilliant and masterful, Marshall's successor, Dean Acheson, could give the president none of the unique credentials that Marshall possessed. What Acheson could offer was absolute loyalty and a sensitivity to the president's requirements surpassing any other of Truman's secretaries of state. He knew that Truman did not want to make foreign policy from the White House; rather, he wanted close consultation and the right to veto final decisions. In Washington, this approach meant daily meetings. When Acheson was away at foreign ministers conferences, he sent the president a personal report at the end of every day, a habit that Truman recorded with satisfaction in his memoirs several years later. Vastly different from Truman in background and capabilities, he nevertheless possessed a temperament so similar to that of his chief that he easily functioned as an alter ego in charge of foreign policy.[3]

He also knew when not to meddle with the president's plans or argue with him. His reactions to two faits accomplis are instructive. Acheson had little enthusiasm for the idea of a broad program of aid to the underdeveloped world, a plan conceived outside normal State Department processes. But rather than try to talk Truman out of it, he let it be dragged out in the planning process and then looked on from afar as it languished in Congress. Point Four, as the program came to be called, would finally get a tiny appropriation of $26.9 million in September 1950.[4]

Confronted with Truman's decision to meet General MacArthur at Wake Island in October 1950, he was persuaded that no good could come of the enterprise. As he later put it, he "begged to be excused" from going along. However, understanding that he would gain nothing but Truman's annoyance, he made no effort to talk the president out of making the trip.[5] By disengaging himself from those relatively few ideas of which he did not approve, Acheson left himself free to serve Truman effectively in those vast areas of foreign policy where they were in agreement.

Acheson's major weakness was lack of support on Capitol Hill. There the hard core of hostility to him was, to be sure, Republican and isolationist, but partisanship and policy differences do not account for the much wider difficulty he had with members of Congress. Most of them had a sense of self-importance and expectations of deference that Acheson could never bring himself to take seriously. With some effort, he could give Tom Connally, Arthur Vandenberg, and a few others the same sort of respect he tendered to Truman, but most legislators sensed a maximum lack of regard. And Vandenberg, while supportive, held well back from any unqualified identification with him.[6]

No member of Congress appears to have known the private Acheson —hard-drinking and humorous in a way that might have gained him many friends on the Hill. Instead, he seemed to most representatives from the provinces akin to a British diplomat in his dress and manner. Robert Donovan remembered his dominant trait as "hauteur, moderated by wit and civility." Marx Leva, an administration colleague, recalled years later that he had a way of giving people with whom he talked "a put-down feeling." Such characteristics were not necessarily serious for a secretary of state, as long as everything was going reasonably well.[7]

As events unfolded, anyone who was secretary of state in the hard years of Truman's second term would have had trouble on the Hill. Yet others—not so grating in manner, more attuned to the sensibilities of the legislators—might have been less a point of attack and more helpful to the president. Acheson was extraordinarily able, but so was Robert Lovett, who was far better liked in Congress; Truman allowed Lovett to go back to New York. In this case, as in many others where he behaved far more egregiously, Truman allowed personal considerations and the need to reward loyal supporters to outweigh what should have been his better judgment. But if not the absolute best choice, Acheson was a superior secretary of state, and his friendship filled an important psychological need for Truman. Unfortunately, he also became an increasingly heavy political liability.

Truman also named a new secretary of defense, Louis Johnson. Johnson's rise was the result in large measure of James Forrestal's emotional collapse under the strain of an impossible job, made all the more difficult by the president's growing lack of confidence in him. Truman wrongly doubted Forrestal's loyalty; he mistook Forrestal's well-founded concern about the growing gap between military capabilities and international commitments for indecisiveness; he confused the secretary's lack of authority with ineptness. At that, the president was charitable compared with Zionists, who resented Forrestal's opposition to the establishment of Israel; partisan Democrats, who thought that he should have campaigned for the president in 1948; and political gossip columnists such as Drew Pearson and Walter Winchell, who disseminated untrue stories that questioned his manhood.

Under attack from all sides, sensing that the president's support was thin, and coping with an emotionally barren personal life, Forrestal quickly disintegrated in the early weeks of Truman's second term. In private conversations, he exhibited classical symptoms of clinical paranoia that left the president with no choice but to replace him. It was to Truman's credit that he did so as graciously as possible. The de facto dismissal was presented as a resignation, accompanied by effusive testimonials and the award of a Distinguished Service Medal. Johnson was sworn in on March 28, 1949. Seven weeks later, James Forrestal threw himself to his death from a window on the sixteenth floor of the Bethesda Naval Hospital.[8]

In style and capabilities, Johnson resembled Truman's earlier prospective secretary of defense, Edwin Pauley. When Truman remarked privately to Jonathan Daniels in November 1949 that Pauley was the sort of "tough, mean son of a bitch" needed to run the defense establishment, he might equally have been describing Johnson.[9] Both men had been successful in private enterprise, both had can-do attitudes, both were accustomed to giving orders and having them followed, both had outsized egos, both had zero tolerance for opposition.

A tall, 250-pound roughneck of a man, Johnson had grown up in small-town West Virginia and moved early into the hurly-burly of politics and public affairs. Like Truman, he had been an army captain in World War I. He had risen quickly through the ranks of the American Legion, serving as its national commander in 1932 and 1933. As Franklin Roosevelt's assistant secretary of war from 1937 to 1940, he had done crucial work pressing for rearmament in the face of the indifference of his isolationist superior, Harry Woodring. Denied promotion to secretary because of Roosevelt's need to appoint Henry Stimson in 1940, Johnson spent World War II as head of the American mission in India.

A major Washington lawyer-lobbyist, he was no stranger to the world of power and its ruthless exercise. Pan-American Airways was one of his clients, and it was widely believed that he had engineered the dismissal of James Landis as chairman of the Civil Aeronautics Board in return for big campaign contributions from it and other airlines. Tough and mean, all right, Johnson was unsentimental, ready to throw his weight around, and unwilling to subordinate himself to any man in the administration except the one who had the power to remove him.[10]

Although his only elective office had been as a member of the West Virginia legislature from 1916 to 1924, he was convinced that his destiny involved far bigger things. If Johnson failed to accomplish all he should, Truman privately told Jonathan Daniels, it would be because he was "running so hard for president." He went on to tell Daniels that the ambition was hardly a recent one: "I remember he came up to me in 1940 and told me that the President had just given him the go sign for the Vice Presidency. I told him Louie you won't get but one vote and that will be your own." In the months before being appointed, Johnson had actively lobbied Truman for Forrestal's dismissal. In January 1949, he told Drew Pearson that the president had privately called Forrestal a "God-damn Wall Street bastard" and a "son of a bitch" after Johnson had criticized the secretary.[11] When Johnson took charge at the Pentagon, no one doubted his next objective.

Still, he was more than a loutish political operator. Benefiting immensely from important National Security Act revisions that relegated the service secretaries to subcabinet status and equipped him with a meaningful staff, Johnson took hold of the Pentagon with a hard grip that impressed many observers. Displaying excellent judgment, he made Steve Early, Roosevelt's old aide, undersecretary (later deputy secretary) of defense. Given firm orders by Truman to hold the line on military spending, Johnson canceled construction of the super aircraft carrier *United States*, quelled a "revolt of the admirals," and accepted the resignation of the secretary of the navy during his first month in office. Many liberals, convinced that the military constituted a bottomless sinkhole of waste, found themselves applauding him.

Truman, however, rather quickly doubted that he had made a brilliant appointment. Like Harry Vaughan, perhaps his closest friend in the administration, Johnson easily offended others without trying. At the end of his first month in office, for example, he mightily irritated the president by holding an impromptu press conference in the White House lobby. He later annoyed Truman by arguing against Leland Olds for the Federal Power Commission and advocating Mon Wallgren instead. After the latter incident, Truman commented to Eben Ayers that "after one or two more things like that Johnson would be quitting."[12]

Far worse than protocol gaffes and unsolicited advice (actually not so bad in the FPC case) was Johnson's open intent to establish himself as top dog in the cabinet by bullying virtually every other member. His most frequent target was Dean Acheson. The most memorable confrontation between the two came at an NSC, State, and Defense meeting on March 22, 1950, to consider a staff draft of NSC-68, the most important document yet to emerge from the National Security Council.

Johnson had reason to be upset. NSC-68 was a State Department–generated document designed to force a dramatic reversal of his (and Truman's) economy policies. Nevertheless, his angry declarations that he had been personally insulted and that State was behaving with disrespect toward Defense did little to advance his cause. Acheson later described him as resembling a table-pounding psychiatric case. The meeting of the nation's two primary national security figures soon adjourned, after fifteen minutes, having accomplished nothing other than to add another layer of hostility to an already envenomed relationship. Truman, never happy with conflict in his official family and probably furious at attacks on his favorite cabinet member, made a supportive phone call to Acheson.[13]

Dissension of this sort was bad enough. Johnson took it to a more serious level—not so surreptitiously sniping at Acheson, especially criticizing his China policy, and behaving as if the State Department were staffed with Communist agents. Harley Kilgore recalled him testifying at a closed Senate committee meeting: "Johnson stared over at a man from the State Department and inquired, 'Is everyone here cleared for security?'" By mid-1950, rumors abounded that he was giving Republican senators material with which they could attack Acheson.[14]

Even so, Truman stuck with Johnson. In part, it was easier to keep him than to fire him. More fundamentally, for all his abrasiveness and temper tantrums, he was doing his job. Despite the resistance of the military services, he was controlling costs in an iron-fisted fashion. The Joint Chiefs had asked for $32 billion. Johnson accepted Truman's limit of $15 billion, then as federal revenues declined during the 1949 recession, he enforced a White House mandate to cut back to $13.5 billion. Truman gave him enthusiastic support. "I am as sure as I sit in the President's chair that we have material on hand, probably rusting in some instances, that will mount up to a half a billion dollars," he told Johnson in April 1950.[15]

Johnson and Truman were playing a dangerous game. Military planners struggled to devise contingency plans that might allow the United States to maintain a foothold in Western Europe and the western Mediterranean if the Russians should attack. Their products were, to put it conservatively, problematical. There was little thought of having to fight on the Asian mainland. With China by now written off and resources stretched so thin, the possibility of committing forces there must have seemed so unlikely as to verge on the bizarre.[16]

III

For all the disarray among his national security aides, Truman could take satisfaction in a string of triumphs that culminated in the establishment of an enduring structure of collective security in Europe. The leadership of Marshall, Acheson, and other makers of American foreign policy served the president well, but above all he had the Soviet Union to thank. The Czech coup, Soviet demands on Finland, and the Berlin blockade had galvanized a drive for Western European cooperation that animated Foreign Ministries from Oslo to Rome. In March 1948, Britain, France, Belgium, the Netherlands, and Luxembourg had signed a mutual-defense pact. Through the rest of the year, negotiations to broaden it proceeded with the United States, Canada, and other European nations.

By April 1949, the United States was a party to an enlarged version of the earlier agreement. This one, now called the North Atlantic Treaty, added Canada, Iceland, Norway, Denmark, Portugal, and (largely at the insistence of France) Italy. Nearly a half-century after the event, with the North Atlantic Treaty Organization (NATO) so immutable a feature of the Western diplomatic and military landscape, it is difficult to re-create the wrenching departure from the past that it represented and the epochal character of the debate that ensued in the Senate.

Just four years earlier, something like the North Atlantic Treaty would have been unthinkable. The reflexive attitude of many senators, especially if they were Republican, was to look for reasons to oppose it. Three issues received the most discussion. The first was the treaty's implicit renunciation of the American tradition against alliances with European nations. The second involved what everyone perceived as the inevitable sequel to ratification: an expensive European rearmament program funded by the United States. The third—and most difficult because it affected the self-definition of individuals who had to approve the pact—was whether the treaty preempted the congressional power to declare war.

In the end, the agreement won overwhelming ratification from yet another incarnation of the coalition that had approved the Greek–Turkish aid program and the Marshall Plan. As before, Truman kept a relatively low profile, confining his public advocacy to a couple of major speeches, answering press conference questions as curtly as possible, letting Acheson serve as administration spokesman, and relying heavily on the good offices of Arthur Vandenberg in the Senate. Traditional isolationism stirred too few emotions to be more than a rhetorical flourish in the debate. The administration resolutely declined to discuss an arms assistance program. Acheson, Vandenberg, and Connally thoroughly obfuscated the war-making question. The opposition soon was confined to a small band of isolationists led by Senator Taft. On July 21, 1949, the Senate voted 82 to 13 for ratification. In brief remarks at the signing ceremony four days later, Truman proclaimed the treaty a "historic step toward a world of peace, a free world, free from fear."[17]

"But it is only one step," he added. Ratification accomplished, the administration swiftly introduced a $1.4 billion military assistance program. Here the going got hard quickly. The initial bill gave the president discretionary powers on so imperial a dimension that Vandenberg, who no doubt welcomed an opportunity to display his independence, led a revolt against it. Truman and Acheson intelligently reformulated the legislation in a fashion that satisfied the critics.

Then economizers hacked away at the amount. In August, the House, in what Acheson would later describe as a "berserk mood," voted to halve the appropriation. Truman fumed privately that too many congressmen were more concerned with getting new post offices than with defending the Western world, but he said nothing untoward in public. The final bill, hammered out in a conference committee after Truman's announcement that the Soviets had tested an atomic bomb, contained only small adjustments and placed no crippling limits on presidential discretion. Signing the measure on October 6, 1949, Truman could feel that he had realized the failed dreams of his old hero Woodrow Wilson.[18]

Other pieces were also falling into place, not at random but as a consequence of shrewdly planned policy decisions. By early May, American and British transport planes, flying around the clock and landing at tight intervals, had been supplying West Berlin for ten months. An awesome display of Western resolve and material resources, the airlift had turned the blockade into a display of Soviet weakness. On May 5, the USSR announced that it would lift the blockade in exchange for a conference on a European settlement.

Aside from saving face, the Soviets hoped to use the meeting as a last-ditch effort to prevent the establishment of a new quasi-independent West German state. Instead, they accomplished nothing. When the foreign ministers met later that month, the Western powers, led by the United States and Great Britain (the French were less enthusiastic), offered only an opportunity to merge the Soviet zone of occupation into a democratic, unified Germany. To no one's surprise, Stalin was unwilling to give up political and economic control over a portion of his postwar empire. The conference ended on June 20 with no agreement and a de facto defeat for Soviet diplomacy. The West proceeded with the establishment of the Federal Republic of Germany on September 21, 1949. The Soviets countered by establishing the German Democratic Republic on October 7. The line that had been drawn by these actions would endure for the next four decades.

In truth, neither side was disappointed by the continuing division of Germany, but the Americans had won a clear moral, economic, and military victory. East Germany from the beginning was nothing more than an instrument of Soviet power, separated from the West only by Soviet troops. West Germany had been established on a consensual basis and was poised to become a showcase of Western capitalism; given its potential industrial power and armed-force capabilities, it was a strategic asset of enormous importance. Yet lest its Western neighbors worry about history repeating itself, NATO provided a means of control.[19]

Progress continued on yet another pillar of America's European policy: the economic unification of Europe, to be built around a Franco-German détente. Pushed along by the far-sighted French statesmen Jean Monnet and Robert Schumann and welcomed by the first postwar German chancellor, Konrad Adenauer, the design that in the distant future would become the European Common Market began ever so slowly to take shape. The Marshall Plan could provide an initial impetus for European recovery, but Truman and Acheson understood well that the lasting success of liberal capitalism on the Continent required a degree of economic unification that previously had been anathema to the mercantilist French. Elated, they quietly encouraged the new initiatives.[20]

Some critics, mostly liberal Democrats, found the president and his secretary of state obstinately rigid. A few suggested that by pushing ahead with NATO and the establishment of West Germany, they had thrown away a chance to negotiate an end to the Cold War. Acheson dismissed such remarks as soft headed. His personal encounter with Andrei Vyshinsky at the May foreign ministers conference had left him persuaded of the futility of conventional diplomacy with the Soviet Union. The only agreements worth making, the secretary declared, were those that were straightforward and self-enforcing, not subject to goodwill, not requiring cooperation, not amenable to being interpreted to death. The task of American foreign policy was to stay with its game plan and continue with the creation of a situation of strength that would give the West dominance in the Cold War. To those demanding a scenario for an eventual settlement, Acheson (who probably did not expect to be an actor in the endgame) had no answer. Given the atmosphere of 1949 and 1950, one may question that he should have.[21]

Truman had no difficulty accepting his secretary's viewpoint. In June 1949, during one of his periodic fits of irritation with the Soviet Union, he jotted down some thoughts on how the United States had attempted to achieve an amiable relationship, only to be rebuffed at every turn, and concluded, "There is only one language they understand, force." In October, during an off-the-record meeting with radio news analysts, he repeated an answer he claimed to have given to a recent caller who asked him to make peace with the Soviets: "All right, we will give them Berlin, we will give them Germany, we will give them Korea, we will give them Japan, we will give them East Asia. Then they will settle. Is that what you want?"[22]

This was not the language of a calculating realpolitiker, but that of an outraged idealist. Far from seeing the Cold War as a quest for some kind of American supremacy, whether military or economic, or as a struggle between communism (in the generic sense) and capitalism, Truman envisioned it as a battle between totalitarianism and freedom—or at its simplest between good and bad men. Furthermore, it was a battle in which ideas, not guns, were the most potent weapons.

In a revealing and wide-ranging confidential discussion with the NATO foreign ministers on April 3, 1949, the president forcefully and articulately asserted that the organization was to be a demonstration of Western resolve, not an instrument for military dominance. The struggle with the Soviet Union was ideological; it could be won only by the sort of democratic economic development that would make Communism unacceptable in the West and discredited to the point of collapse in the East: "We should appreciate that Soviet nationalism is dynamic; it must expand, and the only way to defeat it eventually is not merely to contain it but to carry the ideological war to the Soviet sphere itself."[23]

By the same token, his distaste for totalitarianism did not begin and end with the Soviet variety. Through much of his second term, Truman balked at the reestablishment of diplomatic relations with Spain, although its caudillo, Generalissimo Francisco Franco, possessed impeccable anti-

Soviet credentials and although the United States needed air bases south of the Pyrenees. He was repelled by specific reports of persecution of Protestants and Masons. It took considerable pressure from Catholic groups and their congressional allies, along with persuasion from Acheson, to bring the president around by the end of 1950. His impulses in national security policy doubtless lacked sophistication, but his understanding that it was ultimately about values and the liberties of ordinary people had deep roots in the best American ideals.[24]

IV

By mid-1949, administration triumphs in Europe were being obscured, and ultimately diminished, by what appeared to be a catastrophic defeat in Asia. Throughout the first half of the year, the Communist armies of Mao Zedong moved south in what had become an unstoppable drive for control of the Chinese mainland. The Nationalist capital, Nanking, fell on April 24; Shanghai, about five weeks later. Nationalist leader Chiang Kai-shek retreated to the island of Formosa (Taiwan) and prepared what many American observers assumed would be a futile last stand against an overwhelming amphibious invasion. Mao's triumph was surely a major turning point in twentieth-century world history. At the time, to many Americans it seemed a disaster that required an inquest and a determination of guilt.

The question of what to do about China had simmered throughout Truman's presidency, threatening from time to time to boil over. The most serious episode had been the resignation of United States ambassador Patrick J. Hurley in late 1945. A Republican and an avid supporter of Chiang Kai-shek, Hurley charged before a congressional committee that United States Foreign Service officers in China were pro-Communist. The Marshall mission of 1946 relegated Hurley's complaint to a back burner, but its eventual failure left the problem of China unresolved and politically explosive. Hurley had established a theme to which increasingly bitter Republican partisans would resort during Truman's second term.

Marshall, the Foreign Service, and Truman—all persuaded that Chiang's government was corrupt, incompetent, and incapable of beating the Communists—undertook a progressive disengagement from the Chinese situation. At one level, the policy was realistic. Whether one considered Chiang a third-rate dictator brought down by his own ineffectuality or a paladin of Christian democracy overwhelmed by forces beyond his control, the only honest assessment was that he was on a losing trajectory. The decision to stop aid to Chiang (or to keep it as low as the Republicans would permit) also reflected a real, wholly justifiable priority: Western Europe was infinitely more important to the United States than the mainland of East Asia. American resources were limited; if they were single-mindedly committed to Europe, success was likely. China, by contrast, was a hopeless morass.

The problem was not the policy; it was the near-impossibility of preparing the public, the Congress, the administration itself for its consequences. No matter how unpalatable Chiang was, a Communist regime would seem worse to most of the public. As the Communists swept to power, most Americans were amazed and shocked. Congress was angry. Truman, disgusted with a Nationalist government he would later privately describe as a group of "corrupt bloodsuckers,"[25] was prepared to accept the development. Nonetheless, the administration, lacking realistic contingency plans, found itself adrift and at the mercy of events that consistently ran opposite to its expectations.

These expectations ran roughly as follows: a Communist invasion of Formosa (or possibly an internal collapse there) would put an end to the last vestiges of the Nationalist regime, leaving only Mao's government to recognize. Mao was more a nationalist revolutionary leader than a Communist, perhaps not much of a Communist at all. As a nationalist, he would be at the head of a huge country that had multiple intrinsic conflicts with the Soviet Union; eventually—sooner rather than later—he could be expected to follow the example of Marshal Tito in Yugoslavia, break with the Kremlin, and welcome good relations with the United States. To Truman, as well as to Acheson and State Department analysts, such a possibility seemed more worth pursuing than a strategy of constant attack and harassment against mainland China.[26]

As it was, Mao's forces would never be able to make the 100-mile crossing of the Formosa Strait, occupy the island, and definitively eliminate Chiang. (Since they had earlier taken three months to cross the Yangtze River without opposition, it is hard to understand why diplomatic planners expected them to be able to undertake an operation of so much greater magnitude.) As long as Chiang stubbornly persisted at the head of what amounted to a government-in-exile and proclaimed himself the rightful ruler of China, it was a practical impossibility to withdraw recognition from him.

Once in power, moreover, Mao and his followers behaved as ideologues, not pragmatists. Displaying a vociferous anti-Americanism, they imprisoned the American consul-general in Mukden for months. Having spent the past two decades of their lives deep in the interior of China, they reflexively accepted the Soviet view of the world. Nationalist revolutionaries to be sure, they understandably saw a good relationship with the USSR as essential to the consolidation of their revolution. Thus Mao declared that the new China would lean toward the Soviet Union and proceeded to negotiate Soviet withdrawal from Manchuria; he also freely proclaimed the depravity of American capitalism. On February 14, 1950, Red China and the Soviet Union announced the signing of a mutual-defense treaty.[27]

As the State Department scenario disintegrated before their eyes, Truman and Acheson found themselves in the worst of all possible worlds (or so it must have seemed before the events of November 1950) on the

China issue. The administration belatedly attempted to justify its course with the issuance of a 1,000-page "white paper"; a splendid compilation of documents for scholars, it was an ineffective way of communicating with the public. The Republicans began a drumfire of criticism, partly as a matter of practical politics but even more because the Protestant middle classes, whom they heavily represented, long had possessed a romantic "missionary" attachment to the Chinese. The two major Luce publications, *Time* and *Life*, joined in. From early 1949, public-opinion surveys showed 2 to 1 margins against recognizing a Communist Chinese government.[28]

Through mid-1950, these crosscurrents led to a policy with no clear public sense of direction. Recognition of Communist China was so clearly unfeasible that no administration figure ever broached it. Rather, official State Department rhetoric depicted Mao as a puppet of Stalin. The administration worked with a fair degree of success to prevent recognition by the Western European powers, but suffered an important setback when Britain established diplomatic relations with Mao's government in December 1949. Yet although continuing to recognize the Nationalists as the legitimate government of all of China—and thus a beleaguered ally— the United States was unwilling to offer them any help.

On January 5, 1950, Truman told a press conference that the United States would "not pursue a course which will lead to involvement in the civil conflict in China" and specifically "will not provide military aid or advice to Chinese forces on Formosa." The announcement reflected his sense that the cession of Formosa and the consequent liquidation of the Nationalist government were essential to establishing a relationship with the Chinese Communists in the long run. Almost the whole Republican delegation in Congress responded by advocating some sort of a commitment to the island.[29]

Had Truman and Acheson given away too much? Formosa was defensible and a valuable military asset in the western Pacific. It also held the potential, admittedly much easier to grasp a generation later, of becoming a showcase of capitalist economic development and relative freedom in Southeast Asia. It was all too typical of American policy making in Asia that State Department planners began to grasp the attractiveness of an independent Formosa too late to prevent Chiang from irretrievably establishing himself there. It then became impossible to segregate the island from the Chinese civil war.[30]

The Communist seizure of power in China also raised questions about the commitment of the United States to the pro-American government of South Korea. The country itself was an artificial creation resulting from an arbitrary and presumably temporary division of the Korean peninsula into American and Soviet zones of occupation in 1945. Its leader, Syngman Rhee, a tough, dictatorial nationalist, was little admired in Washington. As part of the steady postwar reduction of the military, the American garrison there had been withdrawn. In early 1950, the House of Representatives rejected by one vote an economic-aid appropriation for South Korea; the vote was later reversed, but its implication of congressional disinterest was inescapable. Militarily and geopolitically, moreover, a small, pro-Western outpost on the periphery of a Red continent had no value.

Acheson had tried to pull the pieces together in an important speech to the National Press Club, delivered on January 12, 1950. He failed badly. Like every other administration pronouncement, this talk was hostage to all the constraints on candor and clear thinking about Asia that had existed since Chiang's flight to Formosa. Acheson's central argument was sound: nationalism was the most powerful force in Asian life; respect for and alignment with it had to be the central theme of American diplomacy in the Far East. The United States, he went on, had always favored and would continue to endorse a free and united China. Given his objectives, these were effective points, but they were quickly vitiated by what had become the mandatory insistence that the Maoist government was subservient to the Soviet Union.

Worse yet was the way in which Acheson attempted to answer the most important question: What were American interests and obligations in the Far East? He stated a "vital interest" in the independence of South Korea and Japan, but went on to assert that the United States was prepared to defend militarily a "defensive perimeter" stretching from the Aleutian Islands through Japan, Okinawa, and the Philippines. South Korea, vital interest or not, did not lie within this imaginary line. Neither, of course, did Formosa.

What if an attack occurred on nations not mentioned in the defensive perimeter? "Their resistance would spark the commitment of the entire civilized world acting under the Charter of the United Nations." To describe this as a muddle would be charitable. The following day, testifying before the Senate Foreign Relations Committee, Acheson conceded that in the event of aggression a Soviet veto in the Security Council probably would foreclose any military assistance to South Korea.

Years later, Acheson's aide, Lucius Battle, would talk of the haste with which the speech had been prepared; yet it was clearly intended to be a major pronouncement. Perhaps this was simply another indication of the low priority American diplomats gave to Asian affairs. Perhaps Acheson, without meaning to encourage aggressors, had come to the logical conclusion that since China had become Communist, South Korea meant little in the larger scheme of things. As things developed, few speeches have so relentlessly haunted any statesman.[31]

V

As Truman and Acheson coped with the shattering collapse of their foreign policy in Asia, the American public watched the dramatic, stunning trials of Alger Hiss. Hiss, a former midlevel State Department official who had become president of the Carnegie Endowment for International

Peace, had been accused of Communist sympathies by Whittaker Chambers, a *Time* editor and admitted former Communist, who testified before the House Committee on Un-American Activities in 1948. When Hiss threatened a libel suit, Chambers enlarged his accusation to espionage; he produced copies of State Department documents that he claimed Hiss had passed to him in 1937 and 1938. In December 1948, after Hiss denied these allegations under oath, a federal grand jury indicted him not for espionage (the statute of limitations had elapsed), but for perjury.[32]

Few legal proceedings in American history have possessed such heavy political implications. The personalities were compelling. Chambers—obese, disheveled, obsessed with the evil of Stalinist Communism—might have been taken for the actor Sidney Greenstreet. Republican conservatives (including Chambers's closest supporter, Richard Nixon) found him brooding and prophetic; Democratic liberals wrote him off as psychotic. Hiss, by contrast, was an all-American type: at forty-four, trim, handsome, youthful, and intensely charming. If Chambers might have been played by Sidney Greenstreet, the role of Hiss would have required a stock Hollywood nice guy, possibly Ronald Reagan. From the beginning, however, an ideological overlay dominated reactions to the principals. Both sides agreed that Chambers had made himself a human representation of anti-Communism and that Hiss was a proxy for the New Deal and the young liberals who had served in it.

Hiss's first trial began on May 31, 1949; it ended on July 7 with a hopelessly deadlocked jury voting 8 to 4 to convict. The second trial started on November 17, 1949. Through the first trial, the fall interval, and the second trial, observers divided bitterly. To most Republicans, a generation of liberalism was under indictment; if Hiss should be convicted, that generation would stand guilty of having failed to protect America and the free world from the spread of a totalitarian Communism at least as bad as Nazism. To the liberal Democrats, Hiss personified the selfless idealism and dedicated public service of the progressive intellectuals; many were convinced that he was the blameless victim of a sinister conspiracy. Truman himself would never repudiate his initial characterization of the charges against Hiss: they amounted to "a red herring."

On January 21, 1950, a federal jury, after sifting through evidence that ran strongly in favor of the prosecution, found Hiss guilty as charged. On January 25, Judge Henry Goddard imposed a sentence of five to ten years at the federal penitentiary in Lewisburg, Pennsylvania.

At a press conference that same day, a reporter asked Secretary of State Acheson to comment on the case. Like many Americans, Acheson had followed the accusations and legal proceedings against Hiss with fascination and at times surely with bewilderment at the complexity of the evidence. Like many, he had been caught up in the emotional debate that made Hiss, never more than a significant second-level official, a surrogate for the foreign policy record of the Democratic party. Unlike all but a handful, he had a personal stake in the case. Hiss's brother, Donald, was his former assistant and a close friend. The secretary's relationship with Alger Hiss had been more distant, but Alger's charm apparently had also won his affection. Although Acheson never said so, in common with almost all of Hiss's friends, he must have entertained the idea that Hiss had been railroaded. In the atmosphere of the time, his attitude was understandable. What remains incomprehensible was his failure to grasp that the public could make no distinction between his personal and official roles; the national interest required suppression of his feelings.

Acheson quite reasonably declined to discuss ongoing legal proceedings, but he pressed on with a statement that was clearly a matter of conscience and deep conviction on the nature of friendship, forgiveness, and loyalty. It included a relevant quotation from the Bible, but eleven of Acheson's own words eclipsed everything else: "I do not intend to turn my back on Alger Hiss."

Meeting with Truman later that day, Acheson offered his resignation. The president naturally refused it, as Acheson surely expected he would. Truman, recalling a matter of personal honor that had motivated an unpopular act of his own five years earlier, told his secretary of state that the episode reminded him of the criticism he had incurred for attending the funeral of a friendless old man just out of the penitentiary.[33]

However personally admirable Truman's attitude may have been, it all the same begged the question of whether American foreign policy was well served. First, there had been China and its aftermath, then Hiss. Acheson had become a liability of the first magnitude, but Truman never contemplated letting him go. The Hiss statement, if it had any effect, made Acheson's position even more secure.

The politics of the situation by early 1950 occupied more and more of Truman's time and attention. Even once-tame Republican moderates such as Senator H. Alexander Smith of New Jersey and Thomas Dewey denounced Acheson and administration policy, although with some reserve and still with a willingness to talk to the State Department.[34] At the other extreme, Senator Joe McCarthy was beginning to attribute the loss of China to Communist subversives within State. On March 21, Senate Republican leader Kenneth Wherry, an unregenerate Nebraska isolationist, called for Acheson's dismissal, describing him as a bad security risk.[35] Senators such as Styles Bridges of New Hampshire and William F. Knowland of California and congressmen such as Walter Judd of Minnesota—all known by and large as mainstream Republicans—were intemperate in their increasingly personal attacks against the secretary.

Truman found it all an outrage. Writing on March 26 to Bridges, who had been a member of his World War II investigating committee, he vented his anger:

> I notice a statement in the press this morning that you are joining the "wolf-hounds" in the attack on Dean Acheson. . . .
> The approach which has been made recently by several Senators has been a most satisfactory one to the Politburo in Moscow. The commu-

nists have never had as much help from all the so-called disloyal people as they have had from these indefensible attacks on Mr. Acheson. . . .

. . . [W]hat you are proposing to do is not only unpatriotic, but is a most dangerous procedure, likely to cause a situation in which young Americans may lose their lives by the thousands. History will no doubt place the blame for that situation right where it belongs.[36]

At a press conference a few days later, Truman authorized use of the following quotation: "The greatest asset that the Kremlin has is the partisan attempt in the Senate to sabotage the bipartisan foreign policy of the United States."[37] Strong stuff, the remark displayed plenty of combativeness. It possessed merit as a tactic to deal with what had become a vocal, orchestrated barrage of personal criticism. But by the spring of 1950, nothing could still the opposition.

Remarkably, Bridges responded to Truman's appeal, met personally with Acheson, and refrained from further attacks on him for about a year.[38] But plenty of other Republicans were ready to pick up the battle-axes, including Senators Wherry and (most ominously) Taft, who was speaking out ever more vociferously on foreign policy. The loss of China had probably been unavoidable. It was a catastrophe all the same; and like all catastrophes, it did not lend itself to smooth management or dispassionate debate. As bad as things were in the spring of 1950, however, the worst was yet to come.

The administration's pillar of strength in Congress, Arthur Vandenberg, was by now in the early stages of a final disease; ill and incapacitated, he could hope only to shift his mantle over to other moderate Republicans. "I cannot presume to accept responsibilities which I am unable to implement," he wrote to Acheson on March 29, 1950. "I do not think you should rely upon a 'broken reed' in your contemporary necessities."[39] Unfortunately for the administration, there was no one in the Senate able to step into Vandenberg's shoes. To make matters worse, it was no secret that Secretary of Defense Johnson was at odds with Acheson on a military commitment to Formosa and its use as an American base.

VI

On September 23, 1949, Truman had been forced to release one more bit of stunning bad news: "We have evidence that within recent weeks an atomic explosion occurred in the U.S.S.R." Just five and a half months earlier in his candid policy discussion with the NATO foreign ministers, he had been able to say that "our best estimate is that we have several years in which we can count on a breathing spell."[40] American nuclear policy had consisted largely of moving ahead with production of increasingly powerful atomic bombs. By mid-1949, McGeorge Bundy estimates, the United States probably possessed more than 200 atomic bombs, many of which possessed an explosive capability five times that of the Hiroshima device.[41] If the Soviets had successfully tested a bomb, they could in a few years achieve rough parity with the United States.

Robert Donovan remembers the public reaction to Truman's announcement as "a quiet sense of dismay and dread"—not hysteria, but a realization that the USSR had neutralized America's biggest military edge and that a civilization-destroying atomic war was now possible. On Capitol Hill, Tom Connally, advocating full funding for arms assistance to the NATO countries, told his colleagues, "Russia has shown her teeth."[42] Within the administration, news of the Soviet A-bomb would set off a dramatic reappraisal of national security policy. For large sectors of the public, it would cause not only fear but widespread confusion expressed in the sense that espionage and treason had provided the necessary secrets to the Soviet Union. It was a quick step to the assumption that spies and traitors might still lurk within the government.

Truman found the development of the Soviet A-bomb difficult to internalize; as late as March 1952, he would privately call the Soviet A-bomb a "phony."[43] But as he understood quite well in his more reflective moments, it was a real, nearly unanswerable challenge to major aspects of his national security policy. The first decision he had to face was whether to authorize production of a super bomb employing thermonuclear fusion rather than nuclear fission. The choice presented horrific moral dilemmas. The super bomb would be as great a leap from the atomic bomb as the original A-bomb had been from the most powerful conventional weapons. A general thermonuclear war would mean the end of human civilization, perhaps of human life itself. Yet given the almost certain prospect that the USSR would move ahead with its own project, how could a president refuse to make an American equivalent?

Truman faced no fait accompli, no unanimous opinion, no prepackaged decision this time around. The Atomic Energy Commission was split 3 to 2 against production. As he had done in 1945, Truman appointed a committee to give him a recommendation. Named on November 19, 1949, it consisted of Dean Acheson, David Lilienthal, and Louis Johnson. The first two detested Johnson, who heartily reciprocated their feelings; Acheson and Lilienthal preserved their friendship, but found themselves in disagreement. The committee proceeded fitfully into January 1950, its principals meeting only twice, its staff work dragging. In the meantime, news of the debate leaked to the public. Numerous politicians, editorialists, and nuclear physicists vented their opinions. On January 5, 1950, at his first press conference of the year, a reporter asked Truman about reports that he would make a decision by February 15. His answer: "I have no comment to make on that." At press conferences on January 19 and 27, there were more questions. Newspapers were filled with stories about the issue, scenarios of impending doom, and accounts of varying accuracy about what was going on inside the administration.

Out of public sight, numerous actors bypassed the special committee. Eminent scientific advisers made their views known on both sides of the issue. General Omar D. Bradley, a soldier Truman much admired, pressed the case for production on behalf of the Joint Chiefs of Staff. No elected politician of any significance was prepared to go to the barricades to defend a negative decision. Senator Brien McMahon, who subsequently would position himself publicly as an emotional advocate of nuclear disarmament, sent Truman a long secret letter arguing that the country had no choice. Still, to assent was a terrible prospect. Was there some chance that if the United States openly renounced the hydrogen bomb, the Soviet Union would follow suit? The great nuclear physicists Enrico Fermi and I. I. Rabi thought it was worth a try. But even if the USSR agreed, was verification possible?[44]

Finally, on January 31, the Acheson-Lilienthal-Johnson committee produced a report that coupled a decision to go ahead with an admonition for "a reexamination of our objectives in peace and war." Lilienthal, who already had decided to leave the government, signed it reluctantly. The three men went to the White House at once, using an appointment that Johnson previously had scheduled for himself. Truman's mind, they discovered, was already made up; he wanted only a final verification that the USSR had the capability to embark on a similar program. Politely but pointedly, he cut short Lilienthal's statement of his personal reservations.

The United States should never use these weapons, he said in remarks aimed primarily at Lilienthal; the country's whole purpose was peace. Yet they had to be made because of the way the Russians were behaving. And there had been so much talk in Congress and everywhere; people had become excited. There was no alternative. As Truman signed an understated two-paragraph press release, he told Lilienthal and the others that he recalled a meeting regarding Greece. At that time, everybody had predicted the end of the world if the United States extended aid; but it had, and the world had not come to an end. It would be the same this time.[45]

Reaction from congressional leaders, opinion shapers, and other influentials was heavily positive. According to the Gallup Poll, the public supported his decision four to one.[46] Critics among nuclear scientists and the intelligentsia disagreed. They were convinced that Truman had made an expedient decision in ignorance of the potential holocaust he might be setting in motion. Many believed that if the United States had displayed self-restraint, so would have the Soviet Union. But years later, Andrei Sakharov, one of the Soviet Union's leading nuclear scientists before he turned to political dissent, asserted that nothing could have stopped Stalin from going ahead: "Any US move toward abandoning or suspending work on a thermonuclear weapon would have been perceived either as a cunning, deceitful maneuver, or as evidence of stupidity or weakness." David Holloway, the most thorough historian of the Soviet nuclear program, agrees.[47]

Truman had taken the measure of his adversary. He also had expressed once again the determined optimism about the future that had been a part of his emotional and intellectual makeup from the time he was old enough to think about such things. His statements about the horror of the atomic bomb make it clear that, as much as any man, he understood what a super bomb could do. Nonetheless, he was convinced that building it was the only way to protect America and that in the end the rational instincts of mankind would prevail. Above all, one thing was certain. This was a decision, quite unlike that involving Hiroshima and Nagasaki, that Harry Truman had looked in the face and made on his own.

VII

It tells much about Truman's outlook and priorities that he found another decision much more difficult. The new Soviet nuclear capability appeared to portend a fundamental shift in the balance of military power and demand a thorough reassessment of Western military capabilities. Even a wholly rearmed Western Europe, bolstered by American occupation troops in West Germany and Austria, would be no match for numerically greater Soviet forces. On April 7, 1950, Truman received a National Security Council paper that addressed the problem.

Truman had authorized NSC-68 the same day he decided to move ahead on the hydrogen bomb. The moving spirit behind the paper was Paul Nitze, the new head of the State Department Policy Planning Staff. Like his boss, Dean Acheson, Nitze was intelligent, capable, pragmatic, blunt, and, most of all, oriented toward the view that usable power was the primary resource of diplomacy. Nitze produced a document that eschewed the complexity, literary elegance, and nuance customarily employed by Nitze's predecessor, George Kennan. It depicted a world divided between forces of freedom and totalitarianism. It asserted that an aggressive, expansionist USSR had the initiative and could be deterred only by a vast expansion of conventional American military power. NSC-68 dismayed Kennan. Its analysis was undeniably simplistic, but its basic recommendations are not so easily dismissed.

Samuel Wells's judgment that NSC-68 was a "shrill but timely" alarm seems a fair estimate. Acheson, with his amiable contempt for the cloistered nature of the academic seminar, would later write, "The task of a public officer seeking to explain and gain support for a major policy is not that of the writer of a doctoral thesis."[48] NSC-68 was aimed at only one person: Harry Truman. Acheson clearly believed that it was necessary, if not to hit the president over the head with a metaphorical two-by-four, at least to be direct, uncomplicated, and unqualified. The document was written with Truman's psychology in mind and designed to persuade him to overcome stubborn, deeply held objections to big defense budgets. Most remarkably, it was primarily a State Department project. State, having initiated and written it, obtained support from the military chiefs and the civilian service secretaries, leaving Louis Johnson isolated and practically compelled to sign it.

In order to appeal to Truman and make Johnson's opposition harder, NSC-68 advanced no cost estimates, a calculated omission that Acheson later defended as dictated by the need to avoid cumbersome, excessive special pleading by every agency or department remotely connected to national security. He also admitted, however, that a section on cost would have "prevented any recommendation to the President."[49]

Truman's reaction was hypercautious. He was not reflexively receptive to NSC-68's analytical framework. His official rhetoric certainly contains the idea that the USSR was bent on world conquest and motivated by ideological zeal; but his basic impulses, expressed in less-prepared comments that reflected his reading of history, ran in other directions. At times, he stressed the malevolence of Soviet leadership. Moreover, he typically saw the USSR as a traditional nation-state rather than an ideologically motivated revolutionary power. For a time, he liked to tell people that Soviet foreign policy actually followed an expansionist line that had been laid down in "the will of Peter the Great." (He had been misinformed by some acquaintance; no such document existed. But the concept that the myth embodied—continuity between the aims of imperial Russia and those of the USSR—could not be as easily dismissed as the testament itself.)[50]

What bothered Truman most was not so much the esoteric problem of motivation as the economic and political consequences of NSC-68. Clearly, implementation would mean a huge increase in the defense budget. Truman, having just gone through an unwanted experience of deficit financing in the 1949 recession, would have been determined to pay the new costs. But how? The document mentioned two possible ways (both positioned as inconspicuously as possible): "reduction of federal expenditures for purposes other than defense and foreign assistance" and "increased taxes."

The prospect of putting the Fair Deal on the shelf and raising taxes had to be daunting enough. Add to that the implicit admission that all the costly programs and entanglements already undertaken—postwar European relief, aid to Greece and Turkey, the Marshall Plan, NATO, European rearmament—were but a down payment on a much more expensive and protracted military buildup that could only detract from the everyday quality of life for the ordinary American. Almost every political and economic instinct within Truman recoiled from such a prescription. Was the need *really* so great and the time so short?

Truman took refuge in a tested technique. He appointed a committee to study the document, produce cost estimates, and make recommendations. July 1, 1950, was to be the deadline for initial estimates; November 1, for final cost figures. At some point during the deliberations, it became accepted that full implementation could mean an increase in defense spending from $13.5 billion to as much as $40 billion. Bureau of the Budget officials declared such a leap an absolute impossibility; Leon Keyserling, without necessarily endorsing NSC-68, said it could be done if the national interest required it.

Truman monitored the ongoing discussion carefully, with a fiscal conservatism his overriding priority. On May 23, he told Budget Director Fred Lawton, as Lawton summarized it, "to continue to raise any questions that we had on this program and that it definitely was not as large in scope as some of the people seemed to think." At this point, perhaps the president would have agreed to add a few billion dollars to defense spending, but he obviously felt no urgency about it. It seemed at least equally likely that, as David Callahan has written, NSC-68, like many policy papers, would "sink quietly from sight."[51]

VIII

China, the Soviet bomb, the H-bomb decision, the Hiss case—all tarnished the luster of what had seemed a spectacularly successful exercise in safeguarding the national security. Another blow came on February 4, when nuclear physicist Klaus Fuchs, one of the veterans of the Manhattan Project, was arrested in Great Britain and charged with having passed information about the atomic bomb to the Soviet Union. These events were bound to have an unsettling effect on Americans; having occurred under Truman and Roosevelt, they could only damage the president and his administration. Hiss, thanks to Acheson's impetuous statement and Truman's "red herring" remark of August 1948, became an embarrassment out of any proportion to the crime for which he had been convicted.

For all those who were unhappy with the direction of things or who wanted to score political points against Truman, Dean Acheson was the perfect target: allegedly soft on Communism, personally faithful to a traitor, possessing no political following of his own, and altogether a cliché representation of a type that in later years would be called "impudent snobs." Angry Republicans, most of them embittered isolationists, saw him as representing all the trends that had disturbed them for the past twenty years: the rise of the welfare state and big government, the dominance of an Ivy League–northeastern establishment, the embrace of a Europe they considered distant and corrupt, the "loss" of China, the specter of international Communism. He would become the focal point of a politics of revenge bent on deposing the Democrats and restoring "true Americanism" in Washington.[52]

On February 9, 1950, a wholly unexpected escalation of the already nasty offensive came from a new source. Speaking in Wheeling, West Virginia, to the Ohio County Women's Republican Club, Senator Joseph R. McCarthy of Wisconsin, declared:

> While I cannot take the time to name all of the men in the State Department who have been named as members of the Communist Party and members of a spy ring, I have here in my hand a list of 205 . . . still working and shaping the policy of the State Department.

Then McCarthy, on a weekend Lincoln Day tour, flew west. He told reporters at the Denver airport that he had a list of "207 bad risks" and declared in Salt Lake City that he "had the names of 57 card-carrying members of the Communist party." From Reno, he sent a telegram to Truman demanding the immediate opening of State Department loyalty files, warning, "Failure on your part to do so will label the Democratic Party as being the bedfellow of international Communism."[53]

What little Truman knew of McCarthy before this weekend would have been unfavorable. During the 5 percenter hearings, the senator had been a nasty questioner of Harry Vaughan and had made snide remarks about Bess. In 1946, McCarthy, waging a demagogic campaign, had defeated the president's respected old friend Robert La Follette, Jr. He exhibited almost every characteristic that offended Truman in a public servant. He was an intemperate boozer, an ill-informed loudmouth, a collector of thinly disguised payoffs from narrow special interests, a troublemaker who managed to offend his senatorial colleagues on a bipartisan basis—the antithesis of the ideal senator in almost every respect.

When McCarthy's telegram was put in front of him, the president drafted a response declaring that the people of Wisconsin must be extremely sorry to have him as a senator, that he was dishonest, insolent, and "not even fit to have a hand in the operation of the Government of the United States." Prudence, whether generated internally or externally, then reigned; the retort was filed away.[54]

What did one do about McCarthy? The State Department issued a statement denying his charges. At a press conference on February 16, Truman declared, "There was not a word of truth in what the Senator said." At that point, there was considerable reason to expect that that would be the end of the controversy. McCarthy had no standing in the Senate, had provided no documentation for his charges, and surely would behave like numerous other Republicans guilty of rhetorical excess in the past. Having fired a few shots, he would back off; the whole flurry would be forgotten in a few weeks.[55]

The expectation was reasonable. McCarthy probably had not intended to touch off a national controversy speaking to a West Virginia women's club. In a matter of days, he had talked about the State Department employing 205 or 207 suspect individuals of some sort, 57 card-carrying Communists, 81 security risks—and had submitted none of his lists to either the administration or the newspapers. How could he be taken seriously?

Yet somehow he not only endured, but seemed to prosper. He never made his lists public. But he began to dribble out a few names, each calling for an investigation that kept him at the center of the Washington scene. On the Hill, the Democrats set up a special subcommittee of the Senate Foreign Relations Committee for the task. It was chaired by Millard Tydings of Maryland, a Democrat who combined hard-edged ability and a political killer instinct with apparently impeccable conservative and anti-Communist credentials. Tydings, who had not been afraid to buck Franklin Roosevelt, had nothing but contempt for McCarthy and was determined to bring him down.

McCarthy's names were preposterous; a few had at most a slight tinge of pink about them. Dorothy Kenyon was a minor member of the American delegation to the United Nations and not even a Foreign Service official. She admitted having belonged to, and resigned from, a number of Popular Front organizations ten years or so in the past, denounced the Soviet Union, and thoroughly cowed the Republican members. Ambassador-at-Large Philip Jessup, who had sporadically been accused of complicity in the loss of China, produced testimonial letters from Generals Marshall and Eisenhower. As David Oshinsky has put it, he "bludgeoned the committee with evidence of his strong anti-Communism."

Other accusations were equally pathetic. Harlow Shapley and Frederick Schumann may have been fellow travelers, but they never had been employed by the State Department. Esther Brunauer, Gustavo Duran, and Haldore Hanson were minor figures against whom no credible evidence existed. John Stewart Service, a career employee of some significance, had leaked some of his classified memoranda on China to the fellow-traveling editor of *Amerasia* magazine in 1945, but had been adjudged not a security risk in three separate loyalty board hearings.

That left Owen Lattimore, a Johns Hopkins professor of Asian politics and sometime consultant to the State Department. McCarthy called him the top Soviet espionage agent in the United States and declared that he would stand or fall on the accusation. By any rational standard, he should have fallen like a ton of bricks. By March 30, 1950, McCarthy himself was admitting, "I have perhaps placed too much stress on the question of whether or not he has been an espionage agent." Yet the show went on into June, one case after another lamely presented, the Democrats unable to bring the hearings to closure. However insubstantial his charges, McCarthy was a shrewd, instinctive demagogue; he spoke to emotions, not to investigative reason. The country as a whole was jittery and uncertain; the Republican right was receptive to charges against the administration; the partisans of Nationalist China were eager for scapegoats. McCarthyism—the term made its way into public discourse that spring—had nothing to do with rationality.

McCarthy remained a force through the spring of 1950 because the Republican right supported him viscerally. Republican moderates were loath to denounce him squarely. Eight of them, led by Margaret Chase Smith of Maine, issued a "declaration of conscience" criticizing McCarthy, but they did so on narrow grounds and without mentioning him by name. They engaged in no follow up; later most of them actually supported one or another of the charges he would make.[56] At least half the Republicans in the Senate actively cheered McCarthy on, including the titular leader Wherry and the de facto leader Taft.

Taft now epitomized the mainstream of his party. With Vandenberg fading, his voice had become far more influential on foreign policy issues. And he was running for the 1952 Republican nomination. A highly educated patrician who might normally have been repelled by McCarthy, he also was a partisan, ideological Republican who had witnessed seventeen years of Democratic rule leading, as he saw it, toward socialist authoritarianism and dangerous, costly entanglements with Europe. From this side of his identity, he found McCarthy compelling and in the end irresistible. "Senator Taft amazed me by admitting publicly . . . that he was egging McCarthy on," Drew Pearson wrote in his diary on March 21. Here, as in so many other respects, "Mr. Republican" was a truly representative figure for his party.[57]

Even so, how far could McCarthy go on a basis of partisan emotion and multiple unsubstantial accusations? The temper tantrum he represented should exhaust itself. Truman and his advisers made a conscious decision not to overreact to his charges and thereby magnify their importance. Thus the president made no major declarations, but neither did he pass up opportunities to tell the world what he thought of McCarthy:

> March 30 [press conference]
> I think that the greatest asset that the Kremlin has is Senator McCarthy.

> April 13 [press conference]
> Mr. President, Senator Taft said this week that you had libeled Senator McCarthy. Would you care to make any comment?
>
> Do you think that is possible? [laughter]
> May we quote that?
> Yes.

> May 4 [press conference]
> Mr. President, will you give us your reaction to McCarthy's description of General Marshall as incompetent?
>
> I have no comment to make on anything McCarthy may say. It isn't worth commenting.[58]

In the Senate, the Tydings investigation moved with infuriating slowness, dealing with one charge after another, examining loyalty investigation files to which Truman reluctantly provided access, and coping with incessant obstructionism by McCarthy himself. Determined to go on the attack, Tydings recruited a few colleagues to criticize McCarthy on the floor of the Senate. The most damaging blow came from Truman's old friend, Dennis Chavez of New Mexico, who as a centrist party man and a Catholic could not easily be impugned. By late June, the Tydings subcommittee staff was getting ready to write a report that would undoubtedly discredit McCarthy and gain at least some support from the more moderate Vandenberg Republicans. There seemed to be cause for optimism.[59]

IX

On Saturday June 24, Truman boarded the presidential airplane, the *Independence*, for a short hop to Baltimore. He made a speech dedicating the new Friendship Airport, and then went on to Missouri. Early that morning, he had written a short letter to Ambassador Stanley Woodward: "I'm going home from Baltimore to see Bess, Margie and my brother and sister, oversee some fence building—not political—order a new roof on the farmhouse and tell some politicians to go to hell. A grand visit—I hope?"[60]

Bess, Madge Wallace, and Margaret were in Independence for an extended summer stay. Once again, Truman and his wife would be separated on their wedding anniversary, which was the coming Wednesday; but at least they could be together for an early observance. The plane touched down at 2:00 P.M., Central Standard Time; in an hour or so, the president was back home at 219 North Delaware, looking forward to a relaxed weekend. His nephew Fred stopped by with his family for a visit. At 6:30, the Trumans and Mrs. Wallace sat down to dinner. Afterward, they all went out on the recently enlarged and screened-in back porch; they chatted, as Margaret recalled, "about everything and nothing in particular."

They had just come back inside when the phone rang. It was 9:20 P.M. Dean Acheson was on the line. It appeared, he said, that the North Korean government had launched a major attack against South Korea.[61]

30

"We've Got to Stop the Sons of Bitches": Korea: The Downward Spiral Begins, June 25, 1950–April 11, 1951

A decade or so after the event, Truman told a television producer that it would not be possible to do an extended show on the decision to fight in Korea. He had taken Acheson's first call on Saturday night, and then had waited overnight for a definitive report. Acheson had called again on Sunday to inform him that the attack was a full-scale invasion. He had said at once, "Dean, we've got to stop the sons of bitches no matter what." The decision had taken about ten seconds, and that was all there was to it.[1] A nice story that carried at least a poetic truth in its description of Truman's reaction, the recollection diminished what was in reality a careful and solemn deliberative process.

The Korean War confronted Truman with the most serious international crisis of his presidency. It wholly rearranged the priorities of his administration, consigned the Fair Deal to limbo, left his presidency in tatters, and did grave damage to his morale. At the end of June 1950, however, it seemed that he had made the only decision possible. Few believed that he was at the beginning of a downward spiral.

II

Through the night in Washington, Acheson, Dean Rusk (now assistant secretary for Far Eastern affairs), and other Department of State officials had monitored the Korean situation. At 3:00 A.M. on Sunday, June 25, the United States formally requested a meeting of the United Nations Security Council. Through the morning, the news continued to be bad. Acting reflexively, Acheson, Rusk, and their associates began to package a decision for the president, one that would mesh perfectly with his temperament.

Back in Missouri, the Trumans went through all the motions of a normal family weekend. Bess and Margaret attended church services. Harry went out to the farm at Grandview, visited with Vivian, and inspected a new electric milking machine. After returning to Independence, he had Assistant Press Secretary Eben Ayers tell reporters that he was concerned but not alarmed about the military action in Korea. Then Acheson's second call came at 12:45 P.M. The UN Security Council was already in session. The secretary recommended an immediate return to Washington.

Truman moved quickly. An hour and a half later, his plane was in the air. As he recalled his thoughts a few years later, they were of the appeasement that had been the prelude to World War II and the necessity for strong action now. He sent Acheson a directive to assemble an evening meeting of top national security officials. Landing at National Airport at 7:15 P.M., he proceeded directly to Blair House. The Security Council, acting with unaccustomed speed in the absence of a boycotting Soviet delegation, had condemned the North Korean invasion and demanded an immediate withdrawal. Already, the issue had broadened from the national interest in South Korea to the problem of whether and how to support the United Nations.[2]

At Blair House, the president met with Acheson, Louis Johnson (himself just off a plane from an inspection trip to the Far East), Chairman of the Joint Chiefs of Staff General Omar D. Bradley, and ten other officials. There was no debate on fundamental issues. Acheson began with a series of recommendations, all of which Truman accepted. Clearly foreshadowing the involvement of American armed forces, they included the resupply of the South Korean army, the use of American air power against the invaders, consideration of further steps, and the deployment of the Seventh Fleet to bar any military action against or from Formosa. The time had come, General Bradley declared, to draw the line. Admiral Forrest Sherman was blunt: the Russians did not want war, he believed, but if they did they could have it. The situation offered the United States a "valuable opportunity" for action. Korea had to be defended because Communist control would create a serious strategic threat to Japan.

Acheson's recommendation on Formosa took on special meaning because Johnson had returned from Tokyo with a memorandum from Far Eastern commander General Douglas MacArthur. It urged protection of Formosa, which MacArthur described as a strategic asset of unique importance, with a critical geopolitical location and potential as an air base that would be the equivalent of ten to twenty aircraft carriers. The

argument was reasonably persuasive, but no one at the meeting was prepared to back MacArthur to the hilt or even to give him great discretion
in reacting to the Korean situation. The Seventh Fleet would provide a
shield without making an irrevocable commitment.

Truman then listed a series of actions to be taken: dispatch of a
military survey group to Korea and elements of the Pacific fleet to Japan,
preparation of contingency plans "to wipe out all Soviet air bases in the
Far East," and estimates of where the next Soviet strike might come. He
was not yet ready, he declared, to make MacArthur the supreme commander of a military effort in Korea. The United States was "working
entirely for the United Nations" and would be prepared to take further
action if UN orders should be flouted.[3]

The Blair House meeting established the tone and assumptions of
the councils that followed: recollections of appeasement in the 1930s, a
determination to stand and fight, and a sense that the whole operation
had been planned in Moscow. The reaction was overly simple, but it
pervaded the Foreign Service. From the American embassy in Paris, Chip
Bohlen—careful, experienced, cautious—telegraphed George Kennan on
June 26 that the attack appeared to be "a very clear case of typical Stalin
methods whereby he initiates action not formally and directly involving
the Soviet Union which he can and will press to the full if only weakness
is encountered." If at all possible, he concluded, the United States should
respond with "the strongest and most vigorous countermeasures."[4]

We know today that the initiative for the invasion came from North
Korean dictator Kim Il Sung, who predicted a near-instant victory, abet-
ted by a revolutionary uprising in the south. Kim's plan nevertheless required approval by Stalin, who may have seen it as a safe, limited probe
of American intentions. Always cautious, Stalin made it clear that if the
North Koreans ran into trouble, they would have to rely on their Chinese comrades for major ground support. He would, however, provide
supply assistance and, after the fall of 1950, air support, behaving very
much in the way Bohlen had expected.[5]

For the United States, the importance of South Korea in the larger
scheme of things might seem murky. Admiral Sherman's argument that a
unified Communist Korea would critically threaten Japan cannot be taken
seriously. For Truman, his major advisers, leading Foreign Service officers, and many European diplomats, the character of the aggression gave
Korea a new, worldwide significance. "You may be sure that all Europeans to say nothing of the Asiatics are watching to see what the United States
will do," Bohlen declared. From the United States embassy in Moscow,
Ambassador Alan Kirk telegraphed that the entire world was focusing on
American reactions and that a failure to act in South Korea's defense would
likely lead many Asian states to undertake a "fundamental reconsideration of [their] orientation" in the Cold War. Averell Harriman, just returned from Europe, advised the president "that the people there had been
gravely concerned lest we fail to meet the challenge."[6]

If these signals simply confirmed the instincts of Truman, Acheson, and others in Washington, they were nonetheless powerful cues to action. If such attitudes were so broadly held in the Western world, was it not likely that they had equal credence in the Communist sphere? South Korea, on June 24 a tiny country of scant significance, suddenly loomed large as a widely understood test of American resolve. "Korea is the Greece of the Far East," Truman told George Elsey on June 26. "If we just stand by, they'll move into Iran and they'll take over the whole Middle East. There's no telling what they'll do, if we don't put up a fight now." In this and other ways, Melvyn Leffler is correct in his assertion that "from the onset of the crisis, Truman's concerns were of a global nature."[7]

III

Despite his later telling of it, the president was not impetuous—far from it. He met with advisers several times in the next five days, examining the situation with caution, exploring options, and moving toward full-scale military intervention with great reluctance. Early on, he had to confront the probability that a commitment to Korea would require mobilization of elements of the National Guard and the reserves. He had done everything he could for five years to prevent this kind of situation, he told his advisory group on the evening of June 26. "I don't want to go to war," he said despairingly.[8]

But neither did he want to let down the United Nations or undermine America's credibility and strategic position in the world. Since almost no one in the American national security apparatus or in European chanceries believed that the USSR was planning a full-scale war, he thought any military action could be limited. The United States atomic stockpile was approaching 500 bombs; 264 aircraft were capable of delivering them. The Soviet atomic position was comparable to America's at the beginning of 1947. The industrial strength of the United States still dwarfed that of the Soviet Union. Despite the overwhelming numerical superiority of its ground forces, the Soviet Union would face destruction in a general war. From Truman down, American leaders bet that Stalin and his Kremlin colleagues would be rational.[9]

As the South Korean army disintegrated under the onslaught of a better-equipped and better-trained foe, a decision for full intervention became unavoidable. On June 27, Truman informed congressional leaders that the United States was committed to the defense of South Korea and would do so with air and naval support; that evening, the UN Security Council, acting under American leadership, called on members to provide military forces to repel the North Korean aggression. At a press conference on June 29, Truman talked of cooperating with the United Nations "to suppress a bandit raid." When a reporter asked him if the effort might be called a "police action," he replied with an easy carelessness, "Yes. That is exactly what it amounts to."[10]

Suppression of bandits. Police action. Such phrases sounded a lot better than "war" and gave Truman an inner reassurance about his course. When he met with congressional leaders on the morning of June 30 to brief them on the sending of ground forces, he was curiously tentative. As George Elsey summarized it, Truman declared that the nation had not yet "committed any troops to actual combat and that our present plan was just to send base troops to Pusan to keep communications and supply lines open." The White House press release, emphasizing air and naval operations, vaguely concluded that "General MacArthur has been authorized to use certain supporting ground units."[11]

Of course, a promise of blood, sweat, and tears in a struggle against North Korea would have been more than a bit hyperbolic. Truman hoped for a quick resolution, and neither he nor his advisers wanted to enmesh Soviet prestige in the situation. One senses, however, a degree of reluctance to face the possible consequences of the commitment and discerns the hope that the United States could fight a quick, dirty little war in Asia without much pain or political disruption at home.

An ominous subtheme ran through the June 30 meeting. Senate Minority Leader Kenneth Wherry, as Elsey described it, "arose, addressed the President as though he were on the Senate Floor, and wanted to know if the President was going to advise the Congress before he sent ground troops into Korea." Truman responded, "I just had to act as Commander-in-Chief, and I did." If there should be a real emergency or a need for large-scale action, he said, he would tell Congress about it. Twice more, Wherry pressed the point. The message was clear enough: the congressional Republicans were not prepared to argue with Truman's decisions— yet. But Wherry's behavior was not encouraging about the prospects for a Capitol Hill debate.[12]

For the moment, the decision to intervene was vastly popular, greeted almost with a sense of relief in the United States and throughout the Western world. No Republican of significance opposed it. From Albany, Thomas Dewey declared his support. On the floor of the Senate, Robert A. Taft—grudgingly, ungraciously, demanding both Acheson's resignation and a congressional vote—said that he would back a declaration of war against North Korea. The Norwegian ambassador, Wilhelm Munthe de Morgenstierne, went to the Department of State to tell Dean Acheson that "he remembered no event which had stirred such unanimous acclaim." Acheson recorded his response to Morgenstierne's assertion that it had been a great moment in history: "I said I thought it was a turning-point in history."[13]

Whether a decision *against* intervention would have been overwhelmingly unpopular is less certain, especially once the dust had settled and it had become clear that dominoes were not falling throughout Asia and Europe. Could Truman have exhibited resolve in other ways? There are no easy answers to these questions. He had done what almost every observer at the time considered the right thing; he had the nation and the non-Communist world behind him. These considerations suggest that the consequences of doing nothing might have been less happy than the "reevaluationists" of the Korean conflict like to believe.[14]

What then of Truman's option not to ask for a declaration of war or its equivalent? The early signs of what might be called adversarial support from Wherry and Taft probably had something to do with it. The Republicans would give him their backing only after ventilating every mistake and failure in American Far Eastern policy, thoroughly trashing his Department of State, and attempting to force Acheson's resignation. Truman asked Acheson for an opinion. The secretary, who understood the probabilities well, met at Blair House with the president, a few cabinet members, military officials, Harriman (who had just been designated special assistant to the president for national security), and Senate Majority Leader Scott Lucas. Acheson recommended a presidential report to be delivered to a joint session of Congress. A resolution in support of American action in Korea could then be introduced by friendly members of Congress.

Lucas, already battered to ineffectiveness in the Eighty-first Congress and facing a tough reelection campaign, observed that Congress was in recess and would not be back for a week. The resolution would pass, he believed, but debate on it might take another week. He displayed no enthusiasm for a long go-round with Wherry, Taft, and like-minded members of the opposition. The proposed resolution was never introduced.[15]

Acheson, with some exaggeration, later assumed unapologetic responsibility for the decision not to seek a functional declaration of war. Actually, it was fully consistent with all of Truman's instincts and reflected the broad view of executive power he had developed from the time Andrew Jackson had been his boyhood hero. A year later, George Elsey commented, "It is quite certain that the President would never have asked for a resolution." A chief executive with a different conception of his constitutional authority would have overruled his advisers, gone to Capitol Hill, endured the debate, and gotten congressional approval.[16]

Probably it was a mistake not to do so, but hardly the enormous error often discerned by retrospective critics. Had the war been brought to a conclusion in November, the president would have been a national hero and the quibbles of congressional adversaries would have been ridiculed. As it was, he became the visible father of a failure; to assume that one or more congressional resolutions would have protected him from his enemies is to wander into a historical theater of the absurd.

IV

The exhilaration of decision and the acclaim of most of the Western world quickly ran up hard and bloodily against reality. The North Koreans, whatever one might call them, were not "bandits." Very well trained, spearheaded by the latest and best Soviet armor, they had cut through the poorly equipped South Korean forces, although not quite with the ease Kim Il Sung had expected. If foredoomed, the South Korean resistance held up long enough to allow for action by the United Nations and for American intervention under its aegis. The first American troops thrown in from Japan on July 1 were ill prepared. Lightly armed, not in combat trim, accustomed to easy occupation duty, they were expendables capable only of delaying an unopposed advance.

Under the command of Major General William F. Dean, units of the Twenty-fourth Division vainly attempted to stop the North Koreans on July 18 at Taejon, ninety miles south of Seoul. Outnumbered, outgunned, they held on for two days, buying time for American reinforcements to land at the southeastern port of Pusan. Dean shouldered a bazooka and went out with antitank squads. At the end of the second day, he ordered the shattered remnants of his forces to retreat. He would not be seen again until September 1953, when he emerged from a North Korean POW camp. Truman would call the defense of Tajeon "one of the finest rear-guard actions in military history." It was also a cruel defeat, endowed with some dignity by the courage of men plucked from a comfortable life and thrown into a war in which they could not prevail.[17]

As the enemy advanced inexorably during the latter half of July, the American forces faced the prospect of a Dunkirk. By the end of the month, the Americans were in a quasi-stabilized "defensive perimeter" hardly bigger than an extended beachhead around Pusan. On July 29, the United States Army commander in Korea, Lieutenant General Walton Walker, issued a "stand or die" order. Throughout August, as supplies and reinforcements came in from Japan and the United States, his men hung on. By mid-August, the Pusan perimeter was stabilized, and it was possible to plan a counteroffensive.[18]

From the beginning of the conflict, MacArthur had contemplated an amphibious invasion at Inchon, halfway up the western side of the Korean peninsula and within easy striking distance of Seoul. The risks, as General Matthew B. Ridgway summarized them seventeen years later, were obvious: rapid thirty-foot tides, shore guns on apparently impregnable Wolmi-do Island dominating a narrow and twisting channel that likely was studded with mines, the possibility of a typhoon. It was easy to imagine a failed attack, rapidly ebbing tides, landing craft filled with combat troops stuck in mudflats and systematically destroyed by land-based artillery. The operation would strip the nation's combat infantry reserve down to one division, the Eighty-second Airborne. A pessimistic Pentagon odds maker declared it a 5,000 to 1 gamble.

Yet MacArthur was insistent and irresistibly persuasive. Seventy years old, he was the most fabled of living American generals. He had been chief of staff of the army from 1930 to 1935, when his nominal superiors in the chain of command had been junior officers. He had led the American resistance against the Japanese at Bataan, had commanded the first

American offensives of the Pacific war, had waded ashore at Leyte to liberate the Philippines, and had ruled Japan since 1945 like a Western shogun. He was revered both by the people he had conquered and by most Americans. He wore five stars on his shoulders. If he seemed often to behave like a Caesar, well perhaps he had earned the right, and perhaps he had a measure of Caesar's genius.

As David McCullough asserts, Truman may also deserve some credit for letting Inchon go forward; but his role was fundamentally passive. He allowed MacArthur to conceive the counterstrike, let the Joint Chiefs review it, kept himself informed, and avoided interference. As with the use of the atomic bomb in 1945, the process was one in which he allowed a prestigious, nearly veto-proof committee to agree on a plan, and then declined to veto it. Given the circumstances, this was model civilian leadership.[19]

At dawn on September 15, 1950, an American invasion force hit stunned North Korean defenders at Inchon. Destroyers and cruisers fired a devastating barrage that silenced enemy gun emplacements on Wolmido. Marine Corsair fighter planes strafed the beach. At 6:30 A.M., a Marine battalion landed, encountered only light resistance, and took the island in less than an hour. American troops and matériel poured ashore, sweeping through the city of Inchon toward Seoul. On September 16, an American tank unit took Kimpo airport, outside the city. Far to the south, General Walker attacked from Pusan. By September 28, North Korean resistance in the vast, ruined city of Seoul ended. In less than two weeks, a shattered enemy was in full retreat.

The superlatives used to describe the Inchon operation—daring, courageous, magnificent, and the like—have been a bit overdone. It was, after all, undertaken against a small country with no effective air or naval power. Never a 5,000 to 1 gamble, never likely to result in the loss of more than a battalion and a destroyer or two if everything had gone wrong, it nevertheless had been a risky venture capped with an unexpected total victory. The success left MacArthur with a sense of his own infallibility—and convinced his superiors that he was right.

It was in a mood of ebullience and impending triumph that Truman and his advisers turned to their next critical decision: whether to cross the thirty-eighth parallel. The correct course was not as clear as retrospective critics would imply. Would it not invite another North Korean attack to stop at the parallel? Was it not consistent with the spirit of the United Nations to crush an outlaw aggressor, unify the Korean people, and hold free elections? Did it make sense to bring successful military operations to a screeching halt along an arbitrary and indefensible line?

But how would the Soviet Union or China react to the possibility of an ally and client state being wiped off the map? From early on in the war, Communist China had been vocal about probable intervention if American troops marched to its border. Yet the State Department was curiously unconcerned, even though the chance of Chinese involvement had popped up in discussions and planning documents almost from the beginning of the war. The Policy Planning Staff was cautious, but not opposed to Korean unification; the department's top Far Eastern officials, Dean Rusk and John Allison, were strong advocates. Almost all officials seemed to think Chinese intervention an abstract possibility rather than a looming terrifying prospect, a matter that could somehow be managed should it happen. In Korea itself, MacArthur, strongly backed by President Syngman Rhee, was eager to move north and unify the country.

On September 11, Truman approved NSC-81/1, which allowed for operations north of the thirty-eighth parallel and contemplated the military occupation of North Korea—*provided that neither China nor the USSR intervened in the war*. Moreover, only South Korean troops were to move all the way to the Chinese and Soviet borders in the far north. If Chinese or Soviet troops moved into North Korea, American forces were to remain south of the thirty-eighth parallel. On September 26, with no indication of Soviet or Chinese involvement, these instructions were sent to MacArthur substantially unchanged. The assumption was that the Communist world would telegraph its intentions and allow for a decent disengagement.[20]

Three days later, with Seoul taken and MacArthur ready to push north, total victory seemed in sight. The United Nations resolution had not authorized the conquest of North Korea, but American officials were not inclined to take the issue back to the Security Council. It seemed natural and easier, to take action rather than to precipitate a messy debate that inevitably would delay an advance and give the enemy a chance to regroup. "We want you to feel unhampered tactically and strategically to proceed north of 38th parallel," Secretary of Defense George Marshall, telegraphed MacArthur. "Evident desire is not to be confronted with necessity of a vote on passage of 38th parallel, rather to find you have found it militarily necessary to do so."[21]

V

Throughout the first half of October, State Department officials planned for the military occupation of the north and the rebuilding of Korea. Yet the fear of Chinese intervention kept appearing despite efforts to exorcise it. At the beginning of the month, Chinese premier Jou En-lai gave the Indian ambassador in Peking a strong warning of intervention if the United States crossed the parallel. The Indian government passed it along to United States ambassador Loy Henderson. Chinese newspapers and Communist party announcements contained similar statements. In mid-October, the Burmese ambassador received a similar communication.

Later on, the administration would argue that it had been misled on intervention by General MacArthur, but he was only a small part of the problem. In Washington, a few midlevel area specialists took the Chinese warnings seriously. The higher ranks at State engaged in wholesale denial.

Dean Acheson set a tone in a meeting with British representatives at the United Nations. Yes, he admitted, there was a risk, but there had been one from the beginning; one must not display hesitation and timidity. What was needed was firm and courageous action, not fright at what probably was a Chinese bluff.[22]

The declaration was vintage Acheson—and a telling indication of the source of his rapport with Truman. Whether as unsuccessful business-man or victorious politician, Truman had never been daunted by risk. Both men demanded movement and accepted gambles. Neither suffi-ciently appreciated the magnitude of this particular one. They shared this unfortunate characteristic with Douglas MacArthur.

On October 13, Truman left Washington for a personal meeting with MacArthur at Wake Island. His motivations appear to have been highly mixed: a desire to meet his Far Eastern commander for the first time, discuss the Korean situation with him face-to-face, and, perhaps most important, secure a good photo opportunity with an American hero against a backdrop of unfolding victory. The upcoming midterm elec-tions—crucial to the future of Truman's Fair Deal—were less than a month away. It appears certain that worry about Chinese intervention was not uppermost in the president's mind. Years later, Charles Murphy described the meeting as primarily a "public relations stunt" with which the president was uncomfortable. Actually, Truman embraced the idea with considerable enthusiasm.[23]

True, he possessed a long-held skepticism about the general's osten-tatious self-promotion and high opinion of himself. In addition, he had been infuriated by MacArthur's open lobbying for an alliance with Nationalist China and the establishment of American bases on Formosa. Toward the end of July, MacArthur had made the equivalent of a state visit to the island, hailed Chiang Kai-shek, and virtually promoted an alliance with him while State Department representatives looked on helplessly. On August 25, he sent a message to the national convention of the Veterans of Foreign Wars extolling the importance of Formosa and lambasting "the threadbare ar-gument by those who advocate appeasement and defeatism in the Pacific that if we defend Formosa we alienate continental Asia."

The declaration was a scarcely disguised slap at Acheson, the State Department Asian specialists, and, by extension, Truman himself. The president, "lips white and compressed" in Acheson's recollection, met the next day with his national security group. He told Secretary of De-fense Johnson to order MacArthur to withdraw the statement. Johnson reluctantly transmitted the directive, and the general complied—after his statement had been reproduced in newspapers and magazines around the world. Truman, as he recalled it, toyed with the idea of relieving MacArthur of his command, but decided against it. As it was, he flew across the Pacific with a jaundiced view of the general.[24]

There would be no confrontation. The Formosa incident was in the past, and triumph was in the air; the dominant tone of the meeting was

cordial banality. Years later, nursing an understandable dislike of
MacArthur, an aging Truman told interviewers that the general had made
him wait and had insulted him by wearing sloppy attire; he, in turn, had
privately reprimanded him. None of this happened. In fact, very little
transpired to justify a 1,900-mile trip for the commanding general of a
major military operation and a 7,500-mile journey for a busy president.

Wake was a tiny island, hardly more than an extended landing strip,
ignored as useless until it had become valuable as a naval and air base
earlier in the century. Its outmanned garrison had offered a gallant resistance to Japan before being overwhelmed in the days following Pearl
Harbor. Truman first saw it gleaming in the sunrise. The press plane
landed first, then another carrying aides and advisers: Averell Harriman
from the White House, Dean Rusk and Philip Jessup from State, Secretary of the Army Frank Pace, General Omar D. Bradley, Admiral Arthur
Radford. (Acheson, who did not attend, had told Truman that while
MacArthur had many of the attributes of a foreign sovereign, and could
be quite as difficult as any, it seemed unwise to treat him as one.) Neither Secretary of Defense Marshall nor his deputy, Robert Lovett, was
along. At about 6:30 A.M., the *Independence* touched down.[25]

MacArthur, who had arrived the previous evening, was waiting. He
asked Harriman what the meeting was about and was told that it had been
called to discuss the consolidation of his brilliant military victory. Quite
possibly relieved, the general was at the foot of the landing steps when
Truman emerged. They greeted each other cordially, and then got into a
dilapidated Chevrolet and rode to a Quonset hut, where they conferred
privately for upward of half an hour. There is no transcript of their talk
but both recounted that goodwill was abundant from the outset.
MacArthur apologized for his message to the Veterans of Foreign Wars.
Truman told him to think no more of it. The general, Truman recalled
six weeks later, said he had been made a "chump" by politicians in the
past, that he had no political ambitions, "that the victory was won in Korea
. . . and that the Chinese Communists would not attack." By January
1951, he could transfer a division of troops from Korea to Europe.

Truman's old pattern of hostility and aggression from afar, geniality
up close, reasserted itself. In his *Memoirs*, he described MacArthur as
"stimulating and interesting," the conversation as "very friendly—I might
say much more so than I had expected." Some years later, MacArthur,
remembering Truman's "courtesy . . . good humor . . . engaging personality . . . [and] quick and witty tongue," would remark, "I liked him from
the start." At about 7:30, they emerged, no longer wary of each other,
and proceeded to a primitive, cinder-block building down the beach for
the plenary conference.[26]

The full meeting was equally friendly and remarkably short, lasting
less than two hours. Bradley, Harriman, Jessup, and Rusk took notes;
Jessup's secretary, Vernice Anderson, seated in the next room behind a
half-open door, jotted down a transcript in shorthand. Much of the dis-

cussion was about the postwar reconstruction of Korea. A fair amount of time was devoted to the prospects for the Pacific area after Korea, with general concern and unanimous head shaking over the lackluster performance of the French in Indochina. About halfway through the conference, Truman asked the question everyone would remember: "What are the chances for Chinese or Soviet interference?"

"Very little," MacArthur replied. An early intervention would have been decisive, but now "if the Chinese tried to get down to Pyongyang there would be the greatest slaughter." As for the Russians, they had no available troops; their air force, while capable, was probably no match for American air power; and any effort to give air support to the Chinese probably would fail for lack of training and coordination. No one probed the general's judgment. Dean Rusk slipped a note to the president suggesting that he slow the meeting down. The president wrote a reply: "Hell, no! I want to get out of here before we get into trouble." At 9:12, the formal conference came to an end. Informal discussions continued for another hour and a half between individual staff people.

MacArthur, anxious to return to Japan before night fell in Tokyo, asked to be excused from a planned luncheon. General Bradley thought that Truman might have been offended; if so, the president did not show it. At the airstrip, Truman awarded MacArthur a Distinguished Service Medal, citing his "vision, judgment, indomitable will, gallantry, and tenacity." The general, plainly elated, was soon off to Tokyo. A communiqué issued to the press stressed the "very complete unanimity of view" shared by the two principals. Shortly thereafter, Truman boarded the *Independence*. *New York Times* newsman Anthony Leviero thought he looked "like an insurance salesman who had at last signed up an important prospect while [MacArthur] appeared dubious over the extent of the coverage."[27]

On October 17, Truman delivered a major speech in San Francisco, full of praise for MacArthur, underscoring their complete accord, and calling on the nation to continue its mission of world leadership. At a press conference in Washington, two days later, he denied that he and MacArthur were in disagreement on Formosa or anything else: "He is loyal to the President in his foreign policy, which I . . . *wish* a lot of your papers were."[28]

Assertion did not, of course, make something so. Still, as American troops rushed up the Korean peninsula toward apparent total victory, neither Truman nor MacArthur wished to search for any continuing disagreements. Thus when MacArthur told the Joint Chiefs that military necessity required him to disregard the prohibition against sending non-Korean forces into the northeastern provinces, no countermand came back from the Pentagon.[29] If Truman unmistakably wished to garb himself in the general's mystique, MacArthur had no wish to challenge his commander to the breaking point. Both contemplated the glow of success and the verdict of history—the tough little president who had possessed the courage to challenge aggression, the military genius who had vanquished the aggressors. Such seemed the certain outcome as trees shed their brightly colored leaves in the warm Washington fall.

In fact, the Chinese Communists, unremittingly suspicious of American intentions, had planned from the beginning to intervene if North Korean troops were thrown back and might well have done so even if American troops had not moved close to Manchuria. In late October, news reports indicated that Chinese troops had moved into the fighting in northern Korea. In Washington, CIA estimates were cautious. They pegged the number of Chinese combatants at 15,000 to 20,000 on November 1, and 30,000 to 40,000 a week later. The Chinese also invaded Tibet and appeared to be establishing a presence in northern Indochina. Intelligence analysts and State Department policy intellectuals struggled with little success to discern the intentions of a nation with which they had no direct contact.[30]

On November 5, two days before the midterm elections, news reports quoted MacArthur's latest public communiqué: "A new and fresh army now faces us, backed up by a possibility of large alien reserves and adequate supplies within easy reach of the enemy but beyond the limits of our present sphere of military action." Privately, he requested permission to bomb the bridges over the Yalu River; with misgivings, Truman granted it.[31]

VI

Even when a quick victory had been in sight, it was clear that Korea had changed the tone of American politics in ways that would have been hard to imagine at the beginning of 1950. Then Truman had been able to hope that his Fair Deal could be resurrected and pushed along by liberal gains in the fall elections. Instead, by late October, he presided over a beleaguered administration, reorganized to end internal high-level discord and pushed by events toward the sharply higher military spending he had wanted to avoid. He faced an electorate obsessed with anti-Communism, willing to listen to the wildest fulminations of Senator McCarthy, and eager to strike out against the Red menace at home. To the extent that voters focused on other issues, the most salient of these were inflation, restrictions on consumption, fear of shortages, and all the irritations that presumably had been left behind with the end of World War II reconversion. For anyone who remembered the politics of 1945 and 1946, the prospect was far from reassuring.

The first and most important act of administrative reorganization was the dismissal of Louis Johnson as secretary of defense and the naming of George Marshall to replace him. In the minds of some observers, Johnson was a convenient scapegoat for American unpreparedness in Korea; however, Truman never would have fired him for aggressively pursuing a presidential mandate. By mid-1950, the obstreperous West Virginian had alienated the president and many other administration figures. As Truman saw it two days after he forced Johnson's resignation, "Potomac fever and a pathological condition" had led to the secretary's demise. Johnson had thrown his weight around arrogantly, alienating most members of the cabinet and the White House, conspiring semipublicly against Dean Acheson, and dealing with Republican right-wingers whom Truman considered "enemy Senators."

Truman met privately with Marshall, won his assent to return to the administration, and then slowly and painfully worked up the will to fire Johnson. By his own account, the president had made up his mind and worked out the arrangement with Marshall by September 1, but he "had to talk to the nation that night and . . . postponed the terrible chore until Monday—and then another week." On September 9, Associated Press correspondent Tony Vaccaro, acting on a tip from Democratic National Chairman William Boyle, reported that Johnson was soon to leave the administration. Would the faithful Boyle have talked to the press without Truman's prompting? Truman wrote of the Vaccaro story in a diary memorandum: "Where it came from no one can find out." His choice of words seems revealing.

On September 11, the president and Johnson faced each other. Truman told him bluntly that he would have to quit. "He was unable to talk," the president recalled. "I've never felt so uncomfortable." When Johnson asked for a couple of days, Truman agreed. The next afternoon, they met again. Johnson's deputy secretary, the tough and always reliable Steve Early, acting in cooperation with the White House, had drafted a letter of resignation that presented Johnson's departure as a patriotic act designed to make way for the unifying presence of Marshall. "He looked like he had been beaten," Truman wrote. He begged the president to change his mind, wept openly when Truman commanded him to sign, and admitted that "he didn't think I'd make him do it."

Truman had summoned the fortitude to do what had to be done for the good of the administration and the country. Turning again to the man whom he most admired, he recalled that thirty-two years earlier on September 12, he had waited with his regiment in reserve as the Saint-Mihiel offensive had pushed the Germans back. Marshall then had been one of Pershing's staff officers. Now "General Marshall and I with positions reversed are still working to save the country and our way of life."[32]

Regrettably, Marshall, ably backstopped by Robert Lovett, was no longer capable of unifying the country. The Republican right now saw him not as a man above politics, but as the secretary of state who had set the stage for the fall of China and the eventual abandonment of all of Asia. Senator Taft, voting against him, called the appointment a "reaffirmation of the tragic policy of this administration in encouraging Chinese communism which brought on the Korean War." Senator William Jenner was blunter: Marshall had been "eager to play the role of a front man for traitors" and was "a living lie." By then, Inchon had occurred, and presumably the United States was moving toward victory. Taft, Jenner, and others had demonstrated that even total triumph would leave no warm glow.[33]

Jenner's rhetoric was so extreme that it was not widely accepted within his own party. Nevertheless, it was a telling measure of the way in which McCarthyite anti-Communism was growing as a force in American politics. As the congressional campaign heated up during the fall, Republican senators attacked Secretary of the Interior Oscar Chapman and Secretary of Agriculture Charles Brannan as pro-Communist. Truman's old friend and informal adviser Max Lowenthal, who had just published a book critical of the FBI, found himself before the House Committee on Un-American Activities. Chapman and Brannan easily refuted the accusations against them. Lowenthal brought along Burton K. Wheeler as his counsel and administered a drubbing to his interrogators. Truman privately blamed the Republican National Committee for the attack on Chapman; whatever the source, an atmosphere in which cabinet officers and presidential confidants had to defend themselves against charges of disloyalty showed the sorry state of the nation's political health.[34]

The most powerful indicator of the new climate was an internal security bill that emerged in the late summer from the Senate Judiciary Committee, controlled by Truman's old enemy Pat McCarran. Based on House-approved legislation sponsored by Republicans Karl Mundt of South Dakota and Richard Nixon of California, the McCarran bill was a blunderbuss document that amalgamated the reasonable with the authoritarian and the unworkable. It required the Department of Justice to register all members of the Communist party; prepare a list of Communist-front organizations; accumulate information about their finances, officials, and membership lists; and see to it that all their literature was prominently labeled "Communist." It barred Communists from employment by the federal government or its defense contractors and prohibited entry into the United States by aliens who advocated a totalitarian form of government.

A group of moderate and liberal Democrats, groping for an alternative that would demonstrate their anti-Communist bona fides, had introduced legislation providing for the summary arrest and internment of suspected subversives during periods of national emergency. After the Senate rejected it, Senate Majority Leader Scott Lucas, mindful of his precarious reelection prospects, moved to add it to McCarran's bill. Only seven liberal Democrats dissented.

The McCarran bill awakened converging emotions within Truman: the personal enmity he long had felt toward the Nevada senator, an intense partisanship rooted in his reading of history, and, above all, a strongly felt Jeffersonian libertarianism that he too long had suppressed in the interests of politics. His administration was not without sin in the eyes of civil libertarians long aghast at the mismanaged loyalty program and the prosecutions of leading Communists. But on this bill, the president—

implicitly comparing himself with Jefferson in 1798 and encouraged in that direction by key aides—was determined to draw the line. He would not, he had told them for months, sign "a sedition bill."

On September 22, he released a long veto message, which he had sent with a personal appeal for consideration to every member of Congress. Its most memorable line asserted: "In a free country, we punish men for the crimes they commit, but never for the opinions they have." Both houses of Congress overrode the veto by enormous majorities; only forty-eight representatives and ten senators voted with the president.[35]

As it turned out, the McCarran Act never amounted to much. Portions of it were ruled unconstitutional; other provisions were ineffective. Only a handful of unfortunate individuals were harmed by it. Still, the conflict of principle was basic. Truman had hurt himself politically, but he could feel with pride that he done the right thing.

VII

The impact of the war at home added to Truman's troubles. Americans had struggled through the Depression, World War II, postwar shortages, inflation, and the 1949 recession. At last, it seemed, they had begun to enjoy the benefits of an emerging prosperity based on widespread abundance and mass consumption. The involvement in Korea posed a new threat to a long-sought stability and comfort. Many people, drawing on the experience of World War II, prepared unrealistically for consumer shortages. The price of staple goods shot up to meet the hysterical demand of hoarders who purchased 100-pound bags of sugar and cases of ground coffee. During the first six months of the war, the Consumer Price Index increased at an annualized rate of 10 percent, with the wholesale prices of most basic commodities escalating much more sharply.[36]

Of course, inflationary pressures were based on more than consumer panic. Even before Chinese intervention, the logic of Korea pointed toward some degree of mobilization; the days of declining defense budgets were clearly over. At the end of September, Truman approved NSC-68, thus committing the nation to a defense buildup of wartime proportions. Although the document itself remained classified and known to only a few Washington insiders, its consequences were manifest to ordinary Americans in a number of ways: supplemental appropriations for defense, requests for higher taxes, and credit restrictions that cut into sales of automobiles and other big-ticket durable goods while pushing marginal buyers out of the residential real-estate market.

In September, Congress passed the Defense Production Act of 1950, giving the president broad, World War II–style authority to allocate strategic raw materials toward defense production and establish wage–price controls. After Truman signed it, he spoke to the nation and soberly outlined the sacrifices that were to come. Confirmed in his own instincts by the advice of Leon Keyserling, he refused to establish a comprehensive economic control system. He hoped that minimal government interference would facilitate the sort of growth needed to accommodate increased defense demands without taking too much from the civilian economy. Nonetheless, a message of at least some deprivation and inconvenience was unavoidable. Inevitably, much of the public read it through the magnifying lenses of the last wartime experience.[37]

It was against this discouraging backdrop that the Democrats fought out the 1950 elections. Republicans assailed the Democrats as responsible for the fall of China and the Korean War; they asserted to various degrees that Truman, Acheson, and their congressional supporters were Communists or pinks or softheaded dupes of the Communist conspiracy. In Illinois, Everett Dirksen went after Scott Lucas as a backer of the "mistakes and blunders" that had led to the fighting in Asia. In California, Richard Nixon lambasted Helen Gahagan Douglas as a "pink lady" who had assisted in the advance of international Communism. Joe McCarthy traveled across the country, speaking conspicuously for one chosen candidate after another. Concentrating his efforts against Millard Tydings, the Maryland senator who had led the effort to discredit him, he distributed a faked photo depicting Tydings in friendly conversation with Communist leader Earl Browder.[38]

Against this offensive, individual Democratic candidates struggled as best they could with no leadership from Truman, who was effectively prevented from campaigning by his role as a wartime leader. Privately, he fully reciprocated the venomous hostility of the Republicans. "I think the antics of McCarthy, Taft and Wherry have had as much as any other one thing to do with bringing on the communist attack in Korea," he wrote to Clinton Anderson in August.[39]

With his emotions running so strong, it was probably just as well that the president was detached from the campaign. His participation consisted of a press conference statement in support of Douglas and one fiery speech the weekend before the election. In the latter, he extolled the Democrats as the party of prosperity and social reform, while lashing out at the "awful mudslinging campaign" of the opposition. It was as if he and his advisers assumed that the issues of 1948 could be replayed effectively. In fact, the simple impact of war had been harmful, and the first indications of Chinese intervention made matters much worse. As the president voted in Independence on November 7 (just three weeks after the Wake Island meeting and six days after the failed attempt on his life), victory in the Far East suddenly was much less a sure thing, a protracted war with China a distinct possibility. Some twenty years later, Richard Bolling, then a young congressman, recalled, "We could feel the ground slipping out from under us."[40]

The returns were devastating. Dirksen and Nixon won handily; Tydings went down, defeated by a near-unknown; Senate Democratic Whip Francis Myers lost in Pennsylvania; reliable administration backer Elbert Thomas was deprived of his seat in Utah. In all, the Republicans picked up five seats in the Senate and twenty-eight in the House. Numerically, the Democratic losses were routine by the normal standards of midterm elections; qualitatively and symbolically, they amounted to a blow between the eyes. McCarthy and McCarthyism loomed ominously large in many of the losses.

McCarthy's impact actually seems to have been less than it appeared. As is always the case, local issues and controversies played a considerable role in many contests; and some of McCarthy's most vocal critics—William Benton, Brien McMahon, Herbert Lehman, Thomas Hennings—prevailed in their contests. Even so, the results spelled an end to any prospect of establishing a liberal congressional coalition responsive to the Fair Deal. Writing to Averell Harriman the following week, Arthur Schlesinger, Jr., commented, "I do not see how the elections can be honestly interpreted except as a triumph for McCarthyism."

And few could doubt that they amounted to a rebuff for the president himself. Truman had begun the day by casting his ballot in Independence; he ended it on the *Williamsburg* somewhere on the Chesapeake Bay. Tired and discouraged, he tossed down one bourbon after another. It was the only occasion on which George Elsey recalled seeing him unmistakably showing the effects of too much to drink. At a National Security Council meeting three weeks later, he accused his most vehement critics of preferring to see the country go down rather than the administration succeed.[41]

VIII

However disappointing the results of the election, victory in Korea still seemed within grasp. On November 7, all contact with Chinese troops, who had fought hard and effectively, ceased. Given the low estimates of their strength, one might assume that they either were exhausted or had recrossed the Yalu River. If their purpose had been to deliver a message to the United Nations forces, it was fatally misunderstood. On November 9, MacArthur responded to indications from the Joint Chiefs that he might be ordered to stop short of the Yalu. To do so, he declared in magisterial fashion, would be abject appeasement.

In retrospect, it is clear that MacArthur should have been told to back off from the northern tier of North Korean provinces, consolidate his forces, unify his divided command on the Korean peninsula, and establish strong defenses for the onslaught to come. Instead, although the earlier surprise had exposed his intelligence as unreliable, he planned a final offensive that would end the war. At the last moment, the Joint Chiefs sent MacArthur a suggestion, not an order, that he should stop short of the Yalu. He dismissed it brusquely, and no further insistence came from Washington. As Acheson had told British diplomats several weeks earlier, leaders did not shrink from risk taking.

MacArthur began the offensive—one that he declared would bring

American troops "home for Christmas"—on November 24. In less than forty-eight hours, it was apparent that the UN forces faced reverses. On November 28, MacArthur told Washington that he faced "an entirely new war" against 250,000 enemy troops, a challenge "that our present strength of force is not sufficient to meet." By December 1, the most optimistic strategy was a retreat to the waist of the peninsula. It was uncertain whether the reeling UN forces could avoid destruction.[42]

Truman inadvertently made things worse with another of his snap replies at a press conference on November 30. Was use of the atomic bomb under active consideration? "There has always been active consideration of its use. I don't want to see it used." Would its use require United Nations authorization? "The military commander in the field will have charge of the use of the weapons, as he always has."[43]

Truman's remarks were palpably at variance with his emotional revulsion against atomic weapons. Neither the State Department nor the Joint Chiefs would recommend using them. Even MacArthur, his later advocacy notwithstanding, never requested them when he had command responsibility.[44]

Understandably, however, the comment sent shock waves through Europe and brought British prime minister Clement Attlee to Washington for urgent consultations. During the talks that followed, Charlie Ross's sudden death hit Truman hard and added a dimension of personal tragedy to the disaster unfolding in Korea. Attlee had come to Washington as a surrogate for other Western European governments, now fearful of a full-scale war between China and the United States and neglect of the Atlantic alliance. Truman, bolstered by Acheson, was determined to hold on in Korea. The logic of alliance compelled some reassurance to Europe; the locus of national power ensured that it would be on American terms.

In fact, neither Truman nor Acheson had considered for a moment abandoning the priority they always had given to Western Europe. But in a way that the impoverished, overextended British found difficult to comprehend, the two men understood that the United States had the capability to fight a limited war in the Far East while strengthening NATO. They correctly realized, moreover, that politics and public opinion in the United States would not tolerate a liquidation of Asian commitments for the sake of a single-minded concentration on the Atlantic alliance.

The talks, more tense than the circumspect diplomatic summaries indicate, began with Truman setting the tone early in his first encounter with Attlee. The United States would not run out on its obligations, even though they were hard to meet. Responding to Attlee's assertion that China was nationalistic and independent of Moscow, Truman declared that whatever the long-run prospects, the Chinese regime was behaving like a Soviet satellite. The only way to meet Communism was to eliminate it. If Korea went, then Indochina, Hong Kong, and Malaya would follow. He wanted to avoid all-out war with China and was not opposed to negotiation, although he doubted the prospects for success. But most of all, he would not voluntarily abandon South Korean allies to the horrors that would await them at the hands of their enemies.[45]

Three days later, Truman and Attlee faced the issue that had impelled the visit in the first place. Contrary to the sensational news accounts of his press conference remarks, Truman assured Attlee that only he could authorize use of the bomb, had not done so, and fully understood the gravity of such a decision. Furthermore, he appreciated that the United States and Britain had always been partners in atomic weaponry; he would not consider use of the weapon without consulting the United Kingdom.

Attlee, pressing harder than was wise, then asked whether this promise could be put in writing. One imagines Truman bristling in a fashion impossible to convey in Philip Jessup's memorandum of the conversation. No, it would not be put in writing, the president replied. If a man's word wasn't any good, it wasn't made any better by writing it down.

Jessup's account concludes: "The Prime Minister expressed his thanks."[46]

Although Attlee's counsel of a withdrawal from Korea was rebuffed, he had made a point that the administration could not ignore. The Europeans were nervous and required strong reassurance; American commitments on the Asian mainland would have to be tightly limited. The result was to write even larger a policy that Truman and Acheson already favored: the United States should hold on in Korea with the goal of ending the war as quickly as possible and without an abject defeat.

In the weeks after the prime minister returned to Britain, American forces in Korea continued to be pushed back. On December 15, speaking somberly to the nation on radio and television, Truman announced that he would declare a state of national emergency. "Our homes, our Nation, all the things we believe in, are in great danger," he declared. The future of civilization depended on American action and resolve. The country would have to accept cutbacks in civilian production, credit controls, higher taxes, and reduced nonmilitary expenditures. It would once again have a World War II–style bureaucracy controlling prices and wages, coordinating defense production, and establishing manpower policy. Appeasement was not the road to peace, he concluded. "The American people have always met danger with courage and determination. I am confident we will do that now, and with God's help we shall keep our freedom."[47]

Over the next few weeks, the military dispatches from Korea brought only more news of retreat and disaster. In the northeast, embattled marines, encircled and cut off, fought their way through ice and snow to evacuation at the port of Hungnam. Major General Oliver P. Smith seemed to epitomize their fighting spirit and briefly captured the nation's imagination when he insisted, "We're just attacking in another direction."[48] On December 22, as the Chinese tide rolled inexorably south, General Walker, the top UN commander in the field, was killed in a jeep accident. When his replacement, General Matthew B. Ridgway, arrived in Taegu on December 26, the enemy was at the thirty-eighth parallel and grouping for an advance on Seoul, which would be abandoned by UN forces on January 3.

IX

MacArthur obviously had displayed bad judgment in launching his "home for Christmas" offensive. In later years, Ridgway would compare it with Custer's at the Little Big Horn. But there had been no questioning from Washington at the time, and Truman was inordinately supportive after the disaster. We could not cause the commanding general in the field to lose face before the enemy, he told the NSC on November 28. At a press conference two days later, he gave MacArthur's actions a blanket endorsement. "He's in very serious trouble," the president wrote in his diary on December 2. "We must get him out of it."[49]

MacArthur neither understood nor reciprocated Truman's solicitude. Well aware that he was a living legend, long accustomed to ignoring Washington, and doubtless psychologically wounded by the defeat inflicted on his command, he denied his own recklessness. Responding to a query from *New York Times* journalist Arthur Krock, he falsely declared that he had received no admonitions from the Joint Chiefs to move toward the Yalu with care. A furious Robert Lovett told Acheson that MacArthur was rewriting history for posterity and labeled the answer "false and mendacious."[50] Increasingly, the general demanded full freedom of action and unlimited resources for all-out retaliation against the Chinese.

At the end of December, he recommended full-scale military action against China: a coastal blockade, intensive bombing of industrial areas, support of Nationalist military operations from Formosa. Truman responded with a long, and in MacArthur's view galling, letter on January 13, 1951. Clearly written by a committee, it contained a long list of objectives that had been served by the UN action in Korea, stressed the importance of maintaining wide international support for the effort, and observed that a final decision about Korea had to be made in the context of the main threat from the Soviet Union. The letter concluded, "The entire nation is grateful for your splendid leadership."[51]

By then, Ridgway was establishing a sound defense line fifty miles south of Seoul. A masterful tactician, a combat-hardened paratrooper, and a charismatic leader, he emerged as a superb field commander. Fifty-five years old but still a fighting man to the core, he established his headquarters close to the front and customarily wore battle gear, including at least one grenade strapped to his chest. (The grenades were not for show, he told a reporter. "They were purely utilitarian.")[52]

At the end of January, he took the offensive, pushing north, smashing a Chinese counteroffensive, and retaking Seoul on March 15. As the advancing UN forces approached the thirty-eighth parallel, European pressures and doubts among military leaders about the wisdom of another drive toward the Yalu combined to establish a wide consensus within the administration that the time had come to push for a negotiated peace that would reestablish the approximate boundaries of June 1950.

Ridgway's drive north both refuted MacArthur's earlier despairing counsel and left him frustrated and bitter at the prospect of a negotiated peace without victory. On March 15, he told a United Press journalist that a line anywhere in the vicinity of the parallel was untenable and that the forces necessary to maintain it would support a drive to the Yalu and the unification of Korea. On March 24, apprised of a planned presidential statement that would propose negotiations to end the war, MacArthur released his own declaration. It proclaimed victory in South Korea, described Chinese military capabilities as hopelessly inferior, threatened an expansion of the war beyond Korea, and offered to meet with the enemy commander-in-chief to arrange what would have amounted to unconditional surrender.

In Washington, Acheson, Lovett, and the Joint Chiefs all reacted in a state of helpless, thunderstruck anger. Truman had to scrap his own statement. In principle, the general should have been dismissed, but his ultimatum had resonated with the public. Instead, the Joint Chiefs sent him a curt reminder that he was not to make statements without prior clearance.

The final blow came on April 5. House Minority Leader Joe Martin read into the *Congressional Record* MacArthur's response to a letter he had sent the general. Martin had called for the establishment of "a second Asiatic front" by the Chinese Nationalists. MacArthur indicated hearty agreement, calling for "maximum counterforce" against the enemy and proclaiming that the loss of Asia would make the fall of Europe inevitable. He concluded, "There is no substitute for victory."[53]

Truman had reacted to the earlier provocations with the stiffest of upper lips, speaking carefully and unresponsively when asked about them by the press. He later wrote that he had made up his mind to fire MacArthur after the March 24 incident, but in fact he still wanted to avoid a final confrontation. With the letter to Martin, however, the general had ventured directly into politics. Truman wrote in his diary, "This looks like the last straw. Rank insubordination."

Yet the president moved slowly and deliberately. Over the next few days, he held a series of meetings, primarily with Acheson, Marshall, Harriman, and General Bradley. All supported dismissal. He consulted also with political friends and congressional leaders: Vice President Barkley, Speaker Rayburn, Senate Majority Leader Ernest McFarland, House Majority Leader John McCormack, Chief Justice Vinson, Secretary of the Treasury John Snyder. The politicians, fully cognizant of the upheaval that would follow, were mixed in their reactions. Truman bucked himself up by drawing a historical analogy to the long-running conflict between Abraham Lincoln and his insubordinate general, George McClellan. On Monday morning, April 9, he made his final decision.

On April 10, he directed Bradley to send the orders relieving MacArthur of all his commands to Secretary of the Army Frank Pace, who was on an inspection trip in Korea; Pace would fly to Tokyo and deliver them to MacArthur personally. That evening, Bradley called to say that there had been a leak and MacArthur's recall would likely soon be in the news. Truman told him to transmit the orders directly to MacArthur through urgent military channels. The new press secretary, Joseph Short, prepared a press release and called a press conference for 1:00 A.M. on April 11. Truman was in bed, perhaps even asleep, when the biggest story of 1951 hit the wires.

Talking with Merle Miller ten years later, Truman remembered his feelings, if not the precise details, passionately. As he recalled it, Bradley had told him that if MacArthur knew he was going to be fired, he probably would resign. Eyes flashing, the old man said he had told Bradley, "The son of a bitch isn't going to resign on me, *I want him fired.*"[54]

31

"It Isn't Polls or Public Opinion Alone of the Moment that Counts. It Is Right and Wrong, and Leadership": Fighting the Tide, 1951–1952

"Quite an explosion. Was expected but I had to act. Telegrams and letters of abuse by the dozens." So Truman wrote in his diary after the dismissal of Douglas MacArthur. His numbers understated an enormous negative reaction that at first was nearly universal. The storm eventually subsided, but it left his standing at a low point from which it never fully recovered.

For more than a year after relieving MacArthur, Truman fought one rearguard battle after another against forces he could barely contain, not quite prevailing but managing to avoid the destruction of his policies and his administration. His resources were slim. To a majority of Americans, he was once again the unprepossessing little man unable to explain his course and in over his head. Intense personal convictions sustained him: his Democratic partisanship, his not unjustified opinion that his enemies were fools and rogues, and, especially, his stubborn conviction that he was right.

Speaking with William Hillman in late 1951 or early 1952, he laid out his feelings eloquently:

I wonder how far Moses would have gone if he had taken a poll in Egypt?

What would Jesus Christ have preached if He had taken a poll in the land of Israel?

Where would the Reformation have gone if Martin Luther had taken a poll?

It isn't polls or public opinion alone of the moment that counts. It is right and wrong, and leadership—men with fortitude, honesty and a belief in the right that make epochs in the history of the world.[1]

II

Joe McCarthy's reaction to the firing of MacArthur was probably the most scurrilous: "The son of a bitch should be impeached," he told reporters as he shaved in a hotel bathroom in Milwaukee. He went on to imply that the president had probably made his decision while drunk on "bourbon and Benedictine." (Truman may have taken as the unkindest cut of all the allegation that he would drink such a spirituous combination.)[2]

Many other initial comments were about as vitriolic:

SENATOR WILLIAM JENNER OF INDIANA: This country today is in the hands of a secret inner coterie which is directed by agents of the Soviet Union.

REPRESENTATIVE O. K. ARMSTRONG OF MISSOURI: The greatest victory for the Communists since the fall of China.

SENATOR RICHARD NIXON OF CALIFORNIA: The happiest group in the country will be the Communists and their stooges.

CHICAGO TRIBUNE: President Truman must be impeached and convicted. . . . [H]e is unfit, morally and mentally, for his high office.[3]

As bitter and partisan as they were, such remarks were close to the first impulses of millions of thunderstruck Americans. Ordinary people knew, or thought they knew, two things about MacArthur: he was a military leader without peer, and he wanted victory instead of bloody stalemate. Some partisan Democrats took the news with as much outrage as the Republicans; many others were dismayed and demoralized.

At the first and most urgent level, Truman had run up against the MacArthur mystique. Few Americans understood that the hero of World War II in the Pacific had a mixed and erratic military record; most gave him far more credit than he deserved for victory over Japan. A consummate master of public relations, MacArthur possessed unparalleled skill at claiming credit for victories while evading blame for defeats. The president, despite his private skepticism, had played the general's game by allowing him to rule Japan for five years, ostentatiously praising him, making the long journey to Wake Island to see him, and refusing to countenance any criticism of him after the disaster of November 1950. Now Truman waited, besieged in Washington, as the old hero flew back to the North American continent for the first time in fourteen years to lead the attack against him.

Truman in addition had to face a deeper and potentially more dangerous level of popular discontent. This involved befuddlement and distress at a new war, possibly the prelude to World War III, just five years after the end of the last great one. By the end of 1950, a "great debate" on American foreign policy already was under way. The argument was polarized fairly consistently between administration Democrats who supported Truman's policy of Europe-first containment, and heartland Republicans who oscillated between continental isolationism and Asia-first militance.

With Arthur Vandenberg gone, the Marshall Plan Republicans who had given so much support to the administration were in disarray, dispirited over the loss of China and the Korean setbacks, unhappy with the abrasive style of Truman and Acheson, more willing to follow natural partisan instincts. For example, Senator H. Alexander Smith of New Jersey—by background, constituency, and temperament—should have been an administration foreign policy supporter. He had backed the Truman Doctrine and the Marshall Plan. Now he talked privately and declaimed publicly about incompetence and pro-Communism in the State Department. He and many other internationalist Republicans might now go along with key aspects of administration foreign policy, but their support was considerably less certain and far more grudging than during the Vandenberg ascendancy.[4]

Many midwestern and western Republicans, heirs to a tradition of isolationism, had never been happy with Truman's diplomacy. Jenner of Indiana, Wherry of Nebraska, Dirksen of Illinois, and numerous others frequently seemed appalled by internationalism itself. Their spiritual leader was Herbert Hoover, who advocated a retreat to the Western Hemisphere. Other Republicans—Asia-firsters—emphasized the importance of the Far East and argued that America's destiny lay with the growth and democratic development of Asia, not with Europe. Whether motivated by a secularized elaboration of the nineteenth-century Protestant missionary interest or by MacArthur's geostrategic rationale, they were strongest in that part of the nation that faced the Pacific. Thus it was natural enough that the emerging leader of the Asia-firsters was William Knowland of California, tough, smart, and intensely partisan.

Somewhere closer to the isolationists and the Asia-firsters than to the Northeasterners stood Robert A. Taft, staking out a foreign policy position for his upcoming presidential candidacy. Taft co-sponsored a Senate resolution demanding congressional authorization for the dispatch of troops to Europe, displayed sympathy toward the Asia-firsters, and struck many observers as a half-hearted isolationist. As usual, he was unwilling to take a categorical position; instead, he seemed to strive for a synthesis of the diverse views within his party. His fears of militarizing the American economy and of overextending American power deserved more than a cavalier dismissal. But other of his arguments—for total victory over Communism at one point, for reduced military expenditures at another—had a way of bumping up awkwardly against each other. Tolerant of McCarthyism, he encouraged the Wisconsin senator to persevere in his attacks.[5]

Taft's militant, emotional partisanship was in many ways the mirror image of Truman's; the two men were civil toward each other but shared a reciprocal dislike that made a Vandenberg-style collaboration impossible. Acheson scarcely bothered to conceal his contempt for Taft. In part because of circumstances, but also because Truman and Acheson had been unable to provide the sort of unifying leadership furnished by Marshall and Lovett in 1947 and 1948, the bipartisan foreign policy was in tatters and the administration under attack from an angry, united Republican opposition.

Arthur Schlesinger, Jr., and others believed that a new isolationism had emerged. The new isolationists, denying international realities, emotionally recoiled from America's post–World War II position as world stabilizer and repository of liberal values. They saw bunglers or conspirators within the government as the source of the nation's troubles; they tended to look for one-shot solutions, whether preventive war or a conference with Stalin. "Until the American people reconciles itself to a future of protracted responsibilities and indefinite crisis, we will continue to have a feedback of McCarthyism," Schlesinger told Averell Harriman. "The people will continue to blame individuals for conditions for which they ought to blame history." Could Truman explain this? He was a great president, Schlesinger averred, but he did not have "the special qualities of a Churchill or a Wilson or a Roosevelt." The observation, made in the wake of the 1950 election disappointment, seemed particularly apt as MacArthur returned to America.[6]

On the evening of April 11, just one day before beginning his seventh year in the presidency, Truman went on the air to defend his policy in Korea and his dismissal of MacArthur. It had been necessary, he declared, to resist aggression. The free world had avoided the mistakes of the 1930s, taught the enemy a costly lesson, and blocked the Communist conquest of the rest of Asia. But it was important to avoid a vast conflict on that continent. "What would suit the ambitions of the Kremlin better than for our military forces to be committed to a full-scale war with China?" MacArthur had been relieved, great general though he was, because he disagreed with the fundamentals of American policy. There would be no appeasement in Korea; neither would the United States touch off a global war: "We know that we are following the great principles of peace, freedom, and justice."[7]

It was a good speech, plausible, reasoned, sincerely delivered. But prepared speeches were still not Truman's forte; he sounded awkward and defensive. Even to many of his supporters, he remained insignificant—pitted against the MacArthur legend. In the atmosphere of April 1951, only a Roosevelt could have crossed swords with the general with much hope of success—and even then the outcome would have been doubtful.

III

MacArthur's return was an amazing spectacle. Far from coming back in disgrace, the general arrived on American soil as a conquering hero. The emperor had made a farewell visit to him in Tokyo; 250,000 Japanese had lined his route to the airport. He neglected no detail in tailoring his image, right down to renaming his personal plane—formerly *SCAP* (Supreme Commander Allied Powers)—the *Bataan.* He landed in Honolulu on April 16 to the cheers of an estimated 100,000 people. His plane touched down in San Francisco at 8:30 P.M. on April 17; his motorcade to downtown crept past 500,000 well-wishers. "The only politics I have is contained in the simple phrase known well to all of you: God Bless America," he said. On April 18, he rode through the financial district in New York, showered by tons of ticker tape, hailed by millions; the parade eclipsed the celebrations of Lindbergh's flight and Eisenhower's return from Europe.[8]

Without bothering to consult the Democratic majority, Joe Martin had invited MacArthur to address Congress. The Democrats apparently never thought about refusing him the opportunity. Truman himself felt compelled to say, "I regard it as fitting that Congress bestow this honor on one of our great military men." When MacArthur stepped off his plane in Washington on April 19, he was greeted by Marshall and the Joint Chiefs, all of whom had recommended his recall. Truman sent a personal representative, General Harry Vaughan.

Someone in the White House with a knack for black humor sketched out a fanciful itinerary for the Washington visit: MacArthur wading ashore from a snorkle submarine, and then parading to the Capitol on an elephant; the beheading of General Vaughan in the Rotunda; the burning of the Constitution; the lynching of Secretary Acheson; the firing of a twenty-one-atomic-bomb salute; and 300 nude Daughters of the American Revolution leaping from the Washington Monument.[9] The actuality was, in its way, nearly as spectacular.

Possessing a gift for self-dramatization not seen in American life since the death of Franklin Roosevelt, MacArthur demonstrated the power of the politics of personality, amplified by the radio microphones and television cameras that brought his speech and his presence to untold millions of Americans. Much of the nation considered his address the most important public event since V-J Day. The general was seventy-one years old and at the end of an exhausting week; nevertheless, he was in complete command. John Spanier remembered him displaying "strength of character, deeply felt convictions, and unshakable self-confidence."

MacArthur's rhetorical and oratorical powers converged to capture the attention, imagination, and emotions of his audience. He stood for no partisan cause, he said. In "the fading twilight of life," he was motivated only by love of country and concern for the splendid fighting sons of America who had served under his command. "Why, my soldiers asked of me, surrender military advantage to an enemy in the field? [Pause] I could not answer." The administration's policy, he declared, was appeasement. There was no substitute for victory. Then, observing that his fifty-two years of military service were ended, he remembered a barracks ballad of his youth:

> "Old soldiers never die; they just fade away." And like the old soldier of that ballad, I now close my military career and just fade away—an old soldier who tried to do his duty as God gave him the light to see that duty. Good-by.[10]

The ovation was akin to an eruption; the congressional eulogies that followed were as overheated as lava from Vesuvius. Richard Rovere recalled Dewey Short as supplying the whitest heat: "We heard God speak here today, God in the flesh, the voice of God." (Short subsequently toned down his remarks a bit for the *Congressional Record*.) Other statements were only slightly less effusive. It was MacArthur's day. No member of Congress dared critize him.[11]

Nor did Truman—at least not in public. Privately, he made his case to friends and potential allies; he also planned a counteroffensive. Writing to General Eisenhower, whom he still liked and admired, he said of MacArthur, "He asked for it, and I gave it to him." As for the Republican attack on him, he told Roy Harper, "They will find they have a bear by the tail."[12]

In the beginning, the bear was not very impressive. Truman had the support of intensely partisan Democrats, ideological liberals, most leading newspapers, and many respected columnists and commentators. But these groups fell well short of a majority. What he and his supporters had to do was to unite the Democratic party as a stable base of support, and then wage a long educational campaign that would encourage a hero-worshiping public to take a skeptical second look at MacArthur. In the month before the general was cashiered, polls had shown plurality public support for ending the war at the thirty-eighth parallel. The upheaval that followed had dealt a blow to that plurality. A well-managed effort had to reestablish it.[13]

Truman rebuilt his base by quietly making peace with the southern Democrats. Even before the dismissal of MacArthur, he appears secretly to have encouraged Richard Russell of Georgia to take the Democratic leadership in the Senate. Russell, content to be the unofficial power broker in the upper chamber, declined and backed Ernest McFarland of Arizona. Senator Robert Kerr of Oklahoma emerged as the toughest and most vocal critic of MacArthur. Probably not coincidentally, Truman's old pal Mon Walgren cast the deciding vote in a Federal Power Commission ruling that in effect was an administrative enactment of the Kerr bill vetoed by Truman a year earlier.

Although the president met with the leaders of Americans for Democratic Action in May 1951 and gave them assurances of his continuing commitment to the Fair Deal and the cause of social welfare, he had little choice but to put his domestic program on the shelf. As a practical matter, such issues as civil rights, repeal of Taft-Hartley, aid to education, national health insurance, and the like were dead on Capitol Hill; they would be soft-pedaled rhetorically and administratively by a White House preoccupied with foreign policy and economic mobilization.[14]

With Press Secretary Joseph Short spearheading the effort, the White House attempted to get out its point of view in a number of ways.[15] Ironically, its most effective venue was a Republican-demanded congressional investigation. The testimony of leading defense and foreign policy officials might not match MacArthur's in eloquence and emotional appeal, but a heavily reported message repeated time and again could hammer its way into the public consciousness. The inquiry, a joint enterprise of the Senate Foreign Relations and Armed Services committees, was chaired by Russell. He barred microphones and cameras in the name of national security, an action that left the information media dependent on printed transcripts and removed the power of personal magnetism from daily newscasts. MacArthur testified first and was rebutted by Marshall, Bradley, the other Joint Chiefs, and Acheson. Subjected for three days to courteous but probing cross-examination by the Democrats, MacArthur could not gloss over the inconsistencies of his record and the dangers of his proposals.

For a month, the administration witnesses emphasized the limits of American power, the military impracticality of MacArthur's recommendations, and, above all, the risks of a wider conflict. Speaking for the Joint Chiefs of Staff, Bradley declared that MacArthur's strategy of carrying the fight to China "would involve us in the wrong war, at the wrong place, at the wrong time and with the wrong enemy." Truman himself, as during the Marshall Plan debate of 1947 and 1948, kept a low profile.[16]

The going was tough, especially for Acheson. When he concluded his long testimony, the last of the hearings, on June 9, someone asked him what he was going to do now that the ordeal was over. He replied, "I have a plan that will test my capacity for the consumption of alcohol, and if another war erupts before I finish, it must be waged without my services." Thereupon, he retired to the home of his good friend Canadian ambassador Hume Wrong and presumably faithfully adhered to his design.[17]

He could feel entitled to do so. He and the others had made their point to a public that had been excited by MacArthur, but was now ready to let him fade away. The general lived in a suite at the Waldorf-Astoria in New York for the rest of his life and served as chairman of the board of Remington-Rand. Too old to run for president, he took only occasional shots at the administration and withdrew completely from politics after 1952.

As for the great debate of early 1951, it was also effectively decided. Neither Truman nor Acheson could claim much popularity, but a weary

America accepted their foreign policy as the best available—if not without continuing anger and frustration. In October 1951, Gallup found 56 percent agreement with the proposition that Korea was a "useless war." In March 1952, 51 percent decried the involvement as a mistake. After April 1951, Truman's approval rating would never exceed 33 percent of the respondents.[18]

IV

The bitter, overheated, partisan debate that had followed MacArthur's dismissal provided yet another lease on life for McCarthyism. The casualty lists from Korea would sustain it for the remainder of Truman's tenure in the White House. To an increasingly passionate opposition, they provided proof positive that Truman and his national security advisers were not dedicated to victory in the struggle against Communism, that they were in fact soft on Communism, and that they might not be disturbed by Red victories abroad.

On May 24, 1951, McCarthy savaged Dean Acheson: "You and your criminal crowd betrayed us. . . . [Y]ou should not only resign from the State Department but you should remove yourself from this country and go to the nation for which you have been struggling and fighting so long." On June 14, the senator went after George Marshall. In a 60,000-word speech, he attacked Marshall as the central figure in "a conspiracy so immense and an infamy so black as to dwarf any previous venture in the history of man." In just two months, McCarthy had accused the president of being a drunk and his two top national security officials of being traitors.

The Marshall talk made the greatest impact. Right-wing, neoisolationist Republicans loved it. GOP moderates, mostly from the Northeast, were disturbed enough to distance themselves; a few were sharply critical. Senator Taft, as had become his established pattern, waffled. Previously beyond politics, Marshall had become just another partisan target.

He got a minimal defense from Democratic senators who in the wake of the 1950 elections were petrified by McCarthy's apparent political power. They did nothing more than walk off the floor when their Wisconsin colleague began to speak. In August, Senator William Benton—wealthy, reckless, and not committed to politics as a career—introduced a resolution to expel McCarthy from the Senate. The silence of his Democratic colleagues was as palpable as their dismay. Benton's resolution never got out of a Democratic-controlled committee.[19]

No one could accuse Truman of fear. He already had made his contempt for McCarthy part of the public record. Yet he also adopted a strategy of silence, turning down one softball question after another at press conferences. Apparently, he and Joe Short had come to believe that the president simply enhanced McCarthy's stature by replying to him. There was something to be said for that judgment, but only if some prominent

Democrat or member of the administration was engaging McCarthy. Through much of the spring and summer of 1951, about the only critics seemed to be moderate Republicans (after McCarthy had committed some special outrage) or a group of journalists and radio commentators who mostly preached to a constituency that was already anti-McCarthy.

Giving McCarthy a free-fire zone, of course, accomplished nothing. The senator went on a tear. He brushed off Benton's charges against him as typical of those that could "be found in the *Daily Worker* almost any day of the week" and undertook a campaign against State Department officials connected in one way or another with the loss of China, a move guaranteed to maximize Republican unity and draw a few renegade Democrats. His most prominent target was State Department official Philip Jessup, whom Truman routinely appointed to the American delegation to the United Nations in September 1951.

The degree of Jessup's affinity for Communism, as Edward Meade Earle reminded Senator H. Alexander Smith, might be gauged by the fact that he admired the ultra-conservative Elihu Root above all other American statesmen and had written a eulogistic biography of him. Nonetheless, a Senate Foreign Relations subcommittee declined to endorse Jessup. Smith, a northeastern moderate, joined in the opposition, claiming that he had done so not because of McCarthy, but because Jessup was "closely identified" with the administration's Far Eastern policy. Like many northeastern moderate Republicans, Smith kept McCarthy at arm's length, but could not resist the lure of the Communist issue or avoid the feeling that some symbolic protest had to be made against a policy that had gone wrong. After Congress adjourned, Truman gave Jessup a recess appointment.[20]

Although McCarthy attracted the greatest denunciation, Pat McCarran was in many respects a more effective player of the politics of anti-Communism. In addition to the fact that Truman and McCarren had long disliked each other, McCarran was the most conservative non-Southerner in the Democratic Senate delegation. Motivated by an intense revulsion against Communism that was derived in large measure from his Catholicism, he was a major booster of the Franco regime in Spain, a vociferous defender of Chiang Kai-shek, and a friend of about any right-wing dictator with anti-Communist credentials. Unbeatable in his native state of Nevada, elected to his fourth Senate term in 1950, he was a shrewd, overbearing, and angry presence who needed no favors from his president and felt not a scintilla of loyalty to his party.

Using his position as chairman of the Senate Judiciary Committee, McCarran investigated almost everyone connected with China policy. He provided what there was in the way of a case against Jessup. He also orchestrated investigations designed to discredit China hands O. Edmund Clubb, John Paton Davies, John Stuart Service, John Carter Vincent, and Owen Lattimore. He investigated the Institute of Pacific Relations, a small think tank of which Jessup had been a trustee, and depicted it as the spearhead of the conspiracy to convey China to the Communists. While not devoid of factual bases, his investigations blurred the difference between poor analysis and treason. They also laid the groundwork for prosecutions and firings of men who were guilty of nothing more than mistaken advice.

By virtue of partisan affiliation, experience, seniority, and force of personality, McCarran could make things happen. He probably really believed that there were traitors in the administration and was dedicated to exposing them. McCarthy, incapable of running a sustained, disciplined investigation, trailed along in his wake. Truman was indignant; Jessup, Davies, and Lattimore were being "persecuted," he told associates. He discovered he could do little about it.

Jessup managed to hang on, as did the presumed ringleader of the Far Eastern sellout, Dean Rusk. The others were not so lucky: Service was dismissed after having survived five loyalty investigations; Clubb, Davies, and Vincent were forced into early retirement with stains on their reputations; Lattimore became a target of the administration's own Justice Department.[21]

When McCarthy went his own way, he was less impressive, tossing out charges that, like lightning, might hit anyone. Led on by anti-Semites, he opposed the nomination of Anna Rosenberg as assistant secretary of defense, only to turn around and vote for her when his charges were demolished. In early 1952, he tossed out oblique attacks at two of Truman's White House aides, David D. Lloyd and Philleo Nash; he also impugned the loyalty of both Leon Keyserling and his wife. The charges were baseless examples of his hit-and-run tactics; yet, as in earlier instances, it seemed to make no difference that they flopped.[22]

On Capitol Hill, J. William Fulbright and Tom Hennings (neither of them up for reelection until 1956) joined Benton as frequent critics of McCarthy. Truman himself, still refusing to mention McCarthy by name, condemned Hitler-style "big lie" tactics, "hate-mongers and character assassins." His most notable speech, delivered on August 14, 1951, at an American Legion gathering, was nationally broadcast. "Everyone in Russia lives in fear of being called an *anti*-Communist," he reminded his audience. "In a dictatorship everybody lives in fear and terror of being denounced and slandered. Nobody dares stand up for his rights." Responding to a letter from Harold Ickes, several days later, he said, "The platform was half-filled with fascists and I was talking to them more than anybody else."[23]

With the American Legion speech, Truman probably hit the best tone of response to McCarthy, but it could do no more than contain him. The senator's charges, however weak, continued to attract attention. Using the technique that Richard Rovere would call the "multiple untruth," he made so many accusations that it was difficult for even the trained journalistic observer to follow them all and easy for the average citizen to assume that below all the smoke there must be some fire.[24]

A Gallup Poll taken just before Truman's American Legion speech found only 15 percent of its respondents willing to state a favorable opinion about McCarthy; 22 percent were unfavorable.[25] By establishing a tone of principled opposition, Truman helped prevent McCarthyism from becoming a mass movement. But the senator's appeal to normally Democratic Catholics was a painful problem; so was the 63 percent of the population that either did not know of McCarthy or had no firm opinion of him. His positive following was dedicated and large enough to have an impact. The way in which he spoke to the emotions and political calculations of many Republicans ensured, moreover, that he would continue to be a center of attention in Washington.

V

"Truman has made a bold and masterly attack upon the virus popularly known as McCarthyism," declared a *New Republic* editorial in April 1952. "Yet every syllable of that attack applies with equal, if not more, pertinence to his own loyalty program."[26] In fact, one could say much the same of the administration's entire approach to the Communist issue.

Truman was aware of problems with the loyalty program. Inside the White House, Counsel Charles Murphy and numerous liberals wanted to reform it. Once the election of 1950 was out of the way, the administration moved to establish a commission of impeccably respectable "wise men" to review the entire problem of dealing with challenges to internal security while protecting constitutional rights. Murphy told Truman that such a body likely would recommend repeal of the McCarran Act, denounce McCarthy, and stem the growing anti-Communist hysteria.

On January 23, 1951, Truman announced the creation of the President's Commission on Internal Security and Individual Rights, gave it the mission of considering "how a free people protect their society from subversive attack without at the same time destroying their own liberties," and specifically mandated an examination of the loyalty program. He asked Herbert Hoover to chair the body; but the old president, vehemently opposed to Truman's foreign and domestic policies, declined. Truman then turned to one of the heroes of World War II, Fleet Admiral Chester Nimitz. The other members were religious leaders, corporate executives, and a leading investment banker.[27]

Could so conservative a group have recommended meaningful reforms in the loyalty program and brought a sense of perspective to the surging fear and loathing of domestic subversion? Historians have tended to assume not; yet conservatives, even fleet admirals, are capable of appreciating libertarian values. In any event, only such a commission could get support for reform. Truman thought the chance was worth taking. His enemies feared he was right. The commission's members and staff required routine congressional legislation exempting them from conflict-of-interest laws. Pat McCarran buried the bill in the Senate Judiciary

Committee and refused to report it out despite a public plea from the president. Never able to begin work, the Nimitz Commission was formally disbanded in October.[28]

In February 1951, just a couple of weeks after Truman announced the establishment of his special commission, William Remington, a Commerce Department official, had been convicted of perjury for having denied that he once was a Communist. To many observers, the Remington affair was a reprise of the Alger Hiss case and Remington's conviction another demonstration of subversive penetration of the administration. Remington, who clearly had been a party fellow traveler in the 1930s and may have passed innocuous information to Elizabeth Bentley during World War II, had been pursued not by McCarthy and McCarran, but by numerous moderate Republicans. Dismissed from the Commerce Department by Secretary Charles Sawyer despite being cleared by the Loyalty Review Board, he had been prosecuted on flimsy charges by second- and third-level Justice Department officials whose determination to convict him exceeded their sense of ethics.

In April, apparently because of Remington's conviction, Truman was persuaded (exactly how and by whom is unclear) to approve a new standard for the dismissal of federal employees. The old wording had allowed involuntary severance from government service if "reasonable grounds exist for belief that the person involved is disloyal." The new wording, taken from the World War II security program, specified dismissal if there was "reasonable doubt" of the person's loyalty. In practice, the new grounds were easier to apply; the number of questionable dismissals increased. Truman privately agonized about these injustices, but with the blocking of the Nimitz Commission and his own signature on the revised loyalty program, he was inescapably locked into the Communist hunt.[29]

Despite his private hostility toward J. Edgar Hoover and the FBI, there was nothing Truman could do but praise the man and the institution constantly as proof that the administration was undertaking the real fight against Communism, whereas Senator McCarthy and his followers were just getting in the way and actually doing Stalin's work by discrediting genuine anti-Communists. Nor was it feasible to try to block federal prosecutions of Communist leaders, even if these were really for political advocacy rather than criminal activity.

After James McGranery became attorney general in May 1952, the Justice Department redoubled its efforts to prosecute Communists. A militant anti-Communist close to J. Edgar Hoover and leaders of the Catholic hierarchy, McGranery expanded the internal security section of the Justice Department's Criminal Division with great fanfare, gave ostentatious publicity to the appointment of Roy Cohn as a special assistant in the battle against subversion, and pushed the arrest of low-level Communist officials under the Smith Act.[30]

In the last year of his presidency, Truman did not preside over a "McCarthyite administration." The government did, however, pursue

Communists to a degree that bore little relevance to national security. (Was a legitimate purpose served by employing the Smith Act against the auto coordinator of the Communist party or the Detroit correspondent of the *Daily Worker*?) The loyalty program became less discriminate, rather than more, about firing federal employees on unsubstantiated suspicion. And despite the president's justifiable conviction that Owen Lattimore was being persecuted, in December 1952, McGranery's Justice Department would secure an indictment of him for perjury. (In 1955, all charges would be summarily dismissed by Judge Luther Youngdahl, a liberal Republican whom Truman had put on the federal bench.)

A strongly felt anti-Communism was, of course, not McCarthyism (a politics of false accusation). Still, obsessive anti-Communism was corrosive and ultimately subversive of the civil liberties that distinguished the United States from the Soviet Union. Truman genuinely appreciated the civil libertarian tradition, but he never came close to imposing his sentiments on key branches of his administration.

VI

Foreign affairs, inevitably affected by McCarthyism and the general mood of anger and frustration that afflicted American politics, continued to exact a heavy toll on Truman's attention and emotions. Despite the opening of truce talks in Korea, the war dragged on and on, butchering Chinese troops by the tens of thousands but also adding American casualties to an ever-growing list. Negotiations for peace bogged down, most notably over the issue of forced repatriation of enemy prisoners; given the certainty of death or inhumane treatment for POWs who resisted a return to Communist authority, the American position was the only moral course. It nonetheless did not prevent the war from continuing to be a running sore in American politics.

A major distraction occurred in Iran. In the spring of 1951, an anti-Western nationalist government under Mohammed Mosadeq came to power, displaced the young pro-American shah, and expropriated the nation's oil reserves, thus effectively wiping out the Anglo-Iranian Oil Company and dealing a severe blow to British interests in the Middle East. From the American perspective, an unfriendly or unstable Iran would be a serious foreign policy reversal at the very spot where Truman had first taken effective action against Soviet expansionism. Apprehension about Mosadeq vied with distaste for what Acheson and other officials considered past British exploitation of the Iranians.

That summer, Averell Harriman spent six futile weeks in Iran attempting to facilitate a settlement between the Iranians and the British. Mosadeq came to America in December. Meeting with Truman and Acheson, he requested aid, as Acheson recalled it, "to fight the British imperialists." The president and secretary made it clear that they were willing to offer developmental aid, but not to join in an anti-British alliance. The following month, January 1952, the United States cut off military aid.

Throughout the year, the administration, increasingly fearful that Iran would wind up behind the Iron Curtain, searched without success for some sort of a midcourse solution that would be acceptable to both sides. The British appeared unwilling to grasp the new realities of the emerging postcolonial world. Mosadeq seemed a whirling dervish with an uncanny knack for spinning away from an agreement just as it seemed sealed; the Americans could not quite bring themselves to believe that xenophobia and crisis were the foundations of his political position in Iran. The controversy, unresolved at the end of Truman's presidency, dealt a blow to American prestige in the Middle East and complicated relations with the British. It would be left to Eisenhower to cut through an impossible knot with a CIA-facilitated coup that would restore the shah.[31]

Largely because of the Korean War, the administration found itself giving direct military assistance to the French struggle in Indochina. Were not the French fighting a holding action against Communism? Was not Indochina another logical object of Chinese expansion? Just as the United States could not, after the beginning of the Korean War, allow Formosa to fall to Communism, neither could it be indifferent to Indochina. Nor was it possible to ignore the demands of a French ally expected to make a heavy military contribution to NATO.

In later years, Acheson freely admitted that the result of all these pressures was "a muddled hodgepodge, directed neither toward edging the French out of an effort to re-establish their colonial role, which was beyond their power, nor helping them hard enough to accomplish it." His defense was that there was no good option. To withhold aid would not have gotten the French out of Indochina; rather, it would have led them to concentrate their military efforts there to the detriment of Western European defenses. It might also have ruptured the alliance, with grave consequences not simply for the immediate defense situation, but also for the prospects of European economic integration.

As it was, the French were infuriating, always wanting more money while rejecting requests for information and turning a deaf ear to advice. By and large, they got their way. By the end of 1952, the United States was paying about 40 percent of the cost of the French military effort in Southeast Asia. The administration made a point of never offering American troops; and even at the peak of assistance, its responsibility for the ultimate American involvement in Vietnam was trivial. All the same, Truman did sanction a fateful first step.[32]

Relations with both Britain and France centered heavily on the consolidation of NATO, which had to be made into a credible alliance and military force. At the working level, this transformation moved imperceptibly in the two years after the beginning of the Korean War, stalled by multiple difficulties with shifting Western European governments, national guns-versus-butter budgetary conflicts, and especially the vexing question of whether and how to rearm West Germany. At the less tangible level of symbolism and leadership, the effort was more successful, thanks to one of Truman's more decisive acts.

In December 1950, Truman recalled General Eisenhower to active duty as NATO supreme commander. Over the next year, Eisenhower functioned effectively as a charismatic symbol of reassurance to the Europeans, his presence alone providing an inspirational guarantee of American resolve. The appointment had been so natural as to have the character of inevitability about it. Still, it displayed once again one of Truman's finest qualities: a willingness to place in key positions individuals who overshadowed him. He delighted in Eisenhower's success. "My faith in him has never wavered and never will," he wrote to Averell Harriman in late 1951.[33]

By then, the administration had taken another major step toward the establishment of a liberal world order by negotiating a peace treaty with Japan. Concluded at a conference in San Francisco in September 1951, over clamorous Soviet opposition, the pact was a triumph on many counts. The participation of John Foster Dulles and other Republicans symbolized the last major achievement of foreign policy bipartisanship under Truman. The practical result was to make a disarmed Japan a dependent ally of the United States and to provide for a continued, strategically vital American military presence there. Thus was secured the position of the United States in the northwestern Pacific.

The Eisenhower appointment aside, Truman's direct engagement in these matters was sporadic. Although important, most did not require his close involvement; in line with his administrative inclinations, the president was content to let Acheson and the State Department handle the burdens of detail and implementation. Truman, of course, remained in close touch with the major issues of American diplomacy. He met almost daily with Acheson, reserved the option of a veto over any policy, and struggled with the infuriating task of attempting to deal with the Communist world while the carnage in Korea continued on its irrational course.

His meetings with numerous foreign leaders in the last years of his presidency likewise were frequently more ceremonial and social occasions than high-level discussions in the mode of Attlee's visit in December 1950. The difference was well exemplified when Winston Churchill, once again prime minister, came to Washington in January 1952. Real, if secondary, differences still existed between the British and American viewpoints on the structure of NATO, the Middle East, and relations with Communist China. Truman participated substantively in the talks; but as Acheson recalled it, he, Anthony Eden, and their aides did most of the work, leaving the president and the prime minister to enjoy each other's company. Truman later described the occasion as "a welcome reunion with an old friend."[34]

On January 5, after a dinner on the *Williamsburg*, Churchill brought up the Potsdam Conference and admitted his initial dismay at seeing

Truman in Roosevelt's position: "I must confess, sir, I held you in very low regard then. I loathed your taking the place of Franklin Roosevelt." He paused for what seemed a very long time, and then resumed: "I misjudged you badly. Since then, you, more than any other man, have saved Western Civilization." Ten years later, one of Truman's aides recalled for Alfred Steinberg the big grin that seemed to spread across the president's face.[35]

VII

Truman's efforts to insert his preferences into policy below the highest levels were sporadic and unsuccessful. He was, for example, outraged at the joint State and Defense decision that the United States would have to normalize relations with Spain and negotiate military bases there. The Spanish regime of Francisco Franco had touched one presidential raw nerve after another. Yet in the end, facing pressure from much of organized American Catholicism and persuasion from Acheson, Marshall, and Bradley, the president had little choice but to give in. Step by step, he acquiesced in diplomatic recognition, financial aid, and negotiations for bases. "I've never been happy about sending an Ambassador to Spain," he told Acheson in August 1951, "and unless Franco changes in his treatment of citizens who do not agree with him religiously I'll be sorely tempted to break off all communication with him in spite of the defense of Europe." Truman's emotions were deeply felt, but he must have known that the threat was an empty one.[36]

For a time, he toyed with the idea of organizing the moral and religious leaders of the world behind the American crusade against Soviet Communism. "I have had special representatives call on the Patriarch of Istanbul," he wrote to Lewis Strauss, "and I myself have talked to the Chief Rabbi of Israel, as well as a great many of the religious leaders of all sects and opinions here in this country." He had, he went on, met with the chief bishop of the German Lutheran Church and with American Catholic cardinals and corresponded with the pope.[37]

But what could come of such an effort? Naturally, all of these spiritual leaders were anti-Communist; nevertheless, for obvious reasons, many of them were unlikely to attach themselves closely to American foreign policy. And what did it matter if they did? The idea of a moral-religious crusade revealed a genuine strain of Protestant idealism that coexisted uneasily in Truman's emotions with his realistic acceptance of military power. Like much fine idealism, it never established itself as a viable way of doing business in the world. It never surfaced publicly.

Another area in which Truman attempted to impose his will involved an emotional but peripheral issue. In 1949, Myron Taylor, the president's "personal representative" to the Vatican, retired from the post, originally established by Franklin Roosevelt during World War II. The Vatican insisted on his replacement by a formally accredited diplomat. After two and a half years of delay, Truman announced in October 1951 that he would nominate General Mark Clark, a Protestant and prominent Mason, as United States ambassador to the Holy See.

The delay had been encouraged by Acheson and probably underwritten by Truman's good political sense in wanting to avoid a heated church–state controversy. With his domestic program dead and the 1952 election on the horizon, the president likely saw the appointment as a worthwhile gesture to a Catholic constituency increasingly drawn to the militant anti-Communism of Joe McCarthy and like-minded Republicans. Instead, it resulted in a withering blast of criticism. Senator Tom Connally, Acheson recalled, was "incoherent with rage." With one voice, Protestant clerics denounced the idea of sending anyone, even a Protestant military hero, as an official diplomat to the Vatican. Shocked at the reaction, Clark withdrew his name.

Truman took refuge in a self-image as a proponent of religious toleration and depicted diplomatic relations with the Vatican as part of his larger international effort to organize the moral forces of religion. Furious after failing to persuade the American leader of the Episcopal Church, he wrote in his diary, "Sorry he couldn't see anything but the Totalitarian Church of Rome as . . . a menace to free religion! What a travesty!" Travesty it was—and not exclusively of Truman's making. The case for his position was respectable, but the nation was not ready for it and the votes not available in the Senate. The United States would not establish formal diplomatic relations with the Vatican until 1984.[38]

Thus the diplomatic scenario played itself out with little room for major presidential involvement. Truman's most important contributions were personnel decisions. These were top-notch: the dismissal of Johnson and the appointment of Marshall, the recall of Eisenhower, the courageous sacking of MacArthur. In September 1951, when Marshall retired, Truman replaced him as secretary of defense with Robert Lovett. Arthur Krock, a columnist not notable for praising Truman, wrote in the *New York Times* that the appointment "was one of those decisions—rare in the record of any President—by which everything good in government and nothing ill was served."[39]

Nonetheless, the fighting in Korea, the difficulties of organizing the Western alliance, the vicious McCarthyite partisanship, and the relentless obstructionism of the Soviet Union all took their toll on a harassed president. In Korea, truce talks continued off and on. The Chinese seemed impervious to horrible losses and used cease-fires as resupply opportunities. The Soviets, hoping to stymie NATO military progress, undertook their own spurious peace offensive. They called for a general East–West conference (which would include Communist China) and held out the hope of a general settlement, complete with atomic disarmament. Neither Acheson nor Truman put any stock in the offer, which resembled previous (and future) Soviet ploys. But (as in later years) the liberal wing of the Democratic party reacted in the fashion of Pavlov's dog; the Europeans also wanted a follow-up. In response, the United States put forth a disarmament proposal at the United Nations. Of course, nothing came of it.

Truman himself remained torn between two beliefs. The first had been forged at Potsdam: that one could do business with Stalin, that subsequent difficulties were a product of Politboro intransigence. The other, born of years of frustration with the USSR and more recent rage at Chinese duplicity, was that the Communists understood only force, that the time might be right to employ the coercive potential of American atomic superiority, that maybe the advocates of preventive war had half a point after all.

By early 1952, the second belief crept into Truman's private thoughts on at least a couple of occasions. For example, he wrote in his diary on January 27, 1952:

> Dealing with Communist Governments is like an honest man trying to deal with a numbers racket king or the head of a dope ring. . . .
>
> It seems to me that the proper approach now would be an ultimatum with a ten day expiration limit, informing Moscow that we intend to blockade the China coast from the Korean border to Indo-China and that we intend to destroy every military base in Manchuria, including submarine bases . . . and if there is any interference we shall eliminate any ports or cities necessary to accomplish our peaceful purposes. . . .
>
> We are tired of these phony calls for peace when there is no intention to make an honest approach to peace. . . .
>
> This means all out war. It means that Moscow, St. Petersburg, Mukden, Vladivostok, Peking, Shanghai, Port Arthur, Dairen, Odessa, Stalingrad, and every manufacturing plant in China and the Soviet Union will be eliminated.
>
> This is the final chance for the Soviet Government to decide whether it desires to survive or not.

And on May 18:

> You've broken every agreement you made at Tehran, Yalta and Potsdam. You have no morals, no honor. . . .
>
> Now do you want an end to hostilities in Korea or do you want China and Siberia destroyed? You may have one or the other, whichever you want. . . . You either accept our fair and just proposal or you will be completely destroyed.
>
> The C. in C.

Such words written by a president are disconcerting, but it seems pretty clear that Truman never seriously expected to act on them, any more than he had expected to hang John L. Lewis or A. F. Whitney in 1946. They stand as a vivid reminder of the depths of the Cold War and of Truman's personal level of frustration as his presidency approached its end.[40]

32

"This Is No Time to Yield to Selfish Interests": Economic Mobilization and Corruption, 1951–1952

The many problems and irritations of economic mobilization contributed mightily to Truman's growing frustration. After December 1950, the skeleton economic control apparatus hastily erected during the previous fall became a much larger bureaucracy, with a resemblance to that of World War II. Its mission of attempting to control prices and wages while allocating resources for the world's largest economy was nearly impossible as a practical matter. It also was politically inflammatory.

The World War II economic bureaucracy, with its serious consumer shortages and rationing, had been much more intrusive, but had found justification in an unprecedented threat to the nation's survival. Even so, popular discontent had been widespread, interest group conflict rampant, and partisan politics bitter. Truman's situation—an inconclusive "small war" and a large defense mobilization against a possible Communist offensive—was much more ambiguous. To the president and many others at the time, however, the distinction was less obvious than it is in retrospect. It was unclear whether in Korea an underprepared United States might be fighting the opening skirmish in World War III. From that perspective, a wartime economy along the lines of 1942 to 1945—enormous military production, civilian shortages, controls, high taxes, an ethos of national sacrifice—seemed absolutely necessary.

Any leader would have experienced difficulty selling such a message in the absence of an actual attack on America itself. Truman tried hard and earnestly, calling time and again for national unity in the face of a lethal threat from Soviet imperialism. Quite sincerely he believed the opposition to be a collection of self-serving scoundrels and plutocrats. "This is no time to yield to selfish interests who scorn equality of sacrifice," he declared in June 1951, while calling for continued strong economic powers.[1]

Sincerity was one thing; political consequences were another. Truman placed himself and his party in a political no-win predicament akin to that of the disastrous reconversion period. Democrats and Republicans had long practiced interest group politics in rallying their electoral coalitions and always had seen selfishness on the other side of the fence. An environment in which the government exercised extraordinary powers over the economy was sure to create especially vehement conflict; the administration would inevitably be the focus of pleading, pressure, and discontent from every interest, large and small, in American society.

Worse yet, Truman found himself presiding over a government that increasingly was caricatured as a happy hunting ground for crooks and grafters. Mobilization created opportunities for influence peddlers, fixers, crooked contractors, and tax evaders, and for dishonest pocket lining inside and outside the administration. Much the same sort of thing had gone on during World War II, but the sense of national emergency had been too great for illicit dealings with the government to be a voting-level issue. In the low-key crisis of Korea, corruption loomed larger than its actual size and was yet another blunt instrument with which an embittered opposition could attack Truman and the Democrats.

II

The pinch on ordinary Americans was small compared with that of World War II. Inflation, after surging at a double-digit rate during the first several months of the Korean conflict, leveled off to a tolerable rate of around 3 percent. Shortages, whether of consumer goods or industrial commodities, evaporated after early waves of scare buying and hoarding. Nevertheless, a pinch existed. Consumers faced credit controls that required larger down payments for home purchases and allowed only fifteen-month (raised to eighteen in mid-1951) payment schedules for new autos. Price ceilings, price rollbacks, and multiple production regulations infuriated business and agriculture. Wage ceilings kept workers behind the ascending curve of inflation. Higher taxes—necessary to control inflation and hold down a rapidly increasing federal budget deficit—affected everyone.

Compared with the ravages of the Depression or the austerity of World War II, these were mosquito bites that diverted attention from a full-employment prosperity and still-rising levels of material abundance. It was Truman's misfortune that the irritations predominated, and a measure of his diminished standing after late 1950 that he could not persuade the nation otherwise.

From the beginning, complaints about economic controls poured into the White House from all sides. Here is a sampling from late 1950 into early 1951: the national commander of AMVETS protested the difficulties that World War II veterans would face in buying homes. Chet Hollifield, a leader of the liberal Democrats in the House of Representatives, told the White House that the Ford dealer in his hometown had sold sixty-seven autos in the month prior to credit controls, only two the next month; that working people could not afford to buy a new car; and that automobiles were a necessity, not a luxury, in southern California. Also citing credit controls, the television industry complained bitterly about a sharp drop-off in sales. Southern cotton growers recruited Truman's friend and biographer Jonathan Daniels to relay a request for generous price ceilings.[2]

"It is a very difficult matter to sit here at this desk and understand the attitude of people toward the emergency with which we are faced," Truman wrote to Daniels in February 1951. "Every segment of the economic setup is interested only in its own selfish interests and is making an effort to grab all the traffic will bear." Four months later, he wrote but did not send a stinging reply to a congressman who claimed that price ceilings on beef were causing shortages. Asserting that the Big Four meat packers were holding their product off the market, Truman declared, "This is a blackmail job and I'm not going to be browbeaten by a bunch of fellows who do not represent the cattle raisers or the cattle feeders and who are out to skin the consumers of meat."[3]

His remarks were understandable. They also were an amalgam of fact and fallacy. The various interests were indeed "selfish" in the sense that none really perceived an overriding national crisis that would temper their normal tendency to maximize rewards for themselves. But the big interests were no more selfish than low- to moderate-income consumers, individual retailers, smaller cotton growers, and cattlemen. The little guys probably felt more pinched than big players who had greater resources.

In protesting this or that government policy that made life somewhat more difficult or bit into profits or kept paychecks from growing, Americans were playing by the usual rules of an interest group democracy in which it was legitimate to try to "get all the traffic will bear." Truman had long instinctively understood such politics; he had played the game brilliantly in 1948 when he reminded voters of all the benefits they had received from the Democrats. By 1951, he was in the uncomfortable position of telling them that they would have to give something up and unable to convince them that it was really necessary to suspend the rules. Going after the big interests was instinctive for him; it also was self-deceptive.

As had been the case during and immediately after World War II, the nation's most visible interest group, and one on which the Democratic party depended heavily, was organized labor. Truman complained privately to confidants that labor had jumped on the same bandwagon as everyone else and was trying to get all it could "while the getting is good," that irresponsible strikes were hampering the defense program.[4] Publicly, he had to be more circumspect.

Democratic administration or not, labor from the beginning felt that the mobilization apparatus was weighted against it. The umbrella agency, the Office of Defense Mobilization (ODM), was headed by Charles E. (Electric Charlie) Wilson, president of General Electric and a leading graduate of the World War II economic bureaucracy. Functioning under its aegis was the Economic Stabilization Agency (ESA) with Eric Johnston (another businessman–World War II economic controller) at the helm. Under ESA's nominal authority was the Office of Price Stabilization (OPS), headed by Michael DiSalle, the former mayor of Toledo, and the Wage Stabilization Board (WSB), a tripartite body composed of representatives of business, labor, and "the public."

On February 15, 1951, the WSB's six business and public representatives voted unanimously to limit wage increases to 10 percent above the levels of January 15. The three labor representatives, claiming that this figure was inadequate to compensate workers for inflation, dissented sharply. They then resigned on orders from the major labor federations. On February 28, labor representatives quit their posts in all the mobilization agencies in protest against what they saw as an antilabor bias. For the next two months, John Steelman and his staff spearheaded an effort to discover just what the labor movement wanted and to bring it back on board.

The revolt drew considerable sympathy among Truman's White House aides and his more liberal cabinet members. The president was less forgiving. Politically, he knew he had to reach an accommodation. Privately, he regarded the unions with the same suspicion that went back to his years as a businessman and county administrator. "There is a conspiracy between labor and management to gouge the country without regard to the public interest," he remarked at a cabinet meeting on February 16. "It is a disgraceful situation."[5]

While all this was going on, Truman had to deal with a national rail strike, as always an especially delicate problem. The switchmen had gone on strike at the beginning of 1951, although their union had agreed to a settlement in December 1950. Truman angrily denounced the strikers at a press conference: "An agreement was signed and they acted like a bunch of Russians. They went back on their signatures." Despite labor attempts to involve him personally, he let the economic mobilization apparatus resolve the job action. On March 1, a new accord, providing cost-of-living adjustments, was achieved.[6]

Throughout March and into April, the impasse over labor's participation in the administration continued. Truman publicly stated his confidence in Wilson while minimizing the seriousness of the situation. Wilson, who had been rather open in his disdain for the labor movement, adopted a more conciliatory approach. Most important, drawing on the precedent of the rail settlement, Eric Johnston on March 8 modified the Wage Stabilization Board's 10 percent rule to allow additional increases for inflation. On April 9, as the MacArthur crisis came to a head, labor representatives agreed to participate in a special mobilization advisory board that would deal directly with the White House. At the end of the month, other union officials returned to the various mobilization agencies.[7]

III

Truman's next step, undertaken in the uproar after MacArthur's dismissal, was to push for stronger economic control authority. He and most of his advisers considered the Defense Production Act of 1950, which had to be renewed by June 30, 1951, barely adequate for the mobilization effort. The nation faced not only a hard push back up the Korean peninsula, but also the emerging need to bankroll the French in Indochina, cope with the possibly serious consequences of the Iranian oil expropriation, and, above all, establish a credible deterrent to the Soviet ground threat in Western Europe. With the World War II experience and fears of a comparable global crisis uppermost in their minds, the president and his aides demanded sweeping authority from Congress to control wages and prices, allocate materials, and construct defense plants—in short, to establish a wartime command economy.

Playing what seemed to be his best card for popular support, Truman emphasized the need to hold down inflation in one statement after another. Inflation had slowed to a crawl by the end of March, but White House economic analysts believed that this was only a "breathing spell" made possible by the imposition of controls at the beginning of the year but unlikely to last without even stronger executive authority. As the defense program escalated in the latter half of the year, moreover, they predicted that inflationary pressures would move apace. Thus Truman found himself trying to mobilize sentiment against a potential threat.

Just sixteen days before the expiration of the Defense Production Act, he went on the air to rouse the public. Declaring that the country was just at the beginning of a two-year process, he read letters from ordinary people suffering from the high cost of living. Warning of an impending crisis, he depicted himself as the opponent of selfish interests (represented, for example, by the National Association of Manufacturers) and emphasized his concern for small business, workers, farmers, and consumers. With men fighting and dying in Korea, with the survival of the nation in question, he asserted, it was wrong to place private concerns above the national interest. Everyone would have to make some small sacrifice; the nation had to work as a team. His administration would promote the spirit of fairness; the opposition would not.[8]

Such was the argument. The congressional response, the Defense Production Act of 1951, demonstrated that it was not convincing. With prices stable and employment at record levels, Congress was motivated less by apprehensions of disaster than by the entreaties of numerous interest groups. Furthermore, most Republicans and southern Democrats had strong ideological objections to massive federal control of the economy. Things moved so slowly on Capitol Hill that Congress had to extend the original act for an extra month. At the end of July, the president found himself forced to sign legislation that actually deprived him of some authority. Calling the bill "the worst I ever had to sign," he denounced it as an engine of inflation and described one key provision as "like a bulldozer, crashing aimlessly through existing price formulas, leaving havoc in its wake."[9]

Tax legislation likewise fell well short of Truman's pay-as-you-go approach to mobilization. Signing the Revenue Act of 1951 in October, the president lamented a failure to raise enough money to cover the cost of the mobilization program and lashed out at "loopholes" such as "excessively liberal capital gains provisions, family partnerships, and excessive depletion allowances."[10] By compelling deficit financing, moreover, the act struck most observers as adding to the already strong inflationary pressures on the economy.

Despite all the administration warnings, runaway inflation never developed. In 1952, the overall Consumer Price Index increased by only 2.2 percent. One explanation for this unexpectedly good news was that defense-production schedules were trimmed back because of shortages and bottlenecks that forced a "stretch-out" of the program. Perhaps higher taxes and stronger controls would have been needed otherwise. It is also possible, however, that a more rigidly controlled economy would have resulted in consumer shortages and an extensive black market with its higher real-world prices.

Truman and other Democrats in 1952 would attempt to turn the unexpected into a political asset, once again reminding Americans that they had never had it so good. The president's final economic report, the work of Leon Keyserling and the Council of Economic Advisers, would count among the achievements of the administration the demonstration that "full employment can be maintained without inflation."[11]

IV

In early 1951, the financial demands of mobilization forced a resolution of a long-simmering struggle for power between the president and the Federal Reserve Board. Independent by law from direct dictation by the president, the Federal Reserve had in practice largely acquiesced in White House–Treasury policy since the New Deal. From the beginning of World War II, it had supported the price of long-term government bonds at par (100 in market terminology) by, in effect, printing money to buy as much federal debt as necessary on the open market. As a result, it had been possible to finance federal activities at a long-term interest rate of 2.5 percent.

Although the creation of large supplies of money carried considerable inflationary potential, World War II had made the risk necessary, and wartime economic controls had at least partly contained price increases. Secretary of the Treasury John Snyder had expected the policy to be continued, and the administration had produced budget surpluses in the immediate postwar years to facilitate it. Snyder talked constantly of the need for stable financial markets; some observers thought his real goal was easy debt management.[12]

Truman himself believed that the government had a moral responsibility to support the price of its bonds and that this was the duty of the Federal Reserve. In addition, low interest rates had long been high on his economic priority list—as befit a boy whose first contemporary hero was William Jennings Bryan, a businessman who felt he had been ruined by a tight-money recession, and an insurgent progressive with a well-nourished resentment of Wall Street. His close friendship with Snyder disposed him to accept uncritically the Treasury's advice on government financing. In 1948, on Snyder's counsel, he had dismissed Marriner Eccles, the most notable Fed chairman to that time, and had appointed Thomas McCabe as new chair.

The Federal Reserve Board had become restless during Truman's first term, but cooperated as long as conservative fiscal policies produced more money than the government expended. Deficit financing during the 1949 recession was expected to be transitory and took place in market conditions that did not pressure long-term federal bonds. As a solid economic recovery set in during the first half of 1950, the Federal Reserve began to take tentative steps toward letting the free market determine the price and interest rates of federal debt instruments. By the end of June, however, it remained uncertain whether a fundamental shift in policy was under way.

The outbreak of the Korean War, the Chinese intervention, the mobilization program, and the prospect of large budget deficits forced the issue. Almost from the beginning, Snyder and Truman were concerned about the board's policy. And with good reason. Two weeks into what still seemed a "police action," Chairman McCabe, more motivated by policy considerations than by his friendship with Snyder, indicated that the Fed wanted to ease away from rigid support. In order to fight inflation, he told the secretary, the board would allow interest rates to go up; the government should price its own debt accordingly.

On August 24, 1950, at Snyder's request, Truman had a long telephone conversation with McCabe. The president followed it up with a curt letter, probably drafted in the Treasury Department and more like an order from the commander-in-chief than a request from the chief executive to the nation's quasi-independent chief banker. The key sentence read, "I think it is imperative that at the earliest possible moment all operations of the Federal Reserve Board and actions relating to the market for Government securities be so adjusted that outstanding United States Government securities sell at par."[13] McCabe returned the letter to the president, but apparently gave assurances that the Fed would honor his request.

Nonetheless, in the fall, the Federal Reserve refused to support one-year Treasury certificates at 1.25 percent. As Snyder looked on in mortification, the rate rose to 1.375, and then to nearly 1.5; the underlying price slipped well below par. Private market investors, forewarned that board support might not be forthcoming, refused to touch the issue; the Fed bought it all, in effect showing that it had the power to dictate the effective yield on short-term federal debt.

Far from reassuring, the action cast doubt on the Federal Reserve's willingness to continue supporting long-term bonds. Throughout the rest of the year and into early 1951, the Treasury became increasingly jittery. At Snyder's instigation, Truman strongly injected himself into the situation, pressuring McCabe with letters, telephone calls, and personal meetings. McCabe responded with pledges to continue supporting long-term bonds at 2.5 percent and to keep one-year yields below 1.5 percent.[14]

By January 1951, the markets, weighed down by increasingly heavy federal debt issues, were displaying signs of skepticism. Long-term bonds that had traded as high as 100 $^{27}/_{32}$ began to slip back toward par. Snyder, who viewed the slightest fluctuation with alarm, believed that the Fed should support federal debt at a price closer to 101 than 100. McCabe and his associates, for their part, increasingly began to view par as unrealistic—at least as long as the interest rate on new issues was only 2.5 percent.

The debate became public and acrimonious. The Treasury acted as if the Federal Reserve had absolute power over the markets and a categorical duty to support government debt instruments at par plus a safety margin of .75 of a point or so; it displayed signs of panic at drops of as little as .03. As the Federal Reserve saw it, Snyder had lost touch with reality. Worried about the inflationary impact of running the printing presses overtime to achieve unrealistically low rates for the Treasury and determined to defend its statutory independence, the board decided that appeasement and accommodation had accomplished little.

Public declarations from both sides and further private conferences were of little benefit. On January 31, the president met at the White House with the entire twelve-man Federal Reserve Open Market Committee, the group responsible for the Fed's government-securities transactions. He recalled that his Liberty Bonds had depreciated from 100 to 80 after World War I and that he had been forced to sell them at a loss. (Apparently, he did not realize that his unhappy experience had no relevance to purchasers of post–World War II savings bonds aimed at the thrifty middle class. These could be cashed in at any time without loss on the initial investment.) He urged the committee to maintain public confidence in government securities.

When McCabe tried to move the discussion from 1921 to 1951, Truman said he did not want to discuss details. The chairman then pledged systematic consultation, but made no commitments. The meeting ended in a friendly and irresolute fashion. Herbert Stein has called it "a masterpiece of deliberate misunderstanding." The Open Market Committee returned to the Federal Reserve Building, debated the issues, and defeated by a vote of 8 to 4 a motion to continue the long-term peg at 2.5 percent—just after the White House had released a statement claiming the committee's support.

A month of recrimination followed, doing nothing for public confidence in either the Treasury or the Federal Reserve. Truman soon discovered that he could not dictate policy. He had a 26 percent approval rating in the polls, little backing in Congress, and no authority to fire any Fed governor. He would be unable to replace McCabe as chairman for a year. The Treasury and the Federal Reserve announced an "accord" on March 4, 1951; it was a collection of fuzzy generalizations about agreement on successful financing and minimal inflationary money creation. The reality behind the accord was that support of government bonds would no longer dominate every other Federal Reserve purpose and that the Treasury would have to pay higher rates.

An unhappy and angry McCabe resigned on March 9, after having exacted the right of approval over his successor. All sides settled on William McChesney Martin, an assistant secretary of the Treasury, well liked by Snyder but in agreement with the Federal Reserve position and determined to be independent. As Martin recalled it twenty-seven years later, Truman made one last effort to get a commitment from him: "He . . . said it just made him sick to think of the bonds going down. He said, 'You will do the very best you can to see that doesn't happen, won't you?' I said I would do my best, but they might go down anyway."[15]

The "showdown" with the Federal Reserve was quixotic at best. Truman never fully understood the issues, uncritically accepted poor advice, got an outcome that ran directly counter to his intentions, and suffered a further erosion of his authority in the process. The result was of great historical importance. With the accord and the appointment of Martin, who would serve as chairman for nearly twenty years, Truman involuntarily launched the Federal Reserve on a course of independence that would make its chairmen more important than the Secretary of the Treasury and at times almost as powerful as the president himself.

It may seem strange that having been outdueled by Thomas McCabe, the president would a month later prevail over the far more imposing Douglas MacArthur. But perhaps not. With McCabe, he displayed consistent wrongheadedness. With MacArthur, he understood what was at stake and was dead right.

V

Few presidents have been as harried as Harry Truman during his last two and a half years in office. Korea, the multiple crises and political irritants of mobilization, the assaults of McCarthy and his followers, the guerrilla warfare with McCarran—all were enormously wearing, and all involved issues of great national significance and political principle. Yet public and political discussion about him increasingly focused on a conglomerate of matters involving his seeming tolerance of minor-league corruption and impropriety.

It was in the end difficult as a matter of principle and politically inexpedient to argue directly with the administration on such big issues as the avoidance of full-scale war with China, all the complexities of mobilization, or the evidentiary merit of McCarthy's allegations. To concentrate on corruption was to fix on an issue that most Americans understood and to take advantage of one of the perennial characteristics of democracy: the personalization of politics. It allowed Truman's opponents to question not his judgment, but his character.

Truman, in turn, played into their hands by displaying a surface lack of concern, consistently moving too slowly to try to set things right, and usually seeming to do so under pressure. His own machine background no doubt had a lot to do with his behavior. His experience had taught him that loyalty to one's friends was a paramount virtue, that seldom was anything achieved by throwing friends overboard to please one's enemies. And a certain fundamental stubbornness impelled him to fight back when his character was impugned. As Robert Donovan, drawing on his personal memories of Truman, has observed, the president was an instinctive counterpuncher when put on the defensive. And by early 1951, he had been on the defensive for so long that he seemed to be carrying a permanent chip on his shoulder.

The long-festering corruption controversy also exposed the defects of Truman's staff organization and perhaps the inadequate size of the White House staff. By the beginning of 1951, he presided over a first-rate group of aides, but it was a relatively small one. No one had the authority to deal with issues and personnel decisions that probably would not go directly to a president today. Charles Murphy assiduously worked to excise the corruption malady; Joe Short at times became almost apoplectic about it. They could push, prod, persuade, but not act in the name of the president. Truman listened to their advice, resisted it, and finally took it—always a step or two behind the public-relations curve.

March 1951 was a crucial month in the Truman presidency. In Korea, Ridgway had turned around a nearly hopeless military situation and was advancing back toward the thirty-eighth parallel. By the end of the month, MacArthur was resisting efforts to end the war there. Critical decisions had to be made. The economic control and mobilization bureaucracy was taking shape, drawing fire from various affected interest groups. Organized labor staged its dramatic walkout from the program. Senators Taft and Wherry were leading the attempt to block the dispatch of infantry divisions to Europe without congressional authorization.

Truman held three press conferences during the month, one of them while vacationing at Key West. He fielded questions involving many of these matters. But others of less consequence yet deep public interest kept coming up. Did he care to make any comment on the Fulbright committee's allegations of favoritism in Reconstruction Finance Corporation loans? On the Kefauver committee crime report? Would Donald Dawson testify before the Fulbright committee? Had the job status of Lauretta Young changed? Did he have any comment on Senator Knowland's suggestion that he ought to get back to Washington and clean house? How about the efforts of various members of Congress to influence the RFC? What did he have to say about ambassador to Mexico William O'Dwyer's admission that when mayor of New York, he had appointed friends and relatives of gangsters to office? Was any change in O'Dwyer's status contemplated? Had the president seen any of the Kefauver hearings on television?

The question about Knowland's remark drew an angry retort: "My house is always clean." More often than not, however, the answer was "no comment." Singly, none of these issues amounted to much. Together, they seemed more portentous than they were. Preoccupied and defensive, Truman had no sense of the number of bullets he was firing through his feet.[16]

The RFC controversy was a good example of the ambiguities. Dawson and various administration officials had done nothing that was not routine for members of Congress, who of course sought RFC loans for friends and associates. Democratic National Chairman William Boyle had received either $1,250 or $1,500 in legal fees from an RFC client and probably had facilitated a loan for it. Arousing Truman's fury, the *St. Louis Post-Dispatch* ran an exposé of the affair and drew national attention to it. Yet as nearly as Charles Murphy could determine, the legal work was genuine and Boyle's fee reasonable. Republican National Chairman Guy Gabrielson had engaged in the same kind of activity.[17]

Harry Vaughan continued to be a target for unfriendly fire. Yet how deep were his improprieties? True, he had interceded with numerous agencies on behalf of friends, acquaintances, and deserving Democrats. He had long since confessed to accepting the infamous, and inoperable, deep-freezes. In 1951, he admitted being offered $150,000 by a businessman for whom he had interceded with the Maritime Commission; he proudly said that he had settled for a box of cigars.[18]

Well-connected influentials had greased business–government relations at least since Daniel Webster had extorted annual retainers from the Bank of the United States. The growth of the federal establishment during the New Deal and World War II had raised the stakes enormously. Donald Dawson's hotel bills or Harry Vaughan's cigars were hardly causes for hanging, but an offer of a six-figure gratuity to a public official had to trouble anyone who read of it. A coating of sleaze seemed to cover the ways in which business was done with the government; inevitably, it rubbed off on many more Democrats than Republicans, because the former had controlled the government since 1933.

VI

The RFC, for example, had been created as a Depression relief agency for business. Managed directly or indirectly by the overbearing Jesse Jones from 1933 to 1945, it had been run in a fashion compatible with private banking standards and had largely avoided political favoritism. Politicians nonetheless had attempted to influence its lending decisions. Truman himself had lobbied it hard for a loan that would bail out the *Kansas City Journal-Post* just before its demise in 1941. Jones, citing a long-standing practice against loans to politically engaged newspapers, had turned him down.[19]

Roosevelt's dismissal of Jones in 1945, along with the end of an emergency-fraught period of depression and war, left the RFC without a clear purpose. In the hands of a mediocre board of directors, it became a monstrous pile of money surrounded by third-rank businessmen and sharp operators, frantically recruiting political types who could help them get a few fistfuls of cash. Perhaps the most pertinent question about the RFC was not whether it was subjected to special influence, but whether it had served its purpose and should be abolished.

On every score, Truman's first impulse was to dig in his heels. His people had done nothing improper. The RFC had made no significant mistakes. And as for doing away with the agency, "we need it in this emergency as badly as we ever have needed it at any time in the past."

All the same, he acted. On February 19, 1951, he submitted to Congress a plan to reorganize the RFC by placing it under a single administrator. When Congress assented, he appointed Stuart Symington. Symington, who had hoped to run the mobilization program, directed his energies toward removing any shadow of suspicion from the agency, right down to dismissing Donald Dawson's wife from a minor clerical position.

Lauretta Young was finally nudged out of her White House job, thereby ending her husband's claim to high-level access. Merle Young's income from various sources in 1950 was estimated at $60,000. Shortly thereafter, he was managing a motel in Florida and under indictment for perjury before the Fulbright committee. Convicted in 1953, he would serve a brief prison term.[20]

Another casualty of the RFC controversy was Bill Boyle. Boyle held no public office; if he had engaged in influence peddling, it was small stuff compared with past and future party chairmen. Even so, pressures for his resignation mounted steadily. In October 1951, he quit, citing ill-health. He was more accurately a victim of his Kansas City background and long relationship with Truman. Boyle's successor, Frank McKinney of Indianapolis, was a banker and organization man who epitomized Truman's ideal: tough, efficient, and honest.[21]

Truman got little credit for cleaning up what RFC malfeasance had existed. The MacArthur controversy obscured his actions; he gave the appearance of acting reluctantly; and the Republicans worked hard to milk the issue. In August, the Fulbright committee issued a report on the RFC that went easy on the administration, but Republican members Homer Capehart and John Bricker launched a broadside attack charging Truman with bringing Pendergast tactics to Washington. Fulbright denounced the minority report but got little credit from Truman. Several months later, the president jotted in his diary that Fulbright had yet to forgive him "for telling him at a Press Club dinner that he'd been a better constitutionalist had he been educated in a land grant American College rather than Oxford."[22]

Meanwhile, the administration and the Democratic party found itself embarrassed by an investigation of politics and organized crime led by Senator Estes Kefauver. For about a year in 1950 and 1951, the Kefauver committee hopped from one city to another, turning over rocks and exposing numerous unpleasant denizens of the underworld—many of them with ties to Democratic politicians.

The entire business disgusted and angered Truman, although it differed only marginally from a number of the inquiries that he had run on both the railroad and war investigating committees. A first-term senator, Kefauver had little standing on Capitol Hill, where he was generally deemed a lightweight and known to have a drinking problem. His investigations had little substantive purpose beyond self-promotion.

The senator undertook one of his early hearings in Kansas City just months after the killing of Charles Binaggio and ten years after the local reform movement had ended the open ties between the mob and the law enforcers. The revelations were low-level stuff: bookmaking, back-room dice tables, a few thuggish types in the liquor and nightclub businesses, county deputy sheriffs allegedly taking payoffs from tavern owners, and so on. The lack of big-time misdeeds left Kefauver with nothing much to do but rake over memories of the bad-old Pendergast days, cast a couple of pebbles at the county sheriff, warn the citizens of a "hard core of racketeers," and distribute a sinister-looking spiderweb diagram displaying the structure of organized crime in the city. Ironically, the most prominent name on it was that of the lamented Binaggio, presumably still running the local underworld from a bunker in Mount St. Mary's Cemetery.[23]

The biggest politician to be skewered was William O'Dwyer; it was widely believed that O'Dwyer, who had resigned as mayor of New York under pressure, had been sent to Mexico at the urging of Bronx boss Ed Flynn, primarily to get him out of the country beyond the reach of subpoenas and possible indictments. Returning to testify before the Kefauver committee on March 19 and 20, 1951, he was subjected to devastating questioning.

Truman not only refused to recall O'Dwyer, but actively expressed confidence in him and seemed to think him about as persecuted as Owen Lattimore or Philip Jessup. "He's a fighter, just like I am," the president declared at a press conference. Although he was never formally charged with any crime, O'Dwyer quickly became yet another appointee beloved by Truman bashers. He remained ambassador until his resignation in December 1952, and then stayed in Mexico for years almost as an exile. He returned to the United States in 1960.[24]

Television, still in its infancy but with a good instinct for a sensational story, picked up the Kefauver hearings. The show played well, featuring characters who often appeared to have been sent over from central casting: Greasy Thumb Guzik, Frank Costello (whose nervous hands and raspy voice fascinated a TV audience denied a look at his face), and the faded glamour girl Virginia Hill, formerly the close companion of late Las Vegas entrepreneur Bugsy Siegel. Truman felt forced to issue a contrived and unconvincing statement detailing his administration's tireless efforts in the struggle against crime. Privately, he seethed about Kefauver's apparent disinterest in Republican-run crime centers and Tennessee hot spots. To an impressed public, the senator began to look more and more like a potential president.[25]

At least, Truman could tell himself, the RFC investigation had not turned up much that was major, and Kefauver had established no direct links to the administration at all. Unfortunately, things got worse. Through 1951, the administration was plagued by revelations of wrongdoing in the Bureau of Internal Revenue and the Tax Division of the Justice Department. Coming at a time when Truman was requesting one round of tax increases after another, reports of tax fixing by venal patronage appointees stirred public anger.

Once again, the administration failed miserably to grasp the public-relations aspect of the issue. It was not that Truman would tolerate crooks. It was that he preferred to believe, until faced with incontrovertible proof to the contrary, that they were not crooks. Rather than meet the problem head on and attempt to control a breaking story, he and his attorney general, J. Howard McGrath, subjected themselves to the political equivalent of water torture.

One by one, local collectors of internal revenue or high officials in their offices either resigned or were dismissed: Jim Finnegan (St. Louis), Denis Delaney (Boston), Joseph Marcelle (Brooklyn), James Olson (alcohol unit, Manhattan), James Johnson (Manhattan), Monroe Dowling (Johnson's successor), James Smyth (San Francisco), Ernest Schino (chief field deputy, San Francisco). Many of them were subsequently indicted and convicted on charges that included bribery, extortion, embezzlement, and tax evasion. Washington executives also fell: Daniel Bolich, assistant commissioner of internal revenue (under congressional investigation, but never convicted of a crime); Assistant Attorney General T. Lamar Caudle, head of the Tax Division (dismissed in December 1951, and convicted of conspiracy in 1956); Charles Oliphant, chief counsel of Internal Revenue (forced to resign for accepting gifts). By the end of 1951, fifty-seven Internal Revenue functionaries had been ousted.[26]

A list of such length might display vigilance. But as forced resignations or firings came one after another, month after month, the cumulative impression was of a tax bureaucracy rotten through and through, a president lax and complacent. It was not until January 1952 that Truman finally proposed a thorough reorganization of the bureau, including civil service status for collectors. By then, he had failed irretrievably to convince the public that he was on top of the scandal rather than just reacting to it.[27]

VII

The president and his aides decided, not unreasonably, that a big part of the problem was Attorney General J. Howard McGrath. Governor of Rhode Island at thirty-seven, solicitor general of the United States at forty-two, United States senator at forty-three, Democratic national chairman at forty-four, and (in 1949) attorney general at forty-six, McGrath had enjoyed a meteoric career. Yet his rise had been based on neither charisma nor extraordinary energy. Good connections, a get-along, go-along attitude, and a powerful patron—venerable Rhode Island senator Theodore Francis Green—had paved the way for him. By the time he became attorney general, McGrath enjoyed not only a fabulously successful political record, but also a net worth of around $4 million, although he came from a family of modest means and had never pursued a career outside the public sector.

The least capable of Truman's four attorneys general, McGrath provided little leadership for the Justice Department. He had been appointed primarily because Truman felt that with Protestant Tom Clark replacing Catholic Supreme Court Justice Frank Murphy, it was necessary to name a Catholic attorney general. It was common knowledge around Washington that McGrath left the administration of the department to his deputy and drank too much. In 1952, his deputy attorney general was A. Dewitt (Gus) Vanech, a third-rate political hanger-on. (McGrath had one excuse: he had promoted Vanech on the request of Matt Connelly, who thereby demonstrated that the White House was also indifferent to the department's talent level.) A confidential memo prepared for Truman in late 1951 declared, "What was once far and away the best legal institution in the United States is now verging on the third rate." The department, it asserted, had become "a headless juggernaut."[28]

By December 1951, Truman finally understood that he had to move. He may have been pushed along by Democratic chairman McKinney, who declared publicly that the president felt some people had sold him down the river and was going to take "drastic action" to clean up the government. At a press conference on December 13, 1951, Truman talked at length, sometimes combatively, sometimes earnestly, about doing whatever was necessary: "Wrongdoers have no house with me, no matter who they are or how big they are."[29]

As he spoke, Truman thought he was in the final stages of establishing a special investigatory commission to be headed by federal judge

Thomas Murphy, the prosecutor of Alger Hiss and a one-time reform police commissioner of New York City. (It was more than passing ironic that Murphy had been appointed New York police commissioner to clean up the mess left by the O'Dwyer administration.) The deal fell through when it appeared that Murphy might have to resign his judgeship.[30]

Truman then moved to replace McGrath. On December 21, he offered the attorney generalship to Wayne Morse, a highly regarded, hyperindependent Republican senator from Oregon. Morse thought it over for a day and declined. Charles Murphy advanced the name of Justin Miller, a highly respected former federal judge. At the last minute, someone dredged up statements that Miller had made in 1936 and 1950 that might have embarrassed the administration. As Murphy recalled it, they involved criticism of the FBI. "I wish you would tell Justin Miller to go back to California," Truman wrote to Murphy. "I certainly can't make a man a member of my Cabinet who has made statements such as the ones attached."[31]

McGrath, who had been told that he would be made ambassador to Spain, fought back. He rallied support from Senator Green and leading Catholic prelates, among them Cardinal Spellman. Not wanting accusations of anti-Catholicism at the beginning of an election year, Truman allowed his attorney general to make one last effort at cleaning up what Republicans were calling "the mess in Washington."[32]

McGrath went to Judge Learned Hand, one of the most distinguished members of the federal judiciary. Hand recommended his son-in-law Newbold Morris, whom McGrath thereupon appointed a special assistant to head the cleanup. On paper, the choice was an inspired one. Morris was an independent Republican and New York City reform politician with a well-established reputation as his own man. Coming down to Washington with a sense of mission and guarantees of unconditional support by McGrath and Truman, Morris announced that he proposed to investigate any and perhaps every branch of the federal government—beginning with the Department of Justice. His chief tool was to be a financial questionnaire that would require federal officials to disclose all outside income. Truman issued an executive order requiring compliance and gave him private reassurances.

In mid-1951, the president had looked over a similar instrument that a congressional committee wanted to distribute to Bureau of Internal Revenue officials. "If one was sent to me for an answer," he told Murphy, "I'd tell the sender to go to hell." Perhaps by the beginning of 1952, he had changed his mind. William Hillman quoted him in *Mr. President* as declaring, "Every public official that gets more than ten thousand dollars a year ought to show exactly what his outside income is, if he has any. . . . I will fight for this vital and urgent change."[33]

A shrewd special investigator would have played such comments for all they were worth and would have cultivated a relationship with the president. Instead, Morris shot off his mouth like a comic-strip New

Yorker. Appearing on NBC's *Meet the Press* on March 2, 1952, he committed one gaffe after another. Why in his opinion had Truman finally ordered the investigation? "Who's to know whether the angel Gabriel appeared to the President?" He would expect the president to fire any federal employee who refused to answer a questionnaire. What if Truman refused? "I'll come home." What was his responsibility to McGrath? He would deputize leading attorneys in seeking indictments and report directly "to the American people through the President." Would he have made O'Dwyer ambassador to Mexico? No—and he would not have appointed Harry Vaughan to the administration either. Truman must have swallowed hard after this performance.[34]

McGrath in the meantime chafed about a special assistant who seemed not simply determined to bypass him, but maybe out to get him. Morris had submitted his questionnaire to the attorney general on the same basis as any other employee of Justice. McGrath refused to respond to it or to allow the document to be distributed. Nor did he respond to a request for correspondence, diaries, appointment books, and telephone records. In Rhode Island on March 16, possibly under the influence of alcohol and implicitly alluding to Morris's Jewish ethnicity, he intimated that the investigation was anti–Irish Catholic. Truman, aware of the potential for a disastrous Catholic–Jewish conflict, stalled, attempted to reassure both parties, and hoped for a way out of the impasse.[35]

The amount of time he had for the issue must have been highly limited. As March turned to April, he was making a final decision against a presidential run, attempting to identify a successor, and facing the possibility of seizing the steel industry. On March 29, he announced that he would not run again. On March 30, he accepted the resignation-in-protest of Defense Mobilization director Charles Wilson. But before he could grapple with a critical economic emergency and initiate a historic constitutional controversy, he had to deal with McGrath and Morris.

On March 28, McGrath told the president that Morris's questionnaire was a violation of personal privacy. By his account, Truman agreed that it should not be sent out. Testifying before a congressional committee on March 31, McGrath publicly aired his disagreement with Morris. On April 1, Charles Murphy advised Truman that the split between McGrath and Morris had probably become irrevocable.[36] On April 2, the attorney general and the president met in the morning. McGrath's terse "no comment" to reporters could not conceal the anger written all over his face. That afternoon, while the president and cabinet waited at National Airport to greet Queen Juliana of the Netherlands, Truman and McGrath were seen shouting at each other.

The next morning, as the president was meeting with his staff, he received the news that McGrath had fired Morris. Press secretary Joe Short and his assistant, Roger Tubby, insisted that McGrath had to go. No one in the room defended the attorney general. Truman then got McGrath on the phone and told him that his resignation would be announced at a scheduled press conference later in the day. Then he called federal judge James McGranery—previously number-two man at Justice, former congressman from Philadelphia, and, most important, a leading Catholic layman with an instantly recognizable Irish name: "Jim, I've got a job for you, and I expect you to take it."

The episode hurt Truman. "I hate to do what I did to Howard," he told his staff. "He was crying at the end." Two weeks later, at the behest of Senator Green, Truman wrote privately to McGrath: "I want you to know that my fondness for you has not changed one bit. Political situations sometimes cause one much pain." If McGrath was interested in some other public post, he would "do anything I can for you." Part political calculation, part genuine sentiment, the letter produced a quick, well-publicized call of thanks from McGrath.[37]

VIII

Even the appointment of McGranery did not conclude the fiasco. McGranery's nomination hung fire on Capitol Hill for nearly two months, as he fended off absurd charges that he might be a bit soft on Communism and negotiated his approval with Pat McCarran. A headless Justice Department defended the steel seizure—and lost ignominiously. Newbold Morris was not brought back to Washington. The corruption cleanup continued in competent and low-key fashion, but the issue remained a bludgeon with which Republicans merrily bashed the president black and blue.

The episode tells historians much about post–New Deal politics and the post–New Deal state. Truman dealt with the corruption issue as a politician of the past. He was perfectly willing to continue a vast bureaucracy with huge sums of money to hand out and countless points of access for supplicants and grafters, and to assume that some impropriety and petty graft were part of the process of government—messy and distasteful perhaps, but unavoidable. If the Republicans carped, it was easy enough (and frequently accurate) to write them off as partisan hypocrites who did the same sorts of things themselves.

What Truman did not understand was the way in which the Democratic party was changing. During the corruption scandals, he found himself criticized both by Fulbright and by the estimable Paul Douglas of Illinois—both learned, professorial Democrats who appealed to a new professional and liberal element of growing importance. The president also faced Estes Kefauver, who had developed considerable appeal to a broader emerging Democratic middle class with no need for the services of the classic machines. Truman never quite qrasped their popularity, just as he never would understand that of the politician who ultimately eclipsed them, Adlai Stevenson. Ultimately, the controversy demonstrates not simply Truman's machine ethic or failure to catch a new drift in American politics, but also his limitations as a public leader capable of setting the agenda of American political debate and defining a tone for the country.

The piddling nature of the Truman "scandals" became not an exculpatory fact, but a reason to regard the administration, and the president who headed it, with contempt. T. Lamar Caudle, Joseph Alsop declared, was not dishonest, just third-rate. "One would have more respect for men like Caudle if they were big thieves on their own," he wrote, "but in fact they are mainly petty favor takers."[38]

Somehow the absence of big-time crooks in Truman's administration became a point used against him by a relatively friendly columnist. Somehow, the character of his most mediocre appointees seemed to be a faithful reflection of the president, while the exemplary nature of his best did not. The caricature was cruel and unfair, but sadly revelatory of the way in which Truman's authority and public standing had declined by the final year of his presidency.

IX

Truman's final struggle involving mobilization policy took shape while he also attempted to cope with McGrath and get McGranery's nomination through the Senate. The 1952 seizure of the steel industry involved important issues of economic stabilization, military readiness, interest group politics, and presidential power. From virtually every angle, the president was at a disadvantage.

Whether from the perspective of civilian consumption or military production, steel was the most important of American industries, the large steel corporations richly profitable and powerful, their managers inflexibly Republican in politics. The United Steelworkers Union was one of the strongest and most politically engaged of American labor groups. Its president, Philip Murray, was also president of the CIO. Children of the New Deal, both organizations were functional adjuncts to the Democratic party. No president of the United States could ignore these circumstances.

On December 31, 1951, the union contract with the companies expired, weeks of negotiations having failed to yield agreement on a new one. The existence of economic control machinery all but invited both sides to throw the issue into the hands of federal agencies. The union doubtless expected sympathetic consideration from a Democratic administration; management, pleading inadequate profits, would demand price increases to cover a wage settlement.

In all, the situation bore an uncomfortable resemblance to the steel labor dispute of early 1946, when a long strike had hampered reconversion and had been settled with a big wage increase and a bulge in the price line. If the similarity occurred to Truman, he doubtless recalled that it had been a no-win experience, and then told himself that the only thing to do with the situation was to face it. On December 22, 1951, he formally referred the dispute to the Wage Stabilization Board and asked both sides to maintain production until a settlement was reached.[39]

For nearly three months, the strike prospect disappeared from public discussion, displaced by the presidential nominating campaigns, political polemics about administration corruption, and the ongoing antics of Senator McCarthy. Then, on March 20, 1952, the WSB voted—business representatives unanimously dissenting—to give labor a generous raise, in the neighborhood of 26 cents an hour in wages and benefits.

The companies, enabled by provisions of the Defense Production Act to claim compensating price increases of $2 to $3 a ton, immediately petitioned the Office of Price Stabilization for an additional $9 to $10. The OPS, now headed by Ellis Arnall, the former liberal Democratic governor of Georgia, turned them down without a dime. Privately, the Council of Economic Advisers told the president that $1 or $2 might be warranted. With the companies unwilling to accept such a settlement and the administration lacking the power to impose it, a strike loomed. Office of Defense Mobilization director Charles Wilson then added a touch of drama by criticizing his two subordinate agencies and arguing for a $4 to $5 price rise. When Truman refused to support him, he resigned on March 30, charging publicly that the administration had become a tool of the labor unions.

Truman released a temperate reply thanking Wilson for his patriotic public service, but defending the WSB–OPS findings as equitable; the steel companies, he believed, were enjoying "extraordinarily high" profits that could easily cover the wage recommendations. Nevertheless, on April 3, with a strike imminent, the administration substantially accepted the Wilson formula. Presumably with the authorization of the president and Acting Director of Defense Mobilization John Steelman, Arnall privately offered the companies $4.50 a ton. In secret negotiations over the next few days, it became clear that they would accept it only if the wage increases were scaled back. The union, having obtained a federal recommendation, would settle for nothing less.[40]

The merits of the dispute, if susceptible to an objective determination, are difficult to master. The public appearance was something else: Truman had aligned himself squarely with labor at the beginning of an election year. The administration, for all the sacrifice it had preached, was endorsing substantial wage increases for some of the more highly paid industrial workers in the nation, while blocking any compensation for the companies. To top it off, the president had been repudiated by his chief mobilization director, had let him go, and then had accepted his formula.

However much Truman thought in terms of mobilizing and consolidating labor support for the Democratic party, he was at least equally concerned with maintaining the defense program, especially the flow of equipment to Korea. Secretary of Defense Lovett, as Truman later summarized him, said that "any curtailment of steel production . . . would endanger the lives of our fighting men."[41] From Truman's point of view, far more sincere than cynical, his primary task was to prevent a strike. Since he held the companies responsible for the impasse, he wanted to pressure them and not seem to punish the union.

The clearest and easiest way to proceed, an eighty-day back-to-work injunction under the Taft-Hartley Act, would be easily obtainable and manifestly legal. It also would be interpreted as a sanction against labor and as proof of the wisdom of prospective Republican presidential candidate Robert A. Taft. The union, moreover, had already stayed on the job without a contract for ninety-nine days. Other possibilities for maintaining production were more ambiguous but rooted in statutory law; they could be found in clauses of the Defense Production Act and the Selective Service Act.

Truman instead was drawn by his lifelong belief in strong executive authority to something more dramatic and more dangerous. On April 8, 1952, he stingingly criticized the steel companies and announced that under his authority as president he was seizing the industry. It is unclear whether the idea had originated with him. He had run it past Chief Justice Vinson in confidence and had obtained Vinson's assessment that a majority of the Supreme Court would support him.[42]

Without questioning Truman's honest belief that the nation faced an emergency calling for decisive action, it is worth remembering that he was also by this time a beaten-down chief executive with a 32 percent approval rating. Seizure on the basis of vague authority was a way of demonstrating to the country, and perhaps to himself, that he could still govern. It was also an action consistent with his entire life experience— a roll of the dice for big stakes with a hell-bent attitude toward risk. Politically and constitutionally, it was about as big a gamble as MacArthur's dash to the Yalu in late 1950.

Truman turned de jure administration of the mills over to Secretary of Commerce Charles Sawyer, who along with Snyder held down the conservative end of his cabinet. "He said he was giving me the dirtiest job he had ever given anyone but he knew I could handle it," Sawyer recalled in his memoirs. Sawyer, of course, actually did not manage the mills; he merely told existing managers to fly the American flag over their plants, stay at their posts, and keep separate books for the seizure period.

A less-than-candid account in his memoirs notwithstanding, Sawyer also initially agreed to issue orders for a partial wage–price increase, thereby presenting both labor and management with a fait accompli that might induce a quick settlement. It is not so clear whether the request came directly from Truman himself or from aides such as Solicitor General Philip Perlman or acting Defense Mobilization director John Steelman. Sawyer publicly threatened the increase, but he never quite got around to implementing it, whether because of conservative second thoughts or—as he argued at the time—because of the technical difficulties in applying a wage increase to the thirty-two different pay scales in existence.[43]

When Murray issued a stinging attack on the commerce secretary for not increasing wages, Truman told Sawyer in writing, "You and I are acquainted with the men who head great organizations. They must be sure that they stand right with their organizations, even if it should take a little demagoguery." Was the comment self-revelatory? It leaves the impression that the president did not exactly place an urgent priority on the wage–price strategy.[44]

Truman did give Sawyer one order that the commerce secretary wisely deflected. On May 2, after being shown a news report to the effect that the president of U.S. Steel might lock out workers rather than accept a government-imposed settlement, a furious president got Sawyer on the phone: "I want you to fire that son-of-a-bitch right away and put a general in charge to run his mills." Sawyer suggested that it would be best not to take an impulsive action based on a news-ticker story and got Lovett to back him up at a later meeting. Truman dropped the demand.

As Sawyer recounted it, Truman was always solicitous, practically begging him to put up with Murray, Perlman, and Steelman, and telling him that he wanted to end the seizure as soon as possible. Yet Truman gave him no responsibility for settlement negotiations. Sawyer especially remembered one discussion in which the president urged him to see the job through: "He said he was going to do something nice for me in the future. I assumed he was thinking of an appointment to the Supreme Court, but I made no comment."[45]

Truman lost his gamble and lost big. The American middle class had never reacted well to seizures of property, whether auto plants by sit-down strikers in the 1930s or Montgomery Ward by Franklin Roosevelt in 1944. The way in which Truman had lashed out at the companies, moreover, made his decision seem punitive and partisan. Business analysts ridiculed the assertion that a big wage increase could be paid without price hikes. Constitutionalists, liberal and conservative, opposed so bold an expression of presidential prerogative. According to Gallup, the seizure had 35 percent approval, 43 percent disapproval.[46]

The courts were no more supportive.

On April 29, District Judge David Pine ruled the seizure unconstitutional. He flatly rejected an assertion by Assistant Attorney General Holmes Baldridge that the inherent authority of the presidency allowed so drastic a step. The administration quickly got a stay of the decision and appealed to the Supreme Court. Steel production, never halted in April, continued through May. On several occasions, Truman affirmed that he would abide by the high court's ruling. "I have no ambition to be a dictator," he told the press on May 1.[47]

On June 2, the final blow came from the Supreme Court. By a 6 to 3 margin, the Court ruled the seizure unconstitutional. Of Truman's four appointees, only Vinson and Minton (both alumni of the World War II executive branch) supported him; they were joined by Stanley Reed. Both Harold Burton and—to Truman's undying rage—Tom Clark voted with a majority that included the "heavyweights" of the Court: Hugo Black, William O. Douglas, Felix Frankfurter, and Robert Jackson. The different emphases and multiple opinions of the majority justices produced no clear constitutional doctrine, but three points appear to have weighed heavily in their thinking: the absence of a formal declaration of war; the existence of the Taft-Hartley Act as a clear, congressionally approved alternative; and the authoritarian potential of a vague appeal to "inherent powers."

Truman returned the companies to private management. A fifty-three-day strike followed, with no appreciable impact on the Korean fighting and probably no serious curtailment of defense production.[48] Nonetheless, utilizing a statement by Lovett to the effect that the job action had damaged the economy as much as a heavy bombing raid, the president brought the parties together toward the end of July and got them to hammer out a settlement. The terms—a 21.5 cent hourly raise for the workers plus formal recognition of a union shop, a $5.20 a ton price increase—were about the same available at the end of March.

If the strike had been unnecessary, it at least did no grave harm to the national interest. Truman put on as good a front as possible after it was over. Hugo Black, who had been in the Senate with him for three years, held a cocktail party for the president and the justices. As William O. Douglas told the story later, things were a bit stiff at first; but after a round or two of drinks, Truman was heard to say, "Hugo, I don't much care for your law, but, by golly, this bourbon is good."[49]

That was Truman at his usual in face-to-face situations. At a remove, he continued to be bitter about the whole fiasco. On July 9, he wrote but did not send a letter to Justice Douglas:

> I am sorry that I didn't have an opportunity to discuss precedents with you before you came to the conclusion you did on that crazy decision that has tied up the country.
> . . . There was no decision by the majority although there were seven opinions against what was best for the country.
> I don't see how a Court made up of so-called "Liberals" could do what that Court did to me.[50]

X

The decisions that officials have to make in times of perceived emergencies are hard and seldom encourage fine distinctions or subtle courses. Yet it is difficult to avoid the conclusion that Truman, having at first grievously underestimated the nation's defense needs, overreacted with a mobilization program that threatened to militarize the nation's economy and with a control apparatus that made the administration the target of every dissatisfied interest group in the country.

At the time, of course, these developments had an aura of inevitability about them. Perhaps because all the World War II examples were so close at hand, it was natural to replay them—from the decision to resist aggression to the adoption of the models of economic mobilization and control that the wartime experience had provided. All the same, President Truman might well have profited from a dialogue with Senator Truman.

Senator Truman had seethed with resentment at the World War II economic controllers, had argued for the needs of the civilian economy, and had skeptically questioned the claims of the military. Acting somewhat like President Roosevelt, President Truman gave unquestioning support to his mobilizers, perhaps assuming that they were a better lot than those of World War II, perhaps believing that there was no alternative. And he did so without the imposing rhetorical skills and charisma that had sustained Roosevelt with the electorate.

Senator Truman had not hesitated to cross swords with an admired figure like Robert Patterson when during the war Patterson had defended such dubious enterprises as the Canol project. By contrast, President Truman did not question Robert Lovett when the latter argued that the defense program and the military effort in Korea would be devastated by a steel strike. One is uncertain whether Truman's missteps were at all avoidable, given his need to make decisions on the basis of incomplete information. There can be no question that they left him and his party with serious wounds.

However poor his judgment, Truman had attempted in good faith to prevent a national emergency. Instead, he had further damaged himself and, to his special chagrin, had to some extent detracted from the authority of the presidency. The steel-seizure case wrote an unhappy end to his effort to mobilize the nation—and in many respects served as a fitting metaphor for its shortcomings.

33

"I Have Served My Country Long, and I Think Efficiently and Honestly": Going Out, 1952

Truman wrote in his diary on April 16, 1950:

> I am not a candidate for nomination by the Democratic convention. . . .
>
> In my opinion, eight years as President is enough and sometimes too much for any man to serve in that capacity.
>
> There is a lure in power. It can get into a man's blood just as gambling and lust for money have been known to do.
>
> This is a Republic. The greatest in the history of the world. I want this country to continue as a Republic. Cincinnatus and Washington pointed the way.

And on May 8, 1950:

> I've said that no third term appeals to me. . . .
>
> Now if we can find a man who will take over. . . .
>
> It seems to me now that the Governor of Illinois has the background and what it takes. Think I'll talk to him.[1]

Truman could have felt in the spring of 1950 that he would bequeath a legacy of accomplishment to whoever followed him. The country was at peace and prosperous; the Western world was united as never before against potential aggression; some elements of his Fair Deal program had survived congressional opposition, and others would follow. Against this record, the early corruption investigations and the initial rantings of Senator McCarthy were nuisances, and NSC-68 was an overwrought claim on national resources that would have to be politely but firmly deflated. With the right leadership, he told himself on May 8, "the Democratic Party can win from now on."

Korea and the downward spiral it set in motion changed all that. From time to time, he was tempted to throw away his diary pledges, stand for reelection, and seek vindication. (The recently passed Twenty-second Amendment to the Constitution specifically exempted the incumbent president.) Step by step, however, he accepted the inevitable. In March 1951, then again in November, he told close aides that he would not run again and that they should plan their futures accordingly. Then more rethinking. Finally, on March 29, 1952, he made his decision public.

II

However much Truman may have been intellectually convinced of the need to give up the presidency, the decision was emotionally difficult. Faced with a Republican candidacy by General Eisenhower and embarrassed by Senator Kefauver, seriously battered by Korea, McCarthyism, the ballooning corruption mess, and all the economic controversies of mobilization, he remained a fighter whose first instinct was to punch back. Perhaps his most unexpected difficulty was his inability to lay hands on a willing and eager Democrat he could support wholeheartedly for the White House. Despite his May 8, 1950, comments on Adlai Stevenson, his first choice was Fred Vinson. Vinson possessed wide experience, administrative talent, and political savvy; loyal to friends and party, he remained the president's most esteemed companion. Truman put the possibility to his old comrade in mid-1950 and received an amiable turndown.[2]

Eisenhower was also on the shopping list. At NATO headquarters in Paris, the general found himself subjected to a steady stream of pleas and demands that he declare for the presidency. Truman still admired him. When Eisenhower returned to the United States for a brief visit, the two men met privately at the White House on November 5, 1951. Three days later, Arthur Krock wrote in the *New York Times* that Truman had offered to support Eisenhower for the Democratic presidential nomination.

Krock's confidential source, William O. Douglas, had walked into a conversation between Truman and Vinson at a White House reception. Truman, as Douglas recalled it, said he had told Eisenhower that "his offer of 1948 held good for 1952"; Eisenhower had responded that his differences with the Democratic party's domestic policies were very large, and things had gotten no further. Eisenhower vehemently denied Krock's story. It seems most likely that Truman had not made a flat-out offer, but had thrown out a line for the general to grab if he was interested. Instead, Eisenhower returned to Paris, enigmatic, uncommunicative, and likely experiencing great inner conflict about his own intentions.[3]

Truman turned again to Vinson, bringing the chief justice down to Key West for a two-week Thanksgiving vacation and making a determined attempt to change his mind. In December, he received a last refusal, based on Vinson's precarious health and his unwillingness to use the Supreme Court as a launching pad for the White House. (He would die in September 1953.)

On December 18, 1951, Truman wrote to Eisenhower:

Dear Ike:

The columnists, the slick magazines and all the political people who like to speculate are saying many things about what is to happen in 1952.

As I told you in 1948 and at our luncheon in [November] 1951, do what you think best for the country. My own position is in the balance. If I do what I want to do I'll go back to Missouri and *maybe* run for the Senate. If you decide to finish the European job (and I don't know who else can) I must keep the isolationists out of the White House. I wish you would let me know what you intend to do. It will be between us and no one else.

I have the utmost confidence in your judgment and your patriotism. My best to you and Mrs. Ike for a happy holiday season.

Most sincerely,

Harry S. Truman

Eisenhower's response was equivocal. He said that although he was deeply touched by the president's letter, he was on military duty in a foreign country. He would not and legally could not seek a political nomination: "Of course a number of people know of my belief that any group of American citizens has a right to fight, politically for any set of principles in which its members believe and to attempt to draft a leader to head the fight!" He was going to remain silent. The possibility of his being drawn into political activity was "so remote as to be negligible." He would maintain that policy "unless and until extraordinary circumstances would place a mandate upon me that, by common consent, would be deemed a duty of transcendent importance."[4]

The letter was a document produced by an incipient candidate. Truman never recorded his reaction to it, but it is entirely possible that his feelings resembled those of a dozen years earlier when Lloyd Stark had assured him that he had no plans to run for the Senate.

On January 7, Eisenhower issued a statement announcing that he was a Republican and affirming that he would accept that party's nomination for president. At the same time, he declared that he would not campaign and intended to stay on the job at NATO. A few days later, Truman told a press conference: "I don't want to stand in his way at all, because I think very highly of him, and if he wants to get out and have all the mud and rotten eggs and rotten tomatoes thrown at him, that is his business." He would not, he told the reporters, support a Republican Eisenhower for president and refused to foreclose a run against him. A few days later, he wrote the general a cordial personal letter, which was answered in kind.

That exchange set the tone for an odd four-month interlude in which Eisenhower stayed on the job, avoided political comment, and wrote occasionally to the president. Truman groused in private, but the interchange between the two was friendly. In the meantime, Eisenhower's American backers, primarily from the Dewey and Stassen wings of the Republican party, fought their way through the primaries, winning several without the formidable presence of their candidate, but finding themselves short of the momentum needed for a convention victory. In April, Eisenhower finally accepted reality and asked to be relieved.[5]

III

If neither Vinson nor Eisenhower, then who? Kefauver, the one Democrat squarely in the race, was never an option in Truman's mind. On January 15, just before announcing his candidacy, Kefauver met with Truman. Despite his seething inner feelings, the president was pleasant—almost fatherly, Kefauver reported to Drew Pearson. Truman, looking back eleven months later, characterized the senator as "intellectually dishonest" and "ignorant of the history of his country." How could he have "had the nerve to ask the President to support him"? Superficially, Kefauver, a tireless campaigner with a quasi-populist appeal, resembled the president. In fact, Truman gagged at the prospect of him heading the Democratic ticket.[6]

Most of the other possibilities also had liabilities. In July, just before the Democratic National Convention, Truman made a list: Richard Russell, a man of "ability and brains" forced to represent the prejudices of Georgia and thus unelectable; Robert Kerr, a strong senator and great speaker irredeemably tied to the oil and gas interests; Vice President Barkley, affectionately called the Veep, a grand, much-loved old wheelhorse of seventy-four, failing physically and not up to the demands of the job; Averell Harriman, "the ablest of them all," but also a Wall Street banker with no electoral experience.[7]

Little wonder that in January, Truman had decided it was time to meet with the governor of Illinois. On January 22, Stevenson, who had just been introduced to a national audience with a *Time* cover story, went to Washington, ostensibly to discuss coal-mine safety problems with John L. Lewis. Word of his off-the-record appointment with the president had been leaked to *Time* by a member of Stevenson's staff. It was an open secret by the time he was ushered into the study of Blair House that evening. Truman was seated in front of a fire and reading the Bible.[8]

The president had known Stevenson since at least 1948, when he had been elected governor by a whopping margin that made possible Truman's own razor-thin victory in the state. The governor's family history—a grandfather who had been vice president to Grover Cleveland, a father who had been prominent in Illinois Democratic politics—impressed him, as doubtless did Stevenson's wide experience, oratorical skill, and

visible talent. Moreover, Stevenson had important backing from key
members of the White House staff, including Charles Murphy, David
Lloyd, and former ADA national director James Loeb.

The two men who confronted each other in the Blair House study
began with feelings of warm mutual admiration, based on observation
from a distance. The meeting provided an opportunity for their first extended private conversation on a matter of great importance. By the time
it was concluded, the feelings of respect remained intact, but (on
Truman's side at least) they were a bit frayed by the realization of how
different the two were in background and temperament.

Stevenson was a patrician in every sense of the word: old family and
old money; inheritor of a tradition of public leadership; educated at
Princeton, Harvard Law School, and Northwestern Law School; fully as
intelligent and well read as Truman and much more articulate; more prone
to see shades of gray in every situation, far less aggressive, and considerably less decisive. On the surface, their foreign and domestic policy positions seemed identical. Actually, Stevenson would have pursued the Cold
War with a somewhat more conciliatory edge; he privately nursed substantial reservations about Truman's Fair Deal that might have precluded
him from consideration had they been widely known.

After the usual pleasantries, Truman quickly got to the point: "I told
him what the presidency is, how it has grown into the most powerful and
the greatest office in the history of the world. I asked him to take it and
told him that if he would agree, he could be nominated." Truman's account, written just after the Democratic National Convention, seven
months later, declares that Stevenson said no. In fact, he appears to have
expressed doubt, and then asked for time to think the offer through. He
told his close friend George Ball that he had "made a hash" of the discussion and left the president thinking him a complete idiot.[9]

Truman may have been a bit exasperated, but he clearly continued
to see Stevenson as the party's best hope. At a press conference a couple
of days later, he told reporters that he and the governor "had a very pleasant visit all around." Someone asked, "You didn't offer him higher office?" Truman evaded a blatant untruth by asking, "How could I?"
Stevenson wrote to congratulate him for his adroit handling of the que-
ries and pledged his own silence. Truman's response indicated nothing
had been closed off: "I hope that sometime in the not too far distant future we may have further conversations on the subject in which we are
both interested."[10]

Charles Murphy, Oscar Chapman, and David Lloyd all talked to
Stevenson over the next few weeks. In the meantime, Truman allowed
party leaders to enter his name in the New Hampshire Democratic primary, but he stayed in Washington while Kefauver tramped through the
snow, shook hands, asked for votes, and attracted attention by wearing a
Tennessee coonskin cap. On March 4, Stevenson flew to Washington to
see an increasingly impatient president. This time, the answer was a flat

no. On March 11, Kefauver won in New Hampshire, beating Truman by a 5 to 4 margin.[11]

The president in the interim had begun to act like an old racehorse who sensed a new season. On February 21, speaking off the cuff to a Masonic breakfast in Washington, he detailed the heavy burdens of the presidency: "an all day and nearly an all night job." Then, with a big smile, he said, "And just between you and me and the gatepost, I like it." Reporters and pundits read such remarks as if they were tea leaves. Truman went off to Key West on March 7 for a twenty-day vacation, interrupted only by a quick trip to New York for a speaking engagement. To all appearances, he had not made up his mind about running. Aides and cabinet members confessed bafflement.[12]

While Truman was in Florida, New York publisher Farrar, Straus and Young released William Hillman's book, *Mr. President*. A compendium of material from Truman's private correspondence, diaries, autobiographical jottings, and interviews with Hillman, the volume was assembled in much the same spirit as an authorized biography by Jonathan Daniels that had appeared in September 1950. It contained a few slightly sensational items: the stiff memo Truman claimed to have to read to James Byrnes in January 1946, a diary entry that excoriated Henry Wallace (rechristened "X"), the sharp letter of 1948 to Bernard Baruch, an endorsement of twelve-year term limits for members of Congress. In the main, however, it presented Truman as a leader who combined dignity with the common touch, wisdom with wit; a large number of handsome illustrations reinforced these points. Many political observers understandably took it as a campaign document.[13]

As Truman mulled over his own future at Key West, he kept up the pressure on Stevenson. Called to Washington again, the governor met with Charles Murphy on the evening of March 14. Afterward, Stevenson wrote a letter to Murphy in which—after paragraphs of protestation—he said that he would not campaign for the Democratic nomination, but would accept a draft.[14]

By March 18, Truman had this information to think about. He surely knew that the time for a decision was near and that if he decided to run, he could not sit in Washington while Kefauver barnstormed the primary states. And although he regularly derided the public-opinion polls, he was well aware that presidential trial runs showed him far behind Eisenhower and Stassen and running even only with Taft, whom he openly described as his favorite Republican candidate.[15]

Bess, who doubtless understood that he had made his contribution to history and could gain little from a third term, discouraged him in the most direct way she knew. She did not believe she could survive another four years in the White House, she told him, and she doubted that he could.

In late March, he met with a group of close friends and advisers—Chief Justice Vinson, Democratic National Chairman McKinney, Charles

Murphy, John Steelman, Matt Connelly, and Joe Short among them. Murphy recalled it as the frankest such meeting he ever had attended. They all tactfully advised the president against the race. Perhaps they reminded him explicitly that he was nearing his sixty-eighth birthday; that his energies were visibly ebbing; that if he served and lived through another term, he would emerge the oldest man, by a margin of four and a half years, to have held the presidency. He thanked them, gave each a newly minted silver dollar, and kept his counsel.

On March 29, a day after his return to Washington, Truman delivered a rip-roaring partisan speech at a gala Jefferson–Jackson Day dinner. Then unexpectedly he concluded, "I shall not be a candidate for reelection. I have served my country long, and I think efficiently and honestly. I shall not accept a renomination. I do not feel that it is my duty to spend another 4 years in the White House."

The shocked crowd was mostly silent for a moment. There were numerous audible gasps, shouts of "No!" and then applause. Harry Vaughan remembered watching Bess: "She looked the way you do when you draw four aces."[16]

IV

Truman was still determined to control the nomination. Stevenson, he believed, could be prevailed on to announce his availability. The governor wrote on March 31, professing his disappointment at Truman's decision and his gratitude for the president's confidence but budging not an inch away from his own noncandidacy. Truman responded on April 4; he asked Stevenson not to make an irrevocable withdrawal. On April 16, Stevenson issued a statement that seemed to do just that: "In view of my prior commitment to run for Governor . . . I could not accept the nomination for any other office this summer." He sent a copy to Truman with an apology. Truman expressed his regrets. Thus the president and his party drifted into the summer.[17]

One of Truman's other ambitions was settled more quickly. As his December 18 letter to Eisenhower indicated, he had toyed seriously with the idea of returning to the Senate, an institution for which he still felt extraordinary affection. He quietly let his friends in Missouri begin a boomlet for him. Had he announced, he would have had the primary field to himself. The people of Missouri probably would have elected him easily over the little-regarded incumbent Republican, James P. Kem.

To return to the Senate over Kem's beaten body and spend another six, maybe twelve, years there—how wonderful a prospect and how likely of accomplishment! Except for one immovable obstacle: Bess wanted nothing more than to return home, spend the rest of her life among her oldest friends, and enjoy the little social activities that meant so much to her.

For eighteen years, Harry and Bess had dealt uneasily with one fundamental point of difference in their lives. Washington had lured him as a center of power and action, as a place in which he could join many of the country's best political leaders in a sense of male comradeship and public service, and as the repository of the nation's heritage. Bess had never liked the capital and had escaped from it as much as she could.

He might happily have lived out the rest of his life there; she insisted on going home. He decided he owed it to her. On April 3, he told a press conference that he would not run for the Senate. Harry Vaughan, perhaps acting with Truman's approval, perhaps not, tried to put together a draft movement. Without an explicit wink or nod from the president, it soon evaporated.[18]

For a presidency that was winding down, Truman's remained intensely busy over the next few months. The steel-seizure crisis and the strike that followed were the dominant issues. He also issued his last two major vetoes.

On May 29, he sent Congress his disapproval of a bill that would have given offshore tidelands oil deposits to adjacent coastal states. The measure had its strongest support from California, Louisiana, and Texas—the three states that would be most enriched by it—and from oil companies that suspected it would be easier to negotiate production agreements with state governments. The bill, Truman declared, "would turn over to certain States, as a free gift, very valuable lands and mineral resources of the United States as a whole. . . . I do not see how any President could fail to oppose it." The veto stuck.[19]

Four weeks later, he unsuccessfully vetoed the McCarran-Walter Immigration Act. In part, the veto was aimed squarely at his old enemy, Pat McCarran; but it also was a principled action that indicated the firmness of Truman's move from the midwestern progressive insurgency of his early days to the New Deal urban liberalism of his political maturity. His message condemned the bill's continuation of discriminatory quotas against Southern and Eastern Europeans and asserted that it denied essential individual rights to resident aliens in a fashion "worse than the infamous Alien Act of 1798." Congress, reflecting the continued political dominance of old-stock Americans and Cold War fears of subversion from the Soviet bloc, overrode the veto by substantial margins. Truman privately called the act "about the worst piece of legislation that has ever been placed on the books."[20]

Steel, tidelands oil, and McCarran-Walter dominated the headline agenda. The routine of the presidency poured in around the edges, filling up every crack of free time. From the beginning of April to mid-July, Truman made trips to Omaha, Nebraska (to inspect major flooding along the upper Missouri River); West Point (to celebrate the academy's sesquicentennial); Annapolis (to balance the visit to West Point); Springfield, Missouri (to attend the Thirty-fifth Division Association reunion); Groton and New London, Connecticut (to lay the keel of the first atomic submarine); and northern Arkansas (to dedicate the Norfork and Bull Shoals dams).[21]

He participated in many brief ceremonies, often doing no more than saying a few words to visiting 4-H members, YMCA officials, business women, archivists, and others able to get a tour of the White House and a little time with the president. Other occasions had more meaning: Distinguished Service Medals for Generals Ridgway and Eisenhower, Congressional Medal of Honor presentations, dedication of a memorial plaque for Leslie Coffelt, a meeting with the surviving members of the task force that had held the line in the early days of the Korean War.

He made formal addresses to the National Conference on Economic and Social Development, the AMVETS, the National Civil Service League, the Americans for Democratic Action, the Electric Consumers Conference, the Jewish National Fund, the Conference on Industrial Safety—all groups that had some claim on the attention of a Democratic president. He held press conferences, one a week without fail.

Always at the back of his mind was the impending Democratic National Convention and the lack of a credible presidential candidate.

V

Kefauver continued to win primaries, but they were still too few to provide the delegates for a majority. Harriman, who would have supported Stevenson, formally entered the race. The most outspoken liberal among the hopefuls, he was also stiff and unexciting. It was a measure of Harriman's limited appeal that Truman gave him a tacit blessing only after receiving a pledge that, as Truman later put it, "when the time came for the convention to nominate its candidate for President I wanted him to be in line to help nominate that man, whoever he was."[22]

Truman still hoped it would be Stevenson, who drew increased attention from Democrats across the country as either the best alternative to Kefauver or simply the best man. And while the governor forswore presidential ambition at every opportunity, he spent a fair amount of time making speeches around the nation, becoming more and more a national figure instead of just another superior state executive. Rather like Truman in 1944, he was happy where he was but willing to accept an honest draft if one came his way. Unlike the Truman of 1944, he also doubtless sensed that an identification with the incumbent president would be of no help to him.[23]

On July 11, the Republican National Convention nominated Eisenhower. The Democratic Convention was to begin on July 21 in Chicago. Confronting a jumble of unpromising candidates, it demanded leadership. Sometime on the day of Eisenhower's victory, Truman met with Democratic National Chairman Frank McKinney, Senate secretary Les Biffle, and political aide Matt Connelly. They considered the claims of the vice president, who had become increasingly open in his ambitions. Truman still regarded Barkley with the same affectionate condescension that long had characterized their relationship. But at least the Veep could unite the party and serve as a caretaker for its aspirations: "We agreed on Barkley for the top place and Oscar Chapman for Vice President. What a position we are facing! But we must face it and meet it. We'll do that." At another meeting on July 13, Truman personally promised Barkley his backing.[24]

What happened next demonstrated Truman's unawareness of the extent to which his power had eroded. A lame-duck president could not dictate to all the professionals and interest group influentials who ultimately determined a nomination. On July 19, Truman's longtime friend David Noyes sent a report from Chicago via William Hillman: Barkley was a sentimental favorite, but almost no one thought he could beat Eisenhower. It was doubtful that he could raise enough money to run a credible campaign. There was no enthusiasm for anyone other than Truman himself or Stevenson. The governor might still be open to a draft. It was imperative for Truman to change the instructions to his alternate in the Missouri delegation, Tom Gavin.[25]

As Truman pondered this intelligence, the Barkley campaign careened toward disintegration. On the morning of July 21, the convention's opening day, Barkley met with sixteen top labor leaders and requested their support. He got a unanimous turndown. They liked him, they said; they hated to do it. But he was too old and not up to the job. Truman later would write that Barkley had made a crucial tactical error: if he had met with each leader individually, he would have gotten the backing he needed. Perhaps. As it was, the labor chiefs delivered a hard judgment that the president should have made.

Shortly afterward, Adlai Stevenson, acting as governor of Illinois, delivered a speech of welcome to the first session of the convention. Typical of Stevenson's best efforts, it was a sprightly blend of wit, eloquence, idealism, and Democratic partisanship. The response from the delegates was electric. In fifteen minutes, wrote James Reston, the man who had been trying to talk himself out of the nomination for five months "talked himself right into the leading candidate's role."[26]

That afternoon, Barkley called Truman and told him that he was withdrawing from the race. At the behest of Secretary of Commerce Charles Sawyer, Truman asked Frank McKinney to arrange an emotional farewell speech for the Veep. On July 23, Barkley appeared before the convention to deliver another of his great old-time partisan orations. Both before and after the speech, the delegates gave him ovations so loud and prolonged that even Franklin Roosevelt might have considered them excessive. Thus it seemed a fine old party leader would fade away with appropriate fanfare. Instead, he left a sour taste in many mouths by allowing supporters to try to nominate him anyway.

Barkley's scant chance of winning was precluded by a call Truman received from Adlai Stevenson on July 24: Would the president be embarrassed if he allowed his name to be placed in nomination? Truman later would write, "I replied with a show of exasperation and some rather vigorous words and concluded by saying to Stevenson, 'I have been trying since January to get you to say that. Why would it embarrass me?'"

"Vigorous words" and annoyance aside, the president went to work to line up professional political support for Stevenson. It was fortunate for the governor, Truman would write in his memoirs, that Barkley had released him; otherwise, the vice president would have been the candidate. In fact, the labor veto of Barkley had demonstrated that Truman could not control the convention. The president facilitated Stevenson's nomination, but he could not have prevented it. In Barkley, the Democrats in Chicago saw their past; in Stevenson, they discerned their future.

On the afternoon of Friday, July 25, the day the convention was to select its candidate, Truman flew to Chicago. Stevenson ran second to Kefauver on a first ballot that concluded shortly after the presidential plane landed. Truman went to his suite at the Blackstone Hotel and worked for a time on the speech he was to make later that night. Then he headed to the Stockyards Inn for a private dinner with Democratic leaders.

Kefauver held his lead on the second ballot, but Stevenson began to close the gap. The convention recessed shortly after 6:00 P.M.; it reconvened a bit before 9:00. Harriman withdrew in favor of Stevenson; so did Governor Paul Dever of Massachusetts. The third-ballot roll call moved slowly but inexorably in Stevenson's direction. At approximately 12:20 A.M., he was nominated.

At 1:45 A.M., Truman and Stevenson walked out on to the platform together. Truman spoke, perhaps a bit overlong, in the fighting fashion of his 1948 acceptance speech; he defended his seven-year record and praised Stevenson. The president told a cheering crowd, "I am going to take off my coat and help him win." Then Stevenson accepted the nomination in a shorter, lower-key, more reflective, and perhaps more uplifting address. Weary but happy and excited, Democrats took heart from a symbolic union of old and new and believed it was possible to win a sixth consecutive presidential election.[27]

VI

With no more than two or three hours of sleep, Truman wrote to Stevenson from his hotel the next morning. The previous night, he said, had been one of the most remarkable of his sixty-eight years.

> You are a brave man. You are assuming the responsibility of the most important office in the history of the world.
>
> You have the ancestral, political and the educational background to do a most wonderful job. If it is worth anything to you, you have my whole hearted support and cooperation.
>
> When the noise and shouting are over, I hope you may be able to come to Washington for a discussion of what is before you.[28]

Stevenson's response was cordial. He was deeply touched, he said. He looked forward to a meeting in Washington. The same day, he wrote to his intimate friend Alicia Patterson: "The line to emphasize is that I am *not* Truman's candidate."[29] Truman had never been a man to relinquish power easily. For both psychological and tactical reasons, Stevenson was determined to take charge of the campaign and keep his distance from the president.

By the time of the Washington meeting on August 12, Stevenson had decided to replace Frank McKinney, one of Truman's most trusted advisers, with Stephen Mitchell. A longtime friend and supporter of the governor, Mitchell was also a political amateur whose only discernible qualification for the job of Democratic national chairman was his Catholicism. He apparently had met not a single member of the party's national committee. His advice to Stevenson, John Bartlow Martin believes, was frequently ill-informed. The president took the dismissal of McKinney as a personal affront and considered Mitchell a major mistake. As his personal campaign manager, Stevenson appointed Wilson Wyatt, a mercurial Kentucky liberal who had been mayor of Louisville and president of Americans for Democratic Action. In Truman's estimate, Wyatt was another amateur. Truman doubtless remembered him for resigning in a huff as housing expediter in 1946.

Stevenson set up his campaign headquarters in Springfield, Illinois, instead of Washington. The move reflected the governor's unavoidable commitment to the state capital and the need to be in close touch with campaign advisers, but it also was intended as a declaration of independence from the Truman White House. Stevenson could have kept a limited staff of close advisers and speech writers in Springfield while setting up the main campaign operation in Washington; instead, he ignored a cadre of experienced Democratic professionals and campaign operatives who could have been valuable to him.

Truman sent out two first-rate young White House staffers, David Bell and Clayton Fritchy, to help with research and speech writing. Oscar Chapman served as primary advance man once the candidate started his speaking tours. Mostly, however, Stevenson relied on smart, well-intentioned, hard-working, grievously inexperienced people who chaotically went about discovering how to run a presidential campaign. Truman was overly sensitive in taking these appointments as a personal rebuff, correct in considering them tactical folly.[30]

As it was, the character of the Stevenson campaign accelerated the movement of a new constituency into the Democratic party: well educated, middle class, moderately liberal, personally devoted to Stevenson, not blindly attached to the labor movement or the old party organization—and unenthusiastic about Truman. Throughout the rest of the 1950s and occasionally afterward, these Democrats (and their children) would become identified with "reform" movements against the old party establishments. Mitchell took pride in these new recruits, but one may question that they amounted to a net gain in 1952, given the alienation of the organization followers and the coolness of labor. Rather, they revealed an emergent fundamental Democratic division—no longer between country and city, as earlier in the century, but between an urban working class and a new middle-class intelligentsia.

Truman's alienation from Stevenson and what he represented had been aroused by the firing of McKinney. It went up a notch when Stevenson, responding to questions from the *Oregon Journal,* fell into the same trap that had earlier caused Truman to be identified with such phrases as "red herring" and "police action." Asked to explain what he would do about "the mess in Washington," he wrote, "As to whether I can clean up the mess in Washington, I would bespeak the careful scrutiny of what I inherited in Illinois and what has been accomplished in three years." The reply had been drafted by a close aide, but Stevenson knew what he was signing; the statement faithfully represented the perspective of his political circle. At about the same time, Democratic vice-presidential candidate, Senator John Sparkman of Alabama, was quoted as saying that the administration had mishandled the steel strike.

Truman, who gave himself credit for the nomination of both Stevenson and Sparkman, drafted, and then put away, angry letters to both. The one to Stevenson, embellished with his sarcastic rendering of "Kefauver," graphically depicts his state of mind:

> It seems to me that the Presidential Nominee and his running-mate are trying to beat the Democratic President instead of the Republicans. . . .
> There is no mess in Washington. . . .
> I've come to the conclusion that if you want to run against your friends, they should retire from the scene and let you do it.
> When you say that you are indebted to no one for your nomination, that makes nice reading in the sabotage press, but gets you no votes because it isn't true. . . .
> I'm telling you to take your crackpots, your high socialites with their noses in the air, run your campaign and win if you can. Cowfever could not have treated me any more shabbily than have you.[31]

Truman came perilously close to going public with his anger in a press conference on August 21. Did he have any comment on Stevenson's remarks? "I have no comment because I know nothing about any 'mess.'" Did he have any feeling of being a target? "I am the key of the campaign. I can't be a target. . . . [T]he Democratic party has to run on the record of the Roosevelt-Truman administrations." What about Governor Stevenson's indication that he wanted to freshen the Democratic party? "I believe there ought to be new blood infused into the Democratic party, but that doesn't mean that we are going back on what the Democratic party has done in the last 20 years." Was he happy with the way Stevenson and Sparkman had begun their campaign? "No comment."[32]

He asked Stevenson to return to Washington for a second meeting, but the Democratic nominee sent Mitchell. The new national chairman and the president met for about fifty minutes. The atmosphere was civil, the discussion about numerous secondary problems rather than the critical divisions between Truman and Stevenson. The president was friendly, Mitchell reported to Stevenson and Wyatt: "I thought his attitude was more wistful or nostalgic than one of disappointment or irritation."

Actually, Truman was seething. It was probably not long after this meeting that he wrote another furious, unsent letter to Stevenson: "I shall go to the dedication of the Hungry Horse Dam in Montana, make a public power speech, get in a plane and come back to Washington and stay there."

In the end, despite his feelings, two considerations dictated his intensive campaigning: Truman's almost reflexive need to get on the trail, and his even greater anger with Dwight D. Eisenhower.[33]

VII

Whatever the gulf between Stevenson and Truman it at least did not involve a rupture of a past close relationship; and, above all, Stevenson was a Democrat. Conversely, Truman felt betrayed by Eisenhower. He had liked and respected the general, had felt a kinship based on their common midwestern backgrounds, and had responded to the common touch that so effectively contrasted Ike with MacArthur. Truman believed that he had advanced Eisenhower's career by making him army chief of staff and supreme commander of NATO. He had offered, however indirectly, to make the general president. Instead, Eisenhower had spurned him, revealed himself to be a Republican, and attacked Truman's record.

As the campaign took shape, molehill grievances developed into mountainous misunderstandings. On August 12, Eisenhower issued a press release criticizing the use of General Bradley and CIA director Walter Bedell Smith to give Stevenson a national security briefing. Truman promptly invited Eisenhower to a White House cabinet luncheon and elaborate briefing of his own, which the general then declined in a lawyer-like response.

Truman responded with a handwritten letter that conveyed a sense of personal injury:

> I am sorry if I caused you embarrassment. . . .
>   Partisan politics should stop at the boundaries of the United States. I am extremely sorry that you have allowed a bunch of screwballs to come between us. . . .
>   From a man who has always been your friend and who always wanted to be!

Eisenhower replied with a friendly longhand letter of his own expressing gratitude for the invitation and stating his "respect and esteem." The incident itself was trivial. Truman's behavior was extraordinarily revealing of the emotions he had invested in his relationship with the general.[34]

Eisenhower's offenses mounted. He achieved a rapproachment with

Robert A. Taft. He and other leading Republicans denounced the policy of containment and advocated "liberation." He endorsed all Republican candidates for reelection, including specifically Joe McCarthy and William Jenner, the two most prominent vilifiers of George C. Marshall. He deleted praise of Marshall, his old mentor, from a speech.

The general's tacit acquiescence in the attacks on Marshall outraged Truman as a matter of principal. But it also added a dimension to his feeling of personal betrayal. If in his heart he felt that Eisenhower owed him little, it was common belief that Eisenhower owed Marshall almost everything. Ike's refusal to speak up for a revered mentor and national leader greatly reinforced Truman's sense that the Republican candidate was guilty of a sin ultimately greater than partisan or policy disagreements: disloyalty. It was this perception that formed the core of an increasingly bitter and vocal resentment.

Truman's first participation in the campaign came on Labor Day, September 1. He left Washington early in the morning, made brief rear-platform speeches in Pittsburgh and Crestline, Ohio, and then ended the day with a major address in Milwaukee. At 8:30 the next morning, he spoke to a railyards crowd in Cincinnati, and then whistle-stopped through West Virginia. The talks were vigorous partisan exercises contrasting the sins of the Republicans with the good deeds of the Democrats, loyally promoting Stevenson, and rarely mentioning Eisenhower. The crowds and the "give-em-hell" cries were ample. The pace was grueling, but the president loved the experience of being away from Washington, talking to real Americans, and being removed from the day-to-day burdens of governing.[35]

Doing little or no coordinating with the Stevenson campaign, Truman took to the rails on a campaign tour that kept him out of Washington for most of October. From September 29 through November 1, he made 202 speeches in twenty-four states. They were more intense versions of his Labor Day efforts and increasingly personal about Eisenhower. On October 9, he told a crowd in Bellefontaine, Ohio:

> The General has gone right down the line and repudiated almost everything he was supposed to stand for. . . .
>
> There was a time when I thought he would make a good President. That was my mistake, and I have found it out the hard way.

On October 17, in Exeter, New Hampshire:

> It is a tragedy to see this man, so competent in the military field, destroying his own reputation by cheap politics.

And on November 1, in St. Louis:

> I knew him; I trusted him. At one time I thought he was qualified to be President. . . .
>
> I cannot but conclude that it would be disastrous for us to elect as President a man who shows so great a willingness to do the purely expedi-

ent thing, in matters that vitally concern our national survival. . . . He has surrendered his moral authority.[36]

Eisenhower, who never had reciprocated Truman's high regard, reacted to the attacks with at least as much animosity as Truman delivered them. Republicans in general cried foul. What was "whistle-stopping"? asked the *Kansas City Star*, perhaps the Midwest's major editorial voice of the moderate, independent Republicanism to which Eisenhower appealed. "In the worst sense it means going out slugging, no matter how reckless or intemperate the charge or statement, accusing the opposition of everything bad, claiming credit for everything good." Joe McCarthy, it added pointedly, was a typical whistle-stopper. "Trumanism," fumed Louis Bromfield, would be defined in future dictionaries "as a mixture of fraud, humbug, corruption, extravagance, waste, incompetence, high taxes and demagoguery."[37]

It was accurate to describe Truman as punching hard and without a lot of attention to the belt line. After Eisenhower endorsed a vehement immigration restrictionist, former senator Chapman Revercomb of West Virginia, the president noted that Dewey had pointedly refused to back Revercomb in 1948 and added, "The Republican candidate for the Presidency cannot escape responsibility for his endorsements. He has had an attack of moral blindness, for today, he is willing to accept the very practices that identified the so-called "master race."[38]

Eisenhower was outraged. Yet Truman's assertion, however excessive the rhetorical flourishes, was accurate. In its truth lay the sting. The Stevenson campaign frequently blanched at the president's words, but they reached working-class and minority constituents who did not identify with the Democratic nominee.

Truman also could point out with substantial accuracy that the opposition had defamed him "as a traitor and a corruptionist."[39] That in the end was why at the age of sixty-eight he subjected himself to a harder campaign than in 1948. The election was less about winning for Stevenson (although he wanted that), or even beating Eisenhower (although that became an increasingly urgent goal); it was about vindication for Truman himself and all the policies he had supported since April 12, 1945.

With every passing day in October, it became apparent that he was fighting a losing battle. From the conventions on, clear-eyed analysts had few doubts about the outcome. Eisenhower ensured his election on October 24 when he declared that he would "go to Korea," inspect the battle zone, and find a way to end the war. On election day, he beat Stevenson by 6.5 million votes.

VIII

"Congratulations on your overwhelming victory," Truman telegraphed Eisenhower the next day. "You should have a representative meet with the Director of the Bureau of the Budget immediately. The *Independence* will be at your disposal if you still desire to go to Korea." Eisenhower ignored the last jab. Thanking the president for his "courteous and generous telegram," he said that any military transport plane would do.[40]

As he analyzed the election returns, Truman could take some comfort in the way they revealed a uniquely personal victory for Eisenhower, the Republicans winning control of Congress by the narrowest of margins. The president understood that no Democrat could have won the presidency against America's most attractive hero. Yet he could not avoid a resentment against Stevenson—his delays, his campaign standoffishness, his relative moderation. "A man running for office must believe in his cause and make the people believe it and in him," Truman mused toward the end of the year.[41]

As hard as it was for Truman to face, however, there could be little doubt that the election result had also been a considerable repudiation of his leadership. From one perspective, this reaction was a puzzle. Economically, the country was better off than ever with full employment, good wages, high profits, strong farm prices, and rapidly rising standards of living. Internationally, the nation was secure, and the administration had successfully protected its interests in Western Europe, the Pacific, and Latin America.

Yet all these objective accomplishments had been overshadowed by frustration with the fall of China, the stalemate in Korea, anxiety about domestic subversion, annoyances with the inconveniences of another war mobilization just five years after the end of the last one, and a sense of malaise about the character and content of the government. To some extent, Truman was a scapegoat for a tired and overlong Democratic ascendancy. Although he was personally a convenient target for partisan Republicans, their slogan—"It's time for a change"—capitalized on a feeling that the Democrats had been in power too long.

One could not gainsay, however, the terribly low approval ratings in the polls. Truman clearly had been unable to allay the anxieties and irritations of the American people. For the most part, his policies had been meritorious. But he had failed at what may be the most critical function of the presidency: defining himself as a leader in whom the public could have confidence and setting a positive tone for the nation.

As had so often been the case, when Truman got past the emotions of the moment, he not only did the right thing but did it generously and splendidly. The last partisan change of power at the White House had occurred when Herbert Hoover had relinquished the office to Franklin Roosevelt. Frosty and bitter, the transition had left the nation rudderless for four months and had brought the Great Depression to its lowest ebb. Since then, the changes in the presidency and the world with which it was engaged had been enormous. Whatever his tendency to identify the presidency with himself, Truman understood that it had become a large and powerful institution, not to be handed over on Inauguration Day with no preparation. He established a model for what has become an established procedure.[42]

He and Eisenhower met only once, leaving high-level aides to handle the transfer of power. Their encounter, on November 18, 1952, was not a pleasant one. The general, Truman thought, "had a chip on his shoulder." They discussed the presidency in private for twenty minutes, with Truman outlining the functions of his major aides. Aside from inquiring whether Truman had a chief of staff, Eisenhower said little. "I think all this went into one ear and out the other," Truman wrote soon afterward. He felt that his guest did not grasp the magnitude of the office or the problems before it.

A seventy-five-minute meeting followed with Dean Acheson, John Snyder, Robert Lovett, and Averell Harriman representing the administration. Eisenhower's two top transition aides, Henry Cabot Lodge, Jr., and Joseph Dodge, joined the president-elect. Devoted almost entirely to foreign policy, the administration presentations covered Korea, Iran, European defense, Southeast Asia, and foreign economic policy. Truman believed that Eisenhower "was overwhelmed when he found what he faced." One doubts that this was the precise emotion felt by a person to whom the title supreme commander had become routine. Eisenhower later wrote in his memoirs that he found the entire exercise unrewarding. Tense though it was, however, it helped lay the basis for necessary transition coordination at the lower levels.[43]

In the days that followed, Truman managed to give his relationship with Eisenhower one more jolt. He remained torn between wishing his successor well and raging at his pledge to go to Korea. "I sincerely wish he didn't have to make the trip. It is an awful risk," he wrote in his diary on November 15. "May God protect him." Typically, however, the more he thought about it, the angrier he got. On December 9, returning from Korea, Eisenhower announced that he would confer with General MacArthur. Two days later at a press conference, the president injected another measure of venom into an already poisoned relationship: he denounced MacArthur and called Eisenhower's trip to Korea "a piece of demagoguery" (once again using a phrase a reporter had put into his mouth).[44]

IX

The final weeks in the White House held measures of sadness and joy. On December 5, Madge Wallace died. Truman eulogized her in his diary as a good mother-in-law and opined that the press would criticize him for spending public money to fly her remains, the family, and himself to Independence for the funeral. No responsible paper or columnist did so.[45]

On January 6, a federal grand jury issued an antitrust indictment against the *Kansas City Star* and a specific criminal count against publisher Roy Roberts. Roberts responded with an angry statement that harshly contrasted federal passivity after the 1946 vote frauds with the zealous pursuit of the paper. The case was in line with emerging antitrust doctrine that prohibited certain kinds of advertising charges, but it was also pretty clearly Truman's last shot at a hated enemy. The Eisenhower administration would drop the criminal charges but pursue the civil case. The *Star* eventually was convicted in the court of Truman's old friend Judge Richard Duncan. It paid a small fine, changed the way in which it sold advertising space, and continued to be an important Kansas City institution.[46]

Also in January, Winston Churchill made a quick trip to the United States to meet briefly with Eisenhower and pay his respects to Truman. Dean Acheson described their conversation as "particularly personal, intimate, and friendly." A small dinner at the British embassy was a gay occasion, replete with a mock trial of Churchill and a piano solo by the president.[47]

Truman believed that he had accomplished a lot. He ticked off a list to his old friend Carl Hatch: reorganization of the administrative office of the presidency, of the national defense establishment, of the State and Treasury departments; creation of the Central Intelligence Agency, the National Security Council, the National Security Resources Board; and precise definitions of responsibilities for aides to the president and members of the cabinet. "I am going to leave the office in better shape than it has ever been left by any President," he declared. Characteristically, he thought in neat administrative-organizational terms fully as much as he had in Jackson County.[48]

On January 15, he delivered a farewell address to the nation over radio and television. It was a graceful, personal recounting of the events and decisions of his presidency and of his reactions to the nature of the job:

> The President—whoever he is—has to decide. He can't pass the buck to anybody. . . . I want you to realize how big a job, how hard a job it is—not for my sake, because I am stepping out of it—but for the sake of my successor. . . . Regardless of your politics, whether you are Republican or Democrat, your fate is tied up with what is done here in this room.

He spoke proudly of the steps he had taken to meet the challenge of Soviet expansionism, including the hard decision to fight in Korea. Free men had failed the test of resolve in the 1930s; "this time we met the test." To those who would have had him initiate an atomic war, he said, "Starting an atomic war is totally unthinkable for rational men." How, then, would the Cold War end? The Communist world looked strong and had great resources, but it also had a fatal flaw: "In the long run the strength of our free society, and our ideals, will prevail over a system that has respect for neither God nor man."

Someday, the world would enter "a wonderful golden age" in which humankind could devote itself to the tasks of peace, to the elimination of poverty and human misery. He talked, as he often had done privately, of making the Tigris and Euphrates Valley bloom, of making Ethiopia into a great corn belt that could feed 100 million people, of turning underdeveloped parts of Latin America into a vast cornucopia. He spoke proudly of the great material progress in American life during his administration.

When Franklin Roosevelt died, Truman concluded, he had felt that a million men were better qualified than he to assume the presidency. The work had fallen to him, and he had tried to give it everything he had. Through it all, he had been sustained by the belief that the people were with him. For that, he would be grateful always.[49]

Inauguration Day, January 20, was clear and beautiful. Truman spent almost two hours in his office taking care of a few minor matters and saying final goodbyes to clerks and Secret Service men. Then he joined the members of the cabinet and their wives in the Red Room to wait for the president-elect and his entourage. The motorcade arrived. An embittered Eisenhower refused to leave his automobile and make the customary courtesy call on the outgoing chief executive. After an awkward pause, the presidential party came out to join them.

Truman rode to the inaugural ceremony in the lead car with Eisenhower, Speaker of the House Joe Martin, and Senator Styles Bridges. He remembered the conversation as innocuous until Eisenhower, misremembering events, said that Secretary of the Army Royall had wanted him to attend the 1949 inaugural and that he had declined because so many of the people who would be cheering Truman had wanted him to run. Truman responded, "Ike I didn't ask you to come—or you'd been here." Bridges gasped, and Martin changed the subject.[50]

After Eisenhower's inauguration, Truman, Bess, and Margaret went to Dean Acheson's house in Georgetown for a luncheon with cabinet members, Chief Justice Vinson, and a few close aides. As the limousine made its way through the city traffic, Margaret, her eyes sparkling, turned to her father and said, "Hello, *Mr.* Truman!" He laughed appreciatively. A crowd of several hundred well-wishers waited outside the Acheson residence. The air inside was thick with sentiment. The deposed old men, many of them probably glad to be relieved of the burdens of power, knew that they would never all be together again. Margaret remembered it as an affair of jokes, laughter, and a few tears.

At 5:30 P.M., the Trumans were driven to Union Station, where the "Ferdinand Magellan" waited to take them to Independence. Thousands of people were there to cheer them. Police and Secret Service men formed a wedge to get them through to the great old railcar. A stream of friends and acquaintances came on to wish them farewell. Truman went back to the rear platform to say a few words to the crowd. As the train began to move, a few voices broke into "Auld Lang Syne." The entire crowd picked it up, providing a thunderous chorus as Harry and Bess waved goodbye.[51]

On across America the next day, there were smaller crowds at one stop after another. Finally at 8:15 P.M., the Trumans arrived in Independence. Ten thousand people greeted them at the station, another 5,000 at 219 North Delaware. The largest such demonstration in the town's history, it left Truman deeply moved. "It was the pay-off," he wrote in his diary, "for thirty years of hell and hard work."[52]

34

"I Took the Grips Up to the Attic": Old Harry, 1953–1972

Truman's departure from the presidency was anything but a retirement. For the next decade, he was active in politics, speaking his mind on issues, excoriating the Republicans, feuding with Eisenhower, and taking issue with almost every viable presidential possibility in the Democratic party.

Yet he also began a process of making himself something beyond a controversial politician. No longer Mr. President, he glided into the role of Mr. Citizen, the plain, unassuming, but wise American democrat. As he grew older and eased out of politics, people increasingly thought of him less as Truman the hot-tongued partisan and more as Old Harry, an American who vividly displayed the spunk and integrity that had made the nation great.

An early sign of what was to come appeared when Mayor Robert Weatherford asked him to describe the first thing he had done after getting settled in Independence. His answer contained no pomposity, no great thoughts, no grand plans. It reflected instead the behavior of an ordinary man back home after a long trip: "I took the grips up to the attic."[1]

II

Three and a half months shy of his sixty-ninth birthday, relieved of the strains of office, Truman was vigorous, determined to defend his record, and eager to be a part of the continuing political dialogue. For the next few years, his schedule was a full one.

The Eisenhower presidency—indeed, the very presence of Eisenhower in the White House—gnawed at him in a way that was not altogether healthy. He understandably took issue with the administration on deeply felt policy positions. He rightly resented mud that was thrown his way. But he also nourished a deeply personal and not altogether rational animosity toward his successor. Eisenhower, demonstrating that he and Truman were more alike than he cared to admit, heartily reciprocated the feeling.

On the policy issues, Truman set the tone early. Addressing a union audience in Detroit on Labor Day, 1953, he delivered a tough speech more in the manner of a leader of the opposition than of a retired chief executive. He accused the Republicans of practicing "trickle-down" economics, pandering to the private electrical utilities, and telling the farmers to "go it alone." Public housing had been "condemned to death." The transfer of offshore oil fields to the states made "Teapot Dome look like petty larceny." Defense cuts jeopardized national security.

Save for the opposition stance, the entire scene might have been taken out of the 1948 campaign. Someone shouted, "Give 'em hell, Harry!" to Truman's obvious delight. If not quite the campaign trail, it was close enough. He replayed the Detroit speech in one form or another for the next seven years.[2]

In November 1953, he got into a nasty brawl with the administration. Eisenhower's attorney general, Herbert Brownell, accused Truman of having appointed Treasury Department official Harry Dexter White to the board of directors of the International Monetary Fund (IMF) in 1947 despite certain evidence that he was a Soviet agent.[3] In fact, the case against White had been at best fuzzy. Truman and Fred Vinson, then secretary of the treasury, had decided to disregard it. White had served at the IMF for a year, rendering no apparent services to the USSR, and resigned in ill health. Publicly accused by Whittaker Chambers and Elizabeth Bentley of espionage in mid-1948, he had denied the charges in testimony before the House Committee on Un-American Activities and died of a heart attack days later. By 1953, the incident was forgotten by almost everyone, including Truman himself. Brownell's exhumation of the case had a strong odor of the McCarthyite politics in which the Eisenhower administration routinely indulged during its first year.[4]

Instead of just declaring that he had received no persuasive evidence against White, Truman swung back wildly, asserting (inaccurately) that he had been given no prior FBI warning whatever about White and that he had discharged White when shown evidence of disloyalty. In a matter of days, the former president was presented with a subpoena commanding his testimony before the Un-American Activities Committee.[5]

On November 16, he responded in a nationally televised speech, which Charles Murphy and William Hillman helped him write. He disingenuously claimed that White had been appointed simply to facilitate a wide-ranging FBI investigation of subversion. He also, fairly enough, accused the Eisenhower administration of "McCarthyism," "shameful demagoguery," and "cheap political trickery." Stating that he would not honor the the committee's subpoena, Truman declared that former presidents were entitled to the same constitutional privileges as sitting ones.

By then, Eisenhower himself was clearly miffed with his attorney general, and no one in Washington was prepared to drag a former president to a political circus in a House hearing room. After riveting national attention for a couple of weeks, the episode dwindled to a minor partisan talking point. As always, an inelegant counterpuncher, Truman nevertheless had displayed considerable nerve in defending the institution of the presidency. He won the controversy by a technical knockout.[6]

Truman's acrimonious feelings for Eisenhower became increasingly personal. Real or imagined, one slight after another—an unreturned telephone call, a consistent failure to consult, routine partisan political attacks—intensified the hostility. He attacked his successor for employing "political assassins," destroying bipartisanship in foreign policy, and engaging in misrepresentation.

To Truman, foremost among these assassins was Vice President Richard Nixon, with whom he refused to be in the same room for years. "He has called me a traitor," Truman said, "and I don't like that." Asked in 1957 about his strained relationship with Eisenhower, he declared, "I just don't give a damn about the situation."[7] Privately, he referred to the new president at one time or another as "pinheaded," "chickenhearted," and "essentially a surly, angry, and disagreeable man."[8]

The nadir of their relationship occurred in May 1959, when Truman turned down an invitation to a White House stag dinner for Winston Churchill. Although in Washington at the time, he pled a previous commitment. Eisenhower allowed his press office to release a toast in which he pointedly noted that many of the guests had canceled important engagements to spend an evening with Sir Winston. Thus Truman passed up his last opportunity to visit with the great Englishman of whom he had become so fond.[9]

III

If not as poisoned as his relationship with Eisenhower, Truman's dealings with Adlai Stevenson were difficult and driven by the same sense of personal betrayal. Unlike Eisenhower, Stevenson was invariably solicitous of Truman and always hopeful of co-opting his support. Still, the older man never forgave Stevenson for the distance he had put between them in 1952. Increasingly, he was put off by their differences in personal style and by the tone of moderation that more and more was prominent in Stevenson's pronouncements.

Truman later recounted an exchange that epitomized their essential differences. He met with Stevenson in July 1956, a month or so before the Democratic National Convention, at the Blackstone Hotel in Chicago. The room was the same in which twelve years earlier Truman had met with Hannegan and others to hear Roosevelt's phone call from San Diego. After a discussion of the political outlook, Stevenson asked, "What am I doing wrong?"

As Truman recalled it, he took the former governor to a window, pointed down to a representative man-in-the-street, and said, "The thing you have got to do is learn how to reach that man."[10]

Whether Truman imagined this episode (as he occasionally imagined others) or whether it actually happened, it was an accurate depiction of the estrangement he felt. In 1956, he encouraged Averell Harriman, narrowly elected governor of New York two years earlier, to run for the presidency. As in 1952, Harriman had impressive assets. Alas, he was still woefully deficient in popular appeal. The contest quickly became one between Stevenson and Kefauver.

When Stevenson came to the convention with more pledged delegates than Kefauver but lacking a majority, Truman issued a public endorsement of Harriman. It attacked Stevenson's "counsel of moderation" and declared "he lacks the kind of fighting spirit that we need to win and keep the party from falling into the hands of . . . a conservative minority group."

The Harriman camp took heart, but the statement did it no good. Stevenson won easily on the first ballot. After Pennsylvania put him over the top, the band in the packed convention hall played "We're Loyal to Illinois" to wild cheers. Then it broke into "The Missouri Waltz." After a moment, Truman stood up in his box, Bess at his side, to receive a rafter-shaking ovation. The Democrats who had rebuffed his choice of a candidate showed him they loved him nevertheless. "An odd gesture it may have been," wrote Russell Baker, "but tonight with the band blaring and the crowd screaming, it was sentimentally perfect."[11]

The next night, although further disgruntled by the selection of Kefauver as the vice-presidential nominee, Truman went to the podium to warm up the crowd for Stevenson's acceptance speech: "Governor Stevenson is a real fighter, and I ought to know. . . . He's given some of us here a pretty good licking." Stevenson responded, "I salute President Harry Truman. I am glad to have you on my side again, sir."

Later on, Truman sent Stevenson a letter of congratulation and exhortation. He had all the qualifications to be president if he would just let them come to the top. He had emerged as a fighter. But the Democratic party could not be a "me-too party"; it had to represent the welfare of all the people. "Now I'm ready to do whatever I can to help the Party and its Leader win," Truman wrote. "I wouldn't blame you if you'd never speak to me again—but let's win the campaign and think of that afterwards."[12] He campaigned hard in the fall, enjoying himself immensely, suppressing persistent doubts about his candidate, and lambasting the Republicans.

Actually, Stevenson never had a chance. As in 1952, he was centrist to the core. No longer a fresh face, he had less appeal to the general public than he had had four years earlier. To many voters, he seemed weak and indecisive, an impression he confirmed by suggesting a unilateral moratorium on nuclear testing. Eisenhower, by contrast, remained a popular figure with a vast following among independents. The Hungarian and Suez crises of that fall, although precipitated in part by his own foreign policy, helped him enormously. On Election Day, the public voted overwhelmingly for the old general in whom it had so much faith. Truman took the results less as a measure of Eisenhower's strength than of Stevenson's ineptness.[13]

Truman's criticism of Stevenson's moderation was deeply felt. Aside from claiming a voice in Democratic presidential politics, he hoped to keep the party moving in the direction he and Roosevelt had led it. He envisioned himself as an elder statesman able to act as a broker between the Capitol Hill moderates, led by Sam Rayburn and Lyndon Johnson, and the liberals, represented by the social democratic wing of the labor movement, the Americans for Democratic Action, and aggressive young legislators like Hubert Humphrey.

To the annoyance of the moderates, Truman joined the Democratic Advisory Council (DAC), an organization established by the party's national chairman, Paul Butler, to provide an alternative, liberal voice to the accommodationist counsels of the congressional leadership. Attending its meetings regularly, he associated genially with old comrades such as Harriman, Dean Acheson, and Leon Keyserling; less comfortably with Butler, Stevenson, Kefauver, and John Kenneth Galbraith among others. He may have hoped to be the dominant figure, but it was Stevenson who raised the money and maintained the highest profile. Policy papers issued by the DAC to some extent foreshadowed Kennedy's New Frontier and Johnson's Great Society. They did not go as far in advocating social spending as Truman would have preferred, but he does not seem to have been unhappy with them.[14]

He persisted in his long-held irritation with dogmatic liberals who had no feel for practical politics, wanted a softer policy toward the USSR, and considered him an irrelevant relic from the past. "Should we quit the Advisory Committee?" he asked Acheson in August 1959. They stayed. But in December, Truman spoke out to a big audience at a DAC dinner in honor of Eleanor Roosevelt. He denounced snobbish "self-appointed guardians of liberal thinking" who abused "many a genuine working liberal." In his typically unsubtle way, he had said that the Democratic party could be successful only through a marriage of the political professionals and the liberal visionaries, that ideals had to be tempered by pragmatism. Not elegantly stated, perhaps articulated on the wrong occasion, these ideas were wiser all the same than many of his listeners understood.[15]

Even more than during Truman's presidency, the newer issue of black civil rights called up conflicting emotions within him. He had no fundamental difficulty with school integration. The basic arguments had after all been developed by his Justice Department. When the state of Arkansas engaged in massive resistance against token desegregation at Little Rock Central High School, he responded to a letter from a justice of the Arkansas Supreme Court: "We must abide by the law of the land. . . . I hope you will join in the effort to put some common sense into the public officials of your great state."

But the sit-ins outraged him fully as much as had the sit-down strikes of the 1930s. In April 1960, he remarked that if anyone attempted such a demonstration in a store he ran, "I'd throw him out." A few days later, he made it clear that he thought businessmen should serve all legitimate customers, but then he tossed off an opinion that the sit-ins were Communist-inspired. The resulting controversy did neither him nor the Democratic party any good. Dean Acheson, writing a long cautionary letter to his old chief a couple of months later, counseled silence: Truman should avoid sounding like an echo of J. Edgar Hoover, "whom you should trust as much as you would a rattlesnake with the silencer on its rattle." The right of free speech, Acheson reminded Truman, did not *compel* one to broadcast his views. Moreover, as reported, these were "wholly out of keeping with your public record." It was good advice. Truman heeded it.[16]

IV

One pragmatic liberal Truman might have been expected to like was John F. Kennedy—a forceful, young slightly left-of-center, Cold Warrior senator with strong ties to the world of traditional Democratic politics. Instead, he thought Kennedy too young, too inexperienced, and too Catholic. No doubt Truman would have looked with disfavor on any young man who seemed embarked on a quest to buy the presidency with a wealthy father's cash. No doubt he found Kennedy's Harvard education and patrician veneer off-putting. Most of all, however, he could not disassociate the son from the father, Joseph P. Kennedy, who had come to represent the worst tendencies of Irish-American Catholicism in his isolationism and McCarthyism. "It's not the Pope I'm afraid of; it's the pop," he said.[17]

In addition, while Truman would have resented being called an anti-Catholic bigot, he did not believe that American Catholics respected full separation of church and state. They were an important segment of the Democratic party, he remarked privately, and a Catholic had to be Democratic national chairman. But he was not ready for a Catholic president.[18]

In May, he endorsed Stuart Symington, possibly envisioning Symington as a stalking horse for Lyndon Johnson, whom he liked and respected even more. On the eve of the Democratic National Convention, with Kennedy holding a commanding lead, Truman announced in a nationally televised press conference that he would not attend in order to protest the closed nature of the proceedings. Misspeaking—and revealing his real preoccupation—he referred to the young candidate as Joseph Kennedy. To many viewers, he seemed a spiteful old man out of touch with reality. He watched from Independence as Kennedy steamrolled to a first-ballot nomination and co-opted Johnson with the vice presidency. Then Truman issued the inevitable declaration of support and called on the party to unite behind its nominee.[19]

Kennedy understood the value of Truman as a partisan icon and traveled to Independence seeking his participation in the campaign. The former president relished the show of deference and, whatever his reservations, thought Kennedy infinitely preferable to the Republican choice: Richard Nixon. At seventy-six, Truman had to maintain a considerably more limited schedule than in past years, but his speeches had as much fire as ever. And his tongue was looser. Speaking to a Democratic dinner at San Antonio, he said, "If you vote for Nixon, you ought to go to hell." He also declared to a news conference that Nixon "never told the truth in his life."

Republican leaders—behaving in a fashion that might be called "shocked, shocked"—demanded a repudiation from Kennedy. Nixon himself put on his most sanctimonious pose during one of the presidential debates, deplored Truman's profanity, and demanded that his opponent put a stop to it. A smiling Kennedy responded that he really could not tell a former president of the United States how to speak, and suggested that Nixon might contact Mrs. Truman. Truman must have enjoyed the exchange. Bess was less amused and let him know about it.[20]

Kennedy's narrow victory pleased Truman enormously. The new president and his beautiful wife invited the Trumans to the White House and thoroughly charmed them. Kennedy consulted Truman on major issues and saw to it that small favors (including a new post office for Independence) were done for him. His assassination stunned the old man, who had grown fond of him, if never quite convinced that he was destined for greatness.

Shaken, Truman refused requests for a press conference, and then flew to Washington to attend Kennedy's funeral. One good thing came out of the terrible event. He and Eisenhower, thrown together by the occasion, seized the opportunity for a long, friendly visit. Characteristically, however, neither permanently revised his opinion of the other.[21]

Truman's relationship with Lyndon Johnson was even more cordial. Its greatest moment came in 1965, when Johnson flew to Independence to sign the Medicare bill and present the eighty-one-year-old former president with Medicare card number 1. The new legislation was far from the universal health proposal that Truman had recommended, but it covered a large group that desperately needed such a program. Truman, fully as much as LBJ, could take it as a moment of triumph. Over the next few years, his health declining but his mind still clear, he watched with misgivings as Johnson led the nation into a quagmire much more agonizing than Korea.[22]

V

Truman's immediate priority after leaving office was to write his memoirs. He worked on this and other projects from an office provided by the federal government in downtown Kansas City. The memoirs had two purposes: to make him financially independent and to deliver a vigorous defense of his presidency. In the end, neither was well achieved.

The contract Truman signed with *Life* for the project was, on the surface, a bonanza, providing in its final form a payment of $600,000. But the cost of assistance (typists, researchers, and ghost writers) was heavy. And most fundamentally, Harry Truman, author, found himself facing the stiff progressive income tax system he always had supported. With the help of Sam Rosenman, who acted as his attorney on the enterprise, he negotiated an arrangement in which the Bureau of Internal Revenue allowed him to save some money by taking his payment in six installments. Even with a favorable ruling, however, he was taxed at 67.5 percent, whereas several years earlier Eisenhower had been allowed to declare his war memoir a capital gain to be taxed at 25 percent. (He either did not know or did not care that Congress had in the interval passed a law to plug this alleged loophole.) In 1957, Truman complained vehemently that he had cleared only $37,000.[23]

Production of the memoirs was a long and difficult process.[24] Truman worked with two ghost writers who were longtime friends: journalist William Hillman and public-relations man David Noyes. Several other assistants participated at one stage or another; probably the most effective was Francis Heller, the young infantry officer who believed in 1945 that the atomic bomb had saved his life. The "ghosts" did extensive oral interviews with Truman and numerous other members of the administration, some of whom also contributed written summaries of issues and actions with which they had been engaged.

In June 1954, midway through the process, Truman suffered his worst health crisis since diptheria had nearly killed him at the age of ten. Stricken with a severe gall-bladder attack, he was rushed to the hospital for emergency surgery. Postoperative complications left him near death for a few days, but he retained an overflowing reservoir of strength and vitality. He rallied, left the hospital twenty days after he had entered it, and recovered swiftly.

Over the next several months, the memoirs developed rapidly—and uncontrollably. By the beginning of 1955, the manuscript amounted to 2 million words; the contract called for 300,000. After renegotiation, Doubleday, which had acquired the book rights, agreed to publish a two-volume work approximately twice that size. The first volume, *Year of Decisions*, was rushed into print that fall. It briefly covered Truman's early career and surveyed his presidency up through the firing of Henry Wallace. The second volume, *Years of Trial and Hope*, came out in early 1956 and gave his account of the rest of his White House years.

The volumes sold well, demonstrating that Truman enjoyed wide affection and respect among his countrymen. Yet they were neither good literature nor good history. The ghosting process, along with Truman's determination to preserve the dignity of the presidency, resulted in depersonalized prose that conveyed little of the emotion, ambition, and raw energy that had seen him through eight difficult years. The relegation of most of those years to the second volume meant that as a history, his account was necessarily episodic. As with most memoirs, the work was unrepentantly self-serving and less than reliable.

VI

Although he remained controversial, Harry Truman out of the presidency was for most Americans a more attractive figure than he had been in it. He resumed the personal, unaffected style that always had come naturally to him, professing and practicing the traditional morality of an older America and providing a reassuring sense of continuity with the past. He liked to cite a quotation from Benjamin Franklin: "In free governments the rulers are the servants and the people their superiors and sovereigns. For the former therefore to return among the latter is not to degrade them but to promote them."[25]

He and Bess lived very much as a retired upper-middle-class couple in the old house at 219 North Delaware. Her two brothers and their wives (Frank and Natalie, and George and May) continued to occupy the bungalows behind, as they had for nearly forty years. Bess's friends and acquaintances recall her as happy and comfortable back in her home, glad to be surrounded by people she had known all her life, gliding naturally into the routine of the Tuesday bridge club and the weekly appointment at a nearby beauty salon. Family lore has it that she was so concerned about money that she insisted on Harry mowing the yard—until he ostentatiously did so one Sunday morning as well-dressed neighbors passed on their way to church. Thereafter, hired help took care of the grounds.[26]

Margaret, living in New York, quietly abandoned her efforts to win acclaim as a contralto and pursued a career as an entertainment personality. In 1956, she married *New York Times* journalist Clifton Daniel. The wedding was at the Episcopal Church in Independence; the reception, at the Truman house. The couple had four sons whom Harry and Bess cherished.

Years later, the eldest of them, Clifton Truman Daniel, recalled an incident that was oddly reminiscent of one in Harry's early life. He was perhaps no more than three, staying with his grandparents while his parents were vacationing. While energetically riding his hobbyhorse, he tipped the wooden animal over and began to cry. Bess started to get out of her chair; Harry told her to sit down. Then he said to the little boy, "You are not hurt. Get up, put the horse back up, and start riding again." Young Clifton obeyed. The old man, probably remembering the time he had fallen off a real pony as a child, may have wondered if his father was somewhere watching.[27]

Although far from rich, the Trumans lived comfortably. They bought full ownership of the Delaware Street house from Bess's brothers, each of whom had been left a one-quarter interest in it. They had managed to save a bit of money; Harry's writing and speaking provided more. For a token sum, Ed Pauley sold him an interest in four producing oil wells. All the Trumans—Harry, Vivian, and Mary Jane—joined the ranks of the financially independent by selling most of the old family farm to a real-estate developer. Nonetheless, both Harry and Bess felt insecure. The "job" of being a former president carried a lot of expenses; federal law provided no remuneration.

Sometimes unbecomingly, Harry lobbied Democratic leaders in Congress for presidential pension legislation. In early 1958, he told Edward R. Murrow in a nationally broadcast television interview, "You know, the United States Government turns its Chief Executives out to grass. They're just allowed to starve. . . . If I hadn't inherited some property that finally paid things through, I'd be on relief right now." Later that year, Congress passed and Eisenhower signed a bill providing generous benefits to former presidents.[28]

Like any comfortable retired couple in good health who wanted to enjoy the years they had left, he and Bess did some traveling, but it was a relatively small part of their life. Within the continental United States, they generally went by train in deference to Bess's fear of flying. The most frequent destination was New York to see Margaret. Their first extended trip after leaving the White House was to Hawaii in the spring of 1953. Accompanied by Margaret, they took the Union Pacific to San Francisco, traveling most of the way in Averell Harriman's private car. They then went to Honolulu by passenger liner.

They spent much of their time as guests at Ed Pauley's lush estate on his privately owned Coconut Island. The navy provided transportation and escort service for an excursion to the island of Hawaii. Like many other Midwesterners, they were enchanted by the lush tropical foliage, spectacular landscapes, Pacific Ocean, hula dancers, great volcanoes, and Edenic myth of an earthly paradise despoiled by the coming of the white man. The trip was memorable. It also established the pattern of an insulated VIP experience that they soon learned was unavoidable.[29]

Their one attempt to travel informally was a bit of a fiasco. A month after they returned from Hawaii, Truman decided to drive the family's new Chrysler to Washington, Philadelphia, and New York. With Bess keeping an eye on the speedometer, they cruised on the open road at fifty-five miles an hour; numerous drivers passed them, waving and shouting greetings. At restaurants and gas stations, they were the center of one hectic scene after another as admirers shook their hands and asked for autographs. Getting in and out of New York, no easy task for the young and alert, was difficult. A patrolman stopped Truman on the Pennsylvania Turnpike to admonish him for an improper lane change. They never drove across the country again.[30]

The most memorable experiences were journeys to Europe in 1956 and 1958. The latter trip, made in the company of Judge Samuel Rosenman and his wife, was in the main a quiet, private vacation. The 1956 trip was a triumphal version of the Grand Tour. Italy: Rome, Naples, Florence, and Venice; an audience with the pope; a tour of the World War II beachheads at Salerno and Anzio ("planned by some squirrel-headed general," Truman remarked); visits to museums and famous sites of classical antiquity; lunch with the great ninety-year-old art critic Bernard Berenson; a gondola ride on a Venice canal. Austria and Germany: Salzburg, Mozart's birthplace, and a cathedral organ recital; Bonn and a meeting with the venerable German chancellor Konrad Adenauer. France: Paris again after thirty-seven years, Versailles, Chartres, the Loire Valley, and the great old château at Chenonceaux. The Low Countries: Brussels, the Hague, Amsterdam, a great exhibition of Rembrandt paintings, lunch with Queen Juliana. England: an honorary degree from Oxford, presented with a three-minute ovation that moved its recipient to tears; Chartwell and a lovely, sentimental visit with Churchill; London, the Houses of Parliament, lunch with Queen Elizabeth and the Duke of Edinburgh.[31]

Did the old man of seventy-two think back to the boy of twelve, captivated by the doings of kings and generals? Never in his wildest fantasies could that boy have imagined that someday the majority of Europeans would think *him* a great man—less grand perhaps than Henri IV, Louis XIV, Gustavus Adolphus, or Napoleon, but more consequential and better for the common people. He had shielded the Europeans from war and despotism, preserved their freedom, and helped them toward prosperity. The achievement merited the acclaim. A dozen such Grand Tours could not begin to repay him for it.

VII

Truman's presidential library was important to him both as a memorial and as a research center for scholarship on his presidency. The only other such institution in the National Archives system was the Franklin D. Roosevelt Library, which might have served as a unique depository for the papers of a unique president had Truman not been determined to push ahead with his. Herbert Hoover, with whom he maintained a cordial personal relationship, soon moved to establish his own library. Eisenhower would follow, as has every president since.

Truman took a keen interest in every aspect of the library's development: fund-raising, architecture, the solicitation of the papers of members of his administration, and the establishment of an affiliated nonprofit institute that would provide generous grants and fellowships for researchers. He attracted to its board of directors such luminaries as Dean

Acheson, Clark Clifford, Averell Harriman, Earl Warren, numerous other members of his administration, and Cyrus Eaton, a Cleveland tycoon he had befriended as a senator investigating the railroads.

He originally had planned to locate the library on the family property at Grandview, but changed his mind when the city of Independence offered a splendid site about a mile from his home. The dedication on July 6, 1957, was a gala civic event that may have evoked memories of the local courthouse dedication a quarter-century earlier; but the far more imposing guest list included Eleanor Roosevelt, President Hoover, Chief Justice Warren, Speaker Rayburn, and Secretary Acheson.

Truman relocated his office to a wing of the library; for years, he was there regularly, handling an extensive correspondence, tending to personal business affairs, receiving important visitors, delivering short talks to students, and usually making himself available to scholars and writers working on some aspect of his administration. From the beginning, the affiliated museum drew hordes of visitors attracted by its proximity to one of America's most heavily traveled cross-country highways.

Scholars were mixed in their evaluation. The presidential papers available in the early years consisted of tons of public-opinion mail and speech drafts supplemented by occasional working papers or the odd piece of personal correspondence. Worried about embarrassing living individuals, Truman maintained tight control over his personal presidential papers until his death. Presenatorial papers remained stashed away and half-forgotten in his home on Delaware Street.

Monroe Billington, one of the early historians to use the library, remarked in 1965 that the president had a habit of striding through the research room and pausing at a table to tell a researcher, "I hope you find what you're looking for." He invariably would move quickly away without waiting for an answer.

Richard Kirkendall, a young professor at the University of Missouri, tried to get started on a multivolume Truman biography. The material was not there, especially for the prepolitical years. "I spent months trying to find out something about his early life," Kirkendall remarked years later. "I wondered why he never wrote any letters."[32]

Truman's availability to researchers was a mixed blessing. To meet with the man was in some sense to take his measure, although one had to remember that the outspoken, temperamental, occasionally profane individual one encountered was not a direct extension of the personality that had lived in the White House. The interviewers, usually scholars interested in public policy, rarely learned much reliable factual information.

Sometimes, Truman took a liking to them. Monte Poen, an older graduate student, had been in the air force, had walked a route as a postman, and seemed more a workingman than a self-important intellectual. Truman regaled him with mostly inaccurate stories of his fight for universal health insurance and described the executive director of the American Medical Association with an innovative and colorful profanity that added an unforgettable phrase to Poen's vocabulary.

Sometimes he was less accommodating. Kirkendall made the mistake of asking him why the United States had "changed objectives" in deciding to cross the thirty-eighth parallel during the Korean War. The answer was prompt and vehement: "We never changed our objectives, young man. Go back and read your history books, and don't bother me again until you have." Kirkendall never interviewed him again.

Eric Goldman, a prominent Princeton historian, wanted to write Truman's biography. Dissatisfied with the way Goldman had treated him and his family in earlier books, he refused all cooperation. *New York Times* journalist Cabell Phillips ran into a similar stone wall while researching his book on the Truman presidency. Unwilling to criticize Truman, Phillips blamed the library, which he called a "sentimental mausoleum in which valuable historical materials are buried beyond the convenient reach of most of the people who need access to them."[33]

Truman himself believed that it would be a half-century before the history of his presidency could be written. If he jealously guarded his extensive personal papers, he also preserved them intact. A few years after his death, they were open to scholars. By the mid-1980s, after Bess was gone, the family papers were also available; the material, which included 1,200 of his letters to her, was worth the wait.

VIII

The activity Truman most enjoyed was speaking to students. The most notable such engagements were at Yale, Cornell, and Columbia; in each case, he spent a few days as a visiting fellow, lecturing to large groups and participating in small informal seminars with selected students and faculty members. He was engaging. Missouri, he liked to tell his audiences, had produced three notorious characters: Mark Twain, Jesse James, and himself. He was the only one left, so they would have to make do with him.

Retaining the mischievous streak of his youth, he liked to shock. At Yale, a star graduate student, Fred Greenstein, was detailed to escort him to a function. Having prepared a little speech of gratitude for the honor, Greenstein attempted to make it, only to be interrupted: "Young feller, I'm an old man, and I have an old man's kidneys. Where can I piss?"

Greenstein recalled him speaking with a small group of faculty and graduate students. Responding to the question of how a Southerner like himself had become a civil rights supporter, he replied eloquently that all Americans had fundamental rights. Then he added, "But personally I don't care to associate with niggers." Charles Blitzer remembers that when he spoke to a large audience, the word "nigger" was never used.[34]

It was good for students to be exposed to a former president. Professors who had spent years developing complex models of the political process found Truman's straightforward views of politics dismayingly simplistic. At Columbia, David B. Truman (no relation), America's premier theorist of interest group politics, lamented to his classes what a pity it was that a man who had such vast practical experience could not get past civics-textbook maxims. Truman's stock talk, "From Precinct to the Presidency," was a good introduction to practical politics for the intelligent undergraduate. Yet, all his professed concern for learning notwithstanding, Truman neither communicated well with scholars nor was interested in most of what they wrote.[35]

With the help of Hillman and Noyes, he produced another book, *Mr. Citizen*, published in 1960. An episodic account of his experiences since leaving the presidency, the book projected far more of his personality than had the memoirs. He appeared as a direct, uncomplicated, appealing man with a sense of humor, attempting to live a normal life (and, incidentally, save the Democratic party from Adlai Stevenson) while under assault from autograph hounds, camera-toting tourists, and Republicans.

Hillman and Noyes also assisted with a few newspaper opinion columns each year from 1957 to 1961; they were widely syndicated by the North American Newspaper Alliance. Truman, Hillman, and Noyes planned a book on the history of the presidency. In 1960 and 1961, they produced hours of taped conversations that were rambling, repetitive, and ultimately unusable. The failure to do the book indicated both the limitations of the two ghosts and the way in which Truman himself was slipping.[36]

At the age of seventy-seven, he became involved in developing a television series. For the better part of a year during 1961 and 1962, he worked with a David Suskind production team that included Robert Alan Aurthur and Merle Miller; their goal was thirteen thirty-minute documentaries. They filmed two episodes, but were unable to sell the series to a major network. Screen Gems took over the project and did a twenty-six-part series that was syndicated in the 1964/1965 season. The films were at best a routine example of the genre, Truman was too old and too stiff to add much life to them.

After Truman's death, Miller published *Plain Speaking*, a book based on his interviews with the president and his associates. It displayed its main character as a crusty old wise man who said what he thought and exemplified the best in traditional American values. Although presented in the form of a transcript of taped interviews, the work was more accurately described by John P. Roche as "a semi-fictional 'oral biography'" that "brought an American original to life."[37]

IX

Roche's remark exemplified the increasing fondness with which much of the American public came to regard the older Harry Truman in the 1960s. Although he made a few Democratic campaign appearances in 1962, he all but ceased to be a partisan figure after the election of Kennedy. A press and a public that had been rough on him as president gained a new appreciation for his better qualities during the administrations of Lyndon Johnson and Richard Nixon. The ultimate indication of his transformation came in 1969, when President Nixon visited the Truman Library, gave it the piano that Truman had used in the White House, and played a tune for his predecessor. Frail, unable to speak well, but choosing his words carefully, Truman thanked his old enemy and proclaimed his reverence for the *office* of the presidency. (Ironically, he later developed a grudging respect for Nixon's management of that office.)[38]

In his last years, Truman was probably overly romanticized. Age accentuated his bad qualities as well as his good ones. He was more inclined than ever to blurt out his prejudices on matters on which he could claim no special authority. A reporter queried him about racial intermarriage in 1963. "Would you want your daughter to marry a Negro?" he replied. Journalists, who got a story out of such utterances, enjoyed his willingness to respond to questions that might best have gone unanswered. They and much of America likewise were entertained by his tendency to employ profanity freely in his old age.[39]

Truman was also more prone to lash out at anyone who annoyed him—whether a college student who betrayed an impudent attitude, a history professor who asked the wrong question, or a television producer trying to make a "play actor" out of him. He indulged his fondness for good bourbon more freely. And he accepted as his due the services of Noyes, Hillman, or some other handler (at Yale it was Dean Acheson), hovering over him, prompting him, flattering him in the classical manner of courtiers throughout history.

Robert Alan Aurthur recalled a documentary filming session in which Truman took questions on the Korean War from army officers at Fort Leavenworth. The president and his host, a major general, had just made a big dent in a bottle of bourbon.

> [Truman] was going only on nervous energy, soon to give out. His answers to the questions reflected his irritation and wrath; he was abrupt, even rude, and worse of all, some of his facts were obviously wrong. At one point, when he referred to the Red Chinese first as the "Yellow Chinee," then as "Chinks," I ran from the room in despair.[40]

But there was always the flip side. In 1970, Thomas Fleming came to Independence to assist Margaret in preparing a biography of her father. The old man was intimidating to the much younger writer. Truman poured big jolts of whiskey for himself and his guest and then asked, "Have you always been a Democrat?" Fleming replied that his family had always voted the straight Democratic ticket. "That's what I wanted to hear!" Truman responded, eyes flashing as he clinked his glass against Fleming's.[41]

More often than not, veneration of the sort Truman had achieved is accompanied by physical decline. In October 1964, he fell in his bathroom and suffered two broken ribs. After that, his visits to the office were irregular. He rarely gave interviews to scholars. A palsy made it impossible for him to write; vertigo left him unsteady and put an end to his daily walks. He stopped attending the Battery D banquet and a birthday luncheon held each year by friends and admirers. He no longer spoke at the few public appearances, mostly Truman Library affairs, that he did make. He wanted, he said, people to remember him as he had been, not as he was. On June 28, 1969, he and Bess quietly observed their fiftieth wedding anniversary.

The artist Thomas Hart Benton, who had created a great mural, *Independence and the Opening of the West*, for the Truman Library, painted Truman's last portrait. He rendered an image of a gnarled old man reading, a stack of books to one side. The work displayed little of Benton's primitivist exaggeration; it was a near-photographic representation of a fast-fading elder.

In April 1970, the twenty-fifth anniversary of his accession to the presidency, Truman attended a luncheon for the board of directors and guests of the Truman Library Institute. The great men of the board—Harriman and Earl Warren among them—had already paid their respects at his home. Now, standing in the reception area, they chatted among themselves while sipping weak highballs. The president was brought in and seated. For what seemed a long time, he sat alone and ignored, holding a cane and sporting a big smile. A historian watched him, tried to screw up the courage to introduce himself, and failed.

In December 1972, shortly after Margaret had published her loving biography, Truman was rushed to the hospital, a victim of the irreversible aging process rather than of some specific malady. On December 26, Wallace Graham, who cared for him to the end, pronounced him dead. He was eighty-eight years, seven months, and eighteen days old. Bess scrapped plans for an elaborate funeral and arranged an Episcopalian service in the auditorium of the Truman Library; a Baptist minister and a Masonic leader also participated. He was buried in the library courtyard.

The epitaph he had prepared was a model of democratic simplicity. It gave the dates of his birth and death, referred to the birth of his daughter, and listed his positions of public trust, from eastern district judge to president of the United States. The marker he prescribed for Bess, who joined him ten years later, would say "First Lady of the United States, 1945–1953."

The honor guard fired its last salute. The widow received the flag. A citizen had come home to his final resting place.

Epilogue

Who He Was, What He Did, and Why We Care

Over the next two decades, Truman became an even more revered American hero. His eulogizers ranged from Chicago, a soft-rock group with a countercultural tinge, to Senator Barry Goldwater, a paladin of the conservative right. In 1992, three presidential candidates all strove to identify with him, and David McCullough's fond biography became a runaway best-seller.

Why, forty years after leaving the presidency as a repudiated incumbent, had Truman become so central a figure in the national mythology?

He was, above all, an archetypical American democrat—reared by a family of middling status within a community that professed egalitarian ideals, compelled to define his own identity in a fluid society. The quest, marked by years of hard work as a farmer and failures in business, finally led him to that most insecure of American endeavors: politics. For thirty years, he earned a living and made a reputation as a professional politician. His climb to the top in this Darwinian world can be seen as a triumph of the values America represented. Thus to celebrate him is to celebrate ourselves.

II

Historians interested in understanding the American experience will learn much from Truman's career, but its lessons go beyond popular wisdom and are far from reassuring. Living, as we all inevitably must, by the ethic of the world of his time, Truman struggled hard and paid a heavy psychological price for his success. A boy who wanted to be a leader was a two-fisted athlete, not a four-eyed sissy who played the piano. A man who owned his own business amounted to something; a man who went into politics was a man who could not manage for himself. The financial penalties of failing as an entrepreneur were perhaps the least worrisome compared with the blows to self-esteem, the readjustment of career goals, and the move to an insecure, low-status occupation.

Truman went into politics not as a good-government independent, but as a "henchman" (to use the term the *Belton Herald* had applied to his father) of a political machine that enjoyed little esteem within the civic establishment. As a county official, he functioned in a political world indifferent to issues and focused single-mindedly on the spoils of power. Genuinely devoted to honesty and efficiency in public service, he uneasily juggled his fealty to boss Tom Pendergast with efforts to hold waste and corruption to a minimum—all the while enduring repeated attack as an organization toady and a failed businessman.

As a county administrator and a United States senator, Truman struggled to walk an uneasy path between the practical demands of real-world politics and the ethical absolutes of disinterested public service. He justified his unrepentant loyalty to the machine by magnifying the boss's virtues while largely ignoring his vices, reluctantly accepting graft and dishonesty as inevitable components of the political process. At the same time, he nurtured a sense of reformers as moral hypocrites, usually unreliable, often seeking personal gain. Although he privately complained about having to give jobs to organization hacks, he freely dispensed patronage to family members and close supporters. He salved his conscience by doing as well as he could for the general public and remaining personally clean.

The psychological toll of so uneasy a series of compromises was high. It was made all the more so by Truman's near-total lack of the indefinable but crucial quality for commanding democratic leadership—charisma. His early hero, Woodrow Wilson, had possessed it; so had Franklin Roosevelt; so did Eisenhower. In each case, a personal magnetism drew millions of enthusiastic followers who voted for a man as much as for a party. Truman had no such good fortune.

Even after escaping the shadow of Tom Pendergast and becoming a leader himself, Truman lived the life of the workaday politician who won elections by campaigning intensively, raising issues, mobilizing a following interested in benefits, and working hard to deliver results when in office. Like most ordinary politicians, he lived with the knowledge that events beyond his control could turn a fickle electorate against him. Unimpressive in appearance and poor as a speaker, he seemed throughout his career to attract disparaging characterizations, the most frequent of which was "little man" or some variant thereof. Political enemies often called him a crook or an incompetent.

How could he avoid acquiring, and constantly honing, a touchiness about himself that at times verged on a personality disorder? Defensive about his business career and his machine ties, solicitous of his family, he possessed a deep need for recognition of his achievements. Above all, he wanted *respect*. His failure to get much of it throughout his political career produced an anger that fueled much of his campaigning and periodically blasted out at random targets.

However natural the syndrome, each outburst renewed a sense that he was erratic and left his authority diminished. An opinionated snappishness that would seem amusing to a later generation was not widely regarded as the stuff of leadership during his presidency. His successes in nearly eight years in the White House are made all the more remarkable by his consistent inability to muster the personal presence that brings success and instinctive acceptance of one's leadership.

III

As much as anything, politics is about the employment of power, a problem Truman faced at several different levels. In politics, this power most frequently involves the organization of support for administrative or legislative agendas, the accumulation of personal and institutional authority, and, above all, the husbanding of the means for election and reelection. Truman was more a master of this game than is commonly understood.

We remember him as a shrill, angry partisan, and his ability to evoke partisan feelings was central to his 1948 victory. Yet at key points in his career, he excelled at building bipartisan coalitions for his objectives, whether bringing the Kansas City business community behind his road-building plans or unifying the Truman Committee or pulling a large number of Republicans behind the Truman Doctrine and the Marshall Plan. Bipartisanship was in truth behind his most important substantive accomplishments.

As a senator, he quickly realized that legislative power had multiple sources. Among his peers, it stemmed from the influence that a conscientious freshman could gain if he worked hard at a chosen speciality. For reelection purposes, power arose from the national attention one could receive from investigating railroads or overseeing the war effort. It also came from the fostering of ties to powerful interest groups, especially the railway brotherhoods.

As an executive, whether at the Jackson County courthouse or the White House, he consciously and consistently sought to channel as much authority to himself as possible. He reminded his cabinet that he regarded each of them as helpers to the president, not as independent operators. Fearing institutions that might dilute his power, he served as his own chief of staff, put an end to informal cabinet luncheons at which he was not present, and rejected a cabinet secretariat. He made the Council of Economic Advisers part of his staff, rebuffing Edwin Nourse's efforts to establish it as a quasi-independent body. In the same spirit, he reminded the members of the newly minted National Security Council that they belonged to *his* council. He vetoed more acts of Congress than any twentieth-century president other than Franklin D. Roosevelt.

Truman found the preservation and exercise of presidential power a frustrating, ongoing struggle, epitomized in his oft-quoted remark that he spent most of his time talking other people into doing what they ought to do anyway. Perhaps the most notable example involved his protracted indirect struggle with Secretary of State George Marshall over Palestine. Yet, however ugly the process, Truman avoided a potentially disastrous confrontation, ultimately dictated policy, and prevailed over a subordinate of considerably greater stature than he. Few will dispute that he left the presidency as strong as he had found it.

At the ultimate level, power can mean the employment of brute force, the willingness to go to war. Truman's life experience gave him an understanding of the limitations of human nature, an acceptance of violence as the ultimate resort in human affairs, and the hope that one could achieve idealistic ends by realistic means. The boy who had venerated great generals, the artillery captain in World War I, the reserve officer, the interventionist of 1940 and 1941, he knew that Nazi thugs could understand only guns and bayonets, that aggressors had to be stopped.

He authorized the use, not just once but twice, of the most awesome and indiscriminate weapon in human history in order to end World War II; then, four and a half years later, he calmly ordered the development of the hydrogen bomb. Here, depending on the viewpoint of the beholder, was a profound realpolitiker, a ruthless warlord, or a morally obtuse scoundrel.

Yet what of the man who told his cabinet that he was withholding a third bomb because he did not want to kill any more kids? Who made it a cornerstone of his nuclear policy to remove atomic weapons from direct military access? Who informed his national security officials during the Berlin crisis that the bomb was not a military weapon but a device to kill women and children? Who forswore its use during the Korean War? Who relentlessly cut military spending until the crises of 1950 forced him in the other direction?

Faced with decisions of war or peace, entrusted with authority over the ultimate in destructive power, he was profoundly ambivalent. Far from an amoral warlord, he was essentially a Niebuhrian liberal who recognized the imperfections of humankind while valuing the sanctity of life. He found the use of power in Korea and the inconclusive conflict there psychologically draining, but never questioned his basic decision to intervene.

IV

What were the purposes of power, whether political or military? For Truman's one-time mentor, Tom Pendergast, power was its own reward. For Truman, it was a means for the protection and extension of deeply internalized values. His politics expressed a loose ideology that provided him with an understanding of the meaning of his own life as well as of the American social-political world.

From his parents and teachers, he learned the values of the straight-arrow Victorian male: monogamy in marriage, courage as a soldier, honesty in transactions with others, a strong belief in the sanctity of agreements (whether between individuals or nations), and a sense of personal honor that led to his discomfort at having to deal with corrupt politicians or make dubious compromises.

His ideology began as a natural expression of the turn-of-the-century neofrontier environment in which he grew up. At its base, it was the Democratic worldview of Jefferson and Jackson, its celebration of small government and individual enterprise underwritten by an optimistic faith in economic opportunity. Over this, Truman layered first the populism of William Jennings Bryan, and then the insurgent progressivism of the early twentieth century as represented by Woodrow Wilson, Robert La Follette, and his friend and colleague Burton Wheeler.

Insurgent progressivism attempted to maintain the values and ethos of the old order while accepting in practice (if often not in theory) such tenets of modernity as efficiency, regulation of business, bigger government, interest group politics, and the bureaucracy that was a by-product of these forces. It marked the way in which farms, small cities, aspiring entrepreneurs, and an insecure middle class attempted to adapt to the twentieth century while preserving the virtues of the nineteenth. By the Great Depression, insurgent progressivism was supplanted by a new style of reformism stemming from the aspirations of big-city working classes and ethnoreligious minorities, based in the labor movement, social-democratic in outlook, and galvanized by the political leadership of Franklin D. Roosevelt.

Truman himself provides a near-ideal case study of the transformation of insurgent progressivism into New Deal–Fair Deal liberalism. He became an advanced "social liberal" and advocate of the regulatory state while remaining a cultural traditionalist who seemed to have been dragged unwillingly into an advanced social-welfare present. However confused such an identity might seem, it probably was a political asset, representing as it did a combination of continuity and change.

From these starting points of personality, experience, values, and ideology, Truman practiced politics skillfully. In America, mass political parties are united by allegiance to a common worldview, but they are also coalitions of diverse interests with special goals and priorities. Successful national political leaders must be ideologists with a clearly articulated, usually polarizing, vision; at the same time, they must be pragmatic, pluralistic coalition builders. At crucial points, notably 1948, Truman transcended his limitations to display startling effectiveness at both endeavors.

These strengths understood, the limitations cannot be swept discreetly away. The political strategy that he pursued throughout his presidency looked to the past, to the resuscitation of a coalition that reflected the impoverished, class conflict–ridden world of the 1930s, and then to the archaic assumption that farmers and urban laborers could achieve a sense of common interest. In an increasingly prosperous and comfortable postwar era, he won reelection by promising to protect what Americans already had, not by offering them a brave new world. When he pushed major new programs all the same, he discovered that the nation did not want them.

His sense of the Democratic party was likewise muddled and impervious to the changing structure of American society. Ideologically, Truman thought of it as the party of liberalism and embraced all the meanings the word had taken on during the age of Roosevelt—a controlled economy, big social-welfare programs, civil rights. Operationally, he wanted the party to be a grand pastiche of northern liberals and southern conservatives; of workers, farmers, and small businessmen; of ethnic minorities and blacks, nativists and segregationists; of energy producers and energy regulators; of machine bosses and good-government reformers; and so on.

The ambition reflected not just Truman's natural bent toward conciliation, but also his instinctive understanding that the party could continue in the majority in no other way. The result was a politics of liberal promise and conservative gridlock that damaged his credibility. His easygoing tolerance of bosses, corrupt machines, and political hacks exacted an even higher price, reeking of an old politics that was discredited and out of date in the independent-minded, affluent society that America came to be in the postwar years.

Truman's foreign policy eventually came to grief because of its inherent contradictions. The frustrating Korean stalemate, which delivered the fatal blow to his presidency, was ultimately the result of a serious disparity between expanding ends and contracting means that characterized the first five years of his presidency. Well into his second term, Truman pursued a policy of ever-widening and sometimes unclear commitments while enforcing a rigid, budget-driven contraction of American military capability. Korea laid bare the inadequacies of these moves, alienating large segments of the American population and alarming the Western allies. The heavy military buildup that followed inflicted economic pain at home while doing nothing to relieve the ongoing bloodletting in Korea.

Yet whatever his mistakes, Truman was magnificently right on what may have been the two most important issues of his time: civil rights and the Soviet challenge.

It went against almost everything in his upbringing for him to conclude that blacks were entitled to equal opportunity. He is still frequently written off as a cynical opportunist and a secret racist. But the political payoff for Truman was at best ambiguous, and he clearly came to believe that although the civil rights movement might be guilty of excesses, its fundamental demands were just. The product of his best inner values and his sense of the national interest, his civil rights program was a noble resolution of contradictory impulses.

Moreover, however unsophisticated it may have been, Truman's understanding of Soviet totalitarianism and imperialism possessed an elemental comprehension and integrity that were impressive when contrasted with the aimless diplomacy of James Byrnes or the ostrich-like fellow-traveling of Henry Wallace. As increasing amounts of available Soviet and Chinese archival material reveal the implacability of Stalin and Mao, Truman's lack of nuance seems less a liability and more a powerful insight. The weak spots of his foreign policy pale beside his mobilization of the Western world against the Communist challenge. Truman was no Churchill, but the achievement was Churchillian in its significance.

V

Despite the waves of radical revisionism that have swept over the historical profession since the 1960s, polls of scholars consistently rank Truman among the top eight presidents in American history. The broader public has made him a mythic figure. His presidency's claims to great impact are irrefutable: containment of Soviet expansionism and the making of the postwar world, preservation of the Rooseveltian Democratic party, definition of the post–New Deal liberal agenda, and contributions to the early black civil rights movement.

Truman liked to define himself in his later years when speaking to students as a politician. Stoutly defending politics as a vocation, he called it the science of government and public service. Rejecting a contrast between politics and statesmanship, he regularly declared that a statesman was simply a dead politician.

But few Americans think of him as just a politician. When asked about his actions as president, most are unlikely to get much beyond use of the atomic bomb and the firing of General MacArthur. They see him as an ordinary man who fought for the interests of their own kind, made great decisions, cared about their welfare, and demonstrated their potential. In the end, it was not *what* he did that made Harry Truman an American icon, but *who* Americans believed him to be.

Notes

Abbreviations

BW/BWT	Bess Wallace/Bess Wallace Truman
CR	*Congressional Record*
FBP	Family, Business, Personal File, Harry S. Truman Papers
FRUS	*Foreign Relations of the United States*
GHDC	General Historical Documents Collections, Harry S. Truman Library
HST	Harry S. Truman
HSTL	Harry S. Truman Library
IE	*Independence Examiner*
JE	*Jackson Examiner*
KCS	*Kansas City Star*
KCT	*Kansas City Times*
LC	Library of Congress
MD	*Missouri Democrat*
Memoirs, 1	Harry S. Truman, *Memoirs by Harry S. Truman*, vol. 1, *Year of Decisions* (Garden City, N.Y.: Doubleday, 1955)
Memoirs, 2	Harry S. Truman, *Memoirs by Harry S. Truman*, vol. 2, *Years of Trial and Hope* (Garden City, N.Y.: Doubleday, 1956)
MHDC	Miscellaneous Historical Documents Collection, Harry S. Truman Library
MT	Margaret Truman
NYT	*New York Times*
OF	Official File, Harry S. Truman Papers
PD	*St. Louis Post-Dispatch*
PPF	President's Personal File, Harry S. Truman Papers
PSF	President's Secretary's File, Harry S. Truman Papers
Public Papers	*Public Papers of the Presidents of the United States: Harry S. Truman, 1945–53* (Washington, D.C.: Government Printing Office, 1961–1966)

SVP   Senatorial and Vice Presidential File, Harry S. Truman Papers

WHMC   Western Historical Manuscripts Collection, University of Missouri/State Historical Society of Missouri

Chapter 1

1. Merle Miller, *Plain Speaking: An Oral Biography of Harry S. Truman* (New York: Berkeley, 1974), 31–32.

2. Information on Truman's forebears is drawn primarily from Jonathan Daniels, *Man of Independence* (Philadelphia: Lippincott, 1950), 30–41, and Alfred Steinberg, *The Man from Missouri* (New York: Putnam, 1962), chaps. 2, 3.

3. The oaths of loyalty are in MHDC Nos. 114, 115. See also Bela Kornitzer, "The Story of Truman," *Parents Magazine*, March 1951, 34–36, 88–94; Miller, *Plain Speaking*, 30, chap. 4; Thomas M. Madden, "Briefed Chronological History of those Lands Located in 'Washington Township' of Jackson County, Missouri, formerly belonging to the 'Solomon Young family' . . . ," attached to Madden to Jonathan Daniels, January 25, 1950, copy in Arthur Mag Papers, HSTL; John Meador, Oral History, HSTL; items in Solomon Young folder, Vertical File, HSTL. For the Civil War claim, see U.S. House of Representatives, 59th Cong., 1st sess., Doc. No. 901, June 20, 1906; and Jackson County Probate Court File No. 2575 (Solomon Young), Jackson County courthouse, Kansas City, Mo.

4. HST, draft material for *Memoirs*, p. 1, HST Papers, Post-Presidential Papers, Memoirs File, HSTL; Steinberg, *Man from Missouri*, 18; Daughters of the American Revolution, *Vital Historical Records of Jackson County* (Kansas City, Mo.: Lowell Press, 1933–1934), 61–64, 75.

5. Miller, *Plain Speaking*, 63; Monte M. Poen, ed., *Letters Home by Harry Truman* (New York: Putnam, 1984), 17–18. The Lamar resident's memory of John Truman was related to me by my late uncle, Luther Summers.

6. Steinberg, *Man from Missouri*, 17; HST to BW, November 7, 1914, FBP.

7. J. C. Truman, interview with author; HST to BW, January 10, 1911, FBP.

8. HST, *Memoirs*, 1:113–15.

9. HST, *Memoirs*, 1:112–23; HST, draft material for *Memoirs*, p. 3, Post-Presidential Papers, Memoirs File; for the description of Harrison Young, see HST, handwritten memorandum, n.d., Personal Notes folder, Post-Presidential Papers, Desk File.

10. On Independence around 1890, see "Solomon Wise" [William Southern, Jr.], in *JE* [weekly edition of the *Independence Examiner*], September 23, 1927; on elections, see "Big Vote in the County," *KCS*, August 5, 1925; for Frank James, see *JE*, November 1, 1912; for Cole Younger, see, for example, *Lee's Summit Journal*, January 13, 1911; for the Quantrill reunion, see, for example, *JE*, July 24, 1908.

11. The most complete account of John Truman's business affairs is in Daniels, *Man of Independence*, chap. 3. The railroad switch story is in Kornitzer, "Story of Truman," 93–94, and was also related by Rufus Burrus, interview with author. On the Simpson-Hunter children, see HST to secretary of the treasury, memorandum, February 19, 1948, PSF. For the lawsuit involving John Truman and his driller, see MHDC No. 465.

12. Solomon Young Probate File; Jackson County Probate File No. 3060 (Harriet Young), Jackson County Courthouse, Independence, Mo.

13. Daniels, *Man of Independence*, 44, 46, 58.

14. HST to C. Raymond Long, July 16, 1953, Post-Presidential Papers, Memoirs File.

15. [William L. C. Palmer,] *Course of Study and Rules and Regulations of the Independence Public Schools* (1909), 131, HSTL; HST, *Memoirs*, 1:118–19, 125.

16. William Hillman, ed., *Mr. President* (New York: Farrar, Straus and Young, 1952), 225.

17. HST, "Two Years in the Army" [handwritten account, ca. 1920, actually mostly about early life and National Guard], FBP; HST, *Memoirs*, 1:122; Mary Paxton Keeley, Oral History, 32–34, HSTL.

18. For the essay, see Poen, *Letters Home*, 16–17; for the Tennyson poem, see John Hersey, *Aspects of the Presidency* (New Haven, Conn.: Ticknor and Fields, 1980), 46–47.

19. HST, *Memoirs*, 1:119–47.

20. HST to BW, May 23, 1911, FBP; HST to A. E. Weston, December 26, 1950; HST to Roy Roberts, June 12, 1950, PSF.

21. HST, interview with Jonathan Daniels, July 28, 1949, Daniels Papers, HST biography materials, University of North Carolina (photocopies at HSTL).

22. Myra Ewin, in *Jackson Daily News*, December 21, 1947, Vertical File, HSTL; HST, *Memoirs*, 1:125.

23. HST, *Memoirs*, 1:115.

24. HST, *Memoirs*, 1:115; HST, memorandum on Pickwick Hotel stationery [hereafter Pickwick memo], May 14, 1934, PSF, Longhand Notes.

25. Mary Ethel Noland, Oral History, 70–71, HSTL; Ron Cockrell, "Historic Structures Report: History and Significance, Harry S. Truman National Historic Site, Independence, Missouri" (Manuscript, National Park Service, Omaha, 1984 [copy at HSTL]).

26. Daniels, *Man of Independence*, 56–68; HST, *Memoirs*, 1:123–24; Commerce Bank employment files of Harry and Vivian Truman, MHDC Nos. 308, 309; Olive Truman, biographical sketch of Ralph Truman, and HST to Ralph Truman, September 17, 1951, Ralph Truman Papers, HSTL, as well as HST to Ralph Truman, February 3, 1923, Post-Presidential Papers, Family Correspondence File; John Hulston, interview with author.

27. HST to Roy Roberts, June 12, 1950, PSF. Spalding went out of business sometime in the 1930s, and none of its records have survived. Truman's dates of attendance can be determined by his typed letter. HST to Mrs. H. L. Young, July 1, 1901, Mary Jane Truman Estate Papers, HSTL, and by his Officer's Qualification Card, January, 1918, Department of the Army Military Personnel Records of Harry S. Truman, 1917–1973, HSTL. For the land sale, see Madden, "Briefed Chronological History."

28. For deed of sale on the Waldo Street house, September 26, 1902, see MHDC No. 151; MHDC Nos. 308, 309; HST to A. E. Weston, December 20, 1950, PSF; HST, *Memoirs*, 1:123–24.

29. HST, Pickwick memo, May 14, 1934, PSF. Daniels cleaned up the foreman's assessment for publication; the unvarnished version is in his notes.

30. MHDC Nos. 308, 309. All prior graduates of Independence High School are listed in [Palmer,] *Course of Study*; Vivian Truman is not among them.

31. MHDC No. 309.

32. MHDC Nos. 308, 309; Robert H. Ferrell, ed., *The Autobiography of Harry S. Truman* (Boulder: Colorado Associated University Presses, 1980), 18–20.

33. On the practical joke, see Robert H. Ferrell, *Truman: A Centenary Remembrance* (New York: Viking, 1984), 39–40; Truman's religious feelings are sprinkled throughout his private memoranda. On his church membership, see Rev. A. C. Chism to HST, April 29, 1942, OF 200, Invitations, Kansas City, and Robert W. Phillips, in *KCS*, December 21, 1976.

34. On the National Guard experience, see HST, "Two Years in the Army," and "The Military Career of a Missourian," SVP. For the Ted Marks incident, see Marks, Oral History, 6–7, HSTL.

35. HST to Roy Roberts, June 12, 1950, PSF.

36. For a discussion of his relationship with Bess Wallace, see Robert Ferrell, Introduction to Ferrell, ed., *Dear Bess: The Letters from Harry to Bess Truman, 1910–1959* (New York: Norton, 1983), esp. 11–14. Truman's one and only mention of Cosby Bailey is in "Two Years in the Army." See also Richard Lawrence Miller, *Truman: The Rise to Power* (New York: McGraw-Hill, 1986), 56.

Chapter 2

1. Both the chapter title and the quotation in this paragraph are from HST's autobiographical memo, "My Impressions of The Senate, The House, Washington, etc.," SVP. The subtitle was used as a heading on stationery ordered by Harry and his father in 1914.

2. This description of the Truman farm rests primarily on Richard S. Kirkendall, "Harry S. Truman: A Missouri Farmer in the Golden Age," *Agricultural History* 14 (October 1974): 467–83, and Truman's many letters to Bess Wallace, 1911–1914, FBP. See also numerous items in Vertical File, HSTL.

3. Jonathan Daniels, *Man of Independence* (Philadelphia: Lippincott, 1950), esp. 75–77; HST, "My Impressions of The Senate"; HST, autobiographical account, 1951, PSF, in *Mr. President*, ed. William Hillman (New York: Farrar, Straus and Young, 1952), 166. On the drought and disease problems, see HST to BW, July 12, 1911, September 17, 30, 1912, FBP. For the surviving remnants of his record keeping and for many receipts from grain and livestock dealers, see Mary Jane Truman Estate Papers, HSTL.

4. Fred Truman, Oral History, Appendices 2–6, HSTL; HST to BW, esp. January 26, September 15, 1911, February 10, May 19, 1913, FBP.

5. HST to BW, March 20, 1914, FBP.

6. Gaylon Babcock, Oral History, 38, HSTL.

7. Stephen Slaughter, "Harry S. Truman as I Knew Him," January 1973, MHDC No. 524; for the insurance application, see FBP.

8. HST, autobiographical memo, May 14, 1934, PSF; HST to BW, December 21, 1911, FBP; Daniels, *Man of Independence*, 76.

9. On Vivian's character, see Mary Ethel Noland, Oral History, 195–98, HSTL.

10. Slaughter, "Harry Truman as I Knew Him"; HST to BW, March 17, 1914, FBP.

11. For example, HST to BW, June 22, October 16, 1911, January 25, 1912, July 29, August 22, 1913, April 7, 1914, FBP.

12. HST to BW, April 1, 1911, January 30, September 9, December 17, 1912, FBP; William D. Tammeus, "Farm Work Helped Mold Truman Character," *KCS*, September 11, 1983.

13. HST to BW, January 6, March 10, 12, 26, April 2, 7, October 22, November 10, 1913, February 17, 24, March 24, 31, May 12, June n.d. [June folder], n.d. [June folder; Robert H. Ferrell, ed., *Dear Bess: The Letters from Harry to Bess Truman, 1910–1959* (New York: Norton, 1983), 169], 1914, FBP; Harriet Young Probate File No. 3060, Jackson County Courthouse, Independence Mo.; Solomon Young Probate File No. 2575, Jackson County Courthouse, Kansas City, Mo.; trial summaries in Record Book No. 603 (March 17–26, 1913), Circuit Court, Division 6; and Record Book No. 207 (February 9–17, 1914), Circuit Court, Division 2, in Jackson County Records Center, Kansas City, Mo.

14. HST to BW, June 16, July 29, October 7, December 14, 1911, January 3, 30, February 27, March 18, July 1, September 17, 23, 1912, May 23, September 30, November 18, 19, 25, 1913, January 12, 20, April n.d. [April folder; Ferrell, ed., *Dear Bess*, 164–65], June n.d. [June folder], 1914, FBP. For Truman's Masonic interests, see "The Masonic Biography of Harry S. Truman," MHDC No. 177.

15. HST to BW, April 8, 1912, November 4, 18, 19, 1913, FBP.

16. HST to BW, May 4, 1914, FBP; Gaylon Babcock, Oral History, 20–21, 49, HSTL.

17. HST to BW, January 6, 1914, FBP.

18. HST to BW, June 22, 1911, FBP.

19. HST to BW, July 10, 12, 1911, FBP.

20. HST to BW, November 4, 1913, FBP.

21. Mary Salisbury Bostian (Agnes's younger sister), Rosalind Gibson (daughter of Harry Allen and Agnes Salisbury), and Rufus Burrus (Independence attorney and political associate of Truman), interviews with author; *JE*, October 30, November 13, 1914, April 23, 1915; Mary Paxton Keeley, quoted in Sue Gentry, in *IE*, November 14, 1991; HST to BW, January 30, 1912, FBP.

22. May Southern Wallace, interview with author; for Southern's career, see Dick Fowler, *Leaders in Our Town* (Kansas City, Mo.: Burd & Fletcher, [1952]), 409–12.

23. HST to BW, April [date uncertain; Ferrell, ed., *Dear Bess*, 164–65], May 12, July [date uncertain; Ferrell, ed., *Dear Bess*, 170–71], 1914, FBP.

24. HST to BW, October 29, 1913, FBP.

25. HST to Ethel and Nellie Noland, October 19, 1911, Mary Ethel Noland Papers, HSTL; HST to BW, October 16, 22, 27, 1911, FBP.

26. HST to BW, n.d. [probably August 1913; Ferrell, ed., *Dear Bess*, 133–34], September 17 [two letters], 30, October 29, November 4, 10, 18, 1913; May 4, 12, 1914, FBP.

27. HST, handwritten reminiscence, July 12, 1960, HST Papers, Desk File, HSTL.

28. Kirkendall, "Truman: Missouri Farmer," 478–79; Lyle W. Dorsett, *The Pendergast Machine* (New York: Oxford University Press, 1968), 54–65; HST to BW, May 23, 1911, March 23, August 6, November 6, 1912, FBP.

29. HST to BW, March 23, August 6, November 6, 1912, January 6, Feb-

ruary 4, May 23, 26[?] [date illegible, probably August 19; Ferrell, ed., *Dear Bess*, 132–33], 1913, FBP; *Belton Herald*, April 24, 1913.

30. HST to BW, December 2, 1913, August 31, 1914, FBP.

31. HST to BW, August 31, September 17, 28, November [date uncertain; Ferrell, ed., *Dear Bess*, 177–78], December 1, 1914, FBP; *IE*, November 3, 1914; Daniels, *Man of Independence*, 74.

Chapter 3

1. The chapter title is from HST to BW, October 29, 1913, FBP.

2. HST to BW, n.d. [January 1915], FBP; MHDC Nos. 27, 44, 160; U.S. Civil Service Commission letter, July 1949, Vertical File, HSTL.

3. HST to Judge Allen Southern, August 3, 1915; roadwork notes, Mary Jane Truman Estate Papers, HSTL. See also *JE*, July 16, 23, 30, August 13, 1915.

4. HST to BW, November 4, 1915, July 25, 30, August 4, 1916, FBP; HST, autobiographical account, 1945, PSF; HST, "My Impressions of The Senate, The House, Washington, etc.," SVP; William Hillman, ed., *Mr. President* (New York: Farrar, Straus and Young, 1952), 196.

5. HST to BW, April 28, 1915; HST to BW [date illegible, probably February 16, 1916], from Fort Worth, Texas, FBP.

6. HST to BW, November 24, 1917; HST to BWT, October 29, 1937, June 30, 1947, FBP.

7. HST to BW, n.d. [probably January 27, 1915], April 28, September 13 [two postcards], November 4, 1915, n.d. [probably February 2, 1916], February 4, 16, 19, 1916, n.d. [probably February 16, 1916], FBP.

8. HST to BW, February 16, March 5, 1916; Articles of Agreement, April 14, May 19, August 5, 1916, FBP. For lead and zinc market prices in early 1916, see *NYT*, January 1, February 1, March 1, 1916, and *PD*, January 3, February 2, March 1, 1916. For the larger situation, see "Lower Metal Prices—the Handwriting on the Wall," *Commercial and Financial Chronicle*, June 17, 1916.

9. HST to BW, March 15, 19, n.d. [probably March 21], 1916; Articles of Incorporation, March 27, 1916; stock certificates, April 14, 1916; list of stockholders, n.d., FBP; Alfred Steinberg, *The Man from Missouri* (New York: Putnam, 1962), 38–39; Michael Shaver to Elizabeth Safly, with attached map, March 9, 1988, Vertical File, HSTL.

10. HST to BW, n.d. [ca. March 22], March 23, April 2, n.d. [April 5 or 6], April 9, 16, 24, 27, 1916; Articles of Agreement [April 14, 1916], FBP.

11. HST to BW, n.d. [April 5 or 6], April 9, 16, 24, 27, 1916, FBP.

12. HST to BW, May 19, 23, 26, FBP.

13. HST to BW, June 10, 24, July 25, 28, 30, August 19, FBP.

14. HST to BW, June 29, July 25, 28, 30, August 4, 5, 22, 29, 1916, FBP.

15. HST to BW, July 30, August 19, 26, 1916, FBP. For market quotations and descriptions, see *PD*, May 1, June 2, July 5, August 2, September 1, 1916.

16. HST to BW, September 7, 1916; C. A. Gish to HST, September 22, 1916, FBP; accounting of expenses on T.C.H. stationery, n.d.[September 1916], and draft of lease agreement to C. L. Windbigler to October 1, 1919, FBP; HST, Pickwick memo, May 14, 1934, PSF, Longhand Notes; HST, "My Impressions of The Senate."

17. HST to BW, August 5, 1916, FBP.

18. HST to BW, June 29, August 19, 29, 1916; last will and testament of Harrison Young, FBP; Harrison Young Probate File No. 15522, Jackson County Courthouse, Kansas City, Mo.

19. [David H. Morgan,] "A Factual Narrative Relating to the Business Activities, etc., of David H. Morgan & Harry S. Truman, 1916–1919," attached to Morgan to HST, August 5, 1951, PSF; Articles of Incorporation [Morgan & Company], December 14, 1916, and Amended Agreement and Declaration of Trust of the Morgan Oil and Refining Company, March 1, 1917, MHDC No. 456.

20. Thomas M. Madden, "Briefed Chronological History of those lands located in 'Washington Township' of Jackson County, Missouri, formerly belonging to the 'Solomon Young family' . . . ," attached to Madden to Jonathan Daniels, January 25, 1950, copy in Arthur Mag Papers, HSTL; J. K. Brelsford, "Memorandum in regard to President's biography," Jonathan Daniels Papers, HSTL (copy in PSF); HST to BW, November 16, 1916, January 12, 23, February 9, 1917, FBP.

21. [Morgan,] "Factual Narrative"; Amended Agreement and Declaration of Trust, MHDC No. 456; "The Foundation of Fortunes" [Morgan Oil and Refining Company prospectus], MHDC No. 45; Morgan & Company advertisement, KCS, April 1, 1917.

22. HST to Mrs. Clara Erickson, February 5, 1917; HST to Mrs. J. H. Best, March 31, 1917, Westbrook Pegler Papers, Herbert Hoover Library, West Branch, Iowa; KCS, April 1, 1917.

23. "Foundation of Fortunes."

24. For a story on the price of crude oil, see NYT, April 18, 1917; "Foundation of Fortunes"; [Morgan,] "Factual Narrative"; HST to BW, January 21, 1919, FBP.

25. Advertisement, business section, KCS, March 4, April 1, 1917.

26. [Morgan,] "Factual Narrative" [includes HST remark to Morgan]; HST to J. H. Conrad, June 26, 1919; HST to David H. Morgan, July 28, 1919, FBP; HST, "My Impressions of The Senate."

Chapter 4

1. The chapter title and opening quotation are from HST, "The Military Career of a Missourian," n.d. [probably 1935], SVP, an important source for this chapter. The remark to Bess is in HST to BW, March 27, 1918, FBP.

2. Enlistment document, Missouri National Guard, June 22, 1917, Department of the Army Military Personnel Records of Harry S. Truman, 1917–1973, HSTL; Jay M. Lee, The Artilleryman: 129th F.A., 1917–1919 (Kansas City: Spencer Press, 1920), 14–15, 268, on which I rely for the history of Truman's regiment; HST to BW, July 14, 1917, FBP; "Examiner Read Eye Chart to Help Truman Join the Army" [newspaper article], April 14, 1945, Mary Ethel Noland Papers, HSTL.

3. HST, Pickwick memos, May 1931, May 14, 1934, PSF, Longhand Notes; HST to BW, July 14, 1914, FBP.

4. HST to BW, October 18, November 8, 11, 17, 1917, FBP.

5. This paragraph is based on news clippings in Vertical File, HSTL, and on the Missouri Valley Room local history collection, Kansas City Public Library. On Thacher, see Nicholas Gilman Thacher to author, October 20, 1988.

6. Richard Lawrence Miller, *Truman: The Rise to Power* (New York: McGraw-Hill, 1986), 109–10.

7. Mary Salisbury Bostian and George W. "Bill" Hamby [no relation to author], interviews with author; HST to BW, October 17, November 3, 1917, FBP.

8. HST to BW, September 30, October 1, 3, 5, 15, 28, November 17, December 14, 1917, January 10, 27, February 1, 3, March 10, 1918, FBP.

9. William Hillman, ed., *Mr. President* (New York: Farrar, Straus and Young, 1952), 171; HST to BW, September 29, 30, October 11, 15, November 17, 24, 1917, January 10, 27, February 1, 3, 1918, FBP.

10. HST, Pickwick memo, May 14, 1934, PSF; HST to BW, October 5, 20, November 5, 24, 1917, January 10, February 7, March 17, 1918, FBP; BW to HST, n.d. [November 1917], MHDC No. 437.

11. Charles Robbins, *Last of His Kind* (New York: Morrow, 1979), 27–28; HST, autobiographical account, 1945, PSF; HST to BW, November 8, 11, 1917, FBP.

12. HST to BW, January 10, February 1, March 10, 1918, FBP; HST, autobiographical account, 1945, PSF.

13. HST, Pickwick memo, May 14, 1934, PSF; HST to BW, February 23, 26, March 5, 1918, FBP.

14. HST to BW, March 20, 21, 24, 26, 27, 28, 1918, FBP; HST, diary, March 30, 1918, FBP; HST to the Nolands, March 26, 1918, Noland Papers; HST, Pickwick memo, May 14, 1934, PSF; Army Military Personnel Records of Harry S. Truman, HSTL.

15. These and the following paragraphs are based primarily on HST to BW, April 14, June 27, 1918, FBP; HST to Ethel and Nellie Noland, May 7, 1918, Noland Papers.

16. William G. Dooley, Jr., *Great Weapons of World War I* (New York: Walker, 1969), 11–12. HST to Ethel and Nellie Noland, May 7, 1918, Noland Papers; HST to BW, April 28, May 5 [two letters], 12, 19, 26, June 2, 8, 1918, FBP.

17. HST to BW, June 14, 19, 27, 30, 1918, FBP.

18. HST, diary, July 4, 1918, FBP.

19. HST, Pickwick memo, May 14, 1934, PSF; HST, autobiographical account, PSF; Robbins, *Last of His Kind*, 28–29; McKinley Wooden [former Chief Mechanic of Battery D], interview with author.

20. Robbins, *Last of His Kind*, 32–33; Merle Miller, *Plain Speaking: An Oral Biography of H. S. Truman* (New York: Berkeley, 1974), 95–100; HST to BW, July 22, 1918, FBP. Truman's "little black book" is in FBP.

21. HST to BW, July 14, 22, 31, August 4, 13, 1918, FBP; HST to the Nolands, August 5, 1918, Noland Papers.

22. HST to BW, September 1, November 23, 1918; [HST,] "The night of the 29th of August . . ." [handwritten account, probably 1919]; HST, diary, August 21–31, 1918; William O'Hare, letter reprinted in *Kansas City Post* [date uncertain], FBP; Commanding Officer, 2nd Bn., 129th F.A. [Marvin Gates] to Commanding Officer, 129th F.A. [Karl Klemm], August 31, 1918, FBP. For Truman's fears about how he would react under fire, see HST to BW, July 31, 1918, FBP. HST–Victor Housholder correspondence, Housholder Papers, HSTL.

23. HST, diary, August 31, 1918, FBP.

24. HST, diary, September 1–6, 1918; HST to BW, November 23, 1918, FBP.

25. HST, diary, September 7–21, 1918, FBP.

26. Eddie Meisburger, "20 Years Ago K. C. Men Made Argonne History," *Kansas City Journal-Post*, September 25, 1938.

27. HST, diary, September 23–October 2, 1918; HST to Jay Lee, n.d. [1919]; HST, "The 129th F.A. . . ." [handwritten]; HST, Operations Report of Battery D . . . , September 26–October 3, 1919; HST, Memorandum of Operations of the 129th F. A. in the Argonne, FBP; Meisburger, "20 Years Ago"; Norman F. Hall, "Five Red Days," *Liberty*, May 14, 1927, 9–12.

28. HST to BW, October 6, 8, 11, November 23, 1918; HST, diary, October 8, 1918, FBP.

29. HST to BW, October 30, November 1, 1918, FBP; HST to Ethel and Nellie Noland, November 1, 1918, Noland Papers.

30. HST, diary, October 18–November 11, 1918, FBP; HST, autobiographical account, 1945, PSF.

31. Major General Peter I. Traub to Commanding Officer, Battery D, October 29, 1918; HST to Commanding General, October 31, 1918; HST to BW, September 5, November 1, 1918, FBP; Marvin Gates, Officer's Rating Card, n.d. [early 1919], and "Report of Discharge of Officer," May 6, 1919, Army Military Personnel Records of Harry S. Truman, HSTL.

32. HST to BW, November 29, December 3, 8, 1918, March 24, 1919; HST, diary, November 26–December 8, 1919, FBP; HST to the Nolands, December 18, 1918, January 20, March 25, 1919, Noland Papers; HST, autobiographical account, 1945, PSF.

33. HST to BW, December 8, 14, 19, 1918, January 11, 26, 27, 1919, FBP; "Training Memorandum No. 5: Care of Horses," n.d. [January 1919], headquarters memoranda, January 15, 18, 1919, and memorandum, February 16, 1919, FBP, Military File.

34. HST to the Nolands, January 20, 1919, Noland Papers.

35. HST to BW, January 26, February 1, April 24, 1919; HST, diary, March 22, 1919, FBP; *KCS*, April 27, 1919.

36. HST to BW, December 26, 1918, FBP; John Thacher to Mrs. Thacher, January 19, 1919, MHDC No. 442; Daniel Shaffer to Myrtle Robinson, December 27, 1918, MHDC No. 462.

37. HST to BW, January 3, 1919, FBP; Wooden and Hamby, interviews with author.

38. Robbins, *Last of His Kind*, 33; Marino Phelps to HST, March 16, 1919, FBP.

39. HST to BW, March 24, 1919; HST, diary, April 20–May 2, 1919, FBP.

Chapter 5

1. *IE*, June 28, 1919; HST to BWT, June 28, 1957, FBP.

2. MT, *Bess W. Truman* (New York: Macmillan, 1986), 81–82. This is an extraordinarily valuable source on which I have relied heavily for Truman's family life. HST to BWT, June 28, 1949, PSF.

3. *IE*, April 7, 1920, January 3, 4, 22, 1921.

4. Ron Cockrell, "Historic Structures Report: History and Significance, Harry S. Truman National Historic Site, Independence, Missouri" (National Park Service, Omaha 1984 [copy at HSTL]), 61–62, 73–74, 83–84; MT, "Memories of a Cherished Home," *NYT*, April 22, 1984.

5. J. C. Truman, interview with author; Ted Marks, Oral History, 27–28, HSTL.

6. On Truman's Masonic activities in the 1920s, see PSF, Subject File, Historical, Personal, Masonic Records and Papers, 1924–1944, especially HST to Joseph S. McIntyre, n.d. [1924]; HST to J. R. McLachlan, September 25, 1926; and HST to Frank R. Jesse, September 25, 1926. For the Kansas City Club, see P. H. Neyhardt [?] to HST, October 3, 1919; HST to W. G. Randall, September 22, 1920, FBP; for the Lakewood Club, see [illegible] [treasurer, Lakewood Golf and Country Club] to HST, December 8, 1920, FBP.

7. HST to Adjutant General of the Army, memorandum [requesting reserve commission], December 4, 1919; HST to James A. Burkhardt, August 14, 1922, FBP; Nicholas Gilman Thacher to author, October 20, 1988.

8. Banquet programs, 1920, 1921; "St. Patrick" to Battery D, n.d. [1921]; E. J. Becker [Elks] to HST, March 22, 1921, FBP; HST to Vere Leigh, August 21, 1951, MHDC No. 385; Harry Murphy, Oral History, 25, HSTL.

9. *Kansas City Journal-Post*, n.d. [September 29 or 30, 1926]; HST to BWT, September 19, 1921, FBP. There is extensive documentation of Truman's 1921 legion work in FBP. See also Thomas J. Heed, "Truman and the Reserve Officers Club of Kansas City," *WhistleStop* [Harry S. Truman Institute Newsletter] 12 (1984): [1–4], and HST to Arthur C. Wahlstadt, February 3, 1950, PPF.

10. On Truman's reserve activities, see the relevant documents in Department of the Army Military Personnel Records of Harry S. Truman, 1917–1973, HSTL; Records from the GAO re Military Service of Harry S. Truman, MHDC No. 116; Rufus Burrus, "Colonel Harry S. Truman as I Knew Him," MHDC No. 173; HST, *Memoirs* interview, p. 11, January 23, 1954, HST Papers, Post-Presidential Papers, Memoirs File, HSTL.

11. On the Reserve Officers Association, see "History of Kansas City Chapter No. 1, Reserve Officers Association," *The Medico*, and "Directory—1937, Reserve Officers Association," Military Career folder, Vertical File, HSTL. From FBP, see news clippings, *KCS*, January 24, 1922, and *Kansas City Journal* or *Post*, n.d. [late January 1922], as well as numerous other items on HST's reserve activities.

12. On Truman's problems after entering the Senate, see the correspondence in Army Military Personnel Records of Harry S. Truman, HSTL.

13. Truman sale display advertisement, *Lee's Summit Journal*, September 18, 1919; Jonathan Daniels, *Man of Independence* (Philadelphia: Lippincott, 1950), 105; Richard Lawrence Miller, *Truman: The Rise to Power* (New York: McGraw-Hill, 1986), 153–54.

14. The various Truman mortgages and quit-claims in 1919 are well summarized in Thomas M. Madden, "Briefed Chronological History of those lands located in 'Washington Township' of Jackson County, Missouri, formerly belonging to the 'Solomon Young family' . . . ," attached to Madden to Jonathan Daniels, January 25, 1950, copy in Arthur Mag Papers, HSTL, and are all on file in deed books B-2005, pp. 42–47; B-1978, pp. 269–71; B-1884, pp. 480–82, Division of Property Records, Jackson County Courthouse, Kansas City, Mo.

15. HST to Box D, 762 Star, November 4, 1919, and attached advertisement, FBP.

16. A copy of the plat map and several pieces of correspondence regarding title and sales are in FBP, as is J. F. Blair [Bank of Belton] to HST, June 29,

1922. Full details are in Jackson County deed books B-2268, pp. 386, 388; B-2321, pp. 102, 105, 349; B-2325, p. 411; B-2326, p. 418; B-2329, p. 82, Jackson County Courthouse, Kansas City, Mo.

17. J. H. Conrad to HST, June 19, 1919; HST to Conrad, June 23, 1919; HST to David H. Morgan, July 28, 1919, FBP; [David H. Morgan,] "A Factual Narrative Relating to the Business Activities, etc., of David H. Morgan & Harry S. Truman, 1916–1919," attached to Morgan to HST, August 5, 1951, PSF; Morgan Oil folder, Vertical File, HSTL; deed book B-2184, p. 55, Jackson County Courthouse, Kansas City, Mo.

18. Exchange Contract, March 26, 1921, FBP; Deed of Trust, April 2, 1921, deed book B-2130, p. 506, Jackson County Courthouse, Kansas City, Mo.; Kansas Warranty Deed, original in deed book 123, p. 527, Recorder's Office, Johnson County Courthouse, Olathe, Kans.; Contract and Lease, HST and Ed Beach, August 5, 1921, FBP.

19. "A Postcard from Old Kansas City," *KCT*, September 5, 1970; the lease is in Eddie Jacobson Papers, HSTL.

20. Truman & Jacobson ledger sheets covering startup and first month of operation, FBP.

21. HST to Vic Housholder, November 28, 1919, FBP. The Truman & Jacobson final-sale flyer gives one a comprehensive idea of the merchandise they handled.

22. See the material and correspondence regarding Oliver Solinger in Jacobson Papers.

23. Invoice ledger, Jacobson Papers.

24. For grain prices, see *KCS*, January 2, 1920, January 3, 1921. The corporate statement and stock offering details are in Jacobson Papers. See also HST to Eddie Jacobson, May 24, 1950; Jacobson to HST, June 12, 1950, PSF; and Articles of Incorporation, deed book B-2154, pp. 263–66, Jackson County Courthouse, Kansas City, Mo.

25. Invoice ledger, Jacobson Papers; *KCS*, July 1, 1921, September 14, 1922. On the bank loans, see Eben Ayers, memorandum [on Truman & Jacobson], July 1951, Ayers Papers, HSTL.

26. Sam O'Neal, in *St. Louis Star-Times*, July 24, 1934, and Eben Ayers, memorandum, July 1951, Ayers Papers, contain extensive research into Truman's debts. There is also considerable correspondence in FBP on the problems with the Johnson County farm. See also deed book 127, p. 180; miscellaneous book 13, p. 572; deed book 134, p. 522, Jackson County Courthouse, Olathe, Kans.

On the Twelfth Street Bank payoff, see Jonathan Daniels, interview with HST, November 12, 1949, Daniels Papers, University of North Carolina, and George Buecking to HST, June 25, 1951, Ayers Papers.

Chapter 6

1. The chapter title is from HST, "My Impressions of The Senate, The House, Washington, etc." SVP. Truman's earliest and arguably most accurate version of Mike Pendergast's visit is in HST, Pickwick memo, May 14, 1934, PSF, Longhand Notes.

2. This discussion is based on Lyle W. Dorsett, *The Pendergast Machine*

(New York: Oxford University Press, 1968), chaps. 1–3, and William Reddig, *Tom's Town* (Philadelphia: Lippincott, 1947), chaps. 1, 2.

3. Joe Shannon, obituary, *KCT*, March 29, 1943.

4. Article on Casimir Welch, *KCS*, January 26, 1930, and his obituary, *KCS*, April 17, 1936.

5. Reddig, *Tom's Town*, 104–15. Miles Bulger's court career is most easily followed in *JE*. See also *KCT*, November 6, 1918, September 22, 29, 30, 1921.

6. For the emergence of the Klan, see, for example, stories and editorials in *JE*, March 3, July 14, September 8, October 13, 1922; *Lee's Summit Journal*, August 31, September 7, 1922; and *KCT*, October 11, 1922. For the Klan's political endorsements in 1922, see *IE*, November 6, 1922.

7. Reddig, *Tom's Town*, 95–98; HST, Pickwick memo ("I have had two wonderful associates . . ."), n.d. [probably fall 1930], PSF; *KCT*, February 21, 1923.

8. *KCT*, January 4, 8, 1922; *Lee's Summit Journal*, March 2, 9, 16, 1922; *JE*, March 3, 1922.

9. *JE*, March 10, 1922; *Lee's Summit Journal*, March 9, 1922; clipping [probably *KCT*], March 8, 1922, FBP; Richard Lawrence Miller, *Truman: The Rise to Power* (New York: McGraw-Hill, 1986), 171.

10. For information on Compton and all other candidates, see *JE*, July 21, 1922, and *Lee's Summit Journal*, July 13, 20, 1922.

11. Montgomery advertisement, *Lee's Summit Journal*, July 13, 1922; Tom Parrent, campaign speech, n.d., FBP.

12. HST to George H. Combs, Jr., August 14, 1922; "Unanimous for Truman" [unidentified clipping], FBP.

13. Editorial, *Marlborough News*, in *JE*, July 7, 1922; "Answer Charges Against Truman," *Kansas City Post* [clipping], n.d., FBP; Eddie McKim, Oral History, 22–23, HSTL.

14. "Endorses Harry Truman" [unidentified clipping], FBP.

15. *JE*, May 12, June 16, 1922; *Lee's Summit Journal*, May 18, 1922.

16. Numerous unidentified clippings in FBP document the character and style of the 1922 campaign. On payments to newspapers, see HST, campaign expense affidavit, August 19, 1922, FBP.

17. "Oak Grove Speech," *Mount Washington News*, July 21, 1922.

18. *JE*, July 21, 28, 1922; *IE*, July 31, August 1, 1922; *JE*, April 28, 1922; *Lee's Summit Journal*, August 3, 1922.

19. *JE*, July 28, 1922; *IE*, August 2, 1922; anti-Montgomery flyer, July 31, 1922, FBP; Brown Harris to HST, January 7, 1947, PSF.

20. *KCT*, August 4, 5, 1922; *KCS*, August 4, 1922; *IE*, August 3, 4, 1922; HST, affidavit, August 9, 1922, FBP.

21. HST to Ralph Truman, August 6, 1922, HST Papers, Post-Presidential Papers, Family Correspondence File, HSTL; *IE*, August 4, 1922.

22. *IE*, August 4, November 6, 8, 1922; clipping, *IE*, n.d., FBP; HST, expense affidavits, August 19, November 24, 1922; *Lee's Summit Journal*, August 31, September 7, November 9, 1922; *JE*, September 6, October 13, November 24, 1922; *KCT*, October 11, 1922, October 27, 1944; *KCS*, November 8, 1922; *Chicago Herald-American*, October 27, 1944; "County to Reed by 1,246" [*KCS* or *KCT* clipping], n.d., FBP; Merle Miller, *Plain Speaking: An Oral Biography of Harry S. Truman* (New York: Berkeley, 1974), 131; Miller, *Rise to Power*, 172–73; HST, appointment book, August 4, 1922, Post-Presidential Papers, Desk File, HSTL.

Chapter 7

1. The chapter title is from HST, Pickwick memo, May 14, 1934, PSF, Longhand Notes.

2. The practical workings of the Jackson County Court during this period are well described in *JE*. For finances, see Arthur Young & Company, audits of Jackson County, 1922–1923, copies in FBP, and Civic Research Institute, "Trends in Jackson County Finance," September 1933, copies in Bryce Smith Papers, HSTL, and Civic Research Institute Papers, WHMC. For payment of the 1920 warrants, see *JE*, January 19, 1923.

3. *JE*, December 1, 8, 15, 22, 1922, July 6, 1923.

4. Thomas J. Heed, "Harry S Truman and the United States Army: Surprising Sources for Progressive Reforms" (Paper presented at the Truman Centennial Symposium, University of Missouri-Kansas City, April 1984); HST to Carl Jenkins, September 16, 1922, FBP.

5. *JE*, January 5, 1923. On Leo Koehler, see *JE*, April 15, December 30, 1921, December 15, 1922, and *KCT*, September 29, 1921.

6. *JE*, January 5, 12, 19, 1923. *Lee's Summit Journal*, January 4, 11, 18, 1923.

7. *JE*, January 26, February 2, 9, 16, March 9, 16, 23, 30, April 6, 1923; *Lee's Summit Journal*, January 18, 25, March 29, April 5, May 24, 1923; *KCT*, February 6, 8, 21, March 3, 9, 10, 13, 19, 20, 1923; *KCS*, March 18, 1923.

8. *JE*, November 17, 24, December 1, 15, 1922, February 16, May 4, June 1, 8, 15, 1923; *KCT*, February 20, 1923; *KCS*, June 1, 2, 1923; Richard Lawrence Miller, *Truman: The Rise to Power* (New York: McGraw-Hill, 1986), 184–85; Fred Boxley to HST, March 8, 1923, FBP; Rufus Burrus, interview with author.

9. *JE*, February 9, March 16, April 27, 1923; *KCT*, February 20, March 13, 1923; Arthur Young audits, 1922–1923, FBP.

10. *JE*, March 9, 30, 1923, January 18, 1924; *KCT*, March 26, 1923; *KCS*, April 5, 1923; Bulger campaign advertisement, *Lee's Summit Journal*, August 1, 1918; Larry Groathaus, "Kansas City Blacks, Harry Truman and the Pendergast Machine," *Missouri Historical Review* 69 (October 1974): 65–82, esp. 71–73.

11. *JE*, January 19, June 29, 1923; *KCT*, February 24, 1923.

12. *JE*, December 7, 14, 1923, January 11, 1924; Miller, *Rise to Power*, 191–93.

13. *JE*, March 23, April 20, 27, July 6, 13, 20, November 9, 1923; *Lee's Summit Journal*, May 24, 1923, January 24, 1924.

14. *JE*, May 11, 1923, March 7, 14, April 25, May 2, 1924; *Lee's Summit Journal*, May 17, June 7, August 2, 1923; *KCS*, May 10, 1923; *KCT*, March 7, 1924; HST, Pickwick memo, May 14, 1934, PSF; HST, "More about government . . . ," n.d., HSTL.

15. HST, appointment books, 1923–1924, FBP; *KCS* and *Kansas City Post*, April 6, 1923. On ideas about rational road planning, see, for example, *JE*, January 5, April 13, 1923, and *Lee's Summit Journal*, April 12, May 3, 17, 1923. For the Stayton–Ash recommendations, see *JE*, May 4, 1923; for the McElroy outburst, see *Lee's Summit Journal*, July 12, 1923. See also J. D. Miller [editor, *Lee's Summit Journal*] to HST, December 26, 1922, April 10, 1923, FBP.

16. *JE*, June 29, July 13, 20, 1923; Arthur Young audit, 1923, FBP; *KCS*, July 9, 1923. For a contrary interpretation, however, see Miller, *Rise to Power*, 200–201; and *Kansas City Journal*, October 8, November 2, 1924.

17. Arthur Young audit, 1923, FBP. For the road overseers, see *JE*, June 29, August 10, 17, 31, September 7, 1923, and *Lee's Summit Journal*, July 12, August 9, October 11, 18, November 15, 1923. For park planning, see *Lee's Summit Journal*, September 21, 1923.

18. *JE*, September 21, 28, December 10, 1923; Ralph Truman to HST, January 23, 1923; HST to Ralph Truman, February 3, 1923, HST Papers, Post-Presidential Papers, Family Correspondence File, HSTL.

19. *JE*, May 23, 1924.

20. *KCT*, March 8, 12, 13, April 9, 1924; *KCS*, March 7, 8, 11, 12, 13, 15, 16, April 9, 1924.

21. Arthur Young audit, 1923; "Statement of the Financial Condition of Jackson County, Missouri, June 30, 1924"; Ray Wilson [Chamber of Commerce] to HST, June 12, 1924, FBP; *JE*, January 11, 18, 25, February 8, 15, March 14, April 4, 18, June 20, July 4, 11, 1924; *KCS*, March 13, 14, July 23, 1924.

22. HST to Chief of Staff, 102nd Div., August 2, 1924, Department of the Army Military Personnel Records of Harry S. Truman, 1917–1973, HSTL; HST, handwritten speeches on stationery of Battery D, 129th Field Artillery [Grandview speech] and Rasbach Hotel, FBP. For the Truman campaign, see *JE*, July 11, 1924, and *Lee's Summit Journal*, July 3, 10, 31, 1924. On the meetings at Grandview and the Wallace farm, see *KCS*, July 27, 1924, and *KCT*, June 26, July 1, 29, 30, 1924. For the institute survey, see *KCT*, July 30, 1924. For endorsements, see *KCS*, July 31, 1924; *JE*, August 1, 1924; and *Independence Sentinel*, June 26, 1924.

23. *JE*, August 8, 1924; Thomas J. Heed, "Prelude to Whistlestop" (Ph.D. diss., Columbia University, 1975), 103, 192–95.

24. *KCS* and *KCT*, April 14–16, 1924; *JE*, August 15, 1924.

25. For the Miles contributions, see County Judge Notebooks, Post-Presidential Papers, Desk File, HSTL. For the Rummel campaign, see *Kansas City Journal*, October 23, 25, 1924.

26. *Kansas City Journal* and *Journal-Post*, September 28–November 4, 1924.

27. *Kansas City Journal*, October 19, 26, 28, 1924; *JE*, October 24, 1924.

28. *JE*, September 5, 12, 25, 1924.

29. HST, handwritten speech on Hotel Victoria stationery, n.d. [the predicted Davis victory is figured on the back of the last page], FBP; Heed, "Prelude to Whistlestop," 219–25; *KCT*, November 1, 1924; *KCS*, November 3, 1924; *JE*, October 31, 1924; Jonathan Daniels, *Man of Independence* (Philadelphia: Lippincott, 1950), 126; Merle Miller, *Plain Speaking: An Oral Biography of Harry S. Truman* (New York: Berkeley, 1974), 130–31.

30. Heed, "Prelude to Whistlestop," 225–35; William Reddig, *Tom's Town* (Philadelphia: Lippincott, 1947), 109–25; Lyle W. Dorsett, *The Pendergast Machine* (New York: Oxford University Press, 1968), 73.

31. *Lee's Summit Journal*, November 13, 1924, January 8, 1925; *JE*, November 21, 1924, January 2, 1925; Civic Research Institute "Trends in Jackson County Finance," 24; *KCS*, December 31, 1924, January 1, 2, 1925.

Chapter 8

1. The chapter title is from HST, Pickwick memo, May 14, 1934, PSF, Longhand Notes.

2. MT, *Bess W. Truman* (New York: Macmillan, 1986), chaps. 7–9, quotes

on 100, 111; May Wallace, interview with author; MT, *Harry S. Truman* (New York: Morrow, 1972), 88–89; *IE*, January 27, July 12, 1930, June 15, 1933, July 12, 13, 1935.

3. For Fred Wallace, see HST, Pickwick memo ("I have had two wonderful associates . . ."), n.d. [probably fall 1930], PSF, and biographical sketch, *MD*, May 17, 1929. For George Wallace, see MT, *Bess Truman*, 118; HST to BWT, April 24, 26, 1934, FBP; and Rufus Burrus, telephone interview with author. For Madge Wallace's dependency, see Richard Lawrence Miller, *Truman: The Rise to Power* (New York: McGraw-Hill, 1986), 337.

4. HST to BWT, February 12, 1931, FBP; deed book B-2135, p. 267, and deed book B-3063, p. 545, Division of Property Records, Jackson County Courthouse, Kansas City, Mo.

5. For Truman's Masonic activities, see, for example, *MD*, November 13, 1925, and *JE*, January 8, 1926; for army reserves, see relevant HST–BWT correspondence, July folders, 1925–1932, August 1933, FBP; for American Legion, see *JE*, February 5, March 12, April 9, 16, August 27, September 3, 1926, and *MD*, April 11, 1930; for the Harpie Club, see Edgar G. Hinde, Oral History, 64–65, HSTL, and Sue Gentry, in *IE*, November 27, 1980.

6. Truman's complete grade record is in MHDC No. 17. A 1923–1924 grade report, the Washington's Birthday banquet program, and numerous class notes and examinations are in FBP. A copy of the law school yearbook is at HSTL.

7. On the early history of the Old Trails Association, see obituaries of its founder, Judge Frank Lowe, in *Lee's Summit Journal*, April 22, 1926, and *MD*, April 23, 1926; see also *Program: Third Annual Convention* [1914], pamphlet on the organization, and map issued by the National Highways Association [1926], FBP. For Truman's election, see *KCT*, July 24, 1926, and *JE*, July 30, 1926.

8. For Truman's Old Trails trips, see *JE*, December 17, 1926; *Dayton Daily News*, November 16, 1926; *MD*, November 19, 1926, April 27, May 4 [text of DAR address], July 6, September 28, 1928, April 19, 1929; "The President, personal (President of the National Old Trails Association, 1928)," April 8, 1946, PSF; and extensive documentation in FBP, which includes the dedication speech at Springfield, Ohio, July 4, 1928.

9. Miller, *Rise to Power*, 207–8; HST, Pickwick memo, May 14, 1934, PSF; HST, autobiographical account, 1945, PSF; HST, *Memoirs*, 1:138. The 1926 average income figure is from George Soule, *Prosperity Decade* (New York: Harper & Row, 1947), 221.

10. Kansas City Trip Files (1951), Eben Ayers Papers, HSTL.

11. For Arthur Elliott and the Farm and Home Savings operation, see Farm and Home folder, H. H. Halverson Papers, HSTL, and articles on Elliott's death in *KCS*, November 28, 1930, and *KCT*, November 29, 1930.

12. A useful brief sketch of Holland may be found in Dick Fowler, *Leaders in Our Town* (Kansas City, Mo.: Burd & Fletcher, [1952]), 205–8.

13 This and the following paragraph are based on material in the Citizens Security Bank File, Lou Holland Papers, WHMC, examined at University of Missouri-Kansas City, and in Halvorson Papers. Paul Cole's gunfight with a bank robber is mentioned in *JE*, August 13, 1926.

14. Agreement between HST and Community Savings and Loan, September 21, 1925; Partnership Agreement, April 21, 1926; Eric O. A. Miller and Co., audit of Harry S. Truman and Co., September 23, 1927; "It Pays to Save!" [flyer]; photograph of Community officials [1927], Halvorson Papers; H. H. Halvorson,

Oral History, 24–32, HSTL, discusses Community Savings. HST to Lou Holland [on Community letterhead], January 26, 1926, Holland Papers, HSTL. For new officers, see C. H. Glenn to Lou Holland, July 27, 1927, Holland Papers, HSTL.

15. Partnership Agreement, April 21, 1926; "Suggested Plan for Operation, Branch Offices, Community Savings & Loan Assn," n.d., Halvorson Papers.

16. Eric Miller audit, September 23, 1927, Halvorson Papers; Jonathan Daniels, *Man of Independence* (Philadelphia: Lippincott, 1950), 136.

17. "Limited Partnership Agreement and Contract," November 1, 1927, and addendum, Halvorson Papers.

18. "Community Investment Company, Balance Sheet covering period Sept. 1st to Dec. 31st, 1927," and "Receipts for January 1928 to January 14th"; H. H. Halvorson to Spencer Salisbury, February 15, 1928; "Suggested Plan for Operation, Branch Offices—Community Savings & Loan Assn," n.d. [February, 1928]; "Community Investment Company . . . Assets & Liabilities as of Feb. 28, 1930"; H. H. Halvorson to Crawford, April 2, 1930; "Community Investment Company, Financial Statements, September 30, 1930," Halvorson Papers.

19. The preceding five paragraphs rest primarily on documents in the Community Savings and Loan and Rural Investment Co. Files, Halvorson Papers, including HST, "Assignment," May 4, 1931; H. H. Halvorson to HST, October 22, 1931; HST to Halvorson, October 28, 1931; and Spencer Salisbury to H. H. Halvorson, December 30, 1931. For Truman's private feelings about Salisbury, see Pickwick memo ("I have had two wonderful associates . . ."), n.d. [probably fall 1930], PSF.

20. Community Savings and Loan, financial statements, August 31, 1931, August 31, 1934, *KCS*, September 16, 1934, Halvorson Papers; Miller, *Rise to Power*, 317–19; Halvorson, Oral History, 43–49, HSTL.

21. On Citizens Security's 1925 difficulties and its transfer to the Truman group, see documents in Citizens Security Bank File, Holland Papers, WHMC; *JE*, February 5, 1926; *KCS*, August 15, 1926. Truman's characterization of Becker is in HST, Pickwick memo ("More about government as it is administered these days"), n.d., PSF.

22. *KCS*, August 15, 1926. On Paul Cole's arrangement with Holland and the other directors, see Citizens Security Bank File, Holland Papers, WHMC.

23. On the transition, see correspondence in Citizens Security Bank File, Holland Papers, WHMC, and *JE*, April 23, 1926.

24. *KCS*, August 13, 15, 17, 19, 22, 1926; *JE*, August 13, 20, 27, October 8, 1926, December 23, 1927; *MD*, August 27, September 10, 1926; March 15, 1929.

Chapter 9

1. The chapter title is slightly altered from HST, Pickwick memo ("I have had two wonderful associates . . .") n.d. [probably fall 1930], PSF.

2. HST, "My Impressions of The Senate, The House, Washington, etc.," SVP; *MD*, December 11, 1925; HST, Pickwick memo ("I have had two wonderful associates . . ."), n.d., PSF.

3. *MD*, March 19, June 4, 1926; HST, "My Impressions of The Senate." For Robert Barr, see *JE*, April 30, May 14, 1926; *Lee's Summit Journal*, June 24, 1926; and *MD*, June 11, 1926.

4. The court's record is easily followed in *JE*, 1925–1926. For election coverage, see *JE*, May 7, August 6, 1926, and *MD*, August 6, 13, September 3, 1926.

5. *Lee's Summit Journal*, December 16, 1926; *JE*, January 7, 1927. For the Salisbury difficulties, see *IE*, March 4, April 4, May 7, 1929, and *MD*, January 24, 1930.

6. On Howard Vrooman and Barr, see primarily HST, Pickwick memos ("I have had two wonderful associates . . ." and "More character sketches"), n.d., PSF, and *MD*, November 16, 1928, February 21, 1930; *JE*, November 30, December 21, 1917, April 9, 1926; HST to George F. Kern, December 15, 1948, PSF.

7. For Thomas Bash, see Pickwick memos ("More character sketches . . ." and "I have had two wonderful associates . . ."), n.d., PSF; *IE*, July 5, December 31, 1928, March 4, May 20, 24, 1929, April 8, 1930; *MD*, October 12, 1928, April 11, May 8, 1930; *KCS*, October 22, 1928.

8. Rufus Burrus, interviews with author; *MD*, July 5, December 27, 1929, September 11, 1936; *KCT*, July 12, 1927.

9. *JE*, February 20, March 20, April 10, November 6, 1925, January 29, February 12, May 14, 28, July 23, July 30, August 6, November 26, 1926; *MD*, August 6, 1926.

10. For the relationship between Leo Koehler and HST, see Rufus Burrus, interviews with author. On discontent with the road overseer system, see "Solomon Wise," in *JE*, May 27, 1927, and editorial, *JE*, July 8, 1927. For Koehler's proposals, see *JE*, January 6, 1928, and *MD*, March 15, 1929.

11. *JE*, February 4, March 4, May 6, 1927; *IE*, May 6, 1927; *KCS*, April 25, 1927.

12. *KCS*, June 13, 1927; *JE*, June 17, 1927; official state road map as of February 1, 1928, in *MD*, March 30, 1928; "Solomon Wise," in *JE*, September 16, 1927.

13. *KCT*, June 14, 1927; *KCS*, May 4, 6, 7, 8, 9, 1928; *KCT*, May 5, 7, 1928; *MD*, May 11, 1928.

14. *JE*, December 9, 1927, January 27, February 3, 1928; *MD*, February 24, March 2, April 27, 1928; HST, statement, June 7, 1927, Lou Holland Papers, HSTL; Rural Jackson County Bond Committee, campaign flyer, FBP.

15. *KCS*, May 9, 1928; *MD*, May 11, 1928.

16. *MD*, May 18, June 15, 29, 1928; *IE*, July 9, 25, August 3, September 18, 1928; *KCS*, September 19, 20, 1928; N. T. Veatch to C. J. McCoy, September 8, 1928, Veatch Papers, HSTL.

17. HST, *Memoirs*, 1:141.

18. HST, Pickwick memo ("I have had two wonderful associates . . .") n.d., PSF; Percy B. Sovey, "T. J. Pendergast: The Man Whose Word Is Good," *Democracy*, July 1935, 4–5.

19. W. T. Kemper, Jr., telephone interview with author; Alfred Steinberg, *The Man from Missouri* (New York: Putnam, 1962), 90; W. M. Spann [highway field engineer] to N. T. Veatch, August 7, 1931, Veatch Papers.

20. *MD*, October 10, 17, 31, 1930; *KCS*, September 14, 21, 1930.

21. *IE*, September 4, 1930; *MD*, October 17, 1930; HST, Pickwick memo ("I have had two wonderful associates . . .") n.d., PSF.

22. Lyle W. Dorsett, *The Pendergast Machine* (New York: Oxford University Press, 1968), 72, 77–78; Walter Matscheck, Oral History, HSTL.

23. *JE*, July 8, 15, 22, August 5, September 5, 23, 1927; *IE*, November 9,

1929; *MD*, December 6, 1929, June 20, July 18, October 24, November 7, 21, 1930. For Public Service Institute involvement, see HST to Walter Matscheck, March 5, 1930; Matscheck to HST, March 7, 1930; "The Jackson County Sewer District Number 1" [study], May 1930; Walter Matscheck to C. W. Atkins, October 6, 1933, Civic Research Institute Papers, WHMC.

24. On zoning, see HST, Pickwick memo ("The Zoning Bills . . ."), n.d., PSF; *KCS*, June 25, 1936. On property assessment, see HST et al., "Proposed Plan of Revaluation . . . ," March 31, 1932, MHDC No. 514; Walter Matscheck to Francis A. Wright, August 4, 1932, Civic Research Institute Papers; *IE*, March 21, 1933; and *PD*, April 13, 1941.

25. Minutes, Subcommittee on County Reorganization; proposed bills for counties of over 400,000 population and for counties of 90,000 to 400,000 population; organizational chart; summary of county government bill, Civic Research Institute Papers. See also *KCS*, May 3, September 24, December 18, 1932; *KCT*, February 26, March 11, May 1, September 26, 1932 [editorial], January 14, 28, February 24, March 21, 1933.

26. HST, speeches, September 25, 1931, November 28, 1931, HST Papers, Presiding Judge File, HSTL; information sheet, agenda, and list of participants for Conference on Financial Administration in Missouri, November 20, 1933, Presiding Judge File; *IE*, September 25, November 28, December 11, 1931.

27. HST, "Ten Year Plan for Independence," *Forward Independence* 1 (October 1930): 3.

28. HST, speeches, February 15, 1929, June 16, 1930, Presiding Judge File; HST, speech, March 10 [1929 or 1930], Holland Papers; HST, Pickwick memo ("The Ideals I've Tried to Make Work"), n.d., PSF.

29. *Results of County Planning* (Independence and Kansas City, Mo.: Jackson County Court, 1932).

30. *KCS*, October 2, 3, 1930; *MD*, October 10, 1930. HST, speech, October 1, 1930, Presiding Judge File.

31. *KCS*, October 31, November 5, 1930.

32. *KCS*, December 14, 1930.

33. *KCS*, November 1, December 10, 11, 13, 15, 17, 1930; *KCT*, December 11, 13, 16, 17, 1930.

34. Quotes from Pickwick memos, PSF.

Chapter 10

1. HST to BWT, February 12, 1932, FBP.

2. *KCS*, January 1, 1931; *MD*, October 24, 31, 1930; *IE*, November 1, 1930; *MD*, August 5, 1932.

3. *MD*, December 4, 1931, December 23, 30, 1932.

4. *IE*, December 22, 31, 1930; *KCS*, December 31, 1930; *MD*, January 2, 9, February 6, 1931; HST to BWT, February 12, 1931, FBP.

5. *KCS* and *KCT*, March 31, April 1, 2, 3, 4, 1931; *MD*, April 24, 1931.

6. *IE*, January 4, 1932; *MD*, January 8, 1932.

7. *IE*, March 29, April 8, 14, 18, May 2, August 27, 1932; *MD*, January 8, April 8, 15, 22, May 13, August 26, September 2, November 25, 1932; *KCT*, April 15, 1932.

8. *MD*, February 3, April 21, 28, May 19, 1933; HST to Guy B. Park,

May 2, 1933, Park Papers, WHMC; "County Budget Bill" [typed summary of bill's provisions], n.d., HST Papers, Presiding Judge File, HSTL; HST to BWT, April 15, 1933, FBP.

9. *MD*, May 5, July 21, August 18, 1933; *IE*, August 9, December 1, 1933.

10. HST to BWT, April 23, 24, May 5, 1933, FBP; *MD*, May 5, August 18, 1933, July 20, October 26, 1934; *KCT*, August 14, 1933.

11. *MD*, November 30, December 21, 28, 1934.

12. HST to BWT, February 12, 1931, FBP.

13. HST to BWT, April 15, 16, 28 [two letters], 1933, FBP; *KCS*, January 30, 1933.

14. *KCT*, June 14, 1932; HST to BWT, April 27, August 21, 1933, FBP.

15. *KCS*, November 6, 1933; *MD*, November 16, 1933; John Barker to HST, September 20, 1949, and HST to Barker, September 26, 1949, PSF.

16. "Family Mortgage from School Funds in an Illegal Amount," James P. Kem Papers, WHMC.

17. MT, *Bess W. Truman* (New York: Macmillan, 1986), 118; HST to BWT, July 7, 1932, FBP; HST to Guy B. Park, October 12, 1933, Park Papers.

18. MT, *Bess W. Truman*, 118; Rufus Burrus, telephone interview with author.

19. *MD*, May 29, 1931.

20. *KCS*, September 18, 1932.

21. HST, speech, September 7, 1933, PSF; *IE*, September 8, 1933.

22. MT, *Boss Truman*, 112, 181; HST to BWT, April 4, 15, May 9, 1933, FBP.

23. *MD*, December 11, 25, 1931, June 3, 1932; *IE*, December 16, 21, 1931; *Kansas City Post*, May 25, 1932; *KCS*, May 25, 1932.

24. Richard Lawrence Miller, *Truman: The Rise to Power* (New York: McGraw-Hill, 1986), 228–30.

25. *MD*, February 20, 27, 1930; *KCS*, March 3, 1931; HST, "County Court House and Tax Reform Suggestion," PSF, Longhand Notes; Lenore K. Bradley, "Building Jackson County," *WhistleStop* 13 (1985): [1–4].

26. *MD*, June 16, August 18, 1933; Ilus Davis [former mayor of Kansas City], telephone interview with author.

27. *KCT*, January 16–20, 1934.

28. *KCS*, December 27, 1934; *MD*, December 28, 1934.

29. William Reddig, *Tom's Town* (Philadelphia: Lippincott, 1947), 250–53; Lazia, obituary, *KCT*, July 11, 1934.

30. Reddig, *Tom's Town*, 141–46; *MD*, February 22, April 12, July 26, September 20, October 18, November 29, December 20, 1929, April 25, July 11, 1930. For the leniency of the local courts, see *KCS*, April 21, 1931.

31. Reddig, *Tom's Town*, 160–61; *Kansas City Post*, July 26, 29, 1931.

32. Reddig, *Tom's Town*, chaps. 4, 5, photo section facing p. 192; *MD*, May 17, 1929; Jerome Beatty, "A Political Boss Talks About His Job," *American Magazine*, February 1933, 30–31, 108–13.

33. Roy Roberts to Jonathan Daniels, June 11, 1949, Daniels Papers, University of North Carolina.

34. *MD*, February 25, 1927, May 25, 1928, July 5, 1929, May 23, June 20, 1930, January 9, 1931, May 5, 1933.

35. *MD*, March 24, April 14, 21, 28, June 16, September 8, 1933, September 14, 21, 1934.

36. *KCS*, June 17, 1933; Reddig, *Tom's Town*, 257–59.

37. *KCT* and *KCS*, August 12, 1933.

38. Civic Research Institute, "Registration and Voting in Kansas City" [typewritten report], 1934, Civic Research Institute Papers, WHMC; Charles Wheeler [former mayor of Kansas City], telephone interview with author.

39. Reddig, *Tom's Town*, 237–43.

40. Reddig, *Tom's Town*, 261; Alfred Steinberg, *The Man from Missouri* (New York: Putnam, 1962), 105–6.

Chapter 11

1. HST, Pickwick memo, May 14, 1934, PSF, Longhand Notes.

2. Franklin D. Mitchell, *Embattled Democracy: Missouri Democratic Politics, 1919–1932* (Columbia: University of Missouri Press, 1968), esp. chap. 1; *The WPA Guide to 1930s Missouri* (reprint, Lawrence: University Press of Kansas, 1986); John M. Fenton, *Politics in the Border States* (New Orleans: Houser Press, 1957).

3. Robert M. Crisler, "Missouri's Little Dixie," *Missouri Historical Review* 42 (April 1948): 130–39.

4. Robert M. Crisler, "Republican Areas in Missouri," *Missouri Historical Review* 42 (July 1948): 299–309.

5. Mitchell, *Embattled Democracy*, 7–8, 100.

6. *Clinton Eye*, September 19, 1929; *IE*, September 27, 1929. The following pages rely heavily on Franklin D. Mitchell, "'Who Is Judge Truman?': The Truman-for-Governor Movement of 1931," *Midcontinent American Studies* 7 (Fall 1966): 3–15.

7. Article, *Clinton Democrat*, in *MD*, September 27, 1929; *IE*, August 19, 20, 1931.

8. James Ruffin to P. T. O'Brien, June 3, 1931, James Ruffin Papers, WHMC; editorial, *Odessa Democrat*, in *MD*, November 21, 1930. Stanley Fike, the teenage editor of the *Inter-City News*, a small goat-controlled paper, wrote an editorial backing Truman at the suggestion of the paper's owner, Less Byam. He may have been Truman's first supporter for the governor's office, but he was an inconsequential one.

9. *KCS*, August 12, 1928.

10. *KCT*, December 18, 1930, May 12, 1931.

11. James Ruffin to M. N. White, May 5, 1931; Southwest Missouri Democratic Club, minutes, May 4, 1931; James Ruffin to Frank Kirtley, May 7, 1931; Ralph Truman to James Ruffin, May 8, 1931 [two letters]; Ruffin to Ralph Truman, May 11, 1931, Ruffin Papers.

12. *Kansas City Post*, April 22, 1931; "Truman for Governor" [editorial], *Kansas City Post*, n.d. [probably same issue], Shannon Scrapbooks, Jackson County Historical Society, Independence, Mo.

13. *MD*, June 3, 1932.

14. *IE*, June 8, 1931.

15. John K. Hulston, *An Ozarks Lawyer's Story* (Republic, Mo.: Western Printing, 1976), 455–59; Will Zorn to Francis Wilson, August 8, 1931, Wilson Papers, WHMC.

16. MT, *Bess W. Truman* (New York: Macmillan, 1986), 117. This account apparently refers to some correspondence that Margaret Truman still possesses.

17. See, for example, Curtis Betts, in *PD*, June 28, 1931.

18. Francis Wilson to Charles W. Dickey, December 10, 1931, Wilson Papers.

19. Wilson to Dickey, December 10, 1931, Wilson Papers.

20. *MD*, May 13, 1932; HST, WDAF radio talk introducing Charles Howell, August 1, 1932, PSF, Addresses, 1929–1933.

21. *Official Manual of the State of Missouri, 1933–34*, 412–23, contains the official primary results.

22. *MD*, October 21, 1932; William Reddig, *Tom's Town* (Philadelphia: Lippincott, 1947), 202–3.

23. *MD*, April 14, 1933; For the 1932 primaries, see *Official Manual of the State of Missouri, 1933 34*, 400 423, and for the size of the new congressional districts, see *Official Manual of the State of Missouri, 1937–38*, 47–51.

24. *MD*, October 27, 1933; editorial, *Ladonia Herald*, in *MD*, November 10, 1933.

25. Bennett Clark to T. J. Pendergast, June 28, 1934, Clark Papers, WHMC; Walter Burr to W. Frank Persons, October 30, 1933, and attached memo signed by Persons, October 18, 1933, Documents from the Records of the U.S. Employment Service (National Archives, Record Group No. 133) Relating to Harry S. Truman, HSTL [hereafter U.S. Employment Service Records].

26. HST to Walter Burr, November 15, 18, 29, December 4, 8, 12, 1933, February 3, 1934; Martin Lewis to Walter Burr, February 17, 1934; HST to Bennett Clark, telegram, December 14, 1933, U.S. Employment Service Records; HST to Guy B. Park, December 5, 1933, Park Papers, WHMC.

27. HST to Walter Burr, November 24, December 12, 15, 21, 1933, March 26, 1934; George Baughman to Walter Burr, February 9, 1934; Burr to HST, March 19, 1934, U.S. Employment Service Records.

28. Walter Burr to HST, December 1, 27, 1933, January 27, March 10, 29, 1934; HST to Burr, December 5, 21, 1933, January 10, 23, February 16, March 7, 1934; T. G. Addison to HST, March 12, 1934, U.S. Employment Service Records.

29. HST to Walter Burr, February 3, 1934; Burr to HST, February 8, 1934; Martin Lewis to Walter Burr, February 17, 1934; [Burr], unsigned memorandum [on conversation between Burr and Lewis], January 24, 1934, U.S. Employment Service Records.

30. HST to Walter Burr, January 10, 1934; Burr to HST, March 19, 1934; HST (by R. B. Browning) to Burr, March 14, 1934, U.S. Employment Service Records; *Monthly Report of the Federal Emergency Relief Administration, January 1 to January 31, 1934* (Washington, D.C.: Government Printing Office, 1934), 20–21.

31. HST, autobiographical account, 1945, PSF; MT, *Bess Truman*, 125–26.

32. HST to BWT, April 23, 1933, FBP.

33. HST to BWT, April 30, May 7, 1933, January 2, 1934, FBP; *MD*, September 15, 1933, March 2, 1934; *IE*, September 22, 1933.

34. *MD*, May 4, 1934; MT, *Bess Truman*, 126; HST, "My Impressions of The Senate, The House, Washington, etc.," SVP.

35. Unsigned, undated memorandum [probably summarizing an interview or a phone conversation with Martin Lewis], beginning "In the summer of 1932?" with handwritten note initialed "WH" at bottom, HST Papers, Post-Presidential Papers, Memoirs File, HSTL.

36. My account of this meeting draws on HST, "My Impressions of The Senate," and HST, autobiographical account, 1945, PSF.

37. *KCS* or *Kansas City Post*, May 14, 1934; *Kansas City Post*, May 15, 1934; *IE*, May 31, 1934; *MD*, May 18, 1934. For Joe Shannon, see the many clippings in the Shannon Scrapbooks. For Miles Bulger, see *KCT*, July 25, 1934; for Spencer Salisbury, see *PD*, August 24, 1934. Ilus Davis, telephone interview with author.

38. *St. Louis Star-Times*, May 16, 1934; *PD*, May 21, 22, 27, 1934.

39. Ross–Pulitzer correspondence, July 25–August 1, 1934, Joseph Pulitzer, Jr., Papers, LC.

40. *MD*, May 25–August 3, 1934. For Truman's support in Jefferson City, see *PD*, July 13, 1934.

41. HST, campaign diary, 1934, HST Papers, Presiding Judge File, HSTL.

42. Richard L. Harkness, in *IE*, June 1, 1934.

43. HST, campaign diary, June 5, 1934, Presiding Judge File.

44. HST to Guy B. Park, June 6, 1934, Park Papers.

45. Harry Pence to Guy B. Park, July 12, 1934, and attached editorial, Park Papers.

46. C. M. Buford to Guy B. Park, July 21, [1934], Park Papers; *PD*, August 24, 1934; *MD*, August 31, September 7, 1934.

47. Guy B. Park to Orestes Mitchell, July 23, 1934; Mitchell to Park, July 25, 1934; Orestes Mitchell to S. G. Thompson, July 26, 1934, Park Papers.

48. *MD*, June 22, July 6, 1934; *KCT*, July 18, 19, 1934; *PD*, July 7, 12, 21, 1934.

49. James Aylward, Oral History, 94, HSTL; *KCT*, July 16, 1934.

50. Hulston, *Ozarks Lawyer's Story*, 462.

51. *KCT*, July 16, 1934; *Paris Mercury*, July 27, 1934.

52. *IE*, August 7, 1934; *PD*, July 7, 1934.

53. *PD*, July 7, 1934; *MD*, July 6, 1934.

54. *PD*, July 7, 10, 12, 1934; *IE*, August 3, 1934.

55. *PD*, July 6, 12, 1934; *KCT*, July 11, 13, 1934; *MD*, June 29, July 13, 20, 1934.

56. Reddig, *Tom's Town*, 261–64; *KCT*, July 10, 11, 1934; *KCS*, July 13, 1934.

57. *PD*, July 26, 1934; *KCT*, July 26, 1934.

58. Jonathan Daniels, *Man of Independence* (Philadelphia: Lippincott, 1950), 169.

59. *PD*, July 7, 1934.

60. *PD*, July 12, 1934.

61. *KCT*, July 28, 1934.

62. *KCT*, July 28, 1934.

63. For form letters, see, for example, HST to "Dear Comrade," July 30, 1934, Mary Ethel Noland Papers, HSTL; HST to Katherine R. Morgan, July 25, 1934, MHDC No. 287; J. L. Rogers [Combined Building Trades Council] to "Organized Labor," July 26, 1934, MHDC No. 287; Gilbert Strode [road overseers association] to "Dear Sir," June 30, 1934, Edwin Halsey Papers, LC; and James Aylward to [no name] [on old-age pensions], n.d., Fred Canfil Papers, HSTL. On Truman's rural newspaper support, see *IE*, June 29, 1934, and numerous pro-Truman editorials reprinted in *MD*. Late analyses of the campaign predicting a Truman victory can be found in Richard L. Harkness, in *IE*, July 20, July 27, 1934, and *KCS*, July 22, 1934.

64. *NYT*, February 21, 1932; Harkness, in *IE*, July 20, 1934; *MD*, July 6, 1934; *KCS*, August 6, 1934; *PD*, August 1, 1934.

65. Howard F. Sachs, "*Hearsay and Impressions*—The Alex F. Sachs Family and Harry S. Truman," January 1978, MHDC No. 312.

66. *Official Manual of the State of Missouri, 1935–36*, 410–11.

67. Olive Truman, "1934 Senatorial Campaign" [manuscript memo], June 9, 1964, and "An Answer to Aylward" [news clipping, probably from *KCS*], July 4, 1934, Ralph E. Truman Papers, HSTL.

68. *PD*, August 8, 1934; *KCS*, August 8, 12, 1934.

69. Bennett Clark to HST, August 17, 1934; HST to Clark, September 3, 1934; Clark to Ewing Cockrell, September 29, 1934, Clark Papers; *MD*, September 14, 21, November 2, 1934; *PD*, November 3, 1934.

70. *PD*, September 19, October 30, 1934; MT, *Bess Truman*, 135.

71. Maurice Milligan to J. L. Milligan, August 16, 1934; Maurice Milligan to Bennett Clark, December 3, 1934; Clark to Maurice Milligan, December 22, 1934, Clark Papers; *MD*, August 10, September 14, 1934.

72. Truman for Senator headquarters, press release, September 12, 1934, Halsey Papers.

73. For Truman's fall campaign speeches, see the file of press releases in PSF, Elections, Senate, 1934.

74. See, for example, Roscoe Patterson, speech, *PD*, November 2, 1934.

75. *Official Manual of the State of Missouri, 1935–36*, 410–11; *PD*, November 7, 1934; *KCS*, November 7, 1934; *MD*, November 23, 1934.

76. *PD*, November 4, 1934; *KCS*, November 7, 1934.

77. *MD*, November 23, 30, December 7, 14, 21, 1934; *IE*, December 11, 1934; *NYT*, December 19, 1934.

78. *MD*, December 21, 28, 1934; *IE*, December 28, 1934, January 1, 1935; MT, *Bess Truman*, 139, 152, 155–56.

Chapter 12

1. HST, *Memoirs*, 1:142–43.

2. MT, *Bess W. Truman* (New York: Macmillan, 1986), 134; Alfred Steinberg, *The Man from Missouri* (New York: Putnam, 1962), 125.

3. *KCS*, May 10, September 8, 1935.

4. *KCS*, December 24, 27, 30, 1936, January 1, 1937; HST to Clinton M. Hester, August 11, 1938, SVP; HST to BWT, June 25, 28, 1936, January 12, February 13, 1937, FBP.

5. *KCT*, January 15, 1935; HST, *Memoirs*, 1:144.

6. *KCS*, July 22, 1937; HST to John J. O'Connor, October 14, 1949, PSF.

7. Thomas J. Pendergast to HST, January 13, 1939, SVP, Pendergast File; *KCS*, July 16, 1939.

8. Thomas J. Pendergast to HST, January 27, February 1, 27, 1939; HST to Pendergast, January 31, February 1, March 1, 1939, SVP, Pendergast File.

9. For Truman's staff as a senator, see "Harry S. Truman's Senate Staff," Vertical File, HSTL.

10. *MD*, January 11, 1935.

11. Donald Dawson, interview with author; Gusti Butinelli, in *Washington Daily News*, March 4, 1960.

12. Vivian Truman File, SVP.

13. HST to BWT, October 25, 1942, FBP; William Kitchen to HST, May 16, 1938, Kitchen Papers, HSTL; HST to BWT, November 17, 1938, FBP.

14. HST to BWT, August 12, 1935, FBP; *KCS*, June 8, 1935; *KCT*, July 6, 1935.

15. Much of this discussion is documented in the Jackson County and Roger Sermon Files, SVP.

16. HST to Roger Sermon, January 15, 1944, SVP; *MD*, November 27, 1936; Postal appointment controversies are thoroughly laid out in ten archival boxes (140–149), SVP.

17. HST to L. T. Slayton, reprinted in *KCS*, October 15, 1936. WPA expenditure figures are in *Official Manual of the State of Missouri, 1937–38*, 832–34. See also Curtis Betts, in *PD*, July 6, 12, 13, 14, 22, 1938, and Fred Canfil to HST, July 22, 1938, Harry Easley Papers, HSTL.

18. *KCS*, April 14, 1935; William Helm, *Harry Truman: A Political Biography* (New York: Duell, Sloan and Pearce, 1947), 7

19. HST, *Memoirs*, 1:145–46.

20. *KCS*, April 14, 1935; HST to BWT, June 18, July 26, 1935, August 5, 1939, FBP.

21. HST, *Memoirs*, 1:144; George H. Hall, in *PD*, June 26, 1949. For "nigga preacher" [James F. Byrnes remark], see HST to BWT, January 6, 1936, FBP; for stories, see HST, diary, April 25, July 28, 1937, January 7, 1938, SVP.

22. HST to BWT, August 5, 1939, FBP; Duke Shoop, in *KCT*, February 2, 1939.

23. Richard Lawrence Miller, *Truman: The Rise to Power* (New York: McGraw-Hill, 1986), chap. 13; HST to BWT, June 15, 17, 20, 1936, FBP; HST to William Kitchen, June 26, 1935, Kitchen Papers.

24. Victor Messall to John W. Snyder, November 17, 1939, SVP; HST to BWT, July 12, 1935, February 10, 1937, September 29, 30, 1939, FBP.

25. Martha Truman to HST, February 14, 1935, SVP.

26. *KCS*, April 5, 1938, June 22, 1939; editorial, *KCT*, May 15, 1939.

27. Mary Jane Truman to HST, February 7, 8, 21, 1935; HST to Mary Jane Truman, May 17, 1935; Victor Messall to Edgar Faris, Jr., September 28, 1935, SVP.

28. Fred Boxley to HST, January 8, 17, 1935; HST to Boxley, January 11, 1935; Eben A. Ayers, memorandum of statements by Omar E. Robinson . . . June 25, 1951, and related materials, Eben Ayers Papers, HSTL; Victor Messall to HST, August 19, 1938; HST to Messall, August 22, 1938, SVP; HST to MT, February 5, 1937, FBP.

29. MT, *Bess Truman*, 135–41.

30. MT, address to joint session of Congress in observance of HST's hundredth birthday, May 8, 1984; Margaret Truman File, FBP; MT with Margaret Cousins, *Souvenir: Margaret Truman's Own Story* (New York: McGraw-Hill, 1956), 37–57.

31. MT, *Bess Truman*, 134–37, 186; Harry Harrison [Harrison Recording Studios] to HST, May 20, 1941; HST to Harrison, May 23, 1941, SVP.

32. MT, *Bess Truman*, 141–44, 149–52, 155–57, 160–61, drawing on letters in FBP, summarizes these tensions well.

33. For comments about early Senate years, see Hot Springs Hospital, clinical record, September 13–23, 1937, and June 27–July 11, 1941, Department of the Army Military Personnel Records of Harry S. Truman, 1917–1973, HSTL;

HST to BWT, December 6, 8, 9, 11, 1935, January 4, 1936, September 11, 12, 15, 20, 21, 1937, FBP.

Chapter 13

1. The chapter title is from HST, speech to the Senate, *CR*, 75th Cong., 1st sess., June 3, 1937, 5274.

2. *KCT*, March 2, 1935; *KCS*, April 14, June 8, 13, 1935.

3. *KCS*, January 29, 1939; Joseph Alsop and Robert Kintner, in *KCS*, January 31, 1939.

4. *KCS*, July 22, 1937; *KCT*, January 22, 1938; HST to BWT, June 11, 1940; HST to MT, June 23, 1941, FBP.

5. *KCS*, April 15, 1935; *KCT*, May 24, 1935, June 6, 1935.

6. *KCT*, February 6, March 2, 5, 13, April 20; *KCS*, February 9, 21, March 10, April 20; HST, speech, April 19, 1937, and form letter, SVP; HST to BWT, February 12, 21, 24, 26, March 10, 1937, FBP.

7. *NYT*, May 13, 14, 1938; *KCT*, March 23, 1938; *KCS*, March 23, 1938.

8. *KCS*, March 23, May 26, August 27, November 26, 1939; HST to BWT, July 5, August 9, September 24, 1939, FBP.

9. *Kansas City Journal-Post*, n.d. [probably January 25, 1936], Shannon Scrapbooks, Jackson County Historical Society, Independence, Mo.; *KCT*, February 1, 1936; HST, speech to St. Louis Chamber of Commerce, February 7, 1936, SVP; *KCT*, January 6, 1938.

10. See, for example, the following speeches: St. Louis Chamber of Commerce, February 7, 1936; WDAF radio, October 30, 1936; Shirtcraft Company, December 19, 1936; Liberty, Missouri, October 11, 1937, Speech File, SVP.

11. *NYT*, January 5, 8, 16 [sec. 9], February 20, March 2, April 7, 20, 30, May 8, 13, 14, 15 [sec. 4; Arthur Krock], 17, June 9 [Krock], 12, 14, 17, 24, 1938; *KCT*, August 19, 1936, May 14, 1938; *CR*, 75th Cong., 3rd sess., May 13, 1938, 6854–58.

12. "Truman of Missouri: A Little Story of the Modest and Capable Western Statesman," *National Aeronautics* 17 (March 1939): 13, 47.

13. Republican National Committee Research Division, "The Legislative Record of Harry S. Truman," p. 9, Harold Gosnell Papers, HSTL; *KCT*, December 5, 1937 [editorial], January 5, July 22, 1939; HST, address to Fraternal Order of Eagles, August 14, 1937; HST, speech on CBS radio, February 7, 1939, SVP.

14. HST, quoted in William Hillman, ed., *Mr. President* (New York: Farrar, Straus and Young, 1952), 235. See also HST to Burton K. Wheeler, November 17, 1951, PSF. The rest of this chapter amounts to an abridgement of my article "'Vultures at the Death of an Elephant': Harry S. Truman, the Great Train Robbery, and the Transportation Act of 1940," *Railroad History* 165 (Autumn 1991): 6–36.

15. On the railroads in the 1920s, see William Morris Leonard, *Railroad Consolidation Under the Transportation Act of 1920* (New York: Columbia University Press, 1946), and Ari Hoogenboom and Olive Hoogenboom, *History of the Interstate Commerce Commission* (New York: Norton, 1975), 94–118.

16. For the Missouri Pacific, see *Moody's Railway Stocks and Bonds, 1937* (New York: Moody's, 1937), 119–22.

17. For Max Lowenthal's early life and career, see his obituary, *NYT*, May

19, 1971; Jacob Potofsky, letter in *NYT*, July 1, 1971; Lowenthal, testimony before the House Committee on Un-American Activities, September 15, 1950. Reaction to *The Investor Pays* (New York: Knopf, 1933) is summarized in *Book Review Digest, 1933* (New York: Wilson, 1934), 584.

18. *NYT*, August 10, November 6, 7, 9, December 7, 8, 9, 10, 14, 15, 1937, January 5, 14, 1938.

19. HST to Ethel Noland, February 2, 1952, Mary Ethel Noland Papers, HSTL.

20. Winthrop Aldrich, sketch in *Current Biography, 1940* (New York: Wilson, 1940), 9–10.

21. *NYT*, October 27, 28, 29, 1937.

22. HST to BWT, October 29, 1937, FBP.

23. *NYT*, November 5, 1937.

24. HST to BWT, November 1, 3, 1937, FBP; *PD*, June 7, October 24, November 2, 14, 1937.

25. HST to BWT, December 12, 1937, FBP.

26. HST to BWT, December 13, 1937, FBP.

27. *CR*, 75th Cong., 1st sess., June 3, 1937, 5271–75.

28. *CR*, 75th Cong., 2nd sess., December 20, 1937, 1912–24, quotation on 1923.

29. *CR*, 75th Cong., 2nd sess., December 20, 1937, 1924.

30. *NYT*, January 7, 21, February 5, 20, 21, March 16, 18, 23, April 4, 6, 1938; editorial, *PD*, February 20, 1938; Leonard, *Railroad Consolidation*, 247–50.

31. *KCT*, February 5, March 5, 1938; *PD*, March 15, 1938.

32. *NYT*, April 22, 25, 27, 28, May 4, 17, 18, 20, 26, June 5, 10, 14, October 15, 1938; *PD*, May 17, 1938; *KCT*, October 15, 1938.

33. *NYT*, December 24, 1938.

34. *KCT*, May 25, 26, 1939; *KCS*, April 6, May 27, 1939 [editorial]; HST to R. K. Keas, May 23, 1939; HST to Carl Giescow, March 7, 1940; HST to L. W. Childress, March 9, 1940; HST to Grant Stauffer, April 26, 1940; Thomas Dysart to HST, May 7, 1940, SVP. Truman's correspondence with L. W. Childress, president of the largest St. Louis–based barge line, is especially worth reading.

35. *NYT*, February 14, March 20, 29, 30, April 1, 14, May 2, June 22, 1939.

36. *NYT*, April 8, 13, 23 [sec. 11], May 4, 24, 26, 27, 28, 1939. For samples of the opposition, see also Frank Parsons to HST, April 20, 1939; G. W. Pettyjohn to HST, April 17, 1939; Harvey C. Fruehauf to HST, May 24, 1939, SVP.

37. *NYT*, July 8, 9 [sec. 3], 15, 17, 18, 23 [sec. 3], 25, 27, 1939.

38. *NYT*, March 8, 9, 11, April 20, 27, 1940.

39. *NYT*, May 10, 1940. See also A. F. Whitney to HST, September 18, 1939; HST to Whitney, September 22, 1939; HST to W. C. Fisher, January 11, 1940; HST to Mrs. W. H. Perry, March 6, 1940, SVP.

40. *NYT*, August 8, 13, 31, September 6, 1940; Ralph L. Dewey, "The Transportation Act of 1940," *American Economic Review* 31 (March 1941): 15–26.

41. See, for example, HST to R. K. Keas, May 23, 1939, SVP.

42. Robert E. Smith [National Conference of Investors] to HST, November 18, 1939, and enclosed summary of the Wheeler-Truman bill; Charles A. Graham [Bank of Le Roy] to HST, June 14, 1940, and enclosure, June 14, 1949, SVP.

Chapter 14

1. HST to BWT, July 5, 1939, FBP.

2. "Lloyd Crow Stark, Governor of Missouri; Chairman, Executive Committee of Governors' Conference; President, Council of State Governments," Lloyd C. Stark Papers, WHMC.

3. For the early Truman–Stark relationship, see MHDC No. 497, a collection of correspondence photocopied from the Stark Papers.

4. HST to Lloyd Stark, telegram, May 20, 1935, Stark Papers.

5. George Everett Slavens, "Lloyd C. Stark as a Political Reformer, 1936–1941" (M.A. thesis, University of Missouri, 1957).

6. *MD*, July 9, 30, August 27, October 15, 22, 29, November 12, December 10, 1937.

7. *KCT*, May 6, 1938.

8. For an overview of the vote fraud prosecutions, see William Reddig, *Tom's Town* (Philadelphia: Lippincott, 1947), 284–94.

9. *PD*, January 11, 23, 27, 1938; *KCS*, January 28, 1938.

10. *KCS*, January 28, 29, 1938; *PD*, January 29, February 3, 1938.

11. *CR*, 75th Cong., 3rd sess., February 15, 1938, 1962–64.

12. *KCT*, February 17, 1938; *PD*, February 16, 1938; *NYT*, February 17, 1938.

13. Maurice Milligan to Westbrook Pegler, September 23, 1949; Westbrook Pegler to Omar Robinson, September 27, 1949; Robinson to Pegler, September 29, 1949, Westbrook Pegler Papers, Herbert Hoover Library, West Branch, Iowa.

14. *KCS*, February 20, March 8, 21, 1938; *KCT*, February 25, 26, March 16, 1938; *PD*, July 27, 1939.

15. *KCS*, April 5, 1938; *KCT*, May 15, 1939; Rufus Burrus, interview with author.

16. Reddig, *Tom's Town*, 303–4; *Missouri Democrat*, April 1, 1938.

17. Elmer Irey, "Tom Pendergast" [manuscript], Pegler Papers and Henry Morgenthau, Jr., Papers, Franklin D. Roosevelt Library, Hyde Park, N.Y. Irey was chief of the Treasury Department Intelligence Unit.

18. Reddig, *Tom's Town*, 311–22.

19. *PD*, April 7, 1939.

20. *PD*, April 7, 1939.

21. Reddig, *Tom's Town*, chap. 6; *KCS*, April 23, 1939.

22. HST to BWT, October 27, 1939, FBP.

23. *KCS*, April 23, June 24, July 7, December 8, 1939, February 1, 1940; *KCT*, May 13, 1939. On Vivian, see HST to David Powell, May 27, 1940, SVP, and HST to BWT, August 13, 15, 1940, FBP.

24. Burton K. Wheeler, *Yankee from the West* (Garden City, N.Y.: Doubleday, 1951), 373; Duke Shoop, in *KCS*, November 19, 1939; HST to John Snyder, November 7, 1939, SVP.

25. Correspondence with Vivian Truman, Canfil, Sermon, Hinde, and Burrus can be found in their files, SVP.

26. John Snyder, Oral History, 16–20, HSTL; on the Snyder–Vardaman relationship, see *St. Louis Globe-Democrat*, February 9, 1937; Harry Vaughan, Oral History, 2–10, HSTL.

27. *KCS*, February 26, 1936; *MD*, September 24, 1937.

28. Lee, Easley, and Wear Files, SVP; see also Harry Easley and Sam Wear Papers, HSTL.

29. Monroe, Nacy, and Van Sant Files, SVP; see also Thomas Van Sant Papers, HSTL. On Nacy's banking ties and machine affiliations, see Curtis Betts, in *PD*, July 8, 1938.

30. Helm and Harper Files, SVP. On Conran, see *PD*, December 12, 1946, and *St. Louis Globe-Democrat*, January 15, 1952, June 3, 1962, September 10, 1966, March 29, 1975; see also J. V. Conran to Jonathan Daniels, October 9, 1949, Daniels Papers, *Man of Independence* materials, University of North Carolina.

31. *PD*, January 26, 1939; *KCT*, January 26, 1939; *KCS*, January 26, 27, 28, 1939; Roger Sermon to Harry Easley, February 20, 1940; Easley to Sermon, March 4, 1940, Easley Papers; HST, *Memoirs*, 1:159.

32. *PD*, February 3, 4, 1940; *KCS*, February 4, 1940.

33. On the foreclosure, see *KCS*, June 14, 15, 1940; *KCT*, July 17, 1940. For the Thirty-fifth Division office, see *PD*, October 22, 1939 (early ed.). On the Masonic office, see HST to BWT, September 28, 1939, FBP, and HST, *Memoirs*, 1:163.

34. HST to BWT, July 24, September 21, 22, 25 [one of two letters], October 3, 4, 1939, FBP; Bennett Clark to Ben Hibbs [editor, *Saturday Evening Post*], March 12, 1952; Bennett Clark to Martin Sommers [*Saturday Evening Post*], March 20, 1952, Clark Papers, WHMC.

35. *PD*, January 7, 8, 1940; HST to John Snyder, January 12, 1940, SVP.

36. Twenty endorsements are listed in "What the United States Senate Thinks of Harry S. Truman," Edwin Halsey Papers, LC. Truman was also endorsed by at least one other colleague: Robert Rice Reynolds of North Carolina (*MD*, July 12, 1940).

37. Edward Keating, "Memorandum for Mr. Jonathan Daniels," Daniels Papers; *PD*, July 25, 1940; Harry Vaughn to Harry Easley, May 30, 1940, Easley Papers. Gary M. Fink, *Labor's Search for Political Order: The Political Behavior of the Missouri Labor Movement, 1890–1940* (Columbia: University of Missouri Press, 1974), 152–59, discusses Stark's support.

38. *PD*, January 14, 1940; *KCS*, July 6, 1940; *KCT*, July 31, August 5, 1940. For Stark, see *St. Louis Globe-Democrat*, June 20, 25, 1940. On this and other issues, see also the file of 1940 Truman press releases, HST Papers, General File, HSTL. On changing sentiment within the state, see, for example, Justice James Douglas to Bennett Champ Clark, June 18, 1940, Clark Papers.

39. Richard Lawrence Miller, *Truman: The Rise to Power* (New York: McGraw-Hill, 1986), 331.

40. William Kitchen to HST, February 18, March 25, 1939; HST to Kitchen, February 21, March 27, 1939, Kitchen Papers, HSTL. For Walton's position and salary, see *Official Manual of the State of Missouri, 1937–38*, 668.

41. *PD*, August 5, 1940.

42. *PD*, April 23, 1939.

43. Spencer Salisbury to Lloyd Stark, August 18, 1938; Spencer Salisbury to A. J. Murphy, Sr., September 3, October 6, 1938, Stark Papers. Richard Farrington to Jonathan Daniels, September 12, 1949, Daniels Papers. For stories on Stark's alienation of state senator Allen McReynolds and influential National Guard officers, see *Kansas City Journal*, May 28, 31, 1939.

44. Lloyd Stark to Bob Hannegan, December 2, 1938, October 20, 1939 [source of quote], Stark Papers; *KCT*, March 2, 1939.

45. See, for example, Thomas Webster to Lloyd Stark, April 19, May 17, 1940; Secretary to Thomas Webster, April 25, 1940; Terrence Philblad to Lloyd Stark, June 29, 1940, Stark Papers.

46. *Kansas City Call*, May 12, October 13, 1939; C. A. Franklin to HST, October 19, 1939; HST to Franklin, October 25, 1939, SVP; Richard E. Kirkendall, *A History of Missouri*, vol. 5, *1919–1953*, gen. ed. William E. Parrish (Columbia: University of Missouri Press, 1986), 195–99; Louis Cantor, *A Prologue to the Protest Movement: The Missouri Sharecropper Roadside Demonstration of 1939* (Durham, N.C.: Duke University Press, 1969).

47. For this speech and a similar one delivered to the National Colored Democratic Association, see *CR*, 76th Cong., 3rd sess., Appendix, 4546–47, 5367–69.

48. For David Berenstein, see *St. Louis Globe-Democrat*, October 25, 1937 [elected president of city Zionist organization], May 13, 1940 [retires as Zionist president], August 31, 1951 [obituary]; John Snyder to HST, March 7, 1940; HST to Snyder, March 11, 1940, SVP.

49. HST to Harry Easley, February 13, 1940, Easley Papers; J. Vivian Truman to Victor Messall, February 17, 1940; Messall to Vivian Truman, February 20, 1940, SVP; HST to Marvin Casteel, February 21, 29, 1940; Fred Canfil to Harry Easley, March 8, 1940, Easley Papers.

50. Harry Easley to HST, April 23, 1940, Easley Papers; Laura Pinnell Hunter to Lloyd Stark, April 4, 1940, Stark Papers. On the WPA situation in Springfield, see J. W. Sanders to Lloyd Stark, July 28, 1939, and H. Everett Ervin, with Charles W. Dickey, "Report # 1," February 12, 1940, Stark Papers. Stark's own assessment is in Lloyd Stark to Franklin D. Roosevelt, August 9, 1940, Roosevelt Papers, PPF 4462, Roosevelt Library.

51. *PD*, April 13, 14, 15, 16, 1940; *KCT*, April 16, 1940; *St. Louis Globe-Democrat*, April 16, 1940. Lloyd Stark to Franklin D. Roosevelt, February 7, 1940, Roosevelt Papers, OF 300 (Missouri); Stark to Roosevelt, March 29, 1940, Roosevelt Papers, PPF 4462; Lloyd Stark, "Memos for the Press," April 11, 12, 1940, Stark Papers.

52. *PD*, April 16, 1940; *St. Louis Star-Times*, April 16, 1940; J. V. Conran to Jonathan Daniels, October 9, 1949, Daniels Papers.

53. *PD*, April 7, 1940; J. P. [Joseph Pulitzer, Jr.] to R. C. [Ralph Couglan], April 23, 24, 1940; R. C. to J. P., April 24, 1940, Joseph Pulitzer, Jr., Papers, LC; [Olive Truman], "Senatorial Election of 1940," Ralph Truman Papers, HSTL. On rabbit support for Maurice Milligan, see *KCT*, April 26, 1940; *KCS*, July 21, 1940; and *PD*, July 24, 25, 1940.

54. Maurice Milligan, speeches, *KCS*, May 19, July 4, 1940; *PD*, May 23, 1940. For comments on Milligan's campaign, see T. H. Van Sant to HST, April 29, May 6, 1940, and William Kitchen to HST, May 17, 1940, SVP, and Curtis Betts, in *PD*, May 26, 1940.

55. *KCT*, April 2, 1940; for the Stark–Roosevelt relationship, see *PD*, July 23, 1939 [withdraws from consideration as secretary of the navy]; Lloyd Stark to Franklin Roosevelt, January 1, 1940, Roosevelt Papers, PPF 4462; Stark to Roosevelt, February 7, 1940, Roosevelt Papers, OF 300 (Missouri); Stark to General E. M. Watson, March 29, 1940, Roosevelt Papers, PPF 4462.

56. *PD*, February 4, 1940; *KCS*, February 5, 1940; HST to Frank McMurray, February 14, 1940; HST to Wilbert McCune, February 14, 1940, SVP. For the CAA fight, see *PD*, April 25, 29, 30, May 1, 14, 1940. On the bridge

bill, see news items in *Railway Age* 108 (January–June 1941): 744, 1067, 1190; and HST to BWT, June 19, 1940, FBP.

57. For FDR quote, see HST to BWT, August 8, 1939, FBP. For news stories put out by other senators, see *KCT*, May 26, 1939, and *KCS*, August 27, 1939. For FDR's declaration of neutrality, see *KCT*, July 31, 1940.

58. *PD*, June 16, 1940; T. H. Van Sant to Jonathan Daniels, n.d.; Frank Monroe to Jonathan Daniels, September 29, 1949; Sam Wear to Jonathan Daniels, n.d., Daniels Papers.

59. *PD*, June 21, 23, 24, 1940; HST to BWT, June 17, 1940, FBP.

60. *PD*, July 18, 1940.

61. *KCT*, February 2, 1938; *PD*, July 23, 1939; *St. Louis Globe-Democrat*, January 4, 1940.

62. *PD*, June 30, July 9, 14, 1940; *St. Louis Globe-Democrat*, July 5, 1940; *KCS*, July 14, 1940; Stark convention flyers, Stark Papers.

63. *PD*, July 16, 17, 18, 19, 1940.

64. Lloyd Stark to Frank Baer, August 1, 1940, Stark Papers; *PD*, July 17, 1940; Maurice Milligan, in *KCT*, July 24, 1940; Bennett Clark, in *KCT*, July 30, 1940; George K. Wallace, in *KCS*, July 21, 23, 1940; Curtis Betts, in *PD*, July 28, 1940.

65. HST, *Memoirs*, 1:161–62; Rufus Burrus, interview with author. HST, itinerary and speech summaries, 1940 Campaign Press Release File, FBP.

66. *By Their Fruits Ye Shall Know Them*, Vertical File, HSTL; HST to Bill Boyle, memorandum, January 9, 1951, William Boyle Papers, HSTL (copy in PSF); *PD*, August 1, 1940; *KCT*, August 1, 1940; Miller, *Rise to Power*, 330–32; James F. Byrnes, *All in One Lifetime* (New York: Harper, 1958), 101; insurance loan documentation, MHDC No. 621.

67. *KCT*, July 25, 1940.

68. Editorials, *PD*, July 25, 1940; editorial, *KCT*, July 29, 1940.

69. *PD*, July 10, August 7, 1940; Lloyd Stark to Mrs. Lawrence McDaniel, April 23, 1940, Stark Papers.

70. *PD*, July 31, August 1, 2, 4, 1940; *KCS*, August 4, 1940.

71. Harry Easley to HST, May 8, 1941, and attached telegrams, Easley Papers; Jonathan Daniels, *Man of Independence* (Philadelphia: Lippincott, 1950), 209–10; *KCT* and *PD*, August 6, 1940.

72. *PD*, August 4, 6, 1940; *KCS*, August 3, 1940.

73. MT, *Bess W. Truman* (New York: Macmillan, 1986), 193; the official results are in *Official Manual of the State of Missouri, 1935–36*, 410–11, and *Official Manual of the State of Missouri, 1941–42*, 366–67.

74. Lloyd Stark to Franklin Roosevelt, August 9, 1944, Roosevelt Papers, PPF 4462; *PD*, August 7, 1940; Lloyd Stark to Stuart Symington, June 11, 1952; Lloyd Stark to Jules James, October 5, 1955, Stark Papers.

75. *MD*, August 16, 1940; HST to BWT, August 10, 1940, FBP.

76. HST to BWT, August 11, 1940, FBP; *KCT*, August 22, 1940.

77. On Milligan's reappointment, see *PD*, August 22, 1940; *KCT*, September 13, 1940; HST to BWT, September 14, 15, 1940, FBP; Bennett Clark to John C. Collett, September 21, 1940, Clark Papers. On Stark, see HST to BWT, August 21, 1940, FBP; Rubey Hulen to Bennett Clark, September 23, 1940, Clark Papers; *PD*, October 31, 1940.

78. HST to BWT, August 29, September 1, 3, 4, 1940, FBP; *KCS*, November 3, 1940.

79. The official returns are in *Official Manual of the State of Missouri, 1941–42*, 240–42.

80. See especially letters to HST from Roger Sermon, Shannon Douglass, and William Kitchen, 1941–1943, SVP.

Chapter 15

1. HST to BWT, March 19, 1941, FBP. The chapter title is from Merle Miller, *Plain Speaking: An Oral Biography of Harry S. Truman* (New York: Berkeley, 1974), 176.

2. HST to Lou Holland, August 15, 1940, February 4, 1941, SVP. Important sources on the Truman committee are in Theodore Wilson, "The Truman Committee, 1941," in *Congress Investigates: A Documented History, 1792–1974*, ed. Arthur M. Schlesinger, Jr., and Roger Bruns (New York: Chelsea House, 1975), 3115–3261; Donald H. Riddle, *The Truman Committee: A Study in Congressional Responsibility* (New Brunswick, N.J.: Rutgers University Press, 1964); Stephen K. Bailey and Howard Samuel, *Congress at Work* (New York: Holt, 1952), 293–321; Roger Willson, "The Truman Committee" (Ph.D. diss., Harvard University, 1966); David A. Skidmore, Jr., "The Truman Committee" (senior honors thesis, Duke University, 1987); and Harry A. Toulmin, *Diary of Democracy: The Senate War Investigating Committee* (New York: Smith, 1947). See also Donald J. Mrozek, "Organizing Small Business During World War II: The Experience of the Kansas City Region," *Missouri Historical Review* 71 (January 1977): 174–92.

3. HST, speech to the Senate, *CR*, 77th Cong., 1st sess., February 10, 1941, 830–38.

4. Wilson, "Truman Committee, 1941," 3121–22.

5. HST to BWT, March 18, 1941, FBP; Wilson, "Truman Committee, 1941," 3122–23; Bailey and Samuel, *Congress at Work*, 297–98.

6. Bailey and Samuel, *Congress at Work*, 299; HST, *Memoirs*, 1:167; Jonathan Daniels, *Man of Independence* (Philadelphia: Lippincott, 1950), 224; list of the committee staff, compiled during the first half of 1942, MHDC No. 296; William Kitchen to HST, February 17, 1941, and HST to Kitchen, February 19, 1941, SVP; for Hugh Fulton's reputation, see *PD*, April 14, 1941.

7. Riddle, *Truman Committee*, Appendix 3, 184, lists the committee staff appointments. See also MHDC Nos. 296, 681, and Walter Hehmeyer, Oral History, 67–70, HSTL. For Matthew Connelly, see Robert S. Allen and William V. Shannon, *The Truman Merry Go-Round* (New York: Vanguard, 1950), 52–53.

8. HST, *Memoirs*, 1:169–70; Wilson, "Truman Committee, 1941," 3128; "The Congressional Mailbag" [transcript, CBS radio program], July 22, 1941, *CR*, 77th Cong. 1st sess., A3628–30, in Wilson, "Truman Committee, 1941," 3154–62 [HST comment on coal strike on 3,156–57]; HST to Lou Holland, May 1, 1941, SVP.

9. *KCS*, May 10, 27, June 9, 12 [quotation], 1941; HST to William Southern, September 9, 1941, SVP.

10. *Senate Report 480, Part 1*, 77th Cong., 1st sess., June 26, 1941 (Serial Set No. 10545); HST, *Memoirs*, 1:175–76; *KCT*, June 27, 1941.

11. *KCT*, May 7, July 5, 23, August 7, 1941; *KCS*, August 14, 1941; *Senate Report 480, Part 2*, 77th Cong., 1st sess., August 14, 1941 (Serial Set No. 10545).

12. *KCS*, June 2, 1941; *KCT*, July 22, 1941.

13. Willson, "Truman Committee," 161–62.

14. See, for example, *KCS*, August 23, 28, September 20, October 1, 19, 29, December 6, 1941; *KCT*, September 9, October 27 [T. E. Alford], 29, November 18, 22, 25, 28, December 4 [Duke Shoop], 1941.

15. HST to BWT, September 30, December 7, 1941, FBP.

16. MT, *Bess W. Truman* (New York: Macmillan, 1986), 207–8; HST to Mary Ethel Noland, December 14, 1941, Mary Ethel Noland Papers, HSTL.

17. *CR*, 77th Cong., 1st sess., December 10, 1941, 9600–9601.

18. MT, *Bess Truman*, 209; HST to BWT, December 21, 1941, FBP; *PD*, January 13, 1942.

19. *CR*, 77th Cong., 2nd sess., January 15, 1942, 380–91; Wilson, "Truman Committee, 1941," 3129–31.

20. HST, *Memoirs*, 1:186; committee staff and payroll, MHDC No. 296.

21. For an example of the crackpots, see HST, *Memoirs*, 1:173. For what appears to be an attempt at settling a score, see [Gerald Nye] to HST, June 6, 1944, Nye Papers, Herbert Hoover Library, West Branch, Iowa.

22. For example, Walter Hehmeyer, George Meader, and Wilbur Sparks, Oral Histories, HSTL; Joseph Ball to David A. Skidmore, Jr., January 19, 1987, MHDC No. 592.

23. Allen Drury, *A Senate Journal, 1943–1945* (New York: McGraw-Hill, 1963), 106.

24. Willson, "Truman Committee," 32.

25. *NYT*, January 11, 1943.

26. *Senate Report 480, Part 5*, 77th Cong., 2nd sess., May 26, 1942 (Serial Set No. 10655).

27. *Senate Report 10, Part 9*, 78th Cong., 1st sess., May 6, 1943 (Serial Set No. 10758); transcript of HST, interview with Richard Harkness, May 6, 1943, SVP; Richard Polenberg, *War and Society* (Philadelphia: Lippincott, 1972), 14–18.

28. *Senate Report 480, Part 11*, 77th Cong., 2nd sess., November 12, 1942 (Serial Set No. 10655); Toulmin, *Diary of Democracy*, chap. 10; "Conferences Relating to the North American Plant at Dallas," Hugh Fulton Papers, HSTL.

29. *Senate Report 480, Part 10*, 77th Cong., 2nd sess., July 16, 1942 (Serial Set No. 10655); Joseph Ball to David A. Skidmore, Jr., January 19, 1987, MHDC No. 592.

30. Neal Helm to HST, November 9, 1942, January 18, 1943, May 12, 1943; HST to Helm, November 16, 1942; William Boyle to Neal Helm, January 23, 1943, SVP; *Senate Report 10, Part 11*, 78th Cong., 1st sess., July 16, 1943 (Serial Set No. 10758).

31. *Senate Report 10, Part 2*, 78th Cong., 1st sess., January 21, 1943 (Serial Set No. 10758); press release on just cited report, n.d., Truman committee records, National Archives; John H. Tolan, Jr., "Confidential Memo on Committee Motivations . . . Prepared for His Commanding Officer, then Commander John A. Kennedy, Jr.," August 2, 1943, GHDC 144.

32. *Senate Report 480, Part 5*, 77th Cong., 2nd sess., January 15, 1942 (Serial Set No. 10655); *KCS*, January 15, February 3, 1942; *KCT*, January 16, 1942; *NYT*, April 29, 1943.

33. *Senate Report 10, Part 12*, 78th Cong., 1st sess., November 5, 1943

(Serial Set No. 10,758); *NYT*, November 6, 20, December 4, 1943; Truman committee, press releases, June 15, July 8, 1944, Truman Committee Records.

34. HST, *Memoirs*, 1:184; Miller, *Plain Speaking*, 177. On the history of the B-26 bomber, see Enzo Angelucci, *The Rand McNally Encyclopedia of Military Aircraft* (New York: Military Press, 1983), 289. On Higgins and the tank lighter controversy, see Toulmin, *Diary of Democracy*, chap. 8; *NYT*, July 23, 24, 1942; *Senate Report 10, Part 16*, 78th Cong., 2nd sess., March 4, 1944, 133–168 (Serial Set No. 10839). Press release: HST to Frank Knox, August 5, 1942, Truman Committee Records; *NYT*, March 17, 1942, April 23, 1943.

35. Toulmin, *Diary of Democracy*, 242–43; Norman M. Littell, *My Roosevelt Years*, ed. Jonathan Dembo (Seattle: University of Washington Press, 1987), 79–89, 94–95, 99–107, 114–15, 139–47.

36. Toulmin, *Diary of Democracy*, chap. 15; Riddle, *Truman Committee*, chap. 6; editorial, *NYT*, July 12, 1943.

37. Riddle, *Truman Committee*, chap. 6; *NYT*, May 20, July 11, 12, 13, August 20, 21, 25, September 1, 2, 3, 5, October 1, 5, 12, 1943, March 7, April 4, 5, 7, 27, 1944.

38. Riddle, *Truman Committee*, chap. 5 [Patterson–Fulton exchange on 101]; *Senate Report 10, Part 14*, 78th Cong., 1st sess., December 21, 1943 (Serial Set No. 10758).

39. Donald Nelson, testimony, January 28, 1942, U.S. Senate, Special Committee Investigating the National Defense Program, *Hearings*, 77th Cong., 2nd sess., January 28, 1942, pt. 104025–43, quote on 4043.

40. "Sleeping Beauty Treatment," *Time*, October 12, 1942, 81–82; *KCT*, January 23, 1943; *NYT*, February 18, 1943; Bruce Catton, *The War Lords of Washington* (New York: Harcourt Brace, 1946), 252–56.

41. Polenberg, *War and Society*, 12–16; Toulmin, *Diary of Democracy*, chaps. 6, 7; *Senate Report 480, Part 7*, 77th Cong., 2nd sess., May 26, 1942, 40 (Serial Set No. 10655); HST to Frank B. Grumbine, June 27, 1942, SVP.

42. *NYT*, May 29, 1943, May 24, June 2, 1944; Truman committee, press releases, March 27, [29], 1943, May 26, 1944, Truman Committee Records.

43. Eliot Janeway, *The Struggle for Survival*, 2nd ed. (New York: Weybright and Talley, 1968), 147.

44. Joseph Ball to David A. Skidmore, January 19, 1987, MHDC No. 592.

45. The committee's final report is *Senate Report 440, Part 6*, 80th Cong., 2nd sess., April 28, 1948, 10 (Serial Set No. 11205).

46. Arthur Krock, in *NYT*, April 30, 1943, July 30, 1944.

47. Curtis Betts to HST, February 26, 1942; HST to Betts, March 2, 1942, SVP; Marquis Childs, in *PD*, November 8, 1942; "Billion-Dollar Watchdog," *Time*, March 8, 1943, 13–15; "The 10 Most Useful Officials in Washington," *Look*, May 16, 1944, 26–27.

48. Drury, *Senate Journal*, 105–6, 182.

Chapter 16

1. The chapter title is from HST to BWT, July 15, 1943, FBP.

2. HST, graduation address, June 2, 1942, Truman Committee Records, National Archives.

3. MT, *Bess W. Truman* (New York: Macmillan, 1986), 202–3, 232–33, 238–39.

4. MT, *Bess Truman*, 214, 219; HST to BWT, July 29, 1943, FBP.

5. MT, *Bess Truman*, 203–4; *New York Herald-Tribune*, July 27, 1944; secretary of the Senate, monthly reports, August 1941–January 1945, Vertical File, HSTL. For some apparent exceptions to the no-honoraria policy, see Frank Waldrop, in *New York Daily News*, August 11, 1944.

6. On assistance to Mamma and Mary Jane, see HST to Vivian Truman, August 11, 1941, January 29, June 18, 1942; Vivian Truman to HST, June 13, 1942; H. H. Halvorson to HST, October 14, 1941, SVP; HST to BWT, November 15, 1941, August 6, 9, November 2, 1942, October 2, 1943, FBP; Fred Klaber to HST, July 23, 1941, with attached proposal by L. C. Miller, agent; HST to Klaber, July 25, 1941; HST to George S. Montgomery, July 25, 1941; HST to James M. Pendergast, August 8, 1941; HST to Russell Gabriel, February 3, 1942; John Snyder to HST, January 3, 1944, SVP.

7. Elizabeth Tyler Ewing to HST, April 8, 1941; HST to Ewing, April 16, 1941, SVP.

8. HST, autobiographical account, 1945, PSF; HST to Lewis Schwellenbach, December 31, 1941, SVP.

9. *PD*, November 9, 1941; *KCT*, October 16, 1941; HST to R. E. Truman, October 14, 1941, January 27, 1942; Bennett Clark to Lt. Gen. Ben Lear, October 11, 1941; George Marshall to HST, December 19, 1941, SVP.

10. Alfred Steinberg, *The Man from Missouri* (New York: Putnam, 1962), 190, 233; *St. Louis Globe-Democrat*, October 6, 1943; *PD*, April 11, 1944; Rufus Burrus, interview with author.

11. HST to Roy Harper, April 28, 1943; Jonathan Daniels, *Man of Independence* (Philadelphia: Lippincott, 1950), 229; J. C. Truman, interview with author; HST to BWT, August 14, 18, 1944, FBP.

12. MT, *Bess Truman*, 200–201.

13. Physician, interview with HST, June 27, 1941, Medical Records, Department of the Army Military Personnel Records of Harry S. Truman, 1917–1973, HSTL.

14. HST to BWT, June 27 [misdated July 27], 28, 30, July 1, 2, 3, 4, 5, 7, 8, 1941, FBP.

15. HST to BWT, June 24, 1941, January 3, July 28, 1942, FBP.

16. Sam Wear to HST, June 14, 1943; HST to Wear, June 22, 1943; HST to Vivian Truman, June 25, 1943, SVP; HST to BWT, July 15, September 7, 1943, FBP.

17. Richard Lawrence Miller, *Truman: The Rise to Power* (New York: McGraw-Hill, 1986), 364–68; T. Willard Hunter, Oral History, HSTL.

18. HST to BWT, November 11, 1939, FBP; HST to Robert Patterson, June 24, 1942; HST to Franklin D. Roosevelt, April 16, 1942; HST to Henry Stimson, June 3, 1943, SVP; HST, statement and attached advance release, April 12, 1943, HST Papers, General File, HSTL. See also the file on *The Forgotten Factor* and the booklet *You Can Defend America: A Morale-Building Program*, SVP.

19. George Seldes to HST, August 8, 1944; HST to Seldes, August 15, 1944, SVP; *PD*, August 11, 1944; N. W. Helm to HST, March 6, 1944, SVP.

20. HST to Carter Harrison, February 29, March 6, 1936, MHDC No. 403. On Truman's thinking about American foreign policy, see Mark Steven Wilburn, "Keeping the Powder Dry: Senator Harry S. Truman and Democratic Interventionism, 1935–1941," *Missouri Historical Review* 84 (April 1990): 311–37,

and Wilson Miscamble, "The Evolution of an Internationalist: Harry S. Truman and American Foreign Policy," *Australian Journal of Politics and History* 23 (August 1977): 268–83.

21. HST, speech at Larchmont, New York, April 20, 1937, SVP.

22. HST, speech at Larchmont, New York, April 20, 1937, SVP.

23. HST, speech to Kiwanis Club, St. Joseph, Missouri, October 27, 1938, SVP.

24. HST, speech at Caruthersville, Missouri, October 8, 1939, SVP.

25. HST to Eddie Meisburger, July 23, 1943, SVP.

26. Wilburn, "Keeping the Powder Dry," 330–36.

27. HST to Luther Ely Smith, February 6, 1941; HST to Charles P. Schafer, May 12, 1941; HST to Rev. Oscar E. Feucht, November 4, 1941, SVP.

28. Robert A. Divine, *Second Chance: The Triumph of Internationalism in America During World War II* (New York: Atheneum, 1967), 91–97, 107–13, 141–54; Miscamble, "Evolution of an Internationalist," 275–80; *NYT*, March 20, 1943; William Boyle to HST, July 23, 1943, SVP.

29. HST to Leonard Williams, August 23, 1943, SVP; Divine, *Second Chance*, 128; an untitled, undated copy of what appears to have been Truman's basic speech on this tour can be found in SVP, Press Release File.

30. The quotations are from a basic speech that Truman used during 1944: "Speech of Senator Harry S. Truman (D. Mo.) to be delivered ——, 1944 at ——," Truman Committee Papers, National Archives. See also HST, speech, January 17, 1944, *CR*, 78th Cong., 2nd sess., Appendix, A265–66.

31. HST to Lillie Knight, February 9, 1943, SVP.

32. HST to Andrew Somers, January 28, 1942; HST, speech to United Rally, Chicago, April 14, [1943]; HST to Peter Bergson, May 7, 1943; Stephen S. Wise to HST, May 20, 1943; HST to Wise, June 1, 1943; HST to Harry Vaughan, April 27, 1943; David Berenstein to HST, October 27, 1943; David Berenstein to William Boyle, February 23, 1944; HST to Phineas Smoller, December 7, 1943; HST to Carl Dubinsky, February 8, 1944, SVP.

33. *NYT*, June 24, 1941; Richard Lowitt, *George W. Norris: The Triumph of a Progressive, 1933–44* (Urbana: University of Illinois Press, 1978), 361.

34. HST to Sumner Blossom, June 2, 1943, SVP; Daniels, *Man of Independence*, 229.

35. HST to Mon Wallgren, December 18, 1945, Wallgren Papers, HSTL; Gary M. Fink and James Hilty, "Prologue: The Senate Voting Record of Harry S. Truman," *Journal of Interdisciplinary History* 4 (Autumn 1973): 207–35.

36. HST to H. C. Newmeyer, April 23, 1943, SVP. See also HST to George M. Rogers, November 4, 1941; HST to Edward D. McKim, November 22, 1941; HST to Brown Harris, May 28, 1942, SVP.

37. *CR*, 77th Cong., 2nd sess., September 30, 1942, 7647. Truman was absent from the Senate, but paired against the Ball amendment.

38. *CR*, 78th Cong., 1st sess., May 5, 1943, 3983; June 25, 1943, 6489; December 9, 1943, 10496–10526.

39. *CR*, 78th Cong., 1st sess., September 21, 1943, 7694–97; HST to W. G. Glover, Sr., January 11, 1944, SVP.

40. HST, correspondence in C. A. Franklin, Negroes, and Recorder of Deeds (Dr. Tompkins) Files, SVP.

41. HST to BWT, October 11, 1943, FBP; HST to Mira Ewin, November 20, 1942; Harry Vaughan to Walter Hilliker, October 31, 1941; Harry

Vaughan to Pvt. James D. Beal, February 13, 1945, SVP; Elmer V. Mosee, untitled story on HST "For Release to COLOR, Inc.," July 28, 1944, attached to Mosee to Robert Hannegan, July 27, 1944, SVP; Richard M. Dalfiume, *Desegregation of the U.S. Armed Forces: Fighting on Two Fronts, 1939–1953* (Columbia: University of Missouri Press, 1969), 135–36.

42. Stephen Kemp Bailey, *Congress Makes a Law: The Story Behind the Employment Act of 1946* (New York: Columbia University Press, 1950), 28–36.

43. HST to Neal Helm, September 11, 1942; HST to Marvin Gates, January 28, 1942, SVP.

44. HST to BWT, June 25, 1942, FBP; *New Republic*, May 8, 1944, esp. 653; *New Republic*, February 5, 1945, esp. 195; Dean R. Brimhall and A. S. Otis, "Consistency of Voting by Our Congressmen," *Journal of Applied Psychology* 32 (February 1948): 1–14. Fink and Hilty, "Prologue: The Senate Voting Record of Harry S. Truman," are in basic agreement with the just cited studies.

Chapter 17

1. The chapter title is Truman's memory of a note that he recalled Robert Hannegan having shown him during the 1944 Democratic National Convention (HST, *Memoirs*, 1:191).

2. HST, statement on the political situation in Missouri, September 9, 1941, enclosed in HST to Oscar Ewing, September 9, 1941, SVP; HST to BWT, September 24, 27, October 3, 5, 1941, FBP.

3. HST to James J. Milligan, April 17, 1941, SVP. For Truman's correspondence with state and local leaders, see the following files in SVP: Blair, James T.; Canfil, Fred; Douglass, Shannon; Easley, Harry; Gabriel, Russell; Henderson, Mitchell; Hinde, Edgar; Jackson County; Kitchen, William; Nacy, Richard; Political Commissions; Political File; Sermon, Roger; Truman, Vivian; Van Sant, T. H.; Walsh, Thomas; Wear, Sam. See also these collections in the Truman Library: Harry Easley, Thomas Van Sant, and Sam Wear.

4. For the election results, see *KCT*, *KCS*, and *PD*, August 2, 3, 1944. For the Clark and Sermon campaigns, see J. V. Conran to HST, July 16, 1944; unsigned memorandum to HST [on Clark–McKittrick contest], June 6, 1944; Hugh Williamson to HST, April 1, 1944; summary of telephone conversation between Fred Canfil and Bill Boyle, January 12, 1944, Canfil File; Fred Canfil to HST, June 17, July 5, 1944; HST to Harry Easley, January 21, 1944; HST to Anne E. Nolen, June 1, 1944, SVP.

5. HST to BWT, August 5, 11, 1942, June 28, October 11, 1943, FBP; HST to Roger Sermon, May 31, 1944, SVP.

6. *PD*, February 25, March 6, 9, 10, 13, April 8, 10, May 4, 8, 1942; HST to Mrs. H. V. Howes, March 5, 1942; HST to Harry Vaughan, May 16, 1942, SVP; HST, *Memoirs*, 1:324.

7. *KCS*, July 11, 1943; *PD*, December 23, 1942, February 3, 12, 21, March 24, 25, April 7, July 8, 1943; Francis Biddle, *In Brief Authority* (Garden City, N.Y.: Doubleday, 1962), 201–4.

8. HST to Francis Biddle, July 13, September 18, 1943; HST to Richard Duncan, telegram, January 12, 1944, SVP, Canfil File.

9. Drew Pearson, in *Washington Post*, June 27, 1943 [accuracy confirmed by HST to BWT, June 27, 1943, FBP].

10. *CR*, 77th Cong., 1st sess., August 14, 1941, 7117–18.

11. Alfred Steinberg, *The Man from Missouri* (New York: Putnam, 1962), 195–96; HST to BWT, August 23, September 27, October 2, 1942, FBP; HST, "We Can Lose the War in Washington," *American Magazine*, November 1942, 22–23, 104–6.

12. *NYT*, March 27, 1944.

13. HST to L. A. Pickard, May 11, 1943, SVP.

14. Allen Drury, *A Senate Journal, 1943–1945* (New York: McGraw-Hill, 1963), 137–38.

15. HST to BWT, July 12, 1943, FBP.

16. HST to Vivian Truman, February 12, 1944, SVP; *NYT*, April 30, 1944.

17. The following account of the 1944 vice-presidential nomination rests primarily on the following sources: James F. Byrnes, *All in One Lifetime* (New York: Harper, 1958), chap. 13; Robert L. Messer, *The End of an Alliance: James F. Byrnes, Roosevelt, Truman, and the Origins of the Cold War* (Chapel Hill: University of North Carolina Press, 1982), chap. 2; Norman D. Markowitz, *Rise and Fall of the People's Century* (New York: Free Press, 1973), chap. 3; Frank Freidel, *Franklin D. Roosevelt: A Rendezvous with Destiny* (Boston: Little, Brown, 1990), chap. 38; Jonathan Daniels, *Man of Independence* (Philadelphia: Lippincott, 1950), chap. 15; and Robert Ferrell's authoritative *Choosing Truman* (Columbia: University of Missouri Press, 1994). I have also consulted Edwin Pauley to Jonathan Daniels, unsigned, undated [1950] memorandum, Jonathan Daniels Papers, University of North Carolina, and PSF.

18. Byrnes, *All in One Lifetime*, 227.

19. Byrnes, *All in One Lifetime*, 228.

20. HST, *Memoirs*, 1:191.

21. Messer, *End of an Alliance*, 29.

22. HST, *Memoirs*, 1:192–93.

23. *NYT*, July 21, 1944; MT, *Bess W. Truman* (New York: Macmillan, 1986), 231.

24. HST to BWT, August 18, 1944, FBP; Steinberg, *Man from Missouri*, 221.

25. Steinberg, *Man from Missouri*, 222–23.

26. Ewing Mitchell's pamphlets *The Four Horsemen of the Pendergast Machine* and *Truman's First Nomination for Senator Was Stolen* can be found in the Ewing Mitchell Papers and the James P. Kem Papers, WHMC.

27. Westbrook Pegler, in *KCT*, August 8, 1944; "Family Mortgage from School Funds in an Illegal Amount" (manuscript), Kem Papers.

28. *Chicago Tribune*, October 28, 1944.

29. Clipping, *Kansas City Jewish Chronicle*, n.d., Vertical File, HSTL.

30. Clipping, *PM*, October 27, 1944, SVP; HST to Mrs. Archibald Reid, August 17, 1944, SVP.

31. For the Official Democratic line on Truman, see Democratic National Committee, press release [1944], Vertical File, HSTL. For a close approximation with a veneer of impartiality, see George Creel, "Truman of Missouri," *Collier's*, September 9, 1944, 24ff. Louis Johnson to Steve [Early], memorandum, n.d., Franklin D. Roosevelt Papers, OF 64, Franklin D. Roosevelt Library, Hyde Park, N.Y. (copy at HSTL). HST, quoted in Drury, *Senate Journal*, 283.

32. *Time*, November 6, 1944, 22–24.

33. HST, *Memoirs*, 1:194.

34. HST to Eddie McKim, February 15, 1945, SVP.

35. MT, *Bess Truman*, 244–45.

36. HST to Lou Holland, February 26, 1945, SVP; "Washington Calling," *Progressive*, April 9, 1945, 6, 16.

37. *KCS*, January 27, 29, 1945.

38. HST, *Memoirs*, 1:198.

39. HST to E. L. Clary, March 30, 1945, SVP.

40. Drury, *Senate Journal*, 374–75.

41. *KCT*, January 26, 30, 1945; *KCS*, January 26, 1945.

42. HST to Franklin Roosevelt, April 5, 1945; Roosevelt to HST, April 7, 1945, Roosevelt Papers (copy in MHDC No. 478 and in HSTL microfilm collection).

43. HST, *Memoirs*, 1:1–4; Drury, *Senate Journal*, 373.

44. HST to Martha and Mary Jane Truman, April 11, 1945, HST Papers, Post-Presidential Papers, Memoirs File, HSTL.

45. This and the following paragraphs are based on HST, diary, April 12, 1945, but probably written in the following few days, PSF; HST, *Memoirs*, 1:4–5; Steinberg, *Man from Missouri*, 233–34.

Chapter 18

1. Jonathan Daniels, *White House Witness, 1942–1945* (Garden City, N.Y.: Doubleday, 1975), 283; Robert J. Donovan, *Conflict and Crisis: The Presidency of Harry S. Truman, 1945–1948* (New York: Norton, 1977), 15, 17.

2. Thomas M. Campbell and George C. Herring, eds., *The Diaries of Edward R. Stettinius, Jr.* (New York: New Viewpoints, 1975), 313–14; Walter Millis, ed., *The Forrestal Diaries* (New York: Viking, 1951), 42–43.

3. MT, *Harry S. Truman* (New York: Morrow, 1973), 210–12; *Forrestal Diaries*, 43.

4. *Stettinius Diaries*, 315–16.

5. HST, diary, April 12, 1945, PSF.

6. The account of Truman's first day in office in this and subsequent paragraphs is based primarily on HST, diary, April 13, 1945 [possibly written later], PSF, and HST, *Memoirs*, 1:chap. 2. There are some minor discrepancies between the two sources that I have tried to sort out by referring to independent evidence.

7. Arthur H. Vandenberg, Jr., and Joe Alex Morris, eds., *The Private Papers of Senator Vandenberg* (Boston: Houghton Mifflin, 1952), 167; Allen Drury, *A Senate Journal, 1943–1945* (New York: McGraw-Hill, 1963), 412–13.

8. Except where otherwise noted, the account of this day is from HST, diary, April 14, PSF, and HST, *Memoirs*, 1:28–35.

9. There are many descriptions of this occasion in addition to Truman's— for example, Drury, *Senate Journal*, 413.

10. Robert E. Sherwood, *Roosevelt and Hopkins* (New York: Harper, 1948), 881; Drury, *Senate Journal*, 414.

11. HST, diary, April 15, 1945 [obviously written later and incorrect on some counts], PSF; Donovan, *Conflict and Crisis*, 18.

12. *Public Papers, 1945*, 1–6; Donovan, *Conflict and Crisis*, 18–19; *NYT*, April 17, 1945.

13. *Public Papers, 1945*, 8–13; Eben Ayers, diary, April 17, 1945, Eben Ayers Papers, HSTL; *NYT*, April 18, 1945; Cabell Phillips, *The Truman Presidency* (New York: Macmillan, 1966), 64.

14. *NYT*, April 17, 1945.

15. George H. Gallup, *The Gallup Poll: Public Opinion, 1935–1971*, 3 vols. (New York: Random House, 1972), 1:512, 537; Robert S. Allen and William V. Shannon, *The Truman Merry Go-Round* (New York: Vanguard, 1950), 49; Donovan, *Conflict and Crisis*, 19–21.

16. HST to BWT, June 6, 1945, FBP.

17. See especially Francis H. Heller, ed., *The Truman White House: The Administration of the Presidency, 1945–1953* (Lawrence: Regents Press of Kansas, 1980).

18. HST, *Memoirs*, 1:18; Charles E. Bohlen, *Witness to History, 1929–1969* (New York: Norton, 1973), 215.

19. HST to Jonathan Daniels, February 26, 1950 [not sent], PSF. For Harold Smith's viewpoint, see his diary, copy at HSTL; for his problems with John Snyder, see Harold Gosnell, *Truman's Crises* (Westport, Conn.: Greenwood Press, 1980), 227–28.

20. Alfred Steinberg, *The Man from Missouri* (New York: Putnam, 1962), 253–54; MT, *Harry Truman*, 215; Merle Miller, *Plain Speaking: An Oral Biography of Harry S. Truman* (New York: Berkeley, 1974), 176, 216.

21. Gosnell, *Truman's Crises*, 232.

22. *Public Papers, 1945*, 16–19; Eben Ayers, diary, April 16, 17, 18–19, 20, 1945, Ayers Papers; Frank Stanton to Robert Underhill, March 16, 1990, and Robert Underhill to Benedict K. Zobrist, April 3, 1990, MHDC No. 683; J. Leonard Reinsch, *Getting Elected: From Radio to Roosevelt to Television and Reagan* (New York: Hippocrene, 1988), 23–32.

23. Donovan, *Conflict and Crisis*, 23. For Ross's career, see Ronald T. Farrar, *Reluctant Servant: The Story of Charles G. Ross* (Columbia: University of Missouri Press, 1968).

24. Graham White, *FDR and the Press* (Chicago: University of Chicago Press, 1979).

25. See, for example, Eben Ayers, diary, April 17, 1945, Ayers Papers.

26. "The New Treasury Secretary," *New Republic*, June 17, 1946, 853–54.

27. *NYT*, May 1, June 13, 1945.

28. MT, *Harry Truman*, 260; *St. Louis Globe-Democrat*, February 4, 1937, May 5, 1945, January 30, March 1, 22, 23, 24, 26, 1946, February 6, 1951; *PD*, May 30, 1948. Jake Vardaman's resignation from the Federal Reserve Board is noted in *NYT*, August 3, 1958.

29. Clark Clifford, with Richard Holbrooke, *Counsel to the President* (New York: Random House, 1991), chap. 2, an account that may be as fascinating for what it omits as what it says; Clark Clifford, conversation with author.

30. William O. Wagnon, Jr., "John Roy Steelman: Native Son to Presidential Advisor," *Arkansas Historical Quarterly* 27 (Autumn 1968): 205–25; John R. Steelman and H. Dewayne Kreager, "The Executive Office as Administrative Coordinator," *Law and Contemporary Problems* 21 (Autumn 1956): 688–709; Steelman, interview for Truman *Memoirs*, December 9, 1954, HST Papers, Post-Presidential Papers, Memoirs File, HSTL.

31. *NYT*, August 31, November 11, December 9, 29, 1945, January 2, 19, 20, 27, February 4, 8, 9, 19, 24 [sec. 6], March 30, August 16, December 22 [sec. 4], 1946.

32. *NYT*, November 13, 14, 26, December 28, 1946; Richard O. Davies, *Housing Reform in the Truman Administration* (Columbia: University of Missouri

Press, 1966), chap. 4; Andrew J. Dunar, *The Truman Scandals and the Politics of Morality* (Columbia: University of Missouri Press, 1984), 82–85.

33. George E. Allen, *Presidents Who Have Known Me*, 2nd ed. (New York: Simon and Schuster, 1960), esp. chaps. 13–15.

34. *NYT*, April 30, 1960.

35. HST to Jonathan Daniels, February 26, 1950 [unsent], PSF, but see also Truman's more charitable evaluations from 1952, available in typewritten form in Post-Presidential Papers, Memoirs File.

36. Eben Ayers, diary, September 14, 1945, Ayers Papers.

37. Sam Rayburn to HST, April 18, 1945, PSF; Francis Biddle, *In Brief Authority* (Garden City, N.Y.: Doubleday, 1962), 365–66; Norman M. Littell, *My Roosevelt Years*, ed. Jonathan Dembo (Seattle: University of Washington Press, 1987), 368; HST to BWT, July 15, 1943, FBP; HST, *Memoirs*, 1:325, is inaccurate in almost every respect.

38. Robert Messer, *The End of an Alliance: James F. Byrnes, Roosevelt, Truman, and the Origins of the Cold War* (Chapel Hill: University of North Carolina Press, 1982), chaps. 3–4, 71–72.

39. *Forrestal Diaries*, 27; Forrestal to the president, memorandum, March 15, 1945, PSF; Jonathan Daniels, *Man of Independence* (Philadelphia: Lippincott, 1950), 305–6, and interviews with HST, Jonathan Daniels Papers, University of North Carolina; Linda Lear, "Edwin Pauley," in *The Harry S. Truman Encyclopedia*, ed. Richard S. Kirkendall (Boston: Hall, 1989), 272–73; HST, appointment diary, May 17, 1945, PSF.

40. Harold Smith, diary, February 8, 1946, HSTL.

41. HST, annotated appointment sheet, May 18, 1945, PSF; Dean Acheson, *Present at the Creation: My Years in the State Department* (New York: Norton, 1969), 184–85; *Forrestal Diaries*, 87, 142; Heller, ed., *Truman White House*, 88–89.

42. Michael S. Sherry, "Unification of the Armed Forces," in *Truman Encyclopedia*, ed. Kirkendall, 11; HST, *Memoirs*, 2:46–53. Demetrios Caraley, *The Politics of Military Unification* (New York: Columbia University Press, 1966), is a classic account. Steven L. Rearden, *History of the Office of the Secretary of Defense: The Formative Years* (Washington, D.C.: Office of the Secretary of Defense, 1984), is exhaustive and nearly definitive.

43. HST, *Memoirs*, 2:55–58; Sherry, "Unification of the Armed Forces," 46; Roy Godson, *The Kremlin and Labor: A Study in National Security Policy* (New York: Crane, Russak, 1977); Harry Ransom, *The Intelligence Establishment* (Cambridge, Mass.: Harvard University Press, 1970).

44. HST, *Memoirs*, 2:59–60; Acheson, *Present at the Creation*, 733–34; Alfred D. Sander, "Truman and the National Security Council, 1945–1947," *Journal of American History* 59 (September 1972): 369–88; Anna Kasten Nelson, "President Truman and the Evolution of the National Security Council," *Journal of American History* 72 (September 1985): 360–78.

Chapter 19

1. For American public opinion, see George H. Gallup, *The Gallup Poll: Public Opinion, 1935–1971*, 3 vols. (New York: Random House, 1972), 1:492–93, 497, 499, 514, 515.

2. Anthony Eden, *The Reckoning* (Boston: Houghton Mifflin, 1965), 621 [quote slightly and probably accurately reworded].

3. HST, diary memo, [probably May 23, 1945], PSF.

4. HST to David Morgan, January 28, 1952, PSF.

5. HST, diary, May 22, 1945, PSF.

6. Truman quotes from HST, diary, July 7, 1945, PSF; Robert Messer, *The End of an Alliance: James F. Byrnes, Roosevelt, Truman, and the Origins of the Cold War* (Chapel Hill: University of North Carolina Press, 1982), 126.

7. *FRUS, 1945,* 3:745–46; 5:210.

8. Thomas M. Campbell and George C. Herring, eds., *The Diaries of Edward R. Stettinius, Jr.* (New York: New Viewpoints, 1975), 318.

9. *FRUS, 1945,* 5:231–34.

10. *Stettinius Diaries,* 325; W. Averell Harriman and Elie Abel, *Special Envoy to Stalin and Churchill* (New York: Random House, 1975), 447.

11. Wilson D. Miscamble, "Anthony Eden and the Truman–Molotov Conversations, April 1945," *Diplomatic History* 2 (Spring 1978): 167–80.

12. *FRUS, 1945,* 5:252–55.

13. *FRUS, 1945,* 5:256–58; Harriman and Able, *Special Envoy,* 447–53; Charles E. Bohlen, *Witness to History, 1929–1969* (New York: Norton, 1973), 222–23.

14. Bohlen, *Witness to History,* 223; Arthur H. Vandenberg, Jr., and Joe Alex Morris, eds., *The Private Papers of Senator Vandenberg* (Boston: Houghton Mifflin, 1952), 176; Harriman and Abel, *Special Envoy,* 453–54, expresses the retrospective reservations of the post-Vietnam Harriman.

15. Abel and Harriman, *Special Envoy,* 477–78; *FRUS: Conference of Berlin, 1945,* 1:8–9.

16. Gallup, *Gallup Poll,* 1:497.

17. George C. Herring, Jr., *Aid to Russia, 1941–1946: Strategy, Diplomacy, and the Origins of the Cold War* (New York: Columbia University Press, 1973), chaps. 8, 9; HST, *Memoirs,* 1:227–28; *Stettinius Diaries,* 358–59; *FRUS, 1945,* 5:998–1004.

18. HST to Eleanor Roosevelt, May 10, 1945, PSF; HST, annotated appointment sheets, May 16, 18, 1945, PSF; Joseph Davies, diary, April 30, 1945, Joseph Davies Papers, LC; John Morton Blum, ed. and intro., *The Price of Vision: The Diary of Henry A. Wallace* (Boston: Houghton Mifflin, 1973), 443–51; Abel and Harriman, *Special Envoy,* 459; Bohlen, *Witness to History,* 225.

19. HST, annotated appointment sheets, May 19, 21, 1945, PSF; HST, diary, May 22, 23, 1945, PSF.

20. [Department of State], memorandum for the president, May 25, 26, 29, 1945, PSF; *FRUS, 1945,* 4:220–314.

21. HST to Eleanor Roosevelt, May 10, 1945, PSF; HST, diary, May 22, 1945, PSF.

22. HST, diary, June 7, 1945, PSF; Eben Ayers, diary, June 6–7, 1945, Eben Ayers Papers, HSTL.

23. *Public Papers, 1945,* 144.

24. Robert Goralski, *World War II Almanac, 1931–1945* (New York: Bonanza, 1981), 398–412.

25. *FRUS: (Potsdam), 1945,* 1:903–10; Barton J. Bernstein, "Writing, Righting, or Wronging the Historical Record: President Truman's Letter on His Atomic-Bomb Decision," *Diplomatic History* 16 (Winter 1992): 163–73.

26. HST, *Memoirs,* 1:10–11, 85, 87; Len Giovannitti and Fred Freed, *The Decision to Drop the Bomb* (New York: Coward-McCann, 1965), 49.

27. Giovannitti and Freed, *Decision to Drop the Bomb,* 58, 63–67.

28. McGeorge Bundy, *Danger and Survival* (New York: Random House, 1988), 70–76, 82–84; *FRUS: (Potsdam), 1945,* 1:909.

29. HST to BWT, July 12, 1945, FBP.

30. *NYT,* June 12, 1945. See also *NYT,* May 3, 22, 1945.

31. *FRUS: Conference of Berlin (Potsdam), 1945,* 1:210–20, 249–50, 1037–41; 2:11–21.

32. Harriman and Abel, *Special Envoy,* 488; Walter Millis, ed., *The Forrestal Diaries* (New York: Viking, 1951), 78; *FRUS: (Potsdam), 1945,* 2:22–23.

33. Bohlen, *Witness to History,* 237–51; HST, diary, July 7, 1945, PSF.

34. HST, diary, July 16, 1945, PSF, Charles Ross File.

35. *FRUS: (Potsdam), 1945,* 2:1, 360.

36. HST, diary, July 16, 17, 1945, PSF, Ross File; *FRUS: (Potsdam), 1945,* 2:43n.3, 1582–87.

37. HST, *Memoirs,* 1:343–414.

38. HST to BWT, July 29, 31, 1945, FBP; HST, *Memoirs,* 1:395.

39. HST, diary, July 18, 1945, PSF, Ross File; HST, diary, August 5, 1945, PSF; HST to BWT, July 18, 20, 22, 31, 1945, FBP; Wallace Graham, interview with author.

40. HST, *Memoirs,* 1:402; HST to BWT, July 20, 22, 25, 29, 31, 1945, FBP; HST, diary, July 30, 1945, PSF, Ross File; Jonathan Daniels, *Man of Independence* (Philadelphia: Lippincott, 1950), 278.

41. *FRUS: (Potsdam), 1945,* 2:1360–70.

42. *FRUS: (Potsdam), 1945,* 2:225, 1361; HST, diary, July 25, 1945, PSF, Ross File.

43. *FRUS: (Potsdam), 1945,* 2:225.

44. *FRUS: (Potsdam), 1945,* 2:47, 81–82, 225, 378–79, 1555–58; HST, *Memoirs,* 1:416.

45. HST to James F. Cate, January 12, 1953 [see also unsent draft and ancillary material], PSF; For a thorough discussion of this document, see Bernstein, "Writing, Righting, or Wronging the Historical Record."

46. *FRUS: (Potsdam), 1945,* 1:877–78.

47. The best treatment of the Konoye mission is Leon V. Sigal, *Fighting to a Finish: The Politics of War Termination in the United States and Japan, 1945* (Ithaca, N.Y.: Cornell University Press, 1988), chap. 2. Kai Bird, in *NYT,* October 9, 1994, incorrectly calls this a surrender offer. For the 1941 Konoye proposal, see Akira Iriye, *The Origins of the Second World War in Asia and the Pacific* (London: Longman, 1987), 157–67.

48. HST, diary, July 18, 1945, PSF, Ross File.

49. *FRUS: (Potsdam), 1945,* 2:1265–67, 1324n., 1372–74.

50. *FRUS: (Potsdam), 1945,* 1272n., 1372–74, 1474–76. Classic works on the atomic decision are Gar Alperowitz, *Atomic Diplomacy: Hiroshima and Potsdam* (New York: Simon and Schuster, 1965, 1985); Herbert Feis, *The Atomic Bomb and the End of World War II* (Princeton, N.J.: Princeton University Press, 1966); and Martin J. Sherwin, *A World Destroyed: The Atomic Bomb and the Grand Alliance* (New York: Knopf, 1975). See also Bundy, *Danger and Survival,* chap. 2, and Gerhard L. Weinberg, *A World at Arms* (New York: Cambridge University Press, 1994), chap. 16. A thorough discussion of the literature may be found in J. Samuel Walker, "The Decision to Use the Bomb," *Diplomatic History* 14 (Winter 1990): 97–114, although it is flawed by a failure even to mention the impact of Okinawa.

51. *FRUS: (Potsdam), 1945,* 2:1293; Robert J. C. Butow, *Japan's Decision to Surrender* (Stanford, Calif.: Stanford University Press, 1954), 145–47.

52. HST, diary, July 25, 1945, PSF, Ross File.

53. HST, *Memoirs*, 1:421; Messer, *End of an Alliance*, 115–16.

54. Feis, *Atomic Bomb*, chap. 9; Butow, *Japan's Decision to Surrender*, 176.

55. *Forrestal Diaries*, 82–84; Wallace, *Price of Vision*, 474.

56. Wallace, *Price of Vision*, 474–75; *Forrestal Diaries*, 83–84.

57. See, for example, Bird, in *NYT*, October 9, 1994, which also manages to misinterpret Truman's July 18 diary entry.

58. See, for example, Robert A. Pape, "Why Japan Surrendered," *International Security* 18 (Fall 1993): 154–201.

59. Francis Heller, conversation with author.

Chapter 20

1. HST to James F. Byrnes, January 5, 1946, PSF.

2. Robert Messer, *The End of an Alliance: James F. Byrnes, Roosevelt, Truman, and the Origins of the Cold War* (Chapel Hill: University of North Carolina Press, 1982), 128–30; John Lewis Gaddis, *The United States and the Origins of the Cold War* (New York: Columbia University Press, 1972), chap. 8; Harold D. Smith, conference with the president, October 5, 1945, Smith diary, HSTL.

3. For the flow of Truman's concerns at staff conferences, see Eben Ayers, diary, September–December, 1945, Eben Ayers Papers, HSTL; for speeches, see *Public Papers, 1945*, 378–81, 404–14, 428–38; for private attitudes on UMT, see Eben Ayers, diary, September 10, 1945; HST, diary, July 26, 1945, PSF, Charles Ross File; for budgetary ideas, see Harold Smith, diary, September 13, 14, 19, December 19, 1945, HSTL.

4. Henry L. Stimson, memorandum for the president, September 11, 1945, PSF.

5. Matthew Connelly, cabinet meeting notes, September 21, 1945, Connelly Papers, HSTL; John Morton Blum, ed. and intro., *The Price of Vision: The Diary of Henry A. Wallace* (Boston: Houghton Mifflin, 1973), 482–85; Eben Ayers, diary, September 24, 1945, Ayers Papers; *Public Papers, 1945*, 381–82, 387–88 [press conference, October 8, 1945].

6. See, for example, HST to Joseph Davies, October 6, 1945, PSF; Wallace, *Price of Vision*, 490.

7. HST to Joseph Davies, October 6, 1945, PSF; Wallace, *Price of Vision*, 490; Dean Acheson, *Present at the Creation: My Years in the State Department* (New York: Norton, 1969), 151–52; David E. Lilienthal, *The Journals of David E. Lilienthal: The Atomic Energy Years, 1945–1950* (New York: Harper & Row, 1964), 10–12.

8. Messer, *End of an Alliance*, 146–48; Acheson, *Present at the Creation*, 163; Harold Smith, diary, November 9, 28, December 5, 1945, HSTL; Wallace, *Price of Vision*, 523–25; Eben Ayers, diary, December 12, 1945, Ayers Papers; [George Elsey], unsigned aide-memoir, January 4, 1946, Elsey Papers, HSTL; W. Averell Harriman and Elie Abel, *Special Envoy to Stalin and Churchill* (New York: Random House, 1945), 530.

9. Harriman and Abel, *Special Envoy*, 524; Bohlen, *Witness to History*, 263.

10. James F. Byrnes, *All in One Lifetime* (New York: Harper, 1958), chap. 22.

11. George F. Kennan, *Memoirs: 1925–1950* (Boston: Little, Brown, 1967), 287.

12. HST, *Memoirs*, 1:547–48; Acheson, *Present at the Creation*, 135–36; Arthur H. Vandenberg, Jr., and Joe Alex Morris, eds., *The Private Papers of Senator Vandenberg* (Boston: Houghton Mifflin, 1952), 229 [entry misdated December 11].

13. HST, *Memoirs*, 1:549.

14. HST, *Memoirs*, 1:549; *NYT*, December 21, 26, 1945; MT, *Bess W. Truman* (New York: Macmillan, 1986), 280; Vandenberg, *Private Papers*, 232–34.

15. MT, *Bess Truman*, 281; HST to BWT, December 28, 1945, PSF.

16. HST, *Memoirs*, 1:549–50; Acheson, *Present at the Creation*, 136; Byrnes, *All in One Lifetime*, 342–43; Eben Ayers, diary, December 29, 1945, Ayers Papers.

17. HST, *Memoirs*, 1:550; Byrnes, *All in One Lifetime*, 342–43.

18. HST to James F. Byrnes, January 5, 1946 [unsent], PSF; for Truman's displeasure at the delay in receiving the Ethridge report, see Eben Ayers, diary, January 5, 1946, Ayers Papers. For Byrnes's "triumphal" presentation of the Moscow agreements, see Byrnes, *All in One Lifetime*, 337, 344–45.

19. Gaddis, *United States and the Origins of the Cold War*, 288–94; George H. Gallup, *The Gallup Poll: Public Opinion, 1935–1971*, 3 vols. (New York: Random House, 1972), 1:523, 565, 567. This compilation does not contain the October survey, which is cited in Gaddis's book.

20. Thomas M. Campbell and George C. Herring, eds., *The Diaries of Edward R. Stettinius, Jr.* (New York: New Viewpoints, 1975), 441–42, 445–48, 451–54; Joseph P. Lash, *Eleanor: The Years Alone* (New York: Norton, 1972), 51–54; Walter Millis, ed., *The Forrestal Diaries* (New York: Viking, 1951), 134.

21. Kennan, *Memoirs*, 292–95, chaps. 12–14, 547–59.

22. Vandenberg, *Private Papers*, 246–51; Gaddis, *United States and the Origins of the Cold War*, 294–96.

23. Gaddis, *United States and the Origins of the Cold War*, 304–6; Byrnes, *All in One Lifetime*, 349–50. Cf. Messer, *End of an Alliance*, chap. 10.

24. Byrnes, *All in One Lifetime*, 353–56; HST, *Memoirs*, 1:552–53; Messer, *End of an Alliance*, 178–80.

25. Jonathan Daniels, *Man of Independence* (Philadelphia: Lippincott, 1950), 279; Robert J. Donovan, *Conflict and Crisis: The Presidency of Harry S. Truman, 1945–1948* (New York: Norton, 1977), 190–91.

26. Fraser Harbutt, *The Iron Curtain* (New York: Oxford University Press, 1986), 197–208; Gallup, *Gallup Poll*, 1:567; HST to Martha and Mary Jane Truman, March 11, 1946, reprinted in MT, *Harry S. Truman* (New York: Morrow, 1973), 312.

27. HST to James F. Byrnes, January 5, 1946, and HST, annotated appointment calendar, March 23, 1946, PSF, cited in Donovan, *Conflict and Crisis*, 194; *FRUS, 1946*, 7:348–49, 372; Bruce R. Kuniholm, *The Origins of the Cold War in the Near East: Great Power Conflict and Diplomacy in Iran, Turkey, and Greece* (Princeton, N.J.: Princeton University Press, 1980), chap. 5.

28. Kuniholm, *Origins of the Cold War in the Near East*, 335–37, 355–62.

29. HST to James F. Byrnes, October 13, 1945, PSF; Eben Ayers, diary, November 1–3, 1945, Ayers Papers; HST, *Memoirs*, 1:552; *FRUS, 1946*, 7:840–42; *Forrestal Diaries*, 192; Acheson, *Present at the Creation*, 194–96.

30. Acheson, *Present at the Creation*, 151–54; Lilienthal, *Journals*, 23–24, 27–31.

31. HST, *Memoirs*, 2:5–16; HST, appointment sheet, March 16, 1946, PSF; Acheson, *Present at the Creation*, 154–56; Lilienthal, *Journals*, 30–83.

32. David Holloway, *Stalin and the Bomb* (New Haven, Conn.: Yale University Press, 1994), 166.

33. HST, *Memoirs*, 2:6, 10, 11.

34. Gallup, *Gallup Poll*, 1:525, 578; Messer, *End of an Alliance*, 137, 190–191.

35. Frank McNaughton, reports to New York office, July 5, 12, 13, 1946, McNaughton Papers, HSTL. For Truman's involvement, see, for example, HST to Tom Stewart, November 9, 1945; HST to J. Parnell Thomas, February 2, 1946; James K. Vardaman, Jr., to HST, memorandum, February 13, 1946, OF 212-A; HST to the secretary of the treasury [Fred Vinson], June 6, 1946, PSF.

36. Quoted in Gaddis, *United States and the Origins of the Cold War*, 331.

37. Arthur Krock, *Memoirs: Sixty Years on the Firing Line* (New York: Funk & Wagnalls, 1968), 389–453. The original manuscript, Clark Clifford to HST, September [24], 1946, and attached report, is in PSF.

38. Krock, *Memoirs*, 393–95, 449.

39. Byrnes, *All in One Lifetime*, 373.

40. See, for example, Wallace, *Price of Vision*, 512–13 [November 13, 1945], 535–39 [December 29, 1945; January 2, 1946].

41. Wallace, *Price of Vision*, 563, 567, 570, 588; HST, *Memoirs*, 1:555–57.

42. HST, diary, September 16, 1946, PSF; Wallace, *Price of Vision*, 612–13; Alonzo L. Hamby, *Beyond the New Deal: Harry S. Truman and American Liberalism* (New York: Columbia University Press, 1973), 128; Donovan, *Conflict and Crisis*, 222–23.

43. *Public Papers, 1946*, 426–29.

44. Wallace, *Price of Vision*, 661–69.

45. HST, diary, September 19, 1946, PSF; Wallace, *Price of Vision*, 617–26.

46. Wallace, *Price of Vision*, 628–32; Charles Ross, diary, September 21, 1946, Ross Papers, HSTL.

47. HST to John Nance Garner, September 21, 1946, PSF.

48. Clark Clifford, with Richard Holbrooke, *Counsel to the President* (New York: Random House, 1991), 123–24; Wallace, *Price of Vision*, 613 [September 12, 1946], 620–21 [September 18, 1946].

Chapter 21

1. The chapter title is from HST, *Memoirs*, 2:1; later quotation from HST, *Memoirs*, 1:482.

2. George H. Gallup, *The Gallup Poll: Public Opinion, 1935–1971*, 3 vols. (New York: Random House, 1972), 1:523.

3. *Public Papers, 1945*, 264–309.

4. HST, *Memoirs*, 1:482–83; Eben Ayers, diary, September 7, 1945, Eben Ayers Papers, HSTL.

5. Francis H. Heller, ed., *The Truman White House: The Administration of the Presidency, 1945–1953* (Lawrence: Regents Press of Kansas, 1980), 227–30.

6. On Truman's program as a whole and his motivation, see Richard E. Neustadt, "Congress and the Fair Deal: A Legislative Balance Sheet," *Public Policy* 5 (1954): 351–81. On the mood of Congress, see reports to *Time*'s New York office by Frank McNaughton (for example, September 28, October 6, November 2, 3, 1945), McNaughton Papers, HSTL. On health insurance, see Monte M. Poen, *Harry S. Truman Versus the Medical Lobby* (Columbia: University of

Missouri Press, 1979), esp. chap. 2; for universal military training, see Eben Ayers, diary, September 8, 10, 1945, Ayers Papers.

7. *Public Papers, 1945*, 10–11. For Truman's private language, see, for example, HST to BWT, June 19, 1946, FBP.

8. Donald McCoy and Richard Ruetten, *Quest and Response: Minority Rights and the Truman Administration* (Lawrence: University Press of Kansas, 1973), 26–29. For primary documentation, see Charles Houston to HST, December 3, 1945; HST to Houston, December 7, 1945; S.I.R. [Samuel I. Rosenman] to HST, memorandum, December 3, 1945; HST to heads of all government departments, December 18, 1945, OF 40. Executive Order No. 9664 is in *Federal Register* 10:15301.

9. MT, *Bess W. Truman* (New York: Macmillan, 1986), 278; HST to Martha and Mary Jane Truman, October 13, 1945, HST Papers, Post-Presidential Papers, Memoirs File, HSTL.

10. On the outgoing governor, see George Killion to Richard Nacy, April 29, 1946; and HST to Richard Nacy, May 15, 1946, SPF.

11. McCoy and Ruetten, *Quest and Response*, 49–54; HST to David Niles, September 20, 1946; HST to Tom Clark, September 20, 1946, PSF.

12. Stephen Kemp Bailey, *Congress Makes a Law: The Story Behind the Employment Act of 1946* (New York: Columbia University Press, 1950), chaps. 1–3; Henry A. Wallace, *Six Million Jobs* (New York: Simon and Schuster, 1945).

13. Frank McNaughton, reports, September 7, 28, November 2, 3, 1945, January 4, 5, 17, 18, July 26, 1946, McNaughton Papers.

14. HST–Vinson exchanges and other material, OF 264.

15. Bailey, *Congress Makes a Law*, chap. 6, Barkley quote on 128n.

16. Alonzo L. Hamby, "Truman, the Liberals, and F.D.R. as Symbol and Myth," *Journal of American History* 56 (March 1970): 859–67.

17. Ansel Luxford to Fred Vinson, memorandum, February 13, 1946, Vinson Papers, University of Kentucky.

18. Edwin Nourse to HST, July 29, 1946, Nourse Papers, HSTL. See especially Nourse's memoranda on his "consultations with the President."

19. Edward Flash, *Economic Advice and Presidential Leadership: The Council of Economic Advisers* (New York: Columbia University Press, 1965). I also have drawn on the papers of John Clark, Leon Keyserling, and Nourse, HSTL.

20. *Public Papers, 1945*, 197–200, 362–66; Richard G. Hewlett and Oscar E. Anderson, Jr., *The New World, 1936–1946*, vol. 1 of *A History of the Atomic Energy Commission* (University Park: Pennsylvania State University Press, 1962), chaps. 12–14.

21. *Public Papers, 1945*, 403.

22. Jonathan Daniels, *White House Witness, 1942–1945* (Garden City, N.Y.: Doubleday, 1975), 287; David E. Lilienthal, *The Journals of David E. Lilienthal: The Atomic Energy Years, 1945–1950* (New York: Harper & Row, 1964), esp. 133–68, 635–36.

23. HST, *Memoirs*, 1:510–12; 2:53–55; *Public Papers, 1945*, 404–13; *Public Papers, 1946*, 509–10.

24. George Q. Flynn, "Selective Service/Universal Military Training," in *The Harry S. Truman Encyclopedia*, ed. Richard S. Kirkendall (Boston: Hall, 1989), 324–25; Gallup, *Gallup Poll*, 1:541, 545–47; Walter Millis, ed., *The Forrestal Diaries* (New York: Viking, 1951), 59–60, 88–89, 93, 243–44, 368–78, 384–89, 394, 397–401, 425–28.

25. Allen Matusow, *Farm Policies and Politics in the Truman Years* (Cambridge, Mass.: Harvard University Press, 1967), is the major source for the famine crisis. My own tone and conclusions, however, are considerably different.

26. Matusow, *Farm Policies*, 5.

27. *Public Papers, 1946*, 107–11.

28. *Public Papers, 1946*, 153, 206–8, 215, 236, 314; Herbert Hoover, overseas trip diary and the "Dear Julius" letters [reports prepared by a close aide], Hoover Papers, Herbert Hoover Library, West Branch, Iowa.

29. Robert J. Donovan, in *The Great Upset of 1948*, prod. Kathleen McCleery, PBS, WETA, Washington, D.C., 1988; Donovan, interview with author.

30. HST to Mon Wallgren, December 18, 1945, PSF (ribbon copy in Wallgren Papers, HSTL).

31. Gallup, *Gallup Poll*, 1:519, 521, 532–33, 539, 567–68, 573, 580–81, 583.

32. Craufurd D. Goodwin, "Attitudes toward Industry in the Truman Administration," in *The Truman Presidency*, ed. Michael Lacey (New York: Cambridge University Press, 1989), 102–3.

33. McNaughton, report to New York office, October 20, 1945, McNaughton Papers.

34. Alonzo L. Hamby, *Beyond the New Deal: Harry S. Truman and American Liberalism* (New York: Columbia University Press, 1973), 67.

35. Robert J. Donovan, *Conflict and Crisis: The Presidency of Harry S. Truman, 1945–1948* (New York: Norton, 1977), 211.

36. HST to Charles Sawyer, May 13, 1946, PSF; *Public Papers, 1946*, 241–42.

37. HST, *Memoirs*, 1:501.

38. *NYT*, May 24, 1946.

39. HST, typed copy of handwritten memo, n.d. [probably spring 1946], Post-Presidential Papers, Memoirs File.

40. HST, handwritten draft [ca. May 23, 1946], Clark Clifford Papers, HSTL, reprinted in Cabell Phillips, *The Truman Presidency* (New York: Macmillan, 1966), 116.

41. *Public Papers, 1946*, 274–80; John Morton Blum, ed. and intro., *The Price of Vision: The Diary of Henry A. Wallace* (Boston: Houghton Mifflin, 1973), 575–77.

42. Wallace, *Price of Vision*, 576.

43. McNaughton, report to New York office, May 25, 1946, McNaughton Papers.

44. *Public Papers, 1946*, 289–97.

45. HST to Sidney Hillman, June 15, 1946, PSF.

46. Harold Smith, conference with HST, May 15, 1946, Smith diary, HSTL.

47. Frank McNaughton, report to New York office, May 4, 1946, McNaughton Papers; HST to BWT, June 14, 1946, FBP.

48. Frank McNaughton, report to New York office, June 28, 1946, McNaughton Papers.

49. *Public Papers, 1946*, 322–34.

50. Frank McNaughton, report to New York office, July 26, 1946, McNaughton Papers.

51. HST to Jim Pendergast, May 21, 1946, PSF; *KCS*, April 19, 1950, and other clippings in Roger Slaughter folder, Vertical File, HSTL.

52. *Public Papers, 1946*, 350–52; *KCT*, July 19, 1946; *KCS*, July 26, 1946.

53. Alfred Steinberg, *The Man from Missouri* (New York: Putnam, 1962), 287–89.

54. Donovan, *Conflict and Crisis*, 235–36.

55. HST, handwritten draft, n.d., October 14 folder, PSF, Speech File.

56. Donovan, *Conflict and Crisis*, 236.

57. HST, diary, September 26, 1946, PSF.

58. On measurements of postwar economic performance, see Richard Vedder and Lowell Gallaway, "The Great Depression of 1946," *Review of Austrian Economics* 5 (1991): 3–32.

59. *NYT*, November 7, 8, 9, 10, 1946; HST, handwritten draft of Gridiron talk, December 14, 1946, PSF.

60. HST to BWT, November 18, 1946, FBP.

Chapter 22

1. *Public Papers, 1947*, 178–79.

2. HST, appointment calendar, February 18, 1947, PSF, reprinted in Robert H. Ferrell, *Off the Record* (New York: Harper & Row, 1980), 108–9.

3. George F. Kennan, *Memoirs: 1925–1950* (Boston: Little, Brown, 1967), 345–46.

4. Dean Acheson, *Present at the Creation: My Years in the State Department* (New York: Norton, 1969), 198–200.

5. For Lincoln MacVeagh's dispatches, see, for example, *FRUS, 1946*, 7:91–92, 97–99, 226–27, 240–45. For conflicting historical viewpoints, see Lawrence Wittner, *American Intervention in Greece, 1943–1949* (New York: Columbia University Press, 1982); Stephen G. Xydis, *Greece and the Great Power: Prelude to the "Truman Doctrine"* (Thessaloniki: Institute for Balkan Studies, 1963); and Bruce R. Kuniholm, *The Origins of the Cold War in the Near East: Great Power Conflict and Diplomacy in Iran, Turkey, and Greece* (Princeton, N.J.: Princeton University Press, 1980).

6. *FRUS, 1947*, 5:29–62; Forrest C. Pogue, *George C. Marshall: Statesman, 1945–1959* (New York: Penguin Books, 1989), 161–65; Acheson, *Present at the Creation*, 219; HST, *Memoirs*, 2:103.

7. *FRUS, 1947*, 5:96–98; Walter Millis, ed., *The Forrestal Diaries* (New York: Viking, 1951), 250–52; HST, *Memoirs*, 2:104–5.

8. *Public Papers, 1947*, 176–80.

9. HST to MT, March 13, 1947, reprinted in MT, *Harry S. Truman* (New York: Morrow, 1972), 343.

10. Chester Kerr to Wilson Wyatt and Leon Henderson [copy received at Department of State, April 9, 1947], Dean Acheson Papers, HSTL, describes a Wallace rally held in New York, March 31, 1947.

11. James T. Patterson, *Mr. Republican: A Biography of Robert A. Taft* (Boston: Houghton Mifflin, 1972), 379–72; see also Taft files, OF 2950, PPF 2253, and PSF.

12. Arthur H. Vandenberg, Jr., and Joe Alex Morris, eds., *The Private Papers of Senator Vandenberg* (Boston: Houghton Mifflin, 1952), 337–52; Frank McNaughton, report to New York office, October 10, 1947, McNaughton Papers,

HSTL; Stephen E. Ambrose, *Nixon: The Education of a Politician, 1913–1962* (New York: Simon and Schuster, 1987), 147–48.

13. *Public Papers, 1947*, 167–72.

14. *Forrestal Diaries*, 263, 266–68; Kennan, *Memoirs*, 325–29; Walter Isaacson and Evan Thomas, *The Wise Men: Six Friends and the World They Made—Acheson, Bohlen, Harriman, Kennan, Lovett, McCloy* (New York: Simon and Schuster, 1986), 405.

15. *Public Papers, 1947*, 265–66.

16. Clark Clifford, with Richard Holbrooke, *Counsel to the President* (New York: Random House, 1991), 139.

17. Herbert Hoover, *An American Epic* (Chicago: Regnery, 1964), 4:245–56; *FRUS, 1947*, 2:394–95; Edwin Pauley to HST, April 15, June 9, 1947, PSF; John Steelman to HST, memorandum, n.d. [March 1947], PSF; *Forrestal Diaries*, 255–56; Michael J. Hogan, *The Marshall Plan* (New York: Cambridge University Press, 1987), 33–35.

18. Pogue, *Marshall: Statesman*, chaps. 3–9, 16; "Digest of Secretary Marshall's Testimony Before Executive Session, Foreign Relations Committee, February 1947," and A. C. Wedemeyer to George Marshall, August 8, 1947, PSF; Kennan, *Memoirs*, 373–74.

19. Isaacson and Thomas, *Wise Men*, 406–7; HST to A. E. Weston, April 25, 1951, PSF.

20. John L. Gaddis, "Harry S. Truman and the Origins of Containment," in *Makers of American Foreign Policy*, ed. Frank Merli and Theodore Wilson (New York: Scribner, 1974), 511.

21. Jack M. Holl and Terrence Fehner, "Military Spending," in *The Harry S. Truman Encyclopedia*, ed. Richard S. Kirkendall (Boston: Hall, 1989), 237–39; Robert Donovan, *Conflict and Crisis: The Presidency of Harry S. Truman, 1945–1948* (New York: Norton, 1977), 143, 200, 261; Robert A. Pollard, *Economic Security and the Origins of the Cold War, 1945–1950* (New York: Columbia University Press, 1985), 22–23; HST to Elbert Thomas, December 2, 1946; HST to Omar Ketchum, December 11, 1946, PSF.

22. HST to Edwin Nourse, March 25, 1948, PSF.

23. John Lewis Gaddis, *Strategies of Containment: A Critical Appraisal of Postwar American National Security Policy* (New York: Oxford University Press, 1982), 359; Pollard, *Economic Security and the Origins of the Cold War*, 153–56, quotation on 156.

24. Gregg Herken, *The Winning Weapon: The Atomic Bomb in the Cold War, 1945–1950* (New York: Knopf, 1980), chaps. 10–13, esp. 260; Victor Housholder, "My Visit to the White House," February 7–8, 1947, Housholder Papers, HSTL.

25. James Shepley and "RTE," report to New York office, May 24, 1947, McNaughton Papers.

26. Pollard, *Economic Security*, 145–48.

27. Alonzo L. Hamby, *Beyond the New Deal: Harry S. Truman and American Liberalism* (New York: Columbia University Press, 1973), esp. chaps. 7–8; Norman O. Markowitz, *The Rise and Fall of the People's Century* (New York: Free Press, 1973), chaps. 7, 8.

28. Frank McNaughton, reports, October 10 [two items], November 7, 21, 1947, McNaughton Papers; Ambrose, *Nixon*, 154–57.

29. H. Bradford Westerfield, *Party Politics and Foreign Policy* (New Haven, Conn.: Yale University Press, 1955), chap. 13.

30. HST, diary, April 3, 1948, PSF; Vandenberg, *Private Papers*, 393–96; Acheson, *Present at the Creation*, 241–42; *NYT*, April 6, 1948; Alan R. Raucher, "Paul Gray Hoffman," in *Truman Encyclopedia*, ed. Kirkendall, 156, and *Paul G. Hoffman: Architect of Foreign Aid* (Lexington: University Press of Kentucky, 1985).

31. *Public Papers, 1948*, 203.

Chapter 23

1. The chapter title is from HST, *Memoirs*, 2:157.

2. HST to David K. Niles, May 13, 1947, PSF.

3. Robert J. Donovan, *Conflict and Crisis: The Presidency of Harry S. Truman, 1945–1948* (New York: Norton, 1977), 322.

4. Merle Miller, *Plain Speaking: An Oral Biography of Harry S. Truman* (Berkeley, 1974), 230–32.

5. Eddie Jacobson, thirteen-page handwritten chronology, n.d. [probably mid-1950], of contacts with the White House and the typewritten explication of them by Frank J. Adler, July 28, 1974, Jacobson Papers, HSTL; Eddie Jacobson to HST, October 3, 1947; HST to Jacobson, October 8, 1947, PSF. For Max Lowenthal, see Michael Cohen, *Truman and Israel* (Berkeley: University of California Press, 1990), 60–69. On the political professionals, see Edward J. Flynn to HST, July 30, 1946; Edwin Pauley to HST, October 9, 1946; Robert Hannegan to HST, October 1, 1946, PSF.

6. Philleo Nash, interview with author; Abram L. Sachar, *The Redemption of the Unwanted: From the Liberation of the Death Camps to the Founding of Israel* (New York: St. Martin's Press, 1983), chap. 8. See, for example, David Niles to HST, memorandum, May 12, 1947; HST to Niles, May 13, 1947; HST to the undersecretary of state [Robert Lovett], August 6, 1947, PSF.

7. HST to Joseph Ball, November 24, 1945, PSF.

8. Dean Acheson, *Present at the Creation: My Years in the State Department* (New York: Norton, 1969), 170.

9. John Morton Blum, ed. and intro., *The Price of Vision: The Diary of Henry A. Wallace* (Boston: Houghton Mifflin, 1973), 607.

10. Evan M. Wilson, *Decision on Palestine* (Stanford, Calif.: Hoover Institution Press, 1979), 97–98; Acheson, *Present at the Creation*, 176–77; Edward Flynn to HST, July 30, 1946, PSF; *Public Papers, 1946*, 442–44; HST, *Memoirs*, 2:154.

11. HST to Edwin Pauley, October 22, 1946; HST to Eleanor Roosevelt, August 23, 1947, PSF.

12. HST to Walter George, October 8, 1946, PSF.

13. Donovan, *Conflict and Crisis*, 322; HST, *Memoirs*, 2:153–54.

14. HST to Martha and Mary Jane Truman, January 19, 1947; HST to Mary Jane Truman, March 21, 1948, HST Papers, Post-Presidential Papers, Memoirs File, HSTL.

15. HST to undersecretary of state, August 6, 1947, PSF; Wilson, *Decision on Palestine*, 116.

16. HST to David Niles, May 13, 1947, PSF.

17. Miller, *Plain Speaking*, 232–33; Joseph P. Lash, *Eleanor: The Years Alone* (New York: Norton, 1972), chap. 5.

18. Walter Laquer, *A History of Zionism* (New York: Holt, Rinehart and Winston, 1972), 573–76; Donovan, *Conflict and Crisis*, 327–28.

19. Walter Isaacson and Evan Thomas, *The Wise Men: Six Friends and the World They Made—Acheson, Bohlen, Harriman, Kennan, Lovett, McCloy* (New York: Simon and Schuster, 1986), 451–52; Clark Clifford, with Richard Holbrooke, *Counsel to the President* (New York: Random House, 1991), 4; Clark Clifford to HST, memorandum, March 6, 8, 1948, in *FRUS, 1948*, 5:687–96.

20. *FRUS, 1948*, 5:637–40, 645, 648–49, 651–54; Senator Francis J. Myers to HST, March 4, 1948; HST to Myers, March 6, 1948, PSF.

21. *FRUS, 1948*, 5:679–81, 697.

22. Donovan, *Conflict and Crisis*, 374–75; Miller, *Plain Speaking*, 234–35; HST, *Memoirs*, 2:160–61.

23. *FRUS, 1948*, 5:742–44; HST, *Memoirs*, 2:161–62; Clifford, *Counsel to the President*, 8–9.

24. HST, diary, March 19, 1948, PSF.

25. Donovan, *Conflict and Crisis*, 377–79.

26. HST to Edwin Pauley, October 22, 1946, PSF.

27. Eleanor Roosevelt to HST, March 22, 1948; HST to Eleanor Roosevelt, March 25, 1948, Eleanor Roosevelt Papers, Franklin D. Roosevelt Library, Hyde Park, N.Y.; *Public Papers, 1948*, 190–92; *FRUS, 1948*, 5:744–46, 748–52, 754, 759–60, 771.

28. *Public Papers, 1948*, 191; *FRUS, 1948*, 5:807–9.

29. *FRUS, 1948*, 5:774, 798–800, 832–33.

30. *FRUS, 1948*, 5:877–79.

31. *FRUS, 1948*, 5:935–36.

32. *FRUS, 1948*, 5:965–69.

33. *FRUS, 1948*, 5:972–80.

34. *FRUS, 1948*, 5:989–93, 1005–7; *Public Papers, 1948*, 258; Isaacson and Thomas, *Wise Men*, 452–53; Clifford, *Counsel to the President*, 18–23.

35. *FRUS, 1948*, 5:1007.

36. Cohen, *Truman and Israel*, 146 (photo).

Chapter 24

1. Charles Ross to Ella Ross, November 13, 1946, Ross Papers, HSTL. The chapter title is from HST, diary, January 6, 1948, PSF.

2. Frank McNaughton, report to New York office, March 28, 1947, McNaughton Papers, HSTL.

3. Robert J. Donovan, *Conflict and Crisis: The Presidency of Harry S. Truman* (New York: Norton, 1977), 239–42; Alonzo L. Hamby, *Beyond the New Deal: Harry S. Truman and American Liberalism* (New York: Columbia University Press, 1973), 170.

4. HST to Richard Duncan, May 18, 1946, PSF.

5. HST to Sherman Minton, November 26, 1946, PSF.

6. HST, diary, December 11, 1946, PSF.

7. Frank McNaughton, reports, esp. January 17, 25, March 1, 7, 28, April 5, 11, 12, May 17, 24, November 16, December 12, 1947, McNaughton Papers; Susan M. Hartmann, *Truman and the 80th Congress* (Columbia: University of Missouri Press, 1971), chaps. 1, 2.

8. Frank McNaughton, report to New York office, March 28, 1947, McNaughton Papers.

9. HST, handwritten draft statement, March 1947, PSF, Mr. and Mrs. Charles Ross File.

10. George H. Gallup, *Gallup Poll: Public Opinion, 1935–1971*, 3 vols. (New York: Random House, 1972), 1:608, 614, 618–19, 621, 623, 626, 638, 648.

11. *Public Papers, 1947*, 3–6.

12. HST to Joseph Ball, January 8, 1947, PSF.

13. Hartmann, *Truman and the 80th Congress*, 79–87; James T. Patterson, *Mr. Republican: A Biography of Robert A. Taft* (Boston: Houghton Mifflin, 1972), chap. 23.

14. Frank McNaughton, report to New York office, May 2, 1947, McNaughton Papers; Hartmann, *Truman and the 80th Congress*, 88–90; *Public Papers, 1947*, 288–301.

15. Frank McNaughton, report to New York office, June 21, 1947, McNaughton Papers; *Public Papers, 1947*, 306–7; HST to Mary Jane Truman, June 28, 1947, HST Papers, Post-Presidential Papers, Memoirs File, HSTL.

16. Hamby, *Beyond the New Deal*, 185.

17. United States Bureau of the Census, *Historical Statistics of the United States, Colonial Times to the Present* (Washington, D.C.: Government Printing Office, 1975), 197–224, food prices on 213.

18. Patterson, *Mr. Republican*, 379–80.

19. *Public Papers, 1947*, 492–98; Patterson, *Mr. Republican*, 383.

20. John D. Clark, unpublished manuscript on the early history of the Council of Economic Advisers, chap. 5, and CEA to HST, November 25, 1947, Clark Papers, HSTL; *Public Papers, 1947*, 532–34; Frank McNaughton, report to New York office, November 21, 1947, McNaughton Papers.

21. Marriner Eccles, congressional testimony, November 25, 1947, and a statement he issued after conferring with John Snyder, December 10, 1947, OF 151; HST to Sherman Minton, February 27, 1948, PSF; Marriner Eccles, *Beckoning Frontiers* (New York: Knopf, 1951), 435–40.

22. Frank McNaughton, report to New York office, March 28, 1947, McNaughton Papers.

23. HST to Harry Mitchell, October 4, 1944; Mitchell to HST, October 12, 1944; HST to Mitchell, November 13, 1944, SVP.

24. Alan Harper, *The Politics of Loyalty: The White House and the Communist Issue, 1946–1952* (Westport, Conn.: Greenwood Press, 1969), chap. 3.

25. George Elsey, note on Clark Clifford conversation with HST, May 2, 1947, Elsey Papers, HSTL.

26. On May 2, 1952, Truman declared that 384 federal employees had been dismissed under the loyalty program; he had no political interest in minimizing the figure (*Public Papers, 1952*, 314). David Caute, however, estimates the higher numbers in the text (*The Great Fear* [New York: Simon and Schuster, 1978], 274–75, 592–93).

27. William Hillman, notes on discussion with HST, December 18, 1954, Post-Presidential Papers, Mr. Citizen File, HSTL.

28. Bernard Sternsher, "Harry Truman," in *Popular Images of American Presidents*, ed. William C. Spragens (Westport, Conn.: Greenwood Press, 1988), 394, 398.

29. Cabell Phillips, *The Truman Presidency* (New York: Macmillan, 1966),

162–65; Hamby, *Beyond the New Deal*, 182–83; Clark Clifford, with Richard Holbrooke, *Counsel to the President* (New York: Random House, 1991), 190–94; Patrick Anderson, *The President's Men* (Garden City, N.Y.: Doubleday, 1968), 134–58.

30. Clark M. Clifford to HST, memorandum, November 19, 1947, Clifford Papers, HSTL; Irwin Ross, *The Loneliest Campaign: The Truman Victory of 1948* (New York: New American Library, 1968), 29–34.

31. Hartmann, *Truman and the 80th Congress*, chap. 4.

32. *Public Papers, 1947*, 263–64; Patterson, *Mr. Republican*, 315–26, 391–92; Monte M. Poen, *Harry S. Truman Versus the Medical Lobby* (Columbia: University of Missouri Press, 1979), 100–101; Richard O. Davies, *Housing Reform in the Truman Administration* (Columbia: University of Missouri Press, 1966), chaps. 5, 6.

33. HST, diary, January 6, 1948, PSF.

34. Hartmann, *Truman and the 80th Congress*, 133; Frank McNaughton, reports to New York office, February 21, March 7, April 26, 1947, July 16, 1948, McNaughton Papers.

35. HST to Mary Jane Truman, June 28, 1947, Post-Presidential Papers, Memoirs File.

36. Mary Jane Truman, interview with Jonathan Daniels, October 2, 1949, Daniels Papers, University of North Carolina.

37. Donovan, *Conflict and Crisis*, 333–34; *Public Papers, 1947*, 311–13.

38. The following paragraphs draw with special profit on Donald McCoy and Richard Ruetten, *Quest and Response: Minority Rights and the Truman Administration* (Lawrence: University Press of Kansas, 1973), chaps. 5, 6.

39. Herblock cartoon, in *Harry S. Truman and the Fair Deal*, ed. Alonzo L. Hamby (Lexington, Mass.: Heath, 1974), 175.

40. Gallup, *Gallup Poll*, 1:722–28.

41. Sternsher, "Harry Truman," 397–98.

42. Gallup, *Gallup Poll*, 1:747–48.

43. Donald Ritchie, *James M. Landis: Dean of the Regulators* (Cambridge, Mass.: Harvard University Press, 1980), 153; Robert Estabrook, "Last of the Brain Trusters," *Nation*, January 17, 1948, 68–70; James Landis, Oral History Memoir, 549–56, Columbia University Oral History Collection.

44. Sternsher, "Harry Truman," 399; Elmo Burns Roper, *You and Your Leaders: Their Actions and Your Reactions* (New York: Morrow, 1957), 132–33; James A. Wechsler, "What Hit Harry Truman?" *Progressive*, May 1948, 9–11.

45. Dwight D. Eisenhower, *Crusade in Europe* (Garden City, N.Y.: Doubleday, 1948), 444; Stephen E. Ambrose, *Eisenhower* (New York: Simon and Schuster, 1983), 1:409, 413–14, 459–60, 463, 477–78.

46. HST to Mary Romine, November 26, 1947, PSF.

Chapter 25

1. *NYT*, June 22, 1948; *Public Papers, 1948*, 356.

2. *Public Papers, 1948*, 261; Ken Hechler, *Working with Truman* (New York: Putnam, 1982), 66–67.

3. *Public Papers, 1948*, 221–24; transcript of Truman's informal remarks, Eben Ayers Papers, HSTL; Eben Ayers, diary, April 17, 1948, Ayers Papers;

HST, *Memoirs*, 2:179; Jonathan Daniels, *Man of Independence* (Philadelphia: Lippincott, 1950), 347–48; Robert A. Donovan, *Conflict and Crisis: The Presidency of Harry S. Truman, 1945–1948* (New York: Norton, 1977), 394.

4. *Public Papers, 1948*, 231–35, 239–43, 245–48, 259–61; HST, diary, May 7, 1948, HST Papers, Post-Presidential Papers, Memoirs File, HSTL; William L. Batt, Jr., to Clark Clifford, memorandum, May 17, 1948, Clifford Papers, HSTL.

5. This account of the Berkeley trip draws especially on Irwin Ross, *The Loneliest Campaign: The Truman Victory of 1948* (New York: New American Library, 1968), chap. 4, and Donovan, *Conflict and Crisis*, 395–402.

6. *Public Papers, 1948*, 284–379, quote on 298.

7. Charles Murphy, Oral History, 9, HSTL.

8. *Public Papers, 1948*, 301, 329; Robert J. Donovan, conversation with author; Clark Clifford, with Richard Holbrooke, *Counsel to the President* (New York: Random House, 1991), 200–202. Newsreel footage of the Pocatello remark can be seen in *The Great Upset of 1948*, prod. Kathleen McCleery, PBS, WETA, Washington, D.C., 1988.

9. Ross, *Loneliest Campaign*, 87–89; Cabell Phillips, *The Truman Presidency* (New York: Macmillan, 1966), 215–16; *NYT*, June 12, 18, 1948; *Public Papers, 1948*, 314.

10. *Public Papers, 1948*, 360; Alfred Steinberg, *The Man from Missouri* (New York: Putnam, 1962), 312; Carleton Kent, Oral History, 53–54, and Richard L. Strout, Oral History, 26–28, HSTL.

11. Forrest C. Pogue, *George C. Marshall: Statesman, 1945–1959* (New York: Penguin Books, 1989), 304; *FRUS, 1948*, 2:928; HST, diary, July 19, 1948, Post-Presidential Papers, Memoirs File.

12. David E. Lilienthal, *The Journals of David E. Lilienthal: The Atomic Energy Years, 1945–1950* (New York: Harper & Row, 1964), 391; Walter Millis, ed., *The Forrestal Diaries* (New York: Viking, 1951), 460–61; David McCullough, *Truman* (New York: Simon and Schuster, 1992), 649–50.

13. *Forrestal Diaries*, 461; *Public Papers, 1948*, 414–16.

14. *Forrestal Diaries*, 487; HST, diary, September 13, 1948, Post-Presidential Papers, Memoirs File.

15. Alonzo L. Hamby, *Beyond the New Deal: Harry S. Truman and American Liberalism* (New York: Columbia University Press, 1973), 224–28.

16. Donovan, *Conflict and Crisis*, 401.

17. Eben Ayers, diary, July 6, 1948, Ayers Papers; *NYT*, July 6, 10, 1948.

18. *NYT*, July 14, 1948.

19. *NYT*, July 13, 1948.

20. HST, diary, July 12, 13, 1948, PSF; Eben Ayers, diary, July 13, 1948, Ayers Papers; MT, *Harry S. Truman* (New York: Macmillan, 1972), 11.

21. HST, diary, July 14, 1948, PSF; Ross, *Loneliest Campaign*, 123–24.

22. Ross, *Loneliest Campaign*, 124; Steinberg, *Man from Missouri*, 317; Eric Sevareid, "The National Conventions in 1948," *NYT Magazine*, May 15, 1988, 10, 12.

23. *Public Papers, 1948*, 406–10.

24. Hamby, *Beyond the New Deal*, 244.

25. HST to General Louis Pick, July 17, 1948, PSF. I thank Ken Hechler for bringing this letter to my attention.

Chapter 26

1. *Time*, September 27, 1948, 23; *NYT*, September 18, 1948.

2. *Public Papers, 1948*, 422; Richard M. Dalfiume, *Desegregation of the U.S. Armed Forces: Fighting on Two Fronts, 1939–1953* (Columbia: University of Missouri Press, 1969), 171–74; Kenneth Royall to HST, September 17, 1948, PSF.

3. *Public Papers, 1948*, 416–22.

4. Earl Latham, *The Communist Controversy in Washington* (Cambridge, Mass.: Harvard University Press, 1966), esp. chaps. 6, 7; Stephen E. Ambrose, *Nixon: The Education of a Politician, 1913–1962* (New York: Simon and Schuster, 1987), chap. 10.

5. *Public Papers, 1948*, 432–34; HST to William Hillman, August 13, 1948, SPF.

6. *NYT*, June 22, 1948.

7. *Public Papers, 1948*, 189.

8. *Public Papers, 1948*, 414, 434n.

9. *Public Papers, 1948*, 610.

10. HST to Bernard Baruch, August 19, 31, 1948; Baruch to HST, August 27, 1948, PSF; *NYT*, December 9, 1950. According to the White House appointments file, Baruch's last meeting with Truman during his presidency was on June 25, 1948.

11. Irwin Ross, *The Loneliest Campaign: The Truman Victory of 1948* (New York: New American Library, 1968), 166–67; Robert A. Donovan, *Conflict and Crisis: The Presidency of Harry S. Truman, 1945–1948* (New York: Norton, 1977), 418–19; Herbert E. Alexander, "Financing Presidential Campaigns," in *History of American Presidential Elections, 1789–1968*, ed. Arthur M. Schlesinger, Jr., and Fred Israel (New York: Chelsea House, 1971), 4:3869–97, 3878; confidential source for the St. Louis story.

12. Donovan, *Conflict and Crisis*, 425; *NYT*, November 4, 1948.

13. *Public Papers, 1948*, 503–8, 743.

14. Clark Clifford, with Richard Holbrooke, *Counsel to the President* (New York: Random House, 1991), 226–30; Clifford, interview in *The Great Upset of 1948*, prod. Kathleen McCleery, PBS, WETA, Washington, D.C., 1988; Eben Ayers, diary, October 2, 1948, Ayers Papers, HSTL; Robert J. Donovan, conversation with author. This account also draws on several journalists' oral histories, HSTL.

15. *Great Upset of 1948*; *NYT*, September 29, 1948; Thomas L. Stokes, "Mood of America, Election Time, 1948," *NYT Magazine*, October 17, 1948, 11, 70–73.

16. *Public Papers, 1948*, 851; *NYT*, October 26, 27, 28, 1948; Stokes, "Mood of America."

17. *NYT*, October 13, 14, 1948.

18. Richard Norton Smith, *Thomas Dewey and His Times* (New York: Simon and Schuster, 1982), 532; Herbert Brownell, quoted in *Great Upset of 1948*.

19. *NYT*, October 31, 1948.

20. *NYT*, October 30, 1948; *Public Papers, 1948*, 920; Donovan, *Conflict and Crisis*, 425–26; Clifford, *Counsel to the President*, 234–35.

21. Ross, *Loneliest Campaign*, 243–44; *Public Papers, 1948*, 400, 935.

22. James G. Patton to HST, July 23, 2948; HST to Patton, August 5, 1948, PSF.

23. This account of the Vinson mission draws most heavily on Forrest C. Pogue, *George C. Marshall: Statesman, 1945–1959* (New York: Penguin Books, 1989), 407–8; but see also Clifford, *Counsel to the President*, 232–34, and Donovan, *Conflict and Crisis*, 424–25.

24. George Elsey, remarks on the 1948 campaign to Politics 203 class at Princeton University, January 11, 1949, Elsey Papers, HSTL.

25. Eliahu Epstein to Clark Clifford, August 3, 1948, Clifford Papers, HSTL.

26. Eben Ayers, diary, September 9, 1948, Ayers Papers; Clark Clifford, draft memorandum, September 11, 1948, Clifford Papers (for archival investigative work on this document, see William Franklin to Daniel J. Reed, July 30, 1973; memorandum of conversation among Franklin, George Elsey, and Clark Clifford, July 25, 1973; memorandum of conversation between Clifford and Franklin, June 20, 1974, Clifford Papers); Chaim Weizmann to HST, memorandum, May 25, 1948, MHDC No. 398; Lloyd Dunne to Harry Vaughan, July 28, 1948; HST to Robert Lovett, August 16, 1948, PSF. Numerous items in the Clifford Papers document the continuing rumors of a deal between the Zionists and the Dewey campaign: for example, Chester Bowles to Clark Clifford, September 23, 1948; Roberta Barrows to Matt Connelly, October 1, 1948; Bartley Crum to Clark Clifford, telegram, October 3, 1948; J. B. C. Howe, memorandum for the record, October 5, 1948; Joseph Keenan to Matthew Connelly, October 23, 1948; and Clark Clifford to HST, October 23, 1948. For a list of major contributors, see Donovan, *Conflict and Crisis*, 419.

27. *Public Papers, 1948*, 843–44, 913, 919–20; Clark Clifford to HST, October 23, 1948, Clifford Papers; HST, *Memoirs*, 2:166–68; John Snetsinger, *Truman, the Jewish Vote, and the Creation of Israel* (Stanford, Calif.: Hoover Institution Press, 1974), chap. 11.

28. George H. Gallup, *The Gallup Poll: Public Opinion, 1935–1971*, 3 vols. (New York: Random House, 1972), 1:766–67; *Public Papers, 1948*, 939–40.

29. Ross, *Loneliest Campaign*, 228; Donovan, *Conflict and Crisis*, 432–35; HST, handwritten account of election evening, n.d., PSF, Longhand Notes.

30. MT, *Bess W. Truman* (New York: Macmillan, 1986), 333–35; *Public Papers, 1948*, 940–42; *Washington Post*, November 5, 6, 1948.

31. Dwight D. Eisenhower to HST, November 18, 1948, PSF.

32. The following comments on the meaning of the 1948 election are drawn in large measure from Ross, *Loneliest Campaign*, chap. 11; Samuel Lubell, *The Future of American Politics* (New York: Harper, 1952), 69–71, 135–36, 196–204, 215–17; various analyses in *NYT*, esp. November 4 [Meyer Berger, James Reston], 7 [Arthur Krock], 8 [Edward H. Collins], 28 [esp. William H. Lawrence], 29 [Lawrence], and 30 [Lawrence]; and my own efforts to read the tea leaves.

Chapter 27

1. See, for example, HST to BWT, December 28, 1945 [unsent], PSF, and HST to BWT, September 13, 1946, FBP; Thomas Jefferson, quoted in Jack Bell, *The Splendid Misery* (Garden City, N.Y.: Doubleday, 1960), frontispiece, 458.

2. MT, *Bess W. Truman* (New York: Macmillan, 1986), 259–61; David McCullough, *Truman* (New York: Simon and Schuster, 1992), 384–86; on the movies, see "All the President's Popcorn," *NYT*, May 23, 1985.

3. McCullough, *Truman*, 593–94, 652, 665, 725, 875–86, is a splendid account of the White House reconstruction.

4. Alfred Steinberg, *The Man from Missouri* (New York: Putnam, 1962), 349.

5. HST, annotated appointment sheets, June 15, September 5, 18, October 15, 1945, February 14, 1946, PSF.

6. Jack Gross to Benedict K. Zobrist, April 20, 1988, MHDC No. 640; White House appointment calendar, November 28, 1948, HSTL.

7. Truman–Housholder correspondence and Housholder account of visit to the White House, Victor Housholder Papers, HSTL; HST to Donald Dawson, memorandum, December 14, 1948, PSF; *KCT*, June 30, 1950; Rufus Burrus and Mary Salisbury Bostian, interviews with author.

8. George Elsey, Leon Kyserling, Philleo Nash, and Richard Neustadt, interviews with author.

9. Roger Jones, Oral History, 15, HSTL.

10. Eben Ayers, diary, May 8, June 28, 1947, December 8, 1950, Ayers Papers, HSTL.

11. Merle Miller, *Plain Speaking: An Oral Biography of Harry S. Truman, 1945–1948* (New York: Berkeley, 1974), 439.

12. This and the following paragraphs on the assassination attempt draw on McCullough, *Truman*, 809–12; Robert J. Donovan, *Tumultuous Years: The Presidency of Harry S. Truman* (New York: Norton, 1982), 291–94; and Robert J. Donovan, *The Assassins* (New York: Popular Library, 1964), 153–81.

13. HST to Ethel Noland, November 17, 1950, PSF; *NYT*, November 7, 1950.

14. Clark Clifford, with Richard Holbrooke, *Counsel to the President* (New York: Random House, 1991), 72.

15. Townsend Hoopes and Douglas Brinkley, *Driven Patriot: The Life and Times of James Forrestal* (New York: Knopf, 1992), 22.

16. Thomas Murray, interview for Truman *Memoirs*, March 16, 1955, HST Papers, Post-Presidential Papers, Memoirs File, HSTL; William Hillman, ed., *Mr. President* (New York: Farrar, Straus and Young, 1952), frontispiece; original copy of prayer in PSF; HST to Edward Pruden, June 13 [?], 1952, MHDC No. 517.

17. HST to BWT, June 15, December 22, 1946, FBP; HST, handwritten speech draft, October 1946 [price controls, radio address, October 14, 1946], PSF.

18. HST, interview for *Memoirs* with Stanley Woodward, February 7, 1955, Post-Presidential Papers, Memoirs File.

19. HST, diary, May 12, 1945; HST to William Benton, April 2, 1947, PSF; Barry Massey, in *Columbus* [Ohio] *Dispatch*, March 30, 1986; HST to Benton, September 16, 1950, MHDC No. 387.

20. HST, diary, November 24, 1952, PSF; MT, *Bess Truman*, 305–7.

21. MT, *Bess Truman*, 297–98, 325.

22. Dean Acheson, *Present at the Creation: My Years in the State Department* (New York: Norton, 1969), 149–50; MT, *Bess Truman*, 282–83.

23. The following paragraphs rest in general on MT, *Bess Truman*, 298–301; the sketch of MT in *Current Biography, 1950* (New York: Wilson, 1950), 575–77; and the extensive Margaret Truman File, PSF.

24. HST to G. Walter Gates, December 7, 1950, PSF.

25. HST to Mary Jane Truman, August 26, 1947, Post-Presidential Papers, Memoirs File; HST to Barbara Heggie, December 20, 1950, PSF; Charles L. Wagner to Westbrook Pegler, September 22, 1949, Pegler Papers, Herbert Hoover Library, West Branch, Iowa.

26. *Washington Post*, December 6, 1950.

27. HST to Paul Hume, December 6, 1950, MHDC No. 517.

28. *NYT*, December 9, 1950, February 28, 1951; HST to G. Walter Gates, December 13, 1950, PSF; "The Music Critic and the President: The Second Time Around," *WhistleStop* 16 (1988): [1–4].

29. HST to Mary Jane and Martha Truman, September 20, 1946; also HST to Martha and Mary Jane Truman, November 9, 1945, and HST to Mary Jane Truman, November 14, 1948, Post-Presidential Papers, Memoirs File; HST to Nellie Noland, October 13, 1950, Mary Ethel Noland Papers, HSTL.

30. HST to J. Vivian Truman, March 5, 1949, PSF.

31. Ralph Truman to HST, April 23, 1951; HST to Ralph Truman, April 25, 1951, PSF.

32. HST to Ethel Noland, June 13, 1946, September 1, 1949, Noland Papers.

33. HST to Nellie Noland, May 9, 1948, October 29, 1949, March 11, 31, 1950; HST to Ethel Noland, August 13, 1949, September 13, November 17, 1950, Noland Papers.

34. The following description of the structure of Missouri politics in the late 1940s and early 1950s rests on my personal impressions; John M. Fenton, *Politics in the Border States* (New Orleans: Hauser, 1957), chaps. 6–8; and Richard S. Kirkendall, *A History of Missouri*, vol. 5, *1919–1953* (Columbia: University of Missouri Press, 1986), chap. 11.

35. HST to Tom Van Sant, April 29, 1950; HST to Forrest Smith, February 25, 1950, PSF.

36. HST to Forrest Smith, February 25, March 6, 1950; Smith to HST, February 28, 1950, PSF; Donald J. Kemper, *Decade of Fear: Senator Hennings and Civil Liberties* (Columbia: University of Missouri Press, 1965), 15–22.

37. HST to Roy Harper, March 1, 1952, PSF; Stuart Symington to Lloyd Stark, August 4, 1952, Stark Papers, WHMC; HST to Richard Duncan, August 12, 1952, PSF; *Official Manual of the State of Missouri, 1953–54*, 1032–33.

38. Lenore Bradley, "The Rise and Fall of the USS Williamsburg," *Whistlestop* 16: (1988): [2–3]; Donald J. MacDonald, "President Truman's Yacht," *Naval History* 4 (Winter 1990): 48–49.

39. Donovan, *Tumultuous Years*, 16; "Harry's Other House," *KCS*, May 24, 1992; Key West trip log, March 12–19, 1947, MHDC No. 682.

40. James David Barber, *The Presidential Character* (Englewood Cliffs, N.J.: Prentice-Hall, 1972).

41. Acheson, *Present at the Creation*, 730.

42. For the "respect-centered character," see Harold Lasswell, "The Democratic Character," in *The Political Writings of Harold Lasswell* (Glencoe, Ill.: Free Press, 1951), 463–525, 495–505.

43. HST to Ralph Truman, August 6, 1922, Post-Presidential Papers, Family Correspondence File; HST, "Members of the 81st Congress . . . " [longhand], 1949, PSF; HST to William Southern, July 8, 1949 [unsent]; HST to Roy Roberts, June 12, 1950, PSF.

44. HST, diary, August 21, 1952, Post-Presidential Papers, Memoirs File.

45. HST to Frank Kent, September 2, 1951; HST to Claude Bowers, December 1, 1948, PSF. See also, for example, HST to Robert Hannegan, September 10, 1946; HST to Arthur Hill, December 14, 1948; HST to Shannon Douglass, February 16, 1948, PSF.

46. HST to Maple T. Harl, February 2, 1949; HST to Edwin Pauley, October 22, 1947, PSF; HST to Mary Jane Truman, October 20, 1946, Post-Presidential Papers, Memoirs File.

47. HST to Roy Roberts, December 30, 1951; Roberts to HST, January 4, 1952; HST to Roberts, January 9, 1952; HST to James Cox, December 29, 1952, PSF.

48. HST to Vivian Truman, July 9, 1947; HST to the attorney general, memorandum, February 24, 1951; HST to Carl Hatch, January 12, 1952; HST to Cliff Johnson, February 13, 1948, PSF. On William Southern, see HST to Mary Jane Truman, October 12, 1946, Post-Presidential Papers, Memoirs File.

49. Francis H. Heller, ed., *The Truman White House: The Administration of the Presidency, 1945–1953* (Lawrence: Regents Press of Kansas, 1980), 138.

50. Monte M. Poen, ed., *Strictly Personal and Confidential: The Letters Harry Truman Never Mailed* (Boston: Little, Brown, 1982).

51. HST to Frank Kent, February 12, 1949; Kent to HST, February 19, 1949; HST to Kent, February 22, 1949; HST to Roy Roberts, June 12, 1950; Roberts to HST, June 26, 1950, PSF. Frank Kent, "How Bad Must It Smell?" [column], August 11, 1951; Westbrook Pegler to Frank Kent, August 8, 1951; Kent to Pegler, August 10, 1951, March 26, 1952, Pegler Papers; Franklin D. Mitchell, "An Act of Presidential Indiscretion: Harry S Truman, Congressman McDonough, and the Marine Corps Incident of 1950," *Presidential Studies Quarterly* 11 (Fall 1981): 565–75.

52. Raymond Brandt, in *PD*, April 23, 1950; cartoon, in *NYT*, May 6, 1952.

53. Roger Tubby, quoted in Donovan, *Tumultuous Years*, 334; Dr. Wallace Graham, interview with author.

Chapter 28

1. *Public Papers, 1949*, 1–7, quote on 7.

2. *Public Papers, 1949*, 109–11; *The Great Upset of 1948*, prod. Kathleen McCleary, PBS, WETA, Washington, D.C., 1988.

3. *Public Papers, 1949*, 111; for this and following descriptive paragraphs, see *NYT*, January 21, 1949.

4. For Tallulah Bankhead, see Eric F. Goldman, *The Crucial Decade—and After: America, 1945–1960* (New York: Vintage Books, 1960), 91–92.

5. HST to Edwin Johnson, October 6, 1949, PSF.

6. Frank McNaughton, report, October 7, 1949, McNaughton Papers, HSTL; HST to Edwin Johnson, October 6, 1949, PSF; James Eastland to HST, July 14, 1949, and HST to Eastland, July 16, 1949, PSF; John Hulston and Philip Lagerquist, conversations with author about Fred Canfil.

7. HST, *Memoirs*, 2:494.

8. Arthur M. Schlesinger, Jr., *A Thousand Days: John F. Kennedy in the White House* (Boston: Houghton Mifflin, 1965), 122; Alonzo L. Hamby, *Beyond the New Deal: Harry S. Truman and American Liberalism* (New York: Columbia

University Press, 1973), 311–21; David McCullough, *Truman* (New York: Simon and Schuster, 1992), 734.

9. The following paragraphs draw on Gallup Polls taken from November 1948, through June 1950. See George H. Gallup, *The Gallup Poll: Public Opinion, 1935–1971*, 3 vols. (New York: Random House, 1972), 2:781, 801, 810, 813–14, 829, 837, 841, 870, 880, 882, 889, 908.

10. Robert S. Allen and William V. Shannon, *The Truman Merry Go-Round* (New York: Vanguard, 1950), 185–86.

11. Robert Messer, *The End of an Alliance: James F. Byrnes, Roosevelt, Truman, and the Origins of the Cold War* (Chapel Hill: University of North Carolina Press, 1982), 219–32; James F. Byrnes, *All in One Lifetime* (New York: Harper, 1958), 398–404.

12. Hamby, *Beyond the New Deal*, 313–14, 342–46; *NYT*, November 30, 1948; *Public Papers, 1949*, 158–59.

13. On the education issue, see Frank McNaughton, report, July 6, 1949, McNaughton Papers; Joseph P. Lash, *Eleanor: The Years Alone* (New York: Norton, 1972), 156–67; HST to Eleanor Roosevelt, September 3, 1949, OF 1502; HST to John Lesinski, n.d. [August 1949], [unsent], PSF.

14. This discussion of agricultural policy draws heavily on Allen Matusow, *Farm Policies and Politics in the Truman Years* (Cambridge, Mass.: Harvard University Press, 1967), chap. 9.

15. HST to the secretary of agriculture, draft memorandum, April 1, 1949, PSF. For a largely accurate perception of Truman's attitude, see Allen and Shannon, *Truman Merry Go-Round*, 117.

16. Frank McNaughton, report, October 7, 1949, McNaughton Papers.

17. Monte M. Poen, *Harry S. Truman Versus the Medical Lobby* (Columbia: University of Missouri Press, 1979), chap. 6; William E. Pemberton, *Bureaucratic Politics: Executive Reorganization During the Truman Administration* (Columbia: University of Missouri Press, 1978), 113–20.

18. Richard O. Davies, *Housing Reform in the Truman Administration* (Columbia: University of Missouri Press, 1966), chap. 8; *Public Papers, 1949*, 381–82.

19. Davies, *Housing Reform in the Truman Administration*, chap. 9, conclusion.

20. *Public Papers, 1949*, 356–67; president's economic reports of January 6 and July 26, 1950, *Public Papers, 1950*, 19–31, 548–60.

21. *Public Papers, 1949*, 518; Edwin Nourse to Robert A. Taft, August 26, 1948; Nourse, diary memoranda, October 17, 22, 23, 1949; Joseph and Stewart Alsop, in *Washington Post*, October 17, 1949, Nourse Papers, HSTL.

22. *Public Papers, 1950*, 22–24.

23. *Public Papers, 1949*, 494–95; Arthur Krock, in *NYT*, February 15, 1950.

24. Frank McNaughton, report, August 19, 1949, McNaughton Papers.

25. Eben Ayers, diary, April 17, 1945, Ayers Papers, HSTL; Andrew J. Dunar, *The Truman Scandals and the Politics of Morality* (Columbia: University of Missouri Press, 1984), chaps. 3, 4; Robert J. Donovan, *Tumultuous Years: The Presidency of Harry S. Truman* (New York: Norton, 1982), 116–18.

26. Drew Pearson, *Diaries: 1949–1959*, ed. Tyler Abell (New York: Holt, Rinehart and Winston, 1974), 24n, 64–65, 78; *Public Papers, 1949*, 142–43; Gallup, *Gallup Poll*, 804–5.

27. Dunar, *Truman Scandals*, 85–94; Donald Dawson, interview with author.

28. *NYT*, February 3, 7, 22, 23, 24, 28, March 2, 6, 13, 1951; Dunar, *Truman Scandals*, 82, 88, 91, 93; Pearson, *Diaries*, 90–91; "Up the Ladder," *Time*, February 12, 1951, 22; Donovan, *Tumultuous Years*, 336–38; McCullough, *Truman*, 863–66.

29. *Public Papers, 1949*, 492; Donovan, *Tumultuous Years*, 339; *Washington Post*, September 30, 1949.

30. *NYT*, April 7, 1950; Dewey Short, in *CR*, 81st Cong., 2nd sess., April 6, 1950, 4938; William Leuchtenburg to James Loeb, Jr., September 28, 1948, Americans for Democratic Action Papers, State Historical Society of Wisconsin, Madison; *Public Papers, 1950*, 250–52.

31. Gallup, *Gallup Poll*, 2:800, 834, 860, 875, 890, 903.

32. See, for example, William Boyle, Jr., to Matthew Connelly, October 14, 1949 [with HST's handwritten comments at the bottom]; HST to John W. McCormack, November 15, 1949; and HST to Claude Bowers, November 19, 1949, PSF.

33. Richard Neustadt, "Congress and the Fair Deal," *Public Policy* 5 (1954): 351–81.

34. Allen and Shannon, *Truman Merry Go-Round*, 97–98, 183–84, 276–77; *Public Papers, 1950*, 257–58; HST to Sam Rayburn, April 6, 1950, MHDC No. 66.

35. Alonzo L. Hamby, "The Vital Center, the Fair Deal, and the Quest for a Liberal Political Economy," *American Historical Review* 77 (June 1972): 653–78.

36. *Public Papers, 1950*, 296–314, 321–416, quote on 410.

Chapter 29

1. *Public Papers, 1949*, 112–16.

2. Forrest C. Pogue, *George C. Marshall: Statesman, 1945–1959* (New York: Penguin Books, 1989), 377, 408.

3. For Dean Acheson's working relationship with Truman, see HST, *Memoirs*, 2:253.

4. Gaddis Smith, *Dean Acheson* (New York: Cooper Square, 1972), 379; Dean Acheson, *Present at the Creation: My Years in the State Department* (New York: Norton, 1969), 265–66.

5. Acheson, *Present at the Creation*, 456; Acheson, meeting with the president, October 9, 1950, Acheson Papers, HSTL.

6. See, for example, Arthur Vandenberg to Clyde Reed, January 12, 1949, Vandenberg Papers, University of Michigan, and Arthur H. Vandenberg, Jr., and Joe Alex Morris, eds., *The Private Papers of Senator Vandenberg* (Boston: Houghton Mifflin, 1952), 500–501. On Congress, see David McLellan, *Dean Acheson: The State Department Years* (New York: Harper & Row, 1976), 140–42.

7. Robert J. Donovan, *Tumultuous Years: The Presidency of Harry S. Truman* (New York: Norton, 1982), 34–35.

8. Townsend Hoopes and Douglas Brinkley, *Driven Patriot: The Life and Times of James Forrestal* (New York: Knopf, 1992), 31, 32; *Public Papers, 1949*, 160, 179–80, 188.

9. Jonathan Daniels, interview with HST, November 12, 1949, Daniels Papers, University of North Carolina.

10. There is no biography of Johnson. Contemporary accounts of his career include *Current Biography, 1942* (New York: Wilson, 1942), 423–26; *Cur-*

rent Biography, 1949 (New York: Wilson, 1949), 298–300; and Robert S. Allen and William V. Shannon, The Truman Merry Go-Round (New York: Vanguard, 1950), 445–66. See also Robert J. Donovan's sketch in Dictionary of American Biography: Supplement 8 (New York: Scribner, 1988), 302–3.

11. Daniels, interview with HST, November 12, 1949, Daniels Papers; Drew Pearson, Diaries: 1949–1959, ed. Tyler Abell (New York: Holt, Rinehart and Winston, 1974), 9.

12. Eben Ayers, diary, April 27, 28, June 8, 9, 1949, Ayers Papers, HSTL.

13. Sidney Souers, "Note on a meeting at the State Department Wednesday, March 23 [March 22], 1950," Souers Papers, HSTL; Acheson, Present at the Creation, 373–74.

14. Alfred Steinberg, The Man from Missouri (New York: Putnam, 1962), 381.

15. HST to the secretary of defense, memorandum, April 20, 1950, PSF.

16. Melvyn P. Leffler, A Preponderance of Power (Stanford, Calif.: Stanford University Press, 1992), 270–77.

17. Public Papers, 1949, 385.

18. Eben Ayers, diary, August 24, 1949, Ayers Papers; Acheson, Present at the Creation, 307–13; Chester J. Pach, Jr., Arming the Free World: The Origins of the United States Military Assistance Program, 1945–1950 (Chapel Hill, University of North Carolina Press, 1991), chap. 7.

19. Leffler, Preponderance of Power, 282–85; Acheson, Present at the Creation, 286–301, 337–43.

20. Leffler, Preponderance of Power, 348–50; Acheson, Present at the Creation, 382–89.

21. McLellan, Dean Acheson, 159–64, 174–85.

22. HST, handwritten notes, June 7, 1949, Clark Clifford Papers, HSTL; Public Papers, 1949, 519.

23. Memorandum of conversation, White House, April 3, 1949, MHDC No. 626.

24. Dean Acheson, conversation with the president, April 19, 1949; HST to Acheson, memorandum, August 2, 1951, with attached letter [Thomas Harkins to Fred Land, July 25, 1951], Acheson Papers; Eben Ayers, diary, May 6, 1949, Ayers Papers; HST to James A. Farley, May 16, 1949, MHDC No. 283; Smith, Acheson, 367–71.

25. HST to Hubert Humphrey, August 31, 1950, PSF. See also HST to A. E. Weston, April 25, 1951, PSF.

26. Acheson, conversation with the president, November 17, 1949, Acheson Papers.

27. Sergei N. Goncharov, John W. Lewis, and Xue Litai, Uncertain Partners: Stalin, Mao, and the Korean War (Stanford, Calif.: Stanford University Press, 1993), chaps. 1–4; Shu Guang Zhang, Deterrence and Strategic Culture (Ithaca, N.Y.: Cornell University Press, 1992), chap. 2. Chen Jian, China's Road to the Korean War (New York: Columbia University Press, 1994), chaps. 1–4, provides a somewhat more nuanced but fundamentally similar analysis of Mao.

28. McLellan, Dean Acheson, 188–209; George H. Gallup, The Gallup Poll: Public Opinion, 1935–1971, 3 vols. (New York: Random House, 1972), 2:831, 881, 915, 924–25.

29. Public Papers, 1950, 11; McLellan, Dean Acheson, 204–9.

30. John Lewis Gaddis, "Korea in American Politics, Strategy, and Diplo-

macy, 1945–50," in *The Origins of the Cold War in Asia*, ed. Yonosuke Nagai and Akira Iriye (Tokyo: University of Tokyo Press, 1977), 277–98, 285.

31. *Bulletin* [Department of State], January 23, 1950, 116; McLellan, *Dean Acheson*, 209–15; Lucius Battle, quoted in Francis H. Heller, ed., *The Korean War: A Twenty-Five-Year Perspective* (Lawrence: Regents Press of Kansas, 1977), 12. On South Korean attempts to get defense guarantees, see Dean Acheson, memorandum of conversation with Pyung Ok Chough, John M. Chang, and Niles W. Bond, July 11, 1949, Acheson Papers.

32. For this and the following paragraphs, see especially Allen Weinstein, *Perjury: The Hiss–Chambers Case* (New York: Knopf, 1978).

33. Acheson, *Present at the Creation*, 359–61.

34. See, for example, Dean Acheson, memorandum of conversation with Alexander Smith, November 30, 1949, and memorandum of conversation with Thomas Dewey, April 10, 1950, Acheson Papers.

35. *NYT*, March 22, 1950, quoted in Acheson, *Present at the Creation*, 364.

36. HST to Styles Bridges, March 26, 1950, PSF.

37. *Public Papers, 1950*, 236.

38. Acheson, *Present at the Creation*, 364, 752n.

39. Arthur Vandenberg to Dean Acheson, March 29, 1950, Acheson Papers.

40. *Public Papers, 1949*, 485; HST, "Memorandum of Conversation . . . April 3, 1949," MHDC No. 626.

41. McGeorge Bundy, *Danger and Survival* (New York: Random House, 1988), 203.

42. Donovan, *Tumultuous Years*, 101, 103.

43. HST, diary, February 29 [March 2], 1952, PSF.

44. Bundy, *Danger and Survival*, 201–29; *Public Papers, 1950*, 14, 116, 118, 134–135; on the public debate, sample *NYT*, January 16–31, 1950.

45. David E. Lilienthal, *The Journals of David E. Lilienthal: The Atomic Energy Years, 1945–1950* (New York: Harper & Row, 1962), 632–33; *Public Papers, 1950*, 138.

46. *NYT*, February 1, 2, 3, 1950; Gallup, *Gallup Poll*, 2:888.

47. David Holloway, *Stalin and the Bomb* (New Haven, Conn.: Yale University Press, 1994), 317–19.

48. Samuel Wells, "Nuclear Weapons and European Security During the Cold War," *Diplomatic History* 16 (Spring 1992): 278–86; Acheson, *Present at the Creation*, 375. See also Ernest May, ed., *Cold War Strategy: NSC-68* (New York: St. Martin's Press, 1992); Paul Y. Hammond, "NSC-68: Prologue to Rearmament," in *Strategy, Politics, and Defense Budgets*, ed. Warner R. Schilling, Paul Y. Hammond, and Glenn H. Snyder (New York: Columbia University Press, 1962), 267–378; and Leffler, *Preponderance of Power*, 355–60.

49. Acheson, *Present at the Creation*, 374–75.

50. J. Garry Clifford, "Harry Truman and Peter the Great's Will," *Diplomatic History* 4 (Fall 1980): 371–85.

51. Fred Lawton, memorandum for the record, May 23, 1950, Fred Lawton Papers, HSTL; Hammon, "NSC-68," chap. 5; David Callahan, *Dangerous Capabilities: Paul Nitze and the Cold War* (New York: HarperCollins, 1990), 120–23.

52. See, for example, Samuel Lubell, *The Revolt of the Moderates* (New York: Harper & Brothers, 1956), 64–74, and Daniel Bell, ed. *The Radical Right* (New York: Doubleday, 1964).

53. David Oshinsky, *A Conspiracy So Immense: The World of Joe McCarthy* (New York: Free Press, 1983), 108–12; Thomas C. Reeves, *The Life and Times of Joe McCarthy: A Biography* (New York: Stein and Day, 1982), 222–27. The following paragraphs draw heavily on these two major biographies.

54. HST to Joseph R. McCarthy, n.d. [unsent], PSF.

55. *Public Papers, 1950*, 163.

56. Oshinsky, *Conspiracy So Immense*, 162–65.

57. Pearson, *Diaries*, 113; James T. Patterson, *Mr. Republican: A Biography of Robert A. Taft* (Boston: Houghton Mifflin, 1972), 445–49.

58. *Public Papers, 1950*, 234, 252, 287.

59. Oshinsky, *Conspiracy So Immense*, 156–57.

60. HST to Stanley Woodward, June 24, 1950, Woodward Papers, HSTL.

61. Eben Ayers, diary, June 24, 1950, Ayers Papers; MT, *Bess W. Truman* (New York: Macmillan, 1986), 355–56; *FRUS, 1950*, 7:125–28.

Chapter 30

1. Robert Alan Aurthur, "The Wit and Sass of Harry S. Truman," *Esquire*, August 1971, 62–67, 115–18, quote on 66.

2. MT, *Harry S. Truman* (New York: Morrow, 1972), 455–58; Eben Ayers, diary, June 24–25, Ayers Papers, HSTL; HST, *Memoirs*, 2:331–33; *FRUS, 1950*, 7:126–157. Burton Kaufmann, *The Korean War* (Philadelphia: Temple University Press, 1986), is a valuable synthesis; chap. 1 has a useful discussion of the decision to intervene.

3. *FRUS, 1950*, 7:157–65.

4. *FRUS, 1950*, 7:174–75.

5. Sergei N. Goncharov, John W. Lewis, and Xue Litai, *Uncertain Partners: Stalin, Mao, and the Korean War* (Stanford, Calif.: Stanford University Press, 1993), esp. chap. 5. For the most sophisticated version of the left-wing fantasy that the war was actually provoked by South Korea, see Joyce Kolko and Gabriel Kolko, *The Limits of Power* (New York: Harper & Row, 1972), 565–87.

6. *FRUS, 1950*, 7:174–76, 185–86, 199; HST, *Memoirs*, 2:340.

7. George Elsey, "President's Conversation with George M. Elsey," June 26, 1950, Elsey Papers, HSTL; Melvyn P. Leffler, *A Preponderance of Power* (Stanford, Calif.: Stanford University Press, 1992), 366.

8. *FRUS, 1950*, 7:183.

9. Leffler, *Preponderance of Power*, 306–8, 369–70; H. Alexander Smith, memorandum of Louis Johnson's meeting in executive session with the Senate Foreign Relations Committee, August 23, 1950, Smith Papers, Princeton University; for various estimates of Soviet intentions, see *FRUS, 1950*, 7:139, 149, 158, 169, 174–77, 185, 203.

10. *FRUS, 1950*, 7:125–270; *Public Papers, 1950*, 504.

11. *Public Papers, 1950*, 513; George Elsey, summary of June 30 meeting, Elsey Papers.

12. George Elsey, summary of June 30 meeting, Elsey Papers.

13. *Public Papers, 1950*, 496; James T. Patterson, *Mr. Republican: A Biography of Robert A. Taft* (Boston: Houghton Mifflin, 1972), 451–54; Dean Acheson, memorandum of conversation with Wilhelm Morgenstierne, June 30, 1950, Acheson Papers, HSTL. See also summaries of reaction in *NYT*, July 2, 1950.

14. Perhaps the two best "reevaluationists," both of them rather ambiva-

lent, are Barton J. Bernstein, "The Truman Administration and the Korean War," in *The Truman Presidency*, ed. Michael Lacey (New York: Cambridge University Press, 1989), 410–44, and Arthur M. Schlesinger, Jr., Introduction to Arthur M. Schlesinger, Jr., and Richard Rovere, *General MacArthur and President Truman: The Struggle for Control of American Foreign Policy* (New Brunswick, N.J.: Transaction, 1992), ix–xvii.

15. *FRUS, 1950*, 7:286–91.

16. Dean Acheson, *Present at the Creation: My Years in the State Department* (New York: Norton, 1969), 414–15; George Elsey, memorandum for Mr. Smith, July 16, 1951, Elsey Papers.

17. HST, *Memoirs*, 2:344; Robert J. Donovan, *Tumultuous Years: The Presidency of Harry S. Truman* (New York: Norton, 1982), 251.

18. There are numerous military histories of the Korean War. Matthew B. Ridgway, *The Korean War* (Garden City, N.Y.: Doubleday, 1967), is to my mind a classic. Among the more recent works, John Toland's *In Mortal Combat* (New York: Morrow, 1991) is a large-scale well-regarded, and extensively researched study.

19. Alfred Steinberg, *The Man from Missouri* (New York: Putnam, 1962), 383–84; David McCullough, *Truman* (New York: Simon and Schuster, 1992), 797; HST, *Memoirs*, 2:358.

20. Leffler, *Preponderance of Power*, 374–77; *FRUS, 1950*, 7:712–21, 781–82.

21. *FRUS, 1950*, 7:826.

22. For Acheson, see *FRUS, 1950*, 7:868–679, and for evaluations of Chinese attentions, see *FRUS, 1950*, 7:839–946.

23. Charles Murphy, Oral History, 67, HSTL, attributes the idea to George Elsey, who denied it in a letter to the author, August 2, 1993.

24. HST to Nellie Noland, October 13, 1950, Mary Ethel Noland Papers, HSTL; George Elsey, memorandum for the file, August 26, 1960, Elsey Papers; HST, *Memoirs*, 2:354–56. See also John Spanier, *The Truman–MacArthur Controversy and the Korean War* (New York: Norton, 1965), in many respects still the best analysis of the Truman–MacArthur dispute.

25. Acheson, *Present at the Creation*, 456, but see also Dean Acheson, meeting with the president, October 9, 1950, Acheson Papers. A fine account of the Wake Island encounter is McCullough, *Truman*, 801–8.

26. HST, "Wake Island" [handwritten memorandum], PSF; HST, *Memoirs*, 2:364–65; Douglas MacArthur, *Reminiscences* (New York: McGraw-Hill, 1964), 361–64.

27. *FRUS, 1950*, 7:948–60; Dean Rusk, *As I Saw It* (New York: Norton, 1990), 169; Spanier, *Truman–MacArthur Controversy*, 112; Anthony Leviero, in *NYT*, October 16, 1950; Dean Acheson, meeting with the president, October 19, 1950, Acheson Papers.

28. *Public Papers, 1950*, 673–80.

29. *FRUS, 1950*, 7:995–96.

30. Goncharov et al., *Uncertain Partners*, chap. 6; Shu Guang Zhang, *Deterrence and Strategic Culture* (Ithaca, N.Y.: Cornell University Press, 1992), 88–106; Chen Jian, *China's Road to the Korean War* (New York: Columbia University Press, 1994), chaps. 5, 6; *FRUS, 1950*, 7:1003–1107.

31. HST, *Memoirs*, 2:372–77; Spanier, *Truman–MacArthur Controversy*, 114–20; *NYT*, November 6, 1950.

32. HST, diary, September 14, 1950, PSF; Donovan, *Tumultuous Years*,

265–67; George Elsey, memorandum for the record [Johnson firing], September 13, 1950, Elsey Papers.

33. Patterson, *Mr. Republican*, 455; Donovan, *Tumultuous Years*, 267; Forrest C. Pogue, *George C. Marshall: Statesman, 1945–1959* (New York: Penguin Books, 1989), 427.

34. HST to Oscar Chapman, memorandum, September 8, 1950, PSF; *Washington Post*, September 16, 1950; House Committee on Un-American Activities, *Hearings Regarding Communism in the U.S. Government, Part 2, August 28, 31, September 1, 15, 1950*, 81st Cong., 2nd sess.

35. Alonzo L. Hamby, *Beyond the New Deal: Harry S. Truman and American Liberalism* (New York: Columbia University Press, 1973), 410–15; cf. Athan Theoharis, *Seeds of Repression: Harry S. Truman and the Origins of McCarthyism* (Chicago: Quadrangle, 1971), 114–20.

36. Figures from *Monthly Labor Review*, June–December, 1950. See also economic report of the president, January 19, 1951, *Public Papers, 1951*, 32, and *NYT*, February 2, 10, May 12, July 2, 1951.

37. *Public Papers, 1950*, 626–31; George Elsey, memorandum for the file [on preparation of president's message to Congress on Korea], July 19, 1950, and memorandum for the file, August 1, 1950, Elsey Papers; William D. Hassett to Aubrey Williams, October 24, 1950, and John Steelman to Congressman Raymond Karst, November 7, 1950, OF 151; Harry Doughty, "Notes on Some Contrasts in the Wage Stabilization Problem: World War II and the Present Emergency" [internal discussion document], November 6, 1950, Harold Enarson Papers, HSTL.

38. Everett McKinley Dirksen to Owen Brewster, July 21, 1950, copy in Smith Papers; Stephen E. Ambrose, *Nixon: The Education of a Politician, 1913–1962* (New York: Simon and Schuster, 1987), chap. 11; David Oshinsky, *A Conspiracy So Immense: The World of Joe McCarthy* (New York: Free Press, 1983), 174–78.

39. HST to Clinton Anderson, August 5, 1950; HST to Max Lowenthal, December 15, 1950, PSF.

40. HST to Clinton Anderson, August 5, 1950, PSF; *Public Papers, 1950*, 697–703; Richard Bolling, interview with author.

41. Arthur Schlesinger, Jr., to Averell Harriman, November 13, 1950, Elsey Papers; Donovan, *Tumultuous Years*, 297–908; *FRUS, 1950*, 7:1247.

42. *FRUS, 1950*, 7:1107–10, 1222–24, 1231–33, 1237–38, 1242–51, 1276–82.

43. *Public Papers, 1950*, 726–27.

44. D. Clayton James, *The Years of MacArthur: Triumph and Disaster, 1945–1964* (Boston: Houghton Mifflin, 1985), 579–81; John Emmerson, memorandum, November 8, 1950, *FRUS, 1950*, 7:1098–1100.

45. *FRUS, 1950*, 7:1361–74.

46. *FRUS, 1950*, 7:1462–65.

47. *Public Papers, 1950*, 741–46.

48. James L. Stokesbury, *A Short History of the Korean War* (New York: Morrow, 1988), 107.

49. *FRUS, 1950*, 7:1245; *Public Papers, 1950*, 724–26; HST, diary, December 2, 1950, PSF.

50. Arthur Krock, in *NYT*, December 1, 1950; [Dean Acheson,] memorandum of conversation with Robert Lovett, December 2, 1950, Acheson Papers.

51. *FRUS, 1950*, 7:1630–33; HST, *Memoirs*, 2:435–36.

52. Matthew Ridgway, obituary, *NYT*, July 27, 1993.

53. *FRUS, 1951*, 7:234, 263–66, 298–99; memorandum of conversation between Dean Acheson and Robert Lovett, March 24, 1951, Acheson Papers; HST, *Memoirs*, 2:443.

54. HST, desk diary, April 5–10, 1951, PSF; HST, *Memoirs*, 2:438–50; *FRUS, 1951*, 7:300–301; HST to David Noyes, April 10, 1951, PSF; [Eben Ayers,] "The MacArthur Dismissal" [memorandum for the file], April 28, 1951, PSF; Merle Miller, *Plain Speaking: An Oral Biography of Harry S. Truman, 1945–1948* (New York: Berkeley, 1974), 329.

Chapter 31

1. HST, diary, April 10, 1951, PSF; William Hillman, ed., *Mr. President* (New York: Farrar, Straus and Young, 1952), 11. A handwritten version of these remarks is in PSF filed with 1954 material and reprinted in Robert H. Ferrell, *Off the Record* (New York: Harper & Row, 1980), 310.

2. David Oshinsky, *A Conspiracy So Immense: The World of Joe McCarthy* (New York: Free Press, 1983), 194–95.

3. John Spanier, *The Truman–MacArthur Controversy and the Korean War* (New York: Norton, 1965), 212; Robert J. Donovan, *Tumultuous Years: The Presidency of Harry S. Truman* (New York: Norton, 1982), 359.

4. H. Alexander Smith's evolving position can be followed in his correspondence and diary, Smith Papers, Princeton University: for example, Smith, memorandum re conference, H.A.S. and Averell Harriman, n.d. [August 24, 1950]; Smith to James Austin, memorandum, August 5, 1950; Smith, [remarks introducing Harold Stassen], October 25, 1950; Smith to William Knowland, November 14, 1950.

5. James T. Patterson, *Mr. Republican: A Biography of Robert A. Taft* (Boston: Houghton Mifflin, 1972), chap. 31.

6. Arthur Schlesinger, Jr., to Averell Harriman, November 13, 1950, George Elsey Papers, HSTL; Norman Graebner, *The New Isolationism* (New York: Ronald, 1956).

7. *Public Papers, 1951*, 223–27.

8. Spanier, *The Truman–MacArthur Controversy*, 213–14; Michael Schaller, *Douglas MacArthur: The Far Eastern General* (New York: Oxford University Press, 1989), 242.

9. "Schedule for Welcoming of General MacArthur," Elsey Papers, reprinted in Schaller, *Douglas MacArthur*, 242–43.

10. Spanier, *Truman–MacArthur Controversy*, 216; the full text of the speech is in Richard Rovere and Arthur Schlesinger, Jr., *General MacArthur and President Truman: The Struggle for Control of American Foreign Policy* (New Brunswick, N.J.: Transaction, 1992), 270–77.

11. Rovere and Schlesinger, *General MacArthur and President Truman*, 15–16.

12. HST to Dwight Eisenhower, April 13, 1951, PSF, cited in Donovan, *Tumultuous Years*, 361; HST to Roy Harper, April 17, 1951, PSF.

13. George H. Gallup, *The Gallup Poll: Public Opinion, 1935–1971*, 3 vols. (New York: Random House, 1972), 2:969, 972–73.

14. Alonzo L. Hamby, *Beyond the New Deal: Harry S. Truman and American Liberalism* (New York: Columbia University Press, 1973), 441–46.

15. See, for example, Kenneth Hechler to John A. Carroll, April 17, 1951; George Elsey, memorandum for the file, April 19, 1951; George Elsey to Theodore Tannenwald, memorandum, May 15, 1951; Elsey to Joseph Short, memorandum, June 28, 1951; Elsey to Beverly Smith, memorandum, July 19, 1951, Elsey Papers.

16. Spanier, *Truman–MacArthur Controversy*, chaps. 12, 13, effectively summarizes the testimony; Bradley's testimony is in Rovere and Schlesinger, *General MacArthur and President Truman*, 284–89, quote on 287.

17. Walter Isaacson and Evan Thomas, *The Wise Men: Six Friends and the World They Made—Acheson, Bohlen, Harriman, Kennan, Lovett, McCloy* (New York: Simon and Schuster, 1986), 551; Dennis Wrong [son of Hume Wrong], conversation with author.

18. Gallup, *Gallup Poll*, 2:1019, 1052–53.

19. On McCarthy's activities in 1951 and early 1952, see Oshinsky, *Conspiracy So Immense*, chaps. 12–15, and Thomas C. Reeves, *The Life and Times of Joe McCarthy: A Biography* (New York: Stein and Day, 1982), chaps. 15, 16.

20. Edward Meade Earle to H. Alexander Smith, September 29, 1951; H. Alexander Smith to Mrs. Helen Baker, November 9, 1951, Smith Papers.

21. Jerome E. Edwards, "Patrick Anthony McCarran," in *The Harry S. Truman Encyclopedia*, ed. Richard S. Kirkendall (Boston: Hall, 1989), 225–26; HST to the attorney general, memorandum, July 5, 1952, Charles Murphy Papers, HSTL; HST to the secretary of defense, memorandum, September 27, 1951, PSF.

22. *NYT*, January 16, 30, April 22, 1952.

23. *Public Papers, 1951*, 461–64; HST to Harold Ickes, August 25, 1951, PSF.

24. Richard Rovere, *Senator Joe McCarthy* (New York: Harper & Row, 1959), 109–10.

25. Gallup, *Gallup Poll*, 2:1003.

26. "Loyalty and Human Freedom," *New Republic*, April 14, 1952, 5–6.

27. Benjamin Kaplan to Charles Murphy, November 9, 1950; Max Kampleman to Charles Murphy, November 20, 1950, Murphy Papers; Charles Murphy to HST, memorandum, November 15, 1950, HST Papers, Murphy Files, HSTL; *Public Papers, 1951*, 119–21, 152–53, 606; Alan Harper, *The Politics of Loyalty: The White House and the Communist Issue, 1946–1952* (Westport, Conn.: Greenwood Press, 1969), chap. 8.

28. *Public Papers, 1951*, 278–79, 605–6.

29. Gary May, *Un-American Activities: The Trials of William Remington* (New York: Oxford University Press, 1994), is a splendid account. See also Athan Theoharis, "The Escalation of the Loyalty Program," in *Policies and Politics of the Truman Administration*, ed. Barton J. Bernstein (Chicago: Quadrangle, 1970), 258–59.

30. On McGranery, see the following material in the James P. McGranery Papers, LC: Personal Correspondence File, which includes numerous letters to and from J. Edgar Hoover and Francis Cardinal Spellman, among other right-wing foes of Communism; Attorney General File, especially press-release folders that document increasing emphasis on anti-Communist activities (for Roy Cohn, see release dated September 4, 1952; for arrest of Communists, September 17, 1952).

31. Dean Acheson, *Present at the Creation: My Years in the State Department* (New York: Norton, 1969), chaps. 52, 71; Rudy Abramson, *Spanning the Century: The Life of Averell Harriman* (New York: Morrow, 1992), chap. 18.

32. Acheson, *Present at the Creation*, chap. 70, quote on 673.

33. HST to Averell Harriman, November 30, 1951, PPF 1191.

34. HST, *Memoirs*, 2:259–60; HST, diary, January 4, 1952, PSF.

35. Alfred Steinberg, *The Man from Missouri* (New York: Putnam, 1962), 11–12.

36. HST to Dean Acheson, memorandum, August 2, 1951, with attached letter [Thomas Harkins to Fred Land, July 25, 1951], PSF and Acheson Papers, HSTL.

37. HST to Lewis Strauss, February 15, 1951, PSF.

38. HST, diary, February 26, 1952, PSF; Acheson, *Present at the Creation*, 574–75.

39. *NYT*, September 13, 1951.

40. HST, diary, January 27, May 18, 1952, PSF.

Chapter 32

1. *Public Papers, 1951*, 335.

2. John Steelman to Harold Russell [AMVETS], November 16, 1950; Chet Hollifield to John Steelman, November 28, 1950; John C. Houston, Jr., to John Steelman, May 3, 1951; J.V.F. to John Steelman, memorandum, May 7, 1951, OF 151; Jonathan Daniels to HST, February 14, 1951, PSF.

3. HST to Jonathan Daniels, February 20, 1951; HST, draft of letter to Harold D. Cooley, June 16, 1951, PSF.

4. HST to Jonathan Daniels, February 20, 1951; HST to John Steelman, memorandum, October 3, 1951, PSF.

5. Robert J. Donovan, *Tumultuous Years: The Presidency of Harry S. Truman* (New York: Norton, 1982), 326. For a far more detailed account of administration–labor problems than possible here, one can follow numerous accounts in the Harold Enarson Papers, HSTL: for example, Enarson to John Steelman, "Basic Issues in the Labor Relations Field" [memorandum], February 15, 1951; Enarson to Steelman, "The Wage Stabilization Board and Labor Disputes: The Textile Strike as Typical Problem" [unsent memorandum, ca. March 5, 1951]; [S.D.B.], "Labor's Controversy with the Administration on the Defense Program," March 23, 1951; [Sam Berger, Harriman's staff,] "Inflation Control Program and the Wage Stabilization Board"; "Friday, March 23 at 11 o'clock I met with Eric Johnston . . ."

6. *Public Papers, 1951*, 143–44, 148–49, 156–57, 173–74; *NYT*, March 2, 1951.

7. *Public Papers, 1951*, 173–77, 186–87, 204; *NYT*, March 9, April 10, May 1, 1951

8. *Public Papers, 1951*, 333–38.

9. "Defense Production Act Amendments of 1951" [unsigned memorandum on stationery of general counsel, Economic Stabilization Agency], July 30, 1951, PSF; *Public Papers, 1951*, 435–36; *NYT*, August 1, 1951.

10. *Public Papers, 1951*, 590.

11. *Public Papers, 1951*, 1183.

12. The following paragraphs are based heavily on Herbert Stein, *The Fiscal Revolution in America* (Chicago: University of Chicago Press, 1969), chap. 12; Donovan, *Tumultuous Years*, 327–31; and "Chronology of Events Relating to the Government Security Market" [unsigned memorandum, probably from the Treasury Department], PSF.

13. HST to Thomas McCabe, August 25, 1950, PSF (copy in John Snyder Papers, HSTL).

14. HST to Thomas McCabe, December 4, 1950; McCabe to HST, December 9, 1950, PSF.

15. Lindley Clark, in *Wall Street Journal*, March 14, 1978.

16. *Public Papers, 1951*, 173–77, 186–94, 201–7.

17. Andrew J. Dunar, *The Truman Scandals and the Politics of Morality* (Columbia: University of Missouri Press, 1984), chap. 5.; Charles Murphy to the president, memorandum [on William Boyle], August 9, 1951; HST to William Benton, August 17, 1951; Franklin Parks to HST, memorandum [summarizing Fulbright's RFC investigations], January 16, 1953, PSF.

18. Dunar, *Truman Scandals*, chaps. 3, 4; *NYT*, October 23, 1951.

19. *PD*, January 24, 1941.

20. HST to Dwight Palmer, February 13, 1951; HST to Frank Boykin, February 14, 1951; HST to Jesse Jones, May 9, 1951, PSF; *Public Papers, 1951*, 158–60, 233; Dunar, *Truman Scandals*, 94–95. On Merle Young, see Donovan, *Tumultuous Years*, 337; *Time*, February 12, 1951, 22; *NYT*, April 9, June 8, 24, 1953.

21. "A Man Who Understands," *Time*, November 12, 1951, 23; "Investigations," *Time*, December 10, 1951, 20; *Current Biography, 1952* (New York: Wilson, 1952), 381–82.

22. *NYT*, August 21, 1951; HST, diary, February 6, 1952, PSF.

23. HST, diary, July 6, December 25, 1952, PSF; "Exhibit # 1—Kansas City Missouri Hearings—1950," PSF, Fred Canfil File; *NYT*, October 1, 1950.

24. *Public Papers, 1951*, 261, 264. On William O'Dwyer's career, see the sketch by David William Vorhees in *Dictionary of American Biography: Supplement 7* (New York: Scribner, 1981), 584–86; *NYT*, August 15, 16, October 12, 1950, March 20, 21, 1951, August 10, November 27, 30, 1952, November 25, 1964 [obituary]; and Drew Pearson, *Diaries: 1949–1959*, ed. Tyler Abell (New York: Holt, Rinehart and Winston, 1974), 295, 300, 346, 443, 446.

25. *Public Papers, 1951*, 201–2. On the Kefauver Committee in general, see especially William H. Moore, *The Kefauver Committee and the Politics of Crime, 1950–52* (Columbia: University of Missouri Press, 1974).

26. This and following paragraphs draw heavily on Dunar, *Truman Scandals*, chap. 6.

27. "Investigations," 20; *Public Papers, 1952–53*, 1–2, 27–31.

28. On McGrath, see Robert S. Allen and William V. Shannon, *The Truman Merry Go-Round* (New York: Vanguard, 1950), 98–110; Donovan, *Tumultuous Years*, 375–76; *Current Biography, 1948* (New York: Wilson, 1948), 399–402; obituary, *NYT*, September 3, 1966; McGrath, interview, March 24, 1955, HST Papers, Post-Presidential Papers, Memoirs File, HSTL. The quotations are from an unsigned, undated memorandum beginning "In our conversation the other day . . . ," PSF, McGrath File.

29. *Public Papers, 1951*, 641–48.

30. *NYT*, December 14, 1951; *Public Papers, 1952–53*, 7; Dunar, *Truman Scandals*, 111–12.

31. Wayne Morse to HST, December 22, 1951; HST to Charles Murphy, memorandum, January 4, 1952, PSF; Donovan, *Tumultuous Years*, 376–77.

32. Alonzo L. Hamby, *Beyond the New Deal: Harry S. Truman and American Liberalism* (New York: Columbia University Press, 1973), 464; Pearson, *Diaries*, 184–86.

33. J. Howard McGrath, interview, March 24, 1955, Post-Presidential Papers, Memoirs File; *Current Biography, 1952*, 441–43; HST to Charles Murphy, memorandum, n.d. [ca. August 24, 1951], Murphy Papers, HSTL; William Hillman, ed., *Mr. President* (New York: Farrar, Straus and Young, 1952), 61–62; Richard Rovere, *The American Establishment* (New York: Harcourt, Brace & World, 1962), 85–112.

34. *NYT*, March 3, 1952.

35. For this and subsequent paragraphs, see Donovan, *Tumultuous Years*, 378–81.

36. Charles Murphy to HST, April 1, 1952, Murphy Papers.

37. HST to J. Howard McGrath, April 17, 1952, attached to HST to Theodore Francis Green, April 18, 1952, PSF.

38. Joseph Alsop, in *PD*, December 17, 1951.

39. *Public Papers, 1951*, 651–53.

40. *Public Papers, 1952*, 226–27; Maeva Marcus, *Truman and the Steel Seizure Case: The Limits of Presidential Power* (New York: Columbia University Press, 1977), 58–74.

41. HST, *Memoirs*, 2:469.

42. *Public Papers, 1952*, 246–51; HST, *Memoirs*, 2:466–74.

43. See the contrasting accounts in Charles Sawyer, *Concerns of a Conservative Democrat* (Carbondale: Southern Illinois University Press, 1968), chap. 18, quote on 257–58, and Richard Neustadt, *Presidential Power and the Modern Presidents* (New York: Free Press, 1990), 21–23, 30–32. Marcus, *Truman and the Steel Seizure Case*, 85–86, is a sound evaluation. For news stories on a possible wage increase, see *Wall Street Journal*, April 17, 19, 1952; *NYT*, April 19, 27, May 2, 1952.

44. Charles Sawyer to HST, May 20, 1952; HST to Sawyer, memorandum, May 22, 1952, PSF.

45. Sawyer, *Concerns of a Conservative Democrat*, 263–66.

46. Edward H. Collins, in *NYT*, April 14, 1951; George H. Gallup, *The Gallup Poll: Public Opinion, 1935–1971*, 3 vols. (New York: Random House, 1972), 2:1065.

47. *Public Papers, 1952*, 307.

48. See, for example, "The Impact of the 1952 Steel Strike," John C. Houston Papers, HSTL.

49. William O. Douglas, *Go East Young Man* (New York: Random House, 1974), 448.

50. HST to William O. Douglas, July 9, 1952 [unsent], PSF.

Chapter 33

1. HST, diary, April 16, May 8, 1950, PSF. The chapter title is from Truman's public declaration of his decision, March 29, 1952 (*Public Papers, 1952*, 225). Truman handles the May 8 diary entry in his *Memoirs* (2:491) as if it had been written toward the end of 1951, although he refers to a May 8 date. The date in the handwritten original is clear and unmistakable.

2. HST, *Memoirs*, 2:489–90.

3. *NYT*, November 8, 1951; Arthur Krock, *Memoirs: Sixty Years on the Firing Line* (New York: Funk & Wagnalls, 1968), 252–54. For the pressure on Eisenhower, leaf almost at random through Louis Galambos et al., eds., *The*

Papers of Dwight David Eisenhower, vol. 12, *NATO and the Campaign of 1952* (Baltimore: Johns Hopkins University Press, 1989), for roughly the last half of 1951. For his denials of the Krock story, see, for example, Dwight Eisenhower to Arthur Hays Sulzberger, November 10, 1951, in *Eisenhower Papers*, 12:701, and William Benton to HST, December 22, 1951, PSF.

4. HST to Dwight Eisenhower, December 18, 1951, PSF; Eisenhower to HST, January 1, 1952, in *Eisenhower Papers*, 12:830–31.

5. *NYT*, January 8, 1952; *Public Papers, 1952–53*, 22. For HST–Eisenhower correspondence, see PSF, Eisenhower File, and *Eisenhower Papers*, 12:907–9, 959–61, 1049–52, 1154–56.

6. Drew Pearson, *Diaries, 1949–1959*, ed. Tyler Abell (New York: Holt, Rinehart and Winston, 1974), 188; HST, diary [on Kefauver], December 25, 1952, HST Papers, Post-Presidential Papers, Memoirs File, HSTL.

7. HST, diary, July 6, 1952, PSF; HST, *Memoirs*, 2:492–94. See also "Memorandum on Senator Kerr's Voting Record," January 28, 1952, and "Comments on the 'Kerr Scorecord,'" February 6, 1952, PSF.

8. This paragraph and much of those that immediately follow are based heavily on John Bartlow Martin, *Adlai Stevenson of Illinois* (Garden City, N.Y.: Doubleday, 1976), 515–28, the most thorough account of Stevenson's career likely to be written.

9. HST, typed copy of diary memo, n.d., beginning "Early in January, 1952, I asked Adlai Stevenson . . . ," Post-Presidential Papers, Memoirs File; HST, *Memoirs*, 2:491–92; Martin, *Adlai Stevenson of Illinois*, 524–25.

10. *Public Papers, 1952–53*, 119; Adlai Stevenson to HST, January 24, 1952; HST to Stevenson, January 29, 1952, PSF.

11. Martin, *Adlai Stevenson of Illinois*, 537–38; HST, *Memoirs*, 2:492. For the Kefauver victory and its impact, see *NYT*, March 12, 13, 1952.

12. *Public Papers, 1952–53*, 168; *NYT*, February 22, March 9 [Arthur Krock], 1952.

13. NYT, March 18, 19, 1952, contains a sampling of comment on *Mr. President* and its purpose.

14. Adlai Stevenson to Mrs. Edison Dick, March 15, 1952; Adlai Stevenson to Charles Murphy, March 17, 1952; Murphy to Stevenson, March 18, 1952, in *The Papers of Adlai Stevenson*, ed. Walter Johnson (Boston: Little, Brown, 1972), 3:532–35.

15. Bernard Sternsher, "Harry Truman," in *Popular Images of American Presidents*, ed. William C. Spragen (New York: Greenwood Press, 1988), 400; *Public Papers, 1952–53*, 20.

16. *Public Papers, 1952–53*, 225; Cabell Phillips, *The Truman Presidency* (New York: Macmillan, 1966), 419; Murphy, Oral History, 354, HSTL; HST, *Memoirs*, 2:488–89; MT, *Bess W. Truman* (New York: Macmillan, 1986), 380–83; Robert J. Donovan, *Tumultuous Years: The Presidency of Harry S. Truman* (New York: Norton, 1982), 392–96; *NYT*, March 30, 1952.

17. Adlai Stevenson to HST, March 31, April 16, 1952; HST to Stevenson, April 4, 22, 1952, PSF.

18. *Public Papers, 1952–53*, 233–34; *NYT*, April 4, 1952; Harry Vaughan to Thomas Van Sant, April 7, 9, 1952, Van Sant Papers, HSTL.

19. *Public Papers, 1952–53*, 379–84.

20. *Public Papers, 1952–53*, 441–47; HST to Max Lowenthal, July 8, 1952, PSF.

21. These and the activities enumerated in the next two paragraphs are documented in *Public Papers, 1952–53*, 228–470.

22. HST, *Memoirs*, 2:493–94. For a more complex account of the Harriman–Truman relationship, see Rudy Abramson, *Spanning the Century: The Life of Averell Harriman* (New York: Morrow, 1992), 491–503.

23. Martin, *Adlai Stevenson of Illinois*, 562–84.

24. HST, diary, July 11, 1952, and diary memo beginning "Early in January . . . ," Post-Presidential Papers, Memoirs File.

25. William Hillman to HST, July 19, 1952, PSF.

26. *Stevenson Papers*, 4:11–14.

27. HST, *Memoirs*, 2:496–97; Martin, *Adlai Stevenson of Illinois*, 592–603; *Public Papers, 1952–53*, 503–9; *Stevenson Papers*, 4:16–19.

28. HST to Adlai Stevenson, July 26, 1952, PSF.

29. Adlai Stevenson to HST, July 27, 1952; Adlai Stevenson to Alicia Patterson, July 27, 1952, in *Stevenson Papers*, 4:20–21.

30. Martin, *Adlai Stevenson of Illinois*, 611–40.

31. HST to Adlai Stevenson [unsent; late August 1952], PSF; HST to John Sparkman [unsent; August 1952], typed copy in Post-Presidential Papers, Memoirs File.

32. *Public Papers, 1952–53*, 530–31.

33. Stephen A. Mitchell to Adlai Stevenson and Wilson Wyatt, memorandum, August 26, 1952, Mitchell Papers, HSTL; HST to Adlai Stevenson [unsent; probably late August or September, 1952], PSF. Robert H. Ferrell, *Off the Record* (New York: Harper & Row, 1980), 266–67, places this document in early August. I doubt that Truman would have been thinking about the Montana Dam speech of October 1 that early; I take the reference to Stevenson declining another invitation for a strategy conference and referring the president to a "crackpot" as likely indicating Mitchell's conference of August 26.

34. HST to Dwight D. Eisenhower, telegram, August 13, 1952, PSF; Eisenhower to HST, August 14, 1952, OF 408; HST to Eisenhower, August 16, 1952, and Eisenhower to HST, August 19, 1952, PSF.

35. *Public Papers, 1952–53*, 548–559, 584.

36. *Public Papers, 1952–53*, 761, 844, 1044.

37. *KCS*, October 5, 1952; *KCT*, October 6, 1952.

38. *Public Papers, 1952–53*, 863, 891.

39. *Public Papers, 1952–53*, 989.

40. HST to Dwight D. Eisenhower, November 5, 1952, and Eisenhower to HST, November 5, 1952, in HST, *Memoirs*, 2:505.

41. HST, diary, November 15, December 22, 1952, PSF.

42. Carl M. Brauer, *Presidential Transitions: Eisenhower Through Reagan* (New York: Oxford University Press, 1986), 14–18.

43. HST, diary, November 20, 1952, PSF; HST, "Memo for the President of the United States," n.d., beginning "Select Secretaries for the White House Staff very carefully," copy in Post-Presidential Papers, Memoirs File; "Memorandum of Meeting at the White House between President Truman and General Eisenhower," Dean Acheson Papers, HSTL; Dwight D. Eisenhower, *The White House Years: Mandate for Change, 1953–56* (Garden City, N.Y.: Doubleday, 1963), 121.

44. HST, diary, November 15, 1952, PSF; *Public Papers, 1952–53*, 1073–76; Donovan, *Tumultuous Years*, 403–4.

45. MT, *Bess Truman*, 392–93; HST, diary, December 6, 1952, PSF.

46. *NYT*, January 7, 9, 10, 1953, January 11, 15, 18, February 8, 22, 23, 24, August 6, 1955, January 24, May 11, June 18, November 16, 26, 1957.

47. Acheson, memorandum of conversation, January 8, 1953, *FRUS, 1952–54,* 6:885–87; Dean Acheson, *Present at the Creation: My Years in the State Department* (New York: Norton, 1969), 715–16.

48. HST to Carl Hatch, December 1, 1952, PSF.

49. *Public Papers, 1952–53,* 1197–1202.

50. HST, diary, January 20, 1953, PSF.

51. Phillips, *Truman Presidency,* 431–32; MT, *Harry S. Truman* (New York: Morrow, 1972), 557–59.

52. HST, diary, January 21, 1953, PSF.

Chapter 34

1. Monte M. Poen, *Letters Home by Harry Truman* (New York: Putnam, 1984), 259.

2. *NYT*, September 8, 1953.

3. *NYT*, November 7, 1953.

4. On the Harry Dexter White case, see Robert J. Donovan, *Conflict and Crisis: The Presidency of Harry S. Truman, 1945–1948* (New York: Norton, 1977), 173–75; David Caute, *The Great Fear* (New York: Simon and Schuster, 1978), 57–58; Whittaker Chambers, *Witness* (New York: Random House, 1952), esp. 414–32; and John M. Blum, ed. *From the Morgenthau Diaries: Years of War* (Boston: Houghton Mifflin, 1967), 188n.

5. *NYT*, November 7, 11, 1953.

6. *NYT*, November 17, 1953; Stephen E. Ambrose, *Eisenhower: The President* (New York: Simon and Schuster, 1984), 137–40.

7. *NYT*, May 11, 1954, August 28, 1955, March 30, 1957, April 15, October 29, 1958.

8. MT, ed., *Where the Buck Stops: The Personal and Private Writings of Harry S. Truman* (New York: Warner, 1989), 62, 68, 72.

9. *NYT*, May 5, 6, 10, 1959.

10. HST, *Mr. Citizen* (New York: Geis, 1960), 74. For Stevenson's efforts at a congenial relationship with Truman, see, for example, Walter Johnson, ed., *The Papers of Adlai Stevenson* (Boston, Little, Brown, 1972), 4:514, 529–30, 561–62.

11. *NYT*, August 12, 16, 17, 1956.

12. *NYT*, August 18, 1956; HST to Adlai Stevenson, August 19, 1956, HST Papers, Post-Presidential Papers, HSTL.

13. See, for example, HST, *Mr. Citizen,* chap. 4, and Merle Miller, *Plain Speaking: An Oral Biography of Harry S. Truman, 1945–1948* (New York: Berkeley, 1974), 24.

14. John Bartlow Martin, *Adlai Stevenson and the World* (Garden City, N.Y.: Doubleday, 1977), 399–402; Herbert Parmet, *The Democrats: The Years After FDR* (New York: Macmillan, 1976), 158–59.

15. HST to Dean Acheson, August 22, 1959, Post-Presidential Papers; *NYT*, December 8, 1959.

16. HST to Edward F. McFaddin, September 29, 1958, Post-Presidential Papers; Dean Acheson to HST, June 27, 1960, Post-Presidential Papers, reprinted in David McCullough, *Truman* (New York: Simon and Schuster, 1992), 971–73; *NYT*, April 18, 19, 1960.

17. Miller, *Plain Speaking*, 199–201.

18. HST, interviews for *Mr. Citizen* with William Hillman and David Noyes, September 11, October 21, 1959, Post-Presidential Papers.

19. *NYT*, May 14, July 3, 11, 16, 1960; author's personal recollections.

20. *NYT*, August 3, 21, October 12, 14, 24, 1960.

21. MT, *Harry Truman*, 573–76, and *Bess W. Truman* (New York: Macmillan, 1986), 418.

22. MT, *Bess Truman*, 418–20.

23. HST to John McCormack, January 10, 1957, Post-Presidential Papers, reprinted with explanatory footnote on tax treatment in Robert H. Ferrell, *Off the Record* (New York: Harper & Row, 1980), 346–47. See also *NYT*, October 29, November 8, 1953, and manuscript documentation on financial aspects of memoirs, Post-Presidential Papers.

24. McCullough, *Truman*, 936–49, provides an excellent account of the production of the memoirs. Primary documentation of business arrangements, interviews, and the enormous first-draft manuscript are all in Post-Presidential Papers, Memoirs File.

25. Miller, *Plain Speaking*, 462.

26. Unless otherwise cited, the personal information in this and the following paragraphs is from MT, *Harry Truman*, chap. 28, and *Bess Truman*, chaps. 28–30.

27. *KCS*, July 3, 1994.

28. *NYT*, February 3, July 31, September 17, 1958; *PD*, May 25, 1954; HST to John McCormack, January 10, 1957, Post-Presidential Papers; HST to Sam Rayburn, January 11, August 26, 1957, August 25, 1958, MHDC No. 66.

29. HST, diary, March 20, 1953, and diary, n.d. [probably April, 1953], Post-Presidential Papers.

30. HST, *Mr. Citizen*, chap. 3; McCullough, *Truman*, 933–35.

31. This trip is lovingly recounted in considerably greater detail in McCullough, *Truman*, 952–59.

32. Monroe Billington, remark made at a panel at the meeting of the Organization of American Historians, HSTL, April 1965; Richard Kirkendall, conversation with author.

33. Monte Poen and Richard Kirkendall, conversations with author; Cabell Phillips, *The Truman Presidency* (New York: Macmillan, 1966), 436–37. Individuals who have seen Truman's personal copy of Eric Goldman's *The Crucial Decade* (New York: Knopf, 1956) tell me that it contains numerous angry marginal comments.

34. James David Barber, Charles Blitzer, and Fred Greenstein, conversations with author; Greenstein to author, September 7, 1989, January 21, 1990.

35. Author's recollection for David Truman comment; HST, "From Precinct to the Presidency," Post-Presidential Papers.

36. The taped conversations are available in Post-Presidential Papers; they apparently form the basis for MT, ed., *Where the Buck Stops*.

37. John P. Roche, "Truman on Tape," *Saturday Review*, February 23, 1974, 20–22.

38. *NYT*, March 22, 1969, and author's recollection for Nixon visit; for opinion on Nixon, see Thomas Fleming, "Eight Days with Harry Truman," *American Heritage* 43 (July–August 1992): 54–59.

39. *NYT*, September 12, 1963.

40. Robert Alan Aurthur, "The Wit and Sass of Harry S. Truman," *Esquire*, August 1971, 62–67, 115–18.

41. Fleming, "Eight Days with Harry Truman."

Bibliographic Essay

Considerations of space (and, at the end of a long book, the reader's patience) do not permit a full listing of every item mentioned in the notes. The purpose of this essay is to indicate the most important sources, not to enumerate each one. It emphasizes the work done specifically for this book and should be supplemented by the bibliographic essay in my book *Beyond the New Deal: Harry S. Truman and American Liberalism* (New York: Columbia University Press, 1973).

Manuscript Collections

The Harry S. Truman Papers, HSTL, were the core resource; among their constituent parts, the most important were the Family, Business, Personal (FBP), Senatorial and Vice-Presidential (SVP), President's Secretary's (PSF), and Post-Presidential files. Other collections of importance at the Truman Library were the papers of Dean Acheson, Eben Ayers, William Boyle, Fred Canfil, John D. Clark, Clark Clifford, Jonathan Daniels (copies of originals at the University of North Carolina), Harry Easley, George Elsey, Harold Enarson, Harold Gosnell, H. H. Halvorson, Lou Holland, Victor Housholder, Eddie Jacobson, Leon Keyserling, William Kitchen, Arthur Mag, Frank McNaughton, Eddie Meisburger, Charles Murphy, Ethel Noland, Edwin Nourse, Charles Ross, Bryce Smith, Mary Jane Truman, Ralph Truman, Thomas Van Sant, N. T. Veatch, and Sam Wear. Also noteworthy were the Department of the Army Military Personnel Records of Harry S. Truman, the Thirty-fifth Division Collection, the General Historical Documents Collection (GHDC), and the Miscellaneous Historical Documents Collection (MHDC).

Among the most useful collections of papers consulted in other depositories were the following from the Western Historical Manuscripts Collection (University of Missouri/State Historical Society of Missouri, used on the Kansas City and Columbia campuses): Civic Research Institute (of Kansas City), Bennett Champ Clark, Russell Dearmont, Lyle W. Dorset, Lou Holland, James P. Kem, Ewing Mitchell, Guy B. Park, and Lloyd C. Stark. A by no means exhaustive investigation of the Truman committee records at the National Archives yielded important insights into that investigative body. At the Library of Congress, I have examined the papers of Joseph Davies, Edwin Halsey, William Leahy, James P. McGranery, and Joseph Pulitzer, Jr. Other collections that merit mention are the papers of Westbrook Pegler (Herbert Hoover Library), Arthur H. Vandenberg (University of Michigan), and H. Alexander Smith (Princeton University).

Personal Interviews

These range from relatively brief and casual conversations to fairly elaborate
interrogatories. I have engaged in an extended dialogue over the years with George
Elsey, by far my kindest and most helpful living source. A few interviews were
conducted by telephone; most, on a face-to-face basis. I identify only those persons not mentioned in the text: Richard Bolling, Mary Salisbury Bostian (sister
of Spencer Salisbury), Rufus Burrus, Oscar Chapman, Clark Clifford, Ilus Davis
(former mayor of Kansas City), Donald Dawson, George Elsey, Edward Flynn
(associate of David Noyes), Rosalind Gibson (niece of Spencer Salisbury and
Mary Salisbury Bostian), Wallace Graham, George W. Hamby, William Hannegan
(son of Robert Hannegan), John Hulston, William T. Kemper, Jr., Leon Keyserling, George Meador (Truman committee staff member, later congressman from
Michigan), Philleo Nash, Richard Neustadt, J. C. Truman, May Southern Wallace,
Raymond Wheeler (former mayor of Kansas City), McKinley Wooden (chief
mechanic, Battery D, 1917–1919).

Oral Histories

The following, all at HSTL, were among the most useful of many I have read
over the years: Eben Ayers, James Aylward, Gaylon Babcock, Richard Bolling,
Clark Clifford, Harry Easley, George Elsey, Tom Evans, Oscar Ewing, Edgar
Faris, Stanley Fike, Edward Folliard, Wallace Graham, Roy Harper, Walter
Hehmeyer, Roger Jones, Mary Paxton Keeley, W. McNeil Lowry, Ted Marks,
Walter Matschek, Edward McKim, John Meador, Charles Murphy, Harry
Murphy, Mary Ethel Noland, Edwin Nourse, Mize Peters, J. Leonard Reinsch,
Samuel I. Rosenman, James Rowe, Jr., James E. Ruffin, Stephen S. Slaughter,
John W. Snyder, Wilbur Sparks, Stephen Spingarn, Richard L. Strout, Fred
Truman, Harry Vaughan, and McKinley Wooden.

Newspapers and Periodicals

It is a practical impossibility to use unindexed daily newspapers on a systematic
basis. My work has been facilitated by the existence of some weekly newspapers
and numerous clipping collections. For Truman's early environment and the
beginnings of his political career, I have profited from stories in the *Jackson Examiner*, the weekly edition of the *Independence Examiner*, with which I have supplemented it on occasion; I also drew on the *Lee's Summit Journal* and the *Belton
Herald*. Unfortunately, no trace remains of the Grandview local paper during
Truman's residence there. The *Missouri Democrat* is a splendid source for
Truman's political career, Kansas City politics, and the rise and fall of the
Pendergast machine from 1925 to 1940.

For the Kansas City and St. Louis daily papers, I did some systematic research on matters that could be dated precisely, but for the most part, I had to
rely on clipping files and guides. These include the Kemper Family Papers and
the Shannon Family Scrapbooks, Jackson County (Mo.) Historical Society; the
Kansas City Star morgue file on Harry and Bess Truman and the *St. Louis Post-
Dispatch* morgue index for Truman, both on microfilm at HSTL; and the
St. Louis Globe-Democrat morgue file, at the St. Louis Mercantile Library. An
enormous clipping file kept by the Truman White House is available at HSTL

on microfilm, and various manuscript collections (for example, FBP) contain useful groups of clippings, sometimes from otherwise inaccessible publications. The HSTL Vertical File, administered for many years with remarkable breadth of vision by Elizabeth Safly, was a vital source of news clippings, useful obituaries, and articles from obscure periodicals.

Published Documents and Memoirs

Truman's own books—*Memoirs by Harry S. Truman*, vol. 1, *Year of Decisions* (Garden City, N.Y.: Doubleday, 1955; *Memoirs by Harry S. Truman*, vol. 2, *Years of Trial and Hope* (Garden City, N.Y.: Doubleday, 1956; and *Mr. Citizen* (New York: Geis, 1960)—are at once essential reading, occasionally revealing, and often frustrating. Compilations of his personal thoughts are most useful. The three leading examples are William Hillman, ed., *Mr. President* (New York: Farrar, Straus and Young, 1952); Merle Miller, *Plain Speaking: An Oral Biography of Harry S. Truman* (New York: Berkeley, 1974); and Margaret Truman, ed., *Where the Buck Stops: The Personal and Private Writings of Harry S. Truman* (New York: Warner, 1989). The leading scholarly editor of Truman material has been Robert H. Ferrell, whose works include *The Autobiography of Harry S. Truman* (Boulder, Colo.: Associated University Presses, 1980); *Dear Bess: The Letters from Harry to Bess Truman, 1910–1959* (New York: Norton, 1983); *Off the Record* (New York: Harper & Row, 1980); and *Truman in the White House: The Diary of Eben A. Ayers* (Columbia: University of Missouri Press, 1992). Monte M. Poen runs a close second with his books *Strictly Personal and Confidential: The Letters Harry Truman Never Mailed* (Boston: Little, Brown, 1982) and *Letters Home by Harry Truman* (New York: Putnam, 1984). I have researched the originals at the Truman Library, but I nonetheless owe Ferrell and Poen a big debt of gratitude for making so many key documents available in a clear, easy-to-use, and readable form.

Public Papers of the Presidents: Harry S. Truman, 1945–53, 8 vols. (Washington, D.C.: Government Printing Office, 1961–1966), and the relevant volumes of *Foreign Relations of the United States, 1945–1953* are indispensible official compilations.

Among memoirs and collections of documents by Truman officials, the most important are Dean Acheson, *Present at the Creation: My Years in the State Department* (New York: Norton, 1969); Walter Millis, ed., *The Forrestal Diaries* (New York: Viking, 1951); David E. Lilienthal, *The Journals of David E. Lilienthal: The Atomic Energy Years, 1945–1950* (New York: Harper & Row, 1964); Clark M. Clifford, with Richard Holbrooke, *Counsel to the President* (New York: Random House, 1991); Charles E. Bohlen, *Witness to History, 1929–1969* (New York: Norton, 1973); W. Averell Harriman and Elie Abel, *Special Envoy to Stalin and Churchill* (New York: Random House, 1975); George F. Kennan, *Memoirs: 1925–1950* (Boston: Little, Brown, 1967); and Charles Sawyer, *Concerns of a Conservative Democrat* (Carbondale: Southern Illinois University Press, 1968).

Other important collections include Walter Johnson, ed., *The Papers of Adlai E. Stevenson*, vols. 2–5 (Boston: Little, Brown, 1972–1975); Drew Pearson, *Diaries, 1949–1959*, ed. Tyler Abell (New York: Holt, Rinehart and Winston, 1974); Arthur H. Vandenberg, Jr., and Joe Alex Morris, eds., *The Private Papers of Senator Vandenberg* (Boston: Houghton Mifflin, 1952); and John Blum, ed., *The Price of Vision: The Diary of Henry A. Wallace* (Boston: Houghton Mifflin, 1973).

Biographies of Truman and Key Works
on His Presidency

Jonathan Daniels, *Man of Independence* (Philadelphia: Lippincott, 1950), is empathetic and nicely written, but limited by lack of perspective and even more by the restrictions placed on Daniels by his status as an authorized biographer. Alfred Steinberg, *The Man from Missouri* (New York: Putnam, 1962), strikes me as a better book than it is usually given credit for being, but its value is lessened by its relative paucity of research and tendency to accept Truman's own account of events. Harold Gosnell, *Truman's Crises* (Westport, Conn.: Greenwood Press, 1980), written by a great political scientist near the end of his career, can be considered little more than a competent survey of its subject's life. David McCullough, *Truman* (New York: Simon and Schuster, 1992), is a nicely told story but (despite its length) episodic and lacking much in the way of historical perspective. Robert H. Ferrell's *Harry S. Truman: A Life* (Columbia: University of Missouri Press, 1994) appeared as my own book was going to press. Margaret Truman's two books, *Harry S. Truman* (New York: Morrow, 1972) and *Bess W. Truman* (New York: Macmillan, 1986), are valuable memoirs written by a loving daughter.

Richard Lawrence Miller, *Truman: The Rise to Power* (New York: McGraw-Hill, 1986), is by far the best account of Truman's pre-presidential life. I have many quibbles with it and believe that it fails to establish a sufficient conceptual framework for interpreting Truman's career; its independent research, however, is admirable. If Miller leans too reflexively in the direction of debunking, he merits recognition as the first historian to ask critical questions about Truman's pre-presidential life. One hopes also that Thomas Heed's exhaustive research into Truman's Jackson County years will someday see the light of day.

I have put together my impressions of Truman's pre-senatorial life and career largely from my own research and, to some extent, my own identity as a Missourian. Neither William Reddig, *Tom's Town* (Philadelphia: Lippincott, 1947), nor Lyle W. Dorsett, *The Pendergast Machine* (New York: Oxford University Press, 1968), provides a fully adequate account of its subject. Franklin W. Mitchell, *Embattled Democracy: Missouri Democratic Politics, 1919–1932* (Columbia: University of Missouri Press, 1968), is a sound study of change and conflict in the Missouri Democratic party from 1920 to 1932; unfortunately, no similar work exists for the 1930s, despite rich sources, or for later decades. Richard S. Kirkendall, *A History of Missouri*, vol. 5, *1919–1953* (Columbia: University of Missouri Press, 1986), is a fine survey but with too broad a sweep to provide much information on matters of political detail.

Truman's Senate years await a strong examination. There is practically no literature on the general topic of transportation policy or on the 1930s railroad investigations. Nor is there an entirely satisfactory work on the World War II Truman committee. On the latter topic, see Donald Riddle, *The Truman Committee: A Study in Congressional Responsibility* (New Brunswick, N.J.: Rutgers University Press, 1964); Roger Willson, "The Truman Committee" (Ph.D. diss., Harvard University, 1966); and Theodore Wilson, "The Truman Committee, 1941," in *Congress Investigates: A Documented History, 1792–1974*, ed. Arthur M. Schlesinger, Jr., and Roger Bruns (New York: Chelsea House, 1975).

The foremost historian of Truman's presidency is Robert J. Donovan, whose works *Conflict and Crisis: The Presidency of Harry S. Truman, 1945–1948* (New

York: Norton, 1977) and *Tumultuous Years: The Presidency of Harry S. Truman* (New York: Norton, 1982) have established a basic and authoritative chronological narration that is unlikely to be surpassed. In keeping with Donovan's vocation as a journalist, however, it is more interested in recounting events than in providing an overarching interpretation. Donald R. McCoy, *The Presidency of Harry S. Truman* (Lawrence: University Press of Kansas, 1984), displays a mastery of the sources at the Truman Library and provides solid coverage in one volume but also lacks an interpretive design. Alonzo L. Hamby, *Beyond the New Deal: Harry S. Truman and American Liberalism* (New York: Columbia University Press, 1973), is perhaps the most strongly interpretive account, although (with the benefit of twenty years of hindsight and perspective) its single-minded focus on the relationship between Truman and organized liberal activists seems inadequate for understanding the dynamics of the Truman presidency. Opposing revisionist views from that period can be found in Barton J. Bernstein, ed., *Policies and Politics of the Truman Administration* (Chicago: Quadrangle, 1970), and in Barton J. Bernstein, "America in War and Peace: The Test of Liberalism," in *Towards a New Past*, ed. Barton J. Bernstein (New York: Pantheon, 1968). Both of us, I am happy to report, find the debate more than a bit stale after two decades.

Readers interested in the scholarly arguments over Truman and his presidency might begin with Richard S. Kirkendall, ed., *The Truman Period as a Research Field: A Reappraisal, 1972* (Columbia: University of Missouri Press, 1974), and Alonzo L. Hamby, *Harry S. Truman and the Fair Deal* (Lexington, Mass.: Heath, 1974), and then move quickly to Michael Lacey, ed., *The Truman Presidency* (New York: Cambridge University Press, 1989). Richard S. Kirkendall, ed., *The Harry S. Truman Encyclopedia* (Boston: Hall, 1989), is a valuable collection of concise articles.

To my mind, the most important interpretations of American foreign policy during the Truman years are two books by John Lewis Gaddis, *The United States and the Origins of the Cold War* (New York: Columbia University Press, 1972) and *Strategies of Containment: A Critical Appraisal of Postwar American National Security Policy* (New York: Oxford University Press, 1982), along with Melvyn P. Leffler, *A Preponderance of Power* (Stanford, Calif.: Stanford University Press, 1992). Other works of special substance include Robert Messer, *The End of an Alliance: James F. Byrnes, Roosevelt, Truman, and the Origins of the Cold War* (Chapel Hill: University of North Carolina Press, 1982); McGeorge Bundy, *Danger and Survival* (New York: Random House, 1988); Robert A. Pollard, *Economic Security and the Origins of the Cold War, 1945–1950* (New York: Columbia University Press, 1985); and Michael Hogan, *The Marshall Plan* (New York: Cambridge University Press, 1987).

Some will protest that I too easily discount the findings of leading revisionists such as Gabriel Kolko, *The Politics of War* (New York: Random House, 1968) and Joyce Kolko and Gabriel Kolko, *The Limits of Power* (New York: Harper, 1972); Lloyd Gardner, *Architects of Illusion* (Chicago: Quadrangle, 1970); and most recently H. W. Brands, *The Devil We Knew* (New York: Oxford University Press, 1994). I have no intention of personally attacking these authors or others who are like-minded; nevertheless, in the end I do not find their major theses credible and believe that their relatively benign attitude toward Stalinism seriously weakens their work.

Index